ABOUT THE AUTHORS

KATHERINE BARBER

HEATHER FITZGERALD

ROBERT PONTISSO

The lexicographers of Oxford University Press Canada's dictionary team have, collectively, over 40 years of experience editing dictionaries and thesauruses. They have lived in six cities in four provinces, and thus bring a wealth of knowledge of both regional and general Canadian English to the task.

In addition to writing Oxford's Canadian dictionaries, the lexicographers are constantly engaged in a reading program to identify new and distinctly Canadian words. They have now read over 9000 Canadian books, magazines, and newspapers.

Katherine Barber, Editor-in-Chief of Canadian dictionaries since 1991, received the Canadian Booksellers Association's Editor of the Year award in 1999, and is well known across Canada for frequent appearances on radio and television. She is also the author of *Six Words You Never Knew Had Something to Do With Pigs*, a lively and entertaining collection of word histories published by Oxford University Press (2006).

Oxford
Canadian
Thesaurus

—— *of* ——

Current
English

Edited by
Katherine Barber
Heather Fitzgerald
Robert Pontisso

Editor-in-chief, Canadian Dictionaries
Katherine Barber

OXFORD
UNIVERSITY PRESS

OXFORD
UNIVERSITY PRESS

70 Wynford Drive, Don Mills, Ontario M3C 1J9
www.oupcanada.com

Oxford University Press is a department of the University of Oxford.
It furthers the University's objective of excellence in research, scholarship,
and education by publishing worldwide in

Oxford   New York
Auckland Cape Town Dar es Salaam Hong Kong Karachi
Kuala Lumpur Madrid Melbourne Mexico City Nairobi
New Delhi Shanghai Taipei Toronto

Oxford is a registered trade mark of Oxford University Press
in the UK and in certain other countries

Published in Canada
by Oxford University Press

Library and Archives Canada Cataloguing in Publication

Oxford Canadian thesaurus of current English / edited by Katherine
Barber, Heather Fitzgerald, Robert Pontisso.

ISBN-10: 0-19-542569-3   ISBN-13: 978-0-19-542569-7

1. English language—Canada—Synonyms and antonyms—Dictionaries.
2. English language—Synonyms and antonyms—Dictionaries.
I. Barber, Katherine, 1959- II. Fitzgerald, Heather, 1972-
III. Pontisso, Robert, 1968-

PE3233.O94 2006   423'.12   C2006-903645-4

Cover Design: Brett J. Miller

6 7 - 11 10 09 08

Printed on 80% recycled paper

Printed in Canada

Features of the Thesaurus

Headword

Number and core synonym to distinguish senses of the entry word

Phrases

Curly brackets showing that the phrase they contain is one complete synonym

Superscript numbers distinguishing homonyms

bush *n.* **1** SHRUB, brier; (bushes) undergrowth, shrubbery. **2** WILDS, wilderness, forest, woodland, timberland, bush country, bushland; backwoods, hinterland(s), backcountry, backlands; *informal* the sticks, boondocks, (*Ont. & Que.*) the back concessions✦, moose pasture✦.

Form of the entry word for which the following synonyms can be substituted

partial *adj.* **1** INCOMPLETE, limited, qualified, imperfect, fragmentary, unfinished. **2** ☞ BIASED.
—OPPOSITES: complete, unbiased.
□ **be partial to** ☞ LIKE[1] 2.

Opposite words

people *n.* **1** HUMAN BEINGS, persons, individuals, humans, mortals, (living) souls, personages, {men, women, and children}; *informal* folks. **2** CITIZENS, subjects, electors, voters, taxpayers, residents, inhabitants, (general) public, citizenry, nation, population. **3** ☞ POPULACE.

Pointer indicating entry and/or sense where synonyms can be found

wind[1] *n.* **1** BREEZE, current of air; gale, hurricane; chinook✦; *informal* blow; *literary* zephyr. **2** BREATH; *informal* puff. **3** FLATULENCE, gas; *formal* flatus.
—RELATED: aeolian.

Canadian synonym

Related words, prefixes, and suffixes

wind[2] *v.* **1** TWIST (AND TURN), bend, curve, loop, zigzag, weave, snake. **2** WRAP, furl, entwine, lace, loop. **3** COIL, roll, twist, twine.

Note on Proprietary Status

This thesaurus includes some words which have or are asserted to have proprietary status as trademarks or otherwise. Their inclusion does not imply that they have acquired for legal purposes a non-proprietary or general significance nor any other judgment concerning their legal status. In cases where the editorial staff have some evidence that a word has proprietary status, this is indicated in the entry for that word, but no judgment concerning the legal status of such words is made or implied thereby.

Aa

abandon *v.* **1** RENOUNCE, relinquish, dispense with, disclaim, disown, disavow, discard, wash one's hands of; give up, drop, jettison, do away with, axe; *informal* ditch, dump, scrap, scrub, junk, deep-six; *formal* forswear. **2** GIVE UP, stop, cease, drop, forgo, desist from, have done with, abstain from, discontinue, break off, refrain from, set aside; *informal* cut out, kick, pack in, quit; *formal* abjure. **3** DESERT, leave, leave high and dry, turn one's back on, cast aside, break up with; jilt, strand, leave stranded, leave in the lurch, throw over; spurn; *informal* walk out on, run out on, leave behind, dump, ditch, drop, finish with, give someone the old heave-ho; *literary* forsake. **4** ☞ LEAVE 1.

abandoned *adj.* **1** DESERTED, forsaken, cast aside/off; jilted, stranded, rejected; *informal* dumped, ditched. **2** UNUSED, disused, neglected, idle; deserted, unoccupied, uninhabited, empty.

abashed *adj.* TAKEN ABACK, disconcerted, discomfited, fazed, floored, disturbed, crestfallen, conscience-stricken. See also EMBARRASSED.

abbreviate *v.* ☞ ABRIDGE. —OPPOSITES: lengthen, expand.

abdicate *v.* RESIGN, retire, stand down, step down, bow out, renounce, relinquish, abandon; give up, surrender, vacate, cede; *archaic* demit.

abduct *v.* KIDNAP, carry off, seize, capture, run away/off with, make off with, spirit away, take/hold hostage/captive/prisoner, hold to ransom; *informal* snatch.

aberrant *adj.* TWISTED, warped, perverted. See also STRANGE 1. —OPPOSITES: normal, typical.

abhorrent *adj.* DETESTABLE, hateful, loathsome, despicable, abominable, execrable, repellent, repugnant, repulsive, revolting, disgusting, distasteful, horrible, horrid, horrifying, awful, heinous, reprehensible, obnoxious, odious, nauseating, offensive, contemptible, damnable, foul, gross, hideous, nasty, sickening, vile, yucky. —OPPOSITES: admirable.

abide *v.* **1** ☞ COMPLY. **2** ☞ BEAR 5. —OPPOSITES: flout, disobey.

ability *n.* **1** CAPACITY, capability, potential, potentiality, power, faculty, aptness, facility; wherewithal, means. **2** ACCOMPLISHMENT; cleverness; qualification, resources; know-how. See also APTITUDE, SKILL.

able *adj.* **1** CAPABLE OF, competent to, equal to, up to, fit to, prepared

to, qualified to; allowed to, free to, in a position to. **2** CAPABLE, competent, efficient, effective. See also GIFTED.
—OPPOSITES: incompetent, incapable.

abnormal *adj.* ☞ STRANGE 1.
—OPPOSITES: normal, typical.

abolish *v.* PUT AN END TO, get rid of, scrap, discard, end, stop, terminate, axe, eradicate, eliminate, exterminate, destroy, annihilate, stamp out, obliterate, wipe out, extinguish, quash, expunge, extirpate; annul, cancel, invalidate, negate, nullify, void, dissolve; rescind, repeal, revoke, overturn; discontinue, remove, excise, drop, jettison, dispense with, abandon; *informal* do away with, ditch, junk, scrub, dump, chop, give something the chop; *formal* abrogate.
—OPPOSITES: retain, create.

abominable *adj.* ☞ TERRIBLE 1, 2.
—OPPOSITES: good, admirable.

aboriginal *adj.* **1** INDIGENOUS, native; original, earliest, first; ancient, primitive, primeval, primordial. **2** NATIVE, indigenous, First Peoples, First Nations, Indian, Inuit, Metis.

abortion *n.* TERMINATION, miscarriage.

abortive *adj.* ☞ UNSUCCESSFUL 1.
—OPPOSITES: successful.

abound *v.* BE PLENTIFUL, be abundant, be numerous, proliferate, superabound, be thick on the ground; *informal* grow on trees.

abrasive *adj.* **1** CORROSIVE, corroding, erosive; caustic, harsh, scratching, coarse. **2** CAUSTIC,

cutting, biting, acerbic; rough, harsh, hard, tough, sharp, grating, curt, brusque, stern, severe; wounding, nasty, cruel, callous, insensitive, unfeeling, unsympathetic, inconsiderate.
—OPPOSITES: kind, gentle.

abridge *v.* SHORTEN, cut, cut short/down, curtail, truncate, trim, crop, clip, pare down, prune; abbreviate, condense, contract, compress, reduce, decrease, shrink; summarize, sum up, abstract, précis, synopsize, give a digest of, put in a nutshell, edit; epitomize.
—OPPOSITES: lengthen.

abrupt *adj.* **1** ☞ SUDDEN. **2** CURT, brusque, blunt, short, sharp, terse, crisp, gruff, rude, discourteous, uncivil, snappish, unceremonious, offhand, rough, harsh; bluff, no-nonsense, to the point; *informal* snappy.
—OPPOSITES: gradual, gentle.

abscond *v.* RUN AWAY, escape, bolt, flee, make off, take flight, take off, decamp, depart, leave; make a break for it, take to one's heels, make a quick getaway, beat a hasty retreat, run for it, make a run for it; disappear, vanish, slip away, split, steal away, sneak away; clear out, duck out, cut and run, skedaddle, skip, scram, head for the hills, do a disappearing act, fly the coop, take French leave, vamoose, go AWOL, go on the lam; *informal* take a powder.

absent *adj.* AWAY, off, out, non-attending, truant; off duty, on holiday, on leave; gone, missing, lacking, unavailable, non-existent; *informal* AWOL, playing hooky, (*Ont.*)

skipping off♣, (*West*) skipping out♣.
—OPPOSITES: present.

absent-minded *adj.* FORGETFUL, distracted, preoccupied, inattentive, vague, abstracted, daydreaming, unheeding, oblivious, distrait, in a brown study, woolgathering; lost in thought, moony, pensive, thoughtful, brooding; *informal* scatterbrained, out of it, out to lunch, miles away, having a mind/memory like a sieve, spacey.

absolute *adj.* **1** COMPLETE, total, utter, out-and-out, outright, entire, full-out, prize, perfect, pure, decided, real, veritable; thorough, thoroughgoing, undivided, unqualified, unadulterated, unalloyed, unmodified, unreserved, downright, undiluted, consummate, unmitigated, sheer, arrant, rank, dyed-in-the-wool. **2** DEFINITE, certain, positive, unconditional, categorical, unquestionable, incontrovertible, undoubted, unequivocal, decisive, conclusive, confirmed, infallible. **3** ☞ UNLIMITED 2.
—OPPOSITES: partial, qualified, limited.

absolve *v.* EXONERATE, discharge, acquit, vindicate; release, relieve, liberate, free, deliver, clear, exempt, let off; forgive, pardon; *formal* exculpate.
—OPPOSITES: blame, condemn.

absorb *v.* **1** SOAK UP, suck up, draw up/in, take up/in, blot up, mop up, sop up. **2** INCORPORATE, assimilate, integrate, take in, subsume, include, co-opt, swallow up. **3** ENGROSS, captivate, occupy, preoccupy, engage, rivet, grip, hold, interest, intrigue, immerse, involve, enthrall, spellbind, fascinate.

absorbent *adj.* POROUS, spongy, sponge-like, permeable, pervious, absorptive; *technical* spongiform.

absorbing *adj.* ☞ INTERESTING.
—OPPOSITES: boring, uninteresting.

abstain *v.* REFRAIN, desist, hold back, forbear; give up, renounce, avoid, shun, eschew, forgo, go without, do without; refuse, decline; *informal* cut out; *formal* abjure.

abstemious *adj.* SELF-DENYING, temperate, abstinent, moderate, self-disciplined, restrained, self-restrained, sober, austere, ascetic, puritanical, Spartan, hair-shirt.
—OPPOSITES: self-indulgent.

abstract *adj.* **1** THEORETICAL, conceptual, notional, intellectual, metaphysical, ideal, philosophical, academic; *rare* ideational. **2** NON-REPRESENTATIONAL, non-pictorial.
—OPPOSITES: actual, concrete.
▶ *n.* SUMMARY, synopsis, précis, resumé, outline, abridgement, digest, summation; wrap-up.

abstruse *adj.* OBSCURE, arcane, esoteric, little known, recherché, rarefied, recondite, difficult, hard, puzzling, perplexing, cryptic, enigmatic, Delphic, complex, complicated, involved, over/above one's head, incomprehensible, unfathomable, impenetrable, mysterious.

absurd *adj.* PREPOSTEROUS, ridiculous, ludicrous, farcical, laughable, risible, idiotic, stupid,

foolish, silly, inane, imbecilic, insane, hare-brained, cockamamie; unreasonable, irrational, illogical, nonsensical, incongruous, pointless, senseless; *informal* crazy, daft, asinine, cockeyed, fatuous, half-baked, implausible, impracticable, lunatic, mad, kooky.
—OPPOSITES: reasonable, sensible.

abundance *n.* PROFUSION, plentifulness, profuseness, copiousness, amplitude, lavishness, bountifulness, bounty; wealth, host, cornucopia, plethora, bonanza, riot; plenty, quantities, scores, multitude; *informal* millions, zillions, hundreds, thousands, lot(s), heap(s), mass(es), whack, stack(s), pile(s), load(s), bags, mountain(s), ton(s), slew, scads, oodles, gobs; *formal* plenitude.
—OPPOSITES: lack, scarcity, dearth.

abundant *adj.* PLENTIFUL, copious, ample, profuse, rich, lavish, abounding, liberal, handsome, generous, bountiful, large, huge, great, bumper, overflowing, prolific, teeming; in plenty, in abundance; inexhaustible, superabundant; extensive, full, fulsome, many, numerous; *informal* galore; *literary* plenteous, bounteous.
—OPPOSITES: scarce, sparse.

abuse *v.* **1** MISUSE, misapply, misemploy; exploit, take advantage of. **2** MISTREAT, maltreat, ill-treat, treat badly; molest, interfere with, indecently assault, sexually abuse, sexually assault; injure, hurt, harm, damage. **3** ☞ INSULT *v.*

▸ *n.* **1** MISUSE, misapplication; exploitation. **2** MISTREATMENT, maltreatment, ill-treatment; molestation, interference, indecent assault, sexual abuse, sexual assault; injury, hurt, harm, damage. **3** INSULTS, curses, jibes, expletives, swear words; swearing, cursing, name-calling; invective, vilification, vituperation, slander; *informal* trash talk.

abusive *adj.* RUDE, vulgar, offensive; scurrilous, blasphemous. See also DEROGATORY.

abut *v.* ADJOIN, be adjacent to, butt against, border, neighbour, join, touch, meet, reach, be contiguous with.

abysmal *adj.* ☞ TERRIBLE 5.

abyss *n.* CHASM, gorge, ravine, canyon, fissure, rift, crevasse, hole, gulf, pit, cavity, void, bottomless pit.

academic *adj.* **1** EDUCATIONAL, scholastic, instructional, pedagogical. **2** SCHOLARLY, studious, literary, well-read, intellectual, clever, erudite, learned, educated, knowledgeable, cultivated, cultured, bookish, highbrow, pedantic, donnish, cerebral; *informal* brainy, inkhorn, bluestocking, egghead, pointy-headed, well-informed, widely read; *dated* lettered. **3** THEORETICAL, conceptual, notional, philosophical, hypothetical, speculative, conjectural, suppositional; impractical, unrealistic, ivory-tower.

▸ *n.* SCHOLAR, lecturer, don, teacher, tutor, professor, fellow,

man/woman of letters,
bluestocking; pedagogue.

accede v. (formal) AGREE TO,
consent to, accept, assent to,
acquiesce in, comply with, go
along with, concur with,
surrender to, yield to, give in to,
give way to, defer to.

accelerate v. **1** SPEED UP, go
faster, gain momentum, increase
speed, pick up speed, gather
speed, put on a spurt. **2** INCREASE,
rise, go up, leap up, surge,
escalate, spiral.
—OPPOSITES: decelerate, delay.

accent n. **1** PRONUNCIATION,
intonation, enunciation,
articulation, inflection, tone,
modulation, cadence, timbre,
manner of speaking, delivery;
brogue, burr, drawl, twang.
2 STRESS, emphasis, accentuation,
force, prominence; beat; technical
ictus. **3** MARK, diacritic.

accentuate v. FOCUS ATTENTION
ON, draw attention to, point up,
underline, underscore, accent,
highlight, spotlight, foreground,
feature, play up, bring to the fore,
heighten, stress, emphasize.

accept v. **1** RECEIVE, take, get,
gain, obtain, acquire. **2** SAY YES TO,
agree to. **3** BELIEVE, regard as true,
give credence to, credit, trust;
informal buy, swallow. **4** GO ALONG
WITH, agree to, consent to,
acquiesce in, concur with, assent
to, acknowledge, comply with,
abide by, follow, adhere to, act in
accordance with, defer to, yield to,
surrender to, bow to, give in to,
submit to, respect; formal accede to.
5 TOLERATE, endure, put up with,
bear, take, submit to, stomach,

swallow; reconcile oneself to,
resign oneself to, get used to,
adjust to, learn to live with, make
the best of; face up to.
—OPPOSITES: refuse, reject.

acceptable adj. SATISFACTORY,
adequate, reasonable, quite good,
fair, decent, good enough,
sufficient, competent, sufficiently
good, fine, not bad, all right,
average, tolerable, passable,
middling, moderate; informal OK,
jake, so-so, {comme ci, comme
ça}, fair-to-middling.

accepted adj. RECOGNIZED,
acknowledged, established,
traditional, orthodox, sanctioned;
usual, customary, common,
current, normal, general,
prevailing, accustomed, familiar,
wonted, popular, expected,
routine, standard, stock.

access n. **1** ENTRANCE, entry, way
in, means of entry; approach,
means of approach. **2** ADMISSION,
admittance, entry, entree, ingress,
right of entry.

accessible adj. **1** REACHABLE,
attainable, approachable;
obtainable, available; informal get-at-
able. **2** APPROACHABLE, friendly,
agreeable, obliging, congenial,
affable, cordial, welcoming,
easygoing, pleasant.

accessory n. **1** ATTACHMENT,
extra, addition, add-on, adjunct,
appendage, appurtenance,
supplement. **2** ☞ ACCOMPLICE.

accident n. **1** MISHAP,
misadventure, unfortunate
incident, mischance, misfortune,
disaster, tragedy, catastrophe,
calamity; technical casualty.
2 ☞ COLLISION. **3** CHANCE, mere

chance, coincidence, twist of fate, freak, hazard; fluke, bit of luck, serendipity; fate, fortuity, fortune, providence, happenstance.

accidental *adj.* FORTUITOUS, chance, adventitious, fluky, coincidental, casual, serendipitous, random; unexpected, unforeseen, unanticipated, unlooked-for, unintentional, unintended, inadvertent, unplanned, unpremeditated, unthinking, unwitting.
—OPPOSITES: intentional, deliberate.

acclaim *v.* PRAISE, applaud, cheer, commend, approve, welcome, pay tribute to, speak highly of, eulogize, compliment, celebrate, sing the praises of, rave about, heap praise on, wax lyrical about, lionize, exalt, admire, hail, extol, honour, hymn; *informal* ballyhoo; *formal* laud.
—OPPOSITES: criticize.

acclimatize *v.* ADJUST, adapt, accustom, accommodate, habituate, acculturate; get used, become inured, reconcile oneself, resign oneself; familiarize oneself; find one's feet, get one's bearings, become seasoned, become naturalized; acclimate.

accommodate *v.* **1** LODGE, house, put up, billet, quarter, board, take in, shelter, give someone a roof over their head; harbour. **2** HELP, assist, aid, oblige; meet the needs/wants of, cater for, fit in with, satisfy.

accommodating *adj.* OBLIGING, co-operative, helpful, eager to help, adaptable, amenable, considerate, unselfish, generous, willing, compliant, kindly, hospitable, neighbourly, kind, friendly, pleasant, agreeable.

accommodation *n.* HOUSING, lodging(s), living quarters, quarters, rooms; place to stay, billet; shelter, a roof over one's head; *informal* digs, pad; *formal* abode, residence, place of residence, dwelling, dwelling place, habitation.

accompany *v.* GO WITH, travel with, keep someone company, tag along with, hang out with, partner, escort, chaperone, attend, show, see, usher, conduct.

accomplice *n.* PARTNER IN CRIME, associate, accessory, abettor, confederate, collaborator, fellow conspirator, co-conspirator; henchman; *informal* sidekick.

accomplish *v.* FULFILL, achieve, succeed in, realize, attain, manage, bring about/off, carry out/through, execute, effect, perform, do, discharge, complete, finish, consummate, conclude; *informal* pull off, nail; *formal* effectuate.

accomplished *adj.* EXPERT, skilled, skilful, masterly, successful, virtuoso, master, consummate, complete, proficient, talented, gifted, adept, adroit, deft, dexterous, able, good, competent, capable, efficient, experienced, seasoned, trained, practised, professional, polished, ready, apt; *informal* great, mean, nifty, crack, ace, wizard; crackerjack, magic.

accomplishment *n.* **1** ACHIEVEMENT, act, deed, exploit, performance, attainment, effort, feat, move, coup. **2** ☞ SKILL.

accord v. **1** GIVE, grant, present, award, vouchsafe; confer on, bestow on, vest in, invest with. **2** CORRESPOND, agree, tally, match, concur, be consistent, harmonize, be in harmony, be compatible, chime in, be in tune, correlate; conform to; *informal* square.
—OPPOSITES: withhold, disagree, differ.
▶ *n.* ☞ TREATY.
□ **of one's own accord**
☞ WILLINGLY.

account *n.* **1** DESCRIPTION, report, version, story, narration, narrative, statement, explanation, exposition, delineation, portrayal, tale; chronicle, history, record, log; view, impression. **2** FINANCIAL RECORD, ledger, balance sheet, financial statement; (**accounts**) books. **3** BILL, invoice, tally; debt, charges; *informal* tab.
□ **account for** EXPLAIN, answer for, give reasons for, rationalize, justify. **on account of** BECAUSE OF, owing to, due to, as a consequence of, thanks to, by/in virtue of, in view of.

accumulate v. GATHER, collect, amass, stockpile, pile up, heap up, store (up), hoard, cumulate, lay in/up; increase, mass, multiply, accrue, snowball; run up.

accumulation *n.* MASS, buildup, pile, heap, stack, collection, stock, store, stockpile, reserve, hoard; amassing, gathering, cumulation, accrual, accretion.

accurate *adj.* CORRECT, precise, exact, right, error-free, perfect; FACTUAL, fact-based, literal,

faithful, true, truthful, true to life, authentic, realistic; *informal* on the mark, bang on, on the money, on the button; *formal* veracious.

accuse v. **1** CHARGE WITH, indict for, arraign for; summons, cite, prefer charges against; impeach for. **2** BLAME FOR, lay/pin the blame on, hold responsible for, inculpate, hold accountable for; condemn for, criticize for, denounce for; *informal* lay at the door of, point the finger at.
—OPPOSITES: absolve, exonerate.

accustomed *adj.*
1 ☞ CUSTOMARY. **2** USED TO, habituated to, acclimatized to, no stranger to, familiar with.

ache *n.* **1** ☞ PAIN *n.* 1. **2** ☞ GRIEF 1.
▶ *v.* HURT, be sore, be painful, be in pain, pain, throb, pound, twinge; smart, burn.

achieve v. ATTAIN, reach, arrive at; realize, bring off/about, pull off, accomplish, carry off/out/through, fulfill, execute, perform, engineer, conclude, complete, finish, consummate; earn, win, gain, acquire, obtain, score, come by, get, secure, clinch, net; *informal* wrap up, wangle, swing; *formal* effectuate.

acid *adj.* **1** ACIDIC, SOUR, tart, bitter, sharp, acrid, pungent, acerbic, vinegary, acetic, acetous. **2** ACERBIC, sarcastic, sharp, sardonic, scathing, cutting, razor-edged, biting, harsh, abrasive, unkind; *informal* bitchy, catty; snarky.
—OPPOSITES: sweet, pleasant.

acknowledge v. **1** ADMIT, accept, grant, allow, concede, accede to, confess, own,

recognize. **2** GREET, salute, address; nod to, wave to, raise one's hat to, say hello to.
3 ANSWER, reply to, respond to.
—OPPOSITES: reject, deny, ignore.

acme n. ☞ PEAK n. 4.
—OPPOSITES: nadir.

acquaint v. FAMILIARIZE, make familiar, make aware of, inform of, advise of, apprise of, let know, get up to date; brief, prime; informal fill in on, clue in on.

acquaintance n. **1** CONTACT, associate, colleague; companion, neighbour. **2** ASSOCIATION, relationship, contact.

acquire v. OBTAIN, come by, get, receive, gain, earn, win, come into, be given; buy, purchase, procure, possess oneself of, secure, pick up, snap up, adopt; gather, collect; informal get one's hands/mitts on, get hold of, land, bag, cop, score.
—OPPOSITES: lose.

acquisition n. PURCHASE, buy, gain, accession, addition, investment, possession.

acquit v. CLEAR, exonerate, find innocent, absolve; discharge, release, free, set free; informal let off (the hook); formal exculpate.
—OPPOSITES: convict.

acrid adj. PUNGENT, bitter, sharp, sour, tart, caustic, harsh, irritating, acid, acidic, vinegary, acetic, acetous; stinging, burning.

acrimonious adj. BITTER, angry, rancorous, caustic, acerbic, scathing, sarcastic, acid, harsh, sharp, cutting; virulent, spiteful, vicious, vitriolic, hostile, venomous, poisonous, nasty, bad-tempered, ill-natured, mean,

malign, malicious, malignant, waspish; ferocious, savage; informal bitchy, catty.

act v. **1** TAKE ACTION, take steps, take measures, move, react. **2** REPRESENT, act on behalf of; stand in for, fill in for, deputize for, take the place of. **3** BEHAVE, conduct oneself, react; formal comport oneself. **4** OPERATE, work, function, serve. **5** PERFORM, play a part, play-act, take part, appear; informal tread the boards, ham it up.
▶ n. **1** DEED, action, feat, exploit, move, gesture, performance, undertaking, stunt, operation; achievement, accomplishment.
2 ☞ LAW 1. **3** PERFORMANCE, turn, routine, number, sketch, skit, shtick. **4** PRETENSE, show, front, facade, masquerade, charade, posture, pose, affectation, sham, fake; informal a put-on.

acting adj. ☞ PROVISIONAL.
—OPPOSITES: permanent.

action n. **1** DEED, act, move, undertaking, exploit, manoeuvre, endeavour, effort, exertion; behaviour, conduct, activity.
2 ENERGY, vitality, vigour, forcefulness, drive, initiative, spirit, liveliness, vim, pep; activity; informal get-up-and-go.
3 EXCITEMENT, activity, happenings, events, incidents; informal goings-on.

activate v. OPERATE, switch on, turn on, start (up), set going, trigger (off), set in motion, initiate, actuate, energize; trip.

active adj. **1** ENERGETIC, lively, sprightly, spry, mobile, vigorous, vital, dynamic, sporty; busy, occupied; informal on the go.

2 HARD-WORKING, busy, industrious, diligent, tireless, contributing, effective, enterprising, involved, enthusiastic, keen, committed, devoted, zealous. **3** ☞ WORKING 2.
—OPPOSITES: listless, passive.

activity *n.* **1** BUSTLE, hustle and bustle, busyness, action, liveliness, movement, life, stir, flurry; happenings, occurrences, proceedings, events, incidents; *informal* toing and froing, comings and goings. **2** PURSUIT, occupation, interest, hobby, pastime, recreation, diversion; venture, undertaking, enterprise, project, scheme, business, entertainment; act, action, deed, exploit.

actual *adj.* REAL, true, genuine, authentic, verified, attested, confirmed, definite, hard, plain, veritable; existing, existent, manifest, substantial, factual, de facto, bona fide; *informal* honest-to-goodness, real live.
—OPPOSITES: notional.

actually *adv.* REALLY, in (actual) fact, in point of fact, as a matter of fact, in reality, in actuality, in truth, if truth be told, to tell the truth; literally; truly, indeed.

acute *adj.* **1** SEVERE, critical, drastic, dire, dreadful, terrible, awful, grave, bad, serious, desperate, dangerous. **2** SHARP, severe, stabbing, piercing, excruciating, agonizing, racking, keen, shooting, searing. **3** KEEN, sharp, good, penetrating, discerning, sensitive.
—OPPOSITES: mild, dull.

adapt *v.* **1** ☞ MODIFY. **2** ADJUST, acclimatize oneself, acclimate, accommodate oneself, habituate oneself, become habituated, get used, orient oneself, reconcile oneself, come to terms, get one's bearings, find one's feet, acculturate, assimilate, blend in, fit in.

add *v.* **1** ATTACH, build on, join, append, affix, connect, annex; include, incorporate, throw/toss in; admix. **2** ☞ TOTAL *v.* **3** AMOUNT TO, constitute; signify, signal, mean, indicate, denote, point to, be evidence of, be symptomatic of; *informal* spell.
—OPPOSITES: subtract.

addict *n.* **1** ABUSER, user; *informal* junkie, druggie, stoner, -head, -freak, pill-popper, dope fiend. **2** ☞ FAN.

addiction *n.* DEPENDENCY, dependence, habit, problem.

addition *n.* **1** ADDING, incorporation, inclusion, introduction. **2** SUPPLEMENT, adjunct, addendum, adhesion✤, appendage, add-on, extra, attachment; rider, appurtenance.
☐ **in addition** ☞ FURTHERMORE.

additional *adj.* EXTRA, added, supplementary, supplemental, further, auxiliary, ancillary; more, other, another, new, fresh; *informal* bonus.

address *n.* **1** HOUSE, flat, apartment, home; *formal* residence, dwelling, dwelling place, habitation, abode, domicile. **2** ☞ SPEECH 3.
▸ *v.* **1** TALK TO, give a talk to, speak to, make a speech to, give a lecture to, lecture, hold forth to; PREACH TO, give a sermon to; *informal* buttonhole, collar. **2** CALL, name, designate; speak to; *formal*

denominate. **3** DIRECT, send, forward, communicate, convey, route, remit.

adept *adj.* ☞ SKILFUL, EXCELLENT.
—OPPOSITES: inept.

adequate *adj.* **1** SUFFICIENT, enough, requisite. **2** ACCEPTABLE, passable, reasonable, satisfactory, tolerable, fair, decent, quite good, pretty good, goodish, moderate, unexceptional, unremarkable, undistinguished, ordinary, average, not bad, all right, middling; *informal* OK, so-so, {comme ci, comme ça}.

adhere *v.* **1** STICK (FAST), cohere, cling, bond, attach; be stuck, be fixed, be glued, be cemented. **2** ☞ OBEY 3.
—OPPOSITES: flout, ignore.

adherent *n.* FOLLOWER, supporter, upholder, defender, advocate, disciple, votary, devotee, partisan, member, friend, stalwart; believer, true believer, worshipper, sectary.
—OPPOSITES: opponent.

adjacent *adj.* ADJOINING, neighbouring, next-door, abutting, contiguous, proximate; (**adjacent to**) close to, near, next to, by, by the side of, bordering on, beside, alongside, attached to, touching, cheek by jowl with.

adjourn *v.* SUSPEND, break off, discontinue, interrupt, prorogue, stay, recess.

adjust *v.* **1** ☞ ADAPT 2. **2** MODIFY, alter, regulate, tune, fine-tune, calibrate, balance; adapt, arrange, rearrange, change, rejig, rework, revamp, remodel, reshape, convert, tailor, improve, enhance, customize; repair, fix, correct,

rectify, overhaul, put right; *informal* tweak.

administer *v.* **1** ☞ MANAGE 1. **2** DISPENSE, issue, give, provide, apply, allot, distribute, hand out, dole out, disburse.

admirable *adj.* COMMENDABLE, praiseworthy, laudable, estimable, meritorious, creditable, exemplary, honourable, worthy, decent, deserving, respectable, worthwhile, good, sterling, fine, masterly, great.
—OPPOSITES: deplorable.

admiration *n.* RESPECT, appreciation, (high) regard, esteem, veneration; commendation, acclaim, applause, praise, compliments, tributes, accolades, plaudits.
—OPPOSITES: scorn.

admire *v.* ESTEEM, approve of, respect, think highly of, rate highly, hold in high regard, have a high opinion of, look up to, regard highly, applaud, praise, commend, acclaim.
—OPPOSITES: despise.

admissible *adj.* VALID, allowable, allowed, permissible, permitted, acceptable, satisfactory, justifiable, defensible, appropriate, well-founded, tenable, sound; legitimate, lawful, legal, licit; *informal* OK, legit, kosher.

admission *n.* **1** ADMITTANCE, entry, entrance, right of entry, access, right of access, ingress; entree. **2** CONFESSION, acknowledgement, mea culpa, acceptance, concession, disclosure, divulgence.

admit v. **1** LET IN, allow entry, allow in, allow to enter, permit entry, take in, usher in, show in, receive, welcome, greet, open the door to. **2** ☞ CONFESS.
—OPPOSITES: exclude, deny.

admonish v. ☞ SCOLD.

adolescent n. ☞ TEENAGER.
▶ adj. TEENAGE, pubescent, young; juvenile; informal teen, tween-ager.
—OPPOSITES: adult, mature.

adopt v. **1** take as one's child, take in, take care of. **2** ESPOUSE, take on/up, embrace, assume; appropriate, arrogate. **3** ☞ SELECT v.
—OPPOSITES: abandon.

adorable adj. LOVABLE, appealing, charming, cute, cuddly, sweet, enchanting, bewitching, captivating, engaging, endearing, dear, darling, delightful, lovely, beautiful, attractive, gorgeous, winsome, winning, fetching; Scottish bonny.
—OPPOSITES: hateful.

adore v. LOVE DEARLY, love, be devoted to, dote on, hold dear, cherish, treasure, prize, think the world of; admire, hold in high regard, look up to, idolize, worship; informal put on a pedestal.
—OPPOSITES: hate.

adorn v. DECORATE, embellish, ornament, enhance; beautify, prettify, grace, bedeck, deck (out), dress (up), trim, swathe, wreathe, festoon, garland, array, emblazon, titivate.
—OPPOSITES: disfigure.

adrift adj. **1** DRIFTING, unmoored, unanchored. **2** LOST, off course; disoriented, confused, at sea; drifting, rootless, unsettled, directionless, aimless, purposeless, without purpose.

adult adj. **1** MATURE, grown-up, fully grown, full-grown, fully developed, of age, of full age. **2** ☞ INDECENT.

adulterate v. MAKE IMPURE, degrade, debase, spoil, taint, contaminate; doctor, tamper with, dilute, water down, weaken; bastardize, corrupt; informal cut, spike, lace, dope.
—OPPOSITES: purify.

advance v. **1** MOVE FORWARD, proceed, press on, push on, push forward, make progress, make headway, gain ground, approach, come closer, draw nearer, near. **2** BRING FORWARD, put forward, move forward. **3** ☞ PROMOTE 2. **4** PROGRESS, make progress, make headway, develop, evolve, make strides, move forward (in leaps and bounds), move ahead; improve, thrive, flourish, prosper.
—OPPOSITES: retreat, hinder, retract.
▶ n. **1** PROGRESS, forward movement; approach. **2** BREAKTHROUGH, development, step forward, step in the right direction, (quantum) leap; find, finding, discovery, invention.
☐ **in advance** BEFOREHAND, before, ahead of time, earlier, previously; in readiness.

advanced adj. STATE-OF-THE-ART, new, modern, developed, cutting-edge, leading-edge, up-to-date, up-to-the-minute, the newest, the latest; progressive, avant-garde, ahead of the times, pioneering, innovative, sophisticated, futuristic, groundbreaking,

innovatory, revolutionary, trail-
blazing.
—OPPOSITES: primitive.

advantage n. 1 BENEFIT, value,
good point, strong point, asset,
plus, bonus, boon, blessing,
virtue; attraction, beauty, profit.
2 UPPER HAND, edge, lead, whip
hand, trump card; superiority,
dominance, ascendancy,
supremacy, power, mastery;
informal inside track.
—OPPOSITES: disadvantage.

advantageous adj. 1 SUPERIOR,
dominant, powerful; good,
fortunate, lucky, favourable.
2 ☞ BENEFICIAL.
—OPPOSITES: disadvantageous,
detrimental.

adventure n. 1 EXCITEMENT,
thrill, stimulation; risk, danger,
hazard, peril, uncertainty,
precariousness. 2 EXPLOIT,
escapade, deed, feat, experience.

adventurous adj. 1 ☞ DARING.
2 RISKY, dangerous, perilous,
hazardous, precarious, uncertain;
exciting, thrilling.
—OPPOSITES: cautious.

adverse adj. 1 UNFAVOURABLE,
disadvantageous, inauspicious,
unpropitious, unfortunate,
unlucky, untimely, untoward.
2 ☞ HARMFUL.
—OPPOSITES: favourable,
beneficial.

adversity n. MISFORTUNE, ill luck,
bad luck, trouble, difficulty,
hardship, distress, disaster,
suffering, affliction, sorrow,
misery, tribulation, woe, pain,
trauma; mishap, misadventure,
accident, upset, reverse, setback,
crisis, catastrophe, tragedy,

calamity, trial, cross, burden,
blow; hard times, trials and
tribulations; informal ill wind.

advertise v. PUBLICIZE, make
public, make known, announce,
broadcast, proclaim, trumpet, call
attention to, bill, promulgate;
promote, market, beat/bang the
drum for, huckster; informal push,
plug, hype, boost; ballyhoo, flack.

advertisement n. AD,
announcement, notice,
commercial, infomercial,
promotion, endorsement, blurb,
write-up; poster, leaflet,
pamphlet, flyer, bill, handbill,
handout, fact sheet, circular,
bulletin, brochure, sign, placard,
junk mail; informal plug, puff,
bumph.

advice n. GUIDANCE, counselling,
counsel, help, direction;
information, recommendations,
guidelines, suggestions, hints,
tips, pointers, ideas, opinions,
views, input, words of wisdom.

advisable adj. JUDICIOUS,
desirable, preferable, well, best,
sensible, prudent, wise,
recommended, suggested;
expedient, politic, advantageous,
beneficial, profitable. See also
APPROPRIATE adj.

advise v. 1 COUNSEL, give
guidance, guide, offer suggestions,
give hints/tips/pointers.
2 ADVOCATE, recommend, suggest,
urge, encourage, enjoin. 3 ☞
TELL 1.

advocacy n. SUPPORT, backing,
promotion, championing;
recommendation, prescription.

advocate n. CHAMPION, upholder,
supporter, backer, defender,

promoter, proponent, exponent, spokesman, spokeswoman, spokesperson, campaigner, lobbyist, fighter, crusader; propagandist, apostle, apologist, booster.
—OPPOSITES: critic.
▶ v. RECOMMEND, prescribe, advise, urge; favour, espouse, endorse, uphold, subscribe to. See also CHAMPION v.

aesthetic adj. ARTISTIC, tasteful, in good taste; graceful, elegant, exquisite, beautiful, attractive, pleasing, lovely.

affable adj. PLEASANT, nice, likeable, personable, charming, jolly, courteous, civil, gracious. See also FRIENDLY 1.
—OPPOSITES: unfriendly.

affair n. **1** ☞ CONCERN n. 3. **2** EVENT, incident, happening, occurrence, eventuality, episode; case, matter, business. **3** RELATIONSHIP, love affair, affaire de coeur, romance, fling, flirtation, dalliance, liaison, involvement, entanglement, intrigue, amour; informal hanky-panky, attachment.

affect[1] v. **1** HAVE AN EFFECT ON, influence, act on, work on, have an impact on, impact; change, alter, modify, transform, form, shape, sway, bias. **2** MOVE, touch, make an impression on, hit (hard), tug at someone's heartstrings; UPSET, trouble, distress, disturb, agitate, shake (up).

affect[2] v. ASSUME, take on, adopt, embrace, espouse.

affected adj. PRETENTIOUS, artificial, contrived, unnatural, stagy, studied, mannered, ostentatious; insincere, unconvincing, feigned, false, fake, sham, simulated; informal la-di-da, phony, pretend, put on.
—OPPOSITES: natural, unpretentious, genuine.

affection n. FONDNESS, love, liking, tenderness, warmth, devotion, endearment, care, caring, attachment, friendship; warm feelings.

affectionate adj. ☞ LOVING.

affiliated adj. ASSOCIATED, allied, related, federated, confederated, amalgamated, unified, connected, linked; in league, in partnership.

affinity n. **1** EMPATHY, rapport, sympathy, accord, harmony, relationship, bond, fellow feeling, like-mindedness, closeness, understanding; liking, fondness; informal chemistry. **2** SIMILARITY, resemblance, likeness, kinship, relationship, association, link, analogy, similitude, correspondence.
—OPPOSITES: aversion, dislike, dissimilarity.

affirm v. DECLARE, state, assert, proclaim, pronounce, attest, swear, avow, guarantee, pledge; formal aver.
—OPPOSITES: deny.

affirmation n. DECLARATION, statement, assertion, proclamation, pronouncement, attestation, confirmation; oath, avowal, guarantee, pledge.
—OPPOSITES: denial.

affirmative adj. POSITIVE, assenting, consenting, corroborative, favourable.
—OPPOSITES: negative.

afflict v. TROUBLE, burden, distress, cause suffering to, beset, harass, worry, oppress; torment, pester, plague, blight, bedevil, rack, smite, curse.

affluent adj. ☞ RICH 1.
—OPPOSITES: poor, impoverished.

afford v. 1 PAY FOR, bear the expense of, have the money for, spare the price of. 2 PROVIDE, supply, furnish, offer, give, make available, yield.

afraid adj. 1 FRIGHTENED, scared, terrified, fearful, petrified, scared witless, scared to death, terror-stricken, terror-struck, frightened/scared out of one's wits, shaking in one's shoes, shaking like a leaf; intimidated, alarmed, panicky; faint-hearted, cowardly; informal scared stiff, in a cold sweat, spooked; chicken. 2 ☞ RELUCTANT.
—RELATED: -phobe.
—OPPOSITES: brave, confident.

aftermath n. REPERCUSSIONS, after-effects, consequences, effects, results, fruits; wake.

afterwards adv. ☞ LATER adv.

age n. 1 ELDERLINESS, old age, oldness, senescence, dotage, seniority, maturity; one's advancing/advanced/declining years; literary eld. 2 ERA, epoch, period, time, eon. 3 (informal) A LONG TIME, days/months/years on end, an eternity, an eon; informal ages and ages, donkey's years, a dog's age, a month of Sundays, forever.

aged adj. ☞ OLD 1.
—OPPOSITES: young.

agent n. 1 REPRESENTATIVE, emissary, envoy, go-between, proxy, negotiator, broker, spokesperson, spokesman, spokeswoman; informal rep. 2 ☞ SPY n.

aggravate v. 1 WORSEN, make worse, exacerbate, inflame, compound; add fuel to the fire/flames, add insult to injury, rub salt in the wound. 2 ☞ ANNOY.
—OPPOSITES: alleviate, improve.

aggressive adj. 1 VIOLENT, confrontational, antagonistic, truculent, belligerent, bellicose, warlike, pugnacious, macho, two-fisted; quarrelsome, argumentative. 2 ASSERTIVE, pushy, forceful, vigorous, energetic, dynamic; bold, audacious; informal in-your-face, feisty.
—OPPOSITES: peaceable, peaceful.

agile adj. NIMBLE, lithe, supple, spry, sprightly, limber, acrobatic, fleet-footed, light-footed, light on one's feet; literary fleet, lightsome.
—OPPOSITES: clumsy, stiff.

agitate v. 1 ☞ UPSET v. 1. 2 CAMPAIGN, strive, battle, fight, struggle, push, press.

agitator n. TROUBLEMAKER, rabble-rouser, agent provocateur, demagogue, incendiary; revolutionary, firebrand, rebel, insurgent, subversive; informal disturber.

agonizing adj. HARROWING, torturous, tormenting; informal hellish. See also EXCRUCIATING.

agony n. PAIN, hurt, suffering, torture, torment, anguish, affliction, trauma; pangs, throes.

agree v. 1 CONCUR, be of the same mind/opinion, see eye to eye, be in sympathy, be united. 2 CONSENT, assent, acquiesce, accept, approve, say yes, give

one's approval, give the nod; *formal* accede. **3** MATCH (UP), jibe, jive, accord, correspond, chime in, conform, coincide, fit, tally, be in harmony/agreement, harmonize, be consistent/equivalent; *informal* square.
—OPPOSITES: differ, contradict.

agreeable *adj.* **1** PLEASANT, pleasing, enjoyable, pleasurable, nice, to one's liking, appealing, charming, delightful. **2** ☞ LIKEABLE.
—OPPOSITES: unpleasant.

agreement *n.* **1** ACCORD, concurrence, consensus; assent, acceptance, consent, acquiescence, endorsement, buy-in. **2** ☞ TREATY. **3** CORRESPONDENCE, consistency, compatibility, accord; similarity, resemblance, likeness, similitude.
—OPPOSITES: discord.

agricultural *adj.* FARM, farming, agrarian; rural, rustic, pastoral, countryside; *literary* georgic, sylvan, Arcadian.
—OPPOSITES: urban.

agriculture *n.* FARMING, cultivation, tillage, tilling, husbandry, land/farm management, horticulture; agribusiness, agronomy.
—RELATED: agri-, agro-.

aid *n.* **1** ASSISTANCE, support, help, backing, co-operation; a helping hand. **2** RELIEF, charity, financial assistance, donations, contributions, subsidies, handouts, subvention, succour; *historical* alms.
—OPPOSITES: hindrance.
▶ *v.* **1** HELP, assist, abet, come to someone's aid, give assistance, lend a hand, be of service; avail, succour, sustain. **2** FACILITATE, promote, encourage, help, further, boost; speed up, hasten, accelerate, expedite.
—OPPOSITES: hinder.

ailing *adj.* ☞ ILL *adj.* 1.
—OPPOSITES: healthy.

ailment *n.* ☞ ILLNESS.

aim *v.* **1** POINT, direct, train, sight, line up; take aim. **2** WORK TOWARDS, be after, set one's sights on, try for, strive for, aspire to, endeavour to achieve; *formal* essay. **3** ☞ INTEND.
▶ *n.* OBJECTIVE, object, goal, end, target, design, desire, desired result, intention, intent, plan, purpose, object of the exercise; ambition, aspiration, wish, dream, hope, raison d'être.

aimless *adj.* PURPOSELESS, goalless, without purpose, haphazard, wandering, without goal, desultory.
—OPPOSITES: purposeful.

air *n.* **1** SKY, atmosphere; heavens, ether. **2** BREEZE, draft, wind; breath/blast of air, gust of wind. **3** EXPRESSION, appearance, look, impression, aspect, aura, mien, countenance, manner, bearing, tone. **4** AFFECTATIONS, pretension, pretentiousness, affectedness, posing, posturing, airs and graces.
—RELATED: aerial, aero-.
▶ *v.* **1** EXPRESS, voice, make public, ventilate, articulate, state, declare, give expression/voice to; have one's say. **2** ☞ BROADCAST 1.

airtight *adj.* **1** SEALED, hermetically sealed, closed/shut tight. **2** ☞ INDISPUTABLE.

airy *adj.* **1** WELL VENTILATED, fresh; spacious, uncluttered; light, bright. **2** NONCHALANT, casual, breezy, flippant, insouciant, heedless.
—OPPOSITES: stuffy.

aisle *n.* PASSAGE, passageway, gangway, walkway, corridor.

alacrity *n.* EAGERNESS, willingness, readiness; enthusiasm, ardour, avidity, fervour, keenness; promptness, haste, swiftness, dispatch, speed.

alarm *n.* **1** FEAR, anxiety, apprehension, trepidation, nervousness, unease, distress, agitation, consternation, disquiet, perturbation, fright, panic. **2** WARNING, alert, siren, alarm bell.
—OPPOSITES: calmness, composure.
▶ *v.* FRIGHTEN, scare, panic, shock; *informal* spook, scare the living daylights out of. See also UPSET *v.* 1.

album *n.* RECORD, CD, recording, disc; LP, vinyl.

alcohol *n.* LIQUOR, intoxicating liquor, strong/alcoholic drink, drink, spirits; *informal* booze, hooch, the hard stuff, firewater, rotgut, moonshine, moose milk✦, grog, tipple, the demon drink, the bottle, sauce, juice.

alcoholic *n.* DIPSOMANIAC, drunk, drunkard, heavy/hard/serious drinker, problem drinker, alcohol-abuser, person with a drinking problem; tippler, sot, inebriate; *informal* boozer, lush, rubby✦, alky, boozehound, dipso, juicer, soak, wino, barfly, sponge.

alert *adj.* **1** VIGILANT, watchful, attentive, observant, wide awake, circumspect; on the lookout, on one's guard/toes, on the qui vive; *informal* heads-up, keeping one's eyes open/peeled, bright-eyed and bushy-tailed. **2** QUICK-WITTED, sharp, bright, quick, keen, perceptive, wide awake, on one's toes; *informal* on the ball, quick on the uptake, all there, with it.
—OPPOSITES: inattentive.
▶ *v.* ☞ WARN 1.

alibi *n.* DEFENCE, justification, explanation, reason; *informal* story, line.

alien *adj.* UNFAMILIAR, unknown, strange, peculiar; exotic, foreign.
—OPPOSITES: native.
▶ *n.* **1** FOREIGNER, non-native, immigrant, (*Atlantic*) come from away✦, emigrant, émigré. **2** EXTRATERRESTRIAL, ET; Martian; *informal* little green man.

align *v.* **1** LINE UP, put in order, put in rows/columns, straighten, place, position, situate, set, range. **2** ☞ ALLY *v.*

alike *adj.* ☞ IDENTICAL.
—OPPOSITES: different.

alive *adj.* LIVING, live, breathing, animate, sentient; *informal* alive and kicking; *archaic* quick.
—OPPOSITES: dead.

allay *v.* REDUCE, diminish, decrease, lessen, assuage, alleviate, ease, relieve, soothe, soften, calm, take the edge off.
—OPPOSITES: increase, intensify.

allegation *n.* CLAIM, assertion, charge, accusation, declaration, statement, contention, deposition, argument, affirmation, attestation, grievance; *formal* averment.

allege v. CLAIM, assert, charge, accuse, declare, state, contend, argue, affirm, maintain, attest, testify, swear; *formal* aver.

allegiance n. ☞ LOYALTY.
—OPPOSITES: disloyalty.

allergic adj. **1** HYPERSENSITIVE, sensitive, sensitized.
2 ANAPHYLACTIC.

alleviate v. REDUCE, ease, relieve, take the edge off, deaden, dull, diminish, lessen, weaken, lighten, attenuate, mitigate, allay, assuage, palliate, damp, soothe, help, soften, temper.
—OPPOSITES: aggravate.

alliance n. ASSOCIATION, union, league, confederation, federation, coalition, consortium, affiliation, partnership.

allot v. ALLOCATE, assign, apportion, distribute, issue, grant; earmark for, designate for, set aside for; hand out, deal out, dish out, dole out, give out; *informal* divvy up.

allow v. **1** ☞ PERMIT. **2** ADMIT, acknowledge, recognize, agree, accept, concede, grant.
—OPPOSITES: prevent, forbid.

allowance n. **1** QUOTA, allocation, allotment, share, ration, grant, limit, portion, slice. **2** PAYMENT, pocket money, sum of money, contribution, grant, subsidy, stipend, maintenance, remittance, financial support, per diem.
☐ **make allowance(s) for 1** TAKE INTO CONSIDERATION, take into account, bear in mind.
2 ☞ EXCUSE v. 1.

alloy n. MIXTURE, mix, amalgam, fusion, meld, blend, compound, combination, composite, union; *technical* admixture.

allude v. REFER, touch on, suggest, hint, imply, mention (in passing), make an allusion to; *formal* advert.

allure n. ATTRACTION, lure, draw, pull, appeal, allurement, enticement, temptation, charm, seduction, fascination.

allusion n. REFERENCE, mention, suggestion, hint, intimation, comment, remark.

ally n. ASSOCIATE, colleague, friend, confederate, partner, supporter.
—OPPOSITES: enemy, opponent.
▸ v. UNITE, combine, join (up), join forces, band together, team up, collaborate, side, align oneself, form an alliance, throw in one's lot, make common cause.
—OPPOSITES: split.

almighty adj. **1** ALL-POWERFUL, omnipotent, supreme, pre-eminent. **2** ☞ HUGE.
—OPPOSITES: powerless, insignificant.

almost adv. NEARLY, (just) about, more or less, practically, virtually, all but, as good as, close to, near, not quite, roughly, not far from/off, for/to all intents and purposes; approaching, bordering on, verging on; *informal* pretty near/much/well; *literary* well-nigh, nigh on.
—RELATED: quasi-.

alone adj. & adv. **1** BY ONESELF, on one's own, all alone, solitary, single, singly, solo, solus; unescorted, partnerless, companionless, by one's lonesome. **2** ☞ LONELY 1.

aloud *adv.* AUDIBLY, out loud, for all to hear.
—OPPOSITES: silently.

also *adv.* ☞ FURTHERMORE.

alter *v.* CHANGE, make changes to, make different, make alterations to, adjust, make adjustments to, adapt, amend, modify, revise, revamp, rework, redo, refine, vary, transform; *informal* tweak; *technical* permute.
—OPPOSITES: preserve

alteration *n.* ☞ CHANGE *n.* 1.

alternate *v.* BE INTERSPERSED, occur in turn/rotation, rotate, follow one another; take turns, take it in turns, work/act in sequence; oscillate, fluctuate.

alternative *adj.* **1** DIFFERENT, other, another, second, possible, substitute, replacement, alternate; standby, emergency, reserve, backup, auxiliary, fallback.
2 ☞ UNCONVENTIONAL.
▸ *n.* OPTION, choice, other possibility; substitute, replacement.

alternatively *adv.* ON THE OTHER HAND, as an alternative, or; otherwise, instead, if not, then again, alternately.

although *conj.* IN SPITE OF THE FACT THAT, despite the fact that, notwithstanding (the fact) that, even though/if, for all that, while, whilst.

altogether *adv.* **1** ☞ COMPLETELY.
2 IN ALL, all told, in toto.
3 ☞ OVERALL *adv.*

always *adv.* **1** EVERY TIME, each time, at all times, all the time, without fail, consistently, invariably, regularly, habitually, unfailingly, religiously, steadily, without exception. **2** CONTINUALLY, continuously, constantly, forever, perpetually, incessantly, ceaselessly, unceasingly, endlessly, the entire time; round-the-clock, night and day, {morning, noon, and night}; *informal* 24-7. **3** ☞ FOREVER 1.
—OPPOSITES: never, seldom, sometimes.

amalgamate *v.* COMBINE, merge, unite, fuse, blend, meld; join (together), join forces, band (together), link (up), team up, go into partnership; *literary* commingle.
—OPPOSITES: separate.

amass *v.* GATHER, collect, assemble; accumulate, aggregate, stockpile, store (up), pile up, heap, cumulate, accrue, lay in/up, garner; *informal* stash (away).
—OPPOSITES: dissipate.

amateur *n.* NON-PROFESSIONAL, non-specialist, layman, layperson, greenhorn; dilettante.
—OPPOSITES: professional, expert.
▸ *adj.* NON-PROFESSIONAL, non-specialist, lay; dilettante; incompetent, unskilful, amateurish.

amaze *v.* ASTONISH, astound, surprise, stun, stagger, shock, stupefy, awe, stop someone in their tracks, leave open-mouthed, leave aghast, take someone's breath away, dumbfound, confound, daze, startle, take aback; *informal* bowl over, flabbergast, blow away; (**amazed**) thunderstruck, at a loss for words, speechless.

amazing *adj.* ASTONISHING, astounding, surprising, stunning, staggering, shocking, startling, stupefying, breathtaking; awesome, awe-inspiring, sensational, remarkable, spectacular, stupendous, phenomenal, extraordinary, incredible, unbelievable; *informal* mind-blowing, mind-boggling, jaw-dropping; *literary* wondrous.

ambassador *n.* ENVOY, plenipotentiary, emissary, (papal) nuncio, representative, high commissioner, consul (general), diplomat; legate.

ambiguous *adj.* EQUIVOCAL, ambivalent, open to debate/argument, arguable, debatable; obscure, unclear, imprecise, vague, abstruse, doubtful, dubious, uncertain.
—OPPOSITES: clear.

ambition *n.* **1** DRIVE, determination, enterprise, initiative, eagerness, motivation, resolve, enthusiasm, zeal, hunger, commitment, a sense of purpose; *informal* get-up-and-go. **2** ☞ GOAL.

ambitious *adj.* **1** ASPIRING, determined, forceful, pushy, enterprising, motivated, enthusiastic, energetic, zealous, committed, purposeful, power-hungry; *informal* go-ahead, go-getting. **2** DIFFICULT, exacting, demanding, formidable, challenging, hard, arduous, onerous, tough.
—OPPOSITES: laid-back.

ambivalent *adj.* EQUIVOCAL, uncertain, inconclusive, irresolute. See also INDECISIVE 2.
—OPPOSITES: unequivocal, certain.

ambush *v.* ATTACK BY SURPRISE, surprise, pounce on, fall upon, lay a trap for, lie in wait for, waylay, bushwhack; ambuscade.

amenable *adj.* CO-OPERATIVE, acquiescent, compliant, accommodating, obliging, biddable, manageable, controllable, governable, persuadable, tractable, responsive, pliant, malleable, complaisant, easily handled; *rare* persuasible.
—OPPOSITES: uncooperative.

amend *v.* REVISE, alter, change, modify, qualify, adapt, adjust; edit, copy-edit, rewrite, redraft, rephrase, reword, rework, revamp.

amenity *n.* FACILITY, service, convenience, resource, appliance, aid, comfort, benefit, feature, advantage.

amiable *adj.* ☞ FRIENDLY 1.
—OPPOSITES: unfriendly, disagreeable.

amnesty *n.* PARDON, pardoning, reprieve; grace; release, discharge.

amorous *adj.* ROMANTIC, lustful, sexual, erotic, amatory, ardent, passionate, impassioned; in love, enamoured, lovesick; lovey-dovey.

amorphous *adj.* SHAPELESS, formless, structureless, indeterminate; vague, nebulous, indefinite.

amount *n.* QUANTITY, number, total, aggregate, sum, quota, group, size, mass, weight, volume, bulk, lot, quantum.
☐ **amount to 1** ADD UP TO, come to, run to, be, make, total. **2** BECOME, grow/develop into, turn out/prove to be.

ample *adj.* **1** ENOUGH, sufficient, adequate, plenty of, more than

enough. **2** ☞ ABUNDANT.
—OPPOSITES: insufficient, meagre.

amputate *v.* CUT OFF, sever, remove (surgically), dismember, saw/chop off.

amuse *v.* **1** ENTERTAIN, make laugh, delight, divert, cheer (up), please, charm, tickle; *informal* tickle pink, crack up. **2** OCCUPY, engage, busy, employ, distract, absorb, engross, hold someone's attention, fascinate, enthrall; interest, entertain, delight, please, divert.
—OPPOSITES: bore.

amusement *n.* **1** MIRTH, merriment, lightheartedness, hilarity, glee, delight, gaiety, joviality, fun; enjoyment, pleasure, high spirits, cheerfulness. **2** ☞ ENTERTAINMENT 1.

amusing *adj.* ☞ FUNNY 1.
—OPPOSITES: boring, solemn.

analogous *adj.* COMPARABLE, parallel, similar, like, akin, corresponding, related, kindred, equivalent.
—OPPOSITES: unrelated.

analysis *n.* EVALUATION, interpretation. See also INVESTIGATION.

analytical, **analytic** *adj.* SYSTEMATIC, logical, scientific, methodical, (well) organized, ordered, orderly, meticulous, rigorous; diagnostic.
—OPPOSITES: unsystematic.

analyze *v.* EXAMINE, inspect, survey, study, scrutinize, look over; investigate, explore, probe, research, go over (with a fine-tooth comb), review, evaluate, break down, dissect, anatomize.

anarchy *n.* LAWLESSNESS, nihilism, mobocracy, revolution, insurrection, disorder, chaos, mayhem, tumult, turmoil.
—OPPOSITES: government, order.

ancestor *n.* **1** FOREBEAR, forefather, predecessor, antecedent, progenitor, primogenitor. **2** FORERUNNER, precursor.
—OPPOSITES: descendant, successor.

ancestry *n.* ANCESTORS, forebears, forefathers, progenitors, antecedents; family tree; lineage, parentage, genealogy, descent, roots, origins, stock, kinship, bloodline, blood, background, extraction, derivation, heredity, line, heritage, pedigree.

anchor *n.* **1** MAINSTAY, cornerstone, linchpin, bulwark, foundation. **2** ☞ ANNOUNCER.
▶ *v.* **1** MOOR, berth, be at anchor. **2** SECURE, fasten, attach, affix, fix.

ancient *adj.* **1** OF LONG AGO, early, prehistoric, primeval, primordial, primitive; *literary* of yore, foregone. **2** OLD, very old, age-old, archaic, time-worn, time-honoured, venerable. **3** OLD, aged, elderly, decrepit, in one's dotage. See also OLD-FASHIONED.
—RELATED: archaeo-, palaeo-.
—OPPOSITES: recent, contemporary.

ancillary *adj.* ADDITIONAL, auxiliary, supporting, helping, extra, supplementary, accessory.
—RELATED: para-.

angelic *adj.* **1** ☞ HEAVENLY 1. **2** INNOCENT, pure, virtuous, good,

saintly, wholesome; beautiful.
—OPPOSITES: demonic, infernal.

anger *n.* RAGE, vexation, exasperation, displeasure, crossness, irritation, irritability, indignation, pique; annoyance, fury, wrath, ire, outrage, irascibility, ill temper/humour, spleen; *informal* slow burn, aggravation; *literary* choler.
—RELATED: irascible.
—OPPOSITES: pleasure, good humour.
▶ *v.* INFURIATE, irritate, exasperate, irk, vex, peeve, madden, put out; enrage, incense, annoy, inflame, antagonize.
—OPPOSITES: pacify, placate.

angle *n.* **1** GRADIENT, slant, inclination. **2** PERSPECTIVE, point of view, viewpoint, standpoint, position, aspect, slant, direction.

angry *adj.* IRATE, mad, annoyed, cross, vexed, irritated, indignant, irked; furious, enraged, infuriated, in a temper, incensed, raging, fuming, seething, beside oneself, choleric, outraged, boiling, hopping mad, incandescent; livid, apoplectic, hot under the collar, up in arms, in high dudgeon, foaming at the mouth, doing a slow burn, steamed up, in a lather, fit to be tied, seeing red, shirty; sore, bent out of shape, ticked off, teed off, cheesed off, PO'd, on the warpath, ranting, raving; *literary* wrathful; *archaic* wroth.
—OPPOSITES: pleased, good-humoured.
☐ **get angry** LOSE ONE'S TEMPER, become enraged, fly into a rage, go berserk, flare up; *informal* go crazy, go bananas, hit the roof, go through the roof, go up the wall, see red, go off the deep end, fly off the handle, blow one's top, blow a fuse/gasket, flip out, have a (hissy) fit, foam at the mouth, explode, go ballistic, flip one's wig, blow one's stack, have a conniption, freak out, go ape, lose control.

angst *n.* ANXIETY, fear, apprehension, worry, foreboding, trepidation, malaise, disquiet, disquietude, unease, uneasiness.

anguish *n.* AGONY, pain, torment, torture, suffering, distress, angst, misery, sorrow, grief, heartache, desolation, despair; *literary* dolour.
—OPPOSITES: happiness.

angular *adj.* **1** SHARP-CORNERED, pointed, V-shaped, Y-shaped. **2** ☞ THIN 3.
—OPPOSITES: rounded, curving.

animate *v.* ☞ ENERGIZE.
—OPPOSITES: depress.
▶ *adj.* ☞ ALIVE.
—OPPOSITES: inanimate.

animated *adj.* ☞ LIVELY 1.
—OPPOSITES: lethargic, lifeless.

animosity *n.* ANTIPATHY, hostility, friction, antagonism, acrimony, enmity, animus, bitterness, rancour, resentment, dislike, ill feeling/will, bad blood, hatred, hate, loathing, abhorrence; malice, spite, spitefulness.
—OPPOSITES: goodwill, friendship.

annex *v.* TAKE OVER, take possession of, appropriate, seize, conquer, occupy.
▶ *n.* EXTENSION, addition; wing; ell.

annihilate *v.* ☞ DESTROY 3.
—OPPOSITES: create.

annotation *n.* NOTE, notation, comment, gloss, footnote; commentary, explanation, interpretation.

announce *v.* **1** MAKE PUBLIC, make known, report, declare, divulge, state, give out, notify, publicize, broadcast, publish, air, advertise, circulate, proclaim, blazon. **2** INTRODUCE, present, name.

announcement *n.* STATEMENT, report, declaration, proclamation, pronouncement; bulletin, communiqué, news flash.

announcer *n.* PRESENTER, anchorman, anchorwoman, anchor, anchorperson; news reader, newscaster, broadcaster; host, master of ceremonies, MC, emcee.

annoy *v.* IRRITATE, vex, make angry/cross, anger, exasperate, irk, gall, pique, put out, antagonize, get on someone's nerves, get to, ruffle someone's feathers, make someone's hackles rise, nettle, displease, upset; rub the wrong way, get under someone's skin, infuriate, madden, pester, provoke, rattle someone's cage, ride, try someone's patience; *informal* aggravate, peeve, hassle, miff, rile, needle, frost, bug, get someone's goat, get someone's back up, get in someone's hair, give someone the gears✲, drive mad/crazy/ bananas, drive around the bend, drive up the wall, tee off, tick off, hack off, piss off, cheese off, burn up, rankle, bother, grate on.
—OPPOSITES: please, gratify.

annoyed *adj.* IRRITATED, cross, angry, vexed, exasperated, irked, piqued, displeased, put out, disgruntled, chagrined, nettled, in a bad mood, in a temper, irate; *informal* aggravated, peeved, frosted, miffed, riled; teed off, ticked off, cheesed off, PO'd, hot under the collar, in a huff, shirty, sore, bent out of shape.

annoying *adj.* IRRITATING, infuriating, exasperating, maddening, trying, tiresome, troublesome, bothersome, nettlesome, obnoxious, irksome, vexing, cursed, vexatious, galling; *informal* aggravating, pesky.

annul *v.* DECLARE INVALID, declare null and void, nullify, invalidate, void, disallow; repeal, reverse, rescind, revoke; *Law* vacate; *formal* abrogate; recall.
—OPPOSITES: restore, enact.

anoint *v.* ☞ CONSECRATE.

anomalous *adj.* ☞ STRANGE 1.
—OPPOSITES: normal, typical.

anonymous *adj.* UNNAMED, of unknown name, nameless, incognito, unidentified, unknown, secret.
—OPPOSITES: known.

answer *n.* **1** REPLY, response, rejoinder, reaction; retort, riposte; *informal* comeback. **2** SOLUTION, remedy, key.
—OPPOSITES: question.
▶ *v.* **1** REPLY, respond, make a rejoinder, rejoin; retort, riposte, return. **2** MATCH, fit, correspond to, be similar to. **3** SATISFY, meet, fulfill, fill, measure up to.

answerable *adj.* ACCOUNTABLE, responsible, liable; subject.

antagonism *n.* OPPOSITION, dissension, rivalry. See also ANIMOSITY 1.

antagonize *v.* AROUSE HOSTILITY IN, alienate. See also ANNOY.

antediluvian *adj.* ☞ OLD-FASHIONED.

anthem *n.* HYMN, song, chorale, psalm, paean.

anthology *n.* COLLECTION, selection, compendium, compilation, treasury, miscellany, potpourri.

anticipate *v.* **1** EXPECT, foresee, predict, be prepared for, bargain on, reckon on; *informal* figure on. **2** LOOK FORWARD TO, await, lick one's lips over.

anticipation *n.* ☞ EXPECTATION 2.

anticlimax *n.* ☞ LETDOWN.

antics *pl. n.* CAPERS, pranks, larks, hijinks, frolicking, skylarking, foolery, tomfoolery.

antidote *n.* **1** ANTITOXIN, antiserum, antivenin. **2** REMEDY, cure, nostrum.

antipathy *n.* AVERSION. See also ANIMOSITY.
—OPPOSITES: liking, affinity.

antique *adj.* **1** OLD, antiquarian, collectable, old-fashioned. **2** ANCIENT, of long ago; *literary* of yore.
—OPPOSITES: modern, state-of-the-art.

antiquity *n.* ANCIENT TIMES, the ancient past, classical times, the distant past.

antiseptic *adj.* **1** DISINFECTANT, germicidal, bactericidal, antibacterial, antibiotic. **2** STERILE, aseptic, germ-free, uncontaminated, disinfected.
—OPPOSITES: contaminated.

anti-social *adj.* UNSOCIABLE, unfriendly, uncommunicative, reclusive, withdrawn; standoffish.

antithesis *n.* ☞ OPPOSITE *n.*

antsy *adj.* AGITATED, anxious, fidgety, jumpy, fretful, restless, stir-crazy, wired.

anxiety *n.* ☞ WORRY *n.* 1.
—OPPOSITES: serenity.

anxious *adj.* **1** WORRIED, concerned, apprehensive, fearful, afraid, scared, frightened, uneasy, perturbed, troubled, bothered, disturbed, distressed, upset, fretful, agitated, nervous, edgy, antsy, unquiet, on edge, tense, overwrought, worked up, keyed up, jumpy, worried sick, with one's stomach in knots, with one's heart in one's mouth; uptight, on tenterhooks, with butterflies in one's stomach, jittery, twitchy, in a stew/twitter/dither/lather/tizz/tizzy, het up; strung out, hag-ridden, having kittens; spooky, squirrelly. **2** EAGER, keen, desirous, impatient.
—OPPOSITES: carefree, unconcerned.

apathetic *adj.* UNINTERESTED, indifferent, unconcerned, unmoved, uninvolved, unemotional, emotionless, dispassionate, lukewarm, unmotivated, half-hearted; *informal* couldn't-care-less; *rare* Laodicean.

aperture *n.* ☞ OPENING 1.

apex *n.* **1** TIP, peak, summit, pinnacle, top, vertex. **2** ☞ PEAK *n.* 4.
—OPPOSITES: bottom, nadir.

apocryphal *adj.* FICTITIOUS, made-up, untrue, fabricated, false, spurious; unverified, unauthenticated, unsubstantiated; bogus.
—OPPOSITES: authentic.

apologetic *adj.* ☞ SORRY 3.
—OPPOSITES: unrepentant.

apology *n.* **1** EXPRESSION OF REGRET. **2** DEFENCE, explanation, justification, apologia.

apostle *n.* **1** DISCIPLE, follower. **2** MISSIONARY, evangelist, proselytizer.

appalling *adj.* SHOCKING, horrific, horrifying, horrible, terrible, awful, dreadful, ghastly, hideous, horrendous, frightful, atrocious, abominable, abhorrent, outrageous, gruesome, grisly, monstrous, heinous, egregious.

apparatus *n.* EQUIPMENT, gear, rig, tackle, gadgetry; appliance, instrument, machine, mechanism, device, contraption, gadget, gizmo, doohickey.

apparel *n.* ☞ CLOTHES.

apparent *adj.* **1** ☞ OBVIOUS. **2** ☞ OSTENSIBLE.
—OPPOSITES: unclear.

apparition *n.* GHOST, phantom, spectre, spirit, wraith; vision, hallucination; *informal* spook, chimera; *literary* phantasm, revenant, shade, visitant, eidolon.

appeal *v.* **1** ☞ IMPLORE. **2** ATTRACT, be attractive to, interest, take someone's fancy, fascinate, tempt, entice, allure, lure, draw.
▶ *n.* **1** PLEA, urgent/earnest request, entreaty, cry, call, petition, supplication, cri de coeur. **2** ATTRACTION, allure, charm;

fascination, magnetism, drawing power, pull.

appealing *adj.* ATTRACTIVE, engaging, alluring, enchanting, captivating, bewitching, fascinating, tempting, enticing, seductive, irresistible, winning, winsome, charming, desirable.
—OPPOSITES: disagreeable, off-putting.

appear *v.* **1** BECOME VISIBLE, come into view/sight, materialize, pop up. **2** ☞ ARRIVE 1. **3** SEEM, look, give the impression, come across as, strike someone as. **4** PERFORM, play, act.
—OPPOSITES: vanish.

appearance *n.* **1** LOOK(S), air, aspect, mien. **2** IMPRESSION, air, image, (outward) show; semblance, facade, veneer, front, pretense.

appease *v.* **1** CONCILIATE, placate, pacify, mollify, propitiate, reconcile, win over. **2** SATISFY, fulfill, gratify, indulge; assuage, relieve.
—OPPOSITES: provoke, inflame.

appendage *n.* **1** ADDITION, attachment, adjunct, addendum, appurtenance, accessory. **2** PROTUBERANCE, projection.

appendix *n.* SUPPLEMENT, addendum, postscript, codicil; coda, epilogue, afterword, tailpiece, back matter; attachment.

appetite *n.* **1** HUNGER, hungriness; taste, palate. **2** ☞ DESIRE 1.

appetizing *adj.* **1** MOUTH-WATERING, inviting, tempting; tasty, delicious, flavourful, toothsome, delectable, succulent;

informal scrumptious, yummy, delish, lip-smacking. **2** APPEALING, attractive, inviting, alluring.
—OPPOSITES: bland, unappealing.

applaud *v.* **1** CLAP, put one's hands together; show one's appreciation; *informal* give someone a big hand. **2** ☞ PRAISE *v.* 1.
—OPPOSITES: boo, criticize.

appliance *n.* DEVICE, machine, instrument, gadget, contraption, apparatus, utensil, implement, tool, mechanism, contrivance, labour-saving device; *informal* gizmo.

applicable *adj.* RELEVANT, appropriate, pertinent, appurtenant, apposite, germane, material, significant, related, connected; fitting, suitable, apt, befitting, to the point, useful, helpful.
—OPPOSITES: inappropriate, irrelevant.

applicant *n.* CANDIDATE, interviewee, competitor, contestant, contender, entrant; claimant, suppliant, supplicant, petitioner, postulant; prospective student/employee, job-seeker, job hunter.

apply *v.* **1** PUT IN AN APPLICATION, put in, try, bid, appeal, petition, sue, register, audition; request, seek, solicit, claim, ask, try to obtain. **2** BE RELEVANT, have relevance, have a bearing, appertain, pertain, relate, concern, affect, involve, cover, deal with, touch; be pertinent, be appropriate, be significant. **3** PUT ON, rub in, work in, spread, smear.

appoint *v.* **1** NOMINATE, name, designate, delegate, install as,

commission, engage, co-opt; select, choose, elect, vote in; *Military* detail. **2** ☞ DETERMINE 3.
—OPPOSITES: reject.

appointment *n.* **1** MEETING, engagement, interview, arrangement, consultation, session; date, rendezvous, assignation; commitment, fixture. **2** JOB, post, position, situation, employment, place, office; *dated* station.

appreciable *adj.* CONSIDERABLE, substantial, significant, sizeable, goodly, fair, reasonable, marked; perceptible, noticeable, visible, discernible; *informal* tidy.
—OPPOSITES: negligible.

appreciate *v.* **1** BE GRATEFUL, be thankful, be obliged, be indebted, be in your debt, be appreciative. **2** VALUE, treasure, admire, respect, hold in high regard, think highly of, think much of. **3** INCREASE, gain, grow, rise, go up, escalate, soar, rocket.
—OPPOSITES: disparage, depreciate, decrease.

appreciative *adj.* **1** ☞ GRATEFUL. **2** SUPPORTIVE, encouraging, sympathetic, responsive; enthusiastic, admiring, approving, complimentary.
—OPPOSITES: ungrateful, disparaging.

apprehensive *adj.* ☞ ANXIOUS 1.
—OPPOSITES: confident.

apprentice *n.* TRAINEE, probationer; pupil, student. See also BEGINNER.
—OPPOSITES: veteran.

apprise *v.* INFORM, tell, notify, advise, brief, make aware, enlighten, update, keep posted, keep up to date; *informal* tip off, clue in, fill in, put wise, bring up to speed.

approach *v.* **1** MOVE TOWARDS, come/go towards, advance towards, inch towards, go/come/draw/move nearer, go/come/draw/move closer, near; close in, gain on; reach, arrive at. **2** SPEAK TO, make a proposal, sound out, proposition. **3** ☞ UNDERTAKE.
—OPPOSITES: leave.
▶ *n.* METHOD, procedure, technique, modus operandi, MO, style, way, manner; strategy, tactic, system, means.

approachable *adj.* ☞ FRIENDLY 1.
—OPPOSITES: aloof.

appropriate *adj.* SUITABLE, proper, fitting, apt, right; relevant, pertinent, apposite; convenient, opportune; seemly, befitting, in keeping, well-suited.
—OPPOSITES: unsuitable.
▶ *v.* SEIZE, commandeer, expropriate, annex, arrogate, sequestrate, sequester, take over, hijack; steal, take; *informal* swipe, nab, (*Nfld*) buck✦, bag, pinch.

approval *n.* ACCEPTANCE, agreement, consent, assent, permission, leave; rubber stamp, sanction, endorsement, ratification, authorization, validation; support, backing, approbation, blessing, say-so; *informal* the go-ahead, the green light, the OK, the thumbs up, the nod.
—OPPOSITES: refusal.

approve *v.* **1** AGREE WITH, endorse, support, back, uphold, subscribe to, recommend, advocate, be in favour of, favour, think well of,

like, appreciate, go for, hold with, take kindly to; be pleased with, admire, applaud, praise. **2** ACCEPT, agree to, give one's blessing to, bless; support, back. See also AUTHORIZE.
—OPPOSITES: condemn, refuse.

approximate *adj.* ESTIMATED, rough, imprecise, inexact, indefinite, broad, loose; *informal* ballpark.
—OPPOSITES: precise.

approximately *adv.* ROUGHLY, (just) about, around, circa, more or less, in the neighbourhood of, in the region of, of the order of, something like, round about, give or take (a few); near to, close to, nearly, almost, approaching; pushing, in the ballpark of, practically, there or thereabouts.
—OPPOSITES: precisely.

apt *adj.* **1** SUITABLE, fitting, appropriate, befitting, relevant, germane, pertinent, applicable, apposite. **2** ☞ LIABLE 2.
—OPPOSITES: inappropriate, unlikely.

aptitude *n.* TALENT, gift, flair, bent, skill, knack, facility, ability, proficiency, capability, potential, capacity, faculty, genius, adeptness.

arbitrary *adj.* CAPRICIOUS, whimsical, random, chance, unpredictable; casual, wanton, unmotivated, motiveless, unreasoned, unsupported, irrational, illogical, groundless, unjustified; personal, discretionary, subjective.
—OPPOSITES: reasoned.

arbitration *n.* ADJUDICATION, judgment, arbitrament;

mediation, conciliation, settlement, intervention.

arbitrator n. ☞ MEDIATOR.

arc n. CURVE, arch, crescent, semicircle, half-moon; curvature, convexity.

arcane adj. MYSTERIOUS, secret; enigmatic, esoteric, cryptic, obscure, abstruse, recondite, recherché, impenetrable, opaque.

arch n. ARCHWAY, vault, span, dome.
▶ v. CURVE, arc.

archetype n. QUINTESSENCE, essence, representative, model, embodiment, prototype, stereotype; original, pattern, standard, paradigm.

ardent adj. ☞ FERVENT.
—OPPOSITES: apathetic.

ardour n. ☞ FERVOUR.

arduous adj. ONEROUS, taxing, difficult, hard, heavy, laborious, labour-intensive, burdensome, strenuous, vigorous, back-breaking; demanding, exacting, tough, challenging, formidable; exhausting, tiring, punishing, gruelling; uphill, steep; informal killing, murderous; toilsome.
—OPPOSITES: easy.

area n. **1** DISTRICT, region, zone, sector, quarter, precinct; locality, locale, neighbourhood, parish, patch; tract, belt; informal neck of the woods, turf. **2** FIELD, sphere, discipline, realm, domain, sector, province, territory, line.

arena n. **1** STADIUM; amphitheatre, coliseum; sportsplex; ground, field, ring, pitch, court; bowl, park; historical circus. See also RINK. **2** SCENE, sphere, realm, province,

domain, sector, forum, territory, world.

argue v. **1** ☞ ASSERT 1. **2** QUARREL, disagree, row, squabble, fall out, bicker, fight, wrangle, dispute, clash, feud, have words, cross swords, lock horns, be at each other's throats; informal spat, scrap. **3** DISPUTE, debate, discuss, controvert, deny, question.

argument n. QUARREL, disagreement, squabble, fight, dispute, wrangle, clash, altercation, feud, contretemps, disputation, falling-out, misunderstanding, difference of opinion; informal tiff, spat, scrap, row, bust-up, blow-up, rhubarb.

argumentative adj. QUARRELSOME, disputatious, captious, contrary, cantankerous, contentious; belligerent, bellicose, combative, antagonistic, truculent, pugnacious.

arid adj. DRY, dried up, bone-dry, waterless, moistureless, parched, scorched, baked, thirsty, droughty, desert; BARREN, infertile.
—OPPOSITES: wet, fertile.

arise v. **1** COME TO LIGHT, become apparent, appear, emerge, crop up, turn up, surface, spring up; occur; literary befall, come to pass. **2** ☞ RESULT V. 1.

aristocracy n. NOBILITY, peerage, gentry, gentility, upper class, ruling class, elite, high society, establishment, haut monde; informal upper crust, top drawer.
—OPPOSITES: working class.

aristocratic adj. **1** NOBLE, titled, upper-class, blue-blooded, high-born, well-born, elite; informal upper-crust, top-drawer. **2** REFINED,

polished, courtly, dignified, posh,
decorous, gracious, fine; haughty,
proud.
—OPPOSITES: working-class,
vulgar.

arm n. BRANCH, section,
department, division, wing,
sector, detachment, offshoot,
extension.
▸ v. EQUIP, provide, supply, furnish,
issue, outfit, fit out.

armaments pl. n. ARMS,
weapons, weaponry, firearms,
guns, ordnance, artillery,
munitions, matériel, hardware.

armistice n. ☞ TRUCE.

armour n. PROTECTIVE COVERING,
armour plate, shield; chain mail,
coat of mail, panoply; armoured
vehicles, tanks; carapace.

army n. ARMED FORCE, military
force, land force, military,
soldiery, infantry, militia; troops,
soldiers; archaic host.
—RELATED: military, martial.

aroma n. ☞ SCENT 1.

arouse v. 1 INDUCE, prompt,
trigger, stir up, bring out, kindle,
fire, spark off, provoke, engender,
cause, foster; literary enkindle.
2 EXCITE, stimulate, titillate; informal
turn on, get going, give a thrill to,
light someone's fire.
—OPPOSITES: allay, pacify, turn
off.

arrange v. 1 ORDER, set out, lay
out, array, position, dispose,
present, display, exhibit; group,
sort, organize, tidy. 2 ORGANIZE, fix
(up), plan, schedule, pencil in,
contrive, settle on, decide,
determine, agree.

arrangement n. 1 POSITIONING,
disposition, order, presentation,

display; grouping, organization,
alignment. 2 PREPARATION, plan,
provision; planning, groundwork.
3 AGREEMENT, deal, understanding,
bargain, settlement, pact, modus
vivendi.

array n. RANGE, collection,
selection, assortment, diversity,
variety; arrangement, assemblage,
lineup, formation; display,
exhibition, exposition.
▸ v. ARRANGE, assemble, group,
order, place, position, set out,
exhibit, lay out, dispose; display.

arrest v. 1 APPREHEND, take into
custody, take prisoner, imprison,
incarcerate, detain, jail, put in jail;
informal pick up, pull in, run in,
pinch, bust, nab, collar. 2 STOP,
halt, check, block, hinder, restrict,
limit, inhibit, impede, curb;
prevent, obstruct; literary stay.
—OPPOSITES: release, start.

arresting adj. STRIKING, eye-
catching, conspicuous, engaging,
engrossing, fascinating,
impressive, imposing, spectacular,
dramatic, breathtaking, dazzling,
stunning, awe-inspiring;
remarkable, outstanding,
distinctive.
—OPPOSITES: inconspicuous.

arrival n. 1 COMING, appearance,
entrance, entry, approach.
2 COMER, entrant, incomer; visitor,
caller, guest.
—OPPOSITES: departure, end.

arrive v. 1 COME, turn up, get
here/there, make it, appear, enter,
present oneself, come along,
materialize; informal show (up), roll
in/up, blow in, show one's face.
2 REACH, get to, come to, make,
make it to, gain, end up at; informal

wind up at. **3** REACH, achieve, attain, gain, accomplish; work out, draw up, put together, strike, settle on; *informal* clinch. **4** HAPPEN, occur, take place, come about; present itself, crop up; *literary* come to pass. **5** EMERGE, appear, surface, come on the scene, dawn, be born, come into being, arise.
—OPPOSITES: depart, leave.

arrogant *adj.* HAUGHTY, conceited, self-important, egotistic, full of oneself, superior; overbearing, pompous, bumptious, presumptuous, imperious, overweening; proud, immodest; *informal* high and mighty, too big for one's britches/boots, big-headed, puffed-up; *rare* hubristic.
—OPPOSITES: modest.

art *n.* **1** SKILL, craft, technique, knack, facility, ability, know-how. **2** CUNNING, artfulness, slyness, craftiness, guile; deceit, duplicity, artifice, wiles.

artful *adj.* **1** SLY, crafty, cunning, wily, scheming, devious, Machiavellian, sneaky, tricky, conniving, designing, calculating; canny, shrewd; deceitful, duplicitous, disingenuous, underhanded; *informal* foxy, shifty; *archaic* subtle. **2** SKILFUL, clever, adept, adroit, skilled, expert.
—OPPOSITES: ingenuous.

article *n.* **1** ITEM, thing, object, artifact, commodity, product. **2** REPORT, account, story, write-up, feature, editorial, item, piece, column, review, commentary. **3** CLAUSE, section, subsection, point, item, paragraph, division, subdivision, part, portion.
▶ *v.* (Cdn) Law APPRENTICE.

articulate *adj.* ELOQUENT, fluent, effective, persuasive, lucid, expressive, silver-tongued; intelligible, comprehensible, understandable.
—OPPOSITES: unintelligible.
▶ *v.* EXPRESS, voice, vocalize, put in words, communicate, state; air, ventilate, vent, pour out; utter, say, speak, enunciate, pronounce; *informal* come out with.

articulated *adj.* HINGED, jointed, segmented; *technical* articulate.

artifice *n.* TRICKERY, deceit, deception, duplicity, guile, cunning, artfulness, wiliness, craftiness, slyness, chicanery; fraud, fraudulence.

artificial *adj.* **1** SYNTHETIC, fake, imitation, mock, ersatz, faux, substitute, pseudo, simulated, replica, reproduction; man-made, manufactured, fabricated, inorganic; plastic; *informal* pretend, phony. **2** INSINCERE, feigned, false, unnatural, contrived, put-on, exaggerated, forced, laboured, strained, hollow; *informal* pretend, phony, bogus.
—OPPOSITES: natural, genuine.

artist *n.* **1** DESIGNER, creator, originator, producer; old master. **2** EXPERT, master, maestro, past master, virtuoso, genius; *informal* pro, ace.
—OPPOSITES: novice.

artistic *adj.* **1** CREATIVE, imaginative, inventive, expressive; sensitive, perceptive, discerning; *informal* artsy. **2** AESTHETIC, aesthetically pleasing, beautiful, attractive, fine; decorative, ornamental; tasteful, stylish, elegant, exquisite.

—OPPOSITES: unimaginative, inelegant.

artistry *n.* CREATIVE SKILL, creativity, art, skill, talent, genius, brilliance, flair, proficiency, virtuosity, finesse, style; craftsmanship, workmanship.

artless *adj.* NATURAL, ingenuous, naive, simple, innocent, childlike, guileless; candid, open, sincere, unaffected.

—OPPOSITES: scheming.

ascend *v.* CLIMB, go up/upwards, move up/upwards, rise (up), clamber (up); mount, scale, conquer; take to the air, take off; rocket.

—OPPOSITES: descend.

ascendancy *n.* ☞ SUPREMACY.

—OPPOSITES: subordination.

ascendant *adj.* RISING (IN POWER), on the rise, on the way up, up-and-coming, flourishing, prospering, burgeoning.

—OPPOSITES: declining.

ascent *n.* **1** CLIMB, scaling, conquest. **2** RISE, climb, launch, takeoff, liftoff, blast-off. **3** (UPWARD) SLOPE, incline, rise, upward gradient, inclination.

—OPPOSITES: descent, drop.

ascertain *v.* FIND OUT, discover, get to know, work out, make out, fathom, learn, deduce, divine, discern, diagnose, see, understand, comprehend; establish, determine, verify, check, confirm; figure out.

ascetic *adj.* AUSTERE, self-denying, abstinent, abstemious, self-disciplined, self-abnegating; simple, puritanical, monastic; reclusive, eremitic, hermitic; celibate, chaste.

—OPPOSITES: sybaritic.

▶ *n.* ABSTAINER, puritan, recluse, hermit, anchorite, solitary; fakir, Sufi, dervish, sadhu; *archaic* eremite.

—OPPOSITES: sybarite.

ascribe *v.* ATTRIBUTE, assign, put down, accredit, credit, chalk up, impute; blame on, lay at the door of; connect with, associate with.

ashamed *adj.* SORRY, shamefaced, abashed, sheepish, guilty, contrite, remorseful, repentant, penitent, regretful, rueful, apologetic; embarrassed, mortified.

—OPPOSITES: proud, pleased.

ashen *adj.* PALE, wan, pasty, grey, ashy, colourless, pallid, anemic, white, waxen, ghostly, bloodless.

asinine *adj.* STUPID, foolish, brainless, mindless, senseless, idiotic, imbecilic, ridiculous, ludicrous, absurd, nonsensical, fatuous, silly, inane, witless, empty-headed; *informal* halfwitted, dim-witted, dumb, moronic.

—OPPOSITES: intelligent, sensible.

ask *v.* **1** INQUIRE, query, want to know; question, interrogate, quiz. **2** PUT (FORWARD), pose, raise, submit. **3** REQUEST, demand; solicit, seek, crave, apply, petition, call, appeal, beg, sue. **4** INVITE, bid, summon, have someone over/round.

—OPPOSITES: answer.

asleep *adj.* **1** SLEEPING, in a deep sleep, napping, catnapping, dozing, drowsing; *informal* snoozing, catching some Z's, zonked, flaked out, hibernating, dead to the world, comatose, in the land of Nod, in the arms of Morpheus;

literary slumbering. **2** NUMB, with no feeling, numbed, benumbed, dead, insensible.
—OPPOSITES: awake.

aspect *n.* **1** FEATURE, facet, side, characteristic, particular, detail; angle, slant. **2** APPEARANCE, look, air, cast, mien, demeanour, expression; atmosphere, mood, quality, ambience, feeling.

aspersions *pl. n.*
▢ **cast aspersions on** VILIFY, disparage, denigrate, defame, run down, impugn, belittle, criticize, condemn, decry, denounce, pillory; malign, slander, libel, discredit; *informal* pull apart, throw mud at, knock, badmouth, dis.

aspiration *n.* ☞ GOAL.

aspire *v.* DESIRE, hope, dream, long, yearn, set one's heart on, wish, want, be desirous of; aim, seek, pursue, set one's sights on.

aspiring *adj.* WOULD-BE, aspirant, hopeful, budding; potential, prospective, future; ambitious, determined, upwardly mobile; *informal* wannabe.

assail *v.* **1** ATTACK, assault, pounce on, set upon/about, fall on, charge, rush, storm; *informal* lay into, tear into, pitch into. **2** PLAGUE, torment, rack, beset, dog, trouble, disturb, worry, bedevil, nag, vex. **3** CRITICIZE, censure, attack, condemn, pillory, revile; *informal* knock, slam.

assassin *n.* MURDERER, killer, gunman; executioner; *informal* hit man, hired gun; *dated* homicide.

assassinate *v.* MURDER, kill, slaughter; eliminate, execute; liquidate; *informal* hit, terminate, knock off; *literary* slay.

assault *v.* **1** ATTACK, hit, strike, punch, beat up, thump; pummel, pound, batter; *informal* clout, wallop, belt, clobber, hammer, bop, sock, deck, slug, plug, lay into, do over, rough up; *literary* smite. **2** ATTACK, assail, pounce on, set upon, strike, fall on, swoop on, rush, storm, besiege. **3** RAPE, sexually assault, molest, interfere with.
▸ *n.* **1** BATTERY, violence; sexual assault, rape. **2** ATTACK, strike, onslaught, offensive, charge, push, thrust, invasion, bombardment, sortie, incursion, raid, blitz, campaign.

assay *n.* EVALUATION, assessment, appraisal, analysis, examination, tests, inspection, scrutiny.
▸ *v.* EVALUATE, assess, appraise, analyze, examine, test, inspect, scrutinize, probe.

assemble *v.* **1** GATHER, collect, get together, congregate, convene, meet, muster, rally. **2** BRING/CALL TOGETHER, gather, collect, round up, marshal, muster, summon; *formal* convoke. **3** CONSTRUCT, build, fabricate, manufacture, erect, set up, put/piece together, connect, join.
—OPPOSITES: disperse, dismantle.

assembly *n.* **1** ☞ GATHERING. **2** CONSTRUCTION, manufacture, building, fabrication, erection.

assent *n.* ACQUIESCENCE, compliance, concurrence, the nod. See also APPROVAL.
—OPPOSITES: dissent, refusal.
▸ *v.* AGREE TO, accept, approve, consent to, acquiesce in, concur in, give one's blessing to, give the nod; sanction, endorse, confirm;

informal give the go-ahead, give the green light, give the OK, OK, give the thumbs up; *formal* accede to.
—OPPOSITES: refuse.

assert *v.* **1** DECLARE, maintain, contend, argue, state, claim, propound, proclaim, announce, pronounce, swear, insist, avow; *formal* aver, opine; *rare* asseverate. **2** INSIST ON, stand up for, uphold, defend, contend, establish, press/push for, stress.

assertive *adj.* CONFIDENT, self-confident, bold, decisive, assured, self-assured, self-possessed, forthright, firm, emphatic; authoritative, strong-willed, forceful, insistent, determined, commanding, pushy; *informal* feisty.
—OPPOSITES: timid.

assess *v.* **1** EVALUATE, judge, gauge, rate, estimate, appraise, consider, get the measure of, determine, analyze; *informal* size up; examine, review. **2** VALUE, calculate, work out, determine, fix, cost, price, estimate.

asset *n.* **1** BENEFIT, advantage, blessing, good point, strong point, selling point, strength, forte, virtue, recommendation, attraction, resource, boon, merit, bonus, plus, pro. **2** PROPERTY, resources, estate, holdings, possessions, effects, goods, valuables, belongings, chattels; capital, wealth, riches.
—OPPOSITES: liability.

assiduous *adj.* DILIGENT, careful, meticulous, thorough, sedulous, attentive, conscientious, punctilious, painstaking, rigorous, particular; persevering.

assign *v.* **1** ALLOCATE, allot, give, set; charge with, entrust with. **2** APPOINT, promote, delegate, commission, post, co-opt; select for, choose for, install in; *Military* detail. **3** EARMARK, designate, set aside, reserve, appropriate, allot, allocate, apportion. **4** ASCRIBE, attribute, put down, accredit, credit, chalk up, impute; pin on, lay at the door of.

assignment *n.* **1** TASK, piece of work, job, duty, chore, mission, errand, undertaking, exercise, business, endeavour, enterprise; project, homework. **2** ALLOCATION, allotment, issuance, designation; sharing out, apportionment, distribution, handing out, dispensation. **3** TRANSFER, making over, giving, handing down, consignment; *Law* conveyance, devise.

assimilate *v.* **1** ABSORB, take in, acquire, soak up, pick up, grasp, comprehend, understand, learn, master; digest, ingest. **2** SUBSUME, incorporate, integrate, absorb, engulf, acculturate; co-opt, adopt, embrace, admit. **3** INTEGRATE, blend in.

assist *v.* **1** HELP, aid, lend a (helping) hand to, oblige, accommodate, serve; collaborate with, work with; support, back (up), second; abet; *informal* pitch in with. **2** FACILITATE, aid, ease, expedite, spur, promote, boost, benefit, foster, encourage, stimulate, precipitate, accelerate, advance, further, forward.
—OPPOSITES: hinder, impede.

assistance *n.* HELP, aid, support, backing, reinforcement, succour,

relief, TLC, intervention, co-operation, collaboration; a (helping) hand, a good turn; *informal* a break, a leg up; social security, benefits, the dole, pogey✤.
—OPPOSITES: hindrance.

assistant *n.* HELPER, deputy, second-in-command, second, number two, right-hand man/woman, aide, attendant, mate, apprentice, junior, auxiliary, subordinate; hired hand, hired help, man/girl Friday; *informal* sidekick, gofer.

associate *v.* **1** LINK, connect, relate, identify, equate, bracket, set side by side. **2** MIX, keep company, mingle, socialize, go around, rub shoulders, rub elbows, fraternize, consort, have dealings; *informal* run around, hobnob, hang out/around.
3 AFFILIATE, align, connect, join, attach, team up, be in league, ally; merge, integrate, confederate.
▶ *n.* PARTNER, colleague, co-worker, workmate, comrade, ally, affiliate, confederate; connection, contact, acquaintance; collaborator; *informal* crony.

association *n.* **1** ALLIANCE, consortium, coalition, union, league, guild, syndicate, federation, confederation, confederacy, conglomerate, co-operative, partnership, affiliation, organization; club, society, congress. **2** RELATIONSHIP, relation, interrelation, connection, interconnection, link, bond, union, tie, attachment, interdependence, affiliation.

assorted *adj.* VARIOUS, miscellaneous, mixed, varied, heterogeneous, varying, diverse, eclectic, multifarious, sundry; *literary* divers.

assortment *n.* MIXTURE, variety, array, mixed bag, mix, miscellany, selection, medley, diversity, ragbag, hodgepodge, mishmash, potpourri, salmagundi, farrago, gallimaufry, omnium-gatherum.

assuage *v.* **1** RELIEVE, ease, alleviate, soothe, mitigate, allay, palliate, abate, suppress, subdue; moderate, lessen, diminish, reduce. **2** SATISFY, gratify, appease, fulfill, indulge, relieve, slake, sate, satiate, quench, check.
—OPPOSITES: aggravate, intensify.

assume *v.* **1** PRESUME, suppose, take it (as given), take for granted, take as read, conjecture, surmise, conclude, deduce, infer, reckon, reason, think, fancy, believe, understand, gather, figure.
2 AFFECT, adopt, impersonate, put on, simulate, feign, fake.
3 ACQUIRE, take on, come to have.
4 ACCEPT, shoulder, bear, undertake, take on/up, manage, handle, deal with.

assumption *n.* SUPPOSITION, presumption, belief, expectation, conjecture, speculation, surmise, guess, premise, hypothesis; conclusion, deduction, inference, illation, notion, impression.

assurance *n.* **1** SELF-CONFIDENCE, confidence, self-assurance, self-possession, nerve, poise, aplomb, level-headedness; calmness, composure, sang-froid, equanimity; *informal* cool, unflappability. **2** WORD (OF HONOUR), promise, pledge, vow, avowal, oath, bond, undertaking,

guarantee, commitment.
—OPPOSITES: self-doubt, uncertainty.

assure v. **1** REASSURE, convince, satisfy, persuade, guarantee, promise, tell; affirm, pledge, swear, vow. **2** ENSURE, secure, guarantee, seal, clinch, confirm; informal sew up.

assured adj. **1** CONFIDENT, self-confident, self-assured, self-possessed, poised, phlegmatic, level-headed; calm, composed, imperturbable, unruffled; informal unflappable, together. **2** GUARANTEED, certain, sure, secure, reliable, dependable, sound; infallible, unfailing; informal surefire.
—OPPOSITES: doubtful, uncertain.

astonish v. ☞ SURPRISE v. 1.

astonishing adj. ☞ AMAZING.

astound v. AMAZE, astonish, stagger, surprise, startle, stun, confound, dumbfound, boggle, stupefy, shock, daze, take aback, leave open-mouthed, leave aghast; informal flabbergast, blow away, bowl over, floor.

astray adv. **1** OFF TARGET, wide of the mark, awry, off course; amiss. **2** INTO WRONGDOING, into error, into sin, into iniquity, away from the straight and narrow.

astute adj. SHREWD, sharp, acute, adroit, quick, clever, crafty, intelligent, bright, smart, canny, intuitive, perceptive, insightful, incisive, sagacious, wise; informal on the ball, quick on the uptake, savvy; heads-up.
—OPPOSITES: stupid.

asylum n. **1** REFUGE, sanctuary, shelter, safety, protection, security, immunity; a safe haven. **2** PSYCHIATRIC HOSPITAL, mental hospital, mental institution; informal madhouse, loony bin, funny farm, nuthouse, bughouse; dated lunatic asylum; archaic bedlam.

asymmetrical adj. LOPSIDED, unsymmetrical, uneven, unbalanced, crooked, awry, askew, skew, misaligned; disproportionate, unequal, irregular; informal cockeyed, wonky.

atheist n. NON-BELIEVER, disbeliever, unbeliever, skeptic, doubter, doubting Thomas, agnostic; nihilist.
—OPPOSITES: believer.

athletic adj. MUSCULAR, muscly, sturdy, strapping, well-built, strong, powerful, robust, able-bodied, vigorous, hardy, lusty, hearty, brawny, burly, broad-shouldered, Herculean; FIT, in good shape, in trim; informal sporty, husky, hunky, beefy; literary thewy.
—OPPOSITES: puny.

athletics pl. n. SPORTS, sporting events, track and field events, track, games, races; contests; working out, exercising.

atmosphere n. **1** AIR, aerospace; sky; literary the heavens, the firmament, the blue, the azure, the ether. **2** AMBIENCE, air, mood, feel, feeling, character, tone, tenor, aura, quality, undercurrent, flavour; informal vibe.

atom n. **1** PARTICLE, molecule, bit, piece, fragment, fraction. **2** GRAIN, iota, jot, whit, mite, scrap, shred, ounce, scintilla, trace, smidgen, modicum.

atone v. MAKE AMENDS, make reparation, make restitution, make up for, compensate, pay, recompense, expiate, redress, make good, offset; do penance.

atrocious adj. **1** BRUTAL, barbaric, barbarous, savage, vicious, beastly; wicked, cruel, nasty, heinous, monstrous, vile, inhuman, black-hearted, fiendish, ghastly, horrible; abominable, outrageous, hateful, disgusting, despicable, contemptible, loathsome, odious, abhorrent, sickening, horrifying, unspeakable, execrable, egregious. **2** APPALLING, dreadful, terrible, very bad, unpleasant, miserable; informal abysmal, dire, rotten, lousy, godawful.
—OPPOSITES: admirable, superb.

atrocity n. ABOMINATION, cruelty, enormity, outrage, horror, monstrosity, obscenity, violation, crime, abuse; barbarity, barbarism, brutality, savagery, inhumanity, wickedness, evil, iniquity.

atrophy v. WASTE AWAY, become emaciated, wither, shrivel (up), shrink; decay, decline, weaken, deteriorate, degenerate.
—OPPOSITES: strengthen, flourish.

attach v. **1** FASTEN, fix, affix, join, connect, link, couple, hook (up), secure, make fast, tie, bind, chain; stick, adhere, glue, bond, fuse, pin, nail, screw, bolt, clamp, clip, hitch; add, append, unite, weld, yoke. **2** ASCRIBE, assign, attribute, accredit, impute. **3** ASSIGN, appoint, allocate, second; Military detail.
—OPPOSITES: detach, separate.

attached adj. **1** SPOKEN FOR, married, engaged, promised in marriage; going out, involved, seeing someone; informal hitched, spliced, shackled, going steady; dated betrothed; formal wed, wedded; literary affianced; archaic espoused. **2** FOND OF, devoted to; informal mad about, crazy about.
—OPPOSITES: single.

attack v. **1** ASSAULT, assail, set upon, beat up; batter, pummel, punch; informal do over, work over, rough up. **2** STRIKE, charge, pounce; bombard, shell, blitz, strafe, fire, besiege. **3** CRITICIZE, censure, condemn, pillory, savage, revile, vilify; informal knock, slam, blast, bash, lay into. **4** ADDRESS, attend to, deal with, confront, apply oneself to, get to work on, undertake, embark on; informal get cracking on.
—OPPOSITES: defend, praise, protect.
▶ n. **1** ASSAULT, onslaught, offensive, strike, blitz, raid, charge, rush, invasion, incursion. **2** FIT, seizure, spasm, convulsion, paroxysm, outburst, bout.
—OPPOSITES: defence, commendation.

attacker n. ASSAILANT, assaulter, aggressor; mugger, rapist, killer, murderer.

attain v. ACHIEVE, accomplish, reach, obtain, gain, procure, secure, get, hook, net, win, earn, acquire; realize, fulfill; informal clinch, bag, snag, wrap up.

attempt v. TRY, strive, aim, venture, endeavour, seek, undertake, make an effort; have a go at, try one's hand at; informal go

all out, bend over backwards, bust a gut, have a crack/shot/stab at, hazard; *formal* essay; *archaic* assay.
▶ *n.* EFFORT, endeavour, try, venture, trial; *informal* crack, go, bid, shot, stab; *formal* essay; *archaic* assay.

attend *v.* **1** BE PRESENT AT, sit in on, take part in; appear at, present oneself at, turn up at, visit, go to; *informal* show up at, show one's face at. **2** PAY ATTENTION, pay heed, be attentive, listen; concentrate, take note, bear in mind, take into consideration, heed, observe, mark. **3** CARE FOR, look after, minister to, see to; tend, treat, nurse, help, aid, assist, succour; *informal* doctor. **4** DEAL WITH, see to, manage, organize, sort out, handle, take care of, take charge of, take in hand, tackle. **5** ESCORT, accompany, chaperone, squire, guide, lead, conduct, usher, shepherd; assist, help, serve, wait on.
—OPPOSITES: miss, disregard, ignore, neglect.

attendant *n.* STEWARD, waiter, waitress, garçon, porter, servant, waitperson, stewardess; escort, companion, retainer, aide, lady in waiting, equerry, chaperone; manservant, valet, butler, maidservant, maid, footman; busboy, houseman; lackey; gas jockey.
▶ *adj.* ACCOMPANYING, associated, related, connected, concomitant, coincident; resultant, resulting, consequent.

attention *n.* **1** CONSIDERATION, contemplation, deliberation,

thought, study, observation, scrutiny, investigation, action. **2** AWARENESS, notice, observation, heed, regard, scrutiny, surveillance. **3** CARE, treatment, ministration, succour, relief, aid, help, assistance.

attentive *adj.* **1** PERCEPTIVE, observant, alert, acute, aware, heedful, vigilant; intent, focused, committed, studious, diligent, conscientious, earnest; wary, watchful; *informal* not missing a trick, on the ball. **2** CONSCIENTIOUS, considerate, thoughtful, kind, caring, solicitous, understanding, sympathetic, obliging, accommodating, courteous, gallant, chivalrous; dutiful, responsible.
—OPPOSITES: inconsiderate.

attire *n.* CLOTHING, clothes, garments, dress, wear, outfits, garb, costume; *informal* gear, duds, getup, threads; *formal* apparel; *archaic* raiment, habiliments.
▶ *v.* DRESS (UP), clothe, garb, robe, array, costume, swathe, deck (out), turn out, fit out, trick out; *archaic* apparel, invest, habit.

attitude *n.* **1** VIEW, viewpoint, outlook, perspective, stance, standpoint, position, inclination, temper, orientation, approach, reaction; opinion, ideas, convictions, feelings, thinking. **2** POSITION, posture, pose, stance, bearing.

attract *v.* **1** DRAW, pull, magnetize. **2** ENTICE, allure, lure, tempt, charm, win over, woo, engage, enthrall, enchant, entrance, captivate, beguile,

bewitch, seduce.
—OPPOSITES: repel.

attractive *adj.* **1** APPEALING, inviting, tempting, irresistible; agreeable, pleasing, interesting. **2** GOOD-LOOKING, beautiful, pretty, sweet, handsome, lovely, stunning, striking, arresting, gorgeous, prepossessing, fetching, captivating, bewitching, beguiling, engaging, charming, enchanting, enticing, appealing, delightful, winning, photogenic, telegenic; sexy, seductive, alluring, tantalizing, irresistible, ravishing, desirable; *informal* drop-dead gorgeous, cute, foxy, hot; *literary* beauteous; *archaic* comely, fair.
—OPPOSITES: uninviting, ugly.

attribute *v.* ASCRIBE, assign, accredit, credit, impute; put down, chalk up, hold responsible, blame, pin on; connect with, associate with.
▶ *n.* **1** QUALITY, characteristic, trait, feature, element, aspect, property, sign, hallmark, mark, distinction. **2** SYMBOL, mark, sign, hallmark, trademark.

attrition *n.* WEARING DOWN/AWAY, weakening, debilitation, enfeebling, sapping, attenuation; abrasion, friction, erosion, corrosion, grinding; deterioration; gradual loss.

attune *v.* ACCUSTOM, adjust, adapt, acclimatize, condition, accommodate, assimilate; acclimate.

audacious *adj.* **1** IMPUDENT, impertinent, insolent, presumptuous, cheeky, irreverent, discourteous, disrespectful, insubordinate, ill-mannered, unmannerly, rude, brazen, shameless, pert, defiant, cocky, bold (as brass); *informal* fresh, lippy, mouthy, saucy, sassy, nervy; *archaic* contumelious. **2** ☞ BRAVE *adj.*
—OPPOSITES: timid, polite.

audacity *n.* IMPUDENCE, impertinence, insolence, presumption, cheek, bad manners, effrontery, nerve, gall, defiance, temerity, boldness, brazenness, cockiness, chutzpah, sass.

audible *adj.* HEARABLE, perceptible, discernible, detectable, appreciable; clear, distinct, loud.
—OPPOSITES: faint.

audience *n.* **1** SPECTATORS, LISTENERS, viewers, onlookers, patrons; crowd, throng, congregation, turnout; house, gallery, stalls. **2** MARKET, PUBLIC, following, fans; listenership, viewership. **3** MEETING, consultation, conference, hearing, reception, interview; *informal* meet-and-greet.

audit *n.* INSPECTION, examination, verification, scrutiny, probe, investigation, assessment, appraisal, evaluation, review, analysis; *informal* going-over, once-over.
▶ *v.* INSPECT, examine, survey, go through, scrutinize, check, probe, vet, investigate, inquire into, assess, verify, appraise, evaluate, review, analyze, study; *informal* give something a/the once-over, give something a going-over.

auditorium *n.* THEATRE, hall, playhouse, assembly room;

chamber, room, arena, stadium, gymnasium.

augment v. INCREASE, add to, supplement, top up, build up, enlarge, expand, extend, raise, multiply, swell, grow; magnify, amplify, escalate; improve, boost; *informal* up, jack up, hike up, bump up.
—OPPOSITES: decrease.

augur v. BODE, portend, herald, be a sign, warn, forewarn, foreshadow, be an omen, presage, indicate, signify, signal, promise, threaten, spell, denote; predict, prophesy; *literary* betoken, foretoken, forebode.

augury n. OMEN, portent, sign, foretoken.

august adj. DISTINGUISHED, respected, eminent, venerable, hallowed, illustrious, prestigious, renowned, celebrated, honoured, acclaimed, esteemed, exalted; great, important, lofty, noble; imposing, impressive, awe-inspiring, stately, grand, dignified.

auspicious adj. FAVOURABLE, propitious, promising, rosy, good, encouraging; opportune, timely, lucky, fortunate, providential, felicitous, advantageous.

austere adj. **1** SEVERE, stern, strict, harsh, steely, flinty, dour, grim, cold, frosty, unemotional, unfriendly; formal, stiff, reserved, aloof, forbidding; grave, solemn, serious, unsmiling, unsympathetic, unforgiving; hard, unyielding, unbending, inflexible; *informal* hard-boiled. **2** ASCETIC, self-denying, self-disciplined, non-indulgent, frugal, Spartan, puritanical, abstemious,

abstinent, self-sacrificing, strict, temperate, sober, simple, restrained; celibate, chaste. **3** PLAIN, simple, basic, functional, modest, unadorned, unembellished, unfussy, restrained; stark, bleak, bare, clinical, Spartan, ascetic; *informal* no frills, bare-bones.
—OPPOSITES: genial, immoderate, ornate.

authentic adj. GENUINE, real, bona fide, true, veritable, simon-pure; legitimate, lawful, legal, valid; *informal* the real McCoy, the real thing, kosher.
—OPPOSITES: fake, unreliable.

authenticate v. **1** VERIFY, validate, prove, substantiate, corroborate, confirm, support, back up, attest to, give credence to. **2** VALIDATE, ratify, confirm, seal, sanction, endorse.

author n. **1** ☞ WRITER.
2 ORIGINATOR, creator, instigator, founder, father, architect, designer, deviser, producer; cause, agent.

authoritarian adj. AUTOCRATIC, dictatorial, despotic, tyrannical, draconian, oppressive, repressive, illiberal, undemocratic; disciplinarian, domineering, overbearing, high-handed, peremptory, imperious, strict, rigid, inflexible; *informal* bossy, iron-fisted.
—OPPOSITES: democratic, liberal.
▸ n. AUTOCRAT, despot, dictator, tyrant; disciplinarian, martinet.

authoritative adj. **1** RELIABLE, dependable, trustworthy, sound, authentic, valid, attested, verifiable; accurate. **2** DEFINITIVE,

most reliable, best; authorized, accredited, recognized, accepted, approved, standard, canonical.
3 ASSURED, confident, assertive; commanding, masterful, lordly; domineering, imperious, overbearing, authoritarian; *informal* bossy.
—OPPOSITES: unreliable, timid.

authority *n.* **1** POWER, jurisdiction, command, control, charge, dominance, rule, sovereignty, supremacy; influence; *informal* clout.
2 AUTHORIZATION, right, power, mandate, prerogative, licence, permission. **3** EXPERT, specialist, aficionado, pundit, guru, sage.

authorize *v.* SANCTION, permit, allow, approve, consent to, assent to; ratify, endorse, validate; *informal* give the green light, give the go-ahead, OK, give the thumbs up, give something the nod, pass, rubber-stamp.
—OPPOSITES: forbid.

authorized *adj.* APPROVED, recognized, sanctioned; accredited, licensed, certified; official, lawful, legal, legitimate.
—OPPOSITES: unofficial.

automatic *adj.* **1** MECHANIZED, mechanical, automated, computerized, electronic, robotic; self-activating. **2** INSTINCTIVE, involuntary, unconscious, reflex, knee-jerk, instinctual, subconscious; spontaneous, impulsive, unthinking; mechanical; *informal* gut.
3 INEVITABLE, unavoidable, inescapable, mandatory, compulsory; certain, definite,

undoubted, assured.
—OPPOSITES: manual, deliberate.

autonomous *adj.* SELF-GOVERNING, self-ruling, self-determining, independent, sovereign, free.

autonomy *n.* SELF-GOVERNMENT, self-rule, home rule, self-determination, independence, sovereignty, freedom.

auxiliary *adj.* **1** ADDITIONAL, supplementary, supplemental, extra, spare, reserve, backup, emergency, fallback, other.
2 ANCILLARY, assistant, support.

available *adj.* **1** OBTAINABLE, accessible, at/to hand, at one's disposal, handy, convenient; on sale, procurable; untaken, unengaged, unused; *informal* up for grabs, on tap, gettable. **2** FREE, unoccupied; present, in attendance; contactable; unattached, single.
—OPPOSITES: busy, engaged.

avant-garde *adj.* INNOVATIVE, original, experimental, left-field, inventive, ahead of the times, cutting/leading/bleeding edge, new, modern, innovatory, advanced, forward-looking, state-of-the-art, trendsetting, pioneering, progressive, bohemian, groundbreaking, trail-blazing, revolutionary; unfamiliar, unorthodox, unconventional; *informal* offbeat, way-out.
—OPPOSITES: conservative.

avarice *n.* GREED, acquisitiveness, cupidity, covetousness, greediness, rapacity, materialism, mercenariness; *informal* money-grubbing, affluenza.
—OPPOSITES: generosity.

avenue *n.* **1** ROAD, street, drive, parade, boulevard, broadway, thoroughfare. **2** LINE, path; method, approach.

average *n.* MEAN, median, mode; norm, standard, rule, par.
▸ *adj.* **1** MEAN, median, modal. **2** ORDINARY, standard, normal, typical, regular. **3** MEDIOCRE, second-rate, undistinguished, ordinary, middle-of-the-road, unexceptional, unexciting, unremarkable, unmemorable, indifferent, pedestrian, lacklustre, forgettable, amateurish; *informal* OK, so-so, {comme ci; comme ça}, fair-to-middling, no great shakes, underwhelming, plain-vanilla.
—OPPOSITES: outstanding, exceptional.

averse *adj.* OPPOSED, against, antipathetic, hostile, ill-disposed, resistant; disinclined, reluctant, unwilling, loath; *informal* anti.
—OPPOSITES: keen.

aversion *n.* DISLIKE, antipathy, distaste, abhorrence, hatred, odium, loathing, detestation, hostility; reluctance, unwillingness, disinclination.
—OPPOSITES: liking.

avert *v.* **1** TURN ASIDE, turn away. **2** PREVENT, avoid, stave off, ward off, forestall, preclude.

avid *adj.* KEEN, eager, enthusiastic, ardent, passionate, zealous; devoted, dedicated, wholehearted, earnest.
—OPPOSITES: apathetic.

avoid *v.* **1** KEEP/STAY AWAY FROM, steer clear of, give a wide berth to, fight shy of. **2** EVADE, dodge, sidestep, escape, run away from; *informal* duck, wriggle out of, get

out of, cop out of. **3** DODGE, duck, get out of the way of. **4** SHUN, stay away from, evade, keep one's distance, elude, hide from; ignore, give the cold shoulder. **5** REFRAIN FROM, abstain from, desist from, eschew.
—OPPOSITES: confront, face up to, seek out.

await *v.* **1** WAIT FOR, expect, anticipate. **2** BE IN STORE FOR, lie ahead of, lie in wait for, be waiting for.

awake *v.* **1** ☞ WAKE 1, 2.
2 ☞ AWAKEN 2. **3** REALIZE, become aware of, become conscious of; *informal* clue in to, get wise to.
▸ *adj.* **1** WAKEFUL, sleepless, restless, restive; *archaic* watchful. **2** VIGILANT, alert, watchful, attentive, on guard.
—OPPOSITES: asleep, oblivious.

awaken *v.* **1** ☞ WAKE 1. **2** AROUSE, rouse, bring out, engender, evoke, incite, trigger, provoke, stir up, stimulate, animate, quicken, kindle; revive; *literary* enkindle.

award *v.* GIVE, grant, accord, assign; confer on, bestow on, present to, endow with, decorate with.
▸ *n.* **1** PRIZE, trophy, medal, decoration; reward. **2** PAYMENT, settlement, compensation. **3** GRANT, scholarship, endowment; bursary.

aware *adj.* **1** CONSCIOUS OF, mindful of, informed about, acquainted with, familiar with, alive to, alert to; *informal* clued in to, wise to, in the know about, hip to; *formal* cognizant of; *archaic* ware of. **2** KNOWLEDGEABLE, enlightened, well-informed, au fait; *informal*

clued in, tuned in, plugged in.
—OPPOSITES: ignorant.

awareness *n.* CONSCIOUSNESS,
recognition, realization;
understanding, grasp,
appreciation, knowledge, insight;
familiarity; *formal* cognizance.

awe *n.* WONDER, wonderment;
admiration, reverence, respect,
esteem; dread, fear.

awesome *adj.* BREATHTAKING, awe-
inspiring, magnificent, wonderful,
amazing, stunning, staggering,
imposing, stirring, impressive;
formidable, fearsome, dreaded;
informal mind-boggling, mind-
blowing, jaw-dropping, excellent,
marvellous; *literary* wondrous; *archaic*
awful.
—OPPOSITES: unimpressive.

awful *adj.* **1** DISGUSTING, horrible,
terrible, dreadful, ghastly, nasty,
vile, foul, revolting, repulsive,
repugnant, odious, sickening,
nauseating; *informal* yucky, gross,
beastly. **2** TERRIBLE, atrocious,
dreadful, frightful, execrable,
abominable; inadequate, inferior,
substandard, lamentable; *informal*
crummy, pathetic, rotten, woeful,
lousy, appalling, abysmal, dire.
3 ILL, unwell, sick, peaky, queasy,
nauseous; poorly; *informal* rough,
lousy, rotten, terrible, dreadful.
4 REMORSEFUL, guilty, ashamed,
contrite, sorry, regretful,
repentant.
—OPPOSITES: wonderful.

awfully *adv.* **1** (*informal*) VERY,
extremely, really, immensely,
exceedingly, thoroughly,
dreadfully, exceptionally,
remarkably, extraordinarily;
informal terrifically, terribly,
seriously, majorly, real, mighty,
awful; *informal, dated* frightfully;
archaic exceeding. **2** VERY BADLY,
terribly, poorly, dreadfully,
atrociously, appallingly,
execrably; *informal* abysmally,
pitifully, diabolically.

awkward *adj.* **1** DIFFICULT, tricky;
cumbersome, unwieldy.
2 INCONVENIENT, inappropriate,
inopportune, unseasonable,
difficult. **3** EMBARRASSING,
uncomfortable, unpleasant,
delicate, tricky, problematic,
troublesome, thorny; humiliating,
compromising; *informal* sticky,
dicey, hairy. **4** UNCOMFORTABLE,
uneasy, tense, nervous, edgy,
unquiet; self-conscious,
embarrassed. **5** CLUMSY, ungainly,
uncoordinated, graceless,
inelegant, gauche, gawky,
wooden, stiff; unskilful,
maladroit, inept, blundering;
informal clodhopping, ham-fisted,
ham-handed, heavy-handed;
informal all thumbs.
—OPPOSITES: easy, convenient, at
ease, graceful.

axe *n.* HATCHET, cleaver,
tomahawk, adze, poleaxe,
broadaxe; *historical* battleaxe,
twibill.
▶ *v.* CANCEL, withdraw, drop, scrap,
discontinue, terminate, end;
informal ditch, dump, pull the plug
on.

Bb

babble *v.* **1** PRATTLE, rattle on, gabble, chatter, jabber, twitter, go on, run on, prate, ramble, burble, blather, blether, gab, yak, yap, yabber, yatter, yammer, blabber, jaw, gas, shoot one's mouth off; natter, waffle, run off at the mouth. **2** ☞ GURGLE.

baby *n.* **1** INFANT, newborn, child, tot, little one; *literary* babe, babe in arms, suckling; papoose; *technical* neonate. **2** SUCK, sissy, wimp, wuss, milquetoast, sook, (*Atlantic*) sooky baby✲; pantywaist.
—RELATED: infantile.
▶ *adj.* ☞ SMALL 1.
—OPPOSITES: large.
▶ *v.* ☞ PAMPER.

babyish *adj.* ☞ CHILDISH 1.
—OPPOSITES: mature.

back *n.* **1** SPINE, backbone, spinal column, vertebral column. **2** REAR, rear side, other side; *Nautical* stern. **3** REVERSE, other side, underside; verso; *informal* flip side.
—RELATED: dorsal, lumbar.
—OPPOSITES: front, head, face.
▶ *adv.* BACKWARDS, behind one, to one's rear, rearwards; away, off.
—OPPOSITES: forward.
▶ *v.* **1** ☞ FINANCE *v.* **2** SUPPORT, endorse, sanction, approve of, give one's blessing to, smile on, favour, advocate, promote, uphold, champion; vote for, ally oneself with, stand behind, stick

by, side with, be on the side of, defend, take up the cudgels for; second; *informal* throw one's weight behind. **3** REVERSE, draw back, step back, move backwards, back off, pull back, retreat, withdraw, give ground, backtrack, retrace one's steps, recede.
—OPPOSITES: oppose, advance.
☐ **back down** BACKTRACK, backpedal. See also SURRENDER 1.
back someone up SUPPORT, stand by, give one's support to, side with, be on someone's side, take someone's side, take someone's part; vouch for.

back-breaking *adj.* ☞ ARDUOUS.

backer *n.* **1** ☞ SUPPORTER 1. **2** SPONSOR, investor, underwriter, financier, patron, benefactor; *informal* angel.

background *n.* **1** BACKDROP, backcloth, surrounding(s), setting, scene. **2** SOCIAL CIRCUMSTANCES, family circumstances; environment, class, culture, tradition; upbringing.
—OPPOSITES: foreground.

backlash *n.* ADVERSE REACTION, adverse response, counterblast, comeback, repercussion; retaliation, reprisal.

backpack *n.* KNAPSACK, rucksack, packsack, pack, day pack, haversack; (*Nfld*) nunny bag✲, kit bag.

backslide v. RELAPSE, lapse, regress, weaken, lose one's resolve, give in to temptation, go astray, fall off the wagon.
—OPPOSITES: persevere.

backward adj. **1** RETROGRADE, retrogressive, regressive, for the worse, in the wrong direction, downhill, negative, reverse. **2** UNDERDEVELOPED, undeveloped; primitive, unsophisticated, benighted.
—OPPOSITES: forward, progressive, advanced.

bad adj. **1** SUBSTANDARD, poor, inferior, second-rate, second-class, unsatisfactory, inadequate, unacceptable, not up to scratch, not up to par, deficient, imperfect, defective, faulty, shoddy, amateurish, careless, negligent, miserable, sorry; incompetent, inept, inexpert, ineffectual; awful, atrocious, appalling, execrable, deplorable, terrible, abysmal, godawful; informal crummy, rotten, pathetic, useless, woeful, bum, lousy, not up to snuff, below par, crude, dismal, dreadful, lame, lamentable, low-grade, low-quality, rubbishy, third-rate, wretched, tinpot, bush-league, crappy, scuzzy, rinky-dink. **2** ☞ HARMFUL. **3** WICKED, evil, sinful, immoral, morally wrong, corrupt, base, black-hearted, reprobate, amoral; criminal, villainous, nefarious, iniquitous, dishonest, dishonourable, unscrupulous, unprincipled; informal crooked, bent, dirty; dated dastardly. **4** ☞ NAUGHTY 1. **5** UNPLEASANT, disagreeable, unwelcome; unfortunate, unlucky, unfavourable; terrible, dreadful, awful, grim, distressing. **6** INAUSPICIOUS, unfavourable, inopportune, unpropitious, unfortunate, disadvantageous, adverse, inappropriate, unsuitable, untoward. **7** ☞ ACUTE 1. **8** ROTTEN, off, decayed, decomposed, decomposing, putrid, putrefied, mouldy, mouldering; sour, spoiled, rancid, rank. **9** GUILTY, conscience-stricken, remorseful, guilt-ridden, ashamed, contrite, sorry, full of regret, regretful, shamefaced.
—OPPOSITES: good, beneficial, virtuous, well-behaved, minor, slight, fresh, unrepentant.

badge n. **1** pin, brooch, button, emblem, crest. **2** SIGN, symbol, indication, signal, mark; hallmark, trademark.

badger v. ☞ PESTER.

bad-tempered adj. ☞ IRRITABLE.

baffle v. ☞ PERPLEX.
—OPPOSITES: enlighten.

bag n. **1** HANDBAG, purse, shoulder bag, clutch bag; sack, pouch; historical reticule. **2** SUITCASE, case, valise, portmanteau, grip, overnighter; duffel bag; satchel. See also BACKPACK.
▶ v. **1** CATCH, land, capture, trap, snare, ensnare; kill, shoot. **2** GET, secure, obtain, acquire, pick up; win, achieve, attain; informal get one's hands on, land, net.

baggage n. LUGGAGE, suitcases, cases, bags.

bait n. ENTICEMENT, lure, decoy, snare, trap, siren, carrot, attraction, draw, magnet, incentive, temptation, inducement; informal come-on.

▶ *v.* TAUNT, tease, goad, pick on, torment, persecute, plague, harry, bother, harass, hound; *informal* needle.

balance *n.* **1** STABILITY, equilibrium, steadiness, footing. **2** COUNTERBALANCE, counterweight, stabilizer, compensation. **3** SCALE(S), weighing machine. **4** REMAINDER, outstanding amount, rest, residue, difference, remaining part.
—OPPOSITES: instability.
▶ *v.* **1** STEADY, stabilize, poise, level. **2** COUNTERBALANCE, balance out, offset, even out/up, counteract, compensate for, make up for. **3** WEIGH, weigh up, compare, evaluate, consider, assess, appraise, judge.

bald *adj.* **1** HAIRLESS, smooth, shaven, depilated; baldheaded; *informal* chrome-domed. **2** PLAIN, simple, unadorned; honest, truthful, realistic, frank, outspoken. See also BLUNT *adj.* 2.
—OPPOSITES: hairy, vague.

ball *n.* **1** SPHERE, globe, orb, globule, spherule, spheroid, ovoid. **2** DANCE, dinner dance, formal, grad✦, prom, masquerade; hoedown, barn dance. **3** GOOD TIME, blast, riot.

ballot *n.* VOTE, poll, election, referendum, plebiscite, show of hands.

ban *v.* **1** PROHIBIT, forbid, veto, proscribe, disallow, outlaw, make illegal, embargo, bar, debar, block, stop, suppress, interdict; *Law* enjoin, restrain. **2** EXCLUDE, banish, expel, eject, evict, drive out, force out, oust, remove, get rid of; *informal* boot out, kick out, turf out.

—OPPOSITES: permit, admit.
▶ *n.* PROHIBITION, veto, proscription, embargo, bar, suppression, stoppage, interdict, interdiction, moratorium, injunction.
—OPPOSITES: permission, admission.

banal *adj.* TRITE, hackneyed, clichéd, platitudinous, vapid, commonplace, ordinary, common, stock, conventional, stereotyped, overused, overdone, overworked, stale, worn out, time-worn, tired, threadbare, hoary, hack, unimaginative, humdrum, ho-hum, unoriginal, uninteresting, dull, trivial; *informal* old hat, corny, cornball, played out.
—OPPOSITES: original.

band *n.* **1** BELT, sash, girdle, strap, tape, ring, hoop, loop, circlet, circle, cord, tie, string, thong, ribbon, fillet, strip; *literary* cincture. **2** STRIPE, strip, streak, line, bar, belt, swathe; *technical* stria, striation. **3** GROUP, gang, mob, pack, body; society, partnership, order, affiliation, institution, federation, clique, set, coterie; *informal* bunch. See also TEAM *n.*, SOCIETY 4. **4** (MUSICAL) GROUP, pop group, ensemble, orchestra; *informal* combo.

bandit *n.* OUTLAW, gunman, gangster, freebooter, hijacker, marauder; *historical* highwayman, footpad. See also THIEF.

bandy¹ *adj.* BOWED, curved, bent; bowlegged, bandy-legged.
—OPPOSITES: straight.

bandy² *v.* SPREAD (ABOUT/AROUND), put about, toss about, discuss, rumour, mention, repeat; *literary* bruit about/abroad.

bang *n.* **1** THUD, thump, bump, crack, crash, smack, boom, clang, clap, knock, tap, clunk, clonk; stamp, stomp, clump, clomp, blam, bam, kaboom, kapow, wham, whump, whomp; report, explosion, detonation. **2** ☞ BUMP *n.* 1.
▶ *v.* ☞ HIT *v.* 1.
▶ *adv.* (*informal*) PRECISELY, exactly, right, directly, immediately, squarely, dead; promptly, prompt, dead on, sharp, on the dot; *informal* smack, slap, smack dab, plumb, on the button, on the nose, spang.

banish *v.* **1** EXILE, deport, expatriate, ostracize, extradite, repatriate, transport; exclude, shut out, ban. See also EVICT. **2** DISPEL, dismiss, disperse, scatter, dissipate, drive away, chase away, shut out, quell, allay.
—OPPOSITES: admit, engender.

bank¹ *n.* **1** EDGE, side, shore, coast, embankment, bankside, levee, border, verge, boundary, margin, rim, fringe; *literary* marge, skirt. **2** SLOPE, rise, incline, gradient, ramp; mound, ridge, hillock, hummock, knoll; bar, reef, shoal, shelf; accumulation, pile, heap, mass, drift. **3** ARRAY, row, line, tier, group, series.
—RELATED: riparian.

bank² *n.* STORE, reserve, accumulation, stock, stockpile, supply, pool, fund, cache, hoard, deposit; storehouse, reservoir, repository, depository.
▶ *v.* DEPOSIT, pay in, invest, lay away.

bankrupt *adj.* **1** INSOLVENT, failed, ruined, in debt, owing money, in the red, in arrears, in receivership; *informal* bust, belly up, broke, cash-strapped, flat broke. **2** BEREFT, devoid, empty, destitute; completely lacking, without, in need of, wanting.
—OPPOSITES: solvent, teeming with.
□ **go bankrupt** FAIL, collapse, fold, go under, founder; go into receivership, go into liquidation, be wound up; *informal* crash, go broke, go bust, go belly up, flop, bomb.

banner *n.* FLAG, standard, ensign, colour(s), pennant, banderole, guidon; *Nautical* burgee.

banquet *n.* ☞ FEAST *n.* 1.
—OPPOSITES: snack.

banter *n.* REPARTEE, witty conversation, raillery, wordplay, cut and thrust, kidding, ribbing, badinage, joshing.

bar *n.* **1** ROD, pole, stick, batten, shaft, rail, paling, spar, strut, crosspiece, beam. **2** BLOCK, slab, cake, tablet, brick, loaf, wedge, ingot. **3** TAVERN, booze can✲, watering hole, pub, cocktail lounge, barroom, beer parlour✲, beverage room✲, taproom, (*Que.*) brasserie✲, gin mill, after-hours club, lounge, parlour✲, nightclub, brew pub, speakeasy, blind pig, barrelhouse, roadhouse, beer cellar, boîte, club, dive, hotel, inn, nineteenth hole, rathskeller, estaminet, cantina, bodega; public house, legion (hall), hostelry, wine bar; *historical* saloon, alehouse. **4** ☞ OBSTACLE.
—OPPOSITES: aid.
▶ *v.* **1** BOLT, lock, fasten, secure, block, barricade, obstruct. **2** PROHIBIT, debar, preclude, forbid,

ban, interdict, inhibit; exclude, keep out; obstruct, hinder, block; *Law* enjoin.
—OPPOSITES: open, admit.

barbarian *n.* SAVAGE, heathen, brute, beast, wild man/woman; ruffian, thug, lout, vandal, boor, hoodlum, hooligan, low-life, Neanderthal, knuckle-dragger, troglodyte; philistine; *informal* roughneck.

barbaric *adj.* ☞ BRUTAL 1.
—OPPOSITES: civilized.

bare *adj.* **1** ☞ NAKED. **2** EMPTY, unfurnished, cleared; stark, austere, Spartan, unadorned, unembellished, unornamented, plain. **3** BASIC, essential, fundamental, plain, straightforward, simple, pure, stark, bald, cold, hard, brutal, harsh.
—OPPOSITES: clothed, furnished.

barely *adv.* HARDLY, scarcely, just, only just, narrowly, by the skin of one's teeth, by a hair's breadth, by a whisker.
—OPPOSITES: easily.

bargain *n.* **1** GOOD BUY; *informal* steal, bargoon✦, deal, giveaway, best buy. **2** ☞ DEAL *n.*
—OPPOSITES: rip-off.

▶ *v.* HAGGLE, negotiate, discuss terms, hold talks, deal, barter, dicker; *formal* treat.

□ **bargain for/on** EXPECT, anticipate, be prepared for, allow for, plan for, reckon with, take into account/consideration, contemplate, imagine, envisage, foresee, predict; count on, rely on, depend on, bank on, plan on, reckon on, figure on.

barrage *n.* **1** BOMBARDMENT, cannonade; gunfire, shelling; salvo, volley, fusillade; *historical* broadside. **2** DELUGE, stream, storm, torrent, onslaught, flood, shower, spate, tide, avalanche, hail, blaze; abundance, mass, profusion.

barrel *n.* CASK, keg, butt, vat, tun, drum, hogshead, kilderkin, barrique, pipe; *historical* firkin.
—RELATED: cooper, stave, hoop.

barren *adj.* **1** UNPRODUCTIVE, infertile, unfruitful, sterile, arid, desert; childless. **2** ☞ FUTILE.
—OPPOSITES: fertile.

barricade *n.* ☞ BARRIER.

▶ *v.* SEAL (UP), close up, block off, shut off/up; defend, protect, fortify, occupy.

barrier *n.* FENCE, railing, barricade, hurdle, bar, blockade, roadblock; obstacle, obstruction, stumbling block, block, impediment, hindrance, curb.

barter *v.* TRADE, swap, exchange, sell. See also BARGAIN *v.*

base *n.* **1** FOUNDATION, bottom, foot, support, stand, pedestal, plinth. **2** BASIS, foundation, bedrock, starting point, source, origin, root(s), core, key component, heart, backbone. **3** HEADQUARTERS, camp, site, station, settlement, post, centre, starting point.
—OPPOSITES: top.

▶ *v.* **1** FOUND, build, construct, form, ground, root. **2** ☞ LOCATE 2.

▶ *adj.* SORDID, low-minded, immoral, improper, unseemly, unscrupulous, unprincipled, wrong, evil. See also DISGRACEFUL.

bashful *adj.* ☞ SHY.

basic *adj.* **1** ☞ FUNDAMENTAL.
2 PLAIN, simple, unsophisticated, straightforward, adequate; unadorned, austere, rudimentary, minimal; crude, makeshift.
—OPPOSITES: secondary, elaborate.

basin *n.* BOWL, dish, pan; sink, washtub.

basis *n.* **1** FOUNDATION, support, base; reasoning, rationale, defence; reason, cause, grounds, argument, justification, motivation. **2** STARTING POINT, base, point of departure, beginning, premise, fundamental point/principle, principal constituent, main ingredient, cornerstone, core, heart, thrust, essence, kernel, nub.

bask *v.* **1** ☞ LOUNGE *v.* **2** REVEL, delight, luxuriate, wallow, take pleasure, rejoice, glory; enjoy, relish, savour, lap up.

bastard *n.* **1** (*archaic*) ILLEGITIMATE CHILD, child born out of wedlock, love child; *dated* by-blow; *archaic* natural child/son/daughter.
2 (*informal*) ☞ JERK *n.* 3.

batch *n.* GROUP, quantity, lot, bunch, mass, cluster, raft, set, collection, bundle, pack; consignment, shipment.

bathe *v.* **1** HAVE/TAKE A BATH, wash; shower. **2** SUFFUSE, permeate, pervade, envelop, flood, cover, wash, fill.

bathos *n.* ANTICLIMAX, letdown, disappointment, disillusionment; absurdity, comedown.

bathroom *n.* WASHROOM, toilet, powder room, urinal, stall, privy, lavatory, latrine, throne room, restroom, men's/women's/ladies' room, WC, water closet, facilities, can, john, biffy, commode, comfort station, porta-potty, outhouse, honey bucket; little girls'/boys' room, loo; *Nautical* head.

baton *n.* **1** STICK, rod, staff, wand.
2 ☞ CUDGEL.

batter *v.* ☞ BEAT *v.* 1.

battle *n.* **1** FIGHT, armed conflict, clash, struggle, skirmish, engagement, fray, duel; war, campaign, crusade; fighting, warfare, combat, action, hostilities; *informal* scrap, dogfight, shootout; brawl. **2** CONFLICT, contest, competition, struggle, turf war, tug-of-war. See also ARGUMENT.
▶ *v.* FIGHT, combat, contend with; resist, withstand, stand up to, confront; war, feud; struggle, strive, work.

bawdy *adj.* RIBALD, indecent, risqué, racy, rude, spicy, sexy, suggestive, titillating, naughty, improper, indelicate, indecorous, off-colour, earthy, barnyard, broad, locker-room, Rabelaisian; pornographic, obscene, vulgar, crude, coarse, lewd, dirty, filthy, smutty, unseemly, salacious, prurient, lascivious, licentious, X-rated, blue, raunchy, nudge-nudge (wink-wink); *euphemistic* adult.
—OPPOSITES: clean, innocent.

bawl *v.* **1** ☞ YELL. **2** ☞ CRY *v.* 1.
—OPPOSITES: whisper.

bay¹ *n.* COVE, inlet, indentation, gulf, bight, basin, fjord, arm; anchorage.

bay² *n.* ALCOVE, recess, niche, nook, oriel, opening, hollow, cavity, inglenook; compartment.

bay³ *v.* ☞ HOWL *v.* 1.
☐ **at bay** AT A DISTANCE, away, off, at arm's length.

bazaar *n.* **1** MARKET, marketplace, souk, mart, exchange. **2** RUMMAGE SALE, fair, carnival, garage sale, yard sale; fundraiser, charity event; flea market, swap meet.

be *v.* **1** EXIST, have being, have existence; live, be alive, have life, breathe, draw breath, be extant. **2** OCCUR, happen, take place, come about, arise, crop up, transpire, fall, materialize, ensue; *literary* come to pass, befall, betide. **3** BE SITUATED, be located, be found, be present, be set, be positioned, be placed, be installed. **4** REMAIN, stay, last, continue, survive, endure, persist, prevail; wait, linger, hold on, hang on; *formal* obtain.

beach *n.* SEASIDE, seashore, water's edge. See also SHORE.

beached *adj.* STRANDED, grounded, aground, ashore, marooned, high and dry, stuck, washed up/ashore.

bead *n.* **1** (**beads**) NECKLACE, rosary, chaplet. **2** DROPLET, drop, blob, dot, dewdrop, teardrop.

beak *n.* BILL, mandible.

beam *n.* **1** JOIST, lintel, rafter, purlin; spar, girder, balk, timber, two-by-four, plank; support, strut; scantling, transom, stringer. **2** RAY, shaft, stream, streak, pencil, finger; flash, gleam, glow, glimmer, glint, flare.
▶ *v.* **1** BROADCAST, transmit, relay, emit, send/put out, disseminate; direct, aim. **2** GRIN, smile, smirk.
—OPPOSITES: frown.

beaming *adj.* GRINNING, smiling, laughing. See also HAPPY 1.
—OPPOSITES: frowning.

bear *v.* **1** CARRY, bring, transport, move, convey, take, fetch, deliver, tote, lug. **2** DISPLAY, exhibit, be marked with, show, carry, have. **3** SUPPORT, carry, hold up, prop up. **4** HARBOUR, foster, entertain, cherish, nurse, nurture, brood over. **5** ENDURE, tolerate, put up with, stand, abide, submit to, experience, undergo, go through, countenance, brave, weather, stomach, support; *informal* hack, swallow; *formal* brook. **6** GIVE BIRTH TO, bring forth, deliver, have, produce, spawn, birth; *literary* beget. **7** PRODUCE, yield, give forth, give, grow, provide, supply.
☐ **bear fruit** YIELD RESULTS, get results, succeed, meet with success, be successful, be effective, be profitable, work, go as planned; *informal* pay off, come off, pan out, do the trick. **bear something in mind** ☞ CONSIDER 4. **bear something out** ☞ CONFIRM 1. **bear with** BE PATIENT WITH, show forbearance towards, make allowances for, tolerate, put up with, endure. **bear witness/testimony to** ☞ TESTIFY 1.

bearable *adj.* TOLERABLE, endurable, supportable, sustainable, sufferable.

bearing *n.* **1** POSTURE, stance, carriage, gait, deportment; *formal* comportment. **2** ☞ DEMEANOUR. **3** RELEVANCE, pertinence, connection, appositeness, germaneness, importance, significance, application. **4** DIRECTION, orientation, course, trajectory, heading. **5** ORIENTATION, sense of direction.

beast *n.* **1** ANIMAL, creature, brute; *informal* critter, varmint. **2** ☞ BRUTE.
—RELATED: bestial.

beastly *adj.* ☞ HORRIBLE 2.
—OPPOSITES: pleasant, kind.

beat *v.* **1** HIT, strike, batter, thump, bang, hammer, punch, knock (around/about), thrash, pound, pummel, slap, smack, rain blows on; assault, attack, abuse; cudgel, bludgeon, club; *informal* wallop, belt, lace/lay into, bash, whack, thwack, clout, clobber, schmuck♣, slug, tan, bop, sock, deck, plug, beat the living daylights out of, give someone a good hiding, rough up; *dated* chastise. **2** HAMMER, forge, form, shape, mould, work, stamp, fashion, model. **3** PULSATE, pulse, palpitate, vibrate, throb; pump, pound, thump, thud, hammer, drum; pitter-patter, flutter, go pit-a-pat, quiver, race. **4** FLAP, flutter, thresh, thrash, wave, vibrate, oscillate. **5** WHISK, mix, blend, whip. **6** ☞ DEFEAT *v.* 1.
▸ *n.* **1** RHYTHM, pulse, metre, time, measure, cadence; stress, accent. **2** PULSE, pulsating, vibration, throb, palpitation, reverberation; pounding, thump, thud, hammering, drumming; pitter-patter. **3** CIRCUIT, round, route, way, path.

beautiful *adj.* ATTRACTIVE, pretty, handsome, good-looking, alluring, prepossessing; lovely, fair, charming, delightful, appealing, engaging, winsome; ravishing, gorgeous, stunning, arresting, glamorous, bewitching, beguiling;

graceful, elegant, exquisite, aesthetic, artistic, decorative, magnificent; *informal* divine, drop-dead gorgeous, killer, cute, foxy; *formal* beauteous; *archaic* comely.
—OPPOSITES: ugly.

beautify *v.* ADORN, embellish, enhance, decorate, ornament, garnish, gild, smarten up, prettify, enrich, glamorize, spruce up, spiff up, deck (out), trick out, grace; *informal* get up, do up, tart up.
—OPPOSITES: spoil, uglify.

beauty *n.* **1** ATTRACTIVENESS, prettiness, good looks, comeliness, allure; loveliness, charm, appeal, heavenliness; winsomeness, grace, elegance, exquisiteness; splendour, magnificence, grandeur, impressiveness, decorativeness; gorgeousness, glamour; *literary* beauteousness, pulchritude. **2** BEAUTIFUL WOMAN, belle, vision, Venus, goddess, beauty queen, picture; *informal* babe, hottie, looker, good looker, beaut, siren, doll, arm candy, lovely, stunner, knockout, bombshell, dish, cracker, peach, eyeful, fox, smasher.
—OPPOSITES: ugliness.

because *conj.* SINCE, as, in view of the fact that, inasmuch as, owing to the fact that, seeing that/as; *informal* on account of, cuz; *literary* for.
—OPPOSITES: despite.

beckon *v.* **1** ☞ WAVE *v.* 3. **2** ENTICE, invite, tempt, coax, lure, charm, attract, draw, call.

become *v.* **1** GROW, get, turn, come to be, get to be; *literary* wax. **2** TURN INTO, change into, be

transformed into, be converted
into. **3** SUIT, flatter, look good on;
set off, show to advantage.

becoming *adj.* FLATTERING,
attractive, lovely, pretty,
handsome, fetching; *archaic*
comely.

bed *n.* **1** cot, cradle, crib, berth,
bunk, divan, futon, four-poster;
informal the sack, the hay. **2** PATCH,
plot, border, strip. **3** BASE,
foundation, support, prop,
substructure, substratum.

beef *n.* **1** MUSCLE, brawn, bulk;
strength, power. **2** ☞ GRIEVANCE 2.
▶ *v.* TOUGHEN UP, strengthen, build
up, reinforce, consolidate,
augment, improve.

befall *v.* (*literary*) HAPPEN TO,
overtake, come upon, be visited
on.

before *prep.* **1** PRIOR TO, previous
to, earlier than, preparatory to, in
preparation for, preliminary to, in
anticipation of, in expectation of;
in advance of, ahead of, leading
up to, on the eve of; until. **2** IN
FRONT OF, in the presence of, in
the sight of. **3** IN PREFERENCE TO,
rather than, sooner than.
—RELATED: pre-.
—OPPOSITES: after.
▶ *adv.* ☞ PREVIOUSLY.
—OPPOSITES: behind.

befriend *v.* MAKE FRIENDS WITH,
make a friend of; look after, help,
protect, stand by.

befuddled *adj.* CONFUSED,
muddled, addled, bewildered,
fazed, perplexed, mixed up,
discombobulated. See also
GROGGY.
—OPPOSITES: clear.

beg *v.* **1** PANHANDLE, ask for money,
seek charity, seek alms; *informal*
sponge, cadge, scrounge, bum,
mooch. **2** ASK FOR, request, plead
for, appeal for, call for, sue for,
solicit, seek, press for. **3** IMPLORE,
entreat, plead with, appeal to,
supplicate, pray to, importune;
ask, request, call on, petition;
literary beseech.

beget *v.* (*literary*) **1** FATHER, sire,
have, bring into the world, give
life to, bring into being, spawn.
2 ☞ CAUSE *v.*

beggar *n.* **1** PANHANDLER,
mendicant, tramp, vagrant,
vagabond, hobo; *informal* scrounger,
sponger, cadger, freeloader, bum,
moocher, mooch, schnorrer.
2 (*informal*) ☞ PERSON.

begin *v.* **1** START, commence, set
about, go about, embark on,
launch into, get down to, take up;
initiate, set in motion, get under
way, institute, inaugurate, get
ahead with; *informal* get cracking
on, get going on, start the ball
rolling, kick off. **2** APPEAR, arise,
become apparent, make an
appearance, spring up, crop up,
turn up, come into existence,
come into being, originate, start,
commence, develop; *literary* come
to pass.
—OPPOSITES: finish, end,
disappear.

beginner *n.* NOVICE, newcomer,
rookie, newbie, fledgling,
neophyte, starter, (raw) recruit,
apprentice, initiate, freshman,
cub; tenderfoot, cheechako, new
kid (on the block), greenhorn,

tyro; learner, trainee; postulant, novitiate.
—OPPOSITES: expert, veteran.

beginning n. **1** DAWN, birth, inception, conception, origination, genesis, emergence, rise, start, commencement, starting point, launch, onset, outset; day one; constitution, debut, establishment, formation, foundation, founding, inauguration, initiation, institution, opening, origin, source, setting up; creation; informal kickoff. **2** ☞ INTRODUCTION 3.
—OPPOSITES: end, conclusion.

begrudge v. RESENT, feel aggrieved about, feel bitter about, be annoyed about, be resentful of, grudge, mind, object to, take exception to, regret.

beguile v. **1** CHARM, attract, enchant, entrance, win over, woo, captivate, bewitch, spellbind, dazzle, hypnotize, mesmerize, seduce. **2** ☞ AMUSE 2.
—OPPOSITES: repel, bore.

behalf
☐ **on behalf of/on someone's behalf 1** AS A REPRESENTATIVE OF, as a spokesperson for, for, in the name of, in place of, on the authority of, at the behest of. **2** IN THE INTERESTS OF, in support of, for.

behave v. **1** CONDUCT ONESELF, act, acquit oneself, bear oneself; formal comport oneself; archaic deport oneself. **2** ACT CORRECTLY, act properly, conduct oneself well, be well-behaved, be good; be polite, show good manners, mind one's manners.
—OPPOSITES: misbehave.

behaviour n. CONDUCT, deportment, bearing, actions, doings; manners, ways; formal comportment.

behold v. (literary) ☞ LOOK v. 1, NOTICE v.

being n. **1** EXISTENCE, living, life, reality, actuality. **2** SOUL, spirit, nature, essence, inner being, inner self, psyche; heart, bosom, breast. **3** CREATURE, life form, living entity, living thing, (living) soul, individual, person, human (being).

belated adj. ☞ LATE adj. 1.
—OPPOSITES: early.

belief n. **1** OPINION, view, conviction, judgment, thinking, way of thinking, idea, impression, theory, conclusion, notion.
2 FAITH, trust, reliance, confidence, credence. **3** IDEOLOGY, principle, ethic, tenet, canon; doctrine, teaching, dogma, article of faith, creed, credo.
—OPPOSITES: disbelief, doubt.

believable adj. ☞ CREDIBLE.

believe v. **1** BE CONVINCED BY, trust, have confidence in, consider honest, consider truthful.
2 REGARD AS TRUE, accept, be convinced by, give credence to, credit, trust, put confidence in; informal swallow, buy, go for.
3 THINK, be of the opinion that, have an idea that, imagine, suspect. See also ASSUME 1.
—OPPOSITES: doubt.

believer n. DEVOTEE, adherent, disciple, follower, supporter.
—OPPOSITES: infidel, skeptic.

belittle v. DISPARAGE, denigrate, run down, deprecate, depreciate, downgrade, play down, trivialize,

minimize, make light of, pooh-pooh, treat lightly, scoff at, sneer at; derogate.
—OPPOSITES: praise, magnify.

belligerent *adj.* **1** ☞ COMBATIVE.
2 WARRING, at war, combatant, fighting, battling.
—OPPOSITES: peaceable, neutral.

belong *v.* **1** BE OWNED BY, be the property of, be the possession of, be held by, be in the hands of.
2 BE A MEMBER OF, be in, be affiliated to, be allied to, be associated with, be linked to, be an adherent of. **3** BE CLASSED, be classified, be categorized, be included, have a place, be located, be situated, be found, lie.

belongings *pl. n.* POSSESSIONS, effects, worldly goods, assets, chattels, property; bags, baggage; *informal* gear, tackle, kit, things, stuff.

beloved *adj.* DARLING, dear, dearest, precious, adored, much loved, cherished, treasured, prized, highly regarded, admired, esteemed, worshipped, revered, venerated, idolized.
—OPPOSITES: hated.
▶ *n.* SWEETHEART, love, darling, dearest, lover, girlfriend, boyfriend, young lady, young man, beau, lady friend, amour, angel, dear, dear one, honey, love of one's life, loved one, sweet; steady, main squeeze, swain; paramour.

belt *n.* **1** SASH, girdle, strap, cummerbund, band; *literary* cincture; *historical* baldric. **2** REGION, area, district, zone, sector, territory; tract, strip, stretch.
▶ *v.* ☞ HIT *v.* 1.

□ **below the belt** UNFAIR, unjust, unacceptable, inequitable; unethical, unprincipled, immoral, unscrupulous, unsporting, sneaky, dishonourable, dishonest, underhanded; *informal* lowdown, dirty.

bemused *adj.* ☞ CONFUSED 1.

bend *v.* **1** CURVE, angle, hook, bow, arch, flex, crook, hump, warp, contort, distort, deform. **2** TURN, curve, incline, swing, veer, deviate, diverge, fork, loop.
3 STOOP, bow, crouch, hunch, lean down/over.
—OPPOSITES: straighten.
▶ *n.* CURVE, turn, corner, jog, correction line✦, kink, dogleg, oxbow, zigzag, angle, arc, crescent, twist, crook, deviation, deflection, loop, hairpin turn, hairpin.
—OPPOSITES: straight.

beneath *prep.* **1** UNDER, underneath, below, at the foot of, at the bottom of; lower than. **2** INFERIOR TO, below, not so important as, lower in status than, subordinate to, subservient to. **3** UNWORTHY OF, unbecoming to, degrading to, below.
—OPPOSITES: above.

benefactor *n.* PATRON, supporter, backer, sponsor; donor, contributor, subscriber, giver; *informal* angel.

beneficial *adj.* ADVANTAGEOUS, favourable, helpful, useful, of use, of benefit, of assistance, valuable, of value, profitable, rewarding, gainful; convenient, expedient.
—OPPOSITES: disadvantageous.

beneficiary *n.* HEIR, heiress, inheritor, legatee; recipient; *Law* devisee.

benefit *n.* **1** GOOD, sake, welfare, well-being, advantage, comfort, ease, convenience; help, aid, assistance; service; profit. **2** ADVANTAGE, reward, merit, boon, blessing, virtue; bonus; value; *informal* perk; *formal* perquisite. **3** SOCIAL SECURITY PAYMENTS, social assistance♣, welfare, the dole; pogey♣, employment insurance♣, unemployment♣, (*Atlantic*) stamps♣; charity, donations, gifts, financial assistance.
—OPPOSITES: detriment, disadvantage.
▸ *v.* **1** BE ADVANTAGEOUS TO, be beneficial to, be of advantage to, be to the advantage of, profit, do good to, be of service to, serve, be useful to, be of use to, be helpful to, be of help to, help, aid, assist, be of assistance to; better, improve, strengthen, boost, advance, further. **2** PROFIT, gain, reap benefits, reap reward, make money; make the most of, exploit, turn to one's advantage, put to good use, do well out of; *informal* cash in, make a killing.
—OPPOSITES: damage, suffer.

benevolent *adj.* ☞ KIND *adj.*, GENEROUS 1.
—OPPOSITES: unkind, tight-fisted.

benign *adj.* **1** KINDLY, warm-hearted, tender-hearted, gentle, compassionate, caring. See also FRIENDLY 1. **2** (*Medicine*) HARMLESS, non-malignant, non-cancerous; *Medicine* benignant.

—OPPOSITES: unfriendly, hostile, malignant.

bent *adj.* TWISTED, crooked, warped, contorted, deformed, misshapen, out of shape, irregular; bowed, arched, curved, angled, hooked, kinked; *informal* pretzelled.
▸ *n.* INCLINATION, leaning, tendency; talent, gift, flair, aptitude, facility, skill, capability.
☐ **bent on** ☞ DETERMINED 1.

bequeath *v.* LEAVE (IN ONE'S WILL), hand on/down, will, make over; pass on, entrust, grant, transfer; donate, give; endow on, bestow on, confer on; *Law* demise, devise, convey.

bequest *n.* LEGACY, inheritance, endowment, settlement; estate, heritage; bestowal; *Law* devise; *Law, dated* hereditament.

berate *v.* ☞ SCOLD
—OPPOSITES: praise.

berserk *adj.* FRENZIED, raving, wild, out of control, amok, on the rampage, frantic, crazy, raging, insane, out of one's mind, hysterical, mad, crazed, maniacal, manic; *informal* bananas, bonkers, nuts, hyper, postal.

berth *n.* **1** ☞ BED 1. **2** MOORING, dock, slip, anchorage; wharf, pier, jetty, quay.
☐ **give someone/something a wide berth** AVOID, shun, keep away from, stay away from, steer clear of, keep at arm's length, have nothing to do with; dodge, sidestep, circumvent, skirt round.

beseech *v.* ☞ IMPLORE.

besiege *v.* **1** LAY SIEGE TO, beleaguer, blockade, surround. **2** SURROUND, mob, crowd round, swarm round, throng round, ring round, encircle. **3** ☞ INUNDATE 2.

besotted adj. ☞ INFATUATED.

best adj. FINEST, greatest, top, foremost, leading, pre-eminent, premier, prime, first, chief, principal, supreme, of the highest quality, superlative, par excellence, unrivalled, second to none, without equal, nonpareil, unsurpassed, peerless, matchless, unparalleled, unbeaten, unbeatable, optimum, optimal, ultimate, incomparable, ideal, perfect; highest, record-breaking; *informal* star, number-one, a cut above the rest, top-drawer, top-level, the Cadillac/Rolls-Royce of.
—OPPOSITES: worst.
▶ *n.* FINEST, choicest, top, cream, choice, prime, elite, crème de la crème, flower, jewel in the crown, nonpareil; *informal* tops, pick of the bunch.
▶ *v.* (*informal*) ☞ DEFEAT 1.

bestial adj. SAVAGE, brutish, brutal, barbarous, barbaric, cruel, vicious, violent, inhuman, subhuman. See also DEPRAVED.
—OPPOSITES: civilized, humane.

bestow v. CONFER ON, grant, accord, afford, endow someone with, vest in, present, award, give, donate, entrust with, vouchsafe.

bestseller n. great success, hit, smash (hit), blockbuster, chart-topper, chartbuster, megahit.
—OPPOSITES: failure, flop.

bet v. **1** WAGER, gamble, stake, risk, venture, hazard, chance; put/lay money, speculate. **2** (*informal*) BE CERTAIN, be sure, be convinced, be confident; expect, predict, forecast, guess.

▶ *n.* **1** WAGER, gamble, stake, ante, exactor♣. **2** (*informal*) OPTION, choice, alternative, course of action, plan.

betray v. **1** BE DISLOYAL TO, be unfaithful to, double-cross, cross, break faith with, inform on/against, give away, denounce, sell out, stab in the back, break one's promise to; *informal* rat on, fink on, sell down the river, squeal on, peach on, rat out, finger. **2** REVEAL, disclose, divulge, tell, give away, leak; unmask, expose, bring out into the open; let slip, let out, let drop, blurt out; *informal* blab, spill, kiss and tell.
—OPPOSITES: be loyal to, hide.

better adj. **1** SUPERIOR, finer, of higher quality; preferable; *informal* a cut above, head and shoulders above. **2** HEALTHIER, fitter, stronger; well, cured, healed, recovered; recovering, on the road to recovery, making progress, improving; *informal* on the mend.
—OPPOSITES: worse, inferior.
▶ *v.* **1** ☞ SURPASS. **2** ☞ IMPROVE 1.
—OPPOSITES: worsen.

beware v. BE ON YOUR GUARD, watch out, look out, be alert, be on the lookout, keep your eyes open/peeled, keep an eye out, keep a sharp lookout, be on the qui vive; take care, be careful, be cautious, watch your step, have a care; *Golf* fore.

bewilder v. ☞ PERPLEX.
—OPPOSITES: enlighten.

bewitch v. ☞ ENCHANT.
—OPPOSITES: repel.

bias n. PREJUDICE, partiality, partisanship, favouritism, unfairness, one-sidedness; bigotry,

intolerance, discrimination, leaning, tendency, inclination, predilection.
—OPPOSITES: impartiality.
▶ *v.* PREJUDICE, influence, colour, sway, weight, predispose; distort, skew, slant.

biased *adj.* PREJUDICED, partial, partisan, one-sided, blinkered; bigoted, intolerant, discriminatory; distorted, warped, twisted, skewed.
—OPPOSITES: impartial.

bid *v.* **1** OFFER, make an offer of, put in a bid of, put up, tender, proffer, propose. **2** TRY TO OBTAIN/ GET, make a pitch/bid for.
▶ *n.* **1** OFFER, tender, proposal. **2** ☞ ATTEMPT.

big *adj.* **1** LARGE, sizeable, substantial, great, huge, immense, enormous, extensive, colossal, massive, mammoth, vast, tremendous, gigantic, giant, monumental, mighty, gargantuan, elephantine, titanic, mountainous, Brobdingnagian; towering, tall, high, lofty, outsize, oversized; goodly; capacious, voluminous, spacious; king-size(d), man-size(d), family-size(d), economy-size(d); *informal* jumbo, whopping, thumping, bumper, mega, humongous, monster, monstrous, ginormous, giant-size(d), astronomical, prodigious, stupendous; *formal* commodious. **2** ☞ LARGE 2. **3** ☞ IMPORTANT 1. **4** GENEROUS, kind, kindly, caring, compassionate, loving. **5** (*informal*) ☞ POPULAR 1.
—OPPOSITES: small, minor.

bigot *n.* CHAUVINIST, partisan, sectarian; racist, sexist, homophobe, dogmatist, jingoist.

bigoted *adj.* PREJUDICED, biased, partial, one-sided, sectarian, discriminatory; opinionated, dogmatic, intolerant, narrow-minded, blinkered, illiberal; racist, sexist, chauvinistic, jingoistic; warped, twisted, distorted.
—OPPOSITES: open-minded.

bill *n.* **1** INVOICE, account, statement, list of charges; check, tab, score. **2** DRAFT LAW, proposed piece of legislation, proposal. **3** BANKNOTE, note.
▶ *v.* **1** INVOICE, charge, debit. **2** DESCRIBE, call, style, label, dub; promote, publicize, talk up, hype.

billow *v.* **1** PUFF UP/OUT, balloon (out), swell, fill (out), belly out. **2** SWIRL, spiral, roll, undulate, eddy; pour, flow.

bind *v.* **1** TIE (UP), fasten (together), hold together, secure, make fast, attach; rope, strap, lash, fetter, truss, hog-tie, tether. **2** ☞ UNITE 1. **3** ☞ HAMPER.
—OPPOSITES: untie, separate.
▶ *n.* PREDICAMENT, difficult/ awkward situation, quandary, dilemma, plight, tight spot/ situation/squeeze, Catch-22, fix, hole, cleft stick.

binding *adj.* IRREVOCABLE, unalterable, inescapable, unbreakable, contractual; compulsory, obligatory, mandatory, incumbent.

birth *n.* **1** CHILDBIRTH, delivery, nativity, birthing; blessed/happy event; *formal* parturition; *dated* confinement, childbed.

2 ☞ BEGINNING 1. **3** ☞ ANCESTRY.
—RELATED: natal.
—OPPOSITES: death, demise, end.
□ **give birth to** HAVE, bear, produce, be delivered of, bring into the world; birth; *informal* drop; *dated* mother; *archaic* bring forth.

bisect *v.* CUT IN HALF, halve, divide/cut/split in two, split down the middle; cross, intersect.

bit *n.* **1** PIECE, portion, segment, section, part; chunk, lump, hunk, slice; fragment, scrap, shred, crumb, grain, speck; spot, drop, pinch, dash, soupçon, modicum; morsel, mouthful, bite, sample; iota, jot, tittle, whit, atom, particle, trace, touch, suggestion, hint, tinge, mite, ounce, scintilla, sliver; snippet, snatch, smidgen, tad, titch. **2** ☞ MOMENT 1.
—OPPOSITES: lot.
□ **a bit** SOMEWHAT, fairly, slightly, rather, quite, a little, moderately; *informal* pretty, sort of, kind of, kinda. **bit by bit** ☞ GRADUALLY.

bitchy *adj.* ☞ MALICIOUS.

bite *v.* **1** SINK ONE'S TEETH INTO, chew, munch, crunch, champ, tear at, snap at. **2** ACCEPT, agree, respond; be lured, be enticed, be tempted; take the bait.
▶ *n.* **1** CHEW, munch, nibble, nip, snap. **2** MOUTHFUL, piece, bit, morsel. **3** SNACK, light meal, soupçon; refreshments. **4** ☞ ZEST 2.

biting *adj.* **1** VICIOUS, harsh, cruel, savage, cutting, sharp, bitter, scathing, caustic, acid, acrimonious, acerbic, stinging; vitriolic, hostile, spiteful, venomous, mean, nasty; *informal*

bitchy, catty. **2** ☞ COLD 1.
—OPPOSITES: mild.

bitter *adj.* **1** SHARP, acid, acidic, acrid, tart, sour, biting, unsweetened, vinegary; *technical* acerbic. **2** RESENTFUL, embittered, aggrieved, begrudging, rancorous, spiteful, jaundiced, ill-disposed, sullen, sour, churlish, morose, petulant, peevish, with a chip on one's shoulder. **3** ☞ PAINFUL 2. **4** ☞ COLD 1. **5** ☞ ACRIMONIOUS.
—OPPOSITES: sweet, magnanimous, content, warm, amicable.

bizarre *adj.* STRANGE, peculiar, odd, funny, curious, weird, outlandish, outré, abnormal, eccentric, unconventional, unusual, unorthodox, queer, extraordinary, far out, idiosyncratic, in left field, kinky, quirky, singular, unfamiliar, zany, wacky, oddball, way out, kooky, freaky, off the wall, offbeat.
—OPPOSITES: normal.

black *adj.* **1** DARK, pitch-black, jet-black, coal-black, ebony, sable, inky. **2** ☞ DARK *adj.* 1. **3** ☞ DISASTROUS. **4** MISERABLE, unhappy, sad, wretched, downcast, dejected, sullen, cheerless, melancholy, morose, gloomy, glum, abject. **5** (*archaic*) ☞ WICKED.
—OPPOSITES: white, clear, bright, joyful.
□ **black out** FAINT, lose consciousness, pass out, swoon; *informal* flake out, go out. **black and white** CATEGORICAL, unequivocal, absolute, uncompromising, unconditional,

unqualified, unambiguous, clear, clear-cut.

blacken v. **1** BLACK, darken; dirty, make sooty, make smoky, stain, grime, soil. **2** ☞ TARNISH 2.

blame v. **1** HOLD RESPONSIBLE/ ACCOUNTABLE, condemn, accuse, find/consider guilty, assign fault/ liability/guilt to, indict, point the finger at, finger, incriminate; *archaic* inculpate. **2** ASCRIBE TO, attribute to, impute to, lay at the door of, put down to; *informal* pin.
—OPPOSITES: absolve.
▶ *n.* RESPONSIBILITY, guilt, accountability, liability, culpability, fault; the rap.

blameless *adj.* ☞ INNOCENT 1.
—OPPOSITES: blameworthy.

bland *adj.* **1** TASTELESS, flavourless, insipid, weak, watery, spiceless, wishy-washy. **2** UNINTERESTING, dull, boring, tedious, monotonous, dry, drab, dreary, wearisome; unexciting, unimaginative, uninspiring, uninspired, lacklustre, vapid, flat, stale, trite, blah, plain-vanilla, white-bread, banal, commonplace, humdrum, ho-hum, vacuous, wishy-washy, colourless, harmless, inoffensive, insipid, mediocre, ordinary, pedestrian, run-of-the-mill, safe, tame.
—OPPOSITES: tangy, interesting.

blank *adj.* **1** EMPTY, unmarked, unused, clear, free, bare, clean, fresh, plain. **2** ☞ EXPRESSIONLESS 1. **3** ☞ CONFUSED 1.
—OPPOSITES: full, expressive.
▶ *n.* SPACE, gap, lacuna.

blasphemous *adj.*
☞ SACRILEGIOUS.
—OPPOSITES: reverent.

blasphemy *n.* PROFANITY, sacrilege, irreligion, irreverence, taking the Lord's name in vain, swearing, curse, cursing, impiety, desecration.
—OPPOSITES: reverence.

blast *n.* **1** EXPLOSION, detonation, discharge, burst. **2** GUST, rush, gale, squall, wind, draft, waft, puff. **3** BLARE, wail, roar, screech, shriek, hoot, honk, beep. **4** GOOD TIME, ball, riot.
▶ *v.* **1** BLOW UP, bomb, blow (to pieces), dynamite, shell, explode. **2** FIRE, shoot, blaze, let fly, discharge. **3** BLARE, boom, roar, thunder, bellow, pump, shriek, screech.

blatant *adj.* ☞ FLAGRANT.
—OPPOSITES: inconspicuous, shamefaced.

blaze *n.* **1** ☞ FIRE *n.* 1. **2** GLARE, gleam, flash, burst, flare, streak, radiance, brilliance, beam.

bleach *v.* TURN WHITE, whiten, turn pale, blanch, lighten, fade, decolorize, peroxide.
—OPPOSITES: darken.

bleak *adj.* **1** BARE, exposed, desolate, stark, desert, lunar, open, empty, windswept; treeless, without vegetation, denuded. **2** UNPROMISING, unfavourable, unpropitious, inauspicious; discouraging, disheartening, depressing, dreary, dim, gloomy, black, dark, grim, hopeless, sombre.
—OPPOSITES: lush, promising.

bleary *adj.* BLURRED, blurry, unfocused; fogged, clouded, dull, misty, watery, rheumy; *archaic* blear.
—OPPOSITES: clear.

blemish *n.* **1** IMPERFECTION, flaw, defect, fault, deformity, discoloration, disfigurement; bruise, scar, pit, pock, scratch, cut, gash; mark, streak, spot, smear, speck, blotch, smudge, smut; birthmark, mole; *Medicine* stigma. **2** TAINT, blot, stain, foible; dishonour, disgrace. See also DEFECT[1].
—OPPOSITES: virtue.
▶ *v.* **1** MAR, spoil, impair, disfigure, blight, deface, mark, scar; ruin. **2** ☞ TARNISH *v.* 2.
—OPPOSITES: enhance.

blend *v.* ☞ MIX *v.* **2** HARMONIZE, go (well), fit (in), be in tune, be compatible; coordinate, match, complement.

blessed *adj.* **1** HOLY, sacred, hallowed, consecrated, sanctified; ordained, canonized, beatified. **2** FAVOURED, fortunate, lucky, privileged, enviable, happy.

blessing *n.* **1** BENEDICTION, invocation, prayer, intercession; grace. **2** ☞ APPROVAL. **3** ☞ GODSEND.
—OPPOSITES: condemnation, affliction.

blight *n.* **1** DISEASE, canker, infestation, fungus, mildew, mould. **2** AFFLICTION, scourge, bane, curse, plague, menace, misfortune, woe, trouble, ordeal, trial, nuisance, pest.
—OPPOSITES: blessing.
▶ *v.* ☞ WRECK 3.

blind *adj.* **1** SIGHTLESS, unsighted, visually impaired, visionless, unseeing; partially sighted, purblind; *informal* as blind as a bat. **2** UNPERCEPTIVE, insensitive, slow, obtuse, uncomprehending; stupid, unintelligent; *informal* dense, dim, thick, dumb, dopey, dozy. **3** UNCRITICAL, unreasoned, unthinking, unconsidered, mindless, undiscerning, indiscriminate.
—OPPOSITES: sighted, perceptive, discerning.
▶ *v.* MAKE BLIND, deprive of sight, render sightless; put someone's eyes out.
▶ *n.* **1** SCREEN, shade, sunshade, shutter, curtain, awning, canopy; louvres, jalousie. **2** DECEPTION, smokescreen, front, facade, cover, pretext, masquerade, feint, camouflage; trick, ploy, ruse, machination.

bliss *n.* JOY, happiness, pleasure, delight, ecstasy, elation, rapture, euphoria.
—OPPOSITES: misery.

blizzard *n.* SNOWSTORM, whiteout, snow squall, flurry, snowfall, blowing snow, snow devil, gale.

bloated *adj.* ☞ SWOLLEN.

blob *n.* **1** ☞ GLOBULE. **2** SPOT, dab, blotch, blot, dot, smudge; *informal* splotch.

block *n.* **1** CHUNK, hunk, lump, wedge, cube, brick, slab, bar, piece. **2** BUILDING, complex, structure, development. **3** BATCH, group, set, quantity. **4** ☞ OBSTACLE. **5** BLOCKAGE, obstruction, stoppage, clog, congestion, occlusion, clot.
—OPPOSITES: aid.
▶ *v.* **1** CLOG (UP), stop up, choke, plug, obstruct, gum up, dam up, bung up, congest, jam, close; *informal* gunge up; *technical* occlude. **2** HINDER, hamper, obstruct, impede, inhibit, restrict, limit;

halt, stop, bar, check, prevent.
—OPPOSITES: facilitate.

blood n. **1** gore, vital fluid; *literary* lifeblood, ichor. **2** ☞ ANCESTRY.
—RELATED: hemal, hematic.

blood-curdling *adj.*
☞ FRIGHTENING.

bloodshed n. SLAUGHTER, massacre, killing, wounding; carnage, butchery, bloodletting, bloodbath; violence, fighting, warfare; *literary* slaying.

bloodthirsty *adj.* MURDEROUS, homicidal, violent, vicious, barbarous, barbaric, savage, brutal, cutthroat; fierce, ferocious, inhuman.

bloody *adj.* **1** BLEEDING; bloodstained, blood-soaked. **2** VICIOUS, ferocious, savage, fierce, brutal, murderous, barbarous, gory; *archaic* sanguinary.

bloom n. **1** ☞ FLOWER 1. **2** PRIME, perfection, acme, peak, height, heyday; salad days. **3** RADIANCE, lustre, sheen, glow, freshness.
▶ v. **1** FLOWER, blossom, open; mature. **2** FLOURISH, thrive, prosper, progress, burgeon.
—OPPOSITES: wither, decline.

blot n. **1** SPOT, dot, mark, blotch, smudge, patch, dab; *informal* splotch. **2** BLEMISH, taint, stain, blight, flaw, fault; disgrace, dishonour.
▶ v. **1** SOAK UP, absorb, sponge up, mop up; dry up/out; dab, pat. **2** ☞ TARNISH v. 2.
—OPPOSITES: honour.
□ **blot something out** ERASE, obliterate, delete, efface, rub out, blank out, expunge, eradicate; cross out, strike out, wipe out.

blotchy *adj.* MOTTLED, dappled, blotched, patchy, spotty, spotted, smudged, marked; *informal* splotchy.

blow v. **1** GUST, bluster, puff, blast, roar, rush, storm. **2** DRIFT, flutter, waft, float, glide, whirl, move. **3** EXHALE, puff, breathe out; emit, expel, discharge, issue. **4** SOUND, blast, toot, pipe, trumpet; play. **5** (*informal*) SPOIL, ruin, bungle, mess up, fudge, muff; WASTE, lose, squander; *informal* botch, screw up, foul up.
▶ n. KNOCK, BANG, hit, punch, thump, smack, crack, rap, karate chop; *informal* whack, thwack, bonk, bash, clout, sock, wallop.
□ **blow over** ABATE, subside, drop off, lessen, ease (off), let up, diminish, fade, dwindle, slacken, recede, tail off, peter out, pass, die down, fizzle out. **blow up**
☞ EXPLODE 1, 2.

blueprint n. PLAN, design, diagram, model, example, drawing, sketch, map, layout, representation.

blues *pl. n.* ☞ DEPRESSION 1.

bluff¹ n. ☞ DECEPTION 2.
▶ v. **1** PRETEND, sham, fake, feign, lie, hoax, pose, posture, masquerade, dissemble. **2** ☞ TRICK v.

bluff² *adj.* HEARTY, genial, good-natured. See also OUTSPOKEN.

bluff³ n. **1** CLIFF, promontory, headland, crag, bank, (*BC, Alta., & North*) ramparts♣, peak, escarpment, scarp. **2** *Cdn* (*Prairies*)
☞ WOOD 2.

blunder n. MISTAKE, error, gaffe, slip, oversight, faux pas, misstep, infelicity; *informal* botch, slip-up,

boo-boo, blooper, boner, flub, goof.
▶ v. **1** MAKE A MISTAKE, err, miscalculate, bungle, trip up, be wrong; *informal* slip up, mess up, screw up, blow it, goof. **2** STUMBLE, lurch, stagger, flounder, struggle, fumble, grope.

blunt *adj.* **1** UNSHARPENED, dull, worn, edgeless; rounded.
2 STRAIGHTFORWARD, frank, plain-spoken, candid, direct, bluff, forthright, unequivocal; BRUSQUE, abrupt, curt, terse, bald, brutal, harsh, severe, austere; stark, unadorned, undisguised, unvarnished; *informal* upfront.
—OPPOSITES: sharp, pointed, subtle.
▶ v. DULL, deaden, dampen, numb, weaken, sap, cool, temper, allay, abate; diminish, reduce, decrease, lessen, deplete.
—OPPOSITES: sharpen, intensify.

blur *v.* **1** CLOUD, fog, obscure, dim, make hazy, unfocus, soften; *literary* bedim; *archaic* blear. **2** OBSCURE, make vague, confuse, muddle, muddy, obfuscate, cloud, weaken.
—OPPOSITES: sharpen, focus.

blurred *adj.* INDISTINCT, blurry, fuzzy, hazy, misty, foggy, cloudy, shadowy, faint; unclear, vague, indefinite, unfocused, obscure, nebulous.

blurt
☐ **blurt something out** BURST OUT WITH, exclaim, call out; DIVULGE, disclose, reveal, betray, let slip, give away; *informal* blab, gush, let on, spill the beans, let the cat out of the bag.

blush *v.* REDDEN, turn/go pink, turn/go red, flush, colour, burn up; feel shy, feel embarrassed.
▶ *n.* FLUSH, rosiness, pinkness, redness, ruddiness, bloom, high colour.

bluster *v.* RANT, rave, thunder, bellow, sound off; be overbearing; *informal* throw one's weight about/around.
▶ *n.* RANTING, thundering, hectoring, bullying; bombast, bravado, bumptiousness, braggadocio.

blustery *adj.* ☞ WINDY 1.
—OPPOSITES: calm.

board *n.* **1** PLANK, beam, panel, slat, batten, timber, lath.
2 COMMITTEE, council, panel, directorate, commission, executive, group. **3** KEEP, maintenance. See also FOOD.
▶ v. **1** GET ON, go aboard, enter, mount, ascend; embark, emplane, entrain; catch; *informal* hop on.
2 LODGE, live, reside, be housed, room; *informal* put up.

boast *v.* BRAG, crow, swagger, swank, gloat, show off; exaggerate, overstate; *informal* talk big, blow one's own horn, sing one's own praises, lay it on thick.

boastful *adj.* BRAGGING, swaggering, bumptious, puffed up, full of oneself; cocky, conceited, arrogant, egotistical; *informal* swanky, big-headed, blowhard; *literary* vainglorious.
—OPPOSITES: modest.

bob *v.* MOVE UP AND DOWN, bounce, toss, skip, dance, jounce; wobble, jiggle, joggle, jolt, jerk; NOD, incline, dip; wag, waggle.

bodily *adj.* PHYSICAL, corporeal, corporal, somatic, fleshly;

concrete, real, actual, tangible.
—OPPOSITES: spiritual, mental.

body *n.* **1** FIGURE, frame, form,
physique, anatomy, skeleton;
soma; *informal* bod. **2** TORSO, trunk.
3 ☞ CORPSE. **4** MAIN PART, central
part, core, heart. **5** QUANTITY,
amount, volume, collection, mass,
corpus.
□ **body and soul** ☞ COMPLETELY.

bog *n.* ☞ MARSH.
□ **bogged down** MIRED, stuck,
entangled, ensnared, embroiled;
hampered, hindered, impeded,
delayed, stalled, detained;
swamped, overwhelmed.

bogus *adj.* ☞ FAKE *adj.*
—OPPOSITES: genuine.

bohemian *n.* NONCONFORMIST,
free spirit, dropout; hippie,
beatnik, boho.
—OPPOSITES: conservative.
▶ *adj.* UNCONVENTIONAL,
nonconformist, unorthodox,
avant-garde, irregular, alternative;
artistic; *informal* boho, artsy, artsy-
fartsy, way-out, offbeat.
—OPPOSITES: conventional.

boisterous *adj.* LIVELY, animated,
exuberant, spirited,
rambunctious; rowdy, unruly,
wild, uproarious, unrestrained,
undisciplined, uninhibited,
uncontrolled, rough, disorderly,
riotous, knockabout; noisy, loud,
clamorous.
—OPPOSITES: restrained, calm.

bold *adj.* **1** ☞ DARING. **2** IMPUDENT,
insolent, impertinent, brazen,
brash, shameless, disrespectful,
presumptuous, audacious,
forward, daring; cheeky, lippy,
fresh, familiar. **3** STRIKING, vivid,
bright, strong, eye-catching,

prominent; gaudy, lurid, garish.
—OPPOSITES: timid, pale.

bolster *v.* STRENGTHEN, reinforce,
boost, fortify, renew; support,
sustain, buoy up, prop up, shore
up, maintain, aid, help; augment,
increase.
—OPPOSITES: undermine.

bolt *n.* **1** BAR, lock, catch, latch,
fastener, deadbolt. **2** RIVET, pin,
peg, screw. **3** FLASH, thunderbolt,
shaft, streak, burst, flare.
▶ *v.* **1** LOCK, bar, latch, fasten,
secure. **2** DASH, dart, run, sprint,
hurtle, career, rush, fly, shoot,
bound; flee; *informal* tear, scoot, leg
it. **3** GOBBLE, gulp, wolf, guzzle,
devour; *informal* demolish, polish
off, shovel down, scarf, snarf.

bomb *n.* **1** EXPLOSIVE, incendiary
(device); missile, projectile; *dated*
blockbuster, bombshell.
2 ☞ FAILURE 2.

bombard *v.* **1** SHELL, pound, blitz,
strafe, bomb; assail, attack,
assault, batter, blast, pelt.
2 ☞ INUNDATE 2.

bombastic *adj.* POMPOUS,
blustering, turgid, verbose,
orotund, high-flown, high-
sounding, overwrought,
pretentious, ostentatious,
grandiloquent; *informal* highfalutin,
puffed up; *rare* fustian.

bonanza *n.* WINDFALL, godsend,
boon, blessing, bonus, stroke of
luck, jackpot.

bond *n.* **1** RELATIONSHIP, tie, link,
friendship, fellowship,
partnership, association,
affiliation, alliance, attachment.
2 ☞ CHAIN *n.* 1. **3** PROMISE, pledge,
vow, oath, word (of honour),
guarantee, assurance; agreement,

contract, pact, bargain, deal.
▸ v. ☞ ATTACH 1.

bondage n. SLAVERY,
enslavement, servitude,
subjugation, subjection,
oppression, domination,
exploitation, persecution;
enthralment, thraldom; historical
serfdom, vassalage.
—OPPOSITES: liberty.

bonus n. 1 BENEFIT, advantage,
boon, blessing, godsend, stroke of
luck, asset, plus, pro, attraction,
gravy. 2 GRATUITY, gift, present,
reward, prize; incentive,
inducement, handout; informal
perk, sweetener; formal perquisite.
—OPPOSITES: disadvantage.

bony adj. ☞ THIN 3.
—OPPOSITES: plump.

book n. 1 VOLUME, tome,
publication, title; novel,
storybook, anthology, treatise,
manual; paperback, hardback.
2 NOTEPAD, notebook, pad, memo
pad, exercise book, scribbler✦,
workbook; logbook, ledger,
journal, diary, scratch pad.
3 ACCOUNTS, records; account
book, record book, ledger, balance
sheet.
▸ v. 1 RESERVE, make a reservation
for, pre-arrange, order; formal
bespeak. 2 ARRANGE, program,
schedule, timetable, line up,
pencil in, slate.

bookish adj. ☞ INTELLECTUAL adj. 2.

booklet n. ☞ PAMPHLET.

boom n. 1 REVERBERATION,
resonance, thunder, echoing,
crashing, drumming, pounding,
roar, rumble, explosion. 2 UPTURN,
upsurge, upswing, increase,
advance, growth, boost,

escalation, improvement, spurt.
—OPPOSITES: slump.
▸ v. REVERBERATE, resound,
resonate; rumble, thunder, blare,
echo; crash, roll, clap, explode,
bang.

boorish adj. COARSE, uncouth,
rude, ill-bred, ill-mannered,
uncivilized, unrefined, rough,
thuggish, loutish, oafish, lubberly,
lumpen; vulgar, common,
uncultured, crass, unsavoury,
gross, brutish, Neanderthal,
knuckle-dragging; informal cloddish.
—OPPOSITES: refined.

boost n. 1 UPLIFT, lift, spur,
encouragement, help, inspiration,
stimulus. 2 INCREASE, expansion,
upturn, upsurge, upswing, rise,
escalation, improvement,
advance, growth, boom; hike,
jump.
—OPPOSITES: decrease.
▸ v. INCREASE, raise, escalate,
improve, strengthen, inflate, push
up, promote, advance, foster,
stimulate, maximize; facilitate,
help, assist, aid; jump-start; informal
hike, bump up.
—OPPOSITES: decrease.

boot v. 1 KICK, punt; propel, drive.
2 START UP, fire up, reboot.

booth n. STALL, stand, kiosk;
cubicle, enclosure.

bootlicker n. ☞ SYCOPHANT.

booty n. LOOT, plunder, pillage,
haul, spoils, stolen goods, ill-
gotten gains, pickings; informal
swag.

booze n. ☞ ALCOHOL.

bordello n. BROTHEL, whorehouse;
cathouse; euphemistic massage
parlour, body-rub parlour✦; archaic
bawdy house, house of ill repute.

border *n.* **1** EDGE, margin, perimeter, circumference, periphery; rim, fringe, verge; sides. **2** FRONTIER, boundary; forty-ninth parallel❖, (*West*) Medicine Line❖; borderline, perimeter; marches, bounds.
▶ *v.* **1** SURROUND, enclose, encircle, circle, edge, fringe, bound, flank. **2** ADJOIN, abut, be next to, be adjacent to, be contiguous with, touch, join, meet, reach.

bore *v.* **1** STULTIFY, pall on, stupefy, weary, tire, fatigue, send to sleep, leave cold; bore to death, bore to tears; *informal* turn off. **2** DRILL, pierce, perforate, puncture, punch, cut; tunnel, burrow, mine, dig, gouge, sink.
▶ *n.* TEDIOUS PERSON/THING, yawn, bother, nuisance, wet blanket.

boring *adj.* TEDIOUS, dull, monotonous, repetitive, unrelieved, unvaried, unimaginative, uneventful; characterless, featureless, colourless, lifeless, insipid, uninteresting, unexciting, uninspiring, unstimulating; unreadable, unwatchable; jejune, flat, bland, dry, stale, tired, banal, lacklustre, stodgy, vapid, dreary, humdrum, mundane; mind-numbing, soul-destroying, wearisome, tiring, tiresome, irksome, trying, frustrating; *informal* deadly, ho-hum, samey, dullsville, dull as dishwater, plain-vanilla.

borrow *v.* take as a loan; lease, hire; *informal* cadge, scrounge, bum, mooch. See also STEAL 1.
—OPPOSITES: lend.

boss *n.* OWNER, proprietor, patron, foreman. See also LEADER.

▶ *v.* ORDER AROUND, dictate to, lord it over, bully, push around, domineer, dominate, pressurize, browbeat; call the shots, lay down the law, bulldoze, walk all over, railroad.

bossy *adj.* DOMINEERING, pushy, overbearing, imperious, officious, high-handed, authoritarian, dictatorial, controlling; *informal* high and mighty.
—OPPOSITES: submissive.

botch *v.* BUNGLE, mismanage, mishandle, make a mess of, mess up, make a hash of, muff, fluff, foul up, screw up, flub.

bother *v.* **1** DISTURB, trouble, inconvenience, burden, discommode, impose on, incommode, put out, put to any trouble, pester, badger, harass, molest, plague, nag, hound, harry, annoy, upset, irritate, hassle, bug, give someone the gears❖, get in someone's hair, get on someone's case, get under someone's skin, ruffle someone's feathers, rag on, ride. **2** MIND, care, concern oneself, trouble oneself, worry oneself; *informal* give a damn, give a hoot. **3** ☞ WORRY *v.* 2.
▶ *n.* NUISANCE, hassle, pain (in the neck), headache, pest, palaver, rigmarole, job, trial, drag, chore, inconvenience, trouble, problem.

bottle *n.* carafe, flask, decanter, canteen, vessel, pitcher, mickey❖, twenty-six❖, forty-ouncer❖ (forty-pounder❖), Texas mickey❖, flagon, magnum, stubby, carboy, demijohn.
  □ **bottle something up**
  ☞ REPRESS 2.

bottleneck *n.* TRAFFIC JAM, jam, congestion, tie-up, holdup, snarl-up, gridlock, logjam, constriction, narrowing, restriction, obstruction, blockage, choke point.

bottom *n.* **1** FOOT, lowest part, lowest point, base; foundation, substructure, underpinning. **2** UNDERSIDE, underneath, undersurface, undercarriage, underbelly. **3** ☞ BUTTOCKS.
—OPPOSITES: top, surface.

bottomless *adj.* UNLIMITED, limitless, boundless, infinite, inexhaustible, endless, never-ending, everlasting; vast, huge, enormous.
—OPPOSITES: limited.

bounce *v.* REBOUND, spring back, ricochet, jounce, carom; reflect.
▸ *n.* BOUND, leap, jump, spring, hop, skip.
□ **bounce back** RECOVER, revive, rally, pick up, be on the mend; perk up, cheer up, brighten up, liven up; *informal* buck up.

bound¹ *adj.* **1** CERTAIN, sure, very likely, destined, fated, doomed. **2** OBLIGATED, obliged, compelled, required, constrained, forced.

bound² *v.* LEAP, jump, spring, bounce, hop; skip, bob, dance, prance, gambol, gallop.

boundary *n.* **1** BORDER, frontier, borderline, partition; cutline✤, fenceline. **2** DIVIDING LINE, divide, division, cut-off point. **3** BOUNDS, confines, limits, margins, edges, fringes; border, periphery, perimeter.

boundless *adj.* ☞ LIMITLESS.
—OPPOSITES: limited.

bountiful *adj.* **1** GENEROUS, magnanimous, munificent, open-handed, unselfish, unstinting, lavish; benevolent, beneficent, charitable. **2** ☞ ABUNDANT.
—OPPOSITES: mean, meagre.

bouquet *n.* **1** BUNCH OF FLOWERS, posy, nosegay, spray, corsage, boutonniere. **2** ☞ FRAGRANCE 1.

bout *n.* **1** ATTACK, fit, spasm, paroxysm, convulsion, eruption, outburst; period, session, spell. **2** CONTEST, match, fight, prizefight, competition, event, meeting, fixture.

bow *v.* **1** INCLINE THE BODY/HEAD, nod, salaam, kowtow, curtsy, bob, genuflect. **2** YIELD, submit, give in, surrender, succumb, capitulate, defer, conform; comply with, accept, heed, observe.

bowl *n.* DISH, basin, pot, crock, mortar; container, vessel, receptacle; *rare* jorum, porringer.
□ **bowl someone over 1** KNOCK DOWN/OVER, fell, floor, prostrate. **2** (*informal*) ☞ AMAZE.

box¹ *n.* CARTON, pack, packet; case, crate, chest, coffer, casket, trunk; container, receptacle.

box² *v.* **1** FIGHT, prizefight, spar; brawl; *informal* scrap. **2** ☞ HIT *v.* 1.

boxer *n.* FIGHTER, pugilist, prizefighter, kick-boxer; *informal* bruiser, scrapper.

boy *n.* LAD, schoolboy, male child, youth, young man, laddie, stripling. See also CHILD.

boycott *n.* BAN, veto, embargo, prohibition, sanction, restriction; avoidance, rejection, refusal.

boyfriend *n.* LOVER, sweetheart, beloved, darling, dearest, young man, man friend, man, guy, escort, suitor; partner, significant other, companion, (main) squeeze, flame, steady, fancy man, toy boy, boy toy, sugar daddy; *literary* swain; *dated* beau; *archaic* paramour.

brace *v.* **1** SUPPORT, shore up, prop up, hold up, buttress, underpin; strengthen, reinforce. **2** STEADY, secure, stabilize, fix, poise; tense, tighten. **3** PREPARE, get ready, gear up, nerve, steel, galvanize, gird, strengthen, fortify; *informal* psych oneself up.

bracing *adj.* ☞ REFRESHING 1.

brag *v.* ☞ BOAST.

brain *n.* **1** CEREBRUM, cerebral matter, encephalon.
2 ☞ INTELLIGENCE 1.
—RELATED: cerebral, encephalic.

brainless *adj.* ☞ STUPID 1.
—OPPOSITES: clever.

branch *n.* **1** BOUGH, limb, arm, offshoot. **2** DIVISION, subdivision, section, subsection, subset, department, sector, part, side, wing. **3** OFFICE, bureau, agency; subsidiary, affiliate, offshoot, satellite.
▶ *v.* FORK, bifurcate, divide, subdivide, split.
□ **branch out** EXPAND, open up, extend; diversify, broaden one's horizons.

brand *n.* MAKE, line, label, marque; type, kind, sort, variety, category, genre, style, ilk, stripe; trade name, trademark, proprietary name.
▶ *v.* **1** MARK, stamp, burn, sear. **2** STIGMATIZE, mark out; denounce, discredit, vilify; label.

brandish *v.* FLOURISH, wave, shake, wield; swing, swish; display, flaunt, show off.

brash *adj.* PUSHY, audacious, brazen, bumptious, impudent, rude. See also COCKY.
—OPPOSITES: meek.

bravado *n.* BOLDNESS, swaggering, bluster; machismo; boasting, bragging, bombast, braggadocio; *informal* showing off.

brave *adj.* COURAGEOUS, valiant, valorous, intrepid, heroic, lion-hearted, bold, fearless, gallant, chivalrous, daring, plucky, audacious; unflinching, unafraid, dauntless, doughty, mettlesome, indomitable, undaunted, venturesome, stout-hearted, spirited; *informal* game, gutsy, spunky, ballsy, daredevil.
—OPPOSITES: cowardly.
▶ *v.* FACE, confront, defy. See also ENDURE 1.

bravery *n.* COURAGE, pluck, valour, intrepidity, nerve, daring, fearlessness, courageousness, audacity, boldness, dauntlessness, stout-heartedness, heroism, gallantry, chivalry; backbone, grit, true grit, spine, spirit, mettle; *informal* guts, balls, cojones, spunk, moxie.

bravo *excl.* WELL DONE, congratulations, brava; encore; *informal* attaboy.

brawl *n.* ☞ FIGHT *n.* 1.

brawny *adj.* ☞ MUSCULAR.
—OPPOSITES: puny, weak.

brazen *adj.* BOLD, SHAMELESS, unashamed, unabashed, unembarrassed; defiant, impudent, impertinent, cheeky, saucy, insolent, in-your-face; barefaced, blatant, flagrant.
—OPPOSITES: timid.

breach *n.* **1** CONTRAVENTION, violation, infringement, infraction, transgression, neglect; *Law* delict. **2** RIFT, schism, division, gulf, chasm; disunion, estrangement, discord, dissension, disagreement; split, break, rupture, scission. **3** BREAK, rupture, split, crack, fracture; opening, gap, hole, fissure.

break *v.* **1** SHATTER, smash, crack, snap, fracture, fragment, splinter, fall to bits, fall to pieces; split, burst; *informal* bust. **2** STOP WORKING, break down, give out, go wrong, malfunction, crash; *informal* go kaput, conk out, be on the blink/fritz, give up the ghost. **3** CONTRAVENE, violate, infringe, breach; defy, flout, disobey, fly in the face of. **4** CUSHION, soften the impact of, take the edge off. **5** EXCEED, surpass, beat, better, cap, top, outdo, outstrip, eclipse. **6** DESTROY, crush, quash, defeat, vanquish, overcome, overpower, overwhelm, suppress, cripple; weaken, subdue, cow, undermine. **7** REVEAL, disclose, divulge, impart, tell; announce, release. **8** FALTER, quaver, quiver, tremble, shake.
—OPPOSITES: repair, keep, resume.
▸ *n.* **1** INTERRUPTION, interval, gap, hiatus; discontinuation, suspension, disruption, cut-off; stop, stoppage, cessation. **2** REST, respite, recess; stop, pause; interval, intermission; *informal* breather, time out, down time; coffee break, (*Nfld*) mug-up♣. **3** RIFT, schism, split, breakup, severance, rupture. **4** OPPORTUNITY, chance, opening.

☐**break away 1** ESCAPE, get away, run away, flee, make off; break free, break loose; *informal* cut and run. **2** LEAVE, secede from, split off from, separate from, part company with, defect from; *Politics* cross the floor. **break down 1** ☞ BREAK *v.* 2. **2** FAIL, collapse, founder, fall through, disintegrate; *informal* fizzle out. **break in 1** COMMIT BURGLARY, break and enter; force one's way in. **2** ☞ INTERRUPT 1. **break something off** END, terminate, stop, cease, call a halt to, finish, dissolve; SUSPEND, discontinue; *informal* pull the plug on. **break up 1** DISPERSE, scatter, disband, part company. **2** SPLIT UP, separate, part (company); divorce.

breakdown *n.* **1** FAILURE, collapse, disintegration, foundering. **2** NERVOUS BREAKDOWN, collapse; *informal* crack-up. **3** ANALYSIS, classification, examination, investigation, dissection.

breakthrough *n.* ADVANCE, development, step forward, success, improvement; discovery, innovation, revolution; breakout.
—OPPOSITES: setback.

breast *n.* (**breasts**) BOSOM(S), bust, chest; *informal* boobs, knockers, bazooms, hooters.

breathe *v.* **1** inhale and exhale, respire, draw breath; puff, pant, blow, gasp, wheeze, huff; *Medicine* inspire, expire. **2** INSTILL, infuse, inject, inspire, impart, imbue.

breathless *adj.* OUT OF BREATH, panting, puffing, gasping, wheezing, hyperventilating;

winded, puffed out, short of breath.

breathtaking adj. ☞ WONDERFUL.

breed v. **1** REPRODUCE, produce/bear/generate offspring, procreate, multiply, propagate; mate. **2** CAUSE, bring about, give rise to, lead to, produce, generate, foster, result in; stir up; *literary* beget.
▶ n. VARIETY, stock, strain; type, kind, sort; brand, genre, generation.

breeze n. **1** GENTLE WIND, puff of air, gust, cat's paw; *Meteorology* light air; *literary* zephyr. **2** ☞ CINCH.

breezy adj. **1** WINDY, fresh, brisk, airy; blowy, blustery, gusty. **2** CASUAL, easy, relaxed, informal. See also CHEERFUL.

brevity n. CONCISENESS, concision, succinctness, economy of language, pithiness, incisiveness, shortness, compactness.
—OPPOSITES: verbosity.

brew v. **1** PREPARE, infuse, make, steep, stew; ferment. **2** DEVELOP, loom, threaten, impend, be imminent, be on the horizon, be in the offing.
▶ n. **1** BEER, ale. **2** ☞ MIXTURE.

bribe v. BUY OFF, pay off, suborn; *informal* grease someone's palm, fix, square.
▶ n. INDUCEMENT, incentive, payoff, kickback, payola, boodle, sweetener, sop.

bridal adj. WEDDING, nuptial, marriage, matrimonial, marital, conjugal.

bridge n. **1** VIADUCT, overpass, fixed link, aqueduct. **2** LINK, connection, bond, tie.
▶ v. JOIN, link, connect, unite; straddle; overcome, reconcile.

bridle v. **1** BRISTLE, take offence, take umbrage, be affronted, be offended, get angry. **2** ☞ CURB.

brief adj. **1** ☞ CONCISE. **2** SHORT, flying, fleeting, hasty, hurried, quick, cursory, perfunctory; temporary, short-lived, momentary, transient; *informal* quickie.
—OPPOSITES: lengthy.
▶ n. SUMMARY, case, argument, contention; dossier.
▶ v. INFORM, tell, update, notify, advise, apprise; prepare, prime, instruct; *informal* fill in, clue in, put in the picture.

briefcase n. ATTACHÉ (CASE), satchel, portfolio, dispatch case.

briefly adv. **1** MOMENTARILY, temporarily, for a moment, fleetingly. **2** ☞ IN SHORT at SHORT.

bright adj. **1** SHINING, brilliant, dazzling, beaming, glaring; sparkling, flashing, glittering, scintillating, gleaming, glowing, luminous, radiant; shiny, lustrous, glossy. **2** ☞ SUNNY. **3** VIVID, brilliant, intense, strong, bold, glowing, rich; gaudy, lurid, garish; COLOURFUL, vibrant; *dated* gay. **4** ☞ INTELLIGENT. **5** PROMISING, rosy, optimistic, hopeful, favourable, propitious, auspicious, encouraging, good, golden.
—OPPOSITES: dull, dark, stupid.

brighten v. **1** ILLUMINATE, light up, lighten, make bright, make brighter, cast/shed light on; *formal* illume. **2** CHEER UP, perk up, rally; be enlivened, feel heartened, be uplifted, be encouraged, take heart; *informal* buck up, pep up.

brilliant *adj.* **1** BRIGHT, intelligent, clever, smart, astute, intellectual; gifted, talented, able, adept, skilful; elite, superior, first-class, first-rate, excellent; *informal* brainy. **2** SUPERB, glorious, illustrious, impressive, remarkable, exceptional. **3** ☞ BRIGHT 1.
—OPPOSITES: stupid, bad, dark.

brim *n.* RIM, lip, brink, edge.
▶ *v.* FULL OF, teeming with, awash in/with, chock full of, loaded with.

bring *v.* **1** CARRY, fetch, bear, take; convey, transport, tote; move, haul, shift, lug. **2** ESCORT, conduct, guide, lead, usher, show, shepherd. **3** CAUSE, produce, create, generate, precipitate, lead to, give rise to, result in; stir up, whip up, promote; *literary* beget.
◻**bring something about** ☞ CAUSE *v.* **bring something in 1** INTRODUCE, launch, inaugurate, initiate, institute. **2** ☞ EARN 1.
bring something off ☞ ACCOMPLISH. **bring someone up** ☞ REAR[1] 1. **bring something up** MENTION, allude to, touch on, raise, broach, introduce; voice, air, suggest, propose, submit, put forward, bring forward, table.

brink *n.* **1** EDGE, verge, margin, rim, lip; border, boundary, perimeter, periphery, limit(s). **2** VERGE, threshold, point.

brisk *adj.* **1** QUICK, rapid, fast, swift, speedy, hurried; energetic, lively, vigorous. **2** BUSY, bustling, lively, hectic; good.
—OPPOSITES: slow, quiet.

bristle *n.* HAIR, whisker; prickle, spine, quill, barb; *Zoology* seta.
▶ *v.* BRIDLE, take offence, take umbrage, be affronted, be offended; get angry, be irritated.

brittle *adj.* BREAKABLE, fragile, delicate; splintery; *formal* frangible.
—OPPOSITES: flexible, resilient.

broach *v.* BRING UP, raise, introduce, talk about, mention, touch on, air.

broad *adj.* **1** EXTENSIVE, wide, vast, immense, great, spacious, expansive, sizeable, sweeping, rolling. **2** COMPREHENSIVE, inclusive, extensive, wide, all-embracing, eclectic, unlimited. **3** GENERAL, non-specific, unspecific, rough, approximate, basic; loose, vague. **4** ☞ OBVIOUS.
—OPPOSITES: narrow, limited, detailed, subtle.

broadcast *v.* **1** TRANSMIT, relay, air, beam, show, televise, telecast, webcast, simulcast, cablecast, screen. **2** ☞ ANNOUNCE 1.

broaden *v.* EXPAND, enlarge, extend, widen; swell; increase, augment, add to, amplify; develop, enrich, improve, build on.

brochure *n.* BOOKLET, pamphlet, leaflet, flyer, handbill, catalogue, handout, prospectus, fact sheet, folder.

broke *adj.* PENNILESS, moneyless, bankrupt, insolvent, ruined, cleaned out, strapped (for cash), down-and-out, without a penny to one's name, without a (red) cent, without two nickels/pennies to rub together, flat broke, bust, hard up; poor, poverty-stricken, impoverished, impecunious, penurious, indigent, in penury, needy, destitute, as poor as a church mouse.

broken-down *adj.*
1 ☞ DILAPIDATED. **2** DEFECTIVE, broken, faulty; not working, malfunctioning, inoperative, non-functioning; *informal* kaput, conked out, done for, had the biscuit✢.

broken-hearted *adj.*
☞ HEARTBROKEN.
—OPPOSITES: overjoyed.

brood *n.* FAMILY; children, offspring, youngsters, progeny; *informal* kids.
▶ *v.* WORRY, fret, agonize, mope, sulk; think, ponder, contemplate, meditate, muse, ruminate.

brook *n.* ☞ STREAM *n.* 1.
▶ *v.* (*formal*) TOLERATE, allow, stand, bear, abide, put up with, endure; accept, permit, countenance; *informal* stomach, stand for, hack.

browbeat *v.* FORCE, coerce, compel, bludgeon. See also INTIMIDATE.

brown *adj.* hazel, chocolate-coloured, coffee-coloured, cocoa-coloured, nut-brown; brunette; sepia, mahogany, umber, burnt sienna; beige, buff, tan, fawn, camel, café au lait, caramel, chestnut.

browse *v.* **1** LOOK AROUND/ROUND, window-shop, peruse. **2** SCAN, skim, glance, look, peruse; thumb, leaf, flick; dip into.

bruise *n.* CONTUSION, lesion, mark, injury; swelling, lump, bump, welt.
▶ *v.* **1** injure, mark, discolour; damage, spoil. **2** UPSET, offend, insult, affront, hurt, wound, injure, crush.

brunt *n.* (*FULL*) FORCE, impact, shock, burden, pressure, weight; effect, repercussions, consequences.

brush *n.* **1** BROOM, sweeper, besom, whisk. **2** ENCOUNTER, clash, confrontation, conflict, altercation, incident; *informal* run-in. **3** UNDERGROWTH, bushes, scrub, underwood, underbrush, brushland, brushwood, shrubs, (*Nfld*) tuckamore✢, chaparral; thicket, copse.
▶ *v.* **1** SWEEP, clean, buff, scrub. **2** ☞ COMB 1. **3** TOUCH, stroke, caress, skim, sweep, graze, contact; kiss.
□ **brush someone off** REBUFF, dismiss, spurn, reject; slight, scorn, disdain; ignore, disregard, snub, cut, turn one's back on, give someone the cold shoulder, freeze out; jilt, cast aside, discard.

brush-off *n.* REJECTION, dismissal, refusal, rebuff, repulse; snub, slight, cut, kiss-off.

brutal *adj.* **1** SAVAGE, cruel, vicious, ferocious, brutish, barbaric, barbarous, wicked, murderous, bloodthirsty, cold-blooded, callous, heartless, ruthless, merciless, sadistic, inhuman; dark, diabolical, fiendish, infernal; heinous, monstrous, abominable, atrocious, bestial, vile, villainous. **2** UNSPARING, unstinting, unembellished, unvarnished, bald, naked, stark, blunt, direct, straightforward, frank, outspoken, forthright, plain-spoken; complete, total.
—OPPOSITES: gentle.

brute *n.* SAVAGE, beast, monster, animal, barbarian, fiend, ogre; sadist; thug, lout, ruffian; *informal* swine, pig.

bubble v. **1** SPARKLE, fizz, effervesce, foam, froth. **2** BOIL, simmer, seethe, gurgle. **3** OVERFLOW, brim over, be filled, gush.

bubbly adj. **1** SPARKLING, bubbling, fizzy, effervescent, gassy, aerated, carbonated; spumante, frothy, foamy. **2** ☞ VIVACIOUS.
—OPPOSITES: still, listless.

buckle n. CLASP, clip, catch, hasp, fastener.
▸ v. **1** FASTEN, do up, hook, strap, secure, clasp, clip. **2** WARP, bend, twist, curve, distort, contort, deform; bulge, arc, arch; crumple, collapse, give way.

bud n. SPROUT, shoot, blossom; Botany plumule.
▸ v. SPROUT, shoot, germinate.

budge v. **1** MOVE, shift, stir, go. **2** GIVE IN, give way, yield, change one's mind, acquiesce, compromise, do a U-turn.

budget n. FINANCIAL PLAN, forecast; accounts, statement, Blue Book✥.
▸ v. ALLOCATE, allot, allow, earmark, designate, set aside.
▸ adj. ☞ INEXPENSIVE.
—OPPOSITES: expensive.

buff v. POLISH, burnish, shine, clean, rub.
▸ n. (informal) AUTHORITY, pundit. See also FAN.

buffer n. CUSHION, bulwark, shield, barrier, guard, safeguard.

buffet[1] n. **1** COLD TABLE, self-service meal, smorgasbord. **2** SIDEBOARD, cabinet, cupboard.

buffet[2] v. BATTER, pound, lash, strike, hit.

buffoon n. ☞ FOOL 1.

bug n. **1** INSECT, mite; informal creepy-crawly, beastie. **2** (informal) BACTERIUM, germ, virus. See also DISEASE. **3** FAULT, error, defect, flaw; virus; informal glitch, gremlin.
▸ v. **1** RECORD, eavesdrop on, spy on, overhear; wiretap, tap, monitor. **2** (informal) ☞ ANNOY.

build v. **1** CONSTRUCT, erect, put up, assemble; make, form, create, fashion, model, shape. **2** ESTABLISH, found, set up, institute, inaugurate, initiate. **3** INCREASE, mount, intensify, escalate, grow, rise.
▸ n. ☞ PHYSIQUE.
□ **build something up 1** BOOST, strengthen, increase, improve, augment, raise, enhance, swell; informal beef up. **2** ACCUMULATE, amass, collect, gather; stockpile, hoard.

building n. STRUCTURE, construction, edifice, erection, pile; property, premises, establishment.
—RELATED: tectonic.

buildup n. **1** INCREASE, growth, expansion, escalation, development, proliferation. **2** ACCUMULATION, accretion.

bulbous adj. BULGING, protuberant, round, fat, rotund; swollen, tumid, distended, bloated.

bulge n. SWELLING, bump, lump, protuberance, prominence, tumescence.
▸ v. SWELL, stick out, puff out, balloon (out), bug out, fill out, belly, distend, tumefy; project, protrude, stand out.

bulk n. **1** SIZE, volume, dimensions, proportions, mass, scale, magnitude, immensity,

vastness. **2** ☞ MAJORITY.
—OPPOSITES: minority.

bulky *adj.* CUMBERSOME,
unmanageable, unwieldy,
ponderous, heavy, weighty. See
also BIG 1.
—OPPOSITES: small, slight.

bulldoze *v.* **1** DEMOLISH, knock
down, tear down, pull down,
flatten, level, raze, clear. **2** FORCE,
push, shove, barge, elbow,
shoulder, jostle, muscle; plunge,
crash, sweep, bundle.

bulletin *n.* **1** REPORT, dispatch,
story, press release, newscast,
flash; statement, announcement,
message, communication,
communiqué. **2** NEWSLETTER,
proceedings; newspaper,
magazine, digest, gazette, review,
tipsheet.

bullish *adj.* CONFIDENT, positive,
assertive, self-assertive, assured,
self-assured, bold, determined;
optimistic, buoyant, sanguine;
informal feisty, upbeat.

bully *n.* PERSECUTOR, oppressor,
tyrant, tormentor, intimidator;
tough guy, bully boy, thug.
▸ *v.* **1** PERSECUTE, oppress,
tyrannize, browbeat, harass,
torment, intimidate, strong-arm,
dominate, bullyrag; *informal* push
around. **2** ☞ PRESSURE *v.*

bulwark *n.* **1** WALL, rampart,
fortification, parapet, stockade,
palisade, barricade, embankment,
earthwork. **2** PROTECTOR, defender,
protection, guard, defence,
supporter, buttress; mainstay,
bastion, stronghold.

bum *n.* (*informal*) **1** ☞ BUTTOCKS.
2 ☞ BEGGAR 1. **3** IDLER, loafer,
slacker, good-for-nothing, ne'er-

do-well, layabout, lounger,
shirker; loser.
▸ *v.* **1** LOAF, lounge, idle, moon,
wander, drift, meander, dawdle;
informal mooch, lallygag. **2** BEG,
borrow; *informal* scrounge, cadge,
sponge, mooch.

bumbling *adj.* BLUNDERING,
bungling, inept, clumsy,
maladroit, awkward, muddled,
klutzy; oafish, clodhopping,
lumbering; botched, schlubby,
ham-handed/fisted.
—OPPOSITES: efficient.

bump *n.* **1** BANG, crash, smash,
smack, crack, jolt, thud, thump,
hit, blow, knock; *informal* whack,
thwack, bash, bonk, wallop.
2 HUMP, lump, ridge, bulge, knob,
protuberance; swelling.
▸ *v.* **1** HIT, crash, smash, smack,
slam, bang, knock, run, plow;
ram, collide with, strike, impact.
2 BOUNCE, jolt, jerk, rattle, shake.

bumpkin *n.* YOKEL, peasant,
provincial, rustic, country cousin,
hayseed, hillbilly, hick, rube; (*Nfld*)
baywop✤, (*Nfld*) bayman✤,
noddy✤.

bumptious *adj.* SELF-IMPORTANT,
conceited, arrogant, self-assertive,
pushy, pompous, overbearing,
cocky, swaggering, proud,
haughty, overweening, egotistical;
informal snooty, uppity.
—OPPOSITES: modest.

bumpy *adj.* **1** UNEVEN, rough,
rutted, rutty, pitted, potholed,
holey; lumpy, rocky. **2** BOUNCY,
rough, uncomfortable, jolting,
lurching, jerky, jarring, bone-
shaking.
—OPPOSITES: smooth.

bunch *n.* **1** BOUQUET, posy, nosegay, spray, corsage; wreath, garland. **2** GROUP, set, circle, company, collection, bevy, band; gang, crowd, load. **3** ASSORTMENT, bundle, collection; many, lots, load, an abundance, job lot.

bundle *n.* BUNCH, roll, clump, wad, parcel, sheaf, bale, bolt; package; pile, stack, heap, mass; *informal* load.
  ▶ *v.* **1** TIE, pack, parcel, wrap, roll, fold, bind, bale, package.
  2 ☞ WRAP 1.

bungle *v.* MISHANDLE, mismanage, mess up, spoil, ruin, blunder, miss, muddle up, forget; *informal* botch, muff, fluff, make a hash of, foul up, screw up, flub, goof up.

bungling *adj.* INCOMPETENT, blundering, amateurish, inept, unskilful, maladroit, clumsy, klutzy, awkward, bumbling; *informal* ham-handed/fisted.

buoy *n.* FLOAT, (*Nfld*) keg✿, marker, beacon.
  ▶ *v.* ☞ HEARTEN.
  —OPPOSITES: depress.

buoyant *adj.* **1** ABLE TO FLOAT, floating, floatable. **2** ☞ CHEERFUL.

burden *n.* **1** ENCUMBRANCE, strain, care, problem, worry, difficulty, trouble, millstone; RESPONSIBILITY, onus, charge, duty, obligation, liability. **2** LOAD, weight, cargo, freight.
  ▶ *v.* LOAD, charge, weigh down, encumber, hamper; overload, overburden; OPPRESS, trouble, worry, harass, upset, distress; haunt, afflict, strain, stress, tax, overwhelm.

burdensome *adj.* TROUBLESOME, worrisome, stressful; vexatious, irksome, trying. See also ONEROUS.

bureau *n.* **1** DESK, writing table, secretaire, escritoire; chest of drawers, cabinet, dresser, commode, tallboy, highboy.
  2 AGENCY, service, office, business, company, firm; DEPARTMENT, division, branch, section.

bureaucracy *n.* RED TAPE, rules and regulations, protocol, officialdom, paperwork.

burglar *n.* ROBBER, housebreaker, cat burglar, thief, raider, looter, safecracker, second-storey man; intruder, prowler.

burglary *n.* BREAK-IN, theft, housebreaking, robbery, raid; *informal* smash and grab, break and enter, heist.

burial *n.* BURYING, interment, committal, entombment; funeral, obsequies; *formal* inhumation.
  —OPPOSITES: exhumation.

burlesque *n.* PARODY, caricature, satire, lampoon, skit, farce; send-up, takeoff, spoof; striptease, strip.

burly *adj.* STRAPPING, well-built, sturdy, brawny, strong, muscular, muscly, thickset, blocky, big, hefty, bulky, stocky, stout, Herculean, hunky, beefy, husky, hulking.
  —OPPOSITES: puny.

burn *v.* **1** BE ON FIRE, be alight, be ablaze, blaze, go up (in smoke), be in flames, be aflame; smoulder, glow. **2** SET FIRE TO, set on fire, set alight, set light to, light, ignite, touch off; incinerate; *informal* torch. **3** SCORCH, singe, sear, char, blacken, brand, sizzle; scald.

4 CONSUME, use up, expend, get/go through, eat up; dissipate.

burning *adj.* **1** BLAZING, flaming, fiery, ignited, glowing, red-hot, smouldering, igneous; raging, roaring. **2** INTENSE, passionate, deep-seated, profound, wholehearted, strong, ardent, fervent, urgent, fierce, eager, frantic, consuming, uncontrollable. **3** IMPORTANT, crucial, significant, vital, essential, pivotal; urgent, pressing, compelling, critical.

burnish *v.* POLISH, shine, buff, rub, gloss.

burrow *n.* HOLE, tunnel, warren, dugout; lair, set, den, earth.
▶ *v.* TUNNEL, dig (out), excavate, grub, mine, bore, channel; hollow out, gouge out.

burst *v.* **1** SPLIT (OPEN), rupture, break, tear. **2** EXPLODE, blow up, detonate, go off. **3** BARGE, charge, plunge, plow, hurtle, career, careen, rush, dash, tear.

bury *v.* **1** INTER, lay to rest, entomb; *informal* put six feet under; *literary* inhume. **2** HIDE, conceal, cover, enfold, engulf, tuck, cup, sink. **3** ABSORB, engross, immerse, occupy, engage, busy, involve.
—OPPOSITES: exhume.

bush *n.* **1** SHRUB, brier; (**bushes**) undergrowth, shrubbery. **2** WILDS, wilderness, forest, woodland, timberland, bush country, bushland; backwoods, hinterland(s), backcountry, backlands; *informal* the sticks, boondocks, (*Ont. & Que.*) the back concessions✦, moose pasture✦.

bushy *adj.* THICK, shaggy, fuzzy, bristly, fluffy, woolly; luxuriant.
—OPPOSITES: sleek, wispy.

business *n.* **1** WORK, line of work, occupation, profession, career, employment, job, position; vocation, calling; field, sphere, trade, métier, craft; *informal* biz, racket, game. **2** ☞ TRADE *n.* 1.
3 COMPANY, firm, concern, enterprise, venture, organization, operation, corporation, undertaking; office, agency, franchise, practice; *informal* outfit.
4 CONCERN, affair, responsibility, duty, function, obligation; problem, worry; *informal* beeswax, bailiwick.
—RELATED: corporate.

businesslike *adj.* PROFESSIONAL, efficient, competent, methodical, disciplined, systematic, orderly, organized, structured, practical, pragmatic, routine, slick.

bust[1] *n.* **1** CHEST, bosom, breasts. **2** SCULPTURE, carving, effigy, statue; head and shoulders.

bust[2] (*informal*) *v.* **1** BREAK, smash, fracture, shatter, crack, disintegrate, snap; split, burst. **2** ☞ ARREST *v.* 1.
☐ **go bust** ☞ GO BANKRUPT at BANKRUPT.

bustle *v.* RUSH, dash, hurry, scurry, scuttle, hustle, scamper, scramble; run, tear, charge; *informal* scoot, beetle, buzz, zoom.

busy *adj.* **1** OCCUPIED (IN), engaged in, involved in, employed in, working at, hard at work (on); rushed off one's feet, hard-pressed, swamped, up to one's neck; on the job, absorbed, engrossed, immersed,

preoccupied; *informal* (as) busy as a bee, on the go, hard at it. **2** UNAVAILABLE, engaged, occupied; working, in a meeting, on duty; *informal* tied up. **3** HECTIC, active, lively; crowded, bustling, abuzz, swarming, teeming, full, thronged.
—OPPOSITES: idle, free, quiet.

busybody *n.* MEDDLER, interferer, mischief-maker, troublemaker; gossip, scandalmonger; eavesdropper; *informal* kibitzer, buttinsky, Nosy Parker, snoop, snooper, yenta.

butt *n.* **1** TARGET, victim, object, subject, dupe; laughingstock. **2** STUB, end, tail end, stump, remnant. **3** (*informal*) ☞ BUTTOCKS.
▶ *v.* **1** ADJOIN, abut, be next to, be adjacent to, border (on); join, touch. **2** RAM, head-butt, bunt; bump, buffet, push, shove.
☐ **butt in** ☞ INTERRUPT 1.

buttocks *pl. n.* REAR (END), backside, seat, bottom, rump, cheeks, behind, derrière, bum, butt, fanny, keister, tush, tail, buns, heinie, arse, ass, caboose; fundament, posterior, haunches, gluteus maximus, sit-upon, stern, wazoo; *Anatomy* nates.

button *n.* **1** FASTENER, stud, toggle; hook, catch, clasp, dome fastener, snap fastener, pin. **2** SWITCH, knob, control; lever, handle; icon, box.

buttress *n.* PROP, support, abutment, brace, shore, pier, reinforcement, stanchion.
▶ *v.* STRENGTHEN, reinforce, fortify, support, bolster, shore up,

underpin, cement, uphold, prop up, defend, sustain, back up.

buxom *adj.* LARGE-BREASTED, big-breasted, bosomy, big-bosomed; shapely, ample, plump, rounded, full-figured, voluptuous, curvaceous, Rubenesque; *informal* busty, built, stacked, chesty, well-endowed, curvy.

buy *v.* PURCHASE, acquire, obtain, get, pick up; take, procure, pay for; invest in; *informal* get hold of, snatch up, snap up, grab, score.
—OPPOSITES: sell.
▶ *n.* (*informal*) PURCHASE, investment, acquisition, gain; deal, value, bargain.

buzz *n.* **1** HUM, humming, buzzing, murmur, drone, zizz. **2** RING, purr, note, tone, beep, bleep, warble, alarm, warning sound. **3** (*informal*) ☞ GOSSIP.
▶ *v.* **1** HUM, drone, bumble, murmur, zizz. **2** PURR, warble, sound, ring, beep, bleep. **3** HUM, throb, vibrate, pulse, bustle, be abuzz.
☐ **buzz off** ☞ SCRAM.

bygone *adj.* PAST, former, olden, earlier, previous, one-time, long-ago, of old, ancient, antiquated; departed, dead, extinct, defunct, out of date, outmoded; *literary* of yore.
—OPPOSITES: present, recent.

bypass *n.* RING ROAD, detour, diversion, alternative route, shortcut.
▶ *v.* **1** GO AROUND, go past, make a detour around; avoid. **2** AVOID, evade, dodge, escape, elude, circumvent, get around, shortcut around, skirt, sidestep, steer clear of; *informal* duck.

by-product *n.* SIDE EFFECT, consequence, entailment, corollary; ramification, repercussion, spinoff, fallout; fruits.

bystander *n.* ONLOOKER, looker-on, passerby, non-participant, observer, spectator, eyewitness, witness, watcher, gawker; *informal* railbird, rubbernecker.

Cc

cabal *n.* CLIQUE, faction, coterie, cell, sect, camarilla, junta; lobby (group), pressure group, ginger group.

cabin *n.* COTTAGE, log cabin, shack, shanty, (Nfld) tilt✦, hut; chalet; cabana; caboose✦; *historical* camboose✦.

cable *n.* ROPE, cord, line, guy, wire, lead; hawser, stay, bridle; choker.

cache *n.* HOARD, store, stockpile, stock, supply, reserve; arsenal; *informal* stash.

cacophony *n.* DIN, racket, noise, clamour, discord, dissonance, discordance, uproar.

cadaverous *adj.* (DEATHLY) PALE, pallid, ashen, grey, whey-faced, sallow, wan, anemic, bloodless, etiolated, corpse-like, deathlike. See also GAUNT.
—OPPOSITES: rosy, plump.

cadence *n.* INTONATION, modulation, lilt, accent, inflection; rhythm, tempo, metre, beat, pulse.

café *n.* COFFEE SHOP, coffee bar, tea room; bistro, brasserie, cafeteria; snack bar, buffet, diner, eatery.

cage *n.* ENCLOSURE, pen, pound; coop, hutch; birdcage, aviary, corral.

cagey *adj.* (*informal*) SECRETIVE, tight-lipped. See also GUARDED.
—OPPOSITES: open.

cajole *v.* ☞ COAX.

cake *n.* BAR, tablet, block, brick, slab, lump.
▶ *v.* COAT, encrust, plaster, cover.

calamitous *adj.* ☞ DISASTROUS.

calamity *n.* DISASTER, catastrophe, tragedy, cataclysm, adversity, tribulation, affliction, misfortune, misadventure.
—OPPOSITES: godsend.

calculate *v.* **1** COMPUTE, work out, reckon, figure, determine, evaluate, quantify; add up/together, count up, tally, total, tote, tot up. **2** INTEND, mean, aim, design.

calculated *adj.* ☞ INTENTIONAL.
—OPPOSITES: unintentional.

calculating *adj.* ☞ CUNNING.
—OPPOSITES: ingenuous.

calibre *n.* **1** QUALITY, merit, distinction, stature, excellence, pre-eminence; ability, expertise, talent, capability, capacity, proficiency; standard, level. **2** BORE, diameter, gauge.

call *v.* **1** CRY (OUT), shout, yell, hail, bellow, roar, bawl, vociferate; *informal* holler. **2** ☞ CONVENE. **3** ☞ NAME *v.* 1.
▶ *n.* **1** CRY, shout, yell, roar, scream, exclamation, vociferation; *informal* holler. **2** PHONE CALL, telephone call, ring; *informal* buzz. **3** APPEAL, request, plea, entreaty. **4** SUMMONS, request. **5** DECISION,

ruling, judgment, verdict.
□ **call for** REQUIRE, need,
necessitate; justify, warrant. **call
something off** ☞ CANCEL 1.

calling *n.* PROFESSION, occupation,
vocation, call, career, work,
employment, job, business, trade,
craft, line (of work); *informal* bag.

callous *adj.* ☞ HEARTLESS.

callow *adj.* ☞ IMMATURE 2.
—OPPOSITES: mature.

calm *adj.* **1** SERENE, tranquil,
relaxed, unruffled, unperturbed,
imperturbable, unflustered,
untroubled; equable, even-
tempered; placid, unexcitable,
unemotional, phlegmatic;
composed, {calm, cool, and
collected}, quiet, sedate, cool-
headed, cool, self-possessed, self-
controlled, at ease, collected;
informal unflappable, unfazed,
easygoing, level-headed, mild,
poised, steady, laid-back,
nonplussed, together, cool (as a
cucumber). **2** WINDLESS, still,
tranquil, serene, (*Nfld*) civil♣,
quiet. **3** TRANQUIL, still, smooth,
(*Nfld*) civil♣, glassy.
—OPPOSITES: excited, nervous,
stormy.
▶ *n.* **1** TRANQUILITY, stillness,
calmness, quiet, quietness,
quietude, peace, peacefulness.
2 ☞ EQUANIMITY.
▶ *v.* SOOTHE, pacify, placate,
mollify, appease, conciliate, quiet
(down), relax.
—OPPOSITES: excite, upset.

calumny *n.* ☞ SLANDER *n.*

camouflage *n.* **1** DISGUISE,
concealment, cover, screen.
2 FACADE, (false) front,
smokescreen, cover-up, mask,
blind, screen, masquerade,
dissimulation, pretense.
▶ *v.* DISGUISE, hide, conceal, keep
hidden, mask, screen, cover (up).

camp[1] *n.* **1** CAMPSITE,
campground, encampment,
bivouac. **2** ☞ FACTION.

camp[2] (*informal*) *adj.* **1** EFFEMINATE,
effete, mincing; *informal* campy,
limp-wristed. **2** EXAGGERATED,
theatrical, affected; *informal* over
the top, camped up.
—OPPOSITES: macho.

campaign *n.* **1** MILITARY
OPERATION(S), manoeuvre(s);
crusade, war, battle, offensive,
attack. **2** CRUSADE, drive, push,
struggle; operation, strategy,
battle plan.
▶ *v.* **1** CRUSADE, fight, battle, push,
press, strive, struggle, lobby.
2 RUN/STAND FOR OFFICE, canvass,
mainstreet♣, barnstorm,
electioneer, stump, go on the
hustings, glad-hand.

can *n.* TIN, canister, bin; garbage
can.
▶ *v.* ☞ DISMISS 1.

cancel *v.* **1** CALL OFF, abandon,
scrap, drop, axe, scrub, nix; end,
terminate. **2** ANNUL, invalidate,
nullify, declare null and void,
void; revoke, rescind, retract,
countermand, withdraw; *Law*
vacate.

cancer *n.* MALIGNANT GROWTH,
cancerous growth, tumour,
malignancy; *technical* carcinoma,
sarcoma, melanoma, lymphoma,
myeloma.

candid *adj.* ☞ OUTSPOKEN.
—OPPOSITES: guarded.

candidate *n.* (JOB) APPLICANT,
job-seeker, interviewee;

contender, competitor, contestant, nominee, hopeful.

candour n. FRANKNESS, openness, honesty, candidness, truthfulness, sincerity, forthrightness, directness, bluntness, straightforwardness, outspokenness; *informal* telling it like it is.

canny adj. SHREWD, astute, smart, sharp, sharp-witted, discerning, penetrating, discriminating, perceptive, perspicacious, wise, worldly-wise, sagacious; cunning, crafty, wily, as sharp as a tack, savvy; *dated* long-headed.
—OPPOSITES: foolish.

canopy n. AWNING, shade, sunshade; marquee; baldachin, tester, chuppah.

cantankerous adj. ☞ IRRITABLE.
—OPPOSITES: affable.

canvass v. 1 ☞ CAMPAIGN v. 2.
2 POLL, question, ask, survey, interview.

canyon n. ☞ GORGE n.

capability n. ABILITY, capacity, power, potential; competence, proficiency, adeptness, aptitude, faculty, wherewithal, experience, skill, skilfulness, talent, flair; *informal* know-how.

capable adj. COMPETENT, able, efficient, effective, proficient, accomplished, adept, handy, experienced, skilful, skilled, talented, gifted; *informal* useful.
—OPPOSITES: incompetent.

capacity n. 1 VOLUME, size, magnitude, dimensions, measurements, proportions.
2 ☞ CAPABILITY. 3 ☞ ROLE 2.

cape¹ n. CLOAK, mantle, cope, wrap, stole, tippet, capelet,

poncho, shawl; *historical* pelisse, mantelet.

cape² n. HEADLAND, promontory, point, spit, head, foreland, horn, hook.

caper v. SKIP, dance, romp, frisk, gambol, cavort, prance, frolic, leap, hop, jump, rollick.

capital n. 1 FIRST CITY, seat of government, metropolis.
2 ☞ MONEY.

capitulate v. ☞ SURRENDER v. 1.
—OPPOSITES: resist, hold out.

caprice n. WHIM, whimsy, vagary, fancy, fad, quirk, eccentricity, foible.

capricious adj. FICKLE, inconstant, changeable, variable, mercurial, volatile, unpredictable, temperamental; whimsical, fanciful, flighty, quirky, faddish.
—OPPOSITES: consistent.

capsize v. OVERTURN, turn over, turn upside down, upend, flip/tip/keel over, turn turtle; *Nautical* pitchpole; *archaic* overset.
—OPPOSITES: right.

capsule n. ☞ PILL.

captain n. 1 COMMANDER, master; *informal* skipper. 2 ☞ LEADER.
▶ v. COMMAND, run, be in charge of, control, manage, govern; *informal* skipper.

caption n. TITLE, heading, wording, head, legend, subtitle; *proprietary* Surtitle, rubric, slogan.

captivate v. ATTRACT, allure; engross. See also ENCHANT.

captive n. ☞ PRISONER.
▶ adj. CONFINED, caged, incarcerated, locked up; jailed, imprisoned, in prison/jail, interned, detained, in captivity,

under lock and key, behind bars, doing time, inside.

captivity *n.* IMPRISONMENT, confinement, internment, incarceration, detention, custody.
—OPPOSITES: freedom.

capture *v.* CATCH, apprehend, seize, arrest; take prisoner/captive, imprison, detain, put/throw in jail, put behind bars, put under lock and key, incarcerate; *informal* nab, collar, bag, pick up.
—OPPOSITES: free.
▶ *n.* ARREST, apprehension, seizure, being taken prisoner/captive, imprisonment.

car *n.* AUTOMOBILE, auto, motor car; *informal* wheels, gas guzzler; jalopy, lemon, beater, junker, clunker, tin Lizzie, rustbucket.

carafe *n.* FLASK, jug, pitcher, decanter, flagon.

cardinal *adj.* ☞ MAIN.
—OPPOSITES: unimportant.

care *n.* **1** SAFEKEEPING, supervision, custody, charge, protection, control, responsibility; guardianship, wardship.
2 ☞ CAUTION *n.* **1. 3** WORRY, anxiety, trouble, concern, stress, pressure, strain; sorrow, woe, hardship.
—OPPOSITES: neglect, carelessness.
▶ *v.* BE CONCERNED, worry (oneself), trouble/concern oneself, bother, mind, be interested; *informal* give a damn/hoot/rap.

career *n.* PROFESSION, occupation, job, vocation, calling, employment, line (of work), walk of life, métier.

carefree *adj.* UNWORRIED, untroubled, blithe, airy, nonchalant, insouciant, happy-go-lucky, free and easy, easygoing,

relaxed, mellow, laid-back.
—OPPOSITES: careworn.

careful *adj.* **1** ☞ CAUTIOUS.
2 ATTENTIVE, conscientious, painstaking, meticulous, diligent, deliberate, assiduous, sedulous, scrupulous, rigorous, punctilious, methodical, detailed, thorough, focused; *informal* persnickety, fussy.
—OPPOSITES: careless, extravagant.

careless *adj.* **1** INATTENTIVE, incautious, negligent, absent-minded, remiss; heedless, irresponsible, impetuous, reckless, foolhardy; cavalier, supercilious, devil-may-care.
2 SHODDY, negligent, disorganized, hasty, hurried. See also SLOPPY 1.
3 THOUGHTLESS, insensitive, indiscreet, unguarded, incautious, inadvertent.
—OPPOSITES: careful, meticulous.

caress *v.* STROKE, touch, fondle, brush, pet, skim, nuzzle.

caretaker *n.* JANITOR, attendant, porter, custodian, concierge, superintendent, super.

careworn *adj.* WORRIED, anxious, strained, stressed, dispirited; drained, drawn, gaunt, haggard.
—OPPOSITES: carefree.

cargo *n.* FREIGHT, load, haul, consignment, delivery, shipment; goods, merchandise, payload, lading.

caricature *n.* CARTOON, parody, satire, lampoon, burlesque; *informal* send-up, takeoff.
▶ *v.* ☞ PARODY *v.*

carnage *n.* ☞ MASSACRE.

carnal *adj.* SEXUAL, sensual, erotic, lustful, lascivious, libidinous, lecherous, licentious; physical,

bodily, corporeal, fleshly.
—OPPOSITES: spiritual.

carnival *n.* **1** ☞ FESTIVAL 1. **2** FAIR, amusement park, fun fair, exhibition♣, ex♣, amusement show, circus, big top.

carp *v.* ☞ COMPLAIN.
—OPPOSITES: praise.

carriage *n.* COACH, car, flatcar.

carry *v.* **1** CONVEY, transfer, move, transport, take, bring, bear, lug, tote, fetch, cart. **2** TRANSMIT, conduct, relay, communicate, dispatch, beam. **3** SUPPORT, sustain, stand. **4** BEAR, accept, assume, undertake, shoulder, take on (oneself). **5** SELL, stock, keep (in stock), offer, have (for sale), retail, supply. **6** ENTAIL, involve, result in, occasion, have as a consequence.
□ **carry something off** WIN, secure, gain, achieve, collect; *informal* land, net, bag, scoop. **carry on 1** CONTINUE, keep (on), go on; persist in, persevere in, stick with/at. **2** (*informal*) ☞ MISBEHAVE. **carry something out 1** CONDUCT, perform, implement, execute. **2** FULFILL, carry through, honour, redeem, make good; keep, observe, abide by, comply with, adhere to, stick to, keep faith with.

cart *n.* SHOPPING CART, bundle buggy, handcart, pushcart, trolley, barrow.
▶ *v.* ☞ CARRY 1.

carton *n.* ☞ BOX¹ *n.*

cartoon *n.* **1** ☞ CARICATURE. **2** COMIC STRIP, comic, funnies, graphic novel. **3** ANIMATED FILM, animation, toon, anime.

cartridge *n.* **1** CASSETTE, canister, container, magazine.

2 BULLET, round, shell, charge, shot.

carve *v.* **1** SCULPT, sculpture; cut, hew, whittle; form, shape, fashion. **2** ☞ ENGRAVE. **3** SLICE, cut up, chop.
□ **carved in stone**
☞ IRREVOCABLE.

cascade *n.* WATERFALL, cataract, falls, rapids, chute♣, white water.
▶ *v.* POUR, gush, surge, spill, stream, flow, issue, spurt.

case¹ *n.* **1** INSTANCE, occurrence, manifestation, demonstration, exposition, exhibition; example, illustration, specimen, sample, exemplification. **2** SITUATION, position, state of affairs. See also SITUATION 2. **3** INVESTIGATION, inquiry, examination, exploration, probe, search, inquest.
4 ☞ LAWSUIT.

case² *n.* **1** ☞ CONTAINER. **2** CASING, cover, covering, sheath, sheathing, envelope, sleeve, jacket, integument.
▶ *v.* ☞ SCOUT *v.* 2.

cash *n.* **1** ☞ MONEY 1. **2** FINANCE, money, resources, funds, assets, the means, the wherewithal.
—OPPOSITES: cheque, credit.
▶ *v.* EXCHANGE, change, convert into cash/money; honour, pay, accept.

cashier *n.* CHECKOUT GIRL/BOY/PERSON, clerk; bank clerk, teller, banker, treasurer, bursar, purser.

cask *n.* ☞ BARREL

cast *v.* **1** ☞ THROW *v.* 1. **2** REGISTER, record, enter, file, vote. **3** EMIT, give off, send out, radiate; project, throw. **4** ☞ MOULD *v.* 1.
▶ *n.* **1** MOULD, die, matrix, shape, casting, model. **2** THROW, toss, fling, pitch, hurl, lob, chuck.

3 TYPE, sort, kind, character, variety, class, style, stamp, nature. **4** ACTORS, performers, players, company, troupe; dramatis personae, characters.

castaway *adj.* SHIPWRECKED, wrecked, stranded, aground, marooned.

caste *n.* (SOCIAL) CLASS, social order, rank, level, stratum, echelon, status; *dated* estate, station.

castigate *v.* ☞ REPRIMAND.
—OPPOSITES: praise, commend.

castle *n.* FORTRESS, fort, stronghold, fortification, keep, citadel.

castrate *v.* NEUTER, geld, cut, desex, unsex, sterilize, fix, alter, doctor; *archaic* emasculate.

casual *adj.* **1** INDIFFERENT, apathetic, uncaring, unconcerned; lackadaisical, blasé, nonchalant, insouciant, offhand, flippant. See also CAREFREE. **2** OFFHAND, spontaneous, unpremeditated, unthinking, unconsidered, impromptu, throwaway, unguarded; *informal* off-the-cuff. **3** ☞ CURSORY. **4** TEMPORARY, part-time, freelance, impermanent, irregular, occasional. **5** ☞ ACCIDENTAL. **6** ☞ INFORMAL 3.
—OPPOSITES: careful, planned, formal.

casualty *n.* VICTIM, fatality, loss, MIA; (**casualties**) dead and injured, missing (in action).

cat *n.* FELINE, tomcat, tom, kitten, mouser; *informal* pussy (cat), puss, kitty; *archaic* grimalkin.

catalogue *n.* DIRECTORY, register, index, list, listing, record, archive, inventory.

▶ *v.* CLASSIFY, categorize, systematize, index, list, archive, make an inventory of, inventory, record, itemize.

catapult *v.* PROPEL, launch, hurl, fling, send flying, fire, blast, shoot.

cataract *n.* ☞ CASCADE *n.*

catastrophe *n.* DISASTER, calamity, cataclysm, holocaust, havoc, ruin, ruination, tragedy; adversity, blight, trouble, trial, tribulation.

catch *v.* **1** SEIZE, grab, snatch, seize/grab/take hold of, grasp, grip, trap, clutch, clench; receive, get, intercept. **2** CAPTURE, seize; apprehend, arrest, take prisoner/captive, take into custody; trap, snare, ensnare; net, hook, land, bag, entrap; *informal* nab, collar, run in, bust. **3** DISCOVER, find, come upon/across, stumble on, chance on; surprise, catch red-handed, catch in the act. **4** ☞ ENGAGE 1. **5** HEAR, perceive, discern, make out. See also UNDERSTAND 1. **6** BECOME INFECTED WITH, contract, get, fall ill with, be taken ill with, develop, come down with, be struck down with.
—OPPOSITES: drop, release, miss.

▶ *n.* **1** HAUL, net, bag, yield. **2** LATCH, lock, fastener, clasp, hasp. **3** TRAP, trick, snare. See also DRAWBACK.

☐ **catch on 1** BECOME POPULAR/FASHIONABLE, take off, boom, flourish, thrive. **2** ☞ UNDERSTAND 1.

catching *adj.* ☞ CONTAGIOUS.

Catch-22 *n.* ☞ DILEMMA.

catchy *adj.* MEMORABLE, unforgettable, haunting; appealing, popular; singable, melodious, tuneful.

categorical *adj.* UNQUALIFIED, unconditional, unequivocal, absolute, explicit, express, unambiguous, definite, direct, downright, outright, emphatic, positive, point-blank, conclusive, without reservations, out-and-out.
—OPPOSITES: qualified, equivocal.

category *n.* CLASS, classification, group, grouping, bracket, heading, set; type, sort, kind, variety, species, breed, brand, make, model; grade, grading, order, rank, ranking.

cater *v.* **1** SERVE, provide for, meet the needs/wants of, accommodate; satisfy, indulge, pander to, gratify. **2** ☞ CONSIDER 4.

catholic *adj.* UNIVERSAL, diverse, diversified, wide, broad, broad-based, eclectic, liberal, latitudinarian; comprehensive, all-encompassing, all-embracing, all-inclusive.
—OPPOSITES: narrow.

catty *adj.* (*informal*) ☞ MALICIOUS.

cause *n.* **1** SOURCE, root, origin, beginning(s), starting point; mainspring, base, basis, foundation, fountainhead; originator, author, creator, producer, agent. **2** REASON, grounds, justification, call, need, necessity, occasion, excuse, pretext. **3** PRINCIPLE, ideal, belief, conviction; object, end, aim, objective, purpose, mission; charity.
—OPPOSITES: effect, result.
▶ *v.* BRING ABOUT, give rise to, lead to, result in, create, produce, generate, engender, spawn, bring on, precipitate, prompt, provoke, trigger, make happen, induce,
inspire, promote, foster; arouse, effect, encourage, instigate, incite, excite, kindle, occasion, rouse, set in motion, stir up, whip up, spark off, touch off; *literary* beget, enkindle.
—OPPOSITES: result from.

caustic *adj.* **1** CORROSIVE, corroding, abrasive, mordant, acid. **2** ☞ SARCASTIC.

caution *n.* **1** CARE, carefulness, heedfulness, heed, attention, attentiveness, alertness, watchfulness, vigilance, circumspection, discretion, prudence. **2** WARNING, injunction. See also REPRIMAND *n.*
▶ *v.* ADVISE, warn, counsel; admonish, reprimand, rebuke, reprove, scold; *informal* give someone a talking-to.

cautious *adj.* CAREFUL, heedful, attentive, alert, watchful, vigilant, circumspect, prudent, wary, on guard; cagey, canny.
—OPPOSITES: reckless.

cavalcade *n.* ☞ PROCESSION.

cavalier *adj.* OFFHAND, indifferent, casual, dismissive, insouciant, unconcerned; supercilious, patronizing, condescending, disdainful, scornful, contemptuous; *informal* couldn't-care-less, devil-may-care.

cave *n.* CAVERN, grotto, underground chamber, pothole; cellar, vault, crypt.
—RELATED: speleology, speleologist; spelunking, spelunker.
☐ **cave in** ☞ COLLAPSE *v.* 1.

cavil *v.* ☞ COMPLAIN.

cavity n. SPACE, chamber, hollow, hole, pocket, pouch; orifice, aperture; socket, gap, crater, pit.

cease v. COME/BRING TO AN END, come/bring to a halt, end, halt, stop, conclude, terminate, finish, draw to a close, wind up, discontinue, suspend, break off.
—OPPOSITES: start, continue.

ceaseless adj. CONTINUAL, constant, continuous; incessant, unceasing, unending, endless, never-ending, interminable, non-stop, round-the-clock, uninterrupted, unremitting, relentless, unrelenting, unrelieved, sustained, persistent, eternal, perpetual.
—OPPOSITES: intermittent.

celebrate v. **1** COMMEMORATE, observe, mark, keep, honour, remember, memorialize. **2** ☞ PARTY v. **3** PRAISE, extol, glorify, eulogize, reverence, honour, pay tribute to; formal laud.

celebrated adj. ACCLAIMED, admired, highly rated, lionized, revered, honoured, esteemed, exalted, vaunted, well-thought-of, ballyhooed; eminent, great, distinguished, prestigious, illustrious, pre-eminent, estimable, notable, of note, of repute; formal lauded.
—OPPOSITES: unsung.

celebration n.
1 COMMEMORATION, observance, marking, keeping. **2** ☞ PARTY n. 1.

celebrity n. **1** FAMOUS PERSON, VIP, very important person, personality, (big) name, famous/household name, star, superstar, celeb, somebody, notable, someone, megastar, big shot, leading light, luminary, personage, giant, icon, legend, phenomenon. **2** ☞ FAME.
—OPPOSITES: obscurity.

celestial adj. **1** (IN) SPACE, heavenly, astronomical, extraterrestrial, stellar, astral, planetary. **2** ETHEREAL, otherworldly. See also DIVINE adj. 1.
—OPPOSITES: earthly, hellish.

celibate adj. UNMARRIED, single, unwed, spouseless; chaste, virginal, virgin, maidenly, maiden, intact, abstinent, self-denying.

cell n. **1** ROOM, cubicle, chamber; dungeon, oubliette, lock-up. **2** COMPARTMENT, cavity, hole, hollow, section.

cement n. MORTAR, grout, concrete. See also GLUE n.
▶ v. ☞ GLUE v.

cemetery n. GRAVEYARD, churchyard, burial ground, burying ground, necropolis, memorial park/garden; informal boneyard; historical potter's field; archaic God's acre.

censor v. CUT, delete parts of, make cuts in, blue-pencil; edit, expurgate, bowdlerize, sanitize; informal clean up.

censorious adj. HYPERCRITICAL, overcritical, fault-finding, disapproving, condemnatory, denunciatory, deprecatory, disparaging, reproachful, reproving, censuring, captious, carping.
—OPPOSITES: complimentary.

censure v. ☞ REPRIMAND v.
▶ n. CONDEMNATION, criticism, attack, abuse. See also REPRIMAND n.
—OPPOSITES: approval.

central *adj.* **1** MIDDLE, centre, halfway, midway, mid, median, medial, mean. **2** ☞ MAIN.

centralize *v.* CONCENTRATE, consolidate, amalgamate, condense, unify, streamline, focus, rationalize.
—OPPOSITES: devolve.

centre *n.* MIDDLE, nucleus, heart, core, hub; middle point, midpoint, halfway point, mean, median.
—OPPOSITES: edge.

ceremonial *adj.* FORMAL, official, state, public; ritual, ritualistic, prescribed, stately, courtly, solemn.
—OPPOSITES: informal.

ceremonious *adj.* DIGNIFIED, majestic, imposing, impressive; regal, imperial, elegant, grand, glorious, splendid, magnificent, resplendent, portentous; *informal* starchy. See also CEREMONIAL.

ceremony *n.* **1** RITUAL, rite, ceremonial, observance; service, sacrament, liturgy, worship, celebration. **2** POMP, protocol, formalities, niceties, decorum, etiquette, punctilio, politesse.

certain *adj.* **1** ☞ SURE 1.
2 UNQUESTIONABLE, sure, definite, beyond question, not in doubt, indubitable, undeniable, irrefutable, indisputable; obvious, evident, recognized, confirmed, accepted, acknowledged, undisputed, undoubted, unquestioned. **3** ☞ DESTINED 1.
4 ☞ UNAVOIDABLE. **5** PARTICULAR, specific, individual, special.
—OPPOSITES: doubtful, possible, unlikely.

certainly *adv.* UNQUESTIONABLY, surely, assuredly, definitely, beyond/without question, without doubt, indubitably, undeniably, irrefutably, indisputably; obviously, patently, evidently, palpably, plainly, clearly, transparently, unmistakably, undoubtedly, absolutely, positively, unequivocally; sure as shootin', for sure.
—OPPOSITES: possibly.
▸ *excl.* YES, definitely, absolutely, sure, by all means, indeed, of course, naturally; affirmative, OK, okay.

certainty *n.* **1** CONFIDENCE, sureness, positiveness, conviction, certitude, assurance, no shadow of a doubt. **2** INEVITABILITY, foregone conclusion; *informal* sure thing, cert, dead cert, no-brainer.
—OPPOSITES: doubt, possibility.

certify *v.* **1** VERIFY, guarantee, attest, validate, confirm, substantiate, endorse, vouch for, testify to; provide evidence, give proof, prove, demonstrate.
2 ACCREDIT, recognize, license, authorize, approve, warrant.

cessation *n.* END, ending, termination, stopping, halting, ceasing, finish, finishing, stoppage, conclusion, winding up, discontinuation, abandonment, suspension, breaking off, cutting short.
—OPPOSITES: start, resumption.

chagrin *n.* EMBARRASSMENT, mortification, humiliation, shame. See also IRRITATION 1.
—OPPOSITES: delight.

chain *n.* **1** (**chains**) FETTERS, shackles, irons, leg irons,

manacles, handcuffs, bonds; *informal* cuffs, bracelets; *historical* bilboes. **2** SERIES, succession, string, sequence, train, course.
▶ *v.* SECURE, fasten, tie, tether, hitch; restrain, shackle, fetter, manacle, handcuff.

chair *v.* PRESIDE OVER, take the chair of; lead, direct, run, manage, control, be in charge of.

chalky *adj.* ☞ PALE *adj.* 1.

challenge *v.* **1** QUESTION, disagree with, dispute, take issue with, protest against, call into question, object to. **2** DARE, summon, throw down the gauntlet to, drop the gloves❖. **3** TEST, tax, strain, make demands on; stretch, stimulate, inspire, excite.

challenging *adj.* DEMANDING, testing, taxing, exacting; stretching, exciting, stimulating, inspiring; difficult, tough, hard, formidable, onerous, arduous, strenuous, rigorous, gruelling, back-breaking, punishing; *formal* exigent.

chamber *n.* **1** ROOM, hall, assembly room, auditorium. **2** COMPARTMENT, cavity.

champion *n.* **1** WINNER, titleholder, gold medallist, titlist; prizewinner, victor; *informal* champ, number one, king. **2** ☞ ADVOCATE.
▶ *v.* ADVOCATE, promote, defend, uphold, support, back; campaign for, lobby for, fight for, crusade for, stick up for.
—OPPOSITES: oppose.

chance *n.* **1** POSSIBILITY, prospect, probability, likelihood, likeliness, expectation, anticipation; risk, threat, danger, fear; hope.
2 OPPORTUNITY, opening, occasion,

turn, time, window (of opportunity); *informal* shot, kick at the can/cat❖. **3** RISK, gamble, venture, speculation, long shot, shot in the dark. **4** ☞ COINCIDENCE 1.
▶ *adj.* ☞ ACCIDENTAL 1.

chancy *adj.* ☞ HAZARDOUS.
—OPPOSITES: predictable.

change *v.* **1** ALTER, make/become different, adjust, adapt, amend, modify, revise, refine; reshape, refashion, redesign, restyle, revamp, rework, remodel, reorganize, reorder; vary, transform, transfigure, transmute, metamorphose, evolve; *informal* tweak, doctor, rejig; *technical* permute. **2** ☞ SWITCH *v.* 2.
—OPPOSITES: preserve, keep.
▶ *n.* **1** ALTERATION, modification, variation, revision, amendment, adjustment, adaptation; remodelling, reshaping, rearrangement, reordering, restyling, reworking; metamorphosis, transformation, evolution, mutation, vagary; *informal* transmogrification.
2 EXCHANGE, substitution, swap, switch, changeover, replacement, alternation, interchange.

changeable *adj.* VARIABLE, inconstant, varying, changing, fluctuating, irregular; erratic, inconsistent, unstable, unsettled, turbulent, protean; fickle, capricious, temperamental, volatile, mercurial, unpredictable, blowing hot and cold, fitful, fluid, mutable, shifting, unreliable, unsteady, vacillating, wavering; *informal* up and down.
—OPPOSITES: constant.

channel *n.* **1** STRAIT(S), sound, narrows, (sea) passage, (*Atlantic*) tickle✦, snye✦. **2** ☞ GUTTER. **3** MEANS, medium, instrument, mechanism, agency, vehicle, route, avenue.
▶ *v.* CONVEY, transmit, conduct, direct, guide, relay, pass on, transfer.

chant *n.* INCANTATION, intonation, singing, song, plainsong, recitative.
▶ *v.* **1** SHOUT, chorus, repeat. **2** SING, intone, incant.

chaos *n.* DISORDER, disarray, disorganization, confusion, mayhem, bedlam, pandemonium, havoc, turmoil, tumult, commotion, disruption, upheaval, uproar, maelstrom, furor; a muddle, a mess, a shambles, a free-for-all; anarchy, lawlessness, entropy; *informal* hullabaloo, hoopla, all hell broken loose. —OPPOSITES: order.

chaotic *adj.* DISORDERLY, disordered, in disorder, in chaos, in disarray, disorganized, topsy-turvy, in pandemonium, in turmoil, in uproar; in a muddle, in a mess, messy, in a shambles; anarchic, lawless.

chap *n.* ☞ GUY.

char *v.* ☞ SCORCH 1.

character *n.* **1** PERSONALITY, nature, disposition, temperament, temper, mentality, makeup; features, qualities, properties, traits; spirit, essence, identity, ethos, complexion, tone, feel, feeling. **2** INTEGRITY, honour, moral strength/fibre, rectitude, uprightness; fortitude, strength, backbone, resolve, grit, willpower; *informal* guts, gutsiness. **3** ☞ REPUTATION. **4** (*informal*) ECCENTRIC, oddity, madcap, crank, individualist, nonconformist, rare bird, oddball, free spirit. **5** PERSONA, role, part.

characteristic *n.* ATTRIBUTE, feature, (essential) quality, property, trait, aspect, element, facet; mannerism, habit, custom, idiosyncrasy, peculiarity, quirk, oddity, foible.
▶ *adj.* TYPICAL, usual, normal, predictable, habitual. See also DISTINCTIVE.

characterize *v.* **1** DISTINGUISH, make distinctive, mark, typify, set apart. **2** ☞ PORTRAY 2.

charade *n.* FARCE, pantomime, travesty, mockery, parody, pretense, act, masquerade.

charge *v.* **1** ASK (IN PAYMENT), levy, demand, want, exact; bill, invoice. **2** ACCUSE, indict, arraign; prosecute, try, put on trial, inculpate. **3** ENTRUST, burden, encumber, saddle, tax. **4** ATTACK, storm, assault, rush, assail, fall on, swoop on, descend on; *informal* lay into, tear into. **5** ☞ PERMEATE.
▶ *n.* **1** FEE, payment, price, tariff, amount, sum, fare, levy. **2** ACCUSATION, allegation, indictment, arraignment. **3** ATTACK, assault, offensive, onslaught, drive, push, thrust. **4** ☞ CARE *n.* 1. **5** WARD, protege, dependant. **6** ☞ THRILL *n.*

charitable *adj.* **1** PHILANTHROPIC, humanitarian, altruistic, benevolent, public-spirited; non-profit; *formal* eleemosynary. **2** ☞ GENEROUS 1.

charity *n.* **1** PHILANTHROPY, humanitarianism, humanity, altruism, public-spiritedness, social conscience, benevolence, beneficence, munificence. **2** GOODWILL, compassion, consideration, concern, kindness, kind-heartedness, tenderness, tender-heartedness, sympathy, indulgence, tolerance, leniency, caritas; *literary* bounteousness.

charm *n.* **1** ATTRACTIVENESS, beauty, glamour, loveliness; appeal, allure, desirability, seductiveness, magnetism, charisma. **2** APPEAL, drawing power, attraction, allure, fascination. **3** ☞ SPELL² 1. **4** TALISMAN, fetish, amulet, mascot, totem, juju.
▸ *v.* **1** DELIGHT, please, win (over), attract, captivate, allure, lure, dazzle, fascinate, enchant, enthrall, enrapture, seduce, spellbind. **2** ☞ COAX.

chart *n.* GRAPH, table, diagram, histogram; *Computing* graphic.
▸ *v.* TABULATE, plot, graph, record, register, represent; make a chart/diagram of.

chase *v.* **1** PURSUE, run after, give chase to, follow; hunt, track, trail; *informal* tail. **2** ☞ BANISH 2.

chasm *n.* CREVASSE, fissure, crevice. See also GORGE *n.*

chaste *adj.* **1** VIRGINAL, virgin, intact, maidenly, unmarried, unwed; celibate, abstinent, self-restrained, self-denying, continent; innocent, virtuous, pure (as the driven snow), sinless, undefiled, unsullied, immaculate; *literary* vestal. **2** NON-SEXUAL, platonic, innocent.

—OPPOSITES: promiscuous, passionate.

chasten *v.* SUBDUE, humble, cow, squash, deflate, abase, flatten, take down a peg or two, put someone in their place, cut down to size, settle someone's hash.

chastise *v.* ☞ SCOLD.
—OPPOSITES: praise.

chastity *n.* CELIBACY, chasteness, virginity, abstinence, self-restraint, self-denial, continence; innocence, purity, virtue, morality.

chat *n.* ☞ DISCUSSION.
▸ *v.* TALK, gossip, chatter, speak, converse, engage in conversation, tittle-tattle, prattle, jabber, babble; *informal* gas, jaw, chew the fat, yap, yak, yabber, yatter, yammer, natter, shoot the breeze/bull, kibitz; *formal* confabulate.

chatty *adj.* ☞ TALKATIVE.
—OPPOSITES: taciturn.

cheap *adj.* **1** ☞ INEXPENSIVE. **2** POOR-QUALITY, second-rate, third-rate, tinpot, substandard, low-grade, inferior, vulgar, shoddy, trashy, tawdry, meretricious, cheapjack, gimcrack, Brummagem, pinchbeck; *informal* rubbishy, chintzy, cheapo, junky, tacky, cheesy, ticky-tacky, kitsch, (*Que.*) kétaine✦, two-bit, dime-store, schlocky. **3** MISERLY, stingy, parsimonious, mean, tight-fisted, niggardly, chintzy, frugal, penny-pinching, cheese-paring, Scrooge-like, close-fisted, el cheapo, grasping.
—OPPOSITES: expensive.

cheapen *v.* DEMEAN, debase, degrade, lower, humble, devalue, abase, discredit, disgrace, dishonour, shame, humiliate, mortify, prostitute.

cheat v. SWINDLE, defraud, deceive, trick, scam, dupe, hoodwink, double-cross, gull; *informal* rip off, con, fleece, shaft, hose, sting, bilk, diddle, rook, gyp, finagle, bamboozle, flim-flam, put one over on, pull a fast one on, sucker, stiff, hornswoggle; *formal* mulct; *literary* cozen.

▶ *n.* SWINDLER, cheater, fraudster, trickster, deceiver, hoaxer, double-dealer, double-crosser, sham, fraud, fake, charlatan, quack, crook, snake oil salesman, mountebank; *informal* con man/artist, scam artist, shark, sharper, phony, flim-flammer, bunco artist; *dated* confidence man.

check v. 1 ☞ INSPECT. 2 MAKE SURE, confirm, verify. 3 HALT, stop, arrest, cut short; bar, obstruct, hamper, impede, inhibit, frustrate, foil, thwart, curb, block, stall, hold up, retard, delay, slow down; *literary* stay.

▶ *n.* 1 TEST, trial, monitoring. See also INSPECTION. 2 CONTROL, restraint, constraint, curb, limitation. 3 BILL, account, invoice, statement, tab.

☐ **check something out** 1 ☞ INSPECT. 2 LOOK AT, survey, regard, inspect, contemplate; *informal* eyeball.

cheek *n.* IMPUDENCE, impertinence, insolence, audacity, cheekiness, presumption, effrontery, gall, pertness, impoliteness, disrespect, bad manners, overfamiliarity, cockiness; answering back, talking back; *informal* brass, lip, mouth, chutzpah, sass, sassiness, nerviness, back talk.

cheeky *adj.* IMPUDENT, impertinent, insolent, presumptuous, audacious, forward, pert, bold (as brass), brassy, brazen, cocky, overfamiliar, discourteous, disrespectful, rude, impolite, bad-mannered; *informal* lippy, mouthy, fresh, saucy, sassy, nervy.
—OPPOSITES: respectful, polite.

cheep v. CHIRP, chirrup, twitter, tweet, peep, chitter, chirr, trill, warble, sing.

cheer *n.* 1 HURRAY, hurrah, whoop, bravo, shout, roar; hosanna, alleluia; (**cheers**) applause, acclamation, clamour, acclaim, ovation. 2 ☞ HAPPINESS.
—OPPOSITES: boo, sadness.

▶ *v.* 1 APPLAUD, hail, salute, shout for, root for, hurrah, hurray, acclaim, clap; encourage, support; bring the house down, holler for, give someone a big hand, put one's hands together for. 2 RAISE SOMEONE'S SPIRITS, make happier, brighten, buoy up, enliven, exhilarate, hearten, gladden, uplift, perk up, boost, encourage, inspirit; *informal* buck up.
—OPPOSITES: boo, depress.

cheerful *adj.* HAPPY, jolly, merry, bright, glad, sunny, joyful, joyous, lighthearted, in good/high spirits, sparkling, bubbly, exuberant, buoyant, ebullient, elated, gleeful; gay, breezy, cheery, jaunty, animated, radiant, smiling; jovial, genial, good-humoured; carefree, unworried, untroubled, without a care in the world; upbeat, chipper, chirpy, peppy, bright-eyed and bushy-tailed, full of beans, bouncy, happy-go-lucky, lively, perky; *formal* blithe, jocund, affable, fun-loving, hail-fellow-well-met, jocose, mirthful, amiable, convivial, friendly, good-natured, high-spirited, outgoing, sociable, vivacious.

—OPPOSITES: sad.

cheerless *adj.* DULL, dismal, bleak, drab, sombre, dark, dim, dingy, funereal; austere, stark, bare, comfortless, unwelcoming, uninviting; miserable, wretched, joyless, depressing, disheartening, dispiriting.

cheery *adj.* ☞ CHEERFUL 1.

cherish *v.* **1** ADORE, hold dear, love, dote on, be devoted to, revere, esteem, admire; think the world of, set great store by, hold in high esteem; care for, tend to, look after, protect, preserve, keep safe. **2** TREASURE, prize, value highly, hold dear. **3** HARBOUR, entertain, possess, hold (on to), cling to, keep in one's mind, foster, nurture.

chest *n.* **1** BREAST, upper body, torso, trunk; bosom, bust; *technical* thorax. **2** ☞ BOX¹.
  □ **get something off one's chest** ☞ CONFESS 2.

chew *v.* MASTICATE, munch, champ, crunch, nibble, gnaw, eat, consume; *formal* manducate.
  □ **chew the fat** (*informal*) ☞ CHAT *v.*

chic *adj.* ☞ FASHIONABLE.

chide *v.* ☞ SCOLD.
  —OPPOSITES: praise.

chief *n.* **1** LEADER, chieftain, grand chief, sachem, sagamore, headman, ruler, overlord, master, commander, seigneur, liege (lord),

potentate, cacique. **2** ☞ LEADER.
  ▶ *adj.* **1** HEAD, leading, principal, premier, prime, top-ranking, highest, foremost, supreme, arch. **2** ☞ MAIN.
  —OPPOSITES: subordinate, minor.

chiefly *adv.* ☞ MAINLY.

child *n.* YOUNGSTER, little one, boy, girl; baby, newborn, infant, toddler; cherub, angel; schoolboy, schoolgirl; minor, junior, preteen; son, daughter, descendant; *informal* kid, kiddie, tot, tyke, young 'un, lad, rug rat, ankle-biter; *derogatory* brat, terrible two, guttersnipe, urchin, gamin, gamine; *literary* babe (in arms); (**children**) offspring, progeny, issue, brood, descendants.
  —RELATED: pedo-.

childbirth *n.* LABOUR, delivery, giving birth, birthing, child-bearing; *formal* parturition; *dated* confinement; *literary* travail; *archaic* childbed.

childhood *n.* INFANCY, babyhood. See also YOUTH 1.
  —OPPOSITES: adulthood.

childish *adj.* **1** IMMATURE, babyish, infantile, juvenile, puerile, adolescent; silly, inane, jejune, foolish, irresponsible. **2** ☞ CHILDLIKE 1.
  —OPPOSITES: mature, adult.

childlike *adj.* **1** YOUTHFUL, young, young-looking, girlish, boyish. **2** UNWORLDLY, unsophisticated, trusting, unsuspicious, unwary, credulous, gullible; uninhibited, natural, spontaneous. See also ARTLESS.

chill *n.* **1** COLDNESS, chilliness, coolness, iciness, rawness, bitterness, nip. **2** UNFRIENDLINESS,

lack of warmth/understanding, chilliness, coldness, coolness.
—OPPOSITES: warmth.

▶ v. MAKE COLD, make colder, cool (down/off); refrigerate, ice.
—OPPOSITES: warm.

□ **chill out** (informal) ☞ RELAX 1.

chilly adj. 1 ☞ COLD 1.
2 ☞ UNFRIENDLY 1.
—OPPOSITES: warm.

chime v. ☞ RING² v.

▶ n. PEAL, pealing, ringing, carillon, toll, tolling; ding-dong, clanging, tintinnabulation; literary knell.

china n. 1 PORCELAIN. 2 DISHES, plates, cups and saucers, tableware, chinaware, dinner service, tea service, crockery.

chink n. ☞ GAP 1.

chip n. 1 FRAGMENT, sliver, splinter, shaving, paring, flake. 2 NICK, crack, scratch, notch; flaw, fault.

▶ v. 1 NICK, crack, scratch; damage, break. 2 WHITTLE, hew, chisel, carve.

□ **chip in** ☞ CONTRIBUTE 1.

chivalrous adj. 1 ☞ GALLANT 2.
2 KNIGHTLY, noble, chivalric; brave, courageous, bold, valiant, valorous, heroic, daring, intrepid.
—OPPOSITES: rude, cowardly.

choice n. 1 SELECTION, election, choosing, picking; decision, say, vote. 2 ☞ OPTION. 3 RANGE, variety, selection, assortment.
4 PREFERENCE, pick, favourite.

▶ adj. ☞ SUPERIOR 4.
—OPPOSITES: inferior.

choose v. ☞ SELECT.

choosy adj. ☞ FASTIDIOUS.

chop v. 1 CUT UP, cut into pieces, chop up, cube, dice, hash; hew, split. 2 CUT, axe, abolish, scrap,

slash, cancel, terminate, ditch, dump, pull the plug on.

choppy adj. ROUGH, turbulent, heavy, heaving, stormy, tempestuous, squally; uneven.
—OPPOSITES: calm.

chorus n. 1 CHOIR, ensemble, choral group, choristers, glee club. 2 REFRAIN.

christen v. CALL, name, dub, style, term, designate, label, nickname, give the name of; baptize; formal denominate.

chronic adj. 1 CONSTANT, continuing, ceaseless, unending, persistent, long-lasting; severe, serious, acute, grave, dire.
2 ☞ INVETERATE.
—OPPOSITES: acute, temporary.

chronicle n. RECORD, written account, history, annals, archive(s); log, diary, journal.

▶ v. ☞ RECORD v. 1.

chronological adj. SEQUENTIAL, consecutive, in sequence, in order (of time).

chubby adj. ☞ FAT 1.
—OPPOSITES: skinny.

chunk n. LUMP, hunk, clump, piece, bit, mass, block, wedge, slab, cake, nugget, ball, brick, cube, pat, knob, clod, gobbet, dollop, wad, bar, Nfld nug✦, square, glob, gob.

church n. PLACE OF WORSHIP, house of God, house of worship; cathedral, minster, abbey, chapel, basilica; synagogue, mosque.
—RELATED: ecclesiastical.

churlish adj. SURLY, sullen, uncharitable. See also IMPOLITE.
—OPPOSITES: polite.

churn v. **1** STIR, agitate, beat, whip, whisk. **2** HEAVE, boil, swirl, toss, seethe; *literary* roil.

cinch n. (*informal*) EASY TASK, child's play, snap, walkover, laugher, piece of cake, picnic, breeze, kids' stuff, cakewalk, pushover, duck soup, five-finger exercise.
—OPPOSITES: challenge.

cinema n. **1** MOVIE THEATRE/HOUSE, multiplex, cinematheque; *historical* nickelodeon. **2** FILMS, movies, pictures, motion pictures.

circle n. **1** RING, band, hoop, circlet; halo, disc; *technical* annulus. **2** GROUP, set, company, coterie, clique; crowd, band; *informal* gang, bunch, crew.
▶ v. **1** WHEEL, move round, revolve, rotate, whirl, spiral. **2** GO ROUND, travel round, circumnavigate; orbit, revolve round. **3** SURROUND, encircle, ring, enclose, encompass; *literary* gird.

circuit n. **1** ☞ LAP. **2** TRACK, racetrack, raceway, running track, course.

circuitous adj. ☞ INDIRECT 2.
—OPPOSITES: direct.

circular adj. ROUND, disc-shaped, ring-shaped, annular.
▶ n. ☞ FLYER 2.

circulate v. **1** SPREAD (ABOUT/AROUND), communicate, propagate; distribute, give out, pass around. See also PUBLICIZE 1. **2** ☞ SOCIALIZE.

circumference n. ☞ PERIMETER.

circumspect adj. WATCHFUL, alert, attentive, heedful, vigilant, leery. See also GUARDED.
—OPPOSITES: unguarded.

circumstances pl. n. **1** SITUATION, conditions, state of affairs, position; (turn of) events, incidents, occurrences, happenings; factors, context, background, environment. **2** THE FACTS, the details, the particulars, how things stand, the lay of the land; *informal* what's what, the score.

circumstantial adj. INDIRECT, inferred, deduced, conjectural; inconclusive, unprovable.

citadel n. FORTRESS, fort, stronghold, fortification, castle.

citation n. **1** ☞ QUOTATION. **2** COMMENDATION, (honourable) mention.

city n. TOWN, municipality, metropolis, megalopolis, megacity; conurbation, urban area, metropolitan area, urban municipality; borough, township; *informal* big smoke, burg.
—RELATED: urban, civic.

civil adj. POLITE, courteous, well-mannered, well-bred, chivalrous, gallant; cordial, genial, pleasant, affable; gentlemanly, ladylike.
—OPPOSITES: rude.

civility n. COURTESY, courteousness, politeness, good manners, graciousness, consideration, respect, politesse, comity.
—OPPOSITES: rudeness.

civilization n. **1** HUMAN DEVELOPMENT, advancement, progress, enlightenment, culture, refinement, sophistication. **2** CULTURE, society, nation, people.

civilize v. ENLIGHTEN, edify, improve, educate, instruct, refine, cultivate, polish, socialize, humanize.

civilized *adj.* POLITE, courteous, well-mannered, civil, gentlemanly, ladylike, mannerly. See also CULTURED.
—OPPOSITES: rude, unsophisticated.

claim *v.* **1** ASSERT, declare, profess, maintain, state, hold, affirm, avow; argue, contend, allege; *formal* aver. **2** REQUEST, ask for, apply for; demand, exact.

clairvoyance *n.* ESP, extrasensory perception, sixth sense, psychic powers, second sight; telepathy.

clamber *v.* SCRAMBLE, climb, scrabble, scravel✦, claw one's way.

clammy *adj.* **1** ☞ SWEATY. **2** DAMP, dank, wet; humid, close, muggy, heavy.
—OPPOSITES: dry.

clamour *n.* ☞ UPROAR 1.
▶ *v.* YELL, shout loudly, bay, scream, roar; call, demand, lobby.

clamp *n.* BRACE, vice, press, clasp; *Music* capo (tasto); *Climbing* jumar.
▶ *v.* **1** FASTEN, secure, fix, attach; screw, bolt. **2** ☞ CLENCH *v.* 2.
☐ **clamp down on** ☞ CRACK DOWN ON at CRACK.

clandestine *adj.* SECRET, covert, furtive, surreptitious, stealthy, cloak-and-dagger, hole-and-corner, closet, backstairs, backroom, underground, undercover; hush-hush.

clarify *v.* MAKE CLEAR, shed/throw light on, elucidate, illuminate; EXPLAIN, explicate, define, spell out, clear up.
—OPPOSITES: confuse.

clash *v.* **1** FIGHT, skirmish, contend, come to blows, come into conflict; do battle. **2** DISAGREE, differ, wrangle, dispute, cross swords, lock horns, be at loggerheads. **3** BE INCOMPATIBLE, not match, not go, be discordant.

clasp *v.* **1** GRASP, grip, clutch, hold tightly; take hold of, seize, grab. **2** ☞ EMBRACE 1.
▶ *n.* **1** FASTENER, fastening, catch, clip, pin; buckle, hasp. **2** EMBRACE, hug, cuddle; grip, grasp.

class *n.* **1** ☞ CATEGORY. **2** KIND, sort, type, variety, genre, brand; species, genus, breed, strain, stripe. **3** SOCIAL DIVISION, social stratum, rank, level, echelon, group, grouping, income group; social status; *dated* estate; *archaic* condition. **4** LESSON; seminar, tutorial, workshop. **5** ☞ STYLE 3.
▶ *v.* ☞ CLASSIFY.

classic *adj.* **1** DEFINITIVE, authoritative; outstanding, first-rate, first-class, best, finest, excellent, superior, masterly. **2** TYPICAL, archetypal, quintessential, vintage; model, representative, perfect, prime, textbook. **3** SIMPLE, elegant, understated; traditional, timeless, ageless.
—OPPOSITES: atypical.

classical *adj.* **1** ancient Greek, Hellenic, Attic; Latin, ancient Roman. **2** TRADITIONAL, long-established; serious, highbrow. **3** SIMPLE, pure, restrained, plain, austere; well-proportioned, harmonious, balanced, symmetrical, elegant.
—OPPOSITES: modern.

classification *n.*
1 CATEGORIZATION, categorizing, classifying, grouping, grading,

ranking, organization, sorting, codification, systematization.
2 ☞ CATEGORY.

classify v. CATEGORIZE, group, grade, rank, rate, order, organize, range, sort, type, codify, bracket, systematize, systemize; catalogue, list, file, index, lump, designate, label, pigeonhole.

classy adj. STYLISH, high-class, superior, exclusive, chic, elegant, smart, sophisticated, upscale, upmarket, high-toned; informal posh, ritzy, plush, swanky.

clause n. SECTION, paragraph, article, subsection; stipulation, condition, proviso, rider.

claw n. TALON, nail, pincer, nipper; technical unguis.
▶ v. SCRATCH, lacerate, tear, rip, scrape, graze, scrob, dig into.

clean adj. **1** WASHED, scrubbed, cleansed, cleaned; spotless, unsoiled, unstained, unsullied, unblemished, immaculate, pristine, dirt-free; hygienic, sanitary, disinfected, sterilized, sterile, aseptic, decontaminated; laundered; informal squeaky clean, as clean as a whistle. **2** ☞ BLANK adj. 1. **3** PURE, clear, fresh, crisp, refreshing; unpolluted, uncontaminated. **4** ☞ VIRTUOUS. **5** FAIR, honest, sporting, sportsmanlike, honourable; informal on the level. **6** (informal) DRUG-FREE, off drugs. See also SOBER adj. 1. **7** COMPLETE, thorough, total, absolute, conclusive, decisive, final, irrevocable. **8** SIMPLE, elegant, graceful, streamlined, smooth.
—OPPOSITES: dirty, polluted.
▶ v. ☞ WASH v. 2.

—OPPOSITES: dirty.
☐ **come clean** (informal) ☞ CONFESS 2.

cleanse v. CLEAN (UP), wash, bathe, rinse, disinfect.

clear adj. **1** UNDERSTANDABLE, comprehensible, intelligible, plain, uncomplicated, explicit, lucid, coherent, simple, straightforward, unambiguous, clear-cut, crystal clear; formal perspicuous. **2** OBVIOUS, evident, plain, crystal clear; sure, definite, unmistakable, manifest, indisputable, patent, incontrovertible, irrefutable, beyond doubt, beyond question; palpable, visible, discernible, conspicuous, overt, blatant, glaring; as plain as day, as plain as the nose on one's face. **3** ☞ TRANSPARENT 1. **4** ☞ SUNNY. **5** UNOBSTRUCTED, unblocked, passable, unrestricted, open, unhindered. **6** UNTROUBLED, undisturbed, unperturbed, unconcerned, having no qualms; peaceful, at peace, tranquil, serene, calm, easy.
—OPPOSITES: vague, opaque, cloudy, obstructed.
▶ adv. **1** AWAY FROM, apart from, at a (safe) distance from, out of contact with. **2** ☞ COMPLETELY.
▶ v. **1** BRIGHTEN (UP), lighten, clear up, become fine/sunny. **2** UNBLOCK, unstop. **3** EVACUATE, empty; leave. **4** REMOVE, take away, carry away, tidy away/up. **5** GO OVER, pass over, sail over; jump (over), vault (over), leap (over), hurdle. **6** ☞ ACQUIT. **7** AUTHORIZE, give permission, permit, allow, pass, accept, endorse, license, sanction, give

approval/consent to; *informal* OK, give the OK, give the thumbs up, give the green light, give the go-ahead.

□ **clear out** (*informal*). ☞ LEAVE¹ 1.

clear something up SOLVE, resolve, straighten out, find an/the answer to; get to the bottom of, explain; *informal* crack, figure out, suss out.

clearance *n.* 1 REMOVAL, clearing, demolition. 2 ☞ PERMISSION. 3 SPACE, room (to spare), margin, leeway, headroom.

clear-cut *adj.* DEFINITE, distinct, clear, well-defined, precise, specific, explicit, unambiguous, unequivocal, black and white, cut and dried.
—OPPOSITES: vague.

clearly *adv.* OBVIOUSLY, evidently, patently, unquestionably, undoubtedly, without doubt, indubitably, plainly, undeniably, incontrovertibly, irrefutably, doubtless, it goes without saying, needless to say.

cleft *n.* SPLIT, slit, crack, fissure, crevice, rift, break, fracture, rent, breach.

clemency *n.* ☞ MERCY.
—OPPOSITES: ruthlessness.

clench *v.* 1 SQUEEZE TOGETHER, clamp together, close/shut tightly. 2 GRIP, grasp, grab, clutch, clasp, hold tightly, seize, press, squeeze.

clergyman, clergywoman *n.* ☞ CLERIC.

cleric *n.* CLERGYMAN, CLERGYWOMAN, pastor, priest, minister, preacher, rabbi, imam, ecclesiastic, vicar, rector, parson, churchman, churchwoman, man/woman of the cloth, man/woman

of God, father, curate, chaplain, curé, canon, Monsignor, bishop, deacon, deaconess, evangelist; *historical* black robe✧; reverend, padre, Holy Joe, sky pilot; divine.

clerical *adj.* 1 OFFICE, desk, backroom; administrative, secretarial. 2 ECCLESIASTICAL, church, priestly, religious, spiritual, sacerdotal; holy, divine.
—OPPOSITES: secular.

clever *adj.* 1 INTELLIGENT, bright, smart, astute, sharp, quick-witted, shrewd; talented, gifted, brilliant, capable, able, competent, apt; educated, learned, knowledgeable, wise; *informal* brainy, savvy. 2 INGENIOUS, canny, cunning, crafty, artful, slick, neat. 3 SKILFUL, dexterous, adroit, adept, deft, nimble, handy; skilled, talented, gifted.
—OPPOSITES: stupid.

cliché *n.* PLATITUDE, hackneyed phrase, commonplace, banality, old saying, maxim, truism, stock phrase, trite phrase; old chestnut.

click *v.* 1 CLACK, snap, snick, tick, pop; clink. 2 (*informal*) BECOME CLEAR, fall into place, come home, make sense, dawn, register, get through, sink in. 3 (*informal*) TAKE TO EACH OTHER, get along, be compatible, be like-minded, feel a rapport, see eye to eye; *informal* hit it off, get on like a house on fire, be on the same wavelength.

client *n.* CUSTOMER, buyer, purchaser, shopper, consumer, user; patient; patron, regular.

cliff *n.* PRECIPICE, rock face, crag, bluff, ridge, escarpment, scar, scarp, ledge, (*BC, Alta., & North*) rampart✧, overhang.

climate *n.* **1** WEATHER CONDITIONS, weather; atmospheric conditions. **2** ATMOSPHERE, mood, feeling, ambience, tenor; tendency, ethos, attitude; milieu; *informal* vibe(s).

climax *n.* ☞ PEAK *n.* 4.
—OPPOSITES: nadir.

climb *v.* **1** ASCEND, mount, scale, scramble up, clamber up, shinny up; go up, walk up; conquer, gain. **2** SLOPE UPWARDS, rise, go uphill, incline upwards. **3** INCREASE, rise, go up; shoot up, soar, rocket.
—OPPOSITES: descend, drop, fall.
▸ *n.* ASCENT, clamber.
—OPPOSITES: descent.

clinch *v.* **1** SECURE, settle, conclude, close, pull off, bring off, complete, confirm, seal, finalize; *informal* sew up, wrap up. **2** SETTLE, decide, determine; resolve; *informal* sort out.
—OPPOSITES: lose.

cling *v.* ☞ ADHERE 1.
☐ **cling (on) to** HOLD ON, clutch, grip, grasp, clasp, attach oneself to, hang on; embrace, hug.

clinic *n.* MEDICAL CENTRE, health centre, (*Que.*) CLSC✤, nursing station✤, (*Nfld*) cottage hospital✤, doctor's office.

clinical *adj.* DETACHED, impersonal, dispassionate, objective, uninvolved, distant; remote, aloof, removed, cold, indifferent, neutral, unsympathetic, unfeeling, unemotional.
—OPPOSITES: emotional.

clip¹ *n.* **1** FASTENER, clasp, hasp, catch, hook, buckle, lock. **2** BROOCH, pin, badge.
▸ *v.* FASTEN, attach, fix, join; pin, staple, tack.

clip² *v.* TRIM, prune, cut, snip, shorten, crop, shear, pare; lop; neaten, shape.
▸ *n.* **1** EXTRACT, excerpt, snippet, cutting, fragment; trailer. **2** (*informal*) SPEED, rate, pace, velocity; *informal* lick.

clique *n.* COTERIE, set, circle, ring, in-crowd, group; club, society, fraternity, sorority; cabal, caucus; *informal* gang, crew.

cloak *n.* CAPE, poncho, shawl, burnoose, cope, ròbe, cowl, djellaba, domino, mantle, wrap, pelisse, serape, tippet; cassock, chasuble, pallium; *historical* cardinal.
▸ *v.* CONCEAL, hide, cover, veil, shroud, mask, obscure, cloud; envelop, swathe, surround.

clog *v.* ☞ BLOCK *v.* 1.

cloistered *adj.* SECLUDED, sequestered, sheltered, protected, insulated; shut off, isolated, confined, incommunicado; solitary, monastic, reclusive.

close¹ *adj.* **1** NEAR, adjacent; in the vicinity of, in the neighbourhood of, within reach of; neighbouring, adjoining, abutting, alongside, on the doorstep, a stone's throw away; nearby, at hand, at close quarters; *informal* within spitting distance; *archaic* nigh. **2** ☞ DENSE 1. **3** EVENLY MATCHED, even, with nothing to choose between them, neck and neck; *informal* even-steven(s). **4** INTIMATE, dear, bosom; close-knit, tight-knit, inseparable, attached, devoted, faithful; special, good, best, fast, firm. **5** STRONG, marked, distinct, pronounced. **6** ☞ CAREFUL 2. **7** VIGILANT, watchful, keen, alert.

8 STRICT, faithful, exact, precise, literal; word for word, verbatim. **9** ☞ MUGGY.
—OPPOSITES: far, distant, slight, loose, fresh.

close² *v.* **1** ☞ SHUT. **2** BLOCK (UP/OFF), stop up, plug, seal (up/off), shut up/off, cork, stopper, bung (up); clog (up), choke, obstruct. **3** NARROW, reduce, shrink, lessen, get smaller, diminish, contract. **4** END, conclude, finish, terminate, wind up, break off, halt, discontinue, dissolve; adjourn, suspend. **5** SHUT DOWN, close down, cease production, cease trading. See also GO BANKRUPT at BANKRUPT. **6** CLINCH, settle, secure, seal, confirm, establish; transact, pull off; complete, conclude, fix, agree, finalize; *informal* wrap up.
—OPPOSITES: open, widen, begin.

closet *n.* CUPBOARD, wardrobe, cabinet, locker.
▸ *adj.* ☞ CLANDESTINE.

clot *n.* LUMP, clump, mass; thrombus, thrombosis, embolus; *informal* glob, gob.
▸ *v.* CONGEAL, thicken, jell; solidify, harden, set, dry.

cloth *n.* **1** FABRIC, material, textile(s), soft goods. **2** RAG, wipe, duster, sponge; flannel, towel.

clothe *v.* ☞ DRESS *v.* 1.

clothes *pl. n.* CLOTHING, garments, attire, garb, dress, wear, costume, outfit, ensemble; *informal* gear, togs, duds, threads, getup, Sunday best, suit, uniform; apparel, vestments.
—RELATED: sartorial.

cloud *n.* MASS, billow; pall, mantle, blanket.
▸ *v.* **1** BECOME CLOUDY, cloud over, become overcast, lower, blacken,

darken. **2** CONFUSE, muddle, obscure, fog, muddy, mar.
□ **on cloud nine** ☞ ECSTATIC.

cloudy *adj.* **1** OVERCAST, clouded; dark, grey, black, leaden, murky; sombre, dismal, heavy, gloomy; sunless, starless; hazy, misty, foggy. **2** MURKY, muddy, milky, dirty, opaque, turbid.
—OPPOSITES: clear.

clout (*informal*) *n.* **1** ☞ SMACK *n.* **2** INFLUENCE, power, weight, sway, leverage, control, say; dominance, authority; *informal* teeth, muscle.

clown *n.* **1** ☞ COMEDIAN. **2** ☞ FOOL *n.* 1.
▸ *v.* FOOL AROUND/ABOUT, play the fool, play about/around, monkey about/around; joke, jest; *informal* mess about/around, lark (about/around), horse about/around, muck about/around.

club¹ *n.* **1** SOCIETY, association, organization, institution, group, circle, band, body, ring, crew; alliance, league, union. **2** NIGHTCLUB, disco, discotheque, bar.

club² *n.* ☞ CUDGEL.
▸ *v.* ☞ BEAT *v.* 1.

clue *n.* EVIDENCE, hint, information, indication, sign, signal, pointer, trace, indicator; lead, tip, tipoff.
□ **clue someone in** ☞ APPRISE.

clump *n.* **1** CLUSTER, thicket, group, bunch, assemblage. **2** LUMP, clod, mass, wad, glob, gob.

clumsy *adj.* **1** AWKWARD, uncoordinated, ungainly; graceless, inelegant; inept, maladroit, unskilful, unhandy, accident-prone, like a bull in a china shop, all thumbs; *informal*

ham-fisted, butterfingered, having two left feet, klutzy.
2 ☞ CUMBERSOME. **3** ☞ TACTLESS.
—OPPOSITES: graceful, elegant, tactful.

cluster *n.* **1** BUNCH, clump, mass, knot, group, collection, clutch, bundle, truss. **2** ☞ HUDDLE *n.*
▶ *v.* CONGREGATE, gather, collect, group, assemble; huddle, crowd, flock.

clutch *v.* GRIP, grasp, clasp, cling to, hang on to, clench, hold.

clutches *pl. n.* POWER, control, domination, command, rule, tyranny; hands, hold, grip, grasp, claws, jaws; custody.

clutter *n.* ☞ MESS 1.

coach[1] *n.* **1** BUS, minibus; *dated* omnibus. **2** CAR, carriage, wagon, compartment, van, Pullman.

coach[2] *n.* INSTRUCTOR, trainer, manager; teacher, tutor, mentor, guru.
▶ *v.* ☞ TEACH.

coagulate *v.* ☞ CLOT *v.*

coalesce *v.* MERGE, unite, join together, combine, fuse, mingle, blend; amalgamate, consolidate, integrate, homogenize, converge.

coalition *n.* ALLIANCE, union, partnership, bloc, caucus; federation, league, association, confederation, consortium, syndicate, combine; amalgamation, merger.

coarse *adj.* **1** ROUGH, scratchy, prickly, wiry. **2** ☞ BOORISH. **3** VULGAR, crude, rude, off-colour, dirty, filthy, smutty, indelicate, improper, unseemly, crass, tasteless, lewd, prurient, blue, farmyard.

—OPPOSITES: soft, delicate, refined.

coast *n.* ☞ SHORE[1].
▶ *v.* FREEWHEEL, cruise, taxi, drift, glide, sail.

coat *n.* **1** OVERCOAT, jacket. **2** FUR, hair, wool, fleece; hide, pelt, skin. **3** LAYER, covering, coating, skin, film, wash; plating, glaze, varnish, veneer, patina; deposit.

coax *v.* PERSUADE, wheedle, cajole, get around, talk into, prevail on; beguile, seduce, inveigle, manoeuvre; *informal* sweet-talk, soft-soap, butter up, twist someone's arm.

cocky *adj.* ARROGANT, conceited, overweening, overconfident, cocksure, self-important, egotistical, presumptuous, boastful, self-assertive; bold, forward, insolent, cheeky, puffed-up.
—OPPOSITES: modest.

coddle *v.* ☞ PAMPER.
—OPPOSITES: neglect.

code *n.* **1** CIPHER, key; hieroglyphics; cryptogram. **2** LAW(S), rules, regulations; constitution, system.

coerce *v.* ☞ PRESSURE *v.*

coffer *n.* **1** STRONGBOX, money box, cash box, money chest, treasure chest, safe; casket, box. **2** FUND(S), reserves, resources, money, finances, wealth, cash, capital, purse; treasury, exchequer; *informal* pork barrel.

cogent *adj.* CONVINCING, compelling, strong, forceful, powerful, potent, weighty, effective; valid, sound, plausible, telling; impressive, persuasive, irresistible, eloquent, credible, influential; conclusive, authoritative, irrefutable; logical, reasoned, rational, reasonable, lucid, coherent, clear.

cogitate v. ☞ CONTEMPLATE 2.

cohere v. STICK TOGETHER, hold together, be united, bind, fuse.

coherent adj. LOGICAL, reasoned, reasonable, rational, sound, cogent, consistent; clear, lucid, articulate; intelligible, comprehensible.
—OPPOSITES: muddled.

cohort n. **1** TROOP, contingent, legion, phalanx. See also REGIMENT. **2** GROUP, grouping, category, class, set, division, batch, list; age group, generation.

coil v. WIND, loop, twist, curl, curve, bend, twine, entwine; spiral, corkscrew.

coin n. **1** penny, nickel, dime, quarter, loonie✽ (loon✽), toonie✽; piece. **2** COINAGE, coins, specie; change.
—RELATED: numismatic.
▸ v. **1** MINT, stamp, strike, cast, punch, die, mould, forge, make. **2** ☞ INVENT 1.

coincide v. **1** OCCUR SIMULTANEOUSLY, happen together, be concurrent, concur, coexist. **2** ☞ CORRESPOND 1.
—OPPOSITES: differ.

coincidence n. ACCIDENT, chance, serendipity, fortuity, luck, providence, happenstance, fate, destiny; a fluke.

coincidental adj. ☞ ACCIDENTAL 1.

cold adj. **1** CHILLY, chill, cool, freezing, icy, snowy, wintry, frosty, frigid, frozen, gelid, glacial, sub-zero, hypothermic, ice-cold, icy-cold; bitter, biting, raw, bone-chilling, arctic, polar; brisk, crisp, fresh, nippy. **2** CHILLY, chilled, cool, freezing, frozen, shivery, numb, benumbed; frozen stiff, frozen to death. **3** INDIFFERENT, unfeeling, unemotional, formal, stiff. See also UNFRIENDLY 1.
—OPPOSITES: hot, warm.

cold-blooded adj. ☞ CRUEL 1.

collaborate v. **1** CO-OPERATE, join forces, team up, band together, work together, participate, combine, ally; pool resources, put —— heads together. **2** COLLUDE, conspire, fraternize, co-operate, consort, sympathize; *informal* be in cahoots.

collaborator n. **1** ☞ COLLEAGUE. **2** QUISLING, collaborationist, colluder, (enemy) sympathizer; traitor, fifth columnist.

collapse v. **1** CAVE IN, fall in, subside, fall down, give (way), crumple, buckle, sag, slump. **2** ☞ FAINT v. **3** BREAK DOWN, fail, fall through, fold, founder, miscarry, come to grief, be unsuccessful; end; *informal* flop, fizzle out.
▸ n. **1** CAVE-IN, subsidence. **2** ☞ BREAKDOWN 1, 2.

collate v. COLLECT, gather, accumulate, assemble; combine, aggregate, put together; arrange, organize.

colleague n. CO-WORKER, fellow worker, workmate, teammate, associate, partner, collaborator, ally, confederate.

collect v. **1** GATHER, accumulate, assemble; amass, stockpile, pile up, heap up, store (up), put by/away, lay by/in, hoard, save; accrue. **2** ☞ CONGREGATE. **3** RAISE,

appeal for, ask for, solicit; obtain, acquire, gather.
—OPPOSITES: disperse, distribute.

collected adj. ☞ CALM adj. 1.
—OPPOSITES: excited, hysterical.

collection n. **1** HOARD, pile, heap, stack, stock, store, stockpile; accumulation, reserve, supply, bank, pool, fund, mine, reservoir. **2** GROUP, crowd, body, assemblage, gathering, throng; knot, cluster; multitude, bevy, party, band, horde, pack, flock, swarm, mob; informal gang, load, gaggle. **3** ☞ ANTHOLOGY.

collective adj. COMMON, shared, joint, combined, mutual, communal, pooled; united, allied, co-operative, collaborative.
—OPPOSITES: individual.

college n. SCHOOL, academy, university, polytechnic, institute, seminary, conservatoire, conservatory.

collide v. **1** CRASH, hit, strike, impact, run into, bump into, meet head-on, cannon into, plow into, barrel into. **2** ☞ CONFLICT v.

collision n. CRASH, accident, impact, smash, bump, hit, smash-up, fender-bender, rear-ender, wreck, pileup.

colloquial adj. INFORMAL, conversational, everyday, non-literary; unofficial, idiomatic, slangy, vernacular, popular, demotic.
—OPPOSITES: formal.

collusion n. CONSPIRACY, connivance, complicity, intrigue, plotting, secret understanding, collaboration, scheming.

colonize v. SETTLE (IN), people, populate; occupy, take over, seize, capture, subjugate.

colony n. SETTLEMENT, dependency, protectorate, satellite, territory, outpost, province.

colossal adj. ☞ HUGE.
—OPPOSITES: tiny.

colour n. **1** HUE, shade, tint, tone, coloration. **2** ☞ BLUSH n. **3** SKIN COLOURING/TONE; race, ethnic group.
—RELATED: chromatic.
▶ v. **1** TINT, dye, stain, paint, pigment, wash. **2** ☞ BLUSH v. **3** INFLUENCE, affect, taint, warp, skew, distort, bias, prejudice.

colourful adj. **1** BRIGHTLY COLOURED, vivid, vibrant, brilliant, radiant, rich; gaudy, glaring, garish; multicoloured, multicolour, rainbow, varicoloured, harlequin, polychromatic, psychedelic, neon, jazzy. **2** VIVID, graphic, lively, animated, dramatic, fascinating, interesting, stimulating, scintillating, evocative.

colourless adj. **1** UNCOLOURED, white, bleached. **2** ☞ PALE adj. 1.
—OPPOSITES: colourful, rosy.

column n. **1** ☞ PILLAR. **2** ☞ ARTICLE 2. **3** LINE, file, queue, procession, train, cavalcade, convoy.

columnist n. ☞ JOURNALIST.

comb v. **1** GROOM, brush, untangle, smooth, straighten, neaten, tidy, arrange; curry. **2** ☞ SEARCH v. 2.

combat n. BATTLE, fighting, action, hostilities, conflict, war, warfare.

combative *adj.* PUGNACIOUS, aggressive, antagonistic, quarrelsome, argumentative, contentious, disputatious, confrontational, hostile, threatening, truculent, belligerent, bellicose, militant; warlike, warmongering, hawkish; *informal* spoiling for a fight, scrappy.
—OPPOSITES: conciliatory.

combination *n.* AMALGAMATION, amalgam, merge, blend, mixture, mix, fusion, marriage, coalition, integration, incorporation, synthesis, composite, compound; alloy; *informal* combo.

combine *v.* **1** AMALGAMATE, integrate, incorporate, merge, mix, fuse, blend; bind, join, marry, unify, assimilate, coalesce, consolidate, desegregate, homogenize, intermingle, meld, mingle, unite. **2** ☞ CO-OPERATE.

combustible *adj.*
☞ INFLAMMABLE.

come *v.* **1** MOVE NEARER, move closer, approach, advance, draw close/closer, draw near/nearer; proceed; *archaic* draw nigh.
2 ARRIVE, get here/there, make it, appear, come on the scene; approach, enter, turn up, come along, materialize; *informal* show (up), roll in/up, blow in, show one's face. **3** BE FROM, be a native of, hail from, originate in; live in, reside in.
—OPPOSITES: go, leave.

□ **come about** ☞ HAPPEN 1. **come across 1** ☞ MEET 1. **2** ☞ SEEM. **come down on.** ☞ REPRIMAND *v.* **come forward** ☞ VOLUNTEER 2. **come off** SUCCEED, work, turn out well, work out, go as planned, produce the desired result, get results. **come out with** UTTER, say, let out, blurt out, burst out with; issue, present. **come through 1** SURVIVE, get through, ride out, weather, live through, pull through; withstand, stand up to, endure, surmount, overcome; *informal* stick out. **2** HELP, be there.
come up ☞ HAPPEN 1.

comeback *n.* **1** ☞ RALLY *n.* 2.
2 RETORT, riposte, return, rejoinder; answer, reply, response.

comedian, comedienne *n.* COMIC, comedienne, funny man/woman, humorist, gagster, stand-up, zany; JOKER, jester, wit, wag, wisecracker, jokester; prankster, clown, fool, buffoon; *informal* laugh, hoot, riot, case, kidder; *informal, dated* card.

comedy *n.* HUMOUR, fun, funny side, comical aspect, absurdity, drollness, farce.
—OPPOSITES: gravity.

comfort *n.* **1** EASE, relaxation, repose, serenity, tranquility, contentment, coziness; luxury, opulence, prosperity; bed of roses.
2 ☞ CONSOLATION.
▶ *v.* CONSOLE, solace, condole with, commiserate with, sympathize with; support, succour, ease, reassure, soothe, calm; cheer, hearten, uplift; *informal* buck up.
—OPPOSITES: distress, depress.

comfortable *adj.* **1** PLEASANT, free from hardship; affluent, well-to-do, luxurious, opulent.
2 ☞ COZY. **3** LOOSE, loose-fitting, casual; *informal* comfy.
—OPPOSITES: hard, Spartan.

comic *adj.* ☞ FUNNY 1.
—OPPOSITES: serious.

▶ *n.* **1** ☞ COMEDIAN. **2** CARTOON, comic book, graphic novel; *informal* funny.

command *v.* **1** ORDER, tell, direct, instruct, call on, require; *literary* bid. **2** BE IN CHARGE OF, be in command of, be the leader of; head, lead, control, direct, manage, supervise, oversee; *informal* head up.
▶ *n.* **1** ☞ INSTRUCTION 2.
2 AUTHORITY, control, charge, power, direction, dominion, guidance; leadership, rule, government, management, supervision, jurisdiction.
3 ☞ KNOWLEDGE 1.

commander *n.* COMMANDER-IN-CHIEF, C in C, commanding officer, CO, officer. See also LEADER.

commemorate *v.* CELEBRATE, pay tribute to, pay homage to, honour, salute, toast; remember, recognize, acknowledge, observe, mark.

commence *v.* BEGIN, start; get the ball rolling, get going, get under way, get off the ground, set about, embark on, launch into, lead off; open, initiate, inaugurate, launch, set in motion; *informal* kick off, get the show on the road.
—OPPOSITES: conclude.

commend *v.* ☞ PRAISE *v.* 1.
—OPPOSITES: criticize.

commendable *adj.* ADMIRABLE, praiseworthy, creditable, laudable, estimable, meritorious, exemplary, deserving, worthy, noteworthy, honourable, respectable, fine, excellent.
—OPPOSITES: reprehensible.

comment *n.* **1** REMARK, observation, statement, utterance; pronouncement, judgment, reflection, opinion, view; criticism. **2** ☞ ANNOTATION.
▶ *v.* **1** REMARK ON, speak about, talk about, discuss, mention.
2 REMARK, observe, reflect, say, state, declare, announce; interpose, interject.

commentary *n.*
1 ☞ DESCRIPTION. **2** EXPLANATION, elucidation, interpretation, exegesis, analysis; assessment, appraisal, criticism; notes, comments.

commerce *n.* TRADE, trading, buying and selling, business, dealing, traffic; (financial) transactions, dealings.

commercial *adj.* **1** TRADE, trading, business, private enterprise, mercantile, sales.
2 ☞ MERCENARY *adj.*
▶ *n.* ☞ ADVERTISEMENT.

commission *n.* **1** PERCENTAGE, brokerage, share, portion, dividend, premium, fee, consideration, bonus; *informal* cut, take, rake-off, slice. **2** TASK, employment, job, project, mission, assignment, undertaking; duty, charge, responsibility. **3** COMMITTEE, board, council, panel, directorate, delegation.
▶ *v.* **1** ENGAGE, contract, charge, employ, hire, recruit, retain, appoint, enlist, book, sign up.
2 ORDER; authorize; *formal* bespeak.
☐ **out of commission** ☞ OUT OF ORDER at ORDER.

commit *v.* **1** CARRY OUT, do, perpetrate, engage in, enact,

execute, effect, accomplish; be responsible for; *informal* pull off.
2 ENTRUST, consign, assign, deliver, give, hand over, relinquish; *formal* commend.
3 PLEDGE, devote, apply, give, dedicate.

commitment *n.*
1 RESPONSIBILITY, obligation, duty, tie, liability; task; engagement, arrangement. **2** ☞ DEVOTION.
3 VOW, promise, pledge, oath; contract, pact, deal; decision, resolution.

committed *adj.* DEVOUT, devoted, dedicated, loyal, faithful, staunch, firm, steadfast, unwavering, wholehearted, keen, passionate, ardent, fervent, sworn, pledged; dutiful, diligent; *informal* card-carrying, hard-core, true blue.
—OPPOSITES: apathetic.

commodious *adj.* ☞ ROOMY.
—OPPOSITES: cramped.

common *adj.* **1** USUAL, ordinary, familiar, regular, frequent, recurrent, everyday; standard, typical, normal, average, conventional, stock, commonplace, run-of-the-mill; *informal* garden variety.
2 WIDESPREAD, general, universal, popular, mainstream, prevalent, prevailing, rife, established, conventional, traditional, orthodox, accepted. **3** COLLECTIVE, communal, community, public, popular, general; shared, combined.
—OPPOSITES: unusual, rare, individual.

commonplace *adj.* **1** ORDINARY, run-of-the-mill, unremarkable, unexceptional, average, mediocre,

pedestrian, prosaic, lacklustre, dull, bland, uninteresting, mundane; hackneyed, trite, banal, clichéd, predictable, stale, tired, unoriginal; *informal* by-the-numbers, boilerplate, plain-vanilla, a dime a dozen, bush-league. **2** ☞ COMMON 1.
—OPPOSITES: original, unusual.

commotion *n.* DISTURBANCE, uproar, tumult, rumpus, ruckus, brouhaha, hoopla, furor, hue and cry, fuss, foofaraw, stir, storm, agitation, bustle, excitement, flurry, fluster; turmoil, disorder, confusion, chaos, mayhem, havoc, pandemonium; unrest, fracas, riot, breach of the peace, donnybrook, ruction, ballyhoo, kerfuffle, hoo-ha, to-do, hullabaloo.

communal *adj.* SHARED, joint, common; COLLECTIVE, co-operative, community, communalist, combined.
—OPPOSITES: private, individual.

communicable *adj.*
☞ CONTAGIOUS.

communicate *v.* **1** CONVEY, tell, impart, relay, transmit, pass on, announce, report, recount, relate, present; divulge, disclose, mention; spread, disseminate, promulgate, broadcast. **2** BE IN TOUCH, be in contact, have dealings, interface, interact, commune, meet, liaise; talk, speak, converse; *informal* have a confab, powwow.

communication *n.*
1 TRANSMISSION, conveyance, divulgence, disclosure; dissemination, promulgation, broadcasting. **2** CONTACT, dealings, relations, connection, association,

socializing, intercourse; correspondence, dialogue, talk, conversation, discussion.
3 ☞ MESSAGE 1.

communicative *adj.*
FORTHCOMING, expansive, expressive, unreserved, uninhibited, vocal, outgoing, frank, open, candid; talkative, chatty, loquacious; *informal* gabby.

communion *n.* ☞ FRIENDSHIP 2.

commute *v.* **1** TRAVEL TO AND FROM WORK, travel to and fro, travel back and forth. **2** REDUCE, lessen, lighten, shorten, cut, attenuate, moderate.
—OPPOSITES: increase.

compact *adj.* **1** DENSE, close-packed, tightly packed; thick, tight, firm. **2** ☞ SMALL 1.
3 ☞ CONCISE.
—OPPOSITES: loose, large, rambling.

companion *n.* **1** ASSOCIATE, partner, escort, compatriot, confederate. See also FRIEND.
2 COMPLEMENT, counterpart, twin, match; accompaniment, supplement, addition, adjunct, accessory.

companionable *adj.*
☞ FRIENDLY 1.

companionship *n.* COMPANY, society, social contact. See also FRIENDSHIP 2.

company *n.* **1** FIRM, business, corporation, establishment, house, agency, office, bureau, institution, organization, operation, concern, enterprise; conglomerate, consortium, syndicate, multinational; *informal* outfit. **2** SOCIETY, association. See also FRIENDSHIP 2. **3** GUESTS,

visitors, callers, people. **4** GROUP, crowd, party, band, assembly, cluster, flock, herd, troupe, throng, congregation; *informal* bunch, gang.

comparable *adj.* SIMILAR, close, near, approximate, akin, equivalent, commensurate, proportional, proportionate; like, matching, homologous.

compare *v.* **1** CONTRAST, juxtapose, collate, differentiate. **2** LIKEN, equate, analogize; class with, bracket with, set side by side with. **3** BE AS GOOD AS, be comparable to, bear comparison with, be the equal of, match up to, be on a par with, be in the same league as, come close to, hold a candle to; match, resemble, emulate, rival, approach.
□**beyond compare**
☞ INCOMPARABLE.

comparison *n.* **1** JUXTAPOSITION, collation, differentiation.
2 ☞ SIMILARITY.

compassion *n.* PITY, sympathy, empathy, fellow feeling, care, concern, solicitude, sensitivity, warmth, love, tenderness, mercy, leniency, tolerance, kindness, humanity, charity, goodwill, heart.
—OPPOSITES: indifference, cruelty.

compassionate *adj.*
SYMPATHETIC, empathetic, understanding, caring, solicitous, sensitive, warm, loving; merciful, lenient, tolerant, considerate, kind, humane, charitable, big-hearted.

compatible *adj.* **1** (WELL) SUITED, well-matched, like-minded, in tune, in harmony; reconcilable.

2 CONSISTENT, congruous, congruent; in keeping.

compel *v.* FORCE, pressure, press; push, urge; dragoon, browbeat, bully, intimidate, strong-arm; oblige, require, make, bind, constrain, leave someone no option, obligate; *informal* lean on, put the screws on.

compelling *adj.* **1** ENTHRALLING, captivating, gripping, riveting, spellbinding, mesmerizing, absorbing, irresistible.
2 ☞ COGENT.
—OPPOSITES: boring, weak.

compensate *v.* **1** RECOMPENSE, repay, pay back, reimburse, remunerate, recoup, requite, indemnify. **2** BALANCE (OUT), counterbalance, counteract, offset, make up for, cancel out, neutralize, negative.

compensation *n.* RECOMPENSE, repayment, reimbursement, remuneration, requital, indemnification, indemnity, redress; damages; *informal* comp.

compete *v.* **1** TAKE PART, participate, play, be a competitor, be involved; enter. **2** CONTEND, vie, battle, fight, wrangle, tussle, jockey, go head to head; strive, struggle, pit oneself against; challenge, take on. **3** ☞ RIVAL *v.*

competent *adj.* CAPABLE, able, proficient, adept, adroit, accomplished, complete, skilful, skilled, gifted, talented, expert; good, excellent; *informal* great, mean, wicked, nifty, ace.
—OPPOSITES: inadequate.

competition *n.* **1** CONTEST, tournament, match, game, meet, heat, trial, bout, event, race,

championship, round robin, tourney; provincials✦, nationals, worlds. **2** ☞ RIVALRY. **3** OPPOSITION, other side, field; enemy; challengers, opponents, rivals, adversaries; *literary* foe.

competitive *adj.* **1** AMBITIOUS, zealous, keen, pushy, combative, aggressive. **2** RUTHLESS, aggressive, fierce; *informal* dog-eat-dog, cutthroat. **3** REASONABLE, moderate. See also INEXPENSIVE.
—OPPOSITES: apathetic, exorbitant.

competitor *n.* **1** CONTESTANT, contender, challenger, participant, entrant, hopeful; runner, player. **2** RIVAL, challenger, opponent, adversary; competition, opposition.
—OPPOSITES: ally.

compile *v.* ASSEMBLE, put together, make up, collate, compose, organize, arrange; gather, collect.

complacent *adj.* SMUG, self-satisfied, self-congratulatory, self-regarding; gloating, triumphant, proud; pleased, satisfied, content, contented.

complain *v.* PROTEST, grumble, whine, bleat, carp, cavil, grouse, make a fuss; object, speak out, criticize, find fault, nag, niggle, quibble; *informal* whinge, kick up a fuss, raise a stink, bellyache, moan, snivel, beef, bitch, sound off, gripe, grouch, kvetch.

complaint *n.* **1** PROTEST, objection, grievance, grouse, cavil, quibble, grumble; charge, accusation, criticism; *informal* beef, gripe, jeremiad, whinge; *Law* plaint. **2** ☞ DISEASE.

complaisant *adj.* WILLING,
acquiescent, agreeable, amenable,
co-operative, accommodating,
obliging; biddable, compliant,
docile, obedient.

complement *n.*
1 ACCOMPANIMENT, companion,
addition, supplement, accessory,
trimming. **2** AMOUNT, total,
contingent, capacity, allowance,
quota.
▶ *v.* ACCOMPANY, go with, round off,
set off, suit, harmonize with;
enhance, complete.

complementary *adj.*
HARMONIOUS, compatible,
corresponding, matching, twin;
supportive, reciprocal,
interdependent.
—OPPOSITES: incompatible.

complete *adj.* **1** ☞ ENTIRE 1.
2 FINISHED, ended, concluded,
completed, finalized;
accomplished, achieved,
discharged, settled, done; *informal*
wrapped up, sewn up, polished
off. **3** ☞ ABSOLUTE 1.
—OPPOSITES: partial, unfinished.
▶ *v.* **1** FINISH, end, conclude,
finalize, wind up; *informal* wrap up,
sew up, polish off. **2** FINISH OFF,
round off, top off, crown, cap,
complement.

completely *adv.* TOTALLY,
entirely, wholly, thoroughly, fully,
utterly, absolutely, perfectly,
unreservedly, unconditionally,
quite, altogether, downright,
clear; in every way, in every
respect, one hundred per cent,
every inch, to the hilt; *informal*
dead, deadly, to the max.

complex *adj.* **1** ☞ COMPLICATED.
2 COMPOUND, composite,
multiplex.
—OPPOSITES: simple.

complicate *v.* MAKE (MORE)
DIFFICULT, make complicated, mix
up, confuse, muddle; *informal* mess
up, screw up, snarl up.
—OPPOSITES: simplify.

complicated *adj.* COMPLEX,
intricate, involved, convoluted,
tangled, impenetrable, knotty,
tricky, thorny, labyrinthine,
tortuous, Gordian; confusing,
bewildering, perplexing, difficult,
elaborate, Byzantine, baroque,
delicate, detailed, entangled,
involuted, ornate, twisted, fiddly.
—OPPOSITES: straightforward.

complication *n.* **1** ☞ DIFFICULTY
1. **2** COMPLEXITY, complicatedness,
intricacy, convolutedness.

compliment *n.* FLATTERING
REMARK, tribute, accolade,
commendation, bouquet, pat on
the back; (**compliments**) praise,
acclaim, admiration, flattery,
blandishments, honeyed words;
informal props, kudos.
—OPPOSITES: insult.
▶ *v.* ☞ PRAISE *v.* 1.
—OPPOSITES: criticize.

complimentary *adj.*
1 FLATTERING, appreciative,
congratulatory, admiring,
approving, commendatory,
favourable, glowing, adulatory;
informal rave. **2** FREE (OF CHARGE),
gratis, for nothing, courtesy, on
the house.
—OPPOSITES: derogatory.

comply *v.* ABIDE BY, observe, obey,
adhere to, conform to, hew to,
follow, respect; agree to, assent to,

go along with, yield to, submit to, defer to; uphold, heed; satisfy, fulfill.
—OPPOSITES: ignore, disobey.

component *n.* CONSTITUENT, ingredient, element, building block; part, piece, bit, strand, portion, unit, feature, aspect, attribute, module, section, segment.

compose *v.* **1** WRITE, formulate, devise, make up, think up, produce, invent, concoct; pen, author, draft; score, orchestrate, choreograph. **2** MAKE UP, constitute, form.

□**compose oneself** CALM DOWN, control oneself, regain one's composure, pull oneself together, collect oneself, steady oneself, keep one's head, relax; *informal* get a grip, keep one's cool, cool one's jets, decompress.

composed *adj.* ☞ CALM *adj.* 1.
—OPPOSITES: excited.

composition *n.* **1** MAKEUP, constitution, configuration, structure, formation, form, framework, fabric, anatomy, organization; *informal* set-up. **2** WRITING, creation, formulation, invention, concoction, orchestration; piece, arrangement. **3** ESSAY, paper, study, piece of writing, theme. **4** ARRANGEMENT, disposition, layout; proportions, balance, symmetry.

compound *n.* **1** ☞ COMBINATION. **2** ENCLOSURE, pound, coop; estate, cloister.
▶ *adj.* COMPOSITE, complex; blended, fused, combined.
—OPPOSITES: simple.

▶ *v.* **1** ☞ COMBINE 1. **2** ☞ WORSEN 1.
—OPPOSITES: alleviate.

comprehend *v.* ☞ UNDERSTAND 1.

comprehensible *adj.* INTELLIGIBLE, understandable, accessible; lucid, coherent, clear, clear-cut, plain, explicit, unambiguous, uncomplicated, straightforward, fathomable, digestible, self-explanatory, simple, user-friendly.
—OPPOSITES: opaque.

comprehensive *adj.* INCLUSIVE, all-inclusive, complete; thorough, full, extensive, all-embracing, exhaustive, detailed, in-depth, encyclopedic, universal, catholic; far-reaching, radical, sweeping, across the board, wholesale; broad, wide-ranging; *informal* wall-to-wall.
—OPPOSITES: limited.

compress *v.* **1** SQUEEZE, press, squash, crush, cram, jam, stuff; tamp, pack, compact; constrict; *informal* scrunch. **2** ☞ ABRIDGE.
—OPPOSITES: expand.

comprise *v.* **1** CONSIST OF, be made up of, be composed of, contain, encompass, incorporate; include; *formal* comprehend. **2** (*informal*) MAKE UP, constitute, form, compose; account for.

compromise *n.* AGREEMENT, understanding, settlement, terms, deal, trade-off, saw-off❖, bargain; middle ground, happy medium, balance.
—OPPOSITES: intransigence.
▶ *v.* **1** MEET EACH OTHER HALFWAY, come to an understanding, make a deal, make concessions, saw off❖, find a happy medium, strike a balance; give and take.

2 UNDERMINE, weaken, damage, harm; jeopardize, prejudice; discredit, dishonour, shame, embarrass.

compulsion *n.* **1** OBLIGATION, constraint, coercion, duress, pressure, intimidation. **2** URGE, impulse, need, desire, drive; obsession, fixation, addiction; temptation.

compulsive *adj.* **1** IRRESISTIBLE, uncontrollable, compelling, overwhelming, urgent; obsessive. **2** OBSESSIVE, obsessional, addictive, uncontrollable. **3** ☞ INVETERATE.

compulsory *adj.* ☞ MANDATORY. —OPPOSITES: optional.

compunction *n.* SCRUPLES, misgivings, qualms, worries, unease, uneasiness, doubts, reluctance, reservations; guilt, regret, contrition, self-reproach.

compute *v.* CALCULATE, work out, reckon, determine, evaluate, quantify; add up, count up, tally, total, totalize, tot up.

comrade *n.* COLLEAGUE, associate, partner, co-worker, workmate. See also FRIEND.

con (*informal*) *v.* ☞ SWINDLE *v.*
▶ *n.* **1** ☞ CONVICT. **2** ☞ SWINDLE *n.*

conceal *v.* **1** HIDE, screen, cover, obscure, block out, blot out, mask, shroud, secrete. **2** HIDE, cover up, disguise, mask, veil; keep secret; suppress, repress, bottle up; *informal* keep a lid on, keep under one's hat. —OPPOSITES: reveal, confess.

concealed *adj.* ☞ HIDDEN 1.

concede *v.* **1** ADMIT, acknowledge, accept, allow, grant, recognize, own, confess; agree.

2 ☞ YIELD *v.* 2.
—OPPOSITES: deny, retain.
□ **concede defeat** ☞ SURRENDER *v.* 1.

conceit *n.* ☞ VANITY 1.
—OPPOSITES: humility.

conceited *adj.* VAIN, narcissistic, self-centred, egotistic, egotistical, egocentric; proud, arrogant, boastful, full of oneself, self-important, immodest, swaggering; self-satisfied, smug; supercilious, haughty, snobbish; *informal* big-headed, too big for one's britches, stuck-up, high and mighty, uppity, snotty; *literary* vainglorious.

conceivable *adj.* IMAGINABLE, possible; plausible, tenable, credible, believable, thinkable, feasible; understandable, comprehensible.

conceive *v.* **1** BECOME PREGNANT, become impregnated. **2** ☞ DEVISE. **3** IMAGINE, envisage, visualize, picture, think, envision; grasp, appreciate, apprehend.

concentrate *v.* **1** FOCUS, direct, centre, centralize. **2** FOCUS ON, pay attention to, keep one's mind on, devote oneself to; be absorbed in, be engrossed in, be immersed in.
▶ *n.* EXTRACT, decoction, distillation.

concentrated *adj.*
1 ☞ CONCERTED 1. **2** CONDENSED, reduced, evaporated, thickened; undiluted, strong.
—OPPOSITES: half-hearted, diluted.

concept *n.* IDEA, notion, conception, abstraction; theory, hypothesis; belief, conviction, opinion; image, impression, picture.

concern v. **1** BE ABOUT, deal with, have to do with, cover; discuss, go into, examine, study, review, analyze; relate to, pertain to. **2** AFFECT, involve, be relevant to, apply to, have a bearing on, impact on; be important to, interest. **3** ☞ WORRY v. 2.
▶ n. **1** ANXIETY, worry, disquiet, apprehensiveness, unease, consternation. **2** SOLICITUDE, consideration, care, sympathy, regard. **3** RESPONSIBILITY, business, affair, charge, duty, job; province, preserve; problem, worry; informal bag, bailiwick. **4** ☞ INTEREST n. 2.
—OPPOSITES: indifference.

concerned adj. **1** ☞ ANXIOUS 1. **2** INTERESTED, involved, affected; connected, related, implicated.

concerning prep. ☞ REGARDING.

concerted adj. **1** STRENUOUS, vigorous, intensive, intense, concentrated; informal all-out. **2** ☞ JOINT adj.
—OPPOSITES: half-hearted, individual.

conciliate v. ☞ PLACATE.
—OPPOSITES: provoke.

concise adj. SUCCINCT, pithy, incisive, brief, short (and to the point), short and sweet; abridged, condensed, compressed, abbreviated, compact, capsule, potted, thumbnail; informal snappy.
—OPPOSITES: lengthy, wordy.

conclude v. **1** ☞ END v. 1. **2** BRING TO AN END, close, wind up, terminate, dissolve; round off; informal wrap up. **3** DEDUCE, infer, gather, judge, decide, conjecture, surmise, extrapolate, figure, reckon.
—OPPOSITES: commence.

conclusion n. **1** END, ending, finish, close, termination, cessation; culmination, denouement, peroration, coda; informal outro. **2** DEDUCTION, inference, interpretation, illation; reasoning; opinion, judgment, verdict; assumption, presumption, supposition.
—OPPOSITES: beginning.

conclusive adj. ☞ INDISPUTABLE.
—OPPOSITES: unconvincing.

concoct v. **1** PREPARE, make, assemble; informal fix, rustle up. **2** ☞ FABRICATE 1.

concomitant adj. ☞ ATTENDANT adj.
—OPPOSITES: unrelated.

concrete adj. **1** ☞ TANGIBLE. **2** DEFINITE, firm, positive, conclusive, definitive; real, genuine, bona fide.
—OPPOSITES: abstract, imaginary.

concur v. AGREE, be in agreement, go along, fall in, be in sympathy; see eye to eye, be of the same mind/opinion.
—OPPOSITES: disagree.

concurrent adj. SIMULTANEOUS, coincident, contemporaneous, parallel.

condemn v. **1** CENSURE, criticize, denounce, revile, blame. See also REPRIMAND v. **2** SENTENCE; convict, find guilty. **3** DOOM, destine, damn; consign, assign.
—OPPOSITES: praise.

condense v. ☞ ABRIDGE.
—OPPOSITES: expand.

condescend v. DEIGN, stoop, descend, lower oneself, demean oneself, humble oneself; vouchsafe, see fit, consent.

condescending *adj.*
☞ SUPERCILIOUS.

condition *n.* **1** STATE, shape, order. **2** CIRCUMSTANCES, surroundings, environment, situation, set-up, setting, habitat. **3** FITNESS, health, form, shape, trim, fettle. **4** ☞ DISEASE. **5** STIPULATION, constraint, prerequisite, precondition, requirement, rule, term, specification, provision, proviso, caveat, demand, qualification, rider.
▶ *v.* **1** TRAIN, teach, educate, guide; accustom, adapt, habituate, mould, inure. **2** IMPROVE, nourish, tone (up), moisturize.

conditional *adj.* CONTINGENT, dependent, qualified, with reservations, limited, provisional, provisory.

condone *v.* DISREGARD, accept, allow, let pass, turn a blind eye to, overlook, forget; forgive, pardon, excuse, let go.
—OPPOSITES: condemn.

conducive *adj.* FAVOURABLE, beneficial, advantageous, opportune, propitious, encouraging, promising, convenient, good, helpful, instrumental, productive, useful.
—OPPOSITES: unfavourable.

conduct *n.* BEHAVIOUR, performance, demeanour; actions, activities, deeds, doings, exploits; habits, manners; *formal* comportment.
▶ *v.* **1** MANAGE, direct, run, administer, organize, coordinate, orchestrate, handle, control, oversee, supervise, regulate, carry out/on. **2** ☞ SHEPHERD *v.*

confer *v.* **1** CONSULT, talk, speak, converse, have a chat, have a tête-à-tête, parley; *informal* have a confab, powwow. **2** ☞ BESTOW.

conference *n.* **1** CONGRESS, meeting, convention, seminar, colloquium, symposium, forum, summit. **2** ☞ DISCUSSION.

confess *v.* **1** ADMIT, acknowledge, reveal, disclose, divulge, avow, declare, profess; own up, tell all; concede, grant. **2** OWN UP, plead guilty, accept the blame; tell the truth, tell all, make a clean breast of it; *informal* come clean, spill the beans, let the cat out of the bag, get something off one's chest, let on, fess (up).
—OPPOSITES: deny.

confidant, confidante *n.* CLOSE FRIEND, bosom friend, best friend; intimate; *informal* buddy, chum, pal, crony, mate.

confide *v.* REVEAL, disclose, divulge, lay bare, betray, impart, declare, intimate, uncover, expose, vouchsafe, tell; confess, admit, give away; *informal* blab, spill.

confidence *n.* **1** ☞ FAITH 1. **2** SELF-ASSURANCE, self-confidence, self-possession, assertiveness; poise, aplomb, phlegm; courage, boldness, mettle, nerve.
—OPPOSITES: skepticism, doubt.

confident *adj.* **1** OPTIMISTIC, hopeful, sanguine; sure, certain, positive, convinced, in no doubt, satisfied, assured, persuaded. **2** SELF-ASSURED, assured, self-confident, positive, assertive, self-possessed, self-reliant, poised; cool-headed, phlegmatic, level-headed, unperturbed, imperturbable, unruffled, at ease; *informal* together, can-do.

confidential *adj.* PRIVATE, personal, intimate, quiet; secret, sensitive, classified, restricted, unofficial, unrevealed, undisclosed, unpublished, off the record, inside; *informal* hush-hush, mum; *formal* sub rosa.

confine *v.* **1** ENCLOSE, incarcerate, imprison, intern, impound, hold captive, trap; shut in/up, keep, lock in/up, coop (up); fence in, hedge in, wall in/up. **2** RESTRICT, limit.

confirm *v.* **1** CORROBORATE, verify, prove, validate, authenticate, substantiate, justify, vindicate; support, uphold, ratify, warrant, back up, bear out. **2** AFFIRM, reaffirm, assert, assure someone, repeat; promise, guarantee. **3** ☞ RATIFY.
—OPPOSITES: contradict, deny.

confiscate *v.* IMPOUND, seize, commandeer, requisition, appropriate, expropriate, sequester, sequestrate, take (away); *Law* distrain.
—OPPOSITES: return.

conflict *n.* **1** DISPUTE, quarrel, squabble, disagreement, dissension, clash; discord, friction, strife, antagonism, hostility, disputation, contention; feud, schism. **2** ☞ WAR.
—OPPOSITES: agreement, peace.
▶ *v.* CLASH, be incompatible, vary, be at odds, be in conflict, differ, diverge, disagree, contrast, collide.

conform *v.* **1** COMPLY WITH, abide by, obey, observe, follow, keep to, hew to, stick to, adhere to, uphold, heed, accept, go along with, fall in with, respect, defer to; satisfy, meet, fulfill. **2** MATCH, fit, suit, answer, agree with, be like, correspond to, be consistent with, measure up to, tally with, square with.
—OPPOSITES: flout, rebel.

confront *v.* **1** CHALLENGE, face (up to), come face to face with, meet, accost, waylay; stand up to, brave, beard, tackle; *informal* collar. **2** ☞ TACKLE *v.* 1.
—OPPOSITES: avoid.

confuse *v.* **1** BEWILDER, baffle, mystify, bemuse, perplex, puzzle, confound; *informal* flummox, faze, stump, fox, discombobulate, bedazzle. **2** COMPLICATE, muddle, jumble, garble, blur, obscure, cloud.
—OPPOSITES: enlighten, simplify.

confused *adj.* **1** BEWILDERED, bemused, puzzled, perplexed, baffled, mystified, nonplussed, muddled, befuddled, dumbfounded, at sea, at a loss, taken aback, disoriented, disconcerted; *informal* flummoxed, bamboozled, clueless, fazed, discombobulated. **2** VAGUE, unclear, indistinct, imprecise, blurred, hazy, woolly, shadowy, dim; imperfect, sketchy. **3** ☞ DISORGANIZED 1.
—OPPOSITES: lucid, clear, precise, neat.

confusion *n.* **1** UNCERTAINTY, incertitude, unsureness, doubt, ignorance; *formal* dubiety. **2** BEWILDERMENT, bafflement, perplexity, puzzlement, mystification, befuddlement; shock, daze, wonder, wonderment, astonishment;

informal bamboozlement, discombobulation. **3** ☞ CHAOS.
—OPPOSITES: certainty, order.

congeal *v.* COAGULATE, clot, thicken, jell, cake, set, curdle.

congenial *adj.* LIKE-MINDED, compatible, kindred, well-suited; companionable, sociable, sympathetic, comradely, convivial, hospitable, genial, personable, agreeable, friendly, pleasant, likeable, amiable, nice, simpatico; enjoyable, pleasurable, satisfying, gratifying, delightful, relaxing, welcoming.
—OPPOSITES: unpleasant.

congenital *adj.* ☞ HEREDITARY 2.
—OPPOSITES: acquired.

congested *adj.* OBSTRUCTED, blocked, clogged, choked; *informal* snarled up, gridlocked. See also CROWDED.
—OPPOSITES: clear.

congratulate *v.* **1** SEND ONE'S BEST WISHES, wish someone good luck, wish someone joy; drink someone's health, toast. **2** ☞ PRAISE *v.* 1.
—OPPOSITES: criticize.

congregate *v.* ASSEMBLE, gather, collect, come together, convene, rally, rendezvous, muster, meet, cluster, group, converge, flock together.
—OPPOSITES: disperse.

conjecture *n.* SPECULATION, guesswork, surmise, fancy, presumption, assumption, theory, postulation, supposition; inference, extrapolation, belief, feeling, guess, hunch, hypothesis, idea, notion, suspicion; estimate;

informal guesstimate, a shot in the dark.
—OPPOSITES: fact.

conjugal *adj.* ☞ MARITAL.

connect *v.* **1** ☞ ATTACH 1. **2** ASSOCIATE, link, couple; identify, equate, bracket, relate to.

connection *n.* **1** LINK, relationship, relation, interconnection, interdependence, association; bond, tie, tie-in, correspondence, parallel, analogy. **2** ATTACHMENT, joint, fastening, coupling.
☐ **in connection with** ☞ REGARDING.

connive *v.* ☞ SCHEME.

connotation *n.* OVERTONE, undertone, undercurrent, implication, hidden meaning, nuance, feeling, hint, echo, vibrations, association, intimation, suggestion, suspicion, insinuation.

conquer *v.* **1** ☞ DEFEAT 1. **2** SEIZE, take (over), appropriate, subjugate, capture, occupy, invade, annex, overrun.

conquest *n.* **1** DEFEAT, vanquishment, annihilation, overthrow, subjugation, rout, mastery, crushing; victory over, triumph over. **2** ☞ OCCUPATION 2.

conscience *n.* SENSE OF RIGHT AND WRONG, moral sense, inner voice; morals, standards, values, principles, ethics, beliefs; compunction, scruples, qualms.

conscientious *adj.* DILIGENT, industrious, punctilious, painstaking, sedulous, assiduous, dedicated, careful, meticulous, thorough, attentive, hard-working, studious, rigorous,

particular; religious, strict.
—OPPOSITES: casual.

conscious adj. **1** AWARE, awake,
alert, responsive, sentient,
compos mentis. **2** AWARE OF, alert
to, mindful of, sensible of; formal
cognizant of. **3** ☞ INTENTIONAL.
—OPPOSITES: unaware.

consecrate v. SANCTIFY, bless,
make holy, make sacred; dedicate
to God, devote, reserve, set apart;
anoint, ordain; formal hallow.

consecutive adj. SUCCESSIVE,
succeeding, following, in
succession, running, in a row, one
after the other, back-to-back,
continuous, straight,
uninterrupted.

consensus n. AGREEMENT,
harmony, concurrence, accord,
unity, unanimity, solidarity; formal
concord.
—OPPOSITES: disagreement.

consent n. ☞ APPROVAL.
—OPPOSITES: dissent.
▶ v. AGREE, assent, yield, give in,
submit; allow, give permission
for, sanction, accept, approve, go
along with.
—OPPOSITES: forbid.

consequence n. **1** RESULT,
upshot, outcome, effect,
repercussion, ramification,
corollary, concomitant, aftermath,
after-effect; fruit(s), product, by-
product, legacy, end result; informal
payoff, spinoff; Medicine sequela.
2 IMPORTANCE, import,
significance, account, substance,
note, mark, prominence, value,
concern, interest; formal moment.
—OPPOSITES: cause.

consequent adj. RESULTING,
resultant, ensuing, consequential;

following, subsequent, successive;
attendant, accompanying,
concomitant; collateral,
associated, related.

conservation n. PRESERVATION,
protection, safeguarding,
safekeeping; care, guardianship,
husbandry, supervision; upkeep,
maintenance, repair, restoration;
ecology, environmentalism.

conservative adj.
1 TRADITIONALIST, traditional,
conventional, orthodox, old-
fashioned, dyed-in-the-wool,
hidebound, unadventurous, set in
one's ways; moderate, middle-of-
the-road, buttoned-down; informal
stick in the mud. **2** CONVENTIONAL,
sober, modest, plain, unobtrusive,
restrained, subtle, low-key,
demure; informal square, straight.
—OPPOSITES: radical, ostentatious.
▶ n. Tory✦, right winger,
reactionary, rightist, diehard;
(Que.) bleu✦, Blue; US Republican.

conserve v. PRESERVE, protect,
save, safeguard, keep, look after;
sustain, prolong, perpetuate;
store, reserve, husband.
—OPPOSITES: squander.

consider v. **1** THINK ABOUT,
contemplate, reflect on, examine,
review; mull over, ponder,
deliberate on, chew over,
meditate on, ruminate on/about,
analyze, explore, inquire into,
investigate, look into, muse on,
take stock of, weigh; assess,
evaluate, appraise; informal size up.
2 DEEM, think, believe, judge,
adjudge, rate, count, find; regard
as, hold to be, reckon to be, view
as, see as. **3** ☞ CONTEMPLATE 1.
4 TAKE INTO CONSIDERATION, take

account of, make allowances for, bear in mind, be mindful of, remember, mind, mark, respect, heed, note, make provision for, cater to.
—OPPOSITES: ignore.

considerable *adj.* **1** SIZEABLE, substantial, appreciable, significant; goodly, fair, hefty, handsome, decent, worthwhile; ample, plentiful, abundant, great, large, generous; *informal* tidy, not to be sneezed at. **2** MUCH, great, a lot of, lots of, a great deal of, plenty of, a fair amount of.
—OPPOSITES: paltry, minor.

considerate *adj.* ATTENTIVE, thoughtful, solicitous, concerned, mindful, heedful; obliging, accommodating, helpful, co-operative, patient; kind, unselfish, compassionate, sympathetic, caring, charitable, altruistic, generous, neighbourly; polite, sensitive, tactful, understanding.

consign *v.* SEND, deliver, hand over, turn over, sentence; confine in, imprison in, incarcerate in, lock up in; *informal* put away, put behind bars.

consist *v.* BE COMPOSED, be made up, be formed; comprise, contain, include, incorporate.

consistent *adj.* **1** CONSTANT, regular, uniform, steady, stable, even, unchanging, undeviating, invariable, unvarying; dependable, reliable, predictable. **2** COMPATIBLE, congruous, consonant, in tune, in line, reconcilable; corresponding to, conforming to.
—OPPOSITES: irregular, incompatible.

consolation *n.* COMFORT, solace, sympathy, compassion, pity, commiseration, condolence, empathy; relief, help, (moral) support, encouragement, reassurance; cheer.

consolidate *v.* STRENGTHEN, secure, stabilize, reinforce, fortify; enhance, improve.

consort *n.* ☞ MATE *n.* 1.
▶ *v.* ☞ ASSOCIATE *v.* 2.

conspicuous *adj.* EASILY SEEN, clear, visible, noticeable, discernible, perceptible, detectable; obvious, manifest, evident, apparent, marked, pronounced, prominent, patent, crystal clear; striking, eye-catching, overt, blatant, writ large; distinct, recognizable, unmistakable, inescapable; *informal* as plain as the nose on one's face, standing/sticking out like a sore thumb.

conspiracy *n.* PLOT, scheme, plan, intrigue, machination, ploy, trick, ruse, subterfuge; *informal* racket.

conspire *v.* ☞ SCHEME *v.*

constant *adj.* **1** ☞ CONTINUOUS. **2** ☞ CONSISTENT 1. **3** ☞ FAITHFUL 1.
—OPPOSITES: fitful, variable, fickle.

constantly *adv.* ☞ ALWAYS 2.
—OPPOSITES: occasionally.

consternation *n.* DISMAY, perturbation, distress, disquiet, discomposure; surprise, amazement, astonishment; alarm, panic, fear, fright, shock.
—OPPOSITES: satisfaction.

constraint *n.* ☞ LIMITATION 1.

construct *v.* BUILD, erect, put up, set up, raise, establish, assemble,

manufacture, fabricate, create, make.
—OPPOSITES: demolish.

construction n. **1** ☞ BUILDING. **2** INTERPRETATION, reading, meaning, explanation, explication, construal; *informal* take.

constructive adj. USEFUL, helpful, productive, positive, encouraging; practical, valuable, profitable, worthwhile.

consult v. SEEK ADVICE FROM, ask, take counsel from, call on/upon, speak to, turn to, have recourse to; *informal* pick someone's brains.

consume v. **1** ☞ EAT 1, DRINK V. 1. **2** USE (UP), utilize, expend; deplete, exhaust; waste, squander, drain, dissipate, fritter away.

contact n. **1** TOUCH, touching; proximity, exposure.
2 ☞ COMMUNICATION 2.
▶ v. GET IN TOUCH WITH, communicate with, make contact with, approach, notify; telephone, phone, call, speak to, talk to, write to, get hold of.

contagious adj. INFECTIOUS, communicable, transmittable, transmissible, transferable, spreadable; *informal* catching; *dated* infective.

contain v. **1** INCLUDE, comprise, take in, incorporate, involve, encompass, embrace; consist of, be made up of, be composed of.
2 ☞ RESTRAIN 1.

container n. RECEPTACLE, vessel, canister, box, *proprietary* Tupperware, holder, repository, tote.

contaminate v. POLLUTE, adulterate; defile, debase, corrupt, taint, infect, foul, spoil, soil, stain,

sully; poison; *literary* befoul.
—OPPOSITES: purify.

contemplate v. **1** LOOK AT, view, regard, examine, inspect, observe, survey, study, scrutinize, scan, stare at, gaze at, eye, check out. **2** THINK ABOUT, ponder, reflect on, consider, mull over, muse on, dwell on, deliberate over, meditate on, ruminate on, chew over, brood on/about, turn over in one's mind; be lost in contemplation/thought, daydream; *informal* put on one's thinking cap; *formal* cogitate.

contemplative adj.
☞ THOUGHTFUL 1.

contemporary adj. **1** OF THE TIME, of the day, contemporaneous, concurrent, coeval, coexisting, coexistent.
2 ☞ MODERN 1. **3** ☞ FASHIONABLE.
—OPPOSITES: old-fashioned, out of date.

contempt n. SCORN, disdain, disrespect, scornfulness, contemptuousness, derision; disgust, loathing, hatred, abhorrence.
—OPPOSITES: respect.

contemptible adj. DESPICABLE, detestable, hateful, reprehensible, deplorable, unspeakable, disgraceful, shameful, ignominious, abject, low, mean, cowardly, unworthy, discreditable, petty, worthless, shabby, cheap, beyond contempt, beyond the pale, sordid, base, beastly, dastardly, dirty, disgusting, dishonourable, foul, lamentable, lowdown, rotten, underhanded, unfair, unprincipled.
—OPPOSITES: admirable.

contemptuous *adj.* SCORNFUL, disdainful, disrespectful, insulting, insolent, derisive, mocking, sneering, scoffing, withering, scathing, snide, disparaging, indifferent, patronizing, slighting; condescending, supercilious, haughty, lordly, proud, superior, arrogant, snobbish, dismissive, aloof; *informal* high and mighty, snotty, sniffy, hoity-toity.
—OPPOSITES: respectful.

contend *v.* 1 COPE WITH, face, grapple with, deal with, take on, pit oneself against. 2 ☞ COMPETE 2. 3 ASSERT, maintain, hold, claim, argue, insist, state, declare, profess, affirm; allege; *formal* aver.

content[1] *adj.* CONTENTED, satisfied, pleased, gratified, fulfilled, happy, cheerful, glad; unworried, untroubled, at ease, at peace, tranquil, serene.
—OPPOSITES: discontented, dissatisfied.

content[2] *n.* 1 (**contents**) CONSTITUENTS, ingredients, components, elements. 2 ☞ SUBJECT *n.* 1.

contented *adj.* ☞ CONTENT[1] *adj.*

contest *n.* 1 ☞ COMPETITION 1. 2 FIGHT, battle, tussle, struggle, competition, race.
▶ *v.* 1 COMPETE FOR, contend for, vie for, fight for, try to win, go for, throw one's hat in the ring. 2 OPPOSE, object to, challenge, take a stand against, take issue with, question, call into question.

contestant *n.* ☞ COMPETITOR 1.

context *n.* CIRCUMSTANCES, conditions, factors, state of affairs, situation, background, scene, setting; frame of reference.

contingency *n.* EVENTUALITY, (chance) event, incident, happening, occurrence, juncture, possibility, fortuity, accident, chance, emergency.

continual *adj.* 1 ☞ REPEATED. 2 ☞ CONTINUOUS.
—OPPOSITES: occasional, temporary.

continue *v.* 1 CARRY ON, proceed, pursue, go on, keep on, persist, press on, persevere, keep at; *informal* stick at, soldier on. 2 ☞ MAINTAIN 1. 3 REMAIN, stay, carry on, keep going. 4 RESUME, pick up, take up, carry on with, return to, recommence.
—OPPOSITES: stop, break off.

continuous *adj.* CONTINUAL, uninterrupted, unbroken, constant, ceaseless, incessant, chronic, steady, sustained, solid, continuing, ongoing, unceasing, without a break, non-stop, round-the-clock, persistent, unremitting, relentless, unrelenting, unrelieved, without respite, endless, unending, never-ending, perpetual, everlasting, eternal, interminable; consecutive, running, without surcease.
—OPPOSITES: intermittent.

contour *n.* OUTLINE, shape, form; lines, curves, figure; silhouette, profile.

contract *n.* AGREEMENT, commitment, arrangement, settlement, understanding, compact, covenant, bond; deal, bargain; *Law* indenture.
▶ *v.* 1 ☞ SHRINK 1. 2 UNDERTAKE, pledge, promise, covenant,

commit oneself, engage, agree, enter an agreement, make a deal. **3** DEVELOP, catch, get, pick up, come down with, be struck down by, be stricken with, succumb to.
—OPPOSITES: expand.
□ **contract something out** SUBCONTRACT, outsource, farm out.

contradict *v.* **1** DENY, refute, rebut, dispute, challenge, counter, controvert; *formal* gainsay. **2** ARGUE AGAINST, go against, challenge, oppose; *formal* gainsay.
—OPPOSITES: confirm, agree with.

contradictory *adj.* OPPOSED, in opposition, opposite, antithetical, contrary, contrasting, conflicting, at variance, at odds, opposing, clashing, divergent, discrepant, different; inconsistent, incompatible, irreconcilable; antagonistic, antipathetic, discordant, inharmonious, mutually exclusive, night and day, poles apart, worlds apart.

contraption *n.* ☞ DEVICE 1.

contrary *adj.* **1** ☞ CONTRADICTORY. **2** ☞ UNREASONABLE 1.
—OPPOSITES: compatible, accommodating.
□ **contrary to** IN CONFLICT WITH, against, at variance with, at odds with, in opposition to, counter to, incompatible with, (diametrically) opposed to, antithetical to, conflicting with, differing from, irreconcilable with, out of keeping with, out of step with.

contrast *n.* DIFFERENCE, dissimilarity, disparity, distinction, contradistinction, divergence, variance, variation, differentiation; contradiction, incongruity, opposition, polarity.

—OPPOSITES: similarity.
▶ *v.* **1** DIFFER FROM, be at variance with, be contrary to, conflict with, go against, be at odds with, be in opposition to, disagree with, clash with. **2** COMPARE, set side by side, juxtapose; measure against.
—OPPOSITES: resemble, liken.

contribute *v.* **1** GIVE, donate, put up, subscribe, hand out, grant, bestow, present, provide, supply, furnish, pay; *informal* chip in, pitch in, fork out, shell out, cough up, kick in, ante up, pony up. **2** PLAY A PART IN, be instrumental in, be a factor in, have a hand in, be conducive to, make for, lead to, cause.

contribution *n.* ☞ DONATION.

contrite *adj.* REMORSEFUL, repentant, penitent, regretful, sorry, apologetic, rueful, sheepish, abashed, hangdog, ashamed, chastened, shamefaced, conscience-stricken, guilt-ridden.

contrived *adj.* FORCED, strained, studied, artificial, affected, put-on, phony, pretended, false, feigned, fake, manufactured, unnatural; laboured, overdone, elaborate.
—OPPOSITES: natural.

control *n.* **1** JURISDICTION, sway, power, authority, command, dominance, government, mastery, leadership, rule, sovereignty, supremacy, ascendancy; charge, management, direction, supervision, superintendence. **2** RESTRAINT, constraint, limitation, restriction, check, curb, brake, rein; regulation. **3** SWITCH, knob, button, dial, handle, lever.
▶ *v.* **1** BE IN CHARGE OF, run,

manage, direct, administer, head, preside over, supervise, superintend, steer; command, rule, govern, lead, dominate, hold sway over, influence, have mastery over, be at the helm; *informal* head up, be in the driver's seat, run the show, rule the roost, wear the pants. **2** ☞ RESTRAIN 1. **3** LIMIT, restrict, curb, cap, constrain.

controversial *adj.* CONTENTIOUS, disputed, at issue, disputable, debatable, arguable, vexed, tendentious; *informal* hot, hot-button.

controversy *n.* DISAGREEMENT, dispute, argument, debate, dissension, contention, disputation, altercation, wrangle, wrangling, quarrel, quarrelling, war of words, storm; cause célèbre, outcry, song and dance, stink, trouble, hot potato, minefield.

conundrum *n.* RIDDLE, puzzle, problem, quandary, dilemma.

convalesce *v.* ☞ RECOVER 1.

convene *v.* SUMMON, call, call together, order; assemble, gather, meet, congregate; *formal* convoke.

convenience store *n.* VARIETY STORE, corner store, (*Que.*) dep✦ (depanneur✦), milk store✦, (*Ont.*) jug milk✦, mini-mart, smoke shop, (*Cape Breton*) dairy✦, confectionery.

convenient *adj.* SUITABLE, appropriate, fitting, fit, suited, opportune, timely, well-timed, favourable, advantageous, seasonable, expedient.

convention *n.* **1** CUSTOM, usage, practice, tradition, way, habit,

norm; rule, code, canon, punctilio; propriety, etiquette, protocol; *formal* praxis. **2** ☞ TREATY. **3** CONFERENCE, meeting, congress, assembly, gathering, summit, convocation, synod, conclave.

conventional *adj.* **1** ORTHODOX, traditional, established, accepted, received, mainstream, prevailing, prevalent, accustomed, customary; old-fashioned. **2** UNORIGINAL, formulaic, predictable, stock, unadventurous, unremarkable; *informal* humdrum, run-of-the-mill. —OPPOSITES: unorthodox, original.

converge *v.* MEET, intersect, cross, connect, link up, coincide, join, unite, merge. —OPPOSITES: diverge.

conversant *adj.* ☞ FAMILIAR 2.

conversation *n.* ☞ DISCUSSION.

convert *v.* **1** CHANGE, turn, transform, metamorphose, transfigure, transmute; alter, adapt, modify, renovate, redesign; *humorous* transmogrify. **2** PROSELYTIZE, evangelize, bring to God, redeem, save, reform, re-educate, cause to see the light.

convey *v.* **1** ☞ TRANSPORT. **2** COMMUNICATE, pass on, make known, impart, relay, transmit, send, hand on, relate, tell, express, reveal, disclose.

convict *v.* FIND GUILTY, sentence. —OPPOSITES: acquit. ▸ *n.* PRISONER, inmate; criminal, offender, lawbreaker, felon; *informal* jailbird, con, crook, lifer, yardbird.

conviction *n.* **1** BELIEF, opinion, view, thought, persuasion, idea, position, stance, article of faith.

2 ☞ CERTAINTY 1.

—OPPOSITES: uncertainty.

convince v. MAKE CERTAIN, persuade, satisfy, prove to; assure, put/set someone's mind at rest; induce, prevail on, talk into.

convincing adj. **1** ☞ COGENT. **2** RESOUNDING, emphatic, decisive, conclusive.

convivial adj. CHEERFUL, jolly, jovial, lively, good-humoured; enjoyable, festive. See also FRIENDLY 1.

convoy n. GROUP, fleet, cavalcade, motorcade, cortège, caravan, line, train.

cook v. **1** PREPARE, make, put together; informal fix, rustle up. **2** ☞ FALSIFY.

cool adj. **1** CHILLY, chill, cold, bracing, brisk, crisp, fresh, refreshing, invigorating, nippy. **2** UNENTHUSIASTIC, lukewarm, tepid, indifferent, uninterested, apathetic, half-hearted; unfriendly, distant, remote, aloof, cold, chilly, frosty, unwelcoming, unresponsive, uncommunicative, undemonstrative, standoffish. **3** ☞ CALM adj. 1. **4** ☞ FASHIONABLE. **5** (informal) ☞ EXCELLENT.

—OPPOSITES: warm, enthusiastic, agitated.

▸ v. **1** CHILL, refrigerate. **2** LESSEN, moderate, diminish, reduce, dampen. **3** CALM DOWN, recover/ regain one's composure, compose oneself, control oneself, pull oneself together, simmer down. —OPPOSITES: heat, inflame, intensify.

▸ excl. EXCELLENT, awesome, great, neat, neat-o, groovy, far-out,

funky, fab, right on, wicked, brilliant; dated keen, swell.

co-operate v. COLLABORATE, work together, work side by side, pull together, band together, join forces, team up, unite, combine, pool resources, make common cause, liaise.

co-operative adj. **1** COLLABORATIVE, collective, combined, common, joint, shared, mutual, united, concerted, coordinated. **2** ☞ ACCOMMODATING.

coordinate v. ORGANIZE, arrange, order, systematize, harmonize, correlate, synchronize, bring together, fit together, dovetail.

cope v. **1** MANAGE, survive, subsist, look after oneself, fend for oneself, shift for oneself, carry on, get by/through, bear up; informal make it, hack it. **2** DEAL WITH, handle, manage, address, face (up to), confront, tackle, come to grips with, get through, weather, come to terms with.

copious adj. ☞ ABUNDANT.

—OPPOSITES: sparse.

copy n. **1** DUPLICATE, facsimile, photocopy, carbon (copy), mimeograph, mimeo; transcript; reprint; proprietary Xerox. **2** REPLICA, reproduction, replication, print, imitation, likeness; counterfeit, forgery, fake; informal knock-off.

▸ v. **1** ☞ DUPLICATE v. 1. **2** IMITATE, reproduce, emulate, follow, echo, mirror, parrot, mimic, ape; plagiarize, steal; informal rip off.

cord n. STRING, thread, thong, lace, ribbon, strap, tape, tie, line, rope, cable, wire, ligature; twine, yarn, elastic, braid, braiding; babiche✦, (West) shaganappi✦.

cordon *n.* BARRIER, line, row, chain, ring, circle; picket line.
▸ *v.* CLOSE OFF, shut off, seal off, fence off, separate off, isolate, enclose, surround.

core *n.* **1** CENTRE, interior, middle, nucleus; recesses, bowels, depths; *informal* innards; *literary* midst.
2 HEART, heart of the matter, nucleus, nub, kernel, marrow, meat, essence, quintessence, crux, gist, pith, substance, basis, fundamentals; *informal* nitty-gritty, brass tacks, nuts and bolts.

corner *n.* **1** BEND, curve, crook, dogleg; turn, turning, jog, junction, fork, intersection; hairpin turn. **2** ☞ REGION.
▸ *v.* **1** DRIVE INTO A CORNER, bring to bay, cut off, block off, trap, hem in, pen in, surround, enclose; capture, catch. **2** ☞ MONOPOLIZE.

corny *adj.* (*informal*) BANAL, trite, hackneyed, commonplace, clichéd, predictable, hoary, stereotyped, platitudinous, tired, stale, overworked, overused, well-worn; mawkish, sentimental, cloying, syrupy, sugary, saccharine, twee; *informal* cheesy, schmaltzy, mushy, slushy, sloppy, cutesy, soppy, cornball, hokey.

corpse *n.* DEAD BODY, body, carcass, skeleton, (mortal) remains; *informal* stiff; *Medicine* cadaver.
—RELATED: necro-.

corpulent *adj.* ☞ FAT *adj.* 1.

correct *adj.* **1** RIGHT, accurate, true, exact, precise, unerring, faithful, strict, faultless, flawless, error-free, perfect, word-perfect; *informal* on the mark, on the nail, bang on, (right) on the money, on the button. **2** PROPER, seemly, decorous, decent, respectable, right, suitable, fit, fitting, befitting, appropriate, apt; approved, accepted, conventional, customary, traditional, orthodox, comme il faut.
—OPPOSITES: wrong, improper.
▸ *v.* **1** ☞ RECTIFY. **2** ADJUST, regulate, fix, set, standardize, normalize, calibrate.

correspond *v.* **1** CORRELATE, agree, be in agreement, be consistent, be compatible, be consonant, accord, be in tune, concur, coincide, tally, tie in, dovetail, fit in, harmonize; match, parallel; *informal* square, jibe, jive. **2** EXCHANGE LETTERS, write, communicate, keep in touch/contact.

correspondence *n.* LETTERS, messages, missives, mail, post; communication.

corroborate *v.* ☞ VERIFY.
—OPPOSITES: contradict.

corrode *v.* **1** RUST, become rusty, tarnish; wear away, disintegrate, crumble, perish, spoil; oxidize. **2** WEAR AWAY, eat away (at), erode, abrade, consume, destroy.

corrupt *adj.* **1** ☞ DISHONEST. **2** UNGODLY, unholy, irreligious, profane, impious, impure; *informal* warped. See also IMMORAL.
—OPPOSITES: honest, pure.
▸ *v.* DEPRAVE, pervert, debauch, degrade, warp, lead astray, defile, pollute, sully, debase, poison.

cosmic *adj.* ☞ INFINITE 1.

cosmopolitan *adj.*
1 MULTICULTURAL, multiracial, international, worldwide, global.
2 SOPHISTICATED, suave, glamorous,

fashionable; *informal* jet-setting, cool, hip, stylish. See also WORLDLY 2.

cost *n.* PRICE, asking price, market price, selling price, unit price, fee, tariff, fare, toll, levy, charge, rental; value, valuation, quotation, rate, worth; *informal* damage.
▶ *v.* BE PRICED AT, sell for, be valued at, fetch, come to, amount to; *informal* set someone back, go for.

costly *adj.* 1 ☞ EXPENSIVE.
2 CATASTROPHIC, disastrous, calamitous, ruinous; damaging, harmful, injurious, deleterious, woeful, awful, terrible, dreadful; *formal* grievous.
—OPPOSITES: cheap.

coterie *n.* ☞ CLIQUE.

cottage *n.* CABIN, lodge, (Que.) chalet✦; shack, shanty; (*Cape Breton*) bungalow✦, bunkhouse✦, bunkie✦, (*Que.*) country house✦.

counsel *n.* 1 ☞ ADVICE.
2 ☞ LAWYER.
▶ *v.* ADVISE, recommend, direct, advocate, encourage, urge, warn, caution; guide, give guidance.

count *v.* 1 ADD UP, add together, reckon up, total, tally, calculate, compute, tot up; census; *formal* enumerate; *dated* cast up.
2 ☞ INCLUDE 2. 3 ☞ CONSIDER 2.
4 MATTER, be of consequence, be of account, be significant, signify, be important, carry weight.
☐ **count on/upon** 1 ☞ DEPEND 2.
2 EXPECT, reckon on, anticipate, envisage, allow for, be prepared for, bargain for/on, figure on.

countenance *n.* ☞ FACE *n.* 1.
▶ *v.* PERMIT, allow, agree to, consent to, give one's blessing to,

go along with, hold with. See also TOLERATE 1, 2.

counter *v.* RESPOND TO, parry, hit back at, answer, retort to.

counteract *v.* 1 ☞ FRUSTRATE 1.
2 OFFSET, counterbalance, balance (out), cancel out, even out, counterpoise, countervail, compensate for, make up for, remedy; neutralize, nullify, negate, invalidate.
—OPPOSITES: encourage, exacerbate.

counterbalance *v.* ☞ OFFSET.

counterfeit *adj.* ☞ FAKE *adj.*
—OPPOSITES: genuine.
▶ *v.* 1 FAKE, forge, copy, reproduce, imitate. 2 FEIGN, simulate, pretend, fake, sham.

counterpart *n.* EQUIVALENT, opposite number, peer, equal, coequal, parallel, complement, analogue, match, twin, mate, fellow, brother, sister; *formal* compeer.

countless *adj.* INNUMERABLE, numerous, untold, legion, without number, numberless, unnumbered, limitless, multitudinous, incalculable; *informal* umpteen, no end of, a slew of, loads of, stacks of, heaps of, masses of, oodles of, zillions of, gazillions of; *literary* myriad.
—OPPOSITES: few.

country *n.* 1 NATION, (sovereign) state, kingdom, realm, territory, domain, province, principality, palatinate, duchy. 2 HOMELAND, native land, fatherland, motherland, the land of one's fathers. 3 COUNTRYSIDE, greenbelt, great outdoors; provinces, rural areas. See also NOWHERE.

coupon n. VOUCHER, token, ticket; *informal* comp, rain check.

courage n. ☞ BRAVERY.
—OPPOSITES: cowardice.

courageous adj. ☞ BRAVE.
—OPPOSITES: cowardly.

course n. **1** ROUTE, way, track, direction, tack, path, line, trail, trajectory, bearing, heading, orbit. **2** PROGRESSION, development, progress, advance, evolution, flow, movement, sequence, order, succession, rise, march, passage, passing. **3** ☞ PROCEDURE. **4** PROGRAM/COURSE OF STUDY, curriculum, syllabus; classes, lectures, studies.
□ **of course** NATURALLY, as you/one would expect, needless to say, certainly, to be sure, as a matter of course, obviously, it goes without saying; by all means; *informal* natch.

court n. **1** COURT OF LAW, law court, bench, bar, judicature, tribunal, chancery. **2** ROYAL HOUSEHOLD, retinue, entourage, train, suite, courtiers, attendants.
▶ v. **1** SEEK, pursue, go after, strive for, solicit. **2** RISK, invite, attract, bring on oneself.

courteous adj. POLITE, well-mannered, civil, respectful, well-behaved, well-bred, well-spoken, mannerly; gentlemanly, chivalrous, gallant; gracious, obliging, considerate, pleasant, cordial, urbane, polished, refined, courtly, civilized.
—OPPOSITES: rude.

courtesy n. POLITENESS, courteousness, good manners, civility, respect, respectfulness; chivalry, gallantry; graciousness, consideration, thought, thoughtfulness, cordiality, urbanity, courtliness.

courtier n. ATTENDANT, lord, lady, lady-in-waiting, steward, page, squire.

cove n. BAY, inlet, fjord, anchorage.

cover v. **1** PROTECT, shield, shelter; hide, conceal, veil. **2** CAKE, coat, encrust, plaster, smother, daub, bedaub, blanket. **3** DEAL WITH, consider, take in, include, involve, comprise, incorporate, embrace. **4** MASK, disguise, hide, camouflage, muffle, block out, stifle, smother.
—OPPOSITES: expose.
▶ n. **1** ☞ COVERING. **2** COATING, coat, covering, layer, carpet, blanket, overlay, dusting, film, sheet, veneer, crust, skin, cloak, mantle, veil, pall, shroud. **3** ☞ SHELTER n. 1.
□ **cover something up** CONCEAL, hide, keep secret/dark, hush up, draw a veil over, suppress, sweep under the carpet, gloss over; *informal* whitewash, keep a/the lid on.

covering n. AWNING, canopy, tarpaulin, cowling, cowl, casing, housing; wrapping, wrapper, cover, envelope, sheath, sleeve, jacket, lid, top, cap.

covert adj. HIDDEN, under-the-table, concealed, private, undercover. See also CLANDESTINE.
—OPPOSITES: overt.

covet v. ☞ DESIRE v.

coward n. WEAKLING, milksop, namby-pamby, mouse; *informal* chicken, scaredy-cat, yellow-belly, sissy, sook, baby, (*Atlantic*) sooky

baby♣, candy-ass, milquetoast.
—OPPOSITES: hero.

cowardly *adj.* ☞ SPINELESS.
—OPPOSITES: brave.

cower *v.* CRINGE, shrink, crouch, recoil, flinch, pull back, draw back, tremble, shake, quake, blench, quail, grovel.

coy *adj.* ARCH, simpering, coquettish, flirtatious, kittenish. See also DEMURE.

cozy *adj.* SNUG, comfortable, warm, homelike, homey, homely, welcoming, pleasant, agreeable; safe, sheltered, secure, down-home, homestyle; *informal* comfy, toasty, snug as a bug (in a rug).

crabby *adj.* ☞ GRUMPY.

crack *n.* **1** SPLIT, break, chip, fracture, rupture; crazing.
2 ☞ GAP 1. **3** ☞ ATTEMPT *n.*
4 (*informal*) JOKE, witticism, quip; *informal* gag, wisecrack, funny. See also JIBE *n.*
▶ *v.* **1** BREAK, split, fracture, rupture, snap. **2** ☞ HIT *v.* **1. 3** BREAK DOWN, give way, cave in, go to pieces, crumble, lose control, yield, succumb. **4** ☞ DECODE.
□ **crack down on** SUPPRESS, prevent, stop, put a stop to, put an end to, stamp out, eliminate, eradicate; clamp down on, get tough on, come down hard on, limit, restrain, restrict, check, keep in check, control, keep under control.

cradle *n.* **1** CRIB, bassinet, cot.
2 BIRTHPLACE, fount, fountainhead, source, spring, fountain, origin, place of origin, seat; *literary* wellspring.
▶ *v.* HOLD, support, pillow, cushion, shelter, protect; rest, prop (up).

craft *n.* **1** ☞ SKILL 1. **2** ACTIVITY, occupation, profession, work, line of work, pursuit. **3** VESSEL, ship, boat; *literary* barque.

crafty *adj.* CUNNING, wily, guileful, artful, devious, sly, tricky, scheming, calculating, designing, sharp, shrewd, astute, canny; duplicitous, dishonest, deceitful; *informal* foxy.
—OPPOSITES: honest.

crag *n.* CLIFF, bluff, ridge, precipice, height, peak, tor, escarpment, scarp.

cram *v.* **1** FILL, stuff, pack, jam, fill to overflowing, fill to the brim, overload; crowd, overcrowd, pile, squash. **2** STUDY, review, bone up.

cramped *adj.* **1** CONFINED, uncomfortable, poky, restricted, constricted, small, tiny, narrow; crowded, packed, congested; *archaic* strait. **2** ☞ ILLEGIBLE.
—OPPOSITES: spacious.

crash *v.* **1** SMASH INTO, collide with, be in collision with, hit, strike, ram, cannon into/against, plow into, meet head-on, run into, impact. **2** SMASH, wreck, write off, total.
▶ *n.* **1** ☞ COLLISION. **2** BANG, smash, smack, crack, bump, thud, clatter, clunk, clonk, clang; report, detonation, explosion; noise, racket, clangour, din. **3** COLLAPSE, failure, bankruptcy.

crass *adj.* STUPID, insensitive, mindless, thoughtless, witless, oafish, boorish, asinine, coarse, gross, graceless, tasteless, tactless, clumsy, heavy-handed, blundering; *informal* ignorant, pig-ignorant.
—OPPOSITES: intelligent.

crate n. ☞ BOX[1].

crater n. HOLLOW, bowl, basin, hole, cavity, depression; *Geology* caldera.

craving n. ☞ LONGING n.

crawl v. **1** CREEP, worm one's way, go on all fours, go on hands and knees, wriggle, slither, squirm, scrabble. **2** ☞ GROVEL.

craze n. FAD, fashion, trend, vogue, enthusiasm, mania, passion, rage, obsession, compulsion, fixation, fetish, fancy, taste, fascination; *informal* thing.

crazy adj. **1** ☞ INSANE 1. **2** ☞ ABSURD. **3** PASSIONATE ABOUT, very keen on, enamoured of, infatuated with, smitten with, devoted to; very enthusiastic about, fanatical about; *informal* wild/mad/nuts about, hog-wild about, gone on.
—OPPOSITES: sane, sensible, apathetic.

creak v. SQUEAK, grate, rasp; groan, complain.

cream n. **1** ☞ LOTION. **2** BEST, finest, pick, flower, crème de la crème, elite.
—OPPOSITES: dregs.

crease n. **1** FOLD, line, ridge; pleat, tuck; furrow, groove, corrugation. **2** ☞ WRINKLE n. 1.
▶ v. CRUMPLE, wrinkle, crinkle, line, scrunch up, rumple, ruck up.

create v. **1** PRODUCE, generate, bring into being, make, fabricate, fashion, build, construct; design, devise, originate, frame, develop, shape, form, forge. **2** BRING ABOUT, give rise to, lead to, result in, cause, breed, generate, engender, produce, make for, promote, foster, sow the seeds of, contribute to. **3** ☞ ESTABLISH 1.
—OPPOSITES: destroy.

creative adj. INVENTIVE, imaginative, innovative, experimental, original; artistic, expressive, inspired, visionary; enterprising, resourceful.

creator n. AUTHOR, writer, designer, deviser, maker, producer; originator, inventor, architect, mastermind, prime mover; *literary* begetter.

creature n. **1** ANIMAL, beast, brute; living thing, living being; *informal* critter. **2** ☞ PERSON.

credentials pl. n. DOCUMENTS, documentation, papers, identity papers, bona fides, ID, ID card, identity card, passport, proof of identity; certificates, diplomas, certification, references.

credible adj. BELIEVABLE, plausible, tenable, able to hold water, conceivable, likely, probable, possible, feasible, reasonable, with a ring of truth, persuasive.

credit n. **1** PRAISE, commendation, acclaim, acknowledgement, recognition, kudos, glory, esteem, respect, thanks, admiration, tributes, gratitude, appreciation; *informal* bouquets, brownie points, full marks. **2** LOAN, advance, (bridge) financing; installments; *informal* plastic.
▶ v. **1** ☞ BELIEVE 2. **2** ASCRIBE, attribute, assign, accredit, chalk up, put down.

creditable adj. ☞ ADMIRABLE.
—OPPOSITES: deplorable.

credulous adj. ☞ GULLIBLE.
—OPPOSITES: suspicious.

creed n. IDEOLOGY, credo, doctrine, teaching, dogma, tenets, canons.

creek n. ☞ STREAM n. 1.

creep v. TIPTOE, steal, sneak, slip, slink, sidle, pad, edge, inch; skulk, prowl.
▸ n. ☞ JERK n. 3.

crest n. 1 COMB, plume, tuft of feathers. 2 ☞ SUMMIT 1. 3 INSIGNIA, regalia, badge, emblem, heraldic device, coat of arms, arms.

crestfallen adj. ☞ DISAPPOINTED.
—OPPOSITES: cheerful.

crevice n. CRACK, fissure, cleft, chink, interstice, cranny, nook, slit, split, rift, fracture, breach; opening, gap, hole.

crime n. 1 OFFENCE, unlawful act, illegal act, felony, misdemeanour, misdeed, wrong; informal no-no.
2 LAW-BREAKING, delinquency, wrongdoing, criminality, misconduct, illegality, villainy; informal crookedness; Law malfeasance.

criminal n. LAWBREAKER, offender, villain, delinquent, felon, convict, malefactor, wrongdoer, culprit, miscreant; thief, burglar, robber, armed robber, gunman, gangster, terrorist; informal crook, con, jailbird, hood, yardbird, perp; Law malfeasant.
▸ adj. 1 UNLAWFUL, illegal, illicit, lawless, felonious, delinquent, fraudulent, actionable, culpable; villainous, nefarious, corrupt, wrong, bad, evil, wicked, iniquitous; informal crooked; Law malfeasant. 2 (informal)
☞ DISGRACEFUL.
—OPPOSITES: lawful.

cringe v. COWER, shrink, recoil, shy away, flinch, wince, blench, draw back; shake, tremble, quiver, quail, quake.

cripple v. 1 ☞ DISABLE 1.
2 DEVASTATE, ruin, destroy, wipe out; paralyze, hamstring, bring to a standstill, put out of action, sideline, put out of business, bankrupt, break.

crisis n. EMERGENCY, disaster, catastrophe, calamity; predicament, plight, mess, trouble, dire straits, difficulty, extremity.

crisp adj. 1 CRUNCHY, crispy, brittle, crumbly, friable, breakable; firm, dry. 2 BRISK, decisive, businesslike, no-nonsense, incisive, to the point, matter of fact, brusque; terse, succinct, concise, brief, short, short and sweet, laconic, snappy.
—OPPOSITES: soft, rambling.

criterion n. STANDARD, specification, measure, gauge, test, scale, benchmark, yardstick, touchstone, barometer; principle, rule, law, canon.

critic n. 1 REVIEWER, commentator, evaluator, analyst, judge, pundit. 2 DETRACTOR, attacker, fault-finder, back-seat driver.

critical adj. 1 CENSORIOUS, condemnatory, condemning, denunciatory, disparaging, disapproving, scathing, fault-finding, judgmental, accusatory, negative, unfavourable; informal nitpicking, picky. 2 ☞ EXPOSITORY.
3 GRAVE, serious, dangerous, risky, perilous, hazardous, precarious, touch-and-go, in the balance,

uncertain, parlous, desperate, dire, acute, life-and-death. **4** ☞ CRUCIAL.
—OPPOSITES: complimentary, unimportant.

criticism *n.* **1** CENSURE, condemnation, denunciation, disapproval, disparagement, opprobrium, fault-finding, attack, broadside, brickbats, potshot, stricture, recrimination; *informal* flak, bad press, panning, put down, knock, slam; *formal* excoriation. **2** EVALUATION, assessment, appraisal, analysis, judgment; commentary, interpretation, explanation, explication, elucidation.

criticize *v.* FIND FAULT WITH, censure, denounce, condemn, attack, lambaste, pillory, rail against, inveigh against, arraign, cast aspersions on, pour scorn on, disparage, denigrate, give bad press to, run down; *informal* knock, pan, maul, slam, slag, roast, hammer, lay into, lace into, flay, crucify, take apart, pull to pieces, pick holes in, pummel, trash, nitpick; *formal* excoriate.
—OPPOSITES: praise.

crockery *n.* ☞ CHINA 2.

crook *n.* **1** ☞ CRIMINAL *n.* **2** BEND, fork, curve, angle.

crooked *adj.* **1** WINDING, twisting, zigzag, meandering, tortuous, serpentine. **2** ☞ DEFORMED. **3** ☞ LOPSIDED. **4** DISHONEST, unscrupulous, unprincipled, untrustworthy, corrupt, corruptible, venal; criminal, illegal, unlawful, nefarious, fraudulent, shady, dodgy.
—OPPOSITES: straight, honest.

crop *n.* **1** HARVEST, year's growth, yield; fruits, produce. **2** BATCH, lot, assortment, selection, collection, supply, intake.
▶ *v.* CUT SHORT, cut, clip, shear, shave, lop off, chop off, hack off; dock, bob.

cross *n.* **1** CRUCIFIX, rood. **2** BURDEN, trouble, worry, trial, tribulation, affliction, curse, bane, misfortune, adversity, hardship, vicissitude; millstone, albatross; misery, woe, pain, sorrow, suffering; *informal* hassle, headache. **3** HYBRID, hybridization, crossbreed, half-breed, mongrel; mixture, amalgam, blend, combination.
▶ *v.* **1** TRAVEL ACROSS, traverse, range over; negotiate, navigate, cover. **2** INTERSECT, meet, join, connect, criss-cross. **3** OPPOSE, resist, defy, obstruct, impede, hinder, hamper; contradict, argue with, quarrel with, stand up to, take a stand against, take issue with; *formal* gainsay.
▶ *adj.* ☞ ANNOYED, IRRITABLE.
—OPPOSITES: pleased.
☐ **cross something out** DELETE, strike out, ink out, score out, edit out, cancel, obliterate.

crossing *n.* ☞ INTERSECTION 2.

crotchety *adj.* ☞ IRRITABLE.
—OPPOSITES: good-humoured.

crouch *v.* SQUAT, bend (down), hunker down, scrunch down, hunch over, stoop, kneel (down); duck, cower.

crowd *n.* **1** THRONG, horde, mass, multitude, host, army, herd, flock, drove, swarm, sea, troupe, pack, press, crush, mob, rabble; collection, company, gathering, assembly, audience, assemblage, congregation; *informal* gaggle, bunch, gang, posse. **2** ☞ CLIQUE. **3** AUDIENCE, spectators, listeners, viewers; house, turnout, attendance, gate; congregation.

▶ *v.* **1** CLUSTER, flock, swarm, mill, throng, huddle, gather, assemble, congregate, converge; scrum♣. **2** SURGE, push one's way, jostle, elbow one's way; squeeze, pile, cram.

crowded *adj.* PACKED, full, filled to capacity, full to bursting, congested, overcrowded, overflowing, teeming, swarming, thronged, populous, overpopulated; busy, crammed, jammed, seething, jam-packed, stuffed, chockablock, chock full, bursting at the seams, wall-to-wall, standing room only, SRO.
—OPPOSITES: deserted.

crown *n.* **1** CORONET, diadem, circlet, tiara; *literary* coronal. **2** MONARCH, sovereign, king, queen, emperor, empress; monarchy, royalty; *informal* royals. **3** HEAD, brow. See also SUMMIT 1.
▶ *v.* **1** ENTHRONE, install; invest, induct. **2** ROUND OFF, cap, be the climax of, be the culmination of, top off, consummate, perfect, complete, put the finishing touch(es) on/to. **3** TOP, cap, tip, head, surmount.

crucial *adj.* PIVOTAL, critical, key, decisive, deciding; life-and-death; all-important, pre-eminent, paramount, essential, vital, central, focal.
—OPPOSITES: unimportant.

crude *adj.* **1** UNREFINED, unpurified, unprocessed, untreated; unpolished; coarse, raw, natural. **2** PRIMITIVE, simple, basic, homespun, rudimentary, rough, rough and ready, rough-hewn, make-do, makeshift, improvised, unfinished, jerry-rigged, jerry-built, slapdash; *dated* rude. **3** ☞ VULGAR 1.
—OPPOSITES: refined, sophisticated.

cruel *adj.* BRUTAL, savage, inhuman, barbaric, barbarous, brutish, bloodthirsty, murderous, vicious, sadistic, wicked, evil, fiendish, diabolical, monstrous, abominable; callous, ruthless, merciless, pitiless, remorseless, uncaring, heartless, stony-hearted, hard-hearted, cold-blooded, cold-hearted, unfeeling, unkind, inhumane, cold, unforgiving; *dated* dastardly; *literary* fell.
—OPPOSITES: compassionate.

cruelty *n.* BRUTALITY, savagery, inhumanity, barbarity, barbarousness, brutishness, sadism, bloodthirstiness, viciousness, wickedness; lack of compassion, callousness, ruthlessness.

cruise *v.* **1** SAIL, voyage, journey. **2** DRIVE SLOWLY, drift; *informal* mosey, toodle.

crumb *n.* ☞ BIT *n.* 1.

crumble *v.* DISINTEGRATE, fall apart, fall to pieces, fall down, break up, collapse, fragment; decay, fall into decay, deteriorate, degenerate, go to rack and ruin, decompose, rot, moulder, perish.

crumple *v.* **1** CRUSH, scrunch up, screw up, squash, squeeze. **2** CREASE, wrinkle, crinkle, rumple, ruck up.

crunch v. MUNCH, chomp, champ, bite into.

crusade n. **1** HOLY WAR; jihad. **2** CAMPAIGN, drive, push, movement, effort, struggle; battle, war, offensive.

crush v. **1** SQUASH, squeeze, press, compress; pulp, mash, macerate, mangle; flatten, trample on, tread on; informal smush. **2** PULVERIZE, pound, grind, break up, smash, crumble; mill. **3** SUPPRESS, put down, quell, quash, stamp out, put an end to, overcome, overpower, defeat, triumph over, break, repress, subdue, extinguish. **4** MORTIFY, humiliate, abash, chagrin, deflate, flatten, demoralize, squash; devastate, shatter; informal shoot down in flames, knock the stuffing out of.

crust n. COVERING, layer, coating, cover, coat, sheet, thickness, film, skin, topping; incrustation, scab.

crusty adj. **1** CRISP, crispy, well baked; crumbly, brittle, friable. **2** ☞ IRRITABLE.
—OPPOSITES: soft, good-natured.

cry v. **1** WEEP, shed tears, sob, wail, cry one's eyes out, bawl, howl, snivel, whimper, squall, mewl, bleat; lament, grieve, mourn, keen, ululate; informal boo-hoo, blubber, turn on the waterworks; literary pule. **2** ☞ YELL.
—OPPOSITES: laugh, whisper.
▶ n. CALL, shout, exclamation, yell, shriek, scream, screech, bawl, bellow, roar, howl, yowl, squeal, yelp, interjection, holler; dated ejaculation.

crypt n. UNDERCROFT. See also TOMB.

cryptic adj. ENIGMATIC, mysterious, confusing, mystifying, perplexing, puzzling, obscure, abstruse, arcane, oracular, Delphic, ambiguous, elliptical, oblique; informal as clear as mud.
—OPPOSITES: clear.

cuddle v. **1** ☞ EMBRACE 1. **2** SNUGGLE, nestle, curl, nuzzle, burrow against.

cudgel n. CLUB, bludgeon, stick, truncheon, baton, shillelagh, mace, blackjack, billy, nightstick.

cue n. SIGNAL, sign, indication, prompt, reminder; nod, word, gesture.

culminate v. COME TO A CLIMAX, come to a head, peak, climax, reach a pinnacle; build up to, lead up to; end with, finish with, conclude with.

culpable adj. TO BLAME, guilty, at fault, in the wrong, answerable, accountable, responsible, blameworthy, censurable.
—OPPOSITES: innocent.

culprit n. GUILTY PARTY. See also OFFENDER.

cult n. SECT, denomination, group, movement, church, persuasion, body, faction.

cultivate v. **1** TILL, plow, dig, hoe, farm, work, fertilize, mulch, weed. **2** win someone's friendship, woo, court, curry favour with, ingratiate oneself with; informal butter up, suck up to.

cultivated adj. ☞ CULTURED.

cultural adj. **1** ETHNIC, racial, folk; societal, lifestyle. **2** AESTHETIC, artistic, intellectual; educational, edifying, civilizing.

culture n. **1** THE ARTS, the humanities, intellectual

achievement; literature, music, painting, philosophy, the performing arts. **2** CIVILIZATION, society, way of life, lifestyle; customs, traditions, heritage, habits, ways, mores, values.

cultured *adj.* CULTIVATED, intellectually/artistically aware, artistic, enlightened, civilized, educated, well-educated, well-read, well-informed, learned, knowledgeable, discerning, discriminating, refined, polished, sophisticated, urbane, cosmopolitan; *informal* artsy.
—OPPOSITES: ignorant.

cumbersome *adj.* UNWIELDY, unmanageable, awkward, clumsy, inconvenient; bulky, large, heavy, hefty, weighty, burdensome; *informal* hulking, clunky.
—OPPOSITES: manageable.

cunning *adj.* CRAFTY, wily, artful, guileful, devious, sly, scheming, designing, calculating, Machiavellian; shrewd, astute, clever, canny; deceitful, deceptive, duplicitous, foxy; *archaic* subtle.
—OPPOSITES: honest.

cup *n.* **1** teacup, coffee cup, demitasse; mug; beaker; *historical* chalice. **2** TROPHY, award, prize.

cupidity *n.* ☞ GREED 1.
—OPPOSITES: generosity.

curb *v.* RESTRAIN, hold back/in, keep back, repress, suppress, fight back, bite back, keep in check, check, control, rein in, contain, bridle, subdue, constrain, hold back, master, quell, smother, stifle; *informal* keep a/the lid on.

curdle *v.* CLOT, coagulate, congeal, solidify, thicken; turn, sour, ferment.

cure *v.* **1** HEAL, restore to health, make well/better; *archaic* cleanse. **2** RECTIFY, remedy, put/set right, right, fix, mend, repair, heal, make better; solve, sort out, be the answer/solution to; eliminate, end, put an end to. **3** ☞ PRESERVE *v.* 3.
▶ *n.* ☞ REMEDY *n.*

curiosity *n.* INTEREST, spirit of inquiry, inquisitiveness.

curious *adj.* **1** INTRIGUED, interested, eager/dying to know, agog; inquisitive. **2** ☞ STRANGE 1.
—OPPOSITES: uninterested, ordinary.

curl *v.* **1** SPIRAL, coil, wreathe, twirl, swirl; wind, curve, bend, twist (and turn), loop, meander, snake, corkscrew, zigzag. **2** CRIMP, perm, wave.
▶ *n.* **1** RINGLET, corkscrew, kink, wave; kiss-curl. **2** SPIRAL, coil, twirl, swirl, twist, corkscrew, curlicue, helix.

curly *adj.* WAVY, curling, curled, crimped, permed, frizzy, kinky, corkscrew.
—OPPOSITES: straight.

current *adj.* **1** CONTEMPORARY, present-day, modern, present, contemporaneous; topical, in the news, live, burning. **2** PREVALENT, prevailing, common, accepted, in circulation, circulating, on everyone's lips, popular, widespread. **3** VALID, usable, up-to-date.
—OPPOSITES: past, out of date.
▶ *n.* FLOW, stream, backdraft, slipstream; airstream, thermal, updraft, draft; undercurrent, undertow, tide.

curse *n.* **1** MALEDICTION, the evil eye, hex, jinx; *formal* imprecation;

literary anathema. **2** EVIL, blight, scourge, plague, cancer, canker, poison. **3** ☞ OBSCENITY.
▶ *v.* **1** PUT A CURSE ON, put the evil eye on, anathematize, damn, hex, jinx; *archaic* imprecate. **2** AFFLICT, trouble, plague, bedevil.
3 ☞ SWEAR 3.

cursory *adj.* PERFUNCTORY, desultory, casual, superficial, token, careless, half-hearted, sketchy; hasty, quick, hurried, rapid, brief, passing, fleeting.
—OPPOSITES: thorough.

curt *adj.* TERSE, brusque, abrupt, clipped, blunt, short, monosyllabic, summary; snappish, snappy, sharp, tart; gruff, offhand, unceremonious, ungracious, rude, impolite, discourteous, uncivil.
—OPPOSITES: expansive.

curtail *v.* REDUCE, cut, cut down, decrease, lessen, pare down, trim, retrench; restrict, limit, curb, rein in; *informal* slash.
—OPPOSITES: increase, lengthen.

curtain *n.* DRAPE, drapery, window treatment, window hanging, screen, blind(s), shade; valance, topper, café curtain.
▶ *v.* CONCEAL, hide, screen, shield; separate, isolate.

curve *n.* BEND, turn, loop, curl, twist, hook; arc, arch, bow, undulation, curvature, meander.
—RELATED: sinuous.
▶ *v.* BEND, turn, loop, wind, meander, undulate, snake, spiral, twist, coil, curl; arc, arch.

curved *adj.* BENT, arched, bowed, crescent, curving, wavy, sinuous, serpentine, meandering,
undulating, curvilinear, curvy.
—OPPOSITES: straight.

cushion *n.* PROTECTION, buffer, shield, defence, bulwark.
▶ *v.* ☞ SOFTEN 1.

custody *n.* CARE, guardianship, charge, keeping, safekeeping, wardship, responsibility, protection, tutelage; custodianship, trusteeship.
☐ **in custody** ☞ CAPTIVE *adj.*

custom *n.* **1** TRADITION, practice, usage, observance, way, convention, formality, ceremony, ritual; sacred cow, unwritten rule; mores; *formal* praxis. **2** ☞ HABIT 1.

customary *adj.* USUAL, traditional, normal, conventional, familiar, accepted, routine, common, everyday, established, time-honoured, regular, prevailing; accustomed, habitual, wonted, ordinary, typical.
—OPPOSITES: unusual.

customer *n.* CONSUMER, buyer, purchaser, patron, client, subscriber; shopper.

cut *v.* **1** GASH, slash, lacerate, sever, slit, pierce, penetrate, wound, injure; scratch, graze, nick, incise, score; lance. **2** CHOP, cut up, slice, dice, cube, mince; carve, hash.
3 TRIM, snip, clip, crop, barber, shear, shave; pare; prune, poll, lop, dock; mow. **4** REDUCE, cut back/down on, decrease, lessen, retrench, trim, slim down; rationalize, downsize, lower, slash, chop. **5** EDIT; bowdlerize, expurgate. See also ABRIDGE.
▶ *n.* **1** GASH, slash, laceration, incision, wound, injury; scratch, graze, nick. **2** (*informal*) SHARE, portion, bit, quota, percentage;

cute | cynical

informal slice, piece of the pie, rake-off, piece of the action.
3 REDUCTION, cutback, decrease, lessening, rollback.
□ **cut back** REDUCE, cut, cut down on, decrease, lessen, retrench, economize on, trim, slim down, scale down; rationalize, downsize, pull/draw in one's horns, tighten one's belt; *informal* slash. **cut someone/something down 1** FELL, chop down, hack down, saw down, hew. **2** ☞ KILL 1. **cut in** ☞ INTERRUPT 1. **cut out** STOP WORKING, stop, fail, give out, break down; *informal* die, give up the ghost, conk out.

cute *adj.* **1** ENDEARING, adorable, lovable, sweet, lovely, appealing, engaging, delightful, dear, darling, winning, winsome, attractive, pretty; *informal* cutesy, twee. **2** ☞ ATTRACTIVE 2.

cutting *adj.* HURTFUL, wounding, barbed, pointed, scathing, acerbic, mordant, caustic, acid, sarcastic, sardonic, snide, spiteful, malicious, mean, nasty, cruel, unkind; *informal* bitchy, catty, snarky.
—OPPOSITES: friendly.

cycle *n.* **1** ROUND, rotation; pattern, rhythm. **2** SERIES, sequence, succession, run; set.

cynical *adj.* SKEPTICAL, doubtful, distrustful, suspicious, disbelieving; pessimistic, negative, world-weary, disillusioned, disenchanted, jaundiced, sardonic.
—OPPOSITES: idealistic.

Dd

dab v. PAT, press, touch, blot, mop, swab; daub, apply, wipe, stroke.
▶ n. DROP, spot, smear, splash, speck, taste, trace, touch, hint, bit.

dabble v. TOY WITH, dip into, flirt with, tinker with, trifle with, play with, dally with.

dabbler n. ☞ AMATEUR n.
—OPPOSITES: professional.

daily adj. EVERYDAY, day-to-day, quotidian, diurnal, circadian.
▶ adv. EVERY DAY, once a day, day after day, diurnally.

dainty adj. **1** DELICATE, fine, neat, elegant, exquisite. **2** ☞ DELICIOUS 1.
—OPPOSITES: unwieldy, unpalatable.
▶ n. DELICACY, tidbit, fancy, luxury, treat; nibble, savoury, appetizer; confection, bonbon, goody, square; archaic sweetmeat.

dally v. **1** ☞ DAWDLE. **2** TRIFLE, toy, amuse oneself, flirt, play fast and loose, philander, carry on, play around.
—OPPOSITES: hurry.

dam n. BARRAGE, barrier, wall, embankment, barricade, obstruction.

damage n. HARM, destruction, vandalism; injury, impairment, desecration, vitiation, detriment; ruin, havoc, devastation.
▶ v. HARM, deface, mutilate, mangle, impair, injure, disfigure, vandalize; tamper with, sabotage; ruin, destroy, wreck, trash; formal vitiate.
—OPPOSITES: repair.

damaging adj. ☞ HARMFUL.

damn v. CONDEMN, censure, criticize, attack, denounce, revile; find fault with, deprecate, disparage; informal slam, lay into, blast.
—OPPOSITES: bless, praise.
▶ excl. DARN, drat, shoot, blast, doggone, goddammit, hell, rats, bugger, geez, tarnation, sugar, fuddle duddle ✤, fiddlesticks.

damp adj. MOIST, moistened, wettish, dampened, dampish; humid, steamy, muggy, clammy, sweaty, sticky, dank, moisture-laden, wet, wetted, rainy, drizzly, showery, misty, foggy, vaporous, dewy.
—OPPOSITES: dry.

dance v. **1** sway, trip, twirl, whirl, pirouette, gyrate; informal bop, disco, rock, boogie, shake a leg, hoof it, cut a/the rug, trip the light fantastic, get down, mosh, groove. **2** ☞ FROLIC.
▶ n. BALL, masquerade, prom, hoedown, disco, (sock) hop.

dandy n. FOP, poseur, man about town, glamour boy, rake; informal sharp dresser, snappy dresser, trendy, hipster, dude, pretty boy; informal, dated swell; dated beau; archaic buck, coxcomb, popinjay.
▶ adj. (informal) ☞ EXCELLENT.

danger *n.* **1** PERIL, hazard, risk, pitfall, jeopardy; menace, threat; perilousness, riskiness, precariousness, uncertainty, instability, insecurity. **2** ☞ CHANCE 1.
—OPPOSITES: safety.

dangerous *adj.* **1** MENACING, threatening, treacherous; savage, wild, vicious, murderous, desperate. **2** ☞ HAZARDOUS.
—OPPOSITES: harmless, safe.

dangle *v.* **1** HANG (DOWN), droop, swing, sway, wave, trail, stream; brandish, flourish. **2** OFFER, hold out; entice/tempt someone with.

dank *adj.* DAMP, musty, chilly, clammy, moist, wet, unaired, humid.
—OPPOSITES: dry.

dappled *adj.* SPECKLED, blotched, blotchy, spotted, spotty, dotted, mottled, marbled, flecked, freckled; piebald, pied, brindle, pinto, calico; patchy, variegated; *informal* splotchy.

dare *v.* **1** BE BRAVE ENOUGH, have the courage; venture, have the nerve, have the temerity, be so bold as, have the audacity; risk, hazard, take the liberty of, stick one's neck out, go out on a limb. **2** CHALLENGE, defy, invite, bid, provoke, goad; throw down the gauntlet.

daring *adj.* BOLD, audacious, intrepid, venturesome, adventurous, fearless, brave, unafraid, undaunted, dauntless, valiant, valorous, heroic, dashing; madcap, rash, reckless, heedless, daredevil, assured, confident, courageous, feisty, plucky,

spirited; *informal* gutsy, spunky, ballsy.

dark *adj.* **1** BLACK, pitch-black, jet-black, inky; unlit, unilluminated; starless, moonless; dingy, gloomy, dusky, shadowy, shady; *literary* Stygian, tenebrous. **2** MYSTERIOUS, secret, hidden, concealed, veiled, covert, clandestine; enigmatic, arcane, esoteric, obscure, abstruse, impenetrable, incomprehensible, cryptic. **3** BRUNETTE, dark brown, chestnut, sable, jet-black, ebony. **4** SWARTHY, dusky, olive, brown, black, ebony; tanned, bronzed. **5** ☞ DISASTROUS. **6** ☞ PESSIMISTIC, DESPONDENT. **7** MOODY, brooding, sullen, dour, scowling, glowering, angry, forbidding, threatening, ominous. **8** EVIL, wicked, sinful, immoral, bad, iniquitous, ungodly, unholy, base; vile, unspeakable, sinister, foul, monstrous, shocking, atrocious, abominable, hateful, despicable, odious, horrible, heinous, execrable, diabolical, fiendish, murderous, barbarous, black; sordid, degenerate, depraved; dishonourable, dishonest, unscrupulous; *informal* lowdown, dirty, crooked, shady.
—OPPOSITES: bright, blond, pale, happy, good.
▸ *n.* **1** DARKNESS, blackness, gloom, murkiness, shadow, shade; dusk, twilight, gloaming. **2** NIGHT, nighttime, darkness; nightfall, evening, twilight, sunset.
—OPPOSITES: light, day.

darken *v.* GROW DARK, blacken, dim, cloud over, lower; shade, fog.

darling *n.* **1** DEAR, dearest, love, lover, sweetheart, sweet, beloved;

informal honey, hon, angel, pet, sweetie, sugar, babe, baby, treasure. **2** FAVOURITE, pet, idol, hero, heroine; *informal* blue-eyed boy/girl.

▶ *adj.* ☞ ADORABLE.

darn *excl.* ☞ DAMN *excl.*

dart *n.* **1** SMALL ARROW, flechette, missile, projectile. **2** ☞ DASH *n.* 1.

▶ *v.* **1** ☞ DASH *v.* 1. **2** DIRECT, cast, throw, shoot, send, flash.

dash *v.* **1** RUSH, race, run, sprint, bolt, dart, gallop, career, charge, shoot, hurtle, careen, hare, fly, speed, zoom, scurry, scuttle, scamper, scramble, bound, leap, dive; *informal* tear, belt, pelt, scoot, zip, whip, hotfoot it, leg it, bomb, barrel, beetle. **2** HURL, smash, crash, slam. See also THROW *v.* 1. **3** SHATTER, destroy, wreck, ruin, crush, devastate, demolish, blight, overturn, scotch, spoil, frustrate, thwart, check; *informal* blow a hole in, put paid to, scupper, scuttle.

—OPPOSITES: dawdle, raise.

▶ *n.* **1** RUSH, race, run, sprint, bolt, dart, leap, charge, bound, dive, break; scramble. **2** PINCH, touch, sprinkle, taste, spot, drop, dab, speck, smattering, sprinkling, splash, bit, modicum, little; *informal* smidgen, tad, lick. **3** ☞ PANACHE.

dashing *adj.* **1** DEBONAIR, devil-may-care, raffish, sporty, spirited, lively, dazzling, energetic, animated, exuberant, flamboyant, dynamic, bold, intrepid, daring, adventurous, plucky, swashbuckling, daredevil, dauntless, fearless, heroic, valiant, valorous; romantic, chivalrous, attractive, gallant. **2** ☞ STYLISH.

data *n.* FACTS, figures, statistics, details, particulars, specifics; information, intelligence, material, input; *informal* info.

date *n.* **1** DAY (OF THE MONTH), occasion, time; year; anniversary. **2** AGE, time, period, era, epoch, century, decade, year. **3** ☞ APPOINTMENT 1. **4** (*informal*) PARTNER, escort, girlfriend, boyfriend, steady.

▶ *v.* (*informal*) GO OUT WITH, take out, go around with, be involved with, see, woo, go steady with; *dated* court.

dated *adj.* ☞ OLD-FASHIONED.

daunt *v.* DISCOURAGE, deter, demoralize, put off, dishearten, dispirit; intimidate, abash, take aback, throw, cow, overawe, awe, frighten, scare, unman, dismay, disconcert, discompose, perturb, unsettle, unnerve; throw off balance; *informal* rattle, faze, shake up.

—OPPOSITES: hearten.

dawdle *v.* LINGER, dally, take one's time, be slow, waste time, idle; lag, trail, straggle, fall behind; delay, procrastinate, stall, dilly-dally, lallygag; *archaic* tarry.

—OPPOSITES: hurry.

dawn *n.* **1** DAYBREAK, sunrise, first light, daylight, cock crow; sun-up. **2** BEGINNING, start, birth, inception, origination, genesis, emergence, advent, appearance, arrival, dawning, rise, origin, onset; unfolding, development, infancy; *informal* kickoff.

—OPPOSITES: dusk, end.

day *n.* **1** DAYTIME, daylight; waking hours. **2** HEYDAY, prime, time; peak, height, zenith, ascendancy;

youth, springtime, salad days.
—RELATED: diurnal.
—OPPOSITES: night, decline.

daze v. STUN, stupefy; knock
unconscious, knock out; *informal*
knock the stuffing out of.
▶ *n.* STUPOR, trance, haze; spin,
whirl, muddle, jumble.

dazzle v. OVERWHELM, overcome,
impress, move, stir, affect, touch,
awe, overawe, leave speechless,
take someone's breath away;
spellbind, hypnotize; *informal* bowl
over, blow away, knock out.

dead adj. **1** PASSED ON/AWAY,
expired, departed, gone, no more;
late, lost, lamented; perished,
fallen, slain, slaughtered, killed,
murdered, lifeless, extinct, cold,
stiff; *informal* (as) dead as a doornail,
six feet under, pushing up daisies;
formal deceased; *euphemistic* with
God, asleep. **2** BARREN, lifeless,
bare, desolate, sterile.
3 ☞ OBSOLETE. **4** NOT WORKING, out
of order, inoperative. **5** ☞ NUMB
adj. **6** EMOTIONLESS, unemotional,
unfeeling. See also DEADPAN.
7 EXTINGUISHED, quashed, stifled;
finished, over, gone, no more;
ancient history. **8** QUIET, sleepy,
slow; *informal* one-horse. See also
BORING.
—OPPOSITES: alive, fertile,
modern, lively.
▶ *adv.* COMPLETELY, absolutely,
totally, utterly, deadly, perfectly,
entirely, quite, thoroughly;
definitely, certainly, positively,
categorically, unquestionably,
undoubtedly, surely.

deaden v. **1** NUMB, dull, blunt,
suppress; alleviate, mitigate,
diminish, reduce, lessen, ease,

soothe, relieve, assuage, kill.
2 MUFFLE, mute, smother, stifle,
dull, dampen; silence, quieten,
soften; cushion, buffer, absorb.
—OPPOSITES: intensify, amplify.

deadlock n. STALEMATE, impasse,
standoff, saw-off✲, logjam;
standstill, halt, (full) stop, dead
end.

deadly adj. **1** FATAL, lethal, mortal,
death-dealing, life-threatening;
dangerous, injurious, harmful,
detrimental, deleterious,
unhealthy; noxious, toxic, killing,
murderous, destructive,
pernicious, poisonous, venomous;
literary deathly. **2** INTENSE, great,
marked, extreme. **3** UNERRING,
unfailing, impeccable, perfect,
flawless, faultless; sure, true,
precise, accurate, exact, bang on.
—OPPOSITES: harmless, mild,
inaccurate.

deadpan adj. BLANK,
expressionless, inexpressive,
impassive, inscrutable, poker-
faced, straight-faced; stony,
wooden, vacant, fixed, lifeless.
—OPPOSITES: expressive.

deafening adj. VERY LOUD, very
noisy, ear-splitting,
overwhelming, almighty, mighty,
tremendous; booming,
thunderous, roaring, resounding,
resonant, reverberating.
—OPPOSITES: quiet.

deal n. AGREEMENT, understanding,
pact, bargain, covenant, contract,
treaty; arrangement, compromise,
settlement; pledge, promise;
terms; transaction, sale, account;
Law indenture.
▶ *v.* **1** COPE WITH, handle, manage,
treat, take care of, take charge of,

take in hand, sort out, tackle, take on; control; act towards, behave towards. **2** TRADE IN, buy and sell; sell, purvey, supply, stock, market, merchandise; traffic, smuggle; *informal* push, flog. **3** DELIVER, administer, dispense, inflict, give, impose; score, land, aim.

dealer *n.* ☞ TRADER.

dear *adj.* **1** BELOVED, loved, adored, cherished, precious; esteemed, respected, worshipped; close, intimate, bosom, best. **2** PRECIOUS, treasured, valued, prized, cherished, special. **3** ☞ ADORABLE. **4** ☞ EXPENSIVE.
—OPPOSITES: hated, disagreeable, cheap.

dearth *n.* LACK, scarcity, shortage, shortfall, want, deficiency, insufficiency, inadequacy, paucity, sparseness, scantiness, rareness; absence.
—OPPOSITES: surfeit.

death *n.* **1** DEMISE, dying, end, passing, loss of life; eternal rest, quietus; murder, assassination, execution, slaughter, massacre; *informal* curtains; *formal* decease; *archaic* expiry. **2** END, finish, termination, extinction, extinguishing, collapse, destruction, eradication, obliteration.
—OPPOSITES: life, birth.

debacle *n.* FIASCO, failure, catastrophe, disaster, mess, ruin; downfall, collapse, defeat; *informal* foul-up, screw-up, hash, botch, washout, snafu.

debase *v.* DEGRADE, devalue, demean, cheapen, prostitute, discredit, drag down, tarnish, blacken, blemish; disgrace, dishonour, shame; damage, harm, undermine.
—OPPOSITES: enhance.

debatable *adj.* ARGUABLE, disputable, questionable, open to question, controversial, contentious; doubtful, dubious, uncertain, unsure, unclear; borderline, inconclusive, moot, unsettled, unresolved, unconfirmed, undetermined, undecided, up in the air, iffy.

debate *n.* DISCUSSION, discourse, parley, dialogue; argument, dispute, wrangle, war of words; argumentation, disputation, dissension, disagreement, contention, conflict; negotiations, talks; *informal* confab, powwow.
▸ *v.* **1** DISCUSS, talk over/through, talk about, thrash out, hash out, argue, dispute; *informal* kick around, bat around. **2** ☞ CONSIDER 1.

debauched *adj.* DISSOLUTE, dissipated, degenerate, corrupt, depraved, sinful, unprincipled, immoral; lascivious, lecherous, lewd, lustful, libidinous, licentious, promiscuous, loose, wanton, abandoned; decadent, profligate, intemperate, sybaritic.
—OPPOSITES: wholesome.

debonair *adj.* SUAVE, urbane, sophisticated, cultured, self-possessed, self-assured, confident, charming, gracious, courteous, gallant, chivalrous, gentlemanly, refined, polished, well-bred, genteel, dignified, courtly; well-groomed, elegant, stylish, smart, dashing; *informal* smooth, sharp, cool, slick, fly.
—OPPOSITES: unsophisticated.

debris *n.* DETRITUS, refuse, rubbish, waste, litter, scrap, dross, chaff, flotsam and jetsam; rubble, wreckage; remains, scraps, dregs, trash, garbage, dreck, junk.

debt *n.* **1** BILL, account, dues, arrears, charges; financial obligation, outstanding payment, money owing; check, tab. **2** INDEBTEDNESS, obligation; gratitude, appreciation, thanks.

decadent *adj.* DISSOLUTE, dissipated, degenerate, corrupt, depraved, sinful, unprincipled, immoral; licentious, abandoned, profligate, intemperate; sybaritic, hedonistic, pleasure-seeking, self-indulgent.

decamp *v.* ☞ ABSCOND.

decay *v.* **1** DECOMPOSE, rot, putrefy, go bad, go off, spoil, fester, perish, deteriorate; degrade, break down, moulder, shrivel, wither. **2** DETERIORATE, degenerate, decline, go downhill, slump, slide, go to rack and ruin, go to seed; disintegrate, fall to pieces, fall into disrepair; fail, collapse; *informal* go to pot, go to the dogs, go into/down the toilet.

deceit *n.* ☞ DECEPTION.
—OPPOSITES: honesty.

deceitful *adj.* **1** ☞ DISHONEST. **2** FRAUDULENT, counterfeit, fabricated, invented, concocted, made up, trumped up, untrue, false, bogus, fake, spurious, fallacious, deceptive, misleading.

deceive *v.* **1** SWINDLE, defraud, cheat, trick, hoodwink, hoax, dupe, take in, mislead, delude, fool, outwit, lead on, inveigle, beguile, double-cross, gull; *informal* con, bamboozle, do, gyp, diddle,

rip off, shaft, pull a fast one on, take for a ride, pull the wool over someone's eyes, sucker, snooker, stiff. **2** BE UNFAITHFUL TO, cheat on, betray, play someone false; *informal* two-time.

decent *adj.* **1** PROPER, correct, appropriate, apt, fitting, suitable; respectable, dignified, decorous, seemly; nice, tasteful; conventional, accepted, standard, traditional, orthodox; comme il faut. **2** HONOURABLE, honest, trustworthy, dependable; respectable, upright, clean-living, virtuous, good; obliging, helpful, accommodating, unselfish, generous, kind, thoughtful, considerate; neighbourly, hospitable, pleasant, agreeable, amiable. **3** ☞ SATISFACTORY.
—OPPOSITES: unpleasant, unsatisfactory.

deception *n.* **1** DECEIT, deceitfulness, duplicity, double-dealing, fraud, cheating, trickery, chicanery, deviousness, slyness, wiliness, guile, bluff, lying, pretense, treachery; *informal* crookedness, monkey business, monkeyshines. **2** TRICK, deceit, sham, fraud, pretense, hoax, fake, blind, artifice, facade, feint, front, stratagem, device, ruse, scheme, dodge, machination, subterfuge; cheat, swindle, bluff, charade, posturing; *informal* con, set-up, scam, flim-flam, bunco.

deceptive *adj.* **1** MISLEADING, illusory, specious, ambiguous; distorted; *literary* illusive. **2** ☞ DECEITFUL 2, DISHONEST.

decide *v.* **1** RESOLVE, determine, make up one's mind, make a decision; elect, choose, opt, plan, aim, have the intention, have in mind, set one's sights on. **2** ADJUDICATE, arbitrate, adjudge, judge; hear, try, examine; rule on.

decided *adj.* **1** DEFINITE, certain, positive, emphatic, undeniable, indisputable, unquestionable; assured, guaranteed. See also MARKED. **2** DETERMINED, resolute, firm, strong-minded, strong-willed, emphatic, dead set, unwavering, unyielding, unbending, inflexible, unshakeable, unrelenting, obstinate, stubborn, rock-ribbed.

decision *n.* **1** RESOLUTION, conclusion, settlement, commitment, resolve, determination; choice, option, selection. **2** VERDICT, finding, ruling, recommendation, judgment, judgment call, pronouncement, adjudication, order, rule, resolve; findings, results; *Law* determination.

decisive *adj.* **1** RESOLUTE, firm, strong-minded, strong-willed, determined; purposeful, forceful, dead set, unwavering, unyielding, unbending, inflexible, unshakeable, obstinate, stubborn, rock-ribbed. **2** DECIDING, conclusive, determining; key, pivotal, critical, crucial, significant, influential, major, chief, principal, prime.

declaration *n.* **1** ANNOUNCEMENT, statement, communication, pronouncement, proclamation, communiqué, edict, advisory. **2** ASSERTION, profession, affirmation, acknowledgement, revelation, disclosure,

manifestation, confirmation, testimony, validation, certification, attestation; pledge, avowal, vow, oath, protestation.

declare *v.* PROCLAIM, announce, state, reveal, air, voice, articulate, express, vent, set forth, publicize, broadcast; assert, maintain, affirm, profess, claim; *informal* come out with.

decline *v.* **1** TURN DOWN, reject, brush aside, refuse, rebuff, spurn, repulse, dismiss; forgo, deny oneself, pass up; abstain from, say no; *informal* give the thumbs down to, give something a miss. **2** DECREASE, reduce, lessen, diminish, dwindle, contract, shrink, fall off, tail off; drop, fall, go down, slump, plummet; *informal* nosedive, take a header, crash. **3** ☞ DETERIORATE 1.
—OPPOSITES: accept, increase, rise. ▸ *n.* REDUCTION, decrease, downturn, downswing, devaluation, depreciation, diminution, ebb, drop, slump, plunge; *informal* nosedive, crash, toboggan slide✲.

decode *v.* DECIPHER, decrypt, work out, solve, interpret, translate; make sense of, get to the bottom of, unravel, unscramble, find the key to; *informal* crack, figure out, suss (out).

decompose *v.* ☞ DECAY 1.

decor *n.* DECORATION, furnishing, ornamentation; colour scheme.

decorate *v.* **1** ORNAMENT, adorn, trim, embellish, garnish, furnish, enhance, grace, beautify, prettify; festoon, garland, bedeck; hang, loop, drape, wreathe; *informal* do up/out. **2** PAINT, WALLPAPER, paper;

refurbish, furbish, renovate, redecorate; *informal* do up, spruce up, do over, fix up, give something a facelift. **3** GIVE A MEDAL TO, honour, cite, reward.

decoration *n.* **1** ORNAMENTATION, adornment, trimming, embellishment, garnishing, gilding; beautification, prettification; enhancements, enrichments, frills, accessories, trimmings, finery, frippery. **2** ☞ DECOR. **3** ORNAMENT, bauble, trinket, knick-knack, spangle; trimming, tinsel.

decorative *adj.* ORNAMENTAL, embellishing, garnishing; fancy, ornate, attractive, pretty, showy. —OPPOSITES: functional.

decorous *adj.* PROPER, seemly, decent, becoming, befitting, tasteful; correct, appropriate, suitable, fitting; tactful, polite, well-mannered, genteel, respectable; formal, restrained, modest, demure, gentlemanly, ladylike. —OPPOSITES: unseemly.

decorum *n.* PROPRIETY, seemliness, decency, good taste, correctness; politeness, courtesy, good manners; dignity, respectability, modesty, demureness. —OPPOSITES: impropriety.

decoy *n.* LURE, bait, red herring; enticement, inducement, temptation, attraction, carrot; snare, trap.

decrease *v.* **1** LESSEN, reduce, drop, diminish, decline, dwindle, fall off; die down, abate, subside, tail off, ebb, wane; plummet, plunge. **2** REDUCE, lessen, lower,

cut (back/down), curtail; slim down, tone down, deplete, minimize, slash. —OPPOSITES: increase. ▸ *n.* REDUCTION, drop, decline, downturn, cut, fall-off, cutback, diminution, ebb, wane. —OPPOSITES: increase.

decree *n.* **1** ORDER, edict, command, commandment, mandate, proclamation, dictum, fiat; law, bylaw, statute, act, order-in-council, cabinet order✦; *formal* ordinance. **2** ☞ RULING *n.* ▸ *v.* ORDER, command, rule, dictate, pronounce, proclaim, ordain; direct, decide, determine.

decrepit *adj.* **1** FEEBLE, infirm, weak, weakly, frail; disabled, incapacitated, crippled, doddering, tottering; old, elderly, aged, ancient, senile; *informal* past it, over the hill, no spring chicken. **2** ☞ DILAPIDATED. —OPPOSITES: strong, sound.

dedicate *v.* **1** DEVOTE, commit, pledge, give, surrender, sacrifice; set aside, allocate, consign. **2** INSCRIBE, address; assign.

dedicated *adj.* COMMITTED, devoted, staunch, firm, steadfast, resolute, unwavering, loyal, faithful, true, dyed-in-the-wool, sworn; wholehearted, sincere, single-minded, enthusiastic, keen, earnest, zealous, ardent, passionate, fervent; *informal* card-carrying, true blue. —OPPOSITES: indifferent.

deduce *v.* CONCLUDE, reason, work out, infer; glean, divine, intuit, understand, assume, presume, conjecture, surmise, reckon; *informal* figure out, suss out.

deduct *v.* SUBTRACT, take away, take off, debit, dock, discount; abstract, remove, knock off. —OPPOSITES: add.

deduction *n.* **1** SUBTRACTION, removal, debit, abstraction. **2** CONCLUSION, inference, supposition, hypothesis, assumption, presumption, illation; suspicion, conviction, belief, reasoning.

deed *n.* **1** ACT, action; feat, exploit, achievement, accomplishment, endeavour, undertaking, enterprise. **2** LEGAL DOCUMENT, contract, indenture, instrument.

deep *adj.* **1** CAVERNOUS, yawning, gaping, huge, extensive; bottomless, fathomless, unfathomable. **2** INTENSE, heartfelt, wholehearted, deep-seated, deep-rooted; sincere, genuine, earnest, enthusiastic, great. **3** SOUND, heavy, intense. **4** PROFOUND, serious, philosophical, complex, weighty; abstruse, esoteric, recondite, mysterious, obscure; intelligent, intellectual, learned, wise, scholarly; discerning, penetrating, perceptive, insightful. **5** RAPT, absorbed, engrossed, preoccupied, immersed, lost, gripped, intent, engaged. **6** LOW-PITCHED, low, bass, rich, powerful, resonant, booming, sonorous. **7** DARK, intense, rich, strong, bold, warm. —OPPOSITES: shallow, superficial, high, light.

deface *v.* VANDALIZE, disfigure, mar, spoil, ruin, sully, damage, blight, impair, trash.

defame *v.* ☞ SLANDER *v.*

defeat *v.* **1** BEAT, vanquish, trounce, triumph over, conquer, be victorious over, get the better of, worst; overcome, overwhelm, overpower, overthrow, subdue, subjugate, quell, quash, crush, rout, outclass, outdo, prevail over; drub, blow out of the water, take to the cleaners, lick, best, hammer, clobber, thrash, paste, demolish, annihilate, wipe the floor with, whip, walk all over, make mincemeat of, massacre, slaughter, cream, shellac, skunk. **2** THWART, frustrate, foil, ruin, scotch, debar, snooker, derail; obstruct, impede, hinder, hamper; *informal* put the kibosh on, put paid to, stymie, scupper, scuttle. **3** REJECT, overthrow, throw out, dismiss, outvote, turn down; *informal* give the thumbs down. ▶ *n.* **1** LOSS, conquest, vanquishment; rout, trouncing; downfall. **2** FAILURE, downfall, collapse, ruin; rejection, frustration, abortion, miscarriage; undoing, reverse. —OPPOSITES: victory, success.

defect¹ *n.* **1** FAULT, flaw, imperfection, deficiency, weakness, weak spot, inadequacy, shortcoming, limitation, failing; kink, deformity, blemish; mistake, error; *informal* glitch; *Computing* bug.

defect² *v.* DESERT, change sides, turn traitor, rebel, renege; abscond, quit, jump ship, escape; break faith; secede from, revolt against; *Military* go AWOL; *Politics* cross the floor; *literary* forsake.

defective *adj.* FAULTY, flawed, imperfect, shoddy, inoperative,

malfunctioning, out of order,
unsound; in disrepair, broken;
informal on the blink, acting up,
kaput, bust, on the fritz.
—OPPOSITES: perfect.

defence n. **1** PROTECTION,
guarding, security, fortification;
resistance, deterrent. **2** BARRICADE,
fortification. **3** VINDICATION,
justification, support, advocacy,
endorsement; apology,
explanation, excuse, alibi, reason.

defenceless adj. POWERLESS,
impotent, weak, susceptible. See
also VULNERABLE 1.
—OPPOSITES: resilient.

defend v. **1** PROTECT, guard,
safeguard, secure, shield; fortify,
garrison, barricade; uphold,
support, watch over. **2** JUSTIFY,
vindicate, argue for, support,
make a case for, plead for; excuse,
explain. **3** SUPPORT, back, stand by,
stick up for, stand up for, argue
for, champion, endorse; *informal*
throw one's weight behind.
—OPPOSITES: attack, criticize.

defendant n. ACCUSED, prisoner
(at the bar); appellant, litigant,
respondent; suspect.
—OPPOSITES: plaintiff.

defensive adj. SELF-JUSTIFYING,
over-sensitive, prickly, paranoid,
neurotic; *informal* uptight, twitchy.

defer v. ☞ POSTPONE.

deference n. RESPECT,
respectfulness, dutifulness;
submissiveness, submission,
obedience, surrender, accession,
capitulation, acquiescence,
complaisance, obeisance.
—OPPOSITES: disrespect.

defiant adj. INTRANSIGENT,
resistant, obstinate,

uncooperative, non-compliant,
recalcitrant; obstreperous,
truculent, dissenting, disobedient,
insubordinate, subversive,
rebellious, mutinous, feisty.
—OPPOSITES: co-operative.

deficiency n. **1** ☞ LACK n.
2 ☞ DEFECT¹.
—OPPOSITES: surplus, strength.

defile v. SPOIL, sully, mar, impair,
debase, degrade; poison, taint,
tarnish; destroy, ruin; desecrate,
profane, violate; contaminate,
pollute, dishonour.
—OPPOSITES: sanctify.

define v. **1** EXPLAIN, expound,
interpret, elucidate, describe,
clarify; give the meaning of, put
into words. **2** DETERMINE, establish,
fix, specify, designate, decide,
stipulate, set out; demarcate,
delineate.

definite adj. **1** EXPLICIT, specific,
express, precise, exact, clear-cut,
direct, plain, outright; fixed,
established, confirmed, concrete.
2 CERTAIN, sure, positive,
conclusive, decisive, firm,
concrete, unambiguous,
unequivocal, clear, unmistakable,
proven; guaranteed, assured, cut
and dried. **3** UNMISTAKABLE,
unequivocal, unambiguous,
certain, undisputed, decided,
marked, distinct.
—OPPOSITES: vague, ambiguous,
indeterminate.

definitely adv. ☞ CERTAINLY.

definition n. **1** MEANING,
denotation, sense; interpretation,
explanation, elucidation,
description, clarification,
illustration. **2** CLARITY, visibility,

sharpness, crispness, acuteness; resolution, focus, contrast.

definitive *adj.* **1** CONCLUSIVE, final, ultimate; unconditional, unqualified, absolute, categorical, positive, definite. **2** AUTHORITATIVE, exhaustive, best, finest, consummate; classic, standard, recognized, accepted, official.

deflect *v.* TURN ASIDE/AWAY, divert, avert, sidetrack; distract, draw away; block, parry, fend off, stave off.

deformed *adj.* MISSHAPEN, distorted, malformed, contorted, out of shape; twisted, crooked, bent, warped, buckled, gnarled; crippled, humpbacked, hunchbacked, bowed, disfigured, grotesque; injured, damaged, mutilated, mangled.

defraud *v.* ☞ SWINDLE *v.*

deft *adj.* POLISHED, slick, professional; clever, shrewd, astute, canny, sharp; *informal* nifty. See also SKILFUL.
—OPPOSITES: clumsy.

defy *v.* **1** ☞ DISOBEY. **2** CHALLENGE, dare.
—OPPOSITES: obey.

degenerate *adj.* CORRUPT, decadent, dissolute, dissipated, debauched, reprobate, profligate; sinful, ungodly, immoral, unprincipled, amoral, dishonourable, disreputable, unsavoury, sordid, low, ignoble.
—OPPOSITES: moral.

degrade *v.* **1** DEBASE, lower, demean, abase, humiliate, downgrade, discredit, shame, dishonour, disgrace; belittle, cheapen, devalue; (**lower oneself**) stoop, sink, descend,

brutalize, dehumanize. **2** BREAK DOWN, deteriorate, degenerate, decay.
—OPPOSITES: dignify.

degree *n.* LEVEL, standard, grade, mark; amount, extent, measure; magnitude, intensity, strength; proportion, ratio.
☐ **by degrees** ☞ GRADUALLY.

dehydrate *v.* DRY (OUT), lose water; desiccate, dehumidify, effloresce.
—OPPOSITES: hydrate.

deign *v.* ☞ CONDESCEND.

deity *n.* ☞ GOD.

dejected *adj.* ☞ SAD 1.

deke *v.* FEINT, fake, dodge, avoid, evade, duck, jink, swerve; dipsy-doodle, stickhandle.

delay *v.* **1** DETAIN, hold up, make late, slow up/down, bog down; hinder, hamper, impede, obstruct. **2** LINGER, dally, drag one's feet, be slow, hold back, dawdle, waste time; procrastinate, stall, hang fire, mark time, temporize, hesitate, dither, shilly-shally, dilly-dally; *archaic* tarry. **3** ☞ POSTPONE.
—OPPOSITES: hurry, advance.
▶ *n.* **1** HOLDUP, wait, detainment; hindrance, impediment, obstruction, setback. **2** POSTPONEMENT, deferral, deferment, stay, respite; adjournment.

delectable *adj.* ☞ DELICIOUS 1.

delegate *n.* REPRESENTATIVE, envoy, emissary, commissioner, agent, deputy, commissary; spokesperson, spokesman/woman; ambassador, plenipotentiary.
▶ *v.* **1** ASSIGN, entrust, pass on, hand on/over, turn over, devolve, depute, transfer. **2** AUTHORIZE,

commission, depute, appoint, nominate, mandate, empower, charge, choose, designate, elect.

delegation *n.* DEPUTATION, legation, (diplomatic) mission, commission; delegates, representatives, envoys, emissaries, deputies; contingent.

delete *v.* REMOVE, cut out, take out, edit out, expunge, excise, eradicate, cancel; cross out, strike out, blue-pencil, ink out, scratch out, obliterate, white out; rub out, erase, efface, wipe out, blot out; *Printing* dele.
—OPPOSITES: add.

deliberate *adj.* **1** ☞ INTENTIONAL. **2** CAREFUL, cautious; measured, regular, even, steady.
—OPPOSITES: accidental, hasty.
▶ *v.* ☞ PONDER.

deliberately *adv.* INTENTIONALLY, on purpose, purposely, by design, knowingly, wittingly, consciously, purposefully; wilfully; *Law* with malice aforethought.

delicate *adj.* **1** FINE, exquisite, intricate, dainty; flimsy, gauzy, filmy, floaty, diaphanous, wispy, insubstantial. **2** SUBTLE, soft, muted; pastel, pale, light.
3 ☞ FRAGILE 1. **4** SICKLY, unhealthy, frail, feeble, weak, debilitated; unwell, infirm; *formal* valetudinarian. **5** DIFFICULT, tricky, sensitive, ticklish, awkward, problematic, touchy, prickly, thorny; embarrassing; *informal* sticky, dicey. **6** CAREFUL, sensitive, tactful, diplomatic, discreet, kid-glove.
—OPPOSITES: coarse, lurid, strong, robust, clumsy.

delicious *adj.* **1** DELECTABLE, mouth-watering, appetizing, tasty, flavourful, toothsome, palatable; succulent, luscious, ambrosial, dainty, tempting; *informal* scrumptious, delish, yummy, nummy, lip-smacking, melt-in-your/the-mouth. **2** DELIGHTFUL, exquisite, lovely, pleasurable, pleasant; *informal* heavenly, divine.
—OPPOSITES: unpalatable, unpleasant.

delight *v.* **1** PLEASE GREATLY, charm, enchant, captivate, entrance, thrill; gladden, gratify, appeal to; entertain, amuse, divert; *informal* send, tickle pink, bowl over. **2** TAKE PLEASURE, revel, luxuriate, wallow, glory; adore, love, relish, savour, lap up, dig.
—OPPOSITES: dismay, disgust, dislike.
▶ *n.* PLEASURE, happiness, joy, glee, gladness; excitement, amusement; bliss, rapture, elation, euphoria.
—OPPOSITES: displeasure.

delighted *adj.* PLEASED, glad, thrilled, overjoyed, ecstatic, elated; enchanted, charmed; amused, diverted. See also HAPPY 1.

delightful *adj.* **1** PLEASANT, lovely, pleasurable, enjoyable; amusing, entertaining, diverting; gratifying, satisfying. See also WONDERFUL. **2** CHARMING, enchanting, captivating, bewitching, appealing; sweet, endearing, cute, lovely, adorable, delectable, delicious, gorgeous, ravishing, beautiful, pretty; *informal* dreamy, divine.

delinquent *n.* OFFENDER, wrongdoer, malefactor, lawbreaker, culprit, criminal;

delirious | demeanour

hooligan, vandal, mischief-maker, ruffian, hoodlum, low-life, punk; young offender.

delirious *adj.* **1** INCOHERENT, raving, babbling, irrational; feverish, frenzied; deranged, demented, unhinged, mad, insane, out of one's mind. **2** HYSTERICAL, wild, frenzied. See also ECSTATIC.

deliver *v.* **1** BRING, take, convey, carry, transport, courier; send, dispatch, remit. **2** HAND OVER, turn over, make over, sign over; surrender, give up, yield, cede; consign, commit, entrust, trust. **3** SAVE, rescue, free, liberate, release, extricate, emancipate, redeem. **4** UTTER, give, make, read, broadcast; pronounce, announce, declare, proclaim, hand down, return, set forth. **5** ADMINISTER, deal, inflict, give; *informal* land. **6** FULFILL, live up to, carry out, carry through, make good.

delivery *n.* **1** CONVEYANCE, carriage, transportation, transport, distribution; dispatch, remittance; haulage, shipment. **2** CONSIGNMENT, load, shipment. **3** ☞ BIRTH 1. **4** SPEECH, pronunciation, enunciation, articulation, elocution; utterance, recitation, recital, execution.

deluge *n.* **1** FLOOD, torrent, spate. **2** DOWNPOUR, torrential rain; thunderstorm, thundershower, rainstorm, cloudburst.
▸ *v.* **1** ☞ FLOOD *v.* 1. **2** INUNDATE, overwhelm, overrun, flood, swamp, snow under, engulf, bombard.

delusion *n.* MISAPPREHENSION, misconception, misunderstanding, mistake, error, misinterpretation, misconstruction; fallacy, illusion, fantasy.

deluxe *adj.* LUXURIOUS, luxury, sumptuous, palatial, opulent, lavish; grand, high-class, quality, exclusive, choice, fancy; expensive, costly, upscale, upmarket; high-end, top-line, top-notch, five-star; *informal* plush, posh, classy, ritzy, swanky, pricey, swank.
—OPPOSITES: basic, cheap.

delve *v.* **1** RUMMAGE, search, hunt, scrabble around, root about/around, ferret, fish about/around in, dig; go through, rifle through. **2** ☞ INVESTIGATE.

demand *n.* **1** REQUEST, call, command, order, dictate, ultimatum, stipulation. **2** REQUIREMENT, need, desire, wish, want; claim, imposition.
▸ *v.* **1** CALL FOR, ask for, request, push for, hold out for; insist on, claim. **2** ORDER, command, enjoin, urge; *literary* bid. **3** ASK, inquire, question, interrogate; challenge. **4** REQUIRE, need, necessitate, call for, involve, entail.

demanding *adj.*
1 ☞ CHALLENGING. **2** NAGGING, clamorous, importunate, insistent; trying, tiresome, hard to please.
—OPPOSITES: easy.

demean *v.* ABASE, humble, humiliate. See also DEBASE.
—OPPOSITES: dignify.

demeanour *n.* MANNER, air, aspect, attitude, appearance, look; bearing, cast, carriage; behaviour, conduct, mien; *formal* comportment.

demolish *v.* **1** KNOCK DOWN, pull down, tear down, bring down, destroy, flatten, raze (to the ground), level, bulldoze, topple; blow up; dismantle, disassemble. **2** DESTROY, ruin, wreck; refute, disprove, discredit, overturn, explode; *informal* poke holes in. —OPPOSITES: construct, strengthen.

demonic, **demoniac** *adj.* DEVILISH, fiendish, diabolical, satanic, Mephistophelean, hellish, infernal; evil, wicked.

demonstrable *adj.* VERIFIABLE, provable, attestable; verified, proven, confirmed; obvious, clear, clear-cut, evident, apparent, manifest, patent, distinct, noticeable; unmistakable, undeniable.

demonstrate *v.* **1** SHOW, indicate, determine, establish, prove, confirm, verify, corroborate, substantiate. **2** GIVE A DEMONSTRATION OF; display, show, illustrate, exemplify, demo. **3** BEAR WITNESS TO, testify to. See also INDICATE 1. **4** PROTEST, rally, march; stage a sit-in, picket, strike, walk out; mutiny, rebel.

demonstration *n.* **1** EXHIBITION, presentation, display, exposition, teach-in, demo, expo. **2** MANIFESTATION, indication, sign, mark, token, embodiment; expression. **3** PROTEST, march, rally, lobby, sit-in; stoppage, strike, walkout, picket (line); *informal* demo.

demonstrative *adj.* EXPRESSIVE, open, forthcoming, communicative, unreserved, emotional, effusive, gushing; affectionate, cuddly, loving, warm, friendly, approachable; *informal* touchy-feely, lovey-dovey, huggy.
—OPPOSITES: reserved.

demoralized *adj.* DISPIRITED, disheartened, downhearted, dejected, downcast, low, depressed, despairing; disconsolate, crestfallen, disappointed, dismayed, daunted, discouraged; crushed, humbled, subdued.

demur *v.* OBJECT, take exception, take issue, protest, cavil, dissent; voice reservations, be unwilling, be reluctant, balk, think twice; drag one's heels, refuse; *informal* kick up a fuss.

demure *adj.* MODEST, unassuming, meek, mild, reserved, retiring, quiet, shy, bashful, diffident, reticent, timid, shrinking, coy; sober, sedate, staid, prim, goody-goody, straitlaced.
—OPPOSITES: brazen.

denial *n.* **1** CONTRADICTION, refutation, rebuttal, repudiation, disclaimer; negation, dissent. **2** REFUSAL, withholding; rejection, rebuff, repulse, veto, turndown; *formal* declination.

denigrate *v.* DISPARAGE, belittle, deprecate, criticize, attack, abuse, insult, revile. See also SLANDER *v.*
—OPPOSITES: extol.

denomination *n.* **1** RELIGIOUS GROUP, sect, cult, movement, body, branch, persuasion, order, school; Church. **2** VALUE, unit, size.

denote *v.* DESIGNATE, indicate, be a mark of, signify, signal, symbolize, represent, mean; typify, characterize, distinguish, mark, identify.

denouement *n.* **1** ☞ FINALE. **2** ☞ OUTCOME.

denounce *v.* **1** CONDEMN, criticize, attack, censure, decry, revile, vilify, discredit, damn, reject; proscribe; malign, rail against, run down, slur; *informal* knock, slam, hit out at, lay into; *formal* castigate. **2** EXPOSE, betray, inform on; incriminate, implicate, cite, name, accuse.
—OPPOSITES: praise.

dense *adj.* **1** THICK, close-packed, tightly packed, closely set, close-set, crowded, cramped, congested, compact, solid, tight; overgrown, jungly, impenetrable, impassable. **2** THICK, heavy, opaque, soupy, murky, smoggy; concentrated, condensed. **3** ☞ STUPID 1.
—OPPOSITES: sparse, thin, clever.

deny *v.* **1** CONTRADICT, repudiate, challenge, contest, oppose; disprove, debunk, explode, discredit, refute, rebut, invalidate, negate, nullify, quash; *informal* poke holes in; *formal* gainsay. **2** REFUSE, turn down, reject, rebuff, repulse, decline, veto, dismiss; *informal* give the thumbs down to, give the red light to, nix.
—OPPOSITES: confirm, accept.

depart *v.* **1** ☞ LEAVE¹ 1. **2** ☞ DEVIATE.
—OPPOSITES: arrive.

departed *adj.* ☞ DEAD *adj.* 1.

department *n.* **1** DIVISION, section, sector, unit, branch, arm, wing; office, bureau, agency, ministry. **2** DOMAIN, territory, province, area, line; responsibility,

duty, function, business, affair, charge, task, concern; *informal* baby, bag, bailiwick.

departure *n.* **1** LEAVING, going, leave-taking, withdrawal, exit, egress, retreat. **2** DEVIATION, divergence, digression, shift; variation, change.

depend *v.* **1** BE CONTINGENT ON, be conditional on, be dependent on, hinge on, hang on, rest on, rely on; be decided by. **2** RELY ON, lean on; count on, bank on, trust (in), have faith in, believe in; pin one's hopes on.

dependable *adj.* RELIABLE, trustworthy, trusty, faithful, loyal, unfailing, sure, steadfast, stable; honourable, sensible, responsible.

dependent *adj.* **1** CONDITIONAL, contingent, based; subject to, determined by, influenced by. **2** RELIANT ON, relying on, counting on; sustained by. **3** RELIANT, needy; helpless, weak, infirm, invalid, incapable; debilitated, disabled.

depict *v.* PORTRAY, represent, picture, illustrate, delineate, reproduce, render; draw, paint; describe, detail, relate.

deplete *v.* EXHAUST, use up, consume, expend, drain, empty, milk; reduce, decrease, diminish.
—OPPOSITES: augment.

deplorable *adj.* **1** ☞ DISGRACEFUL. **2** LAMENTABLE, regrettable, unfortunate, wretched, atrocious, awful, terrible, dreadful, diabolical; sorry, poor, inadequate; *informal* appalling, dire, abysmal, woeful, lousy; *formal* grievous.
—OPPOSITES: admirable.

deplore v. **1** ABHOR, find unacceptable, frown on, disapprove of, take a dim view of, take exception to; detest, despise; condemn, denounce. **2** REGRET, lament, mourn, rue, complain about.
—OPPOSITES: applaud.

deploy v. **1** POSITION, station, post, place, install, locate, situate, site, establish; base; distribute, dispose. **2** USE, utilize, employ, take advantage of, exploit; bring into service, call on, turn to, resort to.

deport v. EXPEL, banish, exile, transport, expatriate, extradite, repatriate; evict, oust, throw out.
—OPPOSITES: admit.

depose v. OVERTHROW, unseat, dethrone, topple, remove, supplant, displace; dismiss, oust, drum out, throw out, expel, eject.

deposit n. **1** ACCUMULATION, sediment; layer, covering, coating, blanket. **2** DOWN PAYMENT, advance payment, prepayment, instalment, retainer, stake.
▶ v. **1** PUT (DOWN), place, set (down), unload, rest; drop; informal dump, park, plonk, plunk. **2** LODGE, bank, house, store, stow, put away; informal stash, squirrel away.

depot n. **1** TERMINAL, terminus, station, garage; headquarters, base. **2** STOREHOUSE, warehouse, store, repository, depository, cache; arsenal, magazine, armoury, ammunition dump, drop-off.

depraved adj. CORRUPT, perverted, deviant, degenerate, debased, immoral, unprincipled; debauched, dissolute, licentious, lecherous, prurient, indecent, sordid; wicked, sinful, vile, iniquitous, nefarious; informal warped, twisted, pervy, sick.

depress v. **1** SADDEN, dispirit, cast down, get down, dishearten, demoralize, crush, shake, desolate, weigh down, oppress, bring down, deject, discourage; upset, distress, break someone's heart, grieve, haunt, harrow; informal give someone the blues. **2** SLOW DOWN, reduce, lower, weaken, impair; limit, check, inhibit, restrict.
—OPPOSITES: encourage.

depressed adj. **1** ☞ SAD 1. **2** WEAK, enervated, devitalized, impaired; inactive, flat, slow, slack, sluggish, stagnant. **3** RUNDOWN, slummy. See also DEPRIVED.
—OPPOSITES: cheerful, strong, prosperous.

depression n. **1** UNHAPPINESS, sadness, melancholy, melancholia, misery, sorrow, woe, gloom, despondency, low spirits, heavy heart, despair, desolation, hopelessness; upset, tearfulness; informal the dumps, the doldrums, the blues, a (blue) funk. **2** RECESSION, slump, decline, downturn, standstill; stagnation; Economics stagflation. **3** HOLLOW, indentation, dent, cavity, concavity, dip, pit, hole, sinkhole, trough, crater; basin, bowl.

deprived adj. DISADVANTAGED, underprivileged, poverty-stricken, impoverished, poor, destitute, needy, distressed, unable to make ends meet.

deputize v. STAND IN, sit in, fill in, cover, substitute, replace, take someone's place, understudy, be a locum, relieve, take over; hold the fort, act for, act on behalf of; *informal* sub.

deputy *n.* SECOND, second-in-command, number two; substitute, stand-in, fill-in, relief, understudy, locum tenens; representative, proxy, agent, spokesperson; *informal* sidekick, locum.

▸ *adj.* ASSISTANT, substitute, stand-in, acting, reserve, fill-in, caretaker, temporary, provisional, stopgap, surrogate, interim; *informal* second-string.

deride *v.* DISDAIN, disparage, denigrate, dismiss, slight; sneer at, scorn, insult; *informal* knock, pooh-pooh. See also RIDICULE *v.*
—OPPOSITES: praise.

derogatory *adj.* DISPARAGING, denigratory, deprecatory, disrespectful, demeaning, belittling; critical, pejorative, negative, scathing, unfavourable, uncomplimentary, unflattering, insulting; offensive, personal, abusive, rude, nasty, mean, hurtful, scornful, snide; defamatory, slanderous, libellous, vituperative; *informal* bitchy, catty.
—OPPOSITES: complimentary.

descend *v.* 1 GO DOWN, come down; drop, fall, sink, dive, plummet, plunge, nosedive. 2 SLOPE, dip, slant, go down, fall away. 3 ☞ STOOP *v.* 2. 4 COME IN FORCE, arrive in hordes; attack, assail, assault, storm, invade, swoop on, charge.
—OPPOSITES: ascend, climb.

descent *n.* 1 DIVE, drop; fall, pitch, nosedive. 2 SLOPE, incline,

dip, drop, gradient, declivity, slant; hill. 3 DECLINE, slide, fall, degeneration, deterioration, regression. 4 ☞ ANCESTRY.

describe *v.* 1 REPORT, recount, relate, tell of, set out, chronicle; detail, catalogue, give a rundown of; explain, illustrate, discuss, comment on. 2 DELINEATE, mark out, outline, trace, draw.

description *n.* ACCOUNT, report, rendition, explanation, illustration; chronicle, narration, narrative, story, commentary; portrayal, portrait; details.

descriptive *adj.* ILLUSTRATIVE, expressive, graphic, detailed, lively, vivid, striking; explanatory, explicative.

desecrate *v.* VIOLATE, profane, defile, debase, degrade, dishonour; vandalize, damage, destroy, deface.

desert[1] *v.* 1 ☞ ABANDON 3. 2 ABSCOND, defect, run away, make off, decamp, flee, turn tail, take French leave, depart, quit, jump ship; *Military* go AWOL.

desert[2] *adj.* ARID, dry, moistureless, parched; scorched, hot; barren, bare, stark, infertile, unfruitful, dehydrated, sterile.
—OPPOSITES: fertile.

deserted *adj.* ABANDONED, evacuated, neglected; desolate, lonely, godforsaken. See also UNINHABITED.
—OPPOSITES: populous.

deserter *n.* ABSCONDER, runaway, fugitive, truant, escapee; renegade, defector, turncoat, traitor.

deserve *v.* MERIT, earn, warrant, rate, justify, be worthy of, be entitled to, have a right to, be qualified for.

deserving *adj.* ☞ ADMIRABLE.

design *n.* **1** PLAN, blueprint, drawing, sketch, outline, map, plot, diagram, draft, representation, scheme, model. **2** PATTERN, motif, device; style, composition, makeup, layout, construction, shape, form. **3** ☞ INTENT *n.*
▶ *v.* **1** PLAN, outline, map out, draft, draw. **2** INVENT, originate, create, think up, come up with, devise, formulate, conceive; make, produce, develop, fashion; *informal* dream up. **3** INTEND, aim; devise, contrive, purpose, plan; tailor, fashion, adapt, gear; mean, destine.

designer *n.* ☞ INVENTOR.

designing *adj.* ☞ SCHEMING.

desire *n.* **1** WISH, want, aspiration, fancy, inclination, impulse; yearning, longing, craving, hankering, hunger, thirst, appetite; eagerness, enthusiasm, avidity, greed, determination; *informal* yen, itch, jones. **2** ☞ LUST 1.
▶ *v.* WANT, wish for, long for, yearn for, crave, hanker after, be desperate for, be bent on, covet, aspire to; fancy; *informal* have a yen for, have a jones for, yen for, hanker after/for.

desolate *adj.* **1** BLEAK, stark, bare, dismal, grim; wild, inhospitable; unfrequented, unvisited, isolated, remote. See also DESERTED. **2** MISERABLE, despondent, devastated, despairing, broken-hearted, grief-stricken, crushed, bereft. See also SAD 1.
—OPPOSITES: populous, joyful.

despair *n.* HOPELESSNESS, disheartenment, discouragement, desperation, distress, anguish, unhappiness; despondency, depression, melancholy, misery, wretchedness; defeatism, pessimism.
—OPPOSITES: hope, joy.
▶ *v.* LOSE HOPE, abandon hope, give up, lose heart, lose faith, be discouraged, be despondent, be demoralized, resign oneself; be pessimistic.

desperate *adj.* **1** DESPAIRING, hopeless; anguished, distressed, wretched, desolate, forlorn, distraught, fraught; out of one's mind, at one's wits' end, beside oneself, at the end of one's rope/tether. **2** LAST-DITCH, last-gasp, eleventh-hour, do-or-die, final; frantic, frenzied, wild; futile, hopeless, doomed. **3** URGENT, pressing, crucial, vital, drastic, extreme; *informal* chronic. **4** IN GREAT NEED OF, urgently requiring, in want of; eager, longing, yearning, hungry, crying out; *informal* dying.

despise *v.* DETEST, hate, loathe, abhor, execrate, deplore, dislike; scorn, disdain, look down on, deride, sneer at, revile; spurn, shun; *formal* abominate.
—OPPOSITES: adore.

despondent *adj.* DISHEARTENED, discouraged, dispirited, downhearted, downcast, crestfallen, down, low, disconsolate, despairing, wretched; melancholy, gloomy, morose, dismal, woebegone, miserable, depressed, dejected, sad; *informal* blue, down in the

mouth, down in the dumps.
—OPPOSITES: hopeful, cheerful.

despotic adj. ☞ TOTALITARIAN.
—OPPOSITES: democratic.

destabilize v. UNDERMINE,
weaken, damage, subvert,
sabotage, unsettle, upset, disrupt.
—OPPOSITES: strengthen.

destination n. JOURNEY'S END,
end of the line; terminus, stop,
stopping place, port of call; goal,
target, end.

destined adj. **1** FATED, ordained,
predestined, meant; certain, sure,
bound, assured, likely; doomed.
2 HEADING, bound, en route,
scheduled; intended, meant,
designed, designated, allotted,
reserved.

destiny n. FATE, providence;
predestination, doom; lot; God's
will, kismet, the stars; luck,
fortune, chance; karma,
serendipity.

destitute adj. ☞ POOR 1.
—OPPOSITES: rich.

destroy v. **1** DEMOLISH, knock
down, level, raze (to the ground),
fell; wreck, ruin, shatter; blast,
blow up, dynamite, explode,
bomb. **2** SPOIL, ruin, wreck,
disfigure, blight, mar, impair,
deface, scar, injure, harm,
devastate, damage, wreak havoc
on. **3** ANNIHILATE, wipe out,
obliterate, wipe off the face of the
earth, eliminate, eradicate,
liquidate, finish off, erase; kill,
put down, put to sleep; slaughter,
massacre, exterminate; informal
take out, rub out, snuff out, waste.
—OPPOSITES: build, preserve,
raise, spare.

destruction n. **1** DEMOLITION,
wrecking, ruination, devastation,
blasting, bombing; wreckage,
ruins. **2** ☞ KILLING. **3** ANNIHILATION,
obliteration, elimination,
eradication, liquidation.

destructive adj. **1** DEVASTATING,
ruinous, disastrous, catastrophic,
calamitous, cataclysmic; harmful,
damaging, detrimental,
deleterious, injurious, crippling;
violent, savage, fierce, brutal,
deadly, lethal. **2** NEGATIVE, hostile,
vicious, unfriendly; unhelpful,
obstructive, discouraging.

desultory adj. CASUAL, cursory,
superficial, token, perfunctory,
half-hearted, lukewarm; random,
aimless, unmethodical,
unsystematic, chaotic. See also
SPORADIC.
—OPPOSITES: keen.

detach v. UNFASTEN, disconnect,
disengage, separate, uncouple,
remove, loose, unhitch, unhook,
undo, free, pull off, cut off, break
off.
—OPPOSITES: attach.

detached adj. INDIFFERENT, aloof,
remote, distant, impersonal;
informal cool. See also DISINTERESTED.

detail n. **1** PARTICULAR, respect,
feature, characteristic, attribute,
specific, aspect, facet, part, unit,
component, constituent; fact,
piece of information, point,
element, circumstance,
consideration. **2** PRECISION,
exactness, accuracy,
thoroughness, carefulness,
scrupulousness, particularity.
3 UNIT, detachment, squad, troop,
contingent, outfit, task force,
patrol.

▶ *v.* DESCRIBE, explain, expound, relate, catalogue, list, spell out, itemize, particularize, identify, specify; state, declare, present, set out, frame; cite, quote, instance, mention, name.

detailed *adj.* COMPREHENSIVE, full, complete, thorough, exhaustive, all-inclusive; elaborate, minute, intricate; explicit, specific, precise, exact, accurate, meticulous, painstaking; itemized, blow-by-blow.
—OPPOSITES: general.

detain *v.* 1 HOLD, take into custody, take (in), confine, lock up, intern. See also ARREST *v.* 1. 2 DELAY, hold up, make late, keep, slow up/down; hinder, hamper, impede, obstruct.
—OPPOSITES: release.

detect *v.* 1 NOTICE, perceive, discern, be aware of, note, make out, spot, recognize, distinguish, remark, identify, diagnose; catch, sense. 2 ☞ UNCOVER 2.

detective *n.* INVESTIGATOR, private investigator, private detective, operative; *informal* private eye, PI, sleuth, snoop, shamus, gumshoe, (private) dick.

detention *n.* CUSTODY, imprisonment, confinement, incarceration, internment, detainment, captivity; arrest; quarantine.

deter *v.* PREVENT, stop, avert, fend off, stave off, ward off, block, halt, check; hinder, inhibit, impede, hamper, obstruct, foil, forestall, counteract, curb.
—OPPOSITES: encourage.

deteriorate *v.* 1 WORSEN, decline, degenerate; fail, slump,

slip, slide, go downhill, wane, ebb; *informal* go to pot, go to the dogs, go into/down the toilet, hit the skids, nosedive. 2 DECAY, degrade, degenerate, break down, decompose, rot, go off, spoil, perish; break up, disintegrate, crumble, fall apart.
—OPPOSITES: improve.

determination *n.* RESOLUTION, resolve, willpower, strength of character, single-mindedness, purposefulness, intentness; staunchness, perseverance, resoluteness, steadfastness, strength of purpose, persistence, firmness, patience, tirelessness, tenacity, staying power, endurance, stamina; strong-mindedness, backbone; stubbornness, intransigence, obduracy, doggedness, obstinacy; spirit, courage, pluck, grit, stout-heartedness; *informal* guts, spunk.

determine *v.* 1 CONTROL, decide, regulate, direct, dictate, govern; affect, influence, mould. 2 RESOLVE, decide, make up one's mind, choose, elect, opt; *formal* purpose. 3 SPECIFY, set, fix, decide on, settle, assign, designate, arrange, choose, establish, ordain, prescribe, decree, appoint. 4 ☞ ASCERTAIN.

determined *adj.* 1 INTENT ON, bent on, set on, insistent on, resolved to, firm about, committed to; single-minded about, obsessive about, fixated on. 2 ☞ RESOLUTE.

deterrent *n.* DISINCENTIVE, discouragement, damper, curb, check, restraint; obstacle, hindrance, impediment,

obstruction, block, barrier, inhibition.
—OPPOSITES: incentive.

detest v. ☞ HATE v. 1.
—OPPOSITES: love.

detestable adj. ☞ ABHORRENT.

detract v. BELITTLE, take away from, diminish, reduce, lessen, minimize, play down, trivialize, decry, depreciate, devalue, deprecate.

detrimental adj. ☞ HARMFUL.
—OPPOSITES: benign.

devastate v. 1 DESTROY, wipe out, lay waste, demolish, annihilate, raze, ruin, wreck, level, flatten, ravage, pillage, sack, despoil. 2 SHATTER, shock, stun, daze, dumbfound, traumatize, crush, overwhelm, overcome, distress.

develop v. 1 GROW, expand, spread; advance, progress, evolve, mature; prosper, thrive, flourish, blossom. 2 EXPAND, augment, broaden, supplement, reinforce; enhance, refine, improve, polish, perfect. 3 START, begin, emerge, erupt, break out, burst out, arise, break, unfold, happen. 4 FALL ILL WITH, be stricken with, succumb to; contract, catch, get, pick up, come down with, become infected with.

development n. 1 EVOLUTION, growth, maturation, expansion, enlargement, spread, progress; success. 2 FORMING, establishment, initiation, instigation, origination, invention, generation. 3 EVENT, occurrence, happening, circumstance, incident, situation, issue.

deviate v. DIVERGE, digress, drift, stray, slew, veer, swerve; get sidetracked, branch off; differ, vary, run counter to, contrast with.

device n. 1 IMPLEMENT, gadget, utensil, tool, appliance, apparatus, instrument, machine, mechanism, invention, contrivance, contraption; informal gizmo, widget, doohickey. 2 ☞ PLOY. 3 EMBLEM, symbol, logo, badge, crest, insignia, coat of arms, escutcheon, seal, mark, design, motif; monogram, hallmark, trademark.

devil n. 1 SATAN, Beelzebub, Lucifer, the Lord of the Flies, the Prince of Darkness; informal Old Nick. 2 EVIL SPIRIT, demon, fiend, bogie; informal spook. 3 ☞ SCAMP.

devilish adj. MISCHIEVOUS, wicked, impish, roguish. See also DIABOLICAL.

devious adj. UNDERHANDED, deceitful, dishonest, dishonourable, unethical, unprincipled, immoral, unscrupulous, fraudulent, dubious, unfair, treacherous, deceptive, duplicitous, evasive, false, shifty, slippery, untrustworthy; crafty, cunning, calculating, artful, conniving, scheming, sly, wily; sneaky, furtive, secret, clandestine, surreptitious, backstairs, cloak-and-dagger, disreputable, covert, snide; informal crooked, shady, dirty, lowdown, double-dealing, not above board.

devise v. CONCEIVE, think up/of, dream up, work out, formulate, concoct; design, invent, coin, originate; compose, construct, fabricate, create, produce, develop; discover, hit on; hatch, contrive; *informal* cook up.

devoted *adj.* LOYAL, faithful, true, staunch, steadfast, constant, committed, dedicated, devout; fond, loving, affectionate, caring, admiring.

devotee *n.* **1** ☞ FAN.
2 ☞ ADHERENT.

devotion *n.* LOYALTY, faithfulness, fidelity, constancy, commitment, adherence, allegiance, dedication; fondness, love, admiration, affection, care.

devour *v.* EAT HUNGRILY, eat greedily, gobble (up/down), guzzle, gulp (down), bolt (down), gorge oneself on, wolf (down), feast on, consume, eat up; *informal* demolish, dispose of, make short work of, polish off, shovel down, stuff oneself with, pig out on, put away; *informal* scarf.

devout *adj.* **1** PIOUS, religious, devoted, dedicated, reverent, God-fearing, spiritual, prayerful; holy, godly, saintly, faithful, dutiful, righteous, churchgoing, orthodox. **2** ☞ DEDICATED.

dexterity *n.* DEFTNESS, adeptness, adroitness, agility, nimbleness, handiness, ability, talent, skill, proficiency, expertise, experience, efficiency, mastery, delicacy, knack, artistry, finesse.

diabolical, diabolic *adj.* DEVILISH, fiendish, satanic, demonic, demoniacal, hellish, infernal, evil, wicked, ungodly, unholy.

diagnose *v.* IDENTIFY, determine, distinguish, recognize, detect, pinpoint.

diagonal *adj.* CROSSWISE, crossways, slanting, slanted, aslant, oblique, angled; cater-cornered, kitty-corner.

diagram *n.* DRAWING, line drawing, sketch, representation, draft, illustration, picture, plan, outline, delineation, figure; *Computing* graphic.

dialect *n.* REGIONAL LANGUAGE, local language/speech, vernacular, patois, idiom; *informal* lingo.

dialectic *n.* DISCUSSION, debate, dialogue, logical argument, reasoning, argumentation, polemics; *formal* ratiocination.

dialogue *n.* ☞ DISCUSSION.

diary *n.* **1** APPOINTMENT BOOK, engagement book, (personal) organizer, daybook, PDA; *proprietary* Filofax. **2** JOURNAL, memoir, chronicle, log, logbook, history, annal, record.

dicey *adj.* ☞ HAZARDOUS.

dictate *v.* **1** PRESCRIBE, lay down, impose, set down, order (about/around), command, decree, ordain, direct, determine, decide, control, govern. **2** ☞ DETERMINE 1.

dictator *n.* AUTOCRAT, absolute ruler, despot, tyrant, oppressor.

dictatorial *adj.* **1** AUTOCRATIC, undemocratic, totalitarian, authoritarian, autarchic, despotic, tyrannical, tyrannous, absolute, unrestricted, unlimited, unaccountable, arbitrary; *informal* iron-fisted. **2** DOMINEERING, autocratic, authoritarian, oppressive, imperious, officious, overweening, overbearing,

peremptory, dogmatic, high and mighty; severe, strict; *informal* bossy, high-handed.
—OPPOSITES: democratic, meek.

diction *n.* ENUNCIATION, articulation, elocution, locution, pronunciation, speech, intonation, inflection; delivery.

dictum *n.* **1** PRONOUNCEMENT, proclamation, direction, injunction, dictate, command, commandment, order, decree, edict, mandate, diktat. **2** ☞ SAYING.

die *v.* **1** PASS AWAY, pass on, lose one's life, expire, breathe one's last, meet one's end, meet one's death, lay down one's life, perish, be killed, fall, decease, go to glory, go the way of all flesh, go to one's last resting place, go to meet one's maker, cross the great divide, slip away; *informal* give up the ghost, kick the bucket, croak, buy it, turn up one's toes, cash in one's chips, shuffle off this mortal coil, bite the big one, check out, buy the farm; *archaic* depart this life. **2** ABATE, subside, drop, lessen, ease (off), let up, moderate, fade, dwindle, peter out, wane, ebb, relent, weaken; melt away, dissolve, vanish, disappear; *archaic* remit. **3** (*informal*) FAIL, cut out, give out, stop, break down, stop working; *informal* conk out, go kaput, give up the ghost.
—OPPOSITES: live, intensify.

diehard *adj.* HARDLINE, reactionary, ultra-conservative, conservative, traditionalist; staunch, steadfast. See also INFLEXIBLE.

differ *v.* **1** CONTRAST WITH, be different from, be dissimilar to, be unlike, vary from, diverge from, deviate from, conflict with, run counter to, be incompatible with, be at odds with, go against, contradict. **2** ☞ DISAGREE 1.
—OPPOSITES: resemble, agree.

difference *n.* **1** DISSIMILARITY, contrast, distinction, differentiation, variance, variation, divergence, disparity, deviation, polarity, gulf, gap, imbalance, contradiction, contradistinction. **2** ☞ ARGUMENT. **3** BALANCE, remainder, rest, remaining amount, residue.
—OPPOSITES: similarity.

different *adj.* **1** DISSIMILAR, unalike, unlike, contrasting, contrastive, divergent, differing, varying, disparate; poles apart, incompatible, mismatched, conflicting, clashing. **2** CHANGED, altered, transformed, new, unfamiliar, unknown, strange. **3** UNUSUAL, out of the ordinary, unfamiliar, novel, new, fresh, original, unconventional, exotic, uncommon.
—OPPOSITES: similar, related, ordinary.

difficult *adj.* **1** HARD, strenuous, arduous, laborious, tough, onerous, burdensome, demanding, punishing, gruelling, back-breaking, exhausting, tiring, fatiguing, wearisome; *informal* hellish, killing. **2** HARD, complicated, complex, involved, impenetrable, unfathomable, over/above one's head, beyond one, puzzling, baffling, perplexing, confusing, mystifying; problematic, intricate, knotty, thorny, ticklish.

3 ☞ TROUBLESOME.

4 ☞ INCONVENIENT.

—OPPOSITES: easy, simple, accommodating.

difficulty *n.* 1 PROBLEM, complication, snag, hitch, catch, drawback, pitfall, handicap, impediment, hindrance, obstacle, hurdle, stumbling block, obstruction, barrier, inconvenience, setback; *informal* fly in the ointment, headache, hiccup, wrench in the works; growing pains. **2** TROUBLE, predicament, plight, hard times, dire straits; quandary, dilemma; *informal* deep water, a fix, a jam, a spot, a scrape, a stew, a hole, a pickle.

—OPPOSITES: ease.

diffident *adj.* SHY, bashful, modest, self-effacing, unassuming, meek, humble, shrinking, reticent, doubtful. See also INSECURE.

—OPPOSITES: confident.

diffuse *v.* SPREAD, spread around, send out, disseminate, scatter, disperse, distribute, put about, circulate, communicate, purvey, propagate, transmit, broadcast, promulgate.

dig *v.* 1 TURN OVER, work, break up; till, harrow, plow, shovel. **2** EXCAVATE, dig out, quarry, hollow out, scoop out, gouge out; cut, bore, tunnel, burrow, mine. **3** ☞ POKE *v.* 1. **4** (**dig up**) ☞ UNCOVER 2.

digest *v.* ASSIMILATE, absorb, take in, understand, comprehend, grasp. See also CONTEMPLATE 2.

dignified *adj.* STATELY, noble, courtly, majestic, distinguished,

proud, august, lofty, exalted, regal, lordly, imposing, impressive, grand; solemn, serious, grave, formal, proper, ceremonious, decorous, reserved, composed, sedate.

dignitary *n.* ☞ VIP.

dignity *n.* 1 STATELINESS, nobility, majesty, regality, courtliness, augustness, loftiness, lordliness, grandeur; solemnity, gravity, gravitas, formality, decorum, propriety, sedateness. **2** ☞ SELF-RESPECT.

digress *v.* DEVIATE, go off on a tangent, get off the subject, get sidetracked, lose the thread, turn aside/away, depart, drift, stray, wander.

dilapidated *adj.* RUNDOWN, tumbledown, ramshackle, derelict, broken-down, in disrepair, shabby, battered, beat-up, rickety, shaky, unsound, crumbling, in ruins, ruined, decayed, decaying, decrepit; neglected, uncared-for, untended, the worse for wear, falling to pieces, falling apart, gone to rack and ruin, gone to seed, fleabag.

dilate *v.* ENLARGE, widen, expand, distend.

—OPPOSITES: contract.

dilemma *n.* QUANDARY, predicament, Catch-22, vicious circle, plight, mess, muddle; difficulty, problem, trouble, perplexity, confusion, conflict; *informal* no-win situation, fix, tight spot/corner.

diligent *adj.* PARTICULAR, punctilious, meticulous, rigorous, careful, thorough, sedulous, earnest, assiduous, attentive, painstaking, studious; tenacious, dedicated, committed, dogged. See also INDUSTRIOUS.

dilute *v.* MAKE WEAKER, weaken, water down; thin out, thin; doctor, adulterate; *informal* cut.

dim *adj.* **1** FAINT, weak, feeble, soft, pale, dull, subdued, muted, wan. **2** DARK, badly lit, ill-lit, dingy, dismal, gloomy, murky. **3** VAGUE, imprecise, imperfect, unclear, indistinct, sketchy, hazy, blurred, shadowy. **4** (*informal*) ☞ STUPID 1.
—OPPOSITES: bright, distinct.
▶ *v.* **1** TURN DOWN, lower, soften, subdue, mute; *literary* bedim. **2** FADE, become vague, dwindle, blur.
—OPPOSITES: brighten, sharpen.

dimension *n.* **1** ☞ SIZE *n.* **2** ASPECT, feature, element, facet, side.

diminish *v.* DECREASE, lessen, decline, reduce, subside, die down, abate, dwindle, fade, slacken off, moderate, let up, ebb, wane, recede, die away/out, peter out, drop (off/away), ease off, fall, grow less, grow smaller, tail off; curtail, cut, restrict, limit.
—OPPOSITES: increase.

diminutive *adj.* ☞ LITTLE 1.
—OPPOSITES: enormous.

din *n.* ☞ NOISE.

dingy *adj.* GLOOMY, dark, dull, badly/poorly lit, murky, dim, dismal, dreary, drab, sombre, grim, cheerless; dirty, grimy, shabby, faded, worn, dowdy, seedy, rundown; *informal* grungy.
—OPPOSITES: bright.

dip *v.* **1** IMMERSE, submerge, plunge, duck, dunk, lower, sink. **2** SINK, set, drop, go/drop down,

fall, descend; disappear, vanish. **3** ☞ DECREASE 1.
—OPPOSITES: rise, increase.
▶ *n.* **1** SWIM, bathe; paddle. **2** SAUCE, relish, dressing. **3** ☞ DECREASE *n.*

diplomacy *n.* **1** STATESMANSHIP, statecraft, negotiation(s), discussion(s), talks, dialogue; international relations, foreign affairs. **2** ☞ TACT.

diplomatic *adj.* TACTFUL, sensitive, subtle, delicate, polite, discreet, thoughtful, careful, judicious, prudent, politic, clever, skilful.
—OPPOSITES: tactless.

direct *adj.* **1** STRAIGHT, undeviating, unswerving; shortest, quickest. **2** NON-STOP, unbroken, uninterrupted, through. **3** ☞ OUTSPOKEN. **4** FACE TO FACE, personal, immediate, first-hand. **5** VERBATIM, word for word, to the letter, faithful, exact, precise, accurate, correct.
▶ *v.* **1** ☞ MANAGE 1. **2** AIM AT, target at, address to, intend for, mean for, design for. **3** GIVE DIRECTIONS, show the way, guide, lead, conduct, accompany, usher, escort.

directive *n.* INSTRUCTION, direction, command, order, charge, injunction, prescription, rule, ruling, regulation, law, dictate, decree, dictum, edict, mandate, fiat; *formal* ordinance.

director *n.* ☞ LEADER.

dirge *n.* ELEGY, lament, threnody, requiem, dead march; *Irish* keen.

dirt *n.* **1** GRIME, filth; dust, soot, smut; muck, mud, mire, sludge, slime, ooze, dross; smudges, stains; *informal* crud, yuck, grunge, gunge. **2** EARTH, soil, loam, clay, silt; ground.

dirty *adj.* **1** SOILED, grimy, grubby, filthy, mucky, stained, unwashed, greasy, smeared, smeary, spotted, smudged, cloudy, muddy, dusty, sooty, smutty; unclean, sullied, impure, tarnished, polluted, contaminated, defiled, foul, unhygienic, unsanitary, sordid, squalid; *informal* cruddy, yucky, icky, grotty, grungy; *literary* befouled, besmirched, begrimed. **2** ☞ INDECENT. **3** DISHONEST, deceitful, unscrupulous, dishonourable, unsporting, ungentlemanly, below the belt, unfair, unethical, unprincipled; crooked, double-dealing, underhanded, sly, crafty, devious, sneaky. **4** MALEVOLENT, resentful, hostile, black, dark; angry, cross, indignant, annoyed, disapproving; *informal* peeved.
—OPPOSITES: clean, innocent, honourable, pleasant.
▸ *v.* SOIL, stain, muddy, blacken, mess up, mark, spatter, bespatter, smudge, smear, splatter; sully, pollute, foul, defile; *literary* befoul, besmirch, begrime.
—OPPOSITES: clean.

disability *n.* HANDICAP, disablement, incapacity, impairment, infirmity, defect, abnormality; condition, disorder, affliction.

disable *v.* **1** INCAPACITATE, put out of action, debilitate; handicap, cripple, lame, maim, immobilize, paralyze. **2** DEACTIVATE, defuse, disarm.

disabled *adj.* HANDICAPPED, incapacitated; debilitated, infirm, out of action; crippled, lame, paralyzed, immobilized, bedridden, paraplegic, quadriplegic; *euphemistic* physically challenged, differently abled.

disadvantage *n.* ☞ DRAWBACK.

disaffected *adj.* DISSATISFIED, disgruntled, discontented, malcontent, frustrated, alienated; disloyal, rebellious, mutinous, seditious, dissident, up in arms; hostile, antagonistic, unfriendly.
—OPPOSITES: contented.

disagree *v.* **1** TAKE ISSUE, challenge, contradict, oppose; be at variance/odds, not see eye to eye, differ, dissent, be in dispute, debate, argue, quarrel, wrangle, clash, be at loggerheads, cross swords, lock horns; *formal* gainsay. **2** ☞ DIFFER 1.

disagreeable *adj.*
1 ☞ UNPLEASANT 1. **2** UNFRIENDLY, unpleasant, nasty, mean, mean-spirited, ill-natured, rude, surly, discourteous, impolite, brusque, abrupt, churlish, disobliging. See also IRRITABLE.
—OPPOSITES: pleasant.

disallow *v.* REJECT, refuse, dismiss, say no to; ban, bar, block, debar, forbid, prohibit; *informal* give the thumbs down to, nix. See also QUASH 1.

disappear *v.* **1** VANISH (INTO THIN AIR), pass from sight, be lost to view/sight, recede from view, become invisible; fade (away), melt away, melt into thin air, be dispelled, clear, dissolve, disperse, evaporate, dematerialize; *literary* evanesce. **2** DIE OUT, die, cease to exist, come to an end, end, pass

away, pass into oblivion, perish, vanish.
—OPPOSITES: materialize.

disappoint v. LET DOWN, fail, dissatisfy, dash someone's hopes; upset, dismay, sadden, disenchant, disillusion, shatter someone's illusions, disabuse.
—OPPOSITES: fulfill.

disappointed adj. UPSET, saddened, let down, cast down, disheartened, downhearted, downcast, depressed, dispirited, discouraged, despondent, dismayed, crestfallen, distressed, chagrined, dejected, desolate, disconsolate, doleful, forlorn, unhappy; disenchanted, disillusioned; displeased, discontented, dissatisfied, frustrated, disgruntled; *informal* choked, bummed (out), miffed, cut up, down in the dumps, down in the mouth.
—OPPOSITES: pleased.

disapproval n. DISAPPROBATION, objection, dislike; dissatisfaction, disfavour, displeasure, distaste; criticism, censure, condemnation, denunciation, deprecation; *informal* the thumbs down.

disapprove v. OBJECT TO, have a poor opinion of, look down one's nose at, take exception to, dislike, take a dim view of, look askance at, frown on, be against, not believe in; deplore, criticize, censure, condemn, denounce, decry, deprecate.

disarray n. ☞ MESS n. 1.

disaster n. **1** CATASTROPHE, calamity, cataclysm, tragedy, act of God, holocaust; accident.

2 ☞ FAILURE 2.
—OPPOSITES: success.

disastrous adj. CATASTROPHIC, calamitous, cataclysmic, tragic; devastating, ruinous, harmful, dire, terrible, awful, woeful, shocking, appalling, dreadful, horrible, horrendous, atrocious, nightmarish, harrowing; costly; black, dark, unfortunate, unlucky, ill-fated, fateful, ill-starred, inauspicious; *formal* grievous.

disbelief n. INCREDULITY, astonishment, amazement, surprise, incredulousness; skepticism, doubt, doubtfulness, dubiousness; cynicism, suspicion, distrust, mistrust; *formal* dubiety.

disburse v. PAY OUT, spend, expend, dole out, dish out, hand out, part with, donate, give; *informal* fork out/over, shell out, lay out, ante up, pony up.

discard v. DISPOSE OF, throw away/out, get rid of, toss out, jettison, scrap, dispense with, cast aside/off; reject, repudiate, abandon, drop, have done with, shed; *informal* chuck (away/out), dump, ditch, junk, get shut of, trash, deep-six.
—OPPOSITES: keep.

discern v. PERCEIVE, make out, pick out, detect, recognize, notice, observe, see, spot; identify, determine, distinguish; *literary* descry, espy.

discernible adj. ☞ NOTICEABLE.

discerning adj. DISCRIMINATING, judicious, shrewd, clever, astute, intelligent, sharp, selective, sophisticated, tasteful, sensitive, perceptive, percipient, perspicacious, wise, aware, knowing.

discharge v. **1** ☞ DISMISS 1.
2 RELEASE, free, set free, let go, liberate, let out. **3** SEND OUT, release, eject, let out, pour out, void, give off. **4** EMIT, exude, ooze, leak. **5** FIRE, shoot, let off; set off, trigger, explode, detonate.
6 ☞ PERFORM 1. **7** PAY, pay off, settle, clear, honour, meet, liquidate, defray, make good; *informal* square.
—OPPOSITES: recruit, imprison, absorb.
▸ *n.* **1** DISMISSAL, release, removal, ejection, expulsion; *Military* cashiering; *informal* the sack, the boot, the axe, a/the pink slip.
2 EMISSION, secretion, excretion, seepage, suppuration; pus, matter; *Medicine* exudate.

disciple *n.* FOLLOWER, apostle, adherent, believer, admirer, devotee, acolyte, votary; pupil, student, learner; upholder, supporter, advocate, proponent, apologist.

disciplinarian *n.* MARTINET, hard taskmaster, authoritarian, stickler for discipline; tyrant, despot, ramrod; *informal* slave-driver.

discipline *n.* **1** CONTROL, training, teaching, instruction, regulation, direction, order, authority, rule, strictness, a firm hand; routine, regimen, drill, drilling; self-control, self-discipline, self-government, self-restraint. **2** FIELD (OF STUDY), branch of knowledge, subject, area; specialty.
▸ *v.* **1** CONTROL, restrain, regulate, govern, keep in check, check, curb, keep a tight rein on, rein in,

bridle, tame, bring into line.
2 PUNISH, penalize, bring to book.
See also REPRIMAND.

disclose *v.* REVEAL, make known, divulge, tell, impart, communicate, pass on; release, make public, broadcast, publish, report, unveil; leak, betray, let slip, let drop, give away; *informal* let on, blab, spill the beans, let the cat out of the bag.
—OPPOSITES: conceal.

discolour *v.* STAIN, mark, soil, dirty, streak, smear, spot, tarnish, sully, spoil, mar, blemish; blacken, char; fade, bleach.

discomfort *n.* **1** PAIN, aches and pains, soreness, tenderness, irritation, stiffness; ache, twinge, pang, throb, cramp.
2 EMBARRASSMENT, discomfiture, unease, uneasiness, awkwardness, discomposure, confusion, nervousness, perturbation, distress, anxiety; chagrin, mortification, shame, humiliation.

disconcert *v.* UNSETTLE, discomfit, throw/catch off balance, take aback, rattle, unnerve, alarm, disorient, perturb, disturb, perplex, confuse, bewilder, baffle, fluster, ruffle, shake, upset, agitate, worry, dismay, surprise, take by surprise, startle, put someone off (their stroke/game), distract; *informal* throw, faze, discombobulate.

disconnect *v.* **1** ☞ DETACH.
2 DEACTIVATE, shut off, turn off, switch off, unplug.
—OPPOSITES: attach.

disconnected *adj.* **1** DETACHED, separate, separated, divorced, cut off, isolated, dissociated, disengaged; apart. **2** ☞ DISJOINTED.

discontented *adj.*
☞ DISSATISFIED.

discord *n.* **1** STRIFE, conflict, friction, hostility, antagonism, antipathy, enmity, bad feeling, ill feeling, bad blood, argument, quarrelling, squabbling, bickering, wrangling, feuding, contention, disagreement, dissension, dispute, difference of opinion, disunity, division, opposition; infighting.
2 DISSONANCE, discordance, disharmony, cacophony.
—OPPOSITES: accord, harmony.

discordant *adj.*
1 ☞ CONTRADICTORY.
2 INHARMONIOUS, tuneless, off-key, dissonant, harsh, jarring, grating, jangling, jangly, strident, shrill, screeching, screechy, cacophonous; sharp, flat.
—OPPOSITES: harmonious.

discount *n.* REDUCTION, deduction, markdown, price cut, cut, rebate.
▶ *v.* **1** DISREGARD, pay no attention to, take no account/notice of, dismiss, ignore, overlook, disbelieve, reject; *informal* take with a pinch of salt, pooh-pooh.
2 ☞ REDUCE 2.

discourage *v.* **1** DETER, dissuade, disincline, put off, talk out of; advise against, urge against.
2 ☞ DISHEARTEN. **3** ☞ PREVENT.
—OPPOSITES: encourage.

discourse *n.* **1** ☞ DISCUSSION.
2 LECTURE, address, speech, oration; sermon, homily. See also PAPER 3.
▶ *v.* ☞ LECTURE 1.

discover *v.* **1** ☞ FIND *v.* 1. **2** FIND OUT, learn, realize, recognize, fathom, see, ascertain, work out, dig up/out, ferret out, root out; *informal* figure out, twig (to), suss out. **3** HIT ON, come up with, invent, originate, devise, design, contrive, conceive of; pioneer, develop.

discovery *n.* **1** REALIZATION, recognition; revelation, disclosure. **2** FIND, finding; invention, breakthrough, innovation.

discredit *v.* **1** BRING INTO DISREPUTE, disgrace, dishonour, damage the reputation of, blacken the name of, put/show in a bad light, reflect badly on, compromise, stigmatize, smear, tarnish, taint, slur. **2** ☞ DISPROVE.

discreet *adj.* CAREFUL, circumspect, cautious, wary, chary, guarded; tactful, diplomatic, prudent, judicious, strategic, politic, delicate, sensitive, kid-glove.

discrepancy *n.* DIFFERENCE, disparity, variance, variation, deviation, divergence, gap, gulf, disagreement, inconsistency, imbalance, dissimilarity, contrast, mismatch, discordance, incompatibility, conflict.
—OPPOSITES: correspondence.

discretion *n.* CIRCUMSPECTION, carefulness, caution, wariness, chariness, guardedness; TACT, tactfulness, diplomacy, delicacy, sensitivity, prudence, judiciousness.

discretionary *adj.* ☞ OPTIONAL.

discriminate *v.* **1** DIFFERENTIATE, distinguish, draw a distinction, tell the difference, tell apart; separate. **2** BE BIASED, be prejudiced; treat differently, treat unfairly, put at a disadvantage, single out; victimize.

discriminating *adj.* DISCERNING, perceptive, astute, shrewd, judicious, perspicacious, insightful, keen; selective, fastidious, tasteful, refined, sensitive, cultivated, cultured, artistic, aesthetic.
—OPPOSITES: indiscriminate.

discrimination *n.* **1** PREJUDICE, bias, bigotry, intolerance, narrow-mindedness, unfairness, inequity, favouritism, one-sidedness, partisanship. **2** (GOOD) TASTE, fastidiousness, refinement, sensitivity, cultivation, culture. See also JUDGMENT 1.
—OPPOSITES: impartiality.

discuss *v.* TALK OVER, talk about, talk through, converse about, debate, confer about, deliberate about, chew over, consider, consider the pros and cons of, thrash out; examine, explore, study, analyze; *informal* kick around, hash out, bat around.

discussion *n.* CONVERSATION, talk, dialogue, discourse, conference, debate, exchange of views, consultation, deliberation; powwow, chat, tête-à-tête, heart-to-heart, huddle; negotiations, parley; *informal* jaw, confab, chit-chat, rap (session), skull session, bull session, chinwag, gabfest; *formal* confabulation, colloquy.

disdainful *adj.* ☞ CONTEMPTUOUS.

disease *n.* ILLNESS, sickness, ill health; infection, ailment, malady, disorder, complaint, affliction, condition, indisposition, upset, problem, trouble, infirmity, disability, defect, abnormality; pestilence, plague, cancer, canker, blight; *informal* bug, virus. *dated* contagion.
—RELATED: pathological.

diseased *adj.* UNHEALTHY, ill, sick, unwell, ailing, sickly, unsound; infected, septic, contaminated, blighted, rotten, bad, abnormal.

disembark *v.* GET OFF, step off, leave, pile out; go ashore, debark, detrain, deplane; land, arrive, alight.

disfigure *v.* MAR, spoil, deface, scar, blemish, uglify; damage, injure, impair, blight, mutilate, deform, maim, ruin; vandalize.
—OPPOSITES: adorn.

disgrace *n.* **1** DISHONOUR, shame, discredit, ignominy, degradation, disrepute, ill repute, infamy, scandal, stigma, opprobrium, obloquy, condemnation, vilification, contempt, disrespect; humiliation, embarrassment, loss of face, debasement. **2** SCANDAL, outrage; discredit, reproach, affront, insult; stain, blemish, blot, black mark; *informal* crime, sin.
—OPPOSITES: honour.
▶ *v.* ☞ SHAME *v.*
—OPPOSITES: honour.

disgraceful *adj.* SHAMEFUL, shocking, scandalous, deplorable, despicable, contemptible, beyond contempt, beyond the pale, dishonourable, discreditable, reprehensible, inexcusable, unpardonable, unforgivable; base, mean, low, blameworthy, unworthy, ignoble, shabby, inglorious, outrageous,

abominable, atrocious, appalling,
dreadful, terrible, disgusting,
shameless, vile, odious,
monstrous, heinous, execrable,
iniquitous, unspeakable,
loathsome, sordid, nefarious;
archaic scurvy.
—OPPOSITES: admirable.

disgruntled *adj.* DISSATISFIED,
discontented, aggrieved, resentful,
fed up, displeased, unhappy,
disappointed, disaffected. See also
ANNOYED.

disguise *v.* CAMOUFLAGE, conceal,
hide, cover up, dissemble, mask,
screen, shroud, veil, cloak; gloss
over, put up a smokescreen.
—OPPOSITES: expose.

disgust *n.* REVULSION,
repugnance, aversion, distaste,
nausea, abhorrence, repulsion,
loathing, detestation, odium,
horror; contempt, outrage.
—OPPOSITES: delight.
▶ *v.* REVOLT, repel, repulse, sicken,
nauseate, turn someone's
stomach, make someone's gorge
rise; *informal* turn off, gross out.

disgusting *adj.* ☞ REPULSIVE.
—OPPOSITES: appealing.

dish *n.* **1** BOWL, plate, platter,
salver, paten; container,
receptacle, casserole, tureen.
2 RECIPE, meal, course; (**dishes**)
food, fare.
☐ **dish something out**
☞ DISTRIBUTE 1.

dishearten *v.* DISCOURAGE,
dispirit, demoralize, cast down,
depress, disappoint, dismay, dash
someone's hopes; put off, deter,
unnerve, daunt, intimidate, cow,
crush.
—OPPOSITES: encourage.

dishevelled *adj.* UNTIDY,
unkempt, scruffy, messy, in a
mess, disordered, disarranged,
rumpled, bedraggled; uncombed,
tousled, tangled, tangly, knotted,
knotty, shaggy, straggly,
windswept, windblown, wild;
slovenly, slatternly, blowsy,
frowzy, mussed (up), mussy.
—OPPOSITES: tidy.

dishonest *adj.* FRAUDULENT,
corrupt, swindling, cheating,
double-dealing; underhanded,
crafty, cunning, devious,
duplicitous, treacherous, unfair,
unjust, dirty, unethical, immoral,
dishonourable, untrustworthy,
unscrupulous, unprincipled,
amoral; criminal, illegal, illicit,
unlawful; false, untruthful,
deceitful, deceiving, disingenuous,
insincere, lying, mendacious,
Machiavellian, calculating,
scheming, bribable, nefarious;
informal crooked, shady, sleazy,
tricky, sharp, shifty, sly, sneaky,
two-faced, hinky; *literary* perfidious.

dishonour *n.* ☞ DISGRACE *n.* 1.
▶ *v.* ☞ SHAME *v.*

dishonourable *adj.*
DISGRACEFUL, shameful,
disreputable, discreditable,
degrading, ignominious, ignoble,
blameworthy, contemptible,
despicable, reprehensible, shabby,
shoddy, sordid, sorry, base, low,
improper, unseemly, unworthy;
unprincipled, unscrupulous,
corrupt, untrustworthy,
treacherous, traitorous; *informal*
shady, dirty; *literary* perfidious;
archaic scurvy.

disillusion *v.* DISABUSE,
enlighten, set straight, open

someone's eyes; disenchant, shatter someone's illusions, disappoint.
—OPPOSITES: deceive.

disinclined *adj.* ☞ RELUCTANT.

disinfect *v.* ☞ STERILIZE 1.

disingenuous *adj.* INSINCERE, dishonest, untruthful, false, deceitful, duplicitous, lying, mendacious; hypocritical.

disintegrate *v.* BREAK UP, break apart, fall apart, fall to pieces, come apart, fragment, fracture, shatter, splinter; explode, blow up, blow apart, fly apart; crumble, deteriorate, decay, decompose, rot, moulder, perish, dissolve, collapse, go to rack and ruin, degenerate; *informal* bust, be smashed to smithereens.

disinterested *adj.* **1** UNBIASED, unprejudiced, impartial, neutral, non-partisan, detached, uninvolved, objective, dispassionate, impersonal, clinical; open-minded, fair, just, equitable, balanced, even-handed, with no axe to grind. **2** ☞ UNINTERESTED.

disjointed *adj.* UNCONNECTED, disconnected, disunited, discontinuous, fragmented, disorganized, disordered, muddled, mixed up, jumbled, garbled, incoherent, confused; rambling, wandering.

dislike *v.* FIND DISTASTEFUL, regard with distaste, be averse to, have an aversion to, have no liking/ taste for, disapprove of, object to, take exception to; hate, detest, loathe, abhor, despise, be unable to bear/stand, shrink from, shudder at, find repellent; *informal*

be unable to stomach; *formal* abominate.

dislocate *v.* PUT OUT OF JOINT; *informal* put out.

disloyal *adj.* UNFAITHFUL, faithless, false, false-hearted, untrue, inconstant, untrustworthy, unreliable, undependable, fickle; treacherous, traitorous, subversive, seditious, unpatriotic, two-faced, double-dealing, double-crossing, deceitful; dissident, renegade; adulterous; *informal* backstabbing, two-timing; *literary* perfidious.

dismal *adj.* **1** ☞ SAD 1. **2** DINGY, dim, dark, gloomy, dreary, drab, dull, bleak, cheerless, depressing, uninviting, unwelcoming.
—OPPOSITES: cheerful, bright.

dismantle *v.* TAKE APART, take to pieces/bits, pull apart, pull to pieces, disassemble, break up, strip (down); knock down, pull down, demolish.
—OPPOSITES: assemble, build.

dismay *v.* APPALL, horrify, shock, shake (up). See also DISCONCERT.
▶ *n.* ALARM, shock, surprise, consternation, concern, perturbation, disquiet, discomposure, distress.
—OPPOSITES: pleasure, relief.

dismiss *v.* **1** GIVE SOMEONE THEIR NOTICE, get rid of, discharge, terminate; lay off, make redundant, sack, give someone the sack, fire, axe, let go, eject, expel, throw out, boot out, give someone the boot/elbow/push, give someone their marching orders, show someone the door, give someone the (old) heave-ho, can, pink-slip, send packing; *Military*

cashier. **2** BANISH, set aside, disregard, shrug off, put out of one's mind; reject, deny, repudiate, spurn.
—OPPOSITES: engage.

disobedient adj. INSUBORDINATE, unruly, wayward, badly behaved, naughty, delinquent, disruptive, troublesome, rebellious, defiant, mutinous, recalcitrant, uncooperative, truculent, wilful, intractable, obstreperous, contrary, difficult, disrespectful, errant, perverse, uncontrollable, undisciplined, unmanageable.

disobey v. DEFY, go against, flout, contravene, infringe, transgress, violate, breach, break; disregard, ignore, pay no heed to.

disobliging adj. UNHELPFUL, uncooperative, unaccommodating, unreasonable, awkward, difficult; discourteous, uncivil, unfriendly.
—OPPOSITES: helpful.

disorder n. **1** ☞ MESS 1. **2** UNREST, disturbance, disruption, upheaval, turmoil, mayhem, pandemonium; violence, fighting, rioting, lawlessness, anarchy; breach of the peace, fracas, rumpus, ruckus, melee. **3** ☞ DISEASE.
—OPPOSITES: tidiness, peace.

disorderly adj. **1** ☞ DISORGANIZED 1. **2** UNRULY, boisterous, rough, rowdy, wild, riotous; disruptive, troublesome, undisciplined, lawless, unmanageable, uncontrollable, out of hand, out of control, rangy✤.
—OPPOSITES: tidy, peaceful.

disorganized adj. **1** DISORDERLY, disordered, unorganized, jumbled, muddled, untidy, messy, chaotic, mixed up, confused, topsy-turvy, haphazard, ragtag; in disorder, in disarray, in a mess, in a muddle, in a shambles. **2** UNMETHODICAL, unsystematic, undisciplined, badly organized, inefficient; haphazard, careless, slapdash; informal sloppy, hit-and-miss.
—OPPOSITES: orderly.

disown v. REJECT, cast off/aside, abandon, renounce, deny; turn one's back on, wash one's hands of, have nothing more to do with; literary forsake.

disparage v. BELITTLE, denigrate, deprecate, trivialize, make light of, undervalue, underrate, play down; ridicule, deride, mock, scorn, scoff at, sneer at; informal pick holes in, knock, slam, pan. See also SLANDER v.
—OPPOSITES: praise, overrate.

disparaging adj. ☞ DEROGATORY.

disparity n. ☞ DISCREPANCY.

dispassionate adj. UNEMOTIONAL, emotionless, impassive, cool, calm, {calm, cool, and collected}, unruffled, unperturbed, composed, self-possessed, self-controlled; objective, detached, disinterested; informal laid-back.

dispatch v. **1** SEND (OFF), post, mail, forward, transmit, email. **2** ☞ KILL 1.
▶ n. **1** ☞ SPEED n. 2.
2 COMMUNICATION, communiqué, bulletin, report, statement, letter, message; news, intelligence; informal memo.

dispense v. **1** ☞ DISTRIBUTE 1. **2** ADMINISTER, deliver, issue, discharge, deal out, mete out. **3** PREPARE, make up.

□**dispense with** WAIVE, omit, drop, leave out, forgo; do away with, give something a miss; manage without, cope without.

disperse v. **1** BREAK UP, split up, disband, scatter, leave, go their separate ways; drive away/off, chase away. **2** DISSIPATE, dissolve, melt away, fade away, clear, lift.
—OPPOSITES: assemble, gather.

displace v. **1** DEPOSE, dislodge, unseat, remove (from office), force out; overthrow, topple, bring down; bump. See also DISMISS 1. **2** REPLACE, take the place of, supplant, supersede.

display n. **1** EXHIBITION, exposition, array, arrangement, presentation, demonstration; spectacle, show, parade, pageant. **2** MANIFESTATION, expression, show. ▶ v. **1** EXHIBIT, show, put on show/view; arrange, array, present, lay out, set out. **2** MANIFEST, show evidence of, reveal; demonstrate, show; formal evince.
—OPPOSITES: conceal.

displease v. ☞ ANNOY.

dispose v. **1** ARRANGE, place, put, position, array, set up, form; marshal, gather, group. **2** INCLINE, encourage, persuade, predispose, make willing, prompt, lead, motivate; sway, influence.
□**dispose of 1** ☞ DISCARD. **2** (informal) ☞ KILL v. 1.

disposed adj. **1** INCLINED, predisposed, minded, in the mood; willing, prepared, ready. **2** LIABLE, apt, likely, prone, tending; capable of.

disprove v. REFUTE, prove false, rebut, falsify, debunk, negate, invalidate, contradict, confound, controvert, negative, discredit, give the lie to, explode; poke holes in, blow out of the water, shoot down; formal confute, gainsay.

dispute n. **1** DEBATE, discussion, disputation, argument, controversy, disagreement, quarrelling, dissension, conflict, friction, strife, discord. **2** ☞ ARGUMENT 1.
—OPPOSITES: agreement.
▶ v. **1** DEBATE, discuss, exchange views. See also ARGUE 2. **2** CHALLENGE, contest, question, call into question, impugn, quibble over, contradict, controvert, argue about, disagree with, take issue with; formal gainsay.
—OPPOSITES: accept.

disquiet v. ☞ UPSET v. 1.

disregard v. IGNORE, take no notice of, pay no attention/heed to; overlook, turn a blind eye to, turn a deaf ear to, shut one's eyes to, gloss over, brush aside, shrug off.
—OPPOSITES: heed.

disrepair n. DILAPIDATION, decrepitude, shabbiness, collapse, ruin; abandonment, neglect, disuse.

disreputable adj. OF BAD REPUTATION, infamous, notorious, louche; dishonourable, dishonest, untrustworthy, unwholesome, villainous, corrupt, immoral; unsavoury, slippery, seedy, sleazy; informal crooked, shady, shifty, dodgy.
—OPPOSITES: respectable.

disrespectful adj. ☞ INSOLENT.

disrupt v. THROW INTO CONFUSION/
DISORDER/DISARRAY, cause
confusion/turmoil in, play havoc
with; disturb, interfere with,
upset, unsettle; obstruct, impede,
hold up, delay, interrupt, suspend;
informal throw a wrench into the
works of.

dissatisfaction n. DISCONTENT,
discontentment, disaffection,
disquiet, unhappiness, malaise,
disgruntlement, vexation,
annoyance, irritation, anger;
disapproval, disapprobation,
disfavour, displeasure.

dissatisfied adj. DISCONTENTED,
malcontent, unsatisfied,
disappointed, disaffected,
unhappy, displeased; disgruntled,
aggrieved, vexed, annoyed,
irritated, frustrated, angry,
exasperated, fed up; *informal*
cheesed off, teed off, ticked off.
—OPPOSITES: contented.

disseminate v. SPREAD,
circulate, distribute, disperse,
promulgate, propagate, publicize,
communicate, pass on, put about,
make known.

dissident n. DISSENTER, objector,
protester; rebel, revolutionary,
recusant, subversive, agitator,
insurgent, insurrectionist,
refusenik.
—OPPOSITES: conformist.

dissimilar adj. DIFFERENT,
differing, unalike, variant,
diverse, divergent, heterogeneous,
disparate, unrelated, distinct,
contrasting; *literary* divers.

dissipate v. 1 ☞ DISAPPEAR 1.
2 ☞ SQUANDER.

dissipated adj. DISSOLUTE,
debauched, decadent,

intemperate, profligate, self-
indulgent, wild, depraved;
licentious, promiscuous; drunken.
—OPPOSITES: ascetic.

dissociate v. SEPARATE, detach,
disconnect, sever, cut off, divorce;
isolate, alienate, disassociate.
—OPPOSITES: relate.

dissolve v. 1 GO INTO SOLUTION,
break down; liquefy, deliquesce,
disintegrate. 2 DISAPPEAR, vanish,
melt away, evaporate, disperse,
dissipate, disintegrate; dwindle,
fade (away), wither; *literary*
evanesce. 3 DISBAND, disestablish,
bring to an end, end, terminate,
discontinue, close down, wind up/
down, suspend; prorogue,
adjourn.

dissuade v. DISCOURAGE, deter,
prevent, divert, stop; talk out of,
persuade against, advise against,
argue out of.
—OPPOSITES: encourage.

distance n. 1 INTERVAL, space,
span, gap, extent; length, width,
breadth, depth; range, reach.
2 ☞ RESERVE n. 5.
▸ v. WITHDRAW, detach, separate,
dissociate, disassociate, isolate.

distant adj. 1 FARAWAY, far-off, far-
flung, remote, out of the way,
outlying. 2 VAGUE, faint, dim,
indistinct, unclear, indefinite,
sketchy, hazy. 3 REMOTE, indirect,
slight. 4 ☞ RESERVED.
5 DISTRACTED, absent-minded,
faraway, detached, distrait, vague;
informal spacey.
—OPPOSITES: near, close.

distasteful adj. ☞ UNPLEASANT 1.
—OPPOSITES: agreeable.

distinct adj. 1 DISCRETE, separate,
different, unconnected; precise,

specific, distinctive, individual, contrasting. **2** ☞ UNMISTAKABLE.
—OPPOSITES: overlapping, indefinite.

distinction *n.* **1** DIFFERENCE, contrast, dissimilarity, variance, variation; division, differentiation, dividing line, gulf, gap.
2 IMPORTANCE, significance, note, consequence; renown, fame, celebrity, prominence, eminence, pre-eminence, repute, reputation, acclaim, account, prestige, standing, stature; merit, worth, greatness, excellence, quality.
—OPPOSITES: similarity, mediocrity.

distinctive *adj.* DISTINGUISHING, characteristic, typical, individual, particular, peculiar, idiosyncratic, defining, singular, unique, exclusive, special; individualized, one's own, personal, personalized.
—OPPOSITES: common.

distinguish *v.* **1** DIFFERENTIATE, tell apart, discriminate between, tell the difference between.
2 ☞ DISCERN. **3** SEPARATE, set apart, make distinctive, make different; single out, mark off, characterize.

distinguished *adj.* EMINENT, famous, renowned, prominent, well-known; esteemed, respected, illustrious, acclaimed, celebrated, great; notable, important, influential.
—OPPOSITES: unknown, obscure.

distract *v.* DIVERT, sidetrack, draw away, disturb, put off.

distracted *adj.* PREOCCUPIED, inattentive, vague, abstracted, distrait, absent-minded, faraway, in a world of one's own; bemused, confused, bewildered; troubled,

harassed, worried, anxious; *informal* miles away, not with it.
—OPPOSITES: attentive.

distraction *n.* **1** DIVERSION, interruption, disturbance, interference, hindrance.
2 AMUSEMENT, entertainment, diversion, recreation, leisure pursuit, divertissement.

distraught *adj.* WORRIED, upset, distressed, fraught; overcome, overwrought, beside oneself, out of one's mind, desperate, hysterical, worked up, at one's wits' end; *informal* in a state, unglued.

distress *n.* **1** ANGUISH, suffering, pain, agony, torment, heartache, heartbreak; misery, wretchedness, sorrow, grief, woe, sadness, unhappiness, desolation, despair.
2 ☞ HARDSHIP.
—OPPOSITES: happiness, prosperity.
▸ *v.* CAUSE ANGUISH/SUFFERING TO, pain, upset, make miserable; trouble, worry, bother, perturb, disturb, disquiet, agitate, harrow, torment.
—OPPOSITES: calm, please.

distribute *v.* **1** GIVE OUT, dispense, issue, supply, deal out, dole out, dish out, hand out/around, pass around; allocate, allot, apportion, share out, divide out/up, parcel out. **2** CIRCULATE, issue, hand out, deliver.
3 DISPERSE, scatter, spread.
—OPPOSITES: collect.

district *n.* NEIGHBOURHOOD, area, region, locality, locale, community, quarter, sector, zone, territory; ward.

distrust v. MISTRUST, be suspicious of, be wary/chary of, be leery of, regard with suspicion, suspect; be skeptical of, have doubts about, doubt, be unsure of/about, have misgivings about, wonder about, disbelieve (in).

disturb v. **1** INTERRUPT, intrude on, butt in on, barge in on; distract, disrupt, bother, trouble, pester, harass; *informal* hassle. **2** DISARRANGE, muddle, rearrange, disorganize, disorder, mix up, interfere with, throw into disorder/confusion, turn upside down. **3** ☞ WORRY 2.

disturbed adj. **1** DISRUPTED, interrupted, fitful, intermittent, broken. **2** TROUBLED, distressed, upset, distraught; unbalanced, unstable, disordered, dysfunctional, maladjusted, neurotic, unhinged; *informal* screwed up.

disturbing adj. WORRYING, perturbing, troubling, upsetting; distressing, discomfiting, disconcerting, disquieting, unsettling, dismaying, alarming, frightening.

disused adj. UNUSED, no longer in use, unemployed, idle; abandoned, deserted, vacated, unoccupied, uninhabited.

ditch n. TRENCH, trough, channel, dike, drain, gutter, gully, watercourse, conduit; *Archaeology* fosse.
▶ v. ☞ DISCARD.

ditzy, **ditsy** adj. SILLY, foolish, giddy, dizzy, spinny✦, light-headed, scatty, scatterbrained, featherbrained, hare-brained, empty-headed, stunned✦,

vacuous, stupid, brainless; skittish, flighty, fickle, capricious, whimsical, inconstant; *informal* dippy, dopey.

dive v. **1** PLUNGE, nosedive, jump headfirst, bellyflop; plummet, fall, drop, pitch, dive-bomb. **2** LEAP, jump, lunge, launch oneself, throw oneself, go headlong, duck.

diverge v. **1** SEPARATE, part, fork, divide, split, bifurcate, go in different directions. **2** DIFFER, be different, be dissimilar; disagree, be at variance/odds, conflict, clash.
—OPPOSITES: converge, agree.

diverse adj. VARIOUS, sundry, manifold, multiple; varied, varying, miscellaneous, assorted, mixed, diversified, divergent, heterogeneous, a mixed bag of, disparate, motley, multifarious, wide-ranging; different, differing, distinct, unlike, dissimilar; *literary* divers, myriad.

diversify v. **1** BRANCH OUT, expand, extend operations. **2** VARY, bring variety to; modify, alter, change, transform; expand, enlarge.

diversion n. **1** DETOUR, bypass, deviation, alternative route. **2** ENTERTAINMENT, amusement, pastime, delight, divertissement; fun, recreation, rest and relaxation, pleasure; *informal* R and R.

divert v. **1** REROUTE, redirect, change the course of, deflect, channel. **2** DISTRACT, sidetrack, disturb, draw away, be a distraction, put off.

diverting adj. ENTERTAINING, amusing, enjoyable, pleasing,

agreeable, delightful, appealing;
interesting, fascinating,
intriguing, absorbing, riveting,
compelling; humorous, funny,
witty, comical.
—OPPOSITES: boring.

divide v. 1 SPLIT (UP), cut up, carve
up; dissect, bisect, halve, quarter;
literary sunder. 2 SEPARATE,
segregate, partition, screen off,
section off, split off. 3 SHARE OUT,
allocate, allot, apportion, portion
out, ration out, parcel out, deal
out, dole out, dish out, distribute,
dispense; *informal* divvy up.
4 ☞ CLASSIFY.
—RELATED: schizo-.
—OPPOSITES: unify, join, converge.
▶ n. BREACH, gulf, gap, split;
borderline, boundary, dividing
line.

divine *adj.* 1 GODLY, angelic,
seraphic, cherubic, saintly,
beatific, godlike; heavenly,
celestial, supernal, holy;
immortal. 2 RELIGIOUS, holy,
sacred, sanctified, consecrated,
blessed, devotional.
3 ☞ EXCELLENT.
—OPPOSITES: mortal.
▶ v. 1 GUESS, surmise, conjecture,
deduce, infer. See also PERCEIVE 1.
2 ☞ PREDICT.

divinity *n.* 1 THEOLOGY, religious
studies, religion, scripture.
2 ☞ GOD.

division *n.* 1 DIVIDING (UP),
breaking up, breakup, carving up,
splitting; partitioning, separation,
segregation; allocation, allotment,
apportionment. 2 DIVIDING LINE,
divide, boundary, borderline,
border, demarcation line.
3 SECTION, subsection, subdivision,

category, class, group, grouping,
set, subset, family; subsidiary,
branch, department. 4 DISUNITY,
disunion, conflict, discord,
disagreement, dissension,
disaffection, estrangement,
alienation, isolation.

divorce *n.* 1 DISSOLUTION,
annulment, (official) separation.
2 SEPARATION, division, split,
disunity, estrangement,
alienation; schism, gulf, chasm.
—OPPOSITES: marriage, unity.
▶ v. DISSOLVE ONE'S MARRIAGE, get a
divorce, separate, break up.

dizzy *adj.* 1 GIDDY, light-headed,
faint, unsteady, shaky, muzzy,
wobbly; *informal* woozy. 2 ☞ DITZY.

do v. 1 CARRY OUT, undertake,
discharge, execute, perform,
accomplish, achieve; bring about/
off, engineer; *informal* pull off; *formal*
effectuate. 2 ACT, behave, conduct
oneself, acquit oneself; *formal*
comport oneself. 3 ☞ DECORATE 1.
4 STYLE, arrange, adjust; brush,
comb, wash, dry, cut; *informal* fix.
5 GRANT, pay, render, give. 6 WORK
OUT, figure out, calculate; solve,
resolve. 7 GET ON/ALONG, progress,
fare, manage, cope; succeed,
prosper.
▶ n. (*informal*) ☞ PARTY *n.* 1.
□ **do away with 1** ☞ ABOLISH.
2 (*informal*) ☞ KILL v. 1. **do
someone/something in** (*informal*)
1 ☞ KILL v. 1. 2 WEAR OUT, tire out,
exhaust, fatigue, weary, overtire,
drain; *informal* shatter, take it out
of. 3 INJURE, hurt, damage. **do
without** ☞ FORGO.

docile *adj.* COMPLIANT, obedient,
pliant, dutiful, submissive,
deferential, unassertive, co-

operative, amenable, accommodating, biddable, malleable.
—OPPOSITES: disobedient, wilful.

dock¹ n. HARBOUR, marina, port, anchorage; wharf, quay, pier, jetty, landing stage.

dock² v. **1** DEDUCT, subtract, remove, debit, take off/away, garnishee; *informal* knock off. **2** REDUCE, cut, decrease.

doctor n. PHYSICIAN, medical practitioner, clinician; general practitioner, GP, consultant, medical officer, MD, medic, intern, resident, specialist; *informal* doc, medico, quack, sawbones; *historical* saddlebag♣.

doctrine n. CREED, credo, dogma, belief, teaching, ideology; tenet, maxim, canon, principle, precept.

document n. PAPER, certificate, deed, contract, legal agreement; *Law* instrument, indenture.
▸ v. RECORD, register, report, log, chronicle, archive, put on record, write down; detail, note, describe.

documentary adj. **1** RECORDED, documented, registered, written, chronicled, archived, on record/paper, in writing. **2** FACTUAL, non-fictional.

dodge v. **1** DART, bolt, dive, lunge, leap, spring. **2** ELUDE, evade, avoid, escape, run away from, lose, shake (off), jink; *informal* give someone the slip, dipsy-doodle around♣, ditch. **3** AVOID, evade, get out of, back out of, sidestep, do an end run; *informal* duck, wriggle out of.
▸ n. **1** DART, bolt, dive, lunge, leap, spring. **2** RUSE, ploy, scheme, tactic, stratagem, subterfuge,

trick, hoax, wile, cheat, deception, blind; swindle, fraud; *informal* scam, con (trick), bunco, grift.

dog n. HOUND, canine, mongrel, cur, (*Nfld*) crackie♣; pup, puppy; *informal* doggy, pooch.
▸ v. PURSUE, follow, track, trail, shadow, hound, plague; *informal* tail.

dogged adj. ☞ TENACIOUS 2.
—OPPOSITES: half-hearted.

dogmatic adj. OPINIONATED, peremptory, assertive, insistent, emphatic, adamant, doctrinaire, authoritarian, imperious, dictatorial, uncompromising, unyielding, inflexible, rigid.

dole n. (*informal*) UNEMPLOYMENT BENEFIT, social security, welfare, pogey♣, EI♣, UI, (*Atlantic*) stamps♣.

doleful adj. ☞ SAD 1.

domestic adj. **1** FAMILY, home, household. **2** DOMESTICATED, tame, pet, household. **3** NATIONAL, state, home, internal.
▸ n. ☞ HELP 3.

dominant adj. **1** PRESIDING, ruling, governing, controlling, commanding, ascendant, supreme, authoritative. **2** ☞ DOMINEERING. **3** ☞ MAIN.
—OPPOSITES: subservient.

dominate v. **1** ☞ CONTROL v. 1. **2** PREDOMINATE, prevail, reign, be prevalent, be paramount, be pre-eminent; *informal* kick butt.

domineering adj. OVERBEARING, authoritarian, imperious, high-handed, autocratic; masterful, dictatorial, despotic, oppressive, iron-fisted, strict, harsh, bossy, peremptory, assertive, authoritative, commanding, pushy.

donate v. GIVE, give/make a donation of, contribute, make a contribution of, gift, pledge, grant, bestow; *informal* chip in, pitch in, kick in.

donation n. GIFT, contribution, present, pledge, handout, grant, offering, subsidy, allowance, endowment; *formal* benefaction; *historical* alms.

donor n. ☞ BENEFACTOR.

doom n. DESTRUCTION, downfall, ruin, ruination; extinction, annihilation, death.

doomed adj. ILL-FATED, ill-starred, cursed, jinxed, foredoomed, damned; *literary* star-crossed.

door n. DOORWAY, portal, opening, entrance, entry, exit.

dope n. (*informal*) 1 (ILLEGAL) DRUGS, narcotics; cannabis, heroin, cocaine. 2 ☞ FOOL n. 1.
▶ v. DRUG, administer drugs to, tamper with, interfere with; sedate.

dormant adj. ASLEEP, sleeping, resting; INACTIVE, passive, inert, latent, quiescent.
—OPPOSITES: awake, active.

dose n. MEASURE, measurement, portion, dosage, shot; *informal* hit, fix.

dot n. SPOT, speck, fleck, speckle; full stop, decimal point, period, pixel.

dote
□ **dote on** INDULGE, spoil, pamper. See also ADORE.

double adj. 1 DUAL, duplex, twin, binary, duplicate, coupled, twofold. 2 AMBIGUOUS, equivocal, dual, two-edged, double-edged, ambivalent, cryptic, enigmatic.
—RELATED: di-, diplo-.

—OPPOSITES: single, unambiguous.
▶ n. LOOK-ALIKE, twin, clone, duplicate, exact likeness, replica, copy, facsimile, doppelgänger; *informal* spitting image, dead ringer.
□ **at/on the double** ☞ FAST adv. 1.

double-cross v. BETRAY, mislead, be disloyal to, be unfaithful to, play false; *informal* sell down the river. See also CHEAT v.

doubt n. 1 UNCERTAINTY, unsureness, indecision, hesitation, dubiousness, suspicion, confusion; queries, questions; *formal* dubiety. 2 INDECISION, hesitation, uncertainty, insecurity, unease, uneasiness, apprehension; hesitancy, vacillation, irresolution.
—OPPOSITES: certainty, conviction.
▶ v. 1 DISBELIEVE, distrust, mistrust, suspect, have doubts about, be suspicious of, have misgivings about, have qualms about, feel uneasy about, feel apprehensive about, query, question, challenge. 2 THINK SOMETHING UNLIKELY, have (one's) doubts about, question, query, be dubious.
—OPPOSITES: trust.
□ **in doubt** ☞ DOUBTFUL 1, 2. **no doubt** ☞ CLEARLY.

doubtful adj. 1 IRRESOLUTE, hesitant, vacillating, dithering, wavering, in doubt, unsure, uncertain, of two minds, shilly-shallying, undecided, in a quandary/dilemma, blowing hot and cold. 2 IN DOUBT, uncertain, open to question, unsure, unconfirmed, not definite, unknown, undecided, unresolved, debatable, in the balance, up in the air; *informal* iffy. 3 ☞ UNLIKELY.

4 ☞ QUESTIONABLE 1.
—OPPOSITES: confident, certain, probable.

dour adj. ☞ STERN.

dowdy adj. UNFASHIONABLE, frumpy, old-fashioned, outmoded, out-of-date, inelegant, shabby, frowzy.
—OPPOSITES: fashionable.

downcast adj. ☞ SAD 1.
—OPPOSITES: elated.

downfall n. UNDOING, ruin, ruination; defeat, conquest, deposition, overthrow; nemesis, destruction, annihilation, elimination; end, collapse, fall, crash, failure; debasement, degradation, disgrace; Waterloo.
—OPPOSITES: rise.

downright adv. THOROUGHLY, utterly, positively, profoundly, really, completely, totally, entirely; unquestionably, undeniably, in every respect, through and through; informal plain.

downside n. ☞ DRAWBACK.
—OPPOSITES: advantage.

downward adj. DESCENDING, downhill, falling, sinking, dipping; earthbound, earthward.

drab adj. **1** COLOURLESS, grey, dull, washed out, muted, lacklustre; dingy, dreary, dismal, cheerless. **2** LAME, tired, sterile, anemic, barren, tame; middle-of-the-road, run-of-the-mill, mediocre, nondescript, unremarkable. See also BORING.
—OPPOSITES: bright, cheerful, interesting.

draft n. PRELIMINARY VERSION, rough outline, plan, skeleton, abstract; blueprint, design, diagram; main points, bare bones.

drag v. **1** HAUL, pull, tug, heave, lug, draw; trail, draw, trawl, tow; informal yank. **2** BECOME TEDIOUS, pass slowly, creep along, hang heavy, wear on, go on too long, go on and on.
□ **drag something out**
☞ PROLONG.

dragoon v. ☞ PRESSURE v.

drain v. **1** DRAW OFF, extract, withdraw, remove, siphon off, pour out, pour off; milk, bleed, tap, void, filter, discharge. **2** FLOW, pour, trickle, stream, run, rush, gush, flood, surge; leak, ooze, seep, dribble, issue, filter, bleed, leach. **3** USE UP, exhaust, deplete, consume, expend, get through, sap, strain, tax; milk, bleed.
—OPPOSITES: fill.
▶ n. SEWER, channel, conduit, ditch, culvert, duct, pipe, gutter, trough; sluice, spillway, race, flume, chute.

dramatic adj. **1** THEATRICAL, thespian, stage, dramaturgical; formal histrionic. **2** NOTABLE, noteworthy, remarkable, extraordinary, exceptional, phenomenal. See also APPRECIABLE. **3** EXCITING, stirring, action-packed, sensational, spectacular; startling, unexpected, tense, gripping, riveting, fascinating, thrilling, hair-raising; rousing, lively, electrifying, impassioned, moving.
4 ☞ STRIKING 1, 2.
—OPPOSITES: insignificant, boring.

dramatist n. PLAYWRIGHT, writer, scriptwriter, screenwriter, scenarist, dramaturge.

dramatize *v.* ☞ EXAGGERATE.

drape *v.* COVER, envelop, swathe, shroud, deck, festoon, overlay, cloak, wind, enfold, sheathe.

drastic *adj.* EXTREME, serious, desperate, radical, far-reaching, momentous, substantial; heavy, severe, harsh, rigorous; oppressive, draconian.
—OPPOSITES: moderate.

draw *v.* **1** SKETCH, make a drawing (of), delineate, outline, draft, rough out, illustrate, render, represent, trace; portray, depict. **2** PULL, haul, drag, tug, heave, lug, trail, tow; *informal* yank. **3** PULL OUT, take out, produce, fish out, extract, withdraw; unsheathe. **4** BREATHE IN, inhale, inspire, respire. **5** ATTRACT, interest, win, capture, catch, engage, lure, entice; absorb, occupy, rivet, engross, fascinate, mesmerize, spellbind, captivate, enthrall, grip.
▶ *n.* **1** ☞ RAFFLE. **2** TIE, dead heat, stalemate, saw-off♣. **3** ☞ ALLURE *n.*
☐ **draw on** CALL ON, have recourse to, avail oneself of, turn to, look to, fall back on, rely on, exploit, use, employ, utilize, bring into play. **draw something out** PROLONG, protract, drag out, spin out, string out, extend, lengthen.

drawback *n.* DISADVANTAGE, snag, downside, stumbling block, catch, hitch, pitfall, fly in the ointment; weak spot/point, weakness, imperfection, defect, fault, flaw; handicap, limitation, trouble, nuisance, difficulty, problem, complication; hindrance, obstacle, impediment, obstruction, inconvenience, discouragement, deterrent; *informal* minus, con, hiccup, wrench in the works.
—OPPOSITES: benefit.

drawing *n.* SKETCH, picture, illustration, representation, portrayal, delineation, depiction, composition, study; diagram, outline, design, plan.
—RELATED: graphic.

dread *v.* FEAR, be afraid of, worry about, be anxious about, have forebodings about; be terrified by, tremble/shudder at, shrink from, quail from, flinch from; *informal* get cold feet about.
▶ *n.* ☞ FEAR *n.* 1.
—OPPOSITES: confidence.

dreadful *adj.* **1** ☞ TERRIBLE 1.
2 UNPLEASANT, disagreeable, nasty, frightful, shocking, awful, abysmal, atrocious, disgraceful, deplorable, very bad, repugnant; poor, inadequate, inferior, unsatisfactory, distasteful; *informal* pathetic, woeful, crummy, rotten, sorry, third-rate, lousy, godawful.
—OPPOSITES: pleasant, agreeable.

dream *n.* **1** nightmare; vision, fantasy, hallucination. **2** DAYDREAM, reverie, trance, daze, stupor, haze. **3** ☞ GOAL.
▶ *v.* **1** FANTASIZE ABOUT, daydream about; WISH FOR, hope for, long for, yearn for, hanker after, set one's heart on; aspire to, aim for, set one's sights on. **2** DAYDREAM, be in a trance, be lost in thought, be preoccupied, be abstracted, stare into space, muse, be in la-la land. **3** THINK, consider, contemplate, conceive.

dreamy *adj.* **1** ☞ IDEALISTIC.
2 DREAMLIKE, vague, dim, hazy, shadowy, faint, indistinct,

unclear. **3** ☞ ATTRACTIVE 2.
—OPPOSITES: practical, clear, ugly.
dreary adj. **1** DULL, drab,
uninteresting, flat, tedious,
wearisome, boring, unexciting,
unstimulating, uninspiring, soul-
destroying; humdrum,
monotonous, uneventful,
unremarkable, featureless, ho-
hum. **2** ☞ SAD 1.
—OPPOSITES: exciting, cheerful.
drench v. SOAK, saturate, wet
through, permeate, douse, souse;
drown, swamp, inundate, flood;
steep, bathe.
dress v. **1** CLOTHE, attire, garb,
deck out, trick out, turn out, fit
out, outfit, costume, array, robe,
swathe; informal get up, doll up.
2 ☞ DECORATE 1. **3** BANDAGE, cover,
bind, wrap, swathe; doctor, care
for.
▶ n. **1** frock, gown, robe, shift.
2 ☞ CLOTHES.
—RELATED: sartorial.
☐ **dress someone down** (informal).
☞ REPRIMAND v.
dribble v. **1** ☞ DROOL v. **2** TRICKLE,
drip, fall, drizzle; ooze, seep.
▶ n. **1** ☞ DROOL n. **2** TRICKLE, drip,
driblet, stream, drizzle; drop,
splash.
drift v. **1** BE CARRIED, be borne;
float, bob, waft, meander.
2 WANDER, meander, stray, putter,
dawdle; digress, deviate. **3** PILE UP,
bank up, heap up, accumulate,
gather, amass.
▶ n. **1** IMPLICATION, intention;
direction, course. See also MEANING
1. **2** PILE, heap, bank, mound,
mass, accumulation.
drill n. **1** TRAINING, instruction,
coaching, teaching; (physical)

exercises, workout. **2** ☞ ROUTINE n.
▶ v. **1** BORE A HOLE IN, make a hole
in; bore, pierce, puncture,
perforate. **2** TRAIN, instruct, coach,
teach, discipline; exercise, put
someone through their paces.
3 INSTILL, hammer, drive, drum,
din, implant, ingrain; teach,
indoctrinate, brainwash.
drink v. **1** SWALLOW, gulp down,
quaff, guzzle, imbibe, sip,
consume; drain, toss off, slug;
informal swig, down, knock back,
put away, swill, chug. **2** DRINK
ALCOHOL, tipple, indulge; carouse;
informal hit the bottle, booze, bend
one's elbow.
▶ n. **1** BEVERAGE, liquid
refreshment; dram, bracer,
nightcap, nip, tot; pint; humorous
libation; archaic potation.
2 ☞ ALCOHOL. **3** SWALLOW, gulp,
sip, draft, slug; informal swig, swill.
drip v. DROP, dribble, trickle,
drizzle, run, splash, plop; leak,
emanate, issue.
drive v. **1** OPERATE, handle,
manage; pilot, steer. **2** CHAUFFEUR,
run, give someone a lift/ride, take,
ferry, transport, convey, carry.
3 HAMMER, screw, ram, sink,
plunge, thrust, propel, knock.
4 FORCE, compel, prompt,
precipitate; oblige, coerce,
pressure, goad, spur, prod.
▶ n. **1** EXCURSION, outing, trip,
jaunt, tour; ride, run, journey;
informal spin. **2** MOTIVATION,
ambition, single-mindedness,
willpower, dedication,
doggedness, tenacity; enthusiasm,
zeal, commitment, aggression,
spirit; energy, vigour, verve,
vitality, pep; informal get-up-and-go.

3 CAMPAIGN, crusade, movement, effort, push, appeal.

◻ **drive at** ☞ SUGGEST 3.

drivel *n.* ☞ NONSENSE.

drool *v.* SALIVATE, dribble, slaver, slobber.

▸ *n.* SALIVA, spit, spittle, dribble, slaver, slobber.

drop *v.* **1** LET FALL, let go of, lose one's grip on; release, unhand, relinquish. **2** ☞ DRIP *v.* **3** FALL, descend, plunge, plummet, dive, nosedive, tumble, pitch; sink, collapse, slump. **4** DECREASE, lessen, reduce, diminish, depreciate; fall, decline, dwindle, sink, slump, plunge, plummet. **5** ABANDON, desert, throw over; renounce, disown, turn one's back on, wash one's hands of; reject, give up, cast off; neglect, shun; *literary* forsake. **6** ☞ OMIT. **7** MENTION, refer to, hint at; bring up, raise, broach, introduce; show off.
—OPPOSITES: lift, rise, increase, keep.

▸ *n.* **1** DROPLET, blob, globule, bead, bubble, tear, dot; *informal* glob. **2** SMALL AMOUNT, little, bit, dash, spot, sprinkle, trickle; dab, speck, modicum; *informal* smidgen, tad. **3** DECREASE, reduction, decline, fall-off, downturn, slump; cut, cutback, curtailment; depreciation.
—OPPOSITES: increase.

drown *v.* **1** ☞ FLOOD *v.* 1. **2** MAKE INAUDIBLE, overpower, overwhelm, override; muffle, deaden, stifle, extinguish.

drowsy *adj.* **1** ☞ TIRED 1. **2** ☞ SOPORIFIC *adj.*
—OPPOSITES: alert, invigorating.

drug *n.* **1** ☞ MEDICINE. **2** NARCOTIC, stimulant, hallucinogen; *informal* dope.

▸ *v.* ANAESTHETIZE, narcotize; poison, lace; knock out, stupefy; *informal* dope, spike, doctor.

drum *v.* **1** TAP, beat, rap, thud, thump; tattoo, thrum. **2** INSTILL, drive, din, hammer, drill, implant, ingrain, inculcate.

◻ **drum someone out** EXPEL, dismiss, throw out, oust; drive out, get rid of; exclude, banish; *informal* give someone the boot.

drum something up ROUND UP, gather, collect; summon, attract; canvass, solicit, petition.

drunk *adj.* ☞ INTOXICATED.
—OPPOSITES: sober.

▸ *n.* ☞ ALCOHOLIC *n.*
—OPPOSITES: teetotaller.

dry *adj.* **1** ☞ ARID. **2** PARCHED, dried, withered, shrivelled, wilted, wizened; crisp, crispy, brittle; dehydrated, desiccated. **3** BARE, simple, basic, fundamental, stark, bald, hard, straightforward. **4** ☞ BORING. **5** WRY, subtle, laconic, sharp; ironic, sardonic, sarcastic, cynical; satirical, mocking, droll; *informal* waggish.
—OPPOSITES: wet, moist, fresh, lively.

▸ *v.* **1** PARCH, scorch, bake; dehydrate, desiccate, dehumidify. **2** DEHYDRATE, desiccate; wither, shrivel.
—OPPOSITES: moisten.

◻ **dry up** DWINDLE, subside, peter out, wane, taper off, ebb, come to a halt/end, run out, give out, disappear, vanish.

dub *v.* NICKNAME, call, name, label, christen, term, tag, entitle, style; designate, characterize, nominate; *formal* denominate.

dubious *adj.* **1** DOUBTFUL, uncertain, unsure, hesitant; undecided, indefinite, unresolved, up in the air; vacillating, irresolute; skeptical, suspicious; *informal* iffy. **2** SUSPICIOUS, suspect, untrustworthy, unreliable, questionable; *informal* shady, fishy, hinky.
—OPPOSITES: certain, trustworthy.

duck *v.* **1** BOB DOWN, bend (down), stoop (down), crouch (down), squat (down), hunch down, hunker down; cower, cringe. **2** DIP, dunk, plunge, immerse, submerge, lower, sink.

duct *n.* TUBE, channel, canal, vessel; conduit, culvert; pipe, pipeline, outlet, inlet, flue, shaft, vent.

due *adj.* **1** OWING, owed, payable; outstanding, overdue, unpaid, unsettled, delinquent. **2** EXPECTED, anticipated, scheduled for, awaited; required. **3** DESERVED BY, merited by, warranted by; appropriate to, fit for, fitting for, right for, proper to. **4** PROPER, correct, rightful, suitable, appropriate, apt; adequate, sufficient, enough, satisfactory, requisite.
▶ *n.* FEE, subscription, charge; payment, contribution.

dulcet *adj.* SWEET, soothing, mellow, honeyed, mellifluous, euphonious, pleasant, agreeable; melodious, melodic, harmonious, musical, rich, soft, tuneful, lilting, lyrical, silvery, golden.
—OPPOSITES: harsh.

dull *adj.* **1** ☞ BORING. **2** ☞ CLOUDY 1. **3** DRAB, dreary, sombre, dark, subdued, muted, lacklustre, faded, washed out, muddy, dingy.

4 MUFFLED, muted, quiet, soft, faint, indistinct; stifled, suppressed. **5** ☞ BLUNT *adj.* 1.
—OPPOSITES: interesting, bright, loud, resonant, sharp.
▶ *v.* LESSEN, decrease, diminish, reduce, dampen, blunt, deaden, allay, ease, soothe, assuage, alleviate.
—OPPOSITES: intensify.

dumb *adj.* **1** MUTE, speechless, tongue-tied, silent, at a loss for words; taciturn, uncommunicative, untalkative, tight-lipped, close-mouthed; *informal* mum. **2** ☞ STUPID 1, 2.
—OPPOSITES: clever.

dumbfound *v.* ☞ SURPRISE *v.* 1.

dummy *n.* **1** MANNEQUIN, model, figure. **2** MOCK-UP, imitation, likeness, look-alike, representation, substitute, sample; replica, reproduction; counterfeit, sham, fake, forgery; *informal* dupe. **3** (*informal*) ☞ IDIOT.

dump *n.* **1** TRANSFER STATION, garbage dump, (*West*) nuisance grounds✦, landfill site, rubbish heap, dumping ground; slag heap. **2** (*informal*) HOVEL, shack, slum; mess; hole, pigsty, dive.
▶ *v.* **1** PUT DOWN, set down, deposit, place, unload; drop, throw down; *informal* stick, park, plonk, plunk. **2** ☞ DISCARD. **3** ☞ ABANDON *v.* 3.

dunce *n.* ☞ FOOL *n.* 1.
—OPPOSITES: genius.

duplicate *n.* ☞ COPY *n.*
▶ *adj.* MATCHING, identical, twin, corresponding, equivalent.
▶ *v.* **1** COPY, photocopy, xerox, reproduce, replicate, reprint, run off. **2** REPEAT, do again, redo, replicate.

duplicity n. DECEITFULNESS, deceit, deception, double-dealing, underhandedness, dishonesty, fraud, fraudulence, sharp practice, chicanery, trickery, subterfuge, skulduggery, treachery; informal crookedness, shadiness, dirty tricks, shenanigans, monkey business; literary perfidy.
—OPPOSITES: honesty.

durable adj. **1** HARD-WEARING, long-lasting, heavy-duty, industrial-strength, tough, resistant, imperishable, indestructible, strong, sturdy. **2** LASTING, long-lasting, long-term, enduring, persistent, abiding; stable, secure, firm, deep-rooted, permanent, undying, everlasting.
—OPPOSITES: delicate, short-lived.

dusk n. TWILIGHT, nightfall, sunset, sundown, evening, (Nfld) duckish✦, close of day; semi-darkness, gloom, murkiness; literary gloaming, eventide.
—OPPOSITES: dawn.

dust n. DIRT, grime, filth, smut, soot; fine powder.
▶ v. WIPE, clean, brush, sweep, mop.

dusty adj. **1** ☞ DIRTY adj. 1. **2** POWDERY, crumbly, chalky, friable; granular, gritty, sandy.
—OPPOSITES: clean.

dutiful adj. CONSCIENTIOUS, responsible, dedicated, devoted, attentive; obedient, compliant, submissive, biddable; deferential, reverent, reverential, respectful, good.
—OPPOSITES: remiss.

duty n. **1** RESPONSIBILITY, obligation, commitment; allegiance, loyalty, faithfulness, fidelity, homage. **2** JOB, task, assignment, mission, function, charge, place, role, responsibility, obligation; dated office. **3** ☞ TAX n.
□ **off duty** NOT WORKING, at leisure, on holiday, on leave, off (work), free.

dwarf n. SMALL PERSON, short person; midget, pygmy, manikin, homunculus.
▶ adj. ☞ SMALL 1.
—OPPOSITES: giant.
▶ v. **1** DOMINATE, tower over, loom over, overshadow, overtop. **2** ☞ SURPASS.

dwell v. (formal) RESIDE, live, be settled, be housed, lodge, stay; informal put up; formal abide, be domiciled.
□ **dwell on** BE PREOCCUPIED BY, be obsessed by, eat one's heart out over; harp on about, discuss at length. See also PONDER.

dwindle v. DIMINISH, decrease, reduce, lessen, shrink; fall off, tail off, drop, fall, slump, plummet; disappear, vanish, die out; informal nosedive.
—OPPOSITES: increase.

dye n. COLOURANT, colouring, colour, dyestuff, pigment, tint, stain, wash.

dynamic adj. ENERGETIC, spirited, active, lively, zestful, vital, vigorous, forceful, powerful, positive; high-powered, aggressive, bold, enterprising; magnetic, passionate, fiery, high-octane; informal go-getting, peppy, full of get-up-and-go, full of vim and vigour, gutsy, spunky, feisty, go-ahead.
—OPPOSITES: half-hearted.

Ee

each *pron.* EVERY ONE, each one, each and every one, all, the whole lot.
▶ *adj.* EVERY, each and every, every single.
▶ *adv.* APIECE, per person, per capita, from each, individually, respectively, severally.

eager *adj.* **1** KEEN, enthusiastic, avid, fervent, ardent, motivated, wholehearted, dedicated, committed, earnest. **2** ANXIOUS, impatient, longing, yearning, wishing, hoping, hopeful; desirous of, hankering after; *informal* itching, dying.
—OPPOSITES: apathetic.

early *adj.* **1** ADVANCE, forward; initial, preliminary, first; pilot, trial. **2** UNTIMELY, premature, unseasonable, before time. **3** PRIMITIVE, ancient, prehistoric, primeval; *literary* of yore.
—OPPOSITES: late, modern.
▶ *adv.* **1** IN THE EARLY MORNING; at dawn, at daybreak, at cock crow. **2** BEFORE THE USUAL TIME; prematurely, too soon, ahead of time, ahead of schedule.
—OPPOSITES: late.

earn *v.* **1** BE PAID, take home, gross, net; receive, get, make, obtain, collect, bring in; *informal* pocket, bank, rake in. **2** DESERVE, merit, warrant, justify, be worthy of; gain, win, secure, establish, obtain, procure, get, acquire.
—OPPOSITES: lose.

earnest *adj.* **1** SERIOUS, solemn, grave, sober, humourless, staid, intense; committed, dedicated, keen, diligent, zealous; thoughtful, cerebral, deep, profound. **2** DEVOUT, heartfelt, wholehearted, sincere, impassioned, fervent, ardent, intense, urgent.

earnings *pl. n.* ☞ INCOME.

earth *n.* **1** WORLD, globe, planet. **2** SOIL, clay, loam; dirt, sod, turf; ground.

earthly *adj.* **1** WORLDLY, temporal, mortal, human; material; carnal, fleshly, bodily, physical, corporeal, sensual. **2** (*informal*) FEASIBLE, possible, likely, conceivable, imaginable.
—OPPOSITES: extraterrestrial, heavenly.

earthy *adj.* **1** DOWN-TO-EARTH, unsophisticated, unrefined, simple, plain, unpretentious, natural. **2** ☞ BAWDY.

ease *n.* **1** EFFORTLESSNESS, no trouble, simplicity; deftness, adroitness, proficiency, mastery. **2** NATURALNESS, casualness, informality, amiability, affability.
▶ *v.* **1** ☞ ALLEVIATE. **2** FACILITATE, expedite, assist, help, aid. **3** GUIDE, manoeuvre, inch, edge; slide, slip, squeeze.

easily *adv.* EFFORTLESSLY, comfortably, simply; with ease, without difficulty, smoothly.

easy *adj.* **1** UNCOMPLICATED, undemanding, unchallenging, effortless, painless, trouble-free, facile, simple, straightforward, elementary, plain sailing; *informal* child's play, kids' stuff, a cinch, no sweat, a breeze, a snap. **2** ☞ EASYGOING. **3** VULNERABLE, susceptible, defenceless; naive, gullible, trusting. **4** NATURAL, casual, informal, unceremonious, unreserved, uninhibited, unaffected, easygoing, amiable, affable, genial, good-humoured; carefree, nonchalant, unconcerned, laid-back. **5** ☞ PROMISCUOUS.

easygoing *adj.* RELAXED, even-tempered, placid, mellow, mild, happy-go-lucky, carefree, free and easy, nonchalant, insouciant, imperturbable; amiable, considerate, undemanding, patient, tolerant, lenient, broad-minded, understanding; good-natured, pleasant, agreeable, easy; *informal* laid-back, unflappable. —OPPOSITES: intolerant.

eat *v.* **1** CONSUME, devour, ingest, partake of; gobble (up/down), bolt (down), wolf (down); swallow, chew, munch, chomp; *informal* guzzle, tuck into, pig out on, scarf, snarf, feast on, snack on, put away, polish off, dispose of. **2** ERODE, corrode, wear away/down/through, burn through, consume, dissolve, disintegrate.

eavesdrop *v.* LISTEN IN, spy; monitor, tap, wiretap, record, overhear, snoop, bug.

ebb *v.* **1** RECEDE, go out, retreat, flow back, fall back/away, subside. **2** DIMINISH, dwindle, wane, fade away, peter out, decline, flag, let up, decrease, weaken, disappear. —OPPOSITES: increase.

ebullient *adj.* ☞ EXUBERANT 1.

eccentric *adj.* UNCONVENTIONAL, uncommon, abnormal, irregular, aberrant, anomalous, odd, queer, strange, peculiar, weird, bizarre, outlandish, freakish, extraordinary; idiosyncratic, quirky, nonconformist, outré; *informal* way out, offbeat, freaky, oddball, wacky, kooky. —OPPOSITES: conventional. ▸ *n.* ODDITY, odd fellow, character, individualist, individual, free spirit; misfit; *informal* oddball, odd duck, weirdo.

echo *n.* REVERBERATION, reflection, ringing, repetition, repeat. ▸ *v.* **1** REVERBERATE, resonate, resound, reflect, ring, vibrate. **2** REPEAT, restate, reiterate; copy, imitate, parrot, mimic.

eclectic *adj.* WIDE-RANGING, broad-based, extensive, comprehensive, encyclopedic; varied, diverse, catholic, all-embracing, multi-faceted, multifarious, heterogeneous, miscellaneous, assorted.

eclipse *v.* **1** BLOT OUT, block, cover, obscure, hide, conceal, obliterate, darken; shade; *Astronomy* occult. **2** OUTSHINE, overshadow, surpass, exceed, outclass, outstrip, outdo, top, trump, transcend, upstage.

economical *adj.* **1** ☞ INEXPENSIVE. **2** THRIFTY, provident, prudent, sensible, frugal, sparing, abstemious; mean, parsimonious, penny-pinching, miserly, stingy.

economize *v.* SAVE (MONEY), cut costs; cut back, make cutbacks, retrench, budget, be frugal, scrimp.

economy *n.* **1** WEALTH, (financial) resources. **2** THRIFT, thriftiness, providence, prudence, careful budgeting, economizing, saving, scrimping, restraint, frugality, abstemiousness.
—OPPOSITES: extravagance.

ecstasy *n.* RAPTURE, bliss, elation, euphoria, transports, rhapsodies; joy, jubilation, exultation.
—OPPOSITES: misery.

ecstatic *adj.* ENRAPTURED, elated, in raptures, euphoric, rapturous, joyful, overjoyed, blissful; on cloud nine, in seventh heaven, walking on air, beside oneself with joy, jumping for joy, delighted, thrilled, exultant, carried away, transported; *informal* over the moon, on top of the world, blissed out, tickled pink.

eddy *n.* SWIRL, whirlpool, vortex, maelstrom.
▶ *v.* SWIRL, whirl, spiral, wind, circulate, twist; flow.

edge *n.* **1** BORDER, boundary, extremity, fringe, margin, side; lip, rim, brim, brink, verge; perimeter, circumference, periphery, limits, bounds. **2** SHARPNESS, severity, bite, sting, asperity, acerbity, acidity, trenchancy; sarcasm, acrimony, malice, spite, venom. **3** ADVANTAGE, lead, head start, the upper hand; *informal* inside track.

—OPPOSITES: middle, disadvantage.

edgy *adj.* TENSE, nervous, on edge, anxious, apprehensive, uneasy, unsettled; twitchy, jumpy, keyed up, restive, skittish, neurotic, insecure; irritable, touchy, tetchy, testy, crotchety, prickly.
—OPPOSITES: calm.

edit *v.* CORRECT, check, copy-edit, improve, emend, polish; modify, adapt, revise, rewrite, reword, rework, redraft; shorten, condense, cut, abridge.

edition *n.* ISSUE, number, volume, impression, publication; version, revision.

educate *v.* TEACH, school, tutor, instruct, coach, train, drill; guide, inform, familiarize with, acquaint with, enlighten; inculcate, indoctrinate; *formal* edify.

educated *adj.* INFORMED, literate, schooled, tutored, well-read, learned, knowledgeable, enlightened; intellectual, academic, erudite, scholarly, cultivated, cultured, sophisticated, bookish, cerebral, highbrow, studious, widely read; *dated* lettered.

eerie *adj.* UNCANNY, sinister, ghostly, unnatural, unearthly, supernatural, otherworldly; strange, abnormal, odd, weird, freakish; creepy, scary, spooky, freaky, frightening.

effect *n.* **1** ☞ CONSEQUENCE 1. **2** IMPACT, action, effectiveness, influence; power, potency, strength; success; *formal* efficacy. **3** SENSE, meaning, theme, drift, import, intent, intention, tenor,

significance, message.
—OPPOSITES: cause.
▶ v. ACHIEVE, accomplish, carry out, realize, manage, bring off, execute, perpetrate, discharge, complete, consummate; cause, bring about, create, produce, make.

effective adj. **1** SUCCESSFUL, effectual, potent, powerful; helpful, beneficial, advantageous, valuable, useful, efficacious; convincing, compelling, strong, forceful, persuasive, plausible. **2** OPERATIVE, in force, in effect; valid; Law effectual.

effeminate adj. WOMANISH, effete, foppish, unmanly, feminine.
—OPPOSITES: manly.

effervescent adj. **1** FIZZY, sparkling, carbonated, aerated, gassy, bubbly. **2** ☞ EXUBERANT 1.

efficient adj. ORGANIZED, methodical, systematic, logical, orderly, businesslike, streamlined, productive, effective, cost-effective.
—OPPOSITES: disorganized.

effigy n. STATUE, statuette, sculpture, model, dummy, figurine; likeness, image.

effort n. **1** ATTEMPT, try, endeavour; informal crack, shot, stab; formal essay. **2** EXERTION, energy, work, endeavour, application, labour, power, muscle, toil, strain; informal sweat, elbow grease.

effrontery n. ☞ AUDACITY.

effusive adj. GUSHING, gushy, unrestrained, extravagant, fulsome, demonstrative, lavish, enthusiastic, lyrical; expansive, wordy, verbose, over the top.
—OPPOSITES: restrained.

egg
☐ **egg someone on** URGE, goad, incite, provoke, push, drive, prod, prompt, induce, impel, spur on; encourage, exhort, motivate, galvanize.

egotistical, **egoistic** adj. SELF-CENTRED, selfish, egocentric, egomaniacal, self-interested, self-seeking, self-absorbed, narcissistic, vain, conceited, self-important; boastful.

egregious adj. SHOCKING, appalling, terrible, awful, horrendous, frightful, atrocious, abominable, abhorrent, outrageous; monstrous, heinous, dire, unspeakable, shameful, unforgivable, intolerable, dreadful, grievous.

eject v. **1** ☞ EMIT. **2** ☞ EVICT.
—OPPOSITES: admit, appoint.

elaborate adj. **1** COMPLICATED, complex, intricate, involved; detailed, painstaking, careful; tortuous, convoluted, serpentine, Byzantine. **2** ORNATE, decorated, embellished, adorned, ornamented, fancy, fussy, busy, ostentatious, extravagant, showy, baroque, rococo, florid.
—OPPOSITES: simple, plain.
▶ v. EXPAND ON, enlarge on, add to, flesh out, embellish.

elastic adj. STRETCHY, elasticized, stretchable, springy, flexible, pliant, pliable, supple, yielding, plastic, resilient.
—OPPOSITES: rigid.

elderly adj. ☞ OLD 1.

elect *v.* VOTE FOR, VOTE IN, return, cast one's vote for; acclaim❧; choose, pick, select.

electric *adj.* EXCITING, charged, electrifying, thrilling, heady, dramatic, intoxicating, dynamic, stimulating, galvanizing, rousing, stirring, moving.

electrify *v.* EXCITE, thrill, stimulate, arouse, rouse, inspire, stir (up), exhilarate, intoxicate, galvanize, move, fire (with enthusiasm).

elegant *adj.* STYLISH, graceful, tasteful, sophisticated, classic, chic, smart, fashionable, modish; refined, dignified, poised, beautiful, lovely, charming, artistic, aesthetic; cultivated, polished, cultured; dashing, debonair, suave, urbane.
—OPPOSITES: gauche.

element *n.* **1** ☞ COMPONENT. **2** TRACE, touch, hint, smattering, soupçon.

elevate *v.* **1** RAISE, lift (up); hoist. **2** PROMOTE, upgrade, advance, move up, raise, prefer; ennoble, exalt, aggrandize.
—OPPOSITES: lower, demote.

elevated *adj.* **1** RAISED, upraised, high up, aloft; overhead. **2** LOFTY, grand, exalted, fine, sublime; inflated, pompous, bombastic, orotund.
—OPPOSITES: lowly.

elf *n.* PIXIE, fairy, sprite, imp, brownie; dwarf, gnome, goblin, hobgoblin; leprechaun, puck, troll.

elicit *v.* OBTAIN, draw out, extract, bring out, evoke, call forth, bring forth, induce, prompt, generate, engender, trigger, provoke; *formal* educe.

eligible *adj.* **1** ENTITLED, permitted, allowed, qualified, able. **2** DESIRABLE, suitable; available.

eliminate *v.* REMOVE, get rid of, put an end to, do away with, end, abolish, stop, terminate, eradicate, destroy, annihilate, stamp out, wipe out, extinguish; erase, efface, excise, expunge.

elite *n.* BEST, pick, cream, crème de la crème, flower, nonpareil, elect; high society; aristocracy, nobility, upper class.
—OPPOSITES: dregs.

eloquent *adj.* FLUENT, articulate, expressive, silver-tongued; persuasive, strong, forceful, powerful, potent, well expressed, effective; smooth-tongued, glib.
—OPPOSITES: inarticulate.

elude *v.* EVADE, avoid, get away from, dodge, escape from, run (away) from; lose, shake off, give the slip to, throw off the scent.

elusive *adj.* **1** DIFFICULT TO FIND; evasive, slippery; *informal* always on the move. **2** INDEFINABLE, intangible, impalpable, ambiguous.

emaciated *adj.* ☞ THIN 3.

emancipate *v.* FREE, liberate, set free, release, deliver, discharge; unchain, unfetter, unshackle, untie, unyoke.
—OPPOSITES: enslave.

emasculate *v.* WEAKEN, enfeeble, debilitate, erode, undermine, cripple; *informal* water down.

embargo *n.* BAN, bar, prohibition, stoppage, interdict, proscription, veto, moratorium; restriction, restraint, block, barrier, impediment, obstruction; boycott.

embarrassed *adj.* MORTIFIED, red-faced, blushing, abashed, shamed, ashamed, shamefaced, humiliated, chagrined, awkward, self-conscious, uncomfortable, sheepish; discomfited, disconcerted, upset, discomposed, flustered.

embed, imbed *v.* IMPLANT, plant, set, fix, lodge, root, insert, place; sink, drive in, hammer in, ram in.

embellish *v.* **1** DECORATE, adorn, ornament; beautify, enhance, grace; trim, garnish, gild; deck, bedeck, festoon, emblazon. **2** ELABORATE, embroider, expand on, exaggerate.

embezzle *v.* MISAPPROPRIATE, steal, thieve, pilfer, purloin, appropriate, defraud someone of, siphon off, pocket; *informal* rob, rip off, skim.

emblazon *v.* ADORN, decorate, ornament, embellish; inscribe.

emblem *n.* SYMBOL, representation, token, image, figure, mark, sign; crest, badge, device, insignia, stamp, seal, heraldic device, coat of arms, shield; logo, trademark, brand.

embody *v.* **1** PERSONIFY, realize, manifest, symbolize, represent, express, concretize, incarnate, epitomize, stand for, typify, exemplify. **2** ☞ ENCOMPASS.

embrace *v.* **1** HUG, take/hold in one's arms, hold, cuddle, clasp to one's bosom, clasp, squeeze, clutch; caress; enfold, encircle, envelop, entwine oneself around;

informal canoodle, clinch. **2** WELCOME, welcome with open arms, accept, take up, take to one's heart, adopt; espouse, support, back, champion.

emend *v.* CORRECT, rectify, repair, fix; improve, enhance, polish, refine, amend; edit, rewrite, revise, change, modify.

emerge *v.* **1** COME OUT, appear, come into view, become visible, surface, materialize, manifest oneself, issue, come forth. **2** BECOME KNOWN, become apparent, be revealed, come to light, come out, turn up.

emergency *n.* CRISIS, urgent situation, extremity, exigency; accident, disaster, catastrophe, calamity; difficulty, plight, predicament, danger.

emigrate *v.* MOVE ABROAD, migrate; relocate, resettle; defect. —OPPOSITES: immigrate.

eminence *n.* FAME, celebrity, illustriousness, distinction, renown, pre-eminence, notability, greatness, prestige, importance, reputation, repute, note; prominence, superiority, stature, standing.

eminent *adj.* ILLUSTRIOUS, distinguished, renowned, esteemed, pre-eminent, notable, noteworthy, great, prestigious, important, influential, outstanding, noted, of note. —OPPOSITES: unknown.

emit *v.* DISCHARGE, release, give out/off, pour out, send forth, throw out, void, vent, issue; emanate, radiate, exude.

emotional *adj.* **1** PASSIONATE, hot-blooded, ardent, fervent,

excitable, temperamental, melodramatic, tempestuous; demonstrative, responsive, tender, loving, feeling, sentimental, sensitive. **2** POIGNANT, moving, touching, affecting, powerful, stirring, emotive, heart-rending, heartwarming, impassioned, dramatic; haunting, pathetic, sentimental; *informal* tear-jerking.
—OPPOSITES: unfeeling.

emotive *adj.* **1** ☞ EMOTIONAL 2. **2** CONTROVERSIAL, contentious, inflammatory; sensitive, delicate, difficult, problematic, touchy, awkward, prickly, ticklish.

emphasis *n.* **1** PROMINENCE, importance, significance, value; stress, weight, accent, attention, priority, pre-eminence, urgency, force. **2** STRESS, accent, accentuation, weight.

emphasize *v.* STRESS, underline, highlight, focus attention on, point up, lay stress on, draw attention to, spotlight, foreground, play up, make a point of; accent, accentuate, underscore; *informal* press home.
—OPPOSITES: understate.

emphatic *adj.* VEHEMENT, firm, wholehearted, forceful, forcible, energetic, vigorous, direct, assertive, insistent; decisive, decided, conclusive; determined, categorical, unqualified, unconditional, unequivocal, unambiguous, absolute, explicit, downright, outright, clear, telling.
—OPPOSITES: hesitant.

empirical *adj.* EXPERIENTIAL, practical, heuristic, first-hand, hands-on; observed, seen.
—OPPOSITES: theoretical.

employ *v.* **1** HIRE, engage, recruit, take on, sign up, sign, enrol, appoint; retain, contract; indenture, apprentice. **2** OCCUPY, engage, involve, keep busy, tie up; absorb, engross, immerse. **3** USE, utilize, make use of; apply, exercise, practise; draw on, resort to, turn to.
—OPPOSITES: dismiss.

employee *n.* WORKER, member of staff, staffer; blue-collar worker, white-collar worker, workman, labourer, (hired) hand; (**employees**) personnel, staff, workforce, human resources.

employer *n.* **1** MANAGER, boss, proprietor, director, chief. **2** COMPANY, firm, business, organization.

empower *v.* AUTHORIZE, entitle, permit, allow, license, sanction, warrant, commission, delegate, qualify, enable, equip.
—OPPOSITES: forbid.

empty *adj.* **1** VACANT, unoccupied, uninhabited, untenanted, bare, desolate, deserted, abandoned; clear, free. **2** MEANINGLESS, hollow, idle, vain, futile, pointless, purposeless, worthless, useless. **3** BLANK, expressionless, vacant, absent, glazed, lifeless.
—OPPOSITES: full, worthwhile.
▸ *v.* **1** UNLOAD, unpack, void; clear, evacuate. **2** REMOVE, take out, extract, pour out, dump out.
—OPPOSITES: fill.

enable *v.* ALLOW, permit, let, give the means to, equip, empower, make able; facilitate; authorize, entitle, qualify.
—OPPOSITES: prevent.

enamoured *adj.* IN LOVE, infatuated, besotted, smitten, captivated, enchanted, fascinated, bewitched, beguiled; keen on, taken with; *informal* mad about, crazy about.

enchant *v.* CAPTIVATE, charm, delight, enrapture, entrance, enthrall, beguile, bewitch, transport, thrill, spellbind, fascinate, hypnotize, mesmerize, rivet, grip, transfix.
—OPPOSITES: bore.

enchanting *adj.* CAPTIVATING, charming, delightful, bewitching, beguiling, adorable, lovely, attractive, appealing, engaging, winning, fetching, winsome, alluring, disarming, irresistible, fascinating.

enclose *v.* **1** SURROUND, circle, ring, girdle, encompass, encircle; confine, close in, shut in, corral, fence in, wall in, hedge in, hem in. **2** INCLUDE, insert, put in; send.

enclosure *n.* PADDOCK, fold, pen, compound, stockade, ring, yard; sty, coop, corral.

encompass *v.* COVER, embrace, include, incorporate, take in, contain, comprise, involve, deal with.

encounter *v.* **1** ☞ MEET 1. **2** EXPERIENCE, hit, run into, come up against, face, be faced with, confront.
▶ *n.* **1** ☞ MEETING 3. **2** BATTLE, fight, clash, confrontation, struggle, skirmish, engagement; *informal* run-in.

encourage *v.* **1** HEARTEN, cheer, buoy up, uplift, inspire, motivate, spur on, stir, stir up, fire up, stimulate, invigorate, vitalize, revitalize, embolden, fortify, rally. **2** PERSUADE, coax, urge, press, push, pressure, pressurize, prod, goad, egg on, prompt, influence, sway. **3** SUPPORT, back, champion, promote, further, foster, nurture, cultivate, strengthen, stimulate; help, assist, aid, boost, fuel.
—OPPOSITES: discourage, dissuade, hinder.

encroach *v.* ☞ INTRUDE.

encumber *v.* BURDEN, load, weigh down, saddle; overwhelm, tax, stress, strain, overload, overburden.

end *n.* **1** EXTREMITY, furthermost part, limit; margin, edge, border, boundary, periphery; point, tip, tail end, tag end, terminus. **2** CONCLUSION, termination, ending, finish, close, resolution, climax, finale, culmination, denouement; epilogue, coda, peroration. **3** AIM, goal, purpose, objective, object; aspiration, wish, desire, ambition. **4** DEATH, dying, demise, passing, expiry; doom, extinction, annihilation, extermination, destruction; downfall, ruin, ruination, Waterloo; *informal* curtains; *formal* decease.
—OPPOSITES: beginning.
▶ *v.* **1** FINISH, conclude, terminate, come to an end, draw to a close, close, stop, cease; culminate, climax. **2** BREAK OFF, call off, bring to an end, put an end to, stop, finish, terminate, discontinue.
—OPPOSITES: begin.

endanger *v.* IMPERIL, jeopardize, risk, put at risk, put in danger; threaten, pose a threat to, be a danger to, damage, injure, harm.

endearing *adj.* LOVABLE, adorable, cute, sweet, dear, delightful, lovely, charming, appealing, attractive, engaging, winning, captivating, enchanting, beguiling, winsome.

endearment *n.*
1 (**endearments**) sweet nothings, sweet talk. **2** AFFECTION, fondness, tenderness, feeling, sentiment, warmth, love, liking, care.

endeavour *v.* ☞ TRY *v.* 1.
▶ *n.* ☞ TRY *n.*

endless *adj.* **1** UNLIMITED, limitless, infinite, inexhaustible, boundless, unbounded, untold, immeasurable, measureless, incalculable; abundant, abounding, great; bottomless. **2** CEASELESS, unceasing, unending, constant, continual, continuous, incessant, interminable, never-ending, non-stop, long-winded, overlong, rambling, tedious, perpetual, persistent, relentless, round-the-clock, sustained, unbroken, uninterrupted, unrelenting, unrelieved, unremitting, without end, everlasting, eternal, enduring, lasting. **3** ☞ COUNTLESS.

endorse *v.* **1** SUPPORT, back, agree with, approve (of), favour, subscribe to, recommend, champion, stick up for, uphold, affirm, sanction. **2** COUNTERSIGN, sign, autograph, authenticate.
—OPPOSITES: oppose.

endow *v.* **1** FINANCE, fund, pay for, subsidize; establish, found, set up, institute. **2** PROVIDE, supply, furnish, equip, invest, gift; give, bestow.

endurance *n.* **1** TOLERATION, tolerance, patience, acceptance, resignation. **2** ☞ STAMINA.

endure *v.* **1** UNDERGO, go through, live through, experience, meet, encounter; cope with, deal with, face, suffer, tolerate, put up with, brave, bear, withstand, sustain, weather. **2** LAST, live, live on, go on, survive, abide, continue, persist, persevere, remain, stay.
—OPPOSITES: fade.

enemy *n.* OPPONENT, adversary, rival, antagonist, combatant, challenger, competitor, opposer, opposition, competition, other side, foe.
—OPPOSITES: ally.

energetic *adj.* **1** ACTIVE, lively, dynamic, zestful, spirited, animated, vital, vibrant, bouncy, bubbly, exuberant, ebullient, perky, frisky, sprightly, tireless, indefatigable, enthusiastic; *informal* peppy, feisty. **2** FORCEFUL, vigorous, high-powered, all-out, determined, bold, powerful, potent; *informal* punchy.
—OPPOSITES: lethargic, half-hearted.

energize *v.* ENLIVEN, liven up, animate, vitalize, invigorate, perk up, excite, electrify, stimulate, stir up, fire up, rouse, motivate, move, drive, spur on, encourage, galvanize, brace, fortify, refresh, rejuvenate, revitalize, wake up, breathe (new) life into, exhilarate, inspire, inspirit, light a fire under, quicken, revive, thrill, vivify; *informal* pep up, buck up, jump-start, kick-start, give a shot in the arm to, turbocharge.

energy *n.* VITALITY, vigour, life, liveliness, animation, vivacity, spirit, spiritedness, verve, enthusiasm, zest, vibrancy, spark, sparkle, effervescence, ebullience, exuberance, buoyancy, sprightliness; strength, stamina, forcefulness, power, dynamism, drive; fire, passion, ardour, zeal; *informal* zip, zing, pep, pizzazz, punch, bounce, oomph, moxie, mojo, go, get-up-and-go, vim and vigour, feistiness.

enfold *v.* ☞ ENVELOP.

enforce *v.* **1** IMPOSE, apply, administer, implement, bring to bear, discharge, execute, prosecute. **2** FORCE, compel, coerce, exact, extort.

engage *v.* **1** CAPTURE, catch, attract, gain, win, hold, grip, grab, seize, captivate, engross, absorb, occupy. **2** EMPLOY, hire, recruit, take on. **3** PARTICIPATE IN, take part in, join in, partake in/of.
—OPPOSITES: lose, dismiss.

engender *v.* ☞ CAUSE *v.*

engine *n.* **1** MOTOR, machine, mechanism. **2** CAUSE, agent, instrument, originator, initiator, generator.

engineer *v.* BRING ABOUT, arrange, pull off, bring off, contrive, manoeuvre, manipulate, negotiate, organize, orchestrate, choreograph, mount, stage, mastermind, originate, direct.

engrave *v.* CARVE, inscribe, cut (in), incise, chisel, chase, score, notch, etch, imprint, impress.

enhance *v.* INCREASE, add to, intensify, heighten, magnify, amplify, inflate, strengthen, build up, supplement, augment, boost, raise, lift, elevate, exalt; improve, enrich, complement.
—OPPOSITES: diminish.

enigma *n.* ☞ MYSTERY 1.

enjoy *v.* **1** LIKE, love, be fond of, be entertained by, take pleasure in, be keen on, delight in, appreciate, relish, revel in, adore, lap up, savour, luxuriate in, bask in, get a kick out of, get a thrill out of; dig. **2** BENEFIT FROM, have the benefit of; be blessed with, be favoured with, be endowed with, be possessed of, possess, own, boast.
—OPPOSITES: dislike, lack.

enjoyable *adj.* ENTERTAINING, amusing, agreeable, pleasurable, diverting, engaging, delightful, pleasant, congenial, convivial, lovely, fine, good, great, delicious, delectable, satisfying, gratifying; marvellous, wonderful, magnificent, splendid; *informal* super, fantastic, fabulous, fab, terrific, magic, groovy.

enlarge *v.* **1** ☞ EXPAND 1. **2** ☞ EXPAND 2.
—OPPOSITES: reduce, shrink.

enlighten *v.* INFORM, tell, make aware, open someone's eyes, notify, illuminate, apprise, brief, update; disabuse, set straight; *informal* clue in, fill in, bring up to speed.

enlist *v.* **1** JOIN UP, join, enrol in, sign up for, volunteer for. **2** ☞ RECRUIT *v.* 1. **3** OBTAIN, engage, secure, win, get, procure.

enliven *v.* CHEER UP, brighten up, liven up, raise someone's spirits, uplift, gladden, buoy up, animate, vivify, vitalize, invigorate, restore, revive, refresh, rejuvenate, stimulate, rouse, boost, exhilarate.

enormous *adj.* HUGE, vast, immense, gigantic, great, giant, massive, colossal, mammoth, tremendous, mighty, monumental, epic, prodigious, mountainous, king-size(d), titanic, towering, elephantine, gargantuan, Brobdingnagian; *informal* mega, monster, humongous, jumbo.
—OPPOSITES: tiny.

enough *adj.* SUFFICIENT, adequate, ample, the necessary; *informal* plenty of.
—OPPOSITES: insufficient.

enquire *v.* ☞ ASK 1.

enrage *v.* ☞ ANGER *v.*

enrapture *v.* ☞ ENCHANT.

ensue *v.* RESULT, follow, develop, proceed, succeed, emerge, stem, arise, derive, issue; occur, happen, take place, come next/after, transpire, supervene; *literary* come to pass.

ensure *v.* MAKE SURE, make certain, see to it; check, confirm, establish, verify, secure, guarantee, assure.

entail *v.* INVOLVE, necessitate, require, need, demand, call for; mean, imply; cause, produce, result in, lead to, give rise to, occasion.

enter *v.* **1** GO IN/INTO, come in/into, get in/into, set foot in, cross the threshold of, gain access to, infiltrate, access. **2** PENETRATE, pierce, puncture, perforate. **3** GET INVOLVED IN, join, throw oneself into, engage in, embark on, take up; participate in, take part in, play a part/role in, contribute to. **4** REACH, move into, get to, begin,

start, commence. **5** ☞ RECORD *v.* 1.
—OPPOSITES: leave.

enterprise *n.* **1** UNDERTAKING, endeavour, venture, exercise, activity, operation, task, business, proceeding; project, scheme, plan, program, campaign. **2** ☞ INITIATIVE. **3** ☞ BUSINESS 3.

enterprising *adj.* RESOURCEFUL, entrepreneurial, imaginative, ingenious, inventive, creative; quick-witted, clever, bright, sharp, sharp-witted; enthusiastic, dynamic, proactive, ambitious, energetic; bold, daring, courageous, adventurous; *informal* go-ahead, take-charge, self-motivated.
—OPPOSITES: unimaginative.

entertain *v.* **1** AMUSE, divert, delight, please, charm, cheer, interest; engage, occupy, absorb, engross. **2** RECEIVE, host, play host/hostess to; wine and dine, feast, cater for, feed, treat, welcome, fete. **3** ☞ CONTEMPLATE 2.
—OPPOSITES: bore, reject.

entertaining *adj.* ☞ ENJOYABLE.

entertainment *n.* **1** AMUSEMENT, pleasure, leisure, recreation, relaxation, fun, enjoyment, interest, diversion. **2** SHOW, performance, presentation, production, extravaganza, spectacle.

enthralling *adj.* ☞ ENCHANTING.

enthusiasm *n.* **1** EAGERNESS, keenness, ardour, fervour, passion, zeal, zest, gusto, energy, verve, vigour, vehemence, fire, spirit, avidity; wholeheartedness, commitment, willingness, devotion, earnestness; *informal* get-up-and-go. **2** INTEREST, passion,

obsession, mania; inclination, preference, penchant, predilection, fancy; pastime, hobby, recreation, pursuit.
—OPPOSITES: apathy.

enthusiast *n.* ☞ FAN.

enthusiastic *adj.* ☞ EAGER 1.

entice *v.* ☞ TEMPT 1.

entire *adj.* **1** WHOLE, complete, total, full; undivided, uncut, unabridged. **2** INTACT, unbroken, undamaged, unscathed, unspoiled, perfect, in one piece. **3** ABSOLUTE, total, utter, out-and-out, wholehearted; unqualified, unreserved, outright.
—OPPOSITES: partial, broken.

entirely *adv.* ABSOLUTELY, completely, totally, wholly, utterly, quite; altogether, in every respect, thoroughly, downright.

entitle *v.* **1** QUALIFY, make eligible, authorize, allow, permit; enable, empower. **2** TITLE, name, call, label, designate, dub.

entity *n.* BEING, creature, individual, organism, life form; person; body, object, article, thing.

entourage *n.* RETINUE, escort, cortège, train, suite; court, staff, bodyguard; attendants, companions, retainers; *informal* posse.

entrails *pl. n.* INTESTINES, bowels, guts, viscera, internal organs, vital organs; offal; *informal* innards.

entrance *n.* **1** ENTRY, way in, entryway, entranceway, access, approach; door, portal, gate, opening; foyer, lobby. **2** APPEARANCE, arrival, entry, ingress, coming. **3** ☞ ADMISSION 1.
—OPPOSITES: exit, departure.

entrant *n.* ☞ COMPETITOR 1.

entreat *v.* IMPLORE, beg, plead with, pray, ask, request; bid, enjoin, appeal to, call on, petition, solicit, importune, beseech.

entrenched *adj.* INGRAINED, established, confirmed, fixed, firm, deep-seated, deep-rooted; unshakeable, indelible, ineradicable, inexorable.

entrepreneur *n.* BUSINESSMAN/ WOMAN, enterpriser, speculator, tycoon, magnate, mogul; dealer, trader; promoter, impresario; *informal* wheeler-dealer, go-getter.

envelop *v.* SURROUND, cover, enfold, engulf, encircle, encompass, cocoon, sheathe, swathe, enclose; cloak, screen, shield, veil, shroud.

envelope *n.* WRAPPER, wrapping, sleeve, cover, covering, casing.

enviable *adj.* DESIRABLE, desired, favoured, sought-after, admirable, covetable, attractive; fortunate, lucky; *informal* to die for.

envious *adj.* JEALOUS, covetous, desirous; grudging, begrudging, resentful; bitter.

environment *n.* **1** HABITAT, territory, domain; surroundings, conditions. **2** SITUATION, setting, milieu, background, backdrop, scene, location; context, framework; sphere, world, realm; ambience, atmosphere.

envisage *v.* ☞ IMAGINE 1.

envy *n.* **1** JEALOUSY, covetousness; resentment, bitterness, discontent. **2** FINEST, best, pride, top, cream, jewel, flower.
▸ *v.* BE ENVIOUS OF, be jealous of; begrudge.

ephemeral *adj.* TRANSITORY, transient, fleeting, passing, short-lived, momentary, brief, short; temporary, impermanent, short-term.
—OPPOSITES: permanent.

epidemic *n.* OUTBREAK, plague, rash, wave, increase, rise.
▸ *adj.* RIFE, rampant, widespread, wide-ranging, extensive, pervasive.

episode *n.* **1** INCIDENT, event, occurrence, happening; occasion, experience, adventure, exploit; matter, affair, thing; interlude, chapter. **2** INSTALMENT, chapter, passage; part, portion, section, component.

epitome *n.* PERSONIFICATION, embodiment, incarnation, paragon; essence, quintessence, archetype, paradigm; exemplar, model, soul, example.

epoch *n.* ERA, age, period, time, span, stage; eon.

equal *adj.* **1** IDENTICAL, uniform, alike, like, the same, equivalent; matching, even, comparable, similar, corresponding; commensurate (with), on a par (with). **2** ☞ EQUITABLE. **3** EVENLY MATCHED, even, balanced, level; on a par, on an equal footing.
—OPPOSITES: different, discriminatory.
▸ *n.* EQUIVALENT, peer, fellow, coequal, like; counterpart, match, parallel.
▸ *v.* **1** BE EQUAL TO, be equivalent to, be the same as; come to, amount to, make, total, add up to. **2** MATCH, reach, parallel, be level with, measure up to.

equality *n.* **1** FAIRNESS, equal rights, equal opportunities, equity, egalitarianism; impartiality, even-handedness; justice. **2** PARITY, similarity, comparability, correspondence; likeness, resemblance; uniformity, evenness, balance.

equanimity *n.* COMPOSURE, calm, level-headedness, self-possession, presence of mind; serenity, tranquility, phlegm, imperturbability, equilibrium, equability, placidness, placidity; poise, assurance, self-confidence, aplomb, sang-froid, nerve; *informal* cool, unflappability.

equilibrium *n.* **1** BALANCE, symmetry, equipoise, parity, equality; stability. **2** ☞ EQUANIMITY.

equip *v.* **1** PROVIDE, furnish, supply, issue, stock, provision, arm, endow. **2** PREPARE, qualify, suit, ready.

equitable *adj.* FAIR, just, impartial, even-handed, unbiased, unprejudiced, egalitarian; disinterested, objective, neutral, non-partisan, open-minded.
—OPPOSITES: unfair.

equivalent *adj.* EQUAL, identical; similar, comparable, corresponding, analogous, commensurate, parallel, synonymous.
▸ *n.* ☞ EQUAL *n.*

equivocal *adj.* AMBIGUOUS, indefinite, noncommittal, vague, imprecise, inexact, inexplicit, hazy; unclear, cryptic, enigmatic; ambivalent, uncertain, unsure, indecisive.
—OPPOSITES: definite.

equivocate v. PREVARICATE, be evasive, be noncommittal, be vague, be ambiguous, dodge the question, beat around the bush, hedge, pussyfoot around; vacillate, waver; temporize, hesitate, hem and haw.

era n. EPOCH, age, period, phase, time, span, eon; generation.

eradicate v. ☞ ELIMINATE.

erase v. DELETE, rub out, wipe off, blot out, cancel; efface, expunge, excise, remove, obliterate, eliminate, cut.

erect adj. **1** UPRIGHT, straight, vertical; standing. **2** ENGORGED, enlarged, swollen, tumescent; hard, stiff.
▸ v. BUILD, construct, put up; assemble, put together, fabricate.

erode v. WEAR AWAY/DOWN, abrade, grind down, crumble; weather; eat away at, dissolve, corrode, rot, decay.

erotic adj. ☞ SEXY 2.

err v. MAKE A MISTAKE, be wrong, be in error, be mistaken, blunder, be incorrect, miscalculate, get it wrong; sin, lapse; informal slip up, screw up, drop the ball, bark up the wrong tree.

errand n. TASK, job, chore, assignment; collection, delivery; mission, undertaking.

erratic adj. UNPREDICTABLE, inconsistent, changeable, variable, inconstant, irregular, fitful, unstable, turbulent, unsettled, changing, varying, fluctuating, mutable; unreliable, undependable, volatile, spasmodic, mercurial, capricious, fickle, temperamental, moody.
—OPPOSITES: consistent.

error n. ☞ MISTAKE n.

erupt v. **1** EMIT LAVA, flare up; explode. **2** BREAK OUT, flare up, start suddenly; ensue, arise, happen; appear.

escapade n. EXPLOIT, stunt, caper, antic(s), spree, shenanigan, adventure, venture; incident, occurrence, event.

escape v. **1** RUN AWAY/OFF, get out, break out, break free, bolt, flee, take flight, make off, take off, abscond, make a run for it, slip away; informal cut and run, fly the coop. **2** GET AWAY FROM, escape from, elude, avoid; dodge, sidestep, circumvent. **3** LEAK, seep, discharge, emanate, issue, spew (out).
▸ n. **1** GETAWAY, breakout, jailbreak, bolt, flight. **2** AVOIDANCE OF, evasion of, circumvention of. **3** LEAK, leakage, spill, seepage, discharge.

eschew v. ABSTAIN FROM, refrain from, give up, forgo, renounce; relinquish, reject, disavow, abandon; forswear, abjure.

escort n. **1** GUARD, bodyguard, protector, attendant, chaperone; entourage, retinue, cortège. **2** COMPANION, partner; hostess, geisha; informal date.
▸ v. CONDUCT, accompany, guide, lead, usher, shepherd.

esoteric adj. ABSTRUSE, obscure, arcane, recherché, rarefied, recondite, abstract; enigmatic, inscrutable, cryptic.

essential adj. **1** CRUCIAL, necessary, key, vital, indispensable, important, all-important, critical, imperative, mandatory, compulsory, obligatory; urgent, pressing, high-priority. **2** BASIC, inherent, fundamental, quintessential, intrinsic, underlying, characteristic, innate, primary, elementary, elemental; central, pivotal.

establish v. **1** SET UP, start, initiate, institute, form, found, create, inaugurate, organize, develop; build, construct, install. **2** PROVE, demonstrate, show, indicate, signal, exhibit, manifest, attest to, evidence, determine, confirm, verify, certify, substantiate.

established adj. **1** ACCEPTED, traditional, orthodox, habitual, set, fixed, official; usual, customary, familiar, routine, typical, conventional. **2** WELL-KNOWN, recognized, esteemed, respected, famous, renowned.

establishment n. **1** FOUNDATION, institution, formation, inception, creation, installation; inauguration. **2** ☞ BUSINESS 3. **3** INSTITUTION, place, premises, institute. **4** THE AUTHORITIES, the powers that be, the system, the ruling class; informal Big Brother.

estate n. **1** PROPERTY, grounds, garden(s), park, land(s). **2** PLANTATION, farm, holding; forest, vineyard; ranch. **3** ☞ ASSET 2.

esteem n. RESPECT, admiration, acclaim, approbation, appreciation; estimation.
▶ v. RESPECT, ADMIRE, value, regard, acclaim, appreciate, like, prize, treasure, favour, revere.

estimate v. CALCULATE ROUGHLY, approximate, guess; evaluate,

judge, gauge, reckon, rate, determine; consider, deem; informal guesstimate, ballpark.
▶ n. **1** ROUGH CALCULATION, approximation, estimation, rough guess; costing, quotation, valuation, evaluation; informal guesstimate. **2** ☞ ESTIMATION 2.

estimation n. **1** ☞ ESTIMATE n. 1. **2** ASSESSMENT, evaluation, judgment; esteem, opinion, view.

estrangement n. ALIENATION, antagonism, antipathy, disaffection, hostility; parting, separation.

estuary n. (RIVER) MOUTH, delta, (BC) slough ♣.

eternal adj. **1** EVERLASTING, never-ending, endless, perpetual, undying, immortal, abiding, permanent, enduring, infinite. **2** ☞ CONTINUOUS.

eternity n. **1** EVER, all time, perpetuity. **2** THE AFTERLIFE, everlasting life, life after death, the hereafter; heaven, paradise, immortality.

ethereal adj. DELICATE, exquisite, dainty, elegant, graceful; fragile, airy, fine, subtle.

ethical adj. MORAL, right-minded, principled, irreproachable; righteous, high-minded, virtuous, good, correct; honourable, reputable, respectable, noble, worthy.

euphoric adj. ☞ ECSTATIC.

evacuate v. **1** REMOVE, clear, move out, take away. **2** LEAVE, vacate, abandon, desert, move out of, quit, flee, depart from, escape from. **3** EXPEL, eject, discharge, excrete, void, empty (out), purge.

evade v. ELUDE, avoid, dodge, escape (from), sidestep; lose, leave behind, shake off, be evasive about; *informal* duck.

evaluate v. ☞ ASSESS 1.

evaporate v. 1 VAPORIZE, become vapour, volatilize. 2 DRY UP/OUT, dehydrate, desiccate, dehumidify. 3 END, pass (away), wear off, vanish, fade, disappear.

evasive adj. EQUIVOCAL, prevaricating, elusive, ambiguous, noncommittal, vague, inexplicit, unclear; roundabout, indirect.

even adj. 1 FLAT, smooth, uniform; unbroken; level, plane. 2 UNIFORM, constant, steady, stable, consistent, regular. 3 EQUAL, the same, identical, similar, comparable. 4 TIED, drawn, level, all square, balanced; neck and neck. 5 EVEN-TEMPERED, balanced, stable, equable, placid, calm, composed, poised, cool, relaxed, easy, imperturbable; *informal* laid-back, unflappable.
—OPPOSITES: bumpy, irregular, unequal, moody.
▸ v. 1 FLATTEN, level, smooth, plane; make uniform. 2 EQUALIZE, make equal, balance, square; standardize.
▸ adv. 1 STILL, yet, more, all the more. 2 INDEED, you could say, veritably, in truth, actually, or rather.
☐ **get even** HAVE ONE'S REVENGE, avenge oneself, take vengeance, even the score, settle the score, hit back, reciprocate, retaliate; *literary* be revenged.

evening n. NIGHT, end of day, close of day; twilight, dusk, nightfall, sunset, sundown.

event n. 1 OCCURRENCE, happening, proceeding, incident, affair, circumstance, occasion, phenomenon; function, gathering; *informal* bash.
2 ☞ COMPETITION 1.

eventful adj. BUSY, action-packed, full, lively, active, hectic, strenuous; momentous, significant, important, historic.
—OPPOSITES: dull.

eventual adj. FINAL, ultimate, concluding, closing, end; resulting, ensuing, consequent, subsequent.

eventually adv. IN THE END, in due course, by and by, in time, finally, at last; ultimately, in the long run, one day, some day, sometime, sooner or later.

everlasting adj. ☞ ETERNAL 1.

everywhere adv. ALL OVER, all around, ubiquitously, far and wide, near and far, high and low; worldwide, globally; *informal* all over the place, everyplace, all over the map.

evict v. EXPEL, eject, oust, remove, dislodge, turn out, throw out, drive out; dispossess, banish, exile, cast out, discharge, force out, dismiss, fire, axe, sack; chuck out, kick out, boot out, bounce, give someone the (old) heave-ho, throw someone out on their ear, turf (out), get rid of, give someone the gate, give someone the bum's rush, give someone their walking papers, give someone their marching orders, send packing, show someone the door.

evidence n. 1 PROOF, confirmation, verification, substantiation, corroboration, affirmation. **2** TESTIMONY, statement, declaration, avowal, submission, claim; *Law* deposition, affidavit. **3** SIGNS, indications, marks, traces; manifestation.

evident *adj.* OBVIOUS, apparent, noticeable, conspicuous, perceptible, visible, discernible, clear, clear-cut, plain, manifest, patent; palpable, tangible, marked, striking, blatant; unmistakable, indisputable.

evil *adj.* **1** WICKED, bad, wrong, immoral, sinful, foul, vile, dishonourable, corrupt, iniquitous, depraved, reprobate, villainous, nefarious, vicious, malicious; malevolent, sinister, demonic, devilish, diabolical, fiendish, dark; monstrous, shocking, despicable, atrocious, heinous, odious, contemptible, horrible, execrable; *informal* lowdown, dirty. **2** CRUEL, mischievous, pernicious, malignant, malign, baleful, vicious; destructive, harmful, hurtful, injurious, detrimental, deleterious, inimical, bad, ruinous. **3** UNPLEASANT, disagreeable, nasty, horrible, foul, disgusting, filthy, vile, noxious. —OPPOSITES: good, beneficial, pleasant.

▸ *n.* **1** WICKEDNESS, bad, badness, wrongdoing, sin, immorality, vice, iniquity, degeneracy, corruption, depravity, villainy, malevolence; *formal* turpitude. **2** HARM, pain, misery, sorrow, suffering, trouble, disaster, misfortune, catastrophe, affliction, woe, hardship.

evoke *v.* BRING TO MIND, conjure up, summon (up), invoke, elicit, induce, kindle, stimulate, stir up, awaken, arouse, call forth; recall, echo, capture.

evolution *n.* **1** DEVELOPMENT, advancement, growth, rise, progress; expansion; transformation. **2** DARWINISM, natural selection.

evolve *v.* DEVELOP, progress, advance; mature, grow, expand, spread; alter, change, transform, adapt, metamorphose; *humorous* transmogrify.

exacerbate *v.* AGGRAVATE, worsen, inflame, compound; intensify, increase, heighten, magnify. —OPPOSITES: reduce.

exact *adj.* **1** PRECISE, accurate, correct, faithful, close, true; literal, strict, perfect, impeccable; explicit, detailed, minute, meticulous, thorough; *informal* bang on. **2** CAREFUL, meticulous, painstaking, punctilious, conscientious, scrupulous, exacting; methodical, organized, orderly. —OPPOSITES: inaccurate, careless. ▸ *v.* DEMAND, require, insist on, request, impose, expect; extract, compel, force, squeeze.

exacting *adj.* ☞ DEMANDING.

exaggerate *v.* OVERSTATE, overemphasize, overestimate, magnify, amplify, aggrandize, inflate; embellish, enhance, embroider, elaborate, overplay, overdo, dramatize; hyperbolize, stretch the truth. —OPPOSITES: understate.

exalted *adj.* **1** HIGH, high-ranking, elevated, superior, lofty, eminent, prestigious, illustrious, distinguished, esteemed. **2** ELATED, exultant, jubilant, joyful, rapturous, ecstatic, blissful, transported, happy, exuberant, exhilarated.

examination *n.* **1** ☞ INSPECTION. **2** TEST, exam, quiz, assessment. **3** *(Law)* INTERROGATION, questioning, cross-examination, inquisition.

examine *v.* **1** ☞ INSPECT. **2** *(Law)* INTERROGATE, question, quiz, cross-examine; *informal* grill, pump.

example *n.* **1** SPECIMEN, sample, exemplar, instance, case, illustration. **2** PRECEDENT, lead, model, pattern, ideal, standard, template, paradigm.

exasperate *v.* INFURIATE, incense, anger, annoy, irritate, madden, enrage, antagonize, provoke, irk, vex, get on someone's nerves; *informal* aggravate, rile, bug.

exasperating *adj.* ☞ INFURIATING.

excavate *v.* DIG (OUT), bore, hollow out, scoop out; burrow, tunnel; uncover, reveal, unearth.

exceed *v.* **1** BE MORE THAN, be greater than, be over, go beyond, overreach, top. **2** SURPASS, outdo, outstrip, outshine, outclass, transcend, beat, better, eclipse, overshadow.

exceedingly *adv.* EXTREMELY, exceptionally, especially, tremendously, very, really, truly, awfully, seriously, totally.

excellence *n.* DISTINCTION, quality, superiority, brilliance, greatness, merit, calibre, eminence, pre-eminence, supremacy; skill, mastery.

excellent *adj.* VERY GOOD, superb, outstanding, exceptional, marvellous, wonderful, magnificent; pre-eminent, perfect, matchless, unbeatable, peerless, supreme, first-rate, first-class, superlative, splendid, fine, beautiful, exemplary, admirable, exquisite, glorious, impressive, noteworthy, remarkable, choice, consummate, crack, premier, prime, unequalled, unparalleled, unrivalled, unsurpassed; *informal* A1, ace, great, super, terrific, fantastic, fabulous, top-notch, smashing, brilliant, wicked, awesome, bang-up, blue-chip, blue-ribbon, high-quality, killer, second to none, skookum, top-grade, top-quality, tremendous, amazing, sensational.
—OPPOSITES: inferior.

except *prep.* EXCLUDING, not including, excepting, omitting, not counting, but, besides, apart from, aside from, barring, bar, other than; with the exception of, save for.
—OPPOSITES: including.

exception *n.* ANOMALY, irregularity, deviation, special case, peculiarity, abnormality, oddity; misfit, aberration.
□ **take exception** OBJECT, take offence, take umbrage, demur, disagree; resent, oppose; *informal* kick up a fuss.

exceptional *adj.* **1** UNUSUAL, uncommon, abnormal, atypical, extraordinary, out of the ordinary, rare, unprecedented, unexpected, surprising; *informal* freaky. **2** OUTSTANDING, extraordinary, remarkable, special, excellent, phenomenal, prodigious; unequalled, unparalleled, unsurpassed, peerless, matchless, nonpareil, first-rate, first-class. —OPPOSITES: normal, average.

excerpt *n.* EXTRACT, part, section, piece, portion, snippet, clip, bit, sample, citation, quotation.

excess *n.* **1** ☞ SURPLUS. **2** REMAINDER, rest, residue; leftovers, remnants. **3** OVERINDULGENCE, intemperance, immoderation, profligacy, lavishness, extravagance, decadence, self-indulgence. —OPPOSITES: lack, restraint.
▸ *adj.* SURPLUS, superfluous, redundant, unwanted, unneeded, excessive; extra.

excessive *adj.* **1** IMMODERATE, intemperate, imprudent, overindulgent, unrestrained, uncontrolled, lavish, extravagant; superfluous. **2** EXORBITANT, extortionate, unreasonable, outrageous, undue, uncalled for, extreme, inordinate, unwarranted, disproportionate.

exchange *n.* **1** INTERCHANGE, trade, trading, swapping, traffic. **2** CONVERSATION, dialogue, talk, discussion, chat.
▸ *v.* TRADE, swap, switch, change, interchange.

excise *v.* **1** CUT OUT/OFF/AWAY, take out, extract, remove. **2** DELETE, cross out/through, strike out, score out, cancel; erase, scratch.

excitable *adj.* TEMPERAMENTAL, mercurial, volatile, emotional, sensitive, high-strung, unstable, nervous, tense, edgy, jumpy, twitchy, uneasy, neurotic; *informal* uptight, wired.

excite *v.* **1** THRILL, exhilarate, animate, enliven, rouse, stir, stimulate, galvanize, electrify, inspirit. **2** AROUSE (SEXUALLY), stimulate, titillate, inflame; *informal* turn someone on. **3** PROVOKE, stir up, rouse, arouse, kindle, trigger (off), incite, cause.

excited *adj.* **1** THRILLED, exhilarated, animated, enlivened, electrified, enthusiastic; *informal* fired up. **2** (SEXUALLY) AROUSED, stimulated, titillated, inflamed; *informal* turned on, horny.

excitement *n.* **1** THRILL, pleasure, delight, joy. **2** EXHILARATION, elation, animation, enthusiasm, eagerness, anticipation.

exciting *adj.* ☞ THRILLING.

exclaim *v.* CRY (OUT), declare, blurt out; call (out), shout, yell.

exclamation *n.* CRY, call, shout, yell, interjection.

exclude *v.* **1** KEEP OUT, deny access to, shut out, debar, disbar, bar, ban, prohibit, ostracize. **2** ELIMINATE, rule out, preclude, foreclose; *formal* except. **3** BE EXCLUSIVE OF, not include, omit, leave out.

exclusive *adj.* **1** SELECT, chic, high-class, elite, fashionable, stylish, elegant, premier, grade A; expensive, upscale, upmarket; *informal* posh, ritzy. **2** NOT INCLUDING, excluding, leaving out, omitting, excepting.
▸ *n.* SCOOP, exposé, special.

excrement *n.* FECES, excreta, stools, droppings; waste matter, ordure, dung; *informal* poo, poop.

excrete *v.* EXPEL, pass, void, discharge, eject, evacuate; defecate, urinate.

excruciating *adj.* AGONIZING, severe, acute, intense, violent, racking, searing, piercing, stabbing, raging; unbearable, unendurable.

excusable *adj.* FORGIVABLE, pardonable, defensible, justifiable; venial.

excuse *v.* 1 FORGIVE, pardon, absolve, exonerate, acquit, make allowances for; *informal* let someone off (the hook); *formal* exculpate. 2 JUSTIFY, defend, condone, vindicate, tolerate, sanction. 3 LET OFF, release, relieve, free.
—OPPOSITES: condemn.
▶ *n.* 1 JUSTIFICATION, defence, reason, explanation, mitigation, vindication. 2 PRETEXT, pretense; *informal* story, alibi. 3 (*informal*) TRAVESTY OF, mockery; *informal* apology for.

execute *v.* 1 PUT TO DEATH, kill. 2 CARRY OUT, accomplish, bring off/about, achieve, complete, perform, engineer, conduct; *informal* pull off.

exemplar *n.* EPITOME, paragon, ideal, textbook example, embodiment, essence, quintessence; paradigm, model.

exemplary *adj.* PERFECT, ideal, model, faultless, flawless, impeccable, irreproachable; excellent, outstanding, admirable, commendable, laudable.
—OPPOSITES: deplorable.

exemplify *v.* 1 TYPIFY, epitomize, represent, be representative of, symbolize. 2 ILLUSTRATE, demonstrate.

exempt *v.* EXCUSE, free, release, exclude, give/grant immunity, spare, absolve; *informal* grandfather.

exercise *n.* 1 PHYSICAL ACTIVITY, a workout, sports, games, aerobics, calisthenics. 2 TASK, piece of work, problem, assignment, activity. 3 USE, utilization, employment; practice, application.
▶ *v.* 1 WORK OUT, do exercises, train. 2 USE, employ, make use of, utilize; practise, apply.

exert *v.* 1 BRING TO BEAR, apply, exercise, employ, use, utilize, deploy. 2 STRIVE, try hard, make an/every effort, endeavour, do one's best/utmost, give one's all, push oneself, drive oneself, work hard; *informal* go all out.

exhaust *v.* 1 TIRE (OUT), wear out, overtire, fatigue, weary, drain; *informal* do in, wipe out, tucker out. 2 USE UP, run through, go through, consume, finish, deplete, spend, empty, drain, run out of; *informal* blow.

exhausting *adj.* TIRING, wearying, taxing, fatiguing, wearing, enervating, draining; arduous, strenuous, onerous, demanding, gruelling.

exhaustion *n.* EXTREME TIREDNESS, fatigue, weariness, burnout.

exhaustive *adj.* COMPREHENSIVE, all-inclusive, complete, full, full-scale, encyclopedic, sweeping, thorough, in-depth.
—OPPOSITES: perfunctory.

exhibit *v.* 1 PUT ON DISPLAY/SHOW, display, show, showcase; set out, lay out, array, arrange. 2 SHOW, reveal, display, manifest; express,

indicate, demonstrate, present; evince.
▶ *n.* ☞ EXHIBITION 1.

exhibition *n.* **1** (PUBLIC) DISPLAY, show, showing, presentation, demonstration, exposition, showcase, exhibit. **2** DISPLAY, show, demonstration, manifestation, expression.

exhilarate *v.* THRILL, excite, intoxicate, elate, delight, enliven, animate, invigorate, energize, stimulate.

exhilaration *n.* ELATION, euphoria, exultation, exaltation, joy, happiness, delight, joyousness, jubilation, rapture, ecstasy, bliss.

exhort *v.* URGE, encourage, call on, enjoin, charge, press; bid, appeal to, entreat, implore, beg; *literary* beseech.

exile *n.* **1** BANISHMENT, expulsion, expatriation, deportation. **2** ÉMIGRÉ, expatriate; displaced person, refugee, deportee; *informal* expat, DP.
▶ *v.* EXPEL, banish, expatriate, deport, drive out, throw out, outlaw.

exist *v.* **1** LIVE, be alive, be living; be. **2** PREVAIL, occur, happen, be found, be in existence; be the case. **3** SURVIVE, subsist, live, support oneself; manage, make do, get by, scrape by, make ends meet.

exit *n.* **1** WAY OUT, door, egress; doorway, gate, gateway, portal. **2** DEPARTURE, leaving, withdrawal, going, decamping, retreat; flight, exodus, escape.
▶ *v.* LEAVE, go (out), depart, withdraw, retreat.

exonerate *v.* ABSOLVE, clear, acquit, find innocent, discharge, release; excuse, exempt; *formal* exculpate.

exorbitant *adj.* EXTORTIONATE, excessive, prohibitive, outrageous, unreasonable, inflated, unconscionable, huge, enormous; *informal* steep.
—OPPOSITES: reasonable.

exotic *adj.* **1** FOREIGN, non-native, faraway, tropical. **2** STRIKING, colourful, eye-catching, flamboyant; unusual, unconventional, out of the ordinary, extravagant, outlandish.

expand *v.* **1** GROW, become/make larger, become/make bigger, enlarge; extend, augment, broaden, widen, lengthen, stretch, thicken; develop, diversify, build up; branch out. **2** ELABORATE ON, enlarge on, go into detail about, flesh out, develop.
—OPPOSITES: shrink, contract.

expanse *n.* AREA, stretch, sweep, tract, swathe, belt, region; sea, carpet, blanket, sheet.

expansive *adj.* **1** WIDE-RANGING, extensive, sweeping, broad, wide, comprehensive, thorough. **2** COMMUNICATIVE, forthcoming, sociable, friendly, outgoing, affable, chatty, talkative, garrulous, effusive, loquacious, voluble.

expect *v.* **1** SUPPOSE, presume, think, believe, imagine, assume, surmise; *informal* guess, reckon, figure. **2** ANTICIPATE, await, look for, hope for; contemplate, bank on; predict, forecast, envisage, envision. **3** REQUIRE, ask for, call for, want, insist on, demand.

expectant *adj.* **1** EAGER, excited, agog, hopeful; in suspense, on tenterhooks. **2** PREGNANT; *informal* expecting, preggers; *dated* in the family way.

expectation *n.* **1** SUPPOSITION, assumption, presumption, conjecture, surmise, calculation, prediction. **2** ANTICIPATION, expectancy, eagerness, excitement, suspense.

expedient *adj.* CONVENIENT, advantageous, useful, of use, beneficial, helpful; practical, pragmatic, politic, prudent.
▸ *n.* MEASURE, means, method, stratagem, scheme, plan, move, tactic, manoeuvre, device, ploy.

expeditious *adj.* SPEEDY, swift, quick, rapid, fast, brisk, efficient; prompt, punctual, immediate, instant.
—OPPOSITES: slow.

expel *v.* **1** ☞ EVICT. **2** BANISH, exile, deport, expatriate.

expend *v.* SPEND, pay out, disburse, dole out, dish out, waste; *informal* fork out, shell out, lay out, cough up.

expendable *adj.* **1** DISPENSABLE, replaceable, non-essential, unnecessary, superfluous. **2** DISPOSABLE, throwaway, single-use.

expensive *adj.* COSTLY, dear, high-priced, overpriced, exorbitant, extortionate, excessive, prohibitive, unreasonable; *informal* steep, pricey, stiff.
—OPPOSITES: cheap, economical.

experience *n.* **1** SKILL, (practical) knowledge, understanding; background, record, history; maturity; *informal* know-how. **2** INCIDENT, occurrence, event, happening, episode; adventure, exploit, escapade. **3** INVOLVEMENT IN, participation in, contact with, acquaintance with, exposure to.
▸ *v.* UNDERGO, encounter, meet, come into contact with, come across, come up against, face, be faced with.

experienced *adj.* KNOWLEDGEABLE, skilful, skilled, expert, accomplished, adept, adroit, master, consummate; proficient, trained, competent; seasoned, practised, mature, veteran, sophisticated, worldly (wise), battle-scarred, battle-weary, established, habituated, hardened, well versed.

experiment *n.* TEST, investigation, trial, examination, observation; assessment, evaluation, appraisal, analysis, study.
▸ *v.* CONDUCT EXPERIMENTS, carry out trials/tests, conduct research; test, trial, do tests on, try out, assess.

experimental *adj.* **1** EXPLORATORY, trial, test, pilot; speculative, conjectural, hypothetical, tentative, preliminary. **2** INNOVATIVE, innovatory, new, original, radical, avant-garde, cutting-edge, alternative.

expert *n.* SPECIALIST, authority, pundit; adept, maestro, virtuoso, (past) master, wizard; connoisseur, aficionado; *informal* ace, buff, pro, whiz.
▸ *adj.* SKILFUL, skilled, adept, accomplished, talented, fine; master, masterly, brilliant,

virtuoso, magnificent, outstanding, great, exceptional, excellent, first-class, first-rate, superb; proficient, good, able, capable, experienced, practised, knowledgeable.
—OPPOSITES: incompetent.

expiate v. ATONE FOR, make amends for, make up for, pay for, redress, make good.

expire v. 1 RUN OUT, become invalid, become void, lapse; END, finish, stop, terminate. 2 ☞ DIE 1. 3 BREATHE OUT, exhale.

explain v. 1 DESCRIBE, make clear/ plain, spell out, put into words; elucidate, expound, explicate, clarify; gloss, interpret. 2 ACCOUNT FOR, give an explanation for, give a reason for; justify, vindicate, legitimize.

explanation n. 1 CLARIFICATION, simplification; description, report, statement; elucidation, exposition, explication; gloss, interpretation, commentary, exegesis. 2 ACCOUNT, reason; justification, excuse, alibi, defence, vindication.

explanatory adj. EXPLAINING, descriptive, describing, illustrative, interpretive.

expletive n. ☞ OBSCENITY.

explicit adj. 1 CLEAR, plain, straightforward, crystal clear; precise, exact, specific, unequivocal, unambiguous; detailed, comprehensive, exhaustive. 2 GRAPHIC, uncensored, candid, full-frontal, hard-core.
—OPPOSITES: vague.

explode v. 1 BLOW UP, detonate, go off, burst (apart), fly apart,

erupt. 2 LOSE ONE'S TEMPER, blow up, get angry, become enraged, get mad; informal fly off the handle, hit the roof, go ballistic, see red, go postal. 3 INCREASE SUDDENLY/ RAPIDLY, mushroom, snowball, escalate, multiply.
—OPPOSITES: defuse.

exploit v. 1 UTILIZE, harness, use, make use of, capitalize on. 2 TAKE ADVANTAGE OF, abuse, impose on, treat unfairly, misuse, ill-treat; informal walk (all) over.
▶ n. FEAT, deed, act, adventure, stunt, escapade; achievement.

explore v. 1 INVESTIGATE, look into, consider; examine, research, survey, scrutinize, study, review; informal check out. 2 TRAVEL, tour, range over; survey, take a look at, inspect.

explosion n. 1 DETONATION, eruption, blowing up. 2 OUTBURST, flare-up, outbreak, eruption, storm, rush, surge; fit, paroxysm, attack.

explosive adj. 1 VOLATILE, inflammable, flammable, combustible, incendiary. 2 FIERY, stormy, violent, angry, hotheaded. 3 TENSE, (highly) charged, overwrought; dangerous, perilous, hazardous, sensitive, delicate, unstable, volatile.

exponent n. ADVOCATE, supporter, proponent, upholder, backer, defender, champion; promoter, propagandist, campaigner, fighter, crusader, enthusiast, apologist.

expose v. 1 REVEAL, uncover, lay bare; make vulnerable, subject, lay open. 2 INTRODUCE TO, make aware of, familiarize with,

acquaint with. **3** UNCOVER, reveal, unveil, unmask, detect, find out; discover, bring to light, make known; denounce, condemn.
—OPPOSITES: cover.

expository *adj.* EXPLANATORY, descriptive, describing, explicative, interpretative.

expression *n.* **1** UTTERANCE, voicing, pronouncement, declaration, articulation, assertion; dissemination, circulation, communication, promulgation. **2** INDICATION, demonstration, show, exhibition, token; communication, illustration, revelation. **3** LOOK, appearance, air, manner, countenance, mien. **4** IDIOM, phrase; proverb, saying, adage, maxim, axiom.

expressionless *adj.*
1 INSCRUTABLE, deadpan, poker-faced; blank, vacant, emotionless, unemotional, inexpressive; glazed, fixed, stony, wooden, impassive, lifeless. **2** DULL, dry, toneless, monotonous, boring, tedious, wooden.

expressive *adj.* **1** ELOQUENT, meaningful, demonstrative, suggestive. **2** EMOTIONAL, passionate, poignant, moving, stirring, evocative, powerful.

expressly *adv.* **1** EXPLICITLY, clearly, directly, plainly, distinctly, unambiguously, unequivocally; absolutely.
2 SOLELY, specifically, particularly, specially, exclusively, explicitly.

extend *v.* **1** EXPAND, enlarge, increase, make larger/bigger; lengthen, widen, broaden; augment, supplement, add to, enhance, develop. **2** CONTINUE,

carry on, run on, stretch (out), reach, lead. **3** PROLONG, lengthen, increase; stretch out, protract, spin out. **4** HOLD OUT, reach out, hold forth; offer, give, outstretch, proffer. **5** OFFER, proffer, give, grant, bestow, accord.
—OPPOSITES: reduce, narrow, shorten.

extensive *adj.* **1** LARGE, large-scale, sizeable, substantial, considerable, ample, expansive, great, vast. **2** COMPREHENSIVE, thorough, exhaustive; broad, wide, wide-ranging, catholic.

extent *n.* **1** AREA, size, expanse, length. **2** DEGREE, scale, level, magnitude, scope.

exterior *adj.* OUTER, outside, outermost, outward, external.
—OPPOSITES: interior.
▸ *n.* OUTSIDE, outer surface, outward appearance, facade.

exterminate *v.* KILL, dispatch; slaughter, butcher, massacre, wipe out, eliminate, eradicate, annihilate; *informal* do away with, bump off, ice.

extinguish *v.* **1** DOUSE, put out, stamp out, smother, beat out. **2** DESTROY, end, finish off, put an end to, terminate.
—OPPOSITES: light.

extol *v.* PRAISE ENTHUSIASTICALLY, acclaim, exalt, eulogize, rave about; *formal* laud.
—OPPOSITES: criticize.

extra *adj.* ADDITIONAL, more, added, supplementary, further, auxiliary, ancillary, subsidiary, secondary, bonus.
▸ *adv.* **1** ☞ EXTREMELY. **2** IN ADDITION, additionally, as well, also, too, besides.

extract *v.* **1** TAKE OUT, draw out, pull out, remove, withdraw; free, release, extricate. **2** WREST, exact, wring, screw, squeeze, extort. **3** SQUEEZE OUT, express, press out, obtain.
▸ *n.* **1** EXCERPT, passage, citation, quotation. **2** DECOCTION, distillation, distillate, abstraction, concentrate, essence, juice.

extraordinary *adj.* REMARKABLE, exceptional, amazing, astonishing, astounding, sensational, stunning, incredible, unbelievable, phenomenal; striking, outstanding, momentous, impressive, singular, memorable, unforgettable, noteworthy, unusual, uncommon, rare, surprising, fantastic, terrific, tremendous, stupendous, great, incomparable, peerless, supreme, unparalleled, fabulous, jaw-dropping, marvellous, splendid, staggering, awesome, magnificent, out of the ordinary, out of this world, unprecedented, wonderful, wondrous.

extravagant *adj.* **1** SPENDTHRIFT, profligate, improvident, wasteful, prodigal, lavish. **2** EXPENSIVE, costly, lavish, high-priced; exorbitant, extortionate, unreasonable; valuable, precious; *informal* pricey. **3** EXCESSIVE, immoderate, exaggerated, gushing, unrestrained, effusive, fulsome.
—OPPOSITES: thrifty, cheap.

extreme *adj.* **1** UTMOST, very great, greatest (possible), maximum, maximal, highest, supreme, great, acute, enormous, severe, high, exceptional, extraordinary. **2** ☞ DRASTIC. **3** RADICAL, extremist, immoderate, fanatical, revolutionary, rebel, subversive, militant.
—OPPOSITES: slight, moderate.
▸ *n.* **1** OPPOSITE, antithesis. **2** LIMIT, extremity, maximum, height, top, zenith, peak.

extremely *adv.* VERY, exceedingly, exceptionally, especially, extraordinarily, in the extreme, tremendously, immensely, vastly, hugely, intensely, acutely, singularly, uncommonly, unusually, decidedly, particularly, supremely, highly, remarkably, really, truly, mightily; *informal* terrifically, awfully, terribly, damn, real, mighty, darned.

exuberant *adj.* **1** EBULLIENT, buoyant, cheerful, jaunty, lighthearted, high-spirited, exhilarated, excited, elated, exultant, euphoric, joyful, cheery, merry, jubilant, energetic, lively, vigorous; *informal* bubbly, bouncy, chipper, chirpy. **2** LUXURIANT, lush, rich, dense, thick, abundant, profuse.
—OPPOSITES: gloomy, restrained.

exultant *adj.* JUBILANT, thrilled, triumphant, delighted, exhilarated, happy, overjoyed, joyous, joyful, gleeful, ecstatic, euphoric, elated, rapturous.

eyesore *n.* MONSTROSITY, blot, mess, scar, blight, disfigurement, blemish, ugly sight.

eyewitness *n.* OBSERVER, onlooker, witness, bystander, spectator, watcher, viewer, passerby, gawker, beholder.

Ff

fabric *n.* **1** CLOTH, material, textile, tissue. **2** STRUCTURE, infrastructure, framework, frame, form, composition, construction, foundations.

fabricate *v.* **1** CONCOCT, make up, dream up, invent, trump up; formulate, hatch; *informal* cook up. **2** MAKE, create, manufacture, produce; construct, build, assemble, put together, form, fashion.

fabulous *adj.* **1** ☞ WONDERFUL. **2** ☞ MYTHICAL.

face *n.* **1** COUNTENANCE, physiognomy, features; (facial) expression, look, appearance, air, manner, bearing, mien; *informal* mug, phiz; puss; *literary* visage. **2** ☞ FROWN *n.* **3** (OUTWARD) APPEARANCE, aspect, nature, image; facade, exterior, appearance.
▶ *v.* **1** LOOK OUT ON, front on to, look towards, be facing, look over/across, overlook, give on to, be opposite (to). **2** ☞ ACCEPT *v.* 5. **3** BE CONFRONTED BY, be faced with, encounter, experience, come into contact with, come up against. **4** BESET, worry, distress, trouble, bother, confront; harass, oppress, vex, irritate, exasperate, strain, stress, tax; torment, plague, blight, bedevil, curse; *formal* discommode.
□ **on the face of it** ☞ OUTWARDLY.

facet *n.* **1** SURFACE, face, side, plane. **2** ASPECT, feature, side, dimension, characteristic, detail, point, ingredient, strand; component, constituent, element.

facetious *adj.* FLIPPANT, flip, glib, frivolous, tongue-in-cheek, ironic, sardonic, joking, jokey, jocular, playful, sportive, teasing, mischievous; witty, amusing, funny, droll, comic, comical, lighthearted, jocose.
—OPPOSITES: serious.

facile *adj.* **1** ☞ SIMPLISTIC. **2** EFFORTLESS, easy, undemanding, painless, trouble-free.

facility *n.* **1** ☞ BATHROOM. **2** AMENITY, resource, service, advantage, convenience, benefit. **3** ESTABLISHMENT, centre, place, station, location, premises. **4** ☞ APTITUDE.

fact *n.* **1** REALITY, actuality, certainty; truth, verity, gospel. **2** DETAIL, particular, item, specific, element, point, factor, feature, characteristic, ingredient, circumstance, aspect, facet; (**facts**) information.
—OPPOSITES: lie, fiction.
□ **in fact** ☞ ACTUALLY.

faction *n.* CLIQUE, coterie, caucus, cabal, bloc, camp, group, grouping, lobby, sector, section, wing, arm, branch, set; ginger group, pressure group.

factor *n.* ELEMENT, part, component, ingredient, strand, constituent, point, detail, item, feature, facet, aspect, characteristic, consideration, influence, circumstance.

factual *adj.* TRUTHFUL, true, accurate, authentic, historical, genuine, fact-based; true-to-life, correct, exact, honest, faithful, literal, verbatim, word for word, well-documented, unbiased, objective, unvarnished; *formal* veridical.
—OPPOSITES: fictitious.

fad *n.* ☞ CRAZE.

fade *v.* **1** BECOME PALE, become bleached, become washed out, lose colour, discolour; grow dull, grow dim, lose lustre. **2** (GROW) DIM, grow faint, fail, dwindle, die away, wane, disappear, vanish, decline, melt away; *literary* evanesce.
—OPPOSITES: brighten, increase.

fail *v.* **1** BE UNSUCCESSFUL, not succeed, fall through, fall flat, collapse, founder, backfire, meet with disaster, come to nothing/ naught, do badly, lose money, be a disaster; *informal* flop, bomb, tank, come a cropper, bite the dust, blow up in someone's face. **2** FLUNK, botch, be unsuccessful in, not pass; not make the grade. **3** LET DOWN, disappoint; desert, abandon, betray, be disloyal to; *literary* forsake. **4** FADE, dim, die away, wane, disappear, vanish. **5** ☞ DETERIORATE 1. **6** ☞ GO BANKRUPT at BANKRUPT.
—OPPOSITES: succeed, pass, thrive.

failing *n.* ☞ SHORTCOMING.

failure *n.* **1** LACK OF SUCCESS, non-fulfillment, defeat, collapse, foundering. **2** FIASCO, debacle, catastrophe, disaster; *informal* flop, megaflop, washout, dead loss, snafu, clinker, clunker, dud, flame-out, no-go, bomb, bust, dog, turkey. **3** LOSER, underachiever, ne'er-do-well, disappointment; *informal* no-hoper, dead loss, dud, writeoff. **4** NEGLIGENCE, dereliction; omission, oversight.
—OPPOSITES: success.

faint *adj.* **1** INDISTINCT, vague, unclear, indefinite, ill-defined, imperceptible, unobtrusive; pale, light, faded. **2** QUIET, muted, muffled, stifled; feeble, weak, whispered, murmured, indistinct; low, soft, gentle. **3** SLIGHT, slender, slim, small, tiny, negligible, remote, vague, unlikely, improbable; *informal* minuscule. **4** DIZZY, giddy, light-headed, unsteady; *informal* woozy.
—OPPOSITES: clear, loud, strong.
▶ *v.* PASS OUT, lose consciousness, black out, keel over, swoon; *informal* flake out, conk out, zonk out, go out like a light.

fair¹ *adj.* **1** JUST, equitable, honest, upright, honourable, trustworthy; impartial, unbiased, unprejudiced, non-partisan, neutral, even-handed; lawful, legal, legitimate; *informal* legit, on the level; on the up and up. **2** ☞ SUNNY. **3** BLOND(E), yellowish, golden, flaxen, light, pale; fair-haired, light-haired. **4** (*archaic*) ☞ BEAUTIFUL. **5** ☞ ADEQUATE 2.
—OPPOSITES: inclement, unfavourable, dark.
☐ **fair and square** HONESTLY,

fairly, without cheating, without foul play, by the book; lawfully, legally, legitimately; *informal* on the level, on the up and up.

fair² *n.* **1** CARNIVAL, exhibition, ex✦, festival. **2** EXHIBITION, exhibit, display, show, presentation, exposition.

fairly *adv.* **1** JUSTLY, equitably, impartially, without bias, without prejudice, even-handedly; lawfully, legally, legitimately, by the book; equally, the same. **2** REASONABLY, passably, tolerably, adequately, moderately, quite, relatively, comparatively; *informal* pretty, kind of, kinda, sort of.

faith *n.* **1** TRUST, belief, confidence, conviction; optimism, hopefulness, hope. **2** ☞ RELIGION.
—OPPOSITES: mistrust.

faithful *adj.* **1** LOYAL, constant, true, devoted, true-blue, unswerving, fast, firm, staunch, steadfast, dedicated, committed; trusty, trustworthy, dependable, reliable. **2** ACCURATE, precise, exact, errorless, unerring, faultless, true, close, strict; realistic, authentic; *informal* on the mark, on the nail, bang on, on the money.
—OPPOSITES: inaccurate.

fake *n.* **1** FORGERY, counterfeit, copy, sham, fraud, hoax, imitation, mock-up, dummy, reproduction, knock-off; *informal* phony, rip-off, dupe. **2** ☞ FRAUD 3.
▶ *adj.* COUNTERFEIT, forged, fraudulent, sham, imitation, pirate(d), false, bogus; invalid, inauthentic; *informal* phony, dud; artificial, synthetic, simulated, reproduction, replica, ersatz, faux,

man-made, dummy, mock; *informal* pretend, pseudo; feigned, faked, put-on, pretended, spurious, assumed, invented, affected; unconvincing.
—OPPOSITES: genuine, authentic.

fall *v.* **1** DROP, descend, come down, go down; plummet, plunge, sink, dive, tumble; cascade. **2** TOPPLE OVER, tumble over, keel over, fall down/over, go head over heels, go headlong, collapse, take a spill, pitch forward; trip (over), stumble, slip; *informal* face plant. **3** DECREASE, decline, diminish, fall off, drop off, lessen, dwindle; subside, recede; plummet, plunge, slump, sink; depreciate, cheapen, devalue; *informal* nosedive, crash. **4** SURRENDER, yield, submit, give in, capitulate, succumb; be taken by, be defeated by, be conquered by. **5** OCCUR, take place, happen, come about; arise; *literary* come to pass.
—OPPOSITES: rise, flood, increase, flourish.
▶ *n.* **1** TUMBLE, trip, spill, topple, slip; collapse; *informal* nosedive, face plant, header, cropper. **2** DECLINE, fall-off, drop, decrease, cut, dip, reduction, downswing; plummet, plunge, slump; *informal* nosedive, toboggan slide✦, crash. **3** DOWNFALL, collapse, ruin, ruination, failure, decline, deterioration, degeneration; destruction, overthrow, demise.
—OPPOSITES: increase, rise, ascent.
☐ **fall apart** ☞ DISINTEGRATE. **fall back** ☞ RETREAT V. **fall behind** ☞ LAG. **fall for 1** FALL IN LOVE WITH, become infatuated with, lose one's heart to, take a fancy to, be

smitten by, be attracted to; *informal* have the hots for. **2** BE DECEIVED BY, be duped by; *informal* go for, buy. **fall out** ☞ ARGUE 2. **fall through** FAIL, be unsuccessful, come to nothing, miscarry, abort, go awry, collapse, founder, come to grief; *informal* fizzle out, flop, fold.

fallacious *adj.* ☞ FALSE 1.
—OPPOSITES: correct.

fallacy *n.* ☞ MISCONCEPTION.

fallout *n.* ☞ AFTERMATH.

fallow *adj.* UNCULTIVATED, unplowed, untilled, unplanted, unsown; unused, dormant, resting, empty, bare.
—OPPOSITES: cultivated.

false *adj.* **1** INCORRECT, untrue, wrong, erroneous, fallacious, flawed, distorted, inaccurate, mistaken, imprecise; untruthful, fictitious, concocted, fabricated, invented, made up, trumped up, unfounded, uncorroborated, groundless, spurious, specious; counterfeit, bogus, forged, fraudulent, phony. **2** FAITHLESS, unfaithful, disloyal, untrue, inconstant, treacherous, traitorous, two-faced, double-crossing, deceitful, dishonest, duplicitous, untrustworthy, unreliable; untruthful; *informal* cheating, two-timing; *literary* perfidious. **3** ☞ FAKE *adj.*
—OPPOSITES: correct, truthful, faithful, genuine.

falsehood *n.* ☞ LIE¹ *n.*
—OPPOSITES: truth.

falsify *v.* FORGE, fake, counterfeit, fabricate; alter, change, doctor, tamper with, interfere with,

massage, fudge, manipulate, fiddle, adulterate, corrupt, misrepresent, misreport, distort, warp, embellish, embroider; *informal* cook.

falter *v.* HESITATE, delay, drag one's feet, stall; waver, vacillate, waffle, be indecisive, be irresolute, blow hot and cold, hem and haw; *informal* sit on the fence, dilly-dally, shilly-shally.

fame *n.* RENOWN, celebrity, stardom, popularity, prominence; note, distinction, esteem, importance, account, consequence, greatness, eminence, prestige, stature, repute; notoriety, infamy.
—OPPOSITES: obscurity.

famed *adj.* ☞ FAMOUS.

familiar *adj.* **1** WELL-KNOWN, widely known, recognized, accustomed, established, popular; common, commonplace, everyday, day-to-day, ordinary, habitual, usual, customary, routine, standard, stock, mundane, run-of-the-mill; *literary* wonted. **2** ACQUAINTED, conversant, versed, knowledgeable, well-informed; skilled, proficient; at home with, no stranger to, au fait/courant with, up on, abreast, up-to-date, up to speed. **3** ☞ BOLD 2.

family *n.* **1** RELATIVES, relations, (next of) kin, kinsfolk, kindred, kith and kin, flesh and blood, nearest and dearest, people, connections; parents; clan, tribe; *informal* folk(s). **2** ☞ ANCESTRY. **3** CHILDREN, little ones, youngsters; offspring, progeny, descendants, scions, heirs; brood; *Law* issue; *informal* kids.

famished *adj.* ☞ HUNGRY 1.

famous *adj.* WELL KNOWN, prominent, famed, popular; renowned, noted, eminent, distinguished, esteemed, celebrated, respected; of distinction, of repute; illustrious, acclaimed, great, legendary, lionized; notorious, infamous.
—OPPOSITES: unknown.

fan *n.* ENTHUSIAST, devotee, admirer, lover; supporter, follower, disciple, adherent, zealot; expert, connoisseur, aficionado; *informal* buff, bum, fiend, freak, nut, addict, junkie, fanatic, groupie.

fanatic *n.* 1 ☞ ZEALOT. 2 (*informal*) ☞ FAN.

fanatical *adj.* 1 ZEALOUS, extremist, extreme, militant, dogmatic, radical, diehard; intolerant, single-minded, blinkered, inflexible, uncompromising, hard-core. 2 ENTHUSIASTIC, eager, keen, fervent, ardent, passionate; obsessive, obsessed, fixated, compulsive; *informal* wild, gung-ho, nuts, crazy, hog-wild.

fanciful *adj.* 1 FANTASTIC, far-fetched, unbelievable, extravagant; ridiculous, absurd, preposterous; imaginary, made-up, make-believe, mythical, fabulous; *informal* tall, hard to swallow. 2 IMAGINATIVE, inventive; whimsical, impractical, dreamy, quixotic.
—OPPOSITES: literal, practical.

fancy *v.* 1 ☞ LIKE¹ 1. 2 THINK, imagine, believe; reckon.
▶ *adj.* ELABORATE, ornate, ornamental, decorative, adorned, embellished, intricate; ostentatious, showy, flamboyant; luxurious, lavish, extravagant, expensive; *informal* flashy, jazzy, ritzy, snazzy, posh, classy; fancy-schmancy.
—OPPOSITES: plain.
▶ *n.* LIKING, taste, inclination; urge, wish, whim, impulse, notion, whimsy, hankering, craving; *informal* yen, itch.

fantastic *adj.* 1 ☞ WONDERFUL. 2 INCREDIBLE, unbelievable, unthinkable, implausible, improbable, unlikely, doubtful, dubious; strange, peculiar, odd, queer, weird, eccentric; visionary, romantic; *informal* crazy, cockeyed, off the wall. See also FANCIFUL. 3 ☞ WEIRD 2.
—OPPOSITES: rational, ordinary.

fantasy *n.* 1 IMAGINATION, fancy, invention, make-believe; creativity, vision; daydreaming, reverie. 2 DREAM, daydream, pipe dream, fanciful notion, wish; fond hope, chimera, delusion, illusion.
—OPPOSITES: realism.

far *adv.* 1 A LONG WAY, a great distance, a good way; afar. 2 ☞ GREATLY.
—OPPOSITES: near.
▶ *adj.* DISTANT, faraway, far-off, remote, out of the way, far-flung, outlying.
—OPPOSITES: near.
☐ **by far** BY A GREAT AMOUNT, by a good deal, by a long way, by a mile, far and away; undoubtedly, without doubt, without question, positively, absolutely, easily; significantly, substantially, appreciably, much. **far and near/**

wide ☞ EVERYWHERE. **go far** ☞ SUCCEED 1.

farcical *adj.* ☞ PREPOSTEROUS.

farewell *excl.* ☞ GOODBYE.

▶ *n.* GOODBYE, valediction, adieu; leave-taking, parting, departure; send-off.

far-fetched *adj.* IMPROBABLE, unlikely, implausible, unconvincing, dubious, doubtful, incredible, unbelievable, unthinkable; contrived, fanciful, unrealistic, ridiculous, absurd, preposterous, beyond belief, hard to believe, highly unlikely, impossible, inconceivable, unimaginable; *informal* hard to swallow, fishy.
—OPPOSITES: likely.

fascinate *v.* INTEREST, captivate, engross, absorb, enchant, enthrall, hold spellbound, entrance, bewitch, transfix, rivet, mesmerize, engage, compel, grip; lure, tempt, entice, draw; charm, attract, intrigue, divert, entertain.
—OPPOSITES: bore.

fashion *n.* **1** VOGUE, trend, craze, rage, mania, fad; style, look; tendency, convention, custom, practice; *informal* thing. **2** CLOTHES, clothing design, couture; *informal* the rag trade. **3** MANNER, way, method, mode, style; system, approach.

▶ *v.* CONSTRUCT, build, make, manufacture, fabricate, tailor, contrive; cast, shape, form, mould, sculpt; forge, hew.
□ **in fashion** ☞ FASHIONABLE.

fashionable *adj.* IN VOGUE, voguish, in fashion, au courant, popular, up-to-date, up-to-the-minute, latest, modern, contemporary, all the rage, du jour, modish, à la mode, trendsetting; stylish, chic; chi-chi, dapper, dashing, elegant, high-fashion, smart, snappy, sophisticated, trim; *informal* trendy, classy, with it, cool, in, the in thing, hot, big, hip, happening, now, sharp, swish, groovy, funky, snazzy, spiffy, tony, kicky, natty, fly.

fast *adj.* **1** SPEEDY, quick, swift, rapid; fast-moving, fast-paced, high-speed, turbo, sporty; accelerated, express, blistering, breakneck, pell-mell; hasty, hurried; *informal* nippy, zippy, blinding, supersonic. **2** SECURE, fastened, tight, firm, closed, shut, to; immovable, unbudgeable. **3** ☞ LOYAL. **4** ☞ PROMISCUOUS.
—OPPOSITES: slow, loose, temporary, chaste.

▶ *adv.* **1** QUICKLY, rapidly, swiftly, speedily, briskly, at speed, at full tilt/speed; hastily, hurriedly, in a hurry, post-haste, pell-mell; like a shot, like a flash, on the double, at the speed of light, at a gallop/run; *informal* lickety-split, PDQ (pretty damn quick), nippily, like (greased) lightning, hell for leather, like mad, like the wind, like a bat out of hell; *literary* apace. **2** SECURELY, firmly, immovably, fixedly.
—OPPOSITES: slowly.

fasten *v.* **1** BOLT, lock, secure, make fast, chain, seal, close, shut. **2** ATTACH, fix, affix, clip, pin, tack; stick, bond, join. **3** TIE (UP), bind, tether, truss, fetter, lash, hitch, anchor, strap, rope. **4** BUTTON (UP), zip (up), do up, close.

—OPPOSITES: unlock, remove, open, untie, undo.

fastidious *adj.* SCRUPULOUS, punctilious, painstaking, meticulous; perfectionist, fussy, finicky, over-particular; critical, overcritical, hypercritical, hard to please, exacting, demanding, difficult; *informal* pernickety, persnickety, nitpicking, choosy, picky, anal.
—OPPOSITES: lax.

fat *adj.* **1** PLUMP, stout, overweight, large, big, chubby, portly, flabby, paunchy, pot-bellied, beer-bellied, meaty, of ample proportions, heavy-set; obese, corpulent, fleshy, gross; *informal* plus-sized, corn-fed, dumpy, full-figured, rotund, well-rounded, zaftig, big-boned, tubby, roly-poly, well-upholstered, beefy, porky, blubbery, chunky, pudgy, bloated, broad in the beam, bulky, heavy, well padded. **2** THICK, big, large, sizeable, considerable, chunky, bulky, substantial; long; generous.
▶ *n.* FATTY TISSUE, adipose tissue, cellulite; blubber; flab.

fatal *adj.* **1** DEADLY, lethal, mortal, death-dealing; terminal, incurable, untreatable, inoperable, malignant; *literary* deathly. **2** ☞ DISASTROUS.
—OPPOSITES: harmless, beneficial.

fatalism *n.* PASSIVE ACCEPTANCE, resignation, stoicism.

fatality *n.* DEATH, casualty, mortality, victim; fatal accident.

fate *n.* **1** DESTINY, providence, the stars, chance, luck, serendipity, fortune, kismet, karma. **2** FUTURE, destiny, outcome, end, lot.
▶ *v.* BE PREDESTINED, be

preordained, be destined, be meant, be doomed; be sure, be certain, be bound, be guaranteed.

fateful *adj.* **1** DECISIVE, critical, crucial, pivotal; momentous, important, key, significant, historic, portentous.
2 ☞ DISASTROUS.
—OPPOSITES: unimportant.

father *n.* **1** DAD; daddy, pop, pa, dada, papa; old man, patriarch, paterfamilias. **2** ORIGINATOR, initiator, founder, inventor, creator, maker, author, architect.
—RELATED: paternal, patri-.

fathom *v.* UNDERSTAND, comprehend, work out, make sense of, grasp, divine, puzzle out, get to the bottom of; interpret, decipher, decode; *informal* make head or tail of, crack, twig, suss (out).

fatigue *n.* TIREDNESS, weariness, exhaustion, enervation, prostration.
—OPPOSITES: energy.
▶ *v.* TIRE (OUT), exhaust, wear out, drain, weary, wash out, overtire, prostrate, enervate; *informal* knock out, take it out of, do in, whack, poop, bush, wear to a frazzle.
—OPPOSITES: invigorate.

fatuous *adj.* SILLY, foolish, stupid, inane, idiotic, vacuous, asinine; pointless, senseless, ridiculous, ludicrous, absurd; *informal* dumb, daft.
—OPPOSITES: sensible.

fault *n.* **1** DEFECT, failing, imperfection, flaw, blemish, shortcoming, weakness, frailty, foible, vice; error, mistake, inaccuracy; *informal* glitch.
2 MISDEED, wrongdoing, offence,

misdemeanour, misconduct,
indiscretion, peccadillo,
transgression.
—OPPOSITES: merit, strength.
▶ *v.* FIND FAULT WITH, criticize,
attack, censure, condemn,
reproach; complain about, quibble
about, moan about; *informal* knock,
slam, gripe about, beef about,
pick holes in.

faultless *adj.* ☞ PERFECT 3.
—OPPOSITES: flawed.

faulty *adj.* **1** ☞ DEFECTIVE 1.
2 DEFECTIVE, flawed, unsound,
inaccurate, incorrect, erroneous,
fallacious, wrong.
—RELATED: dys-.
—OPPOSITES: working, sound.

faux pas *n.* GAFFE, blunder,
mistake, indiscretion,
impropriety, solecism, barbarism;
informal boo-boo, blooper.

favour *n.* **1** SERVICE, good turn,
good deed, (act of) kindness,
courtesy. **2** APPROVAL, approbation,
goodwill, kindness, benevolence.
3 PATRONAGE, backing, support,
assistance.
—OPPOSITES: disservice,
disapproval.
▶ *v.* **1** PREFER, lean towards;
approve (of), advocate, support.
2 BENEFIT, advantage, help, assist,
aid. **3** OBLIGE, honour, gratify,
humour, indulge.
—OPPOSITES: oppose, dislike,
hinder.

favourable *adj.* **1** APPROVING,
commendatory, complimentary,
flattering, glowing, enthusiastic;
good, pleasing, positive; *informal*
rave. **2** ADVANTAGEOUS, beneficial,
in one's favour, good, right,
suitable, fitting, appropriate;

propitious, auspicious, promising,
encouraging. **3** POSITIVE,
affirmative, assenting, agreeing,
approving; encouraging,
reassuring, supportive.
—OPPOSITES: critical,
disadvantageous, negative.

favourite *adj.* BEST-LOVED, most-
liked, favoured, dearest;
preferred, chosen, choice.
▶ *n.* (FIRST) CHOICE, pick,
preference, pet, darling, the apple
of one's eye.

fear *n.* **1** TERROR, fright,
fearfulness, horror, alarm, panic,
agitation, trepidation, dread,
consternation, dismay, distress,
disquiet; anxiety, worry, angst,
unease, uneasiness, apprehension,
apprehensiveness, nervousness,
nerves, perturbation, foreboding;
informal the creeps, the shivers, the
jitters, the willies, the heebie-
jeebies, jitteriness, butterflies (in
the stomach). **2** PHOBIA, aversion,
antipathy, dread, bugbear, bogey,
nightmare, horror, terror; anxiety,
neurosis; *informal* hang-up.
3 ☞ LIKELIHOOD.
▶ *v.* **1** BE AFRAID OF, be fearful of, be
scared of, be apprehensive of,
dread, live in fear of, be terrified
of; be anxious about, worry about,
feel apprehensive about.
2 SUSPECT, have a (sneaking)
suspicion, be inclined to think, be
afraid, have a hunch, think it
likely.

fearful *adj.* **1** AFRAID, frightened,
scared (stiff), scared to death,
terrified, petrified; alarmed,
panicky, nervous, tense,
apprehensive, uneasy, worried

(sick), anxious; *informal* jittery, jumpy. **2** ☞ HORRIBLE 1.

fearless *adj.* BOLD, brave, courageous, intrepid, valiant, valorous, gallant, plucky, lion-hearted, heroic, daring, audacious, indomitable, doughty; unafraid, undaunted, unflinching; *informal* gutsy, spunky, ballsy, feisty. —OPPOSITES: timid, cowardly.

fearsome *adj.* ☞ FRIGHTENING.

feasible *adj.* PRACTICABLE, practical, workable, achievable, attainable, realizable, viable, realistic, sensible, reasonable, within reason; suitable, possible, expedient, doable, within the bounds/realms of possibility. —OPPOSITES: impractical.

feast *n.* **1** BANQUET, celebration meal, (*Que.*) mechoui❖, lavish dinner, (*Atlantic*) scoff❖; treat, entertainment; revels, festivities; *informal* blowout, spread, bunfight. **2** TREAT, delight, joy, pleasure.
▶ *v.* GORGE ON, dine on, eat one's fill of, overindulge in, binge on; eat, devour, consume, partake of; *informal* stuff one's face with, stuff oneself with, pig out on, chow down on.

feat *n.* ACHIEVEMENT, accomplishment, attainment, coup, triumph; undertaking, enterprise, venture, operation, exercise, endeavour, effort, performance, exploit.

feature *n.* **1** CHARACTERISTIC, attribute, quality, property, trait, hallmark, trademark; aspect, facet, factor, ingredient, component, element, theme; peculiarity, idiosyncrasy, quirk. **2** ☞ FACE 1. **3** ARTICLE, piece, item,

report, story, column, review, commentary, write-up.
▶ *v.* **1** PRESENT, promote, make a feature of, give prominence to, focus attention on, spotlight, highlight. **2** STAR, appear, participate, play a part.

federation *n.* CONFEDERATION, confederacy, league; combination, alliance, coalition, union, syndicate, guild, consortium, partnership, co-operative, association, amalgamation; *informal* federacy.

feeble *adj.* **1** WEAK, weakly, weakened, frail, infirm, ill, delicate, sickly, ailing, unwell, poorly, enfeebled, enervated, debilitated, incapacitated, decrepit. **2** INEFFECTIVE, ineffectual, inadequate, unconvincing, implausible, unsatisfactory, poor, weak, flimsy. **3** ☞ SPINELESS. **4** FAINT, dim, weak, pale, soft, subdued, muted. —OPPOSITES: strong, brave.

feed *v.* **1** NOURISH, give food to, provide (food) for, cater for, cook for. **2** GRAZE, browse, crop, pasture; eat, consume food, chow down. **3** STRENGTHEN, fortify, support, bolster, reinforce, boost, fuel, encourage. **4** SUPPLY, provide, give, deliver, furnish, issue.

feel *v.* **1** TOUCH, stroke, caress, fondle, finger, thumb, handle. **2** PERCEIVE, sense, detect, discern, notice, be aware of, be conscious of. **3** EXPERIENCE, undergo, go through, bear, endure, suffer. **4** GROPE, fumble, scrabble, pick. **5** BELIEVE, think, consider (it right), be of the opinion, hold, maintain, judge; *informal* reckon, figure.

▶ *n.* **1** TEXTURE, surface, finish; weight, thickness, consistency, quality. **2** APTITUDE, knack, flair, bent, talent, gift, faculty, ability.
□**feel for** ☞ PITY *v.*

feeling *n.* **1** SENSATION, sense, consciousness. **2** (SNEAKING) SUSPICION, notion, inkling, hunch, funny feeling, feeling in one's bones, fancy, idea; presentiment, premonition; *informal* gut feeling. **3** LOVE, affection, fondness; passion, ardour, desire. **4** ☞ COMPASSION. **5** OPINION, belief, view, impression, intuition, instinct, hunch, estimation, guess. **6** ATMOSPHERE, ambience, aura, air, feel, mood, impression, spirit, quality, flavour; *informal* vibrations, vibes.

feign *v.* SIMULATE, fake, sham, affect, give the appearance of, make a pretense of; pretend, bluff, play-act.

felicitous *adj.* **1** ☞ APT 1.
2 FAVOURABLE, advantageous, good, pleasing.
—OPPOSITES: inappropriate, unfortunate.

fellow *n.* **1** (*informal*) MAN, boy; person, individual, soul; *informal* guy, character, customer, joe, devil, bastard, (esp. *Atlantic*) buddy♣; chap, dude, hombre; *dated* dog. **2** COMPANION, friend, comrade, partner, associate, co-worker, colleague; peer, equal, contemporary, confrere; *informal* chum, pal, buddy.
□**fellow feeling** ☞ COMPASSION.

felon *n.* ☞ CRIMINAL *n.*

feminine *adj.* **1** WOMANLY, ladylike, girlish, girly.
2 EFFEMINATE, womanish, unmanly, effete, epicene; *informal* sissy, wimpy.
—OPPOSITES: masculine, manly.

fence *n.* BARRIER, paling, railing, fencing, enclosure, barricade, stockade, palisade, fenceline.
▶ *v.* **1** ENCLOSE, surround, circumscribe, encircle, circle, encompass; *archaic* compass.
2 CONFINE, pen in, coop up, shut in/up, separate off; enclose, surround, corral.

fend
□**fend for oneself** TAKE CARE OF ONESELF, look after oneself, provide for oneself, manage (by oneself), cope alone, stand on one's own two feet.

ferment *v.* **1** UNDERGO FERMENTATION, brew; effervesce, fizz, foam, froth. **2** ☞ CAUSE *v.*
▶ *n.* FEVER, furor, frenzy, tumult, storm, rumpus; *informal* kerfuffle. See also TURMOIL.

ferocious *adj.* **1** FIERCE, savage, wild, predatory, aggressive, dangerous. **2** BRUTAL, vicious, violent, bloody, barbaric, savage, sadistic, ruthless, cruel, merciless, heartless, bloodthirsty, murderous; *literary* fell. **3** (*informal*) ☞ INTENSE 1.
—OPPOSITES: gentle, mild.

ferry *n.* PASSENGER BOAT/SHIP, ferry boat, car ferry; ship, boat, vessel.
▶ *v.* TRANSPORT, convey, carry, ship, run, take, bring, shuttle.

fertile *adj.* **1** FECUND, fruitful, productive, high-yielding, rich, lush. **2** PRODUCTIVE, prolific. See also IMAGINATIVE.
—OPPOSITES: barren.

fertilize *v.* **1** FEED, mulch, compost, manure, dress, top-dress.

2 POLLINATE, cross-pollinate, cross-fertilize, fecundate.

fertilizer *n.* MANURE, plant food, compost, (*Maritimes*) mussel mud✤, dressing, top dressing, dung.

fervent *adj.* IMPASSIONED, passionate, intense, vehement, ardent, sincere, fervid, fierce, heartfelt, devoted; enthusiastic, zealous, fanatical, wholehearted, avid, eager, keen, committed, dedicated, devout, card-carrying, vigorous, energetic; *informal* mad keen; *literary* perfervid.
—OPPOSITES: apathetic.

fervour *n.* PASSION, ardour, intensity, zeal, vehemence, emotion, warmth, earnestness, avidity, eagerness, keenness, enthusiasm, excitement, animation, vigour, energy, fire, spirit, zest, fervency, gusto.
—OPPOSITES: apathy.

fester *v.* **1** ☞ ROT. **2** RANKLE, eat/gnaw away, brew, smoulder.

festival *n.* **1** FAIR, carnival, fiesta, jamboree, fete, gala, celebrations, festivities, fest. **2** HOLY DAY, feast day, saint's day, commemoration, day of observance.

festive *adj.* JOLLY, merry, joyous, joyful, happy, jovial, lighthearted, cheerful, jubilant, convivial, high-spirited, mirthful, uproarious; celebratory, holiday, carnival; Christmassy.

festoon *n.* GARLAND, chain, lei, swathe, swag, loop.
▶ *v.* ☞ DECORATE 1.

fetch *v.* **1** (GO AND) GET, go for, call for, summon, pick up, collect, bring, carry, convey, deliver, transport, ferry. **2** SELL FOR, bring in, raise, realize, yield, cost, be priced at; *informal* go for.

fetching *adj.* ☞ PRETTY *adj.*

fetish *n.* FIXATION, obsession, compulsion, mania; weakness, fancy, fascination, fad; *informal* thing, hang-up.

feud *n.* VENDETTA, conflict; rivalry, hostility, enmity, strife, discord; quarrel, argument, falling-out.

fever *n.* **1** FEVERISHNESS, (high) temperature, febrility, pyrexia. **2** FERMENT, frenzy, furor; ecstasy, rapture.
—RELATED: febrile.

feverish *adj.* **1** FEBRILE, fevered, hot, burning. **2** FRENZIED, frenetic, hectic, agitated, excited, restless, nervous, worked up, overwrought, frantic, furious, hysterical, wild, uncontrolled, unrestrained.

few *adj.* **1** NOT MANY, hardly any, scarcely any; a small number of, a small amount of, one or two, a handful of; little. **2** SCARCE, scant, meagre, insufficient, in short supply, infrequent, uncommon, rare; negligible.
—OPPOSITES: many, plentiful.

fiasco *n.* FAILURE, disaster, catastrophe, debacle, shambles, farce, mess, wreck; *informal* flop, washout, snafu.
—OPPOSITES: success.

fibre *n.* **1** THREAD, strand, filament; *technical* fibril. **2** ROUGHAGE, bulk.

fickle *adj.* CAPRICIOUS, changeable, variable, volatile, mercurial, mutable; inconstant, undependable, unsteady, unfaithful, faithless, flighty, giddy, skittish; fair-weather.
—OPPOSITES: constant.

fiction *n.* FABRICATION, invention, lies, fibs, untruth, falsehood, fantasy, nonsense.
—OPPOSITES: fact.

fictional *adj.* FICTITIOUS, fictive, invented, imaginary, made up, make-believe, unreal, fabricated, mythical.
—OPPOSITES: real.

fictitious *adj.* 1 FALSE, fake, fabricated, sham; bogus, spurious, assumed, affected, adopted, feigned, invented, made up; *informal* pretend, phony. 2 ☞ FICTIONAL.
—OPPOSITES: genuine.

fidelity *n.* 1 ☞ LOYALTY. 2 ACCURACY, exactness, precision, preciseness, correctness; strictness, closeness, faithfulness, authenticity.
—OPPOSITES: disloyalty.

fidget *v.* 1 MOVE RESTLESSLY, wriggle, squirm, twitch, jiggle, shuffle, be agitated, be jittery. 2 PLAY, fuss, toy, twiddle, fool about/around, fiddle.

fidgety *adj.* ☞ RESTLESS 1.

field *n.* 1 MEADOW, pasture, paddock, grassland, pasture land; *literary* lea, sward; *archaic* glebe. 2 PITCH, ground, sports field, playing field. 3 AREA, sphere, discipline, province, department, domain, sector, branch, subject. 4 SCOPE, range, sweep, reach, extent.
▶ *v.* DEAL WITH, handle, cope with, answer, reply to, respond to.

fiend *n.* 1 DEMON, devil, evil spirit, bogie; *informal* spook. 2 VILLAIN, beast, brute, barbarian, monster, ogre, sadist, evildoer, swine. 3 ☞ ADDICT.

fiendish *adj.* 1 WICKED, cruel, vicious, evil, malevolent, villainous; brutal, savage, barbaric, barbarous, inhuman, murderous, ruthless, merciless; *dated* dastardly. 2 ☞ CUNNING *adj.*

fierce *adj.* 1 FEROCIOUS, savage, vicious, aggressive. 2 AGGRESSIVE, cutthroat, competitive; keen, intense, strong, relentless. 3 ☞ FERVENT.
—OPPOSITES: gentle, mild.

fight *v.* 1 BRAWL, exchange blows, attack/assault each other, hit/punch each other; struggle, grapple, wrestle; *informal* scrap, roughhouse. 2 ENGAGE IN, wage, conduct, prosecute, undertake; meet, clash, skirmish. 3 QUARREL, argue, row, bicker, squabble, fall out, have a row/fight, wrangle, be at odds, disagree, differ, have words, bandy words, be at each other's throats, be at loggerheads; *informal* scrap. 4 OPPOSE, contest, contend with, confront, challenge, combat, dispute, quarrel/argue with.
▶ *n.* 1 BRAWL, fracas, fray, melee, rumpus, skirmish, sparring match, struggle, scuffle, altercation, scrum, clash, disturbance; fisticuffs; *informal* scrap, dust-up, set-to, shindig, punch-up, donnybrook, free-for-all, tussle. 2 BATTLE, engagement, clash, conflict, struggle; war, campaign, crusade, action, hostilities. 3 ☞ ARGUMENT. 4 STRUGGLE, battle, campaign, push, effort.
☐ **fight back** 1 RETALIATE, counterattack, strike back, hit back, respond, reciprocate, return

fire. **2** REPRESS, restrain, suppress, stifle, smother, hold back, fight back, keep in check, curb, control, rein in, choke back; *informal* keep the lid on. **fight someone/ something off** REPEL, repulse, beat off/back, ward off, fend off, keep/hold at bay, drive away/back, force back.

figurative *adj.* METAPHORICAL, non-literal, symbolic, allegorical, representative, emblematic.
—OPPOSITES: literal.

figure *n.* **1** STATISTIC, number, quantity, amount, level, total, sum. **2** DIGIT, numeral, numerical symbol. **3** PRICE, cost, amount, value, valuation. **4** ☞ PHYSIQUE. **5** representative, embodiment, personification, epitome. See also PERSON. **6** SHAPE, pattern, design. **7** DIAGRAM, illustration.
▶ *v.* **1** FEATURE, appear, be featured, be mentioned, be referred to, have prominence. **2** ☞ CALCULATE 1. **3** (*informal*) SUPPOSE, think, believe, consider, expect, take it, suspect, sense; assume, dare say, conclude, presume, deduce, infer, extrapolate, gather, guess.
□ **figure something out**
☞ UNDERSTAND 1.

file¹ *n.* **1** FOLDER, portfolio, binder, *proprietary* Duo-Tang✦. **2** DOSSIER, document, record, report; data, information, documentation.
▶ *v.* CATEGORIZE, classify, organize, put in place/order, order, arrange, catalogue, record, store, archive.

file² *n.* ☞ LINE *n.* 6.
▶ *v.* WALK IN A LINE, march, parade, troop.

fill *v.* **1** MAKE/BECOME FULL, fill up, fill to the brim, top up, charge.

2 CROWD INTO, throng, pack (into), occupy, squeeze into, cram (into); overcrowd, overfill. **3** STOCK, pack, load, supply, replenish, restock, refill. **4** BLOCK UP, stop (up), plug, seal, caulk. **5** PERVADE, permeate, suffuse, be diffused through, penetrate, infuse, perfuse.
—OPPOSITES: empty.
□ **fill in** SUBSTITUTE, deputize, stand in, cover, take over, act as stand-in, take the place of; *informal* sub, pinch-hit. **fill someone in**
☞ TELL 1.

fillip *n.* ☞ STIMULUS.

film *n.* **1** LAYER, coat, coating, covering, cover, sheet, patina, overlay. **2** MOVIE, picture, feature (film), motion picture; *informal* flick, pic.
—RELATED: cinematic.
▶ *v.* RECORD (ON FILM), shoot, capture on film, video.

filter *n.* STRAINER, sifter; riddle; gauze, netting.
▶ *v.* SIEVE, strain, sift, filtrate, clarify, purify, refine, treat.

filth *n.* DIRT, muck, grime, mud, mire, sludge, slime, ooze; excrement, excreta, dung, manure, ordure, sewage; rubbish, refuse, dross; pollution, contamination, filthiness, uncleanness, foulness, nastiness, garbage, crud, grunge, gunge, trash.

filthy *adj.* **1** ☞ DIRTY *adj.* 1. **2** ☞ INDECENT. **3** DESPICABLE, contemptible, nasty, low, base, mean, vile, obnoxious; *informal* dirty (rotten), lowdown, no-good.
—OPPOSITES: clean.

final *adj.* **1** LAST, closing, concluding, finishing, end,

terminating, ultimate, eventual.
2 IRREVOCABLE, unalterable,
absolute, conclusive, irrefutable,
incontrovertible, indisputable,
unchallengeable, binding.
—OPPOSITES: first, provisional.

finale *n.* CLIMAX, culmination; end,
ending, finish, close, conclusion,
termination; denouement,
resolution, epilogue, coda, last
act, final scene.
—OPPOSITES: beginning.

finalize *v.* CONCLUDE, complete,
clinch, settle, work out, secure,
wrap up, wind up; agree on, come
to terms on; *informal* sew up.

finance *n.* **1** FINANCIAL AFFAIRS,
money matters, fiscal matters,
economics, money management,
commerce, business, investment.
2 FUNDS, assets, money, capital,
resources, cash, reserves, revenue,
income; funding, backing,
sponsorship.
▶ *v.* FUND, pay for, back, capitalize,
endow, subsidize, invest in;
underwrite, guarantee, sponsor,
support, be a patron of, contribute
to; *informal* foot the bill for, pick up
the tab for, put up the money for,
bankroll.

financial *adj.* MONETARY, money,
economic, pecuniary, fiscal,
banking, commercial, business,
investment.

find *v.* **1** LOCATE, spot, pinpoint,
unearth, obtain; search out, nose
out, track down, root out; come
across/upon, run across/into,
chance on, light on, bring to light,
happen on, stumble on,
encounter, detect, discover, ferret
out, smoke out, sniff out, uncover,
turn up; *informal* bump into; *literary*

espy. **2** DISCOVER, invent, come up
with, hit on. **3** RETRIEVE, recover,
get back, regain, repossess.
4 OBTAIN, acquire, get, procure,
come by, secure, gain, earn,
achieve, attain. **5** SUMMON (UP),
gather, muster (up), screw up, call
up. **6** DISCOVER, become aware,
realize, observe, notice, note,
perceive, learn.
—OPPOSITES: lose.
▶ *n.* **1** DISCOVERY, acquisition, asset.
2 GOOD BUY, bargain; godsend,
boon.
□ **find out** DISCOVER, become
aware, learn, detect, discern,
perceive, observe, notice, note,
get/come to know, realize; bring
to light, reveal, expose, unearth,
disclose; *informal* figure out, cotton
on, catch on, tumble, get wise,
savvy, twig.

finding *n.* CONCLUSION, decision,
verdict, pronouncement,
judgment, ruling, rule, decree,
order, recommendation, resolve;
Law determination.

fine *adj.* **1** EXCELLENT, first-class,
first-rate, great, exceptional,
outstanding, quality, superior,
splendid, magnificent, exquisite,
choice, select, prime, supreme,
superb, wonderful, superlative, of
high quality, second to none;
informal A1, top-notch, blue-ribbon,
blue-chip, splendiferous.
2 WORTHY, admirable,
praiseworthy, laudable, estimable,
upright, upstanding, respectable.
3 ☞ ACCEPTABLE 1. **4** ☞ HEALTHY.
5 ☞ SUNNY. **6** IMPRESSIVE,
imposing, striking, splendid,
grand, majestic, magnificent,
stately. **7** ELEGANT, stylish,

expensive, smart, chic,
fashionable; fancy, sumptuous,
lavish, opulent; *informal* flashy,
swanky, ritzy, plush. **8** KEEN,
quick, alert, sharp, bright,
brilliant, astute, clever,
intelligent, perspicacious.
9 DELICATE, light, fragile, dainty.
10 INTRICATE, delicate, detailed,
elaborate, meticulous. **11** SUBTLE,
ultra-fine, nice, hairsplitting.
12 DISCERNING, discriminating,
refined, cultivated, cultured,
critical.
—OPPOSITES: poor, unsatisfactory,
ill, inclement, thick, coarse.
▶ *adv.* (*informal*) WELL, all right, not
badly, satisfactorily, adequately,
nicely, tolerably; *informal* OK.
—OPPOSITES: badly.

finicky *adj.* ☞ FASTIDIOUS.

finish *v.* **1** COMPLETE, end,
conclude, stop, cease, terminate,
bring to a conclusion/end/close,
wind up; crown, cap, round off,
put the finishing touches to;
accomplish, discharge, carry out,
do, get done, fulfill; *informal* wrap
up, sew up, polish off. **2** LEAVE,
give up, drop; stop, discontinue,
have done with, complete; *informal*
pack in, quit. **3** END, come to an
end, stop, conclude, come to a
conclusion/end/close, cease.
—OPPOSITES: start, begin,
continue.
▶ *n.* **1** END, ending, completion,
conclusion, close, closing,
cessation, termination; final part/
stage, finale, denouement; *informal*
sewing up, polishing off. **2** VENEER,
lacquer, lamination, glaze,
coating, covering; surface, texture.
—OPPOSITES: start, beginning.

finite *adj.* LIMITED, restricted,
determinate, fixed.

fire *n.* **1** BLAZE, conflagration,
inferno; flames, burning,
combustion. **2** ☞ ENERGY, FERVOUR.
3 GUNFIRE, firing, flak,
bombardment. **4** CRITICISM,
censure, condemnation,
denunciation, opprobrium,
admonishments, brickbats;
hostility, antagonism, animosity;
informal flak.
—RELATED: pyro-.
▶ *v.* **1** SHOOT, discharge, let off, set
off; launch. **2** (*informal*) ☞ DISMISS 1.
3 STIMULATE, stir up, excite,
awaken, arouse, rouse, inflame,
animate, inspire, motivate.

firebrand *n.* RADICAL,
revolutionary, agitator, rabble-
rouser, incendiary, subversive,
troublemaker.

fireproof *adj.* NON-FLAMMABLE,
incombustible, fire resistant,
flame resistant, flame retardant,
heatproof.
—OPPOSITES: inflammable.

firm[1] *adj.* **1** HARD, solid, unyielding,
resistant; solidified, hardened,
compacted, compressed, dense,
stiff, rigid, frozen, set. **2** SECURE,
secured, stable, steady, strong,
fixed, fast, set, taut, tight;
immovable, irremovable,
stationary, motionless. **3** STRONG,
vigorous, sturdy, forceful.
4 RESOLUTE, determined, decided,
resolved, steadfast; adamant,
emphatic, insistent, single-
minded, in earnest, wholehearted;
unfaltering, unwavering,
unflinching, unswerving,
unbending; hardline, committed,
dyed-in-the-wool. **5** CONSTANT,

devoted, loving, faithful, long-standing, steady, steadfast. See also INTIMATE 1. **6** DEFINITE, fixed, settled, decided, established, confirmed, agreed; unalterable, unchangeable, irreversible.
—OPPOSITES: soft, unstable, limp, indefinite.

firm² n. ☞ COMPANY 1.

first adj. **1** EARLIEST, initial, opening, introductory.
2 ☞ FUNDAMENTAL. **3** FOREMOST, principal, highest, greatest, paramount, top, uppermost, prime, chief, leading, main, major; overriding, predominant, prevailing, central, core, dominant; informal number-one.
—OPPOSITES: last, closing.
▶ adv. **1** AT FIRST, to begin with, first of all, at the outset, initially. **2** BEFORE ANYTHING ELSE, first and foremost, now.

first-hand adj. DIRECT, immediate, personal, hands-on, experiential, empirical, eyewitness.
—OPPOSITES: vicarious, indirect.

first-rate adj. ☞ EXCELLENT.

fish v. **1** GO FISHING, angle, cast, trawl, troll. **2** TRY TO GET, seek to obtain, solicit, angle, aim, hope, be after.
☐ **fish someone/something out** ☞ EXTRACT V. 1.

fishy adj. (informal) SUSPICIOUS, questionable, dubious, doubtful, suspect; odd, queer, peculiar, strange; informal funny, shady, crooked, sketchy.

fit¹ adj. **1** SUITABLE, good enough; relevant, pertinent, apt, appropriate, suited, apposite, fitting. **2** COMPETENT, able, capable;

ready, prepared, qualified, trained, equipped. **3** ATHLETIC, muscular, well-built, strong, robust. See also HEALTHY 1.
—OPPOSITES: unsuitable, incapable, unwell.
▶ v. **1** LAY, position, place, fix. **2** EQUIP, provide, supply, fit out, furnish. **3** JOIN, connect, put together, piece together, attach, unite, link, slot. **4** MATCH, suit, be appropriate to, correspond to, tally with, go with, accord with, correlate to, be congruous with, be congruent with, be consonant with.
☐ **fit in** CONFORM, be in harmony, blend in, be in line.

fit² n. **1** ☞ SEIZURE 3. **2** OUTBREAK, outburst, attack, bout, spell. **3** TANTRUM, fit of temper, outburst of anger/rage, frenzy; informal blowout, hissy fit, conniption (fit).

fix v. **1** REPAIR, mend, put right, put to rights, get working, restore (to working order); overhaul, service, renovate, recondition. **2** ☞ ATTACH 1. **3** STICK, lodge, embed, burn, brand. **4** FOCUS, direct, level, point, train. **5** (informal) ARRANGE, put in order, adjust; informal do. **6** (informal) PREPARE, cook, make, get; informal rustle up, whip up. **7** (informal) RIG, arrange fraudulently; tamper with, influence; informal fiddle.
▶ n. (informal) **1** ☞ PREDICAMENT. **2** SOLUTION, answer, resolution, way out, remedy, cure, placebo; informal magic bullet.
☐ **fix something up** ORGANIZE, arrange, make arrangements for, sort out.

fixation n. ☞ MANIA.

fizzy *adj.* EFFERVESCENT, sparkling, carbonated, gassy, bubbly, frothy; spumante, frizzante.
—OPPOSITES: still, flat.

flag¹ *n.* BANNER, standard, ensign, pennant, banderole, streamer, jack, gonfalon; colours.
▶ *v.* INDICATE, identify, point out, mark, label, tag, highlight.

flag² *v.* **1** TIRE, grow tired/weary, weaken, grow weak, wilt, droop, fade, run out of steam. **2** FADE, decline, wane, ebb, diminish, decrease, lessen, dwindle; wither, melt away, peter out, die away/down.
—OPPOSITES: revive.

flagrant *adj.* BLATANT, glaring, obvious, overt, conspicuous, patent, barefaced, naked, shameless, audacious, brazen, undisguised, unconcealed; outrageous, scandalous, shocking, disgraceful, dreadful, terrible, gross.

flair *n.* **1** APTITUDE, talent, gift, instinct, (natural) ability, facility, skill, bent, feel, knack. **2** ☞ STYLE 3.

flamboyant *adj.* **1** EXUBERANT, confident, lively, animated, vibrant, vivacious.
2 ☞ OSTENTATIOUS.

flap *v.* BEAT, flutter, agitate, wave, wag, swing; blow, sway, ripple.
▶ *n.* **1** (*informal*) PANIC, fluster, state, dither, twitter, stew, tizzy.
2 (*informal*) FUSS, commotion, stir, hubbub, storm, uproar; controversy, brouhaha, furor; *informal* to-do, ballyhoo, hoo-ha, kerfuffle.

flash *v.* **1** LIGHT UP, shine, flare, blaze, gleam, glint, sparkle, burn; blink, wink, flicker, shimmer, twinkle, glimmer, glisten, scintillate; *literary* glister, coruscate.
2 ☞ FLAUNT.
▶ *n.* FLARE, blaze, burst; gleam, glint, sparkle, flicker, shimmer, twinkle, glimmer.

flat *adj.* **1** LEVEL, horizontal, smooth, even, uniform, regular, plane. **2** MONOTONOUS, toneless, droning. See also BORING.
3 WITHOUT ENERGY, enervated, sapped, weary, tired out, worn out, exhausted, drained. See also SAD 1. **4** DEFLATED, punctured, burst. **5** OUTRIGHT, direct, absolute, definite, positive, straight, plain, explicit; firm, resolute, adamant, assertive, emphatic, categorical, unconditional, unqualified, unequivocal.
—OPPOSITES: vertical, uneven.
▢ **flat out** HARD, as hard as possible, for all one's worth, to the full/limit, all out; at full speed, as fast as possible, at full tilt, full bore, full throttle; *informal* like crazy, like mad, like the wind.

flatten *v.* **1** MAKE/BECOME FLAT, make/become even, smooth (out/off), level (out/off). **2** COMPRESS, press down, crush, squash, compact, trample. **3** DEMOLISH, raze (to the ground), tear down, knock down, destroy, wreck, devastate, obliterate, total.
4 (*informal*) KNOCK DOWN/OVER, knock to the ground, fell, prostrate; *informal* floor, deck, schmuck❖.

flatter *v.* **1** COMPLIMENT, praise, express admiration for, say nice things about, fawn over; cajole, humour, flannel, blarney; *informal* sweet-talk, soft-soap, brown-nose,

butter up, play/suck up to.
2 HONOUR, gratify, please, delight;
informal tickle pink.
—OPPOSITES: insult, offend.

flattering *adj.* **1** COMPLIMENTARY,
praising, favourable,
commending, admiring,
applauding, appreciative, good;
fulsome, honeyed, sugary,
cajoling, silver-tongued, honey-
tongued; *informal* sweet-talking,
soft-soaping. See also SYCOPHANTIC.
2 BECOMING, enhancing.

flattery *n.* PRAISE, adulation,
compliments, blandishments,
honeyed words; fawning, blarney,
cajolery, encomium; *informal* sweet
talk, soft soap, snow job.

flaunt *v.* SHOW OFF, display
ostentatiously, make a (great)
show of, put on show/display,
parade; brag about, crow about,
vaunt; *informal* flash.

flavour *n.* **1** TASTE, savour, tang.
2 FLAVOURING, seasoning, tastiness,
tang, relish, bite, piquancy,
pungency, spice, spiciness, zest;
informal zing, zip. **3** ☞ ATMOSPHERE
2. **4** IMPRESSION, suggestion, hint,
taste.
▸ *v.* ADD FLAVOUR/FLAVOURING TO,
season, spice (up), ginger up,
enrich; *informal* pep up.

flaw *n.* DEFECT, blemish, fault,
imperfection, deficiency,
weakness, weak spot/point/link,
inadequacy, shortcoming,
limitation, failing, foible; *informal*
glitch.
—OPPOSITES: strength.

flawless *adj.* PERFECT,
unblemished, unmarked,
unimpaired; whole, intact, sound,
unbroken, undamaged, mint,

pristine; impeccable, immaculate,
consummate, accurate, correct,
faultless, error-free, unerring;
exemplary, model, ideal.
—OPPOSITES: flawed.

flee *v.* RUN (AWAY/OFF), run for it,
make a run for it, dash, take
flight, be gone, make off, take off,
take to one's heels, make a break
for it, bolt, beat a (hasty) retreat,
make a quick exit, make one's
getaway, escape; *informal* beat it,
clear off/out, vamoose, skedaddle,
split, leg it, turn tail, scram, light
out, cut out, peel out, take a
powder, make tracks.

fleet *adj.* (*literary*) ☞ AGILE 1.

fleeting *adj.* ☞ TRANSIENT *adj.*
—OPPOSITES: lasting.

flesh
☐ **flesh something out** EXPAND
(ON), elaborate on, add to, build
on, add flesh to, put flesh on (the
bones of), add detail to, expatiate
on, supplement, reinforce,
augment, fill out, enlarge on.

flexible *adj.* **1** PLIABLE, supple,
bendable, pliant, plastic; elastic,
stretchy, whippy, springy,
resilient, bouncy; *informal* bendy.
2 ADAPTABLE, adjustable, variable,
versatile, open-ended, open, free.
3 ☞ ACCOMMODATING.
—OPPOSITES: rigid, inflexible.

flick *v.* **1** CLICK, snap, flip, jerk.
2 SWISH, twitch, wave, wag,
waggle, shake.

flicker *v.* **1** GLIMMER, glint, flare,
dance, gutter; twinkle, sparkle,
blink, wink, flash, scintillate;
literary glister, coruscate. **2** FLUTTER,
quiver, twitch.

flight *n.* **1** AVIATION, flying, air
transport, aerial navigation,

aeronautics. **2** TRAJECTORY, path through the air, track, orbit. **3** FLOCK, skein, covey, swarm, cloud.

□ **take flight** ☞ FLEE.

flimsy *adj.* **1** INSUBSTANTIAL, fragile, breakable, frail, shaky, unstable, wobbly, tottery, rickety, ramshackle, makeshift; jerry-built, badly built, shoddy, chintzy, gimcrack. **2** ☞ GOSSAMER. **3** ☞ FEEBLE 1.
—OPPOSITES: sturdy, thick, sound.

flinch *v.* **1** WINCE, start, shudder, quiver, jerk, shy. **2** SHRINK FROM, recoil from, shy away from, swerve from, demur from; dodge, evade, avoid, duck, balk at, jib at, quail at, fight shy of.

fling *v.* THROW, toss, huck♣, sling, hurl, cast, pitch, lob; *informal* chuck, heave, buzz.

▶ *n.* ☞ AFFAIR 3.

flippant *adj.* FRIVOLOUS, facetious, tongue-in-cheek; disrespectful, irreverent, cheeky, impudent, impertinent; *informal* flip, waggish.
—OPPOSITES: serious, respectful.

flirt *v.* **1** TRIFLE WITH, toy with, tease, lead on. **2** DABBLE IN, toy with, trifle with, amuse oneself with. **3** DICE WITH, court, risk, not fear.

▶ *n.* TEASE, trifler, philanderer, coquette, heartbreaker.

flirtatious *adj.* COQUETTISH, flirty, kittenish, teasing.

flit *v.* DART, dance, skip, play, dash, trip, flutter, bob, bounce.

float *v.* **1** STAY AFLOAT, stay on the surface, be buoyant, be buoyed up. **2** HOVER, levitate, be suspended, hang, defy gravity. **3** DRIFT, glide, sail, slip, slide, waft.
—OPPOSITES: sink, rush.

flock *n.* **1** HERD, drove. **2** FLIGHT, congregation, covey, clutch. **3** CROWD, throng, horde, mob, rabble, mass, multitude, host, army, pack, swarm, sea; *informal* gaggle.

▶ *v.* GATHER, collect, congregate, assemble, converge, mass, crowd, throng, cluster, swarm.

flog *v.* ☞ WHIP *v.* 1.

flood *n.* **1** INUNDATION, swamping, deluge, high water; torrent, overflow, freshet, spate. **2** OUTPOURING, torrent, rush, stream, gush, surge, cascade.
—OPPOSITES: trickle.

▶ *v.* **1** INUNDATE, swamp, deluge, immerse, submerge, drown, engulf; overflow. **2** GLUT, swamp, saturate, oversupply.
—OPPOSITES: trickle.

floor *n.* **1** GROUND, flooring. **2** STOREY, level, deck, tier.

▶ *v.* KNOCK DOWN, knock over, bring down, fell, prostrate.

flop *v.* **1** COLLAPSE, slump, crumple, subside, sink, drop. **2** ☞ FAIL 1.
—OPPOSITES: succeed.

▶ *n.* (*informal*) FAILURE, disaster, debacle, catastrophe, loser; *informal* washout, also-ran, dog, lemon, non-starter, clinker.
—OPPOSITES: success.

floppy *adj.* ☞ LIMP.
—OPPOSITES: erect, stiff.

florid *adj.* **1** ☞ RUDDY. **2** FLOWERY, flamboyant, high-flown, high-sounding, grandiloquent, ornate, fancy, bombastic, elaborate, turgid, pleonastic.
—OPPOSITES: pale, plain.

flounder *v.* **1** STRUGGLE, thrash, flail, twist and turn, splash, stagger, stumble, reel, lurch,

blunder, squirm, writhe.
2 STRUGGLE, be out of one's depth, have difficulty, be confounded, be confused; *informal* be floored, be beaten.
—OPPOSITES: prosper.

flourish *v.* **1** GROW, thrive, prosper, do well, burgeon, increase, multiply, proliferate; spring up, shoot up, bloom, blossom, bear fruit, burst forth, run riot. **2** ☞ BRANDISH.
—OPPOSITES: die, wither.

flout *v.* DEFY, refuse to obey, disobey, break, violate, fail to comply with, fail to observe, contravene, infringe, breach, commit a breach of, transgress against; ignore, disregard.
—OPPOSITES: observe.

flow *v.* **1** RUN, course, glide, drift, circulate; trickle, seep, ooze, dribble, drip, drizzle, spill; stream, swirl, surge, sweep, gush, cascade, pour, roll, rush. **2** ☞ RESULT *v.* 1.
▸ *n.* MOVEMENT, motion, current, flux, circulation; trickle, ooze, percolation, drip; stream, swirl, surge, gush, rush, spate, tide.

flower *n.* **1** BLOOM, blossom, floweret, floret. **2** BEST, finest, pick, choice, cream.
—RELATED: floral, flor-.
—OPPOSITES: dregs.

fluctuate *v.* VARY, change, differ, shift, alter, waver, swing, oscillate, alternate, rise and fall, go up and down, see-saw, yo-yo.

fluent *adj.* ARTICULATE, eloquent, expressive, communicative, coherent, cogent, illuminating, vivid, well-written/spoken; **(be**

fluent in) have a (good) command of.
—OPPOSITES: inarticulate.

fluff *n.* FUZZ, lint, dust, dustballs, dust bunnies.
▸ *v.* ☞ BUNGLE.
—OPPOSITES: succeed in.

fluid *n.* LIQUID, solution; GAS, vapour.
—OPPOSITES: solid.
▸ *adj.* **1** FREE-FLOWING; liquid, liquefied, melted, molten, runny, running; gaseous, gassy.
2 ADAPTABLE, flexible, adjustable, open-ended, open, open to change, changeable, variable.
3 SMOOTH, fluent, flowing, effortless, easy, continuous, seamless; graceful, elegant.
—OPPOSITES: solid, firm.

flunky *n.* MINION, lackey, hireling, subordinate, underling, servant; creature, instrument, cat's paw; *informal* stooge, gofer.

flush *v.* **1** ☞ BLUSH *v.* **2** RINSE, wash, sluice, swill, cleanse, clean.
—OPPOSITES: pale.

fluster *v.* UNSETTLE, make nervous, unnerve, agitate, ruffle, upset, bother, put on edge, disquiet, disturb, worry, perturb, disconcert, confuse, throw off balance, confound; *informal* rattle, faze, throw into a tizzy, discombobulate.
—OPPOSITES: calm.

flutter *v.* **1** FLAP, beat, quiver, agitate, vibrate, whiffle. **2** FLICKER, bat. **3** FLAP, wave, ripple, undulate, quiver; fly.

fly *v.* **1** SOAR, wing, glide, wheel; hover, hang; jet; take wing, take to the air, mount. **2** AIRLIFT, lift, jet. **3** PILOT, operate, control, manoeuvre, steer. **4** DISPLAY, show, exhibit, bear; have hoisted, have run up. **5** ☞ RUN v. 1.

□ **fly at** ☞ TURN ON SOMEONE at TURN.

flyer, flier n. **1** PILOT, airman, aviator. **2** HANDBILL, bill, handout, leaflet, circular, advertisement, junk mail.

foam n. FROTH, spume, surf; fizz, effervescence, bubbles, head; lather, suds.

▸ v. FROTH, spume; fizz, effervesce, bubble; lather; ferment, rise; boil, seethe, simmer.

focus n. **1** CENTRE, focal point, central point, centre of attention, hub, pivot, nucleus, heart, cornerstone, linchpin, cynosure. **2** SUBJECT, theme, concern, subject matter, topic, issue, thesis, point, thread; substance, essence, gist, matter.

▸ v. **1** BRING INTO FOCUS; aim, point, turn. **2** CONCENTRATE, centre, zero in, zoom in; address itself to, pay attention to, pinpoint, revolve around.

□ **in focus** SHARP, crisp, distinct, clear, well-defined, well-focused.
out of focus ☞ BLURRED.

foe n. ENEMY, adversary, opponent, rival, antagonist, combatant, challenger, competitor, opposer, opposition, competition, other side.
—OPPOSITES: friend.

fog n. MIST, smog, murk, haze, ice fog; *literary* brume, fume.

▸ v. STEAM UP, mist over, cloud over, film over, make/become misty.
—OPPOSITES: demist, clear.

foggy adj. **1** MISTY, smoggy, hazy, (Nfld) mauzy✿, murky. **2** DARK, dim, hazy, shadowy, cloudy, blurred, obscure, vague, indistinct, unclear. See also BEFUDDLED.
—OPPOSITES: clear.

foible n. WEAKNESS, failing, shortcoming, flaw, imperfection, blemish, fault, defect, limitation; quirk, kink, idiosyncrasy, eccentricity, peculiarity.
—OPPOSITES: strength.

fold v. **1** DOUBLE (OVER/UP), crease, turn under/up/over, bend; tuck, gather, pleat. **2** ENFOLD, wrap, envelop; take, gather, clasp, squeeze, clutch; embrace. **3** ☞ GO BANKRUPT at BANKRUPT.

▸ n. CREASE, wrinkle, crinkle, pucker, furrow; pleat, gather.

folk n. (informal) **1** PEOPLE, individuals, {men, women, and children}, (living) souls, mortals; citizenry, inhabitants, residents, populace, population; *formal* denizens. **2** ☞ FAMILY 1.

follow v. **1** COME BEHIND, come after, go behind, go after, walk behind. **2** ☞ ACCOMPANY 1. **3** SHADOW, trail, stalk, track, dog, hound; *informal* tail. **4** OBEY, comply with, conform to, adhere to, stick to, keep to, abide by, observe, heed, pay attention to. **5** RESULT, arise, be a consequence of, be caused by, be brought about by, be a result of, come after, develop, ensue, emanate, issue, proceed, spring, flow, originate, stem. **6** ☞ UNDERSTAND 1. **7** ☞ IMITATE 1.
—OPPOSITES: lead, flout, misunderstand.

□ **follow something up**

INVESTIGATE, research, look into, dig into, delve into, make inquiries into, inquire about, ask questions about, pursue, chase up; *informal* check out, scope out.

following *n.* ADMIRERS, supporters, backers, fans, adherents, devotees, advocates, patrons, public, audience, circle, retinue, train.
—OPPOSITES: opposition.
▶ *adj.* **1** NEXT, ensuing, succeeding, subsequent. **2** below, further on; these; *formal* hereunder, hereinafter.
—OPPOSITES: preceding, aforementioned.

foment *v.* ☞ INCITE.

fond *adj.* **1** KEEN ON, partial to, addicted to, enthusiastic about, passionate about; attached to, attracted to, enamoured of, in love with, having a soft spot for; *informal* into, hooked on, gone on, sweet on, struck on. **2** ADORING, devoted, doting, loving, caring, affectionate, warm, tender, kind, attentive. **3** UNREALISTIC, naive, foolish, over-optimistic, deluded, delusory, absurd, vain.
—OPPOSITES: indifferent, unfeeling, realistic.

fondle *v.* CARESS, stroke, pat, pet, finger, tickle, play with; maul, molest; *informal* paw, grope, feel up, touch up, cop a feel of.

food *n.* NOURISHMENT, sustenance, nutriment, fare, bread, daily bread; cooking, cuisine; foodstuffs, edibles, (*Nfld*) prog♣, provender, refreshments, meals, provisions, rations; *informal* eats, eatables, nosh, grub, chow, nibbles, scoff, chuck; *formal*

comestibles; *literary* viands; *dated* victuals.

fool *n.* **1** IDIOT, ass, halfwit, blockhead, jughead, dunce, dolt, dullard, simpleton, clod, dope, hoser♣, ninny, nincompoop, silly, silly-billy, chump, dim-wit, dipstick, dim-bulb, doofus, buffoon, duffer, ignoramus, goober, coot, goon, dumbo, dummy, ditz, dumdum, fathead, numbskull, numbnuts, dunderhead, thickhead, airhead, flake, lamebrain, zombie, cretin, moron, gimp, nerd, imbecile, pea brain, birdbrain, jerk, donkey, noodle, nitwit, twit, goat, dork, twerp, schmuck, bozo, boob, turkey, schlep, chowderhead, dumbhead, bonehead, knucklehead, goofball, goof, goofus, galoot, lummox, klutz, putz, schlemiel, sap, meatball, clown, jackass. **2** LAUGHINGSTOCK, dupe, butt, gull, figure of fun; *informal* stooge, sucker, fall guy, sap.
▶ *v.* **1** ☞ TRICK *v.* **2** PRETEND, make believe, feign, put on an act, act, sham, fake; joke, jest; *informal* kid; have someone on.
☐ **fool around 1** FIDDLE, play (about/around), toy, trifle, meddle, tamper, interfere, monkey around; *informal* mess around, muck about/around. **2** (*informal*) PHILANDER, womanize, flirt, have an affair, commit adultery, cheat; *informal* play around, mess around, carry on, play the field, sleep around.

foolish *adj.* STUPID, silly, idiotic, witless, brainless, mindless, unintelligent, thoughtless, half-baked, imprudent, incautious, injudicious, unwise; ill-advised, ill-

considered, impolitic, rash, reckless, foolhardy, daft; *informal* dumb, dim, dim-witted, halfwitted, thick, hare-brained, crack-brained, crackpot, pea-brained, wooden-headed, dumb-ass.
—OPPOSITES: sensible, wise.

foolproof *adj.* ☞ INFALLIBLE.
—OPPOSITES: flawed.

fop *n.* ☞ DANDY.

foray *n.* ☞ RAID *n.* 1.

forbid *v.* PROHIBIT, ban, outlaw, make illegal, veto, proscribe, disallow, embargo, bar, debar, interdict; *Law* enjoin, restrain.
—OPPOSITES: permit.

forbidding *adj.* 1 HOSTILE, unwelcoming, unfriendly, off-putting, unsympathetic, unapproachable, grim, stern, hard, tough, frosty. 2 THREATENING, ominous, menacing, sinister, brooding, daunting, formidable, fearsome, frightening, chilling, disturbing, disquieting.
—OPPOSITES: friendly, inviting.

force *n.* 1 STRENGTH, power, energy, might, effort, exertion; impact, pressure, weight, impetus. 2 COERCION, compulsion, constraint, duress, oppression, harassment, intimidation, threats; *informal* arm-twisting, bullying tactics. 3 COGENCY, potency, weight, effectiveness, soundness, validity, strength, power, significance, influence, authority; *informal* punch; *formal* efficacy. 4 AGENCY, power, influence, instrument, vehicle, means. 5 BODY, body of people, group, outfit, party, team; detachment, unit, squad; *informal* bunch.

—OPPOSITES: weakness.
▶ *v.* 1 COMPEL, coerce, make, constrain, oblige, impel, drive, pressure, press, push, press-gang, bully, dragoon, bludgeon; *informal* put the screws on, lean on, twist someone's arm. 2 PROPEL, push, thrust, shove, drive, press, pump. 3 EXTRACT, elicit, exact, extort, wrest, wring, drag, screw, squeeze.

forceful *adj.* 1 DYNAMIC, energetic, assertive, authoritative, vigorous, powerful, strong, pushy, driving, determined, insistent, commanding, dominant, domineering; *informal* bossy, in-your-face, go-ahead, feisty. 2 ☞ COGENT.
—OPPOSITES: weak, submissive, unconvincing.

forecast *v.* ☞ PROPHESY.
▶ *n.* PREDICTION, prophecy, forewarning, prognostication, augury, divination, prognosis.

foregoing *adj.* PRECEDING, aforesaid, aforementioned, earlier, above; previous, prior, antecedent.
—OPPOSITES: following.

foreign *adj.* 1 OVERSEAS, exotic, distant, external, alien, non-native. 2 UNFAMILIAR, unknown, unheard of, strange, alien; novel, new.
—RELATED: xeno-.
—OPPOSITES: domestic, native, familiar.

foreigner *n.* ALIEN, non-native, stranger, outsider, (*Atlantic*) come from away✦; immigrant, landed immigrant✦, refugee, settler, newcomer.
—OPPOSITES: native.

foremost *adj.* ☞ BEST *adj.*
—OPPOSITES: minor.

forerunner *n.* **1** ☞ PREDECESSOR.
2 PRELUDE, herald, harbinger, precursor, sign, signal, indication, warning.
—OPPOSITES: descendant.

foreshadow *v.* SIGNAL, indicate, signify, mean, be a sign of, suggest, herald, be a harbinger of, warn of, portend, augur, prefigure, presage, promise, point to, anticipate; *informal* spell; *literary* forebode, foretoken, betoken.

foresight *n.* FORETHOUGHT, (forward) planning, far-sightedness, vision, anticipation, prudence, care, caution, precaution, readiness, preparedness, provision.
—OPPOSITES: hindsight.

forest *n.* WOOD(S), woodland, timberland, trees, bush, plantation; jungle, rainforest, pinewood.
—RELATED: sylvan.

forestall *v.* PRE-EMPT, get in before, steal a march on; anticipate, second-guess. See also PREVENT.

foretell *v.* **1** ☞ PREDICT.
2 ☞ FORESHADOW.

forethought *n.* ☞ FORESIGHT.

forever *adv.* **1** FOR ALWAYS, evermore, for ever and ever, for good, for all time, until the end of time, until hell freezes over, eternally, forevermore, perpetually, in perpetuity; *informal* until the cows come home, until kingdom come, for keeps.
2 ALWAYS, continually, constantly, perpetually, incessantly, endlessly, persistently, repeatedly,

regularly; non-stop, day and night, {morning, noon, and night}; all the time, the entire time; *informal* 24-7.
—OPPOSITES: never, occasionally.

forfeit *v.* LOSE, be deprived of, surrender, relinquish, sacrifice, give up, yield, renounce, forgo; *informal* pass up, lose out on.
—OPPOSITES: retain.

forge *v.* **1** HAMMER OUT, beat into shape, fashion. **2** BUILD, construct, form, create, establish, set up. **3** FAKE, falsify, counterfeit, copy, imitate, reproduce, replicate, simulate.

forgery *n.* **1** COUNTERFEITING, falsification, faking, copying, pirating. **2** ☞ FAKE *n.* 1.

forget *v.* **1** NEGLECT, fail, omit. **2** STOP THINKING ABOUT, put out of one's mind, shut out, blank out, pay no heed to, not worry about, ignore, overlook, take no notice of.
—OPPOSITES: remember.

forgetful *adj.* ABSENT-MINDED, amnesic, amnesiac, vague, disorganized, dreamy, abstracted, with a mind/memory like a sieve; *informal* scatterbrained, scatty.
—OPPOSITES: reliable.

forgive *v.* **1** PARDON, excuse, exonerate, absolve; make allowances for, feel no resentment/malice towards, harbour no grudge against, bury the hatchet with; let bygones be bygones; *informal* let off (the hook); *formal* exculpate. **2** EXCUSE, overlook, disregard, ignore, pass over, allow; turn a blind eye/deaf ear to, wink at, indulge, tolerate.

—OPPOSITES: blame, resent, punish.

forgiveness *n.* PARDON, absolution, exoneration, remission, dispensation, indulgence, clemency, mercy; reprieve, amnesty.

forgiving *adj.* ☞ LENIENT.
—OPPOSITES: merciless, vindictive.

forgo, forego *v.* DO WITHOUT, go without, give up, waive, renounce, surrender, relinquish, part with, drop, sacrifice, abstain from, refrain from, eschew, cut out; *informal* swear off; *formal* forswear, abjure.
—OPPOSITES: keep.

forked *adj.* SPLIT, branching, branched, bifurcate(d), Y-shaped, V-shaped, pronged, divided.
—OPPOSITES: straight.

forlorn *adj.* **1** ☞ SAD 1. **2** DESOLATE, deserted, abandoned, forsaken, forgotten, neglected. **3** ☞ FUTILE.
—OPPOSITES: happy, cared for, hopeful.

form *n.* **1** SHAPE, configuration, formation, structure, construction, arrangement, appearance, exterior, outline, format, layout, design. **2** BODY, shape, figure, stature, build, frame, physique, anatomy. **3** MANIFESTATION, appearance, embodiment, incarnation, semblance, shape, guise. **4** KIND, sort, type, class, classification, category, variety, genre, brand, style; species, genus, family. **5** ☞ PROTOCOL. **6** FITNESS, condition, fettle, shape, trim, health.
—OPPOSITES: content.
▶ *v.* **1** ☞ CONSTRUCT.

2 ☞ FORMULATE 1. **3** SET UP, establish, found, launch, float, create, bring into being, institute, start (up), get going, initiate, bring about, inaugurate. **4** ACQUIRE, develop, get, pick up, contract, slip into, get into. **5** ARRANGE, draw up, line up, assemble, organize, sort, order, range, array, dispose, marshal, deploy. **6** CONSTITUTE, make, make up, compose, add up to.
—OPPOSITES: dissolve, disappear, break.

formal *adj.* **1** CEREMONIAL, ceremonious, ritualistic, ritual, conventional, traditional; stately, courtly, solemn, dignified; elaborate, ornate, dressy; black-tie. **2** ALOOF, reserved, remote, detached, unapproachable; stiff, prim, stuffy, staid, ceremonious, correct, proper, decorous, conventional, precise, exact, punctilious, unbending, inflexible, straitlaced; *informal* buttoned-down, standoffish. **3** OFFICIAL, legal, authorized, approved, validated, certified, endorsed, documented, sanctioned, licensed, recognized, authoritative.
—OPPOSITES: informal, casual, colloquial, unofficial.

formation *n.* **1** ESTABLISHMENT, setting up, start, initiation, institution, foundation, inception, creation, inauguration, launch, flotation. **2** CONFIGURATION, arrangement, pattern, array, alignment, positioning, disposition, order.
—OPPOSITES: destruction, disappearance, dissolution.

former *adj.* **1** ONE-TIME, erstwhile, sometime, ex-, late; PREVIOUS, foregoing, preceding, earlier, prior, past, last. **2** EARLIER, old, past, bygone, olden, long-ago, gone by, long past, of old; *literary* of yore.
—OPPOSITES: future, next, latter.

formidable *adj.* **1** INTIMIDATING, forbidding, daunting, disturbing, alarming, frightening, disquieting, brooding, awesome, fearsome, ominous, foreboding, sinister, menacing, threatening, dangerous. **2** ONEROUS, arduous, taxing, difficult, hard, heavy, laborious, burdensome, strenuous, back-breaking, uphill, Herculean, monumental, colossal; demanding, tough, challenging, exacting; *formal* exigent; *archaic* toilsome. **3** IMPRESSIVE, powerful, mighty, terrific, tremendous, great, complete, redoubtable. See also ACCOMPLISHED.

formula *n.* **1** RECIPE, prescription, blueprint, plan, method, procedure, technique, system; template. **2** PREPARATION, concoction, mixture, compound, creation, substance.

formulate *v.* **1** DEVISE, conceive, work out, think up, lay, draw up, put together, form, produce, fashion, concoct, contrive, forge, hatch, prepare, develop; *informal* dream up. **2** EXPRESS, phrase, word, put into words, frame, couch, put, articulate, convey, say, state, utter.

forsake *v.* (*literary*) **1** ☞ ABANDON *v.* 3. **2** ☞ ABANDON *v.* 1.
—OPPOSITES: keep to, adopt.

forthcoming *adj.* **1** ☞ IMMINENT. **2** AVAILABLE, ready, at hand, accessible, obtainable, at someone's disposal, obtained, given, vouchsafed to someone; *informal* up for grabs, on tap. **3** ☞ COMMUNICATIVE.
—OPPOSITES: past, current, unavailable, uncommunicative.

forthright *adj.* ☞ OUTSPOKEN.
—OPPOSITES: secretive, evasive.

fortify *v.* **1** STRENGTHEN, reinforce, toughen, consolidate, bolster, shore up, brace, buttress. **2** INVIGORATE, strengthen, energize, enliven, liven up, animate, vitalize, rejuvenate, restore, revive, refresh; *informal* pep up, buck up.
—OPPOSITES: weaken, sedate, subdue.

fortitude *n.* COURAGE, bravery, endurance, resilience, mettle, moral fibre, strength of mind, strength of character, strong-mindedness, backbone, spirit, grit, doughtiness, steadfastness, courageousness, pluck, pluckiness, strength, character; *informal* guts, spunk.
—OPPOSITES: faint-heartedness.

fortunate *adj.* **1** LUCKY, favoured, blessed, blessed with good luck, in luck, having a charmed life, charmed, prosperous, successful; sitting pretty, born under a lucky star. **2** FAVOURABLE, advantageous, providential, auspicious, welcome, heaven-sent, beneficial, propitious, fortuitous, opportune, happy, felicitous.
—OPPOSITES: unfortunate, unfavourable.

fortunately *adv.* LUCKILY, by good luck, by good fortune, as luck would have it, propitiously; mercifully, thankfully, happily, opportunely, providentially; thank goodness, thank God, thank heavens, thank the stars.

fortune *n.* **1** CHANCE, accident, coincidence, serendipity, destiny, fortuity, providence, happenstance. **2** LUCK, fate, destiny, predestination, the stars, serendipity, karma, kismet, lot. **3** CIRCUMSTANCES, state of affairs, condition, position, situation; plight, predicament. **4** WEALTH, riches, substance, property, assets, resources, means, possessions, treasure, estate.
—OPPOSITES: pittance.

fortune teller *n.* CLAIRVOYANT, crystal gazer, psychic, prophet, seer, oracle, soothsayer, augur, diviner, sibyl; palmist, palm reader.

forward *adv.* **1** AHEAD, forwards, onwards, onward, on, further. **2** TOWARDS THE FRONT, out, forth, into view. **3** ONWARD, onwards, on, forth; for ever, into eternity; until now.
—OPPOSITES: backwards.
▶ *adj.* **1** MOVING FORWARDS, moving ahead, onward, advancing, progressing, progressive. **2** FRONT, advance, foremost, head, leading, frontal. **3** FUTURE, forward-looking, for the future, prospective. **4** ☞ BOLD 2.
—OPPOSITES: backward, rear, late, shy.
▶ *v.* SEND, dispatch, transmit, carry, convey, deliver, ship.

foster *v.* **1** ENCOURAGE, promote, further, stimulate, advance, forward, cultivate, nurture, strengthen, enrich; help, aid, abet, assist, contribute to, support, back, develop, boost, be a patron of. **2** ☞ REAR[1] 1.
—OPPOSITES: neglect, suppress.

foul *adj.* **1** ☞ REPULSIVE. **2** DIRTY, filthy, mucky, grimy, grubby, muddy, muddied, unclean, unwashed; squalid, sordid, soiled, sullied, scummy; rotten, defiled, decaying, putrid, putrefied, smelly, fetid; *informal* cruddy, yucky, icky, grotty. **3** ☞ UNKIND. **4** INCLEMENT, unpleasant, disagreeable, bad; rough, stormy, squally, gusty, windy, blustery, wild, blowy, rainy, wet. **5** ☞ EVIL *adj.* 1. **6** VULGAR, crude, coarse, filthy, dirty, obscene, indecent, indelicate, naughty, lewd, smutty, ribald, salacious, scatological, offensive, abusive.
—OPPOSITES: pleasant, kind, fair, clean, righteous, mild.
▶ *v.* DIRTY, infect, pollute, contaminate, poison, taint, sully, soil, stain, blacken, muddy, splash, spatter, smear, blight, defile, make filthy.
—OPPOSITES: clean up.

foul-mouthed *adj.* VULGAR, crude, coarse; obscene, rude, smutty, dirty, filthy, indecent, indelicate, offensive, lewd, X-rated, scatological, foul, abusive.

found *v.* **1** ESTABLISH, set up, start (up), begin, get going, institute, inaugurate, launch, float, form, create, bring into being, originate, develop, build. **2** BASE, build, construct; ground in, root in; rest,

hinge, depend.
—OPPOSITES: dissolve, liquidate, abandon, demolish.

foundation n. **1** FOOTING, foot, base, substructure, infrastructure, underpinning; bottom, bedrock, substratum. **2** BASIS, starting point, base, point of departure, beginning, premise; principles, fundamentals, rudiments; cornerstone, core, heart, thrust, essence, kernel. **3** JUSTIFICATION, grounds, defence, reason, rationale, cause, basis, motive, excuse, call, pretext, provocation.

founder n. ORIGINATOR, creator, (founding) father, prime mover, architect, engineer, designer, developer, pioneer, author, planner, inventor, mastermind.

fountain n. JET, spray, spout, spurt, well, fount, cascade.

fracas n. ☞ FIGHT n. 1.

fractious adj. **1** ☞ GRUMPY.
2 WAYWARD, unruly, uncontrollable, unmanageable, out of hand, obstreperous, difficult, headstrong, recalcitrant, intractable; disobedient, insubordinate, disruptive, disorderly, undisciplined; contrary, wilful; formal refractory.
—OPPOSITES: contented, affable, dutiful.

fracture n. CRACK, split, fissure, crevice, break, rupture, breach, rift, cleft, chink, interstice; crazing.
▸ v. BREAK, crack, shatter, splinter, split, rupture; informal bust.

fragile adj. **1** BREAKABLE, easily broken; delicate, dainty, fine, flimsy, frail; eggshell; formal frangible. **2** TENUOUS, shaky,

insecure, unreliable, vulnerable, flimsy.
—OPPOSITES: strong, durable, robust.

fragment n. PIECE, bit, particle, speck; chip, shard, sliver, splinter; shaving, paring, snippet, scrap, offcut, flake, shred, wisp, morsel.
▸ v. BREAK UP, break, break into pieces, crack open/apart, shatter, splinter, fracture; disintegrate, fall to pieces, fall apart.

fragmentary adj. INCOMPLETE, fragmented, disconnected, disjointed, broken, discontinuous, piecemeal, scrappy, bitty, sketchy, uneven, patchy.

fragrance n. **1** SWEET SMELL, scent, perfume, bouquet; aroma, redolence, nose, odour.
2 ☞ PERFUME 1.

fragrant adj. SWEET-SCENTED, sweet-smelling, scented, perfumed, aromatic, perfumy; literary redolent.
—OPPOSITES: smelly.

frail adj. **1** ☞ FEEBLE 1. **2** FRAGILE, breakable, easily damaged, delicate, flimsy, insubstantial, unsteady, unstable, rickety; formal frangible.
—OPPOSITES: strong, robust.

frame n. **1** ☞ FRAMEWORK 1.
2 BODY, figure, form, shape, physique, build, size, proportions.
3 SETTING, mount, mounting.
▸ v. **1** MOUNT, set in a frame.
2 FORMULATE, draw up, draft, plan, shape, compose, put together, form, devise, create, establish, conceive, think up, originate; informal dream up.

framework n. **1** FRAME, substructure, infrastructure,

structure, skeleton, chassis, shell, body, bodywork, casing; support, scaffolding, foundation.
2 STRUCTURE, shape, fabric, order, scheme, system, organization, construction, configuration, composition, warp and woof; *informal* makeup.

frank *adj.* **1** ☞ OUTSPOKEN.
2 ☞ UNDISGUISED.
—OPPOSITES: evasive.

frantic *adj.* PANIC-STRICKEN, panicky, beside oneself, at one's wits' end, distraught, overwrought, worked up, agitated, distressed; frenzied, wild, frenetic, fraught, feverish, hysterical, desperate; *informal* in a state, in a tizzy/tizz, wound up, het up, in a flap, tearing one's hair out.
—OPPOSITES: calm.

fraud *n.* **1** FRAUDULENCE, cheating, swindling, embezzlement, deceit, deception, double-dealing, chicanery, sharp practice.
2 SWINDLE, racket, deception, trick, cheat, hoax; *informal* scam, con, con trick, rip-off, sting, gyp, fiddle, bunco, hustle, grift.
3 IMPOSTER, fake, sham, charlatan, quack, mountebank; swindler, goniff, snake oil salesman, fraudster, racketeer, cheat, confidence trickster; *informal* phony, con man, con artist, scam artist.

fraudulent *adj.* ☞ DISHONEST.
—OPPOSITES: honest.

fraught *adj.* FULL OF, filled with, rife with; attended by, accompanied by.

fray *v.* **1** UNRAVEL, wear, wear thin, wear out/through, become worn.

2 STRAIN, tax, overtax, put on edge.

freak *n.* **1** ANOMALY, aberration, rarity, oddity, unusual occurrence; fluke, twist of fate. **2** (*informal*) ODDITY, eccentric, misfit; crank, lunatic; *informal* oddball, weirdo, nutcase, nut, wacko, kook.
3 ☞ FAN.
▶ *adj.* UNUSUAL, anomalous, aberrant, atypical, unrepresentative, irregular, fluky, exceptional, unaccountable, bizarre, queer, peculiar, odd, freakish; unpredictable, unforeseeable, unexpected, unanticipated, surprising; rare, singular, isolated.
—OPPOSITES: normal.

free *adj.* **1** WITHOUT CHARGE, free of charge, for nothing; complimentary, gratis; *informal* for free, on the house.
2 UNENCUMBERED BY, unaffected by, clear of, without, rid of; exempt from, not liable to, safe from, immune to, excused from; *informal* sans, minus. **3** UNOCCUPIED, not busy, available, between appointments; off duty, off work, off; on vacation, on holiday, on leave; at leisure, with time on one's hands, with time to spare.
4 VACANT, empty, available, unoccupied, not taken, not in use.
5 ON THE LOOSE, at liberty, at large; loose, unconfined, unbound, untied, unchained, untethered, unshackled, unfettered, unrestrained. **6** ALLOWED, permitted; ABLE TO, in a position to, capable of. **7** ☞ GENEROUS 1.
—OPPOSITES: busy, occupied, captive, mean.

▶ *v.* RELEASE, set free, let go, liberate, discharge, deliver; set loose, let loose, turn loose, untie, unchain, unfetter, unshackle, unleash.

—OPPOSITES: confine, trap.

□**free and easy** EASYGOING, relaxed, casual, informal, unceremonious, unforced, natural, open, spontaneous, uninhibited, friendly; tolerant, liberal; *informal* laid-back.

freedom *n.* **1** LIBERTY, liberation, release, deliverance, delivery, discharge; *historical* manumission. **2** INDEPENDENCE, self-government, self-determination, self rule, home rule, sovereignty, non-alignment, autonomy; democracy. **3** EXEMPTION, immunity, dispensation; impunity. **4** RIGHT, entitlement, privilege, prerogative; scope, latitude, leeway, flexibility, space, breathing space, room, elbow room; licence, leave, free rein, a free hand, carte blanche, a blank cheque.

—OPPOSITES: captivity, subjection, liability.

freeze *v.* **1** ICE OVER, ice up, solidify. **2** BE VERY COLD, be numb with cold, turn blue with cold, shiver. **3** STOP DEAD, stop in one's tracks, stop, stand (stock) still, go rigid, become motionless, become paralyzed.

—OPPOSITES: thaw.

freezing *adj.* ☞ COLD 1, 2.

—OPPOSITES: balmy, hot.

freight *n.* **1** ☞ CARGO.

2 TRANSPORTATION, transport, conveyance, carriage, portage, haulage.

frenzy *n.* HYSTERIA, madness, mania, delirium, feverishness, fever, wildness, agitation, turmoil, tumult; wild excitement, euphoria, elation, ecstasy.

frequent *adj.* **1** RECURRENT, recurring, repeated, periodic, continual, one after another, successive; many, numerous, lots of, several. **2** HABITUAL, regular.

—OPPOSITES: occasional.

▶ *v.* VISIT, patronize, spend time in, visit regularly, be a regular visitor to, haunt; *informal* hang out at.

fresh *adj.* **1** CLEAN, blank, empty, clear, white; unused, new, pristine, unmarked, untouched. **2** NEW, recent, latest, up-to-date, modern, modernistic, ultra-modern, newfangled; original, novel, different, innovative, unusual, unconventional, unorthodox; radical, revolutionary; *informal* offbeat. **3** YOUNG, youthful; new, inexperienced, naive, untrained, unqualified, untried, raw; *informal* wet behind the ears. **4** REFRESHED, rested, restored, revived; (as) fresh as a daisy, energetic, vigorous, invigorated, full of vim and vigour, lively, vibrant, spry, sprightly, bright, alert, perky; *informal* full of beans, raring to go, bright-eyed and bushy-tailed, chirpy, chipper. **5** COOL, crisp, refreshing, invigorating, tonic; pure, clean, clear, uncontaminated, untainted. **6** CHILLY, chill, cool, cold, brisk, bracing, invigorating; strong; *informal* nippy. **7** ☞ CHEEKY.

—OPPOSITES: stale, old, tired, warm.

fret v. WORRY, be anxious, feel uneasy, be distressed, be upset, upset oneself, concern oneself; agonize, sigh, pine, brood, eat one's heart out.

friction n. **1** ABRASION, rubbing, chafing, grating, rasping, scraping; resistance, drag. **2** HOSTILITY, animosity, antipathy, enmity, antagonism, resentment, acrimony, bitterness, ill will. See also DISCORD 1.
—OPPOSITES: harmony.

friend n. COMPANION, soul mate, intimate, confidante, confidant, familiar, alter ego, second self, playmate, classmate, schoolmate, workmate; ally, associate; sister, brother; best friend, kindred spirit, bosom buddy, bosom friend; *informal* pal, chum, sidekick, crony, main man, mate, buddy, bud, amigo, compadre, homeboy, homegirl, homie; *archaic* compeer.
—OPPOSITES: enemy.

friendless adj. ALONE, all alone, by oneself, solitary, lonely, with no one to turn to, lone, without friends, companionless, unpopular, unwanted, unloved, abandoned, rejected, forsaken, shunned, spurned, forlorn, lonesome.
—OPPOSITES: popular.

friendliness n. AFFABILITY, amiability, geniality, congeniality, bonhomie, cordiality, good nature, good humour, warmth, affection, demonstrativeness, conviviality, joviality, companionability, sociability, gregariousness, camaraderie, neighbourliness, approachability, accessibility, openness, kindness, kindliness, sympathy, amenability, benevolence.

friendly adj. **1** AFFABLE, amiable, genial, congenial, cordial, warm, affectionate, demonstrative, convivial, companionable, sociable, gregarious, outgoing, comradely, neighbourly, hospitable, approachable, helpful, welcoming, easy to get on with, accessible, communicative, open, unreserved, easygoing, good-natured, good-humoured, kindly, kind, amicable, charming, likeable, nice, personable, pleasant, simpatico, benign, amenable, agreeable, obliging, sympathetic, well-disposed, benevolent, hail-fellow-well-met; *informal* chummy, clubby, buddy-buddy. **2** AMICABLE, congenial, cordial, pleasant, easy, relaxed, casual, informal, unceremonious; close, intimate, familiar.
—OPPOSITES: hostile.

friendship n. **1** RELATIONSHIP, close relationship, attachment, association, bond, tie, link, union. **2** AMITY, camaraderie, friendliness, comradeship, companionship, fellowship, brotherhood, sisterhood, fellow feeling, closeness, togetherness, affinity, rapport, connection, communication, communion, understanding, harmony, unity, accord; intimacy, mutual affection.
—OPPOSITES: enmity.

fright n. **1** ☞ FEAR n. 1. **2** SCARE, shock, surprise, turn, jolt, start; the shivers, the shakes; *informal* the jitters, the heebie-jeebies, the willies, the creeps, the collywobbles, a cold sweat, butterflies (in one's stomach). **3** ☞ EYESORE.

frighten v. ☞ SCARE v.

frightening adj. TERRIFYING, horrifying, alarming, startling, white-knuckle, chilling, spine-chilling, hair-raising, blood-curdling, bone-chilling, disturbing, unnerving, nerve-racking, spine-tingling, intimidating, daunting, formidable, dismaying, disquieting, upsetting, harrowing, traumatic; eerie, sinister, fearsome, nightmarish, macabre, menacing; informal scary, spooky, creepy, hairy.

frightful adj. ALARMING, shocking, terrifying, harrowing, appalling, fearful. See also TERRIBLE 1.

frigid adj. **1** ☞ COLD 1. **2** STIFF, formal, stony, wooden, unemotional, passionless, unfeeling, indifferent, unresponsive, unenthusiastic, austere, distant, aloof, remote, reserved, unapproachable; frosty, cold, icy, cool, unsmiling, forbidding, unfriendly, unwelcoming, hostile; informal offish, standoffish.
—OPPOSITES: hot, friendly.

fringe n. **1** PERIMETER, periphery, border, borderline, margin, rim, outer edge, edge, extremity, limit; outskirts. **2** EDGING, edge, border, trimming, frill, flounce, ruffle; tassels.
—OPPOSITES: middle.
▸ adj. ☞ UNCONVENTIONAL.
—OPPOSITES: mainstream.

frisky adj. LIVELY, bouncy, bubbly, perky, active, energetic, animated,

zestful, full of vim and vigour; playful, coltish, skittish, spirited, high-spirited, exuberant; informal full of beans, zippy, peppy, bright-eyed and bushy-tailed.

frivolity n. LIGHTHEARTEDNESS, levity, joking, jocularity, gaiety, fun, frivolousness, silliness, foolishness, flightiness, skittishness; superficiality, shallowness, flippancy, vacuity, empty-headedness.

frivolous adj. **1** FLIPPANT, glib, facetious, joking, jokey, lighthearted; fatuous, inane, senseless, thoughtless; informal flip. **2** TIME-WASTING, pointless, trivial, trifling, minor, petty, insignificant, unimportant.
—OPPOSITES: sensible, serious.

frolic v. PLAY, amuse oneself, romp, disport oneself, frisk, gambol, cavort, caper, cut capers, scamper, skip, dance, prance, leap about, jump about; dated sport.

front n. **1** FORE, foremost part, forepart, anterior, forefront, nose, head; foreground. **2** FRONTAGE, face, facing, facade; window. **3** FRONT LINE, firing line, vanguard, van; trenches. **4** HEAD, beginning, start, top, lead. **5** APPEARANCE, air, face, manner, demeanour, bearing, pose, exterior, veneer, (outward) show, act, pretense, affectation. **6** COVER, cover-up, false front, blind, disguise, facade, mask, cloak, screen, smokescreen, camouflage.
—OPPOSITES: rear, back.
▸ adj. LEADING, lead, first, foremost; in first place.
—OPPOSITES: last.

frontier *n.* BORDER, boundary, borderline, dividing line, demarcation line; perimeter, limit, edge, rim, bounds.

frosty *adj.* **1** ☞ COLD 1. **2** COLD, frigid, icy, glacial, unfriendly, inhospitable, unwelcoming, forbidding, hostile, stony, stern, steely, hard.

froth *n. & v.* ☞ FOAM.

frown *v.* **1** SCOWL, glower, glare, lower, make a face, look daggers, give someone a black/dirty look; knit/furrow one's brows.
2 DISAPPROVE OF, view with disfavour, dislike, look askance at, not take kindly to, take a dim view of, take exception to, object to, have a low opinion of.
—OPPOSITES: smile.
▶ *n.* GRIMACE, scowl, glower, pout, wince, moue, face.

frugal *adj.* THRIFTY, economical, careful, cautious, prudent, provident, sparing, scrimping; abstemious, abstinent, austere, self-denying, ascetic, monkish, Spartan; parsimonious, miserly, niggardly, cheese-paring, penny-pinching, close-fisted; *informal* tight-fisted, tight, stingy.
—OPPOSITES: extravagant, lavish.

fruitful *adj.* PRODUCTIVE, constructive, useful, of use, worthwhile, helpful, beneficial, valuable, rewarding, profitable, advantageous, gainful, successful, effective, effectual, well-spent.
—OPPOSITES: barren, futile.

fruition *n.* FULFILLMENT, realization, actualization, materialization, achievement, attainment, accomplishment, resolution; success, completion,

consummation, conclusion, close, finish, perfection, maturity, maturation, ripening, ripeness; implementation, execution, performance.

fruitless *adj.* ☞ FUTILE.
—OPPOSITES: productive.

frustrate *v.* **1** THWART, prevent, defeat, foil, block, stop, put a stop to, counter, spoil, check, balk, disappoint, forestall, dash, scotch, quash, crush, derail, snooker; obstruct, impede, hamper, hinder, hamstring, stand in the way of, spike someone's guns, put a crimp in, put paid to, spike, stonewall; *informal* stymie, foul up, screw up, put the kibosh on, do for; *informal* scupper, scuttle. **2** EXASPERATE, infuriate, annoy, anger, vex, irritate, irk, try someone's patience; disappoint, discontent, dissatisfy, discourage, dishearten, dispirit; *informal* aggravate, bug, miff.
—OPPOSITES: help, facilitate.

fudge *v.* ADJUST, manipulate, massage, put a spin on, juggle, misrepresent, misreport, bend; tamper with, tinker with, interfere with, doctor, falsify, distort; *informal* cook, fiddle with.

fuel *n.* **1** GAS, gasoline, diesel, petroleum, propane; power source. **2** ENCOURAGEMENT, ammunition, stimulus, incentive; provocation, goading.

fugitive *n.* ESCAPEE, runaway, deserter, absconder; refugee.
▶ *adj.* ESCAPED, runaway, on the run, on the loose, at large; wanted; *informal* AWOL, on the lam.

fulfill *v.* **1** ACHIEVE, attain, realize, actualize, make happen, succeed in, bring to completion, bring to fruition, satisfy. **2** CARRY OUT, perform, accomplish, execute, do, discharge, conduct; complete, finish, conclude, perfect. **3** MEET, satisfy, comply with, conform to, fill, answer.

full *adj.* **1** CROWDED, packed, crammed, congested; teeming, swarming, thick, thronged, overcrowded, overrun; abounding, bursting, overflowing; *informal* jam-packed, wall-to-wall, stuffed, chockablock, chock full, bursting at the seams, packed to the gunwales, awash. **2** OCCUPIED, taken, in use, unavailable. **3** REPLETE, full up, satisfied, well-fed, sated, satiated, surfeited; gorged, glutted; *informal* stuffed. **4** EVENTFUL, interesting, exciting, lively, action-packed, busy, energetic, active. **5** COMPREHENSIVE, thorough, exhaustive, all-inclusive, all-encompassing, all-embracing, in depth; complete, entire, whole, unabridged, uncut. **6** PLUMP, well-rounded, rounded, buxom, shapely, ample, curvaceous, voluptuous, womanly, Junoesque; *informal* busty, curvy, well-upholstered, well-endowed, zaftig. **7** RICH, intense, full-bodied, strong, deep.
—OPPOSITES: empty, hungry, selective, thin.

fully *adv.* COMPLETELY, entirely, wholly, totally, quite, utterly, perfectly, altogether, thoroughly, in all respects, in every respect, without reservation, without exception, to the hilt.
—OPPOSITES: partly, nearly.

fumble *v.* **1** GROPE, fish, search blindly, scrabble around. **2** STUMBLE, blunder, flounder, lumber, stagger, totter, lurch; feel one's way, grope one's way. **3** MISS, drop, mishandle, bobble.

fume *n.* **1** SMOKE, vapour, gas, effluvium; exhaust; pollution. **2** SMELL, odour, stink, reek, stench, funk; *literary* miasma.
▸ *v.* BE FURIOUS, be enraged, be very angry, seethe, be livid, be incensed, boil, be beside oneself, spit; rage, rant and rave; *informal* be hot under the collar, foam at the mouth, see red.

fun *n.* **1** ENJOYMENT, entertainment, amusement, pleasure; jollification, merrymaking; recreation, diversion, leisure, relaxation; good time, great time; *informal* living it up, a ball. **2** MERRIMENT, cheerfulness, cheeriness, jollity, joviality, jocularity, high spirits, gaiety, mirth, laughter, hilarity, glee, gladness, lightheartedness, levity.
—OPPOSITES: boredom, misery.
▸ *adj.* (*informal*) ENJOYABLE, entertaining, amusing, diverting, pleasurable, pleasing, agreeable, interesting.
□ **make fun of** ☞ TEASE.

function *n.* **1** PURPOSE, task, use, role. **2** RESPONSIBILITY, duty, role, concern, province, activity, assignment, obligation, charge; task, job, mission, undertaking, commission; capacity, post, situation, office, occupation, employment, business. **3** ☞ PARTY *n.* 1.
▸ *v.* **1** WORK, go, run, be in working/running order, operate,

be operative. **2** ACT, serve, operate; perform, work, play the role of, do duty as.

functional *adj.* **1** PRACTICAL, useful, utilitarian, utility, workaday, serviceable; minimalist, plain, simple, basic, modest, unadorned, unostentatious, no-frills, without frills; impersonal, characterless, soulless, institutional, clinical. **2** WORKING, in working order, functioning, in service, in use; going, running, operative, operating, in operation, in commission, in action; *informal* up and running.

fund *n.* **1** COLLECTION, kitty, reserve, pool, purse; endowment, foundation, trust, grant, investment; savings, nest egg; *informal* stash. **2** ☞ MONEY 1. **3** STOCK, store, supply, accumulation, collection, bank, pool; mine, reservoir, storehouse, treasury, treasure house, hoard, repository; *informal* pork barrel.

▶ *v.* FINANCE, pay for, back, capitalize, sponsor, put up the money for, subsidize, underwrite, endow, support, maintain; *informal* foot the bill for, pick up the tab for, bankroll, stake.

fundamental *adj.* BASIC, underlying, core, foundational, rudimentary, elemental, elementary, basal, root; primary, prime, cardinal, first, principal, chief, key, central, vital, essential, quintessential, important, indispensable, necessary, crucial, pivotal, critical; structural, organic, constitutional, inherent, intrinsic.

—OPPOSITES: secondary, unimportant.

fundamentally *adv.* ESSENTIALLY, in essence, basically, at heart, at bottom, deep down, au fond; primarily, above all, first and foremost, first of all; *informal* at the end of the day, when all is said and done, when you get right down to it.

fundraiser *n.* bazaar, bake sale, fowl supper✦, fall supper✦, pancake breakfast, box social, strawberry social, gala; walkathon, skate-a-thon✦.

funereal *adj.* SOMBRE, gloomy, mournful, melancholy, lugubrious, sepulchral, miserable, doleful, woeful, sad, sorrowful, cheerless, joyless, bleak, dismal, depressing, dreary, grave, solemn, serious; *literary* dolorous.

—OPPOSITES: cheerful.

funny *adj.* **1** AMUSING, humorous, witty, comic, comical, droll, facetious, jocular, jokey; hilarious, hysterical, riotous, uproarious; entertaining, diverting, sparkling, scintillating; silly, farcical, slapstick; *informal* side-splitting, rib-tickling, gut-busting, knee-slapping, laugh-a-minute, wacky, zany, waggish, off the wall, a barrel of laughs, a hoot, jocose, laughable, lighthearted, thigh-slapping, tongue-in-cheek, wry, a scream, rich, priceless; *informal, dated* killing. **2** STRANGE, peculiar, odd, queer, weird, bizarre, curious, freakish, freak, quirky; mysterious, mystifying, puzzling, perplexing; unusual, uncommon, anomalous, irregular, abnormal, exceptional, singular, out of the

ordinary, extraordinary.
3 ☞ SUSPECT adj.
—OPPOSITES: serious,
unsurprising, trustworthy.

furious adj. **1** ☞ ANGRY. **2** HEATED,
hot, passionate, fiery, 'lively';
fierce, vehement, violent, wild,
unrestrained, tumultuous,
turbulent, tempestuous, stormy.
—OPPOSITES: calm.

furnish v. **1** FIT OUT, provide with
furniture, appoint, outfit.
2 SUPPLY, provide, equip,
provision, issue, kit out, present,
give, offer, afford, purvey, bestow;
informal fix up.

furniture n. FURNISHINGS, fittings,
movables, appointments, effects;
Law chattels; informal stuff, things.

furor n. COMMOTION, uproar,
outcry, fuss, upset, brouhaha,
foofaraw, palaver, pother,
tempest, agitation,
pandemonium, disturbance,
controversy, hue and cry, row,
storm, trouble, hubbub, rumpus,
tumult, turmoil; stir, excitement;
informal song and dance, to-do, hoo-
ha, hullabaloo, ballyhoo,
kerfuffle, flap, stink.

furrow v. WRINKLE, crease, line,
crinkle, pucker, screw up, scrunch
up, corrugate.

further adj. **1** MORE DISTANT, more
remote, remoter, further away/off,
farther (away/off); far, other,
opposite. **2** ☞ ADDITIONAL.
▶ v. PROMOTE, advance, forward,
develop, facilitate, aid, assist,
help, help along, lend a hand to,
abet; expedite, hasten, speed up,
boost, encourage, cultivate,
nurture, foster.
—OPPOSITES: impede.

furthermore adv. MOREOVER,
further, what's more, also,
additionally, in addition, besides,
as well, too, to boot, on top of
that, over and above that, into the
bargain, by the same token,
likewise.

furtive adj. SIDELONG, sideways,
oblique, indirect; informal hush-
hush, shifty. See also
SURREPTITIOUS.
—OPPOSITES: open.

fury n. **1** RAGE, anger, wrath,
outrage, spleen, temper;
crossness, indignation, umbrage,
annoyance, exasperation; literary
ire, choler. **2** VIRAGO, hellcat,
termagant, spitfire, vixen, shrew,
harridan, dragon, gorgon.
—OPPOSITES: good humour,
mildness.

fuse v. **1** COMBINE, amalgamate,
put together, join, unite, marry,
blend, merge, meld, mingle,
integrate, intermix, intermingle,
synthesize; coalesce, compound,
alloy; technical admix; literary
commingle. **2** BOND, stick, bind,
weld, solder; melt, smelt.
—OPPOSITES: separate.

fuss n. **1** ☞ COMMOTION. **2** BOTHER,
trouble, inconvenience, effort,
exertion, labour; informal hassle.
▶ v. WORRY, fret, be anxious, be
agitated, make a big thing out of;
make a mountain out of a
molehill; informal flap, be in a tizzy,
be in a stew.

fussy adj. FINICKY, particular, over-
particular, fastidious,
discriminating, selective, dainty;
hard to please, difficult, exacting,
demanding; faddish; informal

pernickety, persnickety, choosy, picky.

futile *adj.* FRUITLESS, vain, pointless, purposeless, useless, ineffectual, ineffective, inefficacious, to no effect, of no use, in vain, to no avail, unavailing, for naught, frustrating; unsuccessful, failed, thwarted; unproductive, barren, unprofitable, profitless, unrewarding, wasted, worthless; impotent, hollow, empty, forlorn, idle, hopeless; *archaic* bootless.
—OPPOSITES: useful.

future *n.* DESTINY, fate, fortune; prospects, expectations, chances.
—OPPOSITES: past.

▸ *adj.* **1** LATER, to come, following, ensuing, succeeding, subsequent, coming. **2** TO BE, destined; intended, planned, prospective.
☐ **in future** ☞ HEREAFTER.

fuzzy *adj.* **1** FRIZZY, fluffy, woolly; downy, soft. **2** BLURRY, blurred, indistinct, unclear, bleary, misty, distorted, out of focus, unfocused, lacking definition, nebulous; ill-defined, indefinite, vague, hazy, imprecise, inexact, loose, woolly. **3** CONFUSED, muddled, addled, fuddled, befuddled, groggy, disoriented, disorientated, mixed up, fazed, foggy, dizzy, stupefied, benumbed.

Gg

gadget *n.* ☞ DEVICE 1.

gaffe *n.* INDISCRETION, impropriety, miscalculation, gaucherie, solecism. See also BLUNDER *n.*

gag *n.* ☞ JOKE *n.* 1, PRANK.
▶ *v.* **1** ☞ SILENCE *v.* 1. **2** ☞ RETCH.

gaiety *n.* LIVELINESS, vivacity, animation, effervescence, sprightliness, zest; *informal* chirpiness, bounce, pep. See also HAPPINESS.
—OPPOSITES: misery.

gain *v.* **1** OBTAIN, get, secure, acquire, come by, procure, attain, achieve, earn, win, garner, capture, clinch, pick up, carry off, reap; *informal* land, net, bag. **2** ☞ BENEFIT *v.* 2. **3** PUT ON, increase in. **4** CATCH UP WITH/ON, catch someone up, catch, close (in) on, near. **5** REACH, arrive at, get to, come to, make, attain, set foot on; *informal* hit.
—OPPOSITES: lose.
▶ *n.* **1** PROFIT, advantage, benefit, reward; percentage, takings, yield, return, winnings, receipts, proceeds, dividend, interest; *informal* pickings, cut, take, slice. **2** ☞ INCREASE *n.*
—OPPOSITES: loss, decrease.

gainful *adj.* ☞ PROFITABLE 1.

gait *n.* WALK, step, stride, pace, tread, bearing, carriage; *formal* comportment.

gale *n.* **1** WINDSTORM, strong/high wind, hurricane, tornado, cyclone, whirlwind; storm, squall, tempest, typhoon. **2** PEAL, howl, hoot, shriek, scream, roar; outburst, burst, fit, paroxysm, explosion.

gallant *adj.* **1** ☞ BRAVE *adj.* **2** CHIVALROUS, princely, gentlemanly, honourable, courteous, polite, mannerly, attentive, respectful, gracious, considerate, thoughtful.
—OPPOSITES: cowardly, discourteous.

galvanize *v.* JOLT, shock, startle, impel, stir, spur, prod, urge, motivate, stimulate, electrify, excite, rouse, arouse, awaken; invigorate, fire, animate, vitalize, energize, exhilarate, thrill, catalyze, inspire, light a fire under.

gamble *v.* **1** BET, wager, place/lay a bet on something, stake money on something, back the horses, game; *informal* play the ponies. **2** TAKE A CHANCE, take a risk, take a flier; *informal* stick one's neck out, go out on a limb.
▶ *n.* **1** BET, wager. **2** RISK, chance, hazard, shot in the dark.

game *n.* **1** PASTIME, diversion, entertainment, amusement, distraction, divertissement, recreation, sport, activity. **2** MATCH, contest, tournament,

meet. **3** WILD ANIMALS, wild fowl, big game, country food❖.
▶ *adj.* ☞ READY *adj.* 3.

gang *n.* **1** ☞ CROWD *n.* 1. **2** (*informal*) CIRCLE, social circle, social set, group, clique, in-crowd, coterie, cabal, lot, ring; *informal* crew, rat pack.

gangling, **gangly** *adj.* LANKY, rangy, tall, thin, skinny, spindly, stringy, bony, angular, scrawny, spare; awkward, uncoordinated, ungainly, gawky, inelegant, graceless, ungraceful.
—OPPOSITES: squat.

gangster *n.* HOODLUM, gang member, racketeer, robber, ruffian, thug, tough, villain, lawbreaker, criminal; gunman; Mafioso; *informal* mobster, crook, hit man, hood.

gap *n.* **1** OPENING, aperture, space, breach, chink, slit, slot, vent, crack, crevice, cranny, cavity, hole, orifice, interstice, perforation, break, fracture, rift, rent, fissure, cleft, divide.
2 ☞ PAUSE. **3** OMISSION, blank, lacuna, void, vacuity. **4** CHASM, gulf, rift, split, separation, breach; contrast, difference, disparity, divergence, imbalance.

gape *v.* **1** STARE, stare open-mouthed, stare in wonder, goggle, gaze, ogle; *informal* rubberneck, gawk. **2** OPEN WIDE, open up, yawn; part, split.

garb *n.* CLOTHES, clothing, garments, attire, dress, costume, outfit, wear, uniform, livery, regalia; *informal* gear, getup, togs, duds; *formal* apparel, raiment, vestments.
▶ *v.* ☞ DRESS *v.* 1.

garbage *n.* **1** TRASH, refuse, waste, detritus, litter, junk, scrap; scraps, leftovers, remains, slops, rubbish. **2** ☞ NONSENSE.

garble *v.* MIX UP, muddle, jumble, confuse, obscure, distort, scramble; misstate, misquote, misreport, misrepresent, mistranslate, misinterpret, misconstrue, twist.

garish *adj.* ☞ GAUDY.
—OPPOSITES: drab.

garner *v.* GATHER, collect, accumulate, amass, get (together), assemble, reap.

garrison *n.* **1** TROOPS, militia; armed force, unit, platoon, brigade, squadron, battalion, corps. **2** FORTRESS, fort, fortification, stronghold, citadel, camp, encampment, cantonment, command post, base, station; barracks.

garrulous *adj.* **1** TALKATIVE, loquacious, voluble, verbose, chatty, chattering, gossipy; effusive, expansive, forthcoming, conversational, communicative; *informal* mouthy, gabby.
2 ☞ VERBOSE.
—OPPOSITES: taciturn, concise.

gash *n.* LACERATION, cut, wound, injury, slash, tear, incision; slit, split, rip, rent; scratch, scrape, graze, abrasion; *Medicine* lesion.
▶ *v.* LACERATE, cut (open), wound, injure, hurt, slash, tear, gouge, puncture, slit, split, rend; scratch, scrape, graze, abrade.

gasp *v.* **1** CATCH ONE'S BREATH, draw in one's breath, gulp; exclaim, cry (out). **2** PANT, puff, wheeze, breathe hard, choke, fight for breath.

gate n. GATEWAY, doorway, entrance, entryway; exit, egress, opening; door, portal; barrier, turnstile.

gather v. **1** CONGREGATE, assemble, meet, collect, come/get together, convene, muster, rally, converge; cluster together, crowd, mass, flock together. **2** SUMMON, call together, bring together, assemble, convene, rally, round up, muster, marshal. **3** ☞ COLLECT 1. **4** HARVEST, reap, crop; pick, pluck; collect. **5** UNDERSTAND, believe, think, conclude, deduce, infer, assume, take it, surmise, fancy; hear, hear tell, learn, discover.
—OPPOSITES: disperse.

gathering n. ASSEMBLY, meeting, convention, rally, turnout, congress, convocation, conclave, council, synod, forum; congregation, audience, crowd, group, throng, mass, multitude; informal get-together; formal concourse.

gauche adj. AWKWARD, gawky, inelegant, graceless, ungraceful, ungainly, maladroit, klutzy, inept; unsophisticated, uncultured, uncultivated, unrefined, unworldly.
—OPPOSITES: elegant, sophisticated.

gaudy adj. GARISH, lurid, loud, over-bright, glaring, harsh, violent, showy, glittering, brassy, ostentatious; tasteless, in bad taste, tawdry, vulgar, unattractive, bilious; informal flash, flashy, tacky, kitschy, tinselly, (Que.) kétaine ✤.
—OPPOSITES: drab, tasteful.

gauge n. **1** MEASURE, indicator, barometer, point of reference, guide, guideline, touchstone, yardstick, benchmark, criterion, test, litmus test. **2** SIZE, diameter, thickness, width, breadth; measure, capacity, magnitude; bore, calibre.
▶ v. ☞ MEASURE v.

gaunt adj. HAGGARD, drawn, thin, lean, skinny, spindly, spare, bony, angular, raw-boned, pinched, hollow-cheeked, scrawny, scraggy, as thin as a rake, cadaverous, skeletal, emaciated, skin-and-bones; wasted, withered.
—OPPOSITES: plump.

gawk v. ☞ GAPE 1.

gawky adj. ☞ AWKWARD 5.
—OPPOSITES: graceful.

gay adj. **1** HOMOSEXUAL, lesbian, same-sex; informal queer, camp, pink, lavender, dykey, flaming. **2** (dated) ☞ CHEERFUL 1.

gaze v. STARE, look fixedly, gape, goggle, eye, look, study, scrutinize; ogle, leer; informal gawk, rubberneck.

gear n. (informal) **1** EQUIPMENT, apparatus, paraphernalia, articles, appliances, impedimenta; tools, utensils, implements, instruments, gadgets; stuff, things; kit, rig, tackle, odds and ends, bits and pieces, trappings, appurtenances, accoutrements, regalia. **2** ☞ BELONGINGS.

general adj. **1** WIDESPREAD, common, extensive, universal, wide, popular, public, mainstream; established, conventional, traditional, orthodox, accepted. **2** COMPREHENSIVE, overall, across

the board, blanket, umbrella, mass, wholesale, sweeping, broad-ranging, inclusive, company-wide; universal, global, worldwide, nationwide. **3** MISCELLANEOUS, mixed, assorted, diversified, composite, heterogeneous, eclectic. **4** ☞ CUSTOMARY. **5** BROAD, imprecise, inexact, rough, loose, approximate, unspecific, vague, woolly, indefinite; *informal* ballpark.
—OPPOSITES: restricted, localized, specialist, exceptional, detailed.

generally *adv.* **1** ☞ USUALLY. **2** WIDELY, commonly, extensively, universally, popularly.

generate *v.* CAUSE, give rise to, lead to, result in, bring about, create, make, produce, engender, spawn, precipitate, prompt, provoke, trigger, spark off, stir up, induce, promote, foster.

generosity *n.* LIBERALITY, lavishness, magnanimity, munificence, largesse, open-handedness, unselfishness; kindness, benevolence, altruism, charity, big-heartedness, goodness; *literary* bounteousness.

generous *adj.* **1** LIBERAL, lavish, magnanimous, munificent, giving, open-handed, bountiful, unselfish, ungrudging, extravagant, free, indulgent, beneficent, philanthropic, unsparing, unstinting, prodigal; *literary* bounteous. **2** MAGNANIMOUS, kind, benevolent, altruistic, charitable, noble, big-hearted, honourable, good; unselfish, self-sacrificing. **3** LAVISH, plentiful, copious, ample, liberal, large, great, abundant, profuse, bumper, opulent, prolific; *informal* galore.

—OPPOSITES: mean, selfish, meagre.

genial *adj.* ☞ FRIENDLY 1.
—OPPOSITES: unfriendly.

genius *n.* **1** BRILLIANCE, intelligence, intellect, ability, cleverness, brains, erudition, wisdom, fine mind; artistry, flair. **2** TALENT, gift, flair, aptitude, facility, knack, bent, ability, expertise, capacity, faculty; strength, forte, brilliance, skill, artistry. **3** BRILLIANT PERSON, gifted person, mastermind, Einstein, intellectual, intellect, thinker, brain, mind; prodigy; *informal* egghead, bright spark, brainiac, rocket scientist.
—OPPOSITES: stupidity, dunce.

genteel *adj.* REFINED, respectable, decorous, mannerly, well-mannered, courteous, polite, proper, correct, seemly; well-bred, cultured, sophisticated, ladylike, gentlemanly, dignified, gracious; affected.
—OPPOSITES: uncouth.

gentle *adj.* **1** KIND, tender, sympathetic, considerate, understanding, compassionate, benevolent, good-natured; humane, lenient, merciful, clement; mild, placid, serene, sweet-tempered. **2** LIGHT, soft. **3** GRADUAL, slight, easy.
—OPPOSITES: brutal, strong, steep.

genuine *adj.* **1** AUTHENTIC, real, actual, original, bona fide, true, veritable; attested, undisputed; *informal* the real McCoy/thing. **2** SINCERE, honest, truthful, straightforward, direct, frank, candid, open; artless, natural, unaffected; *informal* straight, upfront, on the level, on the up and up.

—OPPOSITES: bogus, insincere.

germ n. **1** MICROBE, microorganism, bacillus, bacterium, virus; *informal* bug. **2** START, beginning(s), seed, embryo, bud, root, rudiment; origin, source.

germane adj. ☞ RELEVANT.

—OPPOSITES: irrelevant.

gesture n. SIGNAL, sign, motion, indication, gesticulation; show.
▶ v. SIGNAL, motion, gesticulate, wave, indicate.

get v. **1** ACQUIRE, obtain, come by, receive, gain, earn, win, come into, take possession of, be given; buy, purchase, procure, secure; gather, collect, pick up, hook, net, land; achieve, attain; *informal* get one's hands on, get one's mitts on, get hold of, grab, bag, score. **2** ☞ RECEIVE 2. **3** BECOME, grow, turn, go. **4** ☞ FETCH 1. **5** ☞ EARN 1. **6** TRAVEL BY/ON/IN; take, catch, use. **7** SUCCUMB TO, develop, go/come down with; become infected with, catch, contract. **8** UNDERSTAND, comprehend, grasp, see, fathom, follow, perceive, apprehend, unravel, decipher; hear, discern, distinguish; *informal* get the drift of, catch on to, figure out, twig. **9** ☞ ARRIVE 1. **10** PERSUADE, induce, prevail on, influence; talk into. **11** (*informal*) TAKE REVENGE ON, exact/ wreak revenge on, get one's revenge on, avenge oneself on, take vengeance on, get even with, pay back, get back at.

—OPPOSITES: give, send, leave.

☐ **get something across** ☞ COMMUNICATE 1. **get ahead** PROSPER, flourish, thrive, do well; succeed, make it, advance, make good, become rich; *informal* go places, get somewhere. **get at 1** ACCESS, get to, reach, touch. **2** (*informal*) IMPLY, suggest, intimate, insinuate, hint, mean, drive at, allude to. **get back at** ☞ GET 11. **get by** ☞ MANAGE 2. **get lost** ☞ SCRAM. **get out of** EVADE, dodge, shirk, avoid, escape, sidestep; *informal* duck (out of), wriggle out of, cop out of. **get over 1** RECOVER FROM, recuperate from, shrug off, survive. **2** OVERCOME, surmount, get the better of, master, deal with, cope with, sort out; *informal* lick. **get up** GET OUT OF BED, rise, stir, rouse oneself; *informal* surface; *formal* arise.

getaway n. ESCAPE, breakout, bolt for freedom, flight; disappearance, vanishing act.

ghastly adj. **1** TERRIBLE, horrible, grim, awful, dire; frightening, terrifying, horrifying, alarming; distressing, shocking, appalling, harrowing; dreadful, frightful, horrendous, monstrous, gruesome, grisly. **2** ☞ UNPLEASANT 1.

—OPPOSITES: pleasant, charming.

ghost n. SPECTRE, phantom, wraith, spirit, presence; apparition, phantasm, shade; *informal* spook.

ghostly adj. SPECTRAL, ghostlike, phantom, wraithlike, phantasmal, phantasmic; unearthly, unnatural, supernatural; insubstantial, shadowy; eerie, weird, uncanny; frightening, spine-chilling, hairraising, creepy, scary, spooky.

giant n. COLOSSUS, behemoth, Brobdingnagian, mammoth,

monster, leviathan, titan.
—OPPOSITES: dwarf.
▶ *adj.* ☞ HUGE.
—OPPOSITES: miniature.

gibberish *n.* ☞ NONSENSE 1.

gibe *n. & v.* ☞ JIBE.

giddy *adj.* **1** DIZZY, light-headed, faint, weak, vertiginous; unsteady, shaky, wobbly, reeling; *informal* woozy. **2** FLIGHTY, silly, frivolous, skittish, irresponsible, flippant, whimsical, capricious; featherbrained, scatty, thoughtless, heedless, carefree; *informal* dippy, ditsy, ditzy, flaky, spinny✦.
—OPPOSITES: steady, sensible.

gift *n.* **1** PRESENT, handout, donation, offering, bestowal, bonus, award, endowment; tip, gratuity, baksheesh; largesse; *informal* freebie, perk; *formal* benefaction. **2** ☞ TALENT.

gifted *adj.* TALENTED, skilful, skilled, accomplished, expert, consummate, master(ly), virtuoso, first-rate, able, apt, adept, proficient; intelligent, clever, bright, brilliant; precocious; *informal* crack, top-notch, ace.
—OPPOSITES: inept.

gigantic *adj.* ☞ HUGE.
—OPPOSITES: tiny.

giggle *v.* TITTER, snigger, snicker, tee-hee, chuckle, chortle, laugh.

gingerly *adv.* CAUTIOUSLY, carefully, with care, warily, charily, circumspectly, delicately; watchfully, vigilantly, attentively; hesitantly, timidly.
—OPPOSITES: recklessly.

girl *n.* **1** FEMALE CHILD, daughter; schoolgirl; *Scottish* lass, lassie. See also CHILD. **2** YOUNG WOMAN, young lady, miss, mademoiselle; *Scottish* lass, lassie; *informal* chick, gal, grrrl, babe; *literary* maid, damsel.

girlfriend *n.* SWEETHEART, lover, partner, significant other, main squeeze, girl, woman, mistress; fiancée; *informal* steady; betrothed.

girth *n.* **1** CIRCUMFERENCE, perimeter; width, breadth. **2** ☞ STOMACH 1. **3** cinch.

gist *n.* ESSENCE, substance, central theme, heart of the matter, nub, kernel, marrow, meat, burden, crux; thrust, drift, sense, meaning, significance, import; *informal* nitty-gritty.

give *v.* **1** PRESENT WITH, provide with, supply with, furnish with, let someone have; hand (over), offer, proffer; award, grant, bestow, accord, confer, make over; donate, contribute, put up. **2** CONVEY, pass on, impart, communicate, transmit; send, deliver, relay; tell. **3** ENTRUST, commit, consign, assign; *formal* commend. **4** ALLOW, permit, grant, accord; offer. **5** CAUSE, make, create, occasion. **6** ORGANIZE, arrange, lay on, throw, host, hold, have, provide. **7** UTTER, let out, emit, produce, make. **8** ADMINISTER, deliver, deal, inflict, impose. **9** GIVE WAY, cave in, collapse, break, fall apart; bend, buckle.
—OPPOSITES: receive, take.
☐ **give up/in** CAPITULATE, concede defeat, admit defeat, give up, surrender, yield, submit, back down, give way, defer, relent, throw in the towel/sponge. **give something up** STOP, cease, discontinue, desist from, abstain

from, cut out, renounce, forgo; resign from, stand down from; *informal* quit, kick, swear off, leave off, pack in, lay off.

glad *adj.* **1** PLEASED, happy, delighted, thrilled, overjoyed, elated, gleeful; gratified, grateful, thankful; *informal* tickled pink, over the moon. **2** WILLING, eager, happy, pleased, delighted; ready, prepared. **3** PLEASING, welcome, happy, joyful, cheering, heartening, gratifying.
—OPPOSITES: dismayed, reluctant, distressing.

gladden *v.* DELIGHT, please, make happy, elate; cheer (up), hearten, buoy up, give someone a lift, uplift; gratify.
—OPPOSITES: sadden.

glamorous *adj.* **1** BEAUTIFUL, attractive, lovely, bewitching, enchanting, beguiling; elegant, chic, stylish, fashionable; charming, charismatic, appealing, alluring, seductive; *informal* classy, glam. **2** EXCITING, thrilling, stimulating; dazzling, glittering, glossy, colourful, exotic; *informal* ritzy, glitzy, jet-setting.
—OPPOSITES: dowdy, dull.

glamour *n.* **1** BEAUTY, allure, attractiveness; elegance, chic, style; charisma, charm, magnetism, desirability. **2** ALLURE, attraction, fascination, charm, magic, romance, mystique, exoticism, spell; excitement, thrill; glitter; *informal* glitz, glam, tinsel.

glance *v.* **1** LOOK BRIEFLY, look quickly, peek, peep; glimpse; *informal* have a gander. **2** READ QUICKLY, scan, skim, leaf, flick, flip, thumb, browse; dip into. **3** RICOCHET, rebound, be deflected, bounce; graze, clip.
▸ *n.* PEEK, peep, brief look, quick look, glimpse.

glare *v.* ☞ SCOWL.
▸ *n.* **1** SCOWL, glower, angry stare, frown, black look, threatening look, dirty look. **2** BLAZE, dazzle, shine, beam; radiance, brilliance, luminescence.

glass *n.* **1** TUMBLER, drinking vessel; flute, schooner, balloon, goblet, chalice. **2** GLASSWARE, stemware, crystal, crystalware.
—RELATED: vitreous.

glasses *pl. n.* SPECTACLES, eyeglasses, eyewear; *informal* specs; bifocals.

glassy *adj.* **1** SMOOTH, mirror-like, gleaming, shiny, glossy, polished, vitreous; slippery, icy; clear, transparent, translucent; calm, still, flat. **2** EXPRESSIONLESS, glazed, blank, vacant, fixed, motionless; emotionless, impassive, lifeless, wooden, vacuous.
—OPPOSITES: rough, expressive.

glaze *v.* **1** VARNISH, enamel, lacquer, japan, shellac, paint; gloss. **2** BECOME GLASSY, go blank; mist over, film over.
▸ *n.* **1** VARNISH, enamel, lacquer, finish, coating; lustre, shine, gloss. **2** COATING, topping; icing, frosting.

gleam *v.* ☞ GLISTEN.
▸ *n.* **1** GLIMMER, glint, shimmer, twinkle, sparkle, flicker, flash; beam, ray, shaft. **2** SHINE, lustre, gloss, sheen; glint, glitter, glimmer, sparkle; brilliance, radiance, glow; *literary* glister.

glee *n.* DELIGHT, pleasure, happiness, joy, gladness, elation, euphoria; amusement, mirth, merriment; excitement, gaiety, exuberance; relish, triumph, jubilation, satisfaction, gratification.
−OPPOSITES: disappointment.

glib *adj.* SLICK, pat, smooth-talking, fast-talking, silver-tongued, smooth, urbane, disingenuous, insincere, facile, shallow, superficial, flippant; *informal* flip, sweet-talking.
−OPPOSITES: sincere.

glide *v.* 1 SLIDE, slip, sail, float, drift, flow; coast, freewheel, roll; skim, skate. 2 SOAR, wheel, plane; fly.

glimpse *n.* BRIEF LOOK, quick look; glance, peek, peep; sight, sighting.
▶ *v.* CATCH SIGHT OF, notice, discern, spot, spy, sight, pick out, make out; espy, descry.

glint *v.* ☞ GLISTEN.

glisten *v.* SHINE, sparkle, twinkle, glint, glitter, glimmer, shimmer, wink, flash, gleam; *literary* glister.

glitter *v.* ☞ GLISTEN.
▶ *n.* 1 SPARKLE, twinkle, glint, gleam, shimmer, glimmer, flicker, flash; brilliance, luminescence. 2 GLAMOUR, excitement, thrills, attraction, appeal; dazzle; *informal* razzle-dazzle, razzmatazz, glitz, ritziness.

gloat *v.* DELIGHT, relish, take great pleasure, revel, rejoice, glory, exult, triumph, crow; boast, brag, be smug, congratulate oneself, preen oneself, pat oneself on the back; *informal* rub it in.

global *adj.* 1 WORLDWIDE, international, world, intercontinental.
2 COMPREHENSIVE, overall, general, all-inclusive, all-encompassing, encyclopedic, universal, blanket; broad, far-reaching, extensive, sweeping.

globule *n.* DROPLET, drop, bead, tear, ball, bubble, pearl; *informal* blob, glob.

gloom *n.* 1 ☞ DARK *n.* 1.
2 ☞ MELANCHOLY *n.*
−OPPOSITES: light, happiness.

gloomy *adj.* 1 DARK, shadowy, sunless, dim, sombre, dingy, dismal, dreary, murky, unwelcoming, cheerless, comfortless, funereal.
2 ☞ DESPONDENT.
−OPPOSITES: bright, cheerful.

glorious *adj.* 1 ILLUSTRIOUS, celebrated, famous, acclaimed, distinguished, honoured; outstanding, great, magnificent, noble, triumphant.
2 ☞ WONDERFUL.
−OPPOSITES: undistinguished, horrid.

glory *n.* 1 RENOWN, fame, prestige, honour, distinction, kudos, eminence, acclaim, praise; celebrity, recognition, reputation.
2 PRAISE, worship, adoration, veneration, honour, reverence, exaltation, homage, thanksgiving, thanks. 3 MAGNIFICENCE, splendour, resplendence, grandeur, majesty, greatness, nobility; opulence, beauty, elegance.
−OPPOSITES: shame, obscurity, modesty.
▶ *v.* TAKE PLEASURE IN, revel in, rejoice in, delight in; relish,

savour; be proud of, boast about, bask; *informal* get a kick out of, get a thrill out of, kvell.

gloss *n.* **1** ☞ SHEEN. **2** FACADE, veneer, surface, show, camouflage, disguise, mask, smokescreen; window dressing.
▶ *v.* CONCEAL, cover up, hide, disguise, mask, veil; shrug off, brush aside, play down, minimize, understate, make light of; *informal* brush under the carpet.

glossy *adj.* SHINY, gleaming, lustrous, brilliant, shimmering, glistening, satiny, sheeny, smooth, glassy; polished, lacquered, glazed.
—OPPOSITES: dull.

glow *v.* **1** SHINE, radiate, gleam, glimmer, flicker, flare. **2** FLUSH, blush, redden, colour (up), go pink, go scarlet; burn; beam.
▶ *n.* **1** RADIANCE, light, shine, gleam, glimmer, incandescence, luminescence; warmth, heat. **2** FLUSH, blush, rosiness, pinkness, redness, high colour; bloom, radiance.
—OPPOSITES: pallor.

glower *v.* ☞ SCOWL.

glowing *adj.* **1** BRIGHT, shining, radiant, glimmering, flickering, twinkling, incandescent, luminous, luminescent; lit (up), lighted, illuminated, ablaze; aglow, smouldering. **2** ROSY, pink, red, flushed, blushing; radiant, blooming, ruddy, florid; hot, burning. **3** COMPLIMENTARY, favourable, enthusiastic, positive, commendatory, admiring, lionizing, rapturous, rhapsodic, adulatory; fulsome; *informal* rave.

glue *n.* ADHESIVE, fixative, gum, paste, cement; epoxy (resin), size, mucilage, stickum.
▶ *v.* STICK, gum, paste; affix, fix, cement, bond, attach, secure, bind.

glum *adj.* ☞ SAD 1.
—OPPOSITES: cheerful.

glut *n.* ☞ SURPLUS *n.*
—OPPOSITES: dearth.

glutinous *adj.* STICKY, viscous, viscid, tacky, gluey, gummy, treacly; adhesive; *informal* gooey, gloppy.

gluttonous *adj.* GREEDY, gourmandizing, voracious, insatiable, wolfish; *informal* piggish, piggy.

gnarled *adj.* KNOBBLY, knotty, knotted, gnarly, lumpy, bumpy, nodular; twisted, bent, crooked, distorted, contorted, misshapen; arthritic; rough.

gnaw *v.* **1** CHEW, champ, chomp, bite, munch, crunch; nibble, worry. **2** NAG, plague, torment, torture, trouble, distress, worry, haunt, oppress, burden, hang over, bother, fret; niggle.

go *v.* **1** MOVE, proceed, make one's way, advance, progress, pass; walk, travel, journey. **2** EXTEND, stretch, reach; lead. **3** ☞ LEAVE[1] *v.* 1. **4** DISAPPEAR, vanish, be no more, be over, run its course, fade away; finish, end, cease. **5** BE USED UP, be spent, be exhausted, be consumed, be drained, be depleted. **6** ☞ DIE 1. **7** COLLAPSE, give way, fall down, cave in, crumble, disintegrate. **8** BECOME, get, turn, grow. **9** MAKE A SOUND, sound, reverberate, resound; ring, chime, peal, toll, clang. **10** TURN

OUT, work out, develop, come out; result, end (up); *informal* pan out. **11** MATCH, be harmonious, harmonize, blend, be suited, be complementary, coordinate, be compatible. **12** FUNCTION, work, run, operate. **13** BELONG, be kept.
—OPPOSITES: arrive, come, return, clash.

▶ *n.* ATTEMPT, try, effort, bid, endeavour; *informal* shot, stab, crack, bash, whirl, whack; *formal* essay.

☐ **go away.** ☞ GO *v.* 4. **go back on** RENEGE ON, break, fail to honour, default on, repudiate, retract; do an about-face; *informal* cop out (of), rat on. **go down 1** SINK, founder, go under. **2** DECREASE, get lower, fall, drop, decline; plummet, plunge, slump. **3** BE REMEMBERED, be recorded, be commemorated, be immortalized. **go for 1** CHOOSE, pick, opt for, select, decide on, settle on. **2** BE ATTRACTED TO, like, fancy; prefer, favour, choose. **go in for** TAKE PART IN, participate in, engage in, get involved in, join in, enter into, undertake; practise, pursue; espouse, adopt, embrace. **go off 1** EXPLODE, detonate, blow up. **2** GO BAD, go stale, go sour, turn, spoil, go rancid; decompose, go mouldy. **go over 1** ☞ INSPECT. **2** REHEARSE, practise, read through, run through. **go through 1** ☞ UNDERGO. **2** ☞ SPEND 1. **3** SEARCH, look, hunt, rummage, rifle; *informal* frisk. **go under** ☞ GO BANKRUPT at BANKRUPT.

goad *v.* PROVOKE, spur, prod, egg on, hound, badger, incite, rouse, stir, move, stimulate, motivate,

prompt, induce, encourage, urge, inspire; impel, pressure, dragoon.

go-ahead *n.* ☞ PERMISSION.

▶ *adj.* ENTERPRISING, resourceful, innovative, ingenious, original, creative; progressive, pioneering, modern, forward-looking, enlightened; enthusiastic, ambitious, entrepreneurial, high-powered; bold, daring, audacious, adventurous, dynamic; *informal* go-getting.

goal *n.* OBJECTIVE, aim, end, target, design, intention, intent, plan, purpose; (holy) grail; ambition, aspiration, wish, dream, brass ring, desire, hope.

go-between *n.* INTERMEDIARY, middleman, agent, broker, liaison, contact; negotiator, intercessor, mediator.

god *n.* DEITY, goddess, divine being, celestial being, supreme being, divinity, immortal; avatar, creator, demiurge, godhead.

godforsaken *adj.* WRETCHED, miserable, dreary, dismal, depressing, grim, cheerless, bleak, desolate, gloomy; deserted, neglected, isolated, remote, backward.
—OPPOSITES: charming.

godless *adj.* **1** ATHEISTIC, unbelieving, agnostic, skeptical, heretical, faithless, irreligious, ungodly, unholy, impious, profane; infidel, heathen, idolatrous, pagan; satanic, devilish. **2** IMMORAL, wicked, sinful, wrong, evil, bad, iniquitous, corrupt; irreligious, sacrilegious, profane, blasphemous, impious.
—OPPOSITES: religious, virtuous.

godsend *n.* BOON, blessing, bonus, plus, benefit, advantage, help, aid, asset; stroke of luck, windfall, manna (from heaven).
—OPPOSITES: curse.

goggle *v.* ☞ STARE.

good *adj.* **1** FINE, superior, quality; excellent, superb, outstanding, magnificent, exceptional, marvellous, wonderful, first-rate, first-class, sterling; satisfactory, acceptable, up to scratch, up to standard, not bad, all right; *informal* great, OK, A1, jake, hunky-dory, ace, terrific, fantastic, fabulous, fab, top-notch, blue-chip, blue-ribbon, bang-up, skookum, killer, class, awesome, wicked; smashing, brilliant. **2** VIRTUOUS, righteous, upright, upstanding, moral, ethical, high-minded, principled; exemplary, law-abiding, irreproachable, blameless, guiltless, unimpeachable, honourable, scrupulous, reputable, decent, respectable, noble, trustworthy; meritorious, praiseworthy, admirable; whiter than white, saintly, saintlike, angelic; *informal* squeaky clean. **3** WELL-BEHAVED, obedient, dutiful, polite, courteous, respectful, deferential, compliant. **4** RIGHT, correct, proper, decorous, seemly; appropriate, fitting, apt, suitable; convenient, expedient, favourable, opportune, felicitous, timely. **5** ☞ ACCOMPLISHED. **6** CLOSE, intimate, dear, bosom, special, best, firm, valued, treasured; loving, devoted, loyal, faithful, constant, reliable, dependable, trustworthy, trusty, true, unfailing, staunch. **7** HEALTHY, fine, sound, tip-top, hale and hearty, fit, robust, sturdy, strong, vigorous. **8** ENJOYABLE, pleasant, agreeable, pleasurable, delightful, great, nice, lovely; amusing, diverting, jolly, merry, lively; *informal* super, fantastic, fabulous, fab, terrific, grand, brilliant, killer, peachy, ducky. **9** KIND, kind-hearted, good-hearted, generous, charitable, magnanimous, gracious; altruistic, unselfish, selfless. **10** ☞ CONVENIENT. **11** ☞ HEALTHY 2. **12** ☞ DELICIOUS 1. **13** VALID, genuine, authentic, legitimate, sound, bona fide; convincing, persuasive, telling, potent, cogent, compelling. **14** ☞ CONSIDERABLE 1. **15** BEST, smart, smartest, finest, nicest; special, party, Sunday, formal, dressy. **16** FINE, fair, dry; bright, clear, sunny, cloudless; calm, windless; warm, mild, balmy, clement, pleasant, nice.
—OPPOSITES: bad, wicked, naughty, poor, terrible, inconvenient, small, scruffy.
▶ *n.* **1** VIRTUE, righteousness, goodness, morality, integrity, rectitude; honesty, truth, honour, probity; propriety, worthiness, merit; blamelessness, purity. **2** BENEFIT, advantage, profit, gain, interest, welfare, well-being; enjoyment, comfort, ease, convenience; help, aid, assistance, service; behalf.
—OPPOSITES: wickedness, disadvantage.

goodbye *excl.* FAREWELL, adieu, au revoir, ciao, adios; bye, bye-bye, so

long, see you (later), later (skater),
sayonara; bon voyage; cheers.

good-humoured *adj.*
☞ FRIENDLY 1.
—OPPOSITES: grumpy.

good-looking *adj.* ☞
ATTRACTIVE 2.
—OPPOSITES: ugly.

goodly *adj.* LARGE, largish,
sizeable, substantial, considerable,
respectable, significant, decent,
generous, handsome; *informal* tidy,
serious.
—OPPOSITES: paltry.

good-natured *adj.* WARM-
HEARTED, friendly, amiable;
neighbourly, benevolent, kind,
kind-hearted, generous, unselfish,
considerate, thoughtful, obliging,
helpful, supportive, charitable;
understanding, sympathetic,
easygoing, accommodating.
—OPPOSITES: malicious.

goods *pl. n.* **1** MERCHANDISE, wares,
stock, commodities, produce,
products, articles; imports,
exports. **2** PROPERTY, possessions,
effects, chattels, valuables; *informal*
things, stuff, junk, gear, kit, bits
and pieces.

goof *v.* ☞ BLUNDER *v.* 1.
▶ *n.* ☞ FOOL 1.

gorge *n.* RAVINE, canyon, gully,
defile, couloir; chasm, gulf, abyss;
gulch, coulee.
▶ *v.* **1** STUFF, cram, fill; glut, satiate,
overindulge, overfill; *informal* pig
out on. **2** DEVOUR, guzzle, gobble,
gulp (down), wolf; *informal* tuck
into, demolish, polish off, scoff
(down), down, stuff one's face
(with); scarf (down/up).

gorgeous *adj.* **1** ☞ ATTRACTIVE 2.
2 SPECTACULAR, splendid, superb,

wonderful, grand, impressive,
awe-inspiring, awesome, amazing,
stunning, breathtaking,
incredible; *informal* sensational,
fabulous, fantastic.
—OPPOSITES: ugly, drab.

gory *adj.* GRISLY, gruesome,
violent, bloody, brutal, savage;
ghastly, frightful, horrid, fearful,
hideous, macabre, horrible,
horrific; shocking, appalling,
monstrous, unspeakable; *informal*
blood-and-guts.

gossamer *adj.* GAUZY, fine,
diaphanous, delicate, filmy, floaty,
cobwebby, wispy, thin, light,
insubstantial, flimsy; translucent,
transparent; see-through, sheer.

gossip *n.* **1** TITTLE-TATTLE, tattle,
rumour(s), whispers, canards,
tidbits; scandal, hearsay; *informal*
dirt, buzz, scuttlebutt; loose lips.
2 SCANDALMONGER, gossipmonger,
tattler, busybody, muckraker,
flibbertigibbet.
▶ *v.* **1** SPREAD RUMOURS, spread
gossip, tittle-tattle, tattle, talk,
whisper, tell tales; *informal* dish the
dirt. **2** ☞ CHAT *v.*

gouge *v.* SCOOP OUT, hollow out,
excavate; cut (out), dig (out),
scrape (out), scratch (out).

govern *v.* **1** RULE, preside over,
reign over, control, be in charge
of, command, lead, dominate;
run, head, administer, manage,
regulate, oversee, supervise;
informal be in the driver's seat.
2 DETERMINE, decide, control,
regulate, direct, rule, dictate,
shape; affect, influence, sway, act
on, mould, modify, impact on.

government *n.* ADMINISTRATION,
executive, regime, rule, authority,

control, powers that be,
directorate, council, leadership,
management; cabinet, ministry,
Ottawa.

grab v. **1** SEIZE, grasp, snatch, take
hold of, grip, clasp, clutch; take.
2 ☞ ACQUIRE.
▶ n. LUNGE, snatch.

grace n. **1** ELEGANCE, poise,
gracefulness, finesse; suppleness,
agility, nimbleness. **2** COURTESY,
decency, (good) manners,
politeness, decorum, respect, tact.
3 FAVOUR, approval, approbation,
acceptance, esteem, regard,
respect; goodwill, generosity,
kindness, indulgence. **4** BLESSING,
thanksgiving, benediction.
—OPPOSITES: inelegance,
effrontery, disfavour.
▶ v. **1** DIGNIFY, distinguish, honour,
favour; enhance, ennoble, glorify,
elevate, aggrandize, upgrade.
2 ☞ ADORN.

graceful adj. ELEGANT, fluid,
fluent, natural, neat; agile, supple,
nimble, light-footed.

gracious adj. **1** COURTEOUS,
polite, civil, chivalrous, well-
mannered, mannerly, decorous;
tactful, diplomatic; kind,
benevolent, considerate,
thoughtful, obliging,
accommodating, indulgent,
magnanimous; friendly, amiable,
cordial, hospitable. **2** ELEGANT,
stylish, tasteful, graceful;
comfortable, luxurious; informal
swanky, plush. **3** ☞ MERCIFUL.
—OPPOSITES: rude, crude, cruel.

grade n. **1** CATEGORY, set, class,
classification, grouping, group,
bracket. **2** RANK, level, echelon,
standing, position, class, status,

order; step, rung, stratum, tier.
3 MARK, score; assessment,
evaluation, appraisal. **4** YEAR;
class. **5** ☞ GRADIENT 1.
▶ v. **1** CLASSIFY, class, categorize,
bracket, sort, group, arrange,
pigeonhole; rank, evaluate, rate,
value. **2** ASSESS, mark, score,
judge, evaluate, appraise.

gradient n. **1** SLOPE, incline, hill,
rise, ramp, bank; declivity, grade.
2 STEEPNESS, angle, slant, slope,
inclination.

gradual adj. SLOW, measured,
unhurried, cautious; piecemeal,
step-by-step, progressive,
continuous, systematic, steady.
—OPPOSITES: abrupt.

gradually adv. SLOWLY, slowly but
surely, cautiously, gently,
gingerly; piecemeal, little by little,
bit by bit, inch by inch, by
degrees; progressively,
systematically; regularly, steadily.

graduate v. **1** PROGRESS, advance,
move up. **2** CALIBRATE, mark off,
measure out, grade.

graft n. **1** SCION, cutting, shoot,
offshoot, bud, sprout, sprig.
2 TRANSPLANT, implant.
▶ v. **1** AFFIX, join, insert, splice;
attach, add. **2** TRANSPLANT,
implant.

grain n. **1** CEREAL, cereal crops.
2 GRANULE, particle, speck, mote,
mite; bit, piece; scrap, crumb,
fragment, morsel. **3** ☞ TRACE n. 2.
4 TEXTURE, surface, finish; weave,
pattern.

grand adj. **1** MAGNIFICENT,
imposing, impressive, awe-
inspiring, splendid, resplendent,
majestic, monumental; palatial,
stately, large; luxurious,

sumptuous, lavish, opulent, upmarket, upscale; *informal* fancy, posh, plush, classy, swanky, five-star. **2** AMBITIOUS, bold, epic, big, extravagant. **3** AUGUST, distinguished, illustrious, eminent, esteemed, honoured, venerable, dignified, respectable; pre-eminent, prominent, notable, renowned, celebrated, famous; aristocratic, noble, regal, blue-blooded, high-born, patrician; *informal* upper-crust. **4** ☞ EXCELLENT.
—OPPOSITES: inferior, humble, minor, poor.

grandiloquent *adj.* POMPOUS, bombastic, magniloquent, pretentious, ostentatious, high-flown, orotund, florid, flowery; overwrought, overblown, overdone; *informal* highfalutin, purple.
—OPPOSITES: understated.

grandiose *adj.* **1** MAGNIFICENT, impressive, grand, imposing, awe-inspiring, splendid, resplendent, majestic, glorious, elaborate; palatial, stately, luxurious, opulent; *informal* plush, swanky, flash. **2** AMBITIOUS, bold, over-ambitious, extravagant, high-flown, flamboyant; *informal* over the top.
—OPPOSITES: humble, modest.

grant *v.* **1** ALLOW, accord, permit, afford, vouchsafe. **2** GIVE, award, bestow on, confer on, present with, provide with, endow with, supply with. **3** ADMIT, accept, concede, yield, allow, appreciate, recognize, acknowledge, confess; agree.
—OPPOSITES: refuse, deny.
▶ *n.* ENDOWMENT, subvention,

award, donation, bursary, allowance, subsidy, contribution, handout, allocation, gift; scholarship.

granule *n.* GRAIN, particle, fragment, bit, crumb, morsel, mote, speck.

graphic *adj.* **1** VISUAL, symbolic, pictorial, illustrative, diagrammatic; drawn, written. **2** VIVID, explicit, expressive, detailed; uninhibited, powerful, colourful, rich, lurid, shocking; realistic, descriptive, illustrative; telling, effective.
—OPPOSITES: vague.
▶ *n.* *(Computing)* PICTURE, illustration, image, (visual) art; diagram, graph, chart.

grapple *v.* **1** WRESTLE, struggle, tussle; brawl, fight, scuffle, battle. **2** TACKLE, confront, face, deal with, cope with, come to grips with; apply oneself to, devote oneself to.

grasp *v.* **1** GRIP, clutch, clasp, hold, clench; catch, seize, grab, snatch, latch on to. **2** ☞ UNDERSTAND 1. **3** TAKE ADVANTAGE OF, act on; seize, leap at, snatch, jump at, pounce on.
—OPPOSITES: release, overlook.
▶ *n.* **1** GRIP, hold; clutch, clasp, clench; control, power. **2** REACH, scope, power, limits, range; sights.

grasping *adj.* AVARICIOUS, acquisitive, greedy, rapacious, mercenary, materialistic; mean, miserly, parsimonious, niggardly, hoarding, selfish; *informal* tight-fisted, stingy, cheap.

grate *v.* **1** SHRED, pulverize, mince, grind, granulate, crush, crumble. **2** GRIND, rub, rasp, scrape, jar, grit, creak. **3** IRRITATE, set someone's teeth on edge, jar; annoy, nettle, chafe, fret; *informal* aggravate, get on someone's nerves.

grateful *adj.* THANKFUL, appreciative; indebted, obliged, obligated, in your debt, beholden.

gratify *v.* **1** PLEASE, gladden, make happy, delight, make someone feel good, satisfy; *informal* tickle pink, give someone a kick, buck up. **2** ☞ SATISFY 1.
—OPPOSITES: displease, frustrate.

gratis *adv.* FREE (OF CHARGE), without charge, for nothing, at no cost, gratuitously; *informal* on the house, for free.

gratitude *n.* GRATEFULNESS, thankfulness, thanks, appreciation, indebtedness; recognition, acknowledgement, credit.

gratuitous *adj.* UNJUSTIFIED, uncalled for, unwarranted, unprovoked, undue; indefensible, unjustifiable; needless, unnecessary, inessential, unmerited, groundless, senseless, wanton, indiscriminate; excessive, immoderate, inordinate, inappropriate.
—OPPOSITES: necessary.

gratuity *n.* TIP, baksheesh, gift, present, donation, reward, handout; bonus, extra.

grave¹ *n.* ☞ TOMB.

grave² *adj.* **1** SERIOUS, important, weighty, profound, significant, momentous; critical, acute, urgent, pressing; dire, terrible, awful, dreadful. **2** ☞ SOLEMN 2.
—OPPOSITES: trivial, cheerful.

graveyard *n.* ☞ CEMETERY.

gravitate *v.* MOVE, head, drift, be drawn, be attracted; tend, lean, incline.

gravity *n.* **1** SERIOUSNESS, importance, significance, weight, consequence, magnitude; acuteness, urgency, exigence; awfulness, dreadfulness. **2** SOLEMNITY, seriousness, sombreness, sobriety, soberness, severity, grimness, humourlessness, dourness; gloominess.

graze *v.* **1** ☞ SCRAPE *v.* 5. **2** TOUCH, brush, shave, skim, kiss, scrape, clip, glance off.

greasy *adj.* **1** FATTY, oily, buttery, oleaginous. **2** SLIPPERY, slick, slimy, slithery, oily; *informal* slippy. **3** ☞ OBSEQUIOUS.
—OPPOSITES: lean, dry.

great *adj.* **1** CONSIDERABLE, substantial, significant, appreciable, special, serious; exceptional, extraordinary. **2** LARGE, big, extensive, expansive, broad, wide, sizeable, ample; vast, immense, huge, enormous, massive; *informal* humongous, whopping, ginormous. **3** ABSOLUTE, total, utter, out-and-out, downright, thoroughgoing, complete; perfect, positive, prize, sheer, arrant, unqualified, consummate, veritable. **4** PROMINENT, eminent, important, distinguished, illustrious, celebrated, honoured, acclaimed, admired, esteemed, revered, renowned, notable, famous, famed, well-known; leading, top, major, principal, first-rate, matchless, peerless, star. **5** POWERFUL, dominant,

influential, strong, potent, formidable, redoubtable; leading, important, foremost, major, chief, principal. **6** ☞ MAGNIFICENT 1. **7** ENJOYABLE, delightful, lovely, pleasant, congenial; exciting, thrilling; excellent, marvellous, wonderful, fine, splendid, very good; *informal* terrific, fantastic, fabulous, splendiferous, fab, super, grand, cool, hunky-dory, killer, swell.
—OPPOSITES: little, small, minor, modest, poor, unenthusiastic, bad.

greatly *adv.* VERY MUCH, considerably, substantially, appreciably, significantly, markedly, sizeably, seriously, materially, profoundly; enormously, vastly, immensely, tremendously, mightily, abundantly, extremely, exceedingly; *informal* plenty, majorly.
—OPPOSITES: slightly.

greed, greediness *n.* **1** AVARICE, cupidity, acquisitiveness, covetousness, rapacity; materialism, mercenariness; *informal* money-grubbing, affluenza. **2** GLUTTONY, hunger, voracity, insatiability; intemperance, overeating, self-indulgence; *informal* piggishness. **3** ☞ DESIRE *n.* 1.
—OPPOSITES: generosity, temperance, indifference.

greedy *adj.* **1** GLUTTONOUS, ravenous, voracious, intemperate, self-indulgent, insatiable, wolfish; *informal* piggish, piggy. **2** AVARICIOUS, acquisitive, covetous, grasping, materialistic, mercenary, possessive; *informal* money-

grubbing, money-grabbing, grabby. **3** EAGER, avid, hungry, craving, longing, yearning, hankering; impatient, anxious; *informal* dying, itching.

green *adj.* **1** VERDANT, grassy, leafy. **2** ENVIRONMENTAL, ecological, non-polluting, conservation, eco-. **3** INEXPERIENCED, unversed, callow, immature; unripe; new, raw, unseasoned, untried; inexpert, untrained, unqualified, ignorant; simple, unsophisticated, unpolished; naive, innocent, ingenuous, credulous, gullible, unworldly; *informal* wet behind the ears.

green light *n.* ☞ PERMISSION.
—OPPOSITES: the red light, refusal.

greet *v.* **1** SAY HELLO TO, address, salute, hail, halloo; welcome, meet, receive. **2** RECEIVE, acknowledge, respond to, react to, take.

greeting *n.* **1** HELLO, salute, salutation, address; welcome, acknowledgement. **2** BEST WISHES, good wishes, congratulations, felicitations; compliments, regards, respects.
—OPPOSITES: farewell.

grey *adj.* **1** CLOUDY, overcast, dull, sunless, gloomy, dreary, dismal, sombre, bleak, murky. **2** ☞ PALE 1.
—OPPOSITES: sunny, ruddy.

grief *n.* **1** SORROW, misery, sadness, anguish, pain, distress, heartache, ache, heartbreak, agony, torment, affliction, suffering, woe, desolation, dejection, despair; mourning, mournfulness, bereavement, lamentation; *literary* dolour, dole.

2 ☞ NUISANCE.

—OPPOSITES: joy.

grievance *n.* **1** INJUSTICE, wrong, injury, ill, unfairness; affront, insult, indignity. **2** COMPLAINT, criticism, objection, grumble, grouse; ill feeling, bad feeling, resentment, bitterness, pique; *informal* gripe, whinge, moan, grouch, cavil, quibble, niggle, beef, bone to pick.

grieve *v.* **1** MOURN, lament, sorrow, be sorrowful; cry, sob, weep, shed tears, keen, weep and wail, beat one's breast. **2** SADDEN, upset, distress, pain, hurt, wound, break someone's heart.

—OPPOSITES: rejoice, please.

grim *adj.* **1** STERN, forbidding, uninviting, unsmiling, dour, formidable, harsh, steely, flinty, stony; cross, churlish, surly, sour, ill-tempered; fierce, ferocious, threatening, menacing, implacable, ruthless, merciless. **2** ☞ TERRIBLE 1. **3** RESOLUTE, determined, firm, decided, steadfast, dead set; obstinate, stubborn, obdurate, unyielding, intractable, uncompromising, unshakeable, unrelenting, relentless, dogged, tenacious.

—OPPOSITES: amiable, pleasant.

grimy *adj.* ☞ DIRTY 1.

—OPPOSITES: clean.

grind *v.* **1** CRUSH, pound, pulverize, mill, granulate, crumble, smash, press. **2** SHARPEN, whet, hone, file, strop; smooth, polish, sand, sandpaper. **3** RUB, grate, scrape, rasp.

▶ *n.* DRUDGERY, toil, hard work, labour, donkey work, exertion, chores, slog; *literary* travail.

grip *v.* **1** GRASP, clutch, hold, clasp, take hold of, clench, grab, seize, cling to; squeeze, press, glom on to. **2** AFFLICT, affect, take over, beset, rack, convulse. **3** ☞ FASCINATE.

—OPPOSITES: release.

▶ *n.* **1** GRASP, hold; traction. **2** CONTROL, power, hold, stranglehold, chokehold, clutches, command, mastery, influence. **3** UNDERSTANDING, comprehension, grasp, perception, awareness, apprehension, conception; *formal* cognizance.

gripe *v.* ☞ COMPLAIN.

▶ *n.* ☞ GRIEVANCE 2.

grisly *adj.* ☞ GRUESOME.

grit *n.* **1** SAND, dust, dirt; gravel, pebbles, stones, shingle. **2** COURAGE, bravery, pluck, mettle, backbone, spirit, strength of character/will, moral fibre, steel, nerve, fortitude, toughness, hardiness, resolve, resolution, determination, tenacity, perseverance, endurance; *informal* guts, spunk.

groan *v.* **1** MOAN, whimper, cry, call out. **2** ☞ COMPLAIN. **3** CREAK, squeak; grate, rasp.

▶ *n.* MOAN, cry, whimper; creak, squeak.

groggy *adj.* DAZED, muzzy, stupefied, in a stupor, befuddled, fuddled, dizzy, disoriented, disorientated, punch-drunk, shaky, unsteady, wobbly, weak, faint, befogged; *informal* dopey, woozy.

groove *n.* FURROW, channel, trench, trough, canal, gouge, hollow, indentation, rut, gutter, cutting, cut, fissure; *Carpentry* rabbet.

grope *v.* **1** FUMBLE, scrabble, fish, ferret, rummage, feel, search, hunt. **2** ☞ FONDLE.

gross *adj.* **1** ☞ FAT 1. **2** BOORISH, coarse, vulgar, loutish, oafish, thuggish, brutish, philistine, uncouth, crass, common, unrefined, unsophisticated, uncultured, uncultivated; *informal* cloddish. **3** (*informal*) DISGUSTING, repellent, repulsive, abhorrent, loathsome, foul, nasty, obnoxious, sickening, nauseating, stomach-churning, unpalatable; vomitous; *informal* yucky, icky, gut-churning. **4** OUT AND OUT, utter, complete. See also FLAGRANT.
—OPPOSITES: slender, refined, pleasant, net.
▶ *v.* ☞ EARN 1.

grotesque *adj.* **1** MALFORMED, deformed, misshapen, distorted, twisted, gnarled, mangled, mutilated; ugly, unsightly, monstrous, hideous, freakish, unnatural, abnormal, strange, odd, peculiar; *informal* weird, freaky. **2** OUTRAGEOUS, monstrous, shocking, appalling, preposterous; ridiculous, ludicrous, farcical, unbelievable, incredible.
—OPPOSITES: normal.

ground *n.* **1** FLOOR, earth, terra firma; flooring. **2** EARTH, soil, dirt, clay, loam, turf, clod, sod; land, terrain. **3** ESTATE, gardens, lawns, park, parkland, land, acres, property, surroundings, holding, territory. **4** EXCUSE, pretext, motive. See also BASIS 1.
5 SEDIMENT, precipitate, dregs, lees, deposit, residue.

▶ *v.* **1** RUN AGROUND, run ashore, beach, land. **2** BASE, found, establish, root, build, construct, form. **3** ☞ EDUCATE.
☐ **hold one's ground** STAND FIRM, stand fast, make a stand, stick to one's guns, dig in one's heels.

groundless *adj.* BASELESS, without basis, without foundation, ill-founded, unfounded, unsupported, uncorroborated, unproven, empty, idle, unsubstantiated, unwarranted, unjustified, unjustifiable, without cause, without reason, without justification, unreasonable, irrational, illogical, misguided.

groundwork *n.* PRELIMINARY WORK, preliminaries, preparations, spadework, legwork, donkey work; planning, arrangements, organization, homework; basics, essentials, fundamentals, underpinning, foundation.

group *n.* **1** CATEGORY, class, classification, grouping, set, lot, batch, bracket, type, sort, kind, variety, family, species, genus, breed; grade, grading, rank, status. **2** CROWD, party, body, band, company, gathering, congregation, assembly, collection, cluster, flock, pack, troop, contingent, crew, gang; *informal* bunch, pile. **3** FACTION, division, section, clique, coterie, circle, set, ring, camp, bloc, caucus, cabal, fringe movement, splinter group. **4** ASSOCIATION, club, society, league, guild, circle, union. **5** ☞ CLUSTER *n.* 1. **6** BAND, ensemble, act.

▶ *v.* **1** CATEGORIZE, classify, class,

catalogue, sort, bracket, pigeonhole, grade, rate, rank; prioritize, triage. **2** PLACE, arrange, assemble, organize, range, line up, dispose. **3** UNITE, join together/up, team up, gang up, join forces, get together, ally, form an alliance, affiliate, combine; collaborate, work together, pull together, co-operate.

grouse v. ☞ COMPLAIN.

grovel v. BE OBSEQUIOUS, fawn on, kowtow, bow and scrape, toady, truckle, abase oneself, humble oneself; curry favour with, flatter, dance attendance on, make up to, play up to, ingratiate oneself with; *informal* crawl, creep, suck up to, lick someone's boots, brown-nose.

grow v. **1** GET BIGGER, get taller, get larger, increase in size. **2** INCREASE, swell, multiply, snowball, mushroom, balloon, build up, mount up, pile up; *informal* skyrocket. **3** SPROUT, germinate, shoot up, spring up, develop, bud, burst forth, bloom, flourish, thrive, run riot, burgeon. **4** CULTIVATE, produce, propagate, raise, rear, nurture, tend; farm. **5** EXPAND, extend, develop, progress, make progress; flourish, thrive, burgeon, prosper, succeed, boom. **6** ORIGINATE, stem, spring, arise, emerge, issue; develop, evolve. **7** BECOME, get, turn, begin to feel.
—OPPOSITES: shrink, decline.

grown-up n. ADULT, (grown) woman, (grown) man, mature woman, mature man.
—OPPOSITES: child.
▶ *adj.* ☞ ADULT 1.

growth n. **1** INCREASE, expansion, augmentation, proliferation, multiplication, enlargement, mushrooming, snowballing, rise, escalation, buildup.
2 DEVELOPMENT, maturation, growing, germination, sprouting; blooming. **3** EXPANSION, extension, development, progress, advance, advancement, headway, spread; rise, success, boom, upturn, upswing. **4** TUMOUR, malignancy, cancer; lump, excrescence, outgrowth, swelling, nodule; cyst, polyp.
—OPPOSITES: decrease, decline.

grub v. **1** DIG UP, unearth, uproot, root up/out, pull up/out, tear out. **2** RUMMAGE, search, hunt, delve, dig, scrabble, ferret, root, rifle, fish, poke.

grubby *adj.* ☞ DIRTY 1.
—OPPOSITES: clean.

grudge n. GRIEVANCE, resentment, bitterness, rancour, pique, umbrage, dissatisfaction, disgruntlement, bad feelings, hard feelings, ill feelings, ill will, animosity, antipathy, antagonism, enmity, animus; *informal* a chip on one's shoulder.
▶ v. ☞ BEGRUDGE.

gruelling *adj.* EXHAUSTING, tiring, fatiguing, wearying, taxing, draining, debilitating; demanding, exacting, difficult, hard, arduous, strenuous, laborious, back-breaking, harsh, severe, stiff, stressful, punishing, crippling; *informal* killing, murderous, hellish.

gruesome *adj.* GRISLY, ghastly, frightful, horrid, horrifying, hideous, horrible, horrendous, grim, awful, dire, dreadful,

terrible, horrific, shocking,
appalling, disgusting, repulsive,
repugnant, revolting, repellent,
sickening, macabre; loathsome,
abominable, abhorrent, odious,
monstrous, unspeakable; *informal*
sick, gross.
—OPPOSITES: pleasant.

grumble v. ☞ COMPLAIN.

grumpy *adj.* BAD-TEMPERED,
crabby, ill-tempered, short-
tempered, crotchety, tetchy, testy,
waspish, prickly, touchy, irritable,
irascible, crusty, cantankerous,
curmudgeonly, bearish, surly, ill-
natured, churlish, ill-humoured,
peevish, cross, fractious,
disagreeable, pettish; *informal*
grouchy, snappy, chippy,
snappish, shirty, rangy, cranky,
ornery; dour, gloomy, glum,
lugubrious, moody, saturnine,
sour, sullen, unsociable, scowling,
sulky, uncivil, unfriendly,
unpleasant, unsmiling; abrupt,
brusque, curt, gruff.
—OPPOSITES: good-humoured.

guarantee *n.* 1 WARRANTY.
2 PROMISE, assurance, word (of
honour), pledge, vow, oath, bond,
commitment, covenant.
▶ v. 1 UNDERWRITE, put up collateral
for. 2 PROMISE, swear, swear to the
fact, pledge, vow, undertake, give
one's word, give an assurance,
take an oath.

guard v. 1 PROTECT, stand guard
over, watch over, keep an eye on;
cover, patrol, police, defend,
shield, safeguard, keep safe,
secure. 2 BEWARE OF, keep watch
for, be alert to, keep an eye out
for, be on the alert/lookout for.
▶ *n.* 1 SENTRY, sentinel, security

guard, (night) watchman;
protector, defender, guardian;
lookout, watch; garrison.
2 WARDER, warden, keeper; jailer;
informal screw; *archaic* turnkey.

guarded *adj.* CAUTIOUS, careful,
circumspect, wary, chary, on one's
guard, reluctant, reticent,
noncommittal, evasive,
restrained, reserved; *informal* cagey.

guess v. 1 ESTIMATE, hazard a
guess, reckon, gauge, judge,
calculate; hypothesize, postulate,
predict, speculate, conjecture,
surmise; *informal* guesstimate.
2 ☞ SUPPOSE 1.
▶ *n.* HYPOTHESIS, theory, prediction,
postulation, conjecture, surmise,
estimate, belief, opinion,
reckoning, judgment, supposition,
speculation, suspicion,
impression, feeling; *informal*
guesstimate, shot in the dark.

guest *n.* 1 VISITOR, house guest,
caller; company. 2 PATRON, client,
visitor, boarder, lodger, roomer.
—OPPOSITES: host.

guidance *n.* 1 ADVICE, counsel,
direction, instruction,
enlightenment, information;
recommendations, suggestions,
tips, hints, pointers, guidelines.
2 DIRECTION, control, leadership,
management, supervision,
superintendence, charge;
handling, conduct, running,
overseeing.

guileless *adj.* ARTLESS,
ingenuous, naive, open, genuine,
natural, simple, childlike,
innocent, unsophisticated,
unworldly, unsuspicious, trustful,
trusting; honest, truthful, sincere,

straightforward.
—OPPOSITES: scheming.

guilty *adj.* **1** CULPABLE, to blame, at fault, in the wrong, blameworthy, responsible; erring, errant, delinquent, offending, sinful, criminal; *archaic* peccant.
2 ☞ CONTRITE.
—OPPOSITES: innocent, unrepentant.

guise *n.* **1** LIKENESS, outward appearance, appearance, semblance, form, shape, image; disguise. **2** PRETENSE, disguise, front, facade, cover, blind, screen, smokescreen.

gulf *n.* **1** INLET, bay, bight, cove, fjord, estuary, sound. **2** DIVIDE, division, separation, gap, breach, rift, split, chasm, abyss; difference, contrast, polarity.

gullible *adj.* CREDULOUS, naive, easily deceived, easily taken in, exploitable, impressionable, unsuspecting, unsuspicious, unwary, ingenuous, innocent, inexperienced, unworldly, unsophisticated, green; *informal* wet behind the ears, born yesterday.
—OPPOSITES: suspicious.

gulp *v.* **1** SWALLOW, quaff, swill down, down; *informal* swig, (Nfld) glutch✦, knock back, chug, chugalug. **2** ☞ DEVOUR. **3** CHOKE BACK, fight back, hold back/in, suppress, stifle, smother.
—OPPOSITES: sip.

gumption *n.* (*informal*) BACKBONE, pluck, mettle, nerve, courage; astuteness, shrewdness, acumen, sense. See also INITIATIVE.

gun *n.* FIREARM, pistol, revolver, rifle, shotgun, carbine, automatic, handgun, semi-automatic,

machine gun, Kalashnikov, Uzi; six-shooter, piece.

gunman *n.* ARMED ROBBER, gangster, terrorist; sniper, gunfighter; assassin, murderer, killer; *informal* hit man, hired gun, gunslinger, mobster, shootist, hood.

gurgle *v.* BABBLE, burble, tinkle, bubble, ripple, murmur, purl, splash; *literary* plash.

gush *v.* **1** SURGE, burst, spout, spurt, jet, stream, rush, pour, spill, well out, cascade, flood; flow, run, issue. **2** ☞ PRAISE 1.
▶ *n.* SURGE, stream, spurt, jet, spout, outpouring, outflow, burst, rush, cascade, flood, torrent; *technical* efflux.

gusto *n.* ENTHUSIASM, relish, appetite, enjoyment, delight, glee, pleasure, satisfaction, contentment, appreciation, liking; zest, zeal, fervour, verve, keenness, avidity.
—OPPOSITES: apathy, distaste.

gut *n.* **1** STOMACH, belly, abdomen, solar plexus; intestines, bowels, entrails; *informal* tummy, tum, insides, innards. **2** (*informal*) COURAGE, bravery, backbone, nerve, pluck, spirit, boldness, audacity, daring, grit, fearlessness, feistiness, toughness, determination; *informal* spunk, moxie.
—RELATED: visceral, enteric.
▶ *v.* **1** REMOVE THE GUTS FROM, disembowel, draw, eviscerate.
2 DEVASTATE, destroy, demolish, wipe out, lay waste, ravage, consume, ruin, wreck.

gutter *n.* DRAIN, sluice, sluiceway, culvert, spillway, sewer; channel,

conduit, pipe, duct;
eavestrough♣; trough, trench,
ditch, furrow, cut.

guttural *adj.* THROATY, husky,
gruff, gravelly, growly, growling,
croaky, croaking, harsh, rough,
rasping, raspy; deep, low, thick.

guy *n.* (*informal*) MAN, fellow,
gentleman; youth, boy; *informal* lad,
fella, (esp. *Atlantic*) buddy♣, geezer,
gent, dude, joe, Joe Blow, Joe
Schmo, hombre, schmo.

gyrate *v.* ROTATE, revolve, wheel,
turn round, whirl, circle,
pirouette, twirl, swirl, spin,
swivel.

Hh

habit *n.* **1** CUSTOM, practice, routine, wont, pattern, convention, way, norm, tradition, matter of course, rule, policy, usage. **2** ☞ MANNERISM. **3** ADDICTION, dependence, dependency, craving, fixation, compulsion, obsession, weakness. **4** GARMENTS, dress, garb, clothes, clothing, attire, outfit, costume.

habitable *adj.* FIT TO LIVE IN, inhabitable, fit to occupy, in good repair, livable.

habitual *adj.* **1** ☞ CONTINUOUS. **2** INVETERATE, confirmed, compulsive, obsessive, incorrigible, hardened, ingrained, dyed-in-the-wool, chronic, regular; addicted; *informal* pathological. **3** CUSTOMARY, accustomed, regular, usual, normal, set, fixed, established, routine.
—OPPOSITES: occasional, unaccustomed.

habituate *v.* ACCUSTOM, make used, familiarize, adapt, adjust, attune, acclimatize, acculturate, condition; inure, harden; acclimate.

hackneyed *adj.* OVERUSED, overdone, overworked, worn out, time-worn, vapid, stale, tired; trite, banal, hack, clichéd, hoary, commonplace, stock, conventional, predictable; unimaginative, unoriginal, dull,

boring, boilerplate; *informal* old hat.
—OPPOSITES: original.

hag *n.* CRONE, old woman, gorgon; *informal* witch, crow, cow, old bag.

haggard *adj.* DRAWN, tired, exhausted, drained, careworn, unwell, unhealthy, spent, washed out, rundown; gaunt, pinched, peaked, peaky, hollow-cheeked, hollow-eyed, thin, emaciated, wasted, cadaverous.
—OPPOSITES: healthy.

haggle *v.* ☞ BARGAIN *v.*

hail *v.* **1** CALL OUT TO, shout to, halloo, address; greet, say hello to, salute. **2** FLAG DOWN, wave down, signal to. **3** ☞ ACCLAIM *v.* **4** COME FROM, be from, be a native of.

hair *n.* **1** LOCKS, curls, mane, mop; shock of hair, head of hair; tresses. **2** FUR, wool; coat, fleece, pelt; mane.

hair-raising *adj.* ☞ FRIGHTENING.

hairy *adj.* **1** SHAGGY, bushy; woolly, furry, fleecy, fuzzy. **2** BEARDED, moustachioed; unshaven, stubbly, hirsute.

half-baked *adj.* **1** ILL-CONCEIVED, hare-brained, cockamamie, ill-judged, impractical, unrealistic, unworkable, ridiculous, absurd. **2** ☞ STUPID 2.
—OPPOSITES: sensible.

half-hearted *adj.* UNENTHUSIASTIC, cool, lukewarm, tepid, apathetic, indifferent, uninterested, unconcerned, languid, listless; perfunctory, cursory, superficial, desultory, feeble, lacklustre.

halfwitted *adj.* (*informal*). ☞ STUPID 1.

hall *n.* **1** ENTRANCE HALL, hallway, entry, entrance, lobby, foyer, vestibule; atrium, concourse; passageway, passage, corridor, entryway. **2** BANQUET HALL, community centre, assembly room, community hall✦, meeting room, chamber; auditorium, concert hall, theatre.

hallmark *n.* **1** ASSAY MARK, official mark, stamp of authenticity. **2** MARK, characteristic, sign, telltale sign, badge, stamp, trademark, indication, indicator.

hallucinate *v.* HAVE HALLUCINATIONS, see things, be delirious, fantasize; *informal* trip.

hallucination *n.* DELUSION, illusion, figment of the imagination, vision, apparition, mirage, chimera, fantasy; *informal* trip.

halt *v.* **1** ☞ STOP *v.* 3. **2** STOP, bring to a stop/end, put a stop/end to, terminate, end, wind up; suspend, break off, arrest; impede, check, curb, stem, staunch, block, stall, hold back.
—OPPOSITES: start, continue.
▸ *n.* STOP, stoppage, stopping, discontinuation, break, pause, interval, interruption, hiatus; close, end.

hammer *v.* **1** BEAT, forge, shape, form, mould, fashion, make. **2** ☞ BEAT *v.* 1. **3** WORK HARD, labour, slog away, slave away.

hamper *v.* HINDER, obstruct, impede, inhibit, retard, balk, thwart, foil, curb, delay, set back, slow down, hobble, hold up, interfere with; restrict, constrain, trammel, block, check, curtail, frustrate, cramp, bridle, handicap, cripple, hamstring, shackle, fetter, tie hand and foot, tie down; *informal* stymie, hog-tie, throw a wrench in the works of.
—OPPOSITES: help.

hand *n.* **1** palm, fist; *informal* paw, mitt, duke. **2** POINTER, indicator, needle. **3** CONTROL, power, charge, authority; command, responsibility. **4** HELP, a helping hand, assistance, aid, support, succour, relief. **5** WORKER, workman, labourer, operative, hired hand, roustabout, peon.
▸ *v.* PASS, give, reach, let someone have, throw, toss.
☐ **hand something down** PASS ON, pass down; bequeath, will, leave, make over, give, gift, transfer. **hand something over** YIELD, give, give up, pass, grant, surrender, relinquish, cede, turn over. **hands down** ☞ EASILY. **try one's hand** ☞ ATTEMPT *v.*

handbill *n.* ☞ FLYER 2.

handbook *n.* MANUAL, instructions, instruction manual, ABC, how-to guide; almanac, companion, directory; guide, guidebook.

handicap *n.* **1** ☞ DISABILITY. **2** IMPEDIMENT, hindrance, obstacle, barrier, bar, obstruction, encumbrance, constraint, restriction, check, block, curb; disadvantage, drawback, stumbling block, difficulty,

shortcoming, limitation.
▶ v. ☞ HAMPER.
—OPPOSITES: benefit, advantage.

handicapped adj. ☞ DISABLED.

handiwork n. CREATION, product, work, achievement; handicraft, craft.

handle v. 1 HOLD, pick up, grasp, grip, lift; feel, touch, finger; informal paw. 2 CONTROL, drive, steer, operate, manoeuvre, manipulate. 3 DEAL WITH, manage, administer, tackle, take care of, attend to, see to, sort out, take in hand.
▶ n. HAFT, shank, stock, shaft, grip, handgrip, hilt.

hand-me-down adj. ☞ USED.

handsome adj. 1 GOOD-LOOKING, attractive, striking, gorgeous; prepossessing, elegant, stately. 2 SUBSTANTIAL, considerable, sizeable, princely, large, big, ample, bumper; informal tidy, whopping.

handy adj. 1 USEFUL, convenient, practical, easy-to-use, well-designed, user-friendly, user-oriented, helpful, functional, serviceable. 2 READILY AVAILABLE, at hand, to hand, within reach, accessible, ready. 3 SKILFUL, skilled, dexterous, deft, nimble-fingered, adroit, able, adept, proficient, capable.

handyman n. BUILDER, odd-job man, odd jobber, factotum, jack of all trades, do-it-yourselfer, Mr. Fix-it.

hang v. 1 BE SUSPENDED, dangle, hang down, be pendent, swing, sway. 2 PUT UP, fix, attach, affix, fasten, post, display, suspend, pin up. 3 DECORATE, adorn, drape, festoon, bedeck, garland,

ornament. 4 STRING UP, send to the gallows.
□ **hang around/round** (informal) 1 ☞ LOITER. 2 ☞ ASSOCIATE v. 2.

hang on 1 ☞ PERSEVERE. 2 (informal) WAIT, wait a minute, hold on, stop; hold the line; informal hold your horses, sit tight.

hangout n. ☞ HAUNT n.

hang-up n. NEUROSIS, phobia, preoccupation, fixation, obsession; inhibition, mental block, complex.

hanker v. ☞ YEARN.

haphazard adj. RANDOM, unplanned, unsystematic, unmethodical, disorganized, disorderly, irregular, indiscriminate, chaotic, hit-and-miss, arbitrary, aimless, careless, casual, slapdash, slipshod; chance, accidental.

hapless adj. ☞ UNFORTUNATE 1.

happen v. 1 OCCUR, take place, come about; ensue, follow, result, transpire, materialize, arise, crop up, come up, emerge, surface, present itself, arrive, appear, supervene, come to pass, befall; go down. 2 DISCOVER, find, find by chance, come across, chance on, stumble on, hit on.

happening n. OCCURRENCE, event, incident, proceeding, affair, doing, circumstance, phenomenon, episode, experience, occasion, development, eventuality.
▶ adj. ☞ FASHIONABLE.

happiness n. PLEASURE, contentment, satisfaction, cheerfulness, merriment, gaiety, joy, joyfulness, joyousness, gladness, jollity, jolliness, high spirits, joviality, jocularity, conviviality, glee, delight, good spirits, lightheartedness, well-being, enjoyment, mirth; exuberance, exhilaration, elation, ecstasy, jubilation, rapture, bliss, euphoria.

happy *adj.* **1** CHEERFUL, cheery, merry, joyful, jovial, jolly, jocular, gleeful, carefree, untroubled, delighted, smiling, beaming, grinning, in good spirits, in a good mood, lighthearted, pleased, contented, content, satisfied, gratified, buoyant, radiant, sunny, blithe, joyous, beatific; thrilled, elated, exhilarated, ecstatic, blissful, euphoric, overjoyed, exultant, rapturous, in seventh heaven, on cloud nine, walking on air, jumping for joy, jubilant; *informal* chirpy, over the moon, on top of the world, tickled pink, on a high, as happy as a clam; *formal* jocund. **2** GLAD, pleased, delighted; willing, ready, disposed. **3** FORTUNATE, lucky, favourable, advantageous, opportune, timely, well-timed, convenient.
—OPPOSITES: sad, unwilling, unfortunate.

happy-go-lucky *adj.* ☞ EASYGOING.
—OPPOSITES: anxious.

harangue *n.* ☞ TIRADE.
▶ *v.* RANT AT, hold forth to, lecture, shout at; berate, criticize, attack.

harass *v.* **1** PERSECUTE, intimidate, hound, harry, plague, torment, bully, bullyrag, bedevil; pester, bother, worry, disturb, trouble, provoke, stress; *informal* hassle, bug. **2** HARRY, attack, beleaguer, set upon, assail.

harassed *adj.* STRESSED (OUT), strained, worn out, hard-pressed, careworn, worried, troubled, beleaguered, under pressure, hassled.

harbinger *n.* HERALD, sign, indication, signal, portent, omen, augury; forerunner, precursor.

harbour *n.* **1** PORT, dock, haven, marina; mooring, moorage, anchorage; waterfront. **2** REFUGE, safe haven, shelter, sanctuary, retreat.
▶ *v.* **1** SHELTER, conceal, hide, shield, protect, give sanctuary to; take in, put up, accommodate, house. **2** ☞ NURSE *v.* 4.

hard *adj.* **1** FIRM, solid, rigid, stiff, resistant, unbreakable, inflexible, impenetrable, unyielding, solidified, hardened, compact, compacted, dense, close-packed, compressed; steely, tough, strong, stony, rocklike, flinty; *literary* adamantine. **2** ☞ DIFFICULT 1, 2. **3** STRICT, harsh, firm, severe, stern, tough, rigorous, demanding, exacting; callous, unkind, unsympathetic, heartless, unfeeling; intransigent, unbending; pitiless, cruel. **4** FORCEFUL, heavy, strong, sharp, smart, violent, powerful, vigorous, mighty, hefty, tremendous. **5** ADDICTIVE, habit-forming; strong, harmful.
—OPPOSITES: soft, easy lazy, gentle.
▶ *adv.* **1** FORCEFULLY, forcibly, roughly, powerfully, strongly, heavily, sharply, vigorously, energetically. **2** DILIGENTLY, industriously, assiduously, conscientiously, sedulously,

busily, enthusiastically,
energetically, doggedly, steadily.
□ **hard up** ☞ BROKE.

harden v. 1 SOLIDIFY, set, congeal,
clot, coagulate, stiffen, thicken,
cake, cure; freeze, crystallize;
ossify, calcify, petrify. 2 TOUGHEN,
desensitize, inure; deaden, numb.

hard-hitting adj.
UNCOMPROMISING, blunt, forthright,
frank, honest, direct, tough;
critical, unsparing, strongly
worded, straight-talking.

hardline adj. ☞ INFLEXIBLE.
—OPPOSITES: moderate.

hardly adv. SCARCELY, barely, only
just, slightly.

hardship n. PRIVATION,
deprivation, destitution, poverty,
indigence, impoverishment,
austerity, penury, want, need,
neediness; misfortune, distress,
suffering, affliction, trouble, pain,
misery, wretchedness, tribulation,
adversity, trials, dire straits; *literary*
travails.
—OPPOSITES: prosperity, ease.

hard-working adj.
☞ INDUSTRIOUS.
—OPPOSITES: lazy.

hardy adj. ROBUST, healthy, fit,
strong, sturdy, tough, rugged,
hearty, lusty, vigorous, hale and
hearty, fit as a fiddle.
—OPPOSITES: delicate.

harm n. 1 INJURY, hurt, pain,
trauma; damage, impairment,
mischief. 2 EVIL, wrong, ill,
wickedness, iniquity, sin.
—OPPOSITES: benefit.
▸ v. INJURE, hurt, wound, lay a
finger on, maltreat, mistreat,
misuse, ill-treat, ill-use, abuse,
molest; damage, spoil.

harmful adj. DAMAGING, injurious,
detrimental, dangerous,
deleterious, unfavourable,
negative, disadvantageous,
unhealthy, unwholesome, hurtful,
baleful, destructive, adverse,
inimical, prejudicial, ruinous,
undesirable; noxious, hazardous,
poisonous, toxic, deadly, lethal;
bad, evil, malign, malignant,
malevolent, corrupting,
subversive, pernicious.
—OPPOSITES: beneficial.

harmless adj. 1 SAFE, innocuous,
benign, gentle, mild, wholesome,
non-toxic. 2 INOFFENSIVE,
innocuous, unobjectionable,
unexceptionable.
—OPPOSITES: dangerous.

harmonious adj. 1 TUNEFUL,
melodious, melodic, sweet-
sounding, mellifluous, dulcet,
lyrical; euphonious, euphonic,
harmonic, polyphonic. 2 FRIENDLY,
amicable, cordial, amiable,
congenial, easy, peaceful,
peaceable, co-operative;
compatible, sympathetic, united,
attuned, in harmony, in rapport,
in tune, in accord, of one mind.

harmonize v. 1 COORDINATE, go
together, match, blend, mix,
balance; be compatible, be
harmonious, suit each other.
2 COORDINATE, systematize,
correlate, integrate, synchronize,
make consistent, homogenize.
—OPPOSITES: clash.

harmony n. 1 EUPHONY,
polyphony; tunefulness,
melodiousness, mellifluousness.
2 BALANCE, symmetry, congruity,
consonance, coordination,
compatibility. 3 ACCORD,

agreement, peace, amity, friendship, fellowship, co-operation, understanding, consensus, unity, sympathy, rapport, like-mindedness; unison, union, concert, oneness, synthesis; *formal* concord.
—opposites: dissonance, disagreement.

harrowing *adj.* DISTRESSING, distressful, traumatic, upsetting; shocking, disturbing, painful, haunting, appalling, horrifying.

harsh *adj.* **1** GRATING, jarring, rasping, strident, raucous, brassy, discordant; screeching, shrill; rough, coarse, hoarse, gruff, croaky. **2** ☞ TYRANNICAL. **3** SEVERE, stringent, draconian, firm, stiff, hard, stern, rigorous, grim, uncompromising; punitive, cruel, brutal. **4** ☞ RUDE 1. **5** AUSTERE, grim, Spartan, hard, comfortless, inhospitable, stark, bleak, desolate. **6** HARD, severe, cold, bitter, bleak, freezing, icy; arctic, polar, Siberian.
—opposites: soft, subdued, kind, friendly, comfortable, balmy, mild.

harvest *n.* **1** HARVESTING, reaping, picking, collecting. **2** YIELD, crop, vintage; fruits, produce.
▶ *v.* **1** GATHER (IN), bring in, reap, pick, collect. **2** ACQUIRE, obtain, gain, get, earn.

hassle (*informal*) *n.* INCONVENIENCE, bother, nuisance, problem, trouble, struggle, difficulty, annoyance, irritation, fuss; headache, pain (in the neck).
▶ *v.* ☞ HARASS 1.

haste *n.* SPEED, hastiness, hurriedness, swiftness, rapidity,

quickness, briskness.
—opposites: delay.

hasty *adj.* **1** QUICK, hurried, fast, swift, rapid, speedy, brisk. **2** ☞ RASH.
—opposites: slow, considered.

hatch *v.* **1** INCUBATE, brood. **2** DEVISE, conceive, concoct, brew, invent, plan, design, formulate; think up, dream up; *informal* cook up.

hate *v.* **1** LOATHE, detest, despise, dislike, disdain, abhor, execrate; be repelled by, be unable to bear/stand, shudder at, find intolerable, recoil from, shrink from, feel repugnance towards, have a strong aversion to. **2** BE SORRY, be reluctant, be loath, be unwilling, be disinclined; regret, dislike.
—opposites: love.
▶ *n.* ☞ HATRED.

hateful *adj.* DETESTABLE, horrible, horrid, unpleasant, awful, nasty, disagreeable, despicable, objectionable, insufferable, revolting, loathsome, abhorrent, abominable, execrable, odious, disgusting, distasteful, obnoxious, offensive, vile, heinous, ghastly, beastly, godawful.
—opposites: delightful.

hatred *n.* LOATHING, hate, detestation, dislike, distaste, abhorrence, abomination, execration; aversion, hostility, ill will, ill feeling, enmity, animosity, antipathy; revulsion, disgust, contempt, odium, animus, bad feeling, malice, repugnance.

haughty *adj.* PROUD, arrogant, vain, conceited, snobbish, superior, self-important,

pompous, supercilious, condescending, patronizing; scornful, contemptuous, disdainful; *informal* stuck-up, snooty, hoity-toity, uppity.
—OPPOSITES: humble.

haul v. **1** DRAG, pull, tug, heave, lug, hump, draw, tow. **2** TRANSPORT, convey, carry, ship, ferry, move, shift.
▶ n. ☞ BOOTY.

haunt v. **1** FREQUENT, patronize, visit regularly; loiter in, linger in, hang out in. **2** TORMENT, disturb, trouble, worry, plague, burden, beset, beleaguer; prey on, weigh on, gnaw at, weigh heavily on.
▶ n. HANGOUT, stomping ground; territory, domain.

have v. **1** POSSESS, own, be in possession of, be the owner of; be blessed with, boast, enjoy; keep, retain, hold, occupy. **2** COMPRISE, consist of, contain, include, incorporate, be composed of, be made up of; encompass. **3** RECEIVE, get, be given, be sent, obtain, acquire, come by. **4** ORGANIZE, arrange, hold, give, host; entertain, wine and dine. **5** GIVE BIRTH TO, bear, be delivered of, produce. **6** EXPERIENCE, encounter, face, meet, find, run into, go through, undergo. **7** BE SUFFERING FROM, be afflicted by. **8** HARBOUR, entertain, feel, nurse, nurture, sustain, maintain. **9** MAKE, ask to, request to, get to, tell to, require to; order/command to, force to. **10** TOLERATE, endure, bear, support, accept, put up with, go along with, take, countenance; stand, abide, stomach. **11** MUST, be obliged to, be required to, be

compelled to, be forced to, be bound to.
—OPPOSITES: send, give, visit.

haven n. REFUGE, retreat, shelter, sanctuary, asylum; port in a storm, oasis, sanctum.

havoc n. **1** DEVASTATION, destruction, damage, desolation, ruination, ruin; disaster, catastrophe. **2** DISORDER, chaos, disruption, mayhem, bedlam, pandemonium; commotion, furor.

hazard n. DANGER, risk, peril, threat, menace; problem, pitfall.
▶ v. **1** VENTURE, advance, put forward, volunteer, float; conjecture, speculate, surmise. **2** RISK, jeopardize, gamble, stake, bet, chance.

hazardous adj. DANGEROUS, perilous, risky, high-risk, unsafe, unpredictable, precarious, insecure, touch-and-go, chancy, treacherous; *informal* dicey, hairy.
—OPPOSITES: safe, certain.

haze n. **1** MIST, fog, cloud; smoke, vapour, steam. **2** BLUR, daze, confusion, muddle, befuddlement.

hazy adj. **1** MISTY, foggy, cloudy, overcast; smoggy, murky. **2** VAGUE, indistinct, unclear, faint, dim, nebulous, shadowy, blurred, fuzzy, confused.

head n. **1** skull, cranium, crown; *informal* nut, noodle, noggin. **2** BRAIN(S), brainpower, intellect, intelligence; wit(s), wisdom, mind, sense, reasoning, common sense; *informal* savvy, grey matter, smarts. **3** APTITUDE, faculty, talent, gift, capacity, ability; mind, brain. **4** ☞ LEADER. **5** FRONT, beginning, start, fore, forefront; top.
▶ adj. ☞ CHIEF 1.

—OPPOSITES: subordinate.

▶ v. **1** COMMAND, control, lead, run, manage, direct, supervise, superintend, oversee, preside over, rule, govern, captain. **2** MOVE TOWARDS, make for, aim for, go in the direction of; set out for.

□ **head someone/something off 1** INTERCEPT, divert, deflect, redirect, reroute, draw away, turn away. **2** FORESTALL, avert, ward off, fend off, stave off, hold off.

headlong adv. **1** HEADFIRST, on one's head. **2** WITHOUT THINKING, without forethought, precipitously, impetuously, rashly, recklessly, carelessly, heedlessly, hastily.

—OPPOSITES: cautiously.

headquarters pl. n. HEAD OFFICE, main office, HQ, base, nerve centre, war room, mission control, command post, detachment✦.

headstrong adj. ☞ STUBBORN 1.

—OPPOSITES: tractable.

heal v. **1** MAKE BETTER, make well, cure, treat. **2** GET BETTER, get well, be cured, recover, mend, improve. **3** ☞ ALLEVIATE. **4** PUT RIGHT, set right, repair, remedy, resolve, correct, settle; informal patch up.

—OPPOSITES: aggravate, worsen.

health n. **1** WELL-BEING, healthiness, fitness; strength, vigour, wellness. **2** PHYSICAL STATE, physical shape, condition, constitution.

—OPPOSITES: illness.

healthy adj. **1** WELL, in good health, fine, fit, in good trim, in good shape, in fine fettle, in tip-top shape; blooming, thriving, hardy, robust, strong, vigorous, fit

as a fiddle; informal in the pink. **2** HEALTH-GIVING, healthful, good for one; wholesome, nutritious, nourishing; beneficial, salubrious.

—OPPOSITES: ill, unwholesome.

heap n. **1** PILE, stack, mound, mountain, mass, quantity, load, lot, jumble; collection, accumulation, assemblage, store, hoard. **2** ☞ ABUNDANCE.

▶ v. PILE (UP), stack (up), make a mound of; assemble, collect.

hear v. **1** PERCEIVE, make out, discern, catch, get, apprehend; overhear, listen to. **2** BE INFORMED, be told, find out, discover, learn, gather, glean, ascertain, get word, get wind. **3** TRY, judge; adjudicate (on), adjudge, pass judgment on.

hearing n. **1** EARSHOT, hearing range. **2** TRIAL, court case, inquiry, inquest, tribunal; investigation, inquisition.

hearsay n. RUMOUR, gossip, tittle-tattle, tattle, idle talk; stories, tales; informal the grapevine, scuttlebutt.

heart n. **1** EMOTIONS, feelings, sentiments; soul, mind, bosom, breast; love, affection, passion. **2** ☞ COMPASSION. **3** ENTHUSIASM, keenness, eagerness, spirit, determination, resolve, purpose. **4** CENTRE, middle, hub, core, nucleus, eye, bosom. **5** ESSENCE, crux, core, nub, root, substance, kernel.

—RELATED: cardiac, coronary.

—OPPOSITES: edge.

□ **at heart** ☞ FUNDAMENTALLY. **eat one's heart out** PINE, long, ache, brood, mope, fret, sigh, sorrow, yearn, agonize; grieve, mourn, lament. **have a heart** BE

COMPASSIONATE, be kind, be merciful, be lenient, be sympathetic, be considerate, have mercy. **heart and soul** ☞ HEARTILY.

heartache n. ANGUISH, grief, suffering, distress, unhappiness, misery, sorrow, sadness, heartbreak, pain, hurt, agony, angst, despondency, despair, woe, desolation.
—OPPOSITES: happiness.

heartbreaking adj. DISTRESSING, upsetting, disturbing, heart-rending, sad, tragic, painful, traumatic, agonizing, harrowing; pitiful, poignant, plaintive, moving, tear-jerking, gut-wrenching.
—OPPOSITES: comforting.

heartbroken adj. ANGUISHED, devastated, broken-hearted, heavy-hearted, grieving, grief-stricken, inconsolable, crushed, shattered, desolate, despairing; upset, distressed, miserable, sorrowful, sad, downcast, disconsolate, crestfallen, despondent; informal down in the dumps, cut up.

hearten v. CHEER (UP), encourage, raise someone's spirits, boost, buoy up, perk up, ginger up, inspirit, uplift, elate; comfort, reassure; informal buck up.

heartfelt adj. SINCERE, genuine, from the heart; earnest, profound, deep, wholehearted, ardent, fervent, passionate, enthusiastic, eager; honest, bona fide.
—OPPOSITES: insincere.

heartily adv. WHOLEHEARTEDLY, sincerely, genuinely, warmly, profoundly, with all one's heart; eagerly, enthusiastically, earnestly, ardently, heart and soul.

heartless adj. UNFEELING, unsympathetic, unkind, uncaring, unconcerned, insensitive, inconsiderate, hard-hearted, stony-hearted, cold-hearted, mean-spirited; cold, callous, cruel, merciless, pitiless, inhuman.
—OPPOSITES: compassionate.

heat n. 1 WARMTH, hotness, warmness, high temperature; hot weather, warm weather, sultriness, mugginess, humidity; heat wave, hot spell. 2 PASSION, intensity, vehemence, warmth, fervour, fervency; enthusiasm, excitement, agitation; anger, fury.
—RELATED: thermal.
—OPPOSITES: cold, apathy.
▶ v. 1 WARM (UP), heat up, make hot, make warm; reheat, cook. 2 BECOME HOT, become warm, get hotter, get warmer, increase in temperature.
—OPPOSITES: cool.

heated adj. VEHEMENT, passionate, impassioned, animated, spirited, lively, intense, fiery; angry, bitter, furious, fierce, stormy, tempestuous.

heathen n. 1 PAGAN, infidel, idolater, heretic, unbeliever, disbeliever, non-believer, atheist, agnostic, skeptic. 2 PHILISTINE, boor, oaf, ignoramus, lout, yahoo, vulgarian, plebeian.
—OPPOSITES: believer.

heave v. 1 HAUL, pull, lug, drag, draw, tug, heft. 2 THROW, fling, cast, toss, huck✦, hurl, lob, pitch. 3 ☞ VOMIT 1.

heaven *n.* **1** PARADISE, nirvana, Zion; the hereafter, the next world, the next life, Elysium, the Elysian Fields, Valhalla; *literary* the empyrean. **2** BLISS, ecstasy, rapture, contentment, happiness, delight, joy, seventh heaven; paradise, Utopia, nirvana. **3** THE SKY, the skies, the upper atmosphere, the stratosphere, space; *literary* the firmament, the (wide) blue yonder.
—RELATED: celestial.
—OPPOSITES: hell, misery.

heavenly *adj.* **1** DIVINE, holy, celestial, supernal; angelic, seraphic, cherubic. **2** CELESTIAL, cosmic, stellar, astral; planetary. **3** (*informal*) DELIGHTFUL, wonderful, glorious, perfect, excellent, sublime, idyllic, first-class, first-rate; blissful, pleasurable, enjoyable; exquisite, beautiful, lovely; *informal* divine, super, great, fantastic, fabulous, terrific.

heavy *adj.* **1** WEIGHTY, hefty, substantial, ponderous; solid, dense, leaden; burdensome. **2** ☞ FAT 1. **3** FORCEFUL, hard, strong, violent, powerful, vigorous, mighty, hefty, sharp, smart, severe. **4** ☞ ONEROUS. **5** ONEROUS, burdensome, demanding, challenging, difficult, formidable, weighty; worrisome, stressful, trying, crushing, oppressive. **6** DENSE, thick, soupy, murky, impenetrable. **7** SIZEABLE, hefty, substantial, colossal, big, considerable; stiff; *informal* tidy, whopping, steep, astronomical. **8** TEMPESTUOUS, turbulent, rough, wild, stormy, choppy, squally. **9** INTENSE, fierce, vigorous, relentless, all-out, severe, serious. **10** ☞ EXCESSIVE 1.

heavy-handed *adj.* **1** ☞ CLUMSY 1. **2** INSENSITIVE, oppressive, overbearing, high-handed, harsh, stern, severe, tyrannical, despotic, ruthless, merciless.
—OPPOSITES: dexterous, sensitive.

heckle *v.* ☞ JEER *v.*
—OPPOSITES: cheer.

hectic *adj.* FRANTIC, frenetic, frenzied, feverish, manic, busy, active, fast and furious, fast-paced; lively, brisk, bustling, buzzing, abuzz.
—OPPOSITES: leisurely.

hedge *n.* **1** HEDGEROW, bushes; windbreak. **2** SAFEGUARD, protection, shield, screen, guard, buffer, cushion; insurance, security.
▶ *v.* **1** SURROUND, enclose, encircle, ring, border, edge, bound. **2** PREVARICATE, equivocate, vacillate, quibble, hesitate, stall, dodge the issue, be noncommittal, be evasive, be vague, beat around the bush, pussyfoot around; hem and haw.

hedonistic *adj.* SELF-INDULGENT, pleasure-seeking, sybaritic, lotus-eating, epicurean, good-time; unrestrained, intemperate, immoderate, extravagant, decadent.

heed *v.* PAY ATTENTION TO, take notice of, take note of, attend to, listen to; bear in mind, be mindful of, mind, mark, consider, take into account, follow, obey, adhere to, abide by, observe, take to heart, be alert to.
—OPPOSITES: disregard.

▸ *n.* ATTENTION, notice, note, regard; consideration, thought, care.

heedless *adj.* UNMINDFUL, taking no notice, paying no heed, unheeding, neglectful, careless, oblivious, inattentive, absent-minded, blind, deaf; incautious, imprudent, rash, reckless, foolish, frivolous, ill-advised, ill-considered, injudicious, negligent, precipitate, silly, stupid, thoughtless, unguarded, unthinking, unwise, foolhardy, improvident, unwary.

heft *v.* LIFT (UP), raise (up), heave, hoist, haul; carry, lug, tote; *informal* cart, hump.
▸ *n.* WEIGHT, heaviness, bulk.

hefty *adj.* **1** BURLY, heavy, sturdy, strapping, bulky, brawny, husky, strong, muscular, large, big, solid, well-built; portly, stout; *informal* hulking, hunky, beefy.
2 SUBSTANTIAL, sizeable, considerable, huge, large, excessive; stiff, extortionate; *informal* steep, astronomical, whopping.
—OPPOSITES: slight, feeble, light, small.

height *n.* **1** SIZE, tallness, elevation, stature, altitude.
2 ☞ SUMMIT. **3** EPITOME, acme, zenith, quintessence, very limit; ultimate, utmost.
—OPPOSITES: width, nadir.

heighten *v.* **1** RAISE, make higher, lift (up), elevate. **2** INTENSIFY, increase, enhance, add to, augment, boost, strengthen, deepen, magnify, amplify, aggravate, reinforce.
—OPPOSITES: lower, reduce.

heinous *adj.* ODIOUS, wicked, evil, atrocious, monstrous, abominable, detestable, contemptible, reprehensible, despicable, egregious, horrific, terrible, awful, abhorrent, loathsome, hideous, unspeakable, execrable; iniquitous, villainous.
—OPPOSITES: admirable.

hellish *adj.* **1** INFERNAL, Hadean, chthonic; diabolical, fiendish, satanic, demonic; evil, wicked.
2 (*informal*) HORRIBLE, rotten, awful, terrible, dreadful, ghastly, horrid, vile, foul, appalling, atrocious, horrendous, frightful; difficult, unpleasant, nasty, disagreeable; stressful, taxing, tough, hard, frustrating, fraught, traumatic, gruelling.
—OPPOSITES: angelic, wonderful.

help *v.* **1** ASSIST, aid, lend a (helping) hand to, give assistance to, be beneficial, be of assistance, be of use, be useful, be valuable, benefit, do someone a good turn; serve, service, be of service to, be of use to, come to the rescue, pitch in. **2** SUPPORT, contribute to, give money to, donate to; promote, boost, back. **3** RELIEVE, soothe, ease, alleviate, make better, improve, assuage, lessen; remedy, cure, heal.
—OPPOSITES: hinder, impede, worsen.

▸ *n.* **1** ASSISTANCE, aid, a helping hand, support, succour, advice, guidance, TLC; benefit, use, advantage, service, comfort; *informal* a shot in the arm. **2** RELIEF, alleviation, improvement, assuagement, healing; remedy, cure, restorative. **3** DOMESTIC

WORKER, domestic servant, cleaner, cleaning lady, maid, hired help.

helper *n.* ASSISTANT, aide, helpmate, helpmeet, deputy, auxiliary, second, right-hand man/woman, attendant, acolyte; co-worker, teammate, associate, colleague.

helpful *adj.* **1** OBLIGING, eager to please, kind, accommodating, supportive, co-operative; sympathetic, neighbourly, charitable. **2** USEFUL, of use, beneficial, valuable, profitable, advantageous, fruitful, worthwhile, constructive; informative, instructive.

3 ☞ HANDY 1.
—OPPOSITES: unsympathetic, useless, inconvenient.

helping *n.* ☞ SERVING.

helpless *adj.* DEPENDENT, incapable, powerless, impotent, weak; defenceless, vulnerable, exposed, unprotected, open to attack; paralyzed, disabled.
—OPPOSITES: independent.

helter-skelter *adv.* HEADLONG, pell-mell, hotfoot, post-haste, hastily, hurriedly, at full tilt, hell for leather; recklessly, precipitately, heedlessly, wildly; *informal* like a bat out of hell, like the wind, like greased lightning, lickety-split.

▶ *adj.* ☞ DISORGANIZED 1.
—OPPOSITES: orderly.

hem *n.* EDGE, edging, border, trim, trimming.

☐ **hem someone/something in**
1 SURROUND, border, edge, encircle, circle, ring, enclose, skirt, fringe, encompass, corral.

2 RESTRICT, confine, trap, hedge in, fence in; constrain, restrain, limit, curb, check. **hem and haw** HESITATE, dither, vacillate, be indecisive, equivocate, prevaricate, waver, blow hot and cold; *informal* shilly-shally.

herd *n.* **1** drove, flock, pack, fold; group, collection. **2** CROWD, group, bunch, horde, mob, host, pack, multitude, throng, swarm, company.

▶ *v.* **1** DRIVE, shepherd, guide; round up, gather, collect, corral. **2** CROWD, pack, flock.

here *adv.* **1** AT/IN/TO THIS PLACE, at/in/to this spot, at/in/to this location; over here, nearer, closer. **2** PRESENT, in attendance, attending, at hand; available. **3** NOW, at this moment.
—OPPOSITES: absent.

hereafter *adv.* (formal) FROM NOW ON, after this, as of now, from this moment forth, from this day forth, from this day forward, subsequently, in (the) future, hence, henceforth, henceforward; *formal* hereinafter.

hereditary *adj.* **1** INHERITED; bequeathed, willed, handed-down, passed-down, passed-on, transferred; ancestral, family, familial. **2** GENETIC, congenital, inborn, inherited, inbred, innate, inbuilt, natural, inherent.

heresy *n.* DISSENSION, dissent, nonconformity, heterodoxy, unorthodoxy, apostasy, blasphemy, freethinking; agnosticism, atheism, non-belief; idolatry, paganism.

heretic *n.* DISSENTER, nonconformist, apostate,

freethinker, iconoclast; agnostic, atheist, non-believer, unbeliever, idolater, pagan, heathen.
—OPPOSITES: conformist, believer.

heritage n. **1** TRADITION, history, past, background; culture, customs. **2** ANCESTRY, lineage, descent, extraction, parentage, roots, background, heredity, inheritance, birthright.

hermit n. RECLUSE, solitary, loner, ascetic, marabout, troglodyte.

heroic adj. ☞ BRAVE.

heroism n. ☞ BRAVERY.

hesitant adj. UNCERTAIN, undecided, unsure, doubtful, dubious, skeptical; tentative, nervous, reluctant; indecisive, irresolute, hesitating, dithering, vacillating, wavering, waffling, blowing hot and cold; ambivalent, of two minds, hemming and hawing; informal iffy.

hesitate v. **1** PAUSE, delay, wait, shilly-shally, dilly-dally, dither, stall, temporize; be of two minds, be uncertain, be unsure, be doubtful, be indecisive, hedge, equivocate, fluctuate, vacillate, waver, waffle, blow hot and cold, have second thoughts, get cold feet, think twice, hem and haw. **2** BE RELUCTANT, be unwilling, be disinclined, scruple, think twice about, balk at.

hew v. CHOP, hack, cut, lop, axe, cleave, split; fell; carve, chisel, shape, fashion, sculpt, model.

heyday n. ☞ PRIME n.

hidden adj. **1** CONCEALED, secret, undercover, invisible, unseen, out of sight, closeted, covert; secluded, tucked away, private; camouflaged, disguised, masked,

cloaked, obscured. **2** OBSCURE, unclear, veiled, clouded, shrouded, concealed; cryptic, mysterious, secret, abstruse, arcane; ulterior, deep, subliminal, coded.
—OPPOSITES: visible, obvious.

hide v. **1** CONCEAL, secrete, put out of sight; camouflage; lock up, stow away, tuck away, squirrel away, cache, stash. **2** CONCEAL ONESELF, sequester oneself, hide out, take cover, keep out of sight; lie low, go underground; informal hole up, lie doggo. **3** OBSCURE, block out, blot out, obstruct, cloud, shroud, veil, blanket, envelop, eclipse. **4** CONCEAL, keep secret, cover up, keep quiet about, hush up, bottle up, suppress; disguise, dissemble, mask, camouflage.
—OPPOSITES: flaunt, reveal.

hideous adj. UGLY, repulsive, repellent, unsightly, revolting, gruesome, grotesque, monstrous, ghastly; awful, terrible, appalling, dreadful, frightful, horrible, horrendous, horrific, horrifying, shocking, sickening, unspeakable, abhorrent, heinous, abominable, foul, vile, odious, execrable.
—OPPOSITES: beautiful, pleasant.

hiding n. (informal) BEATING, battering, thrashing, thumping, pounding, drubbing, flogging, whipping, caning, spanking; informal licking, pasting.

hierarchy n. PECKING ORDER, order, ranking, chain of command, grading, gradation, ladder, scale, range.

high adj. **1** TALL, lofty, towering, soaring, elevated, giant, big.

2 HIGH-RANKING, high-level, leading, top, top-level, prominent, pre-eminent, foremost, senior; influential, powerful, important, elevated, prime, premier, exalted, ranking. **3** HIGH-MINDED, noble, lofty, moral, ethical, honourable, exalted, admirable, upright, honest, virtuous, righteous. **4** INFLATED, excessive, unreasonable, expensive, costly, exorbitant, extortionate, prohibitive, dear; *informal* steep, stiff, pricey. **5** STRONG, powerful, violent, intense; BLUSTERY, gusty, stiff, howling. **6** LUXURIOUS, lavish, extravagant, grand, opulent; sybaritic, hedonistic, epicurean, decadent; upmarket, upscale; *informal* fancy, classy, swanky. **7** FAVOURABLE, good, positive, approving, admiring, complimentary. **8** HIGH-PITCHED, high-frequency; shrill, sharp, piercing. **9** (*informal*) STONED, intoxicated, inebriated, drugged, impaired❖; *informal* wired, hopped up, wasted, wrecked.
—OPPOSITES: short, lowly, amoral, cheap, light, abstemious, unfavourable, deep, sober, low.
□ **high and dry** DESTITUTE, helpless, in the lurch, in difficulties; abandoned, stranded, marooned. **high and low** ☞ EVERYWHERE.

highbrow *adj.* ☞ INTELLECTUAL *adj.* 2.
—OPPOSITES: lowbrow.
▶ *n.* ☞ INTELLECTUAL *n.*

high-end *adj.* ☞ DELUXE.

high-handed *adj.* IMPERIOUS, arbitrary, peremptory, arrogant, haughty, domineering, supercilious, pushy, overbearing, heavy-handed, lordly, magisterial; inflexible, rigid; autocratic, authoritarian, dictatorial, tyrannical; *informal* bossy, high and mighty.
—OPPOSITES: modest.

high-strung *adj.* ☞ TENSE 2.
—OPPOSITES: easygoing.

hike *n.* WALK, trek, tramp, trudge, slog, footslog, march; ramble, walkabout.
▶ *v.* ☞ WALK *v.*

hilarious *adj.* ☞ FUNNY 1.

hill *n.* HIGH GROUND, prominence, hillock, foothill, hillside, rise, mound, (*Nfld*) tolt❖, mount, knoll, butte, hummock, mesa, coteau, drumlin; (*Maritimes*) cradle-hill❖; bank, bluff, ridge, slope, incline, gradient.

hinder *v.* ☞ HAMPER.

hindrance *n.* ☞ OBSTACLE.

hinge *v.* DEPEND, hang, rest, turn, centre, pivot, be contingent, be dependent, be conditional; be determined by, be decided by, revolve around.

hint *n.* **1** CLUE, inkling, suggestion, indication, indicator, sign, signal, pointer, intimation, insinuation, innuendo, mention, whisper.
2 TIP, suggestion, pointer, clue, guideline, recommendation; advice, help. **3** TRACE, touch, suspicion, suggestion, dash, soupçon, tinge, modicum, whiff, taste, undertone; *informal* smidgen, tad.
▶ *v.* IMPLY, insinuate, intimate, suggest, indicate, signal, give someone to understand; allude to, refer to, drive at, mean, get at.

hip *adj.* ☞ FASHIONABLE.

hire *v.* EMPLOY, engage, recruit, appoint, take on, sign up, enrol, commission, enlist, contract.
—OPPOSITES: dismiss.

historic *adj.* SIGNIFICANT, notable, important, momentous, consequential, memorable, newsworthy, unforgettable, remarkable; famous, famed, celebrated, renowned, legendary; landmark, sensational, groundbreaking, precedent-setting.
—OPPOSITES: insignificant.

historical *adj.* **1** DOCUMENTED, recorded, chronicled, archival; authentic, factual, actual, true. **2** PAST, bygone, ancient, old, former; *literary* of yore.
—OPPOSITES: contemporary.

history *n.* **1** THE PAST, former times, historical events, the olden days, the old days, bygone days, long ago, yesterday, antiquity, days of yore, yesteryear. **2** CHRONICLE, archive, record, diary, report, narrative, account, study, tale, saga; memoir. **3** BACKGROUND, past, life story, biography, experiences, backstory.

hit *v.* **1** STRIKE, slap, smack, spank, cuff, punch, thump, swat; beat, thrash, batter, pound, pummel, box someone's ears; whip, flog, cane; *informal* whack, schmuck✤, wallop, bang, bump, bust, hammer, rap, slam, thud, thwack, welt, whale, whomp, bash, bop, lam, clout, clip, clobber, sock, swipe, crown, beat the living daylights out of, knock someone around, give someone a (good) hiding, belt, tan, lay into, let someone have it, deck, floor, slug, club, cold-cock; *literary* smite. **2** CRASH INTO, run into, smash into, smack into, knock into, bump into, plow into, collide with, meet head-on. **3** DEVASTATE, affect badly, hurt, harm, leave a mark on; upset, shatter, crush, shock, overwhelm, traumatize. **4** OCCUR TO, strike, dawn on, come to.
▸ *n.* SUCCESS, sellout, winner, triumph, sensation; bestseller; *informal* smash (hit), megahit, knockout.
—OPPOSITES: failure.

☐ **hit on/upon 1** DISCOVER, come up with, think of, conceive of, dream up, work out, invent, create, devise, design, pioneer; uncover, stumble on, happen upon, chance on, light on, come upon. **2** FLIRT WITH, show interest in, make eyes at, come on to, chat up.

hoard *n.* CACHE, stockpile, stock, store, collection, supply, reserve, reservoir, fund, accumulation; treasury, treasure house, treasure trove, stash.
▸ *v.* STOCKPILE, store (up), stock up on, put aside, put by, lay by, lay up, set aside, stow away, buy up; cache, amass, collect, save, gather, garner, accumulate, squirrel away, put aside for a rainy day; *informal* stash away, salt away.
—OPPOSITES: squander.

hoarse *adj.* ROUGH, harsh, croaky, croaking, throaty, gruff, husky, growly, gravelly, grating, scratchy, raspy, rasping, raucous.
—OPPOSITES: mellow, clear.

hoax *n.* PRACTICAL JOKE, joke, jest, prank, trick; ruse, deception, fraud, bluff, humbug, confidence trick; *informal* con, spoof, scam, set-up.

hobble *v.* LIMP, walk with difficulty, walk lamely, move unsteadily, walk haltingly; shamble, totter, dodder, stagger, falter, stumble, lurch.

hobby *n.* ☞ PASTIME.

hobnob *v.* (*informal*) ASSOCIATE, mix, fraternize, socialize, keep company, spend time, go around, mingle, consort, network, rub shoulders, rub elbows, schmooze.

hokey *adj.* ☞ CORNY.

hold *v.* **1** CLASP, clutch, grasp, grip, clench, cling to, hold on to; carry, bear. **2** ☞ EMBRACE 1. **3** POSSESS, have, own, bear, carry, have to one's name. **4** SUPPORT, bear, carry, take, keep up, sustain, prop up, shore up. **5** DETAIN, hold in custody, imprison, lock up, put behind bars, put in prison, put in jail, incarcerate, keep under lock and key, confine, constrain, intern, impound; *informal* put away. **6** MAINTAIN, keep, occupy, engross, absorb, interest, captivate, fascinate, enthrall, rivet, mesmerize, transfix; engage, catch, capture, arrest. **7** OCCUPY, have, fill; *informal* hold down. **8** TAKE, contain, accommodate, fit; have a capacity of, have room for. **9** MAINTAIN, consider, take the view, believe, think, feel, deem, be of the opinion; judge, rule, decide; *informal* reckon. **10** BE AVAILABLE, be valid, hold good, stand, apply, remain, exist, be the case, be in force, be in effect. **11** CONVENE, call, summon; conduct, have, organize, run; *formal* convoke. **12** STOP, halt, restrain,

check, cease, discontinue; *informal* break off, give up; hold back, suppress, repress, refrain from using, stifle, withhold.
—OPPOSITES: release, lose, end, resume.
▶ *n.* **1** GRIP, grasp, clasp, clutch. **2** INFLUENCE, power, control, dominance, authority, command, leverage, sway, mastery, dominion. **3** CONTROL, grip, power, stranglehold, chokehold, dominion, authority.
▢ **hold someone back** ☞ HAMPER. **hold something back** ☞ SUPPRESS 2. **hold forth** SPEAK AT LENGTH, talk at length, go on, sound off, declaim, spout, pontificate, orate, preach, sermonize. **hold something off** RESIST, repel, repulse, rebuff, parry, deflect, fend off, stave off, ward off, keep at bay. **hold on 1** WAIT (A MINUTE), just a moment, just a second; stay here, stay put; hold the line; *informal* hang on, sit tight, hold your horses. **2** ☞ PERSEVERE. **hold something over** ☞ POSTPONE. **hold something up 1** SUPPORT, bear, carry, take, keep up, prop up, shore up, buttress. **2** DELAY, detain, make late, set back, keep back, retard, slow up. **3** ROB; *informal* stick up, mug.

holder *n.* **1** CONTAINER, receptacle, case, casing, cover, covering, housing, sheath; stand, rest, rack. **2** BEARER, owner, possessor, keeper; custodian.

hole *n.* **1** OPENING, aperture, gap, space, orifice, vent, chink, breach, break; crack, leak, rift, rupture; puncture, perforation, cut, split,

gash, slit, rent, tear, crevice, fissure. **2** PIT, ditch, trench, cavity, crater, depression, indentation, hollow; well, borehole, excavation, dugout; cave, cavern, pothole. **3** BURROW, lair, den, earth, set; retreat, shelter. **4** FLAW, fault, defect, weakness, shortcoming, inconsistency, discrepancy, loophole; error, mistake. **5** ☞ DUMP *n*. 2.
□ **hole up 1** HIBERNATE, lie dormant. **2** (*informal*) HIDE (OUT), conceal oneself, secrete oneself, shelter, take cover, lie low, lie doggo.

holiday *n*. **1** ☞ VACATION. **2** PUBLIC HOLIDAY, statutory holiday✦, stat holiday✦, festival, celebration; saint's day, holy day.

holiness *adj*. ☞ SANCTITY 1.

hollow *adj*. **1** EMPTY, void, unfilled, vacant. **2** SUNKEN, gaunt, deep-set, concave, depressed, indented. **3** DULL, low, flat, toneless, expressionless; muffled, muted. **4** MEANINGLESS, empty, valueless, worthless, useless, pyrrhic, futile, fruitless, profitless, pointless. **5** ☞ INSINCERE.
—OPPOSITES: solid, worthwhile, sincere.
▸ *n*. **1** ☞ HOLE 2. **2** VALLEY, vale, dale, basin, glen. *literary* dell.
▸ *v*. GOUGE, scoop, dig, shovel, cut; excavate, channel.

holocaust *n*. CATACLYSM, disaster, catastrophe; destruction, devastation, annihilation; massacre, slaughter, mass murder, extermination, extirpation, carnage, butchery; genocide, ethnic cleansing.

holy *adj*. **1** SAINTLY, godly, saintlike, pious, pietistic, religious, devout, God-fearing, spiritual; righteous, good, virtuous, angelic, sinless, pure, numinous, beatific.
2 SACRED, consecrated, hallowed, sanctified, sacrosanct, venerated, revered, divine, religious, blessed, dedicated.
—OPPOSITES: sinful, irreligious, cursed.

home *n*. **1** RESIDENCE, place of residence, house, apartment, flat; accommodation, property, quarters, lodgings, rooms; *informal* pad, place, digs; *formal* domicile, abode, dwelling (place), habitation, pied-à-terre.
2 HOMELAND, native land, hometown, birthplace, roots, fatherland, motherland, mother country, country of origin, the old country. **3** INSTITUTION, nursing home, retirement home, rest home, lodge✦.
□ **bring something home to someone** MAKE SOMEONE REALIZE/ UNDERSTAND, make someone aware; drive home, impress upon someone, draw attention to, focus attention on, underline, highlight, spotlight, emphasize, stress.
home in on FOCUS ON, concentrate on, zero in on, centre on, fix on; highlight, spotlight, target, underline, pinpoint, track, zoom in on.

homeless *adj*. OF NO FIXED ADDRESS, on the streets, vagrant, displaced, dispossessed, destitute, down-and-out.

homely *adj*. **1** UNATTRACTIVE, plain, unprepossessing, unlovely, ill-favoured, ugly; *informal* not much to

look at. **2** ☞ HOMEY 1.
—OPPOSITES: attractive, formal

homemade *adj.* **1** HOMESTYLE, homespun, simple, basic, plain; rustic, folksy; *informal* like mom used to make. **2** HANDMADE, makeshift, jerry-built, rudimentary; crude, rough, unsophisticated.

homey *adj.* **1** COZY, homelike, homely, comfortable, snug, welcoming, informal, relaxed, intimate, warm, pleasant, cheerful, comfy.
2 UNSOPHISTICATED, homely, unrefined, unpretentious, plain, simple, modest, domestic; everyday, ordinary.

homicide *n.* MURDER, killing, slaughter, butchery, massacre; assassination, execution, extermination; *literary* slaying.

homily *n.* SERMON, lecture, discourse, address, lesson, talk, speech, oration.

homosexual *adj.* ☞ GAY 1.
—OPPOSITES: heterosexual.
▸ *n.* GAY, lesbian; *informal* queer, queen, dyke, butch, femme.
—OPPOSITES: heterosexual.

honest *adj.* **1** UPRIGHT, honourable, moral, ethical, principled, righteous, right-minded, respectable; virtuous, good, decent, fair, law-abiding, high-minded, upstanding, incorruptible, truthful, trustworthy, reliable, conscientious, scrupulous, reputable; *informal* on the level, trusty. **2** TRUTHFUL, sincere, candid, frank, open, forthright, ingenuous, straight; straightforward, plain-speaking, matter-of-fact; *informal* upfront, above board, on the level.
—OPPOSITES: unscrupulous, insincere.

honestly *adv.* **1** FAIRLY, lawfully, legally, legitimately, honourably, decently, ethically, in good faith, by the book; openly, on the level, above board. **2** SINCERELY, genuinely, truthfully, truly, wholeheartedly; really, frankly, actually, seriously, to be honest.

honorary *adj.* TITULAR, symbolic, in name only, ceremonial, nominal, unofficial, token.

honour *n.* **1** INTEGRITY, honesty, uprightness, ethics, morals, morality, (high) principles, righteousness, high-mindedness; virtue, goodness, decency, probity, (good) character, scrupulousness, worth, fairness, justness, trustworthiness, reliability, dependability, rectitude, sincerity, truthfulness. **2** DISTINCTION, privilege, glory, kudos, cachet, prestige, merit, credit; importance, illustriousness, notability; respect, esteem, approbation. **3** REPUTATION, (good) name, character, repute, image, standing, stature, status.
4 ACCLAIM, acclamation, applause, accolades, adoration, tributes, compliments; homage, praise.
5 PRIVILEGE, pleasure, pride, joy; compliment, favour. **6** ☞ AWARD *n.* 1.
—OPPOSITES: unscrupulousness, shame.
▸ *v.* **1** ESTEEM, respect, admire, defer to, look up to; appreciate, value, cherish, adore; reverence, revere, venerate, worship.

2 APPLAUD, acclaim, praise, salute, recognize, celebrate, commemorate, commend, hail, lionize, exalt, eulogize, pay homage to, pay tribute to, sing the praises of; *formal* laud. **3** FULFILL, observe, keep, obey, heed, follow, carry out, discharge, implement, execute, effect; keep to, abide by, adhere to, comply with; conform to.
—OPPOSITES: disgrace, criticize, disobey.

honourable *adj.* ☞ HONEST 1.
—OPPOSITES: crooked.

hoodwink *v.* ☞ DECEIVE 1.

hook *n.* FASTENER, fastening, catch, clasp, hasp, clip, pin.
▶ *v.* **1** ATTACH, hitch, fasten, fix, secure, clasp. **2** CURL, bend, crook, loop, curve. **3** CATCH, land, net, take, bag, snare, trap.
☐ **off the hook** (*informal*) OUT OF TROUBLE, in the clear, free, home free; acquitted, cleared, reprieved, exonerated, absolved; *informal* let off.

hooligan *n.* TROUBLEMAKER, (juvenile) delinquent, mischief-maker, vandal; rowdy, ruffian, yahoo.

hoop *n.* RING, band, circle, circlet, bracelet, (hoop) earring, loop.

hooray *excl.* HURRAH, hallelujah, bravo, cowabunga, hot dog, wahoo, yahoo, whoopee, yay, yee-haw, yippee.

hop *v.* JUMP, bound, spring, bounce, leap, vault.
▶ *n.* **1** JUMP, bound, bounce, leap, spring. **2** (*informal*) JOURNEY, distance, ride, drive, run, trip, jaunt; flight.

hope *n.* **1** ASPIRATION, desire, wish, expectation, ambition, aim, goal, plan, design; dream, daydream, pipe dream. **2** CHANCE, prospect, likelihood, probability, possibility.
—OPPOSITES: pessimism.
▶ *v.* **1** EXPECT, anticipate, look for, be hopeful of, pin one's hopes on, want; wish for, dream of. **2** AIM, intend, be looking, have in mind, plan, aspire.

hopeful *adj.* **1** OPTIMISTIC, full of hope, confident, positive, buoyant, sanguine, expectant, bullish, cheerful, upbeat.
2 ☞ PROMISING 1.
▶ *n.* ☞ CANDIDATE.

hopefully *adv.* **1** OPTIMISTICALLY, full of hope, confidently, buoyantly, sanguinely; expectantly. **2** IF ALL GOES WELL, God willing, with (any) luck; most likely, probably; conceivably, feasibly; *informal* touch wood, fingers crossed.

hopeless *adj.* **1** DESPAIRING, desperate, wretched, forlorn, pessimistic, defeatist, resigned; dejected, downhearted, despondent, demoralized.
2 IRREMEDIABLE, beyond hope, lost, beyond repair, irreparable, irreversible; helpless, incurable; impossible, no-win, unwinnable, futile, unworkable, impracticable, useless. **3** BAD, awful, terrible, dreadful, horrible, atrocious; inferior, incompetent, inadequate, unskilled; *informal* pathetic, useless, lousy, rotten.

horde *n.* CROWD, mob, pack, press, crush, gang, group, troop, army, legion, swarm, mass, herd, rabble;

throng, multitude, host, band, flock, drove.

horrible *adj.* **1** DREADFUL, awful, terrible, shocking, appalling, horrifying, horrific, horrendous, hideous, grisly, ghastly, gruesome, gory, harrowing, heinous, vile, unspeakable; nightmarish, macabre, spine-chilling, blood-curdling; loathsome, monstrous, abhorrent, hateful, hellish, execrable, abominable, atrocious, sickening, foul. **2** (*informal*) NASTY, horrid, disagreeable, unpleasant, detestable, awful, dreadful, terrible, appalling, foul, repulsive, repugnant, repellent, ghastly, offensive; obnoxious, hateful, odious, hideous, objectionable, insufferable, vile, loathsome, abhorrent, abominable; *informal* frightful, godawful.
—OPPOSITES: pleasant, agreeable.

horrify *v.* **1** ☞ SCARE *v.* **2** SHOCK, appall, outrage, scandalize, offend; disgust, revolt, nauseate, sicken.

horror *n.* **1** TERROR, fear, fright, alarm, panic; dread, trepidation. **2** HATRED, fear, loathing, abhorrence, dislike; disgust, repugnance, revulsion. **3** DISMAY, consternation, perturbation, alarm, distress; disgust, outrage, shock. **4** AWFULNESS, frightfulness, savagery, barbarity, hideousness; atrocity, outrage. **5** RASCAL, devil, imp, monkey; *informal* terror, scamp, scalawag, tyke, varmint. **6** EYESORE, monstrosity, abomination, blot, disgrace, mess, sight.
—OPPOSITES: delight, satisfaction, beauty.

horse *n.* EQUINE, mount, charger, cob, nag, hack; pony, foal, yearling, colt, stallion, gelding, mare, filly, bronco; *archaic* steed.

horseplay *n.* TOMFOOLERY, fooling around, roughhousing, clowning, buffoonery; pranks, antics, hijinks; *informal* shenanigans, monkey business.

hoser *n.* REDNECK, bubba, Joe Sixpack. See also IDIOT.

hospitable *adj.* WELCOMING, friendly, congenial, genial, sociable, convivial, cordial, courteous; gracious, well-disposed, amenable, helpful, obliging, accommodating, neighbourly, warm, kind, generous, bountiful.

hospital *n.* INFIRMARY, sanatorium, hospice, medical centre, health centre, clinic, nursing station✲, (*Nfld*) cottage hospital✲; *Military* field hospital.

host *n.* **1** PARTY-GIVER, hostess, entertainer. **2** PRESENTER, anchor, anchorman, anchorwoman, announcer, emcee, open-liner✲, master of ceremonies.
—OPPOSITES: guest.
▶ *v.* **1** GIVE, have, hold, throw, put on, provide, arrange, organize. **2** ENTERTAIN, play host/hostess to; receive, welcome; take in, house.

hostage *n.* CAPTIVE, prisoner, detainee, internee; abductee; human shield, pawn, instrument.

hostile *adj.* **1** UNFRIENDLY, unkind, bitter, unsympathetic, malicious, vicious, rancorous, venomous, poisonous, virulent; antagonistic, aggressive, confrontational, belligerent, truculent, warlike. **2** UNFAVOURABLE, adverse, bad, harsh, grim, hard, tough, brutal,

fierce, inhospitable, forbidding, menacing, threatening.
3 OPPOSED, averse, antagonistic, ill-disposed, disapproving of, unsympathetic, antipathetic; opposing, against, inimical; *informal* anti, down on.
—OPPOSITES: friendly, favourable.

hostility *n.* **1** ANTAGONISM, unfriendliness, enmity, malevolence, malice, unkindness, rancour, venom, hatred, loathing; aggression, belligerence.
2 FIGHTING, (armed) conflict, combat, aggression, warfare, war, bloodshed, violence.

hot *adj.* **1** HEATED, piping (hot), sizzling, steaming, roasting, boiling (hot), searing, scorching, scalding, burning, red-hot. **2** VERY WARM, balmy, summery, tropical, scorching, broiling, searing, blistering; sweltering, torrid, sultry, humid, muggy, close, baking, roasting, boiling (hot), sizzling, sticky, stifling, stuffy.
3 SPICY, spiced, highly seasoned, peppery, fiery, strong; piquant, pungent, aromatic, zesty.
4 (*informal*) NEW, fresh, recent, late, up to date, up-to-the-minute; just out, hot off the press. **5** (*informal*)
☞ FASHIONABLE. **6** STOLEN, illegally obtained, purloined, pilfered, illegal, illicit, unlawful; smuggled, fenced, bootleg, contraband.
—OPPOSITES: cold, chilly, mild, old, ugly, lawful.
☐ **hot on the heels/trail of** CLOSE BEHIND, directly after, right after, straight after, hard on the heels of, following closely. **hot under the collar.** ☞ ANGRY.

hotel *n.* INN, motel, boarding house, guest house, bed and breakfast, B & B, hostel, lodge, accommodation, lodging; pension, auberge.

hotheaded *adj.* IMPETUOUS, impulsive, headstrong, reckless, rash, irresponsible, foolhardy, madcap, devil-may-care; excitable, volatile, explosive, fiery, hot-tempered, quick-tempered, unruly, harum-scarum.

house *n.* **1** RESIDENCE, home, place of residence; homestead; a roof over one's head; *formal* habitation, dwelling (place), abode, domicile.
2 HOUSEHOLD, family, occupants; clan, tribe; line, bloodline, lineage, ancestry. **3** FAMILY, clan, tribe; dynasty, line, bloodline, lineage, ancestry, family tree.
4 AUDIENCE, crowd, spectators, viewers, listeners; assembly.
▸ *v.* **1** ACCOMMODATE, give someone a roof over their head, lodge, quarter, board, billet, take in, sleep, put up; harbour, shelter.
2 CONTAIN, hold, store; cover, protect, enclose.

household *n.* FAMILY, house, occupants, residents; clan, tribe; *informal* brood.
▸ *adj.* DOMESTIC, family; everyday, ordinary, common, commonplace, regular, practical, workaday.

hover *v.* **1** BE SUSPENDED, be poised, hang, levitate, float; fly.
2 LINGER, loiter, wait (around); *informal* hang around/about, stick around.

however *adv.* NEVERTHELESS, nonetheless, but, still, yet, though, although, even so, for all that, despite that, in spite of that;

anyway, anyhow, all the same, notwithstanding, be that as it may, just the same, regardless, still and all, that said, at any rate, in any event.

howl *n.* WAIL, cry, yell, yelp, yowl, bark; bellow, roar, clamour, shout, shriek, scream, screech.
▶ *v.* **1** BAY, cry, yowl, bark, yelp.
2 WAIL, cry, yell, yowl, bawl, bellow, shriek, scream, screech, caterwaul, holler. **3** ☞ LAUGH *v.* 1.

hub *n.* **1** PIVOT, axis, fulcrum, centre, middle. **2** CENTRE, core, heart, focus, focal point, nucleus, kernel, nerve centre.
—OPPOSITES: periphery.

huddle *v.* **1** CROWD, cluster, gather, bunch, throng, flock, herd, collect, group, congregate, mass; press, pack, squeeze. **2** CURL UP, snuggle, nestle, hunch up.
—OPPOSITES: disperse.
▶ *n.* CROWD, cluster, bunch, knot, group, throng, flock, press, pack; collection, assemblage; *informal* gang, gaggle.

hue *n.* COLOUR, shade, tone, tint, tinge.

hug *v.* **1** EMBRACE, cuddle, squeeze, clasp, clutch, cradle, cling to, hold close, hold tight, take/fold someone in one's arms, clasp someone to one's bosom.
2 FOLLOW CLOSELY, keep close to, stay near to, follow the course of.
▶ *n.* EMBRACE, cuddle, squeeze, bear hug, clasp, clinch.

huge *adj.* ENORMOUS, vast, immense, large, big, great, boundless, broad, expansive, extensive, immeasurable, infinite, limitless, mighty, sweeping, tremendous, wide; massive, colossal, prodigious, gigantic, gargantuan, mammoth, monumental; giant, towering, elephantine, mountainous, monstrous, titanic; epic, Herculean, Brobdingnagian; *informal* jumbo, mega, monster, king-sized, economy-size(d), oversized, whopping, humongous, honking, hulking, astronomical, cosmic, ginormous.
—OPPOSITES: tiny.

hulking *adj.* (*informal*) LARGE, big, heavy, sturdy, burly, brawny, hefty, strapping; bulky, weighty, massive, ponderous; clumsy, awkward, ungainly, lumbering, lumpish, oafish; *informal* beefy.
—OPPOSITES: small.

hull *n.* **1** FRAMEWORK, body, shell, frame, skeleton, structure; fuselage. **2** SHELL, husk, pod, case, covering, integument, calyx, shuck.

hum *v.* **1** PURR, drone, murmur, buzz, thrum, whirr, throb, vibrate, rumble. **2** sing, croon, murmur, drone. **3** BE BUSY, be active, be lively, buzz, bustle.
□ **hum and haw** ☞ HEM AND HAW at HEM.

human *adj.* **1** MORTAL, flesh and blood; fallible, weak, frail, imperfect, vulnerable, susceptible, erring, error-prone; physical, bodily, fleshly. **2** ☞ HUMANE.
▶ *n.* PERSON, human being, personage, mortal; man, woman; individual, (living) soul, being; Homo sapiens; earthling.

humane *adj.* COMPASSIONATE, kind, considerate, understanding, sympathetic, tolerant; lenient, forbearing, forgiving, merciful,

mild, gentle, tender, clement,
benign, humanitarian,
benevolent, charitable.
—OPPOSITES: cruel.

humble *adj.* **1** MEEK, deferential,
respectful, submissive, diffident,
self-effacing, unassertive; modest,
unassuming, self-deprecating;
subdued, chastened. **2** ☞ LOWLY.
3 MODEST, plain, simple, ordinary,
unostentatious, unpretentious.
—OPPOSITES: proud, noble, grand.
▶ *v.* ☞ HUMILIATE.

humdrum *adj.* MUNDANE, dull,
dreary, boring, tedious,
monotonous, prosaic; unexciting,
uninteresting, uneventful,
unvaried, repetitive,
unremarkable; routine, ordinary,
everyday, day-to-day, workaday,
quotidian, run-of-the-mill,
commonplace, pedestrian; *informal*
plain-vanilla, ho-hum.
—OPPOSITES: remarkable, exciting.

humid *adj.* ☞ MUGGY.

humiliate *v.* EMBARRASS, mortify,
humble, shame, put to shame,
disgrace, chagrin; discomfit,
chasten, abash, deflate, crush,
squash; abase, debase, demean,
degrade, lower; belittle, cause to
feel small, cause to lose face;
informal show up, put down, cut
down to size, take down (a peg or
two), settle someone's hash, put
someone in their place, make
someone eat crow.

humiliation *n.* EMBARRASSMENT,
mortification, shame, indignity,
ignominy, disgrace, discomfiture,
dishonour, degradation, discredit,
belittlement, opprobrium; loss of
face; *informal* blow to one's pride/
ego, slap in the face, kick in the

teeth, comedown.
—OPPOSITES: honour.

humility *n.* MODESTY, humbleness,
meekness, diffidence,
unassertiveness; lack of pride,
lack of vanity; servility,
submissiveness.
—OPPOSITES: pride.

humorous *adj.* ☞ FUNNY 1.
—OPPOSITES: serious.

humour *n.* **1** COMEDY, comical
aspect, funny side, fun,
amusement, funniness, hilarity,
jocularity; absurdity,
ludicrousness, drollness; satire,
irony, farce. **2** JOKES, joking, jests,
jesting, quips, witticisms, funny
remarks, puns, badinage; wit,
wittiness, comedy, drollery; *informal*
gags, wisecracks, cracks, one-
liners. **3** ☞ MOOD 1.
▶ *v.* INDULGE, accommodate, pander
to, cater to, yield to, give way to,
give in to, go along with; pamper,
spoil, baby, overindulge, mollify,
placate, gratify, satisfy.

hump *n.* PROTUBERANCE,
prominence, lump, bump, knob,
protrusion, projection, bulge,
swelling, hunch; growth,
outgrowth.

hunch *v.* CROUCH, huddle, curl;
hunker down, bend, stoop,
slouch, squat, duck.
—OPPOSITES: straighten.
▶ *n.* FEELING, guess, suspicion,
impression, conjecture, inkling,
idea, belief, sixth sense,
supposition, theory, sense, notion,
fancy, intuition, premonition,
presentiment; *informal* gut feeling/
instinct.

hunger *n.* **1** LACK OF FOOD,
hungriness, emptiness; starvation,

malnutrition, famine,
malnourishment,
undernourishment. **2** DESIRE,
craving, longing, yearning,
hankering, appetite, thirst; want,
need; *informal* itch, yen.
□ **hunger after/for** ☞ DESIRE *v.*

hungry *adj.* **1** RAVENOUS, empty, in
need of food, hollow, faint from/
with hunger; starving, starved,
famished; malnourished,
undernourished, underfed; *informal*
peckish. **2** EAGER, keen, avid,
longing, yearning, aching, pining,
greedy; craving, desirous of,
hankering after; *informal* itching,
dying.
—OPPOSITES: full.

hunt *v.* **1** CHASE, stalk, pursue,
course, run down; track, trail,
follow, shadow; *informal* tail.
2 ☞ SEARCH 1.
▶ *n.* **1** CHASE, pursuit. **2** SEARCH,
look, quest.

hurdle *n.* **1** FENCE, jump, barrier,
barricade, bar, railing, rail.
2 ☞ OBSTACLE.

hurl *v.* **1** ☞ THROW *v.* 1. **2** ☞ VOMIT 1.

hurried *adj.* **1** QUICK, fast, swift,
rapid, speedy, brisk, hasty, abrupt;
cursory, perfunctory, brief, short,
fleeting. **2** HASTY, rushed, speedy,
quick; impetuous, impulsive, rash,
incautious, imprudent.
—OPPOSITES: slow, considered.

hurry *v.* **1** BE QUICK, hurry up,
hasten, speed up, press on, push
on; run, dash, rush, race, speed,
fly, career, charge, bolt, hurtle,
pelt, whirl; scurry, scramble,
scuttle, sprint, dart, gallop, shoot;
informal get a move on, move it,
step on it, scoot, bomb, get
cracking, get moving, shake a leg,

tear, hare, zip, zoom, belt, hotfoot
it, hightail it, leg it, get the lead
out. **2** HUSTLE, hasten, push, urge,
drive, spur, goad, prod.
—OPPOSITES: dawdle, delay.

hurt *v.* **1** BE PAINFUL, be sore, be
tender, cause pain, cause
discomfort; ache, smart, sting,
burn, throb. **2** INJURE, wound,
damage, abuse, disable,
incapacitate, maim, mutilate;
bruise, cut, gash, graze, scrape,
scratch, lacerate, break, cripple,
deform, harm, lame, mangle.
3 DISTRESS, pain, wound, sting,
upset, sadden, devastate, grieve,
mortify. **4** HARM, damage, be
detrimental to, weaken, blight,
impede, jeopardize, undermine,
ruin, wreck, sabotage, cripple.
—OPPOSITES: heal, comfort,
benefit.
▶ *n.* DISTRESS, pain, suffering,
injury, grief, misery, anguish,
agony, trauma, woe, upset,
sadness, sorrow; harm, damage,
trouble.
—OPPOSITES: joy.
▶ *adj.* **1** INJURED, wounded, bruised,
grazed, cut, gashed, battered,
sore, painful, aching, smarting,
throbbing. **2** PAINED, injured,
distressed, anguished, upset, sad,
mortified, offended.
—OPPOSITES: pleased.

hurtful *adj.* UPSETTING, distressing,
wounding, painful, injurious;
unkind, cruel, nasty, mean,
malicious, spiteful, vindictive;
cutting, barbed; *informal* catty,
bitchy.

husband *n.* SPOUSE, (life) partner,
mate, consort, man, helpmate,

helpmeet; groom, bridegroom; *informal* hubby, old man, other half.

hush *v.* SILENCE, quieten (down); shush; soothe, calm, pacify; gag, muzzle, muffle, mute; *informal* shut up.

▶ *excl.* BE QUIET, keep quiet, quieten down, be silent, stop talking, hold your tongue; *informal* shut up, sh, hush up, shut your mouth, shut your face, shut your trap, button your lip, pipe down, put a sock in it, give it a rest, save it, not another word.

▶ *n.* ☞ SILENCE *n.* 1.

—OPPOSITES: noise.

☐ **hush up** KEEP SECRET, conceal, hide, suppress, cover up, keep quiet about; obscure, veil, sweep under the carpet; *informal* sit on, keep under one's hat.

hustle *v.* 1 MANHANDLE, push, shove, thrust, frogmarch, whisk, bundle (off). 2 ☞ HURRY *v.* 1.

☐ **hustle and bustle** HURLY-BURLY, bustle, tumult, hubbub, activity, action, liveliness, animation, excitement, agitation, commotion, flurry, whirl; *informal* ballyhoo, hoo-ha, hullabaloo.

hut *n.* SHACK, shanty, (log) cabin, cabana, shelter, shed, lean-to, caboose✤; hovel; fish hut✤, ice hut✤; (Nfld) tilt✤.

hygiene *n.* CLEANLINESS, sanitation, sterility, purity, disinfection; public health, environmental health.

hygienic *adj.* SANITARY, clean, germ-free, disinfected, sterilized, sterile, antiseptic, aseptic, unpolluted, uncontaminated, salubrious, healthy, wholesome, purified.

—OPPOSITES: unsanitary.

hypnotic *adj.* MESMERIZING, mesmeric, spellbinding, entrancing, bewitching, irresistible, magnetic, compelling, enthralling, captivating, charming; soporific, sleep-inducing, sedative, numbing.

hypnotize *v.* 1 MESMERIZE, put into a trance. 2 ENTRANCE, mesmerize, spellbind, enthrall, transfix, captivate, bewitch, charm, absorb, fascinate, magnetize.

hypocrisy *n.* DISSIMULATION, false virtue, cant, posturing, affectation, speciousness, empty talk, insincerity, falseness, deceit, dishonesty, duplicity; sanctimoniousness, sanctimony; *informal* phoniness.

—OPPOSITES: sincerity.

hypothesis *n.* ☞ THEORY 1.

hypothetical *adj.*
☞ THEORETICAL.

—OPPOSITES: actual.

hysteria *n.* FRENZY, feverishness, hysterics, fit of madness, derangement, mania, delirium; panic, alarm, distress.

—OPPOSITES: calm.

hysterical *adj.* 1 OVERWROUGHT, overemotional, out of control, frenzied, frantic, wild, feverish, crazed; beside oneself, driven to distraction, distraught, agitated, berserk, manic, delirious, unhinged, deranged, out of one's mind, raving. 2 ☞ FUNNY 1.

Ii

ice *n.* **1** FROZEN WATER, icicles, (*Nfld*) ice candles ; black ice, frost, rime, glaze. **2** ICE RINK, skating rink, hockey rink, ice pad , ice palace , hockey cushion .
—RELATED: gelid, glacial.
□ **on thin ice** IN A RISKY SITUATION, at risk, in peril, imperilled, living dangerously, living on the edge.

icy *adj.* **1** FROSTY, frozen (over), iced over, ice-bound, ice-covered, iced up; slippery, (*PEI*) glib ; *literary* rimy. **2** ☞ UNFRIENDLY 1.

idea *n.* **1** CONCEPT, notion, conception, thought; image, visualization; hypothesis, postulation. **2** PLAN, scheme, design, proposal, proposition, suggestion, brainchild, vision; aim, intention, purpose, objective, object, goal, target. **3** THOUGHT, theory, view, opinion, feeling, belief, attitude, conclusion; *informal* take.

ideal *adj.* **1** PERFECT, best possible, consummate, supreme, excellent, flawless, faultless, exemplary, classic, model, ultimate, quintessential. **2** ☞ ABSTRACT 1.
—OPPOSITES: bad, concrete, real.
▸ *n.* **1** MODEL, pattern, exemplar, standard, example, paradigm, archetype, prototype; yardstick, lodestar. **2** PRINCIPLE, standard, value, belief, conviction, persuasion.

idealistic *adj.* Utopian, visionary, romantic, optimistic, quixotic, dreamy, unrealistic, impractical, starry-eyed; fanciful, airy-fairy; *informal* with one's head in the clouds.

ideally *adv.* IN A PERFECT WORLD; preferably, if possible, by choice, as a matter of choice, (much) rather; all things being equal, theoretically, hypothetically, in theory, in principle, on paper.

identical *adj.* INDISTINGUISHABLE, (exactly) the same, similar, uniform, twin, duplicate, interchangeable, synonymous, undifferentiated, homogeneous, of a piece, cut from the same cloth; alike, like, matching, like (two) peas in a pod, like Tweedledum and Tweedledee, two of a kind, much of a muchness.

identify *v.* **1** RECOGNIZE, single out, pick out, spot, point out, pinpoint, put one's finger on, put a name to, name, know; discern, distinguish, isolate; locate; remember, recall, recollect; *informal* finger. **2** DETERMINE, establish, ascertain, make out, diagnose, discern, distinguish; verify, confirm; *informal* figure out, get a fix on, peg. **3** ☞ ASSOCIATE 1. **4** EMPATHIZE, be in tune, have a rapport, feel at one, sympathize; be on the same wavelength as,

speak the same language as;
understand, relate to, feel for.

identity *n.* **1** NAME, ID;
specification. **2** INDIVIDUALITY, self,
selfhood; personality, character,
originality, distinctiveness,
singularity, uniqueness.

ideology *n.* ☞ PHILOSOPHY 2.

idiosyncrasy *n.* PECULIARITY,
oddity, eccentricity, mannerism,
trait, singularity, quirk, tic, whim,
vagary, caprice, kink; fetish,
foible, crotchet, habit,
characteristic.

idiot *n.* FOOL, ass, halfwit, dunce,
dolt, ignoramus, simpleton; *informal*
dope, ninny, nincompoop,
chump, dim-wit, dim-bulb,
dumbo, dummy, dumdum, loon,
dork, sap, jackass, blockhead,
jughead, bonehead, knucklehead,
fathead, numbskull, numbnuts,
dumb-ass, doofus, dunderhead,
ditz, lummox, dipstick, thickhead,
meathead, meatball, airhead,
pinhead, lamebrain, cretin,
moron, imbecile, pea brain,
birdbrain, jerk, nerd, donkey,
nitwit, twit, boob, twerp,
schmuck, bozo, hoser♣, turkey,
chowderhead, dingbat.
—OPPOSITES: genius.

idiotic *adj.* ☞ STUPID 2.

idle *adj.* **1** ☞ LAZY. **2** INACTIVE,
unused, unoccupied, unemployed,
disused; out of action, inoperative,
out of service. **3** FRIVOLOUS, trivial,
trifling, vain, minor, petty,
lightweight, shallow, superficial,
insignificant, unimportant,
worthless, paltry, niggling,
peripheral, inane, fatuous;
unnecessary, time-wasting.

—OPPOSITES: industrious,
employed, working, busy.

idler *n.* ☞ LOAFER.

idol *n.* **1** ICON, effigy, statue, figure,
figurine, fetish, totem; graven
image, false god, golden calf.
2 HERO, heroine, star, superstar,
icon, celebrity; favourite, darling;
informal pin-up, heartthrob,
dreamboat, golden boy/girl.

idolize *v.* HERO-WORSHIP, worship,
revere, venerate, deify, lionize;
stand in awe of, reverence, look
up to, admire, adore, exalt; *informal*
put on a pedestal.

idyllic *adj.* PERFECT, wonderful,
blissful, halcyon, happy; ideal,
idealized; heavenly, paradisal,
Utopian, Elysian; peaceful,
picturesque, bucolic, unspoiled;
literary Arcadian.

if *conj.* **1** ON CONDITION THAT,
provided (that), providing (that),
presuming (that), supposing (that),
assuming (that), as long as, given
that, in the event that. **2** WHETHER.
3 ALTHOUGH, albeit, but, yet,
despite being.
▶ *n.* UNCERTAINTY, doubt; condition,
stipulation, provision, proviso,
constraint, precondition,
requirement, specification,
restriction.

ignite *v.* **1** CATCH FIRE, burst into
flames, combust; be set off,
explode. **2** LIGHT, set fire to, set on
fire, set alight, kindle, spark,
touch off; *informal* set/put a match
to. **3** ☞ INCITE.
—OPPOSITES: go out, extinguish.

ignominious *adj.* HUMILIATING,
undignified, embarrassing,
mortifying; ignoble, inglorious;

disgraceful, shameful.
—OPPOSITES: glorious.

ignorant *adj.* UNEDUCATED,
unknowledgeable, untaught,
unschooled, untutored, untrained,
illiterate, unlettered, unlearned,
unread, uninformed,
unenlightened, benighted;
without knowledge, unaware,
unconscious, oblivious,
incognizant, unfamiliar,
unacquainted, ill-informed,
inexperienced, naive, innocent,
green; *informal* in the dark, clueless.
—OPPOSITES: educated,
knowledgeable.

ignore *v.* DISREGARD, take no
notice of, pay no attention to, pay
no heed to; turn a blind eye to,
turn a deaf ear to, tune out, take
no account of; SET ASIDE; break,
contravene, fail to comply with,
fail to observe, disobey, breach,
defy, flout; *informal* pooh-pooh.
—OPPOSITES: acknowledge, obey.

ill *adj.* **1** UNWELL, sick, not (very)
well, ailing, poorly, sickly, peaked,
peaky, indisposed, infirm,
debilitated, delicate, in poor/bad
health; out of sorts, not oneself,
bad, off, rotten, in a bad way;
bedridden, valetudinarian; queasy,
nauseous, nauseated; *informal* under
the weather, laid up, below par,
rough, lousy, pukey, dizzy, woozy.
2 ☞ HOSTILE 1.
—OPPOSITES: well, healthy.
▸ *adv.* **1** POORLY, badly, imperfectly.
2 UNFAVOURABLY, adversely,
inauspiciously. **3** INADEQUATELY,
unsatisfactorily, insufficiently,
imperfectly.
—OPPOSITES: well, auspiciously,

satisfactorily.
☐ **speak ill of** ☞ SLANDER.

ill-advised *adj.* ☞ UNWISE.
—OPPOSITES: judicious.

illegal *adj.* UNLAWFUL, illicit,
illegitimate, criminal, felonious;
unlicensed, unauthorized,
unsanctioned; outlawed, banned,
forbidden, prohibited, proscribed,
taboo; contraband, black-market,
bootleg; *informal* crooked, shady.
—OPPOSITES: lawful, legitimate.

illegible *adj.* UNREADABLE,
indecipherable, unintelligible,
incomprehensible, hieroglyphic;
scrawled, scribbled, crabbed,
cramped.

illegitimate *adj.* BORN OUT OF
WEDLOCK, bastard; *archaic* natural,
misbegotten.
—OPPOSITES: legal, lawful.

ill-fated *adj.* ☞ DOOMED.

illicit *adj.* **1** ☞ ILLEGAL. **2** TABOO,
forbidden, impermissible,
unacceptable.
—OPPOSITES: lawful, legal.

illness *n.* SICKNESS, disease,
ailment, complaint, malady,
affliction, infection, indisposition,
disorder, condition; ill health,
poor health, infirmity; *informal* bug,
virus; *dated* contagion.
—RELATED: -pathy.
—OPPOSITES: good health.

illogical *adj.* IRRATIONAL,
unreasonable, unsound,
unreasoned, unjustifiable;
incorrect, erroneous, invalid,
spurious, faulty, flawed,
fallacious, unscientific; specious,
sophistic, casuistic; absurd,
preposterous, untenable.

illuminating *adj.* ☞ INSTRUCTIVE.

illusion *n.* **1** DELUSION, misapprehension, misconception, false impression; fantasy, fancy, dream, chimera. **2** APPEARANCE, impression, semblance. **3** MIRAGE, hallucination, apparition, figment of the imagination, trick of the light, trompe l'oeil; deception, trick, smoke and mirrors.

illustrate *v.* EXPLAIN, explicate, elucidate, clarify, make plain, demonstrate, show, emphasize; *informal* get across.

illustration *n.* **1** PICTURE, drawing, sketch, figure, image, plate, print, artwork; visual aid. **2** EXEMPLIFICATION, demonstration, showing; example, typical case, case in point, object lesson, analogy.

illustrious *adj.* ☞ EMINENT.

image *n.* **1** ☞ REPRESENTATION 2. **2** PUBLIC PERCEPTION, persona, profile, reputation, stature, standing; face, front, facade, mask, guise.

imaginary *adj.* UNREAL, non-existent, fictional, fictitious, pretend, make-believe, mythical, fabulous, fanciful, illusory, fantastic; made-up, invented, fancied; *archaic* visionary.
—OPPOSITES: real.

imagination *n.* CREATIVE POWER, fancy, mind's eye; CREATIVITY, creativeness; vision, inspiration, inventiveness, invention, resourcefulness, ingenuity, artistry, insight; originality, innovation, innovativeness.

imaginative *adj.* CREATIVE, visionary, inspired, inventive, resourceful, ingenious; original, innovative, innovatory, unorthodox, unconventional; fanciful, whimsical, fantastic; *informal* offbeat, off the wall, zany.

imagine *v.* **1** VISUALIZE, envisage, envision, picture, see in the mind's eye; dream up, think up/of, conjure up, conceive, conceptualize; *formal* ideate. **2** ☞ SUPPOSE 1.

imbue *v.* ☞ INSTILL.

imitate *v.* **1** EMULATE, copy, model oneself on, take as a pattern/model, take as an example, adopt the style of, follow, echo, parrot; *informal* rip off, knock off, pirate. **2** MIMIC, do an impression of, impersonate, ape; parody, caricature, burlesque, travesty; *informal* take off, send up, make like, mock.

imitation *n.* **1** COPY, simulation, reproduction, replica; counterfeit, forgery, rip-off. **2** IMPERSONATION, impression, parody, mockery, caricature, burlesque, travesty, lampoon, pastiche; mimicry, mimicking, imitating, aping; *informal* send-up, takeoff, spoof.
▶ *adj.* ARTIFICIAL, synthetic, simulated, man-made, manufactured, ersatz, substitute; mock, sham, fake, faux, bogus, knock-off, pseudo, phony.
—OPPOSITES: real, genuine.

immature *adj.* **1** UNRIPE, not mature, premature; undeveloped, unformed, unfinished, raw, embryonic. **2** CHILDISH, babyish, infantile, juvenile, adolescent, puerile, sophomoric, foolish, silly, jejune, callow, green, tender, young, inexperienced, unsophisticated, unworldly, naive,

raw, untried; *informal* wet behind the ears.
—OPPOSITES: ripe.

immeasurable *adj.*
☞ INESTIMABLE.

immediate *adj.* **1** INSTANT, instantaneous, swift, prompt, fast, speedy, rapid, brisk, quick, expeditious; sudden, hurried, hasty, precipitate; abrupt, express, lightning, on-the-spot, snappy. **2** CURRENT, present, existing, actual; urgent, pressing, exigent.
—OPPOSITES: delayed, distant.

immediately *adv.* STRAIGHT AWAY, at once, right away, instantly, (right) now, directly, promptly, forthwith, this/that (very) minute, this/that instant, there and then, then and there, on the spot, here and now, without delay, without further ado, post-haste; quickly, as fast as possible, speedily, as soon as possible, ASAP; *informal* pronto, double-quick, on the double, pretty damn quick, PDQ, in/like a flash, like a shot, tout de suite; *humorous* toot sweet; *archaic* forthright.

immense *adj.* ☞ HUGE.
—OPPOSITES: tiny.

immerse *v.* **1** SUBMERGE, dip, dunk, duck, sink, plunge; soak, saturate, marinate, wet, douse, souse, steep. **2** (**absorbed in**) ABSORB, engross, occupy, engage, involve, bury, swamp, lose (oneself in); busy, employ, preoccupy, fixate.

immigrant *n.* NEWCOMER, settler, migrant, emigrant; non-native, foreigner, alien, landed immigrant ♣.
—OPPOSITES: native.

immigrate *v.* ☞ MIGRATE.

imminent *adj.* IMPENDING, close (at hand), near, (fast) approaching, coming, forthcoming, on the way, pending, in the offing, in the pipeline, upcoming, on the horizon, in the air, just around the corner, about to happen, in store, in the wind, nearing, coming down the pike, expected, anticipated, brewing, looming, threatening, menacing; *informal* in the cards.

immobile *adj.* ☞ STATIONARY.
—OPPOSITES: moving.

immodest *adj.* INDECOROUS, improper, indecent, indelicate, immoral; forward, bold, brazen, impudent, shameless, loose, wanton; *informal* fresh, cheeky, saucy, brassy.

immoral *adj.* UNETHICAL, bad, morally wrong, wrongful, wicked, evil, foul, unprincipled, unscrupulous, dishonourable, dishonest, unconscionable, iniquitous, disreputable, corrupt, depraved, vile, villainous, nefarious, base, miscreant; sinful, godless, impure, unchaste, unvirtuous, shameless, degenerate, debased, debauched, dissolute, reprobate, lewd, obscene, perverse, perverted; licentious, wanton, promiscuous, loose; *informal* shady, lowdown, crooked, sleazy.
—OPPOSITES: ethical, chaste.

immortal *adj.* **1** UNDYING, deathless, eternal, everlasting, never-ending, endless, lasting, enduring, ceaseless; imperishable, indestructible, inextinguishable, immutable, perpetual,

immortalize | imperfect

permanent, unfading. **2** TIMELESS, perennial, classic, time-honoured, enduring; famous, famed, renowned, legendary, great, eminent, outstanding, acclaimed, celebrated.

immortalize *v.* COMMEMORATE, memorialize, eternalize; celebrate, deify, exalt, glorify; eulogize, pay tribute to, honour, salute.

immovable *adj.* **1** FIXED, secure, stable, moored, anchored, rooted, braced, set firm, set fast; stuck, jammed, stiff, unbudgeable, four-square. **2** ☞ STATIONARY.
—OPPOSITES: mobile, moving.

immune *adj.* RESISTANT, not subject, not liable, not vulnerable; protected from, safe from, secure against, not in danger of; impervious, invulnerable, unaffected.
—OPPOSITES: susceptible.

immunize *v.* VACCINATE, inoculate, inject; protect from, safeguard against.

impact *n.* **1** COLLISION, crash, smash, bump, bang; knock. **2** EFFECT, influence, significance, meaning; consequences, repercussions, ramifications, reverberations.
▶ *v.* **1** CRASH INTO, smash into, collide with, hit, strike, ram, smack into, bang into, slam into. **2** ☞ AFFECT 1.

impair *v.* HAVE A NEGATIVE EFFECT ON, damage, harm, diminish, reduce, weaken, lessen, decrease, impede, hinder, hobble; *formal* vitiate.
—OPPOSITES: improve, enhance.

impaired *adj.* *(Cdn)* ☞ INTOXICATED.

impartial *adj.* ☞ UNBIASED.
—OPPOSITES: biased, partisan.

impassable *adj.* UNNAVIGABLE, untraversable, impenetrable; closed, blocked, barricaded; dense, thick, blind.

impatient *adj.* **1** RESTLESS, restive, agitated, nervous, anxious, tense, ill at ease, edgy, jumpy, keyed up; *informal* twitchy, jittery, uptight, high-strung. **2** ☞ EAGER 2. **3** ☞ GRUMPY.
—OPPOSITES: calm, reluctant.

impede *v.* ☞ OBSTRUCT 2.
—OPPOSITES: facilitate.

impediment *n.* ☞ OBSTACLE.

impel *v.* FORCE, compel, constrain, oblige, require, make, urge, exhort, press, pressurize, drive, push, spur, prod, goad, incite, prompt, persuade.

impending *adj.* ☞ IMMINENT.

impenetrable *adj.* **1** IMPASSABLE, inaccessible, unnavigable, untraversable; dense, thick, overgrown. **2** ☞ INCOMPREHENSIBLE.

imperceptible *adj.* UNNOTICEABLE, undetectable, indistinguishable, indiscernible, invisible, inaudible, inappreciable, impalpable, unobtrusive, inconspicuous, unseen; tiny, minute, microscopic, infinitesimal; subtle, faint, fine, negligible, inconsequential; indistinct, unclear, indefinite, hard to make out.
—OPPOSITES: noticeable.

imperfect *adj.* FAULTY, flawed, defective, shoddy, unsound, inferior, second-rate, below standard, substandard; damaged, blemished, torn, broken, cracked,

scratched; *informal* not up to scratch, crummy.
—OPPOSITES: flawless.

imperfection *n.* ☞ FLAW.

imperious *adj.* ☞ DOMINEERING.

impersonal *adj.* **1** ALOOF, distant, remote, detached, reserved, withdrawn, unemotional, unsentimental, dispassionate, cold, cool, indifferent, unconcerned; formal, stiff, businesslike; *informal* starchy, standoffish, wooden.
2 ☞ INSTITUTIONAL 2.
—OPPOSITES: biased, warm.

impersonate *v.* ☞ IMITATE 2.

impertinent *adj.* ☞ INSOLENT.
—OPPOSITES: polite.

impetuous *adj.* ☞ RASH.
—OPPOSITES: considered.

impetus *n.* **1** MOMENTUM, propulsion, impulsion, motive force, driving force, drive, thrust; energy, force, power, push, strength. **2** ☞ STIMULUS.

impinge *v.* AFFECT, have an effect, touch, influence, make an impact, leave a mark.

implausible *adj.* ☞ UNLIKELY 2.
—OPPOSITES: convincing.

implement *n.* ☞ TOOL 1.
▶ *v.* EXECUTE, apply, put into effect/action, put into practice, carry out/through, perform, enact; fulfill, discharge, accomplish, bring about, achieve, realize, actualize, phase in; *formal* effectuate.

implicate *v.* ☞ INCRIMINATE.

implication *n.* **1** SUGGESTION, insinuation, innuendo, hint, intimation, imputation.
2 CONSEQUENCE, result, ramification, repercussion, reverberation, effect, significance.

implicit *adj.* IMPLIED, hinted at, suggested; unspoken, unexpressed, undeclared, unstated, tacit, hinted, taken as read, unsaid, unvoiced, unacknowledged, taken for granted; inherent, latent, underlying, inbuilt, incorporated; understood, inferred, deducible.
—OPPOSITES: explicit.

implore *v.* PLEAD WITH, beg, entreat, beseech, appeal to, ask, request, call on; exhort, urge, enjoin, press, push, petition, bid, importune; supplicate.

imply *v.* INSINUATE, suggest, hint, intimate, say indirectly, indicate, give someone to understand.

impolite *adj.* RUDE, bad-mannered, ill-mannered, discourteous, uncivil, disrespectful, inconsiderate, boorish, churlish, ill-bred, ungentlemanly, unladylike, ungracious; insolent, impudent, impertinent, cheeky; loutish, rough, crude, vulgar, indelicate, indecorous, tactless, gauche, uncouth; *informal* ignorant, lippy, saucy; *archaic* contumelious.

important *adj.* **1** SIGNIFICANT, consequential, momentous, of great import, major; critical, crucial, vital, pivotal, decisive, urgent, historic; serious, grave, weighty, material; essential, fundamental; *formal* of great moment. **2** POWERFUL, influential, of influence, well-connected, high-ranking, high-powered; prominent, eminent, pre-eminent, notable, noteworthy, of note;

distinguished, esteemed, respected, prestigious, celebrated, famous, great; *informal* major league.
—OPPOSITES: trivial, insignificant.

impose *v.* **1** FOIST, force, inflict, press, urge; *informal* saddle someone with, land someone with. **2** LEVY, charge, apply, enforce; set, establish, institute, introduce, bring into effect.

imposing *adj.* IMPRESSIVE, striking, arresting, eye-catching, dramatic, spectacular, stunning, awesome, awe-inspiring, formidable, splendid, grand, grandiose, majestic, august.
—OPPOSITES: modest.

impossible *adj.* **1** NOT POSSIBLE, out of the question, unfeasible, impractical, impracticable, non-viable, unworkable; unthinkable, unimaginable, inconceivable, absurd. **2** UNATTAINABLE, unachievable, unobtainable, unwinnable, hopeless, implausible, far-fetched, outrageous, preposterous, ridiculous, absurd, futile.
—OPPOSITES: attainable.

imposter *n.* IMPERSONATOR, masquerader, pretender, imitator, deceiver, hoaxer, trickster, fraudster, swindler; fake, fraud, sham, phony, scammer.

impotent *adj.* ☞ POWERLESS.

impracticable *adj.* UNWORKABLE, unfeasible, non-viable, unachievable, unattainable, unrealizable; impractical, impossible.
—OPPOSITES: workable, feasible.

impractical *adj.* **1** UNREALISTIC, unworkable, unfeasible, non-

viable, impracticable; ill-thought-out, impossible, absurd, wild; *informal* cockeyed, crackpot, crazy. **2** UNSUITABLE, not sensible, inappropriate, unserviceable. **3** ☞ IDEALISTIC.
—OPPOSITES: practical, sensible.

imprecise *adj.* VAGUE, loose, indefinite, inexplicit, indistinct, non-specific, unspecific, sweeping, broad, general; hazy, fuzzy, loosey-goosey, woolly, sketchy, nebulous, ambiguous, equivocal, uncertain.
—OPPOSITES: exact.

impregnate *v.* **1** INFUSE, soak, steep, saturate, drench; permeate, pervade, suffuse, imbue. **2** MAKE PREGNANT, inseminate, fertilize; *informal* get/put in the family way, knock up, get into trouble; *archaic* get with child.

impress *v.* **1** MAKE AN IMPRESSION ON, have an impact on, influence, affect, move, stir, rouse, excite, inspire; dazzle, awe, overawe, take someone's breath away, amaze, astonish; *informal* grab, blow someone away, stick in someone's mind. **2** (**impress upon**) EMPHASIZE TO, stress to, bring home to, instil in, inculcate into, drum into, knock into.
—OPPOSITES: disappoint.

impression *n.* **1** FEELING, feeling in one's bones, sense, fancy, (sneaking) suspicion, inkling, premonition, intuition, presentiment, hunch; notion, idea, funny feeling, gut feeling. **2** OPINION, view, image, picture, perception, judgment, verdict, estimation. **3** IMPERSONATION, imitation; parody, caricature, burlesque, travesty, lampoon; *informal* takeoff, send-up, spoof.

impressionable *adj.* EASILY INFLUENCED, suggestible, susceptible, persuadable, pliable, malleable, pliant, trusting, naive, innocent, wide-eyed, credulous, gullible.

impressive *adj.* MAGNIFICENT, majestic, imposing, splendid, spectacular, grand, awe-inspiring, striking, stunning, breathtaking, memorable, remarkable; admirable, masterly, accomplished, expert, skilled, skilful, consummate; excellent, outstanding, first-class, first-rate, fine, superb; *informal* great, mean, nifty, ace, crackerjack, bang-up, skookum✤, mind-blowing, jaw-dropping.
—OPPOSITES: ordinary, mediocre.

imprison *v.* INCARCERATE, send to prison, jail, lock up, put away, intern, detain, hold prisoner, hold captive; confine, shut up, cage; *informal* put behind bars, clap in irons, put in chains, put under lock and key.
—OPPOSITES: free, release.

improbable *adj.* ☞ UNLIKELY.
—OPPOSITES: certain, believable.

impromptu *adj.* UNREHEARSED, unprepared, unscripted, extempore, extemporized, extemporaneous, improvised, spontaneous, unplanned; *informal* off-the-cuff, offhand, spur-of-the-moment, ad lib.
—OPPOSITES: prepared, rehearsed.

improper *adj.* **1** INAPPROPRIATE, unacceptable, unsuitable, unprofessional, irregular; unethical, corrupt, immoral,

unscrupulous, dishonest, dishonourable. **2** UNSEEMLY, indecorous, unfitting, unladylike, ungentlemanly, indelicate, impolite; indecent, immodest, immoral.
—OPPOSITES: acceptable, decent.

improve *v.* **1** MAKE BETTER, better, ameliorate, advance, further, upgrade, update, refine, enhance, boost, build on, raise, polish, fix (up), amend; *informal* tweak; *formal* meliorate. **2** GET BETTER, advance, progress, develop; make headway, make progress, pick up, look up, turn the corner. **3** ☞ RECOVER 1.
—OPPOSITES: worsen, deteriorate.

improvise *v.* **1** EXTEMPORIZE, ad lib, speak impromptu; *informal* speak off the cuff, speak off the top of one's head, wing it; jam, scat. **2** CONTRIVE, devise, throw together, cobble together, rig up; *informal* whip up, rustle up.

imprudent *adj.* UNWISE, injudicious, incautious, indiscreet, misguided, ill-advised, ill-judged; thoughtless, unthinking, improvident, irresponsible, short-sighted, foolish; rash, reckless, heedless.
—OPPOSITES: sensible.

impulse *n.* ☞ URGE.

impulsive *adj.* **1** ☞ RASH. **2** IMPROMPTU, snap, spontaneous, unpremeditated, spur-of-the-moment, extemporaneous; whimsical.
—OPPOSITES: cautious, premeditated.

impure *adj.* **1** ADULTERATED, mixed, combined, blended, alloyed; *technical* admixed. **2** CONTAMINATED, polluted, tainted, unwholesome,

poisoned; dirty, filthy, foul,
unclean, defiled; unhygienic,
unsanitary; *literary* befouled.
3 ☞ IMMORAL.
—OPPOSITES: clean, chaste.

in *prep.* **1** INSIDE, within, in the
middle of; surrounded by,
enclosed by. **2** INTO, inside.
3 DURING, in the course of, over.
4 TO, per, every, each.
—OPPOSITES: outside.
▶ *adv.* INSIDE, indoors, into the
room, into the house/building.
—OPPOSITES: out.
▶ *adj.* **1** PRESENT, (at) home; inside,
indoors, in the house/room.
2 ☞ FASHIONABLE.
—OPPOSITES: out, unfashionable,
unpopular.
☐ **in for** DUE FOR, in line for;
expecting, about to undergo/
receive. **in on** PRIVY TO, aware of,
acquainted with, informed about/
of, apprised of; *informal* wise to, in
the know about, hip to.

inaccessible *adj.*
1 UNREACHABLE, out of reach,
unapproachable; cut-off, isolated,
remote, insular, in the back of
beyond, out of the way, lonely,
solitary, godforsaken.
2 ☞ INCOMPREHENSIBLE.

inaccurate *adj.* INEXACT,
imprecise, incorrect, wrong,
erroneous, careless, faulty,
imperfect, flawed, defective,
unsound, unreliable; fallacious,
false, mistaken, untrue; *informal*
wide of the mark.

inadequate *adj.* INSUFFICIENT,
deficient, poor, scant, scanty,
scarce, sparse, in short supply;
paltry, meagre, niggardly,
beggarly, limited; *informal* measly,

pathetic; *formal* exiguous.
—OPPOSITES: sufficient.

inadvertent *adj.*
☞ UNINTENTIONAL.
—OPPOSITES: deliberate.

inadvisable *adj.* ☞ UNWISE.

inanimate *adj.* LIFELESS,
insentient, without life, inorganic,
inert; dead, defunct.
—OPPOSITES: living.

inappropriate *adj.* UNSUITABLE,
unfitting, unseemly, unbecoming,
unbefitting, improper, impolite;
incongruous, out of place/keeping,
inapposite, inapt, infelicitous, ill-
suited; ill-judged, ill-advised,
inapplicable, unacceptable; *informal*
out of order/line, ill-considered,
incorrect, indecorous, injudicious,
wrong; *formal* malapropos.
—OPPOSITES: suitable.

inarticulate *adj.* UNINTELLIGIBLE,
incomprehensible, incoherent,
unclear, indistinct, mumbled,
muffled.
—OPPOSITES: silver-tongued,
fluent.

inattentive *adj.* DISTRACTED,
lacking concentration,
preoccupied, absent-minded,
daydreaming, dreamy, abstracted,
distrait; *informal* miles away, spaced
out.
—OPPOSITES: alert.

inauspicious *adj.* UNPROMISING,
unpropitious, unfavourable,
unfortunate, infelicitous, unlucky,
ill-omened, ominous;
discouraging, disheartening,
bleak.
—OPPOSITES: promising.

incapable *adj.* INCOMPETENT,
inept, inadequate, not good
enough, leaving much to be

desired, inexpert, unskilful, ineffective, ineffectual, inefficacious, unequal to the task; unqualified, unequal to the task; unable, incapacitated, helpless, powerless, impotent; *informal* not up to it, not up to snuff, useless, hopeless, pathetic, a dead loss.
—OPPOSITES: competent.

incentive *n.* INDUCEMENT, motivation, motive, reason, stimulus, stimulant, spur, impetus, encouragement, impulse; incitement, goad, provocation; attraction, lure, bait, bribe, draw, pull, reward; *informal* carrot, sweetener.
—OPPOSITES: deterrent.

inception *n.* ☞ BEGINNING 1.
—OPPOSITES: end.

incessant *adj.* ☞ CEASELESS.

incident *n.* **1** EVENT, occurrence, episode, experience, happening, occasion, proceeding, eventuality, affair, business; adventure, exploit, escapade; matter, circumstance, fact, development. **2** DISTURBANCE, fracas, melee, commotion, rumpus, scene; fight, skirmish, clash, brawl, free-for-all, encounter, conflict, ruckus, confrontation, altercation, contretemps; *informal* ruction.

incidental *adj.* LESS IMPORTANT, secondary, subsidiary; minor, peripheral, background, non-essential, inessential, unimportant, insignificant, inconsequential, tangential, extrinsic, extraneous, superfluous.
—OPPOSITES: essential.

incite *v.* STIR UP, whip up, encourage, urge, fan the flames of, stoke up, fuel, kindle, ignite,

inflame, stimulate, instigate, provoke, excite, arouse, awaken, inspire, engender, trigger, spark off, ferment, foment, agitate, rouse, touch off; *literary* enkindle.
—OPPOSITES: discourage, deter.

inclination *n.* ☞ TENDENCY 1.
—OPPOSITES: aversion.

incline *n.* ☞ SLOPE 1.

include *v.* **1** INCORPORATE, comprise, encompass, cover, embrace, involve, take in, number, contain; consist of, be made up of, be composed of; *formal* comprehend. **2** ALLOW FOR, count, take into account, take into consideration.
—OPPOSITES: exclude.

incoherent *adj.* UNCLEAR, confused, unintelligible, incomprehensible, hard to follow, disjointed, disconnected, disordered, mixed up, garbled, jumbled, scrambled, muddled; rambling, wandering, disorganized, illogical; inarticulate, mumbling, slurred.
—OPPOSITES: lucid.

income *n.* EARNINGS, salary, pay, remuneration, wages, stipend; revenue, receipts, takings, profits, gains, proceeds, turnover, yield, dividend, means, take; *formal* emolument.
—OPPOSITES: expenditure.

incomparable *adj.* WITHOUT EQUAL, beyond compare, unparalleled, matchless, peerless, unmatched, without parallel, beyond comparison, second to none, in a class of its own, unequalled, unrivalled, inimitable, nonpareil, par excellence; transcendent, superlative, surpassing, unsurpassed, unsurpassable, supreme, top, best, outstanding, consummate, singular, unique, rare, perfect; *informal* one-in-a-million; *formal* unexampled.

incompatible *adj.* **1** UNSUITED, mismatched, ill-matched. **2** ☞ CONTRADICTORY.
—OPPOSITES: well-matched, consistent.

incompetent *adj.* INEPT, unskilful, unskilled, inexpert, amateurish, unprofessional, bungling, blundering, clumsy, inadequate, substandard, inferior, ineffective, deficient, inefficient, ineffectual, wanting, lacking, leaving much to be desired; incapable, unfit, unqualified; all thumbs, awkward, butterfingered, klutzy, maladroit, unproductive, unsuccessful; *informal* useless, pathetic, ham-fisted, not up to it, not up to scratch, bush league.

incomplete *adj.* **1** UNFINISHED, uncompleted, partial, half-finished, half-done, half-completed. **2** DEFICIENT, insufficient, imperfect, defective, partial, patchy, sketchy, fragmentary, fragmented.

incomprehensible *adj.* UNINTELLIGIBLE, impossible to understand, impenetrable, unclear, indecipherable, inscrutable, beyond one's comprehension, beyond one, beyond one's grasp, complicated, complex, involved, baffling, bewildering, mystifying, unfathomable, puzzling, cryptic, confusing, perplexing; abstruse, esoteric, recondite, arcane,

mysterious, Delphic; *informal* over one's head, all Greek to someone.
—OPPOSITES: intelligible, clear.

inconceivable *adj.* ☞ FAR-FETCHED.
—OPPOSITES: likely.

inconclusive *adj.* INDECISIVE, proving/settling nothing; indefinite, indeterminate, unresolved, unproved, unsettled, still open to question/doubt, debatable, unconfirmed; moot; vague, ambiguous, borderline; *informal* up in the air, left hanging.

incongruous *adj.* **1** OUT OF PLACE, out of keeping, inappropriate, unsuitable, unsuited; wrong, strange, odd, curious, queer, absurd, bizarre. **2** ILL-MATCHED, ill-assorted, mismatched, unharmonious, discordant, dissonant, conflicting, clashing, jarring, incompatible, different, dissimilar, contrasting, disparate.
—OPPOSITES: appropriate, harmonious.

inconsiderate *adj.* THOUGHTLESS, unthinking, insensitive, selfish, self-centred, unsympathetic, uncaring, heedless, unmindful, unkind, uncharitable, ungracious, impolite, discourteous, rude, disrespectful; tactless, undiplomatic, indiscreet, indelicate, remiss.
—OPPOSITES: thoughtful.

inconsistent *adj.* **1** ERRATIC, changeable, unpredictable, variable, varying, changing, inconstant, unstable, irregular, fluctuating, unsteady, unsettled, uneven; self-contradictory,

contradictory, paradoxical; capricious, fickle, flighty, whimsical, unreliable, mercurial, volatile, blowing hot and cold, ever-changing, chameleon-like.
2 (inconsistent with) ☞ CONTRARY TO at CONTRARY.

inconspicuous *adj.* UNOBTRUSIVE, unnoticeable, unremarkable, unspectacular, unostentatious, undistinguished, unexceptional, modest, unassuming, discreet, hidden, concealed; unseen, in the background, low-profile.
—OPPOSITES: noticeable.

inconvenience *n.* disruption, difficulty, disturbance; irritation, annoyance; aggravation, hassle; nuisance, trouble, bother, problem, vexation, worry, trial, bind, bore, irritant, thorn in someone's side; *informal* headache, pain, pain in the neck, pain in the butt, drag.
▶ *v.* ☞ BOTHER 1.

inconvenient *adj.* AWKWARD, difficult, inopportune, untimely, ill-timed, unsuitable, inappropriate, unfortunate.

incorporate *v.* **1** ABSORB, include, subsume, assimilate, integrate, take in, swallow up.
2 ☞ INCLUDE 1.

incorrect *adj.* **1** WRONG, erroneous, in error, mistaken, inaccurate, wide of the mark, off target; untrue, false, fallacious; *informal* out, way out.
2 ☞ INAPPROPRIATE.

incorrigible *adj.* INVETERATE, habitual, confirmed, hardened, dyed-in-the-wool, incurable, chronic, irredeemable, hopeless,

beyond hope; impenitent, unrepentant, unapologetic, unashamed.

increase *v.* **1** GROW, get bigger, get larger, enlarge, expand, swell; rise, climb, escalate, soar, surge, rocket, shoot up, spiral; intensify, strengthen, extend, heighten, stretch, spread, widen; multiply, snowball, mushroom, proliferate, balloon, build up, mount up, pile up, accrue, accumulate; *literary* wax
2 ADD TO, make larger, make bigger, augment, supplement, top up, build up, extend, raise, swell, inflate; magnify, maximize, intensify, strengthen, heighten, amplify; *informal* up, jack up, hike up, bump up, torque up, crank up
—OPPOSITES: decrease, reduce.
▶ *n.* GROWTH, rise, enlargement, expansion, extension, multiplication, elevation, inflation; increment, addition, augmentation; magnification, intensification, amplification, climb, escalation, surge, upsurge, upswing, spiral, spurt, groundswell, leap; *informal* hike.

incredible *adj.* **1** ☞ FAR-FETCHED.
2 MAGNIFICENT, wonderful, marvellous, spectacular, remarkable, phenomenal, prodigious, breathtaking, extraordinary, unbelievable, amazing, stunning, astounding, astonishing, awe-inspiring, staggering, formidable, impressive, supreme, great, awesome, superhuman; *informal* fantastic, terrific, tremendous, stupendous, mind-boggling, mind-blowing, jaw-dropping, out of this world, far-out; *literary* wondrous.

incriminate v. IMPLICATE, involve, enmesh, compromise, embroil; blame, accuse, denounce, inform against, point the finger at; entrap; *informal* frame, set up, stick/pin the blame on, rat on; *archaic* inculpate.

incurable *adj.* **1** UNTREATABLE, inoperable, irremediable; terminal, fatal, mortal; chronic. **2** ☞ INCORRIGIBLE.

incursion *n.* ☞ RAID 1.
—OPPOSITES: retreat.

indecent *adj.* OBSCENE, dirty, filthy, rude, coarse, naughty, vulgar, gross, crude, lewd, salacious, improper, smutty, off-colour, bawdy; pornographic, sexually explicit, offensive, prurient, sordid, scatological, explicit, immoral, profane; ribald, risqué, racy, saucy, suggestive, titillating, porn, porno, X-rated, XXX, raunchy, skin, blue; adult.

indecisive *adj.* **1** ☞ INCONCLUSIVE. **2** IRRESOLUTE, hesitant, tentative, weak; vacillating, equivocating, dithering, wavering, faltering; ambivalent, divided, blowing hot and cold, of two minds, in a dilemma, in a quandary, torn; doubtful, unsure, uncertain; undecided, uncommitted, in doubt; *informal* iffy, sitting on the fence, wishy-washy, hemming and hawing, shilly-shallying, waffly.

indefensible *adj.* INEXCUSABLE, unjustifiable, unjustified, unpardonable, unforgivable; uncalled for, unprovoked, gratuitous, unreasonable, unnecessary; insupportable, unacceptable, unwarranted,
unwarrantable; flawed, wrong, untenable, unsustainable.

indefinite *adj.* **1** INDETERMINATE, unspecified, unlimited, unrestricted, undecided, undetermined, undefined, unfixed, unsettled, unknown, uncertain; limitless, infinite, endless, immeasurable. **2** VAGUE, ill-defined, unclear, imprecise, inexact, loose, general, nebulous, fuzzy, hazy, obscure, ambiguous, equivocal.
—OPPOSITES: fixed, clear.

independence *n.* **1** SELF-GOVERNMENT, self-rule, home rule, separation, self-determination, sovereignty, autonomy, freedom, liberty. **2** SELF-SUFFICIENCY, self-reliance, autonomy, freedom, liberty.

independent *adj.* **1** SELF-GOVERNING, self-ruling, self-determining, sovereign, autonomous, free, non-aligned. **2** SEPARATE, different, unconnected, unrelated, dissociated, discrete. **3** SELF-SUFFICIENT, self-supporting, self-reliant, standing on one's own two feet.
—OPPOSITES: subservient, related, biased.

indescribable *adj.* INEXPRESSIBLE, indefinable, beyond words/description, ineffable, incommunicable; unutterable, unspeakable.

indestructible *adj.* UNBREAKABLE, shatterproof, durable; lasting, enduring, everlasting, perennial, deathless, undying, immortal, inextinguishable, imperishable;

informal heavy-duty, industrial-strength; *literary* adamantine, infrangible.
—OPPOSITES: fragile.

index *n.* ☞ LIST[1].

indicate *v.* **1** POINT TO, be a sign of, be evidence of, evidence, demonstrate, show, testify to, bespeak, be a symptom of, be symptomatic of, denote, connote, mark, signal, signify, suggest, imply, intimate; manifest, reveal, betray, display, reflect, represent, exhibit, express, register; *formal* evince; *literary* betoken. **2** STATE, declare, make known, communicate, announce, mention, express, reveal, divulge, disclose; put it on record; admit, specify, designate, mark, stipulate; show.

indication *n.* ☞ SIGN 1, 2.

indicator *n.* MEASURE, gauge, barometer, guide, index, mark, sign, signal, symptom; bellwether, herald, hint; standard, touchstone, yardstick, benchmark, criterion, point of reference, guideline, test, litmus test.

indifferent *adj.* UNCONCERNED, uninterested, uncaring, casual, nonchalant, offhand, uninvolved, unenthusiastic, apathetic, lukewarm, phlegmatic, blasé, insouciant; unimpressed, bored, unmoved, unresponsive, impassive, dispassionate, detached, cool.
—OPPOSITES: enthusiastic.

indigenous *adj.* NATIVE, original, aboriginal, autochthonous; local, domestic, homegrown; earliest, first.

indignant *adj.* AGGRIEVED, resentful, affronted, disgruntled, displeased, cross, angry, mad, annoyed, offended, exasperated, irritated, piqued, nettled, in high dudgeon, chagrined; *informal* peeved, vexed, irked, put out, miffed, aggravated, riled, in a huff, huffy, ticked off, sore.

indirect *adj.* **1** INCIDENTAL, accidental, unintended, unintentional, secondary, subordinate, ancillary, concomitant. **2** ROUNDABOUT, circuitous, wandering, meandering, serpentine, winding, tortuous, zigzag.

indiscreet *adj.* IMPRUDENT, unwise, impolitic, injudicious, incautious, irresponsible, careless, thoughtless; undiplomatic, indelicate, tactless, insensitive; untimely, infelicitous; immodest, indecorous, unseemly, improper.

indiscriminate *adj.* NON-SELECTIVE, unselective, undiscriminating, uncritical, aimless, hit-or-miss, haphazard, random, arbitrary, unsystematic, undirected; wholesale, general, sweeping, blanket; thoughtless, unthinking, inconsiderate, casual, careless.
—OPPOSITES: selective.

indispensable *adj.* ESSENTIAL, necessary, all-important, of the utmost importance, of the essence, vital, crucial, key, needed, required, requisite, imperative; invaluable.
—OPPOSITES: superfluous.

indisputable *adj.*
INCONTROVERTIBLE, incontestable, undeniable, irrefutable, beyond

dispute, unassailable, unquestionable, beyond question, indubitable, undoubted, not in doubt, beyond doubt, beyond a shadow of a doubt, unarguable, airtight, watertight; unequivocal, unmistakable, certain, sure, definite, definitive, proven, decisive, conclusive, demonstrable, self-evident, clear, clear-cut, plain, obvious, manifest, patent, palpable, categorical, positive, absolute, evident, true.
—OPPOSITES: questionable.

indistinct *adj.* BLURRED, out of focus, fuzzy, hazy, misty, foggy, cloudy, shadowy, dim, nebulous; unclear, obscure, vague, faint, indistinguishable, indiscernible, barely perceptible, hard to see, hard to make out, unintelligible; inaudible, incomprehensible.
—OPPOSITES: clear.

indistinguishable *adj.*
1 ☞ IDENTICAL. **2** ☞ INDISTINCT.
—OPPOSITES: unalike, clear.

individual *adj.* **1** SINGLE, separate, discrete, independent, solo; sole, lone, solitary, isolated.
2 CHARACTERISTIC, distinctive, distinct, typical, particular, peculiar, personal, personalized, special; original, unique, exclusive, singular, idiosyncratic, different, unusual, novel, unorthodox, atypical, out of the ordinary, one of a kind.
▶ *n.* ☞ PERSON.

induce *v.* **1** ☞ PERSUADE.
2 ☞ CAUSE.
—OPPOSITES: dissuade, prevent.

inducement *n.* ☞ INCENTIVE.
—OPPOSITES: deterrent.

indulge *v.* **1** SATISFY, gratify, fulfill, feed, accommodate; yield to, give in to, give way to.
2 WALLOW IN, give oneself up to, give way to, yield to, abandon oneself to, give free rein to; luxuriate in, revel in, lose oneself in.
—OPPOSITES: frustrate.
☐ **indulge oneself** TREAT ONESELF, give oneself a treat; go on a spree. *informal* go to town, splurge.

industrious *adj.* HARD-WORKING, diligent, assiduous, conscientious, steady, painstaking, sedulous, persevering, unflagging, untiring, tireless, indefatigable, studious; busy, as busy as a bee, active, bustling, energetic, on the go, vigorous, determined, dynamic, zealous, productive; with one's shoulder to the wheel, with one's nose to the grindstone.
—OPPOSITES: indolent.

industry *n.* **1** MANUFACTURING, production; construction.
2 BUSINESS, trade, field, line (of business); *informal* racket.

inebriated *adj.* ☞ INTOXICATED.

ineffective *adj.* UNSUCCESSFUL, unproductive, fruitless, unprofitable, abortive, futile, purposeless, useless, worthless, ineffectual, inefficient, inefficacious, inadequate; feeble, inept, lame; *archaic* bootless; powerless, impotent, lame-duck; incompetent, incapable, unfit, weak, poor; hopeless.

ineligible *adj.* UNQUALIFIED, unsuitable, unacceptable, undesirable, inappropriate, unworthy; ruled out, disqualified,

disentitled; *Law* incompetent.
−OPPOSITES: suitable.

inept *adj.* ☞ INCOMPETENT.
−OPPOSITES: competent.

inequality *n.* IMBALANCE,
inequity, inconsistency, variation,
variability; divergence, polarity,
disparity, discrepancy,
dissimilarity, difference; bias,
prejudice, discrimination,
unfairness.

inert *adj.* UNMOVING, motionless,
immobile, inanimate, still,
stationary, static; dormant,
sleeping; unconscious, comatose,
lifeless, insensible, insensate,
insentient; idle, inactive, sluggish,
lethargic, indolent, stagnant,
listless, torpid.
−OPPOSITES: active.

inertia *n.* ☞ LETHARGY.

inescapable *adj.*
☞ UNAVOIDABLE.
−OPPOSITES: avoidable.

inestimable *adj.* IMMEASURABLE,
incalculable, innumerable,
unfathomable, measureless,
countless, untold; limitless,
boundless, unlimited, infinite,
endless, inexhaustible; *informal* no
end of; *literary* myriad.
−OPPOSITES: few.

inevitable *adj.* ☞ UNAVOIDABLE.

inexcusable *adj.*
☞ INDEFENSIBLE.

inexhaustible *adj.* ☞ LIMITLESS.
−OPPOSITES: limited.

inexpensive *adj.* CHEAP, low-
priced, low-cost, modest,
economical, competitive,
affordable, reasonable, budget,
bargain, cut-rate, reduced,
discounted, discount, rock-
bottom, giveaway, bargain-

basement, economy, down-
market, low-end, dirt cheap,
cheap like borscht✦.

inexperienced *adj.* INEXPERT,
unpractised, untrained,
unschooled, unqualified,
unskilled, amateur, rookie,
newbie; ignorant, unversed,
unseasoned; ill-equipped, ill-
prepared; naive, unsophisticated,
callow, immature, green,
unworldly; *informal* wet behind the
ears, raggedy-ass, wide-eyed.

inexplicable *adj.*
UNACCOUNTABLE, unexplainable,
incomprehensible, unfathomable,
impenetrable, insoluble; baffling,
puzzling, perplexing, mystifying,
bewildering, confusing;
mysterious, strange.
−OPPOSITES: understandable.

infallible *adj.* UNFAILING, unerring,
guaranteed, dependable,
trustworthy, reliable, sure,
certain, safe, foolproof, effective;
surefire, airtight, flawless, idiot-
proof, perfect, sound, tried and
tested; *formal* efficacious.

infant *n.* ☞ BABY *n.* 1.

infantile *adj.* ☞ CHILDISH 1.

infatuated *adj.* BESOTTED, in love,
head over heels, obsessed, taken,
lovesick, moonstruck; enamoured
of, attracted to, devoted to,
captivated by, enthralled by,
enchanted by, bewitched by,
under the spell of; *informal* smitten
with, sweet on, keen on, hot on/
for, gone on, all gaga over, hung
up on, mad about, crazy about,
nuts about, stuck on, doting on,
swept off one's feet by, wild
about, carrying a torch for.

infect v. CONTAMINATE, pollute, taint, foul, dirty, blight, damage, ruin; poison.

infectious adj. **1** ☞ CONTAGIOUS. **2** IRRESISTIBLE, compelling, persuasive, contagious, catching.

inferior adj. ☞ BAD 1.
—OPPOSITES: superior, luxury.
▶ n. SUBORDINATE, junior, underling, minion, peon.

infernal adj. HELLISH, nether, subterranean, underworld, chthonic, Tartarean.

infest v. OVERRUN, spread through, invade, infiltrate, pervade, permeate, inundate, overwhelm; beset, plague, swarm.

infidelity n. UNFAITHFULNESS, adultery, cuckoldry, disloyalty, extramarital sex; affair, liaison, fling, amour; informal fooling/ playing around, cheating, two-timing, hanky-panky, a bit on the side; formal fornication.

infinite adj. **1** BOUNDLESS, unbounded, unlimited, limitless, never-ending, interminable; immeasurable, fathomless, imponderable; extensive, vast; immense, great, huge, enormous, massive, colossal, prodigious. **2** ☞ UNLIMITED 2.
—OPPOSITES: limited.

infinitesimal adj. ☞ TINY.
—OPPOSITES: huge.

infirm adj. FRAIL, weak, feeble, debilitated, decrepit, disabled; ill, unwell, sick, sickly, indisposed, ailing.
—OPPOSITES: healthy.

inflame v. **1** ☞ ANGER v.
2 ☞ INCITE.
—OPPOSITES: placate, calm, soothe.

inflammable adj. FLAMMABLE, combustible, incendiary, ignitable; volatile, unstable.
—OPPOSITES: fireproof.

inflammation n. SWELLING, puffiness; redness, heat, burning; rawness, soreness, tenderness; infection, festering.

inflammatory adj.
☞ PROVOCATIVE 1.

inflate v. **1** BLOW UP, fill up, fill with air, aerate, pump up; dilate, distend, swell. **2** ☞ EXAGGERATE.
3 ☞ INCREASE 2.
—OPPOSITES: decrease, understate.

inflexible adj. STUBBORN, obstinate, obdurate, intractable, intransigent, unbending, immovable, unaccommodating; hidebound, single-minded, pigheaded, mulish, uncompromising, adamant, firm, resolute, diehard, dyed-in-the-wool, bloody-minded, determined, hardline, headstrong, inexorable, rigid, stiff-necked, unshakeable, unyielding, implacable, tenacious, uncooperative, unmanageable, unrelenting.
—OPPOSITES: accommodating.

inflict v. ADMINISTER TO, deliver to, deal out to, dispense to, mete out to; impose, exact, wreak; cause to, give to; informal dish out to.

influence n. **1** EFFECT, impact; control, sway, hold, power, authority, mastery, domination, supremacy; guidance, direction; pressure. **2** EXAMPLE TO, (role) model for, guide for, inspiration to. **3** POWER, authority, sway, leverage, weight, pull, standing, prestige, stature, rank; informal clout, muscle, teeth.

▸ *v.* AFFECT, have an impact on, impact, determine, guide, control, shape, govern, decide; change, alter, transform.

influential *adj.* ☞ IMPORTANT 2.

influx *n.* INUNDATION, rush, stream, flood, incursion; invasion, intrusion.

inform *v.* ☞ TELL 1.

informal *adj.* **1** UNOFFICIAL, casual, relaxed, easygoing, unceremonious; open, friendly, intimate; simple, unpretentious, easy; *informal* unstuffy, laid-back, chummy. **2** ☞ COLLOQUIAL. **3** CASUAL, relaxed, comfortable, everyday, sloppy, leisure; *informal* comfy, cazh, sporty.
—OPPOSITES: official, literary, formal.

information *n.* DETAILS, particulars, facts, figures, statistics, data; knowledge, intelligence; instruction, advice, guidance, direction, counsel, enlightenment; news; *informal* info, the lowdown, the dope, the dirt, the inside story, the scoop, the poop.

informative *adj.* ☞ INSTRUCTIVE.

informed *adj.* KNOWLEDGEABLE, enlightened, literate, educated; sophisticated, cultured; briefed, versed, up to date, up to speed, in the know, in the loop, au courant, au fait, switched-on, wise, hip.
—OPPOSITES: ignorant.

informer *n.* INFORMANT, betrayer, traitor, Judas, collaborator, stool pigeon, spy, double agent, infiltrator, plant, tattletale; *informal* rat, squealer, whistle-blower, snake in the grass, snitch, fink, stoolie.

infrequent *adj.* RARE, uncommon, unusual, exceptional, few (and far between), as rare/scarce as hen's teeth; unaccustomed, unwonted; isolated, scarce, scattered; sporadic, irregular, intermittent, seldom; *informal* once in a blue moon.
—OPPOSITES: common.

infuriating *adj.* EXASPERATING, maddening, annoying, irritating, irksome, vexatious, trying, tiresome; *informal* aggravating, pesky, infernal.

ingenious *adj.* INVENTIVE, creative, imaginative, original, innovative, pioneering, resourceful, enterprising, inspired; clever, intelligent, smart, brilliant, masterly, talented, gifted, skilful; astute, sharp-witted, quick-witted, shrewd; elaborate, sophisticated.

ingredient *adj.* ☞ COMPONENT.

inhabit *v.* LIVE IN, occupy; settle (in), people, populate, colonize; dwell in, reside in, tenant, lodge in, have one's home in; *formal* be domiciled in, abide in.

inhabitant *n.* RESIDENT, occupant, occupier, dweller, squatter, settler; local, native, (*Que.*) habitant✦, burgher; (**inhabitants**) population, populace, people, public, community, citizenry, townsfolk, townspeople; *formal* denizen.

inherent *adj.* INTRINSIC, innate, immanent, built-in, indwelling, inborn, ingrained, deep-rooted; essential, fundamental, basic, structural, organic; natural, instinctive, instinctual, congenital, native, deep-seated,

inbred, indelible, integral.
—OPPOSITES: acquired.

inheritance n. LEGACY, bequest, endowment, bestowal, provision; birthright, heritage, patrimony.

inhibit v. IMPEDE, hinder, hamper, hold back, discourage, interfere with, obstruct, slow down, retard; curb, check, suppress, restrict, fetter, cramp, frustrate, stifle, prevent, block, thwart, foil, stop, halt.
—OPPOSITES: assist, encourage, allow.

inhibited adj. SHY, reticent, reserved, self-conscious, diffident, bashful, coy; wary, reluctant, hesitant, insecure, unconfident, unassertive, timid; withdrawn, repressed, constrained, undemonstrative; informal uptight, anal-retentive.

inhospitable adj. UNINVITING, unwelcoming; bleak, forbidding, cheerless, hostile, savage, wild, harsh, inimical; uninhabitable, barren, bare, austere, desolate, stark, Spartan.
—OPPOSITES: welcoming.

initial adj. BEGINNING, opening, commencing, starting, inceptive, embryonic, fledgling; first, early, primary, preliminary, elementary, foundational, preparatory; introductory, inaugural; leadoff.
—OPPOSITES: final.

initiate v. ☞ LAUNCH 3.
—OPPOSITES: finish.

initiative n. SELF-MOTIVATION, resourcefulness, inventiveness, imagination, ingenuity, originality, creativity, enterprise; drive, dynamism, ambition, motivation, spirit, energy, vision;

informal get-up-and-go, pep, moxie, spunk, gumption.

injure v. ☞ HURT 2.

injury n. WOUND, bruise, cut, gash, scratch, graze, abrasion, contusion, lesion; Medicine trauma.

injustice n. UNFAIRNESS, unjustness, inequity; tyranny, repression, exploitation, corruption; bias, prejudice, discrimination, intolerance.

inkling n. IDEA, notion, sense, impression, conception, suggestion, indication, whisper, glimmer, (sneaking) suspicion, fancy, hunch, feeling; hint, clue, intimation, sign; informal the foggiest (idea), the faintest (idea).

inlet n. COVE, bay, (Nfld) angle✦, bight, estuary, fjord, sound, armlet, saltchuck.

innate adj. INBORN, inbred, congenital, inherent, indwelling, natural, native, intrinsic, instinctive, intuitive, unlearned; hereditary, inherited, in the blood, in the family; inbuilt, deep-rooted, deep-seated, hard-wired, connate.
—OPPOSITES: acquired.

inner adj. **1** ☞ INTERNAL 1.
2 PRIVILEGED, restricted, exclusive, private, confidential, intimate.
3 HIDDEN, secret, deep, underlying, unapparent; veiled, unrevealed.
—OPPOSITES: external, apparent.

innocent adj. **1** GUILTLESS, blameless, in the clear, unimpeachable, irreproachable, above suspicion, faultless; honourable, honest, upright, law-abiding; informal squeaky clean.
2 HARMLESS, benign, innocuous,

safe, inoffensive.
—OPPOSITES: guilty, sinful.

innocuous adj. ☞ HARMLESS.
—OPPOSITES: harmful.

innovative adj. ☞ ORIGINAL 1.

innuendo n. INSINUATION, suggestion, intimation, implication, hint, overtone, undertone, allusion, reference; aspersion, slur.

innumerable adj. ☞ COUNTLESS.

inquire v. ☞ ASK 1.

inquiry n. **1** QUESTION, query. **2** ☞ INVESTIGATION.

inquisitive adj. CURIOUS, interested, intrigued, prying, spying, eavesdropping, intrusive, busybody, meddlesome, snooping; inquiring, questioning, probing, searching; informal nosy, Nosy Parker, snoopy.
—OPPOSITES: uninterested.

insane adj. **1** MAD, mentally ill, certifiable, deranged, demented, of unsound mind, out of one's mind, not in one's right mind, sick in the head, crazy, crazed, lunatic, non compos mentis, unhinged, bushed♣, disturbed, raving, psychotic, psychopathic, mentally disordered, schizophrenic, unbalanced, unstable, mad as a hatter, mad as a March hare; informal mental, off one's nut, nuts, nutty (as a fruitcake), nutso, ditzy, out to lunch, spinny, wingy, with a screw loose, off one's rocker, not right in the head, round the bend, stark raving mad, bats, batty, buggy, bonkers, dotty, cuckoo, cracked, loopy, loony, bananas, loco, screwy, schizoid, psycho, touched, gaga, not all there, not

right upstairs, crackers, out of one's tree, meshuga, wacko, gonzo; (**be mad**) have a screw loose, have bats in the/one's belfry; (**go mad**) lose one's reason, lose one's mind, take leave of one's senses, lose one's marbles, crack up. **2** ☞ ABSURD.
—OPPOSITES: sensible.

insecure adj. UNCONFIDENT, uncertain, unsure, doubtful, hesitant, self-conscious, unassertive, diffident, unforthcoming, shy, timid, retiring, timorous, inhibited, introverted; anxious, fearful, worried; informal mousy.
—OPPOSITES: confident.

insensible adj. ☞ UNCONSCIOUS 1.
—OPPOSITES: conscious.

insensitive adj. HEARTLESS, unfeeling, inconsiderate, thoughtless, thick-skinned; hard-hearted, cold-blooded, uncaring, unconcerned, unsympathetic, unkind, callous, cruel, merciless, pitiless.
—OPPOSITES: compassionate.

insert v. PUT, place, push, thrust, slide, slip, load, fit, slot, lodge, install; informal pop, stick.
—OPPOSITES: extract, remove.

inside n. ☞ INTERIOR n. 1.
—OPPOSITES: exterior.
▶ adj. **1** INNER, interior, internal, innermost. **2** ☞ PRIVATE 2.
—OPPOSITES: outer, public.
▶ adv. INDOORS, within, in.

insidious adj. STEALTHY, subtle, surreptitious, cunning, crafty, treacherous, artful, sly, wily, shifty, underhanded, indirect; informal sneaky.

insight *n.* INTUITION, discernment, perception, awareness, understanding, comprehension, apprehension, appreciation, penetration, acumen, perspicacity, judgment, acuity; vision, wisdom, prescience; *informal* savvy.

insignificant *adj.*
☞ UNIMPORTANT.

insincere *adj.* FALSE, fake, hollow, artificial, feigned, pretended, put-on, inauthentic; disingenuous, hypocritical, cynical, deceitful, deceptive, duplicitous, double-dealing, two-faced, lying, untruthful, mendacious; *informal* phony, pretend.

insinuate *v.* ☞ HINT.
☐ **insinuate oneself into** WORM ONE'S WAY INTO, ingratiate oneself with, curry favour with; foist oneself on, introduce oneself into, edge one's way into, insert oneself into; infiltrate, invade, sneak into, manoeuvre oneself into, intrude on, impinge on; *informal* muscle in on.

insist *v.* **1** DEMAND, command, require, dictate; urge, exhort. **2** MAINTAIN, assert, hold, contend, argue, protest, claim, vow, swear, declare, stress, repeat, reiterate; *formal* aver. **3** PERSIST, be determined, stand firm, stand one's ground, be resolute, be intent, be set, be emphatic, be adamant, not take no for an answer; *informal* stick to one's guns.

insistent *adj.* PERSISTENT, determined, adamant, importunate, tenacious, unyielding, dogged, unrelenting, tireless, inexorable; demanding, pushy, forceful, urgent; clamorous, vociferous; emphatic, firm, assertive.

insolent *adj.* IMPERTINENT, impudent, cheeky, ill-mannered, bad mannered, unmannerly, rude, impolite, uncivil, discourteous, disrespectful, insubordinate, contemptuous; audacious, bold, cocky, brazen; insulting, abusive, forward, presumptuous; *informal* fresh, lippy, saucy, pert, sassy, smart-alecky.
—OPPOSITES: polite.

inspect *v.* EXAMINE, check, scrutinize, investigate, vet, test, monitor, survey, study, look over, look at, look into, inquire into, peruse, scan, analyze, explore, probe; assess, appraise, review, audit; *informal* check out, give something a/the once-over.

inspection *n.* EXAMINATION, checkup, survey, scrutiny, probe, exploration, observation, investigation; assessment, appraisal, review, evaluation, analysis, consideration, perusal, study; *informal* once-over, going-over, look-see.

inspector *n.* EXAMINER, checker, scrutineer, investigator, surveyor, assessor, appraiser, reviewer, analyst; observer, overseer, supervisor, monitor, watchdog, ombudsman; auditor.

inspiration *n.* **1** GUIDING LIGHT, example, model, muse, motivation, encouragement, influence, spur, stimulus, lift, boost, incentive, impulse, catalyst. **2** ☞ IMAGINATION. **3** BRIGHT IDEA, revelation, flash; *informal* brainwave, brainstorm, eureka moment.

inspire *v.* **1** STIMULATE, motivate, encourage, influence, rouse, move, stir, energize, galvanize, incite; animate, fire, excite, spark, inspirit, incentivize, affect. **2** AROUSE, awaken, prompt, induce, ignite, trigger, kindle, produce, bring out; *literary* enkindle.

instability *n.* UNRELIABILITY, uncertainty, unpredictability, insecurity, riskiness; impermanence, inconstancy, changeability, variability, fluctuation, mutability, transience.
—OPPOSITES: steadiness.

install *v.* **1** ☞ POSITION *v.* **2** SWEAR IN, induct, instate, inaugurate, invest; appoint; ordain, consecrate, anoint; enthrone, crown. **3** LOAD, store.
—OPPOSITES: remove.

instalment *n.* PART, portion, section, segment, bit; chapter, episode, volume, issue.

instance *n.* EXAMPLE, exemplar, occasion, occurrence, case; illustration.

instant *adj.* **1** ☞ IMMEDIATE 1. **2** PRE-PREPARED, pre-cooked, ready-made, ready-mixed, heat-and-serve, fast; microwaveable.
—OPPOSITES: delayed.
▶ *n.* MOMENT, minute, trice, (split) second, wink/blink/twinkling of an eye, eyeblink, flash, no time (at all), heartbeat; *informal* sec, jiffy, snap.

instigate *v.* SET IN MOTION, get under way, get off the ground, start, commence, begin, initiate,

launch, institute, set up, inaugurate, establish, organize; actuate, generate, bring about; start the ball rolling, kick off; incite, encourage, urge.
—OPPOSITES: halt, dissuade.

instill *v.* INCULCATE, implant, ingrain, impress, imprint, introduce; engender, produce, generate, induce, inspire, promote, foster; drum into, drill into.

instinct *n.* NATURAL TENDENCY, inherent tendency, inclination, urge, drive, compulsion, need; intuition, feeling, hunch, sixth sense, insight; nose.

instinctive *adj.* INTUITIVE, natural, instinctual, innate, inborn, inherent; unconscious, subconscious; automatic, reflex, knee-jerk, mechanical, spontaneous, involuntary, impulsive; *informal* gut, second nature.
—OPPOSITES: learned, voluntary.

institute *v.* ☞ LAUNCH 3.

institutional *adj.* **1** ORGANIZED, established, bureaucratic, conventional, procedural, prescribed, set, routine, formal, systematic, systematized, methodical, businesslike, orderly, coherent, structured, regulated. **2** IMPERSONAL, formal, regimented, uniform, unvaried, monotonous; insipid, bland, uninteresting, dull; unappealing, uninviting, unattractive, unwelcoming, dreary, drab, colourless; stark, Spartan, bare, clinical, sterile, austere.

instruct *v.* **1** ☞ TEACH. **2** ORDER, direct, command, tell, enjoin, require, call on, mandate, charge; *literary* bid.

instruction *n.* **1** TUITION, teaching, coaching, schooling, education, tutelage; lessons, classes, lectures; training, preparation, grounding, guidance. **2** ORDER, command, directive, direction, decree, edict, injunction, mandate, dictate, commandment, bidding, exhortation, request; requirement, stipulation; *informal* marching orders; *literary* behest. **3** DIRECTIONS, key, rubric, specification, how-tos; handbook, manual, guide, tutorial.

instructive *adj.* INFORMATIVE, instructional, informational, illuminating, enlightening, explanatory, revealing; educational, educative, edifying, didactic, pedagogic, heuristic; improving, moralistic, homiletic; useful, helpful.

instructor *n.* ☞ TEACHER.

instrument *n.* **1** ☞ TOOL 1. **2** PAWN, puppet, creature, dupe, cog; tool, cat's paw; *informal* stooge.

instrumental *adj.* **(be instrumental in)** play a part in, contribute to, be a factor in, have a hand in; add to, help, promote, advance, further; be conducive to, make for, lead to, cause.

insubordinate *adj.*
☞ DISOBEDIENT.
—OPPOSITES: obedient.

insufferable *adj.* ☞ UNBEARABLE.

insufficient *adj.* ☞ INADEQUATE.

insular *adj.* NARROW-MINDED, small-minded, blinkered, inward-looking, parochial, provincial, small-town, short-sighted,

hidebound; intolerant, partisan, xenophobic; *informal* redneck.
—OPPOSITES: broad-minded, cosmopolitan.

insulate *v.* PROTECT, save, shield, shelter, screen, cushion, buffer, cocoon; isolate, segregate, sequester, detach, cut off.

insult *v.* ABUSE, be rude to, slight, disparage, discredit, libel, slander, malign, defame, denigrate, cast aspersions on, call someone names, put someone down; offend, affront, hurt, humiliate, wound; *informal* badmouth, dis; *formal* derogate, calumniate.
—OPPOSITES: compliment.
▶ *n.* ABUSIVE REMARK, jibe, affront, slight, barb, slur, indignity; injury, libel, slander, defamation; abuse, disparagement, aspersions; *informal* dig, crack, put-down, slap in the face, kick in the teeth, cheap shot, low blow.

insurgent *n.* ☞ REBEL 1.
—OPPOSITES: loyalist.

intangible *adj.* INDEFINABLE, indescribable, inexpressible, nameless; vague, obscure, abstract, unclear, indefinite, undefined, subtle, elusive.

integral *adj.* **1** ☞ ESSENTIAL 2. **2** BUILT-IN, integrated, incorporated, included. **3** UNIFIED, integrated, comprehensive, composite, combined, aggregate; complete, whole.
—OPPOSITES: peripheral, fragmented.

integrate *v.* ☞ COMBINE 1.
—OPPOSITES: separate.

integrity *n.* ☞ HONOUR *n.* 1.
—OPPOSITES: dishonesty.

intellect n. **1** ☞ INTELLIGENCE 1.
2 ☞ INTELLECTUAL n.

intellectual adj. **1** MENTAL,
cerebral, cognitive, psychological;
rational, abstract, conceptual,
theoretical, analytical, logical;
academic. **2** INTELLIGENT, clever,
academic, educated, well-read,
lettered, erudite, cerebral,
learned, knowledgeable, literary,
bookish, donnish, highbrow,
scholarly, studious, enlightened,
sophisticated, cultured; informal
brainy.
—OPPOSITES: physical, stupid.
▶ n. HIGHBROW, learned person,
academic, bookworm, man/
woman of letters, bluestocking;
thinker, brain, scholar, intellect,
genius, mind, Einstein, polymath,
mastermind; informal egghead,
brains, brainiac, rocket scientist.
—OPPOSITES: dunce.

intelligence n. **1** INTELLECTUAL
CAPACITY, mental capacity,
intellect, mind, brain(s), IQ,
brainpower, judgment, reasoning,
understanding, comprehension;
acumen, wit(s), sense, insight,
perception, penetration,
discernment, smartness,
canniness, astuteness, intuition,
acuity, savvy, cleverness,
brilliance, ability, reason,
thought, wisdom; informal smarts,
grey matter, brain cells,
braininess. **2** ☞ INFORMATION.
3 INFORMATION GATHERING,
surveillance, observation,
reconnaissance, spying,
espionage, infiltration, ELINT,
Humint; informal recon.

intelligent adj. CLEVER, bright,
brilliant, quick-witted, quick on

the uptake, smart, canny, astute,
intuitive, insightful, perceptive,
perspicacious, discerning;
knowledgeable; able, gifted,
talented; ingenious, resourceful;
informal brainy.

intelligible adj.
☞ COMPREHENSIBLE.

intemperate adj. IMMODERATE,
excessive, undue, inordinate,
extreme, unrestrained,
uncontrolled; self-indulgent,
overindulgent, extravagant,
lavish, prodigal, profligate;
imprudent, reckless, wild;
dissolute, debauched, wanton,
dissipated.
—OPPOSITES: moderate.

intend v. PLAN, mean, have in
mind, have the intention, aim,
propose; aspire, hope, expect, be
resolved, be determined; want,
wish, desire, set out; contemplate,
think of, envisage, envision;
design, earmark, designate, set
aside.

intense adj. **1** EXTREME, great,
acute, fierce, severe, high;
exceptional, extraordinary; harsh,
strong, powerful, potent,
overpowering, vigorous; informal
serious. **2** PASSIONATE,
impassioned, ardent, fervent,
zealous, vehement, fiery,
emotional; earnest, eager, keen,
animated, spirited, vigorous,
energetic, fanatical, committed.
—OPPOSITES: mild, apathetic.

intensify v. ESCALATE, increase,
step up, boost, raise, strengthen,
augment, reinforce; pick up, build
up, heighten, deepen, extend,
expand, amplify, magnify;
aggravate, exacerbate, worsen,

inflame, compound.
—OPPOSITES: abate.

intensive adj. THOROUGH, thoroughgoing, in-depth, rigorous, exhaustive; all-inclusive, comprehensive, complete, full; vigorous, strenuous; concentrated, condensed, accelerated; detailed, minute, close, meticulous, scrupulous, painstaking, methodical, careful.
—OPPOSITES: cursory.

intent n. AIM, intention, purpose, objective, object, goal, target; design, end, plan, scheme; wish, desire, hope, dream, ambition, idea, aspiration.
▶ adj. ☞ DETERMINED 1.
□**for/to all intents and purposes** IN EFFECT, effectively, in essence, essentially, virtually, practically; more or less, just about, all but, as good as, in all but name, almost, nearly; informal pretty much, pretty well; literary nigh on.

intention n. ☞ INTENT n.

intentional adj. DELIBERATE, calculated, conscious, intended, planned, volitional, voluntary, meant, studied, knowing, wilful, purposeful, purposive, done on purpose, considered, premeditated, pre-planned, preconceived; rare witting.

interact v. COMMUNICATE, interface, connect, co-operate; meet, socialize, mix, be in contact, have dealings, work together.

intercourse n. 1 DEALINGS, relations, relationships, association, connections, contact; interchange, communication, communion, correspondence; negotiations, transactions; informal doings, truck. 2 SEXUAL INTERCOURSE, sex, lovemaking, sexual relations, intimacy, coupling, mating, copulation, penetration; informal nookie, whoopee, bonking; technical coitus, coition; formal fornication; dated carnal knowledge.

interest n. 1 ATTENTIVENESS, attention, absorption; heed, regard, notice; curiosity, inquisitiveness; enjoyment, delight, enthusiasm. 2 CONCERN, consequence, importance, import, significance, note, relevance, value, weight; formal moment. 3 PURSUIT, pastime, hobby, recreation, diversion, amusement; passion, enthusiasm; informal thing, bag, cup of tea. 4 STAKE, share, claim, investment, stock, equity; involvement, concern. 5 DIVIDENDS, profits, returns; a percentage.
—OPPOSITES: boredom.
▶ v. APPEAL TO, be of interest to, attract, intrigue, fascinate; absorb, engross, rivet, grip, captivate; amuse, divert, entertain; arouse one's curiosity, whet one's appetite; informal float someone's boat, tickle someone's fancy.
—OPPOSITES: bore.

interested adj. 1 ATTENTIVE, intent, absorbed, engrossed, fascinated, riveted, gripped, captivated, rapt, agog; intrigued, inquisitive, curious; keen, eager; informal all ears, nosy, snoopy. 2 ☞ CONCERNED 2.

interesting adj. ABSORBING, engrossing, fascinating, riveting, gripping, consuming, unputdownable, compelling, compulsive, captivating, engaging, enthralling; appealing, attractive; amusing, entertaining, stimulating, lively, thought-provoking, diverting, intriguing, challenging, exciting, thrilling; giving one food for thought, inspirational, inspiring, provocative, refreshing, rousing, sparkling, stirring.

interfere v. **1** IMPEDE, obstruct, stand in the way of, hinder, inhibit, restrict, constrain, hamper, handicap, cramp, check, block; disturb, disrupt, influence, impinge, affect, confuse. **2** ☞ MEDDLE.

interim adj. ☞ PROVISIONAL.
—OPPOSITES: permanent.

interior adj. **1** INSIDE, inner, internal, intramural. **2** INLAND, inshore, upcountry, inner, innermost, central. **3** INNER, mental, spiritual, psychological; private, personal, intimate, secret.
—OPPOSITES: exterior, outer, foreign.
▶ n. **1** INSIDE, inner part/space, depths, recesses, bowels, belly; centre, core, heart, inner part, middle. **2** CENTRE, heartland, hinterland, backcountry, the bush.
—OPPOSITES: exterior, outside.

interject v. INTERPOSE, introduce, throw in, interpolate, add. See also INTERRUPT 1.

interlude n. ☞ PAUSE.

intermediary n. ☞ MEDIATOR.

intermediate adj. IN-BETWEEN, middle, mid, midway, halfway, median, medial, intermediary, intervening, transitional.

interminable adj. ☞ ENDLESS 2.

intermittent adj. SPORADIC, irregular, fitful, spasmodic, broken, fragmentary, discontinuous, isolated, random, patchy, scattered; occasional, periodic, episodic, on and off; informal herky-jerky.
—OPPOSITES: continuous.

internal adj. **1** INNER, interior, inside, intramural, inmost, innermost; central. **2** DOMESTIC, home, interior, civil, local; national, federal, provincial, state. **3** MENTAL, psychological, emotional; personal, private, secret, hidden.
—OPPOSITES: external, foreign.

international adj. GLOBAL, worldwide, intercontinental, universal; multinational.
—OPPOSITES: national, local.

Internet n. WORLD WIDE WEB, web, cyberspace, Net, information (super)highway.

interpret v. **1** EXPLAIN, elucidate, expound, explicate, clarify, illuminate, shed light on. **2** TAKE (TO MEAN), construe, understand, see, regard. **3** TRANSLATE, transliterate, transcribe, paraphrase; decipher, decode, unscramble, make intelligible; understand, comprehend, make sense of, figure out; informal crack.

interrogate v. ☞ QUESTION v. 1.

interrogation n. QUESTIONING, cross-questioning, cross-examination, quizzing; interview, debriefing, inquiry, the third degree; informal grilling; Law examination.

interrupt v. **1** CUT IN (ON), break in (on), barge in (on), intervene (in), put one's oar in, put one's two cents in, poke one's nose in, interject, interfere; *informal* butt in (on), chime in (with). **2** SUSPEND, adjourn, discontinue, break off, put on hold; stop, halt, cease, end, bring to an end/close; *informal* put on ice, put on the back burner.

intersect *v.* CROSS, criss-cross; *technical* decussate.

intersection *n.* **1** CROSSING, criss-crossing; meeting. **2** (ROAD) JUNCTION, T-intersection, interchange, crossroads, corner, cloverleaf.

intervene *v.* INTERCEDE, involve oneself, get involved, interpose oneself, step in; mediate, referee; interfere, intrude, meddle, interrupt.

interview *n.* MEETING, discussion, conference, examination, interrogation; audience, talk, dialogue, exchange, conversation.
▶ *v.* TALK TO, have a discussion/dialogue with; question, interrogate, cross-examine, meet with; poll, canvass, survey, sound out; *informal* grill, pump; *Law* examine.

intimate *adj.* **1** CLOSE, bosom, dear, cherished, faithful, fast, firm, familiar; *informal* chummy. **2** FRIENDLY, warm, welcoming, hospitable, relaxed, informal; cozy, comfortable, snug; *informal* comfy. **3** PERSONAL, private, confidential, secret; innermost, inner, inward, unspoken, undisclosed. **4** SEXUAL, carnal, amorous.
—OPPOSITES: distant, formal.

intimidate *v.* FRIGHTEN, menace, terrify, scare, terrorize, cow,

dragoon, subdue; threaten, browbeat, bully, tyrannize, pressure, harass, harry, hassle, hound; *informal* lean on, bulldoze, railroad, bullyrag, strong-arm.

intolerable *adj.* ☞ UNBEARABLE.
—OPPOSITES: bearable.

intolerant *adj.* **1** BIGOTED, narrow-minded, small-minded, parochial, provincial, illiberal, uncompromising; prejudiced, biased, partial, partisan, discriminatory. **2** ALLERGIC, sensitive, hypersensitive.

intonation *n.* INFLECTION, pitch, tone, timbre, cadence, lilt, accent, modulation, speech pattern.

intoxicated *adj.* DRUNK, inebriated, inebriate, impaired♣, drunken, tipsy, under the influence; *informal* plastered, smashed, bombed, sloshed, sozzled, hammered, sauced, lubricated, well-oiled, wrecked, juiced, blasted, stinko, blitzed, half-cut, fried, gassed, polluted, pissed, tanked (up), soaked, out of one's head/skull, loaded, trashed, buzzed, befuddled, hopped up, besotted, pickled, pixilated, canned, cockeyed, wasted, blotto, blind drunk, roaring drunk, dead drunk, punch-drunk, ripped, stewed, soused, tight, high, merry, the worse for wear, far gone, pie-eyed, in one's cups, three sheets to the wind; *literary* crapulous.
—OPPOSITES: sober.

intricate *adj.* ☞ COMPLICATED.

intrigue *v.* ☞ INTEREST *v.*
▶ *n.* SECRET PLAN, plotting, plot, conspiracy, collusion, conniving, scheme, scheming, stratagem, machination, trickery, sharp

practice, double-dealing, underhandedness, subterfuge; *informal* dirty tricks.

intrinsic *adj.* ☞ INHERENT.

introduce *v.* **1** ☞ LAUNCH 3.
2 PROPOSE, put forward, suggest, table, submit, bring down; raise, broach, bring up, mention, air, float. **3** PRESENT (FORMALLY), make known, acquaint with.
4 ANNOUNCE, present, give an introduction to; start off, begin, open.

introduction *n.* **1** INSTITUTION, establishment, initiation, launch, inauguration, foundation; start, commencement, debut, inception, origination. **2** PRESENTATION; meeting. **3** FOREWORD, preface, preamble, prologue, prelude; opening (statement), beginning; *informal* intro, lead-in, prelims.
4 PRIMER, basic explanation/ account of; the basics, the rudiments, the fundamentals.
5 INITIATION, induction, inauguration, baptism.

introductory *adj.* **1** ☞ INITIAL.
2 ELEMENTARY, basic, rudimentary, primary; initiatory, preparatory, entry-level, survey; *informal* 101.
—OPPOSITES: final, advanced.

introspective *adj.* INWARD-LOOKING, self-analyzing, introverted, introvert, brooding; contemplative, thoughtful, pensive, meditative, reflective; *informal* navel-gazing.

intrude *v.* ENCROACH, impinge, interfere, trespass, infringe, obtrude, invade, violate, disturb, disrupt, interrupt; meddle, barge (in), impose oneself, infiltrate;

informal horn in, muscle in, poke one's nose into.

intruder *n.* TRESPASSER, interloper, invader, infiltrator; burglar, housebreaker, thief, prowler.

intuition *n.* **1** INSTINCT, intuitiveness; sixth sense, clairvoyance, second sight.
2 ☞ HUNCH.

inundate *v.* **1** ☞ FLOOD 1.
2 OVERWHELM, overrun, overload, bog down, swamp, flood, deluge, besiege, snow under, bombard, glut.

invade *v.* **1** OCCUPY, conquer, capture, seize, take (over), annex, win, gain, secure; march into, storm. **2** ☞ INTRUDE. **3** OVERRUN, swarm, overwhelm, inundate.
—OPPOSITES: withdraw.

invalid *adj.* **1** (LEGALLY) VOID, null and void, unenforceable, not binding, illegitimate, inapplicable.
2 FALSE, untrue, inaccurate, faulty, fallacious, spurious, unconvincing, unsound, weak, wrong, wide of the mark, off target; untenable, baseless, ill-founded, groundless; *informal* full of holes.
—OPPOSITES: binding, true.

invaluable *adj.* INDISPENSABLE, crucial, critical, key, vital, necessary, irreplaceable, all-important; immeasurable, incalculable, inestimable, priceless.
—OPPOSITES: dispensable.

invariably *adv.* ☞ ALWAYS 1.
—OPPOSITES: sometimes, never.

invasion *n.* **1** OCCUPATION, capture, seizure, annexation, annexing, takeover; storming,

incursion, attack, assault. **2** INFLUX, inundation, flood, rush, torrent, deluge, avalanche, juggernaut. **3** VIOLATION, infringement, interruption, intrusion, encroachment, disturbance, disruption, breach.
—OPPOSITES: withdrawal.

invent v. **1** ORIGINATE, create, design, devise, contrive, develop, innovate, make up; conceive, think up, dream up, come up with, pioneer; coin. **2** ☞ FABRICATE 2.

invention n. **1** ORIGINATION, creation, innovation, devising, development, design. **2** INNOVATION, creation, design, contraption, contrivance, construction, device, gadget; informal brainchild. **3** FABRICATION, concoction, (piece of) fiction, story, tale; lie, untruth, falsehood, fib, myth, fantasy, make-believe; informal tall tale, cock-and-bull story.

inventive adj. ☞ ORIGINAL 1.
—OPPOSITES: unimaginative.

inventor n. ORIGINATOR, creator, innovator; designer, deviser, developer, planner, maker, producer, builder; author, architect; pioneer, mastermind, father, progenitor.

inventory n. LIST, listing, catalogue, record, register, checklist, log, archive; stock, supply, store.

inverse adj. ☞ REVERSE adj. 2.
▶ n. ☞ OPPOSITE n.

invert v. TURN UPSIDE DOWN, upend, upturn, turn around/about, turn inside out, turn back to front, transpose, reverse, flip (over).

invest v. **1** PUT MONEY INTO, provide capital for, fund, back, finance, subsidize, bankroll, underwrite; buy into, buy shares in; informal grubstake. **2** SPEND, expend, put in, venture, speculate, risk; informal lay out. **3** IMBUE, infuse, charge, steep, suffuse, permeate, pervade.

investigate v. INQUIRE INTO, look into, go into, probe, explore, scrutinize, conduct an investigation into, make inquiries about; inspect, analyze, study, examine, consider, research; informal check out, suss out, scope out, dig, get to the bottom of.

investigation n. EXAMINATION, inquiry, Royal Commission, study, inspection, exploration, consideration, analysis, appraisal; research, scrutiny, perusal; probe, review, (background) check, survey, inquest, hearing.

inveterate adj. CONFIRMED, hardened, incorrigible, addicted, habitual, compulsive, obsessive, hopeless, persistent; informal pathological, chronic; dyed-in-the-wool, diehard, hard-core.

invigorate v. ☞ ENERGIZE.
—OPPOSITES: tire.

invincible adj. INVULNERABLE, indestructible, unconquerable, unbeatable, indomitable, unassailable; impregnable, inviolable.
—OPPOSITES: vulnerable.

invisible adj. UNABLE TO BE SEEN, not visible; undetectable, indiscernible, inconspicuous, imperceptible; unseen, unnoticed, unobserved, hidden, veiled, obscured, out of sight.

invite v. **1** ASK, summon, have someone over, request (the pleasure of) someone's company. **2** ASK FOR, request, call for, appeal for, solicit, seek, summon, welcome. **3** ☞ COURT 2.

inviting adj. TEMPTING, enticing, alluring, beguiling; attractive, appealing, pleasant, agreeable, delightful; appetizing, mouth-watering; fascinating, enchanting, entrancing, captivating, intriguing, irresistible, seductive. —OPPOSITES: repellent.

invoke v. **1** CITE, refer to, adduce, instance; resort to, have recourse to, turn to. **2** APPEAL TO, pray to, call on, supplicate, entreat, solicit, beg, implore; literary beseech. **3** SUMMON, call (up), conjure (up).

involuntary adj. ☞ SPONTANEOUS 2. —OPPOSITES: deliberate.

involve v. **1** REQUIRE, necessitate, demand, call for; entail, mean, imply, presuppose. **2** INCLUDE, count in, bring in, take into account, take note of; incorporate, encompass, touch on, embrace, comprehend, cover. —OPPOSITES: preclude, exclude.

involved adj. **1** ASSOCIATED WITH, connected with, concerned in/with. **2** IMPLICATED, incriminated, inculpated, embroiled, entangled, caught up, mixed up. **3** ☞ COMPLICATED. —OPPOSITES: unconnected, straightforward.

iota n. ☞ TRACE 2.

irate adj. ☞ ANGRY.

ironic adj. **1** SARCASTIC, sardonic, cynical, mocking, satirical, caustic, wry. **2** PARADOXICAL, incongruous. —OPPOSITES: sincere.

irrational adj. UNREASONABLE, illogical, groundless, baseless, unfounded, unjustifiable; absurd, ridiculous, ludicrous, preposterous, silly, foolish, senseless. —OPPOSITES: logical.

irrefutable adj. ☞ INDISPUTABLE.

irregular adj. **1** ASYMMETRICAL, non-uniform, uneven, crooked, misshapen, lopsided, twisted; unusual, peculiar, strange, bizarre; jagged, ragged, serrated, indented. **2** ROUGH, bumpy, uneven, pitted, rutted; lumpy, knobbly, gnarled. **3** ☞ IMPROPER 1. —OPPOSITES: straight, smooth.

irrelevant adj. BESIDE THE POINT, immaterial, not pertinent, not germane, off the subject, unconnected, unrelated, peripheral, extraneous, inapposite, inapplicable; unimportant, inconsequential, insignificant, trivial, tangential, neither here nor there.

irreplaceable adj. ☞ INVALUABLE.

irresistible adj. **1** TEMPTING, enticing, alluring, inviting, seductive; attractive, desirable, fetching, appealing, delightful, captivating, beguiling, enchanting, charming, fascinating, tantalizing, magnetic. **2** ☞ OVERWHELMING 2.

irresolute adj. ☞ INDECISIVE 2. —OPPOSITES: decisive.

irresponsible adj. RECKLESS, rash, careless, thoughtless, foolhardy, foolish, impetuous, impulsive, devil-may-care,

delinquent, derelict, negligent;
unreliable, undependable,
untrustworthy, flighty, immature.
—OPPOSITES: sensible.

irreverent *adj.* DISRESPECTFUL,
disdainful, scornful,
contemptuous, derisive,
disparaging; impertinent,
impudent, cheeky, saucy, flippant,
rude, discourteous; impious,
sacrilegious.
—OPPOSITES: respectful.

irrevocable *adj.* IRREVERSIBLE,
unalterable, unchangeable,
immutable, final, binding,
permanent, carved in stone; *Law*
peremptory.

irritable *adj.* BAD-TEMPERED, short-
tempered, irascible, tetchy, testy,
touchy, grumpy, grouchy, moody,
cranky, ornery, crotchety, shirty,
in a (bad) mood, cantankerous,
curmudgeonly, ill-tempered, ill-
humoured, peevish, cross,
fractious, owly, pettish, crabby,
bitchy, chippy, waspish, prickly,
splenetic, dyspeptic, choleric,
crusty, petulant, sulky, short-
fused, snappish, snappy, snarky,
snippy.
—OPPOSITES: good-humoured.

irritate *v.* ☞ ANNOY.

irritation *n.* **1** ANNOYANCE,
exasperation, vexation,
indignation, impatience,
crossness, displeasure,
dissatisfaction, discontent,
chagrin, pique; anger, rage, fury,
wrath, aggravation, resentment;
literary ire. **2** ☞ NUISANCE.
—OPPOSITES: delight.

isolate *v.* **1** CORDON OFF, seal off,
close off, fence off. **2** separate, set/
keep apart, segregate, detach, cut

off, shut away, keep in solitude,
quarantine, cloister, seclude,
sequester. **3** ☞ IDENTIFY 1.
—OPPOSITES: integrate.

isolated *adj.* **1** ☞ DISTANT 1.
2 SOLITARY, lonely, companionless,
friendless; secluded, cloistered,
segregated, unsociable, reclusive,
hermitic, lonesome. **3** UNIQUE,
lone, solitary; unusual,
uncommon, exceptional,
anomalous, abnormal, untypical,
atypical, freak; *informal* one-off.
—OPPOSITES: accessible, sociable,
common.

issue *n.* **1** MATTER (IN QUESTION),
question, point (at issue), affair,
case, subject, topic; problem, bone
of contention, hot potato.
2 EDITION, number, copy,
instalment, volume, publication.
▶ *v.* **1** SEND OUT, put out, release,
deliver, publish, announce,
pronounce, broadcast,
communicate, circulate,
distribute, disseminate, transmit.
2 ☞ SUPPLY *v.* 2. **3** EMANATE,
emerge, exude, flow (out/forth),
pour (out/forth); be emitted.
—OPPOSITES: withdraw.
□ **at issue** ☞ IN QUESTION at
QUESTION. **take issue** ☞
DISAGREE 1.

itch *n.* **1** tingling, irritation,
prickle, prickling, tickle, tickling,
itchiness. **2** ☞ LONGING.
▶ *v.* **1** tingle, prickle, tickle, be
irritated, be itchy. **2** ☞ WANT.

item *n.* **1** THING, article, object,
artifact, piece, product; element,
constituent, component,
ingredient. **2** REPORT, story,
account, article, piece, write-up,
bulletin, feature.

Jj

jab *v. & n.* ☞ POKE *v.* 1, *n.*

jaded *adj.* SURFEITED, sated, satiated, glutted; dulled, blunted, deadened, inured; unmoved, blasé, apathetic; weary, wearied.
—OPPOSITES: fresh.

jagged *adj.* SPIKY, barbed, ragged, rough, uneven, irregular, broken; jaggy, snaggy; serrated, sawtooth, indented.
—OPPOSITES: smooth.

jail *n.* ☞ PRISON.

jam *v.* **1** ☞ STUFF *v.* 2. **2** CROWD, pack, pile, press, squeeze, squish, cram, wedge; throng, mob, occupy, fill, overcrowd, obstruct, block, congest. **3** STICK, become stuck, catch, seize (up), become trapped. **4** ☞ BLOCK *v.* 1.
5 IMPROVISE, play (music), extemporize, ad lib.
▶ *n.* **1** CONGESTION, holdup, bottleneck, gridlock, backup, tie-up, snarl-up, traffic.
2 ☞ PREDICAMENT.

jar *v.* JOLT, jerk, shake, shock, concuss, rattle, vibrate.

jargon *n.* SPECIALIZED LANGUAGE, slang, cant, idiom, argot, patter; *informal* -speak, -ese, -babble, Newspeak, journalese, bureaucratese, technobabble, psychobabble; double-talk, doublespeak; gibberish, gobbledegook, blather.

jaunt *n.* ☞ TRIP *n.* 1.

jaunty *adj.* ☞ CHEERFUL.
—OPPOSITES: depressed, serious.

jealous *adj.* **1** ENVIOUS, covetous, desirous; resentful, grudging, begrudging, green (with envy). **2** SUSPICIOUS, distrustful, mistrustful, doubting, insecure, anxious; possessive, overprotective. **3** PROTECTIVE, vigilant, watchful, heedful, mindful, careful, solicitous.
—OPPOSITES: proud, trusting.

jeer *v.* TAUNT, mock, scoff at, ridicule, sneer at, deride, insult, abuse, heckle, catcall at, boo, whistle at, jibe at, hiss at.
—OPPOSITES: cheer.
▶ *n.* TAUNT, sneer, insult, shout, jibe, boo, hiss, catcall, raspberry, Bronx cheer; derision, teasing, scoffing, abuse, scorn, heckling, catcalling.
—OPPOSITES: applause.

jell *v.* **1** SET, stiffen, solidify, thicken, harden; cake, congeal, coagulate, clot. **2** TAKE SHAPE, fall into place, come together, take form, work out; crystallize.

jeopardy *n.* DANGER, peril; at risk.

jerk *n.* **1** ☞ YANK. **2** JOLT, lurch, bump, start, jar, bang, bounce, shake, shock. **3** BASTARD, scoundrel, slimeball, son of a bitch, SOB, scumbag, scum-bucket, scuzzball, dirtbag, sleazeball, sleazebag; rascal, rogue, scamp, scalawag, ingrate, miscreant, good-for-nothing, nogoodnik, reprobate, cur, cad, hound, low-life, villain, beast, rat (fink), louse, swine, dog, skunk, heel, snake (in the grass); sleeveen; *archaic* blackguard, knave, varlet, whoreson.

▶ *v.* **1** YANK, tug, pull, wrench, wrest, drag, pluck, snatch, seize, rip, tear. **2** JOLT, lurch, bump, rattle, bounce, shake, jounce.

jerky *adj.* CONVULSIVE, spasmodic, fitful, twitchy, shaky; JOLTING, lurching, bumpy, bouncy, jarring.
—OPPOSITES: smooth.

jet *n.* STREAM, spurt, squirt, spray, spout; gush, rush, surge, burst.

jewel *n.* GEM, gemstone, (precious) stone, brilliant; baguette; sparkler, rock; bijou.

jibe *n.* SNIDE REMARK, cutting remark, taunt, sneer, jeer, insult, barb; *informal* dig, put-down.

▶ *v.* AGREE, be in accord, jive, be consistent, square, fit.

jilt *v.* ☞ ABANDON 3.

jingle *n.* **1** CLINK, chink, tinkle, jangle, ding-a-ling, ring, ding, ping, chime, tintinnabulation. **2** THEME; ditty, song, rhyme, tune; slogan, catchphrase.

▶ *v.* CLINK, chink, tinkle, jangle, ring, ding, ping, chime.

job *n.* **1** OCCUPATION, employment, profession, trade, position, career, (line of) work, livelihood, post, situation, appointment, métier, craft; vocation, calling; vacancy, opening; *humorous* McJob, joe job✦. **2** ☞ TASK. **3** ☞ DUTY 2.
—RELATED: vocational.

jobless *adj.* ☞ UNEMPLOYED.
—OPPOSITES: employed.

jockey *n.* RIDER, horseman, horsewoman, equestrian.

▶ *v.* MANOEUVRE, ease, edge, work, steer; compete, contend, vie; struggle, fight, scramble, jostle.

jocular *adj.* CHEERFUL, cheery, jovial, ludic, merry, playful, teasing. See also FUNNY.
—OPPOSITES: solemn.

jog *v.* **1** RUN SLOWLY, jogtrot, dogtrot, trot, lope. **2** STIMULATE, prompt, stir, activate, refresh; prod, jar, nudge.

▶ *n.* **1** RUN, jogtrot, dogtrot, trot, lope. **2** ☞ BEND *n.*

join *v.* **1** ☞ ATTACH 1. **2** COMBINE, amalgamate, merge, join forces, unify, unite, team up, band together, co-operate, collaborate. **3** SIGN UP WITH, enlist in, enrol in, enter, become a member of, be part of. **4** MEET, reach, abut, touch, adjoin, border on, connect with.

joint *n.* JUNCTURE, junction, join, intersection, confluence, nexus, link, linkage, connection; weld, seam, articulation.

▶ *adj.* COMMON, shared, communal, collective; mutual, co-operative, collaborative, concerted, combined, united, bilateral, multilateral.
—OPPOSITES: separate.

jointly *adv.* ☞ TOGETHER 1.

joke *n.* **1** FUNNY STORY, jest, witticism, quip; pun, play on words, gag, wisecrack, crack, one-liner, rib-tickler, knee-slapper, thigh-slapper, punchline, groaner. **2** ☞ PRANK. **3** FARCE, travesty, waste of time.

▶ *v.* TELL JOKES, jest, banter, quip, wisecrack, josh, fool (around), play a trick, play a (practical) joke, tease, hoax, pull someone's leg, skylark, kid, chaff, have someone on, pull someone's chain.

jolly *adj.* ☞ CHEERFUL.
—OPPOSITES: miserable.

jolt *v.* **1** PUSH, thrust, jar, bump, knock, bang; shake, joggle, jog. **2** BUMP, bounce, jerk, rattle, lurch, shudder, judder, jounce. **3** STARTLE, surprise, shock, stun, shake, take aback; astonish, astound, amaze, stagger, stop someone in their tracks; *informal* rock, floor.
▸ *n.* BUMP, bounce, shake, jerk, lurch.

jostle *v.* BUMP INTO/AGAINST, knock into/against, bang into, cannon into, plow into, jolt; push, shove, elbow, mob, thrust, barge, force, shoulder, bulldoze; STRUGGLE, vie, jockey, scramble.

jot *v.* ☞ WRITE 1.
▸ *n.* ☞ TRACE *n.* 2.

journal *n.* **1** PERIODICAL, magazine, gazette, digest, review, newsletter, bulletin; newspaper, paper, tabloid, broadsheet; daily, weekly, monthly, quarterly. **2** ☞ DIARY *n.* 2.

journalist *n.* REPORTER, correspondent, columnist, writer, commentator, contributor, reviewer, critic; investigative journalist, photojournalist, newspaperman, newspaperwoman, newsman, newswoman, newshound, newshawk, hack, stringer, journo, scribbler, pencil-pusher.

journey *n.* ☞ TRIP *n.* 1.
▸ *v.* ☞ TRAVEL *v.* 1.

jovial *adj.* ☞ CHEERFUL.
—OPPOSITES: miserable.

joy *n.* DELIGHT, great pleasure, joyfulness, jubilation, triumph, exultation, rejoicing, happiness, gladness, glee, exhilaration, exuberance, elation, euphoria, bliss, ecstasy, rapture; enjoyment, felicity, joie de vivre, jouissance; *literary* jocundity.
—OPPOSITES: misery.

joyful *adj.* ☞ HAPPY 1, CHEERFUL.
—OPPOSITES: sad, distressing.

judge *n.* **1** JUSTICE, magistrate, sheriff, jurist. **2** ADJUDICATOR, arbiter, arbitrator, assessor, evaluator, referee, ombudsman, ombudsperson, appraiser, examiner, moderator, mediator.
▸ *v.* **1** FORM THE OPINION, conclude, decide; consider, believe, think, deem, view; deduce, gather, infer, gauge, estimate, guess, surmise, conjecture; regard as, look on as, take to be, rate as, class as; *informal* reckon, figure. **2** TRY, hear; adjudicate, decide, give a ruling/verdict on. **3** ADJUDGE, pronounce, decree, rule, find. **4** ADJUDICATE, arbitrate, mediate, moderate; ASSESS, appraise, evaluate; examine, review.

judgment *n.* **1** DISCERNMENT, acumen, shrewdness, astuteness, (common) sense, perception, perspicacity, percipience, acuity, discrimination, reckoning, wisdom, wit, judiciousness, prudence, canniness, sharpness, powers of reasoning, reason, logic; savvy, horse sense, street smarts, gumption. **2** ☞ RULING. **3** ASSESSMENT, evaluation, appraisal; review, analysis, criticism, critique.

judgmental *adj.* ☞ CRITICAL 1.

judicial *adj.* LEGAL, juridical; official.

judicious *adj.* ☞ PRUDENT.
—OPPOSITES: ill-advised.

jug *n.* PITCHER, carafe, flask, flagon, bottle, decanter, ewer, crock, jar, urn; *historical* amphora.

juggle *v.* HANDLE, manage, deal with, multi-task.

juicy *adj.* **1** SUCCULENT, tender, moist; ripe. **2** SENSATIONAL, lurid, scandalous, spicy.
—OPPOSITES: dry.

jumble *n.* UNTIDY HEAP, clutter, muddle, mess, confusion, disarray, tangle, imbroglio; hodgepodge, mishmash, miscellany, motley collection, mixed bag, medley, jambalaya, farrago, gallimaufry.
▶ *v.* MIX UP, muddle up, disarrange, disorganize, disorder, put in disarray.

jump *v.* **1** LEAP, spring, bound, hop; skip, caper, dance, prance, frolic, cavort. **2** VAULT (OVER), leap over, clear, sail over, hop over, hurdle. **3** ☞ RISE *v.* 3.
▶ *n.* **1** LEAP, spring, vault, bound, hop. **2** ☞ RISE *n.* 1.
□ **jump the gun** (*informal*) ACT PREMATURELY, act too soon, be overhasty, be precipitate, be rash; *informal* be ahead of oneself.

jumpy *adj.* **1** ☞ TENSE 2. **2** JERKY, jolting, lurching, bumpy, jarring; fitful, convulsive.
—OPPOSITES: calm.

junction *n.* **1** ☞ JOINT 1.
2 CONFLUENCE, convergence, meeting point, juncture.

juncture *n.* **1** POINT (IN TIME), time, moment (in time); period,
occasion, phase. **2** ☞ JOINT 1.
3 ☞ JUNCTION 2.

junior *adj.* **1** YOUNGER, youngest.
2 LOW-RANKING, lower-ranking, entry-level, subordinate, lesser, lower, minor, secondary.
—OPPOSITES: senior, older.

junk *n.* RUBBISH, clutter, odds and ends, bric-a-brac, bits and pieces; garbage, trash, refuse, litter, scrap, waste, debris, detritus, dross; *informal* crap.

just *adj.* **1** FAIR, fair-minded, equitable, even-handed, impartial, unbiased, objective, neutral, disinterested, unprejudiced, open-minded, non-partisan; honourable, upright, decent, honest, righteous, moral, virtuous, principled. **2** (WELL) DESERVED, (well) earned, merited; rightful, due, fitting, appropriate, suitable; *formal* condign; *archaic* meet. **3** ☞ JUSTIFIABLE.
—OPPOSITES: unfair, undeserved, unfair.
▶ *adv.* **1** EXACTLY, precisely, absolutely, completely, totally, entirely, perfectly, utterly, wholly, thoroughly, in all respects; *informal* to a T, dead. **2** NARROWLY, only just, by a hair's breadth; barely, scarcely, hardly; *informal* by the skin of one's teeth, by a whisker.
3 ONLY, merely, simply, (nothing) but, no more than.

justice *n.* **1** FAIRNESS, justness, fair play, fair-mindedness, equity, even-handedness, impartiality, objectivity, neutrality, disinterestedness, honesty, righteousness, morals, morality.
2 PUNISHMENT, judgment, retribution, compensation, just

deserts.

□ **do justice to** consider fairly, be worthy of.

justifiable *adj.* VALID, legitimate, sound, warranted, well-founded, justified, just, reasonable; defensible, tenable, supportable, acceptable.

—OPPOSITES: indefensible.

justify *v.* **1** GIVE GROUNDS FOR, give reasons for, give a justification for, explain, give an explanation for, account for; defend, answer

for, vindicate. **2** WARRANT, be good reason for, be a justification for.

jut *v.* STICK OUT, project, protrude, bulge out, overhang.

juvenile *adj.* **1** YOUNG, teenage, adolescent, boyish, girlish, junior, pubescent, prepubescent, youthful. **2** ☞ IMMATURE 2.

—OPPOSITES: adult, mature.

▶ *n.* YOUNG PERSON, youngster, child, teenager, adolescent, youth, boy, girl, minor, junior; *informal* kid, punk.

—OPPOSITES: adult.

Kk

keen *adj.* **1** EAGER, anxious, intent, impatient, determined, ambitious; *informal* raring, itching, dying. **2** ENTHUSIASTIC, avid, eager, ardent, passionate, fervent, impassioned; conscientious, committed, dedicated, zealous. **3** SENSITIVE, acute, discerning, sharp, perceptive, clear. **4** ACUTE, penetrating, astute, incisive, sharp, perceptive, piercing, razor-sharp, perspicacious, shrewd, discerning, clever, intelligent, brilliant, bright, smart, wise, canny, percipient, insightful. **5** ☞ INTENSE 2.
—OPPOSITES: reluctant, unenthusiastic.

keener (*Cdn*) *n.* eager beaver, geek, zealot, a keen/enthusiastic/eager person, joiner.

keep *v.* **1** RETAIN (POSSESSION OF), hold on to, keep hold of, not part with; save, store, conserve, put aside, set aside; *informal* hang on to, stash away. **2** REMAIN, continue to be, stay, carry on being, persist in being. **3** PERSIST IN, keep on, carry on, continue, do something constantly. **4** PRESERVE, keep alive/up, keep going, carry on, perpetuate, maintain, uphold, sustain. **5** STORE, house, stow, put (away), place, deposit.
—OPPOSITES: throw away, break, abandon.
▶ *n.* MAINTENANCE, upkeep, sustenance, board (and lodging), food, livelihood.
☐ **keep at** ☞ PERSEVERE. **keep from** REFRAIN FROM, stop oneself, restrain oneself from, prevent oneself from, forbear from, avoid. **keep on** ☞ CONTINUE 1. **keep up with** KEEP PACE WITH, keep abreast of; match, equal.

keeper *n.* GUARDIAN, custodian, curator, administrator, overseer, steward, caretaker.

keepsake *n.* MEMENTO, souvenir, reminder, remembrance, token; party favour, bomboniere.

key *n.* ANSWER, clue, solution, explanation; basis, foundation, requisite, precondition, means, way, route, path, passport, secret, formula.
▶ *adj.* ☞ MAIN.
—OPPOSITES: peripheral.

kick *v.* BOOT, punt, drop-kick, hoof, strike with the foot.
▶ *n.* **1** BLOW WITH THE FOOT; *informal* boot. **2** (*informal*) THRILL, excitement, stimulation, tingle; fun, enjoyment, amusement, pleasure, gratification; *informal* buzz, high, rush, charge. **3** (*informal*) POTENCY, stimulant effect, strength, power; tang, zest, bite, piquancy, edge, pungency; *informal* punch.
☐ **kick off** ☞ BEGIN *v.* 1. **kick someone out** ☞ EVICT.

kid *v.* **1** JOKE, tease, jest, chaff, be facetious, fool around, pull someone's leg, pull someone's chain, have on, rib. **2** DELUDE, deceive, fool, trick, hoodwink, hoax, beguile, dupe, gull; *informal* con, pull the wool over someone's eyes.

kidnap *v.* ☞ ABDUCT.

kill *v.* **1** MURDER, take/end the life of, assassinate, eliminate, terminate, dispatch, finish off, put to death, execute; slaughter, butcher, massacre, wipe out, annihilate, exterminate, liquidate, mow down, shoot down, cut down, cut to pieces; *informal* bump off, polish off, do away with, do in, knock off, take out, croak, stiff, blow away, dispose of, ice, snuff, rub out, waste, whack, scrag, smoke; *euphemistic* neutralize; *literary* slay. **2** DESTROY, put an end to, end, extinguish, dash, quash, ruin, wreck, shatter, smash, crush, scotch, thwart; *informal* put paid to, put the kibosh on, stymie, scupper, scuttle. **3** ALLEVIATE, assuage, soothe, allay, dull, blunt, deaden, stifle, suppress, subdue. **4** (*informal*) VETO, defeat, vote down, rule against, reject, throw out, overrule, overturn, put a stop to, quash, squash.
—RELATED: -cide.

killer *n.* MURDERER, assassin, slaughterer, butcher, serial killer, gunman; executioner, hit man, cutthroat; homicide.

killing *n.* MURDER, assassination, homicide, manslaughter, elimination, putting to death, putting down, execution; slaughter, massacre, butchery, carnage, bloodshed, extermination, annihilation; *literary* slaying.

killjoy *n.* SPOILSPORT, wet blanket, damper, party-pooper, prophet of doom.

kilter
☐ **off kilter**, **out of kilter** AWRY, off balance, unbalanced, out of order, disordered, confused, muddled, out of tune, out of whack, out of step.

kin *n.* ☞ RELATIVE.

kind *adj.* KINDLY, good-natured, kind-hearted, warm-hearted, caring, affectionate, loving, warm; considerate, helpful, thoughtful, obliging, unselfish, selfless, altruistic, good, attentive; compassionate, sympathetic, understanding, big-hearted, benevolent, benign, friendly, neighbourly, hospitable, well-meaning, public-spirited.
—OPPOSITES: inconsiderate, mean.
▶ *n.* TYPE, sort, nature, manner, variety, class, category, style; calibre, quality, form, group, set, bracket, genre, species, breed, race, family, order, generation, vintage, make, model, brand, stamp, stripe, flavour, ilk, cast, grain, mould.
☐ **kind of** (*informal*) SOMEWHAT, quite, fairly, rather, a little, slightly, a shade; sort of, a bit, kinda, pretty, a touch, a tad.

kindle *v.* **1** ☞ IGNITE 2. **2** ROUSE, arouse, wake, awake, awaken; stimulate, inspire, stir (up), excite, evoke, provoke, fire, inflame, trigger, activate, spark off; *literary* waken, enkindle.
—OPPOSITES: extinguish.

kindred *n.* ☞ RELATIVE.

▸ *adj.* LIKE-MINDED, in sympathy, in harmony, in tune, of one mind, akin, similar, like, compatible; *informal* on the same wavelength.
—OPPOSITES: unrelated, alien.

king *n.* RULER, sovereign, monarch, crowned head, Crown, emperor, prince, potentate, lord.

kink *n.* **1** CURL, twist, twirl, loop, crinkle; knot, tangle, entanglement. **2** FLAW, defect, imperfection, problem, complication, hitch, snag, shortcoming, weakness; *informal* hiccup, glitch. **3** CRICK, stiffness, pinch, knot.

kinky *adj.* **1** (*informal*) PROVOCATIVE, sexy, erotic, titillating, naughty, indecent, immodest. **2** ☞ CURLY.

kit *n.* EQUIPMENT, tools, implements, instruments, gadgets, utensils, appliances, tools of the trade, gear, tackle, hardware, paraphernalia; *informal* things, stuff, the necessaries; *Military* accoutrements.

kitschy *adj.* ☞ TACKY.

klutz *n.* SCHLUB, butterfingers, stumblebum, oaf, galoot, lubber, lug, lummox, hobbledehoy, boor, ape.

knack *n.* **1** GIFT, talent, flair, genius, instinct, faculty, ability, capability, capacity, aptitude, aptness, bent, forte, facility; TECHNIQUE, method, trick, skill, adroitness, art, expertise; *informal* the hang of something. **2** TENDENCY, propensity, habit, proneness, liability, predisposition.

knead *v.* PUMMEL, work, pound, squeeze, shape, mould.

knee-jerk *adj.* IMPULSIVE, automatic, spontaneous, instinctive, mechanical, unthinking, hasty, rash, reckless, impetuous, precipitate.

kneel *v.* FALL TO ONE'S KNEES, get down on one's knees, genuflect; *historical* kowtow.

knife *n.* CUTTING TOOL, blade, cutter.

▸ *v.* ☞ STAB 1, CUT 1.

knit *v.* **1** UNITE, unify, come together, draw together, become closer, bond, fuse, coalesce, merge, meld, blend. **2** FURROW, tighten, contract, gather, wrinkle.

knob *n.* **1** LUMP, bump, protuberance, protrusion, bulge, swelling, knot, node, nodule, ball, boss. **2** DIAL, button.

knock *v.* **1** BANG, tap, rap, thump, pound, hammer; strike, hit, beat. **2** BUMP, bang, hit, strike, crack; injure, hurt, bruise; *informal* bash, thwack.

▸ *n.* **1** TAP, rap, rat-tat-tat, knocking, bang, banging, pounding, hammering, drumming, thump, thud. **2** BUMP, blow, bang, jolt, jar, shock; collision, crash, smash, impact.
☐ **knock someone/something down** FELL, floor, flatten, bring down, knock to the ground; knock over, run over/down; DEMOLISH, pull down, tear down, destroy; raze (to the ground), level, bulldoze. **knock someone out 1** KNOCK UNCONSCIOUS, knock senseless; floor, prostrate, put out cold, KO, kayo. **2** ☞ FATIGUE.

knoll *n.* MOUND, hillock, rise, hummock, hill, drumlin, hump, bank, ridge, elevation, (*Nfld*) tolt✦.

knot *n.* **1** TIE, twist, loop, bow, hitch, half hitch, clove hitch, join, fastening; square knot, reef knot, slip knot, overhand knot, granny knot; tangle, entanglement. **2** NODULE, node; lump, knob, swelling, gall, protuberance, bump, burl.

know *v.* **1** BE AWARE, realize, be conscious, be informed; notice, perceive, see, sense, recognize; *informal* be clued in, savvy. **2** HAVE KNOWLEDGE OF, be informed of, be apprised of; *formal* be cognizant of. **3** BE FAMILIAR WITH, be conversant with, be acquainted with, have knowledge of, be versed in, have mastered, have a grasp of, understand, comprehend; have learned, have memorized, be up to speed on. **4** BE ACQUAINTED WITH, have met, be familiar with; be friends with, be friendly with, be on good terms with, be close to, be intimate with. **5** EXPERIENCE, go through, live through, undergo, taste.

knowing *adj.* **1** SIGNIFICANT, meaningful, eloquent, expressive, suggestive; ARCH. sly, mischievous, impish, teasing, playful. **2** DELIBERATE, intentional, conscious, calculated, wilful, done on purpose, premeditated, planned, preconceived.

knowledge *n.* **1** UNDERSTANDING, comprehension, grasp, command, mastery; expertise, skill, proficiency, expertness, accomplishment, adeptness, capacity, capability; *informal* know-how. **2** ☞ LEARNING. **3** AWARENESS, consciousness, realization, cognition, apprehension, perception, appreciation; *formal* cognizance.
—OPPOSITES: ignorance.

knowledgeable *adj.* **1** WELL-INFORMED, learned, well-read, (well) educated, erudite, scholarly, cultured, cultivated, enlightened. **2** ACQUAINTED, familiar, conversant, au courant, au fait; having a knowledge of, up on, up to date with, up to speed on, abreast of, plugged in, well-grounded.
—OPPOSITES: ill-informed.

known *adj.* RECOGNIZED, well-known, widely known, noted, celebrated, notable, notorious; acknowledged, self-confessed, declared, overt.

LI

label *n.* **1** TAG, ticket, tab, sticker, marker. **2** DESIGNATION, description, tag; name, epithet, nickname, title, sobriquet, pet name, cognomen; *formal* denomination, appellation.
▶ *v.* CATEGORIZE, classify, class, describe, designate, identify; mark, stamp, brand, condemn, pigeonhole, stereotype, typecast; call, name, term, dub, nickname.

laborious *adj.* **1** ☞ ARDUOUS, WEARISOME 1. **2** ☞ LABOURED 1.
—OPPOSITES: easy, effortless.

labour *n.* **1** (HARD) WORK, toil, exertion, industry, drudgery, effort, donkey work, menial work; *informal* slog, grind, sweat, elbow grease, scutwork; *literary* travail, moil. **2** ☞ CHILDBIRTH.
—OPPOSITES: rest.

laboured *adj.* **1** STRAINED, difficult, forced, laborious. **2** CONTRIVED, strained, stilted, forced, stiff, unnatural, artificial, overdone, ponderous, over-elaborate, laborious, unconvincing, overwrought.

lacerate *v.* CUT (OPEN), gash, slash, tear, rip, rend, shred, score, scratch, scrape, graze; wound, injure, hurt.

lack *n.* ABSENCE, want, need, deficiency, dearth, insufficiency, inadequacy, shortage, shortfall, scarcity, paucity, unavailability, deficit, deprivation.
—OPPOSITES: abundance.
▶ *v.* BE WITHOUT, be in need of, need, be lacking, require, want, be short of, be deficient in, be bereft of, be low on, be pressed for, have insufficient; *informal* be strapped for.
—OPPOSITES: have, possess.

lacking *adj.* ☞ WANTING 1, 2.
—OPPOSITES: present, plentiful.

lacklustre *adj.* ☞ MEDIOCRE.

laden *adj.* LOADED, burdened, weighed down, encumbered, overloaded, piled high, fully charged; full, filled, packed, stuffed, crammed; *informal* chock full, chockablock.

lady *n.* **1** ☞ WOMAN 1.
2 NOBLEWOMAN, duchess, countess, peeress, viscountess, baroness; *archaic* gentlewoman.

lag *v.* FALL BEHIND, straggle, fall back, trail (behind), hang back, not keep pace, bring up the rear, dawdle, dilly-dally.
—OPPOSITES: keep up.

laid-back *adj.* RELAXED, easygoing, free and easy, loosey-goosey, casual, nonchalant, unexcitable, imperturbable, unruffled, blasé, cool, equable, even-tempered, insouciant, calm, unperturbed, unflustered, unflappable, unworried, unconcerned, unbothered;

leisurely, unhurried, Type-B; stoical, phlegmatic, tolerant.
—OPPOSITES: uptight.

lair n. DEN, burrow, hole, tunnel, cave.

lake n. POND, pool, tarn, reservoir, slough, lagoon, water, water hole, inland sea, loch; oxbow (lake), pothole (lake), glacial lake; *literary* mere.
—RELATED: lacustrine.

lame adj. **1** LIMPING, hobbling; crippled, disabled, incapacitated; *dated* game. **2** ☞ WEAK 3.
—OPPOSITES: convincing.

lament v. **1** ☞ GRIEVE 1. **2** BEMOAN, bewail, complain about, deplore, rue; protest against, object to, oppose, fulminate against, inveigh against, denounce.
—OPPOSITES: celebrate.

lamentable adj. DEPLORABLE, regrettable, sad, terrible, awful, wretched, woeful, dire, disastrous, grave, appalling, dreadful, pitiful, shameful, sorrowful, unfortunate.
—OPPOSITES: wonderful.

lampoon v. ☞ MOCK 2.
▶ n. ☞ PARODY.

land n. **1** GROUNDS, fields, terrain, territory, open space; property, landholding, acres, acreage, estate, lands, real estate, realty; *historical* demesne. **2** SOIL, earth, loam, topsoil, humus; tillage. **3** ☞ COUNTRY 1. **4** TERRA FIRMA, dry land; coast, coastline, shore.
—RELATED: terrestrial.
▶ v. **1** DISEMBARK, go ashore, debark, alight, get off. **2** TOUCH DOWN, make a landing, come in to land, come down. **3** PERCH, settle, come to rest, alight. **4** ☞ OBTAIN

5 ☞ DEAL v. 3.
—OPPOSITES: sail, take off.

landmark n. **1** MARKER, mark, indicator, beacon, inukshuk, cairn, lobstick✦. **2** TURNING POINT, milestone, watershed, critical point, way station, benchmark.
▶ adj. ☞ HISTORIC.

landscape n. SCENERY, countryside, topography, country, terrain; outlook, view, vista, prospect, aspect, panorama, perspective, sweep; environment, setting, surroundings.

lane n. alley, alleyway, laneway✦, back alley, back lane, byroad, byway, track, road, street.

language n. **1** SPEECH, writing, communication, conversation, speaking, talking, talk, discourse; words, vocabulary. **2** TONGUE, mother tongue, native tongue, heritage language✦; dialect, patois, slang, idiom, jargon, argot, cant; *informal* lingo. **3** WORDING, phrasing, phraseology, style, vocabulary, terminology, expressions, turns of phrase, parlance, form/mode of expression, usages, locutions, choice of words, idiolect; *informal* lingo.
—RELATED: linguistic.

languid adj. **1** RELAXED, unhurried, languorous, slow; listless, lethargic, sluggish, lazy, idle, indolent, apathetic; *informal* laid-back. **2** LEISURELY, languorous, relaxed, restful, lazy. **3** SICKLY, weak, faint, feeble, frail, delicate; tired, weary, fatigued.
—OPPOSITES: energetic.

languish v. WEAKEN, deteriorate, decline; wither, droop, wilt, fade,

waste away, go downhill, rot, be abandoned, be neglected, be forgotten.
—OPPOSITES: thrive.

lanky *adj.* TALL, THIN, slender, slim, lean, lank, skinny, spindly, scrawny, spare, bony, gangling, gangly, gawky, rangy.
—OPPOSITES: stocky.

lap *n.* CIRCUIT, leg, circle, revolution, round; length.

lapse *n.* **1** FAILURE, failing, slip, error, mistake, blunder, fault, omission, hiccup; *informal* slip-up. **2** DECLINE, fall, falling, slipping, drop, deterioration, degeneration, backsliding, regression, retrogression, descent, sinking, slide.
▶ *v.* **1** ☞ EXPIRE 1. **2** ☞ REGRESS.

large *adj.* **1** ☞ BIG 1. **2** BIG, burly, heavy, tall, bulky, thickset, chunky, strapping, hulking, hefty, muscular, brawny, solid, powerful, sturdy, strong, rugged; fat, plump, overweight, chubby, stout, meaty, fleshy, portly, rotund, flabby, paunchy, obese, corpulent; hunky, roly-poly, beefy, tubby, well-upholstered, pudgy, well-fed, big-boned, zaftig, full-figured, buxom, corn-fed, Herculean, broad-shouldered, gigantic, huge, husky, muscly, stark, stocky, thewy, well-built. **3** ABUNDANT, copious, plentiful, ample, liberal, generous, lavish, bountiful, bumper, boundless, good, considerable, superabundant; *literary* plenteous.
—RELATED: macro-, mega-.
—OPPOSITES: small, meagre.
☐ **at large** ☞ LOOSE *adj.* 2. **by and large** ON THE WHOLE, generally, in general, all things considered, all in all, for the most part, in the main, as a rule, overall, almost always, mainly, mostly; on average, on balance.

largely *adv.* ☞ MAINLY.

largesse *n.* ☞ GENEROSITY.
—OPPOSITES: meanness.

lash *v.* **1** FASTEN, bind, tie (up), tether, hitch, knot, rope, make fast. **2** BEAT AGAINST, dash against, pound, batter, strike, hit, knock.
▶ *n.* **1** WHIP, horsewhip, scourge, thong, flail, strap, birch, cane, switch; *historical* cat-o'-nine-tails, cat, knout. **2** STROKE, blow, hit, strike, welt, thwack; *archaic* stripe.
☐ **lash out** CRITICIZE, chastise, censure, attack, condemn, denounce, lambaste, rail at/against, harangue, pillory; berate, upbraid, rebuke, reproach, tear a strip off; *informal* lay into, tear into, blast; *formal* castigate.

last *v.* **1** CONTINUE, go on, carry on, keep on/going, proceed, take; stay, remain, persist. **2** SURVIVE, endure, hold on/out, keep going, persevere; stick it out, hang on; wear well, stand up, bear up; go the distance.
▶ *adj.* **1** REARMOST, hindmost, endmost, at the end, at the back, furthest (back), final, ultimate. **2** CLOSING, concluding, final, ending, end, terminal; later, latter. **3** PREVIOUS, preceding; prior, former. **4** FINAL, only remaining.
—OPPOSITES: first, early, next.
☐ **at last** FINALLY, at long last, after a long time, in the end, eventually, ultimately, in (the fullness of) time. **last hurrah**

SWAN SONG, grand finale, curtain call.

last-ditch *adj.* ☞ DESPERATE 2.

late *adj.* **1** BEHIND SCHEDULE, behind time, behindhand; tardy, running late, overdue, belated, delayed.
2 DEAD, departed, lamented, passed on/away, deceased.
—OPPOSITES: punctual, early.
▶ *adv.* BEHIND SCHEDULE, behind time, behindhand, belatedly, tardily, at the last minute, at the buzzer.
☐ **of late** ☞ LATELY.

lately *adv.* RECENTLY, of late, latterly, in recent times.

latent *adj.* DORMANT, untapped, unused, undiscovered, hidden, concealed, underlying, invisible, unseen, undeveloped, unrealized, unfulfilled, potential.

later *adj.* SUBSEQUENT, following, succeeding, future, upcoming, to come, ensuing, next; *formal* posterior; *archaic* after.
—OPPOSITES: earlier.
▶ *adv.* SUBSEQUENTLY, eventually, then, next, later on, after this/that, afterwards, thereafter, at a later date, in the future, in due course, by and by, in a while, in time.

lateral *adj.* **1** ☞ SIDEWAYS.
2 CREATIVE, inventive, imaginative, original, innovative, non-linear.

latest *adj.* MOST RECENT, newest, just out, just released, fresh, up to date, up-to-the-minute, state-of-the-art, au courant, dernier cri, current, modern, contemporary, fashionable, in fashion, in vogue; newfangled; *informal* in, with it, trendy, hip, hot, big, funky,

happening, cool.
—OPPOSITES: old.

latitude *n.* FREEDOM, scope, leeway, (breathing) space, flexibility, liberty, independence, free rein, licence, room to manoeuvre, wiggle room, freedom of action.
—OPPOSITES: longitude, restriction.

latter *adj.* LATER, closing, end, concluding, final; latest, most recent.
—OPPOSITES: former.

laudable *adj.* ☞ COMMENDABLE.
—OPPOSITES: shameful.

laugh *v.* **1** CHUCKLE, chortle, guffaw, cackle, giggle, titter, twitter, snigger, snicker, yuk, tee-hee, burst out laughing, roar/hoot/howl/shriek with laughter, crack up, dissolve into laughter, split one's sides, be (rolling) on the floor, be doubled up, be killing oneself (laughing); *informal* be in stitches, be rolling in the aisles.
2 (**laugh at**) ☞ RIDICULE.
▶ *n.* CHUCKLE, chortle, guffaw, giggle, titter, twitter, tee-hee, snigger, snicker, yuk, roar/hoot/howl of laughter, shriek of laughter, belly laugh, horse laugh.

laughable *adj.* ☞ RIDICULOUS.

launch *v.* **1** SEND INTO ORBIT, blast off, take off, lift off. **2** ☞ THROW 1.
3 SET IN MOTION, get going, get under way, start, commence, begin, embark on, initiate, inaugurate, set up, organize, introduce, bring into being, bring in, usher in, establish, instigate, institute, originate, pioneer, spark, bring about, found, generate, get off the ground, start

the ball rolling; *informal* kick off, roll out.

lavatory *n.* ☞ BATHROOM.

lavish *adj.* **1** SUMPTUOUS, luxurious, costly, expensive, opulent, grand, splendid, rich, fancy, posh; *informal* fancy-dancy, fancy-schmancy. **2** ☞ GENEROUS 1. **3** ☞ ABUNDANT.
—OPPOSITES: meagre, frugal.
▸ *v.* GIVE FREELY, spend generously, bestow, heap, shower.

law *n.* **1** REGULATION, statute, enactment, act, bill, decree, edict, bylaw, rule, ruling, ordinance, dictum, command, order, directive, pronouncement, proclamation, dictate, diktat, fiat; Criminal Code✤, civil code✤. **2** RULE, regulation, principle, convention, instruction, guideline. **3** PRINCIPLE, rule, precept, directive, injunction, commandment, belief, creed, credo, maxim, tenet, doctrine, canon.
—RELATED: legal, jurisprudence.

lawful *adj.* ☞ LEGAL.
—OPPOSITES: illegal, criminal.

lawless *adj.* UNGOVERNABLE, unruly, disruptive, anarchic, disorderly, rebellious, insubordinate, riotous, mutinous; uncivilized, wild.
—OPPOSITES: orderly, legal.

lawsuit *n.* (LEGAL) ACTION, suit, case, (legal/judicial) proceedings, litigation, trial, assize✤; dispute.

lawyer *n.* counsel, Crown attorney/counsel/prosecutor✤, Queen's Counsel, QC, legal practitioner, legal professional, legal adviser, member of the bar, barrister and solicitor✤, barrister, solicitor, litigator, advocate, attorney; *informal* ambulance chaser, mouthpiece, legal eagle/ beagle.

lax *adj.* SLACK, slipshod, negligent, remiss, careless, heedless, unmindful, slapdash, offhand, casual; easygoing, lenient, permissive, liberal, indulgent, overindulgent.
—OPPOSITES: strict.

laxative *n.* PURGATIVE, enema, cathartic.

lay *v.* **1** PUT (DOWN), place, set (down), deposit, rest, situate, locate, position; *informal* stick, dump, park, plonk. **2** SET IN PLACE, set out/up, establish. **3** ASSIGN, attribute, ascribe, allot, attach. **4** DEVISE, arrange, make (ready), prepare, work out, hatch, design, plan, scheme, plot, conceive, put together, draw up, produce, develop, concoct, formulate, cook up.
□ **lay hands on** CATCH, lay/get hold of, get one's hands on, seize, grab, grasp, capture. **lay into** (*informal*) **1** ☞ ASSAULT *v.* 1. **2** ☞ CRITICIZE. **lay it on thick** (*informal*) EXAGGERATE, overdo it, embellish the truth; flatter, praise, soft-soap, pile it on, sweet-talk. **lay off 1** GIVE UP, abstain from, desist from, cut out. **2** QUIT, pack in, leave off, stop. **lay someone off** ☞ DISMISS 1. **lay something out 1** SPREAD OUT, set out, display, exhibit. **2** OUTLINE, sketch out, rough out, detail, draw up, formulate, work out, frame, draft. **lay waste** ☞ DEVASTATE 1.

layabout *n.* ☞ LOAFER.

layer *n.* COATING, sheet, coat, film, covering, blanket, skin, thickness; stratum, band.

layoff *n.* DISMISSAL, redundancy, discharge; *informal* sacking, firing; downsizing, rationalizing, rightsizing.
—OPPOSITES: recruitment.

laziness *n.* IDLENESS, indolence, slothfulness, sloth, shiftlessness, inactivity, inertia, sluggishness, acedia, lethargy; negligence, slackness, laxity.

lazy *adj.* IDLE, indolent, slothful, work-shy, shiftless, inactive, sluggish, lethargic; remiss, negligent, slack, lax, lackadaisical.
—OPPOSITES: industrious.

lazybones *n.* ☞ LOAFER.

lead *v.* **1** GUIDE, conduct, show (the way), lead the way, usher, escort, steer, pilot, shepherd; accompany, see, take. **2** CAUSE, induce, prompt, move, persuade, influence, drive, condition, make; incline, dispose, predispose.
3 (**lead to**) RESULT IN, cause, bring on/about, give rise to, be the cause of, make happen, create, produce, occasion, effect, generate, contribute to, promote; provoke, stir up, spark off, arouse, foment, instigate; involve, necessitate, entail; *formal* effectuate. **4** BE AT THE HEAD/FRONT OF, head, spearhead; precede. **5** BE THE LEADER OF, be the head of, preside over, head, command, govern, rule, be in charge of, be in command of, be in control of, run, control, direct, be at the helm of; administer, organize, manage; reign over, be in power over; *informal* head up.
6 BE AT THE FRONT OF, be first in, be ahead of, head; outrun, outstrip, outpace, leave behind, draw away from; outdo, outclass, beat; *informal* leave standing.
—OPPOSITES: follow.
▶ *adj.* LEADING, first, top, foremost, front, head; chief, principal, main, premier.
☐ **lead someone on** DECEIVE, mislead, delude, hoodwink, dupe, trick, fool, pull the wool over someone's eyes; *informal* string along, lead up the garden path, take for a ride, fleece, inveigle, hornswoggle, scam.

leader *n.* CHIEF, head, principal; commander, captain; superior, headman; chairman, chairwoman, chairperson, chair; CEO, chief executive (officer), director, proprietor, manager, superintendent, supervisor, overseer, administrator, employer, master, mistress; president, premier, governor; ruler, monarch, king, queen, sovereign, emperor; *informal* boss, skipper, number one, numero uno, kingpin, top dog, (head) honcho, sachem, padrone, big shot/gun/cheese/wheel/kahuna, bigwig, top banana.
—OPPOSITES: follower, supporter.

leadership *n.* GUIDANCE, direction, control, management, superintendence, supervision; organization, government.

leading *adj.* **1** ☞ MAIN. **2** TOP, highest, best, first; front, lead; unparalleled, matchless, star.
—OPPOSITES: subordinate, minor.

leaflet *n.* ☞ PAMPHLET.

league *n.* ☞ ASSOCIATION 1.
☐ **in league with** COLLABORATING

WITH, co-operating with, in alliance with, allied with, conspiring with, hand in glove with; *informal* in cahoots with, in bed with.

leak *v.* **1** SEEP (OUT), escape, ooze (out), secrete, bleed, emanate, issue, drip, dribble, drain; discharge, exude. **2** ☞ DISCLOSE.
▶ *n.* **1** HOLE, opening, aperture, puncture, perforation, gash, slit, nick, rent, break, crack, fissure, rupture. **2** DISCHARGE, leakage, seepage, drip, escape.
3 DISCLOSURE, revelation, exposé, leakage, tipoff.

lean[1] *v.* **1** REST, recline, be supported by. **2** SLANT, incline, bend, tilt, be at an angle, slope, tip, list. **3** TEND, incline, gravitate; have a preference for, have a penchant for, be partial to, have a liking for, have an affinity with.

lean[2] *adj.* **1** SLIM, thin, slender, spare, wiry, lanky, skinny.
2 MEAGRE, sparse, poor, mean, inadequate, insufficient, paltry, scanty, deficient, insubstantial.
—OPPOSITES: fat, abundant, prosperous.

leaning *n.* INCLINATION, tendency, bent, proclivity, propensity, penchant, predisposition, predilection, partiality, preference, bias, attraction, liking, fondness, taste; *informal* yen.

leap *v.* **1** JUMP (OVER), vault (over), spring over, bound over, hop (over), hurdle, clear. **2** SPRING, jump (up), hop, bound.
▶ *n.* JUMP, vault, spring, bound, hop, skip.

learn *v.* **1** ACQUIRE A KNOWLEDGE OF, acquire skill in, become

competent in, become proficient in, grasp, master, take in, absorb, assimilate, digest, familiarize oneself with; study, read up on, be taught, have lessons in; *informal* get the hang of, bone up on.
2 ☞ MEMORIZE. **3** DISCOVER, find out, become aware, be informed, hear (tell); gather, understand, ascertain, establish; *informal* get wind of the fact, suss out, get a line on.

learned *adj.* ☞ ACADEMIC *adj.* 2.

learner *n.* ☞ BEGINNER.

learning *n.* SCHOLARSHIP, knowledge, education, erudition, intellect, enlightenment, illumination, edification, book learning, academic achievement, academic study, culture, letters, information, understanding, wisdom.
—OPPOSITES: ignorance.

lease *v.* **1** RENT, charter. **2** RENT (OUT), let (out), sublet, sublease.

least *adj.* SLIGHTEST, smallest, minutest, tiniest, littlest.

leave[1] *v.* **1** DEPART FROM, go (away) from, withdraw from, retire from, take oneself off from, exit from, take one's leave of, pull out of, quit, be gone from, decamp from, disappear from, vacate, absent oneself from; set off/out, get under way, be on one's way; say one's farewells/goodbyes, make oneself scarce; *informal* push off, shove off, clear out/off, cut and run, split, vamoose, scram, scoot, beat it, skedaddle, take off, make tracks. **2** SET OFF, head, make; set sail, be on one's way, get under way. **3** ☞ ABANDON 3. **4** LEAVE BEHIND, forget, lose, mislay.

5 BEQUEATH, will, endow, hand down, make over.
—OPPOSITES: arrive.

leave² *n.* **1** ☞ PERMISSION.
2 HOLIDAY, vacation, break, time off, furlough, sabbatical, leave of absence.

lecherous *adj.* DEBAUCHED, degenerate, depraved, dissipated, dissolute, filthy, lewd, lubricious. See also LUSTFUL.
—OPPOSITES: chaste.

lecture *n.* **1** SPEECH, talk, address, discourse, disquisition, presentation, oration, lesson; *informal* chalk talk. **2** SCOLDING, chiding, reprimand, rebuke, reproof, reproach, upbraiding, berating, admonishment, sermon; *informal* dressing-down, talking-to, tongue-lashing, earful, roasting; *formal* castigation.
▶ *v.* **1** GIVE A LECTURE/TALK, talk, make a speech, speak, give an address, discourse, hold forth, declaim, expatiate, sermonize, preach; *informal* spout, sound off. **2** TEACH, give instruction, give lessons. **3** ☞ REPRIMAND.

ledge *n.* SHELF, sill, mantel, mantelpiece, shelving; projection, protrusion, overhang, ridge, prominence.

leer *v.* OGLE, look lasciviously, look suggestively, eye, check out; *informal* give someone a/the once-over.

leery *adj.* ☞ WARY 2.
leeway *n.* ☞ LATITUDE.
left *adj.* LEFT-HAND, sinistral; port, larboard; sinister.
—RELATED: levo-.
—OPPOSITES: right, starboard.

leftover *adj.* ☞ SURPLUS *adj.*

leg *n.* **1** (LOWER) LIMB, shank, gam.
2 PART, stage, portion, segment, section, phase, stretch, lap.
□ **pull someone's leg** ☞ TEASE.

legacy *n.* **1** ☞ INHERITANCE.
2 ☞ CONSEQUENCE 1.

legal *adj.* LAWFUL, legitimate, licit, within the law, legalized, valid; permissible, permitted, allowable, allowed, above board, admissible, acceptable; authorized, sanctioned, licensed, constitutional, statutory; *informal* legit.
—OPPOSITES: criminal.

legalize *v.* MAKE LEGAL, decriminalize, legitimize, legitimate, permit, allow, authorize, sanction, license, validate; regularize, normalize; *informal* OK.
—OPPOSITES: prohibit.

legend *n.* **1** MYTH, saga, epic, (folk) tale, (folk) story, fairy tale, fable, mythos, folklore, lore, mythology, fantasy, oral history, folk tradition; urban myth.
2 ☞ CELEBRITY 1.

legendary *adj.* **1** FABLED, heroic, traditional, fairy-tale, storybook, mythical, mythological. **2** FAMOUS, celebrated, famed, renowned, acclaimed, illustrious, esteemed, honoured, exalted, venerable, well-known, popular, prominent, distinguished, great, eminent, pre-eminent, high-profile; *formal* lauded.
—OPPOSITES: historical.

legitimate *adj.* **1** ☞ LEGAL.
2 RIGHTFUL, lawful, genuine, authentic, real, true, proper, authorized, sanctioned, acknowledged, recognized.

3 VALID, sound, well-founded, justifiable, reasonable, sensible, just, fair, bona fide.
—OPPOSITES: illegal, invalid.

legitimize v. VALIDATE, legitimate, permit, authorize, sanction, license, condone, justify, endorse, support; legalize.
—OPPOSITES: outlaw.

leisure n. FREE TIME, spare time, time off; recreation, relaxation, inactivity, pleasure; *informal* R and R, downtime.
—OPPOSITES: work.

leisurely adj. UNHURRIED, relaxed, easy, gentle, sedate, comfortable, restful, undemanding, slow, lazy.
—OPPOSITES: hurried.

lend v. **1** LOAN, let someone use; advance. **2** ADD, impart, give, bestow, confer, provide, supply, furnish, contribute.
—OPPOSITES: borrow.

length n. **1** EXTENT, distance, linear measure, span, reach; area, expanse, stretch, range, scope. **2** PERIOD, duration, stretch, span. □ **at length 1** FOR A LONG TIME, for ages, for hours, interminably, endlessly, ceaselessly, unendingly. **2** THOROUGHLY, fully, in detail, in depth, comprehensively, exhaustively, extensively.

lengthen v. ELONGATE, make longer, extend, prolong, protract, stretch out, drag out; expand, widen, broaden, enlarge; grow/get longer, draw out.
—OPPOSITES: shorten.

lengthy adj. ☞ LONG¹.

lenient adj. MERCIFUL, clement, forgiving, forbearing, tolerant, charitable, humane, indulgent, easygoing, magnanimous,

sympathetic, compassionate, mild, understanding.
—OPPOSITES: severe.

less pron. A SMALLER AMOUNT, not so/as much as, under, below.
—OPPOSITES: more.
▶ *adj.* NOT SO MUCH, smaller, slighter, shorter, reduced; fewer.
▶ *adv.* TO A LESSER DEGREE, to a smaller extent, not so/as much.
▶ *prep.* MINUS, subtracting, excepting, without.
—OPPOSITES: plus.

lessen v. **1** REDUCE, make less/smaller, minimize, decrease; allay, assuage, alleviate, attenuate, palliate, ease, dull, deaden, blunt, moderate, mitigate, dampen, soften, tone down, dilute, weaken. **2** ☞ DIMINISH. **3** DIMINISH, degrade, discredit, devalue, belittle.
—OPPOSITES: increase.

lesser adj. LESS IMPORTANT, minor, secondary, subsidiary, marginal, ancillary, auxiliary, supplementary, peripheral; inferior, insignificant, unimportant, petty.
—OPPOSITES: greater, superior.

lesson n. **1** CLASS, session, seminar, tutorial, lecture, period (of instruction/teaching); chalk talk. **2** WARNING, deterrent, caution; example, exemplar, message, moral.

let v. ☞ PERMIT.
—OPPOSITES: prevent, prohibit.
□ **let someone down** FAIL (TO SUPPORT), disappoint, disillusion; abandon, desert, leave stranded, leave in the lurch. **let go** RELEASE (ONE'S HOLD ON), loose/loosen one's hold on, relinquish; *archaic* unhand. **let someone go**

☞ DISMISS 1. **let someone in**
☞ ADMIT 1. **let someone in on
something** INCLUDE, count in,
admit, allow to share in, let
participate in, inform about, tell
about. **let something off**
DETONATE, discharge, explode, set
off, fire off. **let someone off**
PARDON, forgive, grant an amnesty
to; deal leniently with, be
merciful to, have mercy on;
acquit, absolve, exonerate, clear,
vindicate; *informal* let someone off
the hook; *formal* exculpate. **let on**
(*informal*) PRETEND, feign, affect,
make out, make believe, simulate.
let something out ☞ DISCLOSE.
let someone out RELEASE,
liberate, (set) free, let go,
discharge; set/turn loose, allow to
leave. **let up** ABATE, lessen,
decrease, diminish, subside,
relent, slacken, die down/off, ease
(off), tail off; ebb, wane, dwindle,
fade; stop, cease, finish.

letdown *n.* DISAPPOINTMENT,
anticlimax, comedown, non-event,
fiasco, setback, blow,
disadvantage; *informal* washout.

lethal *adj.* ☞ DEADLY 1.
—OPPOSITES: harmless, safe.

lethargic *adj.* ☞ SLUGGISH 1.

lethargy *n.* SLUGGISHNESS, inertia,
inactivity, inaction, slowness,
torpor, torpidity, lifelessness,
listlessness, languor, laziness,
idleness, indolence, shiftlessness,
sloth, apathy, passivity, weariness,
tiredness, lassitude, fatigue,
inanition, acedia, enervation,
stagnation, stasis; *literary* hebetude.
—OPPOSITES: vigour, energy.

letter *n.* **1** (ALPHABETICAL)
CHARACTER, sign, symbol, mark,
figure, rune; *Linguistics* grapheme.
2 (WRITTEN) MESSAGE, (written)
communication, note, line,
missive, dispatch;
correspondence, news,
information, intelligence, word;
post, mail; *formal* epistle.
—RELATED: epistolary.
□**to the letter** STRICTLY, precisely,
exactly, accurately, closely,
faithfully, religiously,
punctiliously, literally, verbatim,
in every detail.

lettered *adj.* ☞ EDUCATED.
—OPPOSITES: ill-educated.

let-up *n.* ☞ PAUSE.

level *adj.* FLAT, horizontal, smooth,
even, uniform, plane, flush,
plumb.
—OPPOSITES: uneven.
▶ *n.* **1** RANK, standing, status,
position; echelon, degree, grade,
gradation, stage, standard, rung;
class, stratum, group, grouping,
set, classification. **2** QUANTITY,
amount, extent, measure, degree,
volume, size, magnitude,
intensity, proportion. **3** HEIGHT,
altitude, elevation. **4** FLOOR,
storey, deck.
▶ *v.* **1** MAKE LEVEL, level out/off,
make even, even out, make flat,
flatten, smooth (out), make
uniform. **2** RAZE, demolish,
flatten, topple, destroy; tear
down, knock down, pull down,
bulldoze. **3** KNOCK DOWN/OUT, lay
out, flatten, floor, fell; *informal* KO,
kayo. **4** EQUALIZE, make equal,
equal, even (up), make level. **5** AIM,
point, direct, train, focus, turn,
sight, draw a bead on. **6** BE FRANK,
be open, be honest, be above
board, tell the truth, tell all, hide

nothing, be straightforward, be upfront; come clean, set the record straight.

☐ **on the level** GENUINE, straight, honest, above board, fair, true, sincere, straightforward, trustworthy; *informal* upfront, on the up and up.

level-headed *adj.* SENSIBLE, practical, realistic, prudent, pragmatic, wise, reasonable, rational, mature, judicious, sound, sober, businesslike, no-nonsense, composed, calm, {calm, cool, and collected}, confident, well-balanced, equable, cool-headed, self-possessed, having one's feet on the ground; *informal* unflappable, together, grounded.
—OPPOSITES: excitable.

lewd *adj.* ☞ VULGAR 1.
—OPPOSITES: chaste, clean.

liability *n.* 1 ☞ HANDICAP 2.
2 ☞ RESPONSIBILITY 2.

liable *adj.* 1 (LEGALLY) RESPONSIBLE, accountable, answerable, chargeable, blameworthy, at fault, culpable, guilty. 2 LIKELY, inclined, tending, disposed, apt, predisposed, prone, given. 3 EXPOSED, prone, subject, susceptible, vulnerable, in danger of, at risk of.

liar *n.* DECEIVER, fibber, perjurer, false witness, fabricator, equivocator; fabulist; *informal* storyteller.

libel *n. & v.* ☞ SLANDER.

liberal *adj.* 1 PROGRESSIVE, advanced, modern, forward-looking, forward-thinking, progressivist, enlightened, reformist, radical. 2 ☞ TOLERANT. 3 WIDE-RANGING, broad-based,

general. 4 FLEXIBLE, broad, loose, rough, free, general, non-literal, non-specific, imprecise, vague, indefinite. 5 ABUNDANT, copious, ample, plentiful, generous, lavish, luxuriant, profuse, considerable, prolific, rich; *literary* plenteous. 6 ☞ GENEROUS 1, 2.
—OPPOSITES: reactionary, strict, miserly.

liberate *v.* (SET) FREE, release, let out/go, set/let loose, save, rescue; emancipate, enfranchise.
—OPPOSITES: imprison, enslave.

liberty *n.* 1 FREEDOM, independence, free rein, licence, self-determination, free will, latitude. 2 INDEPENDENCE, freedom, autonomy, sovereignty, self government, self rule, self determination; civil liberties, human rights. 3 RIGHT, birthright, prerogative, entitlement, privilege, permission, sanction, authorization, authority, licence, power.
—OPPOSITES: constraint, slavery.

licence *n.* 1 PERMIT, certificate, document, documentation, authorization, warrant; certification, credentials; pass, papers. 2 PERMISSION, authority, right, a free hand, leave, authorization, entitlement, privilege, prerogative; liberty, freedom, power, latitude, scope, free rein, carte blanche, a blank cheque, the go-ahead.

licentious *adj.* ☞ PROMISCUOUS.

lid *n.* COVER, top, cap, covering.
☐ **put a lid on it** ☞ SHUT UP at SHUT. **blow the lid off** EXPOSE, reveal, make known, make public, bring into the open, disclose,

divulge; *informal* spill the beans, blab.

lie¹ *n.* UNTRUTH, falsehood, fib, fabrication, deception, invention, (piece of) fiction, story, cock-and-bull story, flight of fancy, falsification; (little) white lie, half-truth, exaggeration; *informal* tall tale/story, whopper.

—RELATED: mendacious, mendacity.

—OPPOSITES: truth.

▶ *v.* TELL AN UNTRUTH/LIE, fib, dissemble, dissimulate, misinform, mislead, tell a white lie, perjure oneself, commit perjury, prevaricate; *informal* lie through one's teeth, stretch the truth.

□ **give the lie to** ☞ DISPROVE.

lie² *v.* **1** RECLINE, lie down/back, be recumbent, be prostrate, be supine, be prone, be stretched out, sprawl, rest, repose, lounge, loll. **2** BE PLACED, be situated, be positioned, rest, be located, be found, be sited. **3** CONSIST, be inherent, be present, be contained, exist, reside.

—OPPOSITES: stand.

□ **lie low** HIDE (OUT), go into hiding, conceal oneself, keep out of sight, go underground; *informal* hole up.

life *n.* **1** EXISTENCE, being, living, animation; sentience, creation, viability. **2** LIVING BEINGS/CREATURES, the living; human/animal/plant life, fauna, flora, ecosystems; human beings, humanity, humankind, mankind, man. **3** WAY OF LIFE/LIVING, lifestyle, situation, fate, lot. **4** LIFETIME, life span, days, time on earth,

existence. **5** ☞ VERVE. **6** BIOGRAPHY, autobiography, life story/history, profile, chronicle, account, portrait; *informal* bio.

—RELATED: animate, bio-.

—OPPOSITES: death.

lifeless *adj.* **1** ☞ DEAD 1. **2** INANIMATE, without life, inert, insentient. **3** BARREN, sterile, bare, desolate, stark, arid, infertile, uncultivated, uninhabited; bleak, colourless, characterless, soulless. **4** LACKLUSTRE, spiritless, apathetic, torpid, lethargic; dull, monotonous, boring, tedious, dreary, unexciting, expressionless, emotionless, colourless, characterless.

—OPPOSITES: alive, animate, lively.

lifelike *adj.* ☞ REALISTIC 3.

—OPPOSITES: unrealistic.

lift *v.* **1** RAISE, hoist, heave, haul up, heft, raise up/aloft, elevate, hold high; pick up, grab, take up, scoop up, snatch up; winch up, jack up, lever up; *informal* hump; *literary* upheave. **2** BOOST, raise, buoy up, elevate, cheer up, perk up, uplift, brighten up, gladden, encourage, stimulate, revive; *informal* buck up. **3** CANCEL, remove, withdraw, revoke, rescind, annul, void, discontinue, end, stop, terminate. **4** AMPLIFY, raise, make louder, increase. **5** ☞ PLAGIARIZE.

—OPPOSITES: drop, put down.

▶ *n.* **1** (CAR) RIDE, drive. **2** BOOST, fillip, stimulus, impetus, encouragement, spur, push; improvement, enhancement; *informal* shot in the arm, pick-me-up.

light¹ *n.* **1** ILLUMINATION, brightness, luminescence, luminosity,

shining, gleaming, gleam, brilliance, radiance, lustre, glowing, glow, blaze, glare, dazzle; sunlight, moonlight, starlight, lamplight, firelight; ray of light, beam of light; *literary* effulgence, lambency. **2** LAMP, wall light; headlight, headlamp, sidelight; street light, floodlight; lantern; torch, flashlight. **3** DAYLIGHT (HOURS), daytime, day; dawn, morning, daybreak, sunrise; natural light, sunlight.
—RELATED: photo-, lumin-.
—OPPOSITES: darkness.
▶ *v.* SET ALIGHT, set light to, set burning, set on fire, set fire to, put/set a match to, ignite, kindle, spark (off).
—OPPOSITES: extinguish.
▶ *adj.* **1** LIGHT-COLOURED, light-toned, pale, pale-coloured, pastel. **2** FAIR, light-coloured, blond(e), golden, flaxen.
—OPPOSITES: dark, gloomy.
□ **bring something to light** ☞ REVEAL 2. **come to light** BE DISCOVERED, be uncovered, be unearthed, come out, become known, become apparent, appear, materialize, emerge. **in light of** TAKING INTO CONSIDERATION/ACCOUNT, considering, bearing in mind, taking note of, in view of. **light up** BECOME BRIGHT, brighten, lighten, shine, gleam, flare, blaze, glint, sparkle, shimmer, glisten, scintillate. **light something up** ANIMATE, irradiate, brighten, cheer up, enliven. **throw/cast/shed light on** EXPLAIN, elucidate, clarify, clear up, interpret.

light² *adj.* **1** EASY TO LIFT/CARRY, not heavy, lightweight; portable.

2 ☞ THIN 2. **3** NIMBLE, agile, lithe, limber, lissome, graceful; light-footed, fleet-footed, quick, quick-moving, spry, sprightly; *informal* twinkle-toed; *literary* fleet, lightsome. **4** SMALL, modest, simple, easily digested; *informal* low-cal. **5** EASY, simple, undemanding; *informal* cushy. **6** ENTERTAINING, lightweight, diverting, undemanding, frivolous, superficial, trivial. **7** ☞ CHEERFUL. **8** UNIMPORTANT, insignificant, trivial, trifling, petty, inconsequential, superficial. **9** GENTLE, delicate, soft, dainty; faint, indistinct.
—OPPOSITES: heavy.

lighten¹ *v.* MAKE LIGHTER, make brighter, brighten, light up, illuminate, throw/cast light on, shine on, irradiate; *literary* illumine, illume.
—OPPOSITES: darken.

lighten² *v.* **1** MAKE LIGHTER, lessen, reduce, decrease, diminish, ease; alleviate, mitigate, allay, relieve, palliate, assuage. **2** CHEER (UP), brighten, gladden, hearten, perk up, lift, enliven, boost, buoy (up), uplift, revive, restore, revitalize.
—OPPOSITES: increase, depress.

lighthearted *adj.* ☞ CHEERFUL.
—OPPOSITES: miserable.

lightly *adv.* **1** SOFTLY, gently, faintly, delicately. **2** SPARINGLY, slightly, sparsely, moderately. **3** WITHOUT SEVERE PUNISHMENT, easily, leniently, mildly. **4** CARELESSLY, airily, heedlessly, without consideration, indifferently, unthinkingly, thoughtlessly, flippantly, breezily, frivolously.

—OPPOSITES: hard, heavily.

like[1] *v.* **1** BE FOND OF, be attached to, have a soft spot for, have a liking for, have regard for, think well of, admire, respect, esteem; be attracted to, fancy, find attractive, be keen on, be taken with; be infatuated with, carry a torch for, be crazy about, have a crush on, have a thing for, have the hots for, take a shine to. **2** ENJOY, have a taste for, have a preference for, have a liking for, be partial to, find/take pleasure in, be keen on, find agreeable, have a penchant/passion for, find enjoyable; appreciate, love, adore, relish; *informal* have a thing about, be into, be mad about, be hooked on, get a kick out of. **3** FEEL ABOUT, regard, think about, consider.

—OPPOSITES: hate.

like[2] *prep.* **1** SIMILAR TO, the same as, identical to. **2** IN THE SAME WAY/MANNER AS, in the manner of, in a similar way to. **3** SUCH AS, for example, for instance; in particular, namely. **4** CHARACTERISTIC OF, typical of, in character with.

—RELATED: -esque, -ish.

▸ *adj.* SIMILAR, much the same, comparable, corresponding, resembling, alike, analogous, parallel, equivalent, cognate, related, kindred; identical, same, matching.

—OPPOSITES: dissimilar.

likeable *adj.* PLEASANT, nice, friendly, agreeable, affable, amiable, genial, personable, charming, popular, good-natured, engaging, appealing, endearing, convivial, congenial, simpatico, winning, delightful, pleasing, enchanting, lovable, adorable, sweet; *informal* darling, lovely.

—OPPOSITES: unpleasant.

likelihood *n.* PROBABILITY, chance, prospect, possibility, likeliness, odds, feasibility; risk, threat, danger; hope, promise.

likely *adj.* **1** PROBABLE, (distinctly) possible, to be expected, odds-on, plausible, imaginable; expected, anticipated, predictable, predicted, foreseeable; *informal* in the cards, a good/fair/reasonable bet. **2** ☞ PLAUSIBLE. **3** ☞ UNLIKELY 2.

—OPPOSITES: improbable, unbelievable.

▸ *adv.* ☞ PROBABLY.

likeness *n.* **1** ☞ SIMILARITY. **2** SEMBLANCE, guise, appearance, (outward) form, shape, image. **3** ☞ REPRESENTATION 2.

—OPPOSITES: dissimilarity.

liking *n.* FONDNESS, love, affection, penchant, attachment; enjoyment, appreciation, taste, passion; preference, partiality, predilection; desire, fancy, inclination.

limb *n.* **1** ARM, LEG, appendage; *archaic* member. **2** BRANCH, bough, offshoot, shoot.

limber *adj.* LITHE, supple, nimble, lissome, flexible, fit, agile, acrobatic, loose-jointed, loose-limbed.

—OPPOSITES: stiff.

limelight *n.* THE FOCUS OF ATTENTION, public attention/interest, media attention, the public eye, the glare of publicity, prominence, the spotlight, face

time; centre stage.
—OPPOSITES: obscurity.

limit *n.* **1** ☞ BOUNDARY. **2** MAXIMUM, ceiling, limitation, upper limit; restriction, check, control, restraint. **3** UTMOST, breaking point, greatest extent.
▸ *v.* RESTRICT, curb, cap, (hold in) check, restrain, put a brake on, keep within bounds, freeze, regulate, control, govern, moderate, delimit.
☐ **off limits** OUT OF BOUNDS, forbidden, banned, restricted, unacceptable, taboo.

limitation *n.* **1** RESTRICTION, curb, restraint, control, check, damper, rein, condition, constraint, limit, proviso, qualification; bar, barrier, block, deterrent, hindrance, impediment. **2** ☞ SHORTCOMING.
—OPPOSITES: increase, strength.

limited *adj.* **1** RESTRICTED, finite, little, tight, slight, in short supply, short; meagre, scanty, sparse, few, insubstantial, deficient, inadequate, insufficient, paltry, poor, minimal. **2** RESTRICTED, curbed, checked, controlled, restrained, delimited, qualified.
—OPPOSITES: ample, boundless.

limitless *adj.* BOUNDLESS, unbounded, unlimited, illimitable; infinite, endless, never-ending, unending, everlasting, untold, immeasurable, bottomless, fathomless; unceasing, ceaseless, unfailing, interminable, inexhaustible, constant, perpetual.

limp *adj.* SOFT, flaccid, loose, slack, lax, relaxed; floppy, drooping, droopy, sagging, flabby.
—OPPOSITES: firm, energetic.

line *n.* **1** dash, rule, bar, score; underline, underscore, stroke, slash; *technical* stria, striation. **2** ☞ WRINKLE 1. **3** ☞ BOUNDARY. **4** POSITION, formation, defence, fieldwork, front (line); trenches. **5** CORD, rope, string, cable, wire, thread, twine, strand. **6** LINEUP, file, row, queue. **7** ☞ SERIES. **8** COURSE, direction, drift, tack, tendency, trend. **9** BRAND, kind, sort, type, variety, make. **10** ☞ ANCESTRY. **11** SENTENCE, phrase, clause, utterance; passage, extract, quotation, quote, citation.
—RELATED: linear.
▸ *v.* BORDER, edge, fringe, bound, rim.
☐ **in line 1** IN A LINEUP, in a row, in a file, in a queue. **2** IN AGREEMENT, in accord, in accordance, in harmony, in step, in compliance. **3** IN ALIGNMENT, aligned, level, at the same height; abreast, side by side. **4** UNDER CONTROL, in order, in check. **line someone/something up 1** ARRANGE IN LINES, put in rows, arrange in columns, align, range. **2** ASSEMBLE, put together, organize, prepare, arrange, pre-arrange, fix up; book, schedule, timetable. **on the line** AT RISK, in danger, in jeopardy, endangered, imperilled.

linger *v.* **1** WAIT (AROUND), stay (put); remain; loiter, dawdle, dally, take one's time; stick around, hang around, hang on. **2** PERSIST, continue, remain, stay, endure, carry on, last, keep on/up.

link *n.* **1** LOOP, ring, connection, connector, coupling, joint.

2 CONNECTION, relationship, association, linkage, bond, tie, attachment, affiliation.
▶ v. **1** ☞ ATTACH 1. **2** ☞ ASSOCIATE v. 1.

lionize v. ☞ ACCLAIM.
—OPPOSITES: vilify.

lip n. ☞ RIM.
—RELATED: labial, labio-.
☐ **bite one's lip** KEEP QUIET, keep one's mouth shut, say nothing, bite one's tongue.

liquid n. FLUID, moisture; liquor, solution, juice.
▶ adj. **1** FLUID, liquefied; melted, molten, thawed, dissolved; Chemistry hydrous. **2** CONVERTIBLE, disposable, usable, spendable.
—OPPOSITES: solid.

liquidate v. **1** CLOSE DOWN, wind up, put into liquidation, dissolve, disband. **2** CONVERT (TO CASH), cash in, sell off/up.

liquor n. ☞ ALCOHOL.

list¹ n. CATALOGUE, inventory, record, register, roll, file, index, directory, listing, checklist, enumeration.
▶ v. RECORD, register, make a list of, enter; itemize, enumerate, catalogue, file, log, categorize, inventory; classify, group, sort, rank, alphabetize, index.

list² v. ☞ LEAN 2.

listen v. **1** HEAR, pay attention, be attentive, attend, concentrate; keep one's ears open, prick up one's ears; informal be all ears, lend an ear; literary hark; archaic hearken. **2** PAY ATTENTION, take heed, heed, take notice, take note, mind, mark, bear in mind, take into consideration/account, tune in.
☐ **listen in** ☞ EAVESDROP.

listless adj. ☞ SLUGGISH.
—OPPOSITES: energetic.

literal adj. **1** STRICT, factual, plain, simple, exact, straightforward; unembellished, undistorted; objective, correct, true, accurate, genuine, authentic. **2** WORD-FOR-WORD, verbatim, letter-for-letter; exact, precise, faithful, close, strict, accurate.
—OPPOSITES: figurative, loose.

literary adj. **1** FORMAL, written, poetic, dramatic; elaborate, ornate, flowery; informal inkhorn. **2** ☞ ACADEMIC adj. 2.

literate adj. **1** ☞ EDUCATED. **2** KNOWLEDGEABLE, well-versed, savvy, smart, conversant, competent; informal up on, up to speed on, plugged in.
—OPPOSITES: ignorant.

literature n. **1** WRITTEN WORKS, writings, (creative) writing, literary texts, compositions. **2** PUBLICATIONS, published writings, texts, reports, studies. **3** PRINTED MATTER, brochures, leaflets, pamphlets, circulars, flyers, handouts, handbills, bulletins, fact sheets, publicity, propaganda, notices; informal bumph.

lithe adj. AGILE, graceful, supple, limber, loose-limbed, nimble, deft, flexible, lissome, slender, slim, willowy.
—OPPOSITES: clumsy.

litter n. **1** GARBAGE, refuse, junk, waste, debris, scraps, leavings, fragments, detritus, trash, rubbish. **2** BROOD, family.

little adj. **1** SMALL, small-scale, compact, short; mini, miniature, tiny, minute, minuscule; toy,

baby, pocket-sized, undersized, dwarf, midget, wee; *informal* teeny, weeny, teeny-weeny, teensy-weensy, itsy-bitsy, itty-bitty, little-bitty, half-pint, pint-sized, vest-pocket, li'l, knee-high to a grasshopper, micro, microscopic. **2** ☞ SLIGHT 3. **3** YOUNG, younger, junior, small, baby, infant. **4** HARDLY ANY, not much, slight, scant, limited, restricted, modest, little or no, minimal, negligible.
—OPPOSITES: big, large, elder, considerable.

▶ *adv.* HARDLY, barely, scarcely, not much, not at all, (only) slightly.
—OPPOSITES: well, often.

□ **a little 1** SOME, a small amount of, a bit of, a touch of, a soupçon of, a dash of, a taste of, a spot of; a shade of, a suggestion of, a trace of, a hint of, a suspicion of; a dribble of, a splash of, a pinch of, a sprinkling of, a speck of; *informal* a smidgen of, a tad of. **2** SLIGHTLY, faintly, remotely, vaguely; somewhat, a little bit, to some degree. **little by little** ☞ GRADUALLY.

livable *adj.* HABITABLE, inhabitable, fit to live in, in good repair; comfortable, cozy.

live¹ *v.* **1** EXIST, be alive, be, have life; breathe, draw breath, walk the earth. **2** RESIDE, have one's home, have one's residence, be settled; be housed, lodge; inhabit, occupy, populate; *formal* dwell, be domiciled.
—OPPOSITES: die, be dead.

live² *adj.* **1** ☞ ALIVE. **2** IN THE FLESH, personal, in person, not recorded. **3** (RED) HOT, glowing, aglow; burning, alight, flaming, aflame,

blazing, ignited, on fire; *literary* afire. **4** UNEXPLODED, explosive, active; unstable, volatile.
—OPPOSITES: dead, inanimate, recorded.

livelihood *n.* (SOURCE OF) INCOME, means of support, living, subsistence, keep, maintenance, sustenance, nourishment, daily bread, bread and butter; job, work, employment, occupation, vocation.

lively *adj.* **1** ENERGETIC, active, animated, dynamic, full of life, outgoing, spirited, high-spirited, vivacious, enthusiastic, vibrant, buoyant, exuberant, effervescent, cheerful; bouncy, bubbly, perky, sparkling, zestful, alive, eager, ebullient, excited, vigorous; *informal* full of beans, chirpy, chipper, peppy, bright and breezy, bright-eyed and bushy-tailed. **2** BUSY, crowded, bustling, buzzing; vibrant, boisterous, jolly, festive; *informal* hopping. **3** HEATED, vigorous, animated, spirited, enthusiastic, forceful.

liven

□ **liven up** BRIGHTEN UP, cheer up, perk up, revive, rally, pick up, bounce back; *informal* buck up.

liven someone/something up BRIGHTEN UP, cheer up, enliven, animate, raise someone's spirits, perk up, spice up, make lively, wake up, invigorate, revive, refresh, vivify, galvanize, stimulate, stir up, get going; *informal* buck up, pep up.

living *n.* **1** ☞ LIVELIHOOD. **2** WAY OF LIFE, lifestyle, way of living, life; conduct, behaviour, activities, habits.

▶ *adj.* ☞ ALIVE.
—OPPOSITES: dead, extinct.

load *n.* **1** CARGO, freight, consignment, delivery, shipment, goods, merchandise; pack, bundle, parcel; truckload, shipload, boatload, vanload. **2** ☞ LOT 1. **3** COMMITMENT, responsibility, duty, obligation, charge, burden; trouble, worry, strain, pressure.
▶ *v.* **1** FILL (UP), pack, charge, stock, stack, lade. **2** PACK, stow, store, stack, bundle; place, deposit, put away. **3** BURDEN, weigh down, saddle, charge; overburden, overwhelm, encumber, tax, strain, trouble, worry. **4** INSERT, put, place, slot.

loafer *n.* IDLER, (*Atlantic*) hangashore✦, layabout, good-for-nothing, do-nothing, lounger, shirker, sluggard, laggard, malingerer, slugabed, flâneur; *informal* slacker, slob, lazybones, bum; *literary* wastrel.

loan *n.* CREDIT, advance, bridge financing; mortgage, overdraft; lending, moneylending.
▶ *v.* LEND, advance, give credit; give on loan, lease, charter.

loath *adj.* ☞ RELUCTANT.
—OPPOSITES: willing.

loathe *v.* ☞ HATE 1.
—OPPOSITES: love.

loathing *n.* ☞ HATRED.

loathsome *adj.* ☞ ABHORRENT.

local *adj.* **1** COMMUNITY, district, neighbourhood, regional, city, town, municipal, county. **2** NEIGHBOURHOOD, nearby, near, at hand, close by; accessible, handy, convenient. **3** CONFINED, restricted, contained, localized.
—OPPOSITES: national.

▶ *n.* LOCAL PERSON, native, inhabitant, resident.
—OPPOSITES: outsider.

locale *n.* ☞ SETTING 1.

localize *v.* LIMIT, restrict, confine, contain, circumscribe, concentrate, delimit.
—OPPOSITES: generalize.

locate *v.* **1** ☞ FIND 1. **2** SITUATE, site, position, place, base; put, build, establish, found, station, install, settle.

location *n.* POSITION, place, situation, site, locality, locale, spot, whereabouts, point; scene, setting, area, environment; bearings, orientation; venue, address; *technical* locus.

lock *n.* BOLT, catch, fastener, clasp, bar, hasp, latch.
▶ *v.* **1** BOLT, fasten, bar, secure, seal; padlock, latch, chain. **2** JOIN, interlock, intertwine, link, mesh, engage, unite, connect, yoke, mate; couple. **3** BECOME STUCK, stick, jam, become/make immovable, become/make rigid. **4** CLASP, grasp, embrace, hug, squeeze, clench.
—OPPOSITES: unlock, open, separate, divide.
▢ **lock horns** ☞ QUARREL *v.* **lock someone up** ☞ IMPRISON.

lodge *n.* **1** HOUSE, cottage, cabin, outpost camp✦, bush camp✦, chalet, *historical* camboose✦. **2** DEN, lair, hole, set; retreat, haunt, shelter. **3** HALL, clubhouse, meeting room.
▶ *v.* **1** RESIDE, board, stay, live, have lodgings, have rooms, be put up, be quartered, stop, room; *formal* dwell, be domiciled, sojourn; *archaic* abide. **2** ACCOMMODATE, put

up, take in, house, board, billet, quarter, shelter. **3** SUBMIT, register, enter, put forward, advance, lay, present, tender, proffer, put on record, record, table, file.
4 BECOME FIXED, embed itself, become embedded, become implanted, get/become stuck, stick, catch, become caught, wedge.

lofty *adj.* **1** ☞ TOWERING 1. **2** NOBLE, exalted, high, high-minded, worthy, grand, fine, elevated, sublime.
—OPPOSITES: low, short, base, lowly.

log *n.* **1** BRANCH, trunk; piece of wood, deadhead, (*Nfld*) nug♣; (**logs**) timber, firewood, (*Atlantic*) junk♣. **2** RECORD, register, logbook, journal, diary, minutes, chronicle, daybook, record book, ledger, account, tally.
▶ *v.* **1** REGISTER, record, make a note of, note down, write down, jot down, put in writing, enter, file. **2** ATTAIN, achieve, chalk up, make, do, go. **3** CUT DOWN TREES, chop down trees, fell trees, clear cut, harvest trees.
□ **log in** SIGN IN, register, enter, log-on.

logger *n.* LUMBERJACK, lumberman, woodcutter, woodsman, bushman, bushworker♣; *informal* jack; (*BC*) *historical* whistlepunk♣, woodman; powderman, pulp cutter, chaser, faller, high rigger, skidder, handlogger, hooktender, bull of the woods.

logic *n.* REASON, judgment, logical thought, rationality, wisdom,

sense, good sense, common sense, sanity; *informal* horse sense.

logical *adj.* **1** REASONED, well reasoned, reasonable, rational, sound, cogent, well-thought-out, valid; coherent, clear, well-organized, systematic, orderly, methodical, analytical, consistent, objective. **2** NATURAL, reasonable, sensible, understandable; predictable, unsurprising, only to be expected, most likely, likeliest, obvious.
—OPPOSITES: illogical, irrational, unlikely, surprising.

logjam *n.* DEADLOCK, stalemate, saw-off♣, tie; impasse, bottleneck, barrier, block.

loiter *v.* LINGER, wait, skulk; loaf, lounge, idle, laze, waste time, lallygag; *informal* hang around; *archaic* tarry.

lone *adj.* SOLITARY, only, single, solo, unaccompanied, unescorted, alone, by oneself/itself, sole, companionless; detached, isolated.

lonely *adj.* **1** ISOLATED, alone, lonesome, solitary, friendless, with no one to turn to, forsaken, abandoned, rejected, unloved, unwanted, outcast. **2** DESERTED, uninhabited, unfrequented, unpopulated, desolate, isolated, remote, out of the way, secluded, off the beaten track, in the back of beyond, godforsaken, in the middle of nowhere.
—OPPOSITES: popular, sociable, crowded.

long¹ *adj.* LENGTHY, long-lasting, prolonged, extended, extensive; marathon, protracted, overlong, long-drawn-out, dragged out,

lingering, seemingly endless, spun out; verbose, wordy, prolix, long-winded; tedious, boring, interminable.
—OPPOSITES: short, brief.
□ **before long** ☞ SOON 1.

long² v. YEARN, pine, ache, hanker for/after, hunger, thirst, itch, be eager, be desperate; crave, dream of, set one's heart on; *informal* have a yen, (have a) jones, be dying.

longing n. YEARNING, pining, craving, ache, burning, hunger, thirst, appetite, hankering, desire, want, wish, lust, need, urge; *informal* yen, itch, jones.
▶ adj. YEARNING, pining, craving, hungry, thirsty, hankering, wistful, covetous.

long-lasting adj. ENDURING, lasting, abiding, long-lived, long-running, long-established, long-standing, lifelong, deep-rooted, time-honoured, traditional, permanent.
—OPPOSITES: short-lived, ephemeral.

long shot n. **1** GAMBLE, venture, speculation, risk, (outside) chance. **2** UNDERDOG, dark horse, weaker one, little guy, David.

long-winded adj. VERBOSE, wordy, lengthy, long, overlong, prolix, prolonged, protracted, long-drawn-out, interminable; discursive, diffuse, rambling, tortuous, meandering, repetitious, maundering; *informal* windy.
—OPPOSITES: concise, succinct, laconic.

look v. **1** GLANCE, gaze, stare, gape, peer; peep, peek, take a look; watch, observe, view, regard, examine, inspect, eye, scan,

scrutinize, survey, study, contemplate, consider, take in, ogle; *informal* take a gander, rubberneck, goggle, give someone/something a/the once-over, get a load of, eyeball; *literary* behold. **2** COMMAND A VIEW OF, face, overlook, front. **3** SEEM (TO BE), appear (to be), have the appearance/air of being, give the impression of being, give every appearance/indication of being, strike someone as being.
—OPPOSITES: ignore.
▶ n. **1** GLANCE, view, examination, study, inspection, observation, scan, survey, peep, peek, glimpse, gaze, stare; *informal* eyeful, gander, look-see, once-over, squint. **2** EXPRESSION, mien. **3** APPEARANCE, air, aspect, bearing, cast, manner, mien, demeanour, facade, impression, effect. **4** FASHION, style, vogue, mode.
□ **look after** TAKE CARE OF, care for, attend to, minister to, tend, mind, keep an eye on, keep safe, be responsible for, protect; nurse, babysit, house-sit. **look back on** REFLECT ON, think back to, remember, recall, reminisce about. **look down on** DISDAIN, scorn, regard with contempt, look down one's nose at, sneer at, despise. **look for** SEARCH FOR, hunt for, try to find, seek, cast about/around for, try to track down, forage for, scout out, quest for/after. **look into** ☞ INVESTIGATE. **look like** ☞ RESEMBLE. **look on/ upon** REGARD, consider, think of, deem, judge, see, view, count, reckon. **look out** ☞ BEWARE. **look**

something over ☞ INSPECT. **look up to** ☞ ADMIRE.

look-alike n. ☞ DOUBLE n.

loom v. **1** EMERGE, appear, come into view, take shape, materialize, reveal itself. **2** SOAR, tower, rise, rear up; overhang, overshadow, dominate. **3** BE IMMINENT, be on the horizon, impend, threaten, brew, be just around the corner, be in the wind.

loop n. COIL, hoop, ring, circle, noose, oval, spiral, curl, bend, curve, arc, twirl, whorl, twist, hook, helix, convolution.
▶ v. COIL, wind, twist, snake, wreathe, spiral, curve, bend, turn.

loose adj. **1** NOT FIXED IN PLACE, not secure, unsecured, unattached; detached, unfastened, untied; wobbly, unsteady, movable. **2** FREE, at large, at liberty, on the loose, escaped; unconfined, untied, unchained, untethered, stray; fugitive, on the lam, on the run, wanted, AWOL, runaway. **3** VAGUE, indefinite, inexact, imprecise, approximate; broad, general, rough; liberal; informal ballpark. **4** BAGGY, generously cut, slack, roomy; oversized, shapeless, sagging, saggy, sloppy. **5** ☞ PROMISCUOUS.
—OPPOSITES: secure, literal, narrow, tight, chaste, guarded.
▶ v. **1** FREE, set free, unloose, turn loose, set loose, let loose, let go, release; untie, unchain, unfasten, unleash. **2** RELAX, slacken, loosen; weaken, lessen, reduce, diminish, moderate.
—OPPOSITES: confine, tighten.
☐ **let loose**. ☞ LOOSE v. 1. **on the loose** ☞ LOOSE adj. 2.

loosen v. **1** MAKE SLACK, slacken, unstick; unfasten, detach, release, disconnect, undo, unclasp, unlatch, unbolt. **2** BECOME SLACK, slacken, become loose, let go, ease; work loose, work free. **3** WEAKEN, relax, slacken, loose, lessen, reduce, moderate, diminish.
—OPPOSITES: tighten.
☐ **loosen up** ☞ RELAX 1.

loot n. BOOTY, spoils, plunder, stolen goods, contraband, pillage; informal swag, hot goods, ill-gotten gains, take.
▶ v. PLUNDER, pillage, despoil, ransack, sack, raid, rifle, rob, burgle, burglarize.

lop v. CUT, chop, hack, saw, hew, slash, axe; prune, sever, clip, trim, snip, dock, crop.

lopsided adj. CROOKED, askew, awry, off-centre, uneven, out of line, asymmetrical, tilted, at an angle, aslant, slanting; off-balance, off-kilter; informal cockeyed, wonky.
—OPPOSITES: even, level, balanced.

loquacious adj. ☞ TALKATIVE.
—OPPOSITES: reticent, taciturn.

lose v. **1** MISLAY, misplace, be unable to find, lose track of, leave (behind), fail to keep/retain, fail to keep sight of. **2** BE DEPRIVED OF, suffer the loss of; no longer have. **3** ☞ ELUDE. **4** MISS, waste, squander, fail to grasp, fail to take advantage of, let pass, neglect, forfeit; informal pass up, lose out on. **5** BE DEFEATED, be beaten, suffer defeat, be the loser, be conquered, be vanquished, be trounced; informal come a cropper, go down, take a licking, be bested.

—OPPOSITES: find, regain, seize, win.

loser *n.* **1** DEFEATED PERSON, also-ran, runner-up. **2** FAILURE, underachiever, ne'er-do-well, writeoff, has-been; MISFIT, freak, unpopular person; *informal* geek, dweeb, nerd, hoser✦; flop, no-hoper, washout, lemon.
—OPPOSITES: winner, success.

loss *n.* **1** MISLAYING, misplacement, forgetting. **2** DEPRIVATION, disappearance, privation, forfeiture, diminution, erosion, reduction, depletion. **3** DEFICIT, debit, debt, indebtedness, deficiency.
—OPPOSITES: recovery, profit.
□ **at a loss** BAFFLED, nonplussed, mystified, puzzled, perplexed, bewildered, bemused, at sixes and sevens, confused, dumbfounded, stumped, stuck, blank; flummoxed, bamboozled, fazed, floored, beaten, discombobulated.

lost *adj.* **1** MISSING, mislaid, misplaced, vanished, disappeared, gone missing/astray, forgotten, nowhere to be found; absent, not present, strayed; irretrievable, unrecoverable. **2** OFF COURSE, off track, disorientated, having lost one's bearings, going around in circles, adrift, at sea, astray. **3** MISSED, forfeited, neglected, wasted, squandered, gone by the board; *informal* down the drain. **4** BYGONE, past, former, one-time, previous, old, olden, departed, vanished, forgotten, consigned to oblivion, extinct, dead, gone. **5** HOPELESS, beyond hope, futile, forlorn, failed, beyond remedy,

beyond recovery.
—OPPOSITES: current.

lot *n.* **1** (**a lot**) A LARGE AMOUNT, a fair amount, a good/great deal, a great quantity, quantities, an abundance, a wealth, a profusion, a plethora, plenty, a mass, much; many, a great many, a large number, a considerable number, numerous, scores; *informal* hundreds, thousands, millions, billions, gazillions, loads, masses, heaps, a pile, a stack, piles, oodles, stacks, scads, reams, wads, pots, oceans, a mountain, mountains, miles, tons, zillions, more —— than one can shake a stick at, gobs, a bunch, a heap, a ton, a slew, a whack. **2** BATCH, set, collection, group, bundle, quantity, assortment, parcel. **3** FATE, destiny, fortune, doom; situation, circumstances, state, condition, position, plight, predicament. **4** PATCH OF GROUND, piece of ground, plot, area, tract, parcel, plat.
—OPPOSITES: a little, not much, a few, not many.
▶ *adv.* A GREAT DEAL, a good deal, to a great extent, much; often, frequently, regularly.
—OPPOSITES: a little.

lotion *n.* OINTMENT, cream, salve, balm, rub, emollient, moisturizer, lubricant, gel, unguent, liniment.

loud *adj.* **1** NOISY, blaring, booming, deafening, roaring, thunderous, thundering, ear-splitting, ear-piercing, piercing; carrying, clearly audible; lusty, powerful, forceful, stentorian; *Music* forte, fortissimo.
2 VOCIFEROUS, clamorous,

insistent, vehement, emphatic, urgent. **3** ☞ GAUDY.
—OPPOSITES: quiet, soft, gentle, sober, tasteful.

lounge v. LAZE, lie, loll, lie back, lean back, recline, stretch oneself, drape oneself, relax, rest, repose, take it easy, put one's feet up, unwind, luxuriate; sprawl, slump, slouch, flop; loaf, idle, do nothing; *informal* take a load off, kick back.
▸ n. **1** BAR, pub, club, barroom, beer parlour✲, taproom. **2** WAITING AREA, reception room.

lousy adj. **1** ☞ AWFUL 2.
2 ☞ CONTEMPTIBLE. **3** ☞ ILL adj. 1.

lout n. BOOR, hooligan, thug, ruffian, barbarian, oaf, hoodlum, rowdy, lubber; *informal* tough, roughneck, bruiser, yahoo, lug.
—OPPOSITES: gentleman.

lovable adj. ☞ ADORABLE.
—OPPOSITES: hateful, loathsome.

love n. **1** DEEP AFFECTION, fondness, tenderness, warmth, intimacy, attachment, endearment; devotion, adoration, doting, idolization, worship; passion, ardour, desire, lust, yearning, infatuation. **2** LIKING, enjoyment, appreciation, taste, delight, relish, passion, zeal, appetite, zest, enthusiasm, keenness, fondness, soft spot, weakness, bent, leaning, proclivity, inclination, disposition, partiality, predilection, penchant. **3** COMPASSION, care, caring, regard, solicitude, concern, friendliness, friendship, kindness, charity, goodwill, sympathy, kindliness, altruism, unselfishness, philanthropy, benevolence, fellow feeling, humanity. **4** ☞ BELOVED n.
—RELATED: amatory, phil-.

—OPPOSITES: hatred.
▸ v. **1** CARE VERY MUCH FOR, feel deep affection for, hold very dear, adore, think the world of, be devoted to, dote on, idolize, worship; be in love with, be infatuated with, be smitten with, be besotted with; *informal* be mad/crazy/nuts/wild about, have a crush on, carry a torch for. **2** LIKE VERY MUCH, delight in, enjoy greatly, have a passion for, take great pleasure in, derive great pleasure from, relish, savour; have a weakness for, be partial to, have a soft spot for, have a taste for, be taken with; *informal* get a kick out of, have a thing about, be mad/crazy/nuts/wild about, be hooked on, get off on.
—OPPOSITES: hate.
◻ **in love with** INFATUATED WITH, besotted with, enamoured of, smitten with, consumed with desire for; captivated by, bewitched by, enthralled by, entranced by, moonstruck by; devoted to, doting on; *informal* mad/crazy/nuts/wild about.

lovely adj. **1** BEAUTIFUL, pretty, attractive, good-looking, appealing, handsome, adorable, exquisite, sweet, personable, charming; enchanting, engaging, winsome, seductive, sexy, gorgeous, alluring, ravishing, glamorous; *formal* beauteous; *archaic* fair. **2** SCENIC, picturesque, pleasing, easy on the eye; magnificent, stunning, splendid. **3** DELIGHTFUL, very pleasant, very nice, very agreeable, marvellous, wonderful, sublime, superb, magical; *informal* terrific, fabulous,

heavenly, divine, amazing, glorious.
—OPPOSITES: ugly, horrible.

lover *n.* **1** BOYFRIEND, GIRLFRIEND, lady love, beloved, love, darling, sweetheart, inamorata, inamorato; admirer, flame, loved one, steady, suitor, valentine; mistress; partner, significant other, main squeeze, bit on the side, toy boy, boy toy; *dated* beau; *archaic* swain, concubine, paramour. **2** DEVOTEE, admirer, fan, enthusiast, aficionado; *informal* buff, freak, nut, junkie.
—RELATED: -phile.

loving *adj.* AFFECTIONATE, fond, devoted, adoring, doting, solicitous, demonstrative; caring, tender, warm, warm-hearted, close; amorous, ardent, passionate, amatory; *informal* touchy-feely, lovey-dovey.
—OPPOSITES: cold, cruel.

low *adj.* **1** SHORT, small, little; squat, stubby, stunted, dwarf; shallow. **2** CHEAP, economical, moderate, reasonable, modest, bargain, budget, bargain-basement, rock-bottom, cut-rate. **3** SCARCE, scanty, scant, skimpy, meagre, sparse, few, little, paltry; reduced, depleted, diminished. **4** INFERIOR, substandard, poor, bad, low-grade, low-end, below par, second-rate, unsatisfactory, deficient, defective, shoddy. **5** HUMBLE, lowly, low-ranking, plebeian, proletarian, peasant; poor; common, ordinary. **6** UNAMBITIOUS, modest. **7** UNFAVOURABLE, poor, bad, adverse, negative. **8** ☞ CONTEMPTIBLE **9** ☞ VULGAR 3, 1.

10 QUIET, soft, faint, gentle, muted, subdued, muffled, hushed, quietened, whispered, stifled. **11** BASS, baritone, low-pitched, deep, rumbling, booming, sonorous. **12** ☞ SAD 1.
—OPPOSITES: high, expensive, plentiful, superior, noble, favourable, admirable, decent, exalted, loud, cheerful, lively.
▸ *n.* NADIR, low point, lowest point, lowest level, minimum, depth, rock bottom.
—OPPOSITES: high.

lowbrow *adj.* MASS-MARKET, tabloid, popular, lightweight, accessible, unpretentious; uncultured, unsophisticated, trashy, philistine, simplistic, down-market; *informal* dumbed-down, rubbishy.
—OPPOSITES: highbrow, intellectual.

lowdown *n.* FACTS, information, story, intelligence, news, inside story; *informal* info, rundown, the score, the scoop, the word, the dope, the dirt, the skinny.
▸ *adj.* ☞ CONTEMPTIBLE.
—OPPOSITES: kind, honourable.

lower *adj.* **1** SUBORDINATE, inferior, lesser, junior, minor, secondary, lower-level, subsidiary, subservient. **2** BOTTOM, bottommost, nether, under; underneath, further down, beneath.
—OPPOSITES: upper, higher.
▸ *v.* **1** MOVE DOWN, let down, take down, haul down, drop, let fall. **2** SOFTEN, modulate, quieten, hush, tone down, muffle, turn down, mute. **3** REDUCE, decrease, lessen, bring down, mark down,

cut, slash, axe, diminish, curtail, prune, pare (down). **4** SUBSIDE, fall (off), recede, ebb, wane; abate, die down, let up, moderate, diminish, lessen. **5** ☞ DEGRADE 1.
—OPPOSITES: raise, increase.

low-key *adj.* RESTRAINED, modest, understated, muted, subtle, quiet, low-profile, inconspicuous, unostentatious, unobtrusive, discreet, toned-down; casual, informal, mellow, laid-back.
—OPPOSITES: ostentatious, obtrusive.

lowly *adj.* HUMBLE, low, low-born, low-ranking, plebeian, proletarian; common, ordinary, plain, average, modest, simple, inconsequential, insignificant, lower-class, mean, poor, underprivileged, undistinguished, unremarkable; inferior, ignoble, subordinate, obscure.
—OPPOSITES: aristocratic, exalted.

loyal *adj.* FAITHFUL, true, devoted; constant, steadfast, staunch, dependable, reliable, trusted, trustworthy, trusty, dutiful, dedicated, unchanging, unwavering, unswerving; patriotic.
—OPPOSITES: treacherous.

loyalty *n.* ALLEGIANCE, faithfulness, obedience, adherence, homage, devotion, fidelity; steadfastness, staunchness, dependability, reliability, trustworthiness, duty, dedication, commitment; patriotism.
—OPPOSITES: treachery.

lucid *adj.* **1** ☞ CLEAR 1.
2 ☞ RATIONAL 2.
—OPPOSITES: confusing, confused.

luck *n.* **1** GOOD FORTUNE, good luck; fluke, stroke of luck; *informal* lucky break. **2** SUCCESS, prosperity, good fortune, good luck. **3** FORTUNE, fate, destiny, Lady Luck, lot, stars, karma, kismet; fortuity, serendipity; chance, accident, a twist of fate.
—OPPOSITES: bad luck, misfortune.

luckily *adv.* ☞ FORTUNATELY.
—OPPOSITES: unfortunately.

lucky *adj.* **1** ☞ FORTUNATE 1.
2 PROVIDENTIAL, fortunate, advantageous, timely, opportune, serendipitous, expedient, heaven-sent, auspicious; chance, fortuitous, fluky, accidental.
—OPPOSITES: unfortunate.

lucrative *adj.* PROFITABLE, profit-making, gainful, remunerative, money-making, paying, high-income, well-paid, bankable; rewarding, worthwhile; thriving, flourishing, successful, booming.
—OPPOSITES: unprofitable.

ludicrous *adj.* ☞ RIDICULOUS.
—OPPOSITES: sensible.

lukewarm *adj.* **1** TEPID, slightly warm, warmish, at room temperature, chambré.
2 INDIFFERENT, cool, half-hearted, unenthusiastic, tepid, perfunctory.
—OPPOSITES: hot, cold, enthusiastic.

lull *v.* SOOTHE, calm, hush; rock to sleep.
—OPPOSITES: waken, agitate, arouse.
▶ *n.* ☞ PAUSE.
—OPPOSITES: activity.

lumber *n.* TIMBER, wood, boards, planks.

▸ *v.* LURCH, stumble, trundle, shamble, shuffle, waddle; trudge, clump, stump, plod, tramp, tromp, galumph.

lumberjack *n.* ☞ LOGGER.

luminous *adj.* ☞ RADIANT 1.
—OPPOSITES: dark.

lummox *n.* ☞ OAF.

lump *n.* **1** ☞ CHUNK. **2** SWELLING, bump, bulge, protuberance, protrusion, growth, outgrowth, nodule, hump; goose egg. **3** ☞ OAF.

▸ *v.* COMBINE, put, group, bunch, aggregate, unite, pool, merge, collect, throw, consider together.

lunacy *n.* ☞ MADNESS 1, 2.
—OPPOSITES: sanity, sense, prudence.

lunatic *n.* MANIAC, madman, madwoman, imbecile, psychopath, psychotic; fool, idiot; *informal* loony, nut, nutcase, head case, psycho, moron, screwball, crackpot, fruitcake.

▸ *adj.* **1** ☞ MAD 1. **2** ☞ MAD 3.

lunge *n.* THRUST, jab, stab, dive, rush, charge.

▸ *v.* THRUST, dive, spring, launch oneself, rush, make a grab.

lurch *v.* **1** ☞ STAGGER 1. **2** SWAY, reel, list, heel, rock, roll, pitch, toss, jerk, shake, judder, flounder, swerve, teeter.

lure *v.* TEMPT, entice, attract, induce, coax, persuade, inveigle, allure, seduce, win over, cajole, beguile, bewitch, ensnare.
—OPPOSITES: deter, put off.

▸ *n.* TEMPTATION, enticement, attraction, pull, draw, appeal; inducement, allurement,

fascination, interest, magnet; *informal* come-on.

lurid *adj.* **1** BRIGHT, brilliant, vivid, glaring, shocking, fluorescent, flaming, dazzling, intense; gaudy, loud, showy, bold, garish, tacky. **2** SENSATIONAL, sensationalist, exaggerated, over-dramatized, colourful; salacious, graphic, explicit, unrestrained, prurient, shocking; gruesome, gory, grisly; *informal* juicy.
—OPPOSITES: muted, restrained.

lurk *v.* SKULK, loiter, lie in wait, lie low, hide, conceal oneself, take cover, keep out of sight.

luscious *adj.* DELICIOUS, succulent, lush, juicy, mouth-watering, lip-smacking, sweet, tasty, appetizing; *informal* scrumptious, yummy, nummy.

lush *adj.* LUXURIANT, rich, abundant, profuse, exuberant, riotous, prolific, vigorous; dense, thick, rank, rampant; *informal* jungly.
—OPPOSITES: barren, sparse, shrivelled.

lust *n.* **1** SEXUAL DESIRE, sexual appetite, sexual longing, ardour, desire, passion; libido, sex drive, sexuality, biological urge; lechery, lasciviousness, concupiscence; *informal* horniness, the hots, randiness. **2** ☞ DESIRE *n.* 1.
—OPPOSITES: dread, aversion.

lustful *adj.* LECHEROUS, lascivious, libidinous, licentious, salacious, goatish; wanton, unchaste, impure, naughty, immodest, indecent, dirty, prurient; passionate, sensual, sexy, erotic; *informal* horny, randy, raunchy, lusty; *formal* concupiscent.
—OPPOSITES: chaste, pure.

lustrous *adj.* SHINY, shining, satiny, glossy, gleaming, shimmering, burnished, polished; radiant, bright, brilliant, luminous, sheeny; dazzling, sparkling, glistening, twinkling.
—OPPOSITES: dull, dark.

luxuriant *adj.* ☞ LUSH.
—OPPOSITES: barren, sparse.

luxurious *adj.* OPULENT, sumptuous, deluxe, rich, grand, palatial, splendid, magnificent, well appointed, extravagant, fancy, upscale, upmarket, five-star; *informal* plush, posh, classy, ritzy, swanky, swank, expensive, lavish, luxury.
—OPPOSITES: plain, basic.

luxury *n.* **1** OPULENCE, luxuriousness, sumptuousness, grandeur, magnificence, splendour, lavishness, the lap of luxury, a bed of roses, (the land of) milk and honey; *informal* the life of Riley. **2** INDULGENCE, extravagance, self-indulgence, non-essential, treat, extra, frill.
—OPPOSITES: simplicity, necessity.

lying *n.* UNTRUTHFULNESS, fabrication, fibbing, perjury, white lies; falseness, falsity, dishonesty, mendacity, telling stories, invention, misrepresentation, deceit, duplicity; *literary* perfidy.
—OPPOSITES: honesty.

lyrical *adj.* EXPRESSIVE, emotional, deeply felt, personal, subjective, passionate, lyric.

Mm

macabre *adj.* GRUESOME, grisly, grim, gory, morbid, ghastly, unearthly, grotesque, hideous, horrific, shocking, dreadful, loathsome, repugnant, repulsive, sickening.

machine *n.* APPARATUS, appliance, device, contraption, contrivance, mechanism, engine, gadget, tool.
—RELATED: mechanical.

mad *adj.* **1** ☞ INSANE 1. **2** ANGRY, furious, infuriated, irate, raging, enraged, fuming, incensed, seeing red, beside oneself; *informal* livid, sore; *literary* wrathful; (**get mad**) lose one's temper, get in a rage, rant and rave; *informal* explode, go off the deep end, go ape, flip, flip out, flip one's wig. **3** FOOLISH, insane, stupid, lunatic, foolhardy, idiotic, senseless, absurd, impractical, silly, inane, asinine, wild, unwise, imprudent; *informal* crazy, crackpot, crack-brained, daft. **4** (*informal*) ENTHUSIASTIC, passionate; ardent, fervent, avid, fanatical; devoted to, infatuated with, in love with, hot for; *informal* crazy, nuts, wild, hooked on, gone on, nutso. **5** FRENZIED, frantic, frenetic, feverish, wild, hectic, manic.
—OPPOSITES: sane, pleased, sensible, indifferent, calm.

madden *v.* ☞ ANGER.

madman, **madwoman** *n.*
☞ LUNATIC.

madness *n.* **1** INSANITY, mental illness, dementia, derangement; lunacy, instability; mania, psychosis; *informal* craziness. **2** FOLLY, foolishness, stupidity, silliness, idiocy, lunacy, recklessness, foolhardiness, imprudence, irresponsibility, craziness.
—OPPOSITES: sanity, common sense, good sense, calm.

magazine *n.* JOURNAL, periodical, serial, supplement, quarterly, monthly, weekly, newsmagazine; *informal* glossy, mag, zine, fanzine.

magic *n.* **1** SORCERY, witchcraft, wizardry, necromancy, enchantment, the supernatural, occultism, the occult, black magic, the black arts, voodoo, hoodoo, mojo, shamanism; charm, hex, spell, jinx. **2** CONJURING TRICKS, sleight of hand, legerdemain, illusion, prestidigitation.
▶ *adj.* **1** SUPERNATURAL, enchanted, occult. **2** FASCINATING, captivating, charming, glamorous, magical, enchanting, entrancing, spellbinding, magnetic, irresistible, hypnotic.

magician *n.* **1** SORCERER, sorceress, witch, wizard, warlock, enchanter, enchantress,

necromancer, shaman.
2 CONJUROR, illusionist,
prestidigitator.

magnanimous adj. ☞ GENEROUS
1, 2.

magnificent adj. **1** SPLENDID,
spectacular, impressive, striking,
glorious, superb, majestic,
awesome, awe-inspiring,
breathtaking. **2** SUMPTUOUS,
resplendent, grand, impressive,
imposing, monumental, stately,
opulent, luxurious, lavish, rich,
dazzling, beautiful, elegant; informal
splendiferous, ritzy, posh, swanky.
3 MASTERLY, skilful, virtuoso,
brilliant.
—OPPOSITES: uninspiring, modest,
tawdry, poor, weak.

magnitude n. IMMENSITY,
vastness, hugeness, enormity;
size, extent, expanse, greatness,
largeness, bigness.
—OPPOSITES: smallness, triviality.

mail n. POST, letters,
correspondence; postal system,
postal service, post office;
delivery, collection; email; informal
snail mail.

main adj. PRINCIPAL, chief, head,
leading, foremost, most
important, major, ruling,
dominant, central, focal, key,
core, vital, prime, master,
premier, primary, first,
fundamental, basic, supreme,
predominant, (most) prominent,
pre-eminent, highest, paramount,
overriding, cardinal, crucial,
critical, pivotal, salient,
elemental, essential, staple; informal
number-one.
—OPPOSITES: subsidiary, minor.

mainly adv. MOSTLY, for the most
part, in the main, on the whole,
largely, by and large, to a large
extent, predominantly, chiefly,
principally, primarily, basically,
for/to all intents and purposes,
fundamentally, in essence,
substantially; generally, usually,
typically, habitually, commonly,
on average, as a rule, almost
always.

mainstream adj. NORMAL,
conventional, ordinary, orthodox,
conformist, accepted, established,
recognized, common, usual,
prevailing, popular.
—OPPOSITES: fringe.

maintain v. **1** PRESERVE, conserve,
keep, retain, keep going, keep
alive, keep up, prolong,
perpetuate, sustain, carry on,
continue. **2** KEEP IN GOOD
CONDITION, keep in (good) repair,
keep up, service, care for, take
good care of, look after.
3 SUPPORT, provide for, keep,
sustain; nurture, feed, nourish.
4 ☞ ASSERT 1.
—OPPOSITES: break, discontinue,
neglect, deny.

maintenance n.
1 PRESERVATION, conservation,
keeping, prolongation,
perpetuation, carrying on,
continuation, continuance.
2 UPKEEP, service, servicing,
repair(s), care.
—OPPOSITES: breakdown,
discontinuation, neglect.

majestic adj. STATELY, dignified,
distinguished, solemn,
magnificent, grand, splendid,
resplendent, glorious, sumptuous,
impressive, august, noble, awe-

inspiring, monumental, palatial; statuesque, Olympian, imposing, marvellous, sonorous, resounding, heroic.

—OPPOSITES: modest, wretched.

major *adj.* **1** GREATEST, best, finest, most important, chief, main, prime, principal, capital, cardinal, leading, star, foremost, outstanding, first-rate, pre-eminent, arch-; *informal* major league, big league. **2** IMPORTANT, big, significant, weighty, crucial, key, sweeping, substantial.

—OPPOSITES: minor, little, trivial.

majority *n.* LARGER PART/NUMBER, greater part/number, best/better part, most, more than half; plurality, bulk, mass, weight, (main) body, preponderance, predominance, generality, lion's share.

—OPPOSITES: minority.

make *v.* **1** CONSTRUCT, build, assemble, put together, manufacture, produce, fabricate, create, form, fashion, model. **2** FORCE, compel, coerce, press, drive, pressure, oblige, require; have someone do something, prevail on, dragoon, bludgeon, strong-arm, impel, constrain; *informal* railroad. **3** PERFORM, execute, give, do, accomplish, achieve, bring off, carry out, effect. **4** APPOINT, designate, name, nominate, select, elect, vote in, install; induct, institute, invest, ordain. **5** ACQUIRE, obtain, gain, get, realize, secure, win, earn; gross, net, clear; bring in, take (in), rake in. **6** PREPARE, get ready, put together, concoct, cook, dish up, throw together, whip up,

brew; *informal* fix. **7** UTTER, give, deliver, give voice to, enunciate, recite, pronounce. **8** BE, act as, serve as, function as, constitute, do duty for.

—OPPOSITES: destroy, lose.

▶ *n.* BRAND, marque, label.

□ **make believe** PRETEND, fantasize, daydream, build castles in the air, dream, imagine, play-act, play. **make do** SCRAPE BY, get by, manage, cope, survive, muddle through, improvise, make ends meet, keep the wolf from the door, keep one's head above water; *informal* make out; (**make do with**) make the best of, get by on, put up with. **make it 1** SUCCEED, be a success, distinguish oneself, get ahead, make good; *informal* make the grade, arrive. **2** SURVIVE, come through, pull through, get better, recover. **make something out** SEE, discern, distinguish, perceive, pick out, detect, observe, recognize; *literary* descry, espy. **make up** BE FRIENDS AGAIN, bury the hatchet, declare a truce, make peace, forgive and forget, shake hands, become reconciled, settle one's differences, mend fences, call it quits. **make something up 1** CONSTITUTE, form, compose, account for. **2** PREPARE, mix, concoct, put together. **3** INVENT, fabricate, concoct, dream up, think up, hatch, trump up; devise, manufacture, formulate, coin; *informal* cook up. **make up for 1** ATONE FOR, make amends for, compensate for, make recompense for, make reparation for, make redress for, make restitution for, expiate. **2** OFFSET, counterbalance, counteract, compensate for; balance, neutralize, cancel out, even up, redeem. **make up one's mind** DECIDE, come to a decision, make/ reach a decision; settle on a plan of action, come to a conclusion, reach a conclusion; determine, resolve.

make-believe *adj.* ☞ IMAGINARY.
—OPPOSITES: real, actual.

maker *n.* CREATOR, manufacturer, constructor, builder, producer, fabricator, inventor, architect, designer.

makeshift *adj.* TEMPORARY, provisional, interim, stopgap, make-do, standby, rough and ready, improvised, ad hoc, extempore, jury-rigged, jerry-built, thrown together, cobbled together.
—OPPOSITES: permanent.

malice *n.* SPITE, malevolence, ill will, vindictiveness, vengefulness, revenge, malignity, evil intentions, animus, enmity, rancour; *informal* bitchiness, cattiness.
—OPPOSITES: benevolence.

malicious *adj.* SPITEFUL, malevolent, vindictive, vengeful, malign, mean, nasty, hurtful, mischievous, wounding, cruel, unkind; *informal* bitchy, catty; *literary* maleficent.
—OPPOSITES: benevolent.

malign *adj.* HARMFUL, evil, bad, baleful, hostile, inimical, destructive, malignant, injurious; *literary* maleficent.
—OPPOSITES: beneficial.
▸ *v.* DEFAME, slander, libel, blacken someone's name/character, smear,

vilify, speak ill of, cast aspersions on, run down, traduce, denigrate, disparage, slur, abuse, revile; *informal* badmouth, dis, knock; *formal* derogate, calumniate.
—OPPOSITES: praise.

malnutrition *n.* UNDERNOURISHMENT, malnourishment, poor diet, inadequate diet, unhealthy diet, lack of food; hunger, starvation.

maltreat *v.* ☞ MISTREAT.

manage *v.* **1** BE IN CHARGE OF, run, be head of, head, direct, control, be in control of, preside over, lead, govern, rule, command, superintend, supervise, oversee, administer, organize, conduct, operate, handle, orchestrate, coordinate, guide, be at the helm of, be responsible for, regulate, steer; *informal* head up, run the show, call the shots, be in the driver's seat, be in the saddle. **2** COPE, get along/on, make do, be/ fare/do all right, carry on, survive, get by, muddle through/along, fend for oneself, shift for oneself, make ends meet, weather the storm; *informal* make out, hack it. **3** CONTROL, handle, master; cope with, deal with.

manageable *adj.* **1** ACHIEVABLE, doable, practicable, possible, feasible, reasonable, attainable, viable. **2** COMPLIANT, tractable, pliant, pliable, malleable, biddable, docile, amenable, governable, controllable, accommodating, acquiescent, complaisant, yielding.
—OPPOSITES: difficult, impossible.

management *n.*
1 ADMINISTRATION, running,

managing, organization; charge, care, direction, leadership, control, governing, governance, ruling, command, superintendence, supervision, overseeing, conduct, handling, guidance, operation. **2** MANAGERS, employers, directors, board of directors, board, directorate, executives, administrators, administration; owners, proprietors; *informal* bosses, top brass.

mandatory *adj.* COMPULSORY, obligatory, prescribed, required, demanded, statutory, enforced, binding, incumbent; requisite, necessary, imperative, unavoidable, inescapable, essential.
—OPPOSITES: optional.

mangle *v.* MUTILATE, maim, disfigure, damage, injure, crush; hack, cut up, lacerate, tear apart, butcher, maul.

mania *n.* OBSESSION, compulsion, fixation, fetish, fascination, preoccupation, infatuation, passion, enthusiasm, desire, urge, craving; craze, fad, rage; *informal* thing, yen.

maniac *n.* **1** ☞ LUNATIC. **2** (*informal*) ENTHUSIAST, fan, devotee, aficionado; *informal* freak, fiend, fanatic, nut, buff, bum, addict.

manifest *v.* DISPLAY, show, exhibit, demonstrate, betray, present, reveal; *formal* evince.
—OPPOSITES: hide, mask.
▶ *adj.* ☞ OBVIOUS.

manifestation *n.* **1** DISPLAY, demonstration, show, exhibition, presentation. **2** SIGN, indication, evidence, token, symptom,

testimony, proof, substantiation, mark, reflection, example, instance.

manipulate *v.* **1** OPERATE, work; turn, pull. **2** CONTROL, influence, use/turn to one's advantage, exploit, manoeuvre, engineer, steer, direct, gerrymander; twist someone round one's little finger. **3** FALSIFY, rig, distort, alter, change, doctor, massage, juggle, tamper with, tinker with, interfere with, misrepresent; *informal* cook, fiddle.

mankind *n.* THE HUMAN RACE, man, humanity, human beings, humans, Homo sapiens, humankind, people, men and women.

manly *adj.* ☞ MASCULINE 2.
—OPPOSITES: effeminate.

man-made *adj.* ☞ ARTIFICIAL 1.
—OPPOSITES: natural.

manner *n.* **1** WAY, fashion, mode, means, method, system, style, approach, technique, procedure, process, methodology, modus operandi, form. **2** ☞ DEMEANOUR. **3** (**manners**) CORRECT BEHAVIOUR, etiquette, social graces, good form, protocol, politeness, decorum, propriety, gentility, civility, Ps and Qs.

mannered *adj.* AFFECTED, pretentious, unnatural, artificial, contrived, stilted, stiff, forced, put-on, theatrical, precious, stagy, camp; *informal* pseudo.
—OPPOSITES: natural.

mannerism *n.* IDIOSYNCRASY, quirk, oddity, foible, trait, peculiarity, habit, characteristic, tic.

manoeuvre v. **1** STEER, guide, drive, negotiate, navigate, pilot, direct, manipulate, move, work, jockey. **2** INTRIGUE, plot, scheme, plan, lay plans, conspire, pull strings.
▶ n. **1** OPERATION, exercise, activity, move, movement, action. **2** STRATAGEM, tactic, gambit, ploy, trick, dodge, ruse, plan, scheme, operation, device, plot, machination, artifice, subterfuge, intrigue.

manufacture v. **1** MAKE, produce, mass-produce, build, construct, assemble, put together, create, fabricate, turn out, process, engineer. **2** MAKE UP, invent, fabricate, concoct, hatch, dream up, think up, trump up, devise, formulate, frame, contrive; *informal* cook up.

manufacturer n. MAKER, producer, builder, constructor, creator; factory owner, industrialist, captain of industry.

many adj. NUMEROUS, a great/good deal of, a lot of, plenty of, countless, innumerable, scores of, crowds of, droves of, an army of, a horde of, a multitude of, a multiplicity of, multitudinous, multiple, untold, numberless; a quantity of, quite a few, several, various, manifold, sundry, diverse, assorted, multifarious; copious, abundant, profuse, an abundance of, a profusion of; frequent; *informal* lots of, umpteen, loads of, masses of, stacks of, scads of, heaps of, piles of, bags of, tons of, oodles of, dozens of, hundreds of, thousands of, millions of, billions of, zillions of, gazillions of, a slew of, a boatload of, more —— than one can shake a stick at; *literary* myriad, divers.
—RELATED: multi-, poly-.
—OPPOSITES: few.

mar v. ☞ SPOIL 1, RUIN 1.

march v. **1** STRIDE, walk, troop, step, pace, tread; footslog, slog, tramp, tromp, hike, trudge; parade, file, process. **2** ADVANCE, progress, move on, roll on.
▶ n. **1** HIKE, trek, tramp, slog, footslog, walk; route march, forced march. **2** PARADE, procession, cortège; demonstration, protest. **3** PROGRESS, advance, progression, development, evolution; passage.

margin n. **1** EDGE, side, verge, border, perimeter, brink, brim, rim, fringe, boundary, limits, periphery, bound, extremity; *literary* bourn, skirt. **2** GAP, majority, amount, difference.

marginal adj. SLIGHT, small, tiny, minute, insignificant, minimal, negligible.

marginalize v. SIDELINE, trivialize; isolate, cut off, shut out; disenfranchise, alienate, estrange, ghettoize, discriminate against.

marijuana n. CANNABIS, pot, hashish, hash, dope, grass, weed, Mary Jane, bud, BC Bud✿, bhang, hemp, kef, ganja, green, sinsemilla, skunkweed, locoweed.

marital adj. MATRIMONIAL, married, wedded, conjugal, nuptial, marriage, wedding; spousal; connubial.

maritime adj. **1** NAVAL, marine, nautical; seafaring, seagoing, sea, ocean-going. **2** COASTAL, seaside, littoral.

□ *(Cdn)* **the Maritimes** New Brunswick, Prince Edward Island, Nova Scotia; *informal* the East coast, Atlantic provinces.

mark *n.* **1** BLEMISH, streak, spot, fleck, dot, blot, stain, smear, speck, speckle, blotch, smudge, smut, fingermark, fingerprint; bruise, discoloration; birthmark; *informal* splotch; *technical* stigma. **2** LOGO, seal, stamp, imprint, symbol, emblem, device, insignia, badge, brand, trademark, monogram, hallmark, logotype, watermark. **3** POINT, level, stage, degree. **4** SIGN, token, symbol, indication, badge, emblem; symptom, evidence, proof. **5** CHARACTERISTIC, feature, trait, attribute, quality, hallmark, calling card, badge, stamp, property, indicator. **6** GRADE, grading, rating, score, percentage.
▶ *v.* **1** DISCOLOUR, stain, smear, smudge, streak, blotch, blemish; dirty, pockmark, bruise; *informal* splotch; *literary* smirch. **2** INDICATE, label, flag, tick, check off, highlight; show, identify, designate, delineate, denote, specify. **3** CELEBRATE, observe, recognize, acknowledge, keep, honour, solemnize, pay tribute to, salute, commemorate, remember, memorialize. **4** REPRESENT, signify, be a sign of, indicate, herald. **5** CHARACTERIZE, distinguish, identify, typify, brand, stamp. **6** ASSESS, evaluate, grade, appraise, correct.
□ **make one's mark** BE SUCCESSFUL, distinguish oneself, succeed, be a success, prosper, get ahead, make good; *informal* make it, make the grade.

marked *adj.* NOTICEABLE, pronounced, decided, distinct, striking, clear, glaring, blatant, unmistakable, obvious, plain, manifest, patent, palpable, prominent, signal, significant, conspicuous, notable, recognizable, identifiable, distinguishable, discernible, apparent, evident.
—OPPOSITES: imperceptible.

maroon *v.* STRAND, cast away, cast ashore, shipwreck.

marriage *n.* **1** (HOLY) MATRIMONY, wedlock. **2** WEDDING, wedding ceremony, marriage ceremony, nuptials, union.
—RELATED: conjugal, marital, matrimonial.

marry *v.* GET/BE MARRIED, wed, be wed, become man and wife, plight/pledge one's troth; *informal* tie the knot, walk down the aisle, take the plunge, get spliced, get hitched, say 'I do'.

marsh *n.* SWAMP, marshland, bog, peat bog, muskeg, swampland, morass, (*NB & NS*) barren✤, mire, moor, quagmire, slough, fen, fenland, wetland, bayou.

martial *adj.* MILITARY, soldierly, soldier-like, army, naval; warlike, fighting, combative, bellicose, hawkish, pugnacious, militaristic.

marvel *v.* BE AMAZED, be astonished, be surprised, be awed, stand in awe, wonder; stare, gape, goggle, not believe one's eyes/ears, be dumbfounded; *informal* be flabbergasted.
▶ *n.* ☞ WONDER 2.

marvellous *adj.* **1** AMAZING, astounding, astonishing, awesome, breathtaking, sensational, remarkable, spectacular, stupendous, staggering, stunning; phenomenal, prodigious, miraculous, extraordinary, incredible, unbelievable; *literary* wondrous. **2** ☞ EXCELLENT.
—OPPOSITES: commonplace, awful.

masculine *adj.* **1** MALE, man's, men's. **2** VIRILE, macho, manly, muscular, muscly, strong, strapping, well built, rugged, robust, brawny, powerful, red-blooded, vigorous; *informal* hunky.
—OPPOSITES: feminine, effeminate.

mash *v.* PULP, crush, purée, cream, smash, squash, pound, beat, rice.

mask *n.* DISGUISE, false face.
▶ *v.* HIDE, conceal, disguise, cover up, obscure, screen, cloak, camouflage, veil.

mass *n.* **1** PILE, heap, accumulation, aggregation, accretion, concretion, buildup; *informal* batch, wad. **2** ☞ CROWD 1. **3** (**masses**) ☞ POPULACE.
▶ *adj.* WIDESPREAD, general, wholesale, universal, large-scale, extensive, pandemic.

massacre *n.* SLAUGHTER, wholesale/mass slaughter, indiscriminate killing, mass murder, mass execution, annihilation, liquidation, decimation, extermination; carnage, butchery, bloodbath, bloodletting, pogrom, genocide, ethnic cleansing, holocaust, night of the long knives; *literary* slaying.

▶ *v.* SLAUGHTER, butcher, murder, kill, annihilate, exterminate, execute, liquidate, eliminate, decimate, wipe out, mow down, cut down, put to the sword, put to death; *literary* slay.

massage *n.* RUB, rubdown, rubbing, kneading, palpation, manipulation, pummelling; body rub, back rub; shiatsu, reflexology.
▶ *v.* RUB, knead, palpate, manipulate, pummel, work.

master *n.* **1** (*historical*) LORD, overlord, lord and master, ruler, sovereign, monarch, liege (lord), suzerain. **2** ☞ EXPERT *n.*
—OPPOSITES: servant, amateur.
▶ *v.* **1** OVERCOME, conquer, beat, quell, quash, suppress, control, overpower, triumph over, subdue, vanquish, subjugate, prevail over, govern, curb, check, bridle, tame, defeat, get the better of, get a grip on, get over; *informal* lick. **2** ☞ LEARN *v.* 1.
▶ *adj.* ☞ EXPERT *adj.*

masterful *adj.* ☞ EXPERT *adj.*
—OPPOSITES: weak, inept.

mastermind *n.* GENIUS, mind, intellect, author, architect, organizer, originator, prime mover, initiator, inventor; *informal* brain, brains, idea man, bright spark.

masterpiece *n.* PIÈCE DE RÉSISTANCE, chef-d'œuvre, masterwork, magnum opus, finest/best work, tour de force.

match *n.* **1** CONTEST, competition, game, tournament, event, trial, test, meet, matchup; bout, fight, derby; playoff, replay, rematch, engagement, bonspiel. **2** EQUAL, rival, equivalent, peer, counterpart; *formal* compeer.

▸ *v.* **1** GO WITH, coordinate with, complement, suit; be the same as, be similar to. **2** CORRESPOND, be in agreement, tally, agree, match up, coincide, accord, conform, square.

matching *adj.* CORRESPONDING, equivalent, parallel, analogous; coordinating, complementary; paired, twin, identical, like, like (two) peas in a pod, alike.
—OPPOSITES: different, clashing.

mate *n.* **1** (LIFE) PARTNER, husband, wife, spouse, lover, live-in lover, significant other, companion, helpmate, helpmeet, consort; *informal* better half, other half, main squeeze, hubby, missus, missis, old lady, old man. **2** MATCH, fellow, twin, companion, pair, other half, equivalent. **3** (*informal*) ☞ FRIEND.

▸ *v.* BREED, couple, copulate.

material *n.* **1** MATTER, substance, stuff, medium. **2** THINGS, items, articles, stuff, necessaries. **3** FABRIC, cloth, textiles.

▸ *adj.* **1** PHYSICAL, corporeal, tangible, non-spiritual, mundane, worldly, earthly, secular, temporal, concrete, real, solid, substantial. **2** SENSUAL, physical, carnal, corporal, fleshly, bodily, creature. **3** ☞ RELEVANT. **4** SIGNIFICANT, major, important.
—OPPOSITES: spiritual, aesthetic, irrelevant.

materialize *v.* **1** ☞ HAPPEN 1. **2** ☞ APPEAR 1.

maternal *adj.* MOTHERLY, protective, caring, nurturing, loving, devoted, affectionate, fond, warm, tender, gentle, kind, kindly, comforting.

matrimonial *adj.* ☞ MARITAL.

matter *n.* **1** MATERIAL, substance, stuff. **2** AFFAIR, business, proceeding, situation, circumstance, event, happening, occurrence, incident, episode, experience; subject, topic, issue, question, point, point at issue, case, concern. **3** PROBLEM, trouble, difficulty, complication; upset, worry.

▸ *v.* BE IMPORTANT, make any/a difference, be of importance, be of consequence, signify, be relevant, count; *informal* cut any ice.

□ **as a matter of fact** ☞ ACTUALLY. **no matter** IT DOESN'T MATTER, it makes no difference/ odds, it's not important, never mind, don't worry about it.

mature *adj.* **1** ADULT, grown-up, grown, fully grown, full-grown, of age, fully developed, in one's prime, middle-aged. **2** SENSIBLE, responsible, adult, level-headed, reliable, dependable; wise, discriminating, shrewd, sophisticated. **3** RIPE, ripened, mellow; ready to eat/drink.
—OPPOSITES: adolescent, childish.

▸ *v.* **1** BE FULLY GROWN, be full-grown; come of age, reach adulthood, reach maturity. **2** RIPEN, mellow; age. **3** DEVELOP, grow, evolve, bloom, blossom, flourish, thrive.

maudlin *adj.* **1** SENTIMENTAL, over-sentimental, emotional, over-emotional, tearful, lachrymose; *informal* weepy, misty-eyed. **2** ☞ SENTIMENTAL 2.

maverick *n.* INDIVIDUALIST, nonconformist, free spirit, unorthodox person, original, eccentric; rebel, dissenter, dissident, enfant terrible; *informal* cowboy, loose cannon.
—OPPOSITES: conformist.

maxim *n.* ☞ SAYING.

maximum *adj.* GREATEST, highest, biggest, largest, top, topmost, most, utmost, maximal.
—OPPOSITES: minimum.
▶ *n.* UPPER LIMIT, limit, utmost, uttermost, greatest, most, extremity, peak, height, ceiling, top, apex; *informal* max.
—OPPOSITES: minimum.

maybe *adv.* PERHAPS, possibly, conceivably, it could be, it is possible, for all one knows; *literary* peradventure, perchance.

mayhem *n.* ☞ CHAOS.

meadow *n.* FIELD, paddock; pasture, pasture land, prairie; *literary* lea, mead.

meagre *adj.* INADEQUATE, scanty, scant, paltry, limited, restricted, modest, insufficient, sparse, deficient, negligible, skimpy, slender, poor, miserable, pitiful, puny, miserly, niggardly, beggarly; *informal* measly, stingy, pathetic, piddling; *formal* exiguous.
—OPPOSITES: abundant, fat.

mean¹ *v.* **1** SIGNIFY, convey, denote, designate, indicate, connote, show, express, spell out; stand for, represent, symbolize; imply, suggest, intimate, hint at, insinuate, drive at, refer to, allude to, point to; *literary* betoken. **2** ☞ INTEND. **3** ENTAIL, involve, necessitate, lead to, result in, give rise to, bring about, cause, engender, produce. **4** MATTER, be important, be significant.

mean² *adj.* **1** UNKIND, nasty, unpleasant, spiteful, malicious, unfair, cruel, shabby, foul, despicable, contemptible, obnoxious, vile, odious, loathsome, base, low; *informal* horrible, horrid, hateful, rotten, lowdown; beastly. **2** ☞ CHEAP 3. **3** ☞ LOWLY.
—OPPOSITES: generous, kind, luxurious.

meander *v.* **1** ZIGZAG, wind, twist, turn, curve, curl, bend, snake. **2** STROLL, saunter, amble, wander, ramble, drift, maunder; *informal* mosey, tootle, toodle.

meaning *n.* **1** SIGNIFICANCE, sense, signification, import, gist, thrust, drift, implication, tenor, message, essence, substance, purport, intention. **2** DEFINITION, sense, explanation, denotation, connotation, interpretation, nuance. **3** VALUE, validity, worth, consequence, account, use, usefulness, significance, point. **4** EXPRESSIVENESS, significance, eloquence, implications, insinuations.
—RELATED: semantic.

meaningful *adj.* **1** SIGNIFICANT, relevant, important, consequential, telling, material, valid, worthwhile. **2** SINCERE, deep, serious, in earnest, significant, important. **3** EXPRESSIVE, eloquent, pointed, significant, meaning; pregnant, speaking, telltale, revealing, suggestive, charged, loaded.
—OPPOSITES: inconsequential.

meaningless *adj.*

1 UNINTELLIGIBLE, incomprehensible, incoherent. **2** FUTILE, pointless, aimless, empty, hollow, blank, vain, purposeless, valueless, useless, of no use, worthless, senseless, trivial, trifling, unimportant, insignificant, inconsequential.
—OPPOSITES: worthwhile.

means *pl. n.* **1** METHOD, way, manner, mode, measure, technique, expedient, agency, medium, instrument, channel, vehicle, avenue, course, process, procedure. **2** MONEY, resources, capital, income, finance, funds, cash, the wherewithal, assets; wealth, riches, affluence, substance, fortune, property; *informal* dough, bread, moolah.
□ **by all means** ☞ OF COURSE at COURSE. **by means of** USING, utilizing, employing, through, with the help of; as a result of, by dint of, by way of, by virtue of. **by no means** NOT AT ALL, in no way, not in the least, not in the slightest, not the least bit, not by a long shot, certainly not, absolutely not, definitely not, on no account, under no circumstances; *informal* no way.

meanwhile *adv.* **1** FOR NOW, for the moment, for the present, for the time being, meantime, in the meantime, in the interim, in the interval. **2** AT THE SAME TIME, simultaneously, concurrently, the while.

measure *v.* CALCULATE, compute, count, meter, quantify, weigh, size, evaluate, assess, gauge, plumb, determine.

▶ *n.* **1** ACTION, act, course (of action), deed, proceeding, procedure, step, means, expedient; manoeuvre, initiative, program, operation. **2** CERTAIN AMOUNT, degree; some.
□ **for good measure** AS A BONUS, as an extra, into the bargain, to boot, in addition, besides, as well. **measure up** PASS MUSTER, match up, come up to standard, fit/fill the bill, be acceptable; *informal* come up to scratch, make the grade, cut the mustard, be up to snuff.

measured *adj.* **1** REGULAR, steady, even, rhythmic, rhythmical, unfaltering; slow, dignified, stately, sedate, leisurely, unhurried. **2** THOUGHTFUL, careful, carefully chosen, studied, calculated, planned, considered, deliberate, restrained.

mechanical *adj.* **1** MECHANIZED, machine-driven, automated, automatic, power-driven, robotic. **2** AUTOMATIC, unthinking, robotic, involuntary, reflex, knee-jerk, gut, habitual, routine, unemotional, unfeeling, lifeless; perfunctory, cursory, careless, casual.
—OPPOSITES: manual, conscious.

mechanism *n.* MACHINE, piece of machinery, appliance, apparatus, device, instrument, contraption, gadget; *informal* gizmo.

meddle *v.* INTERFERE, butt in, intrude, intervene, pry, fiddle, tamper, tinker, barge into, encroach on, get involved in, impinge on; *informal* poke one's nose in, horn in on, muscle in on, snoop, stick one's oar in, kibitz, fool around, muck around.

mediate v. **1** ARBITRATE, conciliate, moderate, act as peacemaker, make peace; intervene, step in, intercede, act as an intermediary, liaise. **2** RESOLVE, settle, arbitrate in, umpire, reconcile, referee; mend, clear up; *informal* patch up.

mediator n. ARBITRATOR, arbiter, negotiator, conciliator, peacemaker, go-between, middleman, intermediary, moderator, intervenor, intercessor, broker, honest broker, liaison officer; umpire, referee, adjudicator, judge.

medicinal adj. CURATIVE, healing, remedial, therapeutic, restorative, corrective, health-giving; medical.

medicine n. MEDICATION, medicament, drug, prescription, pharmaceutical, dose, treatment, remedy, cure, antidote; nostrum, panacea, cure-all; *informal* meds.
—RELATED: pharmaceutical.

mediocre adj. ORDINARY, average, middling, middle-of-the-road, uninspired, undistinguished, indifferent, unexceptional, unexciting, unremarkable, run-of-the-mill, pedestrian, prosaic, lacklustre, forgettable, amateur, amateurish; *informal* OK, so-so, {comme ci, comme ça}, plain-vanilla, fair-to-middling, no great shakes, not up to much, bush-league.
—OPPOSITES: excellent.

meditate v. CONTEMPLATE, think, consider, ponder, muse, reflect, deliberate, ruminate, chew the cud, brood, mull over; be in a brown study, be deep/lost in thought, debate with oneself;

pray; *informal* put on one's thinking cap; *formal* cogitate.

medium n. **1** MEANS, method, way, form, agency, avenue, channel, vehicle, organ, instrument, mechanism. **2** SPIRITUALIST, necromancer, channeller; fortune teller, clairvoyant, psychic. **3** MIDDLE WAY, middle course, middle ground, middle, mean, median, midpoint; compromise, golden mean.
▶ adj. AVERAGE, middling, medium-sized, middle-sized, moderate, normal, standard.

meek adj. SUBMISSIVE, yielding, obedient, compliant, tame, biddable, tractable, acquiescent, deferential, timid, unprotesting, unresisting, like a lamb to the slaughter; quiet, mild, gentle, docile, lamblike, shy, diffident, unassuming, self-effacing.
—OPPOSITES: assertive.

meet v. **1** ENCOUNTER, meet up with, come face to face with, run into, run across, come across/upon, chance on, happen on, stumble across/on; *informal* bump into. **2** MAKE THE ACQUAINTANCE OF, be introduced to. **3** ASSEMBLE, gather, come together, get together, congregate, convene. **4** CONVERGE, connect, touch, link up, intersect, cross, join. **5** GREET, receive, answer, treat. **6** FULFILL, satisfy, fill, measure up to, match (up to), conform to, come up to, comply with, answer.

meeting n. **1** GATHERING, assembly, conference, congregation, convention, summit, forum, convocation, conclave, council, rally, caucus;

informal get-together.
2 CONSULTATION, audience, interview. **3** ENCOUNTER, contact; appointment, assignation, rendezvous; *literary* tryst.
4 CONVERGENCE, coming together, confluence, conjunction, union, junction, abutment; intersection, T-junction, crossing.

melancholy *adj.* SAD, sorrowful, unhappy, desolate, mournful, lugubrious, gloomy, despondent, dejected, depressed, downhearted, downcast, disconsolate, glum, miserable, wretched, dismal, morose, woeful, woebegone, doleful, joyless, heavy-hearted; *informal* down in the dumps, down in the mouth, blue; *formal* atrabilious.
—OPPOSITES: cheerful.
▶ *n.* SADNESS, sorrow, unhappiness, woe, desolation, melancholia, dejection, depression, despondency, cafard, gloom, gloominess, glumness, misery, wretchedness, despair; *informal* the dumps, the blues.

mellow *adj.* **1** GENIAL, affable, amiable, good-humoured, good-natured, amicable, pleasant, relaxed, easygoing, placid; jovial, jolly, cheerful, happy, merry.
2 DULCET, sweet-sounding, tuneful, melodious, mellifluous; soft, smooth, warm, full, rich.
□ **mellow out** ☞ RELAX 1.

melodious *adj.* TUNEFUL, melodic, musical, mellifluous, dulcet, sweet-sounding, silvery, harmonious, euphonious, lyrical; *informal* easy on the ear.
—OPPOSITES: discordant.

melodramatic *adj.* EXAGGERATED, histrionic, overdramatic, overdone, operatic, sensationalized, over-emotional, overwrought, sentimental, extravagant; theatrical, stagy; *informal* hammy.

melody *n.* TUNE, air, strain, theme, song, refrain, piece of music; *informal* ditty.

melt *v.* **1** LIQUEFY, thaw, defrost, soften, dissolve, deliquesce.
2 VANISH, disappear, fade away, dissolve, evaporate; *literary* evanesce.

member *n.* SUBSCRIBER, associate, affiliate, life member, card-carrying member.

memorable *adj.* UNFORGETTABLE, indelible, catchy, haunting; momentous, significant, historic, notable, noteworthy, important, consequential, remarkable, special, signal, outstanding, extraordinary, striking, vivid, arresting, impressive, distinctive, distinguished, famous, celebrated, renowned, illustrious, glorious.

memorize *v.* COMMIT TO MEMORY, remember, learn by heart, get off by heart, learn, con, learn by rote, become word-perfect in, get something down pat.

memory *n.* **1** ABILITY TO REMEMBER, powers of recall.
2 RECOLLECTION, remembrance, reminiscence; impression.
3 COMMEMORATION, remembrance; honour, tribute, recognition, respect.
—RELATED: mnemonic.

menace *n.* **1** DANGER, peril, risk, hazard, threat; jeopardy.
2 NUISANCE, pest, annoyance,

plague, torment, terror,
troublemaker, mischief-maker,
thorn in someone's side/flesh.
▶ *v.* THREATEN, be a danger to, put
at risk, jeopardize, imperil;
intimidate, terrorize, frighten,
scare, terrify.

mend *v.* REPAIR, fix, put back
together, piece together, restore;
sew (up), stitch, darn, patch,
cobble; rehabilitate, renew,
renovate; *informal* patch up.
—OPPOSITES: break.

menial *adj.* UNSKILLED, lowly,
humble, low-status, inferior,
degrading; routine, humdrum,
boring, dull.

menstruation *n.* PERIOD,
menses, menorrhoea, menstrual
cycle; menarche; *informal* the curse,
monthlies, one's/the time of the
month.

mentality *n.* WAY OF THINKING,
mind set, cast of mind, frame of
mind, turn of mind, mind,
psychology, mental attitude,
outlook, disposition, makeup.

mention *v.* **1** ALLUDE TO, refer to,
touch on/upon; bring up, raise,
broach, introduce, moot. **2** STATE,
say, indicate, let someone know,
disclose, divulge, reveal.
▶ *n.* REFERENCE, allusion, remark,
statement, announcement,
indication.
□ **not to mention** IN ADDITION TO,
as well as; not counting, not
including, to say nothing of, aside
from, besides.

mentor *n.* ADVISER, guide, guru,
counsellor, consultant;
confidant(e).

mercenary *adj.* MONEY-ORIENTED,
grasping, greedy, acquisitive,
avaricious, covetous, bribable,
venal, materialistic; *informal* money-
grubbing.
▶ *n.* SOLDIER OF FORTUNE,
professional soldier, hired soldier,
gunman; *informal* hired gun; *historical*
condottiere.

merchandise *n.* GOODS, wares,
stock, commodities, lines,
produce, products.

merchant *n.* TRADER, dealer,
wholesaler, broker, agent, seller,
buyer, buyer and seller, vendor,
distributor, peddler, retailer,
shopkeeper, storekeeper.

merciful *adj.* FORGIVING,
compassionate, clement, pitying,
forbearing, lenient, humane,
mild, kind, soft-hearted, tender-
hearted, gracious, sympathetic,
humanitarian, liberal, tolerant,
indulgent, generous,
magnanimous, benign,
benevolent.
—OPPOSITES: cruel.

merciless *adj.* RUTHLESS,
remorseless, pitiless, unforgiving,
unsparing, implacable,
inexorable, relentless,
unremitting, inflexible,
inhumane, inhuman,
unsympathetic, unfeeling,
intolerant, rigid, severe, cold-
blooded, hard-hearted, stony-
hearted, heartless, harsh, callous,
cruel, brutal, barbarous,
cutthroat.
—OPPOSITES: compassionate.

mercy *n.* LENIENCY, clemency,
compassion, grace, pity, charity,
forgiveness, forbearance, quarter,
humanity; soft-heartedness,
tender-heartedness, kindness,
sympathy, liberality, indulgence,

tolerance, generosity, magnanimity, beneficence.
—OPPOSITES: ruthlessness, cruelty.

merge *v.* **1** AMALGAMATE, bring together, join, consolidate, conflate, unite, unify, combine, incorporate, integrate, link (up), knit, yoke. **2** MINGLE, blend, fuse, mix, intermix, intermingle, coalesce; *literary* commingle.
—OPPOSITES: separate.

merit *n.* **1** EXCELLENCE, quality, calibre, worth, worthiness, credit, value, distinction, eminence. **2** GOOD POINT, strong point, advantage, benefit, value, asset, plus.
—OPPOSITES: inferiority, fault, disadvantage.
▶ *v.* ☞ DESERVE.

meritorious *adj.*
☞ COMMENDABLE.
—OPPOSITES: discreditable.

merriment *n.* ☞ FUN.

merry *adj.* CHEERFUL, cheery, in high spirits, high-spirited, bright, sunny, smiling, lighthearted, buoyant, lively, carefree, without a care in the world, joyful, joyous, jolly, convivial, festive, mirthful, gleeful, happy, glad, laughing; *informal* chirpy; *formal* jocund; *dated* gay; *literary* blithe.
—OPPOSITES: miserable.

mesh *n.* NETTING, net, network; web, webbing, lattice, latticework.
▶ *v.* HARMONIZE, fit together, match, dovetail.

mesmerize *v.* ENTHRALL, hold spellbound, entrance, dazzle, bedazzle, bewitch, charm, captivate, enchant, fascinate, transfix, grip, hypnotize.

mess *n.* **1** UNTIDINESS, disorder, disarray, disorganization, dishevelment, clutter, shambles, jumble, tangle, heap, muddle, chaos, confusion, hodgepodge; litter, rubbish, junk. **2** ☞ PREDICAMENT. **3** MUDDLE, bungle; *informal* botch, hash, foul-up, snafu.
□ **mess around** fiddle around, play around, fool around; fidget, toy, tamper, tinker, interfere, meddle, monkey around; *informal* piddle around, muck around.
mess up MISMANAGE, mishandle, bungle, fluff, spoil, ruin, wreck; *informal* make a mess of, botch, make a hash of, muck up, foul up, screw up.

message *n.* **1** COMMUNICATION, piece of information, news, note, memorandum, memo, email, letter, missive, report, bulletin, statement, announcement, communiqué, dispatch. **2** MEANING, sense, import, idea; point, thrust, gist, essence, content, subject (matter), substance, implication, drift, lesson.

messenger *n.* MESSAGE-BEARER, courier, runner, envoy, emissary, agent, go-between; postman, letter carrier, mailman, postie; herald, legate.

messy *adj.* **1** DIRTY, filthy, grubby, soiled, grimy; mucky, muddy, slimy, sticky, sullied, spotted, stained, smeared, smudged; *informal* yucky, grungy. **2** DISORDERLY, disordered, in a muddle, chaotic, confused, disorganized, in disarray, disarranged; untidy, cluttered, in a jumble; dishevelled, scruffy, unkempt,

rumpled, matted, tousled, bedraggled, tangled; *informal* like a bomb's hit it. **3** COMPLEX, intricate, tangled, confused, convoluted; unpleasant, nasty, bitter, acrimonious.
—OPPOSITES: clean, tidy.

metamorphosis *n.*
☞ TRANSFORMATION.

method *n.* PROCEDURE, technique, system, practice, routine, modus operandi, process; strategy, tactic, plan.
—OPPOSITES: disorder.

methodical *adj.* ORDERLY, well-ordered, well-organized, (well) planned, efficient, businesslike, systematic, structured, logical, analytic, disciplined; meticulous, punctilious.

meticulous *adj.* CAREFUL, conscientious, diligent, scrupulous, punctilious, painstaking, accurate; thorough, studious, rigorous, detailed, perfectionist, fastidious, methodical, particular.
—OPPOSITES: careless.

microscopic *adj.* ☞ TINY.

middle *n.* CENTRE, midpoint, halfway point, dead centre, focus, hub; eye, heart, core, kernel.
—OPPOSITES: outside.
▶ *adj.* CENTRAL, mid, mean, medium, medial, median, midway, halfway.
—RELATED: meso-.

middle-class *adj.* BOURGEOIS, conventional, mainstream, plain-vanilla; suburban, white-picket-fence, Waspish, WASP, yuppie.

middleman *n.* ☞ MEDIATOR.

middling *adj.* ☞ MEDIOCRE.

might *n.* ☞ POWER 5.

mighty *adj.* ☞ POWERFUL.

migrant *n.* IMMIGRANT, EMIGRANT; nomad, itinerant, traveller, vagrant, transient, rover, wanderer, drifter.
▶ *adj.* TRAVELLING, wandering, drifting, nomadic, roving, roaming, itinerant, vagrant, transient.

migrate *v.* RELOCATE, resettle, move (house), go down the road✦; immigrate; emigrate, go abroad, go overseas, pull up stakes.

mild *adj.* **1** GENTLE, tender, soft-hearted, tender-hearted, sensitive, sympathetic, warm, placid, calm, tranquil, serene, peaceable, good-natured, mild-mannered, amiable, affable, genial, easygoing. **2** SLIGHT, faint, vague, minimal, nominal, moderate, token, feeble. **3** WARM, balmy, temperate, clement.
—OPPOSITES: harsh, strong, severe.

militant *adj.* AGGRESSIVE, violent, belligerent, bellicose, vigorous, forceful, active, fierce, combative, pugnacious; radical, extremist, extreme, zealous, fanatical.
▶ *n.* ACTIVIST, extremist, radical, young turk, zealot; terrorist, freedom fighter, insurgent, guerrilla.

military *adj.* FIGHTING, service, army, armed, defence, martial.
—OPPOSITES: civilian.
▶ *n.* (ARMED) FORCES, services, militia, defence; army, navy, air force, marines.

milky *adj.* PALE, white, milk-white, whitish, off-white, cream, creamy, chalky, pearly, nacreous, ivory, alabaster; cloudy, frosted, opaque.
—OPPOSITES: swarthy.

mill *n.* **1** FACTORY, (processing) plant, works, workshop, shop, foundry. **2** GRINDER, quern, crusher.

mimic *v.* ☞ IMITATE 1, 2.

mince *v.* GRIND, chop up, cut up, dice, hash, chop fine.
□ **not mince (one's) words** TALK STRAIGHT, not beat around the bush, call a spade a spade, speak straight from the heart, pull no punches, not put too fine a point on it, tell it like it is, talk turkey.

mind *n.* **1** ☞ INTELLIGENCE 1. **2** SANITY, mental faculties, senses, wits, reason, reasoning, judgment; *informal* marbles. **3** MEMORY, recollection. **4** INTELLECT, thinker, brain, scholar, academic. **5** INCLINATION, desire, wish, urge, notion, fancy, intention, will.
—RELATED: mental.
▶ *v.* **1** CARE, object, be bothered, be annoyed, be upset, take offence, disapprove, dislike it, look askance; *informal* give a damn, give/care a hoot. **2** BE CAREFUL OF, watch out for, look out for, beware of, be on one's guard for, be wary of. **3** LOOK AFTER, take care of, keep an eye on, attend to, care for, tend, babysit. **4** PAY ATTENTION TO, heed, pay heed to, attend to, take note/notice of, note, mark, listen to, be mindful of; obey, follow, comply with.
□ **be of two minds** ☞ HESITANT.
bear/keep in mind REMEMBER, note, be mindful of, take note of.
cross one's mind ☞ OCCUR 3.
have something in mind THINK OF, contemplate; intend, plan, propose, desire, want, wish. **never**

mind DON'T BOTHER ABOUT, don't worry about, disregard, forget.

mindful *adj.* ☞ AWARE 1.
—OPPOSITES: heedless.

mindless *adj.* **1** ☞ STUPID 1. **2** UNTHINKING, thoughtless, senseless, gratuitous, wanton, indiscriminate, unreasoning. **3** MECHANICAL, automatic, routine; tedious, boring, monotonous, brainless, mind-numbing.

mine *n.* **1** PIT, excavation, quarry, workings, diggings; strip mine, open-pit mine, placer (mine), hardrock mine. **2** RICH SOURCE, repository, store, storehouse, reservoir, gold mine, treasure house, treasury, reserve, fund, wealth, stock.
▶ *v.* QUARRY, excavate, dig (up), extract, remove; strip-mine, pan.

mingle *v.* SOCIALIZE, circulate, fraternize, get together, associate with others; *informal* hobnob, rub elbows.
—OPPOSITES: separate.

miniature *adj.* ☞ SMALL 1.
—OPPOSITES: giant.

minimal *adj.* VERY LITTLE, minimum, the least (possible); nominal, token, negligible.
—OPPOSITES: maximum.

minimize *v.* **1** KEEP DOWN, keep at/to a minimum, reduce, decrease, cut down, lessen, curtail, diminish, prune; *informal* slash. **2** ☞ UNDERVALUE.
—OPPOSITES: maximize, exaggerate.

minimum *n.* LOWEST LEVEL, lower limit, bottom level, rock bottom, nadir; least, lowest, slightest.
—OPPOSITES: maximum.
▶ *adj.* MINIMAL, least, smallest, least

possible, slightest, lowest,
minutest.

minion n. ☞ FLUNKY.

minor adj. **1** ☞ UNIMPORTANT.
2 LITTLE KNOWN, unknown, lesser,
unimportant, insignificant,
obscure, minor-league; *informal*
small-time, two-bit.
—OPPOSITES: major, important.

minute adj. **1** ☞ TINY. **2** NEGLIGIBLE,
slight, infinitesimal, minimal,
insignificant, inappreciable.
3 EXHAUSTIVE, painstaking,
meticulous, rigorous, scrupulous,
punctilious, detailed, precise,
accurate.
—OPPOSITES: huge.

miracle n. WONDER, marvel,
sensation, (supernatural)
phenomenon, mystery.

miraculous adj. SUPERNATURAL,
preternatural, inexplicable,
unaccountable, magical.

mire n. **1** ☞ MARSH. **2** ☞ MUCK 1.
▶ v. **1** BOG DOWN, sink (down).
2 ENTANGLE, tangle up, embroil,
catch up, mix up, involve.

mirror n. LOOKING GLASS, glass.
—RELATED: specular.
▶ v. REFLECT, match, reproduce,
imitate, simulate, copy, mimic,
echo, parallel, correspond to.

misappropriate v. ☞ EMBEZZLE.

misbehave v. BEHAVE BADLY, be
misbehaved, be naughty, be
disobedient, disobey, get up to
mischief, get up to no good; be
bad-mannered, be rude; *informal*
carry on, act up.

miscalculate v. MISJUDGE, make
a mistake (about), calculate
wrongly, estimate wrongly,
overestimate, underestimate,
overvalue, undervalue;

misunderstand; go wrong, err, be
wide of the mark.

miscellaneous adj. VARIOUS,
varied, different, assorted, mixed,
sundry, diverse, disparate;
diversified, motley, multifarious,
ragtag, raggle-taggle,
heterogeneous, eclectic, odd; *literary*
divers.

mischief n. misbehaviour,
mischievousness, misconduct,
naughtiness, bad behaviour,
disobedience; pranks, tricks,
capers, nonsense, devilry, funny
business; *informal* monkey business,
shenanigans, carryings-on.

mischievous adj. ☞ NAUGHTY 1.

misconception n.
MISAPPREHENSION,
misunderstanding, mistake, error,
misinterpretation,
misconstruction, misreading,
misjudgment, miscalculation,
false impression, illusion, fallacy,
delusion.

miserable adj. **1** ☞ UNHAPPY 1.
2 DREARY, dismal, gloomy, drab,
wretched, depressing, grim,
cheerless, bleak, desolate; poor,
shabby, squalid, seedy,
dilapidated; *informal* flea-bitten.
3 UNPLEASANT, disagreeable,
depressing; *informal* rotten.
4 ☞ GRUMPY.
—OPPOSITES: cheerful, lovely.

miserly adj. ☞ CHEAP 3.
—OPPOSITES: generous.

misery n. UNHAPPINESS, distress,
wretchedness, suffering, anguish,
anxiety, angst, torment, pain,
grief, heartache, heartbreak,
despair, despondency, dejection,
depression, desolation, gloom,
melancholy, melancholia, woe,

sadness, sorrow; *informal* the dumps, the blues; *literary* dolour. —OPPOSITES: contentment, pleasure.

misfortune n. PROBLEM, difficulty, setback, trouble, adversity, stroke of bad luck, reversal (of fortune), misadventure, mishap, blow, failure, accident, disaster, catastrophe; sorrow, misery, woe, trial, tribulation, tragedy.

misgiving n. QUALM, doubt, reservation; suspicion, distrust, mistrust, lack of confidence, second thoughts; trepidation, skepticism, unease, uneasiness, anxiety, apprehension, disquiet, question, uncertainty.

misguided adj. ERRONEOUS, fallacious, unsound, misplaced, misconceived, ill-advised, ill-considered, ill-judged, ill-founded, inappropriate, unwise, injudicious, imprudent.

mishap n. ☞ ACCIDENT 1.

mislead v. DECEIVE, delude, take in, lie to, fool, hoodwink, throw off the scent, pull the wool over someone's eyes, misguide, misinform, give wrong information to; *informal* lead up the garden path, take for a ride, give someone a bum steer.

misleading adj. DECEPTIVE, confusing, deceiving, equivocal, ambiguous, fallacious, specious, spurious, false.

misplace v. ☞ LOSE 1.

miss v. **1** FAIL TO HIT, be/go wide of, fall short of. **2** FAIL TO CATCH, drop, fumble, bobble, fluff, flub, mishandle, screw up. **3** BE TOO LATE FOR, fail to catch/get. **4** FAIL TO

SEE/NOTICE, overlook. **5** FAIL TO ATTEND, be absent from, play truant from, cut, skip. **6** LET SLIP, fail to take advantage of, let go/pass, pass up. **7** AVOID, beat, evade, escape, dodge, sidestep, elude, circumvent, steer clear of, find a way round, bypass. **8** PINE FOR, yearn for, ache for, long for, long to see. —OPPOSITES: hit, catch.

misshapen adj. ☞ DEFORMED.

missing adj. LOST, mislaid, misplaced, absent, gone (astray), gone AWOL, unaccounted for; disappeared, vanished; not present, lacking, wanting. —OPPOSITES: present.

mission n. **1** ASSIGNMENT, commission, expedition, journey, trip, undertaking, operation; task, job, labour, work, duty, charge, trust. **2** VOCATION, calling, goal, aim, quest, purpose, function, life's work.

mistake n. ERROR, fault, inaccuracy, omission, slip, blunder, miscalculation, misunderstanding, oversight, misinterpretation, gaffe, faux pas, solecism; *informal* slip-up, boo-boo, blooper, boner, goof, flub.
▶ v. CONFUSE WITH, mix up with, take for, misinterpret as.
□ **be mistaken** BE WRONG, be in error, be under a misapprehension, be misinformed, be misguided; *informal* be barking up the wrong tree. **make a mistake** GO WRONG, err, make an error, blunder, miscalculate; *informal* slip up, make a boo-boo, drop the ball, goof (up).

mistakenly *adv.* **1** WRONGLY, in error, erroneously, incorrectly, falsely, fallaciously, inaccurately. **2** BY ACCIDENT, accidentally, inadvertently, unintentionally, unwittingly, unconsciously, by mistake.
—OPPOSITES: correctly, intentionally.

mistreat *v.* ILL-TREAT, maltreat, abuse, knock about/around, hit, beat, strike, molest, injure, harm, hurt; misuse, mishandle; *informal* beat up, rough up, mess up, kick around.

mistress *n.* LOVER, girlfriend, kept woman; courtesan, concubine, paramour; *informal* bit on the side, the other woman.

mistrust *v.* BE SUSPICIOUS OF, be mistrustful of, be distrustful of, be skeptical of, be wary of, be chary of, distrust, have doubts about, have misgivings about, have reservations about, suspect.
▶ *n.* SUSPICION, distrust, doubt, misgivings, wariness.

misty *adj.* **1** HAZY, foggy, (*Nfld*) mauzy✦, cloudy; smoggy. **2** BLURRY, fuzzy, blurred, clouded, dim, indistinct, unclear, vague.
—OPPOSITES: clear.

misunderstand *v.* MISAPPREHEND, misinterpret, misconstrue, misconceive, mistake, misread; be mistaken, get the wrong idea, receive a false impression; *informal* be barking up the wrong tree, miss the boat.

misunderstanding *n.* **1** MISINTERPRETATION, misconstruction, misreading, misapprehension, misconception, the wrong idea, false impression. **2** ☞ ARGUMENT 1.

misuse *v.* **1** PUT TO WRONG USE, misemploy, embezzle, use fraudulently; abuse, squander, waste. **2** ☞ MISTREAT.
▶ *n.* WRONG USE, embezzlement, fraud; squandering, waste.

mitigate *v.* ALLEVIATE, reduce, diminish, lessen, weaken, lighten, attenuate, take the edge off, allay, ease, assuage, palliate, relieve, tone down.
—OPPOSITES: aggravate.

mix *v.* BLEND, mix up, mingle, combine, put together, jumble; fuse, unite, unify, join, amalgamate, incorporate, meld, marry, coalesce, homogenize, intermingle, intermix; stir, whisk, fold in; *technical* admix; *literary* commingle.
—OPPOSITES: separate.
▶ *n.* ☞ MIXTURE.
☐ **mix something up 1** ☞ MIX *v.* 1. **2** CONFUSE, get confused, muddle (up), get muddled up, mistake. **mixed up in** INVOLVED IN, embroiled in, caught up in.

mixed *adj.* ASSORTED, varied, variegated, miscellaneous, disparate, diverse, diversified, motley, sundry, jumbled, heterogeneous.
—OPPOSITES: homogeneous.

mixed up *adj.* (*informal*) CONFUSED, befuddled, bemused, bewildered, muddled; disturbed, neurotic, unbalanced; *informal* hung up, messed up, at sea.

mixture *n.* BLEND, mix, brew, combination, concoction; composition, compound, alloy, amalgam; mishmash, hodgepodge.

moan *n.* GROAN, wail, whimper, sob, cry.
▶ *v.* **1** GROAN, wail, whimper, sob, cry. **2** ☞ COMPLAIN.

mob *n.* **1** CROWD, horde, multitude, rabble, mass, throng, group, gang, gathering, assemblage. **2** MAFIA, Cosa Nostra, Camorra.
▶ *v.* SURROUND, swarm, besiege, jostle.

mobile *adj.* **1** ABLE TO MOVE (AROUND), moving, walking; *Zoology* motile; *Medicine* ambulant.
2 TRAVELLING, transportable, portable, movable; itinerant, peripatetic.
—OPPOSITES: motionless, static.

mobilize *v.* **1** MARSHAL, deploy, muster, rally, call up, assemble, mass, organize, prepare.
2 GENERATE, arouse, awaken, excite, incite, provoke, foment, prompt, stimulate, stir up, galvanize, encourage, inspire, whip up.

mock *v.* **1** ☞ RIDICULE. **2** PARODY, ape, take off, satirize, lampoon, imitate, impersonate, mimic; *informal* send up.
▶ *adj.* ☞ IMITATION.
—OPPOSITES: genuine.

mockery *n.* **1** ☞ RIDICULE.
2 TRAVESTY, charade, farce, parody.

model *n.* **1** REPLICA, copy, representation, mock-up, dummy, imitation, duplicate, reproduction, facsimile.
2 PROTOTYPE, stereotype, archetype, type, version; mould, template, framework, pattern, design, blueprint. **3** IDEAL, paragon, perfect example/

specimen; perfection, acme, epitome, nonpareil, crème de la crème. **4** FASHION MODEL, supermodel, mannequin. **5** SITTER, poser, subject. **6** VERSION, type, design, variety, kind, sort.
▶ *adj.* **1** REPLICA, toy, miniature, dummy, imitation, duplicate, reproduction, facsimile.
2 PROTOTYPICAL, prototypal, archetypal. **3** IDEAL, perfect, exemplary, classic, flawless, faultless.

moderate *adj.* **1** ☞ MODEST 2.
2 MIDDLE-OF-THE-ROAD, non-extreme, non-radical, centrist.
—OPPOSITES: great, unreasonable, extreme.
▶ *v.* **1** DIE DOWN, abate, let up, calm down, lessen, decrease, diminish; recede, weaken, subside. **2** CURB, control, check, temper, restrain, subdue; repress, tame, lessen, decrease, lower, reduce, diminish, alleviate, allay, appease, assuage, ease, soothe, calm, tone down.
3 CHAIR, take the chair of, preside over.
—OPPOSITES: increase.

moderately *adv.* SOMEWHAT, quite, rather, fairly, reasonably, comparatively, relatively, to some extent; tolerably, passably, adequately; *informal* pretty.

modern *adj.* **1** PRESENT-DAY, contemporary, present, current, 21st-century, latter-day, modern-day, recent. **2** FASHIONABLE, in fashion, in vogue, up to date, all the rage, trendsetting, stylish, styling/stylin', voguish, modish, chic, à la mode; the latest, new, newest, newfangled, modernistic, advanced; *informal*

trendy, cool, in, with it, now, hip, phat, happening, kicky, tony, fly.
—OPPOSITES: past, old-fashioned.

modernize v. UPDATE, bring up to date, streamline, overhaul; renovate, remodel, refashion, revamp.

modest adj. **1** SELF-EFFACING, self-deprecating, humble, unpretentious, unassuming, unostentatious; shy, bashful, self-conscious, diffident, reserved, reticent, coy. **2** MODERATE, fair, limited, tolerable, passable, adequate, satisfactory, acceptable, unexceptional. **3** ordinary, simple, plain, humble, inexpensive, unostentatious, unpretentious. **4** DECOROUS, decent, seemly, demure, proper.
—OPPOSITES: conceited, great, grand.

modify v. ALTER, change, adjust, adapt, amend, revise, reshape, refashion, restyle, revamp, rework, remodel, convert, redesign, refine; informal tweak, doctor.

moist adj. ☞ DAMP.
—OPPOSITES: dry.

molest v. **1** HARASS, harry, hassle, pester, bother, annoy, beset, persecute, torment; informal roust. **2** (SEXUALLY) ABUSE, (sexually) assault, interfere with, rape, violate; grope, paw, fondle.

moment n. **1** LITTLE WHILE, short time, bit, minute, instant, (split) second; informal sec, jiffy. **2** POINT (IN TIME), time, hour. **3** (formal) ☞ CONSEQUENCE 2.

momentary adj. BRIEF, short, short-lived, fleeting, passing, transient, transitory, ephemeral;

literary evanescent.
—OPPOSITES: lengthy.

momentous adj. ☞ IMPORTANT 1.
—OPPOSITES: insignificant.

momentum n. IMPETUS, energy, force, power, strength, thrust, speed, velocity.

money n. **1** (HARD) CASH, ready money; the means, the wherewithal, funds, capital, finances, (filthy) lucre; coins, change, specie, silver, currency, bills, (bank) notes; informal dough, bread, loot, shekels, moolah, dinero, bucks. **2** WEALTH, riches, fortune, affluence, (liquid) assets, savings, resources, reserves, means.
—RELATED: pecuniary, monetary, numismatic.

moneyed adj. ☞ RICH 1.
—OPPOSITES: poor.

monitor n. **1** DETECTOR, scanner, recorder; listening device; security camera. **2** OBSERVER, watchdog, overseer, supervisor. **3** SCREEN, video display terminal, VDT.
▶ v. OBSERVE, watch, track, keep an eye on, keep under observation, keep watch on, keep under surveillance, record, note, oversee; informal keep tabs on.

monopolize v. **1** CORNER, control, take over, gain control/dominance over. **2** DOMINATE, take over; informal hog; keep to oneself, tie up.

monotonous adj. **1** TEDIOUS, boring, dull, uninteresting, unexciting, wearisome, tiresome, repetitive, repetitious, unvarying, unchanging, unvaried, humdrum, ho-hum, routine, mechanical, mind-numbing, soul-destroying;

colourless, featureless, dreary; *informal* deadly, samey, dullsville. **2** TONELESS, flat, uninflected, soporific.
—OPPOSITES: interesting.

monster *n.* **1** FABULOUS CREATURE, mythical creature. **2** BRUTE, fiend, beast, devil, demon, barbarian, savage, animal; *informal* swine, pig.
▶ *adj.* (*informal*) ☞ HUGE.

monstrous *adj.* ☞ HIDEOUS.

monument *n.* MEMORIAL, statue, pillar, column, obelisk, cross; cenotaph, mausoleum, shrine; gravestone, headstone, tombstone, grave marker, plaque.

mood *n.* **1** FRAME/STATE OF MIND, humour, temper; disposition, spirit, tenor. **2** BAD MOOD, (bad) temper, sulk, fit of pique; low spirits, the doldrums, the blues, blue funk; *informal* the dumps, grumps. **3** ATMOSPHERE, feeling, spirit, ambience, aura, character, tenor, flavour, feel, tone.

moody *adj.* TEMPERAMENTAL, emotional, volatile, capricious, changeable, mercurial; grumpy, gloomy, sullen.
—OPPOSITES: cheerful.

mope *v.* BROOD, sulk, be miserable, be despondent, pine, eat one's heart out, fret, grieve; *informal* be down in the dumps/mouth; *literary* repine.

moral *adj.* **1** ETHICAL, social, having to do with right and wrong. **2** VIRTUOUS, good, righteous, upright, upstanding, high-minded, principled, honourable, honest, just, noble, incorruptible, scrupulous, respectable, decent, clean-living, law-abiding.

3 PSYCHOLOGICAL, emotional, mental.
—OPPOSITES: dishonourable.
▶ *n.* **1** LESSON, message, meaning, significance, signification, import, point, teaching. **2** MORAL CODE, code of ethics, moral standards/values, principles, standards, (sense of) morality, scruples.

morale *n.* CONFIDENCE, self-confidence, self-esteem, spirit(s), team spirit, enthusiasm.

morality *n.* **1** ETHICS, rights and wrongs, ethicality. **2** ☞ VIRTUE 1.

more *adj.* ADDITIONAL, further, added, extra, increased, new, other, supplementary.
—OPPOSITES: less, fewer.
▶ *adv.* TO A GREATER EXTENT, further, some more, better.
▶ *pron.* EXTRA, an additional amount/number, an addition, an increase.
—OPPOSITES: less, fewer.
□ **more or less** APPROXIMATELY, roughly, nearly, almost, close to, about, in/of the order of, in the region of.

moreover *adv.* ☞ FURTHERMORE.

moron *n.* ☞ IDIOT.

morsel *n.* MOUTHFUL, bite, nibble, bit, soupçon, taste, spoonful, forkful, sliver, drop, dollop, spot, gobbet, tidbit.

mortal *adj.* **1** PERISHABLE, physical, bodily, corporeal, fleshly, earthly; human, impermanent, transient, ephemeral. **2** DEADLY, fatal, lethal, death-dealing, murderous, terminal.

mortify *v.* ☞ HUMILIATE.

mostly *adv.* **1** MAINLY, for the most part, on the whole, in the main, largely, chiefly, predominantly,

principally, primarily.
2 ☞ USUALLY.

mother *n.* FEMALE PARENT,
materfamilias, matriarch; *informal*
ma, mama, old lady, old woman;
mum, mummy, mom, mommy,
mammy.
—RELATED: maternal, matri-.
—OPPOSITES: child, father.
▶ *v.* **1** LOOK AFTER, care for, take
care of, nurse, protect, tend, raise,
rear; pamper, coddle, cosset, fuss
over. **2** GIVE BIRTH TO, have, bear,
produce, birth.
—OPPOSITES: neglect.

motherly *adj.* ☞ MATERNAL.

motion *n.* **1** MOVEMENT, moving,
locomotion, rise and fall, shifting;
progress, passage, passing, transit,
course, travel, travelling.
2 PROPOSAL, proposition,
recommendation, suggestion.
—RELATED: kinetic.
▶ *v.* GESTURE, signal, direct,
indicate; wave, beckon, nod,
gesticulate.

motionless *adj.* ☞ STILL 1.
—OPPOSITES: moving.

motivate *v.* **1** PROMPT, drive,
move, inspire, stimulate,
influence, activate, impel, push,
propel, spur (on). **2** INSPIRE,
stimulate, encourage, spur (on),
excite, inspirit, incentivize, fire
with enthusiasm.

motive *n.* REASON, motivation,
motivating force, rationale,
grounds, cause, basis, object,
purpose, intention; incentive,
inducement, incitement, lure,
inspiration, stimulus, stimulation,
spur.

motley *adj.* ☞ MISCELLANEOUS.
—OPPOSITES: homogeneous.

mottled *adj.* ☞ SPOTTED.

motto *n.* MAXIM, saying, proverb,
aphorism, adage, saw, axiom,
apophthegm, formula, expression,
phrase, dictum, precept; slogan,
catchphrase, mantra; truism,
cliché, platitude.

mould *n.* **1** CAST, die, form,
matrix, shape, template, pattern,
frame. **2** PATTERN, form, shape,
format, model, kind, type, style;
archetype, prototype.
▶ *v.* **1** SHAPE, form, fashion, model,
work, construct, make, create,
manufacture, sculpt, sculpture;
forge, cast. **2** DETERMINE, direct,
control, guide, lead, influence.

mouldy *adj.* MILDEWED, mildewy,
musty, mouldering, fusty, (*Nfld*)
fousty♦; decaying, decayed,
rotting, rotten, bad, spoiled,
decomposing.

mound *n.* **1** ☞ PILE 1. **2** ☞ HILL.

mount *v.* **1** GO UP, ascend, climb
(up), scale. **2** CLIMB ON TO, jump on
to, clamber on to, get on to. **3** (PUT
ON) DISPLAY, exhibit, present,
install; organize, put on, stage.
4 ORGANIZE, stage, prepare,
arrange, set up; launch, set in
motion, initiate. **5** ☞ INCREASE 1.
6 INSTALL, place, fix, set, put up,
put in position.
—OPPOSITES: descend.

mountain *n.* PEAK, height,
mount, prominence, summit,
pinnacle, alp; (**mountains**) range,
massif, sierra, cordillera.

mountainous *adj.* HILLY, craggy,
rocky, alpine; upland, highland.
—OPPOSITES: flat.

mourn *v.* GRIEVE FOR, sorrow over,
lament for, weep for, wail/keen
over.

mournful *adj.* SAD, sorrowful, doleful, melancholy, melancholic, woeful, grief-stricken, miserable, unhappy, heartbroken, broken-hearted, gloomy, dismal, desolate, dejected, despondent, depressed, downcast, disconsolate, woebegone, forlorn, rueful, lugubrious, joyless, cheerless; *literary* dolorous.
—OPPOSITES: cheerful.

mouth *n.* lips, jaws; maw, muzzle; *informal* trap, chops, kisser, puss.
□ **mouth off** TALK INSOLENTLY TO, be disrespectful to; *informal* lip off.

mouthful *n.* **1** BITE, nibble, taste, bit, piece; spoonful, forkful. **2** SIP, swallow, drop, gulp, slug, swig.

move *v.* **1** GO, walk, proceed, progress, advance; budge, stir, shift, change position. **2** ☞ SHIFT 1. **3** (MAKE) PROGRESS, make headway, advance, develop. **4** TAKE ACTION, act, take steps, do something, take measures; *informal* get moving. **5** RELOCATE, move house, move away, change address/house, leave, go away, go down the road✦, decamp, pull up stakes. **6** AFFECT, touch, impress, shake, upset, disturb, make an impression on. **7** ☞ INSPIRE 1. **8** ☞ PROPOSE 1.
▸ *n.* **1** MOVEMENT, motion, action; gesture, gesticulation. **2** TURN, go; opportunity, chance.
□ **get a move on** ☞ HURRY 1. **on the move** TRAVELLING, in transit, moving, journeying, on the road; *informal* on the go.

movement *n.* **1** MOTION, move; gesture, gesticulation, sign, signal; action, activity. **2** POLITICAL GROUP, party, faction, wing, lobby, camp.

3 CAMPAIGN, crusade, drive, push. **4** PROGRESS, progression, advance.

moving *adj.* **1** IN MOTION, operating, operational, working, going, on the move, active; movable, mobile. **2** AFFECTING, touching, poignant, heartwarming, heart-rending, emotional, disturbing; emotive, sad, sentimental, tear-jerking, tender; inspiring, inspirational, stimulating, stirring.
—OPPOSITES: fixed, stationary.

mow *v.* CUT (DOWN), trim; crop, clip, prune, manicure.

muck *n.* DIRT, grime, filth, mud, slime, mess; *informal* crud, gunk, grunge, gunge, guck, glop.

muddle *v.* **1** CONFUSE, mix up, jumble (up), disarrange, disorganize, disorder, disturb, mess up. **2** BEWILDER, confuse, bemuse, perplex, puzzle, baffle, mystify.
▸ *n.* MESS, confusion, jumble, tangle, mishmash, chaos, disorder, disarray, disorganization, imbroglio, hodgepodge.

muddy *adj.* MUCKY, mud-caked, muddied, dirty, filthy, grimy, soiled; *literary* begrimed; murky, cloudy, turbid, riled; dingy, drab, dull, sludgy.
—OPPOSITES: clean, clear.
▸ *v.* MAKE MUDDY, dirty, soil, spatter, bespatter; *literary* besmirch, begrime.
—OPPOSITES: clarify.

muffle *v.* DEADEN, dull, dampen, mute, soften, quieten, tone down, mask, stifle, smother.

mug *n.* CUP, glass; stein, flagon, tankard; *archaic* stoup.

muggy | muster

▶ *v.* ASSAULT, attack, set upon, beat up, rob; *informal* jump, rough up, lay into, do over.

muggy *adj.* HUMID, close, sultry, sticky, oppressive, airless, stifling, suffocating, stuffy, steamy, clammy, damp, heavy.
—OPPOSITES: fresh.

multiple *adj.* ☞ MANY.
—OPPOSITES: single.

multiply *v.* **1** INCREASE, grow, become more numerous, accumulate, proliferate, mount up, mushroom, snowball; burgeon, expand, explode, skyrocket. **2** BREED, reproduce, procreate.
—OPPOSITES: decrease.

multitude *n.* **1** A LOT, a great/large number, a great/large quantity, host, horde, mass, swarm, abundance, profusion; scores, quantities, droves; *informal* slew, lots, loads, masses, stacks, heaps, piles, tons, dozens, hundreds, thousands, millions, gazillions. **2** CROWD, gathering, assembly, congregation, flock, throng, horde, mob; *formal* concourse. **3** ☞ POPULACE.

munch *v.* CHEW, champ, chomp, masticate, crunch, eat, gnaw, nibble, snack, chow down on.

mundane *adj.* ☞ ORDINARY 2.
—OPPOSITES: extraordinary.

municipal *adj.* CIVIC, civil, metropolitan, urban, city, town, borough.
—OPPOSITES: rural.

murder *n.* KILLING, homicide, assassination, liquidation, extermination, execution, slaughter, butchery, massacre; manslaughter; *literary* slaying.
▶ *v.* ☞ KILL 1.

murderous *adj.* **1** HOMICIDAL, brutal, violent, savage, ferocious, fierce, vicious, bloodthirsty, barbarous, barbaric; fatal, lethal, deadly, mortal, death-dealing; *archaic* sanguinary. **2** ☞ ARDUOUS.

murky *adj.* **1** DARK, gloomy, grey, leaden, dull, dim, overcast, cloudy, clouded, sunless, dismal, dreary, bleak; *literary* tenebrous. **2** DIRTY, muddy, cloudy, turbid, riled, roily.
—OPPOSITES: bright, clear.

murmur *n.* **1** WHISPER, undertone, mutter, mumble. **2** HUM, humming, buzz, buzzing, thrum, thrumming, drone; sigh, rustle; *literary* susurration.
▶ *v.* **1** MUTTER, mumble, whisper, talk under one's breath, speak softly. **2** COMPLAIN, mutter, grumble, grouse; *informal* gripe, moan. **3** RUSTLE, sigh; burble, purl; *literary* whisper.

muscular *adj.* STRONG, brawny, muscly, sinewy, powerfully built, well muscled, burly, strapping, sturdy, powerful, athletic, solid; *Physiology* mesomorphic; *informal* hunky, beefy, muscle-bound; *literary* thewy.

muse *v.* ☞ CONTEMPLATE 2.

mushroom *v.* ☞ MULTIPLY 1.
—OPPOSITES: contract.

musical *adj.* TUNEFUL, melodic, melodious, harmonious, sweet-sounding, sweet, mellifluous, euphonious, euphonic.
—OPPOSITES: discordant.

muster *v.* ASSEMBLE, mobilize, rally, raise, summon, gather (together), mass, collect, convene, call up, call to arms, recruit, conscript, draft; *archaic* levy.

□ **pass muster** ☞ **MEASURE UP** at **MEASURE**.

musty *adj.* MOULDY, stale, fusty, damp, dank, mildewy, (*Nfld*) fousty❖, smelly, stuffy, airless, unventilated; *informal* funky.
—OPPOSITES: fresh.

mutation *n.* ALTERATION, change, variation, modification, transformation, metamorphosis, transmutation; *humorous* transmogrification.

mute *adj.* **1** SILENT, speechless, dumb, unspeaking, tight-lipped, taciturn; *informal* mum, tongue-tied. **2** DUMB, unable to speak; *Medicine* aphasic.
—OPPOSITES: voluble, spoken.
▶ *v.* **1** DEADEN, muffle, dampen, soften, quieten, hush; stifle, smother, suppress. **2** RESTRAIN, soften, tone down, moderate, temper.
—OPPOSITES: intensify.

muted *adj.* **1** MUFFLED, faint, indistinct, quiet, soft, low. **2** SUBDUED, pastel, delicate, subtle, understated, restrained.

mutiny *n.* INSURRECTION, rebellion, revolt, riot, uprising, insurgence, insubordination.
▶ *v.* RISE UP, rebel, revolt, riot, disobey/defy authority, be insubordinate.

mysterious *adj.* **1** PUZZLING, strange, peculiar, curious, funny, queer, odd, weird, bizarre, mystifying, inexplicable, baffling, perplexing, incomprehensible, unexplainable, unfathomable. **2** ENIGMATIC, inscrutable, secretive, reticent, evasive, furtive, surreptitious.
—OPPOSITES: straightforward.

mystery *n.* **1** PUZZLE, enigma, conundrum, riddle, secret, (unsolved) problem. **2** SECRECY, obscurity, uncertainty, mystique. **3** THRILLER, detective story/novel, murder story, crime novel; *informal* whodunit.

mystic, **mystical** *adj.*
1 SPIRITUAL, religious, transcendental, paranormal, otherworldly, supernatural, occult, metaphysical. **2** CRYPTIC, concealed, hidden, abstruse, arcane, esoteric, inscrutable, inexplicable, unfathomable, mysterious, secret, enigmatic.

mystify *v.* ☞ PERPLEX.

myth *n.* **1** (FOLK) TALE, (folk) story, legend, fable, saga, mythos, lore, folklore, mythology. **2** MISCONCEPTION, fallacy, false notion, old wives' tale, fairy story/tale, fiction; *informal* (tall) story/tale, cock-and-bull story, urban myth/legend.

mythical *adj.* **1** LEGENDARY, mythological, fabled, fabulous, folkloric, fairy-tale, storybook; fantastical, imaginary, imagined. **2** IMAGINARY, fictitious, make-believe, fantasy, invented, made-up, non-existent; *informal* pretend.

Nn

nag *v.* **1** HARASS, badger, give someone a hard time, chivvy, hound, harry, criticize, carp, find fault with, keep on at, grumble at, go on at; henpeck, hassle, get on someone's case, ride. **2** TROUBLE, worry, bother, plague, torment, niggle, prey on one's mind; annoy, irritate; *informal* bug, aggravate.

naive *adj.* INNOCENT, unsophisticated, artless, ingenuous, inexperienced, guileless, unworldly, trusting; gullible, credulous, immature, callow, raw, green, wide-eyed; *informal* wet behind the ears, born yesterday.
—OPPOSITES: worldly.

naked *adj.* NUDE, bare, in the nude, stark naked, having nothing on, stripped, unclothed, undressed, au naturel, disrobed, unclad; without a stitch on, in one's birthday suit, in the buff, in the raw, in the altogether, starkers, buck-naked, butt-naked, mother-naked.
—OPPOSITES: clothed.

name *n.* **1** DESIGNATION, label, description, characterization, identity; nickname, epithet, tag, title, honorific, sobriquet; *informal* handle, moniker; *formal* denomination, appellation.
2 ☞ REPUTATION.

—RELATED: nominal, onomastic.
▶ *v.* **1** CALL, give a name to, dub; label, style, term, title, entitle; baptize, christen; *formal* denominate. **2** IDENTIFY, specify. **3** CHOOSE, select, pick, decide on, nominate, designate.

nameless *adj.* UNNAMED, unidentified, anonymous, incognito, unspecified, unacknowledged, uncredited; unknown, unsung, uncelebrated.

nap *v.* DOZE, sleep (lightly), take a nap, catnap, rest, take a siesta; *informal* snooze, catch forty winks, get some shut-eye, catch some zees, catch a few zees.
▶ *n.* (LIGHT) SLEEP, catnap, siesta, doze, lie-down, rest; *informal* snooze, forty winks, shut-eye, beauty sleep, power nap.

narcissism *n.* ☞ VANITY 1.
—OPPOSITES: modesty.

narrate *v.* TELL, relate, recount, describe, chronicle, give a report of, report.

narrow *adj.* **1** SLENDER, slim, slight, spare, attenuated, thin. **2** CONFINED, cramped, tight, restricted, limited, constricted. **3** LIMITED, restricted, circumscribed, small, inadequate, insufficient, deficient.
4 ☞ NARROW-MINDED. **5** STRICT, literal, exact, precise. **6** BY A VERY SMALL MARGIN, close, near, by a

hair's breadth, by a whisker.
—OPPOSITES: wide, broad.

narrow-minded *adj.*
INTOLERANT, illiberal, reactionary, parochial, provincial, insular, small-minded, petty, blinkered, inward-looking, narrow, parish-pump, hidebound, prejudiced, bigoted, redneck.
—OPPOSITES: tolerant.

narrows *pl. n.* STRAIT(S), sound, channel, (*Atlantic*) run✦, waterway, (sea) passage, (*Atlantic*) tickle✦.

nasty *adj.* **1** UNPLEASANT, disagreeable, disgusting, distasteful, awful, dreadful, horrible, terrible, vile, foul, abominable, frightful, loathsome, revolting, repulsive, odious, sickening, nauseating, repellent, repugnant, horrendous, appalling, atrocious, offensive, objectionable, obnoxious, unsavoury, unappetizing, off-putting; noxious, foul-smelling, smelly, stinking, rank, fetid, malodorous, mephitic; *informal* ghastly, horrid, gruesome, diabolical, yucky, skanky, godawful, gross, beastly, grotty, lousy, funky; *literary* miasmal, noisome. **2** ☞ UNKIND. **3** SERIOUS, dangerous, bad, awful, dreadful, terrible, severe; painful, ugly.
4 ☞ ANNOYING.
—OPPOSITES: nice.

nation *n.* COUNTRY, (sovereign/ nation) state, land, realm, kingdom, republic; fatherland, motherland; people, race.

national *adj.* **1** STATE, public, federal, governmental; civic, civil, domestic, internal. **2** NATIONWIDE, general.

—OPPOSITES: local, international.
▸ *n.* CITIZEN, subject, native; voter.

native *n.* INHABITANT, resident, local; citizen, national; aborigine, autochthon; *formal* dweller.
—OPPOSITES: foreigner.
▸ *adj.* **1** INDIGENOUS, original, first, earliest, aboriginal, autochthonous, First Nations✦.
2 DOMESTIC, homegrown, homemade, local; indigenous.
3 ☞ INNATE.
—OPPOSITES: immigrant.

Native Peoples *pl. n.* FIRST PEOPLES, Native Canadians, Native Americans, Aboriginal Peoples, Indigenous Peoples; First Nations, Indians, Inuit, Metis.

natural *adj.* **1** NORMAL, ordinary, everyday, usual, regular, common, commonplace, typical, routine, standard, established, customary, accustomed, habitual.
2 UNPROCESSED, organic, pure, wholesome, unrefined, pesticide-free, additive-free. **3** INNATE, inborn, inherent, native, instinctive, intuitive; hereditary, inherited, inbred, congenital, connate. **4** UNAFFECTED, spontaneous, uninhibited, relaxed, unselfconscious, genuine, open, artless, guileless, ingenuous, unpretentious, without airs. **5** REASONABLE, logical, understandable, (only) to be expected, predictable.
—OPPOSITES: abnormal, artificial, affected.

nature *n.* **1** THE NATURAL WORLD, the environment, Mother Nature, wildlife, flora and fauna, the countryside, Mother Earth; the universe, the cosmos. **2** ESSENCE, inherent/basic/essential qualities, character, complexion.

3 ☞ PERSONALITY 1. **4** ☞ KIND *n.*

naughty *adj.* **1** BADLY BEHAVED, disobedient, bad, misbehaved, misbehaving, wayward, defiant, unruly, insubordinate, wilful, delinquent, undisciplined, uncontrollable, ill-mannered, ungovernable, disorderly, disruptive, fractious, recalcitrant, wild, wicked, obstreperous, difficult, troublesome, awkward, contrary, perverse, incorrigible; mischievous, playful, impish, roguish, rascally, bratty. **2** ☞ INDECENT.
—OPPOSITES: well-behaved, decent.

nausea *n.* SICKNESS, queasiness; vomiting, retching, gagging; upset stomach; travel sickness, seasickness, carsickness, airsickness.

nauseating *adj.* ☞ SICKENING.

nauseous *adj.* SICK, nauseated, queasy, bilious, green around/at the gills, ill, unwell; seasick, carsick, airsick, travel-sick, barfy.

near *adv.* **1** ☞ NEARBY *adv.*
2 ☞ ALMOST.
▶ *prep.* CLOSE TO, close by, a short distance from, in the vicinity of, in the neighbourhood of, within reach of, a stone's throw away from; *informal* within spitting distance of.
▶ *adj.* **1** CLOSE, nearby, close/near at hand, at hand, a stone's throw away, within reach, accessible, handy, convenient; *informal* within spitting distance. **2** ☞ IMMINENT.
—OPPOSITES: far, distant.
▶ *v.* ☞ APPROACH *v.* 1.

nearby *adj.* ☞ NEAR *adj.* 1.
—OPPOSITES: faraway.
▶ *adv.* CLOSE (BY), close/near at hand, near, a short distance away, in the neighbourhood, in the vicinity, at hand, within reach, on the doorstep, (just) round the corner.

nearly *adv.* ☞ ALMOST.

neat *adj.* **1** ☞ TIDY 1, 2. **2** SMART, dapper, trim, well-groomed, well-turned-out, spruce; *informal* natty. **3** WELL-FORMED, regular, precise, elegant, well-proportioned. **4** CLEVER, ingenious, inventive. **5** ☞ WONDERFUL, IMPRESSIVE.
—OPPOSITES: untidy.
▶ *excl.* ☞ COOL *excl.*

necessary *adj.* **1** OBLIGATORY, requisite, required, compulsory, mandatory, imperative, needed, de rigueur; essential, indispensable, vital. **2** INEVITABLE, unavoidable, inescapable, inexorable, ineluctable; predetermined, preordained.

necessity *n.* ☞ REQUIREMENT.

need *v.* **1** REQUIRE, be in need of, have need of, want; be crying out for, be desperate for; demand, call for, necessitate, entail, involve; lack, be without, be short of. **2** HAVE TO, be obliged to, be compelled to.
▶ *n.* **1** NECESSITY, obligation, requirement, call, demand. **2** REQUIREMENT, essential, necessity, want, requisite, prerequisite, demand, desideratum. **3** NEEDINESS, want, poverty, deprivation, privation, hardship, destitution, indigence. **4** DIFFICULTY, trouble, distress; crisis, emergency, urgency,

extremity.

☐ **in need** ☞ POOR 1.

needless *adj.* ☞ UNNECESSARY.
—OPPOSITES: necessary.

negative *adj.* **1** OPPOSING,
opposed, contrary, anti-,
dissenting, saying 'no', in the
negative. **2** ☞ PESSIMISTIC.
3 ☞ HARMFUL.
—OPPOSITES: positive, optimistic,
favourable.

neglect *v.* **1** FAIL TO LOOK AFTER,
leave alone, abandon, desert;
literary forsake. **2** PAY NO ATTENTION
TO, let slide, not attend to, be
remiss about, be lax about, leave
undone, shirk. **3** FAIL, omit, forget.
—OPPOSITES: cherish, remember.
▶ *n.* **1** DISREPAIR, dilapidation,
deterioration, shabbiness, disuse,
abandonment. **2** NEGLIGENCE,
dereliction of duty, carelessness,
heedlessness, unconcern, laxity,
slackness, irresponsibility; *formal*
delinquency. **3** DISREGARD,
ignoring, overlooking; inattention
to, indifference to, heedlessness
to.
—OPPOSITES: care, attention.

negligent *adj.* NEGLECTFUL,
remiss, careless, lax,
irresponsible, inattentive,
heedless, thoughtless, unmindful,
forgetful; slack, sloppy, derelict;
formal delinquent.
—OPPOSITES: dutiful.

negligible *adj.* TRIVIAL, trifling,
insignificant, unimportant,
minor, inconsequential; minimal,
small, slight, inappreciable,
infinitesimal, nugatory, petty;
paltry, inadequate, insufficient,
meagre, pitiful; minuscule,

piddling, measly; exiguous.
—OPPOSITES: significant.

negotiate *v.* **1** DISCUSS TERMS,
talk, consult, parley, confer,
debate; compromise; mediate,
intercede, arbitrate, moderate,
conciliate; bargain, haggle.
2 ARRANGE, broker, work out,
thrash out, agree on; settle,
clinch, conclude, pull off, bring
off, transact; *informal* sort out,
swing. **3** GET ROUND, get past, get
over, clear, cross; surmount,
overcome, deal with, cope with.

neighbourhood *n.* DISTRICT,
area, locality, locale, quarter,
community; part, region, zone;
informal neck of the woods, hood,
nabe, stomping ground.
☐ **in the neighbourhood of**
☞ APPROXIMATELY.

neighbouring *adj.* ☞ ADJACENT.

nemesis *n.* ARCH RIVAL, adversary,
foe, opponent, arch enemy.

nerd *n.* BORE, dork, dweeb, geek,
loser; techie.

nerve *n.* ☞ AUDACITY.
☐ **get on someone's nerves**
☞ ANNOY.

nervous *adj.* **1** ANXIOUS, worried,
apprehensive, on edge, edgy,
tense, stressed, agitated, uneasy,
restless, worked up, keyed up,
overwrought, jumpy; fearful,
frightened, scared, shaky, in a
cold sweat, gun-shy; *informal* with
butterflies in one's stomach,
jittery, twitchy, in a state, uptight,
wired, in a flap, het up, strung
out, high-strung; having kittens,
squirrelly. **2** NEUROLOGICAL, neural.
—OPPOSITES: relaxed, calm.

nestle *v.* SNUGGLE, cuddle, huddle,
nuzzle, settle, burrow.

Net *n.* INTERNET, World Wide Web, web, cyberspace, information (super)highway.

net *n.* **1** NETTING, meshwork, webbing, tulle, fishnet, openwork, lace, latticework. **2** FISHING NET, dragnet, drift net, trawl net, landing net, gill net, cast net, seine, (*Nfld*) linnet✦.
▶ *v.* ☞ CATCH *v.* 2.

nettle *v.* ☞ ANNOY.

network *n.* SYSTEM, complex, nexus, web, webwork.

neurotic *adj.* OVER-ANXIOUS, over-sensitive, nervous, tense, high-strung, strung out, paranoid; obsessive, fixated, hysterical, overwrought, worked up, irrational, twitchy.
—OPPOSITES: stable, calm.

neuter *v.* STERILIZE, castrate, spay, geld, fix, desex, alter, doctor; *archaic* emasculate.

neutral *adj.* **1** ☞ UNBIASED.
2 UNALIGNED, non-aligned, unaffiliated, unallied, uninvolved; non-combatant. **3** PALE, light; colourless, uncoloured, achromatic; indeterminate, insipid, nondescript, dull, drab.
—OPPOSITES: biased, partisan, colourful.

neutralize *v.* COUNTERACT, offset, counterbalance, balance, counterpoise, countervail, compensate for, make up for; cancel out, nullify, negate; equalize.

never-ending *adj.* ☞ ENDLESS.

nevertheless *adv.* ☞ HOWEVER.

new *adj.* **1** RECENTLY DEVELOPED, up to date, latest, current, state-of-the-art, contemporary, advanced, recent, modern, cutting-edge, leading-edge. **2** NOVEL, original, fresh, imaginative, creative, experimental; contemporary, modernist, up to date; newfangled, ultra-modern, avant-garde, futuristic; *informal* way out, far out. **3** UNUSED, brand new, pristine, fresh, in mint condition. **4** DIFFERENT, another, alternative;' unfamiliar, unknown, strange; unaccustomed, untried.
—RELATED: neo-.
—OPPOSITES: old, hackneyed, second-hand.

newcomer *n.* (NEW) ARRIVAL, immigrant, settler; stranger, outsider, (*Atlantic*) come from away✦, foreigner, alien; *informal* johnny-come-lately, new kid on the block.

news *n.* REPORT, announcement, story, account; article, news flash, newscast, headlines, press release, communication, communiqué, bulletin; message, dispatch, statement, intelligence; disclosure, revelation, word, talk, gossip; *informal* scoop; *literary* tidings.

newspaper *n.* PAPER, journal, gazette, tabloid, broadsheet, local (paper), daily (paper), weekly (paper); scandal sheet, rag, tab.

next *adj.* **1** FOLLOWING, succeeding, upcoming, to come.
2 NEIGHBOURING, adjacent, adjoining, next-door, bordering, connected, attached; closest, nearest.
—OPPOSITES: previous.
▶ *adv.* THEN, after, afterwards, after this/that, following that/this, later, subsequently; *formal* thereafter, thereupon.
—OPPOSITES: before.

□ **next to** BESIDE, by, alongside, by the side of, next door to, adjacent to, side by side with; close to, near, neighbouring, adjoining.

nice *adj.* **1** ENJOYABLE, pleasant, agreeable, good, satisfying, gratifying, delightful, marvellous; entertaining, amusing, diverting, lovely, great; likeable, personable, congenial, amiable, affable, genial, friendly, charming, engaging. **2** SUBTLE, fine, delicate, minute, precise, strict, close; careful, meticulous, scrupulous.
—OPPOSITES: unpleasant, nasty, rough.

nicety *n.* SUBTLETY, fine point, nuance, refinement, detail.

nickname *n.* SOBRIQUET, byname, tag, label, epithet, cognomen; pet name, diminutive, endearment; *informal* moniker; *formal* appellation.

nimble *adj.* AGILE, sprightly, light, spry, lively, quick, graceful, lithe, limber; skilful, deft, dextrous, adroit; *informal* nippy, twinkle-toed; *literary* lightsome.
—OPPOSITES: clumsy.

nitpicking *adj.* ☞ PEDANTIC.

no *adv.* absolutely not, most certainly not, of course not, under no circumstances, by no means, not at all, negative, never, not really; *informal* nope, uh-uh, nah, not on your life, no way, no way José, ixnay; *archaic* nay.
—OPPOSITES: yes.

noble *adj.* **1** ARISTOCRATIC, patrician, blue-blooded, high-born, titled. **2** RIGHTEOUS, virtuous, good, honourable, upright, decent, worthy, moral, ethical, reputable; magnanimous, unselfish, generous.
—OPPOSITES: humble, dishonourable, base.
▶ *n.* ARISTOCRAT, nobleman, noblewoman, lord, lady, peer (of the realm), peeress, patrician; aristo.

nod *v.* INCLINE, bob, bow, dip.
▶ *n.* **1** INCLINATION, bob, bow, dip.
2 ☞ APPROVAL 1.

noise *n.* SOUND, din, hubbub, clamour, racket, uproar, tumult, commotion, pandemonium, babel, cacophony, caterwauling, clangour, clatter, outcry, ruckus, rumpus; *informal* hullabaloo.

noisy *adj.* ROWDY, clamorous, loud, boisterous, turbulent, uproarious, riotous, rambunctious, rackety; chattering, talkative, vociferous, shouting, screaming, blaring, booming, deafening, thunderous, tumultuous, ear-splitting, piercing, strident, cacophonous, raucous.
—OPPOSITES: quiet.

nominal *adj.* **1** IN NAME ONLY, titular, formal, official; theoretical, supposed, ostensible, so-called. **2** TOKEN, symbolic; tiny, minute, minimal, small, insignificant, trifling, minuscule, piddling, piffling.
—OPPOSITES: real, considerable.

nonchalant *adj.* CALM, composed, unconcerned, cool, {calm, cool, and collected}, cool as a cucumber; indifferent, blasé, dispassionate, apathetic, casual, insouciant; *informal* laid-back.
—OPPOSITES: anxious.

noncommittal *adj.* EVASIVE, equivocal, guarded, circumspect, reserved; discreet, uncommunicative, tactful, diplomatic, vague; *informal* cagey.

nondescript *adj.* ☞ ORDINARY 2.
—OPPOSITES: distinctive.

nonetheless *adv.* ☞ HOWEVER.

nonsense *n.* RUBBISH, balderdash, gibberish, claptrap, blarney, moonshine, garbage, hogwash, baloney, jive, guff, tripe, drivel, bilge, bull, bunk, BS, bafflegab, piffle, poppycock, hooey, twaddle, gobbledegook, mumbo-jumbo, codswallop, flapdoodle, hot air.
—OPPOSITES: sense, wisdom.
▶ *excl.* BALDERDASH, pshaw, no way, get out of here, phooey, puh-leeze, hooey, poppycock, come off it, like hell.

nonsensical *adj.* FOOLISH, insane, stupid, idiotic, illogical, irrational, senseless, absurd, silly, inane, hare-brained, ridiculous, ludicrous, preposterous; *informal* crazy, crackpot, nutty; daft.
—OPPOSITES: sensible.

non-stop *adj.* ☞ CEASELESS.
▶ *adv.* CONTINUOUSLY, continually, incessantly, unceasingly, ceaselessly, all the time, constantly, perpetually, round the clock, day and night, steadily, relentlessly, persistently; *informal* 24-7.
—OPPOSITES: occasionally.

nook *n.* RECESS, corner, alcove, niche, cranny, bay, inglenook, cavity, cubbyhole, pigeonhole.

normal *adj.* **1** USUAL, standard, ordinary, customary, conventional, habitual, accustomed, expected, wonted; typical, stock, common, everyday, regular, routine, established, set, fixed, traditional, time-honoured. **2** ORDINARY, average, typical, run-of-the-mill, middle-of-the-road,

common, conventional, mainstream, unremarkable, unexceptional, garden-variety, a dime a dozen.
—OPPOSITES: unusual, insane.

normally *adv.* **1** NATURALLY, conventionally, ordinarily; as usual, as normal. **2** ☞ USUALLY.

north *adj.* NORTHERN, northerly, polar, Arctic, boreal.
▶ *n.* ARCTIC, northland, land of the midnight sun, north of sixty, the Barrens.

nose *n.* snout, muzzle, proboscis, trunk; *informal* beak, snoot, schnozz, schnozzola, sniffer.
—RELATED: nasal, rhinal.
☐ **by a nose** (ONLY) JUST, barely, narrowly, by a hair's breadth, by the skin of one's teeth, by a whisker. **on the nose** EXACTLY, precisely, sharp, on the dot, on the button, promptly, prompt, dead on, bang on.

nosedive *v.* FALL, take a header, drop, sink, plunge, plummet, tumble, slump, go down, decline; *informal* crash.
—OPPOSITES: soar, rise.

nostalgic *adj.* WISTFUL, evocative, romantic, sentimental; regretful, dewy-eyed, misty-eyed, maudlin; homesick.

nosy *adj.* PRYING, inquisitive, curious, busybody, spying, eavesdropping, intrusive; *informal* snooping, snoopy.

notable *adj.* **1** NOTEWORTHY, remarkable, outstanding, important, significant, momentous, memorable; marked, striking, impressive; uncommon, unusual, special, exceptional, extraordinary, interesting, singular. **2** ☞ PROMINENT 1.

—OPPOSITES: unremarkable, unknown.

note n. **1** RECORD, entry, item, notation, jotting, memorandum, reminder, aide-mémoire, memo. **2** MINUTES, records, details; report, account, commentary, transcript, proceedings, transactions; synopsis, summary, outline. **3** ANNOTATION, footnote, commentary, comment, marginalia. **4** MESSAGE, communication, letter, line; *formal* epistle, missive. **5** ☞ DISTINCTION 2.
▶ v. **1** BEAR IN MIND, be mindful of, consider, observe, heed, take notice of, pay attention to, take in. **2** MENTION, refer to, touch on, indicate, point out, make known, state. **3** WRITE DOWN, put down, jot down, take down, inscribe, enter, mark, record, register, pencil.

noteworthy adj. ☞ NOTABLE 1.
—OPPOSITES: unexceptional.

nothing n. NOT A THING, not anything, nil, zero; zilch, zip, nada, diddly-squat, squat; *archaic* naught.
—OPPOSITES: something.

notice n. **1** ATTENTION, observation, awareness, consciousness, perception; regard, consideration, scrutiny; watchfulness, vigilance, attentiveness. **2** POSTER, bill, handbill, advertisement, ad, announcement, bulletin; flyer, leaflet, pamphlet; sign, card. **3** NOTIFICATION, (advance) warning, announcement; information, news, communication, word.
▶ v. OBSERVE, perceive, note, see, discern, detect, spot, distinguish, mark, remark; behold, catch sight of, espy, glimpse, make out,

recognize, clap/lay/set eyes on, descry, sight, spy, witness.
—OPPOSITES: overlook.

noticeable adj. DISTINCT, evident, obvious, apparent, manifest, patent, plain, clear, marked, conspicuous, unmistakable, undeniable, pronounced, perceivable, prominent, striking, arresting; perceptible, discernible, detectable, observable, visible, appreciable, palpable, self-evident, tangible, transparent, written all over someone, staring one in the face.

notify v. ☞ TELL 1.

notion n. **1** IDEA, belief, conviction, opinion, view, thought, impression, perception; hypothesis, theory; (funny) feeling, (sneaking) suspicion, hunch. **2** UNDERSTANDING, idea, awareness, knowledge, clue, inkling.

notorious adj. INFAMOUS, scandalous; well known, famous, famed, legendary.

nourishment n. ☞ FOOD.

novel adj. ☞ ORIGINAL 1.
—OPPOSITES: traditional.

novelty n. **1** ORIGINALITY, newness, freshness, unconventionality, unfamiliarity; difference, creativity, innovation, modernity. **2** KNICK-KNACK, trinket, bauble, toy, trifle, gewgaw, gimcrack, ornament, kickshaw.

novice n. ☞ BEGINNER.
—OPPOSITES: expert, veteran.

now adv. **1** AT THE MOMENT, at present, at the present (time/moment), at this moment in time, currently, presently. **2** NOWADAYS, today, these days, in this day and age; in the present climate.

3 ☞ IMMEDIATELY.

☐ **now and again** ☞ SOMETIMES.

nowhere

☐ **the middle of nowhere** BACK OF BEYOND, rural areas, (*Ont. & Que.*) the back concessions✦, backwoods, hinterland, bush, backcountry; *informal* sticks, boondocks, boonies.

noxious *adj.* POISONOUS, toxic, deadly, harmful, dangerous, pernicious, damaging, destructive; unpleasant, nasty, disgusting, awful, dreadful, horrible, terrible; vile, revolting, foul, nauseating, appalling, offensive; malodorous, fetid, putrid; *literary* noisome.

—OPPOSITES: innocuous.

nuance *n.* FINE DISTINCTION, subtle difference; shade, shading, gradation, variation, degree; subtlety, nicety, overtone.

nude *adj.* ☞ NAKED.

nudge *v.* **1** POKE, elbow, dig, prod, jog, jab. **2** TOUCH, bump (against), push (against), run into. **3** PROMPT, encourage, stimulate, prod, galvanize.

▶ *n.* **1** POKE, dig (in the ribs), prod, jog, jab, push. **2** REMINDER, prompt, prompting, prod, encouragement.

nuisance *n.* ANNOYANCE, inconvenience, bore, bother, irritation, problem, trouble, trial, burden; pest, plague, thorn in one's side/flesh, burr under someone's saddle, irritant, torment; *informal* pain (in the neck), hassle, bind, drag, chore, aggravation, headache, menace, nudnik, vexation.

—OPPOSITES: blessing.

numb *adj.* WITHOUT SENSATION, without feeling, numbed, benumbed, desensitized, insensible, senseless, unfeeling; anaesthetized; dazed, stunned, stupefied, paralyzed, crippled, incapacitated, immobilized, frozen.

—OPPOSITES: sensitive.

number *n.* **1** NUMERAL, integer, figure, digit; character, symbol; decimal, unit; cardinal number, ordinal number. **2** AMOUNT, quantity; total, aggregate, tally; quota.

—RELATED: numerical.

☐ **a number of** SEVERAL, various, quite a few, sundry.

numerous *adj.* ☞ MANY.

—OPPOSITES: few.

nurse *n.* CAREGIVER, RN, nurse practitioner, nursing assistant, LPN, health care worker; *informal* Florence Nightingale; VON.

▶ *v.* **1** CARE FOR, take care of, look after, tend, minister to. **2** TREAT, medicate, tend; dress, bandage, soothe, doctor. **3** BREASTFEED, suckle, feed; wet-nurse. **4** HARBOUR, foster, entertain, bear, have, hold (on to), cherish, cling to, retain.

nurture *v.* **1** BRING UP, care for, take care of, look after, tend, rear, raise, support, foster; parent, mother. **2** CULTIVATE, grow, keep, tend. **3** ☞ FOSTER 1.

—OPPOSITES: neglect, hinder.

nut *n.* **1** ☞ LUNATIC. **2** ☞ FAN.

nutritious *adj.* NOURISHING, good for one, full of nutrients, nutritive, nutritional, wholesome, healthy, healthful, beneficial, sustaining.

Oo

oaf *n.* LOUT, boor, barbarian, Neanderthal, churl, bumpkin, hoser✦, yokel; fool, idiot, imbecile, moron; *informal* cretin, ass, goon, yahoo, ape, lump, clod, meathead, meatball, bonehead, knucklehead, lamebrain, palooka, bozo, dumbhead, lummox, klutz, goofus, doofus, turkey, dingbat.

oath *n.* **1** ☞ VOW. **2** ☞ OBSCENITY.

obedient *adj.* COMPLIANT, biddable, acquiescent, tractable, amenable, malleable, pliable, pliant; dutiful, good, law-abiding, deferential, respectful, duteous, well-trained, well-disciplined, manageable, governable, docile, tame, meek, passive, submissive, unresisting, yielding.
—OPPOSITES: rebellious.

obese *adj.* ☞ FAT 1.
—OPPOSITES: thin.

obey *v.* **1** DO WHAT SOMEONE SAYS, carry out someone's orders; submit to, defer to, bow to, yield to. **2** CARRY OUT, perform, act on, execute, discharge, implement, fulfill. **3** COMPLY WITH, adhere to, observe, abide by, act in accordance with, conform to, respect, follow, heed, uphold, keep to, stick to, hew to; play it by the book, toe the line.
—OPPOSITES: defy, ignore.

object *n.* **1** ☞ THING 1. **2** TARGET, butt, focus, recipient, victim.

3 ☞ AIM.
▶ *v.* PROTEST ABOUT, oppose, raise objections to, express disapproval of, take exception to, take issue with, take a stand against, argue against, quarrel with, condemn, draw the line at, demur at, mind, complain about, cavil at, quibble about; beg to differ; *informal* kick up a fuss/stink about.
—OPPOSITES: approve, accept.

objection *n.* PROTEST, protestation, demur, demurral, complaint, expostulation, grievance, cavil, quibble; opposition, argument, counter-argument, disagreement, disapproval, dissent; *informal* niggle.

objectionable *adj.* UNPLEASANT, disagreeable, distasteful, displeasing, off-putting, undesirable, obnoxious, offensive, nasty, horrible, horrid, disgusting, awful, terrible, dreadful, frightful, appalling, insufferable, odious, vile, foul, unsavoury, repulsive, repellent, repugnant, revolting, abhorrent, loathsome, hateful, detestable, reprehensible, deplorable, ghastly; beastly.
—OPPOSITES: pleasant.

objective *adj.* **1** ☞ UNBIASED. **2** FACTUAL, actual, real, empirical, verifiable.
—OPPOSITES: biased, subjective.
▶ *n.* ☞ AIM.

obligation *n.* DUTY, commitment, responsibility; function, task, job, assignment, commission, burden, charge, onus, liability, accountability, requirement, debt.

obligatory *adj.* ☞ MANDATORY.
—OPPOSITES: optional.

oblige *v.* **1** ☞ COMPEL. **2** DO SOMEONE A FAVOUR, accommodate, help, assist, serve; gratify someone's wishes, indulge, humour.

obliging *adj.* ☞ ACCOMMODATING.
—OPPOSITES: unhelpful.

oblique *adj.* **1** ☞ SLANTING. **2** INDIRECT, inexplicit, roundabout, circuitous, circumlocutory, implicit, implied, elliptical, evasive, mealy-mouthed, backhanded. **3** SIDELONG, sideways, furtive, covert, sly, surreptitious.
—OPPOSITES: straight, direct.

obliterate *v.* **1** ERASE, eradicate, expunge, efface, wipe out, blot out, rub out, remove all traces of. **2** DESTROY, wipe out, annihilate, demolish, liquidate, wipe off the face of the earth, wipe off the map; *informal* zap, nuke.

oblivious *adj.* ☞ UNAWARE.
—OPPOSITES: conscious.

obnoxious *adj.* ☞ ANNOYING, UNPLEASANT.
—OPPOSITES: delightful.

obscene *adj.* **1** ☞ INDECENT. **2** SHOCKING, scandalous, vile, foul, atrocious, outrageous, heinous, odious, abhorrent, abominable, disgusting, hideous, repugnant, offensive, repulsive, revolting, repellent, loathsome, nauseating, sickening, awful, dreadful, terrible, frightful.

obscenity *n.* EXPLETIVE, swear word, oath, profanity, vulgarity, curse, four-letter word, dirty word, blasphemy; *informal* cuss, cuss word; *formal* imprecation.

obscure *adj.* **1** UNCLEAR, uncertain, unknown, in doubt, doubtful, dubious, mysterious, hazy, vague, indeterminate, concealed, hidden. **2** ☞ INCOMPREHENSIBLE, CRYPTIC. **3** ☞ UNKNOWN 4.
—OPPOSITES: clear, plain, famous.
▶ *v.* **1** HIDE, conceal, cover, veil, shroud, screen, mask, cloak, cast a shadow over, shadow, block, obliterate, eclipse, darken. **2** CONFUSE, complicate, obfuscate, cloud, blur, muddy; muddy the waters; befog.
—OPPOSITES: reveal, clarify.

obsequious *adj.* SERVILE, ingratiating, sycophantic, fawning, toadying, unctuous, oily, oleaginous, grovelling, cringing, flattering, fulsome, subservient, submissive, slavish; slimy, bootlicking, smarmy.

observant *adj.* ALERT, sharp-eyed, sharp, eagle-eyed, hawk-eyed, having eyes like a hawk, watchful, heedful, aware; on the lookout, on the qui vive, on guard, attentive, vigilant, having one's eyes open/peeled; beady-eyed, not missing a trick, on the ball.
—OPPOSITES: inattentive.

observation *n.* **1** MONITORING, watching, scrutiny, examination, inspection, survey, surveillance, attention, consideration, study. **2** ☞ COMMENT 1.

observe *v.* **1** ☞ NOTICE *v.* **2** ☞ WATCH 1, 2. **3** COMPLY WITH, abide by, keep, obey, adhere to, heed, honour, fulfill, respect, follow, consent to, acquiesce in, accept.

observer *n.* SPECTATOR, onlooker, watcher, looker-on, fly on the wall, viewer, witness; *informal* rubberneck; *literary* beholder.

obsessed *adj.* FIXATED, possessed, consumed, hung up.

obsession *n.* FIXATION, ruling/consuming passion, passion, mania, idée fixe, compulsion, preoccupation, infatuation, addiction, fetish, craze; hobby horse; phobia, complex, neurosis; bee in one's bonnet, hang-up, thing, fad.

obsessive *adj.* ALL-CONSUMING, consuming, compulsive, controlling, fanatical, neurotic, excessive, besetting, tormenting, inescapable, pathological.

obsolete *adj.* OUT OF DATE, outdated, outmoded, old-fashioned, démodé, passé, superseded, vanished; no longer in use, disused, fallen into disuse, superannuated, outworn, antiquated, antediluvian, anachronistic, discontinued, old, dated, archaic, ancient, fossilized, prehistoric, extinct, defunct, dead, bygone.
—OPPOSITES: current, modern.

obstacle *n.* BARRIER, hurdle, stumbling block, obstruction, bar, block, impediment, hindrance, snag, catch, glitch, drawback, hitch, handicap, deterrent, complication, difficulty, problem, disadvantage, curb, check.
—OPPOSITES: advantage, aid.

obstinate *adj.* ☞ STUBBORN 1, INFLEXIBLE.
—OPPOSITES: compliant.

obstruct *v.* **1** BLOCK (UP), clog (up), get in the way of, occlude, cut off, shut off, bung up, choke, dam up; barricade, bar, gunge up. **2** HOLD UP, bring to a standstill, stop, halt; IMPEDE, hinder, interfere with, hamper, hobble, block, interrupt, stand in the way of, frustrate, thwart, balk, inhibit, hamstring, sabotage; slow down, retard, delay, stonewall, restrict, limit, curb, put a brake on, bridle; check, cumber, derail, disrupt, foil, hold back/up, scupper, scuttle, slow (down), stymie, throw a (monkey) wrench in the works.
—OPPOSITES: clear, facilitate.

obtain *v.* GET, acquire, come by, secure, procure, come into the possession of, pick up, be given; gain, earn, achieve, attain; *informal* get hold of, get/lay one's hands on, get one's mitts on, land, bag, be appointed to, carry off, net, swing, win.
—OPPOSITES: lose.

obtuse *adj.* ☞ STUPID 1.
—OPPOSITES: clever.

obvious *adj.* CLEAR, crystal clear, plain, evident, apparent, manifest, patent, conspicuous, pronounced, transparent, palpable, prominent, marked, decided, distinct, noticeable, unmissable, perceptible, visible, discernible; unmistakable, indisputable, self-evident, incontrovertible, incontestable, undeniable, as clear as day, staring someone in the face, writ large; overt, open,

undisguised, unconcealed, frank, glaring, blatant, written all over someone; *informal* as plain as the nose on your face, sticking out like a sore thumb.
—OPPOSITES: imperceptible.

occasion *n.* **1** TIME, instance, juncture, point; event, occurrence, affair, incident, episode, experience; situation, case, circumstance. **2** ☞ PARTY 1. **3** OPPORTUNITY, right moment, chance, opening, window.
▶ *v.* ☞ CAUSE.

occasional *adj.* INFREQUENT, intermittent, irregular, periodic, sporadic, odd, random, uncommon, few and far between, isolated, rare, sometime.
—OPPOSITES: regular, frequent.

occasionally *adv.* ☞ SOMETIMES.
—OPPOSITES: often.

occupation *n.* **1** JOB, profession, line of work, trade, employment, position, post, situation, business, career, métier, vocation, calling, craft, walk of life, racket. **2** CONQUEST, capture, invasion, seizure, takeover, annexation, overrunning, subjugation, subjection, appropriation, acquisition; colonization, rule, control, suzerainty.

occupy *v.* **1** LIVE IN, move into, take up residence in. See also INHABIT. **2** ENGAGE, busy, employ, distract, absorb, engross, preoccupy, hold, interest, involve, entertain, amuse, divert. **3** CAPTURE, seize, take possession of, conquer, invade, overrun, take over, colonize, garrison, annex, subjugate.

occur *v.* **1** ☞ HAPPEN 1. **2** BE FOUND, be present, exist, appear, prevail, present itself, manifest itself, turn up. **3** ENTER ONE'S HEAD/MIND, cross one's mind, come to mind, spring to mind, strike one, hit one, dawn on one, suggest itself.

occurrence *n.* **1** EVENT, incident, happening, phenomenon, affair, matter, circumstance. **2** EXISTENCE, instance, appearance, manifestation, materialization, development; frequency, incidence, rate, prevalence; *statistics* distribution.

odd *adj.* **1** ☞ STRANGE 1. **2** OCCASIONAL, casual, irregular, isolated, random, sporadic, periodic; miscellaneous, various, varied, sundry.
—OPPOSITES: normal, ordinary, regular.

odious *adj.* ☞ REPULSIVE.
—OPPOSITES: delightful.

odour *n.* SMELL, stench, stink, reek, whiff, fetor, funk; *literary* miasma.

offence *n.* **1** CRIME, illegal/unlawful act, misdemeanour, breach of the law, felony, wrongdoing, wrong, misdeed, peccadillo, sin, transgression, infringement, malfeasance; no-no. **2** AFFRONT, slap in the face, insult, outrage, violation. **3** ANNOYANCE, anger, resentment, indignation, irritation, exasperation, wrath, displeasure, hard/bad/ill feelings, disgruntlement, pique, vexation, animosity.
□**take offence** BE OFFENDED, take exception, take something personally, feel affronted, feel

resentful, take something amiss, take umbrage, get upset, get annoyed, get angry, get into a huff.

offend v. HURT SOMEONE'S FEELINGS, give offence to, affront, displease, upset, distress, hurt, wound; annoy, anger, exasperate, irritate, vex, pique, gall, irk, nettle, tread on someone's toes; rub the wrong way; *informal* rile, rattle, peeve, needle, put someone's nose out of joint, put someone's back up.

offender n. WRONGDOER, criminal, lawbreaker, miscreant, malefactor, felon, delinquent, culprit, guilty party, sinner, transgressor, perpetrator; *informal* baddy, crook, perp; *Law* malfeasant.

offensive adj. **1** INSULTING, rude, impertinent, insolent, derogatory, disrespectful, hurtful, wounding, abusive; annoying, exasperating, irritating, galling, provocative, outrageous; discourteous, uncivil, impolite; *formal* exceptionable. **2** ☞ UNPLEASANT 1. **3** ATTACKING, aggressive, hostile, invading, combative, belligerent, on the attack.
—OPPOSITES: complimentary, pleasant, defensive.
▸ n. ATTACK, assault, onslaught, drive, invasion, push, thrust, charge, sortie, sally, foray, raid, incursion, blitz, campaign.

offer v. **1** PUT FORWARD, proffer, give, present, come up with, suggest, recommend, propose, advance, submit, tender, render. **2** BID, tender, put in a bid of, put in an offer of. **3** PROVIDE, afford, supply, give, furnish, present, hold out.
—OPPOSITES: withdraw.
▸ n. **1** PROPOSAL, proposition, suggestion, submission, approach, overture. **2** BID, tender, bidding price.

offering n. CONTRIBUTION, donation, gift, present, handout, charity; *formal* benefaction; *historical* alms.

offhand adj. CASUAL, careless, uninterested, unconcerned, indifferent, cool, nonchalant, blasé, insouciant, cavalier, glib, perfunctory, cursory, unceremonious, ungracious, dismissive, discourteous, uncivil, impolite, terse, abrupt, curt; couldn't-care-less, take-it-or-leave-it.
▸ adv. ON THE SPUR OF THE MOMENT, without consideration, extempore, impromptu, ad lib; extemporaneously, spontaneously; off the cuff, off the top of one's head, just like that.

office n. **1** PLACE OF WORK, place of business, workplace, workroom, workspace, cubicle, cube. **2** BRANCH, division, section, bureau, department; agency. **3** POST, position, appointment, job, occupation, role, situation, function, capacity.

official adj. **1** AUTHORIZED, approved, validated, authenticated, certified, accredited, endorsed, sanctioned, licensed, recognized, accepted, legitimate, legal, lawful, valid, bona fide, proper, ex cathedra, kosher. **2** CEREMONIAL, formal, solemn, ceremonious;

bureaucratic; *informal* stuffed-shirt.
—OPPOSITES: unauthorized, informal.

▶ *n.* OFFICER, office-holder, administrator, executive, appointee, functionary; bureaucrat, mandarin; representative, agent.

offset *v.* COUNTERBALANCE, balance (out), cancel (out), even out/up, counteract, countervail, neutralize, compensate for, make up for, make good, redeem.

offspring *n.* CHILDREN, sons and daughters, progeny, family, youngsters, babies, infants, brood; kids; descendants, heirs, successors; *Law* issue; *derogatory* spawn; *archaic* fruit of one's loins.

often *adv.* FREQUENTLY, many times, many a time, on many/ numerous occasions, a lot, as often as not, repeatedly, again and again; regularly, routinely, usually, habitually, commonly, generally, in many cases/ instances, ordinarily, oftentimes; *literary* oft.
—OPPOSITES: seldom.

oily *adj.* **1** GREASY, oleaginous, sebaceous, pinguid. **2** GREASY, fatty, buttery, swimming in oil/fat. **3** ☞ OBSEQUIOUS.

okay, OK *excl.* ALL RIGHT, right, very well, very good, fine, fair enough; *informal* okey-doke(y).
▶ *adj.* **1** ☞ ACCEPTABLE. **2** ☞ WELL *adj.* 1. **3** ☞ PERMISSIBLE, APPROPRIATE.
—OPPOSITES: unsatisfactory, ill.
▶ *n.* ☞ APPROVAL.
—OPPOSITES: refusal.
▶ *v.* ☞ AUTHORIZE.
—OPPOSITES: refuse, veto.

old *adj.* **1** ELDERLY, aged, older, senior, advanced in years, venerable; in one's dotage, long in the tooth, grey-haired, grizzled, hoary, past one's prime, not as young as one was, ancient, decrepit, doddering, doddery, not long for this world, senescent, senile, superannuated; getting on, past it, over the hill, no spring chicken. **2** ☞ DILAPIDATED. **3** ☞ SHABBY 2, WORN. **4** ANTIQUE, veteran, vintage, classic. **5** BYGONE, past, former, olden, of old, previous, early, earlier, earliest; medieval, ancient, classical, primeval, primordial, prehistoric. **6** ☞ FORMER 1.
—OPPOSITES: young, new, modern.
☐ **old age** DECLINING YEARS, advanced years, age, oldness, winter/autumn of one's life, dotage. **old person** SENIOR CITIZEN, senior, (old-age) pensioner, elder, geriatric, golden ager; crone; Methuselah, old-timer, oldster, old codger.

old-fashioned *adj.* OUT OF DATE, outdated, dated, out of fashion, outmoded, unfashionable, passé, crusty, out, uncool, unstylish, untrendy, démodé, frumpy; outworn, old, old-time, behind the times, archaic, obsolescent, obsolete, ancient, antiquated, superannuated, defunct; medieval, prehistoric, antediluvian, old-fogeyish, conservative, backward-looking, quaint, anachronistic, fusty, moth-eaten, olde worlde, old hat, square, not with it; horse-and-buggy, clunky, rinky-dink.
—OPPOSITES: modern.

omen *n.* PORTENT, sign, signal, token, forewarning, warning, foreshadowing, prediction, forecast, prophecy, harbinger, augury, auspice, presage; writing on the wall, indication, hint; *literary* foretoken.

ominous *adj.* THREATENING, menacing, baleful, forbidding, sinister, inauspicious, unpropitious, portentous, unfavourable, unpromising; black, dark, gloomy.
—OPPOSITES: promising.

omission *n.* EXCLUSION, leaving out; deletion, cut, excision, elimination.

omit *v.* LEAVE OUT, exclude, leave off, take out, miss out, miss, drop, cut; delete, eliminate, rub out, cross out, strike out.
—OPPOSITES: add, include.

omnipotent *adj.* ☞ ALMIGHTY 1.

on
☐ **on and on** FOR A LONG TIME, for ages, for hours, at (great) length, incessantly, ceaselessly, constantly, continuously, continually, endlessly, unendingly, eternally, forever, interminably, unremittingly, relentlessly, indefatigably, without let-up, without a pause/break, without cease.

once
☐ **at once** ☞ IMMEDIATELY. **once in a while** ☞ SOMETIMES.

onerous *adj.* BURDENSOME, arduous, strenuous, difficult, hard, severe, heavy, back-breaking, oppressive, weighty, uphill, effortful, formidable, laborious, Herculean, exhausting, tiring, taxing, demanding, punishing, gruelling, exacting, wearing, wearisome, fatiguing; *archaic* toilsome.
—OPPOSITES: easy.

ongoing *adj.* IN PROGRESS, under way, going on, continuing, taking place, proceeding, progressing, advancing; unfinished.

only *adv.* 1 AT MOST, at best, (only) just, no/not more than; barely, scarcely, hardly. 2 EXCLUSIVELY, solely, to the exclusion of everything else. 3 MERELY, simply, just.
▸ *adj.* SOLE, single, one (and only), solitary, lone, unique; exclusive.

onslaught *n.* ASSAULT, attack, offensive, advance, charge, onrush, rush, storming, sortie, sally, raid, descent, incursion, invasion, foray, push, thrust, drive, blitz, bombardment, barrage, salvo; *historical* broadside.

oops *excl.* WHOOPS, oh dear, oh no, eek, yikes, uh-oh, sorry, silly me, doh, damn, argh, aiyee, whoopsy, oopsy daisy.

open *adj.* 1 NOT SHUT, not closed, unlocked, unbolted, unlatched, off the latch, unfastened, unsecured; ajar, gaping, yawning. 2 FRANK, forthcoming, unreserved. 3 ☞ OVERT. 4 ☞ UNBIASED.
—OPPOSITES: shut.
▸ *v.* 1 UNFASTEN, unlatch, unlock, unbolt, unbar; throw wide. 2 UNWRAP, undo, untie, unseal. 3 ☞ COMMENCE.
—OPPOSITES: close, shut, end.

opening *n.* 1 HOLE, gap, aperture, orifice, vent, crack, slit, slot, chink, interstice. 2 OPPORTUNITY, chance, window (of opportunity), possibility. 3 VACANCY, position, job. **4** BEGINNING, start, commencement, outset; introduction, kickoff. **5** OPENING CEREMONY, official opening, launch, inauguration; opening/ first night, premiere.

open-minded *adj.* UNBIASED, unprejudiced, neutral, non-judgmental, non-discriminatory, objective, disinterested.
—OPPOSITES: prejudiced, narrow-minded.

operate *v.* **1** WORK, make go, run, use, utilize, handle, control, manage; drive, steer, manoeuvre. **2** FUNCTION, work, go, run. **3** ☞ MANAGE 1.

operative *adj.* **1** IN FORCE, in operation, in effect, valid. **2** KEY, significant, relevant, applicable, pertinent, apposite, germane, crucial, critical, pivotal.
—OPPOSITES: invalid.

opinion *n.* BELIEF, judgment, thought(s), (way of) thinking, mind, (point of) view, viewpoint, attitude, stance, position, standpoint.

opponent *n.* **1** RIVAL, adversary, opposer, the opposition, fellow contestant, (fellow) competitor, enemy, antagonist, combatant, contender, challenger; *literary* foe. **2** OPPOSER, objector, dissenter.
—OPPOSITES: ally, supporter.

opportune *adj.* AUSPICIOUS, propitious, favourable, advantageous, golden, felicitous; timely, convenient, suitable, appropriate, apt, fitting.
—OPPOSITES: disadvantageous.

opportunity *n.* (LUCKY) CHANCE, favourable time/occasion/ moment, time, occasion, moment,

opening, option, window (of opportunity), possibility, scope, room, freedom, liberty; shot, kick at the can/cat✦, break, new lease on life.

oppose *v.* BE AGAINST, object to, be hostile to, be in opposition to, disagree with, dislike, disapprove of; resist, take a stand against, put up a fight against, stand up to, fight, challenge; take issue with, dispute, argue with/against, quarrel with; *informal* be anti-.
—OPPOSITES: support.

opposite *adj.* **1** FACING, face to face with, across from; eyeball to eyeball with. **2** CONFLICTING, contrasting, incompatible, irreconcilable, antithetical, contradictory, clashing, at variance, at odds, different, differing, divergent, dissimilar, unalike, disagreeing, opposed, opposing, poles apart.
—OPPOSITES: same.
▶ *n.* REVERSE, converse, antithesis, contrary, inverse, obverse, antipode; the other side of the coin; flip side.

opposition *n.* **1** RESISTANCE, hostility, antagonism, antipathy, objection, dissent, disapproval; defiance, non-compliance, obstruction. **2** OPPONENTS, opposing side, other side/team, competition, opposers, rivals, adversaries.

oppress *v.* PERSECUTE, abuse, maltreat, ill-treat, tyrannize, crush, repress, suppress, subjugate, subdue, keep down, grind down, ride roughshod over.

oppressive *adj.* HARSH, cruel, brutal, repressive, tyrannical,

autocratic, dictatorial, despotic, undemocratic; ruthless, merciless, pitiless.
—OPPOSITES: lenient.

optimistic *adj.* POSITIVE, confident, hopeful, sanguine, bullish, buoyant; upbeat, Pollyannaish.
—OPPOSITES: pessimistic.

optimum *adj.* BEST, most favourable, most advantageous, ideal, perfect, prime, optimal.

option *n.* CHOICE, alternative, possibility, course of action.

optional *adj.* VOLUNTARY, discretionary, elective, non-compulsory, non-mandatory; *Law* permissive.
—OPPOSITES: compulsory.

opulent *adj.* ☞ LUXURIOUS.
—OPPOSITES: Spartan.

order *n.* **1** SEQUENCE, arrangement, organization, disposition, system, series, succession; grouping, classification, categorization, codification, systematization. **2** TIDINESS, neatness, orderliness, organization, method, system; symmetry, uniformity, regularity; routine. **3** PEACE, control, law (and order), lawfulness, discipline, calm, (peace and) quiet, peacefulness, peaceableness. **4** CONDITION, state, repair, shape. **5** COMMAND, instruction, directive, direction, decree, edict, injunction, mandate, dictate, commandment, rescript; law, rule, regulation, diktat; demand, bidding, requirement, stipulation; say-so; behest. **6** ☞ KIND *n.*
—OPPOSITES: chaos.

▶ *v.* **1** INSTRUCT, command, direct,

enjoin, tell, require, charge; *formal* adjure; *literary* bid. **2** DECREE, ordain, rule, legislate, dictate, prescribe. **3** ☞ ORGANIZE 1.

☐ **out of order** NOT WORKING, not in working order, not functioning, broken, broken-down, out of service, out of commission, faulty, defective, inoperative; down; *informal* conked out, bust, (gone) kaput, on the fritz, on the blink, out of whack.

orderly *adj.* **1** ☞ TIDY 1. **2** (WELL) ORGANIZED, efficient, methodical, systematic, meticulous, punctilious; coherent, structured, logical, well-planned, well-regulated, systematized. **3** WELL-BEHAVED, law-abiding, disciplined, peaceful, peaceable.
—OPPOSITES: untidy, disorganized.

ordinary *adj.* **1** USUAL, normal, standard, typical, common, customary, habitual, everyday, regular, routine, day-to-day. **2** AVERAGE, normal, run-of-the-mill, standard, typical, middle-of-the-road, conventional, unremarkable, unexceptional, workaday, undistinguished, nondescript, colourless, commonplace, humdrum, mundane, unmemorable, pedestrian, prosaic, quotidian, uninteresting, uneventful, dull, boring, bland, hackneyed, garden-variety, characterless, faceless, featureless, lacklustre, uninspiring; plain-vanilla, nothing to write home about, no great shakes.
—OPPOSITES: unusual.

☐ **out of the ordinary**
☞ UNCOMMON 1.

organic *adj.* **1** LIVING, live, animate, biological, biotic. **2** PESTICIDE-FREE, additive-free, natural.

organization *n.* **1** PLANNING, arrangement, coordination, administration, organizing, running, management. **2** STRUCTURE, arrangement, plan, pattern, order, form, format, framework, composition, constitution. **3** COMPANY, firm, corporation, institution, group, consortium, conglomerate, agency, association, society; *informal* outfit.

organize *v.* **1** (PUT IN) ORDER, arrange, sort (out), assemble, marshal, put straight, group, classify, collocate, categorize, catalogue, codify, systematize, systemize. **2** MAKE ARRANGEMENTS FOR, arrange, coordinate, sort out, put together, fix up, set up, orchestrate, take care of, see to/about, deal with, manage, conduct, administrate, mobilize; schedule, program.

origin *n.* **1** BEGINNING, start, commencement, origination, genesis, birth, dawning, dawn, emergence, creation, birthplace, cradle; source, basis, cause, root(s); *formal* radix. **2** SOURCE, derivation, root(s), provenance, etymology. **3** ☞ ANCESTRY.

original *adj.* **1** NEW, novel, unusual, unfamiliar, unconventional, unorthodox, different, fresh, imaginative, innovative, innovatory, inventive, modern, avant-garde, pioneering, groundbreaking, revolutionary; rare, unique, singular, unprecedented, creative, cutting-edge, distinctive, ingenious, refreshing; experimental, untested, untried; strange, exotic, newfangled. **2** ☞ AUTHENTIC. ▸ *n.* ARCHETYPE, prototype, source, master.

originate *v.* ARISE, have its origin, begin, start, stem, spring, emerge, emanate.

ornament *n.* DECORATION, adornment, embellishment, ornamentation, trimming, accessories.

ornamental *adj.* ☞ DECORATIVE.

ornate *adj.* ELABORATE, decorated, embellished, adorned, ornamented, fancy, fussy, ostentatious, showy; *informal* flash, flashy.
—OPPOSITES: plain.

orthodox *adj.* **1** CONVENTIONAL, mainstream, conformist, (well) established, traditional, traditionalist, conservative. **2** CONSERVATIVE, traditional, observant, devout, strict.
—OPPOSITES: unconventional.

ostensible *adj.* APPARENT, outward, superficial, professed, supposed, alleged, purported, seeming.
—OPPOSITES: genuine.

ostentatious *adj.* SHOWY, pretentious, conspicuous, flamboyant, gaudy, brash, vulgar, loud, extravagant, fancy, ornate, over-elaborate; flash, flashy, splashy, over the top, glitzy, ritzy, superfly.
—OPPOSITES: restrained.

ostracize *v.* EXCLUDE, shun, spurn, cold-shoulder, reject, shut out, avoid, ignore, snub, cut dead,

keep at arm's length, leave out in the cold; blackball, blacklist.
—OPPOSITES: welcome.

other *adj.* **1** ALTERNATIVE, different. **2** MORE, further, additional, extra, added, supplementary.

outbreak *n.* ERUPTION, flare-up, upsurge, groundswell, outburst, rash, wave, spate, flood, explosion, burst, flurry.

outburst *n.* ERUPTION, explosion, burst, outbreak, flare-up, outflow, rush, flood, storm, outpouring, surge, upsurge, access.

outcast *n.* PARIAH, persona non grata, reject, black sheep, outsider, leper.

outcome *n.* (END) RESULT, consequence, net result, upshot, after-effect, aftermath, conclusion, issue, end (product); *informal* payoff.

outcry *n.* ☞ UPROAR 2.

outdated *adj.* ☞ OLD-FASHIONED.
—OPPOSITES: modern.

outdo *v.* ☞ SURPASS.

outer *adj.* **1** OUTSIDE, outermost, outward, exterior, external, surface. **2** OUTLYING, distant, remote, faraway, furthest, peripheral; suburban.
—OPPOSITES: inner.

outfit *n.* **1** ☞ CLOTHES. **2** KIT, equipment, tools, implements, tackle, apparatus, paraphernalia, things, stuff.
▸ *v.* EQUIP, kit out, fit out/up, rig out, supply, arm; dress, attire, clothe, deck out.

outgoing *adj.* **1** EXTROVERTED, uninhibited, unreserved, demonstrative, affectionate, warm, friendly, genial, cordial, affable, easygoing, sociable,

convivial, lively, gregarious; communicative, responsive, open, forthcoming, frank. **2** DEPARTING, retiring, leaving.
—OPPOSITES: introverted, incoming.

outlandish *adj.* ☞ BIZARRE.
—OPPOSITES: ordinary.

outlaw *n.* FUGITIVE, (wanted) criminal, public enemy, outcast, exile, pariah; bandit, robber.
▸ *v.* ☞ BAN 1.
—OPPOSITES: permit.

outline *n.* **1** SILHOUETTE, profile, shape, contours, form, line, delineation; diagram, sketch; *literary* lineaments. **2** ROUGH IDEA, thumbnail sketch, (quick) rundown, summary, synopsis, resumé, précis; essence, main/key points, gist, (bare) bones, draft, sketch.
▸ *v.* ROUGH OUT, sketch out, draft, give a rough idea of, summarize, précis.

outlook *n.* **1** ☞ PERSPECTIVE. **2** PROSPECTS, expectations, hopes, future.

outlying *adj.* DISTANT, remote, outer, out of the way, faraway, far-flung, inaccessible, off the beaten track.

output *n.* PRODUCTION, amount/quantity produced, yield, gross domestic product, works.

outrage *n.* **1** INDIGNATION, fury, anger, rage, disapproval, wrath, resentment. **2** SCANDAL, offence, insult, injustice, disgrace.
▸ *v.* ENRAGE, infuriate, incense, anger, scandalize, offend, give offence to, affront, shock, horrify, disgust, appall.

outrageous adj. **1** SHOCKING, disgraceful, scandalous, atrocious, appalling, monstrous, heinous; evil, wicked, abominable, terrible, horrendous, dreadful, odious, loathsome, unspeakable; beastly. **2** FAR-FETCHED, (highly) unlikely, doubtful, dubious, questionable, implausible, unconvincing, unbelievable, incredible, preposterous, extravagant, excessive. **3** EYE-CATCHING, flamboyant, showy, gaudy, ostentatious; shameless, brazen, shocking; informal saucy, flashy. **4** ☞ RIDICULOUS 3.

outside n. OUTER/EXTERNAL SURFACE, exterior, outer side/layer, case, skin, shell, covering, facade.
—RELATED: ecto-, exo-, extra-.
▶ adj. EXTERIOR, external, outer, outdoor, out-of-doors.
▶ adv. OUTDOORS, out of doors, alfresco.
—OPPOSITES: inside.

outsider n. STRANGER, visitor, non-member; foreigner, (Atlantic) come from away♣, alien, immigrant, emigrant, émigré; newcomer, parvenu.

outspoken adj. FRANK, direct, straightforward, honest, truthful, sincere, candid, open, forthright, straight, blunt, plain-spoken, no-nonsense, downright, bluff, matter-of-fact, to the point, not afraid to call a spade a spade, upfront.

outstanding adj. **1** ☞ EXCELLENT. **2** TO BE DONE, undone, unattended to, unfinished, incomplete, remaining, pending, ongoing. **3** UNPAID, unsettled, owing, past due, owed, to be paid, payable,

due, overdue, delinquent.
—OPPOSITES: unexceptional.

outwardly adv. EXTERNALLY, on the surface, superficially, on the face of it, for/to all intents and purposes, apparently, ostensibly, seemingly.

outwit v. OUTSMART, outmanoeuvre, outplay, steal a march on, trick, gull, get the better of, euchre; informal outfox, pull a fast one on, put one over on.

overall adj. ALL-INCLUSIVE, general, comprehensive, universal, all-embracing, gross, net, final, inclusive, total; wholesale, complete, across the board, global, worldwide.
▶ adv. GENERALLY (SPEAKING), broadly, in general, altogether, all in all, on balance, on average, for the most part, in the main, on the whole, by and large, to a large extent.

overcome v. **1** ☞ DEFEAT 1. **2** GET/ BRING UNDER CONTROL, control, curb, master, get a grip on, get over.
▶ adj. OVERWHELMED, emotional, moved, affected, speechless.

overconfident adj. COCKSURE, cocky, smug, conceited, self-assured, brash, blustering, overbearing, presumptuous, heading for a fall, riding for a fall; too big for one's britches/boots.

overdue adj. **1** LATE, behind schedule, behind time, delayed. **2** UNPAID, unsettled, owing, owed, payable, due, outstanding, delinquent.
—OPPOSITES: early, punctual.

overflow v. SPILL OVER, flow over, brim over, well over, pour forth, stream forth, flood.
▶ n. SURPLUS, excess, additional people/things, extra people/things, remainder, overspill.

overhead adv. (UP) ABOVE, high up, (up) in the sky, on high, above/over one's head.
—OPPOSITES: below.
▶ adj. AERIAL, elevated, raised, suspended.
—OPPOSITES: underground.

overjoyed adj. ☞ HAPPY 1.
—OPPOSITES: unhappy.

overlook v. **1** FAIL TO NOTICE, fail to spot, miss. **2** DISREGARD, neglect, ignore, pay no attention/heed to, pass over, forget. **3** DELIBERATELY IGNORE, not take into consideration, disregard, take no notice of, make allowances for, turn a blind eye to, excuse, pardon, forgive.

overpowering adj. OVERWHELMING, oppressive, unbearable, unendurable, intolerable, shattering.

overriding adj. DECIDING, decisive. See also MAIN.

oversee v. ☞ SUPERVISE 1, 2.

oversight n. ☞ MISTAKE.

overt adj. UNDISGUISED, unconcealed, plain (to see), clear, apparent, conspicuous, obvious, noticeable, manifest, patent, open, blatant.
—OPPOSITES: covert.

overtake v. PASS, go past/by, get/pull ahead of, leave behind, outdistance, outstrip.

overthrow v. REMOVE (FROM OFFICE/POWER), bring down, topple, depose, oust, displace, unseat, dethrone.

overtone n. ☞ CONNOTATION.

overturn v. **1** ☞ CAPSIZE. **2** CANCEL, reverse, rescind, repeal, revoke, retract, countermand, disallow, override, overrule, veto, quash, overthrow, annul, nullify, invalidate, negate, void, abrogate.

overweight adj. ☞ FAT 1.
—OPPOSITES: skinny.

overwhelm v. **1** SWAMP, submerge, engulf, bury, deluge, flood, inundate. **2** ☞ DEFEAT 1.

overwhelming adj. **1** VERY LARGE, enormous, immense, inordinate, massive, huge. **2** VERY STRONG, forceful, uncontrollable, irrepressible, irresistible, overpowering, compelling, ungovernable.

own adj. PERSONAL, individual, particular, private, personalized, unique.
▶ v. BE THE OWNER OF, possess, be the possessor of, have in one's possession, have (to one's name).
☐ **on one's own** ☞ ALONE 1, 2.
own up ☞ CONFESS 2.

Pp

pace *n.* **1** STEP, stride; gait.
2 SPEED, rate, velocity; clip, lick.
▸ *v.* WALK, stride, tread, march,
pound, patrol.

pacify *v.* PLACATE, appease, calm
(down), conciliate, propitiate,
assuage, mollify, soothe.
—OPPOSITES: enrage.

pack *n.* **1** PACKET, container,
package, box, carton, parcel.
2 ☞ BACKPACK. **3** CROWD, mob,
group, band, troupe, troop, party,
set, clique, gang, rabble, horde,
herd, throng, huddle, mass,
assembly, gathering, host; crew,
bunch.
▸ *v.* **1** FILL (UP), put things in, load.
2 STOW, put away, store, box up.
3 WRAP (UP), package, parcel,
swathe, swaddle, encase, enfold,
envelop, bundle. **4** THRONG, crowd
(into), fill (to overflowing), cram,
jam, squash into, squeeze into.
5 COMPRESS, press, squash,
squeeze, jam, tamp.

packed *adj.* ☞ CROWDED.

pact *n.* AGREEMENT, treaty, entente,
protocol, deal, contract, bargain,
settlement, covenant, concordat,
accord; armistice, truce; pledge,
promise, bond; *formal* concord.

pad *n.* **1** PIECE OF COTTON, dressing,
pack, padding, wadding, wad.
2 ☞ BOOK 2.
▸ *v.* STUFF, fill, pack, wad.

paddle *n.* OAR, scull, blade.
▸ *v.* row gently, pull, scull, canoe,
kayak.

pagan *n.* HEATHEN, idolater,
infidel.
▸ *adj.* HEATHEN, ungodly, irreligious,
infidel, idolatrous.

pain *n.* **1** ACHE, aching, soreness,
throb, throbbing, sting, stinging,
twinge, shooting pain, stab, pang,
cramps; discomfort, irritation,
tenderness. **2** SUFFERING, agony,
torture, torment, discomfort.
3 ☞ GRIEF 1. **4** ☞ NUISANCE. **5** CARE,
effort, bother, trouble.
▸ *v.* SADDEN, grieve, distress,
trouble, perturb, oppress, cause
anguish to.

painful *adj.* **1** ☞ SORE.
2 DISAGREEABLE, unpleasant, nasty,
cruel, awful, bitter, distressing,
upsetting, traumatic, miserable,
sad, heartbreaking, agonizing,
harrowing, tragic.

painstaking *adj.* ☞ CAREFUL 2.
—OPPOSITES: slapdash.

painting *n.* PICTURE, illustration,
portrayal, depiction,
representation, image, artwork;
oil (painting), watercolour, canvas.

pair *n.* SET (OF TWO), matching set,
two of a kind, couple, duo,
twosome; twins.

pale *adj.* **1** WHITE, pallid, pasty,
wan, colourless, anemic,
bloodless, washed out, peaky,

peaked, ashen, chalky, waxen, grey, whitish, white-faced, whey-faced, drained, sickly, sallow, as white as a sheet, deathly pale, ghostly; milky, creamy, cream, ivory, milk-white, alabaster; like death warmed over. **2** LIGHT, light-coloured, pastel, muted, subtle, soft; faded, bleached, washed out. **3** DIM, faint, weak, feeble.
—OPPOSITES: dark.

palpable *adj.* ☞ NOTICEABLE.
—OPPOSITES: imperceptible.

paltry *adj.* SMALL, meagre, trifling, insignificant, negligible, inadequate, insufficient, derisory, pitiful, pathetic, miserable, niggardly, beggarly; *informal* measly, piddling; *formal* exiguous.
—OPPOSITES: considerable.

pamper *v.* SPOIL, indulge, overindulge, cosset, mollycoddle, coddle, pander to, baby, wait on someone hand and foot.

pamphlet *n.* BROCHURE, leaflet, booklet, chapbook, circular, tract, flyer, fact sheet, handbill, mailer, folder, bulletin, handout.

panache *n.* FLAMBOYANCE, confidence, self-assurance, style, flair, élan, dash, verve, zest, spirit, brio, éclat, vivacity, gusto, liveliness, vitality, energy, dynamism; pizzazz, oomph, zip, zing.

pandemonium *n.* ☞ CHAOS.

pander
☐ **pander to** INDULGE, gratify, satisfy, cater to, give in to, accommodate, comply with.

panic *n.* ALARM, anxiety, nervousness, fear, fright, trepidation, dread, terror, agitation, hysteria, consternation,

perturbation, dismay, apprehension; flap, fluster, cold sweat, funk, tizzy.
—OPPOSITES: calm.
▶ *v.* BE ALARMED, be scared, be nervous, be afraid, take fright, be agitated, be hysterical, lose one's nerve, get overwrought, get worked up; flap, get in a flap, lose one's cool, get into a tizzy, freak out, get in a stew, have kittens.

panoramic *adj.* **1** SWEEPING, wide, extensive, scenic, commanding. **2** WIDE-RANGING, extensive, broad, far-reaching, comprehensive, all-embracing.

pant *v.* BREATHE HEAVILY, breathe hard, puff, huff and puff, gasp, wheeze.

pants *pl. n.* TROUSERS, slacks, britches.

paper *n.* **1** writing paper, notepaper, foolscap, vellum. **2** ☞ NEWSPAPER. **3** ESSAY, article, monograph, thesis, work, dissertation, treatise, study, report, analysis, tract, critique, exegesis, review, term paper, theme. **4** (**papers**) DOCUMENTS, certificates, letters, files, deeds, records, archives, paperwork, documentation; ID, credentials.

par
☐ **below par** ☞ BAD 1. **be on a par with** ☞ COMPARE 3. **par for the course** ☞ NORMAL 1. **up to par** ☞ SATISFACTORY.

parade *n.* PROCESSION, march, cavalcade, motorcade, spectacle, display, pageant; review, dress parade, tattoo; march past.
▶ *v.* **1** MARCH, process, file, troop; strut, swagger, stride. **2** ☞ FLAUNT.

paradise *n.* HEAVEN, Eden; Utopia, nirvana.
—OPPOSITES: hell.

paradox *n.* CONTRADICTION (IN TERMS), self-contradiction, inconsistency, incongruity; oxymoron; conflict, anomaly; enigma, puzzle, mystery, conundrum.

parallel *adj.* **1** SIDE BY SIDE, aligned, collateral, equidistant. **2** SIMILAR, analogous, comparable, corresponding, like, of a kind, akin, related, equivalent, matching, homologous.
—OPPOSITES: divergent.
▶ *n.* SIMILARITY, likeness, resemblance, analogy, correspondence, equivalence, correlation, relation, symmetry, parity.
▶ *v.* RESEMBLE, be similar to, be like, bear a resemblance to; correspond to, be analogous to, be comparable/equivalent to, equate with/to, correlate with, imitate, echo, remind one of, duplicate, mirror, follow, match.

paralyze *v.* BRING TO A STANDSTILL, immobilize, bring to a (grinding) halt, freeze, cripple, disable, incapacitate, debilitate.

parameter *n.* FRAMEWORK, variable, limit, boundary, limitation, restriction, criterion, guideline.

paramount *adj.* ☞ PRIMARY.

paranoid *adj.* OVER-SUSPICIOUS, paranoiac, suspicious, mistrustful, fearful, insecure.

parched *adj.* (BONE) DRY, dried up/ out, arid, desiccated, dehydrated, baked, burned, scorched; withered, shrivelled.
—OPPOSITES: soaking.

pardon *n.* **1** ☞ FORGIVENESS. **2** REPRIEVE, amnesty, exoneration, release, acquittal, discharge.
▶ *v.* **1** ☞ FORGIVE 1. **2** EXONERATE, acquit, amnesty; reprieve, release, free; let off.
—OPPOSITES: blame, punish.

pariah *n.* ☞ OUTCAST.

parliament *n.* **1** THE HOUSES OF PARLIAMENT, the (House of) Commons, the House, Ottawa, the Senate, Parliament Hill; *informal* the Hill. **2** LEGISLATURE, legislative assembly, congress, senate, (upper/lower) house, (upper/lower) chamber, diet, assembly.

parochial *adj.* NARROW-MINDED, small-minded, provincial, small-town.

parody *n.* SATIRE, burlesque, lampoon, pastiche, caricature, imitation, mockery; spoof, takeoff, send-up.
▶ *v.* SATIRIZE, burlesque, lampoon, caricature, mimic, imitate, ape, copy, make fun of, take off, send up.

part *n.* **1** BIT, slice, chunk, lump, hunk, wedge, fragment, scrap, piece; portion, proportion, percentage, fraction; section, division, volume, chapter, instalment; component, constituent, element, module. **2** (THEATRICAL) ROLE, character, persona. **3** LINES, words, script, speech; libretto, lyrics, score.
—OPPOSITES: whole.
▶ *v.* SEPARATE, divide (in two), split (in two), move apart.
—OPPOSITES: join.
▶ *adv.* ☞ PARTLY.

—OPPOSITES: completely.

□ **for the most part**. ☞ MOSTLY 1.
in part TO A CERTAIN EXTENT/
DEGREE, to some extent/degree,
partly, partially, slightly, in some
measure, (up) to a point. **part
with** GIVE UP/AWAY, relinquish,
forgo, surrender, hand over,
deliver up, dispose of. **take part**
☞ PARTICIPATE.

partial *adj.* **1** INCOMPLETE, limited,
qualified, imperfect, fragmentary,
unfinished. **2** ☞ BIASED.
—OPPOSITES: complete, unbiased.
□ **be partial to** ☞ LIKE[1] 2.

partially *adv.* ☞ PARTLY.

participate *v.* TAKE PART, engage,
join, get involved, share, play a
part/role, be a participant,
partake, have a hand in, be
associated with; co-operate, help,
assist, lend a hand.

participation *n.* INVOLVEMENT,
part, contribution, association.

particle *n.* (TINY) BIT, (tiny) piece,
speck, spot, fleck; fragment,
sliver, splinter.

particular *adj.* **1** ☞ SPECIFIC 1.
2 (EXTRA) SPECIAL, especial,
exceptional, unusual, singular,
uncommon, notable, noteworthy,
remarkable, unique; *formal*
peculiar. **3** ☞ FASTIDIOUS.
—OPPOSITES: general, careless.
▶ *n.* ☞ DETAIL 1.
□ **in particular** PARTICULARLY,
specifically, especially, specially.

particularly *adv.* **1** ESPECIALLY,
specially, very, extremely,
exceptionally, singularly,
peculiarly, unusually,
extraordinarily, remarkably,
outstandingly, amazingly,
incredibly, really, seriously.

2 SPECIFICALLY, explicitly,
expressly, in particular, especially,
specially.

partisan *n.* GUERRILLA, freedom
fighter, resistance fighter,
underground fighter, irregular
(soldier).
▶ *adj.* BIASED, prejudiced, one-sided,
discriminatory, coloured, partial,
interested, sectarian, factional,
political.
—OPPOSITES: unbiased.

partition *n.* **1** DIVIDING UP,
partitioning, separation, division,
dividing, subdivision, splitting
(up), breaking up, breakup.
2 SCREEN, (room) divider,
(dividing) wall, barrier, panel.
▶ *v.* DIVIDE (UP), subdivide, separate,
split (up), break up; share (out),
parcel out, section off, screen off.

partly *adv.* TO A CERTAIN EXTENT/
DEGREE, to some extent/degree, in
part, partially, a little, somewhat,
not totally, not entirely, relatively,
moderately, (up) to a point, in
some measure, slightly.
—OPPOSITES: completely.

partner *n.* **1** COLLEAGUE, associate,
co-worker, fellow worker,
collaborator, comrade, teammate.
2 SPOUSE, husband, wife, consort,
life partner; lover, girlfriend,
boyfriend, fiancé, fiancée,
significant other, main squeeze,
live-in lover, common-law
husband/wife, man, woman, mate;
informal hubby, missus, old man,
old lady/woman, better half,
intended, other half.

partnership *n.* CO-OPERATION,
association, collaboration,
coalition, alliance, union,

affiliation, relationship, connection.

party *n.* **1** (SOCIAL) GATHERING, (social) function, get-together, celebration, reunion, festivity, jamboree, affair, gala, social event, social occasion, reception, at-home, social; dance, ball, ceilidh, frolic, soiree, carousal, carouse, fete, hoedown, field party❖, shower, bake, cookout, levee; bash, whoop-up❖, meet-and-greet, shindig, rave, do, shebang, bop, hop, bunfight, blast, wingding, (*Atlantic*) time❖. **2** ☞ GROUP 2. **3** FACTION, political party, group, grouping, cabal, junta, bloc, camp, caucus.
▸ *v.* CELEBRATE, have fun, enjoy oneself, have a party, have a good/wild time, go on a spree, rave it up, carouse, make merry, revel, roister; *informal* go out on the town, paint the town red, whoop it up, let one's hair down, make whoopee, live it up, have a ball.

pass *v.* **1** GO, proceed, move, progress, make one's way, travel. **2** OVERTAKE, go past/by, pull ahead of, overhaul, leave behind; *informal* leapfrog. **3** ELAPSE, go by/past, advance, wear on, roll by, tick by. **4** OCCUPY, spend, fill, use (up), employ, while away. **5** HAND (OVER), let someone have, give, reach. **6** ABATE, fade (away), come to an end, blow over, run its course, die out, finish, end, cease, subside. **7** APPROVE, vote for, accept, ratify, adopt, agree to, authorize, endorse, legalize, enact, OK.
—OPPOSITES: stop, fail, reject.
▸ *n.* **1** PERMIT, warrant,

authorization, licence. **2** KICK, hit, throw, set-up, cross, lateral.
☐ **come to pass** ☞ HAPPEN. **pass away/on** ☞ DIE 1. **pass as/for** BE MISTAKEN FOR, be taken for, be accepted as. **pass out** FAINT, lose consciousness, black out. **pass something over** DISREGARD, overlook, ignore, pay no attention to, let pass, gloss over, take no notice of, pay no heed to, turn a blind eye to. **pass something up** TURN DOWN, reject, refuse, decline, give up, forgo, let pass, miss (out on); give something a miss.

passable *adj.* **1** ☞ ADEQUATE 2. **2** NAVIGABLE, traversable, negotiable, unblocked, unobstructed, open, clear.

passage *n.* **1** TRANSIT, progress, passing, movement, motion, travelling. **2** VOYAGE, crossing, trip, journey. **3** WAY (THROUGH), route, path. **4** CORRIDOR, hall, hallway, walkway, aisle. **5** DUCT, orifice, opening, channel; inlet, outlet. **6** ENACTMENT, passing, ratification, royal assent, approval, adoption, authorization, legalization. **7** EXTRACT, excerpt, quotation, quote, citation, reading, piece, selection.

passé *adj.* ☞ OLD-FASHIONED.

passerby *n.* BYSTANDER, eyewitness, witness.

passing *adj.* FLEETING, transient, transitory, ephemeral, brief, short-lived, temporary, momentary.

passion *n.* **1** FERVOUR, ardour, enthusiasm, eagerness, zeal, zealousness, vigour, fire, fieriness, energy, fervency, animation, spirit, spiritedness, fanaticism.

2 LOVE, (sexual) desire, lust, ardour, infatuation, lasciviousness, lustfulness. **3** ENTHUSIASM, love, mania, fascination, obsession, fanaticism, fixation, compulsion, appetite, addiction, thing.
—OPPOSITES: apathy.

passionate adj. **1** INTENSE, impassioned, ardent, fervent, vehement, heated, emotional, heartfelt, eager, excited, animated, spirited, energetic, fervid, frenzied, fiery, wild, consuming, violent. **2** VERY KEEN, very enthusiastic, addicted; mad, crazy, hooked, nuts, nutso. **3** AMOROUS, ardent, hot-blooded, aroused, loving, sexy, sensual, erotic, lustful; informal steamy, hot, red-hot, turned on. **4** EXCITABLE, emotional, fiery, volatile, mercurial, quick-tempered, high-strung, impulsive, temperamental.
—OPPOSITES: apathetic.

passive adj. **1** INACTIVE, non-active, uninvolved. **2** SUBMISSIVE, acquiescent, unresisting, unassertive, compliant, pliant, obedient, docile, tractable, malleable, pliable.
—OPPOSITES: active.

past adj. **1** GONE (BY), over (and done with), no more, done, bygone, former, (of) old, olden, long-ago, of yore. **2** LAST, recent, preceding. **3** ☞ FORMER 1.
—OPPOSITES: present, future.
▶ n. HISTORY, background, life (story).
▶ prep. **1** IN FRONT OF, by. **2** BEYOND, in excess of.
▶ adv. ALONG, by, on.

pastime n. HOBBY, leisure activity/pursuit, sport, game, recreation, amusement, diversion, avocation, entertainment, interest, sideline.

pastor n. ☞ CLERIC.

pastoral adj. RURAL, country, countryside, rustic, agricultural, bucolic; literary sylvan, Arcadian.
—OPPOSITES: urban.

patch n. **1** COVER, covering, pad. **2** BLOTCH, mark, spot, smudge, speckle, smear, stain, streak, blemish; informal splotch. **3** PLOT, area, piece, strip, tract, parcel; bed, allotment, lot, plat. **4** (informal) PERIOD, time, spell, phase, stretch.
▶ v. MEND, repair, put a patch on, sew (up), stitch (up).
□ **patch something up 1** REPAIR, mend, fix hastily, do a makeshift repair on. **2** RECONCILE, make up, settle, remedy, put to rights, rectify, clear up, set right, make good, resolve, square.

patently adv. ☞ CLEARLY.

paternal adj. FATHERLY, fatherlike, patriarchal; protective.

path n. **1** TRAIL, pathway, walkway, track, footpath, trackway, bridleway, bridle path, (West) monkey trail♣, portage trail, lane, alley, alleyway, passage, passageway; sidewalk, bikeway, pedway. **2** ROUTE, way, course; direction, bearing, line; orbit, trajectory.

pathetic adj. **1** ☞ PITIFUL 1. **2** FEEBLE, woeful, sorry, poor, pitiful, lamentable, deplorable, contemptible, inadequate, paltry, insufficient, insubstantial, unsatisfactory.

pathological adj. ☞ INVETERATE.

patience *n.* **1** FORBEARANCE, tolerance, restraint, self-restraint, stoicism; calmness, composure, equanimity, serenity, tranquility, imperturbability, phlegm, understanding, indulgence. **2** PERSEVERANCE, persistence, endurance, tenacity, assiduity, application, staying power, doggedness, determination, resolve, resolution, resoluteness.

patient *adj.* **1** FORBEARING, uncomplaining, tolerant, resigned, stoical; calm, composed, even-tempered, imperturbable, unexcitable, accommodating, understanding, indulgent; unflappable, cool. **2** PERSEVERING, persistent, tenacious, indefatigable, dogged, determined, resolved, resolute, single-minded.
▶ *n.* SICK PERSON, case; invalid, convalescent, outpatient, in-patient.

patriotic *adj.* NATIONALIST, nationalistic, loyalist, loyal; chauvinistic, jingoistic, flag-waving.
—OPPOSITES: traitorous.

patrol *n.* SECURITY GUARD, sentry, sentinel, patrolman; scout, scouting party.
▶ *v.* KEEP GUARD (ON), guard, keep watch (on); police, make the rounds (of); stand guard (over), keep a vigil (on), defend, safeguard.

patron *n.* **1** SPONSOR, backer, financier, benefactor, contributor, subscriber, donor; philanthropist, promoter, friend, supporter; *informal* angel. **2** CUSTOMER, client, frequenter, consumer, user, visitor, guest; regular, habitué.

patronize *v.* **1** TREAT CONDESCENDINGLY, condescend to, look down on, talk down to, put down, treat like a child, treat with disdain. **2** DO BUSINESS WITH, buy from, shop at, be a customer of, be a client of, deal with, trade with, frequent, support.

patronizing *adj.* ☞ SUPERCILIOUS.

pattern *n.* **1** DESIGN, decoration, motif, marking, ornament, ornamentation. **2** SYSTEM, order, arrangement, form, method, structure, scheme, plan, format, framework. **3** MODEL, example, criterion, standard, basis, point of reference, gauge, norm, yardstick, touchstone, benchmark; blueprint, archetype, prototype.

paucity *n.* ☞ SCARCITY.
—OPPOSITES: abundance.

pause *n.* STOP, cessation, break, halt, interruption, check, lull, respite, breathing space, discontinuation, hiatus, gap, interlude, intermission, interval, recess, stoppage, time out; adjournment, suspension, rest, wait, hesitation; *informal* let-up, breather.
▶ *v.* STOP, cease, halt, discontinue, break off, take a break; adjourn, rest, wait, hesitate, falter, waver; take a breather, take five.

pay *v.* **1** REWARD, reimburse, recompense, give payment to, remunerate. **2** ☞ SPEND 1. **3** YIELD, return, produce. **4** BE PROFITABLE, make money, make a profit. **5** BE ADVANTAGEOUS, be of advantage, be beneficial, benefit. **6** BESTOW, grant, give, offer.

▸ *n.* ☞ WAGE.

□ **pay someone back** GET ONE'S REVENGE ON, be revenged on, avenge oneself on, get back at, get even with, settle accounts with, exact retribution on. **pay for** FUND, finance, defray the cost of, settle up for, treat someone to; *informal* foot the bill for, shell out for, fork out for, cough up for, ante up for, pony up for.

payment *n.* **1** REMITTANCE, settlement, discharge, clearance, liquidation. **2** INSTALMENT, premium. **3** SALARY, wages, pay, earnings, fee(s), remuneration, reimbursement, income.

peace *n.* **1** TRANQUILITY, calm, restfulness, peace and quiet, peacefulness, quiet, quietness; privacy, solitude. **2** SERENITY, peacefulness, tranquility, equanimity, calm, calmness, composure, ease, contentment, contentedness. **3** LAW AND ORDER, lawfulness, order, peacefulness, peaceableness, harmony, non-violence; concord.
−OPPOSITES: noise, war.

peaceful *adj.* **1** TRANQUIL, calm, restful, quiet, still, relaxing, soothing, undisturbed, untroubled, private, secluded. **2** SERENE, calm, tranquil, composed, placid, at ease, untroubled, unworried, content.
−OPPOSITES: noisy, agitated.

peak *n.* **1** ☞ SUMMIT 1. **2** ☞ MOUNTAIN. **3** BRIM, visor. **4** HEIGHT, high point/spot, pinnacle, summit, top, climax, culmination, apex, zenith, crowning point, crown, crest,

acme, capstone, apogee, prime, heyday.
▸ *adj.* MAXIMUM, top, greatest, highest; ultimate, best, optimum.

peaky *adj.* PALE, pasty, wan, drained, washed out, drawn, pallid, anemic, ashen, grey, pinched, sickly, sallow, ill, unwell, poorly, indisposed, run down, off; *informal* under the weather, rough, lousy.

peculiar *adj.* **1** ☞ STRANGE 1. **2** CHARACTERISTIC OF, typical of, representative of, indicative of, suggestive of, exclusive to, unique to.
−OPPOSITES: ordinary.

peculiarity *n.* **1** ODDITY, anomaly, abnormality. **2** CHARACTERISTIC, feature, (essential) quality, property, trait, attribute, hallmark, trademark. **3** STRANGENESS, oddness, bizarreness, weirdness, queerness, unexpectedness, unfamiliarity, incongruity; outlandishness, unconventionality, idiosyncrasy, eccentricity, unusualness, abnormality, quirkiness; *informal* wackiness, freakiness.

pedantic *adj.* OVER-SCRUPULOUS, scrupulous, precise, exact, perfectionist, punctilious, meticulous, fussy, fastidious, finicky; dogmatic, purist, literalist, literalistic, formalist; casuistic, casuistical, sophistic, sophistical; captious, hairsplitting, quibbling, nitpicking, persnickety, bookish.

pedestal *n.* PLINTH, base, support, mounting, stand, pillar, column.
□ **put someone on a pedestal** ☞ IDOLIZE.

peek v. (HAVE A) PEEP, have a peek, spy, take a sly/stealthy look, sneak a look; *informal* take a gander.
▶ n. SECRET LOOK, sly look, stealthy look, sneaky look, peep, glance, glimpse, hurried/quick look; gander, squint.

peel v. **1** PARE, skin, take the skin/rind off; hull, shell, husk, shuck. **2** FLAKE (OFF), peel off, come off in layers/strips.
▶ n. RIND, skin, covering, zest; hull, pod, integument, shuck.

peer¹ v. LOOK CLOSELY, try to see, narrow one's eyes, screw up one's eyes, squint.

peer² n. EQUAL, coequal, fellow, confrere; contemporary; *formal* compeer.

peeve v. ☞ ANNOY.

peevish adj. ☞ IRRITABLE.
—OPPOSITES: good-humoured.

pelt n. SKIN, hide, fleece, coat, fur.

pen n. ENCLOSURE, fold, pound, compound, stockade; sty, coop, corral.

penalize v. **1** PUNISH, discipline, inflict a penalty on. **2** HANDICAP, disadvantage, put at a disadvantage, cause to suffer.
—OPPOSITES: reward.

penalty n. **1** PUNISHMENT, sanction, punitive action, retribution; fine, forfeit, sentence; penance. **2** FOUL, infraction.
—OPPOSITES: reward.

penance n. ATONEMENT, expiation, amends; self-punishment, self-mortification, self-abasement; punishment, penalty.

penchant n. LIKING, fondness, preference, taste, relish, appetite, partiality, soft spot, love, passion, desire, fancy, whim, weakness, inclination, leaning, bent, bias, proclivity, predilection, predisposition.

pending adj. **1** UNRESOLVED, undecided, unsettled, awaiting decision/action, undetermined, open, hanging fire, (up) in the air, on ice, ongoing, outstanding, not done, unfinished, incomplete; *informal* on the back burner. **2** ☞ IMMINENT.
▶ prep. AWAITING, until, till, until there is/are.

penetrate v. **1** ☞ PIERCE. **2** REGISTER, sink in, be understood, be comprehended, become clear, fall into place; click.

penitent adj. ☞ SORRY 3.
—OPPOSITES: unrepentant.

penniless adj. ☞ BROKE.

pensive adj. ☞ THOUGHTFUL 1.

people n. **1** HUMAN BEINGS, persons, individuals, humans, mortals, (living) souls, personages, {men, women, and children}; *informal* folks. **2** CITIZENS, subjects, electors, voters, taxpayers, residents, inhabitants, (general) public, citizenry, nation, population. **3** ☞ POPULACE.

perceive v. **1** DISCERN, recognize, become aware of, see, distinguish, realize, grasp, understand, take in, make out, find, identify, hit on, comprehend, apprehend, appreciate, sense, divine; figure out, twig, suss (out), become cognizant of, detect, catch sight of, spot, observe, notice. **2** ☞ REGARD 1.

perceptible adj. ☞ NOTICEABLE.

perception n. **1** RECOGNITION, awareness, consciousness, appreciation, realization, knowledge, grasp, understanding, comprehension, apprehension; *formal* cognizance. **2** IMPRESSION, idea, conception, notion, thought, belief, judgment, estimation.

perceptive *adj.* INSIGHTFUL, discerning, sensitive, intuitive, observant; piercing, penetrating, percipient, perspicacious, penetrative, clear-sighted, far-sighted, intelligent, clever, canny, keen, sharp, sharp-witted, astute, shrewd, quick, smart, acute, discriminating; *informal* on the ball, heads-up, with it.
—OPPOSITES: obtuse.

perfect *adj.* **1** IDEAL, model, without fault, faultless, flawless, consummate, quintessential, exemplary, best, ultimate, copybook; unrivalled, unequalled, matchless, unparalleled, beyond compare, without equal, second to none, too good to be true, Utopian, incomparable, nonpareil, peerless, inimitable, unexcelled, unsurpassed, unsurpassable.
2 FLAWLESS, mint, as good as new, pristine, impeccable, immaculate, superb, superlative, optimum, prime, optimal, peak, excellent, faultless, as sound as a bell, unspoiled, unblemished, undamaged, spotless, unmarred; *informal* tip-top, A1. **3** EXACT, precise, accurate, faithful, correct, unerring, error-free, right, true, strict; impeccable, exemplary; *informal* on the money. **4** IDEAL, just right, right, appropriate, fitting, fit, suitable, apt, made to order, tailor-made; very. **5** ☞ ABSOLUTE 1.
▶ *v.* IMPROVE, better, polish (up),

hone, refine, put the finishing/final touches to, brush up, fine-tune.

perform *v.* **1** CARRY OUT, do, execute, discharge, bring about, bring off, accomplish, achieve, fulfill, complete, conduct, effect, dispatch, work, implement; pull off; effectuate. **2** FUNCTION, work, operate, run, go, respond, behave, act, acquit oneself/itself. **3** STAGE, put on, present, mount, enact, act, produce. **4** APPEAR, play, be on stage, sing, dance, act; busk.
—OPPOSITES: neglect.

performance *n.* **1** SHOW, production, showing, presentation, staging; concert, recital; gig. **2** RENDITION, rendering, interpretation, reading, playing, acting, representation.
3 FUNCTIONING, working, operation running, behaviour, capabilities, capability, capacity, power, potential.

performer *n.* ACTOR, ACTRESS, thespian, artiste, artist, entertainer, trouper, player, musician, singer, dancer, comic, comedian, comedienne.

perfume *n.* **1** FRAGRANCE, scent, eau de toilette, toilet water, eau de cologne, cologne, aftershave. **2** ☞ SCENT 1.

perfunctory *adj.* MECHANICAL, automatic, routine, offhand, inattentive. See also CURSORY.
—OPPOSITES: careful, thorough.

perhaps *adv.* ☞ MAYBE.

peril *n.* ☞ DANGER 1.

perilous *adj.* ☞ HAZARDOUS.
—OPPOSITES: safe.

perimeter *n.* BOUNDARY, border, limits, bounds, confines, edge, margin, fringe(s), periphery, borderline, verge; circumference, outside.

period *n.* **1** TIME, spell, interval, stretch, term, span, phase, bout, run, duration, chapter, stage; while, patch. **2** ERA, age, epoch, time, days, years; *Geology* eon. **3** MENSTRUATION, menstrual flow, menses; *informal* the curse, monthlies, time of the month. **4** POINT, full stop.

periodic *adj.* REGULAR, periodical, at fixed intervals, recurrent, recurring, repeated, cyclical, cyclic, seasonal; occasional, infrequent, intermittent, sporadic, spasmodic, odd.

peripheral *adj.* **1** OUTLYING, outer, on the edge/outskirts, surrounding. **2** ☞ SECONDARY 1.
—OPPOSITES: central.

perish *v.* ☞ DIE 1.

perk[1]
☐ **perk up 1** CHEER UP, brighten up, liven up, take heart; buck up. **2** ☞ RALLY 4.

perk[2] *n.* FRINGE BENEFIT, additional benefit, benefit, advantage, bonus, extra, plus; freebie, perquisite.

perky *adj.* CHEERFUL, lively, vivacious, animated, bubbly, effervescent, bouncy, spirited, high-spirited, in high spirits, cheery, merry, buoyant, ebullient, exuberant, jaunty, frisky, sprightly, spry, bright, sunny, jolly, sparkly, pert; full of beans, bright-eyed and bushy-tailed, chirpy, chipper, peppy.

permanent *adj.* **1** LASTING, enduring, indefinite, continuing, perpetual, everlasting, eternal, abiding, constant, irreparable, irreversible, lifelong, indissoluble, indelible, standing, perennial, unending, endless, never-ending, immutable, undying, imperishable, indestructible, ineradicable; *literary* sempiternal, perdurable. **2** LONG-TERM, stable, secure.
—OPPOSITES: temporary.

permeate *v.* PERVADE, spread through, fill, filter through, diffuse through, imbue, penetrate, pass through, percolate through, perfuse, charge, suffuse, steep, impregnate, inform; SOAK THROUGH, seep through, saturate, transfuse, leach through, flow through, infuse.

permissible *adj.* PERMITTED, allowable, allowed, acceptable, legal, lawful, legitimate, admissible, licit, authorized, sanctioned, tolerated; *informal* legit, OK.
—OPPOSITES: forbidden.

permission *n.* AUTHORIZATION, consent, leave, authority, sanction, licence, dispensation, assent, acquiescence, agreement, approval, seal/stamp of approval, the rubber stamp, warrant, approbation, endorsement, blessing, imprimatur, clearance, allowance, freedom, tolerance, sufferance, empowerment; the go-ahead, the thumbs up, the nod, the OK, the green light, say-so.

permissive *adj.* LIBERAL, broad-minded, open-minded, free, free and easy, easygoing, live-and-let-live, latitudinarian, laissez-faire, libertarian, tolerant, forbearing, indulgent, lenient; overindulgent,

lax, soft.
—OPPOSITES: intolerant, strict.

permit v. ALLOW, let, authorize, give permission/authorization/leave, sanction, grant, give someone the right, license, empower, enable, entitle, qualify; consent to, assent to, give one's consent/assent/blessing, give the nod to, acquiesce in, agree to, tolerate, countenance, admit of; approve of, brook; legalize, legitimate; give the go-ahead to, give the thumbs up to, OK, give the OK to, give the green light to, say the word; *formal* accede to; *archaic* suffer.
—OPPOSITES: ban, forbid.
▸ n. AUTHORIZATION, licence, pass, ticket, warrant, document, certification; passport, visa.

perpetual adj. **1** EVERLASTING, never-ending, eternal, permanent, unending, endless, without end, lasting, long-lasting, constant, abiding, enduring, perennial, timeless, ageless, deathless, undying, immortal; unfailing, unchanging, never-changing, changeless, unfading; *literary* sempiternal, perdurable.
2 ☞ CONTINUOUS. **3** ☞ ENDLESS 2.
—OPPOSITES: temporary, intermittent.

perpetuate v. KEEP ALIVE, keep going, preserve, conserve, sustain, maintain, continue, extend, carry on, keep up, prolong; immortalize, commemorate, memorialize, eternalize.

perplex v. PUZZLE, baffle, mystify, bemuse, bewilder, confound, confuse, addle, disconcert, dumbfound, throw, throw/catch off balance, exercise, worry; flummox, be all Greek to, stump, bamboozle, floor, beat, faze, fox; *informal* discombobulate.

persecute v. **1** OPPRESS, abuse, victimize, ill-treat, mistreat, maltreat, terrorize, tyrannize, torment, torture; martyr.
2 HARASS, hound, plague, badger, harry, intimidate, pick on, pester, bother, devil, bully, victimize, terrorize; *informal* hassle, give someone a hard time, get on someone's case.

persevere v. PERSIST, continue, carry on, go on, keep on, keep going, struggle on, hammer away, be persistent, be determined, see/follow something through, keep at it, press on/ahead, not take no for an answer, be tenacious, stand one's ground, stand fast/firm, hold on, go the distance, stay the course, plod on, stop at nothing, leave no stone unturned; soldier on, hang on, plug away, stick to one's guns, stick to/with it, stick it out, hang in there.
—OPPOSITES: give up.

persist v. **1** ☞ PERSEVERE.
2 CONTINUE, hold, carry on, last, keep on, keep up, remain, linger, stay, endure.

persistent adj. **1** ☞ TENACIOUS 2.
2 ☞ CONTINUOUS.
—OPPOSITES: irresolute, intermittent.

person n. HUMAN BEING, individual, man/woman, child, boy/girl, human, being, (living) soul, mortal, creature; personage, character, customer; *informal* type, sort, cookie, body, dog, bastard, beggar, devil, geezer, guy; *archaic* wight.

□ **in person** PHYSICALLY, in the flesh, in propria persona, personally; oneself; as large as life.

persona *n.* IMAGE, face, public face, character, personality, identity, self; front, facade, guise, exterior, role, part.

personable *adj.* ☞ LIKEABLE.
—OPPOSITES: disagreeable.

personal *adj.* **1** ☞ DISTINCTIVE. **2** PRIVATE, intimate; confidential, secret. **3** DIRECT, empirical, first-hand, immediate, experiential. **4** AD HOMINEM.
—OPPOSITES: public, general.

personality *n.* **1** CHARACTER, nature, disposition, temperament, makeup, persona, psyche, constitution. **2** CHARISMA, magnetism, strength/force of personality, character, charm, presence. **3** ☞ CELEBRITY 1.

personally *adv.* **1** IN PERSON, oneself. **2** FOR MY PART, for myself, to my way of thinking, to my mind, in my estimation, as far as I am concerned, in my view/ opinion, from my point of view, from where I stand, as I see it, if you ask me, my sense is, for my money, in my book; privately; *informal* IMHO (in my humble opinion).

□ **take something personally** TAKE OFFENCE, take something amiss, be offended, be upset, be affronted, take umbrage, take exception, feel insulted, feel hurt.

personify *v.* EPITOMIZE, embody, hypostatize, typify, exemplify, represent, symbolize, stand for, be the incarnation of, put a face on.

personnel *n.* ☞ STAFF.

perspective *n.* OUTLOOK, view, viewpoint, point of view, POV, standpoint, position, stand, stance, angle, slant, attitude, frame of mind, frame of reference, approach, way of looking, interpretation.

persuade *v.* **1** PREVAIL ON, talk into, coax, convince, make, get, induce, win over, bring round, coerce, influence, sway, inveigle, entice, tempt, lure, cajole, wheedle, encourage, inspire, motivate, move, prod into, prompt; sweet-talk, twist someone's arm. **2** CAUSE, lead, move, dispose, incline.
—OPPOSITES: dissuade, deter.

persuasive *adj.* ☞ COGENT.
—OPPOSITES: unconvincing.

pertain *v.* CONCERN, relate to, be related to, be connected with, be relevant to, regard, apply to, be pertinent to, refer to, have a bearing on, appertain to, bear on, affect, involve, touch.

pertinent *adj.* ☞ RELEVANT.
—OPPOSITES: irrelevant.

perturb *v.* ☞ WORRY 2.
—OPPOSITES: reassure.

pervade *v.* ☞ PERMEATE.

pervasive *adj.* PREVALENT, pervading, permeating. See also WIDESPREAD.

perverse *adj.* **1** ☞ UNREASONABLE 1. **2** ILLOGICAL, irrational, unreasonable, wrong, wrong-headed. **3** ☞ PERVERTED.
—OPPOSITES: accommodating, reasonable.

pervert *v.* ☞ CORRUPT *v.*
▶ *n.* DEVIANT, degenerate; perv, dirty old man, sicko.

perverted *adj.* UNNATURAL, deviant, warped, corrupt, twisted, abnormal, unhealthy, depraved, perverse, aberrant, immoral, debauched, debased, degenerate, evil, wicked, vile, amoral, wrong, bad; *informal* sick, sicko, kinky, pervy.

pessimist *n.* DEFEATIST, fatalist, prophet of doom, cynic, doomsayer, doomster, Cassandra; skeptic, doubter, doubting Thomas; misery, killjoy, Job's comforter; *informal* doom (and gloom) merchant, Jeremiah, wet blanket, Chicken Little, gloomy Gus.
—OPPOSITES: optimist, Pollyanna.

pessimistic *adj.* GLOOMY, negative, defeatist, downbeat, cynical, bleak, fatalistic, dark, black, despairing, despondent, depressed, hopeless; suspicious, distrustful, doubting, critical, dismissive.
—OPPOSITES: optimistic.

pest *n.* ☞ NUISANCE.

pester *v.* BADGER, hound, harass, plague, annoy, bother, give someone the gears✤, trouble, keep after, persecute, torment, bedevil, harry, worry, beleaguer, chivvy, nag, hassle, bug, devil, get on someone's case.

pet *n.* FAVOURITE, darling, the apple of one's eye; fair-haired boy/girl.
▶ *adj.* TAME, domesticated, domestic, housebroken, house-trained.
▶ *v.* **1** STROKE, caress, fondle, pat. **2** KISS AND CUDDLE, kiss, cuddle, embrace, caress; *informal* make out, canoodle, neck, smooch, get it on.

petite *adj.* SMALL, dainty, diminutive, slight, little, tiny, elfin, delicate, small-boned, wee, pint-sized.

petition *n.* **1** APPEAL, round robin. **2** ENTREATY, supplication, plea, prayer, appeal, request, invocation, suit; *archaic* orison.

petrified *adj.* ☞ AFRAID 1.

petty *adj.* **1** ☞ TRIVIAL. **2** SMALL-MINDED, mean, ungenerous, shabby, spiteful.
—OPPOSITES: important, magnanimous.

petulant *adj.* ☞ IRRITABLE.
—OPPOSITES: good-humoured.

phantom *n.* ☞ GHOST 1.

phase *n.* STAGE, period, chapter, episode, part, step, point, time, juncture; spell, patch.

phenomenal *adj.*
☞ EXTRAORDINARY.
—OPPOSITES: ordinary.

phenomenon *n.* **1** OCCURRENCE, event, happening, fact, situation, circumstance, experience, case, incident, episode. **2** ☞ WONDER 2.

philanderer *n.* ☞ WOMANIZER.

philanthropic *adj.* CHARITABLE, generous, benevolent, humanitarian, public-spirited, altruistic, magnanimous, munificent, open-handed, bountiful, liberal, generous to a fault, beneficent, caring, compassionate, unselfish, kind, kind-hearted, big-hearted; *formal* eleemosynary.
—OPPOSITES: selfish, mean.

philistine *adj.* UNCULTURED, lowbrow, anti-intellectual, uncultivated, uncivilized, uneducated, unenlightened, commercial, materialist, bourgeois; ignorant, crass, boorish, barbarian.

philosophical *adj.*
1 THEORETICAL, metaphysical.
2 THOUGHTFUL, reflective, pensive, meditative, contemplative, introspective, ruminative; cogitative.

philosophy *n.* **1** THINKING, thought, reasoning. **2** BELIEFS, credo, convictions, ideology, ideas, thinking, notions, theories, doctrine, tenets, principles, views, school of thought; canon(s), creed, ethics, faith, ideals, morals, persuasion, teaching; *informal* ism.

phobia *n.* FEAR, irrational fear, obsessive fear, dread, horror, terror, hatred, loathing, detestation, aversion, antipathy, revulsion; complex, neurosis; *informal* thing, hang-up.

phony *adj.* ☞ FAKE *adj.*
—OPPOSITES: authentic.
▶ *n.* **1** IMPOSTER, sham, fake, fraud, charlatan; *informal* con artist.
2 ☞ FAKE *n.* 1.

photograph *n.* PICTURE, photo, snapshot, shot, image, likeness, print, exposure, slide, transparency, still, enlargement, snap; *informal* mug shot, head shot.

phrase *n.* EXPRESSION, group of words, construction, locution, term, turn of phrase; idiom, idiomatic expression; saying, tag.
▶ *v.* EXPRESS, put into words, put, word, style, formulate, couch, frame, articulate, verbalize.

physical *adj.* **1** BODILY, corporeal, corporal, somatic; carnal, fleshly, non-spiritual. **2** MANUAL, labouring, blue-collar. **3** MATERIAL, concrete, tangible, palpable, solid,

substantial, real, actual, visible.
—OPPOSITES: mental, spiritual.

physician *n.* ☞ DOCTOR.

physique *n.* BODY, build, figure, frame, anatomy, shape, form, proportions; muscles, musculature; *informal* vital statistics, bod.

pick *v.* **1** HARVEST, gather (in), collect, pluck. **2** ☞ SELECT.
3 PROVOKE, start, cause, incite, stir up, whip up, instigate, prompt, bring about.
▶ *n.* CHOICE, selection, option, decision; preference, favourite.
☐ **pick on** BULLY, victimize, tyrannize, torment, persecute, criticize, harass, hound, taunt, tease; *informal* get at, have it in for, be down on, needle. **pick up** ☞ IMPROVE 2, RECOVER 1. **pick someone/something up** LIFT, take up, raise, hoist, scoop up, gather up, snatch up.

picture *n.* **1** PAINTING, DRAWING, sketch, oil painting, watercolour, print, canvas, portrait, portrayal, illustration, artwork, depiction, likeness, representation, image, icon, miniature, landscape; fresco, mural, wall painting.
2 ☞ PHOTOGRAPH.
▶ *v.* **1** DEPICT, photograph, paint, DRAW, sketch, delineate, portray, show, illustrate. **2** VISUALIZE, see in one's mind's eye, conjure up a picture/image of, imagine, see, evoke.

picturesque *adj.* ATTRACTIVE, pretty, beautiful, lovely, scenic, charming, quaint, pleasing, delightful, picture-perfect.
—OPPOSITES: ugly.

pie *n.* PASTRY, tart, tartlet, quiche, pasty, patty, turnover, strudel.

piece *n.* **1** BIT, slice, chunk, segment, section, lump, hunk, wedge, slab, block, cake, bar, cube, stick, length; offcut, sample, fragment, sliver, splinter, wafer, chip, crumb, scrap, remnant, shred, shard, snippet; mouthful, morsel. **2** ☞ COMPONENT. **3** ITEM, article, specimen. **4** ☞ PORTION 2. **5** WORK (OF ART), creation, production; composition, opus. **6** ARTICLE, item, story, report, essay, study, review, composition, column.

piecemeal *adv.* A LITTLE AT A TIME, piece by piece, bit by bit, gradually, slowly, in stages, in steps, step by step, little by little, by degrees, in/by fits and starts.

pier *n.* JETTY, quay, wharf, dock, levee, landing, landing stage.

pierce *v.* PENETRATE, puncture, perforate, prick, lance; stab, spike, stick, impale, transfix, gore, bore through, drill through.

piercing *adj.* **1** SHRILL, ear-splitting, high-pitched, penetrating, strident, loud. **2** BITTER, biting, cutting, penetrating, sharp, keen, stinging, raw; freezing, frigid, glacial, arctic, chill. **3** INTENSE, excruciating, agonizing, sharp, stabbing, shooting, stinging, severe, extreme, fierce, searing, racking. **4** SEARCHING, probing, penetrating, penetrative, shrewd, sharp, keen.

piety *n.* DEVOUTNESS, devotion, piousness, religion, holiness, godliness, saintliness; veneration, reverence, faith, religious duty, spirituality, religious zeal, fervour; pietism, religiosity.

pig *n.* **1** HOG, boar, sow, porker, swine, piglet; piggy. **2** GLUTTON, guzzler, hog, greedy guts. —RELATED: porcine.

pigeonhole *v.* CATEGORIZE, compartmentalize, classify, characterize, label, brand, tag, typecast, ghettoize, designate.

pile *n.* **1** HEAP, stack, mound, pyramid, mass, quantity; collection, accumulation, assemblage, store, stockpile, hoard. **2** ☞ LOT 1.
▶ *v.* **1** HEAP (UP), stack (up). **2** ☞ INCREASE 1. **3** CROWD, climb, pack, squeeze, push, shove.

pill *n.* TABLET, capsule, caplet, cap, gelcap, pellet, lozenge, pastille, horse pill; bolus.

pillage *v.* **1** ☞ PLUNDER 1. **2** ☞ STEAL 1.
▶ *n.* ☞ PLUNDER *n.*

pillar *n.* COLUMN, post, support, upright, baluster, pier, pile, pilaster, stanchion, prop, newel; obelisk, monolith.

pilot *adj.* EXPERIMENTAL, exploratory, trial, test, sample, speculative; preliminary.
▶ *v.* NAVIGATE, guide, manoeuvre, steer, control, direct, captain, shepherd; fly, drive; sail, skipper.

pimple *n.* PUSTULE, boil, swelling, eruption, blackhead, whitehead, carbuncle, blister, spot; *informal* zit; *technical* comedo, papule; (**pimples**) acne, bad skin.

pin *n.* **1** TACK, safety pin, nail, staple, fastener. **2** BOLT, peg, rivet, dowel, screw. **3** BADGE, brooch.
▶ *v.* **1** ATTACH, fasten, affix, fix, tack, clip; join, secure. **2** HOLD,

press, hold fast, hold down; restrain, pinion, immobilize.

pinch v. NIP, tweak, squeeze, grasp.
▶ n. **1** NIP, tweak, squeeze.
2 ☞ TRACE n. 2.
▢ **in a pinch** IF NECESSARY, if need be, in an emergency, just possibly, with difficulty.

pine v. YEARN, long, ache, sigh, hunger, languish; miss, mourn, lament, grieve over, shed tears for, bemoan, rue.

pink adj. ROSE, rosy, rosé, pale red, salmon, coral; flushed, blushing.

pinnacle n. **1** ☞ SUMMIT 1.
2 ☞ PEAK 4.
—OPPOSITES: nadir.

pinpoint v. IDENTIFY, determine, distinguish, discover, find, locate, detect, track down, spot, diagnose, recognize, pin down, home in on, put one's finger on.

pioneer n. **1** ☞ SETTLER.
2 DEVELOPER, innovator, trailblazer, groundbreaker, spearhead; founder, founding father, architect, creator.
▶ v. INTRODUCE, develop, evolve, launch, instigate, initiate, spearhead, institute, establish, found, be the father/mother of, originate, set in motion, create; lay the groundwork, prepare the way, blaze a trail, break new ground.

pious adj. **1** ☞ DEVOUT 1.
2 ☞ SANCTIMONIOUS.
—OPPOSITES: irreligious, sincere.

pipe n. TUBE, conduit, hose, main, duct, line, channel, pipeline, drain; tubing, piping, siphon.
▶ v. **1** SIPHON, feed, channel, run, convey. **2** CHIRP, cheep, chirrup,
twitter, warble, trill, peep, sing, shrill.

pique n. IRRITATION, annoyance, resentment, anger, displeasure, indignation, petulance, ill humour, vexation, exasperation, disgruntlement, discontent; offence, umbrage.
▶ v. STIMULATE, arouse, rouse, provoke, whet, awaken, excite, kindle, stir, galvanize.

pirate n. FREEBOOTER, marauder, raider; privateer; buccaneer, corsair.
▶ v. STEAL, plagiarize, poach, copy illegally, reproduce illegally, appropriate, bootleg; crib, lift, rip off, pinch.

pistol n. ☞ GUN.

pit n. **1** HOLE, ditch, trench, trough, hollow, excavation, cavity, crater, pothole; shaft, mine shaft, sump. **2** POCKMARK, pock, hollow, indentation, depression, dent, dimple.
▢ **the pits** HELL, the worst, the lowest of the low, a nightmare; rock-bottom, extremely bad, awful, terrible, dreadful, deplorable; *informal* appalling, lousy, abysmal.

pitch n. **1** TONE, timbre, key, modulation, frequency. **2** ☞ SLOPE 1. **3** LEVEL, intensity, point, degree, height, extent.
▶ v. **1** ☞ THROW 1. **2** LURCH, toss (about), plunge, roll, reel, sway, rock, keel, list, wallow, labour.
▢ **pitch in** HELP (OUT), assist, lend a hand, join in, participate, contribute, do one's bit, chip in, co-operate, collaborate.

pitfall *n.* HAZARD, danger, risk, peril, difficulty, catch, snag, stumbling block, drawback.

pitiful *adj.* **1** DISTRESSING, sad, piteous, pitiable, pathetic, heart-rending, heartbreaking, moving, touching, tear-jerking; plaintive, poignant, forlorn; poor, sorry, wretched, abject, miserable. **2** WOEFUL, deplorable, awful, terrible, lamentable, hopeless, poor, bad, feeble, pitiable, dreadful, inadequate, below par, laughable; *informal* pathetic, useless, appalling, lousy, abysmal, dire.

pittance *n.* A TINY AMOUNT, next to nothing, very little; peanuts, chicken feed, slave wages, chump change.

pity *n.* **1** COMPASSION, commiseration, condolence, sympathy, fellow feeling, understanding; sorrow, regret, sadness. **2** SHAME, sad thing, bad luck, misfortune; *informal* crime, bummer, sin.
—OPPOSITES: indifference, cruelty.
▶ *v.* FEEL SORRY FOR, feel for, sympathize with, empathize with, commiserate with, condole with, take pity on, be moved by, grieve for.
□ **take pity on** FEEL SORRY FOR, feel sympathy/compassion for, relent, be compassionate towards, be sympathetic towards, have mercy on, help (out), put someone out of their misery.

pivot *n.* FULCRUM, axis, axle, swivel; pin, shaft, hub, spindle, hinge, kingpin.
▶ *v.* ROTATE, turn, swivel, revolve, spin.

pivotal *adj.* ☞ CRUCIAL.

placate *v.* PACIFY, calm, appease, mollify, soothe, assuage, win over, reconcile, conciliate, propitiate, make peace with, humour.
—OPPOSITES: provoke.

place *n.* **1** LOCATION, site, spot, setting, position, situation, area, region, locale; venue; *technical* locus. **2** ☞ HOME 1. **3** SITUATION, position, circumstances; *informal* shoes. **4** STATUS, position, standing, rank, niche; *dated* estate, station.
▶ *v.* **1** PUT (DOWN), set (down), lay, deposit, position, plant, rest, stand, station, situate, leave; *informal* stick, dump, park, plonk, pop, plunk. **2** ☞ IDENTIFY 1.
□ **out of place 1** INAPPROPRIATE, unsuitable, unseemly, improper, untoward, out of keeping, unbecoming, wrong. **2** INCONGRUOUS, out of one's element, like a fish out of water; uncomfortable, uneasy. **put someone in their place** HUMILIATE, take down a peg or two, deflate, crush, squash, humble; *informal* cut down to size, settle someone's hash, make someone eat crow. **take place** ☞ HAPPEN 1. **take the place of** REPLACE, stand in for, substitute for, act for, fill in for, cover for, relieve.

placid *adj.* **1** ☞ CALM 1. **2** QUIET, calm, tranquil, still, peaceful, undisturbed, restful, sleepy.
—OPPOSITES: excitable, bustling.

plagiarize *v.* COPY, infringe the copyright of, pirate, steal, poach, appropriate; *informal* rip off, crib, lift, 'borrow', pinch.

plague *n.* **1** BUBONIC PLAGUE, pneumonic plague, the Black

Death; disease, sickness, epidemic; *dated* contagion; *archaic* pestilence. **2** INFESTATION, epidemic, invasion, swarm, multitude, host. **3** BANE, curse, scourge, affliction, blight.
▶ *v.* **1** AFFLICT, bedevil, torment, trouble, beset, dog, curse. **2** ☞ PESTER.

plain *adj.* **1** ☞ OBVIOUS.
2 INTELLIGIBLE, comprehensible, clear, understandable, coherent, uncomplicated, lucid, unambiguous, simple, straightforward, user-friendly; *formal* perspicuous. **3** CANDID, frank, outspoken, forthright, direct, honest, truthful, blunt, bald, explicit, unequivocal; *informal* upfront. **4** SIMPLE, ordinary, unadorned, unembellished, unornamented, unostentatious, unfussy, basic, modest, unsophisticated, without frills, homespun; restrained, muted; everyday, workaday. **5** HOMELY, unprepossessing, unlovely, ordinary; not much to look at.
—OPPOSITES: obscure, fancy, attractive, pretentious.
▶ *adv.* ☞ DOWNRIGHT.
▶ *n.* GRASSLAND, prairie, flatland, lowland, pasture, meadowland, savannah, steppe; tableland, tundra, pampas, veld.

plaintive *adj.* MOURNFUL, sad, wistful, doleful, pathetic, pitiful, piteous, melancholy, sorrowful, unhappy, wretched, woeful, forlorn, woebegone.

plan *n.* **1** PROCEDURE, scheme, strategy, idea, proposal, proposition, suggestion; project, program, system, method, stratagem, formula, recipe; way, means, measure, tactic. **2** INTENTION, aim, idea, intent, objective, object, goal, target, ambition. **3** BLUEPRINT, drawing, diagram, sketch, layout; illustration, representation.
▶ *v.* **1** ORGANIZE, arrange, work out, design, outline, map out, prepare, schedule, formulate, frame, develop, devise, concoct; plot, scheme, hatch, brew, slate. **2** INTEND, aim, propose, mean, hope, want, wish, desire, envisage; *formal* purpose. **3** DESIGN, draw up, sketch out, map out.

plane *n.* **1** FLAT SURFACE, level surface; horizontal. **2** LEVEL, degree, standard, stratum; position, rung, echelon.

plant *n.* **1** flower, vegetable, herb, shrub, weed, forb; (**plants**) vegetation, greenery, flora, herbage, verdure. **2** FACTORY, works, foundry, mill, workshop, shop.
—RELATED: phyto-, -phyte.
▶ *v.* **1** SOW, scatter, seed; bed out, transplant. **2** PLACE, put, set, position, situate, settle; *informal* plonk. **3** INSTILL, implant, impress, imprint, put, place, introduce, fix, establish, lodge.

plaster *v.* **1** COVER THICKLY, smother, spread, smear, cake, coat, slather. **2** FLATTEN (DOWN), smooth down, slick down.

plate *n.* **1** DISH, platter, salver, paten. **2** PLATEFUL, helping, portion, serving. **3** PANEL, sheet, layer, pane, slab. **4** PLAQUE, sign, tablet, cartouche, brass.

platform *n.* **1** STAGE, dais, rostrum, podium, soapbox.

2 POLICY, program, party line, manifesto, plan, principles, objectives, aims.

platitude n. CLICHÉ, truism, commonplace, banality, old chestnut, bromide, inanity, banal/trite/hackneyed/stock phrase.

platter n. PLATE, dish, salver, paten, tray.

plausible adj. CREDIBLE, reasonable, believable, likely, feasible, tenable, possible, conceivable, imaginable; convincing, persuasive, cogent, sound, rational, logical, thinkable.
—OPPOSITES: unlikely.

play v. **1** AMUSE ONESELF, entertain oneself, enjoy oneself, have fun; relax, occupy oneself, divert oneself; frolic, frisk, romp, caper; *informal* mess about/around, lark (about/around). **2** TAKE PART IN, participate in, be involved in, compete in, do. **3** COMPETE AGAINST, take on, challenge, vie with, face, go up against. **4** ACT (THE PART OF), take the role of, appear as, portray, depict, impersonate, represent, render, perform, enact; *formal* personate. **5** PERFORM, make music, jam. **6** MAKE, produce, reproduce; blow, toot; plunk, bang out; sound. **7** DANCE, flit, ripple, touch; sparkle, glint.
▶ n. **1** AMUSEMENT, entertainment, relaxation, recreation, diversion, distraction, leisure; enjoyment, pleasure, fun, games, fun and games; horseplay, merrymaking, revelry; *informal* living it up. **2** DRAMA, theatrical work; screenplay, comedy, tragedy; production, performance, show, sketch. **3** MOVEMENT, slack, give; room to manoeuvre, scope, latitude.

□ **play around** ☞ FOOL AROUND at FOOL. **play at** PRETEND TO BE, pass oneself off as, masquerade as, profess to be, pose as, impersonate; fake, feign, simulate, affect; *informal* make like. **play something down** MAKE LIGHT OF, make little of, gloss over, de-emphasize, downplay, understate; soft-pedal, tone down, diminish, trivialize, underrate, underestimate, undervalue; disparage, belittle, scoff at, sneer at, shrug off; *informal* pooh-pooh.

playful adj. **1** FRISKY, jolly, lively, full of fun, frolicsome, sportive, high-spirited, exuberant, perky; mischievous, impish, clownish, kittenish, rascally, tricksy; *informal* full of beans. **2** LIGHTHEARTED, in jest, joking, jokey, teasing, humorous, jocular, good-natured, tongue-in-cheek, facetious, frivolous, flippant, arch; waggish.
—OPPOSITES: serious.

playwright n. ☞ DRAMATIST.

plea n. APPEAL, entreaty, supplication, petition, request, call, suit, solicitation.

plead v. **1** BEG, implore, entreat, appeal to, supplicate, importune, petition, request, ask, call on; *literary* beseech. **2** CLAIM, use as an excuse, assert, allege, argue, state.

pleasant adj. **1** ENJOYABLE, pleasurable, nice, agreeable, pleasing, satisfying, gratifying, good; entertaining, amusing, delightful, charming; fine, balmy; *informal* lovely, great. **2** FRIENDLY, agreeable, amiable, nice, genial,

cordial, likeable, amicable, good-humoured, good-natured, personable; hospitable, approachable, gracious, courteous, polite, obliging, helpful, considerate; charming, lovely, delightful, sweet, sympathetic, simpatico.
—OPPOSITES: disagreeable.

please v. MAKE HAPPY, give pleasure to, make someone feel good; delight, charm, amuse, entertain; satisfy, gratify, humour, oblige, content, suit.
—OPPOSITES: annoy.
▶ adv. IF YOU PLEASE, if you wouldn't mind, if you would be so good; kindly, pray; archaic prithee.

pleased adj. HAPPY, glad, delighted, gratified, grateful, thankful, content, contented, satisfied; thrilled, elated, overjoyed; informal over the moon, tickled pink, on cloud nine.
—OPPOSITES: unhappy.

pleasure n. 1 ☞ DELIGHT. 2 JOY, amusement, diversion, recreation, pastime; treat, thrill. 3 ENJOYMENT, fun, entertainment; recreation, leisure, relaxation; informal jollies. 4 HEDONISM, indulgence, self-indulgence, self-gratification, lotus-eating.
☐ **take pleasure in** ☞ ENJOY 1. **with pleasure** GLADLY, willingly, happily, readily; by all means, of course; archaic fain.

pledge n. ☞ PROMISE n. 1.
▶ v. 1 PROMISE, VOW, swear, undertake, engage, commit oneself, declare, affirm, avow. 2 PROMISE (TO GIVE), donate, contribute, give, put up.

plentiful adj. ☞ ABUNDANT.
—OPPOSITES: scarce.

plenty n. PROSPERITY, affluence, wealth, opulence, comfort, luxury; plentifulness, abundance.
▶ pron. A LOT OF, many, a great deal of, a plethora of, enough (and to spare), no lack of, sufficient, a wealth of; informal loads of, lots of, heaps of, stacks of, masses of, tons of, oodles of, scads of, a slew of.

plethora n. ☞ ABUNDANCE.
—OPPOSITES: dearth.

plight n. ☞ PREDICAMENT.

plod v. 1 TRUDGE, walk heavily, clump, stomp, tramp, tromp, lumber, slog. 2 WADE, plow, trawl, toil, labour; slog.

plot n. 1 ☞ CONSPIRACY. 2 STORYLINE, story, scenario, action, thread. 3 PIECE OF GROUND, patch, area, tract, acreage, allotment, lot, plat, homesite.
▶ v. 1 PLAN, scheme, arrange, organize, hatch, concoct, devise, dream up; informal cook up. 2 CONSPIRE, scheme, intrigue, collude, connive. 3 MARK, chart, map, represent, graph.

plow v. 1 TILL, furrow, harrow, cultivate, work, break up. 2 SHOVEL, clear (of snow). 3 TRUDGE, plod, toil, wade, slog.

ploy n. RUSE, tactic, move, device, stratagem, scheme, plot, trick, gambit, plan, manoeuvre, machination, contrivance, expedient, dodge, subterfuge, wile.

plug n. STOPPER, bung, cork, seal, spigot, spile.
▶ v. 1 STOP (UP), seal (up/off), close (up/off), cork, stopper, bung, block

(up/off), fill (up). **2** ☞ PUBLICIZE 2.

□ **plug away** ☞ PERSEVERE.

plummet v. ☞ PLUNGE 2.

plump adj. ☞ FAT 1.
—OPPOSITES: thin.

plunder v. **1** PILLAGE, loot, rob, raid, ransack, despoil, strip, ravage, lay waste, devastate, sack, rape. **2** ☞ STEAL 1.
▶ n. LOOTING, pillaging, plundering, marauding, raiding, ransacking, devastation, sacking; *literary* rapine.

plunge v. **1** DIVE, jump, throw oneself, launch oneself. **2** FALL SHARPLY, plummet, drop, go down, nosedive, tumble, slump. **3** THRUST, jab, stab, sink, stick, ram, drive, push, shove, force.
▶ n. DIVE, jump, nosedive, fall, pitch, drop, plummet, descent.
□ **take the plunge** COMMIT ONESELF, go for it, do the deed, throw caution to the wind(s), risk it, jump in at the deep end, go for broke.

plush adj. ☞ LUXURIOUS.
—OPPOSITES: austere.

pocket n. **1** POUCH, compartment. **2** (ISOLATED) AREA, patch, region, island, cluster, centre.
▶ v. ☞ STEAL 1.

poetic adj. EXPRESSIVE, figurative, symbolic, flowery, artistic, elegant, fine, beautiful; sensitive, imaginative, creative.

poignant adj. ☞ PITIFUL 1, TEARFUL 2.

point n. **1** TIP, (sharp) end, extremity; prong, spike, tine, nib, barb. **2** ☞ DOT. **3** ☞ PLACE 1. **4** TIME, stage, juncture, period, phase. **5** LEVEL, degree, stage, pitch, extent. **6** DETAIL, item, fact, thing, argument, consideration, factor,

element; subject, issue, topic, question, matter. **7** HEART OF THE MATTER, most important part, essence, nub, keynote, core, pith, crux; meaning, significance, gist, substance, thrust, bottom line, burden, relevance; brass tacks, nitty-gritty. **8** ☞ INTENT. **9** ☞ FEATURE 1.
▶ v. **1** AIM, direct, level, train. **2** INDICATE, suggest, evidence, signal, signify, denote, bespeak, reveal, manifest.
□ **point of view** ☞ VIEW 2. **point something out** IDENTIFY, show, designate, draw attention to, indicate, specify, detail, mention.
to the point ☞ RELEVANT.

pointed adj. **1** SHARP, tapering, tapered, conical, jagged, spiky, spiked, barbed; pointy. **2** CUTTING, trenchant, biting, incisive, acerbic, caustic, scathing, venomous, sarcastic; snarky.

pointless adj. ☞ USELESS 1, SENSELESS 2.
—OPPOSITES: valuable.

poise n. **1** GRACE, gracefulness, elegance, balance, control. **2** COMPOSURE, equanimity, self-possession, aplomb, presence of mind, self-assurance, self-control, nerve, calm, sang-froid, dignity; cool, unflappability.
▶ v. **1** BALANCE, hold (oneself) steady, be suspended, remain motionless, hang, hover. **2** PREPARE ONESELF, ready oneself, brace oneself, gear oneself up.

poison n. TOXIN, toxicant, venom; bane.
—RELATED: toxic.

poisonous adj. **1** VENOMOUS, deadly. **2** TOXIC, noxious, deadly,

fatal, lethal, mortal, death-dealing. **3** ☞ MALICIOUS, VICIOUS 2.
—OPPOSITES: harmless, non-toxic, benevolent.

poke v. **1** PROD, jab, dig, nudge, butt, shove, drive, jolt, stab, stick, ram, thrust. **2** STICK OUT, jut out, protrude, project, extend.
▸ n. PROD, jab, dig, elbow, nudge, shove, stab, butt, thrust.

polar adj. ARCTIC, Antarctic, circumpolar, Nearctic.

pole n. POST, pillar; telephone pole, utility pole, hydro pole✳; stanchion, paling, stake, (*Atlantic*) longer✳, stick, support, prop, batten, bar, rail, rod, beam; staff, stave, cane, baton.

police n. the police force, police officers, policemen, policewomen, officers of the law, the forces of law and order, constabulary; *informal* the cops, the Mounties✳, the fuzz, (the long arm of) the law, the boys in blue; coppers, the force, the heat, the pigs.

police officer n. COP, policeman, policewoman, officer (of the law), patrolman; constable, sergeant, inspector, corporal, captain, lieutenant, superintendent; flatfoot, pig.

policy n. PLANS, strategy, stratagem, approach, code, system, guidelines, theory; line, position, stance, attitude.

polish v. **1** SHINE, wax, buff, rub up/down; gloss, burnish; varnish, oil, glaze, lacquer, japan, shellac. **2** ☞ PERFECT V.
▸ n. **1** WAX, glaze, varnish; lacquer, japan, shellac. **2** SHINE, gloss, lustre, sheen, sparkle, patina, finish.

polished adj. **1** SHINY, glossy, gleaming, lustrous, glassy; waxed, buffed, burnished; varnished, glazed, lacquered, japanned, shellacked. **2** EXPERT, accomplished, masterly, masterful, skilful, adept, adroit, dexterous; impeccable, flawless, perfect, consummate, exquisite, outstanding, excellent, superb, superlative, first-rate, fine; *informal* ace. **3** REFINED, cultivated, civilized, well-bred, polite, courteous, genteel, decorous, respectable, urbane, suave, sophisticated.
—OPPOSITES: dull, inexpert, gauche.

polite adj. WELL-MANNERED, civil, courteous, mannerly, respectful, deferential, well-behaved, well-bred, gentlemanly, ladylike, genteel, gracious, urbane; tactful, diplomatic; civilized, refined, cultured, sophisticated, courtly.
—OPPOSITES: rude, uncivilized.

political adj. **1** GOVERNMENTAL, government, constitutional, ministerial, parliamentary, diplomatic, legislative, administrative, bureaucratic; public, civic, state. **2** POLITICALLY ACTIVE, party (political); militant, factional, partisan, ideological.

politics n. **1** GOVERNMENT, affairs of state, public affairs; diplomacy. **2** POLITICAL SCIENCE, civics, statecraft. **3** POWER STRUGGLE, machinations, manoeuvring, opportunism, realpolitik.

poll n. SURVEY, opinion poll, straw poll, canvass, market research, census.

▶ *v.* CANVASS, survey, ask, question, interview, ballot.

pollute *v.* **1** CONTAMINATE, adulterate, taint, poison, foul, dirty, soil, infect; befoul. **2** CORRUPT, poison, warp, pervert, deprave, defile, blight, sully; besmirch.
—OPPOSITES: purify.

pollution *n.* CONTAMINATION, adulteration, impurity; dirt, filth, toxins, infection; smog.

pomp *n.* CEREMONY, ceremonial, solemnity, ritual, display, spectacle, pageantry; show, showiness, ostentation, splendour, grandeur, magnificence, majesty, stateliness, glory, opulence, brilliance, drama, resplendence, splendidness; razzmatazz.

pompous *adj.* SELF-IMPORTANT, imperious, overbearing, domineering, magisterial, pontifical, sententious, grandiose, affected, pretentious, puffed up, arrogant, vain, haughty, proud, conceited, egotistic, supercilious, condescending, patronizing; *informal* snooty, uppity, uppish.
—OPPOSITES: modest.

pond *n.* POOL, water hole, lake, tarn, reservoir, slough, (*Nfld*) steady✦, beaver pond, (*Maritimes*) headpond✦, (*Maritimes*) flowage✦, (*Atlantic*) barachois✦, pothole, (*Nfld*) gully✦, (*Prairies*) dugout✦, tank.

ponder *v.* THINK ABOUT/ON, contemplate, consider, review, reflect on, mull over, meditate on, muse on, deliberate about, cogitate on, dwell on, brood on, ruminate on, chew over, puzzle over, turn over in one's mind.

pool *n.* SUPPLY, reserve(s), reservoir, fund; store, stock, accumulation, cache.
▶ *v.* ☞ COMBINE 1.

poor *adj.* **1** POVERTY-STRICKEN, penniless, moneyless, impoverished, low-income, necessitous, impecunious, indigent, needy, destitute, pauperized, unable to make ends meet, without a sou, in straitened circumstances, distressed, badly off; insolvent, in debt, without a cent (to one's name); *informal* (flat) broke, hard up, cleaned out, strapped, without two coins/cents to rub together, without a red cent, dirt poor; *formal* penurious. **2** ☞ BAD 1. **3** DEFICIENT, lacking, wanting, weak; short of, low on. **4** UNFORTUNATE, unlucky, luckless, unhappy, hapless, ill-fated, ill-starred, pitiable, pitiful, wretched.
—OPPOSITES: rich, superior, good, lucky.

pop
☐ **pop up** APPEAR (SUDDENLY), occur (suddenly), arrive, materialize, come along, happen, emerge, arise, crop up, turn up, present itself, come to light; *informal* show up.

populace *n.* POPULATION, inhabitants, residents, natives; community, country, (general) public, people, nation; common people, man/woman in the street, masses, multitude, rank and file, commonalty, commonality, third estate, plebeians, proletariat; *informal* proles, plebs; Joe Public, John Q. Public; *formal* denizens; *derogatory* the hoi polloi, common herd, rabble, riff-raff.

popular adj. **1** WELL-LIKED, favoured, sought-after, in demand, desired, wanted; commercial, marketable, fashionable, trendy, in vogue, all the rage, hot; in, cool, big. **2** NON-SPECIALIST, non-technical, amateur, layperson's, general, middle-of-the-road; accessible, simplified, plain, simple, easy, straightforward, understandable; mass-market, middlebrow, lowbrow, pop. **3** ☞ COMMON 1, 2. **4** MASS, general, communal, collective, social, collaborative, group, civil, public. —OPPOSITES: highbrow.

population n. INHABITANTS, residents, people, citizens, citizenry, public, community, populace, society, body politic, natives, occupants; denizens.

pornographic adj. ☞ INDECENT. —OPPOSITES: wholesome.

porous adj. PERMEABLE, penetrable, pervious, cellular, holey; absorbent, absorptive, spongy. —OPPOSITES: impermeable.

port n. HARBOUR, dock(s), haven, marina; anchorage, moorage, harbourage, roads.

portable adj. TRANSPORTABLE, movable, mobile, travel; lightweight, compact, handy, convenient.

portion n. **1** PART, piece, bit, section, segment. **2** SHARE, slice, quota, quantum, part, percentage, amount, quantity, ration, fraction, division, allocation, measure; informal cut, rake-off. **3** ☞ SERVING.

portrait n. PAINTING, picture, drawing, sketch, likeness, image, study, miniature; informal oil; formal portraiture.

portray v. **1** PAINT, draw, sketch, picture, depict, represent, illustrate, render. **2** DESCRIBE, depict, characterize, represent, present, delineate, style, brand, evoke, tell of.

pose v. **1** CONSTITUTE, present, create, cause, produce, be. **2** RAISE, ask, put, set, submit, advance, propose, suggest, moot. **3** MODEL, sit. **4** BEHAVE AFFECTEDLY, strike a pose, posture, put on airs; show off.
▶ n. **1** POSTURE, position, stance, attitude, bearing. **2** PRETENSE, act, affectation, facade, show, front, display, masquerade, posture.
☐ **pose as** PRETEND TO BE, impersonate, pass oneself off as, masquerade as, profess to be, represent oneself as; formal personate.

posh adj. SMART, stylish, fancy, high-class, fashionable, chic, luxurious, luxury, deluxe, exclusive, opulent, lavish, grand, showy, upscale, upmarket; informal classy, swanky, snazzy, plush, ritzy, flash, la-di-da, fancy-dancy, fancy-schmancy, swank, tony.

position n. **1** ☞ LOCATION. **2** POSTURE, stance, attitude, pose. **3** SITUATION, state, condition, circumstances; predicament, plight, strait(s). **4** STATUS, place, level, rank, standing; stature, prestige, influence, reputation, importance, consequence, class; dated station. **5** JOB, post, situation, appointment, role, occupation, employment; office, capacity, duty, function; opening, vacancy,

placement. **6** ☞ STANCE 2.
▶ v. PUT, place, locate, situate, set, site, stand, station; plant, stick, install, insert, lodge; arrange, dispose; *informal* plonk, park.

positive *adj.* **1** ☞ FAVOURABLE 3.
2 CONSTRUCTIVE, practical, useful, productive, helpful, worthwhile, beneficial, effective.
3 ☞ OPTIMISTIC. **4** ☞ PROMISING 1.
5 DEFINITE, conclusive, certain, categorical, unequivocal, incontrovertible, indisputable, undeniable, unmistakable, irrefutable, reliable, concrete, tangible, clear-cut, explicit, firm, decisive, real, actual. **6** ☞ SURE 1.
—OPPOSITES: negative, pessimistic, doubtful, unsure.

possess *v.* **1** OWN, have (to one's name), hold. **2** HAVE, be blessed with, be endowed with; enjoy, boast. **3** OBSESS, haunt, preoccupy, consume; eat someone up, prey on one's mind.

possessions *n.* BELONGINGS, things, property, (worldly) goods, (personal) effects, assets, chattels, movables, valuables; stuff, bits and pieces; luggage, baggage; gear, junk.

possessive *adj.* **1** PROPRIETORIAL, overprotective, controlling, dominating, jealous, clingy.
2 COVETOUS, selfish, unwilling to share; grasping, greedy, acquisitive, grabby.

possibility *n.* **1** ☞ CHANCE 1.
2 FEASIBILITY, practicability, chances, odds, probability.
3 ☞ OPTION. **4** POTENTIAL, promise, prospects.

possible *adj.* **1** FEASIBLE, practicable, practical, viable, within the bounds/realms of possibility, attainable, achievable, workable; *informal* doable.
2 CONCEIVABLE, plausible, imaginable, believable, likely, potential, probable, credible; prospective.
—OPPOSITES: unlikely.

possibly *adv.* **1** ☞ MAYBE.
2 CONCEIVABLY, under any circumstances, by any means.

post *n.* POLE, stake, upright, longer✧, shaft, prop, support, picket, strut, pillar, pale, paling, stanchion.
▶ v. AFFIX, attach, fasten, display, pin (up), put up, stick (up), tack (up).

poster *n.* NOTICE, placard, bill, sign, advertisement, playbill.

postpone *v.* PUT OFF/BACK, delay, defer, reschedule, adjourn, shelve, put/hold over, push back, suspend, stay, mothball, take a rain check on; put on ice, put on the back burner, back-burner, put in cold storage.
—OPPOSITES: bring forward.

postulate *v.* PUT FORWARD, suggest, advance, posit, hypothesize, propose; assume, presuppose, presume, take for granted.

posture *n.* **1** POSITION, pose, attitude, stance. **2** BEARING, carriage, stance, comportment.
▶ v. POSE, strike an attitude, strut.

potential *adj.* POSSIBLE, likely, prospective, future, probable; latent, inherent, undeveloped.
▶ *n.* POSSIBILITIES, potentiality, prospects; promise, capability, capacity.

potion n. CONCOCTION, mixture, brew, elixir, philtre, drink, decoction; medicine, tonic.

pottery n. CHINA, crockery, ceramics, earthenware, stoneware.

pouch n. BAG, purse, sack, sac, pocket.

pounce v. JUMP ON, spring, leap, dive, lunge, fall on, set on, attack suddenly; informal jump, mug.

pound[1] v. **1** ☞ BEAT 1. **2** BEAT AGAINST, crash against, batter, dash against, lash, buffet. **3** CRUSH, grind, pulverize, mill, mash, pulp; technical triturate. **4** THROB, thump, thud, hammer, pulse, race, go pit-a-pat.

pound[2] n. ENCLOSURE, compound, pen, yard, corral.

pour v. **1** TIP, let flow, splash, spill, decant; slosh, slop. **2** STREAM, flow, run, gush, course, jet, spurt, surge, spill. **3** ☞ RAIN v. 1.

poverty n. PENURY, destitution, pauperism, pauperdom, beggary, indigence, pen, pennilessness, impoverishment, neediness, need, hardship, impecuniousness.
—OPPOSITES: wealth.

powder n. DUST, fine particles.

powdery adj. FINE, dry, fine-grained, powder-like, dusty, chalky, floury, sandy, crumbly, friable.

power n. **1** ☞ CAPABILITY. **2** CONTROL, authority, influence, dominance, mastery, domination, dominion, sway, weight, leverage; informal clout, teeth, drag; literary puissance. **3** ☞ AUTHORITY 2. **4** ☞ STRENGTH 1. **5** ☞ STRENGTH 7. **6** ENERGY, electrical power, electricity, hydro✦.
—OPPOSITES: inability, weakness.

powerful adj. **1** STRONG, muscular, muscly, sturdy, strapping, robust, brawny, burly, athletic, manly, well built, solid; beefy, hunky; dated stalwart; literary stark, thewy. **2** VIOLENT, forceful, hard, mighty. **3** INTENSE, keen, fierce, passionate, ardent, burning, strong, irresistible, overpowering, overwhelming. **4** STRONG, important, dominant, influential, commanding, potent, forceful, formidable; literary puissant.
—OPPOSITES: weak.

powerless adj. IMPOTENT, helpless, ineffectual, ineffective, useless, weak, feeble; defenceless, vulnerable; lame-duck.

practicable adj. ☞ FEASIBLE.

practical adj. **1** EMPIRICAL, hands-on, actual, active, applied, heuristic, experiential. **2** ☞ FEASIBLE. **3** FUNCTIONAL, sensible, utilitarian, workaday. **4** ☞ REALISTIC 1.
—OPPOSITES: theoretical.

practically adv. ☞ ALMOST.

practice n. **1** APPLICATION, exercise, use, operation, implementation, execution. **2** CUSTOM, procedure, policy, convention, tradition; praxis. **3** TRAINING, rehearsal, repetition, preparation; practice session, dummy run, run-through; dry run. **4** BUSINESS, firm, office, company; informal outfit.
□**in practice** IN REALITY, realistically, practically. **out of practice** RUSTY, unpractised.

practise v. **1** REHEARSE, run through, go over/through, work on/at; polish, perfect. **2** TRAIN, rehearse, prepare, go through one's paces. **3** CARRY OUT, perform, observe.

pragmatic adj. ☞ REALISTIC 1.
—OPPOSITES: impractical.

prairie n. PLAINS, grasslands.

praise v. **1** COMMEND, express admiration for, applaud, approve of, look on with favour, pay tribute to, speak highly/well of, enthuse about, eulogize, compliment, congratulate, salute, honour, sing the praises of, rhapsodize, rave about, go into raptures about, heap praise on, wax lyrical about, make much of, pat on the back, take one's hat off to, lionize, admire, hail, ballyhoo; laud. **2** WORSHIP, glorify, honour, exalt, adore, pay tribute to, give thanks to, venerate, reverence; formal laud.
—RELATED: laudatory.
—OPPOSITES: criticize.
▸ n. **1** APPROVAL, acclaim, admiration, approbation, acclamation, plaudits, congratulations, commendation; tribute, accolade, compliment, a pat on the back, eulogy, panegyric; formal encomium. **2** HONOUR, thanks, glory, worship, devotion, adoration, reverence.

praiseworthy adj.
☞ COMMENDABLE.

prance v. CAVORT, dance, jig, trip, caper, jump, leap, spring, bound, skip, hop, frisk, romp, frolic.

prank n. (PRACTICAL) JOKE, trick, piece of mischief, escapade, stunt, caper, jape, game, hoax, antic; lark.

pray v. SAY ONE'S PRAYERS, make one's devotions, offer a prayer/ prayers.

prayer n. INVOCATION, intercession, devotion; orison; plea, entreaty, petition, supplication.

preach v. **1** PROCLAIM, teach, spread, propagate, expound. **2** ADVOCATE, recommend, advise, urge, teach, counsel. **3** MORALIZE, sermonize, pontificate, lecture, harangue; preachify.
—RELATED: homiletic.

preacher n. ☞ CLERIC.

precarious adj. UNCERTAIN, insecure, unpredictable, risky, parlous, hazardous, dangerous, unsafe; unsettled, unstable, unsteady, shaky; informal dicey, chancy, iffy.
—OPPOSITES: safe.

precaution n. SAFEGUARD, preventative/preventive measure, safety measure, contingency (plan), insurance.

precede v. GO/COME BEFORE, lead (up) to, pave/prepare the way for, herald, introduce, usher in.
—OPPOSITES: follow.

precedence n. PRIORITY, rank, seniority, superiority, primacy, pre-eminence, eminence.
□ **take precedence over** TAKE PRIORITY OVER, outweigh, prevail over, come before.

precedent n. MODEL, exemplar, example, pattern, previous case, prior instance/example; paradigm, criterion, yardstick, standard.

precious adj. **1** VALUABLE, costly, expensive; invaluable, priceless, beyond price. **2** VALUED, cherished, treasured, prized, favourite, dear, dearest, beloved, darling, adored, loved, special. **3** AFFECTED, over-refined, pretentious; la-di-da.

precipitate v. BRING ABOUT/ON, cause, lead to, give rise to, instigate, trigger, spark, touch off, provoke, hasten, accelerate, expedite.
▸ *adj.* HASTY, overhasty, rash, hurried, rushed; impetuous, impulsive, spur-of-the-moment, precipitous, incautious, imprudent, injudicious, ill-advised, reckless, harum-scarum; *informal* previous; *literary* temerarious.

precipitous *adj.* **1** STEEP, sheer, perpendicular, abrupt, sharp, vertical. **2** SUDDEN, rapid, swift, abrupt, headlong, speedy, quick, fast, precipitate.

precise *adj.* **1** EXACT, accurate, correct, specific, detailed, explicit, unambiguous, definite. **2** EXACT, particular, very, specific. **3** METICULOUS, careful, exact, scrupulous, punctilious, conscientious, particular, methodical, strict, rigorous.
—OPPOSITES: inaccurate.

preclude v. PREVENT, make it impossible for, rule out, stop, prohibit, debar, bar, hinder, impede, inhibit, exclude.

preconception *n.* PRECONCEIVED IDEA/NOTION, presupposition, assumption, presumption, prejudgment; prejudice.

predecessor *n.* FORERUNNER, precursor, antecedent.
—OPPOSITES: successor.

predicament *n.* DIFFICULT SITUATION, mess, difficulty, plight, quandary, muddle, mare's nest; hole, fix, jam, pickle, scrape, bind, tight spot/corner, dilemma, dire straits, hot/deep water, imbroglio, problem, stew, tangle, tricky/difficult situation, can of worms.

predict v. FORECAST, foretell, foresee, prophesy, prognosticate, divine, anticipate, tell in advance, envision, envisage; *archaic* augur, presage.

predictable *adj.* FORESEEABLE, (only) to be expected, anticipated, foreseen, unsurprising; inevitable.

predominate v. **1** BE IN THE MAJORITY, preponderate, be predominant, prevail, be most prominent. **2** PREVAIL, dominate, be dominant, carry most weight; override, outweigh.

pre-eminent *adj.* GREATEST, leading, foremost, best, finest, chief, outstanding, excellent, distinguished, prominent, eminent, important, top, famous, renowned, celebrated, illustrious, supreme, marquee.
—OPPOSITES: undistinguished.

preface *n.* INTRODUCTION, foreword, preamble, prologue, prelude; front matter; prelims, intro, lead-in.
▸ v. PRECEDE, introduce, begin, open, start.

prefer v. LIKE BETTER, would rather (have), would sooner (have), favour, be more partial to; choose, select, pick, opt for, go for.

preferable *adj.* BETTER, best, more desirable, more suitable, advantageous, superior, preferred, recommended.

preference n. **1** LIKING, partiality, predilection, proclivity, fondness, taste, inclination, leaning, bias, bent, penchant, predisposition. **2** FAVOURITE, (first) choice, selection; cup of tea, thing, druthers. **3** PRIORITY, favour, precedence, preferential treatment.

pregnant adj. EXPECTING A BABY, expectant, carrying a child; expecting, in the family way, preggers, with a bun in the oven, knocked up; with child.

prejudice n. **1** PRECONCEIVED IDEA, preconception, prejudgment. **2** BIGOTRY, bias, partisanship, partiality, intolerance, discrimination, unfairness, inequality.
▶ v. BIAS, influence, sway, predispose, make biased, make partial, colour.

prejudiced adj. BIASED, bigoted, discriminatory, partisan, intolerant, narrow-minded, unfair, unjust, inequitable, coloured.
—OPPOSITES: impartial.

prejudicial adj. DETRIMENTAL, damaging, injurious, harmful, disadvantageous, hurtful, deleterious.
—OPPOSITES: beneficial.

preliminary adj. PREPARATORY, introductory, initial, opening, prefatory, precursory; early, exploratory.
—OPPOSITES: final.

prelude n. PRELIMINARY, overture, opening, preparation, introduction, start, commencement, beginning, lead-in, precursor.

premature adj. **1** UNTIMELY, (too) early, unseasonable, before time. **2** PRETERM.
—OPPOSITES: overdue.

premeditated adj. PLANNED, intentional, deliberate, pre-planned, calculated, cold-blooded, conscious, pre-arranged.
—OPPOSITES: spontaneous.

premier adj. LEADING, foremost, chief, principal, head, top-ranking, top, prime, primary, first, highest, pre-eminent, nonpareil, senior, outstanding, master, ranking; informal top-notch, blue-ribbon, blue-chip.

premise n. PROPOSITION, assumption, hypothesis, thesis, presupposition, postulation, postulate, supposition, presumption, surmise, conjecture, speculation, assertion, belief.

premonition n. FOREBODING, presentiment, intuition, (funny) feeling, hunch, suspicion, feeling in one's bones; misgiving, apprehension, fear.

preoccupied adj. **1** OBSESSED, concerned, absorbed, engrossed, intent, involved, wrapped up. **2** LOST/DEEP IN THOUGHT, in a brown study, pensive, absent-minded, distracted, abstracted.

preparation n. ARRANGEMENTS, planning, plans, preparatory measures.

prepare v. **1** MAKE/GET READY, put together, draw up, produce, arrange, assemble, construct, compose, formulate. **2** GET READY, make preparations, arrange things, make provision, get everything set. **3** TRAIN, get into shape, practise, get ready; instruct, coach, tutor, drill, prime.

preposterous *adj.* ABSURD, ridiculous, foolish, stupid, silly, ludicrous, farcical, laughable, comical, risible, nonsensical, senseless, insane; outrageous, monstrous; *informal* crazy, hare-brained, cockamamie.
−OPPOSITES: sensible.

prerequisite *adj.* NECESSARY, required, called for, essential, requisite, obligatory, compulsory.
−OPPOSITES: unnecessary.

presence *n.* 1 ATTENDANCE, appearance; company, companionship. 2 CHARISMA, aura, (strength/force of) personality; poise, self-assurance, self-confidence.
−OPPOSITES: absence.

present¹ *adj.* 1 IN ATTENDANCE, here, there, near, nearby, (close/near) at hand, available. 2 CURRENT, present-day, existing.
−OPPOSITES: absent.
▸ *n.* NOW, today, the present time/moment, the here and now.
−OPPOSITES: past, future.

present² *v.* 1 HAND OVER/OUT, give (out), confer, bestow, award, grant, accord. 2 SUBMIT, set forth, put forward, proffer, offer, tender, table. 3 INTRODUCE, make known, acquaint someone with. 4 DEMONSTRATE, show, put on show/display, exhibit, display, launch, unveil.

present³ *n.* GIFT, donation, offering, contribution; *informal* freebie; *formal* benefaction.

presentable *adj.* 1 TIDY, neat, straight, clean, spic and span, in good order, shipshape. 2 SMARTLY DRESSED, tidily dressed, tidy, well-groomed, trim, spruce; natty.

presentation *n.* DEMONSTRATION, talk, lecture, address, speech, show, exhibition, display, introduction, launch, launching, unveiling.

preserve *v.* 1 CONSERVE, protect, maintain, care for, look after. 2 CONTINUE (WITH), conserve, keep going, maintain, uphold, sustain, perpetuate. 3 CONSERVE, bottle, can, freeze, dry, freeze-dry; cure, smoke, pickle.

preside *v.* CHAIR, officiate (at), conduct, lead.
☐ **preside over** ☞ MANAGE 1.

press *v.* 1 PUSH (DOWN), press down, depress, hold down, force, thrust, squeeze, compress. 2 CRUSH, squeeze, squash, mash, pulp, pound, pulverize, macerate. 3 CLUSTER, gather, converge, congregate, flock, swarm, throng, crowd. 4 URGE, put pressure on, force, push, coerce, dragoon, steamroller, browbeat; *informal* lean on, put the screws on, twist someone's arm, railroad, bulldoze. 5 CALL, ask, advocate, clamour, push, campaign, demand, lobby.
▸ *n.* 1 PUBLISHING HOUSE, publisher; printing house/company; printing press. 2 THE MEDIA, the newspapers, the papers, the news media, the fourth estate; journalists, reporters, newspapermen/women, newsmen, pressmen; journos, newshounds, newsies.

pressing *adj.* URGENT, critical, crucial, acute, desperate, serious, grave, life-and-death; important, high-priority.

pressure *n.* **1** PHYSICAL FORCE, load, stress, thrust; compression, weight. **2** COERCION, force, compulsion, constraint, duress; pestering, harassment, nagging, badgering, intimidation, arm-twisting, persuasion. **3** STRESS, strain, tension, trouble, difficulty. ▶ *v.* COERCE, pressurize, put pressure on, press, push, persuade, force, compel, constrain, oblige, impel, bulldoze, hound, harass, nag, harry, badger, goad, pester, browbeat, bully, intimidate, threaten, dragoon, twist someone's arm, strong-arm; railroad, squeeze, lean on, hustle.

prestige *n.* STATUS, standing, stature, reputation, repute, regard, fame, note, renown, honour, esteem, celebrity, importance, prominence, influence, eminence; kudos, cachet; clout.

prestigious *adj.* REPUTABLE, distinguished, respected, esteemed, eminent, august, highly regarded, well-thought-of, acclaimed, authoritative, celebrated, illustrious, leading, renowned.
—OPPOSITES: obscure, minor.

presume *v.* **1** ASSUME, suppose, dare say, imagine, take it, expect, believe, think, surmise, guess, judge, conjecture, speculate, postulate, presuppose. **2** VENTURE, dare, have the audacity/effrontery, be so bold as, take the liberty of.

presumptuous *adj.* BRAZEN, overconfident, arrogant, bold, audacious, forward, familiar, impertinent, insolent, impudent, cocky; cheeky, rude, impolite, uncivil, bumptious; *informal* sassy.

pretend *v.* **1** MAKE AS IF, profess, affect; dissimulate, dissemble, put it on, put on a false front, go through the motions, sham, fake it. **2** PUT ON AN ACT, make believe, play at, act, play-act, impersonate. **3** FEIGN, sham, fake, simulate, put on, counterfeit, affect.

pretentious *adj.* AFFECTED, ostentatious, showy; over-ambitious, pompous, artificial, inflated, overblown, high-sounding, flowery, grandiose, elaborate, extravagant, flamboyant, ornate, grandiloquent, magniloquent, sophomoric; *informal* flashy, highfalutin, la-di-da, pseudo.

pretext *n.* (FALSE) EXCUSE, ostensible reason, alleged reason; guise, ploy, pretense, ruse.

pretty *adj.* ATTRACTIVE, lovely, good-looking, nice-looking, personable, fetching, prepossessing, appealing, charming, captivating, enchanting, delightful, cute, as pretty as a picture; *Scottish* bonny; *informal* easy on the eye, divine; *literary* beauteous; *archaic* fair, comely.
—OPPOSITES: plain, ugly.
▶ *v.* BEAUTIFY, make attractive, make pretty, prettify, titivate, adorn, ornament, smarten; *informal* do oneself up, tart oneself up.

prevail *v.* WIN (OUT/THROUGH), triumph, be victorious, carry the day, come out on top, succeed, prove superior, conquer, overcome; rule, reign.
▢ **prevail on/upon** ☞ PERSUADE.

prevalent *adj.* WIDESPREAD, prevailing, frequent, usual, common, current, popular, general, universal; endemic, rampant, rife.
—OPPOSITES: rare.

prevent *v.* STOP, put a stop to, avert, nip in the bud, fend off, stave off, ward off; hinder, impede, hamper, obstruct, balk, foil, thwart, forestall, counteract, inhibit, curb, restrain, preclude, pre-empt, save, help; disallow, prohibit, forbid, proscribe, exclude, debar, bar; *literary* stay.
—OPPOSITES: allow.

preventive *adj.* PRE-EMPTIVE, deterrent, precautionary, protective; prophylactic.

previous *adj.* FOREGOING, preceding, antecedent; old, earlier, prior, former, ex-, past, last, sometime, one-time, erstwhile; *formal* quondam, anterior.
—OPPOSITES: next.

previously *adv.* FORMERLY, earlier (on), before, hitherto, once, at one time, in the past, in days/times gone by, in bygone days, in times past, in former times; in advance, already, beforehand; *formal* heretofore.

price *n.* **1** COST, charge, fee, fare, levy, amount, sum; outlay, expense, expenditure; valuation, quotation, estimate, asking price; *informal* damage. **2** CONSEQUENCE, result, cost, penalty, sacrifice; downside, snag, drawback, disadvantage, minus.

priceless *adj.* INVALUABLE, of incalculable value/worth, of immeasurable value/worth,

beyond price; irreplaceable, incomparable, unparalleled.
—OPPOSITES: worthless, cheap.

prick *v.* PIERCE, puncture, make/ put a hole in, stab, perforate, nick, jab.
▸ *n.* JAB, sting, pinprick, prickle, stab; pang, twinge.

prickly *adj.* **1** SPIKY, spiked, thorny, barbed, spiny; briery, brambly; rough, scratchy. **2** TINGLY, tingling, prickling.

pride *n.* **1** SELF-ESTEEM, dignity, honour, self-respect, self-worth, self-regard, pride in oneself. **2** PLEASURE, joy, delight, gratification, fulfillment, satisfaction, sense of achievement. **3** ARROGANCE, vanity, self-importance, hubris, conceit, conceitedness, self-love, self-adulation, self-admiration, narcissism, egotism, superciliousness, haughtiness, snobbery, snobbishness; big-headedness; vainglory.
—OPPOSITES: shame, humility.

priest *n.* ☞ CLERIC.

prim *adj.* DEMURE, (prim and) proper, formal, stuffy, straitlaced, prudish; prissy, priggish, puritanical.

primarily *adv.* **1** FIRST (AND FOREMOST), firstly, essentially, in essence, fundamentally, principally, predominantly, basically. **2** MOSTLY, for the most part, chiefly, mainly, in the main, on the whole, largely, to a large extent, especially, generally, usually, typically, commonly, as a rule. ·

primary *adj.* MAIN, chief, key, prime, central, principal,

foremost, first, most important, predominant, paramount, highest, leading, major, of greatest/prime importance, overriding, supreme, top, uppermost; number-one.
—OPPOSITES: secondary.

prime *adj.* **1** ☞ MAIN.
2 FUNDAMENTAL, basic, essential, primary, central. **3** TOP-QUALITY, top, best, first-class, first-rate, grade A, superior, supreme, choice, select, finest; excellent, superb, fine; tip-top, A1, top-notch, blue-ribbon.
—OPPOSITES: secondary, inferior.
▶ *n.* HEYDAY, best days/years, prime of one's life; youth, salad days; peak, pinnacle, high point/spot, zenith.

primitive *adj.* **1** ANCIENT, earliest, first, prehistoric, antediluvian, primordial, primeval, primal. **2** UNCIVILIZED, barbarian, barbaric, barbarous, savage, ignorant, uncultivated. **3** CRUDE, simple, rough (and ready), basic, rudimentary, unrefined, unsophisticated, rude, makeshift.
—OPPOSITES: sophisticated, civilized.

principal *adj.* ☞ MAIN.
—OPPOSITES: minor.

principle *n.* **1** TRUTH, proposition, concept, idea, theory, assumption, fundamental, essential, ground rule. **2** DOCTRINE, belief, creed, credo, (golden) rule, criterion, tenet, code, ethic, dictum, canon, law. **3** MORALS, morality, (code of) ethics, beliefs, ideals, standards; integrity, uprightness, righteousness, virtue, probity,

(sense of) honour, decency, conscience, scruples.

print *v.* **1** IMPRINT, impress, stamp, mark. **2** PUBLISH, issue, release, circulate.
▶ *n.* **1** TYPE, printing, letters, lettering, characters, type size, typeface, font. **2** IMPRESSION, fingerprint, footprint. **3** PRINTED CLOTH/FABRIC, patterned cloth/fabric, chintz.

prior *adj.* EARLIER, previous, preceding, foregoing, antecedent, advance; *formal* anterior.
—OPPOSITES: subsequent.
□ **prior to** BEFORE, until, till, up to, previous to, earlier than, preceding, leading up to; *formal* anterior to.

priority *n.* **1** PRIME CONCERN, most important consideration, primary issue. **2** PRECEDENCE, greater importance, preference, pre-eminence, predominance, primacy, first place.

prison *n.* JAIL, lock-up, penal institution, detention centre, jailhouse, penitentiary, correctional facility, remand centre; *informal* clink, slammer, hoosegow, the big house, stir, jug, brig, can, pen, cooler, pokey, slam.
—RELATED: custodial.

prisoner *n.* CONVICT, detainee, inmate; captive, internee, prisoner of war, POW; *informal* jailbird, con, lifer, yardbird.

pristine *adj.* IMMACULATE, perfect, in mint condition, as new, unspoiled, spotless, flawless, clean, fresh, new, virgin, pure, unused.
—OPPOSITES: dirty, spoiled.

private *adj.* **1** PERSONAL, OWN, individual, special, exclusive, privately owned. **2** CONFIDENTIAL, secret, classified, unofficial, off the record, closet, in camera; backstage, privileged, one-on-one, tête-à-tête, sub-rosa. **3** INTIMATE, personal, secret; innermost, undisclosed, unspoken, unvoiced. **4** RESERVED, introvert, introverted, self-contained, reticent, discreet, uncommunicative, unforthcoming, retiring, unsociable, withdrawn, solitary, reclusive, hermitic. **5** SECLUDED, solitary, undisturbed, concealed, hidden, remote, isolated, out of the way, sequestered. **6** INDEPENDENT; privatized, denationalized; commercial, private-enterprise.
—OPPOSITES: public, open, extrovert, official, state, nationalized.
☐ **in private** IN SECRET, secretly, privately, behind closed doors, in camera; in confidence, confidentially, between ourselves, entre nous, off the record.

privation *n.* DEPRIVATION, hardship, destitution, impoverishment, want, need, neediness, austerity.
—OPPOSITES: plenty, luxury.

privilege *n.* **1** ADVANTAGE, benefit; prerogative, entitlement, right; concession, freedom, liberty. **2** HONOUR, pleasure.

privileged *adj.* **1** WEALTHY, rich, affluent, prosperous; LUCKY, fortunate, elite, favoured; (socially) advantaged. **2** ☞ CONFIDENTIAL.

—OPPOSITES: underprivileged, disadvantaged, public.

prize *n.* AWARD, reward, premium, purse; trophy, medal; honour, accolade, crown, laurels, palm.
▶ *adj.* CHAMPION, award-winning, prize-winning, winning, top, best.
—OPPOSITES: second-rate.
▶ *v.* VALUE, set great store by, rate highly, attach great importance to, esteem, hold in high regard, think highly of, treasure, cherish.

probable *adj.* ☞ LIKELY 1.
—OPPOSITES: unlikely.

probably *adv.* IN ALL LIKELIHOOD, in all probability, presumably, as likely as not, (very/most) likely, ten to one, the chances are, doubtless, no doubt.

probe *n.* INVESTIGATION, inquiry, examination, inquest, exploration, study, analysis.
▶ *v.* **1** EXAMINE, feel, feel around, explore, prod, poke, check. **2** INVESTIGATE, inquire into, look into, study, examine, scrutinize, go into, carry out an inquest into.

problem *n.* **1** DIFFICULTY, trouble, worry, complication, difficult situation; snag, hitch, drawback, stumbling block, obstacle, hurdle, hiccup, setback, catch, glitch; delay, disappointment, hindrance, holdup, impediment, obstruction, reversal, upset; predicament, plight; misfortune, mishap, misadventure; dilemma, quandary; *informal* headache, nightmare. **2** PUZZLE, question, poser, enigma, riddle, conundrum; teaser, brainteaser.
▶ *adj.* ☞ TROUBLESOME 2.
—OPPOSITES: well-behaved, manageable.

problematic *adj.* DIFFICULT, hard, taxing, troublesome, tricky, awkward, controversial, ticklish, complicated, complex, knotty, thorny, prickly, vexed.
—OPPOSITES: easy, simple, straightforward.

procedure *n.* COURSE OF ACTION, plan of action, action plan, policy, series of steps, method, system, strategy, way, approach, formula, mechanism, methodology, MO (modus operandi), technique; routine, drill, practice, operation.

proceed *v.* **1** BEGIN, make a start, get going, move, set something in motion; TAKE ACTION, act, go on, go ahead, make progress, make headway. **2** GO AHEAD, carry on, go on, continue, keep on, get on, get ahead; pursue, prosecute.
—OPPOSITES: stop.

proceedings *pl. n.* **1** REPORT, transactions, minutes, account, record(s); annals, archives. **2** LEGAL ACTION, court/judicial proceedings, litigation; lawsuit, case, prosecution.

process *n.* **1** PROCEDURE, operation, action, activity, exercise, affair, business, job, task, undertaking. **2** ☞ METHOD.

procession *n.* PARADE, march, march past, cavalcade, motorcade, cortège; column, file, train.

proclaim *v.* **1** DECLARE, announce, pronounce, state, make known, give out, advertise, publish, broadcast, promulgate, trumpet, blazon. **2** ASSERT, declare, profess, maintain, protest.

procrastinate *v.* DELAY, put off doing something, postpone action, defer action, be dilatory,

use delaying tactics, stall, temporize, drag one's feet/heels, take one's time, play for time, play a waiting game.

prod *v.* **1** POKE, jab, dig, elbow, butt, stab. **2** ☞ SPUR.

prodigy *n.* GENIUS, mastermind, virtuoso, wunderkind, wonder child, boy wonder; *informal* whiz kid, whiz, wizard.

produce *v.* **1** MANUFACTURE, make, construct, build, fabricate, put together, assemble, turn out, create; mass-produce; *informal* churn out. **2** YIELD, grow, give, supply, provide, furnish, bear, bring forth. **3** CREATE, originate, fashion, turn out; compose, write, pen; paint. **4** PRESENT, offer, provide, furnish, advance, put forward, bring forward, come up with. **5** ☞ CAUSE.
—RELATED: -facient, -genic.
▶ *n.* FOOD, foodstuff(s), products; harvest, crops, fruit, vegetables, greens.

product *n.* **1** ARTIFACT, commodity, manufactured article; creation, invention; (**products**) goods, wares, merchandise, produce. **2** RESULT, consequence, outcome, effect, upshot, fruit, by-product, spinoff.

productive *adj.* **1** PROLIFIC, inventive, creative; energetic. **2** USEFUL, constructive, profitable, fruitful, gainful, valuable, effective, worthwhile, helpful.

profane *adj.* ☞ FOUL 6.
▶ *v.* DESECRATE, violate, defile, treat sacrilegiously.

profanity *n.* ☞ OBSCENITY.

profess v. DECLARE, announce, proclaim, assert, state, affirm, avow, maintain, protest.

profession n. ☞ OCCUPATION 1.

professional adj. **1** WHITE-COLLAR, non-manual. **2** PAID, salaried. **3** ☞ ACCOMPLISHED.
—OPPOSITES: manual, amateur, amateurish.

proficient adj. ☞ EXPERT.
—OPPOSITES: incompetent.

profile n. **1** SIDE VIEW, outline, silhouette, contour, shape, form, figure, lines. **2** DESCRIPTION, account, study, portrait, portrayal, depiction, rundown, sketch, outline.

profit n. (FINANCIAL) GAIN, return(s), yield, proceeds, earnings, winnings, surplus, excess; informal pay dirt, bottom line.
—OPPOSITES: loss.
▶ v. MAKE MONEY, make a profit; informal rake it in, clean up, make a killing, make a bundle, make big bucks, make a fast/quick buck.
—OPPOSITES: lose.
☐ **profit by/from** BENEFIT FROM, take advantage of, derive benefit from, capitalize on, make the most of, turn to one's advantage, put to good use, do well out of, exploit, gain from; informal cash in on.

profitable adj. **1** MONEY-MAKING, profit-making, commercial, successful, solvent, in the black, gainful, remunerative, (financially) rewarding, paying, lucrative, bankable. **2** BENEFICIAL, useful, advantageous, valuable, productive, worthwhile; rewarding, fruitful, illuminating,

informative, constructive, well-spent.
—OPPOSITES: loss-making, fruitless, useless.

profound adj. **1** HEARTFELT, intense, keen, great, extreme, acute, severe, sincere, earnest, deep, deep-seated, overpowering, overwhelming, fervent, ardent. **2** WISE, learned, clever, intelligent, scholarly, sage, erudite, discerning, penetrating, perceptive, astute, thoughtful, insightful, percipient, perspicacious; rare sapient. **3** COMPLEX, abstract, deep, weighty, difficult, abstruse, recondite, esoteric.
—OPPOSITES: superficial.

profuse adj. COPIOUS, prolific, abundant, liberal, unstinting, fulsome, effusive, extravagant, lavish, gushing; informal over the top, gushy.
—OPPOSITES: meagre, sparse.

program n. **1** SCHEDULE, agenda, calendar, timetable; order of events, lineup. **2** plan of action, series of measures, strategy, scheme. **3** BROADCAST, production, show, presentation, transmission, performance, telecast. **4** COURSE, syllabus, curriculum.

progress n. **1** FORWARD MOVEMENT, advance, going, progression, headway, passage. **2** DEVELOPMENT, advance, advancement, headway, step(s) forward; improvement, betterment, growth.
—OPPOSITES: relapse.
▶ v. **1** GO, make one's way, move, move forward, go forward, proceed, advance, go on,

continue, make headway, work one's way. **2** DEVELOP, make progress, advance, make headway, take steps forward, move on, get on, gain ground; improve, get better, come on, come along, make strides; thrive, prosper, blossom, flourish; *informal* be getting there.
—OPPOSITES: relapse.

progressive *adj.* **1** CONTINUING, continuous, increasing, growing, developing, ongoing, accelerating, escalating; gradual, step-by-step, cumulative. **2** MODERN, liberal, advanced, forward-thinking, enterprising, innovative, pioneering, dynamic, bold, avant-garde, reforming, reformist, radical.
—OPPOSITES: conservative, reactionary.
▶ *n.* INNOVATOR, reformer, reformist, liberal, libertarian.

prohibit *v.* ☞ BAN 1.
—OPPOSITES: allow.

prohibitive *adj.* EXORBITANT, excessively high, sky-high, over-inflated; out of the question, beyond one's means; extortionate, unreasonable.

project *n.* **1** PLAN, program, enterprise, undertaking, venture; proposal, idea, concept, scheme. **2** ASSIGNMENT, piece of work, piece of research, task.
▶ *v.* **1** FORECAST, predict, expect, estimate, calculate, reckon.
2 STICK OUT, jut (out), protrude, extend, stand out, bulge out, poke out, thrust out, cantilever.

proliferate *v.* INCREASE RAPIDLY, grow rapidly, multiply, rocket,

mushroom, snowball, burgeon, run riot.
—OPPOSITES: decrease, dwindle.

prolong *v.* LENGTHEN, extend, draw out, drag out, protract, spin out, stretch out, string out, elongate; carry on, continue, keep up, perpetuate.
—OPPOSITES: shorten.

prominent *adj.* **1** IMPORTANT, well-known, leading, eminent, distinguished, notable, noteworthy, noted, illustrious, celebrated, famous, renowned, acclaimed, famed, influential, major-league. **2** CONSPICUOUS, noticeable, easily seen, obvious, unmistakable, eye-catching, pronounced, salient, striking, dominant; obtrusive.
—OPPOSITES: unimportant, unknown, inconspicuous.

promiscuous *adj.* LICENTIOUS, philandering, womanizing, wanton, immoral, unchaste, dissolute, debauched, fast, easy, swinging, sluttish, whorish, bed-hopping, shameless; *dated* loose, fallen, of easy virtue.
—OPPOSITES: chaste.

promise *n.* **1** WORD (OF HONOUR), assurance, pledge, vow, guarantee, oath, bond, undertaking, agreement, commitment, contract, covenant. **2** POTENTIAL, ability, aptitude, capability, capacity. **3** INDICATION, hint, suggestion, sign.
▶ *v.* GIVE ONE'S WORD, swear, pledge, vow, undertake, guarantee, contract, engage, give an assurance, commit oneself, bind oneself, swear/take an oath, covenant; *archaic* plight.

promising adj. **1** GOOD, encouraging, favourable, hopeful, full of promise, auspicious, propitious, bright, rosy, heartening, reassuring, positive. **2** WITH POTENTIAL, budding, up-and-coming, rising, coming, in the making.
—OPPOSITES: unfavourable, hopeless.

promote v. **1** ELEVATE, give promotion to, upgrade, advance, move up; kick upstairs. **2** ENCOURAGE, advocate, further, advance, assist, aid, help, contribute to, foster, nurture, develop, boost, stimulate, forward, work for. **3** ☞ ADVERTISE.
—OPPOSITES: demote, obstruct, play down.

prompt v. INDUCE, make, move, motivate, lead, dispose, persuade, incline, encourage, stimulate, prod, impel, spur on, inspire.
—OPPOSITES: deter.
▸ adj. QUICK, swift, rapid, speedy, fast, direct, immediate, instant, expeditious, early, punctual, in good time, on time, timely.
—OPPOSITES: slow, late.

promptly adv. WITHOUT DELAY, straight away, right away, at once, immediately, now, as soon as possible; QUICKLY, swiftly, rapidly, speedily, fast, expeditiously, momentarily; informal pronto, ASAP, PDQ (pretty damn quick).
—OPPOSITES: late, slowly.

prone adj. SUSCEPTIBLE, vulnerable, subject, open, liable, given, predisposed, likely, disposed, inclined, apt; at risk of.
—OPPOSITES: resistant, immune.

pronounce v. **1** SAY, enunciate, articulate, utter, voice, sound, vocalize, get one's tongue around. **2** ANNOUNCE, proclaim, declare, affirm, assert; judge, rule, decree.

pronounced adj. ☞ NOTICEABLE.
—OPPOSITES: slight.

proof n. EVIDENCE, verification, corroboration, authentication, confirmation, certification, documentation, validation, attestation, substantiation.
▸ adj. RESISTANT, immune, unaffected, invulnerable, impenetrable, impervious, repellent.

prop v. **1** LEAN, rest, stand, balance, steady. **2** HOLD UP, shore up, bolster up, buttress, support, brace, underpin.

propaganda n. INFORMATION, promotion, advertising, publicity, spin; disinformation, the big lie; info, hype, plugging; puff piece.

propel v. **1** MOVE, power, push, drive. **2** THROW, thrust, toss, fling, hurl, launch, pitch, project, send, shoot. **3** SPUR, drive, prompt, precipitate, catapult, motivate, force, impel.

propensity n. ☞ TENDENCY.

proper adj. **1** REAL, genuine, actual, true, bona fide. **2** RIGHT, correct, accepted, orthodox, conventional, established, official, formal, regular, acceptable, appropriate, de rigueur. **3** RESPECTABLE, decorous, seemly, decent, refined, ladylike, gentlemanly, genteel, polite, punctilious.
—OPPOSITES: fake, inappropriate, wrong, unconventional.

property *n.* **1** POSSESSIONS, belongings, things, effects, stuff, gear, chattels, movables, (worldly) goods; resources, assets, valuables, fortune, capital, riches, wealth. **2** BUILDING(S), premises, house(s), land, estates, realty, real estate. **3** QUALITY, attribute, characteristic, feature, power, trait, mark, hallmark.

prophecy *n.* PREDICTION, forecast, prognostication, prognosis, divination, augury.

prophesy *v.* PREDICT, foretell, forecast, foresee, forewarn of, prognosticate.

prophet, prophetess *n.* SEER, soothsayer, fortune teller, clairvoyant, diviner; oracle, augur, sibyl.

proponent *n.* ADVOCATE, champion, supporter, backer, promoter, protagonist, campaigner, booster, cheerleader.

proportion *n.* **1** PART, portion, amount, quantity, bit, piece, percentage, fraction, section, segment, share. **2** RATIO, distribution, relative amount/ number; relationship. **3** BALANCE, symmetry, harmony, correspondence, correlation, agreement. **4** SIZE, dimensions, magnitude, measurements; mass, volume, bulk; expanse, extent, width, breadth.

proposal *n.* PLAN, idea, scheme, project, program, manifesto, motion, proposition, suggestion, submission, trial balloon.

propose *v.* **1** PUT FORWARD, suggest, submit, advance, offer, present, move, come up with, lodge, table, nominate. **2** INTEND,

mean, plan, have in mind/view, resolve, aim, purpose, think of, aspire, want.
—OPPOSITES: withdraw.

prosecute *v.* TAKE TO COURT, bring/institute legal proceedings against, bring an action against, take legal action against, sue, try, impeach, bring to trial, put on trial, put in the dock, bring a suit against, indict, arraign.

prospect *n.* **1** LIKELIHOOD, hope, expectation, anticipation, (good/ poor) chance, odds, probability, possibility, promise; fear, danger. **2** POSSIBILITIES, potential, promise, expectations, outlook. **3** CANDIDATE, possibility. **4** ☞ VIEW 1.

prospective *adj.* POTENTIAL, possible, probable, likely, future, eventual, to-be, soon-to-be, in the making; intending, aspiring, would-be; forthcoming, approaching, coming, imminent.

prosper *v.* FLOURISH, thrive, do well, bloom, blossom, burgeon, progress, do all right for oneself, get ahead, get on (in the world), be successful; *informal* go places.
—OPPOSITES: fail, flounder.

prosperity *n.* SUCCESS, profitability, affluence, wealth, opulence, luxury, the good life, milk and honey, (good) fortune, ease, plenty, comfort, security, well-being.
—OPPOSITES: hardship, failure.

prostitute *n.* CALL GIRL, whore, hooker, sex worker, tart, moll, working girl, courtesan, member of the oldest profession, fille de joie, escort, hustler, chippy; ho, camp follower; gigolo, call boy;

dated streetwalker, lady/woman of the night, scarlet woman, cocotte, strumpet, harlot, trollop, woman of ill repute, wench.

prostrate *adj.* PRONE, lying flat, lying down, stretched out, spread-eagled, sprawling, horizontal, recumbent; *rare* procumbent.
—OPPOSITES: upright.
□**prostrate oneself** THROW ONESELF FLAT/DOWN, lie down, stretch oneself out, throw oneself at someone's feet.

protect *v.* KEEP SAFE, keep from harm, save, safeguard, preserve, defend, shield, cushion, insulate, hedge, shelter, screen, secure, fortify, guard, watch over, look after, take care of, keep; inoculate.
—OPPOSITES: expose, neglect, attack, harm.

protection *n.* **1** DEFENCE, security, shielding, preservation, conservation, safekeeping, safeguarding, safety, sanctuary, shelter, refuge, lee, immunity, insurance, indemnity.
2 SAFEKEEPING, care, charge, keeping, guidance, aegis, auspices, umbrella, guardianship, support, patronage, championship, providence.

protective *adj.* **1** PRESERVATIVE, protecting, safeguarding, shielding, defensive, safety, precautionary, preventive, preventative. **2** SOLICITOUS, caring, warm, paternal/maternal, fatherly/motherly, gallant, chivalrous; overprotective, possessive, jealous.

protest *n.* **1** OBJECTION, complaint, exception, disapproval, challenge, dissent, demurral, remonstration, fuss, outcry.
2 DEMONSTRATION, (protest) march, rally; sit-in, occupation; work-to-rule, industrial action, stoppage, strike, walkout, mutiny, picket, boycott; demo.
—OPPOSITES: support, approval.
▶ *v.* **1** EXPRESS OPPOSITION, object, dissent, take issue, make/take a stand, put up a fight, kick, take exception, complain, express disapproval, disagree, demur, remonstrate, make a fuss; cry out, speak out, rail, inveigh, fulminate; *informal* kick up a fuss/stink.
2 DEMONSTRATE, march, hold a rally, sit in, occupy somewhere; work to rule, take industrial action, stop work, strike, go on strike, walk out, mutiny, picket; boycott something. **3** INSIST ON, maintain, assert, affirm, announce, proclaim, declare, profess, contend, argue, claim, vow, swear (to), stress; *formal* aver.
—OPPOSITES: acquiesce, support, deny.

protocol *n.* ETIQUETTE, conventions, formalities, customs, rules of conduct, procedure, ritual, accepted behaviour, propriety, proprieties, one's Ps and Qs, decorum, good form; tradition, fashion, style, the done thing, the thing to do, punctilio.

prototype *n.* ORIGINAL, first example/model, master, mould, template, framework, mock-up, pattern, sample; DESIGN, guide, blueprint.

protracted *adj.* ☞ LONG¹.

protruding *adj.* STICKING OUT, protuberant, projecting, prominent, jutting, overhanging, beetling, proud, bulging.

proud *adj.* **1** PLEASED, glad, happy, delighted, joyful, overjoyed, thrilled, satisfied, gratified, content. **2** SELF-RESPECTING, dignified, noble, worthy; independent. **3** ARROGANT, conceited, vain, self-important, full of oneself, puffed up, jumped-up, smug, complacent, disdainful, condescending, scornful, supercilious, snobbish, imperious, pompous, overbearing, bumptious, haughty; *informal* big-headed, too big for one's britches/boots, high and mighty, stuck-up, uppity, snooty, highfalutin; *literary* vainglorious; *rare* hubristic.
—OPPOSITES: ashamed, shameful, humble, modest.

prove *v.* **1** SHOW (TO BE TRUE), demonstrate (the truth of), show beyond doubt, manifest, produce proof/evidence; witness to, give substance to, determine, substantiate, corroborate, verify, ratify, validate, authenticate, document, bear out, confirm; *formal* evince. **2** TURN OUT, be found, happen.
—OPPOSITES: disprove.
□ **prove oneself** DEMONSTRATE ONE'S ABILITIES/QUALITIES, show one's (true) mettle, show what one is made of.

proverb *n.* SAYING, adage, saw, maxim, axiom, motto, bon mot, aphorism, apophthegm, epigram, gnome, dictum, precept; words of wisdom.

proverbial *adj.* WELL-KNOWN, famous, famed, renowned, traditional, time-honoured, legendary; notorious, infamous.

provide *v.* **1** SUPPLY, give, issue, furnish, come up with, dispense, bestow, impart, produce, yield, bring forth, bear, deliver, donate, contribute, pledge, advance, spare, part with, allocate, distribute, allot, put up; *informal* fork out, lay out, ante up, pony up. **2** ☞ EQUIP 1. **3** FEED, nurture, nourish; SUPPORT, maintain, keep, sustain, provide sustenance for, fend for, finance, endow. **4** MAKE AVAILABLE, present, offer, afford, give, add, bring, yield, impart.
—OPPOSITES: refuse, withhold.

provided *conj.* IF, on condition that, providing (that), provided that, presuming (that), assuming (that), on the assumption that, as long as, given (that), with the provision/proviso that, with/on the understanding that, contingent on.

providential *adj.* OPPORTUNE, advantageous, favourable, auspicious, propitious, heaven-sent, welcome, golden, lucky, happy, fortunate, felicitous, timely, well-timed, seasonable, convenient, expedient.
—OPPOSITES: inopportune.

provincial *adj.* **1** REGIONAL, state, territorial, district; sectoral, zonal, cantonal. **2** NON-METROPOLITAN, small-town, non-urban, outlying, rural, country, rustic, backwoods, backwater; *informal* one-horse, hick, jerkwater, freshwater.
—OPPOSITES: national, metropolitan, cosmopolitan.

provisional *adj.* INTERIM, temporary, pro tem; transitional,

changeover, stopgap, short-term; deputy, stand-in, fill-in, acting, caretaker; subject to confirmation; pencilled in, working, tentative, contingent, makeshift.
—OPPOSITES: permanent, definite.

proviso *n.* CONDITION, stipulation, provision, clause, rider, qualification, restriction, caveat.

provocative *adj.* **1** INFLAMMATORY, incendiary, controversial, insulting, offensive, annoying, irritating, exasperating, infuriating, maddening, vexing, galling; aggravating, in-your-face. **2** ☞ SEXY 1.
—OPPOSITES: soothing, calming, modest.

provoke *v.* **1** AROUSE, produce, evoke, cause, give rise to, occasion, call forth, elicit, induce, excite, spark off, touch off, kindle, generate, engender, instigate, result in, lead to, bring on, precipitate, prompt, trigger; *literary* beget. **2** GOAD, spur, prick, sting, prod, egg on, incite, rouse, stir, move, stimulate, motivate, excite, inflame, work/fire up, impel.
—OPPOSITES: allay, deter, pacify, appease.

prowess *n.* SKILL, expertise, mastery, facility, ability, capability, capacity, savoir faire, talent, genius, adeptness, aptitude, dexterity, deftness, competence, accomplishment, proficiency, finesse; know-how.
—OPPOSITES: inability, ineptitude.

prowl *v.* MOVE STEALTHILY, slink, skulk, steal, nose, pussyfoot, sneak, stalk, creep, snoop.

prudent *adj.* WISE, well judged, sensible, politic, judicious, sagacious, sage, shrewd, advisable, well-advised, astute, canny, commonsensical, discerning, heads-up, intelligent, percipient, smart, sound.
—OPPOSITES: unwise, reckless.

prudish *adj.* PURITANICAL, priggish, prim, prim and proper, moralistic, pietistic, sententious, censorious, straitlaced, Victorian, old-maidish, fussy, stuffy, strict; goody-goody, starchy.
—OPPOSITES: permissive.

prune *v.* **1** CUT BACK, trim, thin, pinch back, clip, shear, pollard, top, dock. **2** CUT OFF, lop (off), chop off, clip, snip (off), nip off, dock.
—OPPOSITES: increase.

pry *v.* INQUIRE IMPERTINENTLY, be inquisitive, be curious, poke about/around, ferret (about/ around), spy, be a busybody; eavesdrop, listen in, tap someone's phone, intrude; *informal* stick/poke one's nose in/into, be nosy, nose, snoop.
—OPPOSITES: mind one's own business.

pseudo *adj.* BOGUS, sham, phony, artificial, mock, ersatz, quasi-, fake, false, spurious, deceptive, misleading, assumed, contrived, affected, insincere; *informal* pretend, put-on.
—OPPOSITES: genuine.

psych

□ **psych someone out**
☞ DISCONCERT. **psych oneself up**
NERVE ONESELF, steel oneself, brace oneself, summon one's courage, prepare oneself, gear oneself up,

urge oneself on, gird (up) one's loins.

psychological *adj.* MENTAL, emotional, intellectual, inner, cerebral, brain, rational, cognitive.
—OPPOSITES: physical.

pub *n.* ☞ BAR 4.

public *adj.* **1** STATE, national, federal, government; constitutional, civic, civil, official, social, municipal, community, communal, local; nationalized. **2** POPULAR, general, common, communal, collective, shared, joint, universal, widespread. **3** PROMINENT, well-known, important, leading, eminent, distinguished, notable, noteworthy, noted, celebrated, household, famous, famed, influential, major-league. **4** OPEN (TO THE PUBLIC), communal, accessible to all, available, free, unrestricted, community. **5** KNOWN, published, publicized, in circulation, exposed, overt, plain, obvious.
—OPPOSITES: private, obscure, unknown, restricted, secret.
▶ *n.* PEOPLE, citizens, subjects, general public, electors, electorate, voters, taxpayers, residents, inhabitants, citizenry, population, populace, community, society, country, nation, world; everyone.
□ **in public** PUBLICLY, in full view of people, openly, in the open, for all to see, undisguisedly, blatantly, flagrantly, brazenly, overtly.

publication *n.* BOOK, volume, title, work, tome, opus; newspaper, paper, magazine, periodical, newsletter, bulletin, journal, report; organ, booklet, chapbook, brochure, catalogue; daily, weekly, monthly, quarterly, annual; *informal* rag, mag, zine.

publicity *n.* PROMOTION, advertising, propaganda; hype, ballyhoo, puff, puffery, buildup, razzmatazz; plug.

publicize *v.* **1** MAKE KNOWN, make public, publish, announce, report, post, communicate, broadcast, issue, put out, distribute, spread, promulgate, disseminate, circulate, air; disclose, reveal, divulge, leak. **2** ADVERTISE, promote, build up, talk up, push, beat the drum for, boost; *informal* hype, flack, plug, puff (up).
—OPPOSITES: conceal, suppress.

publish *v.* **1** ISSUE, bring out, produce, print. **2** MAKE KNOWN, make public, publicize, announce, report, post, communicate, broadcast, issue, put out, distribute, spread, promulgate, disseminate, circulate, air; disclose, reveal, divulge, leak.

puff *n.* GUST, blast, flurry, rush, draft, waft, breeze, breath.
▶ *v.* BREATHE HEAVILY, pant, blow; gasp, fight for breath.
□ **puff up** BULGE, swell (up), stick out, distend, tumefy, balloon (up/out), expand, inflate, enlarge.

puffy *adj.* SWOLLEN, puffed up, distended, enlarged, inflated, dilated, bloated, engorged, bulging, tumid, tumescent.

pull *v.* **1** TUG, haul, drag, draw, tow, heave, lug, jerk, wrench; *informal* yank. **2** EXTRACT, take out, remove. **3** STRAIN, sprain, wrench, turn, tear; damage.

—OPPOSITES: push.

▸ *n.* **1** TUG, jerk, heave; yank.
2 ATTRACTION: draw, lure, allurement, enticement, magnetism, temptation, fascination, appeal. **3** INFLUENCE, sway, power, authority, say, prestige, standing, weight, leverage, muscle, teeth, clout.

□ **pull someone's leg** TEASE, fool, play a trick on, rag, pull the wool over someone's eyes; kid, rib, take for a ride, have on. **pull something off** ACHIEVE, fulfill, succeed in, accomplish, bring off, carry off, perform, discharge, complete, clinch, fix, effect, engineer. **pull through** GET BETTER, get well again, improve, recover, rally, come through, recuperate. **pull oneself together** REGAIN ONE'S COMPOSURE, recover, get a grip on oneself, get over it; *informal* snap out of it, get one's act together, buck up.

pulp *n.* MUSH, mash, paste, purée, pomace, pap, slop, slush, mulch; gloop, goo, glop.

▸ *v.* MASH, purée, cream, crush, press, liquidize, liquefy, sieve, squash, pound, macerate, grind, mince.

pulsate *v.* PALPITATE, pulse, throb, pump, undulate, surge, heave, rise and fall; beat, thump, drum, thrum; flutter, quiver.

pulse *n.* HEARTBEAT, pulsation, pulsing, throbbing, pounding.

pummel *v.* ☞ BEAT 1.

pump *v.* **1** FORCE, drive, push; suck, draw, tap, siphon, withdraw, expel, extract, bleed, drain.
2 INFLATE, aerate, blow up, fill up;

swell, enlarge, distend, expand, dilate, puff up.

punch *v.* HIT, strike, thump, jab, smash, welt, cuff, clip; batter, buffet, pound, pummel; sock, slug, bop, wallop, clobber, bash, whack, thwack, clout, lam, whomp, cold-cock, boff, bust; *literary* smite.

▸ *n.* BLOW, hit, knock, thump, box, jab, clip, uppercut, hook; *informal* sock, slug, boff, bust, bop, wallop, bash, whack, clout, belt, knuckle sandwich.

punctual *adj.* ON TIME, prompt, on schedule, in (good) time; *informal* on the dot.
—OPPOSITES: late.

puncture *n.* HOLE, perforation, rupture; cut, slit; leak.

▸ *v.* MAKE A HOLE IN, pierce, rupture, perforate, stab, cut, slit, prick, spike, stick, lance; deflate.

pundit *n.* EXPERT, authority, specialist, doyen(ne), master, guru, sage, savant, maven; *informal* buff, whiz.

pungent *adj.* STRONG, powerful, pervasive, penetrating; sharp, acid, sour, biting, bitter, tart, vinegary, tangy; highly flavoured, aromatic, spicy, piquant, peppery, hot.
—OPPOSITES: bland, mild.

punish *v.* **1** DISCIPLINE, bring someone to book, teach someone a lesson; tan someone's hide, come down on (like a ton of bricks). **2** PENALIZE, unfairly disadvantage, handicap, hurt, wrong, ill-use, maltreat.

punishment *n.* PENALTY, penance, sanction, sentence, one's just deserts; discipline, correction,

vengeance, justice, judgment;
informal comeuppance.
—RELATED: punitive, penal.

puny *adj.* UNDERSIZED,
undernourished, underfed,
stunted, slight, small, little; weak,
feeble, sickly, delicate, frail,
fragile; pint-sized.
—OPPOSITES: sturdy.

pupil *n.* STUDENT, scholar;
schoolchild, schoolboy, schoolgirl.

puppet *n.* **1** MARIONETTE; glove
puppet, hand puppet, finger
puppet. **2** PAWN, tool, instrument,
cat's paw, creature, dupe;
mouthpiece, minion, stooge.

purchase *v.* BUY, pay for, acquire,
obtain, pick up, snap up, take,
procure; invest in; *informal* get hold
of, score.
—OPPOSITES: sell.
▸ *n.* ACQUISITION, buy, investment,
order, bargain; shopping, goods.
—OPPOSITES: sale.

pure *adj.* **1** UNADULTERATED,
uncontaminated, unmixed,
undiluted, unalloyed, unblended;
sterling, solid, refined, one
hundred per cent; clarified, clear,
filtered; flawless, perfect, genuine,
real. **2** CLEAN, clear, fresh,
sparkling, unpolluted,
uncontaminated, untainted;
wholesome, natural, healthy;
sanitary, uninfected, disinfected,
germ-free, sterile, sterilized,
aseptic. **3** VIRTUOUS, moral, ethical,
good, righteous, saintly,
honourable, reputable,
wholesome, clean, honest,
upright, upstanding, exemplary,
irreproachable; chaste, virginal,
maidenly; decent, worthy, noble,
blameless, guiltless, spotless,

unsullied, uncorrupted, undefiled;
informal squeaky clean. **4** ☞ SHEER 1.
—OPPOSITES: adulterated,
polluted, immoral, practical.

purely *adv.* ENTIRELY, completely,
absolutely, wholly, exclusively,
solely, only, just, merely.

purge *v.* **1** CLEANSE, clear, purify,
wash, shrive, absolve. **2** REMOVE,
get rid of, expel, eject, exclude,
dismiss, sack, oust, eradicate,
clear out, weed out.

purify *v.* CLEAN, cleanse, refine,
decontaminate; filter, clarify,
clear, freshen, deodorize; sanitize,
disinfect, sterilize.

puritanical *adj.* MORALISTIC,
puritan, pietistic, straitlaced,
stuffy, prudish, prim, priggish;
narrow-minded, sententious,
censorious; austere, severe,
ascetic, abstemious; goody-goody.
—OPPOSITES: permissive.

purpose *n.* **1** ☞ INTENT.
2 INTENTION, aim, object, objective,
goal, end, plan, scheme, target;
ambition, aspiration. **3** FUNCTION,
role, use.
▢ **on purpose** DELIBERATELY,
intentionally, purposely, by
design, wilfully, knowingly,
consciously, of one's own volition;
expressly, specifically, especially,
specially.

purposely *adv.* ☞ ON PURPOSE at
PURPOSE.

pursue *v.* **1** FOLLOW, run after,
chase; hunt, stalk, track, trail,
shadow, hound, course; *informal*
tail. **2** STRIVE FOR, work towards,
seek, search for, aim at/for, aspire
to. **3** WOO, chase, run after, go
after; *dated* court, romance.
4 ENGAGE IN, be occupied in,

practise, follow, prosecute, conduct, ply, take up, undertake, carry on.
—OPPOSITES: avoid, shun.

push v. **1** SHOVE, thrust, propel; send, drive, force, prod, poke, nudge, elbow, shoulder; sweep, bundle, hustle, manhandle. **2** PRESS, depress, bear down on, hold down, squeeze; operate, activate.
—OPPOSITES: pull.
▶ n. **1** SHOVE, thrust, nudge, ram, bump, jolt, butt, prod, poke. **2** ADVANCE, drive, thrust, charge, attack, assault, onslaught, onrush, offensive, sortie, sally, incursion.
□ **push someone around** BULLY, domineer, ride roughshod over, trample on, bulldoze, browbeat, tyrannize, intimidate, threaten, victimize, pick on; *informal* lean on, boss around.

pushy *adj.* ASSERTIVE, self-assertive, overbearing, domineering, aggressive, forceful, forward, bold, bumptious, officious; thrusting, ambitious, overconfident, cocky; bossy.
—OPPOSITES: submissive.

put v. **1** PLACE, set (down), lay (down), deposit, position, settle; leave, plant; *informal* stick, dump, park, plonk, plunk, pop. **2** LAY, pin, place, fix; attribute to, impute to, assign to, allocate to, ascribe to. **3** SUBMIT, present, tender, offer, proffer, advance, suggest, propose. **4** EXPRESS, word, phrase, frame, formulate, render, convey, couch; state, say, utter.
□ **put something aside** SAVE, put by, set aside, deposit, reserve, store, stockpile, hoard, stow,

cache; *informal* salt away, squirrel away, stash away. **put something away 1** ☞ PUT SOMETHING ASIDE. **2** TIDY UP, put back, tidy away, replace, clear away. **put something back** REPLACE, return, restore, put away, tidy away. **put someone down** CRITICIZE, belittle, disparage, deprecate, denigrate, slight, humiliate, shame, crush, squash, deflate; *informal* show up, cut down to size. **put something down 1** WRITE DOWN, note down, jot down, take down, set down; list, record, register, log. **2** SUPPRESS, check, crush, quash, squash, quell, overthrow, stamp out, repress, subdue. **3** DESTROY, put to sleep, put out of its misery, put to death, kill, euthanize. **4** ATTRIBUTE, ascribe, chalk up, impute; blame on. **put something forward**. ☞ PUT 3. **put something off** POSTPONE, defer, delay, put back, adjourn, hold over, reschedule, shelve, table; *informal* put on ice, put on the back burner. **put something on 1** DRESS IN, don, pull on, throw on, slip into, change into; *informal* doll oneself up in. **2** ORGANIZE, stage, mount, present, produce. **3** FEIGN, fake, simulate, mimic, affect, assume. **put one over on** ☞ DECEIVE 1. **put someone out 1** ANNOY, anger, irritate, offend, affront, displease, irk, vex, pique, nettle, gall, upset; *informal* rile, miff, peeve. **2** INCONVENIENCE, trouble, bother, impose on, disoblige; *informal* put someone on the spot; *formal* discommode. **put something out 1** EXTINGUISH, quench, douse, smother; blow

out, snuff out, (*Nfld*) dout✤.
2 ISSUE, publish, release, bring
out, circulate, publicize, post. **put
someone up** ACCOMMODATE,
house, take in, lodge, quarter,
billet; give someone a roof over
their head. **put something up
1** BUILD, construct, erect, raise.
2 DISPLAY, pin up, stick up, hang
up, post. **3** PROVIDE, supply,
furnish, give, contribute, donate,
pledge, pay; *informal* fork out, cough
up, shell out, ante up, pony up.
put upon TAKE ADVANTAGE OF,
impose on, exploit, use, misuse;
informal walk all over. **put
someone up to something**
PERSUADE TO, encourage to, urge
to, egg on to, incite to, goad into.
put up with TOLERATE, take, stand
(for), accept, stomach, swallow,
endure, bear, support, take

something lying down; *informal*
abide, lump it; *formal* brook.
put-down *n.* SNUB, slight, affront,
rebuff, sneer, disparagement,
humiliation, barb, jibe, criticism;
dig.
putrid *adj.* DECOMPOSING, decaying,
rotting, rotten, bad, off, putrefied,
putrescent, rancid, mouldy; foul,
fetid, rank.
puzzle *v.* ☞ PERPLEX.
▶ *n.* ENIGMA, mystery, paradox,
conundrum, poser, riddle,
problem, quandary; stumper.
puzzling *adj.* BAFFLING,
perplexing, bewildering,
confusing, complicated, unclear,
mysterious, enigmatic,
ambiguous, obscure, abstruse,
unfathomable, incomprehensible,
impenetrable, cryptic.
—OPPOSITES: clear.

Qq

quail v. ☞ COWER.

quake v. **1** ☞ SHAKE v. 1.
2 TREMBLE, shake, quiver, shiver; blench, blanch, flinch, shrink, recoil, cower, cringe.

qualification n. **1** CERTIFICATE, diploma, degree, licence, document, warrant; eligibility, acceptability, adequacy; proficiency, skill, ability, capability, aptitude.
2 MODIFICATION, limitation, reservation, stipulation; alteration, amendment, revision, moderation, mitigation; condition, proviso, caveat.

qualified adj. CERTIFIED, certificated, chartered, licensed, professional; trained, fit, competent, accomplished, proficient, skilled, experienced, expert.

qualify v. **1** BE ELIGIBLE, meet the requirements; be entitled to, be permitted. **2** COUNT, be considered, be designated, be eligible. **3** BE CERTIFIED, be licensed; pass, graduate, make the grade, succeed; pass muster. **4** AUTHORIZE, empower, allow, permit, license; equip, prepare, train, educate, teach. **5** MODIFY, limit, restrict, make conditional; moderate, temper, modulate, mitigate.

quality n. **1** STANDARD, grade, class, calibre, condition, character, nature, form, rank, value, level; sort, type, kind, variety. **2** ☞ EXCELLENCE.
3 ☞ FEATURE 1.

qualm n. ☞ MISGIVING.

quantity n. **1** AMOUNT, total, aggregate, sum, quota, mass, weight, volume, bulk; quantum, proportion, portion, part. **2** ☞ LOT 1.

quarrel n. ARGUMENT, disagreement, squabble, fight, dispute, wrangle, clash, altercation, feud, contretemps, disputation, falling-out, war of words, shouting match; informal tiff, slanging match, run-in, hassle, blow-up, row, bust-up.
▶ v. ARGUE, fight, disagree, fall out; differ, be at odds; bicker, squabble, cross swords, lock horns, be at each other's throats.

quarrelsome adj.
☞ ARGUMENTATIVE.
—OPPOSITES: peaceable.

quash v. **1** CANCEL, reverse, rescind, repeal, revoke, retract, countermand, withdraw, overturn, overrule, veto, annul, nullify, invalidate, negate, void, throw out; Law vacate; formal abrogate. **2** PUT AN END TO, put a stop to, stamp out, crush, put down, check, curb, nip in the bud, squash, quell, subdue, suppress, extinguish, stifle; informal squelch,

put the kibosh on, deep-six.
—OPPOSITES: validate.

queasy *adj.* ☞ NAUSEOUS.

quell *v.* **1** PUT AN END TO, put a stop
to, end, crush, put down, check,
crack down on, curb, nip in the
bud, squash, quash, subdue,
suppress, overcome; *informal*
squelch. **2** CALM, soothe, pacify,
settle, quieten, quiet, silence,
allay, assuage, mitigate, moderate;
literary stay.

quench *v.* **1** SATISFY, slake, sate,
satiate, gratify, relieve, assuage,
take the edge off, indulge; lessen,
reduce, diminish, check, suppress,
extinguish, overcome.
2 ☞ EXTINGUISH 1.

quest *n.* **1** SEARCH, hunt;
pursuance of. **2** EXPEDITION,
journey, voyage, trek, travels,
odyssey, adventure, exploration,
search; crusade, mission,
pilgrimage.

question *n.* **1** INQUIRY, query;
interrogation. **2** DOUBT, dispute,
argument, debate, uncertainty,
dubiousness, reservation. **3** ISSUE,
matter, business, problem,
concern, topic, theme, case;
debate, argument, dispute,
controversy.
—RELATED: interrogative.
—OPPOSITES: answer, certainty.
▶ *v.* **1** INTERROGATE, cross-examine,
cross-question, quiz, catechize;
interview, debrief, examine, give
the third degree to; *informal* grill,
pump. **2** QUERY, call into question,
challenge, dispute, cast aspersions
on, doubt, suspect, have
suspicions about, have
reservations about.
☐ **beyond question**

1 ☞ UNDOUBTED. **2** ☞ UNDOUBTEDLY.
in question AT ISSUE, under
discussion, under consideration,
on the agenda, to be decided, for
debate, in dispute. **out of the
question** IMPOSSIBLE,
impracticable, unfeasible,
unworkable, inconceivable,
unimaginable, unrealizable,
unsuitable.

questionable *adj.*
1 CONTROVERSIAL, contentious,
doubtful, dubious, uncertain,
debatable, arguable; unverified,
unprovable, unresolved,
unconvincing, implausible,
improbable; borderline, marginal,
moot; *informal* iffy. **2** SUSPICIOUS,
suspect, dubious, irregular, odd,
strange, murky, dark, unsavoury,
disreputable; *informal* funny, fishy,
shady, iffy.
—OPPOSITES: indisputable, honest.

quibble *n.* CRITICISM, objection,
complaint, protest, argument,
exception, grumble, grouse, cavil;
informal niggle, moan, gripe, beef,
grouch.
▶ *v.* OBJECT TO, find fault with,
complain about, cavil at; split
hairs, chop logic; criticize, query,
fault, pick holes in; *informal* nitpick;
archaic pettifog.

quick *adj.* **1** ☞ FAST *adj.* 1. **2** HASTY,
hurried, cursory, perfunctory,
desultory, superficial, summary;
brief, short, fleeting, transient,
transitory, short-lived, lightning,
momentary, whirlwind, whistle
stop. **3** SUDDEN, instantaneous,
immediate, instant, abrupt,
precipitate.
—OPPOSITES: slow, long.

quicken v. **1** SPEED UP, accelerate, step up, hasten, hurry (up). **2** STIMULATE, excite, arouse, rouse, stir up, activate, galvanize, whet, inspire, kindle; invigorate, revive, revitalize.

quiet adj. **1** SILENT, still, hushed, noiseless, soundless. See also MUTE 1. **2** SOFT, low, muted, muffled, faint, indistinct, inaudible, hushed, whispered, suppressed. **3** PEACEFUL, sleepy, tranquil, calm, still, restful, undisturbed, untroubled; unfrequented. **4** ☞ SECRET adj. 1.
—OPPOSITES: loud, public.
▸ n. PEACEFULNESS, peace, restfulness, calm, tranquility, serenity; silence, quietness, stillness, still, quietude, hush, soundlessness.

quit v. **1** RESIGN FROM, leave, give up, hand in one's notice, stand down from, relinquish, vacate, walk out on, retire from; informal chuck, pack in; pack it in, call it quits, hang up one's skates✦. **2** GIVE UP, stop, cease, discontinue, drop, break off, abandon, abstain from, desist from, refrain from, avoid, forgo; informal pack (it) in, leave off.

quite adv. ☞ SIGNIFICANTLY.

quiver v. **1** TREMBLE, shake, shiver, quaver, quake, shudder. **2** FLUTTER, flap, beat, agitate, vibrate.
▸ n. TREMOR, tremble, shake, quaver, flutter, fluctuation, waver.

quota n. ALLOCATION, share, allowance, limit, ration, portion, dispensation, slice (of the cake); percentage, commission; proportion, fraction, bit, amount, quantity; informal cut, rake-off.

quotation n. CITATION, quote, excerpt, extract, passage, line, paragraph, verse, phrase; reference, allusion.

quote v. **1** RECITE, repeat, reproduce, retell, echo, parrot, iterate; take, extract. **2** CITE, mention, refer to, name, instance, specify, identify; relate, recount; allude to, point out, present, offer, advance.

Rr

race *n.* **1** CONTEST, competition, event, heat, trial(s). **2** COMPETITION, rivalry, contention; quest.
▶ *v.* **1** COMPETE, contend; run.
2 ☞ HURRY 1.

racism *n.* RACIAL DISCRIMINATION, racialism, racial prejudice, xenophobia, chauvinism, bigotry.

racist *n.* RACIAL BIGOT, racialist, xenophobe, chauvinist, supremacist.
▶ *adj.* (RACIALLY) DISCRIMINATORY, racialist, prejudiced, bigoted.

radiant *adj.* **1** SHINING, bright, illuminated, brilliant, gleaming, glowing, ablaze, luminous, luminescent, lustrous, incandescent, dazzling, shimmering, resplendent, fluorescent, phosphorescent, scintillating. **2** ☞ HAPPY 1.
—OPPOSITES: dark, gloomy.

radical *adj.* **1** THOROUGHGOING, thorough, complete, total, comprehensive, exhaustive, sweeping, far-reaching, wide-ranging, extensive, across the board, profound, major, stringent, rigorous. **2** FUNDAMENTAL, basic, essential, quintessential; structural, deep-seated, intrinsic, organic, constitutive.
3 REVOLUTIONARY, progressive, reformist, revisionist, progressivist; extreme, extremist, fanatical, militant, diehard, hard-core.
—OPPOSITES: superficial, minor, conservative.
▶ *n.* REVOLUTIONARY, progressive, reformer, revisionist; militant, zealot, extremist, fanatic, diehard; *informal* ultra.
—OPPOSITES: conservative.

raffle *n.* LOTTERY, lotto, (prize) draw, sweepstake, sweep(s).

rage *n.* **1** ☞ FURY 1. **2** CRAZE, passion, fashion, taste, trend, vogue, fad, enthusiasm, obsession, compulsion, fixation, fetish, mania, preoccupation; *informal* thing.
▶ *v.* **1** BE ANGRY, be furious, be enraged, be incensed, seethe, be beside oneself, rave, storm, fume, spit; *informal* be livid, be wild, foam at the mouth, have a fit, be steamed up. **2** PROTEST ABOUT, complain about, oppose, denounce; fulminate, storm, rail.

ragged *adj.* TATTERED, in tatters, torn, ripped, holey, in holes, moth-eaten, frayed, worn (out), falling to pieces, threadbare, scruffy, shabby; *informal* tatty.

raid *n.* **1** ATTACK, assault, descent, blitz, incursion, sortie, strike; onslaught, storming, charge, advance, foray, push, sally, thrust, offensive, invasion, blitzkrieg.
2 ☞ ROBBERY. **3** SWOOP, search;

informal bust, takedown.
▶ *v.* **1** ATTACK, assault, set upon, descend on, swoop on, blitz, assail, storm, rush. **2** ☞ ROB 1. **3** SEARCH, swoop on; *informal* bust.

rain *n.* **1** RAINFALL, precipitation, raindrops, wet weather; drizzle, shower, rainstorm, cloudburst, torrent, downpour, deluge, storm. **2** SHOWER, deluge, flood, torrent, avalanche, flurry; storm, hail.
—RELATED: pluvial.
▶ *v.* **1** POUR (DOWN), pelt down, tip down, teem down, beat down, lash down, sheet down, rain cats and dogs; fall, drizzle, spit, bucket down. **2** FALL, hail, drop, shower.

rainy *adj.* WET, showery, drizzly, damp, inclement.

raise *v.* **1** LIFT (UP), hold aloft, elevate, uplift, upraise, upthrust; hoist, haul up, hitch up, hoick up. **2** SET UPRIGHT, set vertical; sit up, stand up. **3** INCREASE, put up, push up, up, mark up, escalate, inflate; *informal* hike (up), jack up, bump up. **4** AMPLIFY, louden, magnify, intensify, boost, lift, increase, heighten, augment. **5** GET, obtain, acquire; accumulate, amass, collect, fetch, net, make. **6** RECRUIT, enlist, sign up, conscript, call up, mobilize, rally, assemble, draft. **7** BRING UP, air, ventilate; present, table, propose, submit, advance, suggest, moot, put forward. **8** GIVE RISE TO, occasion, cause, produce, engender, elicit, create, result in, lead to, prompt, awaken, arouse, induce, kindle, incite, stir up, trigger, spark off, provoke, instigate, foment, whip up; *literary* beget. **9** BRING UP, rear, nurture, look after, care for, provide for, mother, parent, tend, cherish; educate, train. **10** BREED, rear, nurture, keep, tend; grow, farm, cultivate, produce.
—OPPOSITES: lower, reduce.

rally *v.* **1** REGROUP, reassemble, re-form, reunite. **2** ☞ MUSTER. **3** GET TOGETHER, band together, assemble, join forces, unite, ally, collaborate, co-operate, pull together. **4** RECOVER, improve, get better, pick up, revive, bounce back, perk up, look up, turn a corner.
—OPPOSITES: disperse, disband, slump.
▶ *n.* **1** (MASS) MEETING, gathering, assembly; demonstration, (protest) march, protest; *informal* demo. **2** RECOVERY, upturn, improvement, comeback, resurgence.
—OPPOSITES: slump.

rambling *adj.* **1** ☞ LONG-WINDED. **2** WINDING, twisting, twisty, tortuous, labyrinthine; sprawling.
—OPPOSITES: concise.

rambunctious *adj.*
☞ DISORDERLY 2.

rampage *v.* RIOT, run riot, go on the rampage, run amok, go berserk; storm, charge, tear.

rampant *adj.* **1** UNCONTROLLED, unrestrained, unchecked, unbridled, widespread; out of control, out of hand, rife. **2** ☞ LUSH.
—OPPOSITES: controlled.

random *adj.* UNSYSTEMATIC, unmethodical, arbitrary, unplanned, undirected, casual, indiscriminate, non-specific, haphazard, stray, erratic; chance, accidental.

—OPPOSITES: systematic.

□ **at random** UNSYSTEMATICALLY, arbitrarily, randomly, unmethodically, haphazardly.

rank¹ *n.* **1** POSITION, level, grade, echelon; class, status, standing; *dated* station. **2** HIGH STANDING, blue blood, high birth, nobility, aristocracy; eminence, distinction, prestige; prominence, influence, consequence, power. **3** ROW, line, file, column, string, train, procession.

▶ *v.* **1** ☞ CLASSIFY. **2** PRIORITIZE, order, organize, arrange, list; triage.

□ **the rank and file 1** OTHER RANKS, soldiers, NCOs, lower ranks, enlisted personnel; men, troops. **2** THE (COMMON) PEOPLE, the proletariat, the masses, the populace, the commonality, the third estate, the plebeians; the hoi polloi, the rabble, the riff-raff, the great unwashed; *informal* the proles, the plebs.

rank² *adj.* **1** ☞ LUSH. **2** OFFENSIVE, unpleasant, nasty, revolting, sickening, obnoxious, noxious; foul, fetid, smelly, stinking, reeking, high, off, rancid, putrid, malodorous; humming; *literary* noisome. **3** DOWNRIGHT, utter, outright, out-and-out, absolute, complete, sheer, arrant, thoroughgoing, unqualified, unmitigated, positive, perfect, patent, pure, total.

—OPPOSITES: sparse, pleasant.

rankle *v.* CAUSE RESENTMENT, annoy, upset, anger, irritate, offend, affront, displease,

provoke, irk, vex, pique, nettle, gall; *informal* rile, miff, peeve, aggravate, hack off, tick off.

ransack *v.* PLUNDER, pillage, raid, rob, loot, sack, strip, despoil; ravage, devastate, turn upside down; scour, rifle, comb, search.

rapid *adj.* QUICK, fast, swift, speedy, expeditious, express, brisk; lightning, meteoric, whirlwind; sudden, instantaneous, instant, immediate; hurried, hasty, precipitate, breakneck, dizzying, headlong; *literary* fleet.

—OPPOSITES: slow.

▶ *n.* fast water, chute✦, whitewater, riffle, (*Nfld & NS*) rattle✦; swift✦.

rapport *n.* AFFINITY, close relationship, (mutual) understanding, bond, empathy, sympathy, accord.

rapture *n.* ☞ JOY.

rare *adj.* **1** INFREQUENT, scarce, sparse, few and far between, thin on the ground, like gold dust; occasional, limited, odd, isolated, unaccustomed, unwonted. **2** UNUSUAL, recherché, uncommon, unfamiliar, atypical, singular. **3** ☞ EXTRAORDINARY.

—OPPOSITES: common, commonplace.

rascal *n.* SCALAWAG, imp, monkey, mischief-maker, wretch; *informal* scamp, tyke, horror, monster, varmint; *archaic* rapscallion.

rash *adj.* RECKLESS, impulsive, impetuous, hasty, foolhardy, incautious, precipitate; careless, heedless, thoughtless, imprudent, foolish; ill-advised, injudicious, ill-judged, misguided, hare-brained, trigger-happy, bullheaded, devil-

may-care, harum-scarum, headstrong, hotheaded, hurried, ill-considered, impromptu, overhasty, precipitous, rushed, spontaneous, spur-of-the-moment; audacious, daredevil, irresponsible, kamikaze, madcap, over-adventurous, unheeding, unwise; *literary* temerarious.
—OPPOSITES: prudent.

rate *n.* **1** PERCENTAGE, ratio, proportion; scale, standard, level. **2** CHARGE, price, cost, tariff, fare, levy, toll; fee, remuneration, payment, wage, allowance. **3** SPEED, pace, tempo, velocity, momentum.
▶ *v.* **1** ASSESS, evaluate, appraise, judge, estimate, calculate, gauge, measure, adjudge; grade, rank, classify, categorize. **2** CONSIDER, judge, reckon, think, hold, deem, find; regard as, look on as, count as. **3** MERIT, deserve, warrant, be worthy of, be deserving of.

rather *adv.* **1** SOONER, by preference, preferably, by choice. **2** QUITE, a bit, a little, fairly, slightly, somewhat, relatively, to some degree, comparatively; *informal* pretty, sort of, kind of, kinda. **3** MORE PRECISELY, to be precise, to be exact, strictly speaking. **4** MORE; as opposed to, instead of. **5** ON THE CONTRARY, au contraire, instead.

ratify *v.* CONFIRM, approve, sanction, endorse, agree to, accept, uphold, authorize, formalize, validate, recognize; sign.
—OPPOSITES: reject.

ratio *n.* PROPORTION, comparative number, correlation, relationship,

correspondence; percentage, fraction, quotient.

ration *n.* ALLOWANCE, allocation, quota, quantum, share, portion, helping; amount, quantity, measure, proportion, percentage.
▶ *v.* CONTROL, limit, restrict; conserve.

rational *adj.* **1** LOGICAL, reasoned, sensible, reasonable, cogent, intelligent, judicious, shrewd, common-sense, commonsensical, sound, prudent; down-to-earth, practical, pragmatic. **2** SANE, compos mentis, in one's right mind, of sound mind; normal, balanced, lucid, coherent, able to think clearly, clear-headed, in possession of one's faculties, sensible, sober; *informal* all there. **3** INTELLIGENT, thinking, reasoning; cerebral, logical, analytical; *formal* ratiocinative.
—OPPOSITES: illogical, insane.

rationalize *v.* **1** JUSTIFY, explain (away), account for, defend, vindicate, excuse. **2** STREAMLINE, reorganize, modernize, update; trim, hone, simplify, downsize, prune.

rattle *v.* **1** CLATTER, patter; clink, clunk. **2** JINGLE, jangle, clink, tinkle. **3** JOLT, bump, bounce, jounce, shake, judder.
4 ☞ DISCONCERT.
▶ *n.* CLATTER, clank, clink, clang; jingle, jangle.

raucous *adj.* HARSH, strident, screeching, piercing, shrill, grating, discordant, dissonant; noisy, loud, cacophonous.
—OPPOSITES: soft, quiet.

ravage *v.* LAY WASTE, devastate, ruin, destroy, wreak havoc on, leave desolate; pillage, plunder, despoil, ransack, sack, loot, rape.

rave v. **1** TALK WILDLY, babble, jabber, talk incoherently. **2** RANT (AND RAVE), rage, lose one's temper, storm, fulminate, fume; shout, roar, thunder, bellow; *informal* fly off the handle, blow one's top, hit the roof, flip one's wig. **3** PRAISE ENTHUSIASTICALLY, go into raptures about/over, wax lyrical about, sing the praises of, rhapsodize over, enthuse about/over, acclaim, eulogize, extol; *informal* ballyhoo; *formal* laud; *archaic* panegyrize.
—OPPOSITES: criticize.
▶ *n.* (*informal*) ENTHUSIASTIC/LAVISH PRAISE, a rapturous reception, tribute, plaudits, acclaim.
—OPPOSITES: criticism.

raw adj. **1** UNCOOKED, fresh. **2** UNPROCESSED, untreated, unrefined, crude, natural; unedited, undigested, unprepared. **3** ☞ INEXPERIENCED. **4** SORE, red, painful, tender; abraded, chafed; *Medicine* excoriated. **5** BLEAK, cold, chilly, bone-chilling, freezing, icy, icy-cold, wintry, bitter, biting; *informal* nippy. **6** STRONG, intense, passionate, fervent, powerful, violent; undisguised, unconcealed, unrestrained, uninhibited. **7** REALISTIC, unembellished, unvarnished, brutal, harsh, gritty.
—OPPOSITES: cooked, processed.
□ **in the raw** ☞ NAKED.

ray *n.* **1** BEAM, shaft, streak, stream. **2** GLIMMER, flicker, spark, hint, suggestion, sign.

reach v. **1** STRETCH OUT, hold out, extend, outstretch, thrust out, stick out. **2** PASS, hand, give, let

someone have. **3** ARRIVE AT, get to, come to; end up at; *informal* make. **4** ATTAIN, get to; rise to, climb to; fall to, sink to, drop to; *informal* hit. **5** ACHIEVE, attain, work out, draw up, put together, negotiate, thrash out, hammer out. **6** GET IN TOUCH WITH, contact, get through to, get, speak to; *informal* get hold of. **7** INFLUENCE, sway, get (through) to, make an impression on, have an impact on.
▶ *n.* **1** GRASP, range. **2** CAPABILITIES, capacity. **3** JURISDICTION, authority, influence; scope, range, compass, ambit.

react v. **1** BEHAVE, act, take it, conduct oneself; respond, reply, answer. **2** REBEL AGAINST, oppose, rise up against.

reactionary adj. RIGHT-WING, conservative, rightist, traditionalist, conventional, redneck, unprogressive.
—OPPOSITES: progressive.
▶ *n.* RIGHT WINGER, conservative, rightist, traditionalist, dinosaur.
—OPPOSITES: radical.

readable adj. **1** LEGIBLE, easy to read, decipherable, clear, intelligible, comprehensible, reader-friendly. **2** ENJOYABLE, entertaining, interesting, absorbing, gripping, enthralling, engrossing, stimulating; *informal* unputdownable.
—OPPOSITES: illegible.

readily adv. **1** ☞ WILLINGLY. **2** EASILY, with ease, without difficulty.
—OPPOSITES: reluctantly.

ready adj. **1** PREPARED, (all) set, organized, primed; *informal* fit, psyched up, geared up.

2 COMPLETED, finished, prepared, organized, done, arranged, fixed, in readiness. **3** WILLING, prepared, pleased, inclined, disposed, predisposed; eager, keen, happy, glad; *informal* game. **4** ABOUT TO, on the point of, on the verge of, close to, liable to, likely to. **5** (EASILY) AVAILABLE, accessible; handy, close/near at hand, to/on hand, convenient, within reach, at the ready, near, at one's fingertips. **6** PROMPT, quick, swift, speedy, fast, immediate, unhesitating; clever, sharp, astute, shrewd, keen, perceptive, discerning.
▶ *v.* PREPARE, get/make ready, organize; gear oneself up; *informal* psych oneself up.

real *adj.* **1** ACTUAL, non-fictional, factual, real-life; historical; material, physical, tangible, concrete, palpable. **2** GENUINE, authentic, bona fide; *informal* kosher, honest-to-goodness/God. **3** TRUE, actual. **4** SINCERE, genuine, true, unfeigned, heartfelt, unaffected. **5** COMPLETE, utter, thorough, absolute, total, prize, perfect.
—OPPOSITES: imaginary, imitation.

realistic *adj.* **1** PRACTICAL, pragmatic, matter-of-fact, down-to-earth, sensible, commonsensical; rational, reasonable, level-headed, clear-sighted, businesslike; *informal* having both/one's feet on the ground, hard-nosed, no-nonsense. **2** ACHIEVABLE, attainable, feasible, practicable, viable, reasonable, sensible, workable; *informal* doable. **3** TRUE (TO LIFE), lifelike, truthful, faithful, unidealized, real-life,

kitchen-sink, naturalistic, graphic, detailed, exact, natural, precise, representational, vivid.
—OPPOSITES: idealistic, impracticable.

reality *n.* **1** THE REAL WORLD, real life, actuality; truth; physical existence. **2** FACT, actuality, truth. **3** VERISIMILITUDE, authenticity, realism, fidelity, faithfulness.
—OPPOSITES: fantasy.

realize *v.* **1** REGISTER, perceive, discern, be/become aware of (the fact that), be/become conscious of (the fact that), notice; understand, grasp, comprehend, see, recognize, work out, fathom, apprehend; *informal* latch on to, cotton on to, savvy, figure out, get (the message); twig, suss; *formal* be/become cognizant of. **2** FULFILL, achieve, accomplish, make a reality, make happen, bring to fruition, bring about/off, carry out/through; *formal* effectuate. **3** MAKE, clear, gain, earn, return, produce. **4** BE SOLD FOR, fetch, go for, make, net.

reap *v.* **1** HARVEST, garner, gather in, bring in. **2** RECEIVE, obtain, get, acquire, secure, realize.

rear[1] *v.* **1** BRING UP, raise, care for, look after, nurture, parent, provide for; educate. **2** BREED, raise, keep, farm, ranch. **3** GROW, cultivate. **4** RAISE, lift (up), hold up, uplift. **5** RISE (UP), tower, soar, loom.

rear[2] *n.* **1** BACK (PART), hind part, back end; *Nautical* stern. **2** (TAIL) END, rear end, back end, tail, tag end. **3** ☞ BUTTOCKS.
—OPPOSITES: front.
▶ *adj.* BACK, end, rearmost; hind,

hinder, hindmost; *technical* posterior.

reason *n.* **1** CAUSE, ground(s), basis, rationale; motive, motivation, purpose, point, aim, intention, objective, goal; explanation, justification, argument, defence, vindication, excuse, pretext. **2** RATIONALITY, logic, logical thought, reasoning, cognition; *formal* ratiocination. **3** SANITY, mind, mental faculties; senses, wits; *informal* marbles. **4** GOOD SENSE, good judgment, common sense, wisdom, sagacity, reasonableness.
▸ *v.* **1** THINK RATIONALLY, think logically, use one's common sense, use one's head/brain; *formal* cogitate, ratiocinate. **2** CALCULATE, come to the conclusion, conclude, reckon, think, judge, deduce, infer, surmise; *informal* figure. **3** TALK ROUND, bring round, win round, persuade, prevail on, convince, make someone see the light.
□ **reason something out** WORK OUT, think through, make sense of, get to the bottom of, puzzle out; *informal* figure out. **with reason** JUSTIFIABLY, justly, legitimately, rightly, reasonably.

reasonable *adj.* **1** SENSIBLE, rational, logical, fair, fair-minded, just, equitable; intelligent, wise, level-headed, practical, realistic; sound, (well) reasoned, valid, commonsensical; tenable, plausible, credible, believable. **2** WITHIN REASON, practicable, sensible; appropriate, suitable. **3** FAIRLY GOOD, acceptable, satisfactory, average, adequate,

fair, all right, tolerable, passable; *informal* OK. **4** ☞ INEXPENSIVE.

reasoned *adj.* ☞ LOGICAL 1.

reassure *v.* PUT/SET SOMEONE'S MIND AT REST, put someone at ease, encourage, inspirit, hearten, buoy up, cheer up; comfort, soothe.
—OPPOSITES: alarm.

rebel *n.* **1** REVOLUTIONARY, insurgent, mutineer, insurrectionist, guerrilla, terrorist, freedom fighter, agitator, anarchist, renegade, subversive. **2** NONCONFORMIST, dissenter, dissident, iconoclast, maverick.
▸ *v.* **1** REVOLT, mutiny, riot, rise up, take up arms, stage/mount a rebellion, be insubordinate. **2** RECOIL, show/feel repugnance. **3** DEFY, disobey, refuse to obey, kick against, challenge, oppose, resist.
—OPPOSITES: obey.

rebellion *n.* **1** UPRISING, revolt, insurrection, mutiny, revolution, insurgence, insurgency; rioting, riot, disorder, unrest. **2** DEFIANCE, disobedience, rebelliousness, insubordination, subversion, subversiveness, resistance.

rebellious *adj.* **1** REBEL, insurgent, mutinous, mutinying, rebelling, rioting, riotous, insurrectionary, insurrectionist, revolutionary. **2** ☞ DISOBEDIENT.

rebound *v.* **1** BOUNCE (BACK), spring back, ricochet, boomerang, carom. **2** RECOVER, rally, pick up, make a recovery. **3** BACKFIRE, boomerang, have unwelcome repercussions; come back to haunt; *archaic* redound on.

rebuke *v. & n.* ☞ REPRIMAND.
—OPPOSITES: praise.

recall v. **1** ☞ REMEMBER 1. **2** BRING TO MIND, call to mind, put one in mind of, call up, conjure up, evoke.
—OPPOSITES: forget.

receive v. **1** BE GIVEN, be presented with, be awarded, collect, garner; get, obtain, gain, acquire; win, be paid, earn, gross, net. **2** BE SENT, be in receipt of, accept (delivery of). **3** BE TOLD, be informed of, be notified of, hear, discover, find out (about), learn; *informal* get wind of. **4** HEAR, listen to; respond to, react to.
5 EXPERIENCE, sustain, undergo, meet with; suffer, bear. **6** GREET, welcome, say hello to.
—OPPOSITES: give, send.

recent adj. **1** NEW, the latest, current, fresh, modern, contemporary, up-to-date, up-to-the-minute. **2** NOT LONG PAST, occurring recently, just gone.
—OPPOSITES: old.

receptive adj. OPEN-MINDED, responsive, amenable, well-disposed, flexible, approachable, accessible.
—OPPOSITES: unresponsive.

recession n. ECONOMIC DECLINE, downturn, depression, slump, slowdown.
—OPPOSITES: boom.

reciprocal adj. **1** GIVEN/FELT IN RETURN, requited, reciprocated. **2** MUTUAL, common, shared, joint, corresponding, complementary.

recite v. **1** REPEAT FROM MEMORY, say aloud, declaim, quote, deliver, render. **2** GIVE A RECITATION, say a poem. **3** ENUMERATE, list, detail, reel off, rhyme off♣; recount,

relate, describe, narrate, give an account of, recapitulate, repeat.

reckless adj. ☞ RASH.
—OPPOSITES: careful.

reckon v. **1** ☞ CALCULATE 1.
2 INCLUDE, count, consider to be, regard as, look on as. **3** (*informal*) BELIEVE, think, be of the opinion/view, be convinced, dare say, imagine, guess, suppose, consider, figure. **4** REGARD AS, consider, judge, hold to be, think of as; deem, rate, gauge, count.
5 EXPECT, anticipate, hope to, be looking to; count on, rely on, depend on, bank on, figure on.
☐ **to be reckoned with** IMPORTANT, of considerable importance, significant; influential, estimable, powerful, strong, potent, formidable, redoubtable. **reckon with 1** DEAL WITH, contend with, face (up to).
2 TAKE INTO ACCOUNT, take into consideration, bargain for/on, anticipate, foresee, be prepared for, consider.

reckoning n. **1** CALCULATION, estimation, count, computation, working out, summation, addition. **2** OPINION, view, judgment, evaluation, estimate, estimation. **3** RETRIBUTION, fate, doom, nemesis, punishment.

recognize v. **1** IDENTIFY, place, know, put a name to; remember, recall, recollect; know by sight.
2 ACKNOWLEDGE, accept, admit; realize, be aware of, be conscious of, perceive, discern, appreciate; *formal* be cognizant of. **3** OFFICIALLY APPROVE, certify, accredit, endorse, sanction, validate. **4** PAY TRIBUTE TO, show appreciation of,

appreciate, be grateful for, acclaim, commend.

recommend *v.* **1** ADVOCATE, endorse, commend, suggest, put forward, propose, nominate, put up; speak favourably of, speak well of, put in a good word for, vouch for; *informal* plug. **2** ADVISE, counsel, urge, exhort, enjoin, prescribe, argue for, back, support; suggest, advocate, propose.

recommendation *n.* **1** ☞ ADVICE. **2** COMMENDATION, endorsement, good word, favourable mention, testimonial; suggestion, tip; *informal* plug.

reconcile *v.* **1** REUNITE, bring (back) together (again), restore friendly relations between, make peace between; pacify, appease, placate, mollify; *formal* conciliate. **2** SETTLE ONE'S DIFFERENCES, make (one's) peace, (kiss and) make up, bury the hatchet, declare a truce. **3** MAKE COMPATIBLE, harmonize, square, make congruent, balance. **4** (COME TO) ACCEPT, resign oneself to, come to terms with, learn to live with, get used to.
—OPPOSITES: estrange, quarrel.

reconsider *v.* RETHINK, review, revise, re-examine, re-evaluate, reassess, reappraise; change, alter, modify; have second thoughts, change one's mind.

record *n.* **1** ACCOUNT(S), document(s), documentation, data, file(s), dossier(s), evidence, report(s); annal(s), archive(s), chronicle(s); minutes, transactions, proceedings, transcript(s); certificate(s), instrument(s), deed(s); register,

log, logbook; *Law* muniment(s). **2** PREVIOUS CONDUCT/PERFORMANCE, track record, (life) history, reputation. **3** REMINDER, memorial, souvenir, memento, remembrance, testament.
▶ *adj.* RECORD-BREAKING, best ever, unsurpassed, unparalleled, unequalled, second to none.
▶ *v.* **1** WRITE DOWN, put in writing, take down, note, make a note of, jot down, put down on paper; document, put on record, enter, minute, register, log, report, chronicle; list, catalogue. **2** INDICATE, register, show, display.
☐ **off the record 1** UNOFFICIAL, confidential, in (strict) confidence, not to be made public. **2** UNOFFICIALLY, privately, in (strict) confidence, confidentially, between ourselves.

recover *v.* **1** RECUPERATE, get better, convalesce, regain one's strength, get stronger, get back on one's feet; be on the mend, make a recovery, be on the road to recovery, pick up, rally, respond to treatment, improve, heal, pull through, bounce back, rebound, make a comeback. **2** RETRIEVE, regain (possession of), get back, recoup, reclaim, repossess, redeem, recuperate, find (again), track down. **3** SALVAGE, save, rescue, retrieve.
—OPPOSITES: deteriorate.

recovery *n.* **1** RECUPERATION, convalescence. **2** IMPROVEMENT, rallying, picking up, upturn, upswing. **3** RETRIEVAL, regaining, repossession, getting back, reclamation, recouping, redemption, recuperation.

—OPPOSITES: relapse, deterioration.

recreation *n.* **1** PLEASURE, leisure, relaxation, fun, enjoyment, entertainment, amusement; play, sport; *informal* R and R, rec; *archaic* disport. **2** ☞ PASTIME.
—OPPOSITES: work.

recruit *v.* **1** ENLIST, call up, conscript, draft, muster in; *archaic* levy. **2** ☞ MUSTER. **3** ☞ HIRE.
—OPPOSITES: disband, dismiss.
▶ *n.* **1** CONSCRIPT, new soldier; *US* draftee, yardbird. **2** NEW MEMBER, new entrant, newcomer, initiate, beginner, novice, tenderfoot, hire; *informal* rookie, newbie, greenhorn.

rectify *v.* CORRECT, (put) right, put to rights, sort out, deal with, amend, remedy, repair, fix, make good, resolve, settle; *informal* patch up.

recuperate *v.* **1** ☞ RECOVER 1. **2** ☞ REGAIN.

recur *v.* HAPPEN AGAIN, reoccur, occur again, repeat (itself); come back (again), return, reappear, appear again.

recurrent *adj.* REPEATED, recurring, repetitive, periodic, cyclical, seasonal, perennial, regular, frequent; intermittent, sporadic, spasmodic.

recycle *v.* REUSE, reprocess, reclaim, recover; salvage, save.

red *adj.* **1** scarlet, vermilion, crimson, ruby, cherry, cerise, cardinal, carmine, wine, blood-red; coral, cochineal, rose; brick-red, maroon, rusty, rufous; reddish; *literary* damask, vermeil, sanguine. **2** FLUSHED, blushing, beet red, reddish, crimson, pink, pinkish, florid, rubicund; ruddy, rosy, glowing; burning, feverish; *literary* rubescent; *archaic* sanguine. **3** reddish, auburn, titian, carroty, ginger, sandy, strawberry blond.

reduce *v.* **1** LESSEN, make smaller, lower, bring down, decrease, diminish, minimize; shrink, narrow, contract, shorten; axe, cut (back/down), make cutbacks in, trim, curtail, slim (down), prune; *informal* chop. **2** DISCOUNT, mark down, lower the price of, cut (in price), make cheaper, put on sale; *informal* slash, knock down.
—OPPOSITES: increase, put up.

reduction *n.* **1** LESSENING, lowering, decrease, diminution, fade-out. **2** CUTBACK, cut, downsizing, scaling down, trimming, pruning, axing, chopping. **3** EASING, lightening, moderation, alleviation. **4** DISCOUNT, markdown, deduction, (price) cut.

redundancy *n.* PLEONASM, repetition, reiteration, tautology, superfluity, duplication.

redundant *adj.* ☞ UNNECESSARY.

reel *v.* **1** ☞ STAGGER 1. **2** BE SHAKEN, be stunned, be in shock, be shocked, be taken aback, be staggered, be aghast, be upset. **3** GO ROUND (AND ROUND), whirl, spin, revolve, swirl, twirl, turn, swim.

refer *v.* **1** MENTION, make reference to, allude to, touch on, speak of/about, talk of/about, write about, comment on, deal with, point out, call attention to. **2** PASS, hand on/over, send on, transfer, remit, entrust, assign. **3** ☞ APPLY 2. **4** DENOTE, describe, indicate,

mean, signify, designate.
5 CONSULT, turn to, look at, have
recourse to.

reference *n.* **1** MENTION OF,
allusion to, comment on, remark
about. **2** SOURCE, citation,
authority, credit; bibliographical
data. **3** REFERRAL, transfer,
remission. **4** TESTIMONIAL,
character reference,
recommendation; credentials.
☐ **with reference to**
☞ REGARDING.

refined *adj.* **1** PURIFIED, processed,
treated. **2** CULTIVATED, cultured,
polished, stylish, elegant,
sophisticated, urbane; polite,
gracious, well-mannered, well-
bred, gentlemanly, ladylike,
genteel. **3** DISCRIMINATING,
discerning, fastidious, exquisite,
impeccable, fine.
—OPPOSITES: crude, coarse.

refinement *n.* **1** PURIFICATION,
refining, processing, treatment,
treating. **2** IMPROVEMENT, polishing,
honing, fine-tuning, touching up,
finishing off, revision, editing,
reworking. **3** STYLE, elegance,
finesse, polish, sophistication,
urbanity; politeness, grace,
graciousness, good manners, good
breeding, gentility; cultivation,
taste, discrimination.

reflect *v.* **1** SEND BACK, throw
back, cast back. **2** ☞ INDICATE 1.
3 THINK ABOUT, give thought to,
consider, give consideration to,
review, mull over, contemplate,
cogitate about/on, meditate on,
muse on, brood on/over, turn over
in one's mind; *archaic* pore on.
☐ **reflect badly on** ☞ DISCREDIT 1.

reflection *n.* **1** SENDING BACK,
throwing back, casting back.
2 (MIRROR) IMAGE, likeness.
3 INDICATION, display,
demonstration, manifestation;
expression, evidence. **4** SLUR,
aspersion, imputation, reproach,
shame, criticism. **5** ☞ THOUGHT 2.
6 OPINION, thought, view, belief,
feeling, idea, impression,
conclusion, assessment; comment,
observation, remark.

reflex *adj.* ☞ INSTINCTIVE.
—OPPOSITES: conscious.

reform *v.* **1** IMPROVE, (make)
better, ameliorate, refine; alter,
make alterations to, change,
adjust, make adjustments to,
adapt, amend, revise, reshape,
refashion, redesign, restyle,
revamp, rebuild, reconstruct,
remodel, reorganize. **2** MEND ONE'S
WAYS, change for the better, turn
over a new leaf, improve.
▸ *n.* IMPROVEMENT, amelioration,
refinement; alteration, change,
adaptation, amendment, revision,
reshaping, refashioning,
redesigning, restyling, revamp,
revamping, renovation,
rebuilding, reconstruction,
remodelling, reorganizing,
reorganization.

refrain *v.* ☞ ABSTAIN.

refresh *v.* **1** REINVIGORATE,
revitalize, revive, restore, fortify,
enliven, perk up, stimulate,
freshen, energize, exhilarate,
reanimate, wake up, revivify,
inspirit; blow away the cobwebs;
informal buck up, pep up. **2** JOG,
stimulate, prompt, prod.
—OPPOSITES: weary.

refreshing *adj.* **1** INVIGORATING, revitalizing, reviving, restoring, restorative, bracing, fortifying, enlivening, inspiriting, stimulating, energizing, exhilarating; FRESH, brisk. **2** WELCOME, stimulating, fresh, imaginative, innovative, innovatory.

refuge *n.* **1** SHELTER, protection, safety, security, asylum, sanctuary. **2** SANCTUARY, shelter, place of safety, (safe) haven, sanctum; retreat, bolthole, hiding place, hideaway, hideout.

refuse¹ *v.* **1** DECLINE, turn down, say no to; reject, spurn, rebuff, dismiss; send one's regrets; *informal* pass up. **2** WITHHOLD, not grant, deny.
—OPPOSITES: accept, grant.

refuse² *n.* ☞ GARBAGE 1.

refute *v.* **1** ☞ DISPROVE. **2** DENY, reject, repudiate, rebut; contradict; *formal* gainsay.

regain *v.* RECOVER, get back, win back, recoup, retrieve, reclaim, repossess; take back, retake, recapture, reconquer.

regard *v.* **1** CONSIDER, look on, view, see, think of, judge, deem, estimate, assess, reckon, adjudge, rate, gauge. **2** ☞ CONTEMPLATE 1.
▶ *n.* **1** CONSIDERATION, care, concern, thought, notice, heed, attention. **2** ☞ ESTEEM. **3** (FIXED) LOOK, gaze, stare; observation, contemplation, study, scrutiny. **4** RESPECT, aspect, point, item, particular, detail, specific; matter, issue, topic, question.
☐ **with regard to.** ☞ REGARDING.

regarding *prep.* CONCERNING, as regards, with/in regard to, with respect to, with reference to, relating to, respecting, dealing with, referring to, re, about, apropos, on the subject of, in connection with, vis-à-vis.

regardless *adv.* ANYWAY, anyhow, in any case, nevertheless, nonetheless, despite everything, in spite of everything, even so, all the same, in any event, come what may.

regiment *n.* UNIT, outfit, force, corps, division, brigade, battalion, squadron, company, platoon.
▶ *v.* ORGANIZE, order, systematize, control, regulate, manage, discipline.

region *n.* DISTRICT, province, territory, division, area, section, sector, zone, belt, part, quarter; *informal* parts, corner.

register *n.* **1** OFFICIAL LIST, listing, roll, roster, index, directory, catalogue, inventory. **2** RECORD, chronicle, log, logbook, ledger, archive; annals, files.
▶ *v.* **1** ☞ RECORD *v.* 1. **2** ENROL, put one's name down, enlist, sign on/up, be enumerated✦, apply. **3** INDICATE. **4** MAKE AN IMPRESSION, get through, sink in, penetrate, have an effect, strike home.

regress *v.* REVERT, retrogress, relapse, lapse, backslide, slip back; deteriorate, decline, worsen, degenerate, get worse, drift, fall, sink, slide, slip; *informal* go downhill.
—OPPOSITES: progress.

regret *v.* BE SORRY ABOUT, feel contrite about, feel remorse about/for, be remorseful about, rue, repent (of), feel repentant about, be regretful at/about.

▶ *n.* **1** ☞ REMORSE. **2** SADNESS, sorrow, disappointment, unhappiness, grief.

—OPPOSITES: satisfaction.

regretful *adj.* SORRY, remorseful, contrite, repentant, rueful, penitent, conscience-stricken, apologetic, guilt-ridden, ashamed, shamefaced.

—OPPOSITES: unrepentant.

regular *adj.* **1** UNIFORM, even, consistent, constant, unchanging, unvarying, fixed. **2** RHYTHMIC, steady, even, uniform, constant, unchanging, unvarying. **3** FREQUENT, repeated, continual, recurrent, periodic, constant, perpetual, numerous. **4** ESTABLISHED, conventional, orthodox, proper, official, approved, bona fide, standard, usual, traditional, tried and tested. **5** METHODICAL, systematic, structured, well-ordered, well-organized, orderly, efficient. **6** USUAL, normal, customary, habitual, routine, typical, accustomed, established.

—OPPOSITES: erratic, occasional.

regulate *v.* **1** CONTROL, adjust, manage. **2** SUPERVISE, police, monitor, check (up on), be responsible for; control, manage, direct, guide, govern.

regulation *n.* **1** ☞ RULE *n.* 1. **2** ADJUSTMENT, control, management, balancing. **3** SUPERVISION, policing, superintendence, monitoring, inspection; control, management, responsibility for.

rehearse *v.* **1** PREPARE, practise, read through, run through/over, go over. **2** TRAIN, drill, prepare,

coach, put someone through their paces.

reinforce *v.* **1** STRENGTHEN, fortify, bolster up, shore up, buttress, prop up, underpin, brace, support. **2** STRENGTHEN, fortify, support; cement, boost, promote, encourage, deepen, enrich, enhance, intensify, improve. **3** AUGMENT, increase, add to, supplement, boost, top up.

reinforcement *n.* **1** STRENGTHENING, fortification, bolstering, shoring up, buttressing, bracing. **2** AUGMENTATION, increase, supplementing, boosting, topping up. **3** ADDITIONAL TROOPS, fresh troops, auxiliaries, reserves; support, backup, help.

reject *v.* **1** TURN DOWN, refuse, decline, say no to, spurn; *informal* give the thumbs down to. **2** REBUFF, spurn, shun, snub, repudiate, cast off/aside, discard, abandon, desert, turn one's back on, have nothing (more) to do with, wash one's hands of; *informal* give someone the brush-off; *literary* forsake.

—OPPOSITES: accept.

rejoice *v.* **1** BE JOYFUL, be happy, be pleased, be glad, be delighted, be elated, be ecstatic, be euphoric, be overjoyed, be as pleased as punch, be jubilant, be in raptures, be beside oneself with joy, be delirious, be thrilled, be on cloud nine, be in seventh heaven; celebrate, make merry; *informal* be over the moon, be on top of the world; *literary* joy; *archaic* jubilate. **2** TAKE DELIGHT, find/take pleasure, feel satisfaction, find joy, enjoy,

revel in, glory in, delight in, relish, savour.
—OPPOSITES: mourn.

relate v. **1** ☞ TELL 2. **2** CONNECT (WITH), associate (with), link (with), correlate (with), ally (with), couple (with). **3** ☞ APPLY 2. **4** HAVE A RAPPORT, get on (well), feel sympathy, feel for, identify with, empathize with, understand; informal hit it off with.

related adj. **1** CONNECTED, interconnected, associated, linked, coupled, allied, affiliated, concomitant, corresponding, analogous, kindred, parallel, comparable, homologous, equivalent. **2** OF THE SAME FAMILY, kin, akin, kindred; formal cognate, consanguineous.
—OPPOSITES: unconnected.

relation n. **1** CONNECTION, relationship, association, link, correlation, correspondence, parallel, alliance, bond, interrelation, interconnection. **2** RELEVANCE, applicability, reference, pertinence, bearing. **3** ☞ RELATIVE n.

relationship n. **1** CONNECTION, relation, association, link, correlation, correspondence, parallel, alliance, bond, interrelation, interconnection. **2** FAMILY TIES/CONNECTIONS, blood ties/relationship, kinship, affinity, consanguinity, common ancestry/lineage. **3** ☞ ROMANCE 2.

relative adj. **1** COMPARATIVE, respective, comparable, correlative, parallel, corresponding. **2** PROPORTIONATE, proportional, in proportion, commensurate, corresponding.

3 MODERATE, reasonable, a fair degree of, considerable, comparative.
▶ n. RELATION, member of someone's/the family, kinsman, kinswoman; (**relatives**) family, (kith and) kin, kindred, kinsfolk, people.

relax v. **1** UNWIND, loosen up, ease up/off, slow down, de-stress, unbend, rest, put one's feet up, take it easy, unbutton, hang loose, chill (out), take a load off, kick back; calm down, lighten up. **2** CALM (DOWN), unwind, loosen up, make less tense/uptight, soothe, pacify, compose. **3** LOOSEN, loose, slacken, unclench, weaken, lessen. **4** BECOME LESS TENSE, loosen, slacken, unknot. **5** MODERATE, modify, temper, ease (up on), loosen, lighten, dilute, weaken, reduce, decrease; informal let up on.
—OPPOSITES: tense, tighten.

relaxation n. **1** (MENTAL) REPOSE, calm, tranquility, peacefulness, loosening up, unwinding. **2** ☞ RECREATION 1. **3** LOOSENING, slackening. **4** MODERATION, easing, loosening, lightening; alleviation, mitigation, dilution, weakening, reduction; informal letting up.

release v. **1** (SET) FREE, let go/out, allow to leave, liberate, set at liberty. **2** UNTIE, undo, loose, let go, unleash, unfetter. **3** MAKE AVAILABLE, free (up), put at someone's disposal, supply, furnish, provide. **4** EXCUSE, exempt, discharge, deliver, absolve; informal let off. **5** MAKE PUBLIC, make known, issue, break, announce, declare, report, reveal,

divulge, disclose, publish, broadcast, circulate, communicate, disseminate, publicize.
—OPPOSITES: imprison, tie up.
▶ *n.* **1** FREEING, liberation, deliverance, bailout; freedom, liberty. **2** ISSUING, announcement, declaration, reporting, revealing, divulging, disclosure, publication, communication, dissemination. **3** ☞ ANNOUNCEMENT.

relent *v.* **1** CHANGE ONE'S MIND, backpedal, do a U-turn, back down, give way/in, capitulate; become merciful, become lenient, agree to something, allow something, concede something; *formal* accede. **2** EASE (OFF/UP), slacken, let up, abate, drop, die down, lessen, decrease, subside, weaken, tail off.

relentless *adj.* **1** PERSISTENT, continuing, constant, continual, continuous, non-stop, never-ending, interminable, incessant, unceasing, endless, unending, unremitting, unrelenting, unrelieved; unfaltering, unflagging, untiring, unwavering, dogged, tenacious, single-minded, tireless, indefatigable; *formal* pertinacious. **2** ☞ MERCILESS.

relevant *adj.* PERTINENT, applicable, suitable, fitting, apposite, apt, material, apropos, to the point, germane; connected, related, linked; appropriate, fit, to the purpose.

reliable *adj.* **1** DEPENDABLE, good, well-founded, authentic, valid, genuine, sound, true. **2** ☞ TRUSTWORTHY.
—OPPOSITES: untrustworthy.

relief *n.* **1** REASSURANCE, consolation, comfort, solace. **2** ALLEVIATION, alleviating, relieving, assuagement, assuaging, palliation, allaying, soothing, easing, lessening, reduction. **3** FREEDOM, release, liberation, deliverance. **4** RESPITE, amusement, diversion, entertainment, jollity, jollification, recreation. **5** HELP, aid, assistance, succour, sustenance, TLC; charity, gifts, donations. **6** REPLACEMENT, substitute, deputy, reserve, cover, stand-in, supply, locum (tenens), understudy.
—OPPOSITES: intensification.

relieve *v.* **1** ☞ ALLEVIATE. **2** COUNTERACT, reduce, alleviate, mitigate; interrupt, vary, stop, dispel, prevent. **3** REPLACE, take over from, stand in for, fill in for, substitute for, deputize for, cover for. **4** (SET) FREE, release, exempt, excuse, absolve, let off, discharge.
—OPPOSITES: aggravate.

religion *n.* FAITH, belief, worship, creed, ideology, (religious) belief/persuasion, doctrine; sect, cult, church, denomination.

religious *adj.* **1** ☞ DEVOUT. **2** SPIRITUAL, theological, scriptural, doctrinal, ecclesiastical, church, churchly, holy, divine, sacred.
—OPPOSITES: atheistic, secular.

relish *n.* ☞ GUSTO.
—OPPOSITES: dislike.
▶ *v.* **1** ENJOY, delight in, love, adore, take pleasure in, rejoice in, appreciate, savour, revel in, luxuriate in, glory in. **2** LOOK FORWARD TO, fancy, anticipate with pleasure.

reluctant *adj.* UNWILLING, disinclined, unenthusiastic, resistant, resisting, opposed, against, averse, antipathetic, ill-disposed, loath; hesitant, unprepared, indisposed, not in favour of.
—OPPOSITES: willing, eager.

rely *v.* **1** DEPEND, count, bank, place reliance, reckon; be confident of, be sure of, believe in, have faith in, trust in; *informal* swear by, figure on. **2** BE DEPENDENT, depend, be unable to manage without.

remain *v.* **1** CONTINUE TO EXIST, endure, last, abide, carry on, persist, stay (around), prevail, survive, live on. **2** STAY (BEHIND/PUT), wait (around), be left, hang on; *informal* hang around. **3** CONTINUE TO BE, stay, keep, persist in being, carry on being. **4** BE LEFT (OVER), be still available, be unused; have not yet passed.

remainder *n.* RESIDUE, balance, remaining part/number, rest, others, those left, remnant(s), surplus, extra, excess, overflow; *technical* residuum.

remark *v.* **1** ☞ COMMENT *v.* 2.
2 COMMENT, mention, refer to, speak of, pass comment on. **3** NOTE, notice, observe, take note of, perceive, discern.
▶ *n.* ☞ COMMENT *n.* 1.

remarkable *adj.*
☞ EXTRAORDINARY.
—OPPOSITES: ordinary.

remedy *n.* **1** TREATMENT, cure, medicine, medication, medicament, drug, antidote, therapy; *archaic* physic. **2** SOLUTION, answer, cure, antidote, curative,

nostrum, panacea, cure-all; *informal* magic bullet.

remember *v.* **1** RECALL, call to mind, recollect, think of; reminisce about, look back on; *archaic* bethink oneself of.
2 ☞ MEMORIZE. **3** BEAR/KEEP IN MIND, be mindful of the fact; take into account, take into consideration.
4 BE SURE, be certain; mind that you, make sure that you.
5 ☞ COMMEMORATE.
—OPPOSITES: forget.

remind *v.* **1** JOG SOMEONE'S MEMORY, help someone remember, prompt. **2** MAKE ONE THINK OF, cause one to remember, put one in mind of, bring/call to mind, evoke.

remiss *adj.* ☞ NEGLIGENT.
—OPPOSITES: careful.

remorse *n.* CONTRITION, deep regret, repentance, penitence, guilt, compunction, ruefulness, contriteness; pangs of conscience, breast-beating.

remorseful *adj.* ☞ SORRY 3.
—OPPOSITES: unrepentant.

remorseless *adj.*
1 ☞ MERCILESS. **2** ☞ RELENTLESS 1.
—OPPOSITES: compassionate.

remote *adj.* **1** ☞ DISTANT 1.
2 ISOLATED, out of the way, off the beaten track, secluded, lonely, in the back of beyond, godforsaken, inaccessible, far-flung, in the backwoods, lonesome; *informal* in the sticks, in the middle of nowhere, cut-off, hinterland, in the back concessions✦, in the boonies/boondocks, outlying, outpost✦. **3** UNLIKELY, improbable, implausible, doubtful, dubious; faint, slight, slim, small, slender.

4 ☞ RESERVED.

—OPPOSITES: close, central.

removal *n.* **1** TAKING AWAY, moving, carrying away. **2** DISMISSAL, ejection, expulsion, ousting, displacement, deposition, ouster; *informal* firing, sacking. **3** WITHDRAWAL, elimination, taking away. **4** DELETION, elimination, erasing, effacing, obliteration. **5** UPROOTING, eradication.

—OPPOSITES: installation.

remove *v.* **1** DETACH, unfasten; pull out, take out, disconnect. **2** TAKE OFF, undo, unfasten. **3** TAKE OUT, produce, bring out, get out, pull out, withdraw. **4** TAKE AWAY, carry away, move, transport; confiscate; *informal* cart off. **5** CLEAN OFF, wash off, wipe off, rinse off, scrub off, sponge out. **6** TAKE OFF, pull off, slip out of, peel off. **7** ☞ DISMISS 1. **8** WITHDRAW, abolish, eliminate, get rid of, do away with, stop, cut, axe. **9** DELETE, erase, rub out, cross out, strike out, score out, deep-six. **10** UPROOT, pull out, eradicate.

—OPPOSITES: attach, insert, replace.

renegade *n.* TRAITOR, defector, deserter, turncoat; rebel, mutineer.

▶ *adj.* TREACHEROUS, traitorous, disloyal, treasonous, rebel, mutinous.

—OPPOSITES: loyal.

renege *v.* DEFAULT ON, fail to honour, go back on, break, back out of, withdraw from, retreat from, welsh on, backtrack on; break one's word/promise.

—OPPOSITES: honour.

renew *v.* **1** RESUME, return to, take up again, come back to, begin again, start again, restart, recommence; continue (with), carry on (with). **2** REAFFIRM, reassert; repeat, reiterate, restate. **3** REVIVE, regenerate, revitalize, reinvigorate, restore, resuscitate, breathe new life into, rekindle. **4** RENOVATE, restore, refurbish, modernize, overhaul, redevelop, rebuild, reconstruct, remodel, bring something up to code; *informal* do up, rehab. **5** EXTEND, prolong. **6** REPLENISH, restock, resupply, top up, replace.

renounce *v.* **1** GIVE UP, relinquish, abandon, abdicate, surrender, waive, forego; *Law* disclaim; *formal* abnegate. **2** ☞ ABANDON 1. **3** REPUDIATE, deny, reject, abandon, wash one's hands of, turn one's back on, disown, spurn, shun; *literary* forsake.

—OPPOSITES: assert, accept.

☐ **renounce the world** BECOME A RECLUSE, turn one's back on society, cloister oneself, hide oneself away.

renovate *v.* MODERNIZE, restore, refurbish, revamp, recondition, rehabilitate, overhaul, redevelop; update, upgrade, refit, bring something up to code; *informal* do up, rehab.

renown *n.* ☞ EMINENCE.

renowned *adj.* FAMOUS, celebrated, famed, eminent, distinguished, acclaimed, illustrious, pre-eminent, prominent, great, esteemed, of note, of repute, well-known, well-thought-of.

—OPPOSITES: unknown.

repair v. **1** ☞ MEND. **2** PUT/SET RIGHT, mend, fix, straighten out, smooth, improve, warm up; *informal* patch up.
□ **beyond repair** IRREPARABLE, irreversible, irretrievable, irremediable, irrecoverable, past hope.

repay v. **1** REIMBURSE, refund, pay back/off, recompense, compensate, indemnify. **2** PAY BACK, return, refund, reimburse. **3** RECIPROCATE, return, requite, recompense, reward.

repeal v. REVOKE, rescind, cancel, reverse, annul, nullify, declare null and void, quash, abolish; *Law* vacate; *formal* abrogate; *archaic* recall.
—OPPOSITES: enact.
▶ *n.* REVOCATION, rescinding, cancellation, reversal, annulment, nullification, quashing, abolition; *formal* abrogation; *archaic* recall.

repeat v. **1** SAY AGAIN, restate, reiterate, go/run through again, recapitulate; *informal* recap. **2** RECITE, quote, parrot, regurgitate; *informal* trot out. **3** DO AGAIN, redo, replicate, rehash, duplicate.
▶ *n.* **1** REPETITION, duplication, replication, duplicate, rehash. **2** RERUN, rebroadcast.
□ **repeat itself** REOCCUR, recur, occur again, happen again.

repeated adj. RECURRENT, frequent, persistent, continual, incessant, constant; regular, periodic, numerous, (very) many, a great many.
—OPPOSITES: occasional.

repel v. **1** FIGHT OFF, repulse, drive back/away, force back, beat back,

push back; hold off, ward off, keep at bay; *archaic* rebut. **2** BE IMPERVIOUS TO, be impermeable to, keep out, resist, be —— proof. **3** ☞ DISGUST v.

repellent adj. ☞ REPULSIVE.
—OPPOSITES: delightful.

repent v. FEEL REMORSE, regret, be sorry, rue, reproach oneself, be ashamed, feel contrite; be penitent, be remorseful, be repentant.

repentant adj. ☞ SORRY 3.
—OPPOSITES: impenitent.

repetitive adj. MONOTONOUS, tedious, boring, humdrum, mundane, dreary, tiresome; unvaried, unchanging, unvarying, recurrent, recurring, repeated, repetitious, routine, mechanical, automatic.

replace v. **1** PUT BACK, return, restore. **2** TAKE THE PLACE OF, succeed, take over from, supersede; oust, overthrow; stand in for, substitute for, deputize for, cover for, relieve; *informal* step into someone's shoes/boots. **3** SUBSTITUTE, exchange, change, swap.
—OPPOSITES: remove.

replacement n. **1** SUCCESSOR; SUBSTITUTE, stand-in, locum, relief, cover. **2** RENEWAL, replacing.

reply v. ☞ ANSWER v. 1.
▶ *n.* ☞ ANSWER n. 1.

report v. **1** ☞ ANNOUNCE 1. **2** COVER, write about, describe, give details of, commentate on; investigate, look into, inquire into. **3** INFORM ON, tattle on; *informal* tell on, squeal on, rat on, peach on. **4** PRESENT ONESELF, arrive, turn up, clock in, sign in, punch in;

informal show up.

▶ *n.* **1** ACCOUNT, review, record, description, statement; transactions, proceedings, transcripts, minutes. **2** NEWS, information, word, intelligence; *literary* tidings. **3** STORY, account, article, piece, item, column, feature, bulletin, dispatch. **4** ASSESSMENT, report card, evaluation, appraisal. **5** RUMOUR, whisper; *informal* buzz.

represent *v.* **1** SYMBOLIZE, stand for, personify, epitomize, typify, embody, illustrate. **2** STAND FOR, designate, denote; *literary* betoken. **3** ☞ DEPICT. **4** CONSTITUTE, be, amount to, be regarded as. **5** BE A TYPICAL SAMPLE OF, be representative of, typify.

representation *n.* **1** PORTRAYAL, depiction, delineation, presentation, rendition. **2** LIKENESS, painting, drawing, picture, illustration, sketch, image, model, figure, figurine, statue, statuette, depiction, photograph, portrait, portrayal, sculpture, study.

representative *adj.*
1 ☞ TYPICAL 1. **2** SYMBOLIC, emblematic. **3** ELECTED, elective, democratic, popular.
—OPPOSITES: atypical, totalitarian.
▶ *n.* **1** SPOKESPERSON, spokesman, spokeswoman, agent, official, mouthpiece. **2** SALESPERSON, salesman, saleswoman, agent; *informal* rep. **3** DELEGATE, commissioner, ambassador, attaché, envoy, emissary, chargé d'affaires, deputy. **4** MEMBER (OF PARLIAMENT), MP, MLA, MPP, MNA, MHA; councillor, alderman,

senator, legislator, lawmaker; voice. **5** DEPUTY, substitute, stand-in, proxy.

repress *v.* **1** ☞ SUPPRESS 1.
2 RESTRAIN, hold back/in, keep back, suppress, keep in check, control, keep under control, curb, stifle, bottle up; conceal, hide; *informal* button up, cork, keep the lid on.

repressed *adj.* **1** OPPRESSED, subjugated, subdued, tyrannized. **2** RESTRAINED, suppressed, held back/in, kept in check, stifled, pent up, bottled up. **3** INHIBITED, frustrated, restrained; *informal* uptight, hung up.
—OPPOSITES: democratic, uninhibited.

reprieve *v.* **1** GRANT A STAY OF EXECUTION TO, pardon, spare, grant an amnesty to, amnesty; *informal* let off (the hook). **2** SAVE, rescue; *informal* take off the hit list.
▶ *n.* STAY OF EXECUTION, remission, pardon, amnesty; *US Law* continuance.

reprimand *v.* REBUKE, admonish, chastise, chide, discipline, upbraid, reprove, reproach, scold, berate, castigate, take to task, lambaste, give someone a piece of one's mind, haul/rake over the coals, give someone a tongue-lashing, give someone hell, lecture, criticize, censure; *informal* give someone a talking-to, tell off, dress down, give someone a dressing-down, give someone an earful, give someone a roasting, rap over the knuckles, rap, slap someone's wrist, bawl out, pitch into, lay into, lace into, blast, tear a strip off, have a go at, zing, give

someone what for, chew out, ream out.
—OPPOSITES: praise.
▶ *n.* REBUKE, reproof, admonishment, admonition, reproach, scolding, upbraiding, censure, obloquy; *informal* rap over the knuckles, slap on the wrist, dressing-down, earful, roasting, tongue-lashing, talking-to; *formal* castigation.
—OPPOSITES: commendation.

reproach *v.* ☞ REPRIMAND *v.*
▶ *n.* ☞ REPRIMAND *n.*
□ **beyond/above reproach** PERFECT, blameless, above suspicion, without fault, faultless, flawless, irreproachable, exemplary, impeccable, immaculate, unblemished, spotless, untarnished, stainless, unsullied, whiter than white; *informal* squeaky clean.

reproachful *adj.* DISAPPROVING, reproving, critical, censorious, disparaging, withering, accusatory, admonitory.
—OPPOSITES: approving.

reproduce *v.* **1** ☞ DUPLICATE *v.* 1. **2** REPEAT, replicate, recreate, redo; simulate, imitate, emulate, mirror, mimic. **3** ☞ BREED *v.* 1.

reproduction *n.* **1** COPYING, duplication, duplicating; photocopying, xeroxing, printing. **2** PRINT, copy, reprint, duplicate, facsimile, carbon copy, photocopy; *proprietary* Xerox. **3** BREEDING, procreation, multiplying, propagation.

repulsive *adj.* REVOLTING, odious, repellent, repugnant, disgusting, offensive, objectionable, vile, foul, abhorrent, loathsome, nauseating, sickening, hateful, detestable, execrable, abominable, monstrous, appalling, reprehensible, deplorable, insufferable, intolerable, despicable, contemptible, unspeakable, atrocious, awful, terrible, dreadful, frightful, obnoxious, unsavoury, unpalatable, unpleasant, disagreeable, nasty, noisome, distasteful, rebarbative; *informal* ghastly, horrible, horrid, gross, godawful, grotesque, hideous, ugly, horrendous, noxious, gruesome, gut-churning, icky, off-putting, putrid, stomach-churning, stomach-turning, vomitous, yucky.
—OPPOSITES: attractive.

reputable *adj.* WELL-THOUGHT-OF, highly regarded, (well) respected, respectable, of (good) repute, prestigious, established; reliable, dependable, trustworthy.
—OPPOSITES: untrustworthy.

reputation *n.* (GOOD) NAME, character, repute, standing, stature, status, position, renown, esteem, prestige; *informal* rep, rap.

request *n.* **1** APPEAL, entreaty, plea, petition, application, demand, call; *formal* adjuration; *literary* behest. **2** BIDDING, entreaty, demand, insistence.
3 REQUIREMENT, wish, desire; choice.
▶ *v.* **1** ASK FOR, appeal for, call for, seek, solicit, plead for, apply for, demand; *formal* adjure. **2** CALL ON, beg, entreat, implore; *literary* beseech.

require *v.* **1** NEED, be in need of. **2** NECESSITATE, demand, call for,

involve, entail. **3** DEMAND, insist on, call for, ask for, expect.
4 ORDER, instruct, command, enjoin, oblige, compel, force.
5 WANT, wish to have, desire; lack, be short of.

required *adj.* **1** ☞ ESSENTIAL 1.
2 DESIRED, preferred, chosen; correct, proper, right.
—OPPOSITES: optional.

requirement *n.* NEED, wish, demand, want, necessity, essential, prerequisite, stipulation.

rescue *v.* **1** SAVE (FROM DANGER), save the life of, come to the aid of; (set) free, release, liberate.
2 RETRIEVE, recover, salvage, get back.
▶ *n.* SAVING, rescuing; release, freeing, liberation, bailout, deliverance, redemption.

research *n.* **1** INVESTIGATION, experimentation, testing, analysis, fact-finding, fieldwork, examination, scrutiny.
2 EXPERIMENTS, experimentation, tests, inquiries, studies.
▶ *v.* ☞ INVESTIGATE.

resemblance *n.* ☞ SIMILARITY.

resemble *v.* LOOK LIKE, be similar to, be like, bear a resemblance to, remind one of, take after, favour, have the look of; approximate to, smack of, have (all) the hallmarks of, correspond to, echo, mirror, parallel.

resent *v.* BEGRUDGE, feel aggrieved at/about, feel bitter about, grudge, be annoyed at/about, be resentful of, dislike, take exception to, object to, take amiss, take offence at, take umbrage at, bear/harbour a grudge about.
—OPPOSITES: welcome.

resentful *adj.* ☞ DISGRUNTLED.

resentment *n.* BITTERNESS, indignation, irritation, pique, dissatisfaction, disgruntlement, discontentment, discontent, resentfulness, bad feelings, hard feelings, ill will, acrimony, rancour, animosity, jaundice; envy, jealousy.

reservation *n.* DOUBT, qualm, scruple; misgivings, skepticism, unease, hesitation, objection.
☐ **without reservation** WHOLEHEARTEDLY, unreservedly, without qualification, fully, completely, totally, entirely, wholly, unconditionally.

reserve *v.* **1** PUT TO ONE SIDE, put aside, set aside, keep (back), save, hold, put on hold, keep in reserve, earmark. **2** BOOK, make a reservation for, order, arrange for, secure; *formal* bespeak; *dated* engage.
3 RETAIN, maintain, keep, hold.
4 DEFER, postpone, put off, delay, withhold.
▶ *n.* **1** STOCK, store, supply, stockpile, pool, hoard, cache.
2 REINFORCEMENTS, the militia, extras, auxiliaries. **3** (*Cdn*) territory, nation; *informal* rez; *US* reservation. **4** NATIONAL/PROVINCIAL PARK, sanctuary, preserve, conservation area, protected area, wildlife park. **5** RETICENCE, detachment, distance, remoteness, coolness, aloofness, constraint, formality; shyness, diffidence, timidity, taciturnity, inhibition; *informal* standoffishness.
6 RESERVATION, qualification, condition, limitation, hesitation, doubt.
▶ *adj.* BACKUP, substitute, stand-in,

relief, replacement, fallback, spare, extra.

□ **in reserve** AVAILABLE, to/on hand, ready, in readiness, set aside, at one's disposal.

reserved *adj.* RETICENT, quiet, private, uncommunicative, unforthcoming, undemonstrative, unsociable, formal, constrained, cool, aloof, detached, distant, remote, unapproachable, unfriendly, withdrawn, secretive, silent, taciturn; shy, retiring, diffident, timid, self-effacing, inhibited, introverted; *informal* standoffish.

—OPPOSITES: outgoing.

resident *n.* ☞ INHABITANT.
▸ *adj.* **1** LIVING, residing, in residence; *formal* dwelling. **2** LIVE-IN, living in.

resign *v.* **1** LEAVE, hand in one's notice, give notice, stand down, step down; *informal* quit, jump ship, hang up one's skates. **2** GIVE UP, leave, vacate, stand down from; *informal* quit, pack in. **3** RECONCILE ONESELF TO, become resigned to, come to terms with, accept.

resist *v.* **1** WITHSTAND, be proof against, combat, weather, endure, be resistant to, keep out. **2** OPPOSE, fight against, refuse to accept, object to, defy, set one's face against, kick against; obstruct, impede, hinder, block, thwart, frustrate. **3** REFRAIN FROM, abstain from, forbear from, desist from, not give in to, restrain oneself from, stop oneself from. **4** STRUGGLE WITH/AGAINST, fight (against), stand up to, withstand, hold off; fend off, ward off.

—OPPOSITES: welcome, submit.

resolute *adj.* DETERMINED, purposeful, resolved, adamant, single-minded, firm, unswerving, unwavering, steadfast, staunch, stalwart, unfaltering, unhesitating, committed, dedicated, persistent, intent, persevering, indefatigable, tenacious, strong-willed, unshakeable; stubborn, dogged, obstinate, obdurate, inflexible, intransigent, immovable, insistent, implacable, unyielding, unrelenting; spirited, brave, bold, courageous, plucky, steely, indomitable, undaunted, rock-ribbed; *informal* gutsy, spunky, feisty; *formal* pertinacious.

—OPPOSITES: half-hearted.

resolution *n.* **1** INTENTION, resolve, decision, intent, aim, plan; commitment, pledge, promise. **2** MOTION, proposal, proposition, resolve. **3** ☞ DETERMINATION. **4** SOLUTION, answer, end, ending, settlement, conclusion.

resolve *v.* **1** SETTLE, sort out, solve, find a solution to, fix, straighten out, deal with, put right, put to rights, rectify; *informal* hammer out, thrash out, figure out. **2** DETERMINE, decide, make up one's mind, make a decision. **3** VOTE, pass a resolution, rule, decide formally, agree.
▸ *n.* ☞ DETERMINATION.

resort *n.* **1** HOLIDAY DESTINATION, (tourist) centre, vacationland. **2** RECOURSE TO, turning to, the use of, utilizing. **3** EXPEDIENT, measure, step, recourse, alternative, option, choice, possibility, hope.

□ **resort to** HAVE RECOURSE TO, fall

back on, turn to, make use of, use, employ, avail oneself of; stoop to, descend to, sink to.

respect *n.* **1** ESTEEM, regard, high opinion, admiration, reverence, deference, honour. **2** DUE REGARD, politeness, courtesy, civility, deference. **3** ASPECT, regard, facet, feature, way, sense, particular, point, detail.
—OPPOSITES: contempt.
▶ *v.* **1** ESTEEM, admire, think highly of, have a high opinion of, hold in high regard, hold in (high) esteem, look up to, revere, reverence, honour. **2** SHOW CONSIDERATION FOR, have regard for, observe, be mindful of, be heedful of; *formal* take cognizance of. **3** ABIDE BY, comply with, follow, adhere to, conform to, act in accordance with, defer to, obey, observe, keep (to).
—OPPOSITES: despise, disobey.
☐ **with respect to/in respect of** ☞ REGARDING.

respectable *adj.* **1** REPUTABLE, of good repute, upright, honest, honourable, trustworthy, decent, good, well-bred, clean-living. **2** FAIRLY GOOD, decent, fair, reasonable, moderately good; substantial, considerable, sizable.
—OPPOSITES: disreputable, paltry.

respected *adj.* VENERABLE, venerated, revered, honoured, esteemed, hallowed, august, distinguished, eminent, great, grand.

respectful *adj.* DEFERENTIAL, reverent, reverential, dutiful; polite, well-mannered, civil, courteous, gracious.
—OPPOSITES: rude.

respite *n.* REST, break, breathing space, interval, intermission, interlude, recess, lull, pause, time out; relief, relaxation, repose; breather, let-up.

respond *v.* **1** ANSWER, reply, rejoin, retort, riposte, counter. **2** REACT, make a response, reciprocate, retaliate.

response *n.* ☞ ANSWER *n.* 1.
—OPPOSITES: question.

responsibility *n.* **1** DUTY, obligation, task, function, job, role, business. **2** BLAME, fault, guilt, culpability, liability. **3** AUTHORITY, control, power, leadership.

responsible *adj.* **1** IN CHARGE OF, in control of, at the helm of, accountable for, liable for. **2** ☞ CULPABLE. **3** IMPORTANT, powerful, executive. **4** ANSWERABLE, accountable. **5** TRUSTWORTHY, sensible, mature, reliable, dependable.

responsive *adj.* QUICK TO REACT, reactive, receptive, open to suggestions, amenable, flexible, forthcoming.

rest[1] *v.* **1** RELAX, take a rest, ease up/off, let up, slow down, have/ take a break, unbend, unwind, recharge one's batteries, be at leisure, take it easy, put one's feet up; lie down, go to bed, have/take a nap, catnap, doze, sleep; *informal* take five, have/take a breather, snatch forty winks, get some shut-eye, take a load off, chill (out), catch some zees. **2** LIE, be laid, repose, be placed, be positioned, be supported by. **3** SUPPORT, prop (up), lean, lay, set, stand, position, place, put. **4** BE BASED, depend, be

dependent, rely, hinge, turn on, be contingent, revolve around.
▸ *n.* **1** REPOSE, relaxation, leisure, respite, time off, breathing space, downtime; sleep, nap, doze; *informal* shut-eye, snooze, lie-down, forty winks. **2** HOLIDAY, vacation, break, breathing space, interval, interlude, intermission, time off/out; *informal* breather. **3** STAND, base, holder, support, rack, frame, shelf. **4** A STANDSTILL, a halt, a stop.

rest² *n.* REMAINDER, residue, balance, remaining part/number/quantity, others, those left, remains, remnant(s), surplus, excess.
▸ *v.* REMAIN, continue to be, stay, keep, carry on being.

restful *adj.* RELAXED, relaxing, quiet, calm, calming, tranquil, soothing, peaceful, placid, reposeful, leisurely, undisturbed, untroubled.
—OPPOSITES: exciting.

restless *adj.* **1** UNEASY, ill at ease, restive, fidgety, edgy, on edge, tense, worked up, nervous, agitated, anxious, on tenterhooks, keyed up; *informal* jumpy, jittery, twitchy, uptight, antsy. **2** SLEEPLESS, wakeful; fitful, broken, disturbed, troubled, unsettled.

restore *v.* **1** REINSTATE, bring back, reinstitute, reimpose, reinstall, re-establish. **2** REPAIR, fix, mend, refurbish, recondition, rehabilitate, rebuild, reconstruct, remodel, overhaul, redevelop, renovate; *informal* do up, rehab. **3** REINVIGORATE, revitalize, revive, refresh, energize, fortify, revivify,

regenerate, stimulate, freshen.
—OPPOSITES: abolish.

restrain *v.* **1** CONTROL, keep under control, check, hold/keep in check, master, curb, suppress, repress, contain, dampen, subdue, smother, choke back, stifle, quell, swallow, bottle up, rein back/in; *informal* keep the lid on. **2** TIE UP, bind, tether, chain (up), fetter, shackle, manacle, put in irons; *informal* hog-tie.

restrained *adj.* **1** SELF-CONTROLLED, self-restrained, not given to excesses, sober, steady, unemotional, undemonstrative. **2** MUTED, soft, discreet, subtle, quiet, unobtrusive, unostentatious, understated, tasteful.

restraint *n.* **1** CONSTRAINT, check, control, restriction, limitation, curtailment; rein, bridle, brake, damper, impediment, obstacle. **2** SELF-CONTROL, self-restraint, self-discipline, control, moderation, prudence, judiciousness, abstemiousness. **3** BELT, harness, strap.

restrict *v.* **1** ☞ LIMIT *v.* 1. **2** HINDER, interfere with, impede, hamper, obstruct, block, check, curb, shackle. **3** CONFINE, limit.

restriction *n.* **1** ☞ LIMITATION 1. **2** REDUCTION, limitation, diminution, curtailment. **3** HINDRANCE, impediment, slowing, reduction, limitation.

result *n.* **1** CONSEQUENCE, outcome, product, upshot, sequel, effect, reaction, repercussion, ramification, conclusion, culmination. **2** ANSWER, solution; sum, total, product. **3** GRADE,

score, mark.
—OPPOSITES: cause.
▶ *v.* **1** FOLLOW, ensue, develop, stem, spring, arise, derive, evolve, proceed; originate, emanate, emerge; occur, happen, take place, come about; be caused by, be brought about by, be produced by, originate in, be consequent on. **2 (result in)** END IN, culminate in, finish in, terminate in, lead to, prompt, precipitate, trigger; cause, bring about, occasion, effect, give rise to, produce, engender, generate; *literary* beget.

resume *v.* RESTART, recommence, begin again, start again, reopen; renew, return to, continue with, carry on with.
—OPPOSITES: suspend, abandon.

resurrect *v.* REVIVE, restore, regenerate, revitalize, breathe new life into, bring back to life, reinvigorate, resuscitate, rejuvenate, stimulate, re-establish, relaunch.

retain *v.* **1** KEEP (POSSESSION OF), keep hold of, hold on to, hang on to. **2** MAINTAIN, keep, preserve, conserve. **3** REMEMBER, memorize, keep in one's mind/memory, store.
—OPPOSITES: give up.

retaliate *v.* FIGHT BACK, hit back, respond, react, reply, reciprocate, counterattack, return like for like, get back at someone, give tit for tat, take reprisals, get even, get one's own back, pay someone back, give someone a taste of their own medicine; have/get/take one's revenge, be revenged, avenge oneself.

retard *v.* DELAY, slow down/up, hold back/up, set back, postpone, put back, detain, decelerate; hinder, hamper, obstruct, impede, check, restrain, restrict, trammel; *literary* stay.
—OPPOSITES: accelerate.

retch *v.* **1** GAG, heave, dry-heave. **2** ☞ VOMIT *v.* 1.

reticent *adj.* RESERVED, withdrawn, introverted, inhibited, diffident, shy; uncommunicative, unforthcoming, unresponsive, tight-lipped, quiet, taciturn, silent, guarded, secretive.
—OPPOSITES: expansive.

retire *v.* **1** GIVE UP WORK, stop working, stop work; pack it in, call it quits, hang up one's skates❖. **2** RETREAT, withdraw, pull back, fall back, disengage, back off, give ground.

retract *v.* **1** PULL IN/BACK, draw in. **2** TAKE BACK, withdraw, recant, disavow, disclaim, repudiate, renounce, reverse, revoke, rescind, go back on, backtrack on, unsay.

retreat *v.* WITHDRAW, retire, draw back, pull back/out, fall back, give way, give ground, beat a retreat.
—OPPOSITES: advance.
▶ *n.* **1** WITHDRAWAL, pulling back. **2** REFUGE, haven, sanctuary; hideaway, hideout, hiding place, escape; *informal* hidey-hole.

retribution *n.* PUNISHMENT, penalty, one's just deserts; revenge, reprisal, requital, retaliation, vengeance, an eye for an eye (and a tooth for a tooth), tit for tat, lex talionis; redress, reparation, restitution, recompense, repayment, atonement, indemnification, amends.

retrieve v. GET BACK, bring back, recover, regain (possession of), recoup, reclaim, repossess, redeem, recuperate.

retrospect
□ **in retrospect** LOOKING BACK, on reflection, in/with hindsight.

return v. **1** GO BACK, come back, arrive back, come home. **2** RECUR, reoccur, occur again, repeat (itself); reappear, appear again. **3** GIVE BACK, hand back; pay back, repay. **4** RESTORE, put back, replace, reinstall.
—OPPOSITES: depart, disappear, keep.
▶ n. **1** HOMECOMING. **2** RECURRENCE, reoccurrence, repeat, repetition, reappearance, revival, resurrection, re-emergence, resurgence, renaissance. **3** GIVING BACK, handing back, replacement, restoration, reinstatement, restitution. **4** YIELD, profit, gain, revenue, interest, dividend, ROI.
—OPPOSITES: departure, disappearance.

reveal v. **1** DIVULGE, disclose, tell, let slip/drop, give away/out, blurt (out), release, leak; make known, make public, broadcast, publicize, circulate, disseminate; *informal* let on. **2** SHOW, display, exhibit, disclose, uncover, unveil; bring to light, lay bare, unearth, expose.
—OPPOSITES: hide.

revel v. CELEBRATE, make merry, have a party, carouse, roister, go on a spree; *informal* party, live it up, whoop it up, make whoopee, rave, paint the town red.

revelation n. DISCLOSURE, surprising fact, announcement, report; admission, confession.

revenge n. ☞ VENGEANCE.

revenue n. INCOME, takings, receipts, proceeds, earnings, sales, avails✦; profit(s).
—OPPOSITES: expenditure.

reverberate v. RESOUND, echo, re-echo, resonate, ring, boom, rumble, vibrate.

revere v. ☞ RESPECT v. 1.
—OPPOSITES: despise.

reverence n. HIGH ESTEEM, high regard, great respect, acclaim, admiration, appreciation, estimation, favour.
—OPPOSITES: scorn.

reverent adj. RESPECTFUL, reverential, admiring, devoted, devout, dutiful, awed, deferential.

reversal n. **1** TURNAROUND, turnabout, about-face, volte-face, change of heart, U-turn, one-eighty, backtracking; *rare* tergiversation. **2** SETBACK, reverse, upset, failure, misfortune, mishap, disaster, blow, disappointment, adversity, hardship, affliction, vicissitude, defeat; bad luck.

reverse v. **1** BACK, back up, drive back/backwards, move back/backwards. **2** SWAP (ROUND), change (round), exchange, interchange, switch (round). **3** ALTER, change; overturn, overthrow, disallow, override, overrule, veto, revoke, repeal, rescind, annul, nullify, void, invalidate; *formal* abrogate.
▶ adj. **1** BACKWARD(S), reversed, inverted, transposed. **2** INVERSE, reversed, opposite, converse,

contrary, counter, antithetical.
▶ *n.* OPPOSITE, contrary, converse, inverse, obverse, antithesis.

review *n.* **1** ANALYSIS, evaluation, assessment, appraisal, examination, investigation, inquiry, probe, inspection, study. **2** RECONSIDERATION, reassessment, re-evaluation, reappraisal; change, alteration, modification, revision. **3** CRITICISM, critique, assessment, evaluation, commentary; *informal* take.
▶ *v.* **1** SURVEY, study, research, consider, analyze, examine, scrutinize, explore, look into, probe, investigate, inspect, assess, appraise; *informal* size up. **2** ☞ RECONSIDER. **3** COMMENT ON, evaluate, assess, appraise, judge, critique, criticize.

revise *v.* **1** ☞ RECONSIDER. **2** AMEND, emend, correct, alter, change, edit, rewrite, redraft, rephrase, rework.

revitalize *v.* REINVIGORATE, re-energize, boost, regenerate, revive, revivify, rejuvenate, reanimate, resuscitate, refresh, stimulate, breathe new life into, give a shot in the arm to, pep up, jump-start, buck up.

revive *v.* **1** RESUSCITATE, bring round, bring back to consciousness. **2** REINVIGORATE, revitalize, refresh, energize, reanimate, resuscitate, revivify, rejuvenate, regenerate, enliven, stimulate. **3** REINTRODUCE, re-establish, restore, resurrect, bring back, regenerate, resuscitate, rekindle.

revoke *v.* CANCEL, repeal, rescind, reverse, annul, nullify, void, invalidate, countermand, retract, withdraw, overrule, override; abrogate.

revolt *v.* ☞ REBEL *v.* 1.
▶ *n.* ☞ REBELLION 1.

revolting *adj.* ☞ REPULSIVE.
—OPPOSITES: attractive, pleasant.

revolution *n.* **1** REBELLION, revolt, insurrection, mutiny, uprising, riot, rioting, insurgence, seizure of power, coup (d'état). **2** DRAMATIC CHANGE, radical alteration, sea change, metamorphosis, transformation, innovation, reorganization, restructuring; *informal* shakeup, shakedown. **3** (SINGLE) TURN, rotation, circle, spin; circuit, lap.

revolutionary *adj.* **1** REBELLIOUS, rebel, insurgent, rioting, mutinous, renegade, insurrectionary, insurrectionist, seditious, subversive, extremist. **2** ☞ ORIGINAL *adj.* 1.
▶ *n.* REBEL, insurgent, revolutionist, mutineer, insurrectionist, agitator, subversive.

revolve *v.* **1** GO ROUND, turn round, rotate, spin. **2** CIRCLE, travel, orbit. **3** BE CONCERNED WITH, be preoccupied with, focus on, centre on/around.

revulsion *n.* ☞ DISGUST.
—OPPOSITES: delight.

reward *n.* RECOMPENSE, prize, award, honour, decoration, bonus, premium, bounty, present, gift, payment; payoff, perk; perquisite.
▶ *v.* RECOMPENSE, pay, remunerate, make something worth someone's while; give an award to.
—OPPOSITES: punish.

rewarding *adj.* SATISFYING, gratifying, pleasing, fulfilling, enriching, edifying, beneficial, illuminating, worthwhile, productive, fruitful.

rhetorical *adj.* STYLISTIC, oratorical, linguistic, verbal.

rhythm *n.* **1** BEAT, cadence, tempo, time, pulse, throb, swing. **2** METRE, measure, stress, accent, cadence.

ribald *adj.* ☞ VULGAR 1.

rich *adj.* **1** WEALTHY, affluent, moneyed, well off, well-to-do, prosperous, opulent, silk-stocking, propertied, upper-class, upscale; *informal* rolling in money/it, in the money, on easy street, loaded, flush, stinking rich, filthy rich, well-heeled, made of money. **2** ☞ LUXURIOUS. **3** PLENTIFUL, abundant, copious, ample, profuse, lavish, liberal, generous, bountiful; *literary* plenteous, bounteous. **4** ☞ FERTILE 1. **5** SONOROUS, full, resonant, deep, clear, mellow, mellifluous, full-throated.
—OPPOSITES: poor.

riches *pl. n.* ☞ WEALTH 1, MONEY.

richly *adv.* SUMPTUOUSLY, opulently, luxuriously, lavishly, gorgeously, splendidly, magnificently; *informal* plushly, classily.

rickety *adj.* SHAKY, unsteady, unsound, unsafe, tumbledown, broken-down, dilapidated, ramshackle, shacky.

rid *v.* CLEAR, free, purge, empty, strip.
☐ **get rid of** ☞ DISCARD.

riddle *n.* PUZZLE, conundrum, brainteaser, (unsolved) problem, question, poser, enigma, mystery, quandary; stumper.

ridicule *n.* MOCKERY, derision, laughter, scorn, scoffing, contempt, jeering, sneering, sneers, jibes, jibing, teasing, taunts, taunting, badinage, chaffing, sarcasm, satire; *informal* kidding, ribbing, joshing, goofing, razzing.
—OPPOSITES: respect.
▶ *v.* DERIDE, mock, laugh at, heap scorn on, jeer at, jibe at, sneer at, treat with contempt, scorn, make fun of, poke fun at, scoff at, send up, satirize, lampoon, burlesque, caricature, parody, tease, taunt, chaff; *informal* kid, rib, josh, razz, pull someone's chain.

ridiculous *adj.* **1** LAUGHABLE, absurd, comical, funny, hilarious, risible, droll, amusing, farcical, silly, ludicrous; *rare* derisible. **2** SENSELESS, silly, foolish, foolhardy, stupid, inane, fatuous, childish, puerile, half-baked, hare-brained, cockamamie, ill-thought-out, crackpot, idiotic. **3** PREPOSTEROUS, nonsensical, senseless, outrageous.
—OPPOSITES: sensible.

riding (*Cdn*) *n.* constituency, electoral district.

rife *adj.* **1** WIDESPREAD, general, common, universal, extensive, ubiquitous, omnipresent, endemic, inescapable, insidious, prevalent. **2** OVERFLOWING, bursting, alive, teeming, abounding.
—OPPOSITES: unknown.

rift *n.* BREACH, division, split, falling-out, estrangement.

rig¹ v. **1** ☞ EQUIP 1. **2** ☞ DRESS v. 1.
3 SET UP, erect, assemble, build;
throw together, cobble together,
put together, whip up, improvise,
contrive.

rig² v. MANIPULATE, engineer,
distort, misrepresent, pervert,
tamper with, doctor; falsify, fake,
trump up; fix, fiddle with.

right adj. **1** JUST, fair, proper,
good, upright, righteous, virtuous,
moral, ethical, honourable,
honest; lawful, legal. **2** CORRECT,
accurate, exact, precise; proper,
valid, conventional, established,
official, formal. **3** SUITABLE,
appropriate, fitting, correct,
proper, desirable, preferable,
ideal; archaic meet.
—OPPOSITES: wrong.
▸ adv. **1** COMPLETELY, fully, totally,
absolutely, utterly, thoroughly,
quite. **2** EXACTLY, precisely,
directly, immediately, just,
squarely, dead; informal bang,
smack, plumb, smack dab.
3 STRAIGHT, immediately,
instantly, at once, straight away,
now, right now. **4** CORRECTLY,
accurately, properly, precisely,
aright, rightly, perfectly. **5** WELL,
properly, justly, fairly, nicely.
—OPPOSITES: wrong, badly.
▸ n. **1** GOODNESS, righteousness,
virtue, integrity, rectitude,
propriety, morality, truth,
honesty, honour, justice, fairness,
equity; lawfulness, legality.
2 ENTITLEMENT, prerogative,
privilege, advantage, due,
birthright, liberty, authority,
power, licence, permission,
dispensation, leave, sanction,
freedom.

—OPPOSITES: wrong.
□ **in the right** JUSTIFIED,
vindicated. **right away** AT ONCE,
straight away, (right) now, this
(very) minute, this instant,
immediately, instantly, directly,
forthwith, without further ado,
promptly, quickly, without delay,
as soon as possible, ASAP, in short
order; informal straight off, pronto,
lickety-split.

righteous adj. GOOD, virtuous,
upright, upstanding, decent;
ethical, principled, moral, high-
minded, law-abiding, honest,
honourable, blameless,
irreproachable, noble; saintly,
angelic, pure.
—OPPOSITES: sinful. .

rightful adj. ☞ LEGITIMATE 2.

rigid adj. **1** STIFF, hard, firm,
inflexible, unbending, unyielding,
inelastic. **2** STRICT, severe, stern,
stringent, rigorous, inflexible,
uncompromising, intransigent.
—OPPOSITES: flexible, lenient.

rigorous adj. **1** METICULOUS,
conscientious, punctilious,
careful, diligent, attentive,
scrupulous, painstaking, exact,
precise, accurate, thorough, .
particular, strict, demanding,
exacting; informal pernickety,
persnickety. **2** STRICT, severe,
stern, stringent, tough, harsh,
rigid, relentless, unsparing,
inflexible, draconian,
intransigent, uncompromising,
exacting.
.—OPPOSITES: slapdash, lax, mild.

rim n. BRIM, edge, lip, border, side,
margin, brink, fringe, boundary,
perimeter, limits, periphery.

ring¹ *n.* CIRCLE, band, loop, hoop, halo, disc.
▶ *v.* ☞ SURROUND.

ring² *v.* TOLL, sound, peal, chime, clang, bong, ding, dong, jingle, tinkle; *literary* knell.
▶ *n.* CHIME, toll, peal, clang, clink, ding, jingle, tinkle, tintinnabulation, sound; *literary* knell.

rink *n.* skating rink, hockey rink, ice rink, arena, ice pad❖, ice palace❖, *dated* hockey cushion❖.

rinse *v.* WASH (OUT), clean, cleanse, bathe; dip, drench, splash, swill, sluice, hose down.

riot *n.* UPROAR, commotion, upheaval, disturbance, furor, tumult, melee, scuffle, fracas, fray, brawl, free-for-all; violence, fighting, vandalism, mayhem, turmoil, lawlessness, anarchy, violent protest.
▶ *v.* (GO ON THE) RAMPAGE, run riot, fight in the streets, run wild, run amok, go berserk; raise hell.

rip *v.* & *n.* ☞ TEAR *v.* 1.

ripe *adj.* **1** MATURE, ripened, full grown, ready to eat; luscious, juicy, tender, sweet. **2** READY, fit, suitable, right. **3** OPPORTUNE, advantageous, favourable, auspicious, propitious, promising, good, right, fortunate, benign, providential, felicitous, seasonable; convenient, suitable, appropriate, apt, fitting.
—OPPOSITES: unsuitable, young.

rip-off *n.* FRAUD, cheat, deception, swindle, confidence trick; *informal* con, scam, flim-flam, gyp, rip, gouge, shakedown, bunco.

rise *v.* **1** MOVE UP/UPWARDS, come up, make one's/its way up, arise, ascend, climb, mount, soar. **2** LOOM, tower, soar, rise up, rear (up). **3** GO UP, increase, soar, shoot up, surge, leap, jump, rocket, escalate, climb, skyrocket, spiral. **4** STAND UP, get to one's feet, get up, jump up, leap up; *formal* arise. **5** GET UP, get out of bed, rouse oneself, stir, bestir oneself, be up and about; rise and shine, surface; arise. **6** MAKE PROGRESS, climb, advance, get on, work one's way, be promoted. **7** ORIGINATE, begin, start, emerge; issue from, spring from, flow from, emanate from. **8** SLOPE UPWARDS, go uphill, incline, climb.
—OPPOSITES: fall, descend, drop.
▶ *n.* **1** INCREASE, hike, leap, upsurge, upswing, upturn, climb, escalation. **2** PROGRESS, climb, promotion, elevation, aggrandizement.

risk *n.* **1** CHANCE, uncertainty, unpredictability, precariousness, instability, insecurity, perilousness, riskiness. **2** POSSIBILITY, chance, probability, likelihood, danger, peril, threat, menace, fear, prospect.
—OPPOSITES: safety, impossibility.
▶ *v.* **1** ENDANGER, imperil, jeopardize, hazard, gamble (with), chance; put on the line, put in jeopardy. **2** CHANCE, stand a chance of.
☐ **at risk** IN DANGER, in peril, in jeopardy, under threat.

risky *adj.* ☞ HAZARDOUS.

rite *n.* CEREMONY, ritual, ceremonial; service, sacrament, liturgy, worship, office; act, practice, custom, tradition, convention, institution, procedure.

ritual *n.* CEREMONY, rite, ceremonial, observance; service, sacrament, liturgy, worship; act, practice, custom, tradition, convention, formality, procedure, protocol.

rival *n.* **1** OPPONENT, challenger, competitor, contender; adversary, antagonist, enemy; foe. **2** EQUAL, match, peer, equivalent, counterpart, like.
—OPPOSITES: ally.
▶ *v.* MATCH, compare with, compete with, vie with, equal, measure up to, be in the same league as, be on a par with, touch, challenge, keep up with, keep pace with, come close to; hold a candle to.
▶ *adj.* COMPETING, opposing, contending.

rivalry *n.* COMPETITIVENESS, competition, contention, vying; opposition, conflict, feuding, antagonism, friction, enmity; *informal* keeping up with the Joneses.

river *n.* WATERCOURSE, waterway, tributary, stream, rivulet, brook, inlet, rill, runnel, freshet; bourn; creek.
—RELATED: fluvial, fluvio-.

road *n.* STREET, thoroughfare, roadway, avenue, broadway, bypass, ring road, trunk road, byroad; lane, crescent, drive, parade, row, highway, freeway, parkway, boulevard, throughway, expressway, autoroute, turnpike, interstate.

roam *v.* WANDER, rove, ramble, drift, walk, traipse; range, travel, tramp, traverse, trek; cruise, mosey; perambulate.

roar *n.* **1** SHOUT, bellow, yell, cry, howl; clamour; holler. **2** BOOM, crash, rumble, roll, thundering. **3** GUFFAW, howl, hoot, shriek, gale, peal.
▶ *v.* **1** BELLOW, yell, shout, bawl, howl; holler. **2** BOOM, rumble, crash, roll, thunder. **3** GUFFAW, laugh, hoot; *informal* split one's sides, be rolling in the aisles, be doubled up, crack up, be in stitches, die laughing. **4** SPEED, zoom, whiz, flash; belt, tear, zip, bomb.

rob *v.* **1** BURGLE, burglarize, steal from, hold up, break into; raid, loot, plunder, pillage; knock off, stick up. **2** STEAL FROM; mug, jump, clip. **3** CHEAT, swindle, defraud; do out of, con out of, fleece; stiff. **4** OVERCHARGE; rip off, sting, have, gouge. **5** DEPRIVE, strip, divest; deny.

robber *n.* ☞ THIEF.

robbery *n.* BURGLARY, theft, thievery, stealing, breaking and entering, home invasion, housebreaking, larceny, shoplifting, purse snatching; embezzlement, fraud; holdup, break-in, raid; *informal* mugging, smash-and-grab, stickup, heist, B and E.

robe *n.* **1** CLOAK, kaftan, djellaba, wrap, mantle, cape, kimono, wrapper. **2** GARB, regalia, costume, finery; garments, clothes; *formal* apparel; *archaic* raiment, habiliments, vestments. **3** VESTMENT, surplice, cassock, soutane, rochet, alb, dalmatic, chasuble, tunicle, Geneva gown;

canonicals. **4** DRESSING GOWN, bathrobe, housecoat, kimono, wrapper, cover-up.

robust *adj.* **1** STRONG, vigorous, sturdy, tough, powerful, solid, muscular, sinewy, rugged, hardy, strapping, brawny, burly, husky; healthy, (fighting) fit, hale and hearty, lusty, in fine fettle, energetic, stalwart; *informal* beefy, hunky. **2** DURABLE, resilient, tough, hard-wearing, long-lasting, sturdy, strong.
—OPPOSITES: frail, fragile.

rock *v.* **1** MOVE TO AND FRO, move back and forth, sway, see-saw; roll, pitch, plunge, toss, lurch, reel, list; wobble, oscillate. **2** SHAKE, vibrate, quake, tremble. **3** STUN, shock, stagger, astonish, startle, surprise, shake (up), take aback, throw, unnerve, disconcert.

rocky[1] *adj.* STONY, pebbly, shingly; rough, bumpy; craggy, mountainous.

rocky[2] *adj.* **1** UNSTEADY, shaky, unstable, wobbly, tottery, rickety, flimsy. **2** DIFFICULT, problematic, precarious, unstable, unreliable, undependable; *informal* iffy, up and down.
—OPPOSITES: steady, stable.

rod *n.* **1** BAR, stick, pole, baton, staff; shaft, strut, rail, spoke. **2** STAFF, mace, sceptre.

rogue *n.* **1** ☞ SCOUNDREL. **2** ☞ RASCAL.

role *n.* **1** PART; character, cameo. **2** CAPACITY, position, job, post, office, duty, responsibility, mantle, place; function, part.

roll *v.* **1** BOWL, turn over and over, spin, rotate. **2** WHEEL, push, trundle. **3** PASS, go by, slip by, fly by, elapse, wear on, march on. **4** FLOW, run, course, stream, pour, spill, trickle. **5** WIND, coil, fold, curl; twist. **6** LURCH, toss, rock, pitch, plunge, sway, reel, list, keel. **7** RUMBLE, reverberate, echo, resound, boom, roar, grumble.
▶ *n.* **1** CYLINDER, tube, scroll; bolt. **2** REEL, spool. **3** BREAD ROLL, bun, bagel, hoagie, kaiser. **4** LIST, register, directory, record, file, index, catalogue, inventory; census. **5** RUMBLE, reverberation, echo, boom, clap, crack, roar, grumble.
□ **roll in** (*informal*) POUR IN, flood in, flow in. **roll something out** UNROLL, spread out, unfurl, unfold, open (out), unwind, uncoil.

romance *n.* **1** LOVE, passion, ardour, adoration, devotion; affection, fondness, attachment. **2** LOVE AFFAIR, relationship, liaison, courtship, attachment; flirtation, dalliance. **3** LOVE STORY, novel; romantic fiction; *informal* tear-jerker, bodice-ripper. **4** MYSTERY, glamour, excitement, exoticism, mystique; appeal, allure, charm.

romantic *adj.* **1** ☞ LOVING. **2** ☞ SENTIMENTAL 2. **3** IDYLLIC, picturesque, fairy-tale; beautiful, lovely, charming, pretty. **4** IDEALISTIC, idealized, romanticized, unrealistic, fanciful, impractical; head-in-the-clouds, starry-eyed, optimistic, hopeful, visionary, Utopian, fairy-tale.
—OPPOSITES: unsentimental, realistic.
▶ *n.* IDEALIST, sentimentalist, romanticist; dreamer, visionary,

Utopian, Don Quixote, fantasist, fantast.

—OPPOSITES: realist.

room *n.* **1** SPACE; headroom, legroom; area, expanse, extent; *informal* elbow room. **2** SCOPE, capacity, leeway, latitude, freedom; opportunity, chance.

roomy *adj.* SPACIOUS, capacious, sizeable, generous, big, large, extensive; voluminous, ample; *formal* commodious.

—OPPOSITES: cramped.

root *n.* **1** rootstock, tuber, rootlet; *Botany* rhizome, radicle. **2** SOURCE, origin, germ, beginnings, genesis; cause, reason, basis, foundation, bottom, seat; core, heart, nub, essence; *informal* ground zero. **3** ORIGINS, beginnings, family, ancestors, predecessors, heritage; birthplace, homeland.

—RELATED: radical, rhizo-.

▶ *v.* **1** TAKE ROOT, grow roots, establish, strike, take. **2** PLANT, bed out, sow. **3** RUMMAGE, hunt, search, rifle, delve, forage, dig, nose, poke.

☐ **put down roots** SETTLE, establish oneself, set up home. **root something out 1** UPROOT, deracinate, pull up, grub out. **2** ERADICATE, eliminate, weed out, destroy, wipe out, stamp out, extirpate, abolish, end, put a stop to. **3** UNEARTH, dig up, bring to light, uncover, discover, dredge up, ferret out, expose. **take root 1** GERMINATE, sprout, establish, strike, take. **2** BECOME ESTABLISHED, take hold; develop, thrive, flourish.

rot *v.* **1** DECAY, decompose, become rotten; disintegrate, crumble,

perish. **2** GO BAD, go off, spoil; moulder, putrefy, fester.

—RELATED: sapro-.

—OPPOSITES: improve.

▶ *n.* **1** DECAY, decomposition, mould, mildew, blight, canker; putrefaction. **2** DETERIORATION, decline; corruption, cancer.

rotate *v.* **1** REVOLVE, go round, turn (round), spin, gyrate, whirl, twirl, swivel, circle, pivot. **2** ALTERNATE, take turns, change, switch, interchange, exchange, swap; move around.

rotten *adj.* **1** DECAYING, rotting, bad, off, decomposing, putrid, putrescent, perished, mouldy, mouldering, mildewy, rancid, festering, fetid; maggoty, wormy. **2** ☞ DISHONEST.

—OPPOSITES: fresh, honourable.

rough *adj.* **1** UNEVEN, irregular, bumpy, lumpy, knobbly, stony, rocky, rugged, rutted, pitted, rutty. **2** COARSE, bristly, scratchy, prickly; shaggy, hairy, bushy. **3** DRY, leathery, weather-beaten; chapped, calloused, scaly, scabrous. **4** VIOLENT, brutal, vicious; AGGRESSIVE, belligerent, pugnacious, thuggish; boisterous, rowdy, disorderly, unruly, riotous. **5** CARELESS, clumsy, inept, unskilful. **6** BOORISH, loutish, oafish, brutish, coarse, crude, uncouth, vulgar, unrefined, unladylike, ungentlemanly, uncultured; unmannerly, impolite, discourteous, uncivil, ungracious, rude. **7** TURBULENT, stormy, tempestuous, violent, heavy, heaving, choppy. **8** (*informal*) DIFFICULT, hard, tough, bad, unpleasant; demanding, arduous.

9 (*informal*) HARSH, hard, tough, stern, severe, unfair, unjust; insensitive, nasty, cruel, unkind, unsympathetic, brutal, heartless, merciless. **10** PRELIMINARY, hasty, quick, sketchy, cursory, basic, crude, rudimentary, raw, unpolished; incomplete, unfinished. **11** ☞ APPROXIMATE *adj*.
—OPPOSITES: smooth, sleek, gentle, careful, refined, calm, easy, kind, exact.

round *adj*. **1** CIRCULAR, disc-shaped, ring-shaped; spherical, spheroidal, globular, globe-shaped; cylindrical; bulbous, rounded, rotund; *technical* annular, discoid. **2** PLUMP, chubby, fat, full. **3** SONOROUS, resonant, rich, full, mellow, mellifluous, orotund.
—OPPOSITES: thin, reedy.
▶ *n*. **1** BALL, sphere, globe, orb, circle, disc, ring, hoop; *technical* annulus. **2** CIRCUIT, beat, route, tour. **3** STAGE, level; heat, game, bout, contest; go-round. **4** SUCCESSION, sequence, series, cycle. **5** BULLET, cartridge, shell, shot.

roundabout *adj*. **1** ☞ INDIRECT 2. **2** INDIRECT, oblique, circuitous, circumlocutory, periphrastic, digressive, long-winded; evasive.
—OPPOSITES: direct.

rouse *v*. **1** WAKE (UP), awaken, arouse; *formal* waken. **2** WAKE UP, awake, awaken, come to, get up, rise, bestir oneself; *formal* arise. **3** STIR UP, excite, galvanize, electrify, stimulate, inspire, inspirit, move, inflame, agitate, goad, provoke; incite, spur on, light a fire under. **4** PROVOKE, annoy, anger, infuriate, madden,

incense, vex, irk; *informal* aggravate. **5** AROUSE, awaken, prompt, provoke, stimulate, pique, trigger, spark off, touch off, kindle, elicit.
—OPPOSITES: calm, pacify, allay.

routine *n*. PROCEDURE, practice, pattern, drill, regimen; program, schedule, plan; formula, method, system; customs, habits; wont.
▶ *adj*. ☞ STANDARD *adj*. 1.
—OPPOSITES: unusual.

rowdy *adj*. ☞ DISORDERLY 2.
—OPPOSITES: peaceful.

rub *v*. **1** MASSAGE, knead; stroke, pat. **2** APPLY, smear, spread, work in. **3** CHAFE, pinch; hurt, be painful.
▶ *n*. **1** MASSAGE, rubdown. **2** POLISH, wipe, clean. **3** PROBLEM, difficulty, trouble, drawback, hindrance, impediment; snag, hitch, catch.
☐ **rub it in** (*informal*) EMPHASIZE, stress, underline, highlight; go on, harp on; *informal* rub someone's nose in it. **rub off on** BE TRANSFERRED TO, be passed on to, be transmitted to, be communicated to; affect, influence. **rub someone the wrong way** ☞ ANNOY.

rubbish *n*. **1** ☞ GARBAGE 1. **2** ☞ NONSENSE.

ruddy *adj*. ROSY, red, pink, roseate, rubicund; healthy, glowing, fresh; flushed, blushing; florid; *literary* rubescent.
—OPPOSITES: pale.

rude *adj*. **1** ILL-MANNERED, bad-mannered, impolite, discourteous, uncivil, unmannerly; impertinent, insolent, impudent, disrespectful, cheeky; churlish, curt, brusque, brash, offhand, short, sharp; offensive, insulting, derogatory,

disparaging, abusive; tactless, undiplomatic, uncomplimentary. **2** VULGAR, coarse, smutty, dirty, filthy, crude, lewd, obscene, off-colour, offensive, indelicate, tasteless; risqué, naughty, ribald, bawdy, racy; *informal* blue; *euphemistic* adult. **3** ABRUPT, sudden, sharp, startling; unpleasant, nasty, harsh.
—OPPOSITES: polite, clean.

rueful *adj.* ☞ REGRETFUL.

ruffle *v.* **1** DISARRANGE, tousle, rumple, disorder, mess up, tangle; *informal* muss up. **2** ☞ ANNOY.
—OPPOSITES: smooth, soothe.

rugged *adj.* **1** ROUGH, uneven, bumpy, rocky, stony, pitted, jagged, craggy. **2** ROBUST, durable, sturdy, strong, tough, resilient. **3** WELL-BUILT, burly, strong, muscular, muscly, brawny, strapping, husky, hulking; tough, hardy, robust, sturdy, lusty, solid; *informal* hunky, beefy. **4** STRONG, craggy, rough-hewn; manly, masculine; irregular, weathered.
—OPPOSITES: smooth, flimsy, weedy, delicate.

ruin *n.* **1** DISINTEGRATION, decay, disrepair, dilapidation, ruination; destruction, demolition, wreckage. **2** REMAINS, remnants, fragments, relics; rubble, debris, wreckage. **3** ☞ DOWNFALL. **4** BANKRUPTCY, insolvency, penury, poverty, destitution, impoverishment, indigence; failure.
—OPPOSITES: preservation, triumph, wealth.
▶ *v.* **1** WRECK, destroy, spoil, mar, blight, shatter, dash, torpedo, scotch, mess up; sabotage; *informal*

screw up, foul up, put the kibosh on, nix, scupper, scuttle. **2** BANKRUPT, make insolvent, impoverish, pauperize, wipe out, break, cripple, devastate; bring someone to their knees. **3** DESTROY, devastate, lay waste, ravage; raze, demolish, wreck, wipe out, flatten.
—OPPOSITES: save, rebuild.
☐ **in ruins 1** DERELICT, ruined, in disrepair, falling to pieces, dilapidated, tumbledown, ramshackle, decrepit, decaying, ruinous. **2** DESTROYED, ruined, in pieces, over, finished; *informal* in tatters, on the rocks, has had the biscuit✦, done for.

ruined *adj.* **1** DERELICT, in ruins, dilapidated, ruinous, tumbledown, ramshackle, decrepit, falling to pieces, crumbling, decaying, disintegrating. **2** DESTITUTE, impoverished, bankrupt, pauperized, wiped out, wrecked, cleaned out.

ruinous *adj.* **1** ☞ DISASTROUS. **2** ☞ EXORBITANT.

rule *n.* **1** REGULATION, ruling, directive, order, act, law, bylaw, statute, edict, canon, mandate, command, dictate, decree, fiat, injunction, commandment, stipulation, requirement, guideline, direction; *formal* ordinance. **2** PROCEDURE, practice, protocol, convention, norm, routine, custom, habit, wont; *formal* praxis. **3** PRECEPT, principle, standard, axiom, truth, maxim. **4** CONTROL, jurisdiction, command, power, dominion; government, administration, sovereignty, leadership, supremacy, authority; raj.

—RELATED: hegemonic, -cracy, -archy.

▶ v. **1** GOVERN, preside over, control, lead, dominate, run, head, administer, manage. **2** BE IN POWER, be in control, be in command, be in charge, govern; reign, be monarch, be sovereign. **3** DECREE, order, pronounce, judge, adjudge, ordain; decide, find, determine, resolve, settle. **4** PREVAIL, predominate, be the order of the day, reign supreme; *formal* obtain.

□ **as a rule** USUALLY, generally, in general, normally, ordinarily, customarily, for the most part, on the whole, by and large, in the main, mainly, mostly, commonly, typically. **rule something out** EXCLUDE, eliminate, disregard; preclude, prohibit, prevent, disallow.

ruling n. JUDGMENT, decision, adjudication, finding, verdict; pronouncement, resolution, decree, injunction.

▶ adj. **1** GOVERNING, controlling, commanding, supreme, leading, dominant, ascendant, reigning. **2** MAIN, chief, principal, major, prime, dominating, foremost; predominant, central, focal; *informal* number-one.

run v. **1** SPRINT, race, dart, rush, dash, hasten, hurry, scurry, scamper, bolt, fly, gallop, career, charge, shoot, hurtle, speed, zoom, go like lightning, go hell-bent for leather, go like the wind, go like a bat out of hell; jog, trot; *informal* tear, pelt, scoot, hotfoot it,

leg it, belt, zip, whip, bomb, hightail it, barrel. **2** ☞ FLEE. **3** COMPETE, take part, participate. **4** GO, pass, slide, move, travel. **5** CAST, pass, skim, flick. **6** EXTEND, stretch, reach, continue. **7** FLOW, pour, stream, gush, flood, cascade, roll, course, spill, trickle, drip, dribble, leak. **8** BE IN CHARGE OF, manage, direct, control, head, govern, supervise, superintend, oversee; operate, conduct, own. **9** CARRY OUT, do, perform, execute. **10** OPERATE, function, work, go; idle. **11** STAND FOR, be a candidate for, be a contender for; re-offer✦. **12** PUBLISH, print, feature, carry, put out, release, issue. **13** SMUGGLE, traffic in, deal in. **14** CHASE, drive, hound.

▶ n. **1** SPRINT, jog, dash, gallop, trot. **2** SERIES, succession, sequence, string, chain, streak, spell, stretch, spate. **3** DEMAND FOR, rush on.

□ **run across** MEET (BY CHANCE), come across, run into, chance on, stumble on, happen on; *informal* bump into. **run down** DECLINE, degenerate, go downhill, go to seed, decay, go to rack and ruin; *informal* go to pot, go to the dogs. **run into 1** COLLIDE WITH, hit, strike, crash into, smash into, plow into, ram, impact. **2** MEET (BY CHANCE), run across, chance on, stumble on, happen on; *informal* bump into. **3** EXPERIENCE, encounter, meet with, be faced with, be confronted with. **4** REACH, extend to, be as much as. **run on 1** CONTINUE, go on, carry on, last, keep going, stretch. **2** TALK INCESSANTLY, talk a lot, go on, chatter on, ramble on; *informal* yak, gab, run off at the mouth. **run out 1** BE USED UP, dry up, be exhausted, be finished, peter out. **2** BE OUT OF; use up, consume, eat up; *informal* be fresh out of. **3** EXPIRE, end, terminate, finish; lapse. **run over 1** OVERFLOW, spill over, brim over. **2** EXCEED, go over, overshoot, overreach. **3** RECAPITULATE, repeat, run through, go over, reiterate, review; look over, read through; *informal* recap. **run through 1** SQUANDER, spend, fritter away, dissipate, waste, go through, consume, use up; *informal* blow. **2** PERVADE, permeate, suffuse, imbue, inform. **3** ☞ RUN OVER 3. **4** REHEARSE, practise, go over, repeat; *informal* recap. **run to 1** AMOUNT TO, add up to, total, come to, equal, reach, be as much as. **2** AFFORD, stretch to, manage. **3** TEND TO, become, get, grow.

rural *adj.* COUNTRY, countryside, bucolic, rustic, pastoral; agricultural, agrarian; *literary* sylvan, georgic.
—OPPOSITES: urban.

rush *v.* **1** HURRY, dash, run, race, sprint, bolt, dart, gallop, career, charge, shoot, hurtle, careen, hare, fly, speed, zoom, scurry, scuttle, scamper, hasten; *informal* tear, belt, pelt, scoot, zip, whip, hotfoot it, leg it, bomb, hightail it. **2** FLOW, pour, gush, surge, stream, cascade, run, course. **3** PUSH,

hurry, hasten, speed, hustle, press, force.
▸ *n.* **1** DASH, run, sprint, dart, bolt, charge, scramble, break. **2** HUSTLE AND BUSTLE, commotion, hubbub, hurly-burly, stir; busy time. **3** DEMAND, clamour, call, request; run on. **4** HURRY, haste, urgency. **5** SURGE, flow, flood, spurt, stream; thrill, flash; *informal* charge, jolt, kick. **6** GUST, draft. **7** CHARGE, onslaught, attack, assault, onrush. **8** ATTACK, breakout.

rushed *adj.* **1** HASTY, fast, speedy, quick, swift, rapid, hurried. **2** PRESSED FOR TIME, busy, in a hurry, run off one's feet.

rustle *v.* **1** SWISH, whoosh, swoosh, whisper, sigh. **2** STEAL, thieve, take; abduct, kidnap; *informal* swipe.
▸ *n.* SWISH, whisper, rustling; *literary* susurration, susurrus.
□ **rustle something up** (*informal*) PREPARE HASTILY, throw together, make; *informal* fix.

rusty *adj.* **1** RUSTED, corroded, oxidized; tarnished, discoloured. **2** REDDISH-BROWN, rust-coloured, chestnut, auburn, tawny, russet, coppery, copper, Titian, red, ginger, gingery. **3** OUT OF PRACTICE, below par; unpractised, deficient, impaired, weak.

rut *n.* **1** FURROW, groove, trough, ditch, hollow, pothole, crater. **2** BORING ROUTINE, humdrum existence, habit, dead end.

ruthless *adj.* ☞ MERCILESS.
—OPPOSITES: merciful.

Ss

sabotage *n.* VANDALISM,
wrecking, destruction,
impairment, incapacitation,
damage; subversion, obstruction,
disruption, spoiling,
undermining; *informal* a wrench in
the works.
▶ *v.* VANDALIZE, wreck, damage,
destroy, cripple, impair,
incapacitate; obstruct, disrupt,
spoil, ruin, undermine, threaten,
subvert.

sacred *adj.* **1** ☞ HOLY 2.
2 RELIGIOUS, spiritual, devotional,
church, ecclesiastical.
3 SACROSANCT, inviolable,
inviolate, invulnerable,
untouchable, protected, defended,
secure.
—RELATED: hiero-.
—OPPOSITES: secular, profane.

sacrifice *n.* **1** RITUAL SLAUGHTER,
offering, oblation, immolation.
2 (VOTIVE) OFFERING, burnt
offering, gift, oblation.
3 SURRENDER, giving up,
abandonment, renunciation,
forfeiture, relinquishment,
resignation, abdication.
▶ *v.* **1** OFFER UP, immolate,
slaughter. **2** GIVE UP, abandon,
surrender, forgo, renounce,
forfeit, relinquish, resign,
abdicate; betray.

sacrilege *n.* DESECRATION,
profanity, blasphemy, impiety,

irreligion, unholiness,
irreverence, disrespect,
profanation.
—OPPOSITES: piety.

sacrilegious *adj.* PROFANE,
blasphemous, impious, sinful,
irreverent, irreligious, unholy,
disrespectful.

sad *adj.* **1** UNHAPPY, sorrowful,
dejected, depressed, downcast,
downhearted, miserable, down,
despondent, despairing,
disconsolate, dispirited,
discouraged, disheartened, heavy-
hearted, low, morose, desolate,
wretched, abject, glum, gloomy,
doleful, dismal, melancholy,
mournful, woebegone, woeful,
forlorn, crestfallen, heartbroken,
inconsolable, tearful, upset; *informal*
blue, down in the mouth, down in
the dumps, in a blue funk, in the
doldrums, blah; *literary* dolorous,
heartsick. **2** TRAGIC, unhappy,
unfortunate, awful, miserable,
wretched, sorry, pitiful, pathetic,
traumatic, heartbreaking, heart-
rending, harrowing.
3 UNFORTUNATE, regrettable, sorry,
deplorable, lamentable, pitiful,
shameful, disgraceful.
—OPPOSITES: happy, cheerful,
fortunate.

sadden *v.* ☞ DEPRESS 1.

sadness *n.* UNHAPPINESS, sorrow,
dejection, depression, misery,

despondency, despair, desolation, wretchedness, regret, gloom, gloominess, dolefulness, melancholy, mournfulness, woe, heartache, grief; *informal* the blues; *literary* dolour.

safe *adj.* **1** SECURE, protected, shielded, sheltered, guarded, out of harm's way. **2** UNHARMED, unhurt, uninjured, unscathed, all right, well, in one piece, out of danger, home free; *informal* OK. **3** SECURE, sound, impregnable, unassailable, invulnerable. **4** CAUTIOUS, circumspect, prudent, attentive; unadventurous, conservative, unenterprising. **5** HARMLESS, innocuous, benign, non-toxic, non-poisonous.
—OPPOSITES: insecure, dangerous, reckless, harmful.

safeguard *n.* PROTECTION, defence, guard, screen, buffer, preventive, precaution, provision, security; surety, cover, insurance, indemnity.
▶ *v.* ☞ PROTECT.
—OPPOSITES: jeopardize.

safety *n.* **1** WELFARE, well-being, protection, security. **2** SECURITY, soundness, dependability, reliability. **3** SHELTER, sanctuary, refuge.

sag *v.* **1** SINK, slump, loll, flop, crumple. **2** DIP, droop; bulge, bag. **3** ☞ DECLINE *v.* 2.

saga *n.* **1** EPIC, chronicle, legend, folk tale, romance, history, narrative, adventure, myth, fairy story. **2** LONG STORY, rigmarole; chain of events; *informal* spiel.

sailor *n.* SEAMAN, seafarer, mariner; boatman, yachtsman, hand; *informal* (old) salt, sea dog,

rating, bluejacket, matelot, shellback.

saintly *adj.* ☞ HOLY 1.
—OPPOSITES: ungodly.

sake *n.* **1** PURPOSE, reason, aim, end, objective, object, goal, motive. **2** BENEFIT, advantage, good, well-being, welfare, interest, profit.

salary *n.* ☞ WAGE.

sale *n.* **1** SELLING, vending; dealing, trading. **2** DEAL, transaction. **3** MARKDOWN, discount, blowout, clearance (sale), fire sale, sell-off, liquidation (sale).
—OPPOSITES: purchase.
☐ **for sale** ON THE MARKET, on sale, available, purchasable, obtainable.

salute *n.* **1** GREETING, salutation, gesture of respect, obeisance, acknowledgement, welcome, address. **2** TRIBUTE, testimonial, homage, toast, honour, eulogy; celebration of, acknowledgement of.
▶ *v.* **1** GREET, address, hail, welcome, acknowledge, toast; make obeisance to. **2** ☞ HONOUR *v.* 2.

salvage *v.* **1** RESCUE, save, recover, retrieve, raise, reclaim. **2** RETAIN, preserve, conserve; regain, recoup, redeem, snatch.
▶ *n.* **1** RESCUE, recovery, reclamation. **2** REMAINS, debris, wreckage, rubble, remnants, flotsam and jetsam, scrap.

salvation *n.* **1** REDEMPTION, deliverance, reclamation. **2** LIFELINE, preservation; means of escape, help, saving, saviour.
—OPPOSITES: damnation.

same *adj.* **1** IDENTICAL, selfsame, very same, one and the same.

2 MATCHING, identical, alike, duplicate, carbon copy, twin; indistinguishable, interchangeable, corresponding, equivalent, parallel, like, comparable, similar, congruent, concordant, consonant. **3** SELFSAME; aforesaid, aforementioned. **4** UNCHANGING, unvarying, unvaried, invariable, consistent, uniform, regular.
—RELATED: homo-.
—OPPOSITES: another, different, dissimilar, varying.
☐ **all the same** ☞ HOWEVER.

sample n. **1** ☞ SPECIMEN. **2** CROSS SECTION, variety, sampling, test.
▶ v. TRY (OUT), taste, test, put to the test, experiment with; appraise, evaluate, test drive; *informal* check out.

sanctimonious adj. SELF-RIGHTEOUS, holier-than-thou, pious, pietistic, churchy, moralizing, preachy, smug, superior, priggish, hypocritical, insincere; *informal* goody-goody.

sanction n. **1** PENALTY, punishment, deterrent; punitive action, discipline, restriction; embargo, ban, prohibition, boycott. **2** AUTHORIZATION, consent, leave, permission, authority, warrant, licence, dispensation, assent, acquiescence, agreement, approval, approbation, endorsement, accreditation, ratification, validation, blessing, imprimatur; *informal* the go-ahead, the OK, the green light.
—OPPOSITES: reward, prohibition.
▶ v. **1** AUTHORIZE, permit, allow, warrant, accredit, license, endorse, approve, accept, back,

support; *informal* OK. **2** PUNISH, discipline someone for.
—OPPOSITES: prohibit.

sanctity n. **1** HOLINESS, godliness, blessedness, saintliness, spirituality, piety, piousness, devoutness, righteousness, goodness, virtue, purity; *formal* sanctitude. **2** INVIOLABILITY; importance, paramountcy.

sanctuary n. **1** ☞ REFUGE. **2** SAFETY, protection, shelter, immunity, asylum. **3** RESERVE, park, reservation, preserve.

sane adj. **1** OF SOUND MIND, in one's right mind, compos mentis, lucid, rational, balanced, stable, normal; *informal* all there, together. **2** ☞ SENSIBLE.
—OPPOSITES: mad, foolish.

sanitary adj. ☞ HYGIENIC.

sanity n. **1** MENTAL HEALTH, faculties, reason, rationality, saneness, stability, lucidity; sense, wits, mind. **2** (COMMON) SENSE, wisdom, prudence, judiciousness, rationality, soundness, sensibleness.

sarcasm n. DERISION, mockery, ridicule, scorn, sneering, scoffing; irony; cynicism.

sarcastic adj. SARDONIC, ironic, ironical; derisive, snide, scornful, contemptuous, mocking, sneering, jeering; caustic, scathing, trenchant, cutting, biting, bitter, sharp, acerbic, abrasive, vitriolic; *informal* snarky, smart-alecky.

satire n. **1** PARODY, burlesque, caricature, lampoon, skit; *informal* spoof, takeoff, send-up. **2** MOCKERY, ridicule, derision, scorn, caricature; irony, sarcasm.

satirical *adj.* MOCKING, ironic, ironical, satiric, sarcastic, sardonic; caustic, trenchant, mordant, biting, cutting, stinging, acerbic; critical, irreverent, disparaging, disrespectful.

satirize *v.* MOCK, ridicule, deride, make fun of, poke fun at, parody, lampoon, burlesque, caricature, take off; criticize; *informal* send up.

satisfaction *n.* **1** CONTENTMENT, pleasure, gratification, fulfillment, enjoyment, happiness, pride; self-satisfaction, smugness, complacency. **2** FULFILLMENT, gratification; appeasement, assuaging.

satisfactory *adj.* ADEQUATE, all right, acceptable, good enough, sufficient, reasonable, quite good, competent, fair, decent, average, passable, tolerable; fine, in order, up to scratch/snuff, up to the mark, up to standard, up to par, suitable; *informal* OK, jake, hunky-dory, so-so, {comme ci, comme ça}.
—OPPOSITES: inadequate, poor.

satisfy *v.* **1** FULFILL, gratify, meet, fill; indulge, cater to, pander to; appease, assuage; quench, slake, satiate, sate, take the edge off. **2** CONVINCE, persuade, assure; reassure, put someone's mind at rest. **3** COMPLY WITH, meet, fulfill, answer, conform to; measure up to, come up to; suffice, be good enough, fit/fill the bill. **4** REPAY, pay (off), settle, make good, discharge, square, liquidate, clear.
—OPPOSITES: frustrate.

savage *adj.* **1** FEROCIOUS, fierce; wild, untamed, untameable, undomesticated, feral. **2** VICIOUS,

brutal, cruel, sadistic, ferocious, fierce, violent, bloody, murderous, homicidal, bloodthirsty. **3** ☞ SCATHING.
—OPPOSITES: tame, mild.
▸ *n.* **1** BARBARIAN, wild man, wild woman, primitive. **2** BRUTE, beast, monster, barbarian, sadist, animal.
▸ *v.* **1** MAUL, attack, tear to pieces, lacerate, claw, bite. **2** ☞ CRITICIZE.

save *v.* **1** RESCUE, come to someone's rescue, save someone's life; set free, free, liberate, deliver, extricate; bail out; *informal* save someone's bacon/neck/skin. **2** PRESERVE, keep safe, keep, protect, safeguard; salvage, retrieve, reclaim, rescue. **3** PUT ASIDE, set aside, put by, put to one side, save up, keep, retain, reserve, conserve, stockpile, store, hoard, save for a rainy day; *informal* salt away, squirrel away, stash away, hang on to. **4** PREVENT, obviate, forestall, spare; stop; avoid, avert.

saving *n.* **1** REDUCTION, cut, decrease, economy. **2** NEST EGG, money for a rainy day, life savings, RRSP; capital, assets, funds, resources, reserves.

savour *v.* ☞ RELISH *v.* 1.
▸ *n.* **1** SMELL, aroma, fragrance, scent, perfume, bouquet; TASTE, flavour, tang, smack. **2** TRACE, hint, suggestion, touch, smack. **3** PIQUANCY, interest, attraction, flavour, spice, zest, excitement, enjoyment, shine; *informal* zing, pizzazz, sparkle.

savoury *adj.* **1** SALTY, spicy, piquant, tangy. **2** ☞ APPETIZING. **3** ACCEPTABLE, pleasant,

respectable, wholesome, honourable, proper, seemly.
—OPPOSITES: sweet, unappetizing.

say v. **1** SPEAK, utter, voice, pronounce, give voice to, vocalize. **2** DECLARE, state, announce, remark, observe, mention, comment, note, add; reply, respond, answer, rejoin; *informal* come out with. **3** CLAIM, maintain, assert, hold, insist, contend; allege, profess; *formal* opine, aver. **4** EXPRESS, put into words, phrase, articulate, communicate, make known, put/get across, convey, verbalize; reveal, divulge, impart, disclose; imply, suggest. **5** RECITE, repeat, utter, deliver, perform, declaim, orate. **6** INDICATE, show, read. **7** ESTIMATE, judge, guess, hazard a guess, predict, speculate, surmise, conjecture, venture; *informal* reckon. **8** SUPPOSE, assume, imagine, presume, hypothesize, postulate, posit.
▶ n. **1** CHANCE TO SPEAK, turn to speak, opinion, view, voice; *informal* two cents, two cents' worth. **2** INFLUENCE, sway, weight, voice, input, share, part.

saying n. PROVERB, maxim, aphorism, axiom, adage, saw, tag, motto, epigram, dictum, expression, phrase, formula; slogan, catchphrase, mantra; platitude, cliché, commonplace, truism, chestnut.
□ **it goes without saying** OF COURSE, naturally, needless to say, it's taken for granted, it's understood/assumed, it's taken as read, it's an accepted fact; obviously, self-evidently, manifestly; *informal* natch.

scale n. **1** HIERARCHY, ladder, ranking, pecking order, order, spectrum; succession, sequence, series. **2** RATIO, proportion, relative size. **3** EXTENT, size, scope, magnitude, dimensions, range, breadth, compass, degree, reach.
▶ v. CLIMB, ascend, clamber up, shin (up), scramble up, mount, shinny (up).
□ **scale something down** REDUCE, cut down, cut back, cut, decrease, lessen, lower, trim, slim down, prune. **scale something up** INCREASE, expand, augment, build up, add to; step up, boost, escalate.

scaly adj. **1** *technical* squamous, squamate, lamellate. **2** DRY, flaky, flaking, scurfy, rough, scabrous, mangy, scabious.

scamp n. (*informal*) RASCAL, monkey, devil, imp, rogue, wretch, mischief-maker; *informal* scalawag, horror, monster, tyke, varmint, rapscallion; *archaic* scapegrace.

scan v. **1** SCRUTINIZE, examine, study, inspect, survey, search, scour, sweep, look at, stare at, gaze at, eye, watch; *informal* check out, scope (out). **2** GLANCE THROUGH, look through, have a look at, run/cast one's eye over, skim through, flick through, flip through, leaf through, thumb through.
▶ n. **1** INSPECTION, scrutiny, examination, survey. **2** GLANCE, look, flick, browse. **3** EXAMINATION, screening, MRI, ultrasound.

scandal n. **1** WRONGDOING, impropriety, misconduct, immoral behaviour, unethical behaviour; offence, transgression, crime, sin; skeleton in the closet; *informal* -gate. **2** DISGRACE, outrage, injustice; (crying) shame.

3 MALICIOUS GOSSIP, malicious rumour(s), slander, libel, calumny, defamation, aspersions, muckraking; *informal* dirt.

scandalize v. SHOCK, appall, outrage, horrify, disgust; offend, affront, insult.
—OPPOSITES: impress.

scandalous *adj.*
1 ☞ DISGRACEFUL. **2** DISCREDITABLE, disreputable, dishonourable, improper, unseemly, sordid.
3 SCURRILOUS, malicious, slanderous, libellous, defamatory.

scanty *adj.* **1** ☞ MEAGRE.
2 ☞ SKIMPY 1.
—OPPOSITES: ample, plentiful.

scar n. **1** CICATRIX, mark, blemish, disfigurement, discoloration; pockmark, pock, pit; lesion, stigma; birthmark, nevus.
2 TRAUMA, damage, injury.
▶ v. **1** DISFIGURE, mark, blemish; pockmark, pit; stigmatize.
2 DAMAGE, spoil, mar, deface, injure. **3** TRAUMATIZE, damage, injure; distress, disturb, upset.

scarce *adj.* **1** IN SHORT SUPPLY, scant, scanty, meagre, sparse, hard to find, hard to come by, insufficient, deficient, inadequate; at a premium, paltry, negligible; *informal* not to be had for love or money; *formal* exiguous. **2** RARE, few and far between, thin on the ground; uncommon, unusual.
—OPPOSITES: plentiful.

scarcely *adv.* **1** HARDLY, barely, only just; almost not. **2** ☞ SELDOM.
3 SURELY NOT, not, hardly,

certainly not, not at all, on no account, under no circumstances, by no means, noway.
—OPPOSITES: often.

scarcity n. SHORTAGE, dearth, lack, insufficiency, paucity, meagreness, sparseness, poverty; deficiency, inadequacy, deficit, rarity, shortfall, sparsity; unavailability, absence.

scare v. FRIGHTEN, startle, alarm, terrify, petrify, unnerve, intimidate, terrorize, cow, chill, daunt, dismay, disturb, panic, shake, shock, unman; strike terror into, put the fear of God into, chill someone to the bone/marrow, make someone's blood run cold; *informal* frighten/scare the living daylights out of, scare stiff, scarify, frighten/scare someone out of their wits, scare witless, frighten/scare to death, scare the pants off, make someone's hair stand on end, make someone jump out of their skin, make someone's hair curl, spook, scare the bejesus out of, give someone the heebie-jeebies.
▶ n. FRIGHT, shock, start, turn, jump; *informal* heart attack.

scary *adj.* ☞ FRIGHTENING.

scathing *adj.* WITHERING, blistering, searing, devastating, fierce, ferocious, savage, severe, stinging, biting, cutting, mordant, trenchant, virulent, caustic, vitriolic, scornful, sharp, bitter, harsh, unsparing.
—OPPOSITES: mild.

scatter v. **1** THROW, strew, toss, fling; sprinkle, spread, distribute, sow, broadcast, disseminate.

2 ☞ DISPERSE 1.
—OPPOSITES: gather, assemble.

scatterbrained adj. ☞ ABSENT-
MINDED.

scenario n. **1** PLOT, outline,
synopsis, storyline, framework;
screenplay, script, libretto; formal
diegesis. **2** SEQUENCE OF EVENTS,
course of events, chain of events,
situation. **3** SETTING, background,
context, scene, milieu.

scene n. **1** LOCATION, site, place,
position, point, spot; locale,
whereabouts; technical locus.
2 BACKGROUND, setting, context,
milieu, backdrop, mise en scène.
3 INCIDENT, event, episode,
happening. **4** VIEW, vista, outlook,
panorama, sight; landscape,
scenery. **5** FUSS, exhibition of
oneself, performance, tantrum,
commotion, disturbance, upset,
furor, brouhaha; informal to-do.
6 ARENA, stage, sphere, world,
milieu, realm, domain; area of
interest, field, province, preserve.
□ **behind the scenes** SECRETLY,
in secret, privately, in private,
behind closed doors,
surreptitiously; informal on the
quiet, on the q.t.; formal sub rosa.

scenery n. **1** ☞ LANDSCAPE.
2 STAGE SET, set, mise en scène,
backdrop, drop curtain.

scenic adj. PICTURESQUE, pretty,
pleasing, attractive, lovely,
beautiful, charming, pretty as a
picture, easy on the eye;
impressive, striking, spectacular,
breathtaking; panoramic.

scent n. **1** SMELL, fragrance,
aroma, perfume, redolence,
savour, odour; bouquet, nose.

2 SPOOR, trail, track; Hunting foil,
wind.

schedule n. **1** PLAN, program,
timetable, scheme. **2** TIMETABLE,
agenda, diary, calendar, timeline;
itinerary.
▶ v. ARRANGE, organize, plan,
program, timetable, set up, line
up, slate.

scheme n. **1** ☞ PLAN n. 1. **2** PLOT,
intrigue, conspiracy; ruse, ploy,
stratagem, manoeuvre,
subterfuge; machinations; informal
game, racket, con, scam.
3 ARRANGEMENT, system,
organization, configuration,
pattern, format; technical schema.
▶ v. PLOT, hatch a plot, conspire,
collude, collaborate, intrigue,
connive, manoeuvre, plan; informal
be in cahoots.

scheming adj. CUNNING, crafty,
calculating, devious, designing,
conniving, wily, sly, tricky, artful,
guileful, slippery, slick,
manipulative, Machiavellian,
unscrupulous, disingenuous;
duplicitous, deceitful,
underhanded, treacherous,
double-dealing; informal crooked,
foxy.
—OPPOSITES: ingenuous, honest.

scholar n. ACADEMIC, intellectual,
learned person, man/woman of
letters, mind, intellect, savant,
polymath, highbrow,
bluestocking; authority, expert;
informal egghead.

scholarly adj. **1** ☞ ACADEMIC adj. 2.
2 ☞ ACADEMIC adj. 1.
—OPPOSITES: uneducated,
illiterate.

scholarship *n.* **1** ☞ LEARNING.
2 GRANT, award, endowment,
payment, bursary.

school *n.* **1** EDUCATIONAL
INSTITUTION; academy, college,
university; seminary; alma mater.
2 DEPARTMENT, faculty, division.
3 GROUP, set, circle; followers,
following, disciples, apostles,
admirers, devotees, votaries;
proponents, adherents. **4** WAY OF
THINKING, persuasion, creed, credo,
doctrine, belief, faith, opinion,
point of view; approach, method,
style.
—RELATED: scholastic.

scientific *adj.* **1** technological,
technical; research-based,
knowledge-based, empirical.
2 SYSTEMATIC, methodical,
organized, well-organized,
ordered, orderly, meticulous,
rigorous; exact, precise, accurate,
mathematical; analytical, rational.

scintillating *adj.* **1** SPARKLING,
shining, bright, brilliant,
gleaming, glittering, twinkling,
shimmering, glistening; *literary*
glistering. **2** BRILLIANT, dazzling,
exciting, exhilarating,
stimulating; sparkling, lively,
vivacious, vibrant, animated,
ebullient, effervescent; witty,
clever; *literary* coruscating.
—OPPOSITES: dull, boring.

scoff *v.* ☞ RIDICULE.

scold *v.* REBUKE, reprimand,
reproach, reprove, admonish,
remonstrate with, chastise, chide,
criticize, upbraid, berate, take to
task, read someone the riot act,
give someone a piece of one's
mind, haul/rake someone over the
coals, censure, chasten, lambaste,

lecture, reprehend; *informal* tell off,
dress down, give someone an
earful, rap over the knuckles, slap
someone's wrist, zing, let
someone have it, bawl out, give
someone hell, tear a strip off
someone, give someone what for,
give someone a roasting/tongue-
lashing, chew out, ream out, light
into, blow up at, come down on
someone (like a ton of bricks),
have a go at, have someone's guts
for garters, take to the woodshed,
tear a strip off, blast, give
someone a dressing-down, give
someone a talking-to, tear into;
formal castigate.
—OPPOSITES: praise.

scope *n.* **1** EXTENT, range, breadth,
width, reach, sweep, purview,
span, horizon; area, sphere, field,
realm, compass, orbit, ambit,
terms/field of reference,
jurisdiction; confine, limit; gamut.
2 OPPORTUNITY, freedom, latitude,
leeway, capacity, liberty, room (to
manoeuvre), elbow room;
possibility, chance.

scorch *v.* **1** BURN, sear, singe,
char, blacken, discolour; toast.
2 DRY UP, desiccate, parch, wither,
shrivel; burn, bake.

score *n.* **1** RESULT, outcome; total,
sum total, tally, count. **2** RATING,
grade, mark, percentage.
3 GRIEVANCE, bone to pick, axe to
grind, grudge, complaint; dispute
bone of contention. **4** (*informal*) THE
SITUATION, the position, the facts,
the truth of the matter, the (true)
state of affairs, the picture, how
things stand, the lay of the land;
informal what's what.
▸ *v.* NET, bag, rack up, chalk up,

tally, notch, record; get, gain, achieve, make.

scorn *n.* CONTEMPT, derision, contemptuousness, disdain, derisiveness, mockery, sneering.
—OPPOSITES: admiration, respect.
▶ *v.* DERIDE, hold in contempt, treat with contempt, pour/heap scorn on, look down on, look down one's nose at, disdain, curl one's lip at, mock, scoff at, sneer at, jeer at, laugh at, laugh out of court; disparage, slight; dismiss, thumb one's nose at; *informal* turn one's nose up at.
—OPPOSITES: admire, respect.

scornful *adj.* ☞ CONTEMPTUOUS.
—OPPOSITES: admiring, respectful.

scoundrel *n.* ROGUE, rascal, miscreant, good-for-nothing, reprobate; cheat, swindler, scam artist, fraudster, trickster, charlatan; *informal* villain, bastard, beast, son of a bitch, SOB, rat, louse, swine, dog, skunk, heel, snake (in the grass), wretch, scumbag, scum-bucket, scuzzball, sleazeball, sleazebag, sleeveen, rat fink; *informal, dated* hound; *dated* cad; *archaic* blackguard, knave, varlet, whoreson, picaroon.

scourge *n.* AFFLICTION, bane, curse, plague, menace, evil, misfortune, burden, cross to bear; blight, cancer, canker.
—OPPOSITES: blessing, godsend.

scout *n.* 1 LOOKOUT, outrider, advance guard, vanguard; spy. 2 RECONNAISSANCE, reconnoitre; exploration, search, expedition; *informal* recon. 3 TALENT SPOTTER, talent scout; *informal* bird dog.
▶ *v.* 1 SEARCH, look, hunt, ferret about/around, root about/around.

2 RECONNOITRE, explore, make a reconnaissance of, inspect, investigate, spy out, survey; examine, scan, study, observe; *informal* check out, case.

scowl *v.* GLOWER, frown, glare, grimace, lower, look daggers at, give someone a black look; make a face, pull a face, turn the corners of one's mouth down, pout; *informal* give someone a dirty look.
—OPPOSITES: smile, grin.

scram *v.* (*informal*) GO AWAY, leave, get out; go, get moving, be off (with you), shoo; *informal* skedaddle, split, scat, run along, beat it, get lost, shove off, buzz off, push off, clear off, bug off, take a powder, take a hike; *literary* begone.

scrap *n.* 1 FRAGMENT, piece, bit, snippet, shred; offcut, oddment, remnant. 2 BIT, speck, iota, particle, ounce, whit, jot, atom, shred, scintilla, tittle, jot or tittle; *informal* smidgen, tad. 3 LEFTOVERS, leavings, crumbs, scrapings, remains, remnants, residue, odds and ends, bits and pieces. 4 WASTE, rubbish, refuse, litter, debris, detritus; flotsam and jetsam, garbage, trash; *informal* junk.
▶ *v.* 1 THROW AWAY, throw out, dispose of, get rid of, toss out, throw on the scrap heap, discard, remove, dispense with, lose, decommission, recycle, break up, demolish; *informal* chuck (away/out), ditch, dump, junk, get shut of, trash, deep-six. 2 ABANDON, drop, abolish, withdraw, throw out, do away with, put an end to, cancel, axe, jettison; *informal* ditch, dump,

junk, can.

—OPPOSITES: keep, preserve.

scrape v. **1** ABRADE, grate, sand, sandpaper, scour, scratch, rub, file, rasp. **2** GRATE, creak, rasp, grind, scratch. **3** RAKE, drag, pull, tug, draw. **4** SCOOP OUT, hollow out, dig (out), excavate, gouge out. **5** GRAZE, scratch, abrade, scuff, rasp, skin, rub raw, cut, lacerate, bark, chafe; *Medicine* excoriate.

▶ n. **1** GRATING, creaking, grinding, rasp, rasping, scratch, scratching. **2** ☞ SCRATCH n. 1. **3** (*informal*) PREDICAMENT, plight, tight corner/ spot, ticklish/tricky situation, problem, crisis, mess, muddle; *informal* jam, fix, stew, bind, hole, hot water, a pretty/fine kettle of fish.

□ **scrape by** MANAGE, cope, survive, muddle through/along, make ends meet, get by/along, make do, keep the wolf from the door, keep one's head above water, eke out a living; *informal* make out.

scratch v. **1** SCORE, abrade, scrape, scuff. **2** GRAZE, scrape, abrade, skin, rub raw, cut, lacerate, bark, chafe; wound; *Medicine* excoriate. **3** CROSS OUT, strike out, score out, delete, erase, remove, eliminate, expunge, obliterate. **4** WITHDRAW, pull out of, back out of, bow out of, stand down.

▶ n. **1** GRAZE, scrape, abrasion, cut, laceration, wound. **2** SCORE, mark, line, scrape.

scream v. & n. SHRIEK, screech, yell, howl, shout, bellow, bawl, cry, call, yelp, squeal, wail, squawk; *informal* holler.

screen n. **1** PARTITION, (room) divider. **2** DISPLAY, monitor, video display terminal, VDT, cathode-ray tube, CRT. **3** MESH, net, netting. **4** BUFFER, protection, shield, shelter, guard, windbreak.

▶ v. **1** PARTITION OFF, divide off, separate off, curtain off. **2** CONCEAL, hide, veil; shield, shelter, shade, protect, guard, safeguard. **3** VET, check, check up on, investigate; *informal* check out. **4** CHECK, test, examine, investigate. **5** SHOW, broadcast, transmit, air, televise, telecast, put on the air.

scribble v. SCRAWL, write hurriedly, write untidily, scratch, dash off, jot (down); doodle.

▶ n. SCRAWL, squiggle(s), jottings; doodle, doodlings.

scrimp v. ECONOMIZE, skimp, scrimp and save, save; be thrifty, be frugal, tighten one's belt, cut back, husband one's resources, watch one's pennies, pinch (the) pennies.

script n. **1** HANDWRITING, writing, hand, penmanship, calligraphy. **2** TEXT, screenplay; libretto, score; lines, dialogue, words.

scrounge v. BEG, borrow; *informal* cadge, sponge, bum, touch someone for, mooch.

scruffy adj. SHABBY, worn, down-at-(the)-heel, ragged, tattered, mangy, dirty; untidy, unkempt, bedraggled, messy, dishevelled; *informal* tatty, the worse for wear, ratty, raggedy, scuzzy.

—OPPOSITES: smart, tidy.

scrupulous adj. **1** ☞ METICULOUS. **2** ☞ HONEST 1.

—OPPOSITES: careless, dishonest.

scrutinize v. EXAMINE, inspect, survey, study, look at, peruse; investigate, explore, probe, inquire into, go into, check (out), consider, eye, observe, regard, watch; *informal* eyeball.

scrutiny n. EXAMINATION, inspection, survey, study, perusal; investigation, exploration, probe, inquiry; *informal* going-over.

sculpture n. MODEL, carving, statue, statuette, figure, figurine, effigy, bust, head, likeness.

scum n. **1** FILM, layer, covering, froth; filth, dross, dirt. **2** (*informal*) DESPICABLE PEOPLE, the lowest of the low, the dregs of society, vermin, riff-raff, low-lifes; *informal* the scum of the earth, dirt.

seal n. **1** SEALANT, sealer, adhesive, caulking. **2** ☞ EMBLEM.
▸ v. **1** ☞ FASTEN 1. **2** STOP UP, seal up, make airtight/watertight, cork, stopper, plug. **3** CLOSE OFF, shut off, cordon off, fence off, isolate. **4** ☞ CLINCH 1.

search v. **1** HUNT, look, seek, forage, fish about/around, look high and low, cast about/around, ferret about/around, root about/around, rummage about/around. **2** LOOK THROUGH, hunt through, explore, scour, rifle through, go through/over, sift through, comb, sweep, probe, go through with a fine-tooth comb; turn upside down, turn inside out, leave no stone unturned in. **3** EXAMINE, inspect, check, frisk.
▸ n. HUNT, look, quest; pursuit, manhunt.

seasoned adj. ☞ EXPERIENCED.
—OPPOSITES: inexperienced.

second adj. **1** NEXT, following, subsequent, succeeding. **2** ADDITIONAL, extra, alternative, another, spare, backup, fallback, alternate. **3** ANOTHER, new; repeat of, copy of, carbon copy of.
—OPPOSITES: first.
▸ v. FORMALLY SUPPORT, give one's support to, vote for, back, approve, endorse.

secondary adj. **1** LESS IMPORTANT, subordinate, lesser, minor, peripheral, incidental, ancillary, subsidiary, non-essential, inessential, of little account, unimportant, immaterial, marginal, tangential. **2** ACCOMPANYING, attendant, concomitant, consequential, resulting, resultant.
—OPPOSITES: primary, main.

second-hand adj. **1** ☞ USED. **2** INDIRECT, derivative; vicarious.
—OPPOSITES: new, direct.

secret adj. **1** CONFIDENTIAL, top secret, classified, undisclosed, unknown, private, under wraps; *informal* hush-hush; *formal* sub rosa. **2** HIDDEN, concealed, disguised; invisible. **3** ☞ CLANDESTINE. **4** CRYPTIC, encoded, coded; mysterious, abstruse, recondite, arcane, esoteric, cabbalistic. **5** SECLUDED, private, concealed, hidden, unfrequented, out of the way, tucked away. **6** ☞ SECRETIVE.
—OPPOSITES: public, open.
▸ n. **1** CONFIDENTIAL MATTER, confidence, private affair; skeleton in the closet. **2** MYSTERY, enigma, paradox, puzzle, conundrum, poser, riddle. **3** RECIPE, (magic) formula,

blueprint, key, answer, solution.
□ **in secret** ☞ SECRETLY 1.

secrete v. PRODUCE, discharge, emit, excrete, release, send out.
—OPPOSITES: absorb.

secretive adj. UNCOMMUNICATIVE, secret, unforthcoming, playing one's cards close to one's chest, reticent, reserved, silent, quiet, tight-lipped, close-mouthed, taciturn.
—OPPOSITES: open, communicative.

secretly adv. 1 IN SECRET, in private, privately, behind closed doors, in camera, behind the scenes, under cover, under the counter, behind someone's back, furtively, stealthily, on the sly, on the quiet, conspiratorially, covertly, clandestinely, on the side; informal on the q.t., off the record, hush-hush; formal sub rosa. 2 PRIVATELY, in one's heart (of hearts), deep down.

sectarian adj. FACTIONAL, separatist, partisan, parti pris; doctrinaire, dogmatic, extreme, fanatical, rigid, inflexible, bigoted, hidebound, narrow-minded.
—OPPOSITES: tolerant, liberal.

section n. 1 PART, piece, bit, segment, component, division, portion, element, unit, constituent. 2 SUBDIVISION, part, subsection, division, portion, bit, chapter, passage, clause. 3 DEPARTMENT, area, part, division. 4 ☞ SECTOR 2.

sector adj. 1 PART, branch, arm, division, area, department, field, sphere. 2 DISTRICT, quarter, part, section, zone, region, area, belt.

secular adj. NON-RELIGIOUS, lay, temporal, worldly, earthly, profane; formal laic.
—OPPOSITES: holy, religious.

secure adj. 1 FASTENED, fixed, secured, done up; closed, shut, locked. 2 ☞ SAFE 2. 3 CERTAIN, assured, reliable, dependable, settled, fixed.
—OPPOSITES: loose, vulnerable, uncertain.
▶ v. 1 FIX, attach, fasten, affix, connect, couple. 2 ☞ FASTEN 1. 3 TIE UP, moor, make fast; anchor. 4 PROTECT, make safe, fortify, strengthen; undergird. 5 ASSURE, ensure, guarantee, protect, confirm, establish. 6 OBTAIN, acquire, gain, get, get possession of; informal get hold of, land.

sedate adj. 1 SLOW, steady, dignified, unhurried, relaxed, measured, leisurely, slow-moving, easy, easygoing, gentle. 2 CALM, placid, tranquil, quiet, uneventful; boring, dull.
—OPPOSITES: exciting, fast.

sedative adj. TRANQUILIZING, calming, calmative, relaxing, soporific, narcotic; depressant; Medicine neuroleptic.
▶ n. TRANQUILIZER, calmative, sleeping pill, narcotic, opiate; depressant; informal trank, downer.

sedentary adj. SITTING, seated, desk-bound, stationary; inactive, lethargic, lazy, idle.
—OPPOSITES: active.

sediment n. DREGS, lees, precipitate, deposit, grounds; residue, remains; silt, alluvium; technical residuum.

seduce v. 1 persuade to have sex; euphemistic have one's (wicked) way with, take advantage of; *dated* debauch. **2** ATTRACT, allure, lure, tempt, entice, beguile, inveigle, manoeuvre.

seductive *adj.* ☞ SEXY 1.

see *v.* **1** DISCERN, spot, notice, catch sight of, glimpse, catch/get a glimpse of, make out, pick out, spy, distinguish, detect, perceive, note; *informal* clap/lay/set eyes on, clock; *literary* behold, descry, espy. **2** WATCH, look at, view; catch. **3** INSPECT, view, look round, tour, survey, examine, scrutinize; *informal* give something a/the once-over. **4** ☞ UNDERSTAND 1. **5** FIND OUT, discover, learn, ascertain, determine, establish. **6** ENSURE, make sure/certain, see to it, take care, mind. **7** FORESEE, predict, forecast, prophesy, anticipate, envisage, picture, visualize. **8** ENCOUNTER, meet; run into/across, come across, stumble on/across, happen on, chance on; *informal* bump into. **9** MEET, meet up with, get together with, socialize with. **10** ☞ CONSULT. **11** GO OUT WITH, date, take out, be involved with; *informal* go steady with; *dated* court.

□ **see through** UNDERSTAND, get/ have the measure of, read like a book; *informal* be wise to, have someone's number, know someone's (little) game. **see to** ATTEND TO, deal with, see about, take care of, look after, sort out, fix, organize, arrange.

seek *v.* **1** SEARCH FOR, try to find, look for, be on the lookout for, be after, hunt for, be in quest of. **2** TRY TO OBTAIN, work towards, be intent on, aim at/for. **3** ASK FOR,

request, solicit, call for, entreat, beg for, petition for, appeal for, apply for, put in for. **4** TRY, attempt, endeavour, strive, work, do one's best; *formal* essay.

seem *v.* APPEAR (TO BE), have the appearance/air of being, give the impression of being, look, look as though one is, look like, show signs of, look to be; come across as, strike someone as, sound.

seep *v.* OOZE, trickle, exude, drip, dribble, flow, issue, escape, leak, drain, bleed, filter, percolate, soak.

see-through *adj.*
☞ TRANSPARENT.
—OPPOSITES: opaque.

segment *n.* **1** PIECE, bit, section, part, chunk, portion, division, slice; fragment, wedge, lump. **2** PART, section, sector, division, portion, constituent, element, unit, compartment; branch, wing.
▶ *v.* DIVIDE (UP), subdivide, separate, split, cut up, carve up, slice up, break up; segregate, divorce, partition, section.
—OPPOSITES: amalgamate.

segregate *v.* SEPARATE, set apart, keep apart, isolate, quarantine, closet; partition, divide, detach, disconnect, sever, dissociate; marginalize, ghettoize.
—OPPOSITES: amalgamate.

seize *v.* **1** GRAB, grasp, snatch, take hold of, get one's hands on; grip, clutch; nab. **2** CAPTURE, take, overrun, occupy, conquer, take over. **3** ☞ CONFISCATE. **4** ☞ ABDUCT.
—OPPOSITES: relinquish, release.

seizure *n.* **1** CAPTURE, takeover, annexation, invasion, occupation, colonization. **2** CONFISCATION,

appropriation, expropriation, sequestration; *Law* distraint.
3 CONVULSION, fit, spasm, paroxysm; *Medicine* ictus; *dated* apoplexy.

seldom *adv.* RARELY, infrequently, hardly (ever), scarcely (ever), almost never; now and then, occasionally, sporadically; *informal* once in a blue moon.
—OPPOSITES: often.

select *v.* CHOOSE, pick (out), single out, sort out, take; opt for, decide on, settle on, fix on, determine, nominate, appoint, elect, vote for, name, sift out.
▶ *adj.* **1** ☞ SUPERIOR 4. **2** EXCLUSIVE, elite, favoured, privileged; wealthy; *informal* posh.
—OPPOSITES: inferior.

selection *n.* **1** CHOICE, pick; option, preference. **2** RANGE, array, diversity, variety, assortment, mixture. **3** ANTHOLOGY, assortment, collection, assemblage, compilation; miscellany, medley, potpourri.

selective *adj.* DISCERNING, discriminating, discriminatory, critical, exacting, demanding, particular; fussy, fastidious; *informal* choosy, persnickety, picky, finicky.

self-centred *adj.* ☞ EGOTISTICAL.

self-confidence *n.* MORALE, confidence, self-assurance, assurance, assertiveness, self-reliance, self-possession, composure.

self-conscious *adj.* EMBARRASSED, uncomfortable, uneasy, nervous; unnatural, inhibited, gauche, awkward; modest, shy, diffident, bashful,

retiring, shrinking.
—OPPOSITES: confident.

self-control *n.* SELF-DISCIPLINE, restraint, self-possession, willpower, composure, coolness; moderation, temperance, abstemiousness; *informal* cool.

self-denial *n.* SELF-SACRIFICE, selflessness, unselfishness; self-discipline, asceticism, self-deprivation, abstemiousness, abstinence, abstention; moderation, temperance.
—OPPOSITES: self-indulgence.

self-indulgent *adj.*
☞ HEDONISTIC.
—OPPOSITES: abstemious.

selfish *adj.* EGOCENTRIC, egotistic, egotistical, egomaniacal, self-centred, self-absorbed, self-obsessed, self-seeking, self-serving, wrapped up in oneself; inconsiderate, thoughtless, unthinking, uncaring, uncharitable; mean, miserly, grasping, greedy, mercenary, acquisitive, opportunistic; *informal* looking after number one.
—OPPOSITES: altruistic.

selfless *adj.* UNSELFISH, altruistic, self-sacrificing, self-denying; considerate, compassionate, kind, noble, generous, magnanimous, ungrudging, charitable, benevolent, open-handed.
—OPPOSITES: inconsiderate.

self-respect *n.* SELF-ESTEEM, self-regard, self-worth, amour-propre, faith in oneself, pride, dignity, morale, self-confidence.

self-restraint *n.* ☞ SELF-CONTROL.
—OPPOSITES: self-indulgence.

self-righteous adj.
1 ☞ SANCTIMONIOUS. 2 ☞ SMUG.
—OPPOSITES: humble.

self-sacrifice n. ☞ SELF-DENIAL.

sell v. 1 PUT UP FOR SALE, offer for sale, put on sale, dispose of, vend, auction (off); trade, barter. 2 TRADE IN, deal in, traffic in, stock, carry, offer for sale, peddle, hawk, retail, market. 3 GO, be bought, be purchased; move, be in demand. 4 COST, be priced at, retail at, go for, be. 5 PROMOTE; persuade someone to accept, talk someone into, bring someone round to, win someone over to, win approval for.
—OPPOSITES: buy.
□ **sell out 1** HAVE NONE LEFT, be out of stock, have run out; informal be fresh out, be cleaned out. 2 BE BOUGHT UP, be depleted, be exhausted. 3 ABANDON ONE'S PRINCIPLES, prostitute oneself, sell one's soul, betray one's ideals, be untrue to oneself; debase oneself, degrade oneself, demean oneself.
sell someone out ☞ BETRAY 1.
sell someone short ☞ UNDERVALUE.

seller n. VENDOR, retailer, purveyor, supplier, trader, merchant, dealer; shopkeeper, salesperson, salesman, saleswoman, sales rep(resentative), sales assistant, sales associate, clerk, shop assistant, travelling salesperson, peddler; hawker; auctioneer.

send v. 1 DISPATCH, post, mail, address, consign, direct, forward; transmit, convey, communicate; telephone, phone, broadcast, radio, fax, email; dated telegraph, wire, cable. 2 CALL, summon, contact; ask for, request, order. 3 PROPEL, project, eject, deliver, discharge, spout, fire, shoot, release; throw, let fly; informal chuck.
—OPPOSITES: receive.

senile adj. DODDERING, doddery, decrepit, senescent, declining, infirm, feeble; aged, long in the tooth, in one's dotage; mentally confused, having Alzheimer's (disease), having senile dementia; informal past it, gaga.

senior adj. 1 OLDER, elder. 2 SUPERIOR, higher-ranking, high-ranking, more important; top, chief, ranking.
—OPPOSITES: junior, subordinate.

sensation n. 1 FEELING, sense, awareness, consciousness, perception, impression. 2 COMMOTION, stir, impact; interest, excitement; informal splash, to-do, hoopla. 3 TRIUMPH, success, sellout; talking point; informal smash (hit), hit, winner, crowd-pleaser, knockout, blockbuster.

sensational adj. 1 SHOCKING, scandalous, appalling; amazing, startling, astonishing, staggering; stirring, exciting, thrilling, electrifying, red-hot; fascinating, interesting, noteworthy, significant, remarkable, momentous, historic, newsworthy. 2 OVER-DRAMATIZED, dramatic, melodramatic, exaggerated, sensationalist, sensationalistic; graphic, explicit, lurid; informal juicy. 3 (informal) GORGEOUS, stunning, wonderful, exquisite, lovely, radiant,

delightful, charming, enchanting, captivating; striking, spectacular, remarkable, outstanding, arresting, eye-catching; marvellous, superb, excellent, fine, first-class; *informal* great, terrific, tremendous, super, fantastic, fabulous, fab, heavenly, divine, knockout, hot, red-hot, delectable, scrumptious, awesome, magic, wicked, killer, out of this world, smashing, brilliant.
—OPPOSITES: dull, understated, unremarkable.

sense *n.* **1** SENSORY FACULTY, feeling, sensation, perception; sight, hearing, touch, taste, smell. **2** FEELING, awareness, sensation, consciousness, recognition. **3** APPRECIATION, awareness, understanding, comprehension, discernment; *informal* nose. **4** WISDOM, common sense, sagacity, discernment, perception; wit, intelligence, cleverness, shrewdness, judgment, reason, logic, brain(s); *informal* gumption, horse sense, savvy, (street) smarts. **5** PURPOSE, point, reason, object, motive; use, value, advantage, benefit. **6** MEANING, definition, import, signification, significance, purport, implication, nuance; drift, gist, thrust, tenor, message.
—OPPOSITES: stupidity.
▶ *v.* DISCERN, feel, observe, notice, recognize, pick up, be aware of, distinguish, make out, identify; comprehend, apprehend, see, appreciate, realize; suspect, have a funny feeling about, have a hunch, divine, intuit; *informal* catch on to, twig.

senseless *adj.* **1** ☞ UNCONSCIOUS 1. **2** POINTLESS, futile, useless, needless, unavailing, in vain, purposeless, meaningless, unprofitable; absurd, foolish, insane, stupid, idiotic, ridiculous, ludicrous, mindless, illogical.
—OPPOSITES: conscious, wise.

sensible *adj.* PRACTICAL, realistic, responsible, reasonable, commonsensical, rational, logical, sound, balanced, sober, no-nonsense, pragmatic, level-headed, thoughtful, down-to-earth, wise, prudent, judicious, sagacious, shrewd.
—OPPOSITES: foolish.

sensitive *adj.* **1** RESPONSIVE TO, reactive to, sentient of, sensitized to; aware of, conscious of, alive to; susceptible to, affected by, vulnerable to; attuned to. **2** DELICATE, fragile; tender, sore, raw. **3** TACTFUL, careful, thoughtful, diplomatic, delicate, subtle, kid-glove; sympathetic, compassionate, understanding, intuitive, responsive, insightful. **4** ☞ TOUCHY 1. **5** ☞ TOUCHY 2.
—OPPOSITES: impervious, resilient, clumsy, thick-skinned, uncontroversial.

sensual *adj.* **1** PHYSICAL, carnal, bodily, fleshly, animal; hedonistic, epicurean, sybaritic, voluptuary. **2** ☞ SEXY 1.
—OPPOSITES: spiritual, passionless.

sensuous *adj.* **1** AESTHETICALLY PLEASING, gratifying, rich, sumptuous, luxurious; sensory, sensorial. **2** SEXUALLY ATTRACTIVE, sexy, seductive, voluptuous, luscious, lush.

sentiment | serious

sentiment *n.* **1** VIEW, feeling, attitude, thought, opinion, belief. **2** SENTIMENTALITY, sentimentalism, mawkishness, emotionalism; emotion, sensibility, soft-heartedness, tender-heartedness; *informal* schmaltz, mush, slushiness, corniness, cheese, soppiness, sappiness.

sentimental *adj.* **1** NOSTALGIC, tender, emotional, affectionate. **2** MAWKISH, over-emotional, cloying, sickly, saccharine, sugary; romantic, touching, twee; *informal* slushy, mushy, weepy, tear-jerking, schmaltzy, lovey-dovey, gooey, drippy, cheesy, corny, soppy, cornball, sappy, hokey. **3** SOFT-HEARTED, tender-hearted, soft; *informal* soppy.
—OPPOSITES: practical, gritty.

separate *adj.* **1** UNCONNECTED, unrelated, different, distinct, discrete; detached, divorced, disconnected, independent, autonomous. **2** SET APART, detached, fenced off, cut off, segregated, isolated; free-standing, self-contained.
—OPPOSITES: linked, attached.
▸ *v.* **1** SPLIT (UP), break up, part, pull apart, divide; *literary* sunder. **2** ☞ DETACH. **3** PARTITION, divide, come between, keep apart; bisect, intersect. **4** ISOLATE, partition off, section off; close off, shut off, cordon off, fence off, screen off. **5** PART (COMPANY), go their separate ways, split up; say goodbye; disperse, disband, scatter. **6** FORK, divide, branch, bifurcate, diverge. **7** SPLIT UP, break up, part, be estranged, divorce. **8** ISOLATE, set apart, segregate; distinguish, differentiate, dissociate; sort out, sift out, filter out, remove, weed out. **9** BREAK AWAY FROM, break with, secede from, withdraw from, leave, quit, dissociate oneself from, resign from, drop out of, repudiate, reject.
—OPPOSITES: unite, join, link, meet, merge, marry.

separatist *n.* sovereignist✦ (or sovereigntist✦), Péquiste✦, indépendantiste✦.

sequel *n.* **1** FOLLOW-UP, continuation. **2** ☞ CONSEQUENCE.

sequence *n.* ☞ SUCCESSION 1.

serene *adj.* **1** ☞ CALM 1. **2** ☞ PEACEFUL 1.
—OPPOSITES: agitated, turbulent.

series *n.* SUCCESSION, sequence, string, chain, run, round; spate, wave, rash; set, course, cycle; row, line; *formal* concatenation.

serious *adj.* **1** ☞ SOLEMN 2. **2** IMPORTANT, significant, consequential, momentous, weighty, far-reaching, major, grave; urgent, pressing, crucial, critical, vital, life-and-death, high-priority. **3** CAREFUL, detailed, in-depth, deep, profound, meaningful. **4** INTELLECTUAL, highbrow, heavyweight, deep, profound, literary, learned, scholarly; *informal* heavy. **5** SEVERE, grave, bad, critical, acute, terrible, dire, dangerous, perilous, parlous; *formal* grievous. **6** IN EARNEST, earnest, sincere, wholehearted, genuine; committed, resolute, determined.
—OPPOSITES: lighthearted, trivial, superficial, lowbrow, minor, half-hearted.

sermon *n.* **1** HOMILY, address, speech, talk, discourse, oration; lesson. **2** LECTURE, tirade, harangue, diatribe; speech, disquisition, monologue; reprimand, reproach, reproof, admonishment, admonition, remonstration, criticism; *informal* talking-to, dressing-down, earful; *formal* castigation.

serve *v.* **1** WORK FOR, be in the service of, be employed by; obey. **2** BE OF SERVICE TO, be of use to, help, assist, aid, make a contribution to, do one's bit for, do something for, benefit. **3** BE A MEMBER OF, work on, be on, sit on, have a place on. **4** CARRY OUT, perform, do, fulfill, complete, discharge; spend. **5** DISH UP/OUT, give out, distribute; present, provide, supply; eat. **6** ATTEND TO, deal with, see to; ASSIST, help, look after. **7** PRESENT, deliver, give, hand over. **8** ACT AS, function as, do the work of, be a substitute for.

service *n.* **1** WORK, employment, employ, labour. **2** FAVOUR, kindness, good turn, helping hand; (**services**) ASSISTANCE, help, aid, offices, ministrations. **3** USE, usage; functioning. **4** OVERHAUL, tune-up, maintenance check, servicing. **5** CEREMONY, ritual, rite, observance; liturgy, sacrament; *formal* ordinance. **6** AMENITY, facility, resource, utility. **7** ☞ MILITARY *n.*
▶ *v.* OVERHAUL, check, go over, maintain; repair, mend, recondition.
□ **be of service** ☞ HELP *v.* 1.

serving *n.* PORTION, helping, plateful, plate, bowlful; amount, quantity, ration, chunk, hunk, piece, slab, slice, wedge.

session *n.* **1** MEETING, sitting, *Law* assize✦, assembly, conclave, plenary; hearing; conference, discussion, forum, symposium, caucus. **2** PERIOD, time, spell, stretch, bout. **3** ACADEMIC YEAR, school year; term, semester.

set¹ *v.* **1** PUT (DOWN), place, lay, deposit, position, settle, leave, stand, plant, posit; *informal* stick, dump, park, plonk, plunk. **2** FIX, embed, insert; mount. **3** ADORN, ornament, decorate, embellish; *literary* bejewel. **4** ASSIGN, allocate, give, allot, prescribe. **5** APPLY, address, direct, aim, turn, focus, concentrate. **6** DECIDE ON, select, choose, arrange, schedule; fix (on), settle on, determine, designate, name, appoint, specify, stipulate. **7** ADJUST, regulate, synchronize; calibrate; put right, correct; program, activate, turn on. **8** SOLIDIFY, harden, stiffen, thicken, jell, cake, congeal, coagulate, clot; freeze, crystallize.
—OPPOSITES: melt, rise.
□ **set about** ☞ BEGIN 1. **set someone apart** DISTINGUISH, differentiate, mark out, single out, separate, demarcate. **set something apart** ISOLATE, separate, segregate, put to one side. **set something aside** **1** SAVE, put by, put aside, put away, lay by, keep, reserve; store, stockpile, hoard, stow away, cache, withhold; *informal* salt away, squirrel away, stash away. **2** PUT DOWN, cast aside, discard, abandon, dispense with. **3** DISREGARD, put aside, ignore,

forget, discount, shrug off, bury.
4 ☞ OVERTURN 2. **set something down 1** WRITE DOWN, put in writing, jot down, note down, make a note of; record, register, log. **2** FORMULATE, draw up, establish, frame; lay down, determine, fix, stipulate, specify, prescribe, impose, ordain. **set off** SET OUT, start out, sally forth, leave, depart, embark, set sail; *informal* hit the road. **set something off 1** DETONATE, explode, blow up, touch off, trigger; ignite. **2** GIVE RISE TO, cause, lead to, set in motion, occasion, bring about, initiate, precipitate, prompt, trigger (off), spark (off), touch off, provoke, incite. **3** ENHANCE, bring out, emphasize, show off, throw into relief; complement. **set something out 1** ARRANGE, lay out, put out, array, dispose, display, exhibit. **2** PRESENT, set forth, detail; state, declare, announce; submit, put forward, advance, propose, propound. **set someone up 1** ESTABLISH, finance, fund, back, subsidize. **2** (*informal*) FALSELY INCRIMINATE, frame, entrap. **set something up 1** ERECT, put up, construct, build, raise, elevate. **2** ESTABLISH, start, begin, initiate, institute, found, create. **3** ARRANGE, organize, fix (up), schedule, timetable, line up. **4** ESTABLISH, form, strike ♣.

set² *n*. **1** GROUP, collection, series; assortment, selection, compendium, batch, number; arrangement, array. **2** ☞ CLIQUE. **3** SCENERY, setting, backdrop,

flats; mise en scène. **4** SESSION, time; stretch, bout, round.

set³ *adj*. **1** FIXED, established, predetermined, hard and fast, pre-arranged, prescribed, specified, defined; unvarying, unchanging, invariable, unvaried, rigid, inflexible, cast iron, strict, ironclad, settled, predictable; routine, standard, customary, regular, usual, habitual, accustomed, wonted. **2** INFLEXIBLE, rigid, fixed, firm, deep-rooted, deep-seated, ingrained, entrenched. **3** STOCK, standard, routine, rehearsed, well-worn, formulaic, conventional. **4** READY, prepared, organized, equipped, primed; *informal* geared up, psyched up. **5** DETERMINED TO, intent on, bent on, hell-bent on, resolute about, insistent about. **6** OPPOSED TO, averse to, hostile to, resistant to, antipathetic to, unsympathetic to; *informal* anti.
—OPPOSITES: variable, flexible, original, unprepared, uncertain.

setback *n*. ☞ PROBLEM 1.
—OPPOSITES: breakthrough.

setting *n*. **1** SURROUNDINGS, position, situation, environment, background, backdrop, milieu, environs, habitat; spot, place, location, locale, site, scene, locality, neighbourhood, venue, area, region, district. **2** MOUNT, fixture, surround.

settle *v*. **1** RESOLVE, sort out, solve, clear up, end, fix, work out, iron out, straighten out, set right, rectify, remedy, reconcile; *informal* patch up. **2** PUT IN ORDER, sort out, tidy up, arrange, organize, order, clear up. **3** DECIDE ON, set, fix,

agree on, name, establish, arrange, appoint, designate, assign; choose, select, pick. **4** PAY, settle up, square, clear, defray. **5** ACCEPT, agree to, assent to; *formal* accede to. **6** MAKE ONE'S HOME, set up home, take up residence, put down roots, establish oneself; live, move to, emigrate to. **7** COLONIZE, occupy, inhabit, people, populate. **8** APPLY ONESELF TO, get down to, set about, attack; concentrate on, focus on, devote oneself to. **9** CALM DOWN, quieten down, be quiet, be still; *informal* shut up. **10** CALM, quieten, quiet, soothe, pacify, quell; sedate, tranquilize. **11** SIT DOWN, seat oneself, install oneself, ensconce oneself, plant oneself; *informal* park oneself, plonk oneself. **12** LAND, come to rest, alight, descend, perch; *archaic* light. **13** SINK, subside, fall, gravitate.
—OPPOSITES: agitate, rise.

settlement *n.* **1** AGREEMENT, deal, arrangement, resolution, bargain, understanding, pact. **2** RESOLUTION, settling, solution, reconciliation. **3** COMMUNITY, colony, outpost, encampment, post; village, commune; *historical* plantation, clearing✥. **4** COLONIZATION, settling, populating; *historical* plantation. **5** PAYMENT, discharge, liquidation, clearance.

settler *n.* COLONIST, colonizer, frontiersman, frontierswoman, pioneer, bushwhacker; immigrant, newcomer; *historical* homesteader.
—OPPOSITES: native.

sever *v.* **1** CUT OFF, chop off, detach, disconnect, dissever,

separate, part; amputate; *literary* sunder. **2** CUT (THROUGH), rupture, split, pierce. **3** BREAK OFF, discontinue, suspend, end, terminate, cease, dissolve.
—OPPOSITES: join, maintain.

severe *adj.* **1** ☞ ACUTE 1. **2** FIERCE, violent, strong, powerful, intense; tempestuous, turbulent. **3** HARSH, bitter, cold, bleak, freezing, icy, arctic, extreme; *informal* brutal. **4** ☞ EXCRUCIATING. **5** ☞ CHALLENGING. **6** ☞ SCATHING. **7** HARSH, stern, hard, inflexible, uncompromising, unrelenting, merciless, pitiless, ruthless, draconian, oppressive, repressive, punitive; brutal, cruel, savage. **8** ☞ STERN. **9** ☞ AUSTERE 3.
—OPPOSITES: minor, gentle, mild, easy, lenient, friendly, ornate.

sex *n.* **1** SEXUAL INTERCOURSE, intercourse, lovemaking, making love, sex act, (sexual) relations; mating, copulation; *informal* nookie, whoopee, the horizontal mambo, a roll in the hay, quickie; *formal* fornication; *technical* coitus, coition; *dated* carnal knowledge. **2** THE FACTS OF LIFE, reproduction; *informal* the birds and the bees. **3** GENDER.
□**have sex** HAVE SEXUAL INTERCOURSE, make love, sleep with, go to bed; mate, copulate; seduce, rape; *informal* do it, go all the way, know in the biblical sense; get it on; *euphemistic* be intimate; *literary* ravish; *formal* fornicate.

sexuality *n.* **1** SENSUALITY, sexiness, seductiveness, desirability, eroticism, physicality; sexual appetite, passion, desire, lust. **2** SEXUAL ORIENTATION, sexual preference, leaning, persuasion; heterosexuality, homosexuality, lesbianism, bisexuality.

sexy *adj.* **1** SEXUALLY ATTRACTIVE, seductive, desirable, alluring, toothsome, sensual, sultry, slinky, provocative, tempting, tantalizing, vampish, come-hither, coquettish, flirtatious; nubile, voluptuous, luscious, lush, hot, beddable, foxy, cute. **2** EROTIC, sexually explicit, arousing, exciting, stimulating, hot, titillating, suggestive, racy, naughty, ribald, risqué, adult, X-rated; rude, pornographic, crude, lewd; *informal* raunchy, steamy, porno, blue, skin, XXX. **3** (SEXUALLY) AROUSED, sexually excited, amorous, lustful, passionate; *informal* horny, hot, turned on, sexed up, randy.

shabby *adj.* **1** RUNDOWN, down-at-the-heel, scruffy, dilapidated, ramshackle, tumbledown; seedy, slummy, insalubrious, squalid, sordid, flea-bitten; *informal* crummy, scuzzy, grotty, shacky. **2** SCRUFFY, old, worn out, threadbare, ragged, frayed, tattered, battered, faded, moth-eaten, mangy; *informal* tatty, ratty, the worse for wear, raggedy. **3** ☞ CONTEMPTIBLE.

—OPPOSITES: smart, honourable.

shade *n.* **1** SHADOW(S), shadiness, shelter, cover; cool. **2** COLOUR, hue, tone, tint, tinge. **3** NUANCE, gradation, degree, difference, variation, variety; nicety, subtlety; undertone, overtone. **4** BLIND, curtain, screen, cover, covering; awning, canopy.

—OPPOSITES: light.

▶ *v.* **1** CAST A SHADOW OVER, shadow, shelter, cover, screen; darken. **2** DARKEN, colour in, pencil in, block in, fill in; cross-hatch.

□ **put someone/something in the shade** ☞ SURPASS.

shadow *n.* **1** SILHOUETTE, outline, shape, contour, profile. **2** SHADE, darkness, twilight; gloom, murkiness. **3** (BLACK) CLOUD, pall; gloom, blight; threat. **4** TRACE, scrap, shred, crumb, iota, scintilla, jot, whit, grain; *informal* smidgen, smidge, tad. **5** TRACE, hint, suggestion, suspicion, ghost, glimmer.

shady *adj.* **1** SHADED, shadowy, dim, dark; sheltered, screened, shrouded; leafy; *literary* bosky, tenebrous. **2** (*informal*) SUSPICIOUS, suspect, questionable, dubious, doubtful, disreputable, untrustworthy, dishonest, devious, dishonourable, underhanded, unscrupulous, irregular, unethical; *informal* fishy, murky.

—OPPOSITES: bright, honest.

shake *v.* **1** VIBRATE, tremble, quiver, quake, shiver, shudder, judder, jiggle, wobble, rock, sway; convulse. **2** JIGGLE, joggle, agitate; *informal* waggle. **3** BRANDISH, wave, flourish, swing, wield; *informal* waggle. **4** UPSET, distress, disturb, unsettle, disconcert, discompose, disquiet, unnerve, trouble, throw off balance, agitate, fluster; shock, alarm, frighten, scare, worry; *informal* rattle. **5** WEAKEN, undermine, damage, impair, harm; reduce, diminish, decrease.

—OPPOSITES: soothe, strengthen.

shakeup *n.* (*informal*) REORGANIZATION, restructuring,

reshuffle, change, overhaul,
makeover; upheaval, shakedown,
housecleaning.

shaky *adj.* **1** TREMBLING, shaking,
tremulous, quivering, quivery,
unsteady, wobbly, weak; tottering,
tottery, teetering, doddery; *informal*
trembly. **2** ☞ UNSTABLE 1.
3 UNRELIABLE, untrustworthy,
questionable, dubious, doubtful,
tenuous, suspect, flimsy, weak,
unsound, unsupported,
unsubstantiated, unfounded;
informal iffy.
—OPPOSITES: steady, stable, sound.

shallow *adj.* SUPERFICIAL, facile,
simplistic, oversimplified; flimsy,
insubstantial, lightweight, empty,
trivial, trifling; surface, skin deep,
two-dimensional, frivolous,
foolish, silly, Mickey Mouse.
—OPPOSITES: profound.

sham *n.* **1** PRETENSE, fake, act,
fiction, simulation, fraud, feint,
lie, counterfeit; humbug.
2 ☞ FRAUD 3.
▶ *adj.* ☞ FAKE *adj.*
—OPPOSITES: genuine.

shame *n.* **1** ☞ HUMILIATION. **2** GUILT,
remorse, contrition, compunction.
3 PITY, misfortune, sad thing; bad
luck; *informal* bummer, crime, sin,
crying shame.
—OPPOSITES: pride, honour.
▶ *v.* DISGRACE, dishonour, discredit,
degrade, debase, bring into
disrepute; stigmatize, taint, stain,
tarnish, sully, besmirch, blacken,
drag through the mud.
—OPPOSITES: honour.

shameful *adj.* ☞ DISGRACEFUL.
—OPPOSITES: admirable.

shameless *adj.* FLAGRANT,
blatant, barefaced, overt, brazen,
brash, audacious, outrageous,
undisguised, unconcealed,
transparent; immodest,
indecorous; unabashed,
unashamed, unblushing,
unrepentant.
—OPPOSITES: modest.

shape *n.* FORM, appearance,
configuration, formation,
structure; figure, build, physique,
body; contours, lines, outline,
silhouette, profile.
—RELATED: morpho-.
▶ *v.* **1** FORM, fashion, make, mould,
model, cast; sculpt, sculpture,
carve, cut, whittle. **2** DETERMINE,
form, fashion, mould, define,
develop; influence, affect.
☐ **shape up** IMPROVE, get better,
progress, show promise; develop,
take shape, come on, come along.
take shape BECOME CLEAR,
become definite, become tangible,
crystallize, come together, fall
into place.

shapeless *adj.* **1** FORMLESS,
amorphous, unformed, indefinite.
2 BAGGY, saggy, ill-fitting, sacklike,
oversized, unshapely, formless.

shapely *adj.* WELL-PROPORTIONED,
clean-limbed; curvaceous,
voluptuous, Junoesque; attractive,
sexy; *informal* curvy; *archaic* comely.

share *n.* PORTION, part, division,
quota, quantum, allowance,
ration, allocation, measure, due;
percentage, commission,
dividend; helping, serving; *informal*
cut, slice.
▶ *v.* **1** SPLIT, divide, go halves on;
informal go fifty-fifty, go Dutch.
2 APPORTION, divide up, allocate,
portion out, ration out, parcel out,
measure out; carve up, divvy up.

3 PARTICIPATE IN, take part in, play a part in, be involved in, contribute to, have a hand in, partake in.

sharp *adj.* **1** KEEN, razor-edged; sharpened, honed.
2 ☞ EXCRUCIATING. **3** TANGY, piquant, strong; ACIDIC, acid, sour, tart, pungent, acrid, bitter, acidulous. **4** LOUD, piercing, shrill, high-pitched, penetrating, harsh, strident, ear-splitting, deafening.
5 ☞ COLD **1**. **6** ☞ ACRIMONIOUS.
7 INTENSE, acute, keen, strong, bitter, fierce, heartfelt, overwhelming. **8** SUDDEN, abrupt, rapid; steep, precipitous.
9 ☞ PERCEPTIVE.
—OPPOSITES: blunt, mild, sweet, soft, kind, indistinct, gradual, slow, weak, stupid, naive.

sharpen *v.* **1** HONE, whet, strop, grind, file. **2** IMPROVE, brush up, polish up, better, enhance; hone, fine-tune, perfect.

shatter *v.* **1** SMASH, break, splinter, crack, fracture, fragment, disintegrate, shiver; *informal* bust.
2 ☞ QUASH **2**. **3** DEVASTATE, shock, stun, daze, traumatize, crush, distress.

shave *v.* **1** CUT OFF, snip off; crop, trim, barber. **2** PLANE, pare, whittle, scrape. **3** REDUCE, cut, lessen, decrease, pare down, shrink.

shed *v.* **1** DROP, scatter, spill.
2 SLOUGH OFF, cast off, moult.
3 TAKE OFF, remove, shrug off, discard, doff, climb out of, slip out of, divest oneself of, peel off.
4 SPILL, discharge. **5** ☞ DISCARD.

6 CAST, radiate, diffuse, disperse, give out.
—OPPOSITES: don, keep.

sheen *n.* SHINE, lustre, gloss, patina, shininess, burnish, polish, shimmer, brilliance, radiance.

sheer *adj.* **1** UTTER, complete, absolute, total, pure, downright, out-and-out, arrant, thorough, thoroughgoing, patent, veritable, unmitigated, plain. **2** PRECIPITOUS, steep, vertical, perpendicular, abrupt, bluff, sharp. **3** DIAPHANOUS, gauzy, filmy, floaty, gossamer, thin, translucent, transparent, see-through, insubstantial.
—OPPOSITES: gradual, thick.

shell *n.* **1** CARAPACE, exterior; armour; *Zoology* exoskeleton. **2** POD, husk, hull, casing, case, covering, integument, shuck. **3** PROJECTILE, bomb, explosive; grenade; bullet, cartridge. **4** FRAMEWORK, frame, chassis, skeleton; hull, exterior.
—RELATED: conchoidal, concho-.
▶ *v.* **1** HULL, pod, husk, shuck.
2 BOMBARD, fire on, shoot at, attack, bomb, blitz, strafe.

shelter *n.* **1** PROTECTION, cover, screening, shade; safety, security, refuge, sanctuary, asylum.
2 SANCTUARY, refuge, home, haven, safe house, interval house✤, transition house✤; harbour, port in a storm.
—OPPOSITES: exposure.
▶ *v.* **1** ☞ PROTECT. **2** TAKE SHELTER, take refuge, seek sanctuary, take cover; *informal* hole up.
—OPPOSITES: exposure.

sheltered *adj.* **1** PROTECTED, screened, shielded, covered; shady; cozy. **2** SECLUDED, cloistered, isolated, protected, withdrawn, sequestered, reclusive; privileged, secure, safe, quiet.

shepherd v. USHER, steer, herd, lead, take, escort, guide, conduct, marshal, walk; show, see, chaperone.

shift v. **1** MOVE, carry, transfer, transport, convey, lug, haul, fetch, switch, relocate, reposition, rearrange; *informal* cart. **2** MOVE, slide, slip, be displaced. **3** VEER, alter, change, turn, swing round. —OPPOSITES: keep.
▶ n. **1** MOVEMENT, move, transference, transport, transposition, relocation. **2** ☞ CHANGE n. 1. **3** STINT, stretch, spell of work.

shifty adj. (*informal*) ☞ DEVIOUS. —OPPOSITES: honest.

shine v. **1** EMIT LIGHT, beam, radiate, gleam, glow, glint, glimmer, sparkle, twinkle, glitter, glisten, shimmer, flash, flare, glare, fluoresce; *literary* glister, coruscate. **2** POLISH, burnish, buff, wax, gloss. **3** EXCEL, be outstanding, be brilliant, be successful, stand out.

shiny adj. ☞ LUSTROUS. —OPPOSITES: matte.

shirk v. **1** EVADE, dodge, avoid, get out of, sidestep, shrink from, shun, skip, miss; neglect; *informal* duck (out of), cop out of, cut. **2** AVOID ONE'S DUTY, be remiss, be negligent, play truant, swing the lead, slack off; *informal* goof off, play hooky.

shirker n. DODGER, truant, absentee, layabout, good-for-nothing, loafer, idler; *informal* slacker, bum, lazybones.

shiver v. & n. TREMBLE, quiver, shake, shudder, quaver, quake.

shock n. **1** BLOW, upset, disturbance; surprise, revelation, a bolt from the blue, thunderbolt, bombshell, rude awakening, eye-opener; *informal* whammy, wake-up call. **2** FRIGHT, scare, jolt, start; *informal* turn. **3** TRAUMA, prostration; collapse, breakdown. **4** VIBRATION, reverberation, shake, jolt, jar, jerk; impact, blow.
▶ v. APPALL, horrify, outrage, revolt, disgust, nauseate, sicken; traumatize, distress, upset, disturb, disquiet, unsettle; stun, rock, stagger, astound, astonish, amaze, startle, surprise, dumbfound, shake, take aback, throw, unnerve.

shoot v. **1** GUN DOWN, mow down, hit, wound, injure; put a bullet in, pick off, bag, fell, kill; *informal* pot, blast, pump full of lead, plug. **2** FIRE, open fire, aim, snipe, let fly; bombard, shell. **3** DISCHARGE, fire, launch, loose off, let fly, emit. **4** ☞ RACE v. 2. **5** FILM, photograph, take, snap, capture, record, tape; videotape, video.

shop n. **1** STORE, (retail) outlet, boutique, emporium, department store, big box store, supermarket, superstore, chain store, market, mart, trading post, mini-mart, convenience store, (*Que*) depanneur♦. **2** WORKSHOP, workroom, plant, factory, works, mill, yard.
▶ v. GO SHOPPING, buy, purchase, get, acquire, obtain, pick up, snap up, procure, stock up on.

shore¹ n. SEASHORE, lakeshore, lakefront, bayfront, beach,

foreshore, sand(s), shoreline, waterside, waterfront, front, coast, coastline, seaboard; *literary* strand.
—RELATED: littoral.

shore² v. PROP UP, hold up, bolster, support, brace, buttress, strengthen, fortify, reinforce, underpin.

short adj. **1** SMALL, little, tiny; *informal* teeny. **2** SMALL, little, petite, tiny, diminutive, stubby, elfin, dwarfish, midget, pygmy, Lilliputian, minuscule, miniature, slight; *informal* pint-sized, teeny, knee-high to a grasshopper; *Scottish* wee. **3** CONCISE, brief, succinct, compact, summary, economical, crisp, pithy, epigrammatic, laconic, thumbnail, capsule, abridged, abbreviated, condensed, synoptic, summarized, contracted, truncated; *formal* compendious. **4** BRIEF, momentary, temporary, short-lived, impermanent, cursory, fleeting, passing, fugitive, lightning, transitory, transient, ephemeral, quick. **5** ☞ SCARCE 1.
—OPPOSITES: long, tall, plentiful.
▶ adv. ABRUPTLY, suddenly, sharply, all of a sudden, all at once, unexpectedly, without warning, out of the blue.
□ **in short** BRIEFLY, in a word, in a nutshell, in précis, in essence, to come to the point; in conclusion, in summary, to sum up. **short of** DEFICIENT IN, lacking, wanting, in need of, low on, short on, missing; *informal* strapped for, pushed for, minus.

shortage n. ☞ SCARCITY.
—OPPOSITES: abundance.

shortcoming n. DEFECT, fault, flaw, imperfection, deficiency, limitation, failing, drawback, weakness, weak point, foible, frailty, vice.
—OPPOSITES: strength.

shorten v. **1** ☞ ABRIDGE. **2** curtail, truncate.
—OPPOSITES: extend.

shortly adv. ☞ SOON 1.

short-sighted adj. **1** MYOPIC, near-sighted; *informal* as blind as a bat. **2** NARROW-MINDED, unimaginative, small-minded, insular, parochial, provincial, improvident.
—OPPOSITES: far-sighted, imaginative.

short-tempered adj.
☞ IRRITABLE.
—OPPOSITES: placid.

shot n. **1** report of a gun, crack, bang, blast; (**shots**) gunfire. **2** BULLETS, cannonballs, pellets, ammunition. **3** STROKE, hit, strike; kick, throw, pitch, lob. **4** INJECTION, inoculation, immunization, vaccination, booster; *informal* jab, needle.
□ **a shot in the arm** (*informal*) BOOST, tonic, stimulus, spur, impetus, encouragement. **a shot in the dark** (WILD) GUESS, surmise, supposition, conjecture, speculation.

shout v. ☞ YELL.
—OPPOSITES: whisper.
▶ n. YELL, cry, call, roar, howl, bellow, bawl, clamour, vociferation, shriek, scream; *informal* holler.

shove v. **1** PUSH, thrust, propel, drive, force, ram, knock, elbow, shoulder; jostle, hustle,

manhandle. **2** PUSH (ONE'S WAY),
force one's way, barge (one's way),
elbow (one's way), shoulder one's
way.
▸ *n.* PUSH, thrust, bump, jolt.

show *v.* **1** BE VISIBLE, be seen, be in
view, be obvious. **2** DISPLAY,
exhibit, put on show/display, put
on view, parade, uncover, reveal.
3 MANIFEST, exhibit, reveal,
convey, communicate, make
known; express, proclaim, make
plain, make obvious, disclose,
betray; *formal* evince.
4 DEMONSTRATE, explain, describe,
illustrate; teach, instruct, give
instructions. **5** PROVE,
demonstrate, confirm, show
beyond doubt; substantiate,
corroborate, verify, establish,
attest, certify, testify, bear out;
formal evince. **6** ESCORT,
accompany, take, conduct, lead,
usher, guide, direct, steer,
shepherd.
—OPPOSITES: conceal.
▸ *n.* **1** DISPLAY, array, exhibition,
presentation, exposition,
spectacle. **2** EXHIBITION, exposition,
fair, extravaganza, spectacle,
exhibit. **3** (THEATRICAL)
PERFORMANCE, musical, play,
opera, ballet. **4** APPEARANCE,
display, impression, ostentation,
image. **5** PRETENSE, outward
appearance, (false) front, guise,
semblance, pose, parade.
□ **show off** (*informal*) BEHAVE
AFFECTEDLY, put on airs, put on an
act, swagger around, swank, strut,
strike an attitude, posture; draw
attention to oneself; *informal* cop an
attitude. **show something off**
DISPLAY, show to advantage,

exhibit, demonstrate, parade,
draw attention to, flaunt. **show
up 1** BE VISIBLE, be obvious, be
seen, be revealed. **2** (*informal*)
☞ ARRIVE 1. **show someone/
something up 1** EXPOSE, reveal,
make visible, make obvious,
highlight. **2** (*informal*) ☞ HUMILIATE.

showdown *n.* CONFRONTATION,
clash, faceoff.

shower *n.* **1** (LIGHT) FALL, drizzle,
sprinkling, misting. **2** VOLLEY, hail,
salvo, bombardment, barrage,
fusillade, cannonade. **3** AVALANCHE,
deluge, flood, spate, flurry;
profusion, abundance, plethora.
▸ *v.* **1** RAIN, fall, hail. **2** DELUGE,
flood, inundate, swamp, engulf;
overwhelm, overload, snow under.
3 LAVISH, heap, bestow freely.

show-off *n.* (*informal*) EXHIBITIONIST,
extrovert, poser, poseur, peacock,
swaggerer, self-publicist, braggart;
informal showboat, blowhard,
grandstander.

showy *adj.* OSTENTATIOUS,
conspicuous, pretentious,
flamboyant, gaudy, garish, brash,
vulgar, loud, extravagant, fancy,
ornate, over-elaborate, kitsch,
kitschy; *informal* flash, flashy, glitzy,
ritzy, swanky, fancy-dancy, fancy-
schmancy.
—OPPOSITES: restrained.

shrewd *adj.* ASTUTE, sharp-witted,
sharp, smart, acute, intelligent,
clever, canny, perceptive,
perspicacious, sagacious, wise;
informal on the ball, savvy, heads-
up; *formal* sapient.
—OPPOSITES: stupid.

shrill *adj.* HIGH-PITCHED, piercing,
high, sharp, ear-piercing, ear-

splitting, penetrating, screeching, shrieking, screechy.

shrine *n.* **1** HOLY PLACE, temple, church, chapel, tabernacle, sanctuary, sanctum. **2** MEMORIAL, monument.

shrink *v.* **1** GET SMALLER, become/ grow smaller, contract, diminish, lessen, reduce, decrease, dwindle, decline, fall off, drop off. **2** DRAW BACK, recoil, back away, retreat, withdraw, cringe, cower, quail. **3** RECOIL, shy away, demur, flinch, have scruples, have misgivings, have qualms, be loath, be reluctant, be unwilling, be averse, fight shy of, be hesitant, be afraid, hesitate, balk at.
—OPPOSITES: expand, increase.

shrivel *v.* WITHER, shrink; wilt; dry up, desiccate, dehydrate, parch, frazzle.

shuffle *v.* **1** SHAMBLE, drag one's feet, totter, dodder. **2** SCRAPE, drag, scuffle, scuff. **3** MIX (UP), mingle, rearrange, jumble.

shun *v.* AVOID, evade, eschew, steer clear of, shy away from, fight shy of, keep one's distance from, give a wide berth to, have nothing to do with; snub, give someone the cold shoulder, cold-shoulder, ignore, look right through; reject, rebuff, spurn, ostracize; *informal* give someone the brush-off, freeze out, give someone the bum's rush.
—OPPOSITES: welcome.

shut *v.* CLOSE, pull/push to, slam, fasten; put the lid on, bar, lock, secure.
—OPPOSITES: open, unlock.
▫**shut down** CEASE ACTIVITY, close (down), cease operating, cease trading, be shut (down); turn off,

switch off; *informal* fold; power down. **shut something in** CONFINE, enclose, impound, shut up, pen (in/up), fence in, immure, lock up/in, cage, imprison, intern, incarcerate, corral. **shut up** (*informal*) BE QUIET, keep quiet, hold one's tongue, keep one's lips sealed; stop talking, quieten (down); *informal* keep mum, button your lip, hush up, cut the crap, shut it, shut your face/mouth/trap, put a sock in it, give it a rest, save it, hold your tongue, not another word, pipe down, put a lid on it.

shy *adj.* BASHFUL, diffident, farouche, timid, sheepish, reserved, reticent, introverted, retiring, self-effacing, withdrawn, timorous, mousy, nervous, insecure, unconfident, inhibited, repressed, self-conscious, embarrassed, apprehensive, hesitant, reluctant, shrinking, blushing, coy, demure.
—OPPOSITES: confident.

shyness *n.* BASHFULNESS, diffidence, sheepishness, reserve, introversion, reticence, timidity, timidness, timorousness, mousiness, lack of confidence, self-consciousness, embarrassment, coyness, demureness.

sick *adj.* **1** ☞ ILL *adj.* 1. **2** ☞ NAUSEOUS. **3** FED UP, bored, tired, weary.
—OPPOSITES: well.

sickening *adj.* NAUSEATING, stomach-turning, stomach-churning, repulsive, revolting, disgusting, repellent, repugnant, appalling, obnoxious, nauseous, vile, nasty, foul, loathsome, offensive, objectionable, off-putting, distasteful, obscene, gruesome, grisly, vomitous; *informal* gross; *formal* rebarbative.

sickly *adj.* **1** EDGE, ☞ UNHEALTHY 2.
2 PALE, wan, pasty, sallow, pallid, ashen, anemic. **3** INSIPID, pale, light, light-coloured, washed out, faded.
—OPPOSITES: healthy.

sickness *n.* **1** ☞ DISEASE.
2 ☞ NAUSEA.

side *n.* **1** EDGE, border, verge, boundary, margin, fringe(s), flank, bank, perimeter, extremity, periphery, (outer) limit, limits, bounds; *literary* marge, bourn.
2 DISTRICT, quarter, area, region, part, neighbourhood, sector, section, zone, ward. **3** SURFACE, face, plane. **4** ☞ OPINION. **5** FACTION, camp, bloc, party, wing. **6** TEAM, squad, lineup.
—RELATED: lateral.
—OPPOSITES: centre, end.
▶ *adj.* **1** LATERAL, wing, flanking.
2 SUBORDINATE *adj.* 2.
—OPPOSITES: front, central.
☐ **side by side** ALONGSIDE (EACH OTHER), beside each other, abreast, shoulder to shoulder, close together; in collaboration, in solidarity. **take someone's side** SUPPORT, take someone's part, side with, be on someone's side, stand by, back, give someone one's backing, be loyal to, defend, champion, ally (oneself) with, sympathize with, favour.

sidelong *adj.* INDIRECT, oblique, sideways, sideward; surreptitious, furtive, covert, sly.
—OPPOSITES: overt.

sidetrack *v.* ☞ DISTRACT.

sideways *adv.* **1** TO THE SIDE, laterally. **2** EDGEWISE, sidewards, side first, edgeways, end on, broadside. **3** OBLIQUELY, indirectly, sidelong; covertly, furtively, surreptitiously, slyly.
▶ *adj.* **1** LATERAL, sideward, horizontal, side to side.
2 ☞ SIDELONG.

sift *v.* **1** SIEVE, strain, screen, filter, riddle; *archaic* bolt. **2** SEPARATE OUT, filter out, sort out, put to one side, weed out, get rid of, remove.
3 SEARCH THROUGH, look through, examine, inspect, scrutinize, pore over, investigate, analyze, dissect, review.

sight *n.* **1** EYESIGHT, vision, eyes, faculty of sight, visual perception.
2 VIEW, glimpse, glance, look.
3 RANGE OF VISION, field of vision, view. **4** LANDMARK, place of interest, monument, spectacle, view, marvel, wonder.
—RELATED: optical, visual.
▶ *v.* ☞ GLIMPSE *v.*
☐ **set one's sights on** ASPIRE TO, aim at/for, try for, strive for/towards, work towards.

sign *n.* **1** INDICATION, signal, symptom, pointer, suggestion, intimation, mark, manifestation, demonstration, token, evidence; *literary* sigil. **2** PORTENT, omen, warning, forewarning, augury, presage; promise, threat.
3 GESTURE, signal, wave, gesticulation, cue, nod. **4** NOTICE, signpost, signboard, warning sign, road sign, traffic sign, guidepost, marquee. **5** SYMBOL, mark, cipher, letter, character, figure, hieroglyph, ideogram, rune, emblem, device, logo.

▶ *v.* **1** WRITE ONE'S NAME ON, autograph, endorse, initial, countersign, ink; *formal* subscribe. **2** ENDORSE, validate, certify, authenticate, sanction, authorize; agree to, approve, ratify, adopt, give one's approval to; *informal* give something the go-ahead, give something the green light, give something the thumbs up. **3** WRITE, inscribe, pen. **4** RECRUIT, hire, engage, employ, take on, appoint, sign on/up, enlist. **5** ☞ SIGNAL *v.* 1.

☐ **sign on/up** ENLIST, take a job, join (up), enrol, register, volunteer. **sign something over** TRANSFER, make over, hand over, bequeath, pass on, transmit, cede; *Law* devolve, convey.

signal *n.* **1** GESTURE, sign, wave, gesticulation, cue, indication, warning, motion. **2** INDICATION, sign, symptom, hint, pointer, intimation, clue, demonstration, evidence, proof. **3** CUE, prompt, impetus, stimulus; *informal* go-ahead.

▶ *v.* **1** GESTURE, sign, give a sign to, direct, motion; wave, beckon, nod. **2** INDICATE, show, express, communicate, proclaim, declare. **3** MARK, signify, mean, be a sign of, be evidence of, herald; *literary* betoken, foretoken.

significance *n.* **1** IMPORTANCE, import, consequence, seriousness, gravity, weight, magnitude, momentousness, substance, note; *formal* moment. **2** ☞ MEANING 1.

significant *adj.* **1** NOTABLE, noteworthy, worthy of attention, remarkable, important, of importance, of consequence; impressive, interesting, marked, memorable, outstanding, singular, striking; serious, crucial, weighty, momentous, epoch-making, uncommon, unusual, rare, extraordinary, exceptional, special; *formal* of moment. **2** MEANINGFUL, expressive, eloquent, suggestive, knowing, telling.

significantly *adv.* NOTABLY, remarkably, outstandingly, importantly, crucially, materially, appreciably; markedly, considerably, obviously, conspicuously, strikingly, signally.

signify *v.* **1** BE EVIDENCE OF, be a sign of, mark, signal, mean, spell, be symptomatic of, herald, indicate; *literary* betoken. **2** MEAN, denote, designate, represent, symbolize, stand for; *literary* betoken.

silence *n.* **1** QUIETNESS, quiet, quietude, still, stillness, hush, tranquility, noiselessness, soundlessness, peacefulness, peace (and quiet). **2** SPEECHLESSNESS, wordlessness, dumbness, muteness, taciturnity. **3** SECRETIVENESS, secrecy, reticence, taciturnity.
—OPPOSITES: sound.

▶ *v.* **1** QUIETEN, quiet, hush, shush; gag, muzzle, censor. **2** MUFFLE, deaden, soften, mute, smother, dampen, damp down, mask, suppress, reduce. **3** STOP, put an end to, put a stop to.

silent *adj.* **1** COMPLETELY QUIET, still, hushed, inaudible, noiseless, soundless. **2** SPEECHLESS, quiet, unspeaking, dumb, mute, taciturn, uncommunicative, tight-

lipped; *informal* mum. **3** UNSPOKEN,
wordless, unsaid, unexpressed,
unvoiced, tacit, implicit,
understood.
—OPPOSITES: audible, noisy.

silly *adj.* **1** FOOLISH, stupid,
unintelligent, idiotic, brainless,
mindless, witless, imbecilic,
doltish; imprudent, thoughtless,
rash, reckless, foolhardy,
irresponsible; mad,
scatterbrained, featherbrained;
frivolous, giddy, inane, immature,
childish, puerile, empty-headed;
brain-dead, dumb, fatuous,
moronic, vacant, vacuous, vapid,
informal crazy, dotty, scatty, loopy,
wingy♣, ditzy, spinny♣, screwy,
thick, thick-headed, birdbrained,
pea-brained, dopey, dim, dim-
witted, halfwitted, dippy,
blockheaded, boneheaded,
lamebrained, daft; *dated* tomfool.
2 ☞ UNWISE. **3** ☞ TRIVIAL.
—OPPOSITES: sensible.

similar *adj.* **1** ALIKE, (much) the
same, indistinguishable, almost
identical, homogeneous,
homologous; *informal* much of a
muchness. **2** COMPARABLE, like,
corresponding, homogeneous,
equivalent, analogous. **3** LIKE,
much the same as, comparable to.
—OPPOSITES: different, unlike.
☐ **be similar to** ☞ RESEMBLE.

similarity *n.* RESEMBLANCE,
likeness, sameness, similitude,
comparability, correspondence,
correlation, parallel, parity,
equivalence, homogeneity,
indistinguishability, uniformity;
archaic semblance.

similarly *adv.* LIKEWISE, in similar
fashion, in like manner,

comparably, correspondingly,
uniformly, indistinguishably,
analogously, homogeneously,
equivalently, in the same way, the
same, identically.

simple *adj.* **1** STRAIGHTFORWARD,
easy, uncomplicated, uninvolved,
effortless, painless, undemanding,
elementary, child's play; *informal* as
easy as pie, as easy as ABC, a piece
of cake, a cinch, no sweat, a
pushover, kids' stuff, a breeze,
duck soup, a snap. **2** CLEAR, plain,
straightforward, intelligible,
comprehensible, uncomplicated,
accessible; *informal* user-friendly.
3 PLAIN, unadorned, undecorated,
unembellished, unornamented,
basic, unsophisticated, no-frills;
classic, understated, uncluttered,
restrained. **4** UNPRETENTIOUS,
unsophisticated, ordinary,
unaffected, unassuming, natural,
honest-to-goodness, cracker-
barrel.
—OPPOSITES: difficult, complex,
fancy.

simplistic *adj.* FACILE, superficial,
oversimplified; shallow, jejune,
naive; glib.

simply *adv.* **1** STRAIGHTFORWARDLY,
directly, clearly, plainly,
intelligibly, lucidly,
unambiguously. **2** PLAINLY, without
adornment, without decoration,
without ornament/
ornamentation, soberly, unfussily,
classically. **3** UNPRETENTIOUSLY,
modestly, quietly. **4** MERELY, just,
purely, solely, only. **5** UTTERLY,
absolutely, completely, positively,
really; *informal* plain. **6** WITHOUT
DOUBT, unquestionably,

undeniably, incontrovertibly, certainly, categorically.

simultaneous *adj.* CONCURRENT, happening at the same time, contemporaneous, concomitant, coinciding, coincident, synchronous, synchronized.

sin *n.* **1** IMMORAL ACT, wrong, wrongdoing, act of evil/ wickedness, transgression, crime, offence, misdeed, misdemeanour; *archaic* trespass. **2** WICKEDNESS, wrongdoing, wrong, evil, evildoing, sinfulness, immorality, iniquity, vice, crime. **3** (*informal*) SCANDAL, crime, disgrace, outrage.
—OPPOSITES: virtue.
▶ *v.* COMMIT A SIN, commit an offence, transgress, do wrong, commit a crime, break the law, misbehave, go astray; *archaic* trespass.

sincere *adj.* **1** ☞ HEARTFELT. **2** ☞ GENUINE 2.

sincerely *adv.* GENUINELY, honestly, really, truly, truthfully, wholeheartedly, earnestly, fervently.

sinful *adj.* IMMORAL, wicked, (morally) wrong, wrongful, evil, bad, iniquitous, corrupt, criminal, nefarious, depraved, degenerate.
—OPPOSITES: virtuous.

sing *v.* **1** croon, carol, trill, chant, intone, chorus; *informal* belt out. **2** WARBLE, trill, chirp, chirrup, cheep, peep.

singer *n.* VOCALIST, soloist, songster, songstress, cantor, chorister; *informal* songbird; siren, diva, chanteuse, torch singer, chansonnier; *literary* troubadour, minstrel.

single *adj.* **1** ONE (ONLY), sole, lone, solitary, by itself/oneself, unaccompanied, alone. **2** INDIVIDUAL, separate, distinct, particular. **3** UNMARRIED, unwed, unwedded, unattached, available, free, a bachelor, a spinster; partnerless, husbandless, wifeless; separated, divorced, widowed; *informal* solo.
—OPPOSITES: double, married.
□ **single someone/something out** SELECT, pick out, choose, decide on; target, earmark, mark out, separate out, set apart/aside.

single-minded *adj.* ☞ TENACIOUS 2.
—OPPOSITES: half-hearted.

singular *adj.* **1** ☞ EXTRAORDINARY. **2** ☞ STRANGE.

sinister *adj.* **1** MENACING, threatening, ominous, forbidding, baleful, frightening, alarming, disturbing, disquieting, dark, black; *formal* minatory; *literary* direful. **2** EVIL, wicked, criminal, corrupt, nefarious, villainous, base, vile, malevolent, malicious; *informal* shady.
—OPPOSITES: innocent.

sink *v.* **1** BECOME SUBMERGED, be engulfed, go down, drop, fall, descend. **2** FOUNDER, go under, submerge. **3** SCUTTLE, send to the bottom; scupper. **4** DESTROY, ruin, wreck, put an end to, demolish, smash, shatter, dash; *informal* put the kibosh on, put paid to, scupper; *archaic* bring to naught. **5** DESCEND, drop, go down/ downwards. **6** LOWER ONESELF, flop, collapse, fall, drop down, slump; *informal* plonk oneself. **7** FALL, drop, become/get quieter,

become/get softer. **8** STOOP, lower oneself, descend. **9** DETERIORATE, decline, fade, grow weak, flag, waste away; be at death's door, be on one's deathbed, be slipping away; *informal* go downhill, be on one's last legs, be giving up the ghost.
—OPPOSITES: float, rise.
□ **sink in** REGISTER, be understood, be comprehended, be grasped, get through.

sinner n. WRONGDOER, evildoer, transgressor, miscreant, offender, criminal; *archaic* trespasser.

sit v. **1** TAKE A SEAT, seat oneself, be seated, perch, ensconce oneself, plump oneself, flop; *informal* take the load/weight off one's feet, plonk oneself, take a load off. **2** PUT (DOWN), place, set (down), lay, deposit, rest, stand; *informal* stick, dump, park, plonk.
—OPPOSITES: stand.
□ **sit back** RELAX, unwind, lie back; *informal* let it all hang out, veg out, hang loose, chill (out), take a load off.

site n. ☞ LOCATION.

situation n. **1** CIRCUMSTANCES, (state of) affairs, state, condition. **2** THE FACTS, how things stand, the lay of the land, what's going on; *informal* the score, the scoop. **3** ☞ LOCATION.

size n. DIMENSIONS, measurements, proportions, magnitude, largeness, bigness, area, expanse, extent; breadth, width, length, height, depth, volume, capacity; immensity, hugeness, vastness.
□ **size someone/something up** (*informal*) ASSESS, appraise, form an estimate of, take the measure of,

judge, take stock of, evaluate, suss out.

sketch n. **1** (PRELIMINARY) DRAWING, outline; diagram, design, plan; *informal* rough. **2** ☞ OUTLINE n. 2. **3** DESCRIPTION, portrait, profile, portrayal, depiction. **4** SKIT, scene, piece, act, item, routine.
▶ v. **1** DRAW, make a drawing of, draw a picture of, pencil, rough out, outline. **2** DESCRIBE, outline, give a brief idea of, rough out; summarize, précis.

sketchy *adj.* INCOMPLETE, patchy, fragmentary, cursory, perfunctory, scanty, vague, imprecise, imperfect; hurried, hasty.
—OPPOSITES: detailed.

skilful *adj.* EXPERT, accomplished, skilled, masterly, master, virtuoso, consummate, proficient, talented, gifted, adept, adroit, deft, dexterous, able, good, competent, capable, brilliant, handy; *informal* mean, wicked, crack, ace, wizard, crackerjack, pro.

skill n. **1** EXPERTISE, skilfulness, expertness, adeptness, adroitness, deftness, dexterity, ability, proficiency, prowess, mastery, competence, capability, aptitude, artistry, art, virtuosity, talent, flair. **2** ACCOMPLISHMENT, strength, gift.
—OPPOSITES: incompetence.

skilled *adj.* EXPERIENCED, trained, qualified, proficient, practised, accomplished, expert, skilful, talented, gifted, adept, adroit, deft, dexterous, able, good, competent; *informal* crack, crackerjack.
—OPPOSITES: inexperienced.

skimp v. ☞ STINT v.

skimpy adj. **1** REVEALING, short, low, low-cut; flimsy, thin, see-through, indecent. **2** MEAGRE, scanty, sketchy, limited, paltry, deficient, sparse.

skinny adj. ☞ THIN 3.

skip v. **1** ☞ CAPER **2** OMIT, leave out, miss out, dispense with, pass over, skim over, disregard; *informal* give something a miss. **3** PLAY TRUANT FROM, miss, cut, (*Ont.*) skip off❖, (*West*) skip out❖; *informal* play hooky from, ditch.

sky n. the upper atmosphere; *literary* the heavens, the firmament, the blue, the (wide) blue yonder, the welkin, the azure, the empyrean.
—RELATED: celestial.

slack adj. **1** LOOSE, limp, hanging, flexible. **2** FLACCID, flabby, loose, sagging, saggy. **3** SLUGGISH, slow, quiet, slow-moving, flat, depressed, stagnant. **4** LAX, negligent, remiss, careless, slapdash, slipshod, lackadaisical, inefficient, casual; *informal* sloppy, slap-happy.
—OPPOSITES: tight, taut.
▸ n. **1** LOOSENESS, play, give. **2** SURPLUS, excess, residue, spare capacity. **3** LULL, pause, respite, break, hiatus, breathing space; *informal* let-up, breather.
▸ v. (*informal*) IDLE, shirk, be lazy, be indolent, waste time, lounge about; *informal* goof off.
□ **slack off 1** DECREASE, subside, let up, ease off, abate, diminish, die down, fall off. **2** RELAX, take things easy, let up, ease up/off, loosen up, slow down; *informal* hang loose, chill (out). **slack up** SLOW (DOWN), decelerate, reduce speed.

slacker n. ☞ LOAFER.

slam v. **1** BANG, shut/close with a bang, shut/close noisily, shut/close with force. **2** CRASH INTO, smash into, collide with, hit, strike, ram, plow into, run into, bump into, impact. **3** (*informal*) ☞ CRITICIZE.

slander n. DEFAMATION (OF CHARACTER), character assassination, calumny, libel; scandalmongering, malicious gossip, disparagement, denigration, aspersions, vilification, obloquy; lie, slur, smear, false accusation; *informal* mudslinging, badmouthing, trash-talk; *archaic* contumely.
▸ v. DEFAME, malign, libel, blacken someone's name, sully someone's reputation, speak ill/evil of, give someone a bad name, traduce, smear, cast aspersions on, drag someone's name through the mud, besmirch, tarnish, taint, tell lies about, stain, impugn someone's character/integrity, vilify, denigrate, disparage, run down, stigmatize, discredit, decry, slur, blacken, damage, impugn; *informal* dis, badmouth, do a hatchet job on, drag through the mud; *formal* derogate, calumniate.

slanderous adj. DEFAMATORY, denigratory, disparaging, libellous, pejorative, false, misrepresentative, scurrilous, scandalous, malicious, abusive, insulting; *informal* mudslinging.
—OPPOSITES: complimentary.

slant v. **1** SLOPE, tilt, incline, be at an angle, tip, cant, lean, dip, pitch, shelve, list, bank. **2** BIAS, distort, twist, skew, weight, give a bias to.

▸ *n.* **1** SLOPE, incline, tilt, gradient, pitch, angle, cant, camber, inclination. **2** POINT OF VIEW, viewpoint, standpoint, stance, angle, perspective, approach, view, attitude, position; bias, leaning.

slanting *adj.* OBLIQUE, sloping, at an angle, on an incline, inclined, tilting, tilted, slanted, aslant, diagonal, canted, cambered, angled, askew.

slap *v.* ☞ HIT 1.
▸ *n.* SMACK, blow, thump, cuff, clout, punch, spank; *informal* whack, thwack, wallop, clip, bash.

slapdash *adj.* CARELESS, slipshod, hurried, haphazard, unsystematic, untidy, messy, hit-or-miss, negligent, neglectful, lax; *informal* sloppy, slap-happy.
—OPPOSITES: meticulous.

slaughter *v.* ☞ MASSACRE *v.*
▸ *n.* **1** ☞ MASSACRE *n.* **2** CARNAGE, bloodshed, bloodletting, bloodbath.

slave *n.* **1** *historical* serf, vassal, thrall; *archaic* bondsman, bondswoman. **2** DRUDGE, servant, lackey, joe-boy; *informal* gofer. **3** DEVOTEE, worshipper, adherent; fan, lover, aficionado; *informal* fanatic, freak, nut, addict.
—RELATED: servile.
—OPPOSITES: freeman, master.

slavery *n.* **1** BONDAGE, enslavement, servitude, thraldom, thrall, serfdom, vassalage. **2** DRUDGERY, toil, (hard) slog, hard labour, grind; *literary* travail; *archaic* moil.
—OPPOSITES: freedom.

sleek *adj.* **1** SMOOTH, glossy, shiny, shining, lustrous, silken, silky.

2 STREAMLINED, trim, elegant, graceful. **3** WELL-GROOMED, stylish, wealthy-looking, suave, sophisticated, debonair.

sleep *n.* NAP, doze, siesta, catnap, beauty sleep; *informal* snooze, forty winks, a bit of shut-eye, power nap; *literary* slumber.
▸ *v.* BE ASLEEP, doze, take a siesta, take a nap, catnap, sleep like a log; *informal* snooze, catch/snatch forty winks, get some shut-eye, put one's head down, catch some zees; *humorous* be in the land of Nod, be in the arms of Morpheus; *literary* slumber.
—OPPOSITES: wake up.
☐**go to sleep** FALL ASLEEP, get to sleep; *informal* drop off, nod off, drift off, crash out, flake out, sack out. **put an animal to sleep** PUT DOWN, destroy, euthanize.

sleepy *adj.* **1** DROWSY, tired, somnolent, languid, languorous, heavy-eyed, asleep on one's feet; lethargic, sluggish, enervated, torpid; *informal* dopey; *literary* slumberous. **2** SOPORIFIC, sleep-inducing, somnolent. **3** QUIET, peaceful, tranquil, placid, slow-moving; dull, boring.
—OPPOSITES: awake, alert.

slender *adj.* ☞ THIN 3.
—OPPOSITES: plump.

slick *adj.* **1** EFFICIENT, smooth, smooth-running, polished, well-organized, well-run, streamlined. **2** GLIB, smooth, fluent, plausible. **3** SUAVE, urbane, polished, assured, self-assured, smooth-talking, glib; *informal* smarmy. **4** SHINY, glossy, shining, sleek, smooth, oiled. **5** SLIPPERY, wet, greasy; *informal* slippy.

slide v. **1** GLIDE, move smoothly, slip, slither, skim, skate; skid, slew. **2** TRICKLE, run, flow, pour, stream. **3** CREEP, steal, slink, slip, tiptoe, sidle. **4** SINK, fall, drop, descend; decline, degenerate.
▶ n. FALL, decline, drop, slump, downturn, downswing.
—OPPOSITES: rise.
□ **let things slide** NEGLECT, pay little/no attention to, not attend to, be remiss about, let something go downhill.

slight adj. **1** SMALL, modest, tiny, minute, inappreciable, negligible, insignificant, minimal, remote, slim, faint; informal minuscule; formal exiguous. **2** MINOR, inconsequential, trivial, unimportant, lightweight, superficial, shallow. **3** SLIM, slender, petite, diminutive, small, delicate, dainty.
—OPPOSITES: considerable.
▶ v. INSULT, snub, rebuff, repulse, spurn, treat disrespectfully, give someone the cold shoulder, scorn; informal give someone the brush-off, freeze out.
—OPPOSITES: respect.
▶ n. INSULT, affront, snub, rebuff; informal put-down, dig.
—OPPOSITES: compliment.

slim adj. **1** ☞ THIN 3. **2** SLIGHT, small, slender, faint, poor, remote, unlikely, improbable.
—OPPOSITES: plump.

slimy adj. **1** SLIPPERY, greasy, muddy, mucky, sludgy, wet, sticky; informal slippy, gunky, gooey. **2** (informal) ☞ OBSEQUIOUS.

slink v. ☞ CREEP.

slip v. **1** SLIDE, skid, glide; fall (over), lose one's balance, tumble.

2 FALL, drop, slide. **3** ☞ CREEP.
4 DECLINE, deteriorate, degenerate, worsen, get worse, fall (off), drop; informal go downhill, go to the dogs, go to pot. **5** DROP, go down, sink, slump, decrease, depreciate.
6 PASS, elapse, go by/past, roll by/past, fly by/past, tick by/past.
7 PUT, tuck, shove; informal pop, stick, stuff. **8** PUT ON, pull on, don, dress/clothe oneself in; change into. **9** TAKE OFF, remove, pull off, doff, peel off. **10** UNTIE, unfasten, undo.
▶ n. **1** FALSE STEP, misstep, slide, skid, fall, tumble. **2** ☞ MISTAKE.

slippery adj. **1** ICY, greasy, oily, glassy, smooth, slimy, wet; informal slippy. **2** EVASIVE, unreliable, unpredictable; devious, crafty, cunning, unscrupulous, wily, tricky, artful, slick, sly, sneaky, scheming, untrustworthy, deceitful, duplicitous, dishonest, treacherous, two-faced, snide; informal shady, shifty.

slit n. **1** CUT, incision, split, slash, gash, laceration. **2** OPENING, gap, chink, crack, aperture, slot.
▶ v. CUT, slash, split open, slice open, gash, lacerate, make an incision in.

slither v. SLIDE, slip, glide, wriggle, crawl; skid.

sliver n. SPLINTER, shard, shiver, chip, flake, shred, scrap, shaving, paring, piece, fragment.

slogan n. CATCHPHRASE, jingle, byword, motto; informal tag line, buzzword, mantra.

slope n. **1** GRADIENT, incline, angle, slant, inclination, pitch, decline, ascent, declivity, rise, fall, tilt, tip, downslope, upslope, grade, downgrade, upgrade, bank, descent, dip, hill, ramp. **2** HILL, hillside, hillock, bank, sidehill, escarpment, scarp; *literary* steep. **3** PISTE, run, trail.

▸ *v.* SLANT, incline, tilt; drop away, fall away, decline, descend, shelve, lean; rise, ascend, climb.

sloppy *adj.* **1** CARELESS, slapdash, slipshod, lackadaisical, haphazard, lax, slack, slovenly; *informal* slap-happy. **2** BAGGY, loose-fitting, loose, generously cut; shapeless, sack-like, oversized.

slot *n.* **1** APERTURE, slit, crack, hole, opening. **2** SPOT, time, period, niche, space; *informal* window.

▸ *v.* INSERT, put, place, slide, slip.

slow *adj.* **1** UNHURRIED, leisurely, steady, sedate, slow-moving, plodding, dawdling, sluggish, sluggardly, lead-footed. **2** LONG-DRAWN-OUT, time-consuming, lengthy, protracted, prolonged, gradual. **3** ☞ STUPID 1.
4 ☞ RELUCTANT.
—OPPOSITES: fast.

▸ *v.* **1** REDUCE SPEED, go slower, decelerate, brake. **2** TAKE IT EASY, relax, ease up/off, take a break, slack off, let up; *informal* chill (out), hang loose. **3** HOLD BACK/UP, delay, retard, set back; restrict, check, curb, inhibit, impede, obstruct, hinder, hamper; *archaic* stay.
—OPPOSITES: accelerate.

slowly *adv.* **1** AT A SLOW PACE, without hurrying, unhurriedly, steadily, at a leisurely pace, at a snail's pace; *Music* adagio, lento, largo. **2** GRADUALLY, bit by bit, little by little, slowly but surely, step by step.
—OPPOSITES: quickly.

sluggish *adj.* **1** LETHARGIC, listless, lacking in energy, lifeless, inert, inactive, slow, torpid, languid, apathetic, weary, tired, fatigued, sleepy, drowsy, enervated, languorous, spiritless; lazy, idle, indolent, slothful, sluggardly, logy; *Medicine* asthenic; *informal* dozy, dopey. **2** INACTIVE, quiet, slow, slack, flat, depressed, stagnant.
—OPPOSITES: vigorous.

slump *v.* **1** SIT HEAVILY, flop, flump, collapse, sink, fall; *informal* plonk oneself. **2** FALL STEEPLY, plummet, tumble, drop, go down; *informal* crash, nosedive. **3** DECLINE, deteriorate, degenerate, worsen, slip; *informal* go downhill.

▸ *n.* **1** STEEP FALL, drop, tumble, downturn, downswing, slide, *informal* toboggan slide✦, decline, decrease, nosedive. **2** RECESSION, economic decline, depression, slowdown, stagnation.
—OPPOSITES: rise, boom.

slur *v.* MUMBLE, speak unclearly, garble.

▸ *n.* INSULT, slight, slander, slanderous statement, aspersion, smear, allegation.

sly *adj.* ☞ CUNNING.
▢ **on the sly** IN SECRET, secretly, furtively, surreptitiously, covertly, clandestinely, on the quiet, behind someone's back; *informal* on the q.t.

smack *n.* SLAP, hit, clout, cuff, blow, spank, rap, swat, crack, thump, punch, karate chop; *informal* whack, thwack, clip, wallop, swipe, bop, belt, bash, sock.

▸ *v.* **1** SLAP, hit, strike, spank, swat, clout, thump, punch, swat; box someone's ears; *informal* whack, clip, wallop, swipe, bop, belt, bash, sock, boff, slug, bust. **2** BANG, slam, crash, thump; sling, fling; *informal* plonk, plunk.

small *adj.* **1** LITTLE, compact, bijou, tiny, miniature, mini; minute, microscopic, minuscule; small-scale, toy, baby, dwarf, pygmy; poky, cramped, boxy; SHORT, petite, diminutive, elfin; puny, undersized, stunted, dwarfish, midget, Lilliputian; *informal* teeny (weeny), teensy (weensy), vest-pocket, itsy-bitsy, itty-bitty, bite-sized, pocket, pocket-sized, half-pint, little-bitty, pint-sized, scaled-down; *Scottish* wee. **2** SLIGHT, minor, unimportant, trifling, trivial, insignificant, inconsequential, negligible, nugatory, infinitesimal; *informal* minuscule, piffling, piddling. **3** ☞ MEAGRE.
—RELATED: micro-, mini-, nano-.
—OPPOSITES: big, tall, major, ample, substantial.

small-minded *adj.* NARROW-MINDED, petty, mean-spirited, uncharitable; close-minded, short-sighted, myopic, blinkered, inward-looking, unimaginative, parochial, provincial, insular, small-town; intolerant, illiberal, conservative, hidebound, dyed-in-the-wool, set in one's ways, inflexible; prejudiced, bigoted.
—OPPOSITES: tolerant.

smart *adj.* **1** ☞ CLEVER.
2 ☞ FASHIONABLE.
—OPPOSITES: stupid.
▶ *v.* STING, burn, tingle, prickle; hurt, ache.

smash *v.* **1** BREAK, shatter, splinter, crack, shiver; *informal* bust. **2** CRASH INTO, collide with, hit,

strike, ram, smack into, slam into, plow into, run into, bump into, impact. **3** ☞ HIT *v.* 1. **4** ☞ DESTROY.
▶ *n.* (*informal*) SUCCESS, sensation, sellout, triumph; *informal* (smash) hit, blockbuster, winner, knockout, barnburner, biggie.

smear *v.* **1** STREAK, smudge, mark, soil, dirty; *informal* splotch; *literary* besmear. **2** COVER, coat, grease; *literary* bedaub. **3** SPREAD, rub, daub, slap, slather, smother, plaster, slick; apply; *literary* besmear.
4 ☞ SLANDER *v.*
▶ *n.* **1** STREAK, smudge, daub, dab, spot, patch, blotch, mark; *informal* splotch. **2** ☞ SLANDER *n.*

smell *n.* ODOUR, aroma, fragrance, scent, perfume, redolence; bouquet, nose; stench, fetor, stink, reek, whiff, hum; *informal* funk; *literary* miasma.
—RELATED: osmic, olfactory.
▶ *v.* **1** SCENT, get a sniff of, detect. **2** SNIFF, nose. **3** STINK, reek, have a bad smell, whiff.

smelly *adj.* FOUL-SMELLING, stinking, reeking, fetid, malodorous, pungent, rank, noxious, mephitic; off, gamy, high; musty, fusty; *informal* stinky, humming, funky; *literary* miasmic, noisome.

smitten *adj.* **1** STRUCK DOWN, laid low, suffering, affected, afflicted, plagued, stricken. **2** ☞ INFATUATED.

smooth *adj.* **1** EVEN, level, flat, plane; unwrinkled, featureless; glassy, glossy, silky, polished. **2** CALM, still, tranquil, undisturbed, unruffled, even, flat, waveless, like a millpond. **3** STEADY, regular, uninterrupted, unbroken, fluid, fluent;

straightforward, easy, effortless, trouble-free, seamless. **4** SUAVE, urbane, sophisticated, polished, debonair; courteous, gracious, glib, slick, ingratiating, unctuous; *informal* smarmy.
−OPPOSITES: uneven, rough, lumpy, irregular, gauche.
▶ *v.* **1** FLATTEN, level (out/off), even out/off; press, roll, steamroll, iron, plane. **2** EASE, facilitate, clear the way for, pave the way for, expedite, assist, aid, help, oil the wheels of, lubricate.

smother *v.* **1** SUFFOCATE, asphyxiate, stifle, choke. **2** EXTINGUISH, put out, snuff out, dampen, douse, stamp out, choke. **3** SMEAR, daub, spread, cover; *literary* besmear, bedaub. **4** OVERWHELM, inundate, envelop, cocoon. **5** STIFLE, muffle, strangle, repress, suppress, hold back, fight back, bite back, swallow, contain, bottle up, conceal, hide; bite one's lip; *informal* keep a/the lid on.

smug *adj.* SELF-SATISFIED, self-congratulatory, complacent, superior, pleased with oneself, self-approving.

snag *n.* **1** ☞ DIFFICULTY 1. **2** TEAR, rip, hole, gash, slash; run.
▶ *v.* CATCH, get caught, hook.

snap *v.* **1** BREAK, fracture, splinter, come apart, split, crack; *informal* bust. **2** FLARE UP, lose one's self-control, freak out, go to pieces, get worked up; *informal* crack up, lose one's cool, blow one's top, fly off the handle. **3** BITE; gnash its teeth. **4** SAY ROUGHLY, say brusquely, say abruptly, say angrily, bark, snarl, growl; retort, rejoin, retaliate; round on

someone; *informal* jump down someone's throat.
▶ *n.* **1** CLICK, crack, pop. **2** PERIOD, spell, time, interval, stretch, patch. **3** EASY TASK; *informal* a piece of cake, cinch, breeze, child's play, kid's stuff, duck soup.
☐ **snap out of it** (*informal*) RECOVER, get a grip, pull oneself together, get over it, get better, cheer up, perk up; *informal* buck up. **snap something up** BUY EAGERLY, accept eagerly, jump at, take advantage of, grab, seize (on), grasp with both hands, pounce on.

snappy *adj.* (*informal*) **1** ☞ IRRITABLE. **2** succinct, memorable, catchy, neat, clever, crisp, pithy, witty, incisive, brief, short. **3** ☞ FASHIONABLE.
−OPPOSITES: peaceable, long-winded, slovenly.

snatch *v.* **1** ☞ GRAB *v.* 1. **2** (*informal*) ☞ STEAL *v.* 1. **3** (*informal*) ☞ ABDUCT. **4** SEIZE, pluck, wrest, achieve, secure, obtain; scrape.
▶ *n.* **1** PERIOD, spell, time, fit, bout, interval, stretch. **2** FRAGMENT, snippet, bit, scrap, part, extract, excerpt, portion.

sneak *v.* **1** CREEP, slink, steal, slip, slide, sidle, edge, move furtively, tiptoe, pussyfoot, pad, prowl. **2** SMUGGLE, bring/take surreptitiously, bring/take secretly, bring/take illicitly, spirit, slip. **3** STEAL, take furtively, take surreptitiously; *informal* snatch.

sneer *n.* **1** SMIRK, curl of the lip, disparaging smile, contemptuous smile, cruel smile. **2** JIBE, barb, jeer, taunt, insult, slight, affront, slur; *informal* dig.

▶ *v.* **1** SMIRK, curl one's lip, smile disparagingly, smile contemptuously, smile cruelly. **2** SCOFF AT, scorn, disdain, mock, jeer at, hold in contempt, ridicule, deride, insult, slight, slur.

snicker *v. & n.* GIGGLE, titter, snigger, chortle, simper, laugh.

sniff *v.* **1** INHALE, breathe in; snuffle. **2** SMELL, scent, get a whiff of.

snip *v.* **1** CUT, clip, slit, nick, notch. **2** CUT OFF, trim (off), clip, prune, chop off, lop (off), dock, crop, sever, detach, remove, take off. ▶ *n.* **1** CUT, slit, nick, notch, incision. **2** SCRAP, snippet, cutting, shred, remnant, fragment, sliver, bit, piece.

snippet *n.* PIECE, bit, scrap, fragment, particle, shred; excerpt, extract.

snobbish *adj.* ELITIST, snobby, superior, supercilious; arrogant, haughty, disdainful, condescending; pretentious, affected; *informal* snooty, uppity, high and mighty, la-di-da, stuck-up, hoity-toity, snotty.

snoop (*informal*) *v.* **1** PRY, inquire, be inquisitive, be curious, poke about/around, be a busybody, poke one's nose into; interfere (in/with), meddle (in/with), intrude (on); *informal* be nosy. **2** INVESTIGATE, explore, search, nose, have a good look; prowl around. ▶ *n.* SEARCH, nose, look, prowl, ferret, poke, investigation.

snub *v.* REBUFF, spurn, repulse, cold-shoulder, brush off, give the cold shoulder to, keep at arm's length; ignore; insult, slight, affront, humiliate; *informal* freeze out, stiff. ▶ *n.* REBUFF, repulse, slap in the face; humiliation, insult, slight, affront; *informal* brush-off, kiss-off, put-down.

snug *adj.* **1** COZY, comfortable, warm, welcoming, restful, reassuring, intimate, sheltered, secure; *informal* comfy. **2** TIGHT, skin-tight, close-fitting, form-fitting, figure-hugging, slinky. —OPPOSITES: bleak, loose.

snuggle *v.* NESTLE, curl up, huddle (up), cuddle up, nuzzle, settle.

soak *v.* **1** IMMERSE, steep, submerge, submerse, dip, dunk, bathe, douse, marinate, souse. **2** DRENCH, wet through, saturate, waterlog, deluge, inundate, submerge, drown, swamp. **3** PERMEATE, penetrate, percolate, seep into, spread through, infuse, impregnate. **4** ABSORB, suck up, blot (up), mop (up), sponge up, sop up.

soar *v.* **1** FLY, wing, ascend, climb, rise; take off, take flight. **2** GLIDE, plane, float, drift, wheel, hover. **3** INCREASE, escalate, shoot up, rise, spiral; *informal* go through the roof, skyrocket. —OPPOSITES: plummet.

sober *adj.* **1** NOT DRUNK, clear-headed; teetotal, abstinent, abstemious, dry; *informal* on the wagon. **2** SERIOUS, solemn, sensible, thoughtful, grave, sombre, staid, level-headed, businesslike, down-to-earth, commonsensical, pragmatic, conservative; unemotional, dispassionate, objective, matter-of-

fact, no-nonsense, rational, logical, straightforward. **3** SOMBRE, subdued, severe; conventional, traditional, quiet, drab, plain.
—OPPOSITES: drunk, frivolous, sensational, flamboyant.
▶ *v.* **1** QUIT DRINKING, dry out, become sober. **2** MAKE SERIOUS, subdue, calm down, quieten, steady; bring down to earth, make someone stop and think, give someone pause for thought.

sociable *adj.* FRIENDLY, affable, companionable, gregarious, convivial, amicable, cordial, warm, genial; communicative, responsive, forthcoming, open, outgoing, extrovert, hail-fellow-well-met, approachable; *informal* chummy, clubby.
—OPPOSITES: unfriendly.

social *adj.* **1** COMMUNAL, community, collective, group, general, popular, civil, public,. societal. **2** RECREATIONAL, leisure, entertainment, amusement. **3** GREGARIOUS, interactional; organized.
—OPPOSITES: individual.
▶ *n.* PARTY, gathering, function, get-together, soiree; celebration, reunion, jamboree; *informal* bash, shindig, (*Atlantic*) time♣, do, bunfight.

socialist *adj.* LEFT-WING, progressive, leftist, labour, CCF/NDP♣, anti-corporate, antiglobalization; radical, revolutionary, militant; communist; *informal* lefty, red.
—OPPOSITES: conservative.
▶ *n.* LEFT-WINGER, leftist, progressive, progressivist, NDPer♣; radical, revolutionary;

communist, Marxist; *informal* lefty, red.
—OPPOSITES: conservative.

socialize *v.* INTERACT, converse, be sociable, mix, mingle, get together, meet, fraternize, consort; entertain, go out; *informal* hobnob.

society *n.* **1** THE COMMUNITY, the (general) public, the people, the population; civilization, humankind, mankind, humanity. **2** CULTURE, community, civilization, nation, population. **3** HIGH SOCIETY, polite society, the upper classes, the elite, the smart set, the beautiful people, the beau monde, the haut monde; *informal* the upper crust, the top drawer. **4** ASSOCIATION, club, group, circle, fellowship, guild, lodge, fraternity, brotherhood, sisterhood, sorority, league, union, alliance. **5** COMPANY, companionship, fellowship, friendship, comradeship, camaraderie.

soft *adj.* **1** MUSHY, squashy, pulpy, pappy, slushy, squelchy, squishy, doughy; *informal* gooey. **2** SWAMPY, marshy, boggy, miry, oozy; heavy, squelchy. **3** SQUASHY, spongy, compressible, supple, springy, pliable, pliant, resilient, malleable. **4** VELVETY, smooth, fleecy, downy, furry, silky, silken, satiny. **5** GENTLE, light, mild, moderate. **6** DIM, low, faint, subdued, muted, mellow. **7** PALE, pastel, muted, understated, restrained, subdued, subtle.
8 ☞ QUIET *adj.* 2.
—OPPOSITES: hard, firm, rough, strong, harsh, lurid, strident.

soften v. **1** ALLEVIATE, ease, relieve, soothe, allay, take the edge off, assuage, cushion, moderate, mitigate, palliate, diminish, blunt, deaden, dull. **2** DIE DOWN, abate, subside, moderate, let up, calm, diminish, slacken, weaken.
□ **soften someone up** CHARM, win over, persuade, influence, weaken, disarm, sweeten, butter up, soft-soap.

soggy adj. MUSHY, squashy, pulpy, slushy, squelchy, squishy; swampy, marshy, boggy, miry; soaking, soaked through, wet, saturated, drenched.

soil¹ n. **1** EARTH, loam, dirt, clay, gumbo; ground. **2** TERRITORY, land, domain, dominion, region, country.

soil² v. **1** DIRTY, stain, splash, spot, spatter, splatter, smear, smudge, sully, spoil, foul; informal muck up; literary begrime. **2** DISHONOUR, damage, sully, stain, blacken, tarnish, taint, blemish, defile, blot, smear, drag through the mud; literary besmirch.

soldier n. FIGHTER, trooper, serviceman, servicewoman; warrior; US GI; peacekeeper, blue helmet/beret; archaic man-at-arms.
□ **soldier on** (informal).
☞ PERSEVERE.

solemn adj. **1** DIGNIFIED, ceremonious, ceremonial, stately, formal, courtly, majestic; imposing, awe-inspiring, splendid, magnificent, grand. **2** SERIOUS, grave, sober, sombre, unsmiling, stern, grim, dour, humourless, pensive, meditative, thoughtful. **3** SINCERE, earnest, honest, genuine, firm, heartfelt,
wholehearted, sworn.
—OPPOSITES: frivolous, lighthearted, insincere.

solicit v. **1** ASK FOR, request, seek, apply for, put in for, call for, press for, beg, plead for. **2** ASK, petition, importune, implore, plead with, entreat, appeal to, lobby, beg, supplicate, call on, press; literary beseech.

solid adj. **1** HARD, rock-hard, rigid, firm, solidified, set, frozen, concrete. **2** PURE, 24-carat, unalloyed, unadulterated, genuine. **3** CONTINUOUS, uninterrupted, unbroken, non-stop, undivided. **4** WELL-BUILT, sound, substantial, strong, sturdy, durable. **5** WELL-FOUNDED, valid, sound, reasonable, logical, authoritative, convincing, cogent, plausible, credible, reliable. **6** DEPENDABLE, reliable, firm, unshakeable, trustworthy, stable, steadfast, staunch, constant, rock-steady.
—OPPOSITES: liquid, alloyed, broken, flimsy, untenable, unreliable.

solidarity n. UNANIMITY, unity, like-mindedness, agreement, accord, harmony, consensus, concurrence, co-operation, cohesion; formal concord.

solo adj. UNACCOMPANIED, single-handed, companionless, unescorted, unattended, unchaperoned, independent, solitary; alone, on one's own, by oneself.
—OPPOSITES: accompanied.

solution n. **1** ANSWER, result, resolution, way out, fix, panacea; key, formula, explanation, interpretation. **2** MIXTURE, mix, blend, compound, suspension, tincture, infusion, emulsion.

solve v. RESOLVE, answer, work out, find a solution to, find the key to, puzzle out, fathom, decipher, decode, clear up, straighten out, get to the bottom of, unravel, piece together, explain; *informal* figure out, crack.

sometimes adv. OCCASIONALLY, from time to time, now and then, every so often, once in a while, on occasion, at times, off and on, at intervals, periodically, sporadically, spasmodically, intermittently, now and again, on and off.

soon adv. **1** SHORTLY, presently, in the near future, before long, in a little while, in a minute, in a moment, in an instant, in a bit, in the twinkling of an eye, in no time, before you know it, any minute (now), any day (now), by and by; *informal* pronto, in a jiffy; *dated* directly, anon. **2** EARLY, quickly, promptly, speedily, punctually.

soothe v. **1** CALM (DOWN), pacify, comfort, hush, quiet, subdue, settle (down), lull, tranquilize, appease, conciliate, mollify. **2** ☞ ALLEVIATE.
—OPPOSITES: agitate, aggravate.

sophisticated adj.
1 ☞ ADVANCED. **2** WORLDLY, worldly-wise, experienced, enlightened, cosmopolitan, knowledgeable; urbane, cultured, cultivated, civilized, polished, refined; elegant, stylish; *informal* cool.
—OPPOSITES: crude, naive.

soporific adj. SLEEP-INDUCING, sedative, somnolent, calmative, tranquilizing, narcotic, opiate; drowsy, sleepy; *Medicine* hypnotic.
—OPPOSITES: invigorating.

sordid adj. **1** SLEAZY, dirty, seedy, seamy, unsavoury, tawdry, cheap, debased, degenerate, dishonourable, disreputable, discreditable, contemptible, ignominious, shameful, abhorrent. **2** SQUALID, slummy, insalubrious, dirty, filthy, mucky, grimy, shabby, messy, soiled, scummy, unclean; *informal* cruddy, grungy, crummy, scuzzy; grotty.
—OPPOSITES: respectable, immaculate.

sore adj. PAINFUL, hurting, hurt, aching, throbbing, smarting, stinging, agonizing, excruciating; inflamed, irritated, sensitive, tender, raw, bruised, wounded, injured.
▶ n. INFLAMMATION, swelling, lesion; wound, scrape, abrasion, cut, laceration, graze, contusion, bruise; ulcer, boil, abscess, carbuncle.

sorrow n. **1** ☞ SADNESS.
2 TROUBLE, difficulty, problem, adversity, misery, woe, affliction, trial, tribulation, misfortune, pain, setback, reverse, blow, failure, tragedy.
—OPPOSITES: joy.

sorrowful adj. ☞ SAD 1.

sorry adj. **1** ☞ SAD 1. **2** FULL OF PITY, sympathetic, compassionate, moved, consoling, empathetic, concerned. **3** REGRETFUL, remorseful, contrite, repentant, rueful, penitent, apologetic, abject, guilty, ashamed, sheepish,

shamefaced, conscience-stricken, in sackcloth and ashes.
—OPPOSITES: glad, unsympathetic, unrepentant.

sort n. ☞ KIND n.

▶ v. CLASSIFY, class, categorize, catalogue, grade, group; organize, arrange, order, marshal, assemble, systematize, systemize, pigeonhole, sort out.

so-so adj. (informal) MEDIOCRE, indifferent, average, middle-of-the-road, middling, moderate, ordinary, adequate, fair; uninspired, undistinguished, unexceptional, unremarkable, run-of-the-mill, lacklustre, {comme ci, comme ça}; informal no great shakes, not up to much, okay.

soul n. **1** SPIRIT, psyche, (inner) self, inner being, life force, vital force; individuality, makeup, subconscious, anima; Philosophy pneuma; Hinduism atman. **2** EMBODIMENT, personification, incarnation, epitome, quintessence, essence; model, exemplification, exemplar, image, manifestation. **3** ☞ PERSON. **4** INSPIRATION, feeling, emotion, passion, animation, intensity, fervour, ardour, enthusiasm, warmth, energy, vitality, spirit.

sound¹ n. **1** NOISE, note; din, racket, row, hubbub; resonance, reverberation. **2** UTTERANCE, cry, word, noise, peep. **3** MUSIC, tone, notes. **4** IDEA, thought, concept, prospect, description.
—RELATED: acoustic, sonic, aural, audio-, sono-.
—OPPOSITES: silence.

▶ v. **1** MAKE A NOISE, resonate, resound, reverberate, go off, blare; ring, chime, peal. **2** BLOW, blast, toot, blare; operate, set off; ring. **3** PRONOUNCE, verbalize, voice, enunciate, articulate, vocalize, say. **4** UTTER, voice, deliver, express, speak, announce, pronounce. **5** APPEAR, look (like), seem, strike someone as being, give every indication of being, come across as.

sound² adj. **1** HEALTHY, in good condition, in good shape, fit, hale and hearty, in fine fettle; undamaged, unimpaired. **2** WELL-BUILT, solid, substantial, strong, sturdy, durable, stable, intact, unimpaired. **3** WELL-FOUNDED, valid, reasonable, logical, weighty, authoritative, reliable, well-grounded. **4** RELIABLE, dependable, trustworthy, fair; good, sensible; wise, judicious, sagacious, shrewd, perceptive. **5** SOLVENT, debt-free, in the black, in credit, creditworthy, secure, solid. **6** DEEP, undisturbed, uninterrupted, untroubled, peaceful.
—OPPOSITES: unhealthy, unsafe, unreliable, insolvent, light.

sour adj. **1** ACID, acidic, acidy, acidulated, tart, bitter, sharp, vinegary, pungent; technical acerbic. **2** BAD, off, turned, curdled, rancid, high, rank, foul, fetid; (of beer) skunky♣. **3** EMBITTERED, resentful, rancorous, jaundiced, bitter; nasty, spiteful, irritable, peevish, fractious, cross, crabby, crotchety, cantankerous, disagreeable, petulant, querulous, grumpy, bad-tempered, ill-humoured, sullen, surly, sulky, churlish; informal snappy, grouchy, shirty, cranky.

—OPPOSITES: sweet, fresh, amiable.

source *n.* **1** SPRING, origin, headspring, headwater(s); *literary* wellspring. **2** ORIGIN, birthplace, spring, fountainhead, fount, starting point, ground zero; history, provenance, derivation, root, beginning, genesis, start, rise; author, originator, initiator, inventor. **3** REFERENCE, authority, material, document, informant.

sow *v.* **1** PLANT, scatter, spread, disperse, strew, disseminate, distribute, broadcast; drill, seed. **2** CAUSE, bring about, occasion, create, lead to, produce, spread, engender, generate, prompt, initiate, precipitate, trigger, provoke; culminate in, entail, necessitate; foster, foment; *literary* beget.

space *n.* **1** ROOM, capacity, area, volume, expanse, extent, scope, latitude, margin, leeway, play, clearance. **2** AREA, expanse, stretch, sweep, tract. **3** GAP, interval, opening, aperture, cavity, cranny, fissure, crack, interstice, lacuna.

▸ *v.* POSITION, arrange, range, array, dispose, lay out, locate, situate, set, stand.

span *n.* **1** EXTENT, length, width, reach, stretch, spread, distance, range. **2** PERIOD, space, time, duration, course, interval.

▸ *v.* **1** BRIDGE, cross, traverse, pass over. **2** LAST, cover, extend, spread over, comprise.

spare *adj.* **1** EXTRA, supplementary, additional, second, other, alternative, alternate; emergency, reserve,

backup, relief, fallback, substitute; fresh. **2** SURPLUS, superfluous, excessive, extra; redundant, unnecessary, inessential, unessential, unneeded, uncalled for, dispensable, disposable, expendable, unwanted; *informal* going begging. **3** FREE, leisure, own.

▸ *v.* **1** AFFORD, do without, manage without, dispense with, part with, give, provide. **2** PARDON, let off, forgive, reprieve, release, free; leave uninjured, leave unhurt; be merciful to, show mercy to, have mercy on, be lenient to, have pity on.

sparkle *v.* **1** GLITTER, glint, glisten, twinkle, flash, blink, wink, shimmer, shine, gleam; *literary* coruscate, glister. **2** BE LIVELY, be vivacious, be animated, be ebullient, be exuberant, be bubbly, be effervescent, be witty, be full of life.

▸ *n.* GLITTER, glint, twinkle, flicker, shimmer, flash, shine, gleam; *literary* coruscation.

sparse *adj.* SCANT, scanty, scattered, scarce, infrequent, few and far between; meagre, paltry, skimpy, limited, in short supply.

—OPPOSITES: abundant.

speak *v.* **1** TALK, say anything/something; utter, state, declare, tell, voice, express, pronounce, articulate, enunciate, vocalize, verbalize. **2** CONVERSE, have a conversation, talk, communicate, chat, pass the time of day, have a word, gossip; *informal* have a confab, chew the fat; natter, shoot the breeze; *formal* confabulate.

3 GIVE A SPEECH, talk, lecture, hold forth, discourse, expound, expatiate, orate, sermonize, pontificate, declaim; *informal* spout, spiel, speechify, jaw, sound off. **4** MENTION, talk about, discuss, refer to, remark on, allude to, describe. **5** INDICATE, show, display, register, reveal, betray, exhibit, manifest, express, convey, impart, bespeak, communicate, evidence; suggest, denote, reflect; *formal* evince.

speaker *n.* SPEECH-MAKER, lecturer, talker, speechifier, orator, declaimer, rhetorician; spokesperson, spokesman/woman, mouthpiece; reader, lector, commentator, broadcaster, narrator; *informal* tub-thumper, spieler; *historical* demagogue, rhetor.

special *adj.* **1** EXCEPTIONAL, unusual, singular, uncommon, notable, noteworthy, remarkable, outstanding, unique. **2** DISTINCTIVE, distinct, individual, particular, characteristic, specific, peculiar, idiosyncratic. **3** MOMENTOUS, significant, memorable, signal, important, historic, festive, gala, red-letter. **4** SPECIFIC, particular, purpose-built, tailor-made, custom-built/made.
—OPPOSITES: ordinary, general.

specialist *n.* EXPERT, authority, pundit, professional; connoisseur; master, maestro, adept, virtuoso; *informal* pro, buff, ace, whiz, hotshot, maven.
—OPPOSITES: amateur.

specialty *n.* **1** FORTE, strong point, strength, métier, strong suit, talent, skill, bent, gift,

speciality; *informal* bag, thing, cup of tea. **2** DELICACY, speciality, fine food/product, traditional food/product.

species *n.* TYPE, kind, sort; genus, family, order, breed, strain, variety, class, classification, category, set, bracket; style, manner, form, genre; generation, vintage.

specific *adj.* **1** PARTICULAR, specified, fixed, set, determined, distinct, definite; single, individual, peculiar, discrete, express, precise. **2** DETAILED, explicit, express, clear-cut, unequivocal, precise, exact, meticulous, strict, definite.
—OPPOSITES: general, vague.

specify *v.* STATE, name, identify, define, describe, set out, frame, itemize, detail, list, spell out, enumerate, particularize, cite, instance; stipulate, prescribe.

specimen *n.* SAMPLE, example, instance, illustration, demonstration, exemplification, representative piece; bit, snippet, swatch; model, prototype, pattern, dummy, pilot, trial, taster, taste, tester.

spectacle *n.* **1** DISPLAY, show, pageant, parade, performance, exhibition, extravaganza, spectacular. **2** SIGHT, vision, scene, prospect, vista, picture. **3** EXHIBITION, laughingstock, fool, curiosity.

spectacular *adj.* **1** IMPRESSIVE, magnificent, splendid, dazzling, sensational, dramatic, remarkable, outstanding, memorable, unforgettable. **2** STRIKING, picturesque, eye-

catching, breathtaking, arresting, glorious; *informal* out of this world.
—OPPOSITES: unimpressive, dull.

spectator *n.* WATCHER, viewer, observer, onlooker, looker-on, bystander, witness; commentator, reporter, monitor; *literary* beholder.
—OPPOSITES: participant.

speculate *v.* **1** CONJECTURE, theorize, hypothesize, guess, surmise; think, wonder, muse. **2** GAMBLE, take a risk, venture, wager; invest, play the market.

speculative *adj.* **1** CONJECTURAL, suppositional, theoretical, hypothetical, putative, academic, notional, abstract; tentative, unproven, unfounded, groundless, unsubstantiated. **2** RISKY, hazardous, unsafe, uncertain, unpredictable; *informal* chancy, dicey, iffy.

speech *n.* **1** SPEAKING, talking, verbal expression, verbal communication. **2** DICTION, elocution, articulation, enunciation, pronunciation; utterance, words. **3** TALK, address, lecture, discourse, oration, disquisition, peroration, deliverance, presentation; sermon, homily; monologue, soliloquy; *informal* spiel. **4** LANGUAGE, tongue, parlance, idiom, dialect, vernacular, patois; *informal* lingo, patter, -speak, -ese.
—RELATED: lingual, oral, phono-, -phone, -phasia.

speechless *adj.* LOST FOR WORDS, at a loss (for words), dumbstruck, dumbfounded, bereft of speech, tongue-tied, inarticulate, mute,
dumb, voiceless, silent; *informal* mum.
—OPPOSITES: verbose.

speed *n.* **1** RATE, pace, tempo, momentum. **2** RAPIDITY, swiftness, speediness, quickness, dispatch, promptness, immediacy, briskness, sharpness; haste, hurry, precipitateness; acceleration, velocity; *informal* lick, clip; *literary* celerity.
—RELATED: tacho-, tachy-.
▶ *v.* **1** HURRY, rush, dash, run, race, sprint, bolt, dart, gallop, career, charge, shoot, hurtle, careen, hare, fly, zoom, scurry, scuttle, scamper, hasten; *informal* tear, belt, pelt, scoot, zip, zap, whip, hotfoot it, bomb, hightail it. **2** HASTEN, expedite, speed up, accelerate, advance, further, promote, boost, stimulate, aid, assist, facilitate.
—OPPOSITES: slow, hinder.

speedy *adj.* **1** RAPID, swift, quick, fast; prompt, immediate, expeditious, express, brisk, sharp; whirlwind, lightning, meteoric; hasty, hurried, precipitate, breakneck, rushed; *informal* PDQ (pretty damn quick), snappy, quickie. **2** FAST, high-speed; *informal* nippy, zippy, peppy; *literary* fleet.
—OPPOSITES: slow.

spell¹ *v.* SIGNAL, signify, mean, amount to, add up to, constitute; portend, augur, herald, bode, promise; involve; *literary* betoken, foretoken, forebode.
☐ **spell something out** EXPLAIN, make clear, make plain, elucidate, clarify; specify, itemize, detail, enumerate, list, expound, particularize, catalogue.

spell² *n.* **1** INCANTATION, charm, conjuration, formula; (**spells**) magic, sorcery, witchcraft, hex, mojo, curse. **2** INFLUENCE, (animal) magnetism, charisma, allure, lure, charm, attraction, enticement; magic, romance, mystique.
□ **cast a spell on** BEWITCH, enchant, entrance; curse, jinx, witch, hex.

spell³ *n.* **1** PERIOD, time, interval, season, stretch, run, course, streak, patch. **2** BOUT, fit, attack.

spend *v.* **1** PAY (OUT), dish out, expend, disburse; squander, waste, fritter away; use up, consume, exhaust, deplete; lavish; fork out, ante up, lay out, shell out, cough up, drop, blow, splurge, pony up. **2** PASS, occupy, fill, take up, while away.

spendthrift *n.* PROFLIGATE, prodigal, squanderer, waster; *informal* big spender.
—OPPOSITES: miser.
▸ *adj.* PROFLIGATE, improvident, wasteful, extravagant, prodigal.
—OPPOSITES: frugal.

spent *adj.* **1** USED UP, consumed, exhausted, finished, depleted, drained; *informal* burnt out.
2 ☞ TIRED 1.

sphere *n.* **1** GLOBE, ball, orb, spheroid, globule, round; bubble. **2** AREA, field, compass, orbit; range, scope, extent. **3** DOMAIN, realm, province, field, area, territory, arena, department.

spicy *adj.* **1** HOT, peppery, piquant, picante; spiced, seasoned; tasty, zesty, strong, pungent.
2 ENTERTAINING, colourful, lively, spirited, exciting, piquant, zesty; risqué, racy, scandalous, ribald, titillating, bawdy, naughty, salacious, dirty, smutty; *informal* raunchy, juicy, saucy.
—OPPOSITES: bland, boring.

spill *v.* **1** KNOCK OVER, tip over, upset, overturn. **2** OVERFLOW, flow, pour, run, slop, slosh, splash; leak, escape; *archaic* overbrim. **3** STREAM, pour, surge, swarm, flood, throng, crowd.
▸ *n.* **1** SPILLAGE, leak, leakage, overflow, flood. **2** FALL, tumble; *informal* header, cropper, nosedive.

spin *v.* **1** REVOLVE, rotate, turn, go round, whirl, gyrate, circle. **2** WHIRL, wheel, twirl, turn, swing, twist, swivel, pirouette, pivot. **3** REEL, whirl, go round, swim. **4** TELL, recount, relate, narrate, weave, concoct, invent, fabricate, make up.
—RELATED: rotary.
▸ *n.* **1** ROTATION, revolution, turn, whirl, twirl, gyration. **2** SLANT, angle, twist, bias. **3** TRIP, jaunt, outing, excursion, journey; drive, ride, run, turn, airing, joyride.
□ **spin something out** PROLONG, protract, draw out, drag out, string out, extend, carry on, continue; fill out, pad out.

spineless *adj.* WEAK, weak-willed, weak-kneed, feeble, soft, ineffectual, irresolute, indecisive; COWARDLY, timid, timorous, fearful, faint-hearted, pusillanimous, craven, unmanly, namby-pamby, lily-livered, chicken-hearted; *informal* wimpish, wimpy, sissy, wussy, chicken, yellow, yellow-bellied, gutless.
—OPPOSITES: bold, brave, strong-willed.

spiral *adj.* COILED, helical, corkscrew, curling, winding, twisting, whorled; *technical* voluted, helicoid, helicoidal.

▶ *n.* COIL, helix, corkscrew, curl, twist, gyre, whorl, scroll; *technical* volute, volution.

▶ *v.* **1** COIL, wind, swirl, twist, wreathe, snake, gyrate; *literary* gyre. **2** SOAR, shoot up, rocket, increase rapidly, rise rapidly, escalate, climb; *informal* skyrocket, go through the roof. **3** DETERIORATE, decline, degenerate, worsen, get worse; *informal* go downhill, take a nosedive, go to pot, go to the dogs, hit the skids, go down the tubes.

—OPPOSITES: fall, improve.

spirit *n.* **1** SOUL, psyche, (inner) self, inner being, inner man/ woman, mind, ego, id; *Philosophy* pneuma. **2** GHOST, phantom, spectre, apparition, wraith, presence; *informal* spook; *literary* shade. **3** ATTITUDE, frame of mind, way of thinking, point of view, outlook, thoughts, ideas. **4** MOOD, frame of mind, state of mind, emotional state, humour, temper. **5** MORALE, esprit de corps. **6** ETHOS, prevailing tendency, motivating force, essence, quintessence; atmosphere, mood, feeling, climate; attitudes, beliefs, principles, standards, ethics. **7** COURAGE, bravery, pluck, valour, strength of character, fortitude, backbone, mettle, stout-heartedness, determination, resolution, resolve, fight, grit; *informal* guts, spunk, sand, moxie. **8** ENTHUSIASM, eagerness, keenness, liveliness, vivacity,

vivaciousness, animation, energy, verve, vigour, dynamism, zest, dash, élan, panache, sparkle, exuberance, gusto, brio, pep, fervour, zeal, fire, passion; *informal* get-up-and-go. **9** REAL/TRUE MEANING, true intention, essence, substance.

—OPPOSITES: body, flesh.

spirited *adj.* ☞ LIVELY 1, 3.

—OPPOSITES: timid, apathetic, lifeless.

spiritual *adj.* **1** NON-MATERIAL, incorporeal, intangible; inner, mental, psychological; transcendent, ethereal, otherworldly, mystic, mystical, metaphysical; *rare* extramundane. **2** RELIGIOUS, sacred, divine, holy, church, ecclesiastical, devotional.

—OPPOSITES: physical, secular.

spit *v.* **1** EXPECTORATE; *informal* hawk, hork, gob. **2** SNAP, say angrily, hiss. **3** SIZZLE, hiss; crackle, sputter. **4** RAIN LIGHTLY, drizzle, sprinkle.

▶ *n.* SPITTLE, saliva, sputum, slobber, dribble, gob.

spite *n.* ☞ MALICE.

—OPPOSITES: benevolence.

spiteful *adj.* ☞ MALICIOUS.

—OPPOSITES: benevolent.

splash *v.* **1** SPRINKLE, spray, shower, splatter, slosh, slop, squirt; daub; wet. **2** SPATTER, bespatter, splatter, speck, speckle, blotch, smear, stain, mark; *informal* splotch. **3** SWASH, wash, break, lap; dash, beat, lash, batter, crash, buffet; *literary* plash. **4** PADDLE, wade, slosh; wallow; *informal* splosh. **5** BLAZON, display, spread, plaster, trumpet, publicize; *informal* splatter.

▶ *n.* **1** SPOT, blob, dab, daub,

smudge, smear, speck, fleck;
mark, stain; *informal* splotch.
2 DROP, dash, bit, spot, soupçon,
dribble, driblet. **3** PATCH, burst,
streak.
splendid *adj.* **1** MAGNIFICENT,
sumptuous, grand, impressive,
imposing, superb, spectacular,
resplendent, opulent, luxurious,
deluxe, rich, fine, costly,
expensive, lavish, ornate,
gorgeous, glorious, dazzling,
elegant, regal, handsome,
beautiful; stately, majestic,
princely, noble, proud, palatial;
informal plush, posh, swanky, spiffy,
ritzy, splendiferous, swank; *literary*
brave. **2** ☞ EXCELLENT.
—OPPOSITES: modest, awful.
splendour *n.* MAGNIFICENCE,
sumptuousness, grandeur,
impressiveness, resplendence,
opulence, luxury, richness,
fineness, lavishness, ornateness,
glory, beauty, elegance; majesty,
stateliness; *informal* ritziness,
splendiferousness.
—OPPOSITES: ordinariness,
simplicity, modesty.
splinter *n.* SLIVER, shiver, chip,
shard; fragment, piece, bit, shred;
(**splinters**) matchwood, flinders.
▶ *v.* SHATTER, break into tiny pieces,
smash, smash into smithereens,
fracture, split, crack, disintegrate,
crumble.
split *v.* **1** BREAK, chop, cut, hew,
lop, cleave; snap, crack. **2** BREAK
APART, fracture, rupture, fissure,
snap, come apart, splinter. **3** TEAR,
rip, slash, slit; *literary* rend. **4** DIVIDE,
separate, sever; bisect, partition;
literary tear asunder. **5** SHARE (OUT),
divide (up), apportion, allocate,

allot, distribute, dole out, parcel
out, measure out; carve up, slice
up; *informal* divvy up. **6** FORK, divide,
bifurcate, diverge, branch.
7 BREAK UP, separate, part, part
company, become estranged;
divorce, get divorced. **8** (*informal*)
☞ LEAVE[1] sense 1.
—RELATED: fissile, schizo-.
—OPPOSITES: mend, join, unite,
pool, converge, get together,
marry.
▶ *n.* **1** CRACK, fissure, cleft, crevice,
break, fracture, breach. **2** RIP, tear,
cut, rent, slash, slit. **3** DIVISION, rift,
breach, schism, rupture, partition,
separation, severance, scission,
breakup. **4** BREAKUP, split-up,
separation, parting,
estrangement, rift; divorce.
—OPPOSITES: marriage.
spoil *v.* **1** MAR, damage, impair,
blemish, disfigure, blight, flaw,
deface, scar, injure, harm; ruin,
destroy, wreck; be a blot on the
landscape. **2** RUIN, wreck, destroy,
upset, undo, mess up, make a
mess of, dash, sabotage, scotch,
torpedo; *informal* foul up, louse up,
muck up, screw up, put the
kibosh on, scupper, scuttle, do
for, throw a wrench in the works
of, deep-six; *archaic* bring to
naught. **3** OVERINDULGE, pamper,
indulge, mollycoddle, cosset,
coddle, baby, wait on hand and
foot, kill with kindness; nanny.
4 GO BAD, go off, go rancid, turn,
go sour, go mouldy, go rotten, rot,
perish.
—OPPOSITES: improve, enhance,
further, help, neglect, be strict
with, keep.
spoilsport *n.* ☞ KILLJOY.

spoken *adj.* VERBAL, oral, vocal, viva voce, uttered, said, stated; unwritten; by word of mouth. —OPPOSITES: non-verbal, written.

sponsor *n.* BACKER, patron, promoter, benefactor, supporter, partner, contributor, subscriber, friend, guarantor, underwriter, donor.
▶ *v.* ☞ FINANCE.

spontaneous *adj.* **1** UNPLANNED, unpremeditated, unrehearsed, impulsive, impetuous, unstudied, impromptu, spur-of-the-moment, extempore, extemporaneous; unforced, voluntary, unconstrained, unprompted, unbidden, unsolicited; *informal* off-the-cuff. **2** REFLEX, automatic, mechanical, natural, knee-jerk, involuntary, unthinking, unconscious, instinctive, instinctual, uncontrollable, unintentional, visceral; *informal* gut. —OPPOSITES: planned, calculated, conscious, voluntary, inhibited.

sporadic *adj.* OCCASIONAL, infrequent, irregular, periodic, scattered, patchy, isolated, odd; intermittent, spasmodic, fitful, desultory, erratic, unpredictable. —OPPOSITES: frequent, steady, continuous.

spot *n.* **1** MARK, patch, dot, fleck, smudge, smear, stain, blotch, blot, splash; *informal* splotch. **2** PLACE, location, site, position, point, situation, scene, setting, locale, locality, area, neighbourhood, region; venue; *technical* locus. **3** POSITION, place, slot, space.
▶ *v.* **1** ☞ NOTICE. **2** STAIN, mark, fleck, speckle, smudge, streak, splash, spatter; *informal* splotch.

spotless *adj.* **1** PERFECTLY CLEAN, ultra-clean, pristine, immaculate, shining, shiny, gleaming, spic and span. **2** UNBLEMISHED, unsullied, untarnished, untainted, unstained, pure, whiter than white, innocent, impeccable, blameless, irreproachable, above reproach; *informal* squeaky clean. —OPPOSITES: dirty, tarnished, impure.

spotted *adj.* MOTTLED, dappled, speckled, flecked, freckled, freckly, dotted, stippled, brindle(d); *informal* splotchy.

spout *v.* **1** SPURT, gush, spew, erupt, shoot, squirt, spray; disgorge, discharge, emit, belch forth. **2** HOLD FORTH, sound off, go on, talk at length, expatiate; *informal* mouth off, speechify, spiel.

sprawl *v.* **1** STRETCH OUT, lounge, loll, lie, recline, drape oneself, slump, flop, slouch. **2** SPREAD, stretch, extend, be strung out, be scattered, straggle, spill.

spray *n.* **1** SHOWER, sprinkling, sprinkle, jet, mist, drizzle; spume, spindrift; foam, froth. **2** ATOMIZER, vaporizer, aerosol, sprinkler; nebulizer.
▶ *v.* **1** SPRINKLE, shower, spatter; scatter, disperse, diffuse; mist; douche; *literary* besprinkle. **2** SPOUT, jet, gush, spurt, shoot, squirt.

spread *v.* **1** LAY OUT, open out, unfurl, unroll, roll out; straighten out, fan out; stretch out, extend; *literary* outspread. **2** EXTEND, stretch, open out, be displayed, be exhibited, be on show; sprawl. **3** SCATTER, strew, disperse, distribute. **4** DISSEMINATE, circulate, pass on, put about, communicate,

diffuse, make public, make known, purvey, broadcast, publicize, propagate, promulgate; repeat; *literary* bruit about/abroad. **5** SMEAR, daub, plaster, slather, lather, apply, put; smooth, rub. **6** COVER, coat, layer, daub, smother; butter.
—OPPOSITES: fold up, suppress.
▸ *n.* **1** EXPANSION, proliferation, extension, growth; dissemination, diffusion, transmission, propagation. **2** SPAN, width, extent, stretch, reach. **3** EXPANSE, area, sweep, stretch. **4** RANGE, span, spectrum, sweep; variety. **5** (*informal*) LARGE/ELABORATE MEAL, feast, banquet; *informal* blowout, nosh.

sprightly *adj.* SPRY, lively, agile, nimble, energetic, active, full of energy, vigorous, spirited, animated, vivacious, frisky; *informal* full of vim and vigour.
—OPPOSITES: doddery, lethargic.

spring *v.* **1** LEAP, jump, bound, vault, hop. **2** FLY, whip, flick, whisk, kick, bounce. **3** ORIGINATE, derive, arise, stem, emanate, proceed, issue, evolve, come. **4** APPEAR SUDDENLY, appear unexpectedly, materialize, pop up, shoot up, sprout, develop quickly; proliferate, mushroom. **5** ANNOUNCE SUDDENLY/ UNEXPECTEDLY, reveal suddenly/ unexpectedly, surprise someone with.
▸ *n.* **1** LEAP, jump, bound, vault, hop; pounce. **2** SPRINGINESS, bounciness, bounce, resilience, elasticity, flexibility, stretch, stretchiness, give. **3** BUOYANCY, bounce, energy, liveliness,

jauntiness, sprightliness, confidence. **4** SOURCE, geyser; *literary* wellspring, fount. **5** ORIGIN, source, fountainhead, root, roots, basis; *informal* ground zero.
—RELATED: vernal.

sprinkle *v.* **1** SPLASH, trickle, spray, shower; spatter. **2** SCATTER, strew; drizzle, pepper. **3** DREDGE, dust. **4** DOT, stipple, stud, fleck, speckle, spot, pepper; scatter, cover.

sprout *v.* GERMINATE, put/send out shoots, bud, burgeon, grow, develop, spring up, shoot up, come up, appear.

spur *n.* ☞ STIMULUS.
—OPPOSITES: disincentive, discouragement.
▸ *v.* STIMULATE, encourage, prompt, propel, prod, induce, impel, motivate, move, galvanize, inspire, incentivize, urge, drive, egg on, stir; incite, goad, provoke, prick, sting, light a fire under.
—OPPOSITES: discourage.

spurn *v.* REJECT, rebuff, scorn, turn down, treat with contempt, disdain, look down one's nose at, despise; snub, slight, jilt, dismiss, brush off, turn one's back on; give someone the cold shoulder, cold-shoulder; *informal* turn one's nose up at, give someone the brush-off, kick in the teeth, give someone the bum's rush.
—OPPOSITES: welcome, accept.

spurt *v.* SQUIRT, shoot, jet, erupt, gush, pour, stream, pump, surge, spew, course, well, spring, burst; disgorge, discharge, emit, belch forth, expel, eject.
▸ *n.* **1** SQUIRT, jet, spout, gush, stream, rush, surge, flood,

cascade, torrent. **2** BURST, fit, bout, rush, spate, surge, attack, outburst, blaze. **3** BURST OF SPEED, turn of speed, sprint, rush, burst of energy.

spy *n.* SECRET AGENT, intelligence agent, double agent, undercover agent, operative, informant, mole, sleeper, plant, scout, fifth columnist; *informal* snooper, spook; *archaic* intelligencer.

▶ *v.* **1** BE A SPY, gather intelligence, work for the secret service; *informal* snoop. **2** OBSERVE FURTIVELY, keep under surveillance/observation, watch, keep a watch on, keep an eye on. **3** ☞ NOTICE.

squander *v.* WASTE, misspend, misuse, throw away, fritter away, spend recklessly, spend unwisely, spend like water; expend, use up, consume, run through; *informal* blow, go through, splurge, drop, pour down the drain.

—OPPOSITES: manage, make good use of, save.

square *adj.* **1** QUADRILATERAL, rectangular, oblong, right-angled, at right angles, perpendicular; straight, level, parallel, horizontal, upright, vertical, true, plane. **2** LEVEL, even, drawn, equal, tied; neck and neck, nip and tuck, side by side, evenly matched; *informal* even-steven(s). **3** FAIR, honest, just, equitable, straight, true, upright, above board, ethical, decent, proper; *informal* on the level. **4** (*informal*) OLD-FASHIONED, behind the times, out of date, conservative, traditionalist, conventional, conformist, bourgeois, straitlaced, fogeyish,

stuffy; *informal* stick-in-the-mud, fuddy-duddy.

—OPPOSITES: crooked, uneven, underhanded, trendy.

squash *v.* **1** CRUSH, squeeze, flatten, compress, press, smash, distort, pound, trample, stamp on; pulp, mash, cream, liquidize, beat, pulverize; *informal* squish, squoosh. **2** FORCE, ram, thrust, push, cram, jam, stuff, pack, compress, squeeze, wedge, press.

squat *v.* **1** CROUCH (DOWN), hunker (down), sit on one's haunches, sit on one's heels. **2** OCCUPY ILLEGALLY, set up residence, dwell, settle, live.

▶ *adj.* STOCKY, thickset, dumpy, stubby, stumpy, short, small.

squeak *n. & v.* **1** PEEP, cheep, pipe, piping, squeal, tweet, yelp, whimper. **2** SCREECH, creak, scrape, grate, rasp, jar, groan.

squeeze *v.* **1** COMPRESS, press, crush, squash, pinch, nip, grasp, grip, clutch, flatten. **2** EXTRACT, press, force, express. **3** FORCE, thrust, cram, ram, jam, stuff, pack, wedge, press, squash. **4** CROWD, crush, cram, pack, jam, squash, wedge oneself, shove, push, force one's way. **5** EXTORT, force, extract, wrest, wring, milk; *informal* bleed someone of something.

squirm *v.* **1** WRIGGLE, wiggle, writhe, twist, slide, slither, turn, shift, fidget, jiggle, twitch, thresh, flounder, flail, toss and turn. **2** WINCE, shudder, feel embarrassed, feel ashamed.

squirt *v.* **1** SPURT, shoot, spray, fountain, jet, erupt; gush, rush, pump, surge, stream, spew, well, spring, burst, issue, emanate; emit, belch forth, expel, eject. **2** SPLASH, wet, spray, shower, spatter, splatter, sprinkle; *literary* besprinkle.

stab v. **1** KNIFE, run through, skewer, spear, bayonet, gore, spike, stick, impale, transfix, pierce, prick, puncture; *literary* transpierce. **2** LUNGE, thrust, jab, poke, prod, dig.
▶ n. **1** KNIFE WOUND, puncture, incision, prick, cut, perforation. **2** LUNGE, thrust, jab, poke, prod, dig, punch. **3** TWINGE, pang, throb, spasm, cramp, dart, prick, flash, thrill. **4** (*informal*) ATTEMPT, try, effort, endeavour; guess; *informal* go, shot, crack, bash, whack; *formal* essay.

stability n. **1** FIRMNESS, solidity, steadiness, strength, security, safety. **2** BALANCE OF MIND, mental health, sanity, normality, soundness, rationality, reason, sense. **3** STEADINESS, firmness, solidity, strength, durability, lasting nature, enduring nature, permanence, changelessness, invariability, immutability, indestructibility, reliability, dependability.

stable adj. **1** FIRM, solid, steady, secure, fixed, fast, safe, moored, anchored, stuck down, immovable. **2** WELL-BALANCED, of sound mind, compos mentis, sane, normal, right in the head, rational, steady, reasonable, sensible, sober, down-to-earth, matter-of-fact, having both one's feet on the ground; *informal* all there. **3** SECURE, solid, strong, steady, firm, sure, steadfast,

unwavering, unvarying, unfaltering; established, abiding, durable, enduring, lasting, permanent, reliable, dependable.
—OPPOSITES: loose, wobbly, unbalanced, rocky, lasting, changeable.

stack n. **1** HEAP, pile, mound, mountain, pyramid, tower. **2** CHIMNEY, smokestack, funnel, exhaust pipe.
—OPPOSITES: few, little.
▶ v. **1** HEAP (UP), pile (up), make a heap/pile/stack of; assemble, put together, collect, hoard, store, stockpile. **2** LOAD, fill (up), lade, pack, charge, stuff, cram; stock.
—OPPOSITES: empty.

staff n. EMPLOYEES, workers, workforce, personnel, human resources, manpower, labour.
▶ v. MAN, people, crew, work, operate, occupy.

stage n. **1** PHASE, period, juncture, step, point, time, moment, instant, level. **2** PART, section, portion, stretch, leg, lap, circuit. **3** PLATFORM, dais, stand, grandstand, staging, apron, rostrum, podium; bandstand, bandshell; catwalk. **4** THEATRE, drama, dramatics, dramatic art, thespianism; *informal* the boards. **5** SCENE, setting; context, frame, sphere, field, realm, arena, backdrop; affairs.
▶ v. **1** PUT ON, present, produce, mount, direct; perform, act, give. **2** ORGANIZE, arrange, coordinate, lay on, put together, get together, set up; orchestrate, choreograph, mastermind, engineer; take part in, participate in, join in.

stagger *v.* **1** LURCH, walk unsteadily, reel, sway, teeter, totter, stumble, wobble, blunder, weave. **2** ☞ AMAZE.

stagnant *adj.* **1** STILL, motionless, static, stationary, standing, dead, slack; FOUL, stale, putrid, smelly. **2** INACTIVE, sluggish, slow-moving, lethargic, static, flat, depressed, declining, moribund, dying, dead, dormant.
—OPPOSITES: flowing, fresh, active, vibrant.

staid *adj.* SEDATE, respectable, quiet, serious, serious-minded, steady, conventional, traditional, unadventurous, unenterprising, set in one's ways, sober, proper, decorous, formal, stuffy, stiff, priggish; *informal* starchy, buttoned-down, stick-in-the-mud.
—OPPOSITES: frivolous, daring, informal.

stain *v.* **1** DISCOLOUR, blemish, soil, mark, muddy, spot, spatter, splatter, smear, splash, smudge, blotch, blacken; *literary* imbrue. **2** DAMAGE, injure, harm, sully, blacken, tarnish, taint, smear, bring discredit to, dishonour, drag through the mud; *literary* besmirch. **3** COLOUR, tint, dye, tinge, pigment, colour-wash.
▶ *n.* **1** MARK, spot, spatter, splatter, blotch, smudge, smear. **2** BLEMISH, injury, taint, blot, smear, discredit, dishonour; damage. **3** TINT, colour, dye, tinge, pigment, colourant, colour wash.

stake¹ *n.* POST, pole, stick, spike, upright, support, prop, strut, pale, paling, picket, pile, piling, cane.
▶ *v.* PROP UP, tie up, tether, support, hold up, brace, truss.

☐ **stake something out 1** MARK OFF/OUT, demarcate, measure out, delimit, fence off, section off, close off, shut off, cordon off. **2** (*informal*) OBSERVE, watch, keep an eye on, keep under observation, keep watch on, monitor, keep under surveillance; *informal* keep tabs on, keep a tab on, case.

stake² *n.* **1** BET, wager, ante. **2** PRIZE MONEY, purse, pot, winnings. **3** COMPETITION, contest, battle, challenge, rivalry, race, running, struggle, scramble. **4** SHARE, interest, ownership, involvement.
▶ *v.* BET, wager, lay, put on, gamble, chance, venture, risk, hazard.

stale *adj.* **1** OLD, past its best, off, dry, hard, musty, rancid. **2** STUFFY, close, musty, fusty, stagnant, frowzy. **3** FLAT, turned, spoiled, off, insipid, tasteless. **4** HACKNEYED, tired, worn out, overworked, threadbare, warmed-up, banal, trite, clichéd, platitudinous, unoriginal, unimaginative, uninspired, flat; out of date, outdated, outmoded, passé, archaic, obsolete; warmed-over; *informal* old hat, corny, unfunny, played out.
—OPPOSITES: fresh, original.

stalk¹ *n.* STEM, shoot, trunk, stock, cane, bine, bent, straw, reed.
—RELATED: cauline.

stalk² *v.* **1** CREEP UP ON, trail, follow, shadow, track down, go after, be after, course, hunt; *informal* tail. **2** STRUT, stride, march, flounce, storm, stomp, sweep.

stall *n.* **1** STAND, table, counter, booth, kiosk. **2** PEN, coop, sty, corral, enclosure, compartment.

▶ v. **1** OBSTRUCT, impede, interfere with, hinder, hamper, block, interrupt, hold up, hold back, thwart, balk, sabotage, delay, stonewall, check, stop, halt, derail, put a brake on; *informal* stymie. **2** STOP, fizzle, flatline, die, reach an impasse, hit a roadblock. **3** USE DELAYING TACTICS, play for time, temporize, gain time, procrastinate, hedge, beat around the bush, drag one's feet, delay, filibuster, stonewall, give someone the runaround, rag the puck✦. **4** DELAY, divert, distract; HOLD OFF, stave off, fend off, keep off, ward off, keep at bay.

stalwart *adj.* STAUNCH, loyal, faithful, committed, devoted, dedicated, dependable, reliable, steady, constant, trusty, solid, hard-working, steadfast, redoubtable, unwavering.
—OPPOSITES: disloyal, unfaithful, unreliable.

stamina *n.* ENDURANCE, staying power, tirelessness, fortitude, strength, energy, toughness, determination, tenacity, perseverance, grit.

stamp *v.* **1** TRAMPLE, step, tread, tramp, stomp; CRUSH, squash, flatten. **2** STOMP, stump, clomp, clump. **3** IMPRINT, print, impress, punch, inscribe, emboss, brand, frank. **4** FIX, inscribe, etch, carve, imprint, impress.

▶ *n.* **1** MARK, hallmark, indication, sign, seal, sure sign, telltale sign, quality, smack, smell, savour, air. **2** TYPE, kind, sort, variety, class, category, classification, style, description, condition, calibre,

status, quality, nature, ilk, kidney, cast, grain, mould, stripe.

□ **stamp something out** PUT AN END/STOP TO, end, stop, crush, put down, crack down on, curb, nip in the bud, scotch, squash, quash, quell, subdue, suppress, extinguish, stifle, abolish, get rid of, eliminate, eradicate, beat, overcome, defeat, destroy, wipe out; *informal* put the kibosh on, clean house.

stampede *n.* CHARGE, panic, rush, flight, rout.

▶ v. BOLT, charge, flee, take flight; race, rush, career, sweep, run.

stance *n.* **1** POSTURE, body position, pose, attitude. **2** ATTITUDE, stand, point of view, viewpoint, opinion, way of thinking, outlook, standpoint, position, angle, perspective, approach, line, policy.

stand *v.* **1** BE ON ONE'S FEET, be upright, be erect, be vertical. **2** RISE, get/rise to one's feet, get up, straighten up, pick oneself up, find one's feet, be upstanding; *formal* arise. **3** BE, exist, be situated, be located, be positioned, be sited, have been built. **4** PUT, set, set up, erect, upend, place, position, locate, prop, lean, stick, install, arrange; *informal* park. **5** REMAIN IN FORCE, remain valid/effective/ operative, remain in operation, hold, hold good, apply, be the case, exist. **6** WITHSTAND, endure, bear, put up with, take, cope with, handle, sustain, resist, stand up to. **7** (*informal*) ENDURE, tolerate, bear, put up with, take, abide, support, countenance; *informal* swallow, stomach; *formal* brook.

—OPPOSITES: sit, lie, sit down, lie down.

▶ *n.* **1** ATTITUDE, stance, point of view, viewpoint, opinion, way of thinking, outlook, standpoint, position, approach, thinking, policy, line. **2** OPPOSITION, resistance, objection, hostility, animosity. **3** BASE, support, mounting, platform, rest, plinth, bottom; tripod, rack, trivet.

□ **stand by** WAIT, be prepared, be in (a state of) readiness, be ready for action, be on full alert, wait in the wings. **stand by someone/ something 1** REMAIN/BE LOYAL TO, stick with/by, remain/be true to, stand up for, support, back up, defend, stick up for. **2** ABIDE BY, keep (to), adhere to, hold to, stick to, observe, comply with. **stand for 1** MEAN, be an abbreviation of, represent, signify, denote, indicate, symbolize. **2** (*informal*) PUT UP WITH, endure, tolerate, accept, take, abide, support, countenance; *informal* swallow, stomach; *formal* brook. **3** ADVOCATE, champion, uphold, defend, stand up for, support, back, endorse, be in favour of, promote, recommend, urge. **stand in** SUBSTITUTE, fill in, sit in, do duty, take over, act as deputy, be deputized, act as locum, be a proxy, cover, hold the fort, step into the breach; replace, relieve, take over from; sub, fill someone's shoes, step into someone's shoes, pinch-hit. **stand out** BE NOTICEABLE, be visible, be obvious, be conspicuous, stick out, be striking, be distinctive, be prominent, attract attention, catch the eye, leap out, show up; *informal* stick/stand out like a sore thumb. **stand up** REMAIN/BE VALID, be sound, be plausible, hold water, hold up, stand questioning, survive investigation, bear examination, be verifiable. **stand up for** SUPPORT, defend, back, back up, stick up for, champion, promote, uphold, take someone's part, take the side of, side with. **stand up to 1** DEFY, confront, challenge, resist, take on, put up a fight against, argue with, take a stand against. **2** WITHSTAND, survive, come through (unscathed), outlast, outlive, weather, ride out, ward off.

standard *n.* **1** QUALITY, level, grade, calibre, merit, excellence. **2** GUIDELINE, norm, yardstick, benchmark, measure, criterion, guide, touchstone, model, pattern, example, exemplar. **3** PRINCIPLE, ideal; (**standards**) code of behaviour, code of honour, morals, scruples, ethics.

▶ *adj.* **1** NORMAL, usual, typical, stock, common, ordinary, customary, conventional, wonted, established, settled, set, fixed, traditional, prevailing. **2** DEFINITIVE, established, classic, recognized, accepted, authoritative, most reliable, exhaustive.

—OPPOSITES: unusual, special.

standardize *v.* SYSTEMATIZE, make consistent, make uniform, make comparable, regulate, normalize, bring into line, equalize, homogenize, regiment.

standoff *n.* DEADLOCK, stalemate, impasse, saw-off✦; draw, tie, dead heat; suspension of hostilities, lull.

staple *adj.* MAIN, principal, chief, major, primary, leading, foremost, first, most important, predominant, dominant, (most) prominent, basic, standard, prime, premier; *informal* number-one.

stare *v.* GAZE, gape, goggle, glare, ogle, peer; *informal* gawk, rubberneck.

start *v.* ☞ BEGIN.
—OPPOSITES: finish, stop, clear up, wind up, give up, arrive, stay, close down.
▸ *n.* ☞ BEGINNING 1.
—OPPOSITES: end, finish.

startle *v.* SURPRISE, frighten, scare, alarm, give someone a shock/fright/jolt, make someone jump; PERTURB, unsettle, agitate, disturb, disconcert, disquiet; *informal* give someone a turn, make someone jump out of their skin, freak someone out.
—OPPOSITES: put at ease.

startling *adj.* SURPRISING, astonishing, amazing, unexpected, unforeseen, staggering, shocking, stunning; extraordinary, remarkable, dramatic; disturbing, unsettling, perturbing, disconcerting, disquieting; frightening, alarming, scary.
—OPPOSITES: predictable, ordinary.

state¹ *n.* **1** CONDITION, shape, situation, circumstances, position; predicament, plight. **2** (*informal*) FLUSTER, frenzy, fever, fret, panic, state of agitation/anxiety; *informal* flap, tizzy, dither, stew, sweat.

3 COUNTRY, nation, land, sovereign state, nation state, kingdom, realm, power, republic, confederation, federation.
4 GOVERNMENT, parliament, administration, regime, authorities.

state² *v.* EXPRESS, voice, utter, put into words, declare, say, affirm, assert, announce, make known, put across/over, communicate, air, reveal, disclose, divulge, proclaim, present, expound; set out, set down; *informal* come out with.

stately *adj.* DIGNIFIED, majestic, ceremonious, courtly, imposing, impressive, solemn, awe-inspiring, regal, elegant, grand, glorious, splendid, magnificent, resplendent; slow-moving, measured, deliberate.

statement *n.* DECLARATION, expression of views/facts, affirmation, assertion, announcement, utterance, communication, proclamation, presentation, expounding; account, testimony, evidence, report, bulletin, communiqué.

static *adj.* **1** UNCHANGED, fixed, stable, steady, unchanging, changeless, unvarying, invariable, constant, consistent.
2 ☞ STATIONARY.
—OPPOSITES: variable, mobile, active, dynamic.

stationary *adj.* STATIC, parked, stopped, motionless, immobile, unmoving, still, stock-still, at a standstill, at rest; not moving a muscle, like a statue, rooted to the spot, frozen, transfixed,

paralyzed, inactive, inert, lifeless, inanimate.
—OPPOSITES: moving, shifting.

statue *n.* SCULPTURE, figure, effigy, statuette, figurine, idol; carving, bronze, graven image, model; bust, head.

stature *n.* **1** HEIGHT, tallness; size, build. **2** REPUTATION, repute, standing, status, position, prestige, distinction, eminence, pre-eminence, prominence, importance, influence, note, fame, celebrity, renown, acclaim.

status *n.* **1** STANDING, rank, ranking, position, social position, level, place, estimation; *dated* station. **2** ☞ PRESTIGE. **3** STATE, position, condition, shape, stage.

staunch *adj.* ☞ STALWART.
—OPPOSITES: disloyal, unfaithful, unreliable.

stay *v.* **1** REMAIN (BEHIND), stay behind, stay put; wait, linger, stick, be left, hold on, hang on, lodge; *informal* hang around/round; *archaic* bide, tarry. **2** CONTINUE (TO BE), remain, keep, persist in being, carry on being, go on being. **3** VISIT, spend time, put up, stop (off/over); holiday; lodge, room, board, have rooms, be housed, be accommodated, be quartered, be billeted, vacation; *formal* sojourn; *archaic* bide.
—OPPOSITES: leave.
▶ *n.* VISIT, stop, stopoff, stopover, overnight, break, holiday, vacation; *formal* sojourn.

steadfast *adj.* **1** ☞ LOYAL.
2 ☞ RESOLUTE.
—OPPOSITES: disloyal, irresolute.

steady *adj.* **1** STABLE, firm, fixed, secure, fast, safe, immovable,

unshakeable, dependable; anchored, moored, jammed, rooted, braced. **2** MOTIONLESS, still, static, stationary, unmoving. **3** FIXED, intent, unwavering, unfaltering. **4** SENSIBLE, level-headed, rational, settled, mature, down-to-earth, full of common sense, reliable, dependable, sound, sober, serious-minded, responsible, serious. **5** CONSTANT, unchanging, regular, consistent, invariable; continuous, continual, unceasing, ceaseless, perpetual, unremitting, unwavering, unfaltering, unending, endless, round-the-clock, all-year-round. **6** REGULAR, usual, established, settled, firm, devoted, faithful.
—OPPOSITES: unstable, loose, shaky, darting, flighty, immature, fluctuating, sporadic, occasional.
▶ *v.* **1** STABILIZE, hold steady; brace, support; balance, poise; secure, fix, make fast. **2** CALM, soothe, quieten, compose, settle; subdue, quell, control, get a grip on.

steal *v.* **1** PURLOIN, thieve, take, take for oneself, help oneself to, loot, pilfer, run off with, abscond with, carry off, shoplift; embezzle, misappropriate, pillage; have one's fingers/hand in the till; *informal* walk off with, rob, swipe, snatch, (*Nfld*) buck✤, nab, nick, rip off, lift, 'liberate', 'borrow', filch, snaffle, snitch, pinch, heist; *formal* peculate. **2** ☞ PLAGIARIZE.
3 SNATCH, sneak. **4** CREEP, sneak, slink, slip, slide, glide, tiptoe, sidle, slope, edge.

stealing *n.* ☞ THEFT.

stealthy *adj.* ☞ SURREPTITIOUS.
—OPPOSITES: open.

steep *adj.* **1** PRECIPITOUS, sheer, abrupt, sharp, perpendicular, vertical, bluff, vertiginous. **2** SHARP, sudden, precipitate, precipitous, rapid. **3** (*informal*) ☞ EXPENSIVE.
—OPPOSITES: gentle, gradual, reasonable.

steer *v.* **1** GUIDE, direct, manoeuvre, drive, pilot, navigate; *Nautical* con, helm. **2** manoeuvre, stickhandle✦. **3** GUIDE, conduct, direct, lead, take, usher, shepherd, marshal, herd.

step *n.* **1** PACE, stride. **2** FOOTSTEP, footfall, tread. **3** GAIT, walk, tread. **4** SHORT DISTANCE, stone's throw, spitting distance; *informal* {a hop, skip, and jump}. **5** STAIR, tread; (**steps**) STAIRS, staircase, stairway. **6** RUNG, tread. **7** COURSE OF ACTION, measure, move, act, action, initiative, manoeuvre, operation, tactic. **8** ADVANCE, development, move, movement; breakthrough. **9** STAGE, level, grade, rank, degree; notch, rung.
▶ *v.* **1** WALK, move, tread, pace, stride. **2** TREAD, stamp, trample; squash, crush, flatten.
□ **step in 1** INTERVENE, intercede, involve oneself, become/get involved, take a hand. **2** STAND IN, sit in, fill in, cover, substitute, take over; replace, take someone's place.

stereotyped *adj.* STOCK, conventional, stereotypical, standard, formulaic, predictable; hackneyed, clichéd, cliché-ridden, banal, trite, unoriginal; typecast; *informal* corny, old hat.
—OPPOSITES: unconventional, original.

sterile *adj.* **1** INFERTILE, unable to reproduce/conceive, unable to have children/young; *archaic* barren. **2** UNPRODUCTIVE, infertile, unfruitful, barren. **3** ASEPTIC, sterilized, germ-free, antiseptic, disinfected; uncontaminated, unpolluted, pure, clean; sanitary, hygienic.
—OPPOSITES: fertile, productive, septic.

sterilize *v.* **1** DISINFECT, fumigate, decontaminate, sanitize; pasteurize; clean, cleanse, purify; *technical* autoclave. **2** make infertile, hysterectomize, vasectomize, have one's tubes tied, have a tubal ligation, have a salpingectomy. **3** NEUTER, castrate, spay, geld, cut, fix, desex, alter, doctor.
—OPPOSITES: contaminate.

stern *adj.* SERIOUS, unsmiling, frowning, severe, forbidding, grim, unfriendly, austere, dour, gruff, surly, sullen, stony, flinty, steely, unrelenting, unforgiving, unbending, unsympathetic, disapproving.
—OPPOSITES: genial, friendly, lenient, lax.

stick[1] *n.* **1** PIECE OF WOOD, twig, small branch. **2** WALKING STICK, cane, staff, alpenstock, crook, crutch. **3** CANE, pole, post, stake, upright. **4** CLUB, cudgel, bludgeon, shillelagh; truncheon, baton; cane, birch, switch, rod.
□ **the sticks** (*informal*) THE COUNTRY, the countryside, rural areas, the provinces; the backwoods, (*Ont. & Que.*) the back concessions✦, the back of beyond, the wilds, the hinterland, moose pasture✦, a backwater, the backcountry, the

backland, the middle of nowhere, the boondocks, the boonies, hicksville.

stick² *v.* **1** THRUST, push, insert, jab, poke, dig, plunge. **2** PIERCE, penetrate, puncture, prick, stab. **3** ADHERE, cling, be fixed, be glued. **4** AFFIX, attach, fasten, fix; paste, glue, gum, tape, Scotch-tape, pin, tack. **5** BECOME TRAPPED, become jammed, jam, catch, become wedged, become lodged, become fixed, become embedded. **6** REMAIN, stay, linger, dwell, persist, continue, last, endure, burn. **7** BE UPHELD, hold, be believed; *informal* hold water. **8** (*informal*) PUT (DOWN), place, set (down), lay (down), deposit, position; leave, stow; *informal* dump, park, pop, plonk, plunk. □**stick out 1** PROTRUDE, jut (out), project, stand out, extend, poke out; bulge, overhang. **2** BE NOTICEABLE, be visible, be obvious, be conspicuous, stand out, be obtrusive, be prominent, attract attention, catch the eye, leap out, show up; *informal* stick/stand out like a sore thumb. **stick to** ABIDE BY, keep, adhere to, hold to, comply with, fulfill, make good, stand by. **stick up for** SUPPORT, take someone's side, side with, be on the side of, stand by, stand up for, take someone's part, defend, come to the defence of, champion, speak up for, fight for.

sticky *adj.* **1** (SELF-)ADHESIVE, gummed; *technical* adherent. **2** GLUTINOUS, viscous, viscid, gluey, tacky, gummy, treacly, syrupy; mucilaginous; *informal* gooey, icky, gloppy. **3** ☞ MUGGY. **4** AWKWARD,

difficult, tricky, ticklish, problematic, delicate, touch-and-go, touchy, embarrassing, sensitive, uncomfortable; *informal* hairy.
—OPPOSITES: dry, fresh, cool, easy.

stiff *adj.* **1** RIGID, hard, firm, inelastic, inflexible. **2** SEMI-SOLID, viscous, viscid, thick, stiffened, firm. **3** ACHING, achy, painful; arthritic, rheumatic; *informal* creaky, rusty. **4** ☞ FORMAL 2. **5** ☞ HARSH 3.
—OPPOSITES: flexible, plastic, limp, runny, supple, limber, relaxed, informal, lenient, mild.

stifle *v.* **1** ☞ SUFFOCATE. **2** SUPPRESS, smother, restrain, fight back, choke back, gulp back, check, swallow, curb, silence. **3** CONSTRAIN, hinder, hamper, impede, hold back, curb, check, restrain, prevent, inhibit, suppress.
—OPPOSITES: let out, encourage.

still *adj.* **1** MOTIONLESS, unmoving, not moving a muscle, stock-still, immobile, inanimate, like a statue, as if turned to stone, rooted to the spot, transfixed, static, stationary; paralyzed, frozen. **2** ☞ QUIET *adj.* 1. **3** CALM, flat, even, smooth, placid, tranquil, pacific, waveless, glassy, like a millpond, unruffled, stagnant.
—OPPOSITES: moving, active, noisy, rough.
▶ *adv.* ☞ HOWEVER.

stilted *adj.* STRAINED, forced, contrived, constrained, laboured, stiff, self-conscious, awkward, unnatural, wooden.

—OPPOSITES: natural, effortless, spontaneous.

stimulant n. **1** TONIC, restorative; antidepressant; informal pep pill, upper, pick-me-up, bracer, happy pill. **2** STIMULUS, incentive, encouragement, impetus, inducement, boost, spur, prompt; informal shot in the arm.
—OPPOSITES: sedative, downer, deterrent.

stimulate v. ENCOURAGE, act as a stimulus/incentive/impetus/spur to, prompt, prod, move, motivate, trigger, spark, spur on, galvanize, activate, kindle, fire, fire with enthusiasm, fuel, whet, nourish; inspire, inspirit, rouse, excite, animate, electrify, jump-start, light a fire under.
—OPPOSITES: discourage.

stimulating adj. **1** RESTORATIVE, tonic, invigorating, bracing, energizing, reviving, refreshing, revitalizing, revivifying. **2** ☞ INTERESTING.
—OPPOSITES: sedative, uninspiring, uninteresting, boring.

stimulus n. SPUR, stimulant, encouragement, impetus, catalyst, boost, prompt, prod, incentive, incitement, inducement, inspiration, springboard; motivation, impulse; informal shot in the arm, kick up the backside.
—OPPOSITES: deterrent, discouragement.

stingy adj. ☞ CHEAP 3.
—OPPOSITES: generous, liberal.

stink v. REEK, smell (foul/bad/disgusting), stink/smell to high heaven; informal hum.
▶ n. **1** STENCH, reek, fetor, foul/bad

smell; informal funk; literary miasma. **2** (informal) FUSS, commotion, rumpus, ruckus, trouble, outcry, uproar, brouhaha, furor; informal song and dance, to-do, kerfuffle, hoo-ha.

stint v. SKIMP, scrimp, be economical, economize, be sparing, hold back, be frugal; be mean, be parsimonious; limit, restrict; informal be stingy, be mingy, be tight.
▶ n. SPELL, stretch, turn, session, term, shift, tour of duty.

stipulate v. SPECIFY, set down, set out, lay down; demand, require, insist on, make a condition of, prescribe, impose; Law provide.

stipulation n. ☞ CONDITION n. 5.

stir v. **1** MIX, blend, agitate; beat, whip, whisk, fold in, cut in, toss. **2** MOVE SLIGHTLY, change one's position, shift. **3** DISTURB, rustle, shake, move, flutter, agitate. **4** GET UP, get out of bed, rouse oneself, rise; WAKE (UP), awaken; informal rise and shine, surface, show signs of life; formal arise; literary waken. **5** MOVE, budge, make a move, shift, go away; leave. **6** AROUSE, rouse, fire, kindle, inspire, stimulate, excite, awaken, quicken; literary waken. **7** ☞ SPUR v.
—OPPOSITES: go to bed, retire, go to sleep, stultify, stay, stay put.
▶ n. ☞ COMMOTION.
☐ **stir something up** WHIP UP, work up, foment, fan the flames of, trigger, spark off, precipitate, excite, provoke, incite, ignite.

stirring adj. ☞ THRILLING.
—OPPOSITES: boring, pedestrian.

stocky adj. THICKSET, sturdy, heavily built, chunky, burly,

strapping, brawny, solid, heavy,
heavy-set, hefty, beefy, blocky.
—OPPOSITES: slender, skinny.

stomach n. **1** ABDOMEN, belly,
gut, middle; *informal* tummy, tum,
breadbasket, insides. **2** PAUNCH,
pot-belly, beer belly, beer gut,
Molson muscle✦, girth, pot,
tummy, spare tire, middle-aged
spread. **3** APPETITE, taste, hunger,
thirst; inclination, desire, relish,
fancy.
—RELATED: gastric.
▸ v. **1** DIGEST, keep down, manage
to eat/consume, tolerate, take.
2 TOLERATE, put up with, take,
stand, endure, bear; *informal* hack,
abide.

stoop v. **1** BEND (OVER/DOWN), lean
over/down, crouch (down).
2 LOWER ONESELF, sink, descend,
resort, demean oneself, debase
oneself; go as far as, sink as low
as.
▸ n. **1** HUNCH, round shoulders;
curvature of the spine; *Medicine*
kyphosis. **2** PORCH, steps,
platform, veranda, terrace.

stop v. **1** PUT AN END/STOP/HALT TO,
bring to an end/stop/halt/close/
standstill, end, halt; finish,
terminate, wind up, discontinue,
cut short, interrupt, nip in the
bud; deactivate, shut down.
2 CEASE, discontinue, desist from,
break off; give up, abandon,
abstain from, cut out; *informal* quit,
leave off, knock off, pack in, lay
off, give over. **3** PULL UP, draw up,
come to a stop/halt, come to rest,
pull in, pull over; park.
4 CONCLUDE, come to an end/stop/
standstill, cease, end, finish, draw
to a close, be over, terminate;

pause, break off; peter out, fade
away. **5** STEM, staunch, hold back,
check, curb, block, dam; *archaic*
stay. **6** PREVENT, hinder, obstruct,
impede, block, bar, preclude;
dissuade from. **7** ☞ FRUSTRATE 1.
8 BLOCK (UP), plug, close (up), fill
(up); seal, caulk, bung up; *technical*
occlude.
—OPPOSITES: start, begin,
continue, allow, encourage,
expedite, open.
▸ n. **1** HALT, end, finish, close,
standstill; cessation, conclusion,
stoppage, discontinuation.
2 BREAK, stopover, stopoff, stay,
visit; *formal* sojourn.
—OPPOSITES: start, beginning,
continuation.

store n. **1** STOCK, supply,
stockpile, hoard, cache, reserve,
bank, pool; *informal* war chest, pork
barrel. **2** STOREROOM, storehouse,
repository, depository, stockroom,
depot, warehouse, magazine;
informal lock-up. **3** SUPPLIES,
provisions, stocks, necessities;
food, rations, provender;
materials, equipment, hardware;
Military matériel, accoutrements;
Nautical chandlery. **4** SHOP, (retail)
outlet, boutique, department
store, chain store, emporium;
supermarket, hypermarket,
superstore, megastore, big box
store. See also CONVENIENCE STORE.
▸ v. KEEP, keep in reserve,
stockpile, lay in, put/set aside, put
away/by, put away for a rainy day,
save, collect, accumulate, hoard,
cache; *informal* squirrel away, salt
away, stash away.
—OPPOSITES: use, discard.
☐ **set (great) store by** VALUE,

attach great importance to, put a high value on, put a premium on; THINK HIGHLY OF, hold in (high) regard, have a high opinion of; *informal* rate.

storm *n.* **1** TEMPEST, squall; gale, hurricane, tornado, cyclone, typhoon; thunderstorm, thundershower, rainstorm, monsoon, hailstorm, snowstorm, ice storm, blizzard; dust storm, black blizzard, windstorm. **2** VOLLEY, salvo, fusillade, barrage, cannonade; shower, spray, hail, rain. **3** ☞ FUROR.

stormy *adj.* **1** BLUSTERY, squally, windy, gusty, blowy; rainy, thundery, snowy, blizzardy; wild, tempestuous, turbulent, violent, rough, foul. **2** ANGRY, heated, fiery, fierce, furious, passionate, lively. —OPPOSITES: calm, fine, peaceful.

story *n.* **1** TALE, narrative, anecdote, report, account, history; legend, fable, myth, parable, allegory, saga; *informal* yarn. **2** PLOT, storyline, scenario, libretto. **3** NEWS ITEM, news report, reportage, article, feature, piece, photo essay. **4** RUMOUR, piece of gossip, whisper; speculation. **5** TESTIMONY, statement, report, account, version. **6** ☞ LIE[1] *n.*

stout *adj.* **1** ☞ FAT *adj.* 1. **2** STRONG, sturdy, solid, substantial, robust, tough, durable, hard-wearing. **3** DETERMINED, vigorous, forceful, spirited; staunch, steadfast, stalwart, firm, resolute, unyielding, dogged; brave, bold, courageous, valiant, valorous, gallant, fearless, doughty, intrepid; *informal* gutsy, spunky. —OPPOSITES: thin, flimsy, feeble.

straight *adj.* **1** UNSWERVING, undeviating, linear, as straight as an arrow, unbending. **2** LEVEL, even, in line, aligned, square; vertical, upright, perpendicular; horizontal. **3** IN ORDER, (neat and) tidy, neat, shipshape, orderly, spic and span, organized, arranged, sorted out, straightened out. **4** HONEST, direct, frank, candid, truthful, sincere, forthright, straightforward, plain-spoken, blunt, unequivocal, unambiguous; *informal* upfront. **5** LOGICAL, rational, clear, lucid, sound, coherent. **6** SUCCESSIVE, in succession, consecutive, in a row, running. **7** UNDILUTED, neat, pure, straight up. **8** (*informal*) RESPECTABLE, conventional, conservative, traditional, old-fashioned, straitlaced; *informal* stuffy, square, fuddy-duddy. —OPPOSITES: winding, crooked, untidy, evasive.

▸ *adv.* **1** RIGHT, directly, squarely, full; *informal* smack, bang, spang, smack dab. **2** DIRECTLY, right, by a direct route. **3** RIGHT AWAY, straight away, immediately, directly, at once; *archaic* straightway. **4** FRANKLY, directly, candidly, honestly, forthrightly, plainly, point-blank, bluntly, flatly, without beating about the bush, without mincing words, unequivocally, unambiguously, in plain English, to someone's face, straight up. **5** LOGICALLY, rationally, clearly, lucidly, coherently, cogently.

☐ **go straight** REFORM, mend one's ways, turn over a new leaf, get back on the straight and

narrow. **straight away** AT ONCE,
right away, (right) now, this/that
(very) minute, this/that instant,
immediately, instantly, directly,
forthwith, without further/more
ado, promptly, quickly, without
delay, then and there, here and
now, as soon as possible, ASAP, as
quickly as possible, in short order;
informal straight off, PDQ, pretty
damn quick, pronto, lickety-split;
archaic straightway.

straighten v. **1** MAKE STRAIGHT,
adjust, arrange, rearrange, (make)
tidy, spruce up. **2** PUT/SET RIGHT,
sort out, clear up, settle, resolve,
put in order, regularize, rectify,
remedy; *informal* patch up. **3** STAND
UP (STRAIGHT), stand upright.

straightforward *adj.* **1** ☞ EASY
1. **2** ☞ HONEST 2.
—OPPOSITES: complicated.

strain v. **1** OVERTAX, overwork,
overextend, overreach, drive too
far, overdo it; exhaust, wear out;
informal knock oneself out. **2** INJURE,
damage, pull, wrench, twist,
sprain. **3** STRUGGLE, labour, toil,
make every effort, try very hard,
break one's back, push/drive
oneself to the limit; *informal* pull
out all the stops, go all out, bust a
gut. **4** MAKE EXCESSIVE DEMANDS ON,
overtax, be too much for, test, tax,
put a strain on. **5** PULL, tug, heave,
haul, jerk; *informal* yank.
▶ *n.* **1** TENSION, tightness, tautness.
2 INJURY, sprain, wrench, twist.
3 PRESSURE, demands, burdens;
stress; *informal* hassle. **4** STRESS,
(nervous) tension; exhaustion,
fatigue, pressure of work,
overwork. **5** SOUND, music;
melody, tune.

strained *adj.* **1** AWKWARD, tense,
uneasy, uncomfortable, edgy,
difficult, troubled. **2** DRAWN,
careworn, worn, pinched, tired,
exhausted, drained, haggard.
3 FORCED, constrained, unnatural;
artificial, insincere, false, affected,
put-on.
—OPPOSITES: friendly.

strand *n.* **1** THREAD, filament,
fibre; length, ply. **2** ELEMENT,
component, factor, ingredient,
aspect, feature, strain.

stranded *adj.* **1** BEACHED,
grounded, run aground, high and
dry; shipwrecked, wrecked,
marooned. **2** HELPLESS, without
resources, in difficulties; in the
lurch, abandoned, deserted.

strange *adj.* **1** UNUSUAL, odd,
curious, peculiar, funny, bizarre,
weird, uncanny, queer,
unexpected, unfamiliar, atypical,
anomalous, out of the ordinary,
extraordinary, puzzling,
mystifying, mysterious,
perplexing, baffling,
unaccountable, inexplicable,
singular, freakish, incongruous,
surprising; suspicious,
questionable; eerie, unnatural;
fishy, creepy, spooky, eccentric,
unconventional, unorthodox,
outlandish, quirky, idiosyncratic,
zany, wacky, way out, freaky,
kooky, offbeat, off the wall,
screwy, wacko, aberrant,
abnormal, deviant, perverse,
perverted, twisted, warped,
mutant, unhealthy, distorted,
different, exceptional, freak,
irregular, oddball, out of the way,
outré, rare, remarkable,
uncommon. **2** UNFAMILIAR,

unknown, new. **3** ILL, unwell, poorly, peaky; *informal* under the weather, funny, peculiar, lousy, off; *dated* queer. **4** ILL AT EASE, uneasy, uncomfortable, awkward, self-conscious.
—OPPOSITES: ordinary, familiar.

stranger *n.* NEWCOMER, new arrival, visitor, outsider, newbie.
□ **a stranger to** UNACCUSTOMED TO, unfamiliar with, unused to, new to, fresh to, inexperienced in; *archaic* strange to.

strangle *v.* **1** THROTTLE, choke, garrotte; *informal* strangulate. **2** SUPPRESS, smother, stifle, repress, restrain, fight back, choke back. **3** HAMPER, hinder, impede, restrict, inhibit, curb, check, constrain, squash, crush, suppress, repress.

strategic *adj.* PLANNED, calculated, tactical, politic, judicious, prudent, shrewd.

strategy *n.* MASTER PLAN, grand design, game plan, plan (of action), action plan, policy, program; tactics.

stray *v.* **1** WANDER OFF, go astray, get separated, get lost. **2** DIGRESS, deviate, wander, get sidetracked, go off on a tangent, veer off; get off the subject. **3** BE UNFAITHFUL, have affairs, cheat, philander; *informal* play around, play the field.
▸ *adj.* **1** HOMELESS, lost, strayed, gone astray, abandoned. **2** RANDOM, chance, freak, unexpected, isolated, lone, single.

streak *n.* **1** BAND, line, strip, stripe, vein, slash, ray. **2** MARK, smear, smudge, stain, blotch; *informal* splotch. **3** ELEMENT, vein, touch, strain; trait, characteristic.

4 PERIOD, spell, stretch, run, patch.
▸ *v.* **1** STRIPE, band, fleck. **2** MARK, daub, smear; *informal* splotch.

stream *n.* **1** CREEK, river, rivulet, rill, runnel, streamlet, freshet; tributary, watercourse; bourn; brook. **2** JET, flow, rush, gush, surge, torrent, flood, cascade, outpouring, outflow; *technical* efflux. **3** SUCCESSION, flow, series, string.
▸ *v.* **1** FLOW, pour, course, run, gush, surge, flood, cascade, spill. **2** POUR, surge, charge, flood, swarm, pile, crowd. **3** FLUTTER, float, flap, fly, blow, waft, wave.

strength *n.* **1** POWER, brawn, muscle, muscularity, burliness, sturdiness, robustness, toughness, hardiness; vigour, force, might, forcefulness, powerfulness; punch, beef; *literary* thew. **2** HEALTH, fitness, vigour, stamina.
3 ☞ FORTITUDE. **4** ROBUSTNESS, sturdiness, firmness, toughness, soundness, solidity, durability.
5 POWER, influence, dominance, ascendancy, supremacy; *informal* clout; *literary* puissance. **6** INTENSITY, vehemence, force, forcefulness, depth, ardour, fervour. **7** COGENCY, forcefulness, force, weight, power, potency, persuasiveness, soundness, validity. **8** STRONG POINT, advantage, asset, forte, aptitude, talent, skill; specialty. **9** SIZE, extent, magnitude.
—OPPOSITES: weakness.

strengthen *v.* **1** FORTIFY, make strong/stronger, build up, give strength to. **2** REINFORCE, make stronger, buttress, shore up, underpin. **3** TOUGHEN, temper, anneal. **4** BECOME STRONG/

STRONGER, gain strength, intensify, pick up. **5** FORTIFY, bolster, make stronger, boost, reinforce, harden, stiffen, toughen, fuel. **6** REDOUBLE, step up, increase, escalate; *informal* up, crank up, beef up.

7 REINFORCE, lend more weight to; support, substantiate, back up, confirm, bear out, corroborate.
—OPPOSITES: weaken.

strenuous *adj.* ☞ ARDUOUS. **2** VIGOROUS, energetic, zealous, forceful, strong, spirited, intense, determined, resolute, tenacious, tireless, indefatigable, dogged; *formal* pertinacious.
—OPPOSITES: easy, half-hearted.

stress *n.* **1** STRAIN, pressure, (nervous) tension, worry, anxiety, trouble, difficulty; *informal* hassle. **2** EMPHASIS, importance, weight. **3** EMPHASIS, accent, accentuation; beat; *Prosody* ictus. **4** PRESSURE, tension, strain.
▶ *v.* **1** ☞ EMPHASIZE. **2** PLACE THE EMPHASIS ON, emphasize, place the accent on. **3** OVERSTRETCH, overtax, push to the limit, pressure, make tense, worry, harass; *informal* hassle.
—OPPOSITES: play down.

stressful *adj.* DEMANDING, trying, taxing, difficult, hard, tough; fraught, traumatic, pressured, tense, frustrating.
—OPPOSITES: relaxing.

stretch *v.* **1** BE ELASTIC, be stretchy, be tensile. **2** PULL (OUT), draw out, extend, lengthen, elongate, expand. **3** PROLONG, lengthen, make longer, extend, spin out. **4** BE SUFFICIENT FOR, be enough for, cover; afford, have the money for. **5** PUT A STRAIN ON, overtax, overextend, drain, sap.

6 BEND, strain, distort, exaggerate, embellish. **7** REACH OUT, hold out, extend, outstretch, proffer; *literary* outreach. **8** EXTEND, straighten (out). **9** LIE DOWN, recline, lean back, be recumbent, sprawl, lounge, loll. **10** EXTEND, spread, continue.
—OPPOSITES: shorten.
▶ *n.* **1** EXPANSE, area, tract, belt, sweep, extent. **2** PERIOD, time, spell, run, stint, session, shift. **3** (*informal*) (PRISON) SENTENCE, rap.

strict *adj.* **1** PRECISE, exact, literal, faithful, accurate, rigorous, careful, meticulous, pedantic. **2** STRINGENT, rigorous, severe, harsh, hard, rigid, tough, ironclad, demanding, exacting, firm, hard and fast, inflexible, tight. **3** STERN, severe, harsh, uncompromising, authoritarian, firm, austere.
—OPPOSITES: loose, liberal.

strife *n.* CONFLICT, friction, discord, disagreement, dissension, dispute, argument, quarrelling, wrangling, bickering, controversy; ill/bad feeling, falling-out, bad blood, hostility, animosity.
—OPPOSITES: peace.

strike *v.* **1** ☞ HIT *v.* **1.** **2** CRASH INTO, collide with, hit, run into, bump into, smash into, impact. **3** ATTACK, set upon someone, fall on someone, assault someone. **4** AFFECT, afflict, attack, hit. **5** OCCUR TO, come to (mind), dawn on one, hit, spring to mind, enter one's head. **6** SEEM TO, appear to, come across to, give the impression to. **7** TAKE INDUSTRIAL ACTION, go on strike, down tools, walk out, picket, walk the picket line, hit the bricks.

▶ *n.* **1** INDUSTRIAL ACTION, walkout, job action, stoppage. **2** (AIR) ATTACK, assault, bombing, raid. **3** FIND, discovery.

striking *adj.* **1** NOTICEABLE, obvious, conspicuous, evident, marked, notable, unmistakable, strong; remarkable, extraordinary, incredible, amazing, astounding, astonishing, staggering. **2** IMPRESSIVE, imposing, grand, splendid, magnificent, spectacular, breathtaking, superb, marvellous, wonderful, stunning, staggering, sensational, awesome, awe-inspiring, dramatic. **3** ☞ ATTRACTIVE 2.
—OPPOSITES: unremarkable.

stringent *adj.* ☞ STRICT 2.

strip *v.* **1** UNDRESS, strip off, take one's clothes off, unclothe, disrobe, strip naked. **2** PEEL, remove, take off, scrape, rub, clean. **3** TAKE AWAY FROM, dispossess, deprive, confiscate, divest, relieve. **4** DISMANTLE, disassemble, take to bits/pieces, take apart. **5** EMPTY, clear, clean out, plunder, rob, burgle, burglarize, loot, pillage, ransack, despoil, sack.
—OPPOSITES: dress.

strive *v.* ☞ TRY 1.

stroke *n.* **1** BLOW, hit, thump, punch, slap, smack, cuff, knock; *informal* wallop, clout, whack, thwack, bash, swipe; *archaic* smite. **2** SHOT, hit, strike. **3** MOVEMENT, action, motion. **4** FEAT, accomplishment, achievement, master stroke. **5** MARK, line. **6** DETAIL, touch, point.

7 THROMBOSIS, seizure; *Medicine* ictus.
▶ *v.* CARESS, fondle, pat, pet, touch, rub, massage, soothe.

stroll *v. & n.* ☞ WALK.

strong *adj.* **1** POWERFUL, muscular, brawny, powerfully built, strapping, sturdy, burly, meaty, robust, athletic, tough, rugged, lusty, strong as an ox/horse; *informal* beefy, hunky, husky; *dated* stalwart. **2** FORCEFUL, determined, spirited, self-assertive, tough, tenacious, indomitable, formidable, redoubtable, strong-minded; *informal* gutsy, feisty. **3** SECURE, well-built, indestructible, well fortified, well protected, impregnable, solid. **4** DURABLE, hard-wearing, heavy-duty, industrial-strength, tough, sturdy, well-made, long-lasting. **5** FORCEFUL, powerful, vigorous, fierce, intense. **6** KEEN, eager, passionate, fervent. **7** INTENSE, forceful, passionate, ardent, fervent, fervid, deep-seated; *literary* perfervid. **8** KEEN, eager, enthusiastic, dedicated, staunch, loyal, steadfast. **9** COMPELLING, cogent, forceful, powerful, potent, weighty, convincing, sound, valid, well-founded, persuasive, influential. **10** FIRM, forceful, drastic, extreme. **11** MARKED, striking, noticeable, pronounced, distinct, definite, unmistakable, notable. **12** LOUD, powerful, forceful, resonant, sonorous, rich, deep, booming. **13** INTENSE, deep, rich, bright, brilliant, vivid, dazzling, glaring. **14** CONCENTRATED, undiluted, potent.
—OPPOSITES: weak, gentle, mild.

structure *n.* 1 ☞ BUILDING.
2 CONSTRUCTION, form, formation, shape, composition, anatomy, makeup, constitution; organization, system, arrangement, design, framework, configuration, pattern.
▸ *v.* ARRANGE, organize, design, shape, construct, build, put together.

struggle *v.* 1 ☞ TRY *v.* 1. 2 FIGHT, grapple, wrestle, scuffle, brawl, spar; *informal* scrap. 3 COMPETE, contend, vie, fight, battle, jockey. 4 SCRAMBLE, flounder, stumble, fight/battle one's way, labour.
▸ *n.* 1 ENDEAVOUR, striving, effort, exertion, labour; campaign, battle, crusade, drive, push.
2 FIGHT, scuffle, brawl, tussle, wrestling bout, skirmish, fracas, melee; breach of the peace; *informal* scrap, dust-up, punch-up, bust-up.
3 CONFLICT, fight, battle, confrontation, clash, skirmish; hostilities, fighting, war, warfare, campaign. 4 CONTEST, competition, fight, clash; rivalry, friction, feuding, conflict, tug-of-war, turf war. 5 EFFORT, trial, trouble, stress, strain, battle; *informal* grind, hassle.

stubborn *adj.* 1 OBSTINATE, headstrong, wilful, strong-willed, pigheaded, obdurate, difficult, contrary, perverse, recalcitrant, inflexible, uncompromising, unbending, bullheaded, dogged, self-willed; *informal* stiff-necked, bloody-minded, balky; *formal* pertinacious, refractory, contumacious. 2 INDELIBLE,

permanent, persistent, tenacious, resistant.
—OPPOSITES: compliant.

stuck *adj.* 1 FIXED, fastened, attached, glued, pinned.
2 IMMOVABLE, stuck fast, jammed.
3 BAFFLED, beaten, at a loss, at one's wits' end; *informal* stumped, bogged down, flummoxed, fazed, bamboozled.

student *n.* 1 SCHOLAR, undergraduate, graduate, grad student, post-doctoral fellow; freshman, frosh, sophomore.
2 PUPIL, schoolchild, schoolboy, schoolgirl, scholar. 3 TRAINEE, apprentice, probationer, recruit, intern, novice; *informal* rookie.

studious *adj.* 1 ☞ ACADEMIC *adj.* 2.
2 ☞ DILIGENT.

study *n.* 1 LEARNING, education, schooling, academic work, scholarship, tuition, research; *informal* cramming. 2 INVESTIGATION, inquiry, research, examination, analysis, review, survey. 3 ESSAY, article, work, review, paper, dissertation, disquisition.
▸ *v.* 1 WORK, review; *informal* cram, hit the books. 2 LEARN, read, be taught. 3 ☞ INVESTIGATE.
4 ☞ SCRUTINIZE.

stuff *n.* 1 ITEMS, articles, objects, goods, equipment; *informal* things, bits and pieces, odds and ends.
2 BELONGINGS, (personal) possessions, effects, goods (and chattels), paraphernalia; *informal* gear, things. 3 FACTS, information, data, subject.
▸ *v.* 1 FILL, pack, pad, upholster.
2 SHOVE, thrust, push, ram, cram, squeeze, force, jam, pack, pile, stick. 3 (*informal*) FILL, gorge,

overindulge; gobble, devour, wolf; *informal* pig out, make a pig of oneself. **4** BLOCK, bung, congest, obstruct.

stuffy *adj.* **1** AIRLESS, close, musty, stale. **2** STAID, sedate, sober, prim, priggish, straitlaced, conformist, conservative, old-fashioned; *informal* square, straight, starchy, fuddy-duddy. **3** BLOCKED, stuffed up, bunged up.
—OPPOSITES: airy, clear.

stump *v.* ☞ PERPLEX.

stun *v.* **1** ☞ DAZE. **2** ☞ ASTOUND.

stunning *adj.* **1** ☞ EXTRAORDINARY. **2** ☞ BEAUTIFUL.
—OPPOSITES: ordinary.

stupid *adj.* **1** UNINTELLIGENT, ignorant, dense, foolish, dull-witted, slow-witted, stunned✦, slow, mindless, simple-minded, vacuous, vapid, idiotic, imbecilic, imbecile, obtuse, doltish; thick, dim, dim-witted, dumb, dopey, dozy, moronic, cretinous, pea-brained, halfwitted, soft in the head, dumb-ass, slow on the uptake, uncomprehending, brain-dead, boneheaded, thick-headed, wooden-headed, muttonheaded, chowderheaded, empty-headed, fatheaded, daft, asinine, birdbrained, brainless, dippy, featherbrained, feeble-minded, pig-ignorant, witless. **2** FOOLISH, silly, unintelligent, idiotic, scatterbrained, nonsensical, senseless, unthinking, ill-advised, ill-considered, unwise, injudicious; inane, absurd, ludicrous, ridiculous, laughable, risible, fatuous, asinine, mad, insane, lunatic; *informal* crazy, dopey, cracked, half-baked, dim-witted, cockeyed, hare-brained, lamebrained, nutty, batty, cuckoo, loony, loopy, dumb-ass.
—OPPOSITES: intelligent, sensible.

stupidity *n.* **1** LACK OF INTELLIGENCE, foolishness, denseness, brainlessness, ignorance, slow-wittedness, doltishness, slowness; *informal* thickness, dimness, dopiness, doziness. **2** FOOLISHNESS, folly, silliness, idiocy, brainlessness, senselessness, injudiciousness, ineptitude, inaneness, inanity, absurdity, ludicrousness, ridiculousness, fatuousness, madness, insanity, lunacy, craziness.

sturdy *adj.* **1** STRAPPING, well-built, muscular, athletic, strong, hefty, brawny, powerful, solid, burly, rugged, robust, tough, hardy, lusty; *informal* husky, beefy, meaty; *dated* stalwart; *literary* thewy. **2** ROBUST, strong, strongly made, well built, solid, stout, tough, resilient, durable, long-lasting, hard-wearing. **3** VIGOROUS, strong, stalwart, firm, determined, resolute, staunch, steadfast.
—OPPOSITES: weak.

style *n.* **1** MANNER, way, technique, method, methodology, approach, system, mode, form, modus operandi; *informal* MO. **2** TYPE, kind, variety, sort, genre, school, brand, pattern, model. **3** FLAIR, stylishness, elegance, grace, gracefulness, poise, polish, suaveness, sophistication, urbanity, chic, dash, panache, élan; (good) taste, discernment, refinement, quality; *informal* class, pizzazz. **4** COMFORT, luxury,

elegance, opulence, lavishness.
5 FASHION, trend, vogue, mode.
stylish *adj.* FASHIONABLE, modish,
voguish, modern, up to date;
smart, sophisticated, elegant,
chic, dapper, dashing, trim,
debonair; *informal* trendy, natty,
classy, nifty, ritzy, snazzy, fly,
kicky, tony, spiffy, swish.
—OPPOSITES: unfashionable.
suave *adj.* ☞ DEBONAIR.
—OPPOSITES: unsophisticated.
subdue *v.* **1** ☞ DEFEAT. **2** ☞ CURB.
subject *n.* **1** THEME, subject
matter, topic, issue, question,
concern, point; argument, thesis;
substance, essence, gist, thrust,
material, content, text, ideas.
2 BRANCH OF STUDY, discipline,
field.
▶ *v.* PUT THROUGH, treat with,
expose to.
☐ **subject to 1** CONDITIONAL ON,
contingent on, dependent on.
2 SUSCEPTIBLE TO, liable to, prone
to, vulnerable to, predisposed to,
at risk of. **3** BOUND BY, constrained
by, accountable to.
subjective *adj.* PERSONAL,
individual, emotional, instinctive,
intuitive.
—OPPOSITES: objective.
sublime *adj.* **1** EXALTED, elevated,
noble, lofty, awe-inspiring,
majestic, magnificent, glorious,
superb, wonderful, marvellous,
splendid; *informal* fantastic,
fabulous, terrific, heavenly,
divine, out of this world.
2 SUPREME, total, complete, utter,
consummate.
submission *n.* **1** YIELDING,
capitulation, acceptance, consent,
compliance. **2** SURRENDER,

capitulation, resignation, defeat.
3 COMPLIANCE, submissiveness,
acquiescence, passivity,
obedience, docility, deference,
subservience, servility, subjection.
4 PRESENTATION, presenting,
proffering, tendering, proposal,
proposing. **5** PROPOSAL,
suggestion, proposition,
recommendation. **6** ARGUMENT,
assertion, contention, statement,
claim, allegation.
—OPPOSITES: defiance, resistance.
submissive *adj.* COMPLIANT,
yielding, acquiescent, unassertive,
passive, obedient, biddable,
dutiful, docile, pliant; *informal*
under someone's thumb.
submit *v.* **1** GIVE IN/WAY, yield, back
down, cave in, capitulate;
surrender, knuckle under. **2** BE
GOVERNED BY, abide by, be
regulated by, comply with, accept,
adhere to, be subject to, agree to,
consent to, conform to. **3** PUT
FORWARD, present, offer, proffer,
tender, propose, suggest, float;
put in, send in, register.
4 CONTEND, assert, argue, state,
claim, posit, postulate.
—OPPOSITES: resist, withdraw.
subordinate *adj.* **1** LOWER-
RANKING, junior, lower, supporting.
2 SECONDARY, lesser, minor,
subsidiary, subservient, ancillary,
auxiliary, peripheral, marginal;
supplementary, accessory.
—OPPOSITES: senior.
▶ *n.* JUNIOR, assistant, second (in
command), number two, right-
hand man/woman, deputy, aide,
underling, minion; *informal*
sidekick, second banana.
—OPPOSITES: superior.

subscription n. MEMBERSHIP FEE, dues, annual payment, charge, season ticket.

subsequent adj. FOLLOWING, ensuing, succeeding, later, future, coming, to come, next.
—OPPOSITES: previous.
□ **subsequent to** FOLLOWING, after, at the close/end of.

subside v. 1 ABATE, let up, quieten down, calm, slacken (off), ease (up), relent, die down, recede, lessen, soften, diminish, decline, dwindle, weaken, fade, wane, ebb. 2 RECEDE, ebb, fall, go down, get lower, abate. 3 SINK, settle, cave in, collapse, crumple, give way.
—OPPOSITES: intensify, rise.

subsidize v. GIVE MONEY TO, pay a subsidy to, contribute to, invest in, sponsor, support, fund, finance, underwrite; informal shell out for, fork out for, cough up for; bankroll.

subsidy n. GRANT, allowance, endowment, contribution, donation, handout; backing, support, sponsorship, finance, funding; formal benefaction.

subsist v. SURVIVE, live, stay alive, exist, eke out an existence; support oneself, manage, get along/by, make (both) ends meet.

substance n. 1 MATERIAL, matter, stuff. 2 SOLIDITY, body, corporeality; density, mass, weight, shape, structure. 3 MEANINGFULNESS, significance, importance, import, validity, foundation; formal moment. 4 CONTENT, subject matter, theme, message, essence.

substantial adj. 1 REAL, true, actual; physical, solid, material, concrete, corporeal. 2 CONSIDERABLE, real, significant, important, notable, major, valuable, useful. 3 SIZEABLE, considerable, significant, large, ample, appreciable, goodly. 4 STURDY, solid, stout, thick, strong, well built, durable, long-lasting, hard-wearing. 5 HEFTY, stout, sturdy, large, solid, bulky, burly, well built, portly.

substantially adv. 1 ☞ GREATLY. 2 ☞ MAINLY.
—OPPOSITES: slightly.

substitute n. REPLACEMENT, deputy, relief, proxy, reserve, surrogate, cover, stand-in, locum (tenens), understudy; informal sub, pinch-hitter.
▶ adj. ACTING, supply, replacement, deputy, relief, reserve, surrogate, stand-in, temporary, caretaker, interim, provisional.
—OPPOSITES: permanent.
▶ v. 1 EXCHANGE, replace, use instead of, use as an alternative to, use in place of, swap. 2 DEPUTIZE, act as deputy, act as a substitute, stand in, cover; replace, relieve, take over from; informal sub, fill someone's boots/ shoes.

subtle adj. 1 UNDERSTATED, muted, subdued; delicate, faint, pale, soft, indistinct. 2 FINE, fine-drawn, nice, hairsplitting.

subversive adj. DISRUPTIVE, troublemaking, inflammatory, insurrectionary; seditious, revolutionary, rebellious, rebel, renegade, dissident.
▶ n. TROUBLEMAKER, dissident, agitator, revolutionary, renegade, rebel.

succeed *v.* **1** TRIUMPH, achieve success, be successful, do well, flourish, thrive, prosper; *informal* make it, make the grade, make a name for oneself, make one's mark, go places. **2** BE SUCCESSFUL, turn out well, work (out), be effective; *informal* come off, pay off. **3** REPLACE, take the place of, take over from, follow, supersede; *informal* step into someone's shoes. **4** INHERIT, assume, acquire, attain; *formal* accede to. **5** FOLLOW, come after, follow after.
—OPPOSITES: fail, precede.

success *n.* **1** FAVOURABLE OUTCOME, triumph. **2** PROSPERITY, affluence, wealth, riches. **3** TRIUMPH, bestseller, blockbuster, sellout; *informal* (smash) hit, megahit, winner. **4** STAR, superstar, celebrity, big name, household name; *informal* celeb, megastar.
—OPPOSITES: failure.

successful *adj.* **1** VICTORIOUS, triumphant; fortunate, lucky; effective. **2** PROSPEROUS, affluent, wealthy, rich; doing well, famous, eminent, top. **3** FLOURISHING, thriving, booming, buoyant, doing well, profitable, money-making, lucrative.

succession *n.* **1** SEQUENCE, series, progression, chain, cycle, round, string, train, line, run, flow, stream. **2** ACCESSION, elevation, assumption.
□ **in succession** ONE AFTER THE OTHER, in a row, consecutively, successively, in sequence; running.

suck *v.* **1** SIP, sup, siphon, slurp, draw, drink. **2** DRAW, pull, breathe, gasp; inhale, inspire. **3** IMPLICATE IN, involve in, draw into; *informal* mix up in.

sudden *adj.* UNEXPECTED, unforeseen, unanticipated, unlooked-for; immediate, instantaneous, instant, precipitous, surprising, startling, precipitate, abrupt, rapid, swift, quick, hasty.

suddenly *adv.* IMMEDIATELY, instantaneously, instantly, straight away, all of a sudden, all at once, promptly, abruptly, swiftly; unexpectedly, without warning, without notice, out of the blue; *informal* straight off, in a flash, like a shot.
—OPPOSITES: gradually.

suffer *v.* **1** HURT, ache, be in pain, feel pain; be in distress, be upset, be miserable. **2** BE AFFLICTED BY, be affected by, be troubled with, have. **3** UNDERGO, experience, be subjected to, receive, endure, face. **4** BE IMPAIRED, be damaged, deteriorate, decline.

sufficient *adj.* ☞ ENOUGH.
—OPPOSITES: inadequate.

suffocate *v.* CHOKE (TO DEATH), asphyxiate, smother, stifle; throttle, strangle.

suggest *v.* **1** PROPOSE, put forward, recommend, advocate; advise, urge, encourage, counsel. **2** INDICATE, lead to the belief, argue, demonstrate, show; *formal* evince. **3** HINT, insinuate, imply, intimate, indicate, allude to; refer to, mean, intend; *informal* put ideas into one's head, get at. **4** CONVEY, express, communicate, impart, imply, intimate, smack of, evoke, conjure up; *formal* evince.

suggestion n. **1** PROPOSAL, proposition, motion, submission, recommendation; advice, counsel, hint, tip, clue, idea, trial balloon. **2** ☞ HINT n. 3.

suggestive adj. **1** ☞ INDECENT. **2** REDOLENT, evocative, reminiscent; characteristic, indicative, typical.

suit v. **1** BECOME, work for, look good on, look attractive on, flatter. **2** BE CONVENIENT FOR, be acceptable to, be suitable for, meet the requirements of; informal fit the bill. **3** MAKE APPROPRIATE TO/FOR, tailor, fashion, adjust, adapt, modify, fit, gear, design.

suitable adj. ☞ APPROPRIATE. —OPPOSITES: inappropriate.

sulk v. MOPE, brood, be sullen, have a long face, be in a bad mood, be in a huff, be grumpy, be moody; informal be down in the dumps.

sulky adj. SULLEN, surly, moping, pouting, moody, sour, piqued, petulant, brooding, broody, disgruntled, ill-humoured, in a bad mood, out of humour, fed up, put out; bad-tempered, grumpy, huffy, glum, gloomy, morose; informal grouchy, crabby, cranky. —OPPOSITES: cheerful.

sullen adj. SURLY, sulky, pouting, sour, morose, resentful, glum, moody, gloomy, grumpy, bad-tempered, ill-tempered; unresponsive, uncommunicative, farouche, uncivil, unfriendly. —OPPOSITES: cheerful.

sum n. **1** AMOUNT, quantity, volume. **2** AMOUNT OF MONEY, price, charge, fee, cost. **3** (SUM) TOTAL, grand total, tally, aggregate, summation. **4** ENTIRETY, totality, total, whole, aggregate, summation, beginning and end. —OPPOSITES: difference.

summarize v. SUM UP, abridge, condense, encapsulate, outline, give an outline of, put in a nutshell, recapitulate, give/make a summary of, give a synopsis of, précis, synopsize, give the gist of; informal recap.

summary n. SYNOPSIS, précis, resumé, abstract, digest, encapsulation, abbreviated version; outline, sketch, rundown, review, summing-up, overview, recapitulation, epitome; informal recap.

summit n. **1** (MOUNTAIN) TOP, peak, crest, crown, apex, tip, pinnacle, cap, hilltop. **2** ☞ PEAK 4. —OPPOSITES: base, nadir.

summon v. **1** SEND FOR, call for, request the presence of; ask, invite. **2** CONVENE, assemble, order, call, announce; formal convoke. **3** MUSTER, gather, collect, rally, screw up. **4** CALL TO MIND, call up/forth, conjure up, evoke, recall, revive, arouse, kindle, awaken, spark (off). **5** CONJURE UP, call up, invoke.

sumptuous adj. LAVISH, luxurious, opulent, magnificent, resplendent, gorgeous, splendid, grand, lavishly appointed, palatial, rich; informal plush, ritzy. —OPPOSITES: plain.

sundry adj. ☞ DIVERSE.

sunny adj. BRIGHT, sunshiny, sunlit, clear, fine, fair, cloudless, without a cloud in the sky, dry, sun-drenched.

superb *adj.* ☞ EXCELLENT.
—OPPOSITES: poor, inferior.

supercilious *adj.* ARROGANT, haughty, conceited, disdainful, overbearing, pompous, condescending, superior, patronizing, imperious, proud, snobbish, snobby, smug, scornful, sneering; *informal* hoity-toity, high and mighty, uppity, snooty, stuck-up, snotty, snot-nosed, jumped up, too big for one's britches/boots.

superficial *adj.* **1** SURFACE, exterior, external, outer, outside, slight. **2** SHALLOW, surface, skin deep, artificial; empty, hollow, meaningless. **3** CURSORY, perfunctory, casual, sketchy, desultory, token, slapdash, offhand, rushed, hasty, hurried. **4** APPARENT, seeming, outward, ostensible, cosmetic, slight. **5** TRIVIAL, lightweight, two-dimensional. **6** FACILE, shallow, flippant, empty-headed, trivial, frivolous, silly, inane.
—OPPOSITES: deep, thorough.

superfluous *adj.* **1** SURPLUS (TO REQUIREMENTS), redundant, unneeded, excess, extra, (to) spare, remaining, unused, left over, in excess, waste. **2** UNNECESSARY, unneeded, redundant, uncalled for, unwarranted.
—OPPOSITES: necessary.

superior *adj.* **1** HIGHER-RANKING, higher-level, senior, higher, higher-up. **2** BETTER, more expert, more skilful; worthier, fitter, preferred. **3** FINER, better, higher-grade, of higher quality, greater; accomplished, expert. **4** GOOD-QUALITY, high-quality, first-class, first-rate, top-quality; choice, select, exclusive, prime, prize, fine, excellent, best, choicest, finest, hand-picked, high-grade, premier, quality, special; *informal* A1, blue-chip, blue-ribbon, grade A, tip-top, top, top-notch. **5** HIGH-CLASS, upper-class, select, exclusive, upscale, upmarket, five-star; *informal* classy, posh. **6** ☞ SUPERCILIOUS.
—OPPOSITES: junior, inferior.

superlative *adj.* ☞ EXCELLENT.
—OPPOSITES: mediocre.

supernatural *adj.* **1** PARANORMAL, psychic, magic, magical, occult, mystic, mystical, superhuman, supernormal; *rare* extramundane. **2** GHOSTLY, phantom, spectral, otherworldly, unearthly, unnatural.

supervise *v.* **1** OVERSEE, superintend, be in charge of, preside over, direct, manage, run, look after, be responsible for, govern, organize, administer, handle, micromanage. **2** WATCH, oversee, keep an eye on, observe, monitor, mind; invigilate.

supervision *n.* **1** ADMINISTRATION, management, control, charge; superintendence, regulation, government, governance. **2** OBSERVATION, guidance, custody, charge, safekeeping, care, guardianship; control.

supervisor *n.* MANAGER, director, overseer, controller, superintendent, governor, chief, head; steward, foreman; *informal* boss.

supplant *v.* **1** REPLACE, supersede, displace, take over from, substitute for, override. **2** OUST, usurp, overthrow, remove, topple, unseat, depose, dethrone; succeed, come after; *informal* fill someone's shoes/boots.

supple *adj.* **1** LITHE, limber, lissome, willowy, flexible, loose-limbed, agile, acrobatic, nimble, double-jointed. **2** PLIANT, pliable, flexible, soft, bendable, workable, malleable, stretchy, elastic, springy, yielding, rubbery.
—OPPOSITES: stiff, rigid.

supplement *n.* **1** ADDITION, accessory, supplementation, supplementary, extra, add-on, adjunct, appendage; *Computing* peripheral. **2** SURCHARGE, addition, increase. **3** APPENDIX, addendum, adhesion✤, end matter, tailpiece, codicil, postscript, addition, coda. **4** PULLOUT, insert, extra section.
▶ *v.* ☞ AUGMENT.

supplementary *adj.*
1 ☞ ADDITIONAL. **2** APPENDED, attached, added, extra, accompanying.

supply *v.* **1** GIVE, contribute, provide, furnish, donate, bestow, grant, endow, impart; dispense, disburse, allocate, assign; *informal* fork out, shell out. **2** PROVIDE, furnish, endow, serve, confer; equip, arm; fit out. **3** SATISFY, meet, fulfill, cater for.
▶ *n.* **1** STOCK, store, reserve, reservoir, stockpile, hoard, cache; storehouse, repository; fund, mine, bank. **2** PROVISIONS, stores, stocks, rations, food, foodstuffs, eatables, produce, necessities; *informal* eats; *formal* comestibles.

support *v.* **1** HOLD UP, bear, carry, prop up, keep up, brace, shore up, underpin, buttress, reinforce,

undergird, sustain. **2** PROVIDE FOR, maintain, sustain, keep, take care of, look after. **3** COMFORT, encourage, sustain, buoy up, hearten, fortify, console, solace, reassure; *informal* buck up.
4 SUBSTANTIATE, back up, bear out, corroborate, confirm, attest to, verify, prove, validate, authenticate, endorse, ratify, undergird. **5** HELP, aid, assist; contribute to, back, subsidize, fund, finance, underwrite, sponsor; *informal* bankroll. **6** BACK, champion, help, assist, aid, abet, favour, encourage; vote for, stand behind, defend; sponsor, second, promote, endorse, sanction; *informal* throw one's weight behind.
7 ADVOCATE, promote, champion, back, espouse, be in favour of, recommend, defend, subscribe to.
—OPPOSITES: neglect, contradict, oppose.
▶ *n.* **1** PILLAR, post, prop, upright, crutch, plinth, brace, buttress; base, substructure, foundation, underpinning. **2** MAINTENANCE, keep, sustenance, subsistence; alimony. **3** ENCOURAGEMENT, friendship, strength, consolation, solace, succour, relief. **4** COMFORT, help, assistance, tower of strength, prop, mainstay.
5 CONTRIBUTIONS, backing, donations, money, subsidy, funding, funds, finance, capital, underwriting, sponsorship.
6 BACKING, help, assistance, aid, endorsement, approval, endorsation✤; votes, patronage.
7 ADVOCACY, backing, promotion, championship, espousal, defence, recommendation.

supporter *n.* **1** ADVOCATE, backer, adherent, promoter, champion, defender, upholder, crusader, proponent, campaigner, apologist; *informal* cheerleader, booster. **2** BACKER, helper, adherent, follower, ally, voter, disciple; member. **3** ☞ SPONSOR. **4** FAN, follower, enthusiast, devotee, admirer; *informal* buff, addict, groupie.

supportive *adj.* **1** ENCOURAGING, caring, sympathetic, reassuring, understanding, concerned, helpful, kind, kindly. **2** IN FAVOUR OF, favourable to, pro, on the side of, sympathetic to, well-disposed to, receptive to.

suppose *v.* **1** ASSUME, presume, expect, dare say, take it (as read); believe, think, fancy, suspect, sense, trust; imagine, (let's) say; hypothesize, theorize, speculate; guess, surmise, reckon, figure, conjecture, deduce, infer, gather; *formal* opine. **2** REQUIRE, presuppose, imply, assume; call for, need.

supposed *adj.* **1** APPARENT, ostensible, seeming, alleged, putative, reputed, rumoured, claimed, purported; professed, declared, assumed, presumed. **2** MEANT, intended, expected; required, obliged.

supposition *n.* ☞ CONJECTURE.

suppress *v.* **1** SUBDUE, repress, crush, quell, quash, squash, stamp out; defeat, conquer, overpower, put down, crack down on; end, stop, terminate, halt. **2** CONCEAL, restrain, stifle, smother, bottle up, hold back, control, check, curb, contain, bridle, inhibit, keep a rein on, put a lid on. **3** CENSOR, keep secret, conceal, hide, hush up, gag, withhold, cover up, stifle; ban, proscribe, outlaw; sweep under the carpet.
—OPPOSITES: incite, reveal.

supremacy *n.* ASCENDANCY, predominance, primacy, dominion, hegemony, authority, mastery, control, power, rule, sovereignty, command, domination, leadership, influence; dominance, superiority, advantage, the upper hand, the whip hand, the edge; distinction, greatness.

supreme *adj.* **1** HIGHEST RANKING, chief, head, top, foremost, principal, superior, premier, first, prime; greatest, dominant, predominant, pre-eminent. **2** ☞ EXTRAORDINARY. **3** ULTIMATE, final, last; utmost, extreme, greatest, highest.
—OPPOSITES: subordinate, insignificant.

sure *adj.* **1** CERTAIN, positive, convinced, confident, definite, assured, satisfied, persuaded, in no doubt; unhesitating, unwavering, unshakeable. **2** BOUND, likely, destined, fated. **3** GUARANTEED, unfailing, infallible, unerring, assured, certain, inevitable; *informal* surefire.
—OPPOSITES: uncertain, unlikely.

surge *n.* **1** GUSH, rush, outpouring, stream, flow. **2** INCREASE, rise, growth, upswing, upsurge, groundswell, escalation, leap. **3** RUSH, uprush, storm, torrent, blaze, outburst, eruption.
▶ *v.* **1** GUSH, rush, stream, flow, burst, pour, cascade, spill,

overflow, sweep, roll.
2 ☞ INCREASE n.

surly adj. ☞ GRUMPY.
—OPPOSITES: pleasant.

surmise v. ☞ SUPPOSE 1.

surmount v. **1** OVERCOME, conquer, prevail over, triumph over, beat, vanquish; clear, cross, pass over; resist, endure. **2** CLIMB OVER, top, ascend, scale, mount. **3** CAP, top, crown, finish.
—OPPOSITES: descend.

surpass v. EXCEL, exceed, transcend; outdo, outshine, outstrip, outclass, overshadow, eclipse; improve on, top, trump, cap, beat, better, outperform; be a cut above, be head and shoulders above, get ahead of, get the better of, leave behind, outmanoeuvre, put in the shade, run rings round, upstage; leapfrog.

surplus n. EXCESS, surfeit, superabundance, superfluity, oversupply, glut, profusion, plethora; remainder, residue, remains, leftovers.
—OPPOSITES: dearth.
▸ adj. EXCESS, leftover, unused, remaining, extra, additional, spare; superfluous, redundant, unwanted, unneeded, dispensable, expendable.
—OPPOSITES: insufficient.

surprise n. **1** ASTONISHMENT, amazement, wonder, incredulity, bewilderment, stupefaction, disbelief. **2** SHOCK, bolt from the blue, bombshell, revelation, rude awakening, eye-opener, wake-up call, shocker.
▸ v. **1** ASTONISH, amaze, startle, astound, stun, stagger, shock; leave open-mouthed, take

someone's breath away, dumbfound, stupefy, daze, take aback, shake up; informal bowl over, floor, flabbergast. **2** TAKE BY SURPRISE, catch unawares, catch off guard, catch red-handed, catch in the act, catch out.

surprised adj. ASTONISHED, amazed, astounded, startled, stunned, staggered, nonplussed, shocked, taken aback, stupefied, dumbfounded, dumbstruck, speechless, thunderstruck, confounded, shaken up; informal bowled over, flabbergasted, floored, flummoxed.

surprising adj. UNEXPECTED, unforeseen, unpredictable; astonishing, amazing, startling, astounding, staggering, incredible, extraordinary, breathtaking, remarkable; informal mind-blowing.

surrender v. **1** CAPITULATE, give in, give (oneself) up, give way, yield, concede (defeat), submit, climb down, back down, cave in, relent, reconsider, crumble; lay down one's arms, raise the white flag, throw in the towel/sponge. **2** GIVE UP, relinquish, renounce, forgo, forswear; cede, abdicate, waive, forfeit, sacrifice; hand over, turn over, yield, resign, transfer, grant.
—OPPOSITES: resist, seize.
▸ n. CAPITULATION, submission, yielding, succumbing, acquiescence; fall, defeat, resignation.

surreptitious adj. SECRET, secretive, stealthy, clandestine, sneaky, sly, furtive; concealed, hidden, undercover, covert,

veiled, cloak-and-dagger, hole-and-corner, backstairs, backroom.
—OPPOSITES: blatant.

surround v. ENCIRCLE, enclose, encompass, ring, girdle; fence in, hem in, confine, bound, circumscribe, cut off, seal off; besiege, trap.

surroundings pl. n. ENVIRONMENT, setting, milieu, background, backdrop; conditions, circumstances, situation, context; vicinity, locality, habitat, environs.

surveillance n. OBSERVATION, scrutiny, watch, view, inspection, supervision; spying, espionage, infiltration, reconnaissance; *informal* bugging, wiretapping, recon, stakeout.

survey v. **1** LOOK AT, look over, observe, view, contemplate, regard, gaze at, stare at, eye; scrutinize, examine, inspect, scan, study, consider, review, take stock of; *informal* size up; *literary* behold. **2** INTERVIEW, question, canvass, poll, cross-examine, investigate, research, study, probe, sample. ▶ n. **1** STUDY, review, consideration, overview; scrutiny, examination, inspection, appraisal. **2** POLL, review, investigation, inquiry, study, probe, questionnaire, census, research.

survive v. **1** REMAIN ALIVE, live, sustain oneself, pull through, get through, hold on/out, make it, keep body and soul together. **2** CONTINUE, remain, persist, endure, live on, persevere, abide, go on, carry on, be extant, exist. **3** OUTLIVE, outlast; live longer than.

susceptible adj. **1** IMPRESSIONABLE, credulous, gullible, innocent, ingenuous, naive, easily led; defenceless, vulnerable; persuadable, tractable; sensitive, responsive, thin-skinned. **2** OPEN TO, receptive to, vulnerable to; an easy target for. **3** LIABLE TO, prone to, subject to, inclined to, predisposed to, disposed to, given to, at risk of. —OPPOSITES: skeptical, immune, resistant.

suspect v. **1** HAVE A SUSPICION, have a feeling, feel, (be inclined to) think, fancy, reckon, guess, surmise, conjecture, conclude, have a hunch; suppose, presume, deduce, infer, sense, imagine; fear. **2** DOUBT, distrust, mistrust, have misgivings about, be skeptical about, have qualms about, be suspicious of, be wary of, harbour reservations about. ▶ adj. SUSPICIOUS, dubious, doubtful, untrustworthy; odd, queer; *informal* fishy, funny, shady, sketchy.

suspend v. **1** ADJOURN, interrupt, break off, postpone, delay, defer, shelve, put off, intermit, prorogue, hold over, hold in abeyance; cut short, discontinue, dissolve, disband, terminate, table; *informal* put on ice, put on the back burner, mothball, take a rain check on. **2** EXCLUDE, debar, remove, eliminate, expel, eject. **3** HANG, sling, string; swing, dangle.

suspense n. TENSION, uncertainty, doubt, anticipation, expectation, expectancy, excitement, anxiety,

apprehension, strain.
☐**in suspense** EAGERLY, agog, with bated breath, on tenterhooks; on edge, anxious, edgy, jumpy, keyed up, uneasy, antsy, uptight, jittery.

suspicion n. 1 ☞ HUNCH.
2 ☞ MISGIVING.

suspicious adj. 1 ☞ WARY 2.
2 DISREPUTABLE, unsavoury, dubious, suspect, funny-looking, slippery; informal shifty, shady.
3 ☞ QUESTIONABLE 1.
—OPPOSITES: trusting, honest, innocent.

sustain v. 1 ☞ SUPPORT 1.
2 COMFORT, help, assist, encourage, succour, support, give strength to, buoy up, carry, cheer up, hearten; informal buck up.
3 ☞ MAINTAIN 1. 4 NOURISH, feed, nurture; maintain, preserve, keep alive, keep going, provide for.
5 UNDERGO, experience, suffer, endure. 6 UPHOLD, validate, ratify, vindicate, confirm, endorse; verify, corroborate, substantiate, bear out, prove, authenticate, back up, evidence, justify.

sustained adj. ☞ CONTINUOUS.
—OPPOSITES: sporadic.

swap v. EXCHANGE, trade, barter, interchange, bargain; switch, change, replace.
▶ n. EXCHANGE, interchange, trade, switch, trade-off, substitution; informal switcheroo.

sway v. 1 SWING, shake, oscillate, undulate, move to and fro, move back and forth. 2 STAGGER, wobble, rock, lurch, reel, roll, list, stumble, pitch. 3 ☞ PERSUADE.
4 RULE, govern, dominate, control, guide.

▶ n. 1 SWING, roll, shake, oscillation, undulation. 2 CLOUT, influence, power, weight, authority, control.

swear v. 1 PROMISE, vow, pledge, give one's word, take an oath, undertake, guarantee; Law depose; formal aver. 2 INSIST, avow, pronounce, declare, proclaim, assert, profess, maintain, contend, emphasize, stress; formal aver.
3 CURSE, blaspheme, utter profanities, utter oaths, use bad language, take the Lord's name in vain; informal cuss; archaic execrate.

swearing n. BAD LANGUAGE, strong language, cursing, blaspheming, blasphemy; profanities, obscenities, curses, oaths, expletives, swear words; informal cussing, four-letter words; formal imprecation.

sweat n. PERSPIRATION, moisture, dampness, wetness; Medicine diaphoresis.
▶ v. 1 PERSPIRE, swelter, glow; be damp, be wet; secrete. 2 WORK (HARD), work like a Trojan, labour, toil, slog, slave, work one's fingers to the bone; informal plug away; archaic drudge. 3 WORRY, agonize, fuss, panic, fret, lose sleep; informal be on pins and needles, be in a state, be in a flap, be in a stew, torture oneself, torment oneself.

sweaty adj. PERSPIRING, sweating, clammy, sticky, glowing; Medicine diaphoretic; moist, damp.

sweep v. 1 BRUSH, clean, wipe, mop, dust. 2 REMOVE, brush, clean, clear, whisk. 3 CARRY, pull, drag, tow. 4 ENGULF, overwhelm, flood.
5 GLIDE, sail, breeze, drift, flit, flounce; stride, stroll, swagger.

6 GLIDE, sail, rush, race, streak, speed, fly, zoom, whiz, hurtle; *informal* tear, whip. **7** SEARCH, probe, check, explore, go through, scour, comb.

▸ *n.* **1** GESTURE, stroke, wave, movement. **2** SEARCH, hunt, exploration, probe. **3** EXPANSE, tract, stretch, extent, plain. **4** RANGE, span, scope, compass, reach, spread, ambit, gamut, spectrum, extent.

sweeping *adj.*
1 ☞ COMPREHENSIVE.
2 OVERWHELMING, decisive, thorough, complete, total, absolute, out-and-out, unqualified, landslide. **3** WHOLESALE, blanket, generalized, all-inclusive, unqualified, indiscriminate, universal, oversimplified, imprecise. **4** BROAD, extensive, expansive, vast, spacious, boundless, panoramic.
—OPPOSITES: limited, narrow, focused, small.

sweet *adj.* **1** SUGARY, sweetened, saccharine; sugared, honeyed, candied, glacé; sickly, cloying. **2** FRAGRANT, aromatic, perfumed; *literary* ambrosial. **3** ☞ DULCET. **4** ☞ PLEASANT 1. **5** ☞ LIKEABLE. **6** CUTE, lovable, adorable, endearing, charming, attractive, dear.
—OPPOSITES: sour, savoury, harsh, disagreeable.

▸ *n.* DESSERT, treat, dainty, cake, cookie, pastry.

sweetheart *n.* **1** ☞ DARLING.
2 ☞ LOVER 1.

swell *v.* **1** EXPAND, bulge, distend, inflate, dilate, bloat, puff up, balloon, fatten, fill out, tumefy.

2 GROW, enlarge, increase, expand, rise, escalate, multiply, proliferate, snowball, mushroom. **3** BE FILLED, be bursting, brim, overflow. **4** INCREASE, enlarge, augment, boost, top up, step up, multiply. **5** GROW LOUD, grow louder, amplify, crescendo, intensify, heighten.
—OPPOSITES: shrink, decrease, quieten.

swelling *n.* BUMP, lump, bulge, protuberance, enlargement, distension, prominence, protrusion, node, nodule, tumescence; boil, blister, bunion, carbuncle.

swerve *v.* VEER, deviate, skew, diverge, sheer, weave, zigzag, change direction; *Sailing* tack.
▸ *n.* CURVE, curl, deviation, twist.

swift *adj.* **1** PROMPT, rapid, sudden, immediate, instant, instantaneous; abrupt, hasty, hurried, precipitate, headlong. **2** FAST, rapid, quick, speedy, high-speed, fast-paced, brisk, lively; express, breakneck; fleet-footed; *informal* nippy, supersonic.
—OPPOSITES: slow, leisurely.

swindle *v.* DEFRAUD, cheat, trick, dupe, deceive, double-cross, fool, hoax, hoodwink, bilk, bamboozle, embezzle; *informal* fleece, con, sting, hose, diddle, rip off, take for a ride, pull a fast one on, put one over on, take to the cleaners, gull, stiff, euchre, hornswoggle; shaft, rook, gyp, sucker, snooker; *literary* cozen.

▸ *n.* FRAUD, trick, deception, deceit, cheat, sham, artifice, ruse, dodge, racket, wile; sharp practice; *informal* con, fiddle, diddle, rip-off, flim-flam, bunco.

swindler *n.* FRAUDSTER, fraud, (confidence) trickster, cheat, rogue, mountebank, charlatan, imposter, hoaxer; *informal* con man, con artist, scam artist, shyster, goniff, shark, sharp, hustler, phony, crook, snake oil salesman.

swing *v.* **1** SWAY, oscillate, move back and forth, move to and fro, wave, wag, rock, flutter, flap. **2** BRANDISH, wave, flourish, wield, shake, wag, twirl. **3** CURVE, bend, veer, turn, bear, wind, twist, deviate, slew, skew, drift, head. **4** CHANGE, fluctuate, shift, alter, oscillate, waver, alternate, see-saw, yo-yo, vary. **5** (*informal*) ACCOMPLISH, achieve, obtain, acquire, get, secure, net, win, attain, bag, hook; *informal* wangle, land.
▶ *n.* **1** OSCILLATION, sway, wave. **2** CHANGE, move; turnaround, turnabout, reversal, about face, volte face, change of heart, U-turn, sea change. **3** TREND, tendency, drift, movement. **4** FLUCTUATION, change, shift, variation, oscillation.

swirl *v.* WHIRL, eddy, billow, spiral, circulate, revolve, spin, twist; flow, stream, surge, seethe.

switch *n.* **1** BUTTON, lever, control, dial, rocker. **2** CHANGE, move, shift, transition, transformation; reversal, turnaround, U-turn, changeover, transfer, conversion; substitution, exchange. **3** BRANCH, twig, stick, rod.
▶ *v.* **1** CHANGE, shift; reverse; *informal* chop and change. **2** EXCHANGE, change, swap, interchange,

alternate, trade, substitute, replace, rotate.

swollen *adj.* DISTENDED, expanded, enlarged, bulging, inflated, dilated, bloated, puffed up, puffy, tumescent, tumid; inflamed, varicose.

swoop *v.* **1** DIVE, descend, sweep, pounce, plunge, pitch, nosedive; rush, dart, speed, zoom. **2** RAID, pounce on, attack, assault, assail, charge, bust.

sycophant *n.* bootlicker, brown-noser, browner♣, toady, lickspittle, flatterer, flunky, lackey, yes-man, stooge, cringer, suck♣, suck-up.

sycophantic *adj.* OBSEQUIOUS, servile, subservient, deferential, grovelling, toadying, fawning, flattering, ingratiating, cringing, unctuous, slavish; *informal* smarmy, bootlicking, brown-nosing.

symbol *n.* **1** EMBLEM, token, sign, representation, figure, image; metaphor, allegory; icon. **2** SIGN, character, mark, letter, ideogram. **3** LOGO, emblem, badge, stamp, trademark, crest, insignia, coat of arms, seal, device, monogram, hallmark, flag, motif, icon.

symbolic *adj.* **1** EMBLEMATIC, representative, typical, characteristic, symptomatic. **2** FIGURATIVE, representative, illustrative, emblematic, metaphorical, allegorical, parabolic, allusive, suggestive; meaningful, significant.
—OPPOSITES: literal.

symbolize *v.* REPRESENT, stand for, be a sign of, exemplify; denote, signify, mean, indicate, convey, express, imply, suggest, allude to; embody, epitomize, encapsulate, personify, typify; *literary* betoken.

symmetrical *adj.* REGULAR, uniform, consistent; evenly shaped, aligned, equal; mirror-image; balanced, proportional, even.

sympathetic *adj.*
1 COMPASSIONATE, caring, concerned, solicitous, empathetic, understanding, sensitive; commiserative, pitying, consoling, comforting, supportive, encouraging; considerate, kind, tender-hearted. **2** LIKEABLE, pleasant, agreeable, congenial, friendly, genial, simpatico. **3** IN FAVOUR OF, in sympathy with, pro, on the side of, supportive of, encouraging of; well-disposed to, favourably disposed to, receptive to.
—OPPOSITES: unfeeling, opposed.

sympathize *v.* **1** PITY, feel sorry for, show compassion for, commiserate, offer condolences to, feel for, show concern, show interest; console, comfort, solace, soothe, support, encourage; empathize with, identify with, understand, relate to. **2** AGREE WITH, support, be in favour of, go along with, favour, approve of, back, side with.

sympathy *n.* **1** COMPASSION, caring, concern, solicitude, empathy; commiseration, pity, condolence, comfort, solace, support, encouragement; consideration, kindness.
2 RAPPORT, fellow feeling, affinity, empathy, harmony, accord,

compatibility; fellowship, camaraderie. **3** AGREEMENT, favour, approval, approbation, support, encouragement, partiality; association, alignment, affiliation.
—OPPOSITES: indifference, hostility.

symptom *n.* **1** MANIFESTATION, indication, indicator, sign, mark, feature, trait; *Medicine* prodrome.
2 EXPRESSION, sign, indication, mark, token, manifestation; portent, warning, clue, hint; testimony, evidence, proof; result, consequence, product.

symptomatic *adj.* INDICATIVE, characteristic, suggestive, typical, representative, symbolic.

synthetic *adj.* ☞ ARTIFICIAL 1.
—OPPOSITES: natural.

system *n.* **1** STRUCTURE, organization, arrangement, complex, network; *informal* set-up.
2 METHOD, methodology, technique, process, procedure, approach, practice; means, way, mode, framework, modus operandi; scheme, plan, policy, program, regimen, formula, routine. **3** ORDER, method, orderliness, systematization, planning, logic, routine. **4** THE ESTABLISHMENT, the administration, the authorities, the powers that be; bureaucracy, officialdom; the status quo.

systematic *adj.* STRUCTURED, methodical, organized, orderly, planned, systematized, regular, routine, standardized, standard; logical, coherent, consistent; efficient, businesslike, practical.
—OPPOSITES: disorganized.

Tt

taboo *adj.* FORBIDDEN, prohibited, banned, proscribed, interdicted, outlawed, illegal, illicit, unlawful, restricted, off limits; unmentionable, unspeakable, unutterable, unsayable, ineffable; rude, impolite.
—OPPOSITES: acceptable.

tacit *adj.* ☞ IMPLICIT.
—OPPOSITES: explicit.

taciturn *adj.* UNTALKATIVE, uncommunicative, reticent, reserved, unforthcoming, quiet, secretive, tight-lipped, close-mouthed; silent, mute, dumb, inarticulate; withdrawn.
—OPPOSITES: talkative.

tackle *v.* **1** COME TO GRIPS WITH, address, face, get to work on, set one's hand to, approach, take on, attend to, see to, try to sort out, grapple with; deal with, take care of, handle, manage, confront; *informal* have a crack at, have a go at. **2** CONFRONT, face up to, take on, contend with, challenge, attack; seize, grab, grapple with, intercept, block, stop; bring down, floor, fell; *informal* have a go at.

tacky *adj.* TAWDRY, tasteless, kitsch, kitschy, (*Que.*) kétaine , vulgar, crude, garish, gaudy, showy, trashy, cheesy, cheap, common, second-rate.
—OPPOSITES: tasteful.

tact *n.* DIPLOMACY, tactfulness, sensitivity, understanding, thoughtfulness, consideration, care, politeness, delicacy, discretion, prudence, judiciousness, subtlety, savoir faire.

tactful *adj.* DIPLOMATIC, discreet, considerate, sensitive, understanding, thoughtful, delicate, judicious, politic, perceptive, subtle; courteous, polite, decorous, respectful.

tactic *n.* **1** STRATEGY, scheme, stratagem, plan, manoeuvre; method, expedient, gambit, move, approach, tack; device, trick, ploy, dodge, ruse, machination, contrivance. **2** STRATEGY, policy, campaign, battle plans, game plans, manoeuvres, logistics; generalship, organization, planning, direction, orchestration.

tactless *adj.* INSENSITIVE, inconsiderate, thoughtless, indelicate, undiplomatic, ill-judged, impolitic, indiscreet, unsubtle, clumsy, heavy-handed, graceless, awkward, inept, gauche; blunt, frank, outspoken, abrupt, gruff, rough, crude, coarse; imprudent, injudicious, unwise; rude, impolite, uncouth, discourteous, crass, tasteless, disrespectful, boorish.

tag *n.* **1** LABEL, ticket, badge, mark, marker, tab, sticker, stub, counterfoil, flag. **2** ☞ NAME 1.
▶ *v.* **1** LABEL, mark, ticket, identify, flag, indicate. **2** ☞ LABEL *v.*
3 FOLLOW, trail; come after, go after, shadow, dog; accompany, attend, escort; *informal* tail.

take *v.* **1** LAY HOLD OF, get hold of; grasp, grip, clasp, clutch, grab. **2** REMOVE, pull, draw, withdraw, extract, fish. **3** EXTRACT, quote, cite, excerpt, derive, abstract, copy, cull. **4** DRINK, imbibe; consume, swallow, eat, ingest. **5** CAPTURE, seize, catch, arrest, apprehend, take into custody; carry off, abduct. **6** ☞ STEAL 1. **7** SUBTRACT, deduct, remove; discount; *informal* knock off, minus. **8** OCCUPY, use, utilize, fill, hold; reserve, engage; *informal* bag. **9** ACCEPT, undertake. **10** PICK, choose, select; prefer, favour, opt for, vote for. **11** CONSIDER, contemplate, ponder, think about, mull over, examine, study, meditate over, ruminate about. **12** WRITE, note (down), jot (down), scribble, scrawl, record, register, document, minute. **13** BRING, carry, bear, transport, convey, move, transfer, shift, ferry; *informal* cart, tote. **14** ESCORT, accompany, help, assist, show, lead, guide, see, usher, convey. **15** RECEIVE, obtain, gain, get, acquire, collect, accept, be awarded; secure, come by, win, earn, pick up, carry off; *informal* land, bag, net, scoop. **16** ACT ON, take advantage of, capitalize on, use, exploit, make the most of, leap at, jump at, pounce on, seize, grasp, grab, accept. **17** DERIVE,
draw, acquire, obtain, get, gain, extract, procure; experience, undergo, feel. **18** RECEIVE, respond to, react to, meet, greet; deal with, cope with. **19** REGARD AS, consider to be, view as, see as, believe to be, reckon to be, imagine to be, deem to be. **20** ENDURE, bear, tolerate, stand, put up with, abide, stomach, accept, allow, countenance, support, shoulder; *formal* brook; *archaic* suffer. **21** CARRY OUT, do, complete, write ♣, conduct, perform, execute, discharge, accomplish, fulfill. **22** STUDY, learn, have lessons in; take up, pursue; *informal* do. **23** LAST, continue for, go on for, carry on for; require, call for, need, necessitate, entail, involve. **24** BE EFFECTIVE, take effect, hold, root, be productive, be effectual, be useful; work, operate, succeed, function; *formal* be efficacious.
—OPPOSITES: give, free, add, refuse, miss.
▶ *n.* **1** CATCH, haul, bag, yield, net. **2** REVENUE, income, gain, profit; takings, proceeds, returns, receipts, winnings, pickings, earnings, spoils; purse. **3** VIEW OF, reading of, version of, interpretation of, understanding of, account of, analysis of, approach to.
☐ **take after** RESEMBLE, look like; remind one of, make one think of, recall, conjure up, suggest, evoke; *informal* favour, be a chip off the old block. **take something apart**
1 DISMANTLE, pull to pieces, pull apart, disassemble, break up; tear down, demolish, destroy, wreck. **2** (*informal*) ☞ CRITICIZE. **take**

someone back 1 EVOKE, remind one of, conjure up, summon up; echo, suggest. **2** BE RECONCILED TO, forgive, pardon, excuse, exonerate, absolve; let bygones be bygones, bury the hatchet. **take something back 1** RETRACT, withdraw, renounce, disclaim, unsay, disavow, recant, repudiate; *formal* abjure. **2** RETURN, bring back, give back, restore. **take something down** WRITE DOWN, note down, jot down, set down, record, commit to paper, register, draft, document, minute, pen. **take someone in 1** ACCOMMODATE, board, house, feed, put up, admit, receive; harbour. **2** ☞ DECEIVE 1. **take something in 1** COMPREHEND, understand, grasp, follow, absorb; *informal* get. **2** INCLUDE, encompass, embrace, contain, comprise, cover, incorporate, comprehend, hold. **take off 1** ☞ FLEE. **2** BECOME AIRBORNE, take to the air, take wing; lift off, blast off. **take someone on 1** COMPETE AGAINST, oppose, challenge, confront, face, fight, vie with, contend with, stand up to. **2** ☞ HIRE. **take something on** ☞ UNDERTAKE. **take one's time** ☞ DAWDLE. **take someone out 1** GO OUT WITH, escort, partner, accompany, go with; romance, woo; *informal* date, see, go steady with; *dated* court. **2** (*informal*) ☞ KILL 1. **take something over** ASSUME CONTROL OF, take charge of, take command of. **take to 1** MAKE A HABIT OF, resort to, turn to, have recourse to; start, commence. **2** LIKE, get on with, be friendly towards; *informal*

take a shine to. **3** BECOME GOOD AT, develop an ability for; like, enjoy. **take something up 1** ENGAGE IN, practise; begin, start, commence. **2** CONSUME, fill, absorb, use, occupy; waste, squander. **3** RESUME, recommence, restart, carry on, continue, pick up, return to.

tale *n.* **1** ☞ STORY 1. **2** ☞ LIE¹.

talent *n.* FLAIR, aptitude, facility, gift, knack, technique, touch, bent, ability, expertise, capacity, faculty; strength, forte, genius, brilliance; dexterity, skill, artistry.

talented *adj.* ☞ GIFTED.
—OPPOSITES: inept.

talk *v.* **1** SPEAK, chat, chatter, gossip, prattle, babble, rattle on, blather; *informal* yak, gab, jaw, chew the fat, natter, rap. **2** UTTER, speak, say, voice, express, articulate, pronounce, verbalize, vocalize. **3** CONVERSE, communicate, speak, confer, consult; negotiate, parley; *informal* have a confab, chew the fat, rap; *formal* confabulate. **4** MENTION, refer to, speak about, discuss. **5** CONFESS, speak out/up, reveal all, tell tales, give the game away, open one's mouth; *informal* come clean, blab, squeal, let the cat out of the bag, spill the beans, sing, rat. **6** GOSSIP, pass comment, make remarks; criticize.
▶ *n.* **1** CHATTER, gossip, prattle, jabbering, babbling, gabbling; *informal* yakking, gabbing, nattering. **2** ☞ DISCUSSION. **3** ☞ LECTURE. **4** ☞ GOSSIP *n.* 1. **5** (*informal*) BOASTING, bragging, idle talk, bombast, braggadocio; *informal* hot air, mouth. **6** SPEECH, language, slang, idiom, idiolect;

words; *informal* lingo, -ese.

□ **talk back** ANSWER BACK, be impertinent, be cheeky, be rude, be lippy; contradict, argue with, disagree with. **talk down to** CONDESCEND TO, patronize, look down one's nose at, put down. **talk someone into something** ☞ PERSUADE.

talkative *adj.* CHATTY, loquacious, garrulous, voluble, conversational, communicative; gossipy, babbling, blathering; long-winded, wordy, verbose, prolix; gabby, mouthy, motor-mouthed, talky, expansive, gassy, gossiping, having the gift of the gab, unreserved, windy, able to talk the hind leg off a donkey.
—OPPOSITES: taciturn.

tall *adj.* **1** BIG, large, huge, towering, colossal, gigantic, giant, monstrous; leggy; *informal* long. **2** HIGH, big, lofty, towering, elevated, sky-high; multi-storey.
—OPPOSITES: short, low, wide.

tame *adj.* **1** DOMESTICATED, domestic, docile, tamed, broken, trained; gentle, mild; pet, housebroken, house-trained. **2** (*informal*) AMENABLE, biddable, co-operative, willing, obedient, tractable, acquiescent, docile, submissive, compliant, meek. **3** ☞ BLAND 2.
—OPPOSITES: wild, uncooperative, exciting.

▶ *v.* **1** DOMESTICATE, break, train, master, subdue. **2** SUBDUE, curb, control, calm, master, moderate, overcome, discipline, suppress, repress, mellow, temper, soften, bridle, get a grip on; *informal* lick.

tamper *v.* **1** INTERFERE, monkey around, meddle, tinker, fiddle,

fool around, play around; doctor, alter, change, adjust, damage, deface, vandalize; *informal* mess around, muck about/around. **2** INFLUENCE, get at, rig, manipulate, bribe, corrupt, bias; *informal* fix.

tangible *adj.* TOUCHABLE, palpable, material, physical, real, substantial, corporeal, solid, concrete; visible, noticeable; actual, definite, clear, clear-cut, distinct, manifest, evident, unmistakable, perceptible, discernible.
—OPPOSITES: abstract.

tangled *adj.* KNOTTED, knotty, ravelled, entangled, snarled (up), twisted, matted, tangly, messy; tousled, unkempt; *informal* mussed up.
—OPPOSITES: simple.

tape *n.* **1** BINDING, ribbon, string, braid. **2** ADHESIVE TAPE, sticky tape, masking tape, duct tape; *proprietary* Scotch Tape. **3** (AUDIO/VIDEO) CASSETTE, (tape) recording, reel, spool; video, VHS.

▶ *v.* **1** BIND, stick, fix, fasten, secure, attach; tie, strap. **2** CORDON, seal, close, shut, mark, fence; isolate, segregate. **3** RECORD, tape-record, capture on tape; video. **4** BIND, wrap, bandage.

taper *v.* **1** NARROW, thin (out), come to a point, attenuate. **2** DECREASE, lessen, dwindle, diminish, reduce, decline, die down, peter out, wane, ebb, slacken (off), fall off, let up, thin out.
—OPPOSITES: thicken, increase.

target *n.* **1** MARK, bull's eye, goal. **2** PREY, quarry, game, kill.

3 OBJECTIVE, goal, aim, end; plan, intention, intent, design, aspiration, ambition, ideal, desire, wish. **4** VICTIM, butt, recipient, focus, object, subject.

▶ *v.* **1** PICK OUT, single out, earmark, fix on; attack, aim at, fire at. **2** AIM, direct, level, intend, focus.

□ **on target 1** ACCURATE, precise, unerring, sure, on the mark. **2** ON SCHEDULE, on track, on course, on time.

tarnish *v.* **1** DISCOLOUR, rust, oxidize, corrode, stain, dull, blacken. **2** SULLY, blacken, stain, blemish, blot, taint, soil, drag through the mud/mire, ruin, disgrace, mar, damage, harm, hurt, undermine, dishonour, stigmatize, bring discredit to; slander, defame; *literary* besmirch.
—OPPOSITES: polish, enhance.

▶ *n.* **1** DISCOLORATION, oxidation, rust; film. **2** SMEAR, stain, blemish, blot, taint, stigma.

tart *adj.* **1** SOUR, sharp, acid, acidic, zesty, tangy, piquant; lemony, acetic. **2** ACERBIC, sharp, biting, cutting, astringent, caustic, trenchant, incisive, barbed, scathing, sarcastic, acrimonious, nasty, rude, vicious, spiteful, venomous.
—OPPOSITES: sweet, kind.

task *n.* JOB, duty, chore, charge, assignment, detail, mission, engagement, occupation, undertaking, exercise, business, responsibility, burden, endeavour, enterprise, venture, errand, operation, piece of work, project.
□ **take someone to task** REBUKE, reprimand, reprove, reproach,

remonstrate with, upbraid, scold, berate, castigate, lecture, censure, criticize, admonish, chide, chasten, arraign; *informal* tell off, bawl out, give someone a dressing-down.

taste *n.* **1** FLAVOUR, savour, relish, tang, smack. **2** MOUTHFUL, drop, bit, sip, nip, swallow, touch, soupçon, dash, modicum. **3** PALATE, taste buds, appetite, stomach. **4** LIKING, love, fondness, fancy, desire, preference, penchant, predilection, inclination, partiality; hankering, appetite, hunger, thirst, relish. **5** EXPERIENCE, impression; exposure to, contact with, involvement with. **6** JUDGMENT, discrimination, discernment, tastefulness, refinement, finesse, elegance, grace, style. **7** DECORUM, propriety, etiquette, politeness, delicacy, nicety, sensitivity, discretion, tastefulness.
—RELATED: gustatory.
—OPPOSITES: dislike.

▶ *v.* **1** SAMPLE, test, try, savour; sip, sup. **2** PERCEIVE, discern, make out, distinguish. **3** HAVE A FLAVOUR, savour, smack, be reminiscent; suggest. **4** CONSUME, drink, partake of; eat, devour. **5** EXPERIENCE, encounter, come face to face with, come up against, undergo; know.

tasteful *adj.* AESTHETICALLY PLEASING, in good taste, refined, cultured, elegant, stylish, smart, chic, attractive, exquisite.
—OPPOSITES: tasteless.

tasteless *adj.* **1** FLAVOURLESS, bland, insipid, unappetizing, savourless, watery, weak. **2** VULGAR, crude, tawdry, garish,

gaudy, loud, trashy, showy,
ostentatious, cheap, chintzy,
inelegant, tacky, kitsch, (Que.)
kétaine❖. **3** CRUDE, vulgar,
indelicate, uncouth, crass,
tactless, gauche, undiplomatic,
indiscreet, inappropriate,
offensive.
—OPPOSITES: tasty, tasteful,
seemly.

tasty adj. ☞ DELICIOUS.
—OPPOSITES: bland.

tattle v. **1** GOSSIP, chatter, chat,
prattle, babble, jabber, gabble,
rattle on; informal chinwag, jaw,
yak, gab, natter, tittle-tattle, chit-
chat. **2** INFORM; report, talk, tell
all, spill the beans; informal squeal,
sing, let the cat out of the bag.

taunt n. JEER, jibe, sneer, insult,
barb, catcall; (**taunts**) teasing,
provocation, goading, derision,
mockery; informal dig, put-down.
▶ v. JEER AT, sneer at, scoff at, poke
fun at, make fun of, get at, insult,
tease, chaff, torment, goad,
ridicule, deride, mock, heckle,
ride; informal rib, needle.

taut adj. **1** TIGHT, stretched, rigid.
2 FLEXED, tense, hard, solid, firm,
rigid, stiff. **3** FRAUGHT, strained,
stressed, tense; informal uptight.
—OPPOSITES: slack, relaxed.

tawdry adj. GAUDY, flashy, showy,
garish, loud; tasteless, vulgar,
trashy, kétaine❖, junky,
cheapjack, shoddy, shabby,
gimcrack, chintzy; informal tacky,
cheesy, kitschy, schlocky.
—OPPOSITES: tasteful.

tax n. DUTY, excise, customs, dues;
levy, tariff, toll, impost, tithe,
charge, fee; payment, rate.
—RELATED: fiscal.

—OPPOSITES: rebate.
▶ v. STRAIN, stretch, overburden,
overload, encumber, push too far;
overwhelm, try, wear out,
exhaust, sap, drain, weary,
weaken.

teach v. **1** EDUCATE, instruct,
school, tutor, coach, train;
enlighten, illuminate, verse, edify,
indoctrinate; drill, discipline;
guide, inform, prepare, prime.
2 GIVE LESSONS IN, lecture in, be a
teacher of; demonstrate, instill,
inculcate. **3** TRAIN, show, guide,
instruct, explain to, demonstrate
to, break in, ground, inculcate,
initiate.
—RELATED: didactic, pedagogic.

teacher n. EDUCATOR, tutor,
instructor, master, mistress,
governess, educationist,
preceptor; coach, trainer; lecturer,
professor, don; guide, mentor,
guru, counsellor; substitute
teacher, sub, supply teacher❖;
informal teach; formal pedagogue;
historical schoolman, schoolmarm.

team n. GROUP, squad, company,
party, crew, troupe, band, side,
lineup, phalanx; informal bunch,
gang, posse.
▶ v. JOIN (FORCES), collaborate, get
together, work together; unite,
combine, co-operate, link, ally,
associate.

tear v. **1** RIP UP, rip in two, pull to
pieces, shred. **2** LACERATE, cut
(open), gash, slash, scratch, hack,
pierce, stab; injure, wound.
3 DIVIDE, split, sever, break up,
rupture; literary rend, sunder,
cleave. **4** SNATCH, grab, seize, rip,
wrench, wrest, pull, pluck, yank,
drag, heave, peel, pry, tug.

5 (*informal*) ☞ RUSH 1.
—OPPOSITES: unite.
▸ *n.* RIP, hole, split, slash, slit, snag, cut, gash, laceration, rent.
□ **tear something down**
☞ DEMOLISH 1.

tearful *adj.* **1** CLOSE TO TEARS, emotional, upset, distressed, sad, unhappy; in tears, with tears in one's eyes, choked up, crying, weeping, sobbing, snivelling; *informal* weepy, teary, misty-eyed; *formal* lachrymose. **2** EMOTIONAL, upsetting, distressing, sad, heartbreaking, sorrowful; poignant, moving, touching, tear-jerking; *literary* dolorous.
—OPPOSITES: cheerful.

tease *v.* MAKE FUN OF, poke fun at, chaff, laugh at; taunt, bait, goad, pick on, jeer at, scoff at; deride, mock, ridicule; *informal* give someone the gears❖, send up, rib, kid, josh, have on, pull someone's leg, pull someone's chain, razz.

technique *n.* **1** METHOD, approach, procedure, system, modus operandi, MO, way; means, strategy, tack, tactic, line; routine, practice. **2** SKILL, ability, proficiency, expertise, mastery, talent, genius, artistry, craftsmanship; aptitude, adroitness, deftness, dexterity, facility, competence; performance, delivery; *informal* know-how.

tedious *adj.* ☞ BORING.
—OPPOSITES: exciting.

teem *v.* BE FULL OF, be filled with, be alive with, be brimming with, abound in, be swarming with, be aswarm with; be packed with, be crawling with, be overrun by,

bristle with, seethe with, be thick with; be jam-packed with, be chockablock with, be chock full of.

teenage *adj.* ADOLESCENT, teenaged, youthful, young, juvenile, teen.

teenager *n.* ADOLESCENT, youth, young person, youngster, minor, juvenile, teen, teenybopper.

tell *v.* **1** INFORM, notify, apprise, let know, make aware, acquaint with, advise, put in the picture, brief, fill in; alert, warn; *informal* clue in/ up. **2** RELATE, recount, narrate, unfold, report, recite, describe, sketch, weave, spin; utter, voice, state, declare, communicate, impart, divulge. **3** INSTRUCT, order, command, direct, charge, enjoin, call on, require; *literary* bid. **4** ASSURE, promise, give one's word, swear, guarantee. **5** REVEAL, show, indicate, be evidence of, disclose, convey, signify. **6** GIVE THE GAME AWAY, talk, tell tales, tattle; *informal* spill the beans, let the cat out of the bag, blab. **7** INFORM ON, tell tales on, give away, denounce, sell out; *informal* blow the whistle on, rat on, peach on, squeal on, finger. **8** ASCERTAIN, determine, work out, make out, deduce, discern, perceive, see, identify, recognize, understand, comprehend; *informal* figure out, suss out. **9** DISTINGUISH, differentiate, discriminate. **10** TAKE ITS TOLL, leave its mark; affect.
□ **tell someone off** (*informal*)
☞ REPRIMAND *v.*

telling *adj.* REVEALING, significant, weighty, important, meaningful,

influential, striking, potent, powerful, compelling.
—OPPOSITES: insignificant.

temper n. **1** (FIT OF) RAGE, fury, fit of pique, tantrum, (bad) mood, sulk, huff; informal grump, snit, hissy fit. **2** ANGER, fury, rage, annoyance, vexation, irritation, irritability, ill humour, spleen, pique, petulance, testiness, tetchiness, crabbiness; literary ire, choler. **3** COMPOSURE, equanimity, self-control, self-possession, sangfroid, calm, good humour; informal cool.
□ **lose one's temper** ☞ GET ANGRY at ANGRY.

temperament n. DISPOSITION, nature, character, personality, makeup, constitution, mind, spirit; stamp, mettle, mould; mood, frame of mind, attitude, outlook, humour.

temperamental adj. VOLATILE, excitable, emotional, mercurial, capricious, erratic, unpredictable, changeable, inconsistent; hotheaded, fiery, quick-tempered, irritable, irascible, impatient; touchy, moody, sensitive, over-sensitive, high-strung, neurotic, melodramatic.
—OPPOSITES: placid.

temporary adj. **1** NON-PERMANENT, short-term, interim; provisional, pro tem, makeshift, stopgap; acting, fill-in, stand-in, caretaker. **2** BRIEF, short-lived, momentary, fleeting, passing.
—OPPOSITES: permanent, lasting.

tempt v. **1** ENTICE, persuade, convince, inveigle, induce, cajole, coax, woo; informal sweet-talk. **2** ALLURE, attract, appeal to, whet

the appetite of; lure, seduce, beguile, tantalize, draw.
—OPPOSITES: discourage, deter.

tempting adj. **1** ☞ IRRESISTIBLE 1. **2** ☞ APPETIZING 1.
—OPPOSITES: off-putting, uninviting.

tenacious adj. **1** FIRM, tight, fast, clinging; strong, forceful, powerful, unshakeable, immovable, iron. **2** PERSEVERING, persistent, determined, dogged, strong-willed, tireless, indefatigable, resolute, resolved, purposeful, patient, unflagging, staunch, steadfast, untiring, unwavering, unswerving, unshakeable, unyielding, relentless, unrelenting, insistent, single-minded; stubborn, intransigent, obstinate, obdurate, stiff-necked; rock-ribbed; pertinacious.
—OPPOSITES: weak, irresolute.

tend[1] v. **1** BE INCLINED, be apt, be disposed, be prone, be liable, have a tendency, have a propensity. **2** INCLINE, lean, gravitate, move; prefer, favour, trend.

tend[2] v. LOOK AFTER, take care of, care for, minister to, attend to, see to, wait on; watch over, keep an eye on, mind, protect, watch, guard, supervise; nurse, nurture, cherish.
—OPPOSITES: neglect.

tendency n. **1** PROPENSITY, proclivity, proneness, aptness, likelihood, inclination, disposition, predisposition, bent, leaning, penchant, predilection, susceptibility, liability; readiness; habit. **2** TREND, movement, drift, swing, gravitation, direction, course; orientation, bias.

tender adj. **1** CARING, kind, kindly, kind-hearted, soft-hearted, tender-hearted, compassionate, sympathetic, warm, warm-hearted, solicitous, fatherly, motherly, maternal, gentle, mild, benevolent, generous, giving, humane. **2** AFFECTIONATE, fond, loving, emotional, warm, gentle, soft; amorous, adoring; informal lovey-dovey. **3** EASILY CHEWED, chewable, soft; succulent, juicy; tenderized, fork-tender. **4** ☞ SORE.
—OPPOSITES: hard-hearted, callous, tough.

tense adj. **1** TAUT, tight, rigid, stretched, strained, stiff. **2** ANXIOUS, nervous, on edge, edgy, antsy, strained, stressed (out), under pressure, agitated, uptight, ill at ease, fretful, uneasy, restless, strung out, worked up, wound up, het up, keyed up, overwrought, jumpy, high-strung, on tenterhooks, with one's stomach in knots, worried, apprehensive; panicky, jittery, twitchy, spooky, squirrelly, a bundle of nerves, fidgety, in a tizz/tizzy. **3** NERVE-RACKING, stressful, anxious, worrying, fraught, charged, strained, nail-biting, white-knuckle, suspenseful, uneasy, difficult, uncomfortable; exciting, cliffhanging, knife-edge.
—OPPOSITES: slack, calm.
▸ v. TIGHTEN, tauten, tense up, flex, contract, brace, stiffen; screw up, knot, strain, stretch.
—OPPOSITES: relax.

tension n. **1** TIGHTNESS, tautness, rigidity; pull, traction. **2** STRAIN, stress, anxiety, pressure; worry, apprehensiveness, apprehension, agitation, nerves, nervousness, jumpiness, edginess, restlessness; suspense, uncertainty, anticipation, excitement; informal heebie-jeebies, butterflies (in one's stomach), collywobbles. **3** STRAINED RELATIONS, strain; ill feeling, friction, antagonism, antipathy, hostility, enmity.

tentative adj. **1** PROVISIONAL, unconfirmed, pencilled in, iffy, preliminary, to be confirmed, subject to confirmation; speculative, conjectural, sketchy, untried, unproven, exploratory, experimental, trial, test, pilot. **2** HESITANT, uncertain, cautious, timid, hesitating, faltering, shaky, unsteady, halting; wavering, unsure.
—OPPOSITES: definite, confident.

term n. **1** WORD, expression, phrase, turn of phrase, idiom, locution; name, title, designation, label, moniker; formal appellation, denomination, descriptor. **2** LANGUAGE, mode of expression, manner of speaking, phraseology, terminology; words, expressions. **3** CONDITIONS, stipulations, specifications, provisions, provisos, qualifications, particulars, small print, details, points. **4** RATES, prices, charges, costs, fees; tariff. **5** PERIOD, period of time, time, length of time, spell, stint, duration; stretch, run; period of office, mandate✤, incumbency. **6** SESSION, semester, trimester, quarter; intersession.
☐ **come to terms 1** REACH AN AGREEMENT/UNDERSTANDING, make a

deal, reach a compromise, meet each other halfway. **2** ACCEPT, come to accept, reconcile oneself to, learn to live with, become resigned to, make the best of; face up to.

terminal *adj.* **1** INCURABLE, untreatable, inoperable; fatal, mortal, deadly. **2** INCURABLE, dying; near death, on one's deathbed, on one's last legs, with one foot in the grave. **3** FINAL, last, concluding, closing, end.

terminate *v.* **1** BRING TO AN END, end, abort, curtail, bring to a close/conclusion, close, conclude, finish, stop, put an end to, wind up/down, wrap up, discontinue, cease, kill, cut short, axe, can; *informal* pull the plug on. **2** FIRE, downsize; *informal* can, cut. **3** END ITS JOURNEY, finish up, stop.
—OPPOSITES: begin, start, continue.

terminology *n.* PHRASEOLOGY, terms, expressions, words, language, lexicon, parlance, vocabulary, wording, nomenclature; usage, idiom; jargon, cant, argot; *informal* lingo, -speak, -ese.

terrible *adj.* **1** DREADFUL, awful, appalling, horrific, horrifying, horrible, horrendous, horrid, atrocious, abominable, deplorable, abhorrent, frightful, shocking, alarming, hideous, ghastly, grisly, grim, dire, unspeakable, gruesome, monstrous, sickening, heinous, vile; serious, grave, acute, calamitous; depressing, distressing, upsetting; *formal* grievous. **2** REPULSIVE, disgusting, awful, dreadful, ghastly, horrid, horrible, execrable, vile, foul, abominable, frightful, loathsome, revolting, nasty, odious, repugnant, nauseating, repellent, horrendous, hideous, appalling, offensive, objectionable, obnoxious, gruesome, putrid, noisome, yucky, godawful, gross; disagreeable, distasteful, hateful, reprehensible, unpleasant, wretched. **3** SEVERE, extreme, intense, acute, excruciating, agonizing, unbearable, intolerable, unendurable. **4** ☞ UNKIND. **5** VERY BAD, dreadful, awful, deplorable, atrocious, hopeless, worthless, useless, poor, pathetic, pitiful, lamentable, appalling, abysmal, disgraceful, frightful, rotten, shameful, woeful; *informal* lame, lousy, dire, brutal, painful, crappy, crummy, the pits. **6** ☞ ILL 1. **7** GUILTY, conscience-stricken, remorseful, guilt-ridden, ashamed, chastened, contrite, sorry, sick, bad, awful.
—OPPOSITES: minor, slight, pleasant, wonderful.

terrific *adj.* ☞ EXCELLENT.

terrorist *n.* EXTREMIST, fanatic; revolutionary, radical, insurgent, guerrilla, anarchist, freedom fighter; bomber, suicide bomber, gunman, assassin, hijacker.

terrorize *v.* PERSECUTE, victimize, torment, harass, tyrannize, intimidate, menace, threaten, bully, browbeat; scare, frighten, terrify, petrify.

test *n.* **1** TRIAL, experiment, test case, case study, pilot study, trial run, tryout, dry run; check, examination, assessment,

evaluation, appraisal, investigation, inspection, analysis, scrutiny, study, probe, exploration; screening; *technical* assay. **2** EXAM, examination, quiz.
▸ *v.* **1** TRY OUT, put to the test, put through its paces, experiment with, pilot; check, examine, assess, evaluate, appraise, investigate, analyze, scrutinize, study, probe, explore, trial; sample; screen; *technical* assay. **2** PUT A STRAIN ON, strain, tax, try; make demands on, stretch, challenge.

testify *v.* **1** GIVE EVIDENCE, bear witness, be a witness, give one's testimony, attest; *Law* make a deposition. **2** ATTEST, swear, state on oath, state, declare, assert, affirm; allege, submit, claim; *Law* depose. **3** BE EVIDENCE/PROOF OF, attest to, confirm, prove, corroborate, substantiate, bear out, evidence; show, demonstrate, establish, bear witness to, speak to, indicate, reveal, bespeak.

testimony *n.* **1** EVIDENCE, sworn statement, attestation, affidavit; statement, declaration, assertion, affirmation; allegation, submission, claim; *Law* deposition. **2** TESTAMENT, proof, evidence, attestation, witness; confirmation, verification, corroboration; demonstration, illustration, indication.

testy *adj.* ☞ IRRITABLE.
—OPPOSITES: good-humoured.

text *n.* **1** BOOK, work, written/printed work, document. **2** WORDS, wording, writing; content, body, main body; narrative, story.
3 TEXTBOOK, book, material.

4 PASSAGE, extract, excerpt, quotation, verse, line; reading.

texture *n.* FEEL, touch; appearance, finish, surface, grain; quality, consistency; weave, nap.

thank *v.* EXPRESS (ONE'S) GRATITUDE TO, express one's thanks to, offer/extend thanks to, say thank you to, show one's appreciation to, credit, recognize, bless.

thankful *adj.* GRATEFUL, appreciative, filled with gratitude, relieved.

thankless *adj.* **1** UNENVIABLE, difficult, unpleasant, unrewarding; unappreciated, unrecognized, unacknowledged.
2 ☞ UNGRATEFUL.
—OPPOSITES: rewarding, grateful.

thanks *pl. n.* GRATITUDE, appreciation; acknowledgement, recognition, credit.
□ **thanks to** AS A RESULT OF, owing to, due to, because of, through, as a consequence of, on account of, by virtue of, by dint of, by reason of.

thaw *v.* ☞ MELT 1.
—OPPOSITES: freeze.
▸ *n.* **1** (spring) breakup✢, debacle, ice-out. **2** IMPROVEMENT, relaxation, coming to terms, rapprochement, détente.

theatre *n.* **1** PLAYHOUSE, auditorium, amphitheatre; cinema, movie theatre/house, *proprietary* Cineplex; *dated* nickelodeon. **2** ACTING, performing, the stage; drama, the dramatic arts, dramaturgy, the thespian art; show business, Broadway; *informal* the boards, show biz. **3** HALL, room, auditorium.

4 SCENE, arena, field/sphere/place of action.

theatrical *adj.* **1** STAGE, dramatic, thespian, dramaturgical; show-business; *informal* showbiz; *formal* histrionic. **2** EXAGGERATED, ostentatious, stagy, showy, melodramatic, overacted, overdone, histrionic, over-the-top, artificial, affected, mannered; *informal* hammy, ham, camp.

theft *n.* ROBBERY, stealing, thieving, larceny, thievery, shoplifting, burglary, misappropriation, appropriation, embezzlement; raid, holdup; *informal* smash and grab, heist, stickup; five-finger discount, rip-off; *formal* peculation.
—RELATED: kleptomania.

theme *n.* **1** SUBJECT, topic, subject matter, matter, thesis, argument, text, burden, concern, thrust, message; thread, motif, keynote. **2** MELODY, tune, air; motif, leitmotif.

then *adv.* **1** AT THAT TIME, in those days; at that point (in time), at that moment, on that occasion. **2** NEXT, after that, afterwards, subsequently, later. **3** IN ADDITION, also, besides, as well, additionally, on top of that, over and above that, moreover, furthermore, what's more, to boot; too. **4** IN THAT CASE, that being so, it follows that.

theoretical *adj.* HYPOTHETICAL, abstract, conjectural, academic, suppositional, speculative, notional, what-if, assumed, presumed, untested, unproven, unsubstantiated, conjectured,

putative, supposed.
—OPPOSITES: actual, real.

theorize *v.* SPECULATE, conjecture, hypothesize, philosophize, postulate, propose, posit, suppose.

theory *n.* **1** HYPOTHESIS, thesis, conjecture, supposition, speculation, postulation, postulate, theorem, proposition, premise, surmise, assumption, presupposition; opinion, view, belief, contention; concept, idea, notion, possibility. **2** PRINCIPLES, ideas, concepts; philosophy, ideology, system of ideas, science.
☐ **in theory** IN PRINCIPLE, on paper, in the abstract, all things being equal, in an ideal world; hypothetically, theoretically, supposedly.

therefore *adv.* CONSEQUENTLY, SO, as a result, hence, thus, accordingly, for that reason, ergo, that being the case, on that account; *formal* whence; *archaic* wherefore.

thesis *n.* **1** THEORY, contention, argument, line of argument, proposal, proposition, idea, claim, premise, assumption, hypothesis, postulation, supposition. **2** DISSERTATION, essay, paper, treatise, disquisition, composition, monograph, study.

thick *adj.* **1** STOCKY, sturdy, stubby, chunky, blocky, hefty, thickset, burly, beefy, meaty, big, solid; fat, stout, plump. **2** PLENTIFUL, abundant, profuse, luxuriant, bushy, rich, riotous, exuberant; rank, rampant; dense, impenetrable, impassable. **3** VISCOUS, gooey, syrupy, firm, stiff, heavy; clotted, coagulated,

viscid, semi-solid, gelatinous; concentrated. **4** DENSE, heavy, opaque, impenetrable, soupy, murky.
—OPPOSITES: thin, slender, sparse.

thief n. ROBBER, burglar, housebreaker, cat burglar, rustler, shoplifter, pickpocket, purse snatcher, sneak thief, pilferer, mugger; embezzler, swindler; plunderer, looter, pillager, raider; criminal; kleptomaniac; bandit, pirate, highwayman; informal crook; literary brigand.

thieve v. ☞ STEAL 1.

thin adj. **1** NARROW, fine, attenuated. **2** LIGHTWEIGHT, light, fine, delicate, floaty, flimsy, diaphanous, gossamer, insubstantial; sheer, gauzy, filmy, transparent, see-through; paper-thin. **3** SLIM, lean, slender, rangy, willowy, svelte, sylphlike, spare, slight; SKINNY, underweight, scrawny, waiflike, scraggy, bony, angular, raw-boned, hollow-cheeked, gaunt, skin-and-bones, emaciated, skeletal, wasted, pinched, undernourished, underfed; lanky, spindly, gangly, gangling, weedy; informal anorexic, like a bag of bones. **4** SPARSE, scanty, wispy, thinning. **5** WATERY, weak, dilute, diluted; runny. **6** WEAK, faint, feeble, small, soft; reedy. **7** INSUBSTANTIAL, flimsy, slight, feeble, lame, poor, weak, tenuous, inadequate, insufficient, unconvincing, unbelievable, implausible.
—OPPOSITES: thick, broad, fat, abundant.

thing n. **1** OBJECT, article, item, artifact, commodity; device, gadget, instrument, utensil, tool, implement; entity, body; informal whatsit, whatchamacallit, thingummy, thingy, thingamabob, thingamajig, doohickey, doodad, dingus. **2** BELONGINGS, possessions, stuff, property, worldly goods, (personal) effects, trappings, paraphernalia, bits and pieces, luggage, baggage, bags; informal gear, junk; Law goods and chattels. **3** EQUIPMENT, apparatus, gear, kit, tackle, stuff; implements, tools, utensils; accoutrements. **4** ACTIVITY, act, action, deed, undertaking, exploit, feat; task, job, chore. **5** THOUGHT, notion, idea; concern, matter, worry, preoccupation. **6** REMARK, statement, comment, utterance, observation, declaration, pronouncement. **7** INCIDENT, episode, event, happening, occurrence, phenomenon. **8** MATTERS, affairs, circumstances, conditions, relations; state of affairs, situation, life. **9** CHARACTERISTIC, quality, attribute, property, trait, feature, point, aspect, facet, quirk. **10** FACT, piece of information, point, detail, particular, factor. **11** FACT OF THE MATTER, fact, point, issue, problem. **12** PERSON, soul, creature, wretch; informal devil, bastard. **13** PHOBIA, fear, dislike, aversion, problem; obsession, fixation; complex, neurosis; informal hang-up. **14** PENCHANT, preference, taste, inclination, partiality, predilection, soft spot, weakness, fondness, fancy, liking, love; fetish, obsession, fixation. **15** WHAT

ONE LIKES, what interests one; *informal* one's cup of tea, one's bag, what turns one on. **16** FASHION, trend, rage.

think *v.* **1** BELIEVE, be of the opinion, be of the view, be under the impression; expect, imagine, anticipate; surmise, guess, fancy; conclude, determine, reason; *informal* reckon, figure; *formal* opine. **2** DEEM, judge, hold, reckon, consider, presume, estimate; regard as, view as. **3** PONDER, reflect, deliberate, consider, meditate, contemplate, muse, ruminate, be lost in thought, be in a brown study, brood; concentrate, brainstorm, rack one's brains; put on one's thinking cap, sleep on it; *formal* cogitate. **4** RECALL, remember, recollect, call to mind, think back to. **5** IMAGINE, picture, visualize, envisage, consider; dream about, fantasize about.
□ **think better of** HAVE SECOND THOUGHTS ABOUT, think twice about, think again about, change one's mind about; reconsider, decide against; *informal* get cold feet about. **think something over** CONSIDER, contemplate, deliberate about, mull over, ponder, chew over, chew on, reflect on, muse on, ruminate on. **think something up** DEVISE, dream up, conjure up, come up with, invent, create, concoct, make up; hit on.

thinker *n.* THEORIST, philosopher, scholar, savant, sage, intellectual, intellect, ideologist, ideologue; mind, brain, brainiac, genius.

thirst *n.* **1** THIRSTINESS, dryness; dehydration. **2** CRAVING, desire, longing, yearning, hunger, hankering, keenness, eagerness, lust, appetite; *informal* yen, itch.

thorough *adj.* **1** RIGOROUS, in-depth, exhaustive, thoroughgoing, minute, detailed, close, meticulous, methodical, careful, complete, comprehensive, full, extensive, widespread, sweeping, all-embracing, all-inclusive. **2** METICULOUS, scrupulous, assiduous, conscientious, painstaking, methodical, careful, diligent, industrious, hard-working.
—OPPOSITES: superficial, cursory, careless.

thought *n.* **1** IDEA, notion, opinion, view, impression, feeling, theory; judgment, assessment, conclusion. **2** THINKING, contemplation, musing, pondering, consideration, reflection, introspection, deliberation, rumination, meditation, brooding, reverie, concentration; *formal* cogitation.

thoughtful *adj.* **1** PENSIVE, reflective, contemplative, musing, meditative, introspective, philosophical, ruminative, absorbed, engrossed, rapt, preoccupied, deep/lost in thought, in a brown study, brooding; *formal* cogitative. **2** ☞ CONSIDERATE.
—OPPOSITES: vacant, inconsiderate.

thoughtless *adj.*
1 ☞ INCONSIDERATE. **2** ☞ HEEDLESS.
—OPPOSITES: considerate, careful.

threaten *v.* ☞ MENACE *v.*

thrifty *adj.* ☞ FRUGAL.
—OPPOSITES: extravagant.

thrill *n.* (FEELING OF) EXCITEMENT,
stimulation, adrenaline rush,
pleasure, tingle; fun, enjoyment,
amusement, delight, joy; *informal*
buzz, high, rush, kick, charge.
▶ *v.* EXCITE, stimulate, arouse,
rouse, inspire, delight, exhilarate,
intoxicate, stir, charge up,
electrify, galvanize, move, fire
(with enthusiasm), fire someone's
imagination; *informal* give someone
a buzz, give someone a kick, give
someone a charge.
—OPPOSITES: bore.

thrilling *adj.* EXCITING, stirring,
action-packed, breathtaking, rip-
roaring, spine-tingling, gripping,
riveting, fascinating, dramatic,
hair-raising, mind-blowing;
rousing, stimulating, moving,
inspiring, inspirational,
electrifying, heady, arousing,
compelling, exhilarating,
intoxicating, invigorating,
powerful.
—OPPOSITES: boring.

throb *v.* PULSATE, beat, pulse,
palpitate, pound, thud, thump,
drum, thrum, trip-hammer, pitter-
patter, go pit-a-pat, quiver.
▶ *n.* PULSATION, beat, beating, pulse,
palpitation, pounding, thudding,
thumping, drumming,
thrumming.

throttle *v.* **1** CHOKE, strangle,
strangulate, garrotte, gag.
2 SUPPRESS, inhibit, stifle, control,
restrain, check, contain, choke
off, put a/the lid on; stop, put an
end to, end, stamp out.

throughout *prep.* **1** ALL OVER,
across, in every part of,
everywhere in, all through, right
through, all around. **2** ALL

THROUGH, all, for the duration of,
for the whole of, until the end of.

throw *v.* **1** HURL, toss, fling,
huck✦, pitch, cast, lob, launch,
catapult, project, propel; bowl;
informal chuck, heave, sling, peg, let
fly with, shoot, fire. **2** DELIVER,
give, land. **3** DIRECT, cast, send,
dart, shoot. **4** DISCONCERT,
unnerve, fluster, ruffle, agitate,
discomfit, put off, throw off
balance, discountenance, unsettle,
confuse; *informal* rattle, faze,
flummox, baffle, befuddle,
discombobulate.
▢ **throw something away**
1 ☞ DISCARD. **2** ☞ SQUANDER.
throw someone out ☞ EVICT.
throw something out
1 ☞ DISCARD. **2** REJECT, dismiss,
turn down, refuse, disallow, veto;
informal give the thumbs down to.
throw up (*informal*) ☞ VOMIT *v.* 1.

thrust *v.* SHOVE, push, force,
plunge, stick, drive, propel, ram,
poke, jam.
▶ *n.* **1** SHOVE, push, lunge, poke.
2 ADVANCE, push, drive, attack,
assault, onslaught, offensive,
charge, sortie, foray, raid, sally,
invasion, incursion. **3** FORCE,
propulsive force, propulsion,
power, impetus, momentum.
4 GIST, substance, drift, burden,
meaning, sense, theme, message,
import, tenor.

thug *n.* RUFFIAN, goon, hooligan,
bully boy, vandal, hoodlum,
gangster, criminal; tough, bruiser,
heavy, enforcer, lout, hired gun,
hood.

thwart *v.* ☞ FRUSTRATE 1.
—OPPOSITES: facilitate.

tidy *adj.* **1** NEAT, neat and tidy, orderly, well-ordered, in (good) order, well-kept, shipshape, in apple-pie order, immaculate, spic and span, uncluttered, straight, trim, spruce. **2** NEAT, trim, spruce, dapper, well-groomed, organized, well-organized, methodical, meticulous; fastidious; *informal* natty. **3** (*informal*) LARGE, sizeable, considerable, substantial, generous, significant, appreciable, handsome, respectable, ample, decent, goodly.
—OPPOSITES: messy.
▸ *v.* PUT IN ORDER, clear up, sort out, straighten (up), clean up, spruce up.

tie *v.* **1** BIND, tie up, tether, hitch, strap, truss, fetter, rope, chain, make fast, moor, lash, attach, fasten, fix, secure, join, connect, link, couple. **2** DO UP, lace, knot. **3** LINK, connect, couple, relate, join, marry; make conditional on, bind up with. **4** DRAW, be equal, be even, be neck and neck.
▸ *n.* **1** LACE, string, cord, fastening, fastener. **2** NECKTIE, bow tie, string tie, bolo tie. **3** BOND, connection, link, relationship, attachment, affiliation, allegiance, friendship; kinship, interdependence. **4** DRAW, dead heat, deadlock, saw-off✦.
☐ **tie in** BE CONSISTENT, tally, agree, be in agreement, accord, concur, fit in, harmonize, be in tune, dovetail, correspond, match; square, jibe.

tight *adj.* **1** FIRM, fast, secure, fixed, clenched. **2** TAUT, rigid, stiff, tense, stretched, strained.
—OPPOSITES: slack, loose.

time *n.* **1** HOUR. **2** MOMENT, point (in time), occasion, hour, minute, second, instant, juncture, stage. **3** WHILE, spell, stretch, stint, span, season, interval, period (of time), length of time, duration, space, phase, stage, term, patch. **4** ERA, age, epoch, period, years, days; generation, date. **5** LIFETIME, life, life span, days, time on earth, existence. **6** HEYDAY, day, best days/years, glory days, prime, peak, Golden Age. **7** CONDITIONS, circumstances; life, state of affairs, way of the world. **8** RHYTHM, tempo, beat; metre, measure, pattern.
—RELATED: chronological, temporal.
☐ **ahead of one's time**
☞ ADVANCED.

timeless *adj.* LASTING, enduring, classic, ageless, permanent, perennial, abiding, unfailing, unchanging, unvarying, never-changing, changeless, unfading, unending, undying, immortal, eternal, everlasting, immutable.
—OPPOSITES: ephemeral.

timely *adj.* OPPORTUNE, well-timed, at the right time, convenient, appropriate, expedient, seasonable, felicitous.
—OPPOSITES: ill-timed.

timid *adj.* APPREHENSIVE, fearful, easily frightened, afraid, faint-hearted, timorous, nervous, scared, frightened, cowardly, pusillanimous, spineless; shy, diffident, self-effacing; *informal* wimpish, wimpy, yellow, chicken, mousy, gutless, sissy, lily-livered.
—OPPOSITES: bold.

tinker v. FIDDLE WITH, adjust, fix, try to mend, play about with, fool with, futz with; tamper with, interfere with, mess about with, meddle with.

tint n. **1** SHADE, colour, tone, hue, pigmentation, tinge, cast, tincture, flush, blush, wash. **2** DYE, colouring, rinse, highlights, lowlights.

tiny adj. MINUTE, minuscule, microscopic, infinitesimal, very small, little, imperceptible, indiscernible, mini, diminutive, miniature, scaled down, baby, toy, dwarf, pygmy, peewee, Lilliputian; informal teeny, teeny-weeny, teensy, teensy-weensy, itty-bitty, itsy-bitsy, eensy, eensy-weensy, little-bitty, bite-sized, pint-sized; Scottish wee.
—OPPOSITES: huge.

tip¹ n. POINT, end, extremity, head, sharp end, spike, prong, tine, nib; top, summit, apex, cusp, crown, crest, pinnacle, vertex.

tip² v. **1** OVERTURN, turn over, topple (over), fall (over); keel over, capsize, flip, turn turtle; Nautical pitchpole. **2** UPSET, overturn, topple over, turn over, knock over, push over, upend, capsize, roll, flip. **3** LEAN, tilt, list, slope, bank, slant, incline, pitch, cant, heel, careen.

tip³ n. **1** GRATUITY, baksheesh; present, gift, reward. **2** PIECE OF ADVICE, suggestion, word of advice, pointer, recommendation; clue, (helpful) hint, tipoff; word to the wise.

tirade n. DIATRIBE, harangue, rant, onslaught, attack, polemic, denunciation, broadside, fulmination, condemnation, censure, invective, criticism, tongue-lashing; blast; lecture; literary philippic.

tire v. **1** WEAKEN, grow weak, flag, wilt, droop; deteriorate. **2** ☞ FATIGUE v. **3** WEARY, get fed up, get sick, get bored, get impatient; informal have had it up to here, have had enough.

tired adj. **1** EXHAUSTED, worn out, weary, fatigued, dog-tired, dead beat, bone-tired, bone-weary, ready to drop, drained, zonked, wasted; sleepy, dopey, dozy, drowsy, groggy, languid, lethargic, listless, sluggish, snoozy, somnolent, torpid, yawning, enervated, jaded; informal done in, bushed, whipped, bagged, knocked out, wiped out, pooped, tuckered out. **2** FED UP WITH, weary of, bored with/by, sick (to death) of; informal up to here with. **3** HACKNEYED, overused, overworked, worn out, stale, clichéd, hoary, stock, stereotyped, predictable, unimaginative, unoriginal, uninspired, dull, boring, routine; informal old hat, corny.
—OPPOSITES: energetic, lively, fresh.

tireless adj. INDEFATIGABLE, energetic, vigorous, industrious, hard-working, determined, enthusiastic, keen, zealous, spirited, dynamic, dogged, tenacious, persevering, untiring, unwearying, unremitting, unflagging, indomitable.
—OPPOSITES: lazy.

tiresome *adj.* **1** ☞ BORING.
2 ☞ ANNOYING.
—OPPOSITES: interesting, pleasant.

tiring *adj.* EXHAUSTING, wearying, fatiguing, enervating, draining, sapping, stressful, wearing, crushing; demanding, exacting, taxing, trying, challenging, burdensome, arduous, gruelling, punishing, grinding, onerous, difficult, hard, tough, heavy, laborious, back-breaking, strenuous, rigorous.

title *n.* **1** NAME, heading, legend, label, caption, inscription.
2 PUBLICATION, work, book, newspaper, paper, magazine, periodical. **3** DESIGNATION, name, form of address, honorific; epithet, rank, office, position, job title; *informal* moniker, handle, tag; *formal* appellation, denomination; sobriquet. **4** CHAMPIONSHIP, crown, first place; laurels, palm.
5 OWNERSHIP, proprietorship, possession, holding, freehold, entitlement, right, claim.

toast *n.* TRIBUTE, salute, salutation.
▶ *v.* DRINK (TO) THE HEALTH OF, drink to, salute, honour, pay tribute to.

together *adv.* **1** WITH EACH OTHER, in conjunction, jointly, mutually, in co-operation, co-operatively, in collaboration, in partnership, in combination, in league, in tandem, side by side, hand in hand, shoulder to shoulder, cheek by jowl; in collusion, hand in glove; *informal* in cahoots.
2 SIMULTANEOUSLY, at the same time, at one and the same time, at once, all together, as a group, in unison, in concert, in chorus, as

one, with one accord.
—OPPOSITES: separately.

token *n.* **1** SYMBOL, sign, emblem, badge, representation, indication, mark, manifestation, expression, pledge, demonstration, recognition; evidence, proof.
2 MEMENTO, souvenir, keepsake, reminder, remembrance, memorial.
▶ *adj.* SYMBOLIC, emblematic; perfunctory, slight, nominal, minimal, minor, mild, superficial, inconsequential.

tolerable *adj.* **1** ☞ BEARABLE.
2 ☞ ADEQUATE 2.
—OPPOSITES: unacceptable.

tolerance *n.* **1** ACCEPTANCE, toleration; open-mindedness, broad-mindedness, forbearance, liberality, liberalism; patience, charity, indulgence, understanding. **2** ENDURANCE, resilience, resistance, immunity.

tolerant *adj.* OPEN-MINDED, forbearing, broad-minded, liberal, unprejudiced, unbiased; patient, long-suffering, understanding, forgiving, charitable, lenient, indulgent, permissive, easygoing, lax, laid-back.
—OPPOSITES: intolerant.

tolerate *v.* **1** ALLOW, permit, condone, accept, swallow, countenance; *formal* brook.
2 ENDURE, put up with, bear, take, stand, support, stomach, deal with; abide.

toll *n.* **1** CHARGE, fee, payment, levy, tariff, tax. **2** NUMBER, count, tally, total, sum total, grand total, sum; record, list. **3** ADVERSE EFFECT(S), detriment, harm, damage, injury, impact, hurt; cost, price, loss, disadvantage, suffering, penalty.

tomb *n.* BURIAL CHAMBER, sepulchre, mausoleum, vault, crypt, catacomb; ossuary; last/final resting place, grave, barrow, burial mound; *historical* charnel house.
—RELATED: sepulchral.

tone *n.* **1** TIMBRE, sound, sound quality, voice, voice quality, colour, tonality. **2** MOOD, air, spirit, feel, sound, flavour, note, attitude, character, nature, manner, temper; tenor, vein, drift, gist. **3** NOTE, signal, beep, bleep. **4** SHADE, colour, hue, tint, tinge.
□ **tone something down** SOFTEN, lighten, mute, subdue, mellow; MODERATE, modify, modulate, mitigate, temper, dampen.

tonic *n.* **1** STIMULANT, restorative, refresher, medicine; *informal* pick-me-up. **2** STIMULANT, boost, fillip; *informal* shot in the arm, pick-me-up.

tool *n.* **1** IMPLEMENT, utensil, instrument, device, apparatus, gadget, appliance, machine, contrivance, contraption; *informal* gizmo. **2** PUPPET, pawn, creature, cat's paw; minion, lackey, instrument, organ; *informal* stooge.

top *n.* **1** SUMMIT, peak, pinnacle, crest, crown, brow, head, tip, apex, vertex. **2** SWEATER, jersey, sweatshirt, vest, pullover; T-shirt, tank top, shirt; blouse. **3** HIGH POINT, height, peak, pinnacle, zenith, acme, culmination, climax, prime.
—OPPOSITES: bottom, base.
▸ *adj.* **1** HIGHEST, topmost,

uppermost. **2** ☞ BEST *adj.* 1.
3 UPPER, chief, principal, main, leading, highest, highest-ranking, ruling, commanding, most powerful, most important.
4 PRIME, excellent, superb, superior, choice, select, top-quality, top-grade, first-rate, first-class, grade A, best, finest, premier, superlative, second to none, nonpareil; *informal* A1, top-notch, blue-ribbon, blue-chip, number-one. **5** MAXIMUM, maximal, greatest, utmost.
—OPPOSITES: bottom, lowest, minimum.
▸ *v.* **1** EXCEED, surpass, go beyond, better, best, beat, outstrip, outdo, outshine, eclipse, go one better than, cap. **2** LEAD, head, be at the top of. **3** COVER, cap, coat, smother; finish, garnish.

topic *n.* ☞ SUBJECT *n.* 1.

topical *adj.* CURRENT, up-to-date, up-to-the-minute, contemporary, recent, relevant; newsworthy, in the news.
—OPPOSITES: out of date.

torment *n.* **1** ☞ AGONY. **2** ORDEAL, affliction, scourge, curse, plague, bane, thorn in someone's side/flesh, cross to bear; sorrow, tribulation, trouble.
▸ *v.* **1** TORTURE, afflict, rack, harrow, plague, haunt, bedevil, distress, agonize. **2** TEASE, taunt, bait, harass, provoke, goad, plague, bother, trouble, persecute; *informal* needle.

torn *adj.* **1** RIPPED, rent, cut, slit; ragged, tattered, in tatters, in ribbons. **2** ☞ INDECISIVE 2.

torrent *n.* **1** FLOOD, deluge, inundation, spate, cascade,

cataract, rush, stream, current, flow, overflow, tide. **2** OUTBURST, outpouring, stream, flood, volley, barrage, tide, spate.
—OPPOSITES: trickle.

tortuous *adj.* **1** TWISTING, twisty, twisting and turning, winding, windy, zigzag, sinuous, snaky, serpentine, meandering, circuitous. **2** CONVOLUTED, complicated, complex, labyrinthine, tangled, tangly, involved, confusing, difficult to follow, involuted, lengthy, overlong, circuitous.
—OPPOSITES: straight, straightforward.

torture *n.* **1** INFLICTION OF PAIN, abuse, ill-treatment, maltreatment, persecution; sadism. **2** TORMENT, agony, suffering, pain, anguish, misery, distress, heartbreak, affliction, scourge, trauma, wretchedness; hell, purgatory.
▶ *v.* **1** INFLICT PAIN ON, ill-treat, abuse, mistreat, maltreat, persecute. **2** TORMENT, rack, afflict, harrow, plague, agonize, scourge, crucify.

toss *v.* **1** ☞ THROW 1. **2** PITCH, lurch, rock, roll, plunge, reel, list, keel, sway, wallow, flounder.

total *adj.* **1** ENTIRE, complete, whole, full, comprehensive, combined, aggregate, gross, overall, final. **2** COMPLETE, utter, absolute, thorough, out-and-out, outright, all-out, sheer, perfect, consummate, arrant, positive, rank, unmitigated, unqualified, unreserved, categorical.
—OPPOSITES: partial.
▶ *v.* **1** ADD UP TO, amount to, come

to, run to, make, work out to. **2** ADD (UP), count, calculate, reckon, tot up, tally up, compute, work out.

totalitarian *adj.* AUTOCRATIC, undemocratic, one-party, dictatorial, tyrannical, despotic, fascist, oppressive, repressive, draconian, illiberal; authoritarian, autarchic, absolute, absolutist; dystopian.
—OPPOSITES: democratic.

touch *v.* **1** BE IN CONTACT WITH, come into contact with, meet, join, connect with, converge with, be contiguous with, be against. **2** PRESS LIGHTLY, tap, pat; feel, stroke, fondle, caress, pet; brush, graze, put a hand to. **3** COMPARE WITH, rival, compete with, come/ get close to, be on a par with, equal, match, be a match for, be in the same class/league as, measure up to; better, beat; *informal* hold a candle to. **4** HANDLE, hold, pick up, move; meddle with, play about with, fiddle with, interfere with, tamper with, disturb, lay a finger on; use, employ, make use of. **5** AFFECT, impact, have an effect/impact on, make a difference to, change. **6** AFFECT, move, tug at someone's heartstrings; leave an impression on, have an effect on.
▶ *n.* **1** TAP, pat; stroke, caress; brush, graze; hand. **2** SKILL, skilfulness, expertise, dexterity, deftness, adroitness, adeptness, ability, talent, flair, facility, proficiency, mastery, knack, technique, approach, style.
3 TRACE, bit, grain, hint, suggestion, suspicion, scintilla,

tinge, overtone, undertone, note; dash, taste, drop, dab, dribble, pinch, speck, soupçon. **4** DETAIL, feature, point; addition, accessory. **5** CONTACT, communication, correspondence; connection, association, interaction.
—RELATED: tactile.

touching adj. ☞ MOVING 2.

touchy adj. **1** SENSITIVE, over-sensitive, hypersensitive, easily offended, thin-skinned, high-strung, tense; irritable, dyspeptic, tetchy, testy, crotchety, peevish, waspish, querulous, bad-tempered, petulant, pettish, cranky, fractious, choleric. **2** DELICATE, sensitive, tricky, ticklish, thorny, prickly, embarrassing, awkward, difficult; contentious, controversial.
—OPPOSITES: affable.

tough adj. **1** DURABLE, strong, resilient, sturdy, rugged, solid, stout, long-lasting, heavy-duty, industrial-strength, well-built, made to last. **2** CHEWY, leathery, gristly, stringy, fibrous. **3** ROBUST, resilient, strong, hardy, rugged, flinty, fit; stalwart, tough as nails. **4** STRICT, stern, severe, stringent, rigorous, hard, firm, hard-hitting, uncompromising; unsentimental, unsympathetic. **5** ARDUOUS, onerous, strenuous, gruelling, exacting, difficult, demanding, hard, taxing, tiring, exhausting, punishing, laborious, stressful, back-breaking, Herculean. **6** DIFFICULT, hard, heavy, knotty, thorny, tricky.
—OPPOSITES: soft, weak, easy.

tour n. **1** TRIP, excursion, journey, expedition, jaunt, outing; trek, safari. **2** VISIT, inspection, guided tour.
▸ v. **1** TRAVEL AROUND, explore, discover, vacation in, holiday in. **2** VISIT, go around, walk round, inspect; informal check out.

tourist n. VACATIONER, traveller, sightseer, visitor, backpacker, globetrotter, day tripper, out-of-towner.
—OPPOSITES: local.

tournament n. ☞ COMPETITION 1.

tow v. PULL, haul, drag, draw, tug, lug.
□ **in tow** IN ATTENDANCE, by one's side, alongside, in one's charge; accompanying, following, tagging along.

towering adj. **1** HIGH, tall, lofty, soaring, sky-high, multi-storey; giant, gigantic, enormous, huge, massive; informal ginormous. **2** OUTSTANDING, pre-eminent, leading, foremost, finest, top, surpassing, supreme, great, incomparable, unrivalled, unsurpassed, peerless.

toxic adj. ☞ POISONOUS.
—OPPOSITES: harmless.

trace v. **1** TRACK DOWN, find, discover, detect, unearth, turn up, hunt down, ferret out. **2** DRAW, outline, mark, sketch. **3** OUTLINE, map out, follow, sketch out, delineate, depict, show, indicate.
▸ n. **1** VESTIGE, sign, mark, indication, evidence, clue; trail, tracks, marks, prints, footprints, spoor; remains, remnant, relic. **2** BIT, touch, hint, suggestion, suspicion, shadow, whiff, whisper; drop, dash, tinge, soupçon, scintilla, ounce, speck, spot, crumb, shred, iota, jot, whit,

scrap; smidgen, tad, grain, atom, mite, titch.

track n. **1** PATH, pathway, footpath, lane, trail, (West) monkey trail♣, route, portage trail, way, course. **2** COURSE, racetrack, raceway; velodrome. **3** TRACES, marks, prints, footprints, trail, spoor. **4** COURSE, path, line, route, way, trajectory, wake. **5** RAIL, line, railway line, steel♣. **6** SONG, recording, number, piece.
▶ v. FOLLOW, trail, trace, pursue, shadow, stalk, keep an eye on, keep in sight; *informal* tail.
□ **keep track of** MONITOR, follow, keep up with, keep an eye on; keep in touch with, keep up to date with; *informal* keep tabs on.
track down DISCOVER, find, detect, hunt down/out, unearth, uncover, turn up, dig up, ferret out, bring to light. **on track** ON COURSE, on an even keel, on schedule.

trade n. **1** COMMERCE, buying and selling, dealing, traffic, trafficking, business, marketing, merchandising; dealings, transactions, deal-making. **2** EXCHANGE, transaction, swap, handover. **3** CRAFT, occupation, job, career, profession, business, line (of work), métier, vocation, calling, walk of life, field; work, employment, livelihood.
—RELATED: mercantile.
▶ v. **1** DEAL, buy and sell, traffic, market, merchandise, peddle, vend, hawk, flog. **2** OPERATE, run, do business. **3** SWAP, exchange, switch; barter, trade in.

trader n. DEALER, merchant, buyer, seller, buyer and seller, marketeer, merchandiser, broker, agent; distributor, vendor, hawker, peddler, salesman/woman, purveyor, supplier, trafficker; shopkeeper, retailer, wholesaler; wheeler-dealer.

tradition n. **1** HISTORICAL CONVENTION, unwritten law, mores; oral history, lore, folklore. **2** CUSTOM, practice, convention, ritual, observance, way, usage, habit, institution.

traditional adj. **1** LONG-ESTABLISHED, customary, time-honoured, established, classic, accustomed, standard, regular, normal, conventional, usual, orthodox, habitual, set, fixed, routine, ritual; old, age-old, ancestral. **2** HANDED-DOWN, folk, unwritten, oral.

tragedy n. DISASTER, calamity, catastrophe, cataclysm, misfortune, mishap, blow, trial, tribulation, affliction, adversity.

tragic adj. **1** DISASTROUS, calamitous, catastrophic, cataclysmic, devastating, terrible, dreadful, awful, appalling, dismal, horrendous; fatal, deadly, mortal, lethal. **2** SAD, unhappy, pathetic, moving, distressing, depressing, painful, harrowing, heart-rending, piteous, wretched, sorry; melancholy, doleful, mournful, miserable, gut-wrenching. **3** REGRETTABLE, shameful, terrible, horrible, awful, deplorable, lamentable, piteous, dreadful, grievous.
—OPPOSITES: fortunate, happy.

trail n. **1** SERIES, string, chain, succession, sequence; aftermath, wake. **2** TRACK, spoor, path, scent;

traces, marks, signs, prints, footprints. **4** LINE, column, train, file, procession, string, chain, convoy; lineup. **5** PATH, pathway, way, footpath, walk, (*West*) monkey trail✲, track, portage trail, course, route.
▸ *v.* **1** DRAG, sweep, swish, be drawn; dangle, hang (down), droop. **2** HANG, droop, fall, spill, cascade. **3** FOLLOW, pursue, track, shadow, stalk, hunt (down); *informal* tail. **4** LOSE, be down, be behind, lag behind. **5** FADE, tail off/away, grow faint, die away, dwindle, taper off, subside, peter out, fizzle out.

train *v.* **1** ☞ TEACH. **2** STUDY, learn, prepare, take instruction. **3** EXERCISE, do exercises, work out, get into shape, practise, prepare. **4** AIM, point, direct, level, focus; take aim, zero in on.

trait *n.* ☞ CHARACTERISTIC.

traitor *n.* BETRAYER, backstabber, double-crosser, renegade, Judas, quisling, fifth columnist; turncoat, defector, deserter; collaborator, informer, fink, mole, snitch, double agent; *informal* snake in the grass, two-timer.

trample *v.* **1** TREAD, tramp, stamp, stomp, walk over; squash, crush, flatten. **2** TREAT WITH CONTEMPT, disregard, show no consideration for, abuse; encroach on, infringe.

trance *n.* DAZE, stupor, hypnotic state, half-conscious state, dream, reverie, fugue state.

tranquil *adj.* **1** PEACEFUL, calm, calming, still, serene, placid, restful, quiet, relaxing, undisturbed, limpid, pacific. **2** ☞ CALM **1**.
—OPPOSITES: busy, excitable.

tranquilizer *n.* ☞ SEDATIVE.
—OPPOSITES: stimulant.

transcend *v.* **1** GO BEYOND, rise above, cut across. **2** ☞ SURPASS.

transfer *v.* **1** MOVE, convey, take, bring, shift, remove, carry, transport; transplant, relocate, resettle. **2** HAND OVER, pass on, make over, turn over, sign over, consign, devolve, assign, delegate.

transform *v.* CHANGE, alter, convert, metamorphose, transfigure, transmute, mutate; revolutionize, overhaul; remodel, reshape, redo, reconstruct, rebuild, reorganize, rearrange, rework, renew, revamp, remake, retool; *informal* transmogrify, morph.

transformation *n.* CHANGE, alteration, mutation, conversion, metamorphosis, transfiguration, transmutation, sea change; revolution, overhaul; remodelling, reshaping, redoing, reconstruction, rebuilding, reorganization, rearrangement, reworking, renewal, revamp, remaking, remake; *informal* transmogrification, morphing.

transient *adj.* TRANSITORY, temporary, short-lived, short-term, ephemeral, impermanent, brief, short, momentary, fleeting, passing, cursory, here today and gone tomorrow; *literary* evanescent, fugitive.
▸ *n.* HOBO, tramp, vagrant, vagabond, street person, homeless person, down-and-out; drifter, derelict, bum, bag lady.
—OPPOSITES: permanent.

translate *v.* **1** RENDER, put, express; transcribe, transliterate; interpret. **2** RENDER, paraphrase, reword, rephrase, convert, decipher, decode, gloss, explain. **3** ADAPT, change, convert, transform, alter, turn, transmute; *informal* transmogrify, morph.

transmission *n.* SPREAD, transferral, communication, conveyance; dissemination, circulation, transference.

transmit *v.* **1** TRANSFER, pass on, hand on, communicate, convey, impart, channel, carry, relay, forward, dispatch; disseminate, spread, circulate. **2** BROADCAST, relay, send out, air, televise.

transparent *adj.* **1** CLEAR, crystal clear, see-through, translucent, pellucid, limpid, glassy, vitreous. **2** SEE-THROUGH, sheer, filmy, gauzy, diaphanous, translucent. **3** ☞ OBVIOUS.
—OPPOSITES: opaque, obscure.

transport *v.* CONVEY, carry, bring, take, transfer, move, shift, shuttle, send, deliver, bear, ship, ferry, haul; *informal* cart.

trap *n.* **1** SNARE, net, mesh, deadfall, leghold (trap), pitfall. **2** TRICK, ploy, ruse, deception, subterfuge; booby trap, ambush, set-up.
▸ *v.* **1** SNARE, entrap, ensnare, lay a trap for; capture, catch, bag, corner, ambush. **2** CONFINE, cut off, corner, shut in, pen in, hem in; imprison, hold captive. **3** TRICK, dupe, deceive, lure, inveigle, beguile, fool, hoodwink; catch out, trip up.

trash *n.* **1** ☞ LITTER 1. **2** JUNK, dross, dreck, drivel, nonsense, trivia, pulp (fiction), pap, garbage, rubbish; *informal* crap, schlock.
▸ *v.* **1** WRECK, ruin, destroy, wreak havoc on, devastate; vandalize, tear up, bust up, smash; *informal* total. **2** ☞ CRITICIZE.

traumatic *adj.* DISTURBING, shocking, distressing, upsetting, heartbreaking, painful, scarring, jolting, agonizing, hurtful, stressful, damaging, injurious, harmful, awful, terrible, devastating, harrowing.

travel *v.* **1** JOURNEY, tour, take a trip, voyage, explore, go sightseeing, backpack, cruise, drive, fly, go, go on an expedition, hike, make one's way, ride, roam, rove, sail, trek; *archaic* peregrinate. **2** JOURNEY THROUGH, cross, traverse, cover; roam, wander, rove, range, trek. **3** MOVE, be transmitted.
▸ *n.* JOURNEYS, expeditions, trips, tours, excursions, voyages, treks, safaris, explorations, wanderings, odysseys, pilgrimages, jaunts, junkets; travelling, touring, sightseeing, backpacking, globe-trotting, gallivanting; *archaic* peregrinations.

traveller *n.* TOURIST, vacationer, tripper, holidaymaker, sightseer, visitor, globetrotter, backpacker; pilgrim, wanderer, drifter, nomad, migrant; passenger, commuter, fare.

treacherous *adj.* **1** TRAITOROUS, disloyal, faithless, unfaithful, duplicitous, deceitful, deceptive, false, backstabbing, double-crossing, double-dealing, two-faced, weaselly, untrustworthy, unreliable; apostate, renegade,

two-timing; *literary* perfidious.
2 ☞ HAZARDOUS.
—OPPOSITES: loyal, faithful,
reliable.

treason *n.* TREACHERY, disloyalty,
betrayal, faithlessness; sedition,
subversion, mutiny, rebellion;
high treason, lèse-majesté;
apostasy; *literary* perfidy.
—OPPOSITES: allegiance, loyalty.

treasure *n.* **1** RICHES, valuables,
jewels, gems, gold, silver, precious
metals, money, cash; wealth,
fortune; treasure trove. **2** VALUABLE
OBJECT, valuable, work of art,
masterpiece, precious item.
3 (*informal*) PARAGON, gem, angel,
find, star, one of a kind, one in a
million.
▶ *v.* CHERISH, hold dear, prize, value
greatly; adore, dote on, love, be
devoted to, worship, venerate.

treat *v.* **1** BEHAVE TOWARDS, act
towards; deal with, handle; *literary*
use. **2** REGARD, consider, view,
look upon, think of. **3** TACKLE, deal
with, handle, discuss, present,
explore, investigate, approach;
consider, study, analyze. **4** GIVE
MEDICAL CARE TO, nurse, care for;
tend, help, give treatment to,
attend to, administer to;
medicate. **5** CURE, heal, remedy;
fight, combat. **6** BUY, take out for,
give; pay for; entertain, wine and
dine; foot the bill for, pick up the
tab for. **7** REGALE WITH, entertain
with/by, fete with, amuse with,
divert with.
▶ *n.* **1** CELEBRATION, entertainment,
amusement; surprise; party,
excursion, outing, special event.
2 PRESENT, gift; delicacy, luxury,
indulgence, extravagance, guilty

pleasure; *informal* goodie.
3 PLEASURE, delight, boon, thrill,
joy.

treatment *n.* **1** BEHAVIOUR
TOWARDS, conduct towards;
handling of, dealings with,
management of. **2** MEDICAL CARE,
therapy, nursing, ministrations;
medication, drugs, medicaments;
cure, remedy. **3** DISCUSSION,
handling, investigation,
exploration, consideration, study,
analysis, critique; approach,
methodology.

treaty *n.* AGREEMENT, settlement,
pact, deal, entente, concordat,
accord, protocol, convention,
contract, covenant, bargain,
pledge; concord, compact.

tremble *v.* **1** SHAKE, shake like a
leaf, quiver, twitch, jerk; quaver,
waver. **2** SHAKE, shudder, judder,
quake, wobble, rock, vibrate,
move, sway, totter, teeter.

trend *n.* **1** TENDENCY, movement,
drift, swing, shift, course, current,
direction, progression,
inclination, leaning; bias, bent.
2 FASHION, vogue, style, mode,
craze, mania, rage; *informal* fad,
thing, flavour of the month.

trendy *adj.* ☞ FASHIONABLE.
—OPPOSITES: unfashionable.

trial *n.* **1** COURT CASE, case,
assize✦, lawsuit, suit, hearing,
inquiry, tribunal, litigation, (legal/
judicial) proceedings, legal action;
court martial; appeal, retrial.
2 TEST, tryout, experiment, pilot
study; examination, check,
assessment, evaluation, appraisal;
trial/test period, trial/test run,
beta test, dry run. **3** ☞ NUISANCE.
4 ☞ ADVERSITY.

tribute *n.* **1** ACCOLADE, praise, commendation, salute, testimonial, homage, eulogy, paean, panegyric, toast; congratulations, compliments, plaudits, appreciation; gift, present, offering; bouquet; *formal* encomium. **2** TESTIMONY, indication, manifestation, testament, evidence, proof, attestation.
—OPPOSITES: criticism, condemnation.
□**pay tribute to** PRAISE, sing the praises of, speak highly of, commend, acclaim, tip one's hat to, applaud, salute, honour, show appreciation of, recognize, acknowledge, pay homage to, extol; *formal* laud.

trick *n.* **1** STRATAGEM, ploy, ruse, scheme, device, manoeuvre, contrivance, machination, artifice, wile, dodge; deceit, deception, trickery, subterfuge, shenanigan, chicanery, swindle, hoax, fraud, confidence trick, con (trick), set-up, rip-off, game, scam, sting, flim-flam, bunco. **2** PRACTICAL JOKE, joke, prank, jape, spoof, gag, put-on. **3** FEAT, stunt; (**tricks**) SLEIGHT OF HAND, legerdemain, prestidigitation; magic. **4** ILLUSION, optical illusion, figment of the imagination; mirage. **5** KNACK, art, skill, technique; secret, short cut.
▸ *v.* DECEIVE, delude, hoodwink, mislead, take in, dupe, fool, double-cross, cheat, defraud, swindle, catch out, gull, hoax, bamboozle, con, diddle, rook, put one over on, pull a fast one on, pull the wool over someone's eyes, take for a ride, shanghai,

shaft, flim-flam, sucker, snooker, stiff, euchre, hornswoggle; *literary* cozen.

trickery *n.* DECEPTION, deceit, dishonesty, cheating, duplicity, double-dealing, legerdemain, sleight of hand, guile, craftiness, deviousness, subterfuge, skulduggery, chicanery, fraud, fraudulence, swindling; *formal* pettifoggery; *informal* monkey business, funny business.
—OPPOSITES: honesty.

trickle *v.* DRIP, dribble, ooze, leak, seep, percolate, spill.
—OPPOSITES: pour, gush.
▸ *n.* DRIBBLE, drip, thin stream, rivulet.

tricky *adj.* DIFFICULT, awkward, problematic, delicate, ticklish, sensitive, embarrassing, touchy; risky, uncertain, precarious, touch-and-go; thorny, knotty, sticky, dicey.

trim *v.* **1** CUT, crop, bob, shorten, clip, snip, shear, barber; neaten, shape, tidy up. **2** CUT OFF, remove, take off, chop off, lop off; prune. **3** REDUCE, decrease, cut down, cut back on, scale down, prune, slim down, pare down, dock. **4** SHORTEN, abridge, condense, abbreviate, telescope, truncate. **5** DECORATE, adorn, ornament, embellish; edge, pipe, border, hem, fringe.
▸ *n.* **1** DECORATION, trimming, ornamentation, adornment, embellishment; border, edging, piping, rickrack, hem, fringe, frill, frippery. **2** HAIRCUT, cut, barbering, clip, snip; pruning, tidying up.
▸ *adj.* **1** NEAT, tidy, neat and tidy, orderly, in (good) order,

uncluttered, well-kept, well-maintained, shipshape, spruce, in apple-pie order, immaculate, spic and span. **2** SLIM, in shape, slender, lean, sleek, willowy, lissome, svelte; streamlined.
—OPPOSITES: untidy, messy.

trinket n. KNICK-KNACK, bauble, ornament, curio, trifle, toy, novelty, gewgaw, tchotchke.

trip v. **1** STUMBLE, lose one's footing, catch one's foot, slip, lose one's balance, fall (down), tumble, topple, take a spill, wipe out. **2** MAKE A MISTAKE, miscalculate, make a blunder, blunder, go wrong, make an error, err; informal slip up, screw up, make a boo-boo, goof up, mess up, fluff.
▶ n. **1** EXCURSION, outing, jaunt; HOLIDAY, visit, tour, journey, expedition, voyage; drive, run, ride, day out, day trip, road trip, cruise, junket, spin, crossing, flight, globe-trotting, odyssey, passage, pilgrimage, travels, trek, wandering; peregrination. **2** STUMBLE, slip, misstep, false step; fall, tumble, spill.

trite adj. ☞ BANAL.
—OPPOSITES: original, imaginative.

triumphant adj. **1** VICTORIOUS, successful, winning, conquering, all-conquering; undefeated, unbeaten. **2** JUBILANT, exultant, elated, rejoicing, joyful, joyous, delighted, gleeful, proud, gloating.
—OPPOSITES: unsuccessful, despondent.

trivial adj. UNIMPORTANT, banal, trite, commonplace, insignificant, inconsequential, minor, of no account, of no consequence, of no

importance; incidental, inessential, non-essential, petty, trifling, trumpery, pettifogging, footling, small, slight, little, inconsiderable, negligible, paltry, nugatory, piddling, picayune, nickel-and-dime, penny-ante, frivolous, piffling, silly; Mickey Mouse.
—OPPOSITES: important, significant, serious.

trouble n. **1** PROBLEMS, difficulty, bother, inconvenience, worry, concern, anxiety, distress, stress, strife, agitation, harassment, hassle, unpleasantness. **2** PROBLEM, misfortune, difficulty, trial, tribulation, trauma, burden, pain, woe, grief, heartache, misery, affliction, vexation, suffering. **3** EFFORT, inconvenience, fuss, bother, exertion, work, labour; pains, care, attention, thought. **4** ☞ NUISANCE.
▶ v. **1** ☞ WORRY v. **2**. **2** BE AFFLICTED BY, be burdened with; suffer from, be cursed with, be plagued by. **3** WORRY, upset oneself, fret, be anxious, be concerned, concern oneself.

troublemaker n. RABBLE-ROUSER, rogue, scourge, agitator, agent provocateur, ringleader; incendiary, firebrand, demagogue; scandalmonger, gossipmonger, meddler, nuisance, mischief-maker, hellraiser; informal badass.

troublesome adj. **1** ANNOYING, irritating, exasperating, maddening, infuriating, irksome, pesky, vexatious, vexing, bothersome, nettlesome, tiresome, worrying, worrisome, disturbing, upsetting, niggling,

nagging; difficult, awkward, problematic, taxing; *informal* aggravating. **2** DIFFICULT, awkward, trying, demanding, uncooperative, rebellious, unmanageable, unruly, obstreperous, perverse, contrary, disruptive, badly behaved, disobedient, naughty, recalcitrant; fussy, finicky; *formal* refractory.
—OPPOSITES: simple, co-operative.

truce *n.* CEASEFIRE, armistice, suspension of hostilities, peace, entente; respite, lull; *informal* let-up.

true *adj.* **1** CORRECT, accurate, right, verifiable, in accordance with the facts, what actually/really happened, well-documented, the case, so; literal, factual, unvarnished. **2** GENUINE, authentic, real, actual, bona fide, proper; honest-to-goodness, kosher, legit, the real McCoy. **3** RIGHTFUL, legitimate, legal, lawful, authorized, bona fide, de jure. **4** SINCERE, genuine, real, unfeigned, heartfelt, hearty, from the heart. **5** LOYAL, faithful, constant, devoted, staunch, steadfast, true-blue, unswerving, unwavering; trustworthy, trusty, reliable, dependable. **6** ACCURATE, true to life, faithful, telling it like it is, fact-based, realistic, close, lifelike.
—OPPOSITES: untrue, false, disloyal, inaccurate.

trust *n.* CONFIDENCE, belief, faith, certainty, assurance, conviction, credence; reliance.
—OPPOSITES: distrust, mistrust, doubt.
▶ *v.* **1** PUT ONE'S TRUST IN, have faith in, have (every) confidence in, believe in, pin one's hopes/faith on, confide in. **2** RELY ON, depend on, bank on, count on, be sure of. **3** HOPE, expect, take it, assume, presume, suppose. **4** ENTRUST, consign, commit, give, hand over, turn over, assign.
—OPPOSITES: distrust, mistrust, doubt.

trustworthy *adj.* RELIABLE, dependable, honest, honourable, upright, principled, true, truthful, as good as one's word, ethical, virtuous, incorruptible, unimpeachable, above suspicion; responsible, sensible, level-headed; loyal, faithful, staunch, steadfast, trusty; safe, sound, reputable, discreet; *informal* on the level, straight-up.
—OPPOSITES: unreliable.

truth *n.* VERACITY, truthfulness, verity, sincerity, candour, honesty; accuracy, correctness, validity, factuality, authenticity.
—OPPOSITES: lies, fiction, falsehood.

truthful *adj.* **1** HONEST, sincere, trustworthy, genuine; candid, frank, straight-shooting, open, forthright, straight, upfront, on the level, on the up and up. **2** ☞ TRUE 1.
—OPPOSITES: deceitful, untrue.

try *v.* **1** ATTEMPT, endeavour, venture, make an effort, exert oneself, strive, do one's best, do one's utmost, move heaven and earth; undertake, aim, take it upon oneself, have a go, give it one's best shot, bend over backwards, bust a gut, do one's damnedest, pull out all the stops, go all out, knock oneself out; *formal*

essay. **2** TEST, put to the test,
sample, taste, inspect, investigate,
examine, appraise, evaluate,
assess; *informal* check out, give
something a whirl, test drive.
3 TAX, strain, test, stretch, sap,
drain, exhaust, wear out.
4 ADJUDICATE, consider, hear,
adjudge, examine.
▸ *n.* ATTEMPT, effort, endeavour;
informal go, shot, crack, stab; *formal*
essay.

trying *adj.* **1** STRESSFUL, taxing,
demanding, difficult, tough, hard,
pressured, frustrating, fraught;
arduous, gruelling, tiring,
exhausting; *informal* hellish.
2 ☞ ANNOYING.
—OPPOSITES: easy,
accommodating.

tumble *v.* **1** FALL (OVER/DOWN),
topple over, lose one's balance,
keel over, take a spill, go
headlong, go head over heels, trip
(up), stumble; *informal* come a
cropper. **2** HURRY, rush, scramble,
scurry, bound, pile, bundle. **3**
CASCADE, fall, flow, pour, spill,
stream. **4** PLUMMET, plunge, fall,
dive, nosedive, drop, slump, slide,
decrease, decline, crash.
—OPPOSITES: rise.
▸ *n.* **1** FALL, trip, spill; *informal*
nosedive. **2** DROP, fall, plunge,
dive, nosedive, slump, decline,
collapse, crash; toboggan slide❖.
—OPPOSITES: rise.

tumour *n.* CANCEROUS GROWTH,
malignant growth, cancer,
malignancy; lump, growth,
swelling, fibroid; *Medicine*
carcinoma, sarcoma.
—RELATED: onco-, -oma.

tune *n.* MELODY, air, strain, theme;
song, jingle, ditty.
▸ *v.* **1** ADJUST, fine-tune, tune up.
2 ATTUNE, adapt, adjust, fine-tune;
regulate, modulate.

tuneful *adj.* ☞ MELODIOUS.

turbulent *adj.* **1** TEMPESTUOUS,
stormy, unstable, unsettled,
tumultuous, chaotic; violent,
anarchic, lawless. **2** ROUGH,
stormy, tempestuous, storm-
tossed, heavy, violent, wild,
roiling, raging, seething, choppy,
agitated, boisterous.
—OPPOSITES: peaceful, calm.

turmoil *n.* CONFUSION, upheaval,
turbulence, tumult, disorder,
disturbance, agitation, ferment,
unrest, disquiet, trouble,
disruption, chaos, mayhem;
uncertainty.
—OPPOSITES: peace.

turn *v.* **1** GO AROUND, revolve,
rotate, spin, roll, circle, wheel,
whirl, twirl, gyrate, swivel, pivot.
2 CHANGE DIRECTION, change
course, make a U-turn, about-face,
turn about/round, pull a U-ey, do a
one-eighty. **3** GO ROUND, round,
negotiate, take. **4** BEND, curve,
wind, veer, twist, meander, snake,
zigzag. **5** AIM AT, point at, level at,
direct at, train on. **6** SPRAIN, twist,
wrench; hurt. **7** BECOME, develop
into, turn out to be; be
transformed into, metamorphose
into, descend into, grow into.
8 BECOME, go, grow, get.
9 CONVERT, change, transform,
make; adapt, modify, rebuild,
reconstruct. **10** REACH, get to,
become, hit. **11** TAKE UP, become
involved in, go into, enter,
undertake. **12** MOVE ON TO, go on

to, proceed to, consider, attend to, address; take up, switch to.
▶ *n.* **1** ROTATION, revolution, spin, whirl, gyration, swivel. **2** CHANGE OF DIRECTION, veer, divergence. **3** BEND, corner, turning, turnoff, junction, crossroads.
4 OPPORTUNITY, chance, say; stint, time; try, go, shot, kick at the can/cat✦, stab, crack. **5** SERVICE, deed, act; favour, kindness.
▢**in turn** ONE AFTER THE OTHER, one by one, one at a time, in succession, successively, sequentially. **turn of events** DEVELOPMENT, incident, occurrence, happening, circumstance, surprise. **turn against someone** BECOME HOSTILE TO, take a dislike to, betray, double-cross. **turn someone away** SEND AWAY, reject, rebuff, repel, cold-shoulder; *informal* send packing. **turn someone in** BETRAY, inform on, denounce, sell out, stab someone in the back; blow the whistle on, rat on, squeal on, finger. **turn someone off** PUT OFF, leave cold, repel, disgust, revolt, offend; disenchant, alienate; *bore, gross out.* **turn on** DEPEND ON, rest on, hinge on, be contingent on, be decided by. **turn someone on** ☞ AROUSE 2. **turn someone on to** INTRODUCE SOMEONE TO, get someone into, pique someone's interest in. **turn on someone** ATTACK, assault, pounce on, set upon, set about, let fly at, turn on, round on, lash out at, hit out at, belabour, fall on; *informal* lay into, tear into, lace into, sail into, pitch into, wade into, let someone have it, jump, have a go at, light into, bite someone's head off, jump down someone's throat. **turn out 1** COME, be present, attend, appear, turn up, arrive; assemble, gather, show up. **2** TRANSPIRE, emerge, come to light, become apparent, become clear. **3** HAPPEN, occur, come about; develop, proceed; work out, come out, end up, pan out, result. **turn up 1** BE FOUND, be discovered, be located, reappear. **2** ARRIVE, appear, present oneself, show (up), show one's face. **3** PRESENT ITSELF, offer itself, occur, happen, crop up, appear.

twilight *n.* **1** DUSK, sunset, sundown, nightfall, evening, close of day; *literary* eventide, gloaming. **2** HALF-LIGHT, semi-darkness, gloom. **3** DECLINE, waning, ebb; autumn, final years, tail end.
—OPPOSITES: dawn.
▶ *adj.* SHADOWY, dark, shady, dim, gloomy, obscure, crepuscular, twilit.

twin *n.* DUPLICATE, double, carbon copy, exact likeness, mirror image, replica, look-alike, doppelgänger, clone; counterpart, match, pair; *informal* dead ringer, spitting image.
▶ *adj.* **1** MATCHING, identical, matched, paired. **2** TWOFOLD, double, dual; related, linked, connected; corresponding, parallel, complementary, equivalent.
▶ *v.* COMBINE, join, link, couple, pair.

twist *v.* **1** CRUMPLE, crush, buckle, mangle, warp, deform, distort. **2** CONTORT, screw up. **3** WRING, squeeze. **4** TURN (AROUND), swivel (around), spin (around), pivot, rotate, revolve. **5** WRIGGLE, squirm, worm one's way, wiggle. **6** SPRAIN, wrench, turn. **7** DISTORT, misrepresent, change, alter, pervert, falsify, warp, skew, misinterpret, misconstrue, misstate, misquote; garble. **8** TWIDDLE, adjust, turn, rotate, swivel. **9** WIND, twirl, coil, curl, wrap. **10** INTERTWINE, twine, interlace, weave, plait, braid, coil, wind. **11** WIND, bend, curve, turn, meander, weave, zigzag, swerve, snake.

▶ *n.* **1** TURN, twirl, spin, rotation; flick. **2** BEND, curve, turn, zigzag, kink. **3** CONVOLUTION, complication, complexity, intricacy; surprise, revelation. **4** INTERPRETATION, slant, outlook, angle, approach, treatment; variation, change, difference.

twitch *v.* JERK, convulse, have a spasm, quiver, tremble, shiver, shudder.

▶ *n.* **1** SPASM, convulsion, quiver, tremor, shiver, shudder, small movement; tic. **2** PULL, tug, tweak, yank, jerk. **3** PANG, twinge, dart, stab, prick.

type *n.* **1** ☞ KIND *n.* **2** PRINT, font, typeface, face, characters, lettering, letters.

typical *adj.* **1** REPRESENTATIVE, classic, quintessential, archetypal, model, prototypical, stereotypical, paradigmatic. **2** NORMAL, average, ordinary, standard, regular, routine, run-of-the-mill, conventional, unremarkable, unsurprising, unexceptional, blah. **3** CHARACTERISTIC, in keeping, usual, normal, par for the course, predictable, true to form; customary, habitual.
—OPPOSITES: atypical, unusual, exceptional, uncharacteristic.

typify *v.* EPITOMIZE, exemplify, characterize, be representative of; personify, embody, be emblematic of.

tyrannical *adj.* DICTATORIAL, despotic, autocratic, oppressive, repressive, totalitarian, undemocratic, illiberal; authoritarian, high-handed, imperious, harsh, strict, ironhanded, iron-fisted, severe, cruel, brutal, ruthless.
—OPPOSITES: liberal.

tyrant *n.* DICTATOR, despot, autocrat, authoritarian, oppressor; slave-driver, martinet, bully, megalomaniac.

Uu

ugly *adj.* **1** UNATTRACTIVE,
unappealing, unpleasant, hideous,
unlovely, unprepossessing,
unsightly, horrible, frightful,
awful, ghastly, vile, revolting,
repellent, repulsive, repugnant;
grotesque, disgusting, monstrous,
misshapen, deformed, disfigured;
homely, plain, not much to look
at. **2** UNPLEASANT, nasty,
disagreeable, alarming, tense,
charged, serious, grave;
dangerous, perilous, threatening,
menacing, hostile, ominous,
sinister. **3** HORRIBLE, despicable,
reprehensible, nasty, appalling,
objectionable, offensive,
obnoxious, vile, dishonourable,
rotten, vicious, spiteful.
—OPPOSITES: beautiful, pleasant.

ultimate *adj.* **1** EVENTUAL, final,
concluding, terminal, end;
resulting, ensuing, consequent,
subsequent. **2** ☞ FUNDAMENTAL.
3 ☞ BEST.
▶ *n.* UTMOST, optimum, last word,
height, epitome, peak, pinnacle,
acme, zenith, nonpareil, dernier
cri, ne plus ultra.

ultimately *adv.* **1** EVENTUALLY, in
the end, in the long run, at
length, finally, sooner or later, in
time, in the fullness of time,
when all is said and done, one
day, some day, sometime, over the
long haul; *informal* when push
comes to shove. **2** FUNDAMENTALLY,

basically, primarily, essentially, at
heart, deep down.

unable *adj.* POWERLESS, impotent,
at a loss, inadequate,
incompetent, unfit, unqualified,
incapable.

unacceptable *adj.* INTOLERABLE,
insufferable, unsatisfactory,
inadmissible, inappropriate,
unsuitable, undesirable,
unreasonable, insupportable;
offensive, obnoxious,
disagreeable, disgraceful,
deplorable, beyond the pale, bad;
a bit much, too much.
—OPPOSITES: satisfactory.

unanimous *adj.* ☞ UNITED 3.
—OPPOSITES: divided.

unauthorized *adj.* UNOFFICIAL,
unsanctioned, unlicensed,
unwarranted, unapproved,
bootleg, pirated; wildcat;
disallowed, prohibited, out of
bounds, banned, barred,
forbidden, outlawed, illegal,
illegitimate, illicit, proscribed.
—OPPOSITES: official.

unavoidable *adj.* INESCAPABLE,
inevitable, inexorable, assured,
sure, certain, predestined,
predetermined, fated, ineluctable;
necessary, compulsory, required,
obligatory, mandatory; destined,
fixed.

unaware *adj.* IGNORANT,
unknowing, unconscious,

heedless, unmindful, oblivious, incognizant, unsuspecting, uninformed, unenlightened, unwitting, innocent; inattentive, unobservant, unperceptive, blind; *informal* in the dark.
—OPPOSITES: conscious.

unbearable *adj.* INTOLERABLE, insufferable, insupportable, unendurable, unacceptable, unmanageable, overpowering, beyond endurance, unsupportable; too much (to bear).
—OPPOSITES: tolerable.

unbelievable *adj.* ☞ FAR-FETCHED.
—OPPOSITES: credible.

unbiased *adj.* IMPARTIAL, unprejudiced, neutral, non-partisan, disinterested, detached, dispassionate, objective, value-free, open-minded, equitable, even-handed, fair, open.
—OPPOSITES: prejudiced.

unbounded *adj.* UNLIMITED, boundless, limitless, illimitable; unrestrained, unrestricted, unconstrained, uncontrolled, unchecked, unbridled, rampant; untold, immeasurable, endless, unending, interminable, everlasting, infinite, inexhaustible.
—OPPOSITES: limited.

uncertain *adj.* **1** UNKNOWN, debatable, open to question, in doubt, undetermined, unsure, in the balance, up in the air; unpredictable, unforeseeable, incalculable; risky, chancy, dicey; *informal* iffy. **2** VAGUE, unclear, fuzzy, ambiguous, unknown, unascertainable, obscure, arcane.

3 ☞ CHANGEABLE. **4** UNSURE, doubtful, dubious, undecided, irresolute, hesitant, blowing hot and cold, vacillating, vague, unclear, ambivalent, of two minds. **5** HESITANT, tentative, faltering, unsure, unconfident.
—OPPOSITES: predictable, sure, confident.

uncomfortable *adj.* **1** PAINFUL, disagreeable, intolerable, unbearable, confining, cramped. **2** UNEASY, awkward, nervous, tense, ill at ease, strained, edgy, restless, embarrassed, troubled, worried, anxious, fraught, rattled, twitchy, discombobulated, antsy.
—OPPOSITES: relaxed.

uncommon *adj.* **1** UNUSUAL, abnormal, rare, atypical, unconventional, unfamiliar, strange, odd, curious, extraordinary, outlandish, novel, singular, peculiar, bizarre; alien, weird, oddball, offbeat; scarce, few and far between, exceptional, isolated, infrequent, irregular, seldom seen, out of the ordinary. **2** ☞ EXCEPTIONAL 2.

unconditional *adj.*
☞ WHOLEHEARTED.

unconscious *adj.* **1** INSENSIBLE, senseless, insentient, insensate, comatose, inert, knocked out, stunned; motionless, immobile, prostrate; *informal* out cold, out like a light, out of it, down for the count, passed out, dead to the world, blacked out, zonked out. **2** HEEDLESS, unmindful, disregarding, oblivious to, insensible to, impervious to, unaffected by, unconcerned by, indifferent to; unaware,

unknowing, ignorant of,
incognizant of. **3** SUBCONSCIOUS,
latent, suppressed, subliminal,
sleeping, dormant, inherent,
instinctive, involuntary,
uncontrolled, spontaneous;
unintentional, unthinking,
unwitting, inadvertent; *informal* gut.
—OPPOSITES: aware, voluntary.

unconventional *adj.* UNUSUAL,
irregular, unorthodox, unfamiliar,
uncommon, unwonted, out of the
ordinary, atypical, singular,
alternative, different; new, novel,
innovative, groundbreaking,
pioneering, original,
unprecedented; eccentric,
idiosyncratic, quirky, odd,
strange, bizarre, weird,
outlandish; curious; abnormal,
anomalous, aberrant,
extraordinary; nonconformist,
bohemian, avant-garde,
experimental, extreme, fringe,
innovatory, peripheral, radical,
way out; *informal* far out, offbeat, off
the wall, wacky, madcap, oddball,
zany, hippie, kooky, wacko, left-
field, off-off Broadway.
—OPPOSITES: orthodox.

uncouth *adj.* UNCIVILIZED,
uncultured, uncultivated,
unrefined, unpolished,
unsophisticated, bush-league,
common, plebeian, low, rough,
rough-hewn, coarse, loutish,
boorish, oafish, troglodyte;
churlish, uncivil, rude, impolite,
discourteous, disrespectful,
unmannerly, bad-mannered, ill-
bred, indecorous, crass, indelicate;
vulgar, crude, raunchy.
—OPPOSITES: refined.

uncover *v.* **1** EXPOSE, reveal, lay
bare; unwrap, unveil; strip,
denude. **2** DETECT, discover, come
across, stumble on, chance on,
find, turn up, unearth, dig up,
dredge up, root out, ferret out;
expose, unveil, unmask, disclose,
reveal, lay bare, make known,
make public, bring to light, blow
the lid off, blow the whistle on,
pull the plug on.

undeniable *adj.* ☞ INDISPUTABLE.
—OPPOSITES: questionable.

underestimate *v.* UNDERRATE,
undervalue, lowball, do an
injustice to, be wrong about, sell
short, play down, understate;
minimize, de-emphasize,
underemphasize, diminish, gloss
over, trivialize; miscalculate,
misjudge, misconstrue, misread.
—OPPOSITES: exaggerate.

undergo *v.* GO THROUGH,
experience, undertake, face,
submit to, be subjected to, come
in for, receive, sustain, endure,
brave, bear, tolerate, stand,
withstand, weather.

underground *adj.*
1 SUBTERRANEAN, buried, sunken,
subsurface, basement.
2 ☞ CLANDESTINE. **3** ALTERNATIVE,
radical, revolutionary,
unconventional, unorthodox,
avant-garde, counterculture,
experimental, innovative.

underhanded *adj.* ☞ DEVIOUS.

underline *v.* **1** UNDERSCORE,
mark, pick out, emphasize,
highlight. **2** ☞ EMPHASIZE.

undermine *v.* SUBVERT, undercut,
sabotage, threaten, weaken,
compromise, diminish, reduce,

impair, mar, spoil, ruin, damage, hurt, injure, cripple, sap, shake.

understand v. **1** COMPREHEND, grasp, take in, see, apprehend, ascertain, follow, make sense of, fathom, absorb, learn, see the light; unravel, decipher, get to the bottom of, interpret; *informal* work out, figure out, make head or tail of, get one's head around, get the drift of, get the picture/message, catch on to, cotton on to, latch on to, get, twig, crack, suss (out). **2** APPRECIATE, recognize, realize, acknowledge, know, be aware of, be conscious of; *informal* be wise to; *formal* be cognizant of. **3** BELIEVE, gather, take it, hear (tell), notice, see, learn; conclude, infer, assume, surmise, fancy.

understanding n.
1 COMPREHENSION, apprehension, grasp, mastery, appreciation, assimilation, absorption; knowledge, awareness, insight, skill, expertise, proficiency; *informal* know-how; *formal* cognizance.
2 BELIEF, perception, view, conviction, feeling, opinion, intuition, impression, assumption, supposition, inference, interpretation.
3 ☞ COMPASSION. **4** AGREEMENT, arrangement, deal, bargain, settlement, pledge, pact, compact, contract, covenant, bond, meeting of minds.
—OPPOSITES: ignorance, indifference.
▶ *adj.* COMPASSIONATE, sympathetic, sensitive, considerate, tender, kind, thoughtful, tolerant, patient, forbearing, lenient, merciful, forgiving, humane;

approachable, supportive, perceptive.

undertake v. TACKLE, take on, assume, accept, shoulder, handle, manage, deal with, be responsible for; engage in, take part in, go about, set about, get down to, come to grips with, embark on; attempt, try, endeavour; *informal* have a go at; *formal* essay.

undervalue v. UNDERRATE, underestimate, play down, downplay, understate, underemphasize, diminish, minimize, downgrade, reduce, brush aside, gloss over, trivialize, underprice; *informal* sell short.

undesirable *adj.* ☞ UNPLEASANT.
—OPPOSITES: pleasant, agreeable.

undisciplined *adj.* UNRULY, disorderly, disobedient, badly behaved, recalcitrant, restive, wayward, delinquent, rebellious, refractory, insubordinate, disruptive, errant, out of control, uncontrollable, wild, naughty; disorganized, unsystematic, unmethodical, lax, slapdash, slipshod, sloppy.

undisguised *adj.* OBVIOUS, evident, patent, manifest, transparent, overt, unconcealed, unmistakable, undeniable, plain, clear, clear-cut, explicit, naked, visible, perceptible, palpable; blatant, flagrant, glaring, bold.

undistinguished *adj.*
☞ ORDINARY 2.
—OPPOSITES: extraordinary.

undo v. **1** UNFASTEN, unbutton, unhook, untie, unlace; unlock, unbolt; loosen, disentangle, extricate, release, detach, free, open; disconnect, disengage,

separate. **2** REVOKE, overrule, overturn, repeal, rescind, reverse, retract, countermand, cancel, annul, nullify, invalidate, void, negate; *Law* vacate; *formal* abrogate. **3** RUIN, undermine, subvert, overturn, scotch, sabotage, spoil, impair, mar, destroy, wreck, eradicate, obliterate; cancel out, neutralize, thwart, foil, frustrate, hamper, hinder, obstruct; *informal* blow, put the kibosh on, foul up, scupper, scuttle, muck up.
—OPPOSITES: fasten, ratify, enhance.

undoubted *adj.* UNDISPUTED, unchallenged, unquestioned, indubitable, incontrovertible, irrefutable, incontestable, sure, certain, unmistakable; definite, accepted, acknowledged, recognized.

undoubtedly *adv.* DOUBTLESS, indubitably, doubtlessly, no doubt, without (a) doubt, unquestionably, without question, indisputably, undeniably, incontrovertibly, clearly, obviously, patently, certainly, definitely, surely, of course, indeed.

undue *adj.* ☞ EXCESSIVE.

uneasy *adj.* **1** ☞ ANXIOUS.
2 ☞ WORRYING. **3** TENSE, awkward, strained, fraught; precarious, unstable, insecure.
—OPPOSITES: calm, stable.

unemployed *adj.* JOBLESS, out-of-work, between jobs, unwaged, unoccupied, redundant, laid off, idle; on welfare, on pogey✦, on EI✦, on the dole.

unethical *adj.* IMMORAL, amoral, unprincipled, unscrupulous,

dishonourable, dishonest, wrong, deceitful, unconscionable, unfair, fraudulent, underhanded, wicked, evil, sneaky, corrupt; unprofessional, improper.

uneven *adj.* **1** BUMPY, rough, lumpy, stony, rocky, rugged, potholed, rutted, pitted, jagged. **2** IRREGULAR, unequal, unbalanced, misaligned, lopsided, askew, crooked, wonky, asymmetrical, unsymmetrical. **3** INCONSISTENT, variable, varying, fluctuating, irregular, erratic, patchy; choppy, unsteady. **4** ONE-SIDED, unequal, unfair, unjust, inequitable, ill-matched, unbalanced, David and Goliath.
—OPPOSITES: flat, regular, equal.

unexpected *adj.* UNFORESEEN, unanticipated, unpredicted, unlooked-for, sudden, abrupt, surprising, unannounced.

unfair *adj.* **1** UNJUST, inequitable, prejudiced, biased, discriminatory; one-sided, unequal, uneven, unbalanced, partisan, partial, skewed. **2** UNDESERVED, unmerited, uncalled for, unreasonable, unjustified. **3** UNSPORTSMANLIKE, unsporting, dirty, below the belt, underhanded, dishonourable. **4** INCONSIDERATE, thoughtless, insensitive, selfish, spiteful, mean, unkind, unreasonable; hypercritical, overcritical.
—OPPOSITES: just, justified.

unfaithful *adj.* **1** ADULTEROUS, faithless, fickle, untrue, inconstant; unchaste, cheating, philandering, two-timing. **2** DISLOYAL, treacherous, traitorous, untrustworthy,

unreliable, undependable, fair-weather, false, two-faced, double-crossing, deceitful; *literary* perfidious.
—OPPOSITES: loyal.

unfamiliar *adj.* 1 UNKNOWN, new, strange, foreign, alien; unexplored, uncharted. 2 ☞ UNCOMMON 1. 3 UNACQUAINTED, unused, unaccustomed, unversed, inexperienced, uninformed, unschooled, unenlightened, ignorant, not cognizant, new to, a stranger to.

unfashionable *adj.* OUT, out of date, outdated, old-fashioned, outmoded, out of style, dated, unstylish, passé, démodé, unhip, uncool, nerdy, dowdy, frumpy, lame, unsexy, old hat, square.

unfavourable *adj.* 1 ADVERSE, critical, hostile, inimical, unfriendly, unsympathetic, negative, scathing; discouraging, disapproving, uncomplimentary, unflattering. 2 GLOOMY, adverse, inauspicious, unpropitious, disadvantageous; unsuitable, inappropriate, inopportune.
—OPPOSITES: positive.

unfeeling *adj.* ☞ UNSYMPATHETIC 1.
—OPPOSITES: compassionate.

unfit *adj.* 1 UNQUALIFIED, unsuitable, unsuited, inappropriate, unequipped, inadequate, not designed; incapable of, unable to, not up to, not equal to, unworthy of; *informal* not cut out for, not up to scratch. 2 UNHEALTHY, out of shape, in poor condition/shape.
—OPPOSITES: suitable.

unflattering *adj.*
1 UNFAVOURABLE, uncomplimentary, harsh, unsympathetic, critical, negative, hostile, scathing. 2 UNATTRACTIVE, unbecoming, unsightly, ugly, homely, plain, ill-fitting.
—OPPOSITES: complimentary, becoming.

unfortunate *adj.* 1 UNLUCKY, hapless, jinxed, out of luck, luckless, wretched, miserable, forlorn, poor, pitiful; *informal* down on one's luck. 2 ☞ ADVERSE 1. 3 REGRETTABLE, inappropriate, unsuitable, infelicitous, unbecoming, inopportune, tactless, injudicious.
—OPPOSITES: lucky, auspicious.

unfriendly *adj.* 1 HOSTILE, disagreeable, antagonistic, aggressive; ill-natured, unpleasant, surly, sour, uncongenial; inhospitable, forbidding, unneighbourly, unwelcoming, unkind, unsympathetic; unsociable, anti-social; aloof, stiff, cold, cool, chilly, frosty, frigid, glacial, lukewarm, distant, unapproachable; *informal* standoffish, starchy. 2 UNFAVOURABLE, unhelpful, disadvantageous, unpropitious, inauspicious, hostile. 3 HARMFUL, damaging, destructive, disrespectful.
—OPPOSITES: amiable, favourable.

ungrateful *adj.* UNAPPRECIATIVE, unthankful, thankless, ungracious, churlish, ingrate.
—OPPOSITES: thankful.

unhappy *adj.* 1 SAD, miserable, sorrowful, dejected, despondent, disconsolate, crestfallen, desolate, devastated, dismal, distressed, grief-stricken, sorry for oneself,

morose, broken-hearted,
heartbroken, hurting, down,
downcast, dispirited,
downhearted, depressed,
melancholy, mournful, gloomy,
glum, lugubrious, despairing,
doleful, forlorn, woebegone,
woeful, wretched, long-faced,
joyless, cheerless; *informal* down in
the dumps/mouth, blue.
2 UNFORTUNATE, unlucky, luckless;
ill-starred, ill-fated, doomed;
regrettable, lamentable; *informal*
jinxed; *literary* star-crossed.
3 ☞ DISSATISFIED.
—OPPOSITES: cheerful.

unhealthy *adj.* **1** ☞ HARMFUL.
2 SICKLY, ill, unwell, in poor
health, ailing, sick, indisposed,
weak, wan, sallow, frail, delicate,
infirm, washed out, rundown.
3 UNWHOLESOME, morbid, macabre,
twisted, abnormal, warped,
depraved, unnatural; *informal* sick,
wrong.

unimaginable *adj.* UNTHINKABLE,
inconceivable, indescribable,
incredible, unbelievable, unheard
of, unthought of, untold, mind-
boggling, undreamed of, beyond
one's wildest dreams.

unimportant *adj.* INSIGNIFICANT,
inconsequential, insubstantial,
immaterial, trivial, minor, venial,
trifling, of little/no importance, of
little/no consequence, of no
account, no-account, irrelevant,
peripheral, extraneous, petty,
paltry, frivolous, inconsiderable,
meaningless, negligible, nugatory,
pointless, worthless, derisory,
weightless, small; *informal* piddling.

uninhabited *adj.* UNPOPULATED,
unpeopled, unsettled, vacant,
empty, unoccupied; unlived-in,
untenanted.

uninhibited *adj.* **1** UNRESTRAINED,
unrepressed, abandoned, wild,
reckless; unrestricted,
uncontrolled, unchecked,
intemperate, wanton, loose;
informal gung-ho. **2** UNRESERVED,
unrepressed, liberated,
unselfconscious, free and easy,
free-spirited, relaxed, informal,
open, outgoing, extrovert,
outspoken, candid, frank,
forthright; *informal* upfront.
—OPPOSITES: repressed.

unintentional *adj.* UNINTENDED,
accidental, inadvertent,
involuntary, unwitting,
unthinking, unpremeditated,
unconscious; random, fortuitous,
serendipitous; careless, negligent,
uncalculated, unplanned, fluky.
—OPPOSITES: deliberate.

uninterested *adj.* INDIFFERENT,
unconcerned, incurious,
uninvolved, unmoved,
unresponsive, apathetic,
lukewarm, unenthusiastic, bored;
informal couldn't-care-less.

uninteresting *adj.* ☞ BORING.
—OPPOSITES: exciting.

union *n.* **1** UNIFICATION, uniting,
joining, merging, merger, fusion,
fusing, amalgamation, coalition,
combination, synthesis, blend,
blending, mingling; MARRIAGE,
wedding, alliance; coupling.
2 ASSOCIATION, labour union, trade
union, league, guild,
confederation, federation,
brotherhood, organization.
—OPPOSITES: separation, parting.

unique *adj.* **1** DISTINCTIVE, distinct,
individual, special, idiosyncratic;

single, sole, lone, unrepeatable,
solitary, exclusive, rare,
uncommon, unusual, sui generis;
informal one-off, one-of-a-kind, once-
in-a-lifetime, one-shot.
2 ☞ EXCEPTIONAL. **3** PECULIAR,
specific, limited.

unit *n.* **1** COMPONENT, element,
building block, constituent;
subdivision. **2** QUANTITY, measure,
denomination. **3** DETACHMENT,
contingent, division, company,
squadron, corps, regiment,
brigade, platoon, battalion; cell,
faction.

unite *v.* **1** UNIFY, join, link,
connect, combine, amalgamate,
fuse, weld, bond, wed, marry,
bring together, knit together,
splice. **2** JOIN TOGETHER, join
forces, combine, band together,
ally, co-operate, collaborate, work
together, pull together, team up,
hitch up, hook up, twin.
—OPPOSITES: divide.

united *adj.* **1** UNIFIED, integrated,
amalgamated, joined, merged;
federal, confederate. **2** COMMON,
shared, joint, combined,
communal, co-operative,
collective, collaborative,
concerted. **3** UNANIMOUS, in
agreement, agreed, in unison, of
the same opinion, like-minded, as
one, in accord, in harmony, in
unity.

unity *n.* **1** UNION, unification,
integration, amalgamation;
coalition, federation,
confederation. **2** HARMONY, accord,
co-operation, collaboration,
agreement, consensus, solidarity;
formal concord, concordance.
3 ONENESS, singleness, wholeness,

uniformity, homogeneity.
—OPPOSITES: division, discord.

universal *adj.* GENERAL,
ubiquitous, comprehensive,
common, omnipresent, all-
inclusive, all-embracing, across
the board; global, worldwide,
international, widespread; *formal*
catholic.

unjust *adj.* **1** ☞ UNFAIR 1.
2 WRONGFUL, unfair, undeserved,
unmerited, unwarranted, uncalled
for, unreasonable, unjustifiable,
undue, gratuitous.
—OPPOSITES: fair.

unjustifiable *adj.*
1 ☞ INDEFENSIBLE.
2 ☞ GROUNDLESS.
—OPPOSITES: reasonable.

unkind *adj.* UNCHARITABLE,
unpleasant, disagreeable, nasty,
mean, mean-spirited, cruel,
vindictive, vicious, spiteful,
malicious, callous, unsympathetic,
unfeeling, uncaring, unsparing,
hurtful, ill-natured, hard-hearted,
cold-hearted; unfriendly, uncivil,
inconsiderate, insensitive, hostile;
base, malevolent, despicable,
contemptible; *informal* horrible,
horrid, rotten, bitchy, catty.

unknown *adj.* **1** UNCERTAIN,
undisclosed, unrevealed, secret;
undetermined, undecided,
unresolved, unsettled, unsure,
unascertained. **2** UNEXPLORED,
uncharted, unmapped,
untravelled, undiscovered,
unfamiliar, unheard of, new,
novel, strange. **3** UNIDENTIFIED,
anonymous, unnamed, nameless;
faceless, hidden. **4** OBSCURE,
unrecognized, unheard of,
unsung, overlooked, unheralded,

minor, insignificant, unimportant, forgotten, little known, nameless, undistinguished.
—OPPOSITES: familiar.

unlikely *adj.* **1** IMPROBABLE, doubtful, dubious. **2** IMPLAUSIBLE, improbable, questionable, unconvincing, far-fetched, unrealistic, incredible, unbelievable, inconceivable, unimaginable; absurd, preposterous; *informal* tall.
—OPPOSITES: probable, believable.

unlimited *adj.* **1** ☞ LIMITLESS. **2** UNRESTRICTED, unconstrained, unrestrained, unchecked, unbridled, unbounded, boundless, infinite; total, unqualified, unconditional, absolute, supreme.
—OPPOSITES: finite, restricted.

unloved *adj.* UNWANTED, uncared-for, friendless, unvalued; rejected, unwelcome, shunned, spurned, neglected, abandoned.

unlucky *adj.* **1** UNFORTUNATE, luckless, out of luck, jinxed, hapless, ill-fated, ill-starred, unhappy; *informal* down on one's luck; *literary* star-crossed. **2** UNFAVOURABLE, inauspicious, unpropitious, ominous, cursed, ill-fated, ill-omened, unfortunate, disadvantageous.
—OPPOSITES: fortunate, favourable.

unmistakable *adj.* DISTINCTIVE, distinct, telltale, indisputable, indubitable, undoubted, unambiguous, unequivocal; plain, clear, clear-cut, definite, obvious, unmissable, evident, self-evident, manifest, patent, pronounced, as plain as the nose on your face, as clear as day.

unnatural *adj.* **1** ABNORMAL, unusual, uncommon, extraordinary, strange, odd, peculiar, unorthodox, exceptional, irregular, atypical, untypical; freakish, freaky, uncanny. **2** ☞ ARTIFICIAL 1. **3** ☞ PERVERTED.
—OPPOSITES: normal.

unnecessary *adj.* UNNEEDED, inessential, not required, uncalled for, useless, unwarranted, unwanted, undesired, dispensable, unimportant, optional, extraneous, gratuitous, expendable, disposable, redundant, pointless, purposeless, excessive, needless, non-essential, superfluous.
—OPPOSITES: essential.

unpalatable *adj.* **1** UNAPPETIZING, unappealing, unsavoury, inedible, uneatable; disgusting, rancid, revolting, nauseating, tasteless, flavourless, gross. **2** DISAGREEABLE, unpleasant, regrettable, unwelcome, lamentable, hard to swallow, hard to take.
—OPPOSITES: tasty.

unparalleled *adj.*
☞ EXCEPTIONAL.

unpleasant *adj.* **1** DISAGREEABLE, irksome, troublesome, annoying, irritating, vexatious, displeasing, distressing, nasty, horrible, terrible, awful, dreadful, hateful, miserable, invidious, objectionable, offensive, obnoxious, repugnant, repulsive, repellent, revolting, abominable, foul, frightful, horrid, odious, off-putting, disgusting, distasteful,

detestable, nauseating, sickening, unpalatable, unsavoury, vile, abhorrent, loathsome, undesirable, beastly, ghastly, godawful, gross. **2** UNLIKABLE, unlovable, disagreeable; unfriendly, rude, impolite, obnoxious, nasty, spiteful, mean, mean-spirited; insufferable, unbearable, annoying, irritating.
—OPPOSITES: agreeable, likable.

unpopular *adj.* DISLIKED, friendless, unliked, unloved, loathed, despised; unwelcome, avoided, ignored, rejected, outcast, shunned, spurned, cold-shouldered, ostracized; unfashionable, unhip, out.

unpredictable *adj.*
1 UNFORESEEABLE, uncertain, unsure, doubtful, dubious, iffy, dicey, in the balance, up in the air. **2** ☞ VOLATILE.

unpremeditated *adj.* UNPLANNED, spontaneous, unprepared, impromptu, spur-of-the-moment, unrehearsed, ad lib, improvised, extemporaneous; *informal* off-the-cuff, off the top of one's head.
—OPPOSITES: planned.

unprepared *adj.* **1** UNREADY, off (one's) guard, surprised, taken aback; caught napping, caught flat-footed, caught with one's pants down. **2** UNWILLING, disinclined, loath, reluctant, resistant, opposed.
—OPPOSITES: ready, willing.

unpretentious *adj.*
1 UNAFFECTED, modest, unassuming, without airs, natural, straightforward, open, honest, sincere, frank, ingenuous.

2 SIMPLE, plain, modest, humble, unostentatious, unsophisticated, folksy, no-frills.

unprincipled *adj.* IMMORAL, unethical, amoral, unscrupulous, Machiavellian, dishonourable, dishonest, deceitful, devious, corrupt, crooked, wicked, evil, villainous, shameless, base, low; libertine, licentious.
—OPPOSITES: ethical.

unprofessional *adj.* IMPROPER, unethical, unprincipled, unscrupulous, dishonourable, disreputable, unseemly, unbecoming, indecorous; AMATEURISH, amateur, unskilled, unskilful, inexpert, unqualified, inexperienced, incompetent, second-rate, inefficient.

unpromising *adj.*
☞ INAUSPICIOUS.
—OPPOSITES: auspicious.

unquestionable *adj.*
☞ INDISPUTABLE.

unreal *adj.* ☞ IMAGINARY.

unrealistic *adj.* **1** IMPRACTICAL, impracticable, unfeasible, non-viable; unreasonable, irrational, illogical, senseless, silly, foolish, fanciful, idealistic, quixotic, romantic, starry-eyed, airy-fairy, blue-sky, pie in the sky.
2 UNLIFELIKE, unnatural, non-representational, abstract; unbelievable, implausible.
—OPPOSITES: pragmatic, lifelike.

unreasonable *adj.*
1 UNCOOPERATIVE, unhelpful, disobliging, unaccommodating, awkward, contrary, difficult; obstinate, obdurate, wilful, headstrong, pigheaded, cussed, intractable, intransigent,

inflexible, stubborn, obstructive, perverse, recalcitrant, refractory, balky, bloody-minded, bullheaded, mulish, self-willed; irrational, illogical, prejudiced, intolerant. **2** UNACCEPTABLE, preposterous, outrageous, ridiculous; excessive, impossible, immoderate, disproportionate, undue, inordinate, intolerable, unjustified, unwarranted, uncalled for.

unreliable *adj.* **1** UNDEPENDABLE, untrustworthy, irresponsible, fickle, fair-weather, capricious, erratic, unpredictable, inconstant, faithless, temperamental. **2** QUESTIONABLE, open to doubt, doubtful, dubious, suspect, unsound, tenuous, uncertain, fallible; risky, chancy, inaccurate; *informal* iffy, dicey.

unrestricted *adj.* UNLIMITED, open, free, freewheeling, clear, unhindered, unimpeded, unhampered, unchecked, unqualified, unrestrained, unconstrained, unblocked, unbounded, unconfined, rampant. —OPPOSITES: limited.

unscrupulous *adj.*
☞ UNPRINCIPLED.

unselfish *adj.* ☞ SELFLESS.

unshakeable *adj.* STEADFAST, resolute, staunch, firm, decided, determined, unswerving, unwavering; unyielding, inflexible, dogged, obstinate, obdurate, tenacious, persistent, indefatigable, tireless, unflagging, unremitting, unrelenting, relentless.

unskilled *adj.* UNTRAINED, unqualified; manual, blue-collar, labouring, menial; inexpert, inexperienced, unpractised, amateurish, unprofessional.

unsophisticated *adj.*
1 UNWORLDLY, naive, unrefined, simple, innocent, ignorant, green, immature, callow, inexperienced, childlike, artless, guileless, ingenuous, natural, unaffected, unassuming, unpretentious; *informal* cheesy. **2** SIMPLE, crude, low-tech, basic, rudimentary, primitive, rough and ready, homespun, bush-league; straightforward, uncomplicated, uninvolved.

unspoiled *adj.* IMMACULATE, perfect, pristine, virgin, unimpaired, unblemished, unharmed, undamaged, untouched, unmarked, untainted, as good as new/before.

unstable *adj.* **1** UNSTEADY, rocky, wobbly, tippy; rickety, shaky, unsafe, insecure, precarious. **2** ☞ VOLATILE 1. **3** UNBALANCED, of unsound mind, mentally ill, deranged, demented, disturbed, unhinged, volatile. —OPPOSITES: steady, firm.

unsuccessful *adj.* **1** FAILED, ineffective, ineffectual, to no effect, fruitless, profitless, unproductive, abortive; vain, futile, unavailing, to no avail, useless, pointless, worthless, luckless. **2** UNPROFITABLE, loss-making. **3** FAILED, losing, beaten; unlucky, out of luck.

unsuitable *adj.*
1 ☞ INAPPROPRIATE. **2** INOPPORTUNE, infelicitous, inappropriate, wrong, unfortunate; *formal* malapropos.

—OPPOSITES: appropriate, opportune.

unsure *adj.* **1** UNCONFIDENT, unassertive, insecure, hesitant, diffident, anxious, apprehensive. **2** UNDECIDED, irresolute, dithering, equivocating, vacillating, of two minds, wishy-washy, in a quandary. **3** DUBIOUS, doubtful, skeptical, uncertain, unconvinced. **4** NOT FIXED, undecided, uncertain.
—OPPOSITES: confident.

unsuspecting *adj.* UNSUSPICIOUS, unwary, unaware, unconscious, ignorant, unwitting, trusting, gullible, credulous, ingenuous, naive, wide-eyed.
—OPPOSITES: wary.

unsympathetic *adj.*
1 UNCARING, unconcerned, unfriendly, unfeeling, apathetic, insensitive, indifferent, unkind, pitiless, thoughtless, heartless, hard-hearted, stony, callous. **2** OPPOSED, against, (dead) set against, antagonistic, ill-disposed; *informal* anti. **3** UNLIKEABLE, dislikable, disagreeable, unpleasant, unappealing, off-putting, objectionable, unsavoury; unfriendly.
—OPPOSITES: caring.

unthinkable *adj.* UNIMAGINABLE, inconceivable, unbelievable, incredible, beyond belief, implausible, preposterous.

untidy *adj.* **1** SCRUFFY, tousled, dishevelled, unkempt, messy, disordered, disarranged, messed up, rumpled, bedraggled, uncombed, ungroomed, straggly, ruffled, tangled, matted, windblown; *informal* mussed up, raggedy. **2** DISORDERED, messy, in a mess, disorderly, disorganized, in disorder, cluttered, in a muddle, muddled, in chaos, chaotic, haywire, topsy-turvy, in disarray, at sixes and sevens; *informal* higgledy-piggledy, like a bomb went off.
—OPPOSITES: neat, orderly.

untrue *adj.* **1** FALSE, untruthful, fabricated, made up, invented, concocted, trumped up; erroneous, wrong, incorrect, inaccurate; fallacious, fictitious, unsound, unfounded, baseless, misguided. **2** ☞ DISLOYAL.
—OPPOSITES: correct, faithful.

unusual *adj.* ☞ UNCOMMON 1.
—OPPOSITES: common.

unwelcome *adj.* **1** UNWANTED, uninvited, excluded, rejected. **2** UNDESIRABLE, undesired, unpopular, unfortunate, disappointing, upsetting, distressing, disagreeable, displeasing; regrettable, deplorable, objectionable, lamentable.

unwilling *adj.* ☞ RELUCTANT.

unwise *adj.* INJUDICIOUS, ill-advised, ill-judged, imprudent, inexpedient, foolish, silly, inadvisable, impolitic, misguided, foolhardy, irresponsible, crazy, idiotic, irrational, mindless, senseless, stupid, thoughtless, impetuous, rash, hasty, overhasty, ill-considered, reckless.
—OPPOSITES: sensible.

unworthy *adj.* **1** UNDESERVING, ineligible, unqualified, unfit. **2** UNBECOMING, unsuitable, inappropriate, unbefitting, unfitting, unseemly, improper; discreditable, shameful,

dishonourable, despicable, ignoble, contemptible, reprehensible.
—opposites: deserving, becoming.

upbraid v. ☞ REPRIMAND.

upgrade v. **1** IMPROVE, modernize, update, bring up to date, make better, ameliorate, reform; rehabilitate, recondition, refurbish, spruce up, renovate, rejuvenate, overhaul; bring up to code. **2** PROMOTE, give promotion to, elevate, move up, raise.
—opposites: downgrade, demote.

upheaval n. DISRUPTION, disturbance, trouble, turbulence, disorder, confusion, turmoil, pandemonium, chaos, mayhem, cataclysm, shakeup, debacle; revolution, change, craziness.

uphold v. **1** CONFIRM, endorse, sustain, approve, agree to, support; champion, defend. **2** MAINTAIN, sustain, continue, preserve, protect, champion, defend, keep, hold to, keep alive, keep going, back (up), stand by.
—opposites: overturn, oppose.

upkeep n. ☞ MAINTENANCE 2.

upright adj. **1** ☞ VERTICAL. **2** ☞ HONEST 1.
—opposites: horizontal, dishonourable.

uproar n. **1** TURMOIL, disorder, confusion, chaos, commotion, disturbance, rumpus, ruckus, tumult, turbulence, mayhem, pandemonium, bedlam, noise, din, clamour, hubbub, racket; shouting, yelling, babel; informal hullabaloo, hoo-ha, brouhaha. **2** OUTCRY, furor, protest; fuss, reaction, backlash, commotion, hue and cry; informal hullabaloo,

stink, kerfuffle, firestorm.
—opposites: calm.

upset v. **1** DISTRESS, trouble, perturb, dismay, concern, disturb, discompose, unsettle, disconcert, disquiet, worry, make uneasy/anxious, bother, agitate, fluster, throw, ruffle, unnerve, shake; hurt, sadden, grieve; informal rattle, faze; discombobulate. **2** KNOCK OVER, overturn, upend, tip over, flip, topple (over); spill. **3** DISRUPT, interfere with, disturb, throw out, throw into confusion, throw off balance, mess with/up. **4** DEFEAT, beat, topple; surprise, embarrass.
▸ adj. **1** DISTRESSED, troubled, perturbed, dismayed, disturbed, unsettled, disconcerted, worried, bothered, anxious, agitated, flustered, ruffled, unnerved, shaken, unstrung; hurt, saddened, grieved; informal cut up, choked. **2** DISTURBED, unsettled, queasy, bad, hurting, poorly.
—opposites: unperturbed, calm.

upstart n. PARVENU, arriviste, nouveau riche, status seeker, social climber, a jumped-up ——, johnny-come-lately.

up to date adj. **1** MODERN, contemporary, the latest, state-of-the-art, cutting-edge, leading-edge, new, present-day, up-to-the-minute; advanced; mod. **2** INFORMED, up to speed, in the picture, in touch, au fait, au courant, conversant, familiar, knowledgeable, acquainted, aware, clued in.
—opposites: out of date, old-fashioned.

urbane adj. SUAVE, sophisticated, debonair, worldly, cultivated, cultured, civilized, cosmopolitan; smooth, polished, refined, self-possessed; courteous, polite, well-mannered, mannerly, civil, charming, gentlemanly, gallant. —OPPOSITES: uncouth, unsophisticated.

urge *v.* **1** ENCOURAGE, exhort, enjoin, press, entreat, implore, call on, appeal to, beg, plead with, coax; egg on, prod, prompt, spur, goad, incite, push, pressure, pressurize; *formal* adjure; *literary* beseech. **2** SPUR (ON), force, drive, impel, propel. **3** ADVISE, counsel, advocate, recommend, suggest, advance.
▸ *n.* DESIRE, wish, need, compulsion, longing, yearning, hankering, craving, appetite, hunger, thirst; fancy, impulse, impetus; *informal* yen, itch.

urgent *adj.* **1** ACUTE, pressing, dire, desperate, critical, serious, grave, intense, crying, burning, compelling, extreme, exigent, high-priority, top-priority; life-and-death. **2** INSISTENT, persistent, importunate, earnest, pleading, begging.

use *v.* **1** UTILIZE, make use of, avail oneself of, employ, work, operate, wield, ply, apply, manoeuvre, manipulate, put to use, put/press into service. **2** EXERCISE, employ, bring into play, practise, apply, exert, bring to bear. **3** TAKE ADVANTAGE OF, exploit, manipulate, take liberties with, impose on, abuse; capitalize on, profit from, trade on, milk; *informal* walk all over. **4** CONSUME, get/go through, exhaust, deplete, expend, spend; waste, fritter away, squander,

dissipate, run out of.
▸ *n.* **1** UTILIZATION, usage, application, employment, operation, manipulation. **2** ADVANTAGE, benefit, service, utility, usefulness, help, good, gain, avail, profit, value, worth, point, object, purpose, sense, reason. **3** NEED, necessity, call, demand, requirement.

used *adj.* SECOND-HAND, pre-owned, nearly new, old; worn, hand-me-down, cast-off, recycled, warmed-over.
—OPPOSITES: new.
☐ **used to** ACCUSTOMED TO, no stranger to, familiar with, at home with, in the habit of, an old hand at, experienced in, versed in, conversant with, acquainted with.

useful *adj.* **1** FUNCTIONAL, practical, handy, convenient, utilitarian, serviceable, of use, of service. **2** BENEFICIAL, advantageous, helpful, worthwhile, profitable, rewarding, productive, constructive, valuable, fruitful.
—OPPOSITES: useless, disadvantageous.

useless *adj.* **1** FUTILE, to no avail, (in) vain, pointless, to no purpose, unavailing, hopeless, ineffectual, ineffective, to no effect, fruitless, unprofitable, profitless, unproductive; *archaic* bootless. **2** UNUSABLE, broken, kaput, defunct, dud, faulty. **3** (*informal*) INCOMPETENT, inept, ineffective, incapable, unemployable, inadequate, hopeless, no-account, bad; *informal* pathetic.
—OPPOSITES: useful, beneficial, competent.

usual *adj.* HABITUAL, customary, accustomed, wonted, normal, routine, regular, standard, typical, established, set, settled, stock, conventional, traditional, expected, predictable, familiar; average, general, ordinary, everyday.
—OPPOSITES: exceptional.

usually *adv.* NORMALLY, generally, habitually, customarily, routinely, typically, ordinarily, commonly, conventionally, traditionally; as a rule, in general, more often than not, in the main, mainly, mostly, for the most part, most of the time, by and large, on the whole, nine times out of ten.

usurp *v.* **1** SEIZE, take over, take possession of, take, commandeer, wrest, assume, expropriate. **2** OUST, overthrow, remove, topple, unseat, depose, dethrone; supplant, replace.

Vv

vacant *adj.* **1** EMPTY, unoccupied, available, not in use, free, unfilled; uninhabited, untenanted. **2** BLANK, expressionless, unresponsive, emotionless, impassive, uninterested, vacuous, empty, absent, glazed, glassy; unintelligent, dull-witted, dense, brainless, empty-headed.
—OPPOSITES: full, occupied, expressive.

vacation *n.* HOLIDAY, trip, tour, break, leave, leave of absence, time off, recess, furlough, sabbatical; *formal* sojourn.

vague *adj.* **1** INDISTINCT, indefinite, indeterminate, unclear, ill-defined; hazy, fuzzy, misty, blurred, blurry, out of focus, faint, shadowy, dim, obscure, nebulous, amorphous, diaphanous. **2** IMPRECISE, rough, approximate, inexact, non-specific, generalized, ambiguous, equivocal, hazy, woolly. **3** HAZY, uncertain, undecided, unsure, unclear, unsettled, indefinite, indeterminate, unconfirmed, up in the air, speculative, sketchy. **4** ABSENT-MINDED, forgetful, dreamy, abstracted, with one's head in the clouds, scatty, scattered, not with it.
—OPPOSITES: clear, precise, certain.

vain *adj.* **1** ☞ CONCEITED. **2** ☞ FUTILE.
—OPPOSITES: modest, successful.

valid *adj.* **1** WELL-FOUNDED, sound, reasonable, rational, logical, justifiable, defensible, viable, bona fide; cogent, effective, powerful, potent, convincing, credible, forceful, strong, solid, weighty. **2** LEGALLY BINDING, lawful, legal, legitimate, official, signed and sealed, contractual; in force, current, in effect, effective; *informal* legit. **3** LEGITIMATE, authentic, authoritative, reliable, bona fide.

validate *v.* **1** PROVE, substantiate, corroborate, verify, support, back up, bear out, lend force to, confirm, justify, vindicate, authenticate. **2** RATIFY, endorse, approve, agree to, accept, authorize, legalize, legitimize, warrant, license, certify, recognize.
—OPPOSITES: disprove.

valuable *adj.* **1** PRECIOUS, costly, pricey, expensive, dear, high-priced, high-cost, high-end, upscale, big-ticket; worth its weight in gold, priceless. **2** USEFUL, helpful, beneficial, invaluable, crucial, productive, constructive, effective, advantageous, worthwhile, worthy, important.
—OPPOSITES: cheap, worthless, useless.

value n. **1** PRICE, cost, worth; market price, monetary value, face value. **2** WORTH, usefulness, advantage, benefit, gain, profit, good, help, merit, helpfulness, avail; importance, significance. **3** PRINCIPLES, ethics, moral code, morals, standards, code of behaviour.
▶ v. **1** EVALUATE, assess, estimate, appraise, price, put/set a price on. **2** THINK HIGHLY OF, have a high opinion of, hold in high regard, rate highly, esteem, set (great) store by, put stock in, appreciate, respect; prize, cherish, treasure.

valued adj. CHERISHED, treasured, dear, prized; esteemed, respected, highly regarded, appreciated, important.

vanguard n. FOREFRONT, advance guard, spearhead, front, front line, fore, van, lead, cutting edge; avant-garde, leaders, founders, founding fathers, pioneers, trailblazers, trendsetters, innovators, groundbreakers.
—OPPOSITES: rear.

vanity n. **1** CONCEIT, narcissism, self-love, self-admiration, self-absorption, self-regard, egotism; pride, arrogance, boastfulness, cockiness, swagger, conceitedness, hubris, smugness; big-headedness, egoism, self-centredness, self-obsession, self-importance, self-satisfaction; *literary* vainglory. **2** FUTILITY, uselessness, pointlessness, worthlessness, fruitlessness.
—OPPOSITES: modesty.

variable adj. ☞ CHANGEABLE.
—OPPOSITES: constant.

variation n. **1** DIFFERENCE, dissimilarity; disparity, contrast, discrepancy, imbalance; *technical* differential. **2** CHANGE, alteration, modification; diversification. **3** DEVIATION, variance, divergence, departure, fluctuation. **4** VARIANT, form, alternative form; development, adaptation, alteration, mutation, transformation, diversification, modification.

varied adj. ☞ DIVERSE.

variety n. **1** DIVERSITY, variation, diversification, heterogeneity, multifariousness, change, choice, difference. **2** ☞ ASSORTMENT. **3** ☞ KIND n.
—OPPOSITES: uniformity.

various adj. ☞ DIVERSE.

vary v. **1** DIFFER, be different, be dissimilar, conflict. **2** FLUCTUATE, rise and fall, go up and down, change, alter, shift, swing, deviate, differ. **3** MODIFY, change, alter, transform, adjust, regulate, control, tweak, set; diversify, reshape.

vast adj. ☞ HUGE.

vehement adj. PASSIONATE, forceful, ardent, impassioned, heated, spirited, urgent, fervent, violent, fierce, fiery, strong, forcible, powerful, emphatic, vigorous, intense, earnest, keen, enthusiastic, zealous.
—OPPOSITES: mild, apathetic.

veneer n. **1** SURFACE, lamination, layer, overlay, *proprietary* Arborite♣, facing, covering, finish, exterior, cladding, laminate. **2** FACADE, front, false front, show, outward display, appearance, impression, semblance, guise, disguise, mask, masquerade, pretense, camouflage, cover, window dressing.

vengeance *n.* REVENGE, retribution, retaliation, payback, requital, reprisal, satisfaction, an eye for an eye (and a tooth for a tooth).

vent *n.* DUCT, flue, shaft, well, passage, airway; outlet, inlet, opening, aperture, hole, gap, orifice.
▶ *v.* RELEASE, air, give vent to, give free rein to, let out, pour out, express, give expression to, voice, give voice to, verbalize, ventilate, discuss, talk over, communicate.

ventilate *v.* AIR, aerate, air out, oxygenate, fan; freshen, cool.

venture *n.* ENTERPRISE, undertaking, project, initiative, scheme, operation, endeavour, speculation, plunge, gamble, gambit, experiment.
▶ *v.* **1** SET OUT, go, travel, journey. **2** PUT FORWARD, advance, proffer, offer, volunteer, air, suggest, submit, propose, moot. **3** DARE, be/make so bold as, presume; take the liberty of, stick one's neck out, go out on a limb.

verbal *adj.* ORAL, spoken, stated, said, verbalized, expressed; unwritten, by word of mouth.

verbatim *adv.* WORD FOR WORD, letter for letter, line for line, to the letter, literally, exactly, precisely, accurately, closely, faithfully.

verbose *adj.* WORDY, loquacious, garrulous, talkative, voluble; long-winded, flatulent, lengthy, prolix, tautological, pleonastic, periphrastic, circumlocutory,

circuitous, wandering, discursive, digressive, rambling; *informal* mouthy, gabby, waffly, motor-mouthed.
—OPPOSITES: succinct, laconic.

verdict *n.* JUDGMENT, adjudication, decision, finding, ruling, decree, resolution, pronouncement, conclusion, opinion; *Law* determination.

verify *v.* SUBSTANTIATE, confirm, prove, corroborate, back up, bear out, justify, support, uphold, attest to, testify to, vouch for, give credence to, validate, authenticate, ratify, endorse, certify.
—OPPOSITES: refute.

versatile *adj.* ADAPTABLE, flexible, all around, multi-faceted, multi-talented, resourceful; adjustable, multi-purpose, all-purpose, handy.

version *n.* **1** ACCOUNT, report, statement, description, record, story, rendering, interpretation, explanation, understanding, reading, impression, side, take. **2** EDITION, translation, impression. **3** FORM, sort, kind, type, variety, variant, model.

vertical *adj.* UPRIGHT, erect, perpendicular, plumb, straight up and down, on end, standing, upstanding, bolt upright.
—OPPOSITES: horizontal.

verve *n.* ENTHUSIASM, vigour, energy, pep, dynamism, élan, vitality, vivacity, buoyancy, liveliness, animation, zest, sparkle, charisma, spirit, ebullience, exuberance, life, brio, gusto, eagerness, keenness, passion, zeal, relish, feeling, ardour, fire; bounce, drive, punch;

informal zing, zip, vim, pizzazz, oomph, mojo, moxie, get-up-and-go.

very *adv.* EXTREMELY, exceedingly, exceptionally, extraordinarily, tremendously, immensely, hugely, intensely, acutely, abundantly, singularly, uncommonly, decidedly, particularly, supremely, highly, remarkably, really, truly, mightily, ever so; *informal* terrifically, awfully, fearfully, terribly, devilishly, majorly, seriously, mega, ultra, damn, damned; dead, real, way, mighty, awful, darned; *archaic* exceeding.
—OPPOSITES: slightly.
▸ *adj.* **1** EXACT, actual, precise. **2** MERE, simple, pure; sheer.

veteran *n.* OLD HAND, old sweat, past master, doyen, vet; *informal* old-timer, old stager, old warhorse.
—OPPOSITES: novice.
▸ *adj.* LONG-SERVING, seasoned, old, hardened; adept, expert, well trained, practised, experienced, senior; *informal* battle-scarred.

veto *n.* REJECTION, dismissal; prohibition, proscription, embargo, ban, interdict, check; *informal* thumbs down, red light.
—OPPOSITES: approval.
▸ *v.* REJECT, turn down, throw out, dismiss; prohibit, forbid, interdict, proscribe, disallow, embargo, ban, rule out, say no to; *informal* kill, put the kibosh on, give the thumbs down to, give the red light to.
—OPPOSITES: approve.

vex *v.* ☞ ANNOY.

vibrant *adj.* **1** SPIRITED, lively, full of life, energetic, vigorous, vital, full of vim and vigour, animated, sparkling, effervescent, vivacious,

dynamic, stimulating, exciting, passionate, fiery; *informal* peppy, feisty. **2** VIVID, bright, striking, brilliant, strong, rich, colourful, bold. **3** RESONANT, sonorous, reverberant, resounding, ringing, echoing; strong, rich, full, round.
—OPPOSITES: lifeless, pale.

vibrate *v.* **1** QUIVER, shake, tremble, shiver, shudder, judder, throb, pulsate, rattle; rock, wobble, oscillate, waver, swing, sway, move to and fro.
2 REVERBERATE, resonate, resound, ring, echo.

vibration *n.* TREMOR, shaking, quivering, quaking, judder, juddering, shuddering, throb, throbbing, pulsation.

vice *n.* **1** IMMORALITY, wrongdoing, wickedness, badness, evil, iniquity, villainy, corruption, misconduct, misdeeds; sin, sinfulness, ungodliness; depravity, degeneracy, dissolution, dissipation, debauchery, decadence, lechery, perversion; crime, transgression; *formal* turpitude; *archaic* trespass.
2 SHORTCOMING, failing, flaw, fault, bad habit, defect, weakness, deficiency, limitation, imperfection, blemish, foible, frailty.
—OPPOSITES: virtue.

vicinity *n.* NEIGHBOURHOOD, surrounding area, locality, locale, (local) area, district, region, quarter, zone; environs, surroundings, precincts; *informal* neck of the woods.

vicious *adj.* **1** BRUTAL, ferocious, savage, violent, dangerous, ruthless, remorseless, merciless,

heartless, callous, cruel, harsh,
cold-blooded, inhuman, fierce,
barbarous, barbaric, brutish,
bloodthirsty, fiendish, sadistic,
monstrous, murderous,
homicidal. **2** MALICIOUS,
malevolent, malignant, malign,
spiteful, hateful, vindictive,
venomous, poisonous, rancorous,
mean, cruel, bitter, cutting,
acrimonious, hostile, nasty;
defamatory, slanderous; *informal*
catty.
—OPPOSITES: gentle, kindly.

victim *n.* **1** SUFFERER, injured
party, casualty; fatality, loss; loser.
2 TARGET, object, subject, focus,
recipient, butt. **3** LOSER, prey,
stooge, dupe, sucker, quarry, fool,
fall guy, chump; *informal* patsy, sap.
4 SACRIFICE, (burnt) offering,
scapegoat.

victimize *v.* PERSECUTE, pick on,
push around, bully, abuse,
discriminate against, ill-treat,
mistreat, maltreat, terrorize,
hector; exploit, prey on, take
advantage of, dupe, cheat, double-
cross, get at, have it in for, give
someone a hard time, hassle, lean
on, gang up on.

view *n.* **1** OUTLOOK, prospect,
panorama, vista, scene, aspect,
perspective, spectacle, sight;
scenery, landscape. **2** OPINION,
point of view, viewpoint, belief,
judgment, thinking, notion, idea,
conviction, persuasion, attitude,
feeling, sentiment, concept,
hypothesis, theory; stance,
standpoint, philosophy, doctrine,
dogma, approach, take. **3** SIGHT,
perspective, vision, visibility.
▸ *v.* **1** LOOK AT, eye, observe, gaze

at, stare at, ogle, contemplate,
watch, scan, regard, take in,
survey, inspect, scrutinize; *informal*
check out, get a load of, eyeball;
literary espy, behold. **2** CONSIDER,
regard, look upon, see, perceive,
judge, deem, reckon.
□ **in view of** CONSIDERING, bearing
in mind, taking into account, on
account of, in the light of, owing
to, because of, as a result of,
given. **on view** ON DISPLAY, on
exhibition, on show.

vigorous *adj.* **1** ROBUST, healthy,
hale and hearty, strong, sturdy,
fit; hardy, tough, athletic;
bouncing, thriving, flourishing,
blooming; energetic, lively, active,
perky, spirited, vibrant, vital,
zestful; *informal* peppy, bouncy, in
the pink. **2** STRENUOUS, powerful,
forceful, spirited, mettlesome,
determined, aggressive, two-
fisted, driving, eager, zealous,
ardent, fervent, vehement,
passionate; tough, robust,
thorough, blunt, hard-hitting;
informal punchy.
—OPPOSITES: weak, feeble.

vigour *n.* ROBUSTNESS, health,
hardiness, strength, sturdiness,
toughness; bloom, radiance,
energy, life, vitality, virility, verve,
spirit; zeal, passion,
determination, dynamism, zest,
pep, drive, force; *informal* oomph,
get-up-and-go, zing, piss and
vinegar.
—OPPOSITES: lethargy.

vile *adj.* FOUL, nasty, unpleasant,
bad, disagreeable, horrid,
horrible, dreadful, abominable,
atrocious, offensive, obnoxious,
odious, unsavoury, repulsive,

disgusting, distasteful, loathsome, hateful, nauseating, sickening; disgraceful, appalling, shocking, sorry, shabby, shameful, dishonourable, execrable, heinous, abhorrent, deplorable, monstrous, wicked, evil, iniquitous, nefarious, depraved, debased; contemptible, despicable, reprehensible; *informal* gross, godawful, lowdown, lousy; *archaic* scurvy.
—OPPOSITES: pleasant.

vilify v. DISPARAGE, denigrate, defame, run down, revile, abuse, speak ill of, criticize, condemn, denounce; malign, slander, libel, slur; *informal* tear apart/into, lay into, slam, badmouth, dis, crucify; *formal* derogate, calumniate.
—OPPOSITES: commend.

vindicate v. 1 ACQUIT, clear, absolve, exonerate; discharge, liberate, free; *informal* let off (the hook); *formal* exculpate. 2 JUSTIFY, warrant, substantiate, ratify, authenticate, verify, confirm, corroborate, prove, defend, support, back up, bear out, evidence, endorse.

vindictive adj. VENGEFUL, revengeful, unforgiving, resentful, acrimonious, bitter; spiteful, mean, rancorous, venomous, malicious, malevolent, nasty, mean-spirited, cruel, unkind; *informal* catty.
—OPPOSITES: forgiving.

violate v. 1 CONTRAVENE, breach, infringe, break, transgress, overstep, disobey, defy, flout; disregard, ignore, trample on. 2 INVADE, trespass upon, encroach upon, intrude upon; disrespect.

3 ☞ DESECRATE.
—OPPOSITES: respect.

violence n. 1 BRUTALITY, brute force, ferocity, savagery, cruelty, sadism, barbarity, brutishness. 2 FIGHTS, bloodshed, brawling, disorder, rioting, hostility, turbulence, mayhem; *informal* punch-ups. 3 FORCEFULNESS, force, power, strength, might, savagery, ferocity, brutality. 4 INTENSITY, severity, strength, force, vehemence, power, potency, fervency, ferocity, fury, fire.

violent adj. 1 BRUTAL, vicious, savage, rough, aggressive, (physically) abusive, threatening, fierce, physical, wild, ferocious; barbarous, barbaric, thuggish, pugnacious, cutthroat, homicidal, murderous, cruel. 2 POWERFUL, forceful, hard, sharp, smart, strong, vigorous, mighty, hefty; savage, ferocious, brutal, vicious. 3 INTENSE, extreme, strong, powerful, vehement, intemperate, unbridled, uncontrollable, ungovernable, inordinate, consuming, passionate. 4 GORY, gruesome, grisly, full of violence.
—OPPOSITES: gentle, weak, mild.

VIP n. CELEBRITY, famous person, very important person, personality, big name, star, superstar; dignitary, luminary, leading light, pillar of society, worthy, grandee, lion, notable, personage; *informal* heavyweight, celeb, bigwig, big shot, big cheese, honcho, top dog, megastar, big wheel, (big) kahuna, big fish, somebody, big chief, big enchilada, big gun, supremo, top banana, top brass, mucky-muck, high muckamuck.

virtue *n.* **1** GOODNESS, virtuousness, righteousness, morality, integrity, dignity, rectitude, honour, decency, respectability, nobility, worthiness, purity; principles, ethics. **2** STRONG POINT, good point, good quality, asset, forte, attribute, strength, talent, feature. **3** MERIT, advantage, benefit, usefulness, strength, efficacy, plus, point.
—OPPOSITES: vice, failing, disadvantage.

virtuous *adj.* RIGHTEOUS, good, pure, whiter than white, saintly, angelic, moral, ethical, upright, upstanding, high-minded, principled, exemplary; law-abiding, irreproachable, blameless, guiltless, unimpeachable, immaculate, honest, honourable, reputable, laudable, decent, respectable, noble, worthy, meritorious; *informal* squeaky clean.

visible *adj.* PERCEPTIBLE, perceivable, seeable, observable, noticeable, detectable, discernible; in sight, in/on view, on display; evident, apparent, manifest, transparent, plain, clear, conspicuous, obvious, patent, unmistakable, unconcealed, undisguised, prominent, salient, striking, glaring.

vision *n.* **1** EYESIGHT, sight, observation, (visual) perception; eyes; view, perspective. **2** APPARITION, hallucination, illusion, mirage, spectre,

phantom, ghost, wraith, manifestation; *literary* phantasm, shade. **3** DREAM, daydream, reverie; plan, hope; fantasy, pipe dream, delusion. **4** IMAGINATION, creativity, inventiveness, innovation, inspiration, intuition, perception, insight, foresight, prescience. **5** BEAUTIFUL SIGHT, feast for the eyes, pleasure to behold, delight, dream, beauty, picture, joy, marvel; *informal* sight for sore eyes, stunner, knockout, looker, eye-catcher, peach.

visionary *adj.* INSPIRED, imaginative, creative, inventive, ingenious, enterprising, innovative; insightful, perceptive, intuitive, prescient, discerning, shrewd, wise, clever, resourceful; idealistic, romantic.

visual *adj.* **1** OPTICAL, optic, ocular, eye; vision, sight. **2** VISIBLE, perceptible, perceivable, discernible.
▸ *n.* GRAPHIC, visual aid, image, illustration, diagram, display, show and tell.

vital *adj.* **1** ESSENTIAL, of the essence, critical, crucial, key, indispensable, integral, all-important, imperative, mandatory, requisite, urgent, pressing, burning, compelling, high-priority, life-and-death. **2** MAJOR, main, chief; essential, necessary. **3** LIVELY, energetic, active, sprightly, spry, spirited, vivacious, exuberant, bouncy, enthusiastic, vibrant, zestful, sparkling.
—OPPOSITES: unimportant, minor, listless.

vitality *n.* ☞ VERVE.

vivacious *adj.* LIVELY, spirited, bubbly, ebullient, buoyant, sparkling, lighthearted, jaunty, merry, happy, jolly, full of fun, cheery, cheerful, perky, animated, sunny, breezy, carefree, bright, enthusiastic, irrepressible, vibrant, vital, zestful, energetic, effervescent, dynamic; *informal* peppy, bouncy, upbeat, chirpy.
—OPPOSITES: dull.

vivid *adj.* **1** BRIGHT, colourful, brilliant, radiant, vibrant, glaring, strong, bold, deep, intense, rich, warm. **2** GRAPHIC, evocative, realistic, lifelike, faithful, authentic, clear, detailed, lucid, eloquent, striking, arresting, impressive, colourful, rich, dramatic, lively, stimulating, interesting, fascinating, scintillating; memorable, powerful, stirring, moving, telling, haunting.
—OPPOSITES: dull, vague.

vocal *adj.* **1** VOCALIZED, voiced, uttered, articulated, oral; spoken, viva voce, said. **2** VOCIFEROUS, outspoken, forthright, plain-spoken, expressive, blunt, frank, candid, open; vehement, strident, vigorous, emphatic, insistent, forceful, zealous, clamorous, loud-mouthed.

vocation *n.* CALLING, life's work, mission, purpose, function, avocation; profession, occupation, career, job, employment, trade, craft, business, line (of work), métier.

vogue *n.* FASHION, trend, fad, craze, rage, enthusiasm, passion, obsession, mania; fashionableness, popularity,

currency, favour; *informal* trendiness.
□ **in vogue** FASHIONABLE, voguish, stylish, modish, up-to-date, up-to-the-minute, du jour, modern, current; prevalent, popular, in favour, in demand, sought-after, all the rage; chic, chi-chi, smart, tony, kicky, le dernier cri; trendy, hip, cool, big, happening, now, in, with it.

voice *n.* **1** POWER OF SPEECH. **2** EXPRESSION, utterance, verbalization, vocalization. **3** OPINION, view, feeling, wish, desire, will, vox populi, vox pop. **4** SAY, influence, vote, input, role, representation, seat at the table. **5** SPOKESPERSON, speaker, champion, representative, mouthpiece, intermediary; forum, vehicle, instrument, channel, organ, agent.
▸ *v.* EXPRESS, vocalize, communicate, articulate, declare, state, assert, reveal, proclaim, announce, publish, publicize, make public, make known, table, air, vent; utter, say, speak; *informal* come out with.

void *n.* VACUUM, emptiness, nothingness, nullity, blankness, vacuity; (empty) space, gap, cavity, chasm, abyss, gulf, pit, black hole.
▸ *v.* INVALIDATE, annul, nullify; negate, quash, cancel, countermand, repeal, revoke, rescind, retract, withdraw, reverse, undo, abolish; *Law* vacate; *formal* abrogate.
—OPPOSITES: validate.
▸ *adj.* **1** EMPTY, vacant, blank, bare, clear, free, unfilled, unoccupied, uninhabited. **2** DEVOID OF, empty

of, vacant of, bereft of, free from; lacking, wanting, without, with nary a. **3** INVALID, null, ineffective, non-viable, useless, worthless, nugatory.
—OPPOSITES: full, occupied, valid.

volatile adj. **1** UNPREDICTABLE, changeable, variable, inconstant, inconsistent, erratic, irregular, unstable, turbulent, blowing hot and cold, varying, shifting, fluctuating, fluid, mutable; mercurial, capricious, whimsical, fickle, flighty, impulsive, temperamental, high-strung, excitable, emotional, fiery, moody, tempestuous. **2** TENSE, strained, fraught, uneasy, uncomfortable, charged, explosive, inflammatory, turbulent; informal nail-biting, ready to blow. **3** EVAPORATIVE, vaporous; explosive, inflammable; unstable, labile.
—OPPOSITES: stable, calm.

volume n. **1** BOOK, publication, tome, hardback, paperback, title; manual, almanac, compendium. **2** CAPACITY, cubic measure, size, magnitude, mass, bulk, extent; dimensions, proportions, measurements. **3** QUANTITY, amount, proportion, measure, mass, bulk. **4** LOUDNESS, sound, amplification; informal decibels.

voluminous adj. CAPACIOUS, roomy, spacious, ample, full, big, large, bulky, extensive, sizeable, generous; billowing, baggy, loose-fitting; formal commodious.

voluntary adj. **1** OPTIONAL, discretionary, elective, non-compulsory, volitional; Law permissive. **2** UNPAID, unsalaried,

unwaged, for free, without charge, for nothing; honorary, volunteer; Law pro bono (publico).
—OPPOSITES: compulsory, paid.

volunteer v. **1** OFFER, tender, proffer, put forward, put up, venture. **2** OFFER ONE'S SERVICES, present oneself, make oneself available, come forward, sign up.

voluptuous adj. CURVACEOUS, shapely, ample, buxom, full-figured; seductive, alluring, comely, sultry, sensuous, sexy, womanly; informal bodacious, hot, curvy, busty, stacked, built, slinky; formal Junoesque, Rubenesque.

vomit v. **1** BE SICK, spew, heave, retch, gag, get sick; informal throw up, puke, purge, hurl, barf, upchuck, ralph. **2** REGURGITATE, bring up, spew up, cough up, lose; throw up, puke, spit up.

voracious adj. INSATIABLE, unquenchable, unappeasable, prodigious, uncontrollable, compulsive, gluttonous, greedy, esurient, rapacious; enthusiastic, eager, keen, avid, desirous, hungry, ravenous; informal piggish.

vow n. OATH, pledge, promise, bond, covenant, commitment, avowal, profession, affirmation, attestation, assurance, guarantee; word (of honour).
▶ v. SWEAR, pledge, promise, avow, undertake, engage, make a commitment, give one's word, guarantee.

vulgar adj. **1** RUDE, indecent, indelicate, offensive, distasteful, coarse, crude, ribald, risqué, naughty, suggestive, racy, earthy, off-colour, bawdy, obscene, profane, lewd, salacious, smutty,

dirty, filthy, pornographic, porno, X-rated, XXX; *informal* sleazy, raunchy, blue, locker-room; saucy, salty; *euphemistic* adult. **2** TASTELESS, crass, tawdry, ostentatious, flamboyant, overdone, showy, gaudy, garish, brassy, kitsch, loud; *informal* flash, flashy, tacky, (*Que.*) kétaine✦. **3** IMPOLITE, ill-mannered, unmannerly, rude, indecorous, unseemly, ill-bred, boorish, uncouth, crude, rough; unsophisticated, unrefined, common, low-minded; unladylike, ungentlemanly.
—OPPOSITES: tasteful, decorous.

vulnerable *adj.* **1** IN DANGER, in peril, in jeopardy, at risk, endangered, unsafe, unprotected, unguarded; open to attack, assailable, exposed, wide open; undefended, unfortified, unarmed, defenceless, helpless. **2** EXPOSED TO, open to, liable to, prone to, prey to, susceptible to, subject to, an easy target for.
—OPPOSITES: resilient.

Ww

wad *n.* **1** ☞ CHUNK. **2** BUNDLE, roll, pile, stack, sheaf, bankroll.

waddle *v.* TODDLE, dodder, totter, wobble, shuffle; duckwalk.

wade *v.* **1** PADDLE, wallow, dabble. **2** PLOW, plod, trawl, labour, toil; study, browse; *informal* slog.
□ **wade in** (*informal*) SET TO WORK, buckle down, go to it, put one's shoulder to the wheel; *informal* plunge in, dive in, jump in, get cracking.

wag *v.* **1** SWING, swish, switch, sway, shake, quiver, twitch, whip, bob; *informal* waggle. **2** SHAKE, wave, wiggle, flourish, brandish.

wage *n.* PAY, payment, remuneration, salary, stipend, fee, honorarium; income, revenue; profit, gain, reward; earnings, paycheque, pay packet, reimbursement, compensation; *formal* emolument.
▶ *v.* ENGAGE IN, carry on, conduct, execute, pursue, prosecute, proceed with.

wail *n.* ☞ HOWL.
▶ *v.* ☞ HOWL 2.

wait *v.* **1** STAY (PUT), remain, rest, stop, halt, pause; linger, loiter, dally; *informal* stick around, hang out, hang around, kill time, waste time, kick one's heels, twiddle one's thumbs; *archaic* tarry. **2** HOLD ON, hold back, bide one's time, hang fire, mark time, stand by, sit

tight, hold one's horses. **3** AWAIT; anticipate, look forward, long, pine, yearn, expect, be ready. **4** BE POSTPONED, be delayed, be put off, be deferred; *informal* be put on the back burner, be put on ice.
▶ *n.* DELAY, holdup, interval, interlude, intermission, pause, break, stay, cessation, suspension, stoppage, halt, interruption, lull, respite, recess, moratorium, hiatus, gap, rest.
□ **wait on someone** SERVE, attend to, tend, cater for/to; minister to, take care of, look after, see to. **wait up 1** STAY AWAKE, stay up, keep vigil. **2** STOP, slow down, hold on, wait for me.

waive *v.* **1** RELINQUISH, renounce, give up, abandon, surrender, cede, sign away, yield, reject, dispense with, abdicate, sacrifice, refuse, turn down, spurn. **2** DISREGARD, ignore, overlook, set aside, forgo, drop.

wake *v.* **1** AWAKE, waken, awaken, rouse oneself, stir, come to, come round, bestir oneself; get up, get out of bed; *formal* arise. **2** ROUSE, arouse, waken. **3** ACTIVATE, stimulate, galvanize, enliven, animate, stir up, spur on, buoy, invigorate, revitalize; *informal* perk up, pep up.

walk *v.* STROLL, saunter, amble, trudge, plod, dawdle, hike, tramp, tromp, slog, stomp, trek, march, stride, sashay, glide, troop, patrol, wander, ramble, tread, prowl, promenade, roam, traipse; stretch one's legs; *informal* mosey, hoof it; *formal* perambulate.

▶ *n.* **1** STROLL, saunter, promenade; ramble, hike, tramp, march; turn; *dated* constitutional. **2** PATH, pathway, walkway, sidewalk. **3** ☞ GAIT.

wall *n.* **1** BARRIER, partition, enclosure, screen, panel, divider; bulkhead. **2** FORTIFICATION, rampart, barricade, bulwark, stockade. **3** OBSTACLE, barrier, fence; impediment, hindrance, block, roadblock, check.
—RELATED: mural.

wallow *v.* **1** LOLL ABOUT/AROUND, roll about/around, lie about/around, splash about/around; slosh, wade, paddle; *informal* splosh. **2** ROLL, lurch, toss, plunge, pitch, reel, rock, flounder, keel, list; labour. **3** LUXURIATE, bask, take pleasure, take satisfaction, indulge (oneself), delight, revel, glory; enjoy, like, love, relish, savour; *informal* get a kick out of, get off on.

wan *adj.* **1** ☞ PALE 1. **2** ☞ DIM 1.
—OPPOSITES: flushed, bright.

wander *v.* **1** STROLL, amble, saunter, walk, dawdle, potter, ramble, meander; roam, rove, range, drift, prowl; *informal* traipse, mosey, tootle, mooch. **2** STRAY, depart, diverge, veer, swerve, deviate, digress, drift, get sidetracked.

wane *v.* DECLINE, diminish, decrease, dwindle, shrink, tail off, ebb, fade (away), lessen, peter out,

fall off, recede, slump, flag, weaken, give way, wither, crumble, evaporate, disintegrate, die out; *literary* evanesce.
—OPPOSITES: wax, grow.

want *v.* DESIRE, wish for, hope for, aspire to, fancy, care for, like; long for, yearn for, crave, hanker after, hunger for, thirst for, cry out for, covet; need; *informal* have a yen for, have a jones for, be dying for, ache for, be eager, burn, be itching for, pine, set one's sights on.

wanting *adj.* **1** DEFICIENT, inadequate, lacking, insufficient, imperfect, unacceptable, unsatisfactory, flawed, faulty, defective, unsound, substandard, inferior, second-rate, poor, shoddy. **2** WITHOUT, lacking, deprived of, devoid of, bereft of, in need of, out of; deficient in, short on, low on; *informal* minus.
—OPPOSITES: sufficient.

wanton *adj.* **1** DELIBERATE, wilful, malicious, spiteful, wicked, cruel; gratuitous, unprovoked, motiveless, arbitrary, groundless, unjustifiable, needless, unnecessary, uncalled for, senseless, pointless, purposeless, meaningless, empty, random; capricious. **2** PROMISCUOUS, immoral, immodest, indecent, shameless, unchaste, fast, loose, impure, abandoned, lustful, lecherous, lascivious, libidinous, licentious, dissolute, debauched, degenerate, corrupt, whorish, disreputable.
—OPPOSITES: justifiable, chaste.

war *n.* CONFLICT, warfare, combat, fighting, (military) action,

bloodshed, struggle; battle, skirmish, fight, clash, engagement, encounter; offensive, attack; campaign, crusade; hostilities; jihad.
—RELATED: belligerent, martial.
—OPPOSITES: peace.

wares pl. n. ☞ MERCHANDISE.

warlike adj. AGGRESSIVE, belligerent, warring, bellicose, pugnacious, combative, bloodthirsty, jingoistic, hostile, threatening, quarrelsome; militaristic, militant, warmongering.

warm adj. 1 HOT, cozy, snug; informal toasty. 2 BALMY, summery, sultry, hot, mild, temperate; sunny, fine. 3 HEATED, tepid, lukewarm. 4 ☞ HOSPITABLE.
—OPPOSITES: cold, chilly, hostile.

warm-blooded adj.
1 HOMEOTHERMIC. 2 PASSIONATE, ardent, red-blooded, emotional, intense, impetuous, lively, lusty, spirited, fiery, tempestuous.
—OPPOSITES: poikilothermic, reserved.

warmth n. 1 HEAT, warmness, hotness, fieriness; coziness.
2 ☞ FRIENDLINESS. 3 ☞ ENTHUSIASM 1.

warn v. 1 NOTIFY, alert, apprise, inform, tell, make someone aware, forewarn, remind, give notice, put on one's guard; informal tip off, clue in. 2 ADVISE, exhort, urge, counsel, caution.

warning n. 1 (ADVANCE) NOTICE, forewarning, alert; hint, signal, sign, alarm bells; informal tipoff, heads-up, red flag. 2 CAUTION, advisory, notification, information; exhortation,

injunction; advice. 3 OMEN, premonition, foreboding, prophecy, prediction, forecast, token, portent, signal, sign; literary foretoken. 4 EXAMPLE, deterrent, lesson, caution, exemplar, message, moral. 5 ADMONITION, caution, remonstrance, reprimand, censure; informal dressing-down, talking-to.

warp v. 1 BUCKLE, twist, bend, distort, deform, misshape, skew, curve, bow, contort. 2 CORRUPT, twist, pervert, deprave, lead astray.
—OPPOSITES: straighten.

warrant n. 1 AUTHORIZATION, order, licence, permit, document; writ, summons, subpoena; mandate, decree, fiat, edict.
2 VOUCHER, slip, ticket, coupon, pass.
▶ v. JUSTIFY, vindicate, call for, sanction, validate; permit, authorize; deserve, excuse, account for, legitimize; support, license, approve of; merit, qualify for, rate, be worthy of, be deserving of.

wary adj. 1 CAUTIOUS, careful, circumspect, on one's guard, chary, guarded, hesitant, alert, on the lookout, on one's toes, on the qui vive; attentive, heedful, watchful, vigilant, observant; informal wide awake. 2 SUSPICIOUS, chary, leery, careful, distrustful, mistrustful, disbelieving, skeptical, doubtful, dubious; anxious, worried, apprehensive, uncertain, unsure.
—OPPOSITES: inattentive, trustful.

wash v. 1 CLEAN ONESELF; bathe, bath, shower, soak, freshen up;

formal perform one's ablutions.
2 CLEAN, cleanse, rinse, launder, scour; shampoo, lather, sponge, scrub, wipe, mop; sluice, douse, swab, disinfect, hose down; *literary* lave. **3** SPLASH, lap, splosh, dash, crash, break, beat, surge, ripple, roll. **4** SWEEP, carry, convey, transport.

▶ *n.* **1** CLEAN, shower, dip, bath, soak; *formal* ablutions. **2** LAUNDRY, washing. **3** LOTION, salve, preparation, rinse, liquid; liniment. **4** BACKWASH, wake, trail, path. **5** SURGE, flow, swell, sweep, rise and fall, roll, splash. **6** PAINT, stain, film, coat, coating; tint, glaze.

waste *v.* **1** SQUANDER, misspend, misuse, fritter away, throw away, lavish, dissipate, throw around; *informal* blow, splurge. **2** GROW WEAK, grow thin, shrink, decline, wilt, fade, flag, deteriorate, degenerate, languish. **3** EMACIATE, atrophy, wither, debilitate, shrivel, shrink, weaken, enfeeble.
—OPPOSITES: conserve, thrive.

▶ *adj.* **1** UNWANTED, excess, superfluous, left over, scrap, useless, worthless; unusable, unprofitable. **2** UNCULTIVATED, barren, desert, arid, bare; desolate, void, uninhabited, unpopulated; wild.

▶ *n.* **1** MISUSE, misapplication, abuse; extravagance, wastefulness, lavishness. **2** GARBAGE, rubbish, trash, refuse, litter, debris, flotsam and jetsam, dross, junk, detritus, scrap; dregs, scraps; sewage, effluent. **3** DESERT, wasteland, the Barrens✦, the Barren Lands✦, wilderness, wilds, emptiness.

wasteful *adj.* PRODIGAL, profligate, uneconomical, inefficient, extravagant, lavish, excessive, imprudent, improvident, intemperate; spendthrift; needless, useless.
—OPPOSITES: frugal.

wasteland *n.* WILDERNESS, desert; wilds, wastes, badlands, moose pasture✦.

watch *v.* **1** OBSERVE, view, look at, eye, gaze at, stare at, gape at, peer at; contemplate, survey, keep an eye on; inspect, scrutinize, scan, examine, study, ogle, gawk at, regard, mark; *informal* check out, get a load of, eyeball; *literary* behold. **2** SPY ON, keep in sight, track, monitor, survey, follow, keep under surveillance; *informal* keep tabs on, stake out. **3** LOOK AFTER, mind, keep an eye on, take care of, supervise, tend, attend to; guard, safeguard, protect, babysit. **4** GUARD, protect, shield, defend, safeguard; cover, patrol, police. **5** BE CAREFUL, mind, be aware of, pay attention to, consider, pay heed to.
—OPPOSITES: ignore, neglect.

watchful *adj.* OBSERVANT, alert, vigilant, attentive, awake, aware, heedful, sharp-eyed, eagle-eyed, hawk-eyed; on the lookout, on the qui vive, wary, cautious, careful, chary.

watchman *n.* SECURITY GUARD, custodian, warden; sentry, guard, patrolman, lookout, sentinel, scout, watch.

watertight *adj.* **1** IMPERMEABLE, impervious, (hermetically) sealed; waterproof, water-repellent, water-resistant. **2** INDISPUTABLE,

unquestionable, incontrovertible, irrefutable, unassailable, impregnable; foolproof, sound, flawless, airtight, bulletproof, conclusive.
—OPPOSITES: leaky, flawed.

watery *adj.* **1** LIQUID, fluid, aqueous; *technical* hydrous. **2** WET, damp, moist, sodden, soggy, squelchy, slushy, soft; saturated, waterlogged; boggy, marshy, swampy, miry, muddy. **3** THIN, runny, weak, sloppy, dilute, diluted; tasteless, flavourless, insipid, bland. **4** PALE, wan, faint, weak, feeble; *informal* wishy-washy, washy. **5** TEARFUL, teary, weepy, moist, rheumy; *formal* lachrymose.
—OPPOSITES: dry, thick, bright.

wave *v.* **1** BRANDISH, shake, swish, move to and fro, move up and down, wag, sweep, swing, flourish, wield; flick, flutter; *informal* waggle. **2** RIPPLE, flutter, undulate, stir, flap, sway, billow, shake, quiver, move. **3** GESTURE, gesticulate, signal, beckon, motion.
▶ *n.* **1** GESTURE, gesticulation; signal, sign, motion; salute. **2** BREAKER, roller, comber, boomer, ripple, whitecap, bore, big kahuna; (**waves**) swell, surf, froth; backwash. **3** FLOW, rush, surge, flood, stream, tide, deluge, spate. **4** SURGE, rush, stab, dart, upsurge, groundswell; thrill, frisson; feeling. **5** CURL, kink, corkscrew, twist, ringlet, coil. **6** ripple, vibration, oscillation.

waver *v.* **1** FLICKER, quiver, twinkle, glimmer, wink, blink. **2** FALTER, wobble, tremble, quaver, shake. **3** ☞ HESITATE.

way *n.* **1** METHOD, process, procedure, technique, system; plan, strategy, scheme; means, mechanism, approach. **2** MANNER, style, fashion, mode; modus operandi, MO. **3** PRACTICE, wont, habit, custom, policy, procedure, convention, routine, modus vivendi; trait, attribute, peculiarity, idiosyncrasy; conduct, behaviour, manner, style, nature, personality, temperament, disposition, character. **4** ROUTE, course, direction; road, street, track, path. **5** DOOR, gate, exit, entrance, entry; route. **6** DISTANCE, length, stretch, journey; space, interval, span. **7** TIME, stretch, term, span, duration. **8** DIRECTION, bearing, course, orientation, line, tack. **9** RESPECT, regard, aspect, facet, sense, angle; detail, point, particular. **10** STATE, condition, situation, circumstances, position; predicament, plight; *informal* shape.
☐ **by the way** INCIDENTALLY, by the by, in passing, en passant, as an aside. **give way 1** YIELD, back down, surrender, capitulate, concede defeat, give in, submit, succumb; acquiesce, agree, assent; *informal* throw in the towel/sponge, cave in. **2** COLLAPSE, give, cave in, fall in, come apart, crumple, buckle. **3** BE REPLACED BY, be succeeded by, be followed by, be supplanted by.

wayward *adj.* ☞ WILFUL 2.

weak *adj.* **1** FRAIL, feeble, delicate, fragile; infirm, sick, sickly, debilitated, incapacitated, ailing, indisposed, decrepit; tired, fatigued, exhausted, anemic; *informal* weedy. **2** INADEQUATE, poor,

…le; defective, faulty, deficient, …mperfect, substandard. **3** UNCONVINCING, untenable, tenuous, implausible, unsatisfactory, poor, inadequate, feeble, flimsy, lame, hollow; *informal* pathetic, sorry. **4** SPINELESS, craven, cowardly, pusillanimous, timid; irresolute, indecisive, ineffectual, inept, effete, meek, tame, ineffective, impotent, soft, faint-hearted; *informal* yellow, weak-kneed, gutless, chicken. **5** DIM, pale, wan, faint, feeble, muted. **6** INDISTINCT, muffled, muted, hushed, low, faint, thin. **7** WATERY, diluted, dilute, watered down, thin, tasteless, flavourless, bland, insipid, wishy-washy. **8** UNENTHUSIASTIC, feeble, half-hearted, lame. —OPPOSITES: strong, powerful, convincing, resolute, bright, loud.

weaken *v.* **1** ENFEEBLE, debilitate, incapacitate, sap, enervate, tire, exhaust, wear out; wither, cripple, disable, emasculate. **2** REDUCE, decrease, diminish, soften, lessen, moderate, temper, dilute, blunt, mitigate. **3** DECREASE, dwindle, diminish, wane, ebb, subside, peter out, fizzle out, tail off, decline, falter. **4** IMPAIR, undermine, erode, eat away at, compromise; invalidate, negate, discredit.

weakness *n.* **1** FRAILTY, feebleness, enfeeblement, fragility, delicacy; infirmity, sickness, sickliness, debility, incapacity, impotence, indisposition, decrepitude, vulnerability. **2** FAULT, flaw, defect, deficiency, weak point, failing,

shortcoming, weak link, imperfection, Achilles heel, foible. **3** FONDNESS, liking, partiality, preference, love, penchant, soft spot, predilection, inclination, taste, eye; enthusiasm, appetite; susceptibility. **4** TIMIDITY, cowardliness, pusillanimity; indecision, irresolution, ineffectuality, ineptitude, impotence, meekness, powerlessness, ineffectiveness. **5** UNTENABILITY, implausibility, poverty, inadequacy, transparency; flimsiness, hollowness. **6** INDISTINCTNESS, faintness, feebleness, lowness; dimness, paleness.

wealth *n.* **1** AFFLUENCE, prosperity, riches, means, substance, fortune; money, cash, lucre, capital, treasure, finance; assets, possessions, resources, funds; property, stock, reserves, securities, holdings; *informal* wherewithal, dough, moolah. **2** ☞ ABUNDANCE. —OPPOSITES: poverty, dearth.

wealthy *adj.* ☞ RICH 1. —OPPOSITES: poor.

wear *v.* **1** DRESS IN, be clothed in, have on, sport, model; put on. **2** BEAR, have (on one's face), show, display, exhibit; give, put on, assume. **3** ERODE, abrade, rub away, grind away, wash away, crumble (away), wear down; corrode, eat away (at), dissolve. **4** LAST, endure, hold up, bear up, prove durable. ▸ *n.* **1** USE, wearing, service, utility, value; *informal* mileage. **2** CLOTHES, clothing, garments, dress, attire, garb, wardrobe; *informal* getup, gear, togs, duds, kit; *formal* apparel; *literary* array. **3** DAMAGE, friction, erosion, attrition, abrasion; weathering.

☐ **wear off** FADE, diminish, lessen, dwindle, decrease, wane, ebb, peter out, fizzle out, pall, disappear, run out. **wear out** DETERIORATE, become worn, wear thin, fray, become threadbare, wear through.

wearisome *adj.* **1** ☞ TIRING. **2** ☞ BORING. **3** labour-intensive, time-consuming.

weary *adj.* **1** ☞ TIRED 1, 2. **2** ☞ TIRING.
—OPPOSITES: fresh, keen, refreshing.

weave *v.* **1** ENTWINE, lace, twist, knit, intertwine, braid, plait, loop. **2** THREAD, wind, wend; dodge, deke, dipsy-doodle♦, zigzag.

web *n.* **1** MESH, net, lattice, latticework, lacework, webbing; gauze, gossamer. **2** NETWORK, nexus, complex, set, chain; tissue. **3** INTERNET, World Wide Web, information superhighway, cyberspace, Net.
▸ *adj.* ONLINE, Internet, virtual, digital, cyber-, web-based, e-.

wedge *n.* **1** DOORSTOP, chock, block, stop. **2** HUNK, segment, triangle, slice, section; chunk, lump, slab, block, piece.
▸ *v.* SQUEEZE, cram, jam, ram, force, push, shove; *informal* stuff.

weigh *v.* **1** MEASURE THE WEIGHT OF, put on the scales; heft. **2** HAVE A WEIGHT OF, tip the scales at, weigh in at. **3** OPPRESS, lie heavy on, burden, hang over, gnaw at, prey on (one's mind); trouble, worry, bother, disturb, get down,

depress, haunt, nag, torment, plague. **4** ☞ CONSIDER 1. **5** BALANCE, evaluate, compare, juxtapose, contrast, measure.

weight *n.* **1** HEAVINESS, mass, load, burden, pressure, force; poundage, tonnage, pounds, kilos. **2** INFLUENCE, force, leverage, sway, pull, importance, significance, consequence, value, substance, power, authority; *informal* clout. **3** BURDEN, load, millstone, albatross, encumbrance; trouble, worry, pressure, strain. **4** PREPONDERANCE, majority, bulk, body, lion's share, predominance; most, almost all.

weird *adj.* **1** ☞ EERIE. **2** BIZARRE, quirky, outlandish, eccentric, unconventional, unorthodox, idiosyncratic, surreal, crazy, peculiar, odd, strange, queer, freakish, zany, madcap, outré; *informal* wacky, freaky, way-out, offbeat, off the wall, wacko.
—OPPOSITES: normal, conventional.

welcome *n.* GREETING, salutation; reception, hospitality; the red carpet.
▸ *v.* **1** GREET, salute, receive, meet, usher in. **2** BE PLEASED BY, be glad about, approve of, appreciate, embrace; *informal* give the thumbs up to.
▸ *adj.* PLEASING, agreeable, encouraging, gratifying, heartening, promising, favourable, pleasant, refreshing; gladly received, wanted, appreciated, popular, desirable.

welfare *n.* **1** WELL-BEING, health, comfort, security, safety, protection, prosperity, success, fortune; interest, good. **2** SOCIAL ASSISTANCE, social security, benefit, public assistance; pension, credit, (income) support; sick pay, unemployment (benefit), EI❖; *informal* the dole, pogey❖.

well¹ *adv.* **1** SATISFACTORILY, nicely, correctly, properly, fittingly, suitably, appropriately; decently, fairly, kindly, generously, honestly. **2** HARMONIOUSLY, agreeably, pleasantly, nicely, happily, amicably, amiably, peaceably; *informal* famously. **3** SKILFULLY, ably, competently, proficiently, adeptly, deftly, expertly, admirably, excellently. **4** INTIMATELY, thoroughly, deeply, profoundly, personally. **5** CAREFULLY, closely, attentively, rigorously, in depth, exhaustively, in detail, meticulously, scrupulously, conscientiously, methodically, completely, comprehensively, fully, extensively, thoroughly, effectively. **6** ADMIRINGLY, highly, approvingly, favourably, appreciatively, warmly, enthusiastically, positively, glowingly. **7** COMFORTABLY, in (the lap of) luxury, prosperously. **8** QUITE POSSIBLY, conceivably, probably; undoubtedly, certainly, unquestionably. **9** CONSIDERABLY, very much, a great deal, substantially, easily, comfortably, significantly. **10** EASILY, comfortably, readily, effortlessly. —OPPOSITES: badly, negligently, disparagingly, barely.
▸ *adj.* **1** HEALTHY, fine, fit, robust, strong, vigorous, blooming, thriving, hale and hearty, in good

shape, in good condition, in fine fettle; *informal* in the pink. **2** SATISFACTORY, all right, fine, in order, as it should be, acceptable; *informal* OK, hunky-dory. —OPPOSITES: poorly, unsatisfactory.

well² *n.* **1** BOREHOLE, bore, spring, water hole; gusher. **2** SOURCE, supply, fount, reservoir, wellspring, mine, fund, treasury.
▸ *v.* FLOW, spill, stream, run, rush, gush, roll, cascade, flood, spout; seep, trickle; burst, issue.

well-bred *adj.* ☞ POLITE.

well-known *adj.* **1** ☞ FAMILIAR 1. **2** ☞ FAMOUS. —OPPOSITES: obscure.

wet *adj.* **1** DAMP, moist, soaked, drenched, saturated, sopping, dripping, soggy; waterlogged. **2** RAINY, raining, pouring, teeming, inclement, showery, drizzly, drizzling; damp; humid, muggy. **3** STICKY, tacky; fresh. —OPPOSITES: dry.
▸ *v.* DAMPEN, damp, moisten; sprinkle, spray, splash, spritz; soak, saturate, flood, douse, souse, drench. —OPPOSITES: dry.
▸ *n.* **1** WETNESS, damp, moisture, moistness, sogginess; wateriness. **2** RAIN, drizzle, precipitation; spray, dew, damp.

whim *n.* **1** IMPULSE, urge, notion, fancy, foible, caprice, conceit, vagary, inclination. **2** CAPRICIOUSNESS, whimsy, caprice, volatility, fickleness, idiosyncrasy.

whimper *n. & v.* WHINE, cry, sob, moan, snivel, wail, groan; mewl, bleat.

whimsical *adj.* **1** FANCIFUL, playful, mischievous, waggish, quaint, curious, droll; eccentric, quirky, idiosyncratic, unconventional. **2** VOLATILE, capricious, fickle, changeable, unpredictable, variable, erratic, mercurial, mutable, inconstant, inconsistent, unstable, protean.

whine *n. & v.* **1** WHIMPER, cry, mewl, howl, yowl. **2** HUM, drone. **3** COMPLAIN(T), grouse, grumble, murmur; *informal* gripe, moan, grouch, bellyache, beef.

whip *n.* LASH, scourge, strap, belt, rod, bullwhip; *historical* cat-o'-nine-tails.
▸ *v.* **1** FLOG, scourge, flagellate, lash, strap, cane, belt, thrash, beat, tan someone's hide. **2** WHISK, beat. **3** ROUSE, stir up, excite, galvanize, electrify, stimulate, inspire, fire up, get someone going, inflame, agitate, goad, provoke. **4** (*informal*) ☞ DASH *v.* 1. **5** (*informal*) PULL, whisk, snatch, pluck, jerk.

whirl *v.* **1** ROTATE, circle, wheel, turn, revolve, orbit, spin, twirl. **2** ☞ HURRY 1. **3** SPIN, reel, swim.
▸ *n.* **1** SWIRL, flurry, eddy. **2** HURLY-BURLY, activity, bustle, rush, flurry, fuss, turmoil, merry-go-round. **3** SPIN, daze, stupor, muddle, jumble; confusion; *informal* dither.

whirlwind *n.* **1** TORNADO, hurricane, typhoon, cyclone, vortex, twister, dust devil. **2** MAELSTROM, welter, bedlam, mayhem, babel, swirl, tumult, hurly-burly, commotion, confusion.
▸ *adj.* ☞ RAPID.

whisper *v.* **1** MURMUR, mutter, mumble, speak softly, breathe; hiss. **2** (*literary*) RUSTLE, murmur, sigh, moan, whoosh, whirr, swish, blow, breathe.
—OPPOSITES: roar.
▸ *n.* **1** MURMUR, mutter, mumble, low voice, undertone; susurration. **2** (*literary*) RUSTLE, murmur, sigh, whoosh, swish. **3** RUMOUR, story, report, speculation, insinuation, innuendo, suggestion, hint; *informal* buzz. **4** ☞ WHIT.

white *adj.* **1** COLOURLESS, bleached, natural; snowy, milky, chalky, ivory. **2** PALE, pallid, wan, ashen, bloodless, waxen, chalky, pasty, washed out, drained, drawn, ghostly, deathly. **3** SNOWY, grey, silver, silvery, hoary, grizzled. **4** CAUCASIAN, European.

white-collar *adj.* CLERICAL, administrative, professional, executive, salaried, office.

whiz *n.* GENIUS, virtuoso, ace, master, prodigy, hotshot, wizard, magician.
▸ *v.* ZOOM, flash, zip, whip, hurtle, fly.

whole *adj.* **1** ENTIRE, complete, full, unabridged, uncut. **2** INTACT, in one piece, unbroken; undamaged, unmarked, perfect.
—OPPOSITES: incomplete.
☐ **on the whole** OVERALL, all in all, all things considered, for the most part, in the main, in general, generally (speaking), as a (general) rule, by and large; normally, usually, more often than not, almost always, most of the time, typically, ordinarily.

wholehearted *adj.* COMMITTED, positive, emphatic, devoted,

dedicated, enthusiastic, unshakeable, unswerving; unqualified, unstinting, unreserved, without reservations, unconditional, unequivocal, unmitigated; complete, full, total, absolute.
—opposites: half-hearted.

wholesome *adj.* **1** ☞ HEALTHY 2.
2 GOOD, ethical, moral, clean, virtuous, pure, innocent, chaste; uplifting, edifying, proper, correct, decent, harmless; *informal* squeaky clean.

wholly *adv.* **1** ☞ COMPLETELY.
2 EXCLUSIVELY, only, solely, purely, alone.

wicked *adj.* EVIL, sinful, immoral, (morally) wrong, wrongful, bad, iniquitous, corrupt, base, mean, vile; villainous, nefarious, erring, foul, monstrous, shocking, outrageous, atrocious, abominable, depraved, reprehensible, hateful, detestable, despicable, odious, contemptible, horrible, heinous, egregious, execrable, fiendish, vicious, murderous, black-hearted, barbarous; criminal, illicit, unlawful, illegal, lawless, felonious, dishonest, unscrupulous; *Law* malfeasant; *informal* crooked; *dated* dastardly.
—opposites: virtuous.

wide *adj.* **1** BROAD, extensive, spacious, vast, spread out. **2** FULLY OPEN, dilated, gaping, staring, wide open. **3** COMPREHENSIVE, broad, extensive, diverse, full, ample, large, large-scale, wide-ranging, exhaustive, general, all-inclusive. **4** OFF TARGET, off the mark, inaccurate.

—opposites: narrow.
▶ *adv.* **1** FULLY, to the fullest/furthest extent, as far/much as possible. **2** OFF TARGET, inaccurately.
□ **wide open 1** AGAPE, yawning, open wide, fully open. **2** UNDECIDED, unpredictable, uncertain, unsure, in the balance, up in the air; *informal* anyone's guess. **3** VULNERABLE, exposed, unprotected, defenceless, undefended, at risk, in danger.

widen *v.* **1** BROADEN, make/become wider, open up/out, expand, extend, enlarge. **2** INCREASE, augment, boost, swell, enlarge.

widespread *adj.* GENERAL, extensive, universal, common, global, worldwide, international, omnipresent, ubiquitous, across the board, blanket, sweeping, wholesale; predominant, prevalent, rife, broad, rampant, pervasive.
—opposites: limited.

width *n.* **1** BREADTH, broadness, wideness, thickness, span, diameter, girth. **2** RANGE, breadth, compass, scope, span, spectrum, scale, extent, extensiveness, comprehensiveness.
—opposites: length, narrowness.

wield *v.* **1** BRANDISH, flourish, wave, swing; use, employ, handle. **2** EXERCISE, exert, hold, maintain, command, control.

wild *adj.* **1** UNTAMED, undomesticated, feral; fierce, ferocious, savage, untameable. **2** UNCULTIVATED, native, indigenous. **3** PRIMITIVE, uncivilized, uncultured; savage, barbarous, barbaric. **4** UNINHABITED,

unpopulated, uncultivated;
rugged, rough, inhospitable,
desolate, barren. **5** STORMY,
squally, tempestuous, turbulent.
6 ☞ DISHEVELLED. **7** UNCONTROLLED,
unrestrained, out of control,
undisciplined, unruly, rowdy,
disorderly, riotous. **8** VERY EXCITED,
delirious, in a frenzy; tumultuous,
passionate, vehement,
unrestrained. **9** (*informal*)
DISTRAUGHT, frantic, beside
oneself, in a frenzy, hysterical,
deranged, berserk; *informal* mad,
crazy. **10** (*informal*) ☞ ANGRY.
11 (*informal*) ENAMOURED, very
enthusiastic, very keen,
infatuated, smitten; *informal* crazy,
blown away, mad, nuts.
12 MADCAP, ridiculous, ludicrous,
foolish, rash, stupid, foolhardy,
idiotic, absurd, silly, ill-
considered, senseless,
nonsensical; impractical,
impracticable, unworkable; *informal*
crazy, crackpot, cockeyed, hare-
brained, cockamamie, loopy.
13 RANDOM, arbitrary, haphazard,
uninformed.
—OPPOSITES: tame, cultivated,
calm, disciplined.

wilderness *n.* **1** WILDS, wastes,
bush, bush country, bushland,
inhospitable region; desert,
backcountry, boondocks, boonies,
outback, moose pasture✤; the
great outdoors, the Barrens✤, the
Barren Lands✤. **2** WASTELAND, no
man's land.

wilful *adj.* **1** DELIBERATE,
intentional, done on purpose,
premeditated, planned, conscious.
2 HEADSTRONG, strong-willed,
stubborn, obstinate, pigheaded,

obstreperous, ungovernable,
obdurate, perverse, contrary,
disobedient, insubordinate,
undisciplined; rebellious, defiant,
uncooperative, recalcitrant,
unruly, wild, unmanageable,
erratic; difficult, impossible; *formal*
refractory, contumacious.
—OPPOSITES: accidental,
amenable, docile.

will *n.* **1** ☞ DETERMINATION. **2** DESIRE,
wish, preference, inclination,
intention, intent, choice, volition.
3 (LAST WILL AND) TESTAMENT,
bequest.
▶ *v.* **1** WANT, wish, please, see/think
fit, think best, like, choose, prefer.
2 ☞ DECREE. **3** ☞ BEQUEATH.

willing *adj.* **1** READY, prepared,
disposed, inclined, of a mind,
minded; happy, glad, pleased,
agreeable, amenable; *informal* game.
2 READILY GIVEN, willingly given,
ungrudging, volunteered.
—OPPOSITES: reluctant.

willingly *adv.* VOLUNTARILY, of
one's own free will, of one's own
accord; readily, without
reluctance, ungrudgingly,
cheerfully, happily, gladly, with
pleasure.

willingness *n.* READINESS,
inclination, will, desire, alacrity.

wilt *v.* **1** DROOP, sag, become limp,
flop; wither, shrivel (up).
2 LANGUISH, flag, droop, become
listless, tire, wane.
—OPPOSITES: flourish.

wily *adj.* **1** ☞ SHREWD. **2** ☞ CRAFTY.
—OPPOSITES: naive.

win *v.* **1** TAKE, be the victor in, be
the winner of, come first in, take
first prize in, triumph in, be
successful in. **2** COME FIRST, be the

winner, be victorious, carry/win the day, come out on top, succeed, triumph, prevail. **3** SECURE, gain, garner, collect, pick up, walk away/off with, carry off; *informal* land, net, bag, scoop. **4** CAPTIVATE, steal, snare, capture.
—OPPOSITES: lose.
▶ *n.* VICTORY, triumph, conquest.
—OPPOSITES: defeat.

wind¹ *n.* **1** BREEZE, current of air; gale, hurricane; chinook✤; *informal* blow; *literary* zephyr. **2** BREATH; *informal* puff. **3** FLATULENCE, gas; *formal* flatus.
—RELATED: aeolian.

wind² *v.* **1** TWIST (AND TURN), bend, curve, loop, zigzag, weave, snake. **2** WRAP, furl, entwine, lace, loop. **3** COIL, roll, twist, twine.

windfall *n.* BONANZA, jackpot, pennies from heaven, piece of luck.

windy *adj.* **1** BREEZY, blowy, fresh, blustery, gusty; wild, stormy, squally, tempestuous, boisterous; howling, roaring. **2** WINDSWEPT, exposed, open to the elements, bare, bleak.
—OPPOSITES: still, sheltered.

wink *v.* **1** BLINK, flutter, bat. **2** SPARKLE, twinkle, flash, glitter, gleam, shine, scintillate.

winner *n.* VICTOR, champion, conqueror, vanquisher, hero; medallist; *informal* champ, top dog, world-beater.
—OPPOSITES: loser.

winning *adj.* **1** VICTORIOUS, successful, triumphant, vanquishing, conquering; first, first-place, top, leading. **2** ENGAGING, charming, appealing, endearing, sweet, cute, winsome,
attractive, pretty, prepossessing, fetching, lovely, lovable, adorable, delightful, disarming, captivating, bewitching.

wintry *adj.* **1** BLEAK, cold, chilly, chill, frosty, freezing, icy, snowy, blizzardy, arctic, glacial, bitter, raw; *informal* nippy. **2** UNFRIENDLY, unwelcoming, cool, cold, frosty, frigid, dismal, cheerless.
—OPPOSITES: summery, warm.

wipe *v.* **1** RUB, mop, sponge, swab; clean, dry, polish, towel. **2** RUB OFF, clean off, clear up, remove, get rid of, take off, erase, efface. **3** OBLITERATE, expunge, erase, blot out. **4** ERASE, delete, trash, zap, kill, nuke.
▶ *n.* RUB, mop, sponge, swab; clean, polish.
❑ **wipe someone/something out** DESTROY, annihilate, eradicate, eliminate; slaughter, massacre, kill, exterminate; demolish, raze to the ground; *informal* take out, zap, waste; *literary* slay.

wiry *adj.* **1** SINEWY, tough, athletic, strong; lean, spare, thin, stringy, skinny. **2** COARSE, rough, strong; curly, wavy.
—OPPOSITES: flabby, smooth.

wisdom *n.* **1** SAGACITY, intelligence, sense, common sense, shrewdness, astuteness, smartness, judiciousness, judgment, prudence, circumspection; logic, rationale, rationality, soundness, advisability. **2** KNOWLEDGE, learning, erudition, sophistication, scholarship, philosophy; lore.
—OPPOSITES: folly.

wise *adj.* **1** SAGE, sagacious, intelligent, clever, learned, knowledgeable, enlightened; astute, smart, shrewd, sharp-witted, canny, knowing; sensible, prudent, discerning, discriminating, sophisticated, judicious, perceptive, insightful, perspicacious; rational, logical, sound, sane; *formal* sapient.
2 ☞ SENSIBLE.
—OPPOSITES: foolish.

wish *v.* **1** DESIRE, want, hope for, covet, dream of, long for, yearn for, crave, hunger for, lust after; aspire to, set one's heart on, seek, fancy, hanker after; *informal* have a yen for, itch for; *archaic* be desirous of. **2** WANT, desire, feel inclined, feel like, care; choose, please, think fit.
▶ *n.* **1** ☞ DESIRE *n.* 1. **2** REQUEST, requirement, bidding, instruction, direction, demand, entreaty, order, command; want, desire; will; *literary* behest.

wishy-washy *adj.* FEEBLE, ineffectual, weak, vapid, effete, gutless, spineless, limp, namby-pamby, spiritless, indecisive, characterless; pathetic.

wistful *adj.* NOSTALGIC, yearning, longing; plaintive, regretful, rueful, melancholy, mournful, elegiac; pensive, reflective, contemplative.

wit *n.* **1** ☞ INTELLIGENCE.
2 WITTINESS, humour, funniness, drollery, esprit; repartee, badinage, banter, wordplay; jokes, witticisms, quips, puns.
3 ☞ COMEDIAN.

witch *n.* **1** SORCERESS, enchantress, hex. **2** (*informal*) HAG, crone, harpy, harridan; *informal* battleaxe.

withdraw *v.* **1** REMOVE, extract, pull out, take out; take back, take away. **2** ABOLISH, cancel, lift, set aside, end, stop, remove, reverse, revoke, rescind, repeal, annul, void. **3** RETRACT, take back, go back on, recant, disavow, disclaim, repudiate, renounce, abjure; back down, climb down, backtrack, backpedal, do a U-turn, eat one's words. **4** LEAVE, pull out of, evacuate, quit, (beat a) retreat from. **5** PULL OUT OF, back out of, bow out of; get cold feet. **6** RETIRE, retreat, adjourn, decamp; leave, depart, absent oneself; *formal* repair; *dated* remove; *literary* betake oneself.
—OPPOSITES: insert, introduce, deposit, enter.

wither *v.* **1** SHRIVEL (UP), dry up; wilt, droop, go limp, fade, perish; shrink, waste away, atrophy.
2 ☞ DIMINISH.
—OPPOSITES: thrive, grow.

withhold *v.* **1** HOLD BACK, keep back, refuse to give; retain, hold on to; hide, conceal, keep secret; *informal* sit on. **2** SUPPRESS, repress, hold back, fight back, choke back, control, check, restrain, contain.

withstand *v.* ☞ RESIST 1.

witless *adj.* FOOLISH, stupid, unintelligent, idiotic, brainless, mindless; fatuous, inane.

witness *n.* OBSERVER, onlooker, eyewitness, spectator, viewer, watcher; bystander, passerby.
▶ *v.* **1** SEE, observe, watch, view, notice, spot; be present at, attend; *literary* behold; *informal* get a look at.
2 UNDERGO, experience, go

through, see; enjoy; suffer.
3 COUNTERSIGN, sign, endorse,
validate; notarize.

witty adj. HUMOROUS, amusing,
droll, funny, comic, comical;
jocular, facetious, waggish,
tongue-in-cheek; sparkling,
scintillating, entertaining; clever,
quick-witted.

wizard n. **1** SORCERER, warlock,
magus. **2** GENIUS, expert, master,
virtuoso.

woe n. **1** ☞ MISERY. **2** TROUBLE,
difficulty, problem, trial,
tribulation, misfortune, setback,
reverse, adversity, disaster,
hardship, regret.
—OPPOSITES: joy.

woeful adj. **1** ☞ SAD. **2** TRAGIC, sad,
miserable, cheerless, gloomy,
sorry, pitiful, pathetic, traumatic,
depressing, heartbreaking, heart-
rending, tear-jerking.
3 LAMENTABLE, awful, terrible,
atrocious, disgraceful, deplorable,
shameful, hopeless, dreadful;
substandard, poor, inadequate,
inferior, unsatisfactory.
—OPPOSITES: cheerful, excellent.

woman n. **1** LADY, girl, female;
matron; informal chick, dame,
broad, gal; literary maid, maiden,
damsel; archaic wench.
2 ☞ GIRLFRIEND.

womanizer n. PHILANDERER,
Casanova, Don Juan, Romeo,
Lothario, ladies' man, playboy,
seducer, rake, roué, libertine,
lecher; skirt chaser, lady-killer,
lech, wolf, stud.

wonder n. **1** AWE, admiration,
wonderment, fascination;
surprise, astonishment,
stupefaction, amazement.

2 MARVEL, miracle, phenomenon,
sensation, spectacle, beauty;
curiosity; nonpareil; doozy,
humdinger, phenom, prodigy,
rarity, ripsnorter, stunner,
something else.
▶ v. **1** PONDER, think about,
meditate on, reflect on, muse on,
puzzle over, speculate about,
conjecture; be curious about.
2 ☞ MARVEL.

wonderful adj. MARVELLOUS,
magnificent, superb, spectacular,
glorious, sublime, lovely,
delightful, fine; amazing,
astounding, astonishing, awe-
inspiring, wondrous,
breathtaking, exceptional, jaw-
dropping, mind-blowing, mind-
boggling, phenomenal,
remarkable, stupendous,
unbelievable, unheard of,
unimaginable, unthinkable,
untold; exciting, thrilling; informal
super, great, fantastic, stunning,
terrific, tremendous, sensational,
incredible, fabulous, fab, out of
this world, heavenly, divine,
awesome, neat.
—OPPOSITES: awful.

woo v. **1** PAY COURT TO, pursue,
chase (after); dated court, romance,
seek the hand of, set one's cap at,
make love to. **2** SEEK, pursue,
curry favour with, try to win, try
to attract, try to cultivate.
3 ENTICE, tempt, coax, persuade,
wheedle; informal sweet-talk.

wood n. **1** TIMBER, lumber, planks,
planking; logs, sawlogs. **2** FOREST,
woodland, trees; copse, coppice,
grove, bush, woodlot, (Prairies)
bluff♣, (Atlantic) droke♣, stand,
clump.

wooded *adj.* FORESTED, treed, tree-covered.

wooden *adj.* **1** WOOD, timber, woody; ligneous. **2** STILTED, stiff, unnatural, awkward, leaden; dry, flat, stodgy, lifeless, passionless, spiritless, soulless. **3** EXPRESSIONLESS, impassive, poker-faced, emotionless, blank, vacant, unresponsive.

word *n.* **1** TERM, name, expression, designation, locution, vocable; *formal* appellation. **2** REMARK, comment, observation, statement, utterance, pronouncement. **3** SCRIPT, lyrics, libretto. **4** PROMISE, word of honour, assurance, guarantee, undertaking; pledge, vow, oath, bond. **5** TALK, conversation, chat, tête-à-tête, heart-to-heart, one-to-one, man-to-man; discussion, consultation. **6** NEWS, information, communication, intelligence; message, report, communiqué, dispatch, bulletin; *informal* info, dope; *literary* tidings. **7** RUMOUR, hearsay, talk, gossip; *informal* the grapevine, the word on the street, (*esp. North*) the moccasin telegraph✦. **8** INSTRUCTION, order, command; signal, prompt, cue, tipoff; *informal* go-ahead, thumbs up, green light. **9** COMMAND, order, decree, edict; bidding, will. **10** MOTTO, watchword, slogan, catchword, buzz word.
  —RELATED: verbal, lexical.
▶ *v.* PHRASE, express, put, couch, frame, formulate, style; say, utter.

wordy *adj.* ☞ LONG-WINDED, VERBOSE.

work *n.* **1** LABOUR, toil, slog, drudgery, exertion, effort, industry, service; tasks, jobs, duties, assignments, projects; chores; *informal* grind, sweat, elbow grease. **2** ☞ JOB. **3** COMPOSITION, piece, creation; opus, oeuvre. **4** WRITINGS, oeuvre, canon, output.
  —OPPOSITES: leisure.
▶ *v.* **1** TOIL, labour, exert oneself, slave (away); keep at it, put one's nose to the grindstone; *informal* slog (away), beaver away, plug away, put one's back into it, knock oneself out, sweat blood. **2** BE EMPLOYED, have a job, earn one's living, do business. **3** CULTIVATE, farm, till, plow. **4** FUNCTION, go, run, operate; *informal* behave. **5** OPERATE, use, handle, control, manipulate, run. **6** SUCCEED, work out, turn out well, go as planned, get results, be effective; *informal* come off, pay off, do/turn the trick. **7** BRING ABOUT, accomplish, achieve, produce, perform, create, engender, contrive, effect.
  —OPPOSITES: rest, fail.

workable *adj.* PRACTICABLE, feasible, viable, possible, achievable; realistic, reasonable, sensible, practical; *informal* doable.
  —OPPOSITES: impracticable.

worker *n.* EMPLOYEE, staff member; workman, labourer, hand, operative, operator; proletarian; artisan, craftsman, craftswoman; wage earner, breadwinner.

working *adj.* **1** EMPLOYED, in (gainful) employment, in work, waged. **2** FUNCTIONING, operating, running, active, operational, in operation, functional, serviceable; *informal* up and running.
  —OPPOSITES: unemployed, faulty.

workmanship *n.*
CRAFTSMANSHIP, artistry, craft, art, artisanship, handiwork; skill, expertise, technique.

world *n.* **1** EARTH, globe, planet, sphere. **2** PLANET, moon, star, heavenly body, orb. **3** SPHERE, society, circle, arena, milieu, province, domain, orbit, preserve, realm, field, discipline, area, sector. **4** EVERYONE, everybody, people, mankind, humankind, humanity, the (general) public, the population.

worldly *adj.* **1** EARTHLY, terrestrial, temporal, mundane; mortal, human, material, materialistic, physical, carnal, fleshly, bodily, corporeal, sensual.
2 SOPHISTICATED, experienced, worldly-wise, knowledgeable, knowing, enlightened, shrewd, mature, seasoned, cosmopolitan, streetwise, street-smart, urbane, cultivated, cultured.
—OPPOSITES: spiritual, naive.

worn *adj.* SHABBY, worn out, threadbare, tattered, in tatters, falling to pieces, ragged, frayed, well-used, well-thumbed, moth-eaten, scruffy; *informal* tatty, the worse for wear, raggedy, dog-eared.

worried *adj.* ☞ ANXIOUS.

worry *v.* **1** FRET, be concerned, be anxious, agonize, brood, panic, lose sleep, get worked up, get stressed, get in a flap, get in a state, stew, torment oneself.
2 TROUBLE, bother, make anxious, disturb, distress, upset, concern, disquiet, fret, agitate, unsettle, perturb, scare, fluster, stress, tax, torment, plague, bedevil; prey on

one's mind, weigh down, gnaw at, rattle, bug, get to, dig at, nag, alarm, discomfit, disconcert, discountenance, dismay, exercise, ruffle, throw, unnerve.
▶ *n.* **1** ANXIETY, perturbation, distress, concern, uneasiness, unease, disquiet, fretfulness, restlessness, nervousness, nerves, agitation, edginess, tension, stress; apprehension, fear, dread, trepidation, misgiving, angst.
2 PROBLEM, cause for concern, issue; nuisance, pest, plague, trial, trouble, vexation, bane, bugbear; *informal* pain (in the neck), headache, hassle, stress.

worrying *adj.* ALARMING, worrisome, daunting, perturbing, niggling, nagging, bothersome, troublesome, unsettling, nerve-racking; distressing, disquieting, upsetting, traumatic, problematic; *informal* scary, hairy.

worsen *v.* **1** AGGRAVATE, exacerbate, compound, add to, intensify, increase, magnify, heighten, inflame, augment; *informal* add fuel to the fire.
2 ☞ DETERIORATE.
—OPPOSITES: improve.

worship *n.* **1** REVERENCE, veneration, adoration, glorification, glory, exaltation; devotion, praise, thanksgiving, homage, honour. **2** SERVICE, religious rite, prayer, praise, devotion, religious observance. **3** ADMIRATION, adulation, idolization, lionization, hero-worship.
▶ *v.* REVERE, reverence, venerate, pay homage to, honour, adore, praise, pray to, glorify, exalt,

extol; hold dear, cherish, treasure, esteem, adulate, idolize, deify, hero-worship, lionize; follow, look up to; *informal* put on a pedestal; *formal* laud.

worth *n.* **1** VALUE, price, cost; valuation, quotation, estimate. **2** BENEFIT, advantage, use, value, virtue, utility, service, profit, help, aid; desirability, appeal; significance, sense. **3** WORTHINESS, merit, value, excellence, calibre, quality, stature, eminence, consequence, importance, significance, distinction.

worthless *adj.* **1** VALUELESS; poor quality, inferior, second-rate, third-rate, low-grade, cheap, shoddy, tawdry, cheesy; *informal* crummy. **2** USELESS, no use, ineffective, ineffectual, fruitless, unproductive, unavailing, pointless, nugatory, valueless, inadequate, deficient, meaningless, senseless, insubstantial, empty, hollow, trifling, petty, inconsequential, lame, paltry, pathetic, no-account. **3** GOOD-FOR-NOTHING, ne'er-do-well, useless, despicable, contemptible, low, ignominious, corrupt, villainous, degenerate, shiftless, feckless; *informal* no-good, lousy. —OPPOSITES: valuable, useful.

worthwhile *adj.* VALUABLE, useful, of use, of service, beneficial, rewarding, advantageous, positive, helpful, profitable, gainful, fruitful, productive, lucrative, constructive, effective, effectual, meaningful, worthy.

worthy *adj.* ☞ VIRTUOUS. —OPPOSITES: disreputable.

☐ **be worthy of** DESERVE, merit, warrant, rate, justify, earn, be entitled to, qualify for.

wound *n.* **1** ☞ INJURY. **2** INSULT, blow, slight, offence, affront; hurt, damage, injury, pain, distress, grief, anguish, torment. ▸ *v.* ☞ HURT.

wrap *v.* **1** SWATHE, bundle, swaddle, muffle, cloak, enfold, envelop, encase, cover, fold, wind, shroud, drape. **2** PARCEL (UP), package, pack (up), bundle (up); gift-wrap.

wreck *v.* **1** DEMOLISH, crash, smash up, damage, destroy; vandalize, deface, desecrate, write off, trash, total. **2** SHIPWRECK, sink, capsize, run aground. **3** RUIN, spoil, disrupt, undo, put a stop to, frustrate, blight, crush, quash, dash, destroy, scotch, shatter, devastate, sabotage; *informal* mess up, screw up, foul up, put paid to, scupper, scuttle, stymie, put the kibosh on, nix.

wrench *n.* TUG, pull, jerk, jolt, heave; *informal* yank. ▸ *v.* **1** TUG, pull, jerk, wrest, heave, twist, pluck, grab, seize, snatch; *informal* yank. **2** SPRAIN, twist, turn, strain, crick, pull; injure, hurt.

wretched *adj.* **1** ☞ UNHAPPY. **2** ☞ ILL. **3** HARSH, hard, grim, stark, difficult; poor, impoverished; pitiful, pathetic, miserable, cheerless, sordid, shabby, seedy, unhealthy, insalubrious, dilapidated; *informal* scummy. **4** UNFORTUNATE, unlucky, luckless, ill-starred, blighted, hapless, poor, pitiable, downtrodden, oppressed; *literary* star-crossed. **5** DESPICABLE,

contemptible, reprehensible, base, vile, loathsome, hateful, detestable, odious, ignoble, shameful, shabby, worthless; *informal* dirty, rotten, lowdown, lousy. **6** TERRIBLE, awful, dire, atrocious, dreadful, bad, poor, lamentable, deplorable; *informal* godawful.
—OPPOSITES: cheerful, well, comfortable, fortunate, excellent.

wriggle *v.* SQUIRM, writhe, wiggle, jiggle, jerk, thresh, flounder, flail, twitch, twist and turn; snake, worm, slither.

wring *v.* **1** TWIST, squeeze, screw, scrunch, knead, press, mangle. **2** EXTRACT, elicit, force, exact, wrest, wrench, squeeze.

wrinkle *n.* **1** CREASE, fold, pucker, line, crinkle, furrow, ridge, groove; *informal* crow's feet, laugh line. **2** DIFFICULTY, snag, hitch, drawback, imperfection, problem.
▶ *v.* CREASE, pucker, gather, line, crinkle, crimp, crumple, rumple, ruck up, scrunch up.

write *v.* **1** NOTE (DOWN), write down, jot down, put down, put in writing, take down, record, register, log, list; inscribe, sign, scribble, scrawl, pencil. **2** COMPOSE, draft, think up, formulate, compile, pen, dash off, produce. **3** CORRESPOND, write a letter, communicate, get/stay in touch, keep in contact, email; *informal* drop someone a line.

writer *n.* AUTHOR, wordsmith, man/woman of letters, penman; novelist, essayist, biographer; journalist, columnist, correspondent; scriptwriter, playwright, dramatist,

dramaturge, tragedian; poet; *informal* scribbler, scribe, pencil-pusher, hack.

writing *n.* **1** HANDWRITING, hand, script, print; penmanship, calligraphy; *informal* scribble, scrawl, chicken scratch. **2** WORKS, compositions, books, publications, oeuvre; papers, articles, essays.

wrong *adj.* **1** INCORRECT, mistaken, in error, erroneous, inaccurate, inexact, imprecise, fallacious, wide of the mark, off target, unsound, faulty; *informal* out. **2** INAPPROPRIATE, unsuitable, inapt, inapposite, undesirable; ill-advised, ill-considered, ill-judged, impolitic, injudicious, infelicitous, unfitting, out of keeping, improper; *informal* out of order. **3** ILLEGAL, unlawful, illicit, criminal, dishonest, dishonourable, corrupt; unethical, immoral, bad, wicked, sinful, iniquitous, nefarious, blameworthy, reprehensible; *informal* crooked. **4** AMISS, awry, out of order, not right, faulty, flawed, defective.
—OPPOSITES: right, correct, appropriate, legal.
▶ *adv.* INCORRECTLY, wrongly, inaccurately, erroneously, mistakenly, in error.
▶ *n.* **1** IMMORALITY, sin, sinfulness, wickedness, evil; unlawfulness, crime, corruption, villainy, dishonesty, injustice, wrongdoing, misconduct, transgression. **2** MISDEED, offence, injury, crime, transgression, violation, peccadillo, sin; injustice, outrage, atrocity; *Law* tort; *archaic* trespass.

—OPPOSITES: right.

▸ v. **1** ILL-USE, mistreat, do an injustice to, do wrong to, ill-treat, abuse, harm, hurt, injure.
2 MALIGN, misrepresent, do a disservice to, impugn, defame, slander, libel.

wrongful *adj.* UNJUSTIFIED, unwarranted, unjust, unfair, undue, undeserved, unreasonable, groundless, indefensible, inappropriate, improper, unlawful, illegal, illegitimate.
—OPPOSITES: rightful.

Yy

yank *v.* (*informal*) JERK, pull, tug, wrench; snatch, seize.

yarn *n.* **1** THREAD, cotton, wool, fibre, filament; ply. **2** (*informal*) STORY, tale, anecdote, saga, narrative; *informal* tall tale/story, fish story, cock-and-bull story, shaggy-dog story, spiel.

yearn *v.* LONG, pine, crave, desire, want, wish, hanker, covet, lust, pant, hunger, burn, thirst, ache, eat one's heart out, have one's heart set on; *informal* have a yen, have a jones, itch.

yell *v.* CRY (OUT), call (out), shout, howl, yowl, wail, scream, shriek, screech, yelp, squeal; roar, bawl, bark, trumpet, thunder, bellow, ejaculate, exclaim, vociferate; *informal* holler.

yen *n.* (*informal*) HANKERING, yearning, longing, craving, urge, desire, want, wish, hunger, thirst, lust, appetite, ache; fancy, inclination; *informal* itch.

yield *v.* **1** PRODUCE, bear, give, supply, provide, afford, return, bring in, earn, realize, generate, deliver, offer, pay out. **2** RELINQUISH, surrender, cede, concede, remit, part with, hand over; make over, bequeath, leave. **3** SURRENDER, capitulate, submit, relent, admit defeat, back down, climb down, give in, give up the struggle, lay down one's arms, raise/show the white flag, throw in the towel/sponge. **4** GIVE IN TO, give way to, submit to, bow down to, comply with, agree to, consent to, go along with; grant, permit, allow; *informal* cave in to; *formal* accede to. **5** BEND, give, give way.
—OPPOSITES: withhold, resist, defy.
▶ *n.* PROFIT, gain, return, dividend, earnings.

yoke *n.* **1** HARNESS, collar, coupling. **2** TYRANNY, oppression, domination, hegemony, enslavement, servitude, subjugation, subjection, bondage, thrall; bonds, chains, fetters, shackles. **3** BOND, tie, connection, link.
▶ *v.* **1** HARNESS, hitch, couple, tether, fasten, attach, join. **2** UNITE, join, marry, link, connect; tie, bind, bond.

yokel *n.* ☞ BUMPKIN.

young *adj.* **1** YOUTHFUL, juvenile; junior, adolescent, teenage; in the springtime of life, in one's salad days. **2** IMMATURE, childish, inexperienced, unsophisticated, naive, unworldly; *informal* wet behind the ears. **3** FLEDGLING, developing, budding, in its infancy, emerging.
—OPPOSITES: old, elderly, mature.
▶ *n.* **1** OFFSPRING, progeny, family, babies. **2** YOUNG PEOPLE, children,